CW00925782

Warehouse Management with SAP S/4HANA®

SAP PRESS is a joint initiative of SAP and Rheinwerk Publishing. The know-how offered by SAP specialists combined with the expertise of Rheinwerk Publishing offers the reader expert books in the field. SAP PRESS features first-hand information and expert advice, and provides useful skills for professional decision-making.

SAP PRESS offers a variety of books on technical and business-related topics for the SAP user. For further information, please visit our website: *www.sap-press.com*.

Namita Sachan, Aman Jain

Warehouse Management with SAP S/4HANA®

Editor Meagan White
Acquisitions Editor Emily Nicholls
Copyeditor Julie McNamee
Cover Design Graham Geary
Photo Credit Shutterstock.com: 165783872/© SasaStock, 237161533/© Quang Ho
Layout Design Vera Brauner
Production Kelly O'Callaghan
Typesetting SatzPro, Krefeld (Germany)
Printed and bound in the United States of America, on paper from sustainable sources

ISBN 978-1-4932-1915-5

2nd edition 2020

Library of Congress Cataloging-in-Publication Data
Names: Sachan, Namita, author. | Jain, Aman, 1983- author.
Title: Warehouse management with SAP S/4HANA : embedded and decentralized EWM / Namita Sachan, Aman Jain.
Description: 2nd edition. | Boston : Rheinwerk Publishing, 2020. | Includes index.
Identifiers: LCCN 2019052860 (print) | LCCN 2019052861 (ebook) | ISBN 9781493219155 (hardcover) | ISBN 9781493219162 (ebook)
Subjects: LCSH: Warehouses--Management--Data processing. | Business logistics. | SAP HANA (Electronic resource)
Classification: LCC HF5485 .S2355 2020 (print) | LCC HF5485 (ebook) | DDC 658.7/85028553--dc23
LC record available at https://lccn.loc.gov/2019052860
LC ebook record available at https://lccn.loc.gov/2019052861

Contents at a Glance

Dear Reader,

When I was young, I had a great big plastic container of beads. There must have been hundreds of glass, plastic, and wooden beads organized by color and type in a matrix of small slots. The caddy was two-tiered, so the lid opened to reveal a top shelf that nested above the bottom one. Being a highly organized—if somewhat strange—small child, on several occasions I dumped the whole thing out on the floor and then spent many happy hours resorting every bead into its proper place.

This is the fifth warehouse management book I've edited here at SAP PRESS, and every time I dig into chapters about picking and packing, I can't help but think of my bead container. In many ways, my warehouse in miniature had many of the same considerations as a real warehouse: like should go with like, and fast-moving goods (in my case, the prettiest beads) should be stored on the top shelf within easy reach. Although my chaotic dumping motion hardly resembles goods issue, my careful putaway effort mimicked a more elegant goods receipt process on a larger scale.

So whether your warehouse is child-sized like my bead caddy or large enough to fill a whole city block, I hope you enjoy this book! If you care to share your feedback about *Warehouse Management with SAP S/4HANA*, your comments and suggestions are the most useful tools to help us make our books the best they can be. Please feel free to contact me and share any praise or criticism you may have.

Thank you for purchasing a book from SAP PRESS!

Meagan White
Editor, SAP PRESS

meaganw@rheinwerk-publishing.com
www.sap-press.com
Rheinwerk Publishing · Boston, MA

Contents

13 Advanced Production Integration 611

20 Value-Added Services 765

Appendices

Foreword

More than 1,800 companies in more than 65 countries from various industries already use SAP Extended Warehouse Management (SAP EWM) for their warehouses.

SAP EWM is a best-of-breed solution that is integral to building an intelligent warehouse covering a broad range from small warehouses to high-end automated warehouses (production supply warehouses, distribution centers, and cross-dock warehouses). It optimizes core warehouse processes; simplifies and automates redundant or complex process steps; enhances visibility in warehouse operations through integration with other applications, such as SAP Transportation Management and SAP Manufacturing Execution, or global track-and-trace software; and increases engagement and user productivity by integrating wearables, mobile devices, and modern radio-frequency identification (RFID) technology with SAP EWM.

To offer our customers a road map to SAP S/4HANA was a logical next step in our product strategy. With SAP S/4HANA 1511, we offered the possibility to connect SAP EWM to SAP S/4HANA in the same way as it connected to SAP ERP. Since SAP S/4HANA 1610, SAP EWM became an embedded part of the core of SAP S/4HANA Enterprise Management. As embedded EWM is deployed on the same system as SAP S/4HANA, it avoids master data duplication by directly accessing core enterprise process data. Since May 2019, with the release of SAP S/4HANA 1809 Feature Pack 2, we made available a new decentralized deployment option for EWM. However, our biggest release in 2019 was SAP S/4HANA 1909. With SAP S/4HANA 1909, we've bridged the feature gaps between decentralized EWM on SAP S/4HANA and the standalone SAP EWM 9.5. This release also brought many innovative functionalities and improvements to SAP EWM, both for the decentralized EWM and embedded EWM options, such as the following:

- **Synchronous backflush posting**
  With this feature, the components used to produce a set amount of goods will be deducted from the warehouse management system with the receiving of the finished goods in the warehouse.
- **Simplified Kanban**
  For the Kanban process, we've reduced the number of steps a warehouse clerk has to complete. In the previous Kanban approach from an EWM-managed warehouse, the replenishment would trigger warehouse requests in EWM, which then would need to be converted into picking tasks. Because this takes more time and

effort than is required, the 1909 release introduces a new Kanban control type that will significantly reduce process steps and increase the automation of redundant and monotonous tasks.

- **Harmonized production supply areas and control cycles**
  We improved our users' experience in maintaining production supply areas and control cycles by deepening the integration between the production modules in the central SAP S/4HANA system and embedded EWM. This allows for direct replication of the SAP S/4HANA production supply area into embedded EWM as well as the harmonization of the control cycles in both application areas. For our users, this means that less effort is required to maintain that data in both systems and the risks of data errors (and the costs that result) are greatly reduced.
- **Using transportation equipment in production supply**
  We've added a new functionality by which a customer can use distribution equipment to support multistep supply of components to the production supply area.
- **Core data services (CDS) analytics for warehouse orders and warehouse tasks**
  With our new app for analytics, users can take an overview of key performance indicators (KPIs) relevant to their warehouse operations, for example, the total number of open warehouse tasks to be processed on the current date.

Those are just a few examples of how we continue to innovate our warehouse management solution. We'll continue investing in warehouse capabilities to optimize your supply chain operations, which is essential to staying competitive in fulfilling increasingly complex customer requirements.

Looking at the number of customers from various industries and countries, it's clear that both embedded EWM and decentralized EWM can be used flexibly: with its architecture, it provides the ability to map complex warehouse processes down to the level of the conveyor system, to control these processes, and to take into account custom requirements during implementation. When implementing EWM, regardless of the deployment option, it's imperative to adapt the software in such a way that you'll be able to benefit from future innovations from SAP. To take full advantage of this architecture, understanding the foundations of this product's capabilities is essential.

This book will help you become acquainted with the basic principles of the SAP EWM architecture so that you can make the best decisions for your own implementation. You should pay special attention to quality management and performance, staying close to the standard way of processing to ensure that your implementation supports your supply chain sustainably and efficiently and that you can benefit from future innovations that are already planned.

I hope you enjoy reading this book and wish you many more successful implementations of EWM in SAP S/4HANA. The authors of this book have shared their many years of practical experience from their implementations, development, and optimization of embedded EWM and decentralized EWM with you.

Jörg Michaelis
Chief Product Owner of SAP EWM, SAP SE

Preface

Modern times require businesses to be more efficient and responsive. Companies are trying to simplify their business models by connecting people, devices, and business networks, thus improving business efficiency while reducing IT costs. SAP S/4HANA combines SAP ERP offerings to run day-to-day business processes with portions of other SAP Business Suite products such as SAP Supplier Relationship Management (SAP SRM) and SAP Customer Relationship Management (SAP CRM). It also helps businesses simplify their business models by leveraging its two key capabilities—an advanced in-memory platform based on SAP HANA and a personalized user experience with SAP Fiori—among other things.

SAP released its first version of the embedded EWM solution with SAP S/4HANA 1610 in October 2016. This provided customers with the option of choosing embedded EWM or standalone SAP EWM depending on their business and IT requirements. Embedded EWM leverages all the advantages of having "one system," thus improving the system's functional capabilities and providing an improved user experience. With SAP S/4HANA 1809 FPS 02 came decentralized EWM in SAP S/4HANA, which can simultaneously integrate with multiple ERP applications (most commonly SAP ERP and SAP S/4HANA) rather than integrating with the central SAP S/4HANA application only.

This book covers both the business processes supported by embedded EWM in SAP S/4HANA 1909 and the underlying system configurations required to drive those capabilities.

Target Audience

We hope the information included in this publication will help companies, warehousing professionals, and SAP EWM practitioners around the world to further their knowledge and understanding of the integration of complex warehousing requirements with this enterprise technology solution. Each chapter begins with a high-level overview before delving into configuration details that should be helpful to both first-time users and existing SAP EWM users. Various configurations and business processes have been explained using system screenshots wherever possible to give you a feel for what the setup will look like on your end system.

We've also tried to highlight some key points about where embedded EWM and decentralized EWM in SAP S/4HANA vary in scope from the standalone SAP EWM solution for those of you who are already familiar with the SAP EWM. This will help you clarify your expectations for embedded EWM and decentralized EWM, be aware of your options, and make key decisions.

Objective

The purpose of this book is to cover the scope of the embedded EWM solution in SAP S/4HANA 1909, the business processes contained in it, and how they can be implemented. Because SAP has proposed to provide support for SAP ERP only until 2025, it becomes imperative for businesses to be aware of the functionalities available within the embedded EWM application available in SAP S/4HANA so that they can make clear decisions about their business roadmaps and embark on their SAP S/4HANA transformation journeys in a more decisive way. Various types of illustrations such as flowcharts, diagrams, and system screenshots will help clarify the business processes and how they're set up in the system. This book will cover all aspects of embedded EWM setup, including integration requirements, master data, and deployment of business processes. Towards the end, we also cover integration with other SAP applications, such as SAP Transportation Management and SAP Global Trade Services, and deployment of SAP Fiori apps for embedded EWM in SAP S/4HANA, to help you discover how to leverage these integrations to further streamline your business processes.

Structure of the Book

This book is comprised of 25 chapters. The book starts with an introduction to SAP S/4HANA and warehouse management benefits, deployment options, and feature sets. The book begins with the basic setup and integration that must be performed at the outset of the project and setting up the organizational structure and master data. From there, the book dedicates one chapter each to the key processes (inbound, outbound, and internal) and subprocesses (physical inventory, resource management, and so on) for basic warehousing. Next, the book covers the advanced/extended warehouse management processes supported by embedded EWM. The underlying master data and organizational structure remains the same. Within each chapter, the basic definitions are explained, followed by step-by-step instructions for configuring the given business processes in the system. Where possible, we've shown the end-to-end business process in the warehouse using system screenshots so that you can visualize how the process will be executed in the system.

The structure of the book is as follows:

- **Chapter 1: Warehouse Management in SAP**
  This chapter brings together the two key concepts of this book: warehouse management and SAP S/4HANA. It explains warehouse management benefits, deployment options, and feature sets available to customers when deploying embedded EWM with SAP S/4HANA.
- **Chapter 2: Organizational Structures**
  This chapter describes the different organizational units required for executing warehouse management processes as part of an organization's larger logistics operations.
- **Chapter 3: First Steps in Implementing EWM in SAP S/4HANA**
  This chapter describes the basic configurations required to set up the system landscape for enabling data integration between SAP S/4HANA and the embedded EWM application.
- **Chapter 4: Warehouse Structures**
  This chapter describes the different units that define a warehouse structure in embedded EWM and how to map them. These components help businesses model their physical warehouses in embedded EWM to support various warehousing operations.
- **Chapter 5: Master Data**
  This chapter describes various master data that needs to be created in SAP S/4HANA and the embedded EWM application. This data includes business partners, products, storage bins, and so on.
- **Chapter 6: Cross-Process Settings**
  Some definitions are used across warehouse management process and so should be discussed before you focus on core processes like inbound, outbound, and internal warehouse processes. This chapter describes definitions used across processes, including necessary configurations required to set them up.

- **Chapter 7: Inbound Processing**
  Two of the most important warehouse management processes are goods receipt and putaway. This chapter explains the general inbound process and configuration for items received from vendors or customers using step-by-step instructions. The chapter also explains in detail how to unload and handle goods receipt and how to create and confirm single- and multistep putaway tasks to optimize bin capacity and material flow.
- **Chapter 8: Outbound Processing**
  In this chapter we cover outbound processing, or movement of stock out of the warehouse. We cover the general business processes and configurations for outbound delivery, stock removal, picking, loading, and pick denial using step-by-step instructions.
- **Chapter 9: Internal Warehouse Processes**
  Organizations often need to move stock within the warehouse. This chapter explains the different mechanisms for stock movements in the warehouse, including ad hoc movements, replenishment, posting changes, and stock transfer and the configurations required to set them up.
- **Chapter 10: Physical Inventory**
  Inventory management is a key component in warehouse management. This chapter describes how a physical inventory is set up and performed using different counting methods in embedded EWM.
- **Chapter 11: Resource Management**
  This chapter describes the use of resource management in embedded EWM, which helps improve warehouse efficiency by streamlining resources and workload. We cover different components of resource management like semi-system-guided processing, task interleaving, and pick, pack, and pass, which help optimize resources and processes in the warehouse.
- **Chapter 12: Warehouse Monitoring and Reporting**
  This chapter explains monitoring and reporting of warehouse processes in SAP S/4HANA. The embedded EWM warehouse monitor tool is the single source of truth for monitoring and stock movement in the warehouse, and the graphical warehouse layout provides a graphical view of stock position in the warehouse. We cover the configuration details required to set these tools up and to customize them based on user requirements.

- **Chapter 13: Advanced Production Integration**
  Embedded EWM uses advanced production integration to integrate the supply of raw materials for the production process and receipt of finished goods in the embedded EWM-managed warehouse. In this chapter, we cover the process of advanced production integration and configurations required to set it up.
- **Chapter 14: Radio Frequency Framework**
  Embedded EWM provides a standard solution using the radio frequency (RF) framework by displaying application data on an RF device using menus and screens. In this chapter, we discuss how to configure RF in embedded EWM to integrate business operations with RF in the warehouse.
- **Chapter 15: Cross-Docking**
  This chapter describes cross-docking, a practice that optimizes the routing of goods in the warehouse. We cover the planned and opportunistic cross-docking processes that can be used with embedded EWM and the configurations required to set them up.
- **Chapter 16: Wave Management**
  Wave management improves picking for multiple deliveries leaving the warehouse. Waves can be combined or split based on different criteria like route, activity area, or product. This chapter explains how to set up and use wave management in embedded EWM.
- **Chapter 17: Slotting and Rearrangement**
  Slotting is a practice that facilitates inventory optimization in the warehouse by identifying the right bin for a product based on product characteristics. This chapter outlines how to set up and use this functionality.
- **Chapter 18: Shipping and Receiving**
  This chapter covers the concepts and configurations required to set up and monitor shipping and receiving in the warehouse. We cover key concepts such as vehicles, shipments, and yard management in detail.
- **Chapter 19: Labor Management**
  Labor management helps users plan labor time and resources in the warehouse. It covers the different ways in which workload can be calculated and how labor activities can be monitored in embedded EWM. This chapter explains how to activate, configure, and use key labor management functionality.
- **Chapter 20: Value-Added Services**
  This chapter provides step-by-step instructions for configuring and using value-added services (VAS) functionality to enhance products in the warehouse.

- **Chapter 21: Kitting**
  This chapter covers kitting and the various kitting methods that can be set up in embedded EWM, including kit to order, kit to stock, and reverse kitting.
- **Chapter 22: Cartonization Planning**
  Cartonization planning is an advanced warehouse management practice that improves the packing and shipping of goods from the warehouse. This chapter explains the concept of cartonization planning and how to set up and use various functionalities, including how to create planned shipping handling units manually or automatically.
- **Chapter 23: SAP Dock Appointment Scheduling**
  This chapter explains SAP Dock Appointment Scheduling, which helps plan the arrivals of vehicles in the warehouse from both the warehouse and carrier perspectives. We also cover the configurations required to set it up.
- **Chapter 24: Material Flow System**
  As organizations grow, they implement advanced functionalities for optimized material flow in the warehouse. Automated warehouses provide one such optimization by using carousels, vertical lift modules, and automated storage and retrieval systems. In this chapter, we discuss the concept of material flow systems, which allow users to connect an automated warehouse to embedded EWM via programmable logic controllers.
- **Chapter 25: Integration with Other SAP Solutions**
  Warehousing and transportation are closely connected. This chapter will cover embedded EWM integration with SAP Transportation Management functionality, both embedded and standalone. We also cover integration with SAP Global Trade Services.

We hope this book will help the SAP EWM community to understand embedded EWM as a solution and equip you with the tools to carry out full-fledged embedded EWM implementations.

References

The content at the following links has been referenced by the authors during the writing of this book and should be referred to for more information:

1. **Concepts, definitions, and industry terminology**
   - *http://www.apics.org*

2. **SAP S/4HANA product and release information**
   - *www.sap.com/s4hana*
   - *https://rapid.sap.com/bp*
   - *https://launchpad.support.sap.com/*
   - *https://fioriappslibrary.hana.ondemand.com/*

Acknowledgments

We would like to thank the following colleagues for encouraging us to go forward with this project and for providing support throughout the journey and making it a success:

- Duncan Baldry, Leadership (Accenture UK)
- Dr. Alexander Zeier, Leadership (Accenture Germany)
- Dirk Appelhoff, Leadership (Accenture Germany)
- Swanand Bhedasgaonkar, Capgemini India

We also want to thank warehousing subject matter experts Duncan Baldry, Accenture UK and Dhiren Shah, Unilever India, for reviewing various chapters and providing us with their valuable feedback.

Our thanks to the technical team for providing us with the SAP S/4HANA system and resolving any technical issues as and when they appeared.

Our sincere thanks to everyone at Rheinwerk Publishing and especially Meagan White, the editor of this book, for her immense support and dedication throughout this work. Also, our sincere thanks to Emily Nicholls for selecting this project and helping convert it from an idea to an actual book.

We extend a special thanks to Jörg Michaelis, SAP EWM chief product owner at SAP SE, for sharing his views on SAP EWM and the inspiring foreword.

Our sincere thanks to our friends and family for their relentless patience and support throughout the duration of this project. We dedicate this book to our loving son Vihaan Jain and to our parents Virender Kumar Jain, Sadhana Jain, and Asha Sachan for their blessings, which is of paramount importance as well as for accepting our prolonged period of absence during the creation of this book.

Chapter 1
Warehouse Management in SAP

Warehouse management is a key component in supply chain management. In this chapter, we review SAP's warehouse management solutions and their benefits, deployment options, and available features.

As supply chains expand globally, they put operational and cost pressures on companies to maintain visibility into their inventory and shipping processes via tracking. For more than 40 years, SAP has been working with thousands of customers to resolve complex IT challenges. SAP has launched many packaged applications, such as SAP ERP, and integration solutions, such as SAP Supplier Relationship Management (SAP SRM) and SAP Customer Relationship Management (SAP CRM), to cater to various business processes. SAP S/4HANA brings these applications together on a single platform and database, resulting in a massive reduction in costs. All this helps to simplify business processes by providing seamless integration with various application areas.

In this introduction to warehouse management, we first outline in Section 1.1 the process of warehouse management and the warehousing challenges faced by businesses today. Section 1.2 then describes the SAP warehouse management solutions, including the evolution of warehousing solutions offered by SAP over time and the various deployment options available. Section 1.3 covers the various migration scenarios that may precede business planning to migrate to embedded Extended Warehouse Management (EWM) in SAP S/4HANA (embedded EWM) and how they can be handled. In Section 1.4, we'll cover the deployment options available: embedded EWM, decentralized Extended Warehouse Management on SAP S/4HANA (decentralized EWM), and stock room management. Section 1.5 covers a key feature in embedded EWM: division of available functionalities among end users based on business requirements and licensing mechanisms.

1.1 What Is Warehouse Management?

A *warehouse management system* (WMS) is a software application that a company uses to manage its day-to-day warehousing operations. This includes stock monitoring, managing incoming and outgoing stock, and performing maintenance work on stock in the warehouse. A clear overview of stock and open requirements enables businesses to manage staffing and utilization of available resources, produce more efficient material requirements planning (MRP), and keep an optimum stock level in the warehouse.

A WMS can be a standalone application or a built-in application within the company's enterprise resource planning (ERP) system. A company's requirements for a WMS can vary depending on the scale of business and the complexity of business processes. The underlying functionality of a WMS is to receive orders and help execute picking or stock putaway. WMSs have evolved over time to cater to changing, complex, and data-intensive business requirements. The functions of a WMS not only carry out day-to-day warehouse operations but also help carry out these operations faster and better. These systems are adopting next-generation technologies such as pick by voice and the Internet of Things (IoT) to improve warehousing operations.

The warehouse management process itself incorporates controlling the storage and movement of goods in the warehouse and processing related transactions, such as picking, putaway, and internal warehouse movements. In the multi-echelon model for distribution, there may be multiple levels of warehouses, including a central warehouse, a regional warehouse (serviced by the central warehouse), and sometimes retail warehouses (serviced by the regional warehouses). Complex warehouse management also uses automatic identification and data-capture technology, such as barcode scanners, mobile computers, wireless local area networks (LANs), and potentially radio-frequency identification (RFID) to monitor the flow of products efficiently.

Because we operate in a world of increasing complexity and constant change, warehouse management faces a host of challenges. Expanding omnichannel markets are forcing manufacturers and distributors to change how they sell to consumers. Customers today demand perfect orders. Failure to meet service levels leads not only to fines and chargebacks from powerful retail customers but also costs incurred to correct the imperfect orders.

Another challenge companies are facing is that the value of the order (order size) is decreasing while the number of orders continues to increase. This puts pressure on the company's logistical capabilities because it still needs its available-to-promise (ATP) inventory, but all at a larger order-volume level. Companies need to automate repetitive tasks to save time spent on individual orders.

Figure 1.1 shows some of the challenges in warehouse management in the real world. Given these factors, manufacturers and distributors are faced with escalating costs and complexity that drive demands for greater productivity in warehouse operations. Poor order management, excessive labor costs, and inefficient warehousing operations all exacerbate the problem.

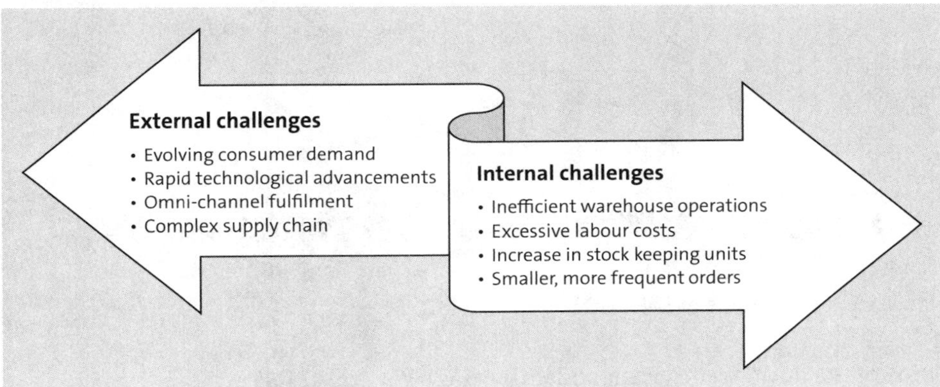

External challenges
• Evolving consumer demand
• Rapid technological advancements
• Omni-channel fulfilment
• Complex supply chain
Internal challenges
• Inefficient warehouse operations
• Excessive labour costs
• Increase in stock keeping units
• Smaller, more frequent orders

Figure 1.1 Warehouse Management Challenges

1.2 Warehouse Management with SAP

Warehouse management in SAP focuses on providing inventory accuracy, optimized utilization of warehouse space, and streamlined picking and putaway. SAP's warehousing solutions have evolved over time to cater to changing business requirements. In 1993, SAP launched SAP ERP Warehouse Management (WM) as a submodule of Materials Management (MM) in SAP R/3. This release evolved over time to support storage units, a warehouse monitor, HR integration, decentralized WM, radio frequency (RF), and task and resource management.

In 2005, SAP released version 5.0 of its SAP Supply Chain Management (SAP SCM) software and, with it, the first version of its SAP Extended Warehouse Management (SAP EWM) software. SAP EWM's system architecture was significantly different from that of WM, and it focused on the needs of high-volume, automated, and complex warehouses. Released as an add-on for SAP SCM, SAP EWM provided you with the option to deploy your warehouse management applications on a decentralized system. Figure 1.2 highlights some of the key features of decentralized SAP EWM.

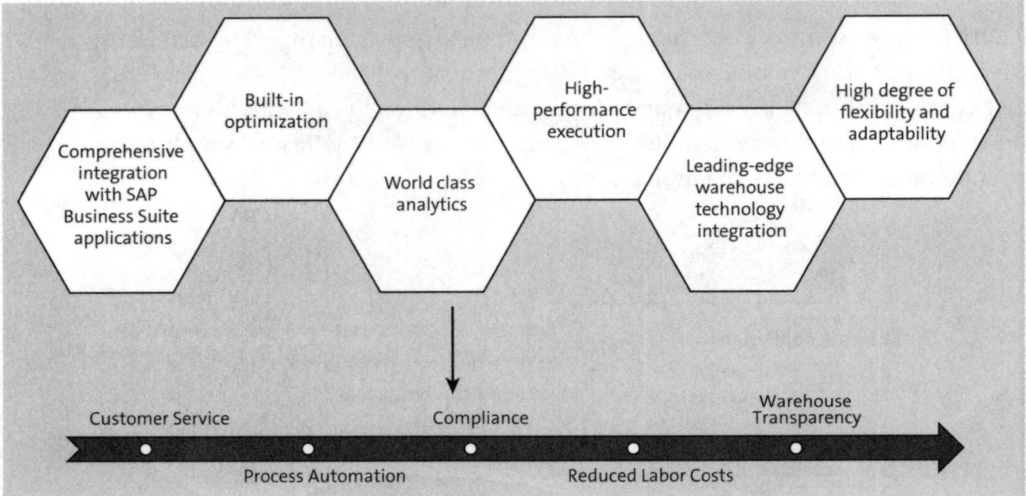

Figure 1.2 Key Features of SAP EWM

Some of the business drivers for adopting SAP EWM are as follows:

- Provides support for a full range of complex warehouse processes
- Enables flexible, automated support for warehouse and distribution logistics, as well as inventory tracking and management
- Allows you to manage product movement within warehouses, from goods receipt to goods issue
- Allows you to leverage sophisticated features that can scale as you grow
- Optimizes warehouse resource and asset utilization
- Provides support for the latest technologies, as follows:
  - Runs on SAP HANA to handle throughput of up to one million items per day
  - Supports supply chain execution platforms such as transit warehouses, warehouse billing, and so on
  - Enables user-friendly rendition of real-time business insights and intelligence on any mobile device via SAP Fiori-driven user interfaces (UIs)

> **Note**
>
> SAP will no longer offer usage rights for WM after December 31, 2025. Support for decentralized WM will also only continue until December 2025. Decentralized EWM and embedded EWM in SAP S/4HANA seem to be the key focus areas of SAP in its warehouse management solutions space. This acts as another driver for businesses to investigate leveraging the functionalities of embedded EWM to optimize their warehouse operations further.

Figure 1.3 shows some of the functional capabilities of SAP EWM. We'll discuss these in detail in subsequent chapters.

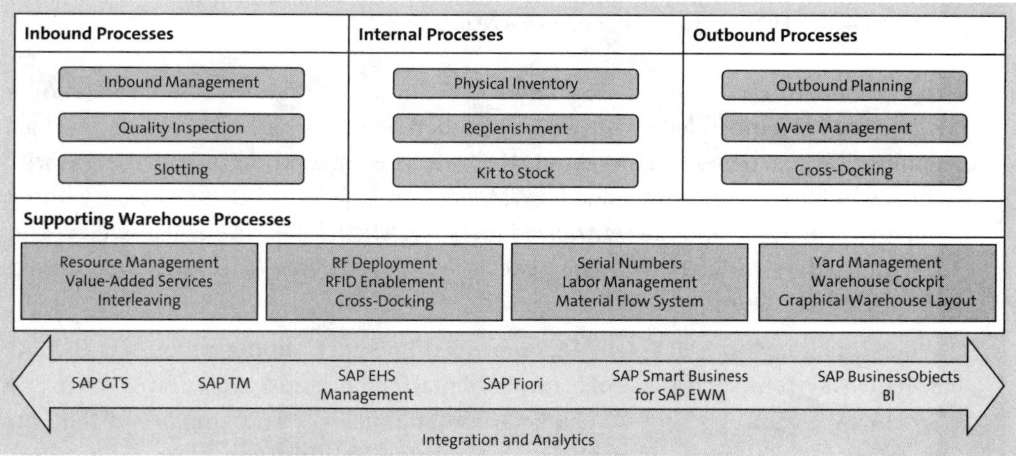

Figure 1.3 SAP EWM Functional Capabilities

With the introduction of embedded EWM—the topic of this book—in SAP S/4HANA, embedded EWM gained key benefits from the SAP S/4HANA landscape that differentiate it from all other deployment options, as shown in Figure 1.4.

Until SAP S/4HANA 1511, decentralized SAP EWM was able to connect with the SAP S/4HANA 1511 on-premise solution using a sidecar approach. This involves connecting the SAP S/4HANA system with SAP EWM as a decentralized system deployed on a separate server platform, which can be an SAP SCM server or SAP NetWeaver.

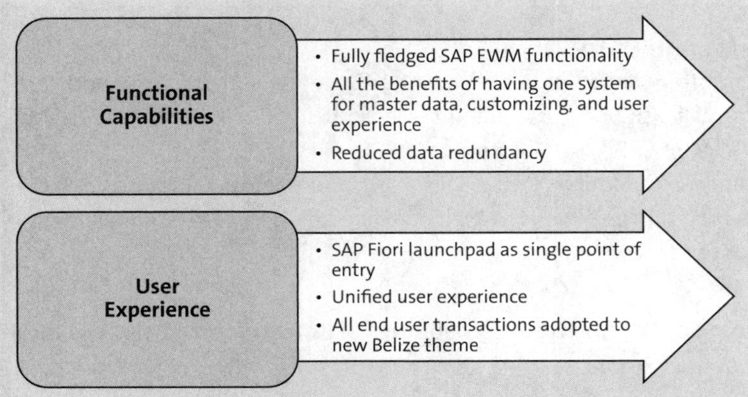

Figure 1.4 Key Highlights of Embedded EWM in SAP S/4HANA

In October 2016, SAP launched SAP S/4HANA Supply Chain for extended warehouse management (embedded EWM), which included integration of EWM as an embedded application component in SAP S/4HANA 1610. This integration provided users with the benefits of using embedded EWM processes within SAP S/4HANA without deploying any add-on or decentralized instance, which helps SAP S/4HANA leverage the transparency, high performance execution, and efficient distribution and storage offered by SAP EWM.

When integrated in SAP S/4HANA, embedded EWM gets all the benefits of the SAP S/4HANA system, such as use of centralized master data and features provided in SAP S/4HANA (e.g., support for 40-character material fields). Removing use of the Core Interface (CIF) for sending material master, batch, and business master data eliminates data redundancy. Embedded EWM in SAP S/4HANA also provides reduced data redundancy and enables direct read of actual data by skipping the creation of delivery request objects, eliminating the quality inspection engine from quality management processes, and replacing expected goods receipt objects, to name a few. (We'll discuss these further in subsequent chapters.) Embedded EWM in SAP S/4HANA also leverages the SAP Fiori Belize theme, which enhances product capabilities.

Note

For simplicity, we'll refer to SAP S/4HANA Supply Chain for EWM as *embedded EWM* throughout this book.

This integration continues to exist in SAP S/4HANA 1909, and SAP has provided certain improvements over the existing integration, for example:

- Comprehensive embedded EWM and quality management integration to support quality management processes in the warehouse
- Use of core data services (CDS) views for embedded EWM for dashboards and analytics with SAP Smart Business or SAP Fiori apps for warehouse experts
- New capabilities for setting up labor structures and standards to support advanced labor tracking
- New e-commerce enhancements and enhanced warehouse optimization

Tip

The sidecar approach as an option for integration with SAP S/4HANA is recommended for complex and automated warehouses and distribution centers. Embedded EWM in SAP S/4HANA is recommended for small- and mid-sized warehouses that are less complex and have less data throughput.

Note

Embedded EWM in SAP S/4HANA offers many other distinctions from decentralized EWM. To learn more about the differences between embedded EWM in SAP S/4HANA 1909 and SAP EWM 9.5, see SAP Note 2806070.

Note

Throughout this book, we've tried to highlight some of the key differences that users familiar with standalone SAP EWM should note while trying to use embedded EWM in SAP S/4HANA. This will help you identify the changes introduced by embedded deployment.

1.3 SAP S/4HANA Conversion and Migration

There are three conversion paths for customers moving to SAP S/4HANA, as follows:

- **System conversion**
  This business-led migration from an existing SAP ERP system to SAP S/4HANA allows users to leverage their existing business process implementation in SAP ERP. The transition path requires a technical upgrade and a complete migration of SAP ERP to SAP S/4HANA. It offers the following benefits:
  - Migration without reimplementation
  - No disruption for existing business processes
  - Reevaluation of customization and existing process flows
- **Landscape transformation**
  This scenario is for businesses that want to consolidate their business landscapes or carve out select entities, such as company codes, and reimplement them on SAP S/4HANA. This migration approach offers the following benefits:
  - Selective data transformation for a phased approach, focusing on the parts of the business with the highest returns on investment (ROIs)
  - Possibility of consolidation or selective data migration, helping lead to lower total cost of investment
  - Reimagined business processes based on the latest innovations
- **New implementation**
  This scenario refers to a new implementation or reimplementation by new SAP customers planning to move to SAP S/4HANA or those already on SAP ERP that want to move to SAP S/4HANA through a greenfield implementation. This option enables businesses to standardize and simplify their landscapes and then retire their old landscapes after implementation is complete. This migration scenario offers the following benefits:
  - Reengineering and process simplification based on ready-to-run business processes
  - Predefined migration objects and best practices available with guided configuration
  - Reduced time-to-value and customer total cost of ownership

Table 1.1 shows the possible scenarios and provides recommendations for some of the migration approaches.

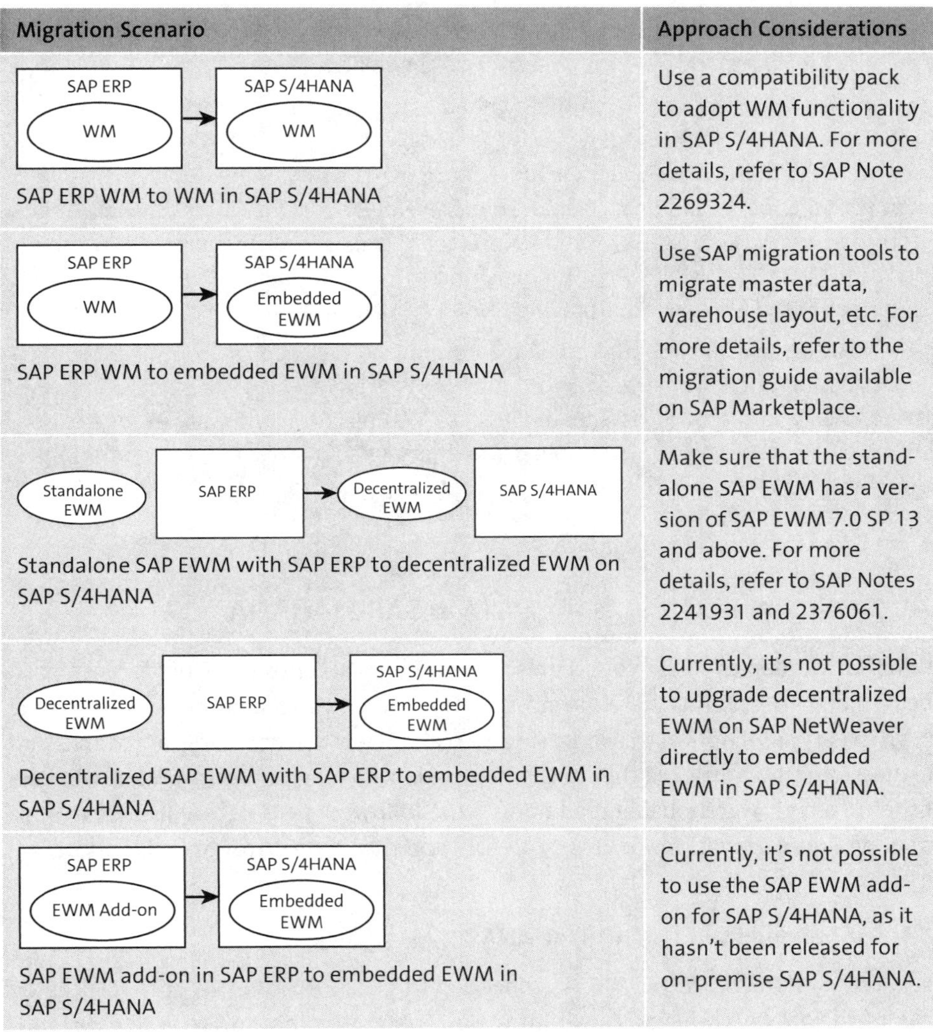

Migration Scenario	Approach Considerations
SAP ERP WM to WM in SAP S/4HANA	Use a compatibility pack to adopt WM functionality in SAP S/4HANA. For more details, refer to SAP Note 2269324.
SAP ERP WM to embedded EWM in SAP S/4HANA	Use SAP migration tools to migrate master data, warehouse layout, etc. For more details, refer to the migration guide available on SAP Marketplace.
Standalone SAP EWM with SAP ERP to decentralized EWM on SAP S/4HANA	Make sure that the standalone SAP EWM has a version of SAP EWM 7.0 SP 13 and above. For more details, refer to SAP Notes 2241931 and 2376061.
Decentralized SAP EWM with SAP ERP to embedded EWM in SAP S/4HANA	Currently, it's not possible to upgrade decentralized EWM on SAP NetWeaver directly to embedded EWM in SAP S/4HANA.
SAP EWM add-on in SAP ERP to embedded EWM in SAP S/4HANA	Currently, it's not possible to use the SAP EWM add-on for SAP S/4HANA, as it hasn't been released for on-premise SAP S/4HANA.

Table 1.1 Embedded EWM and SAP EWM with SAP S/4HANA: Migration Scenarios

Compatibility Packs

Users can continue to use both WM (using a compatibility pack) and embedded EWM on an SAP S/4HANA client. However, it isn't possible to run the same warehouse with both WM and embedded EWM. It's also possible to have a mix of WM and SAP EWM warehouses, running on centralized and decentralized WM and SAP EWM.

Due to the large WM customer base, the WM solution is still available within on-premise SAP S/4HANA as a compatibility package solution.

Compatibility packs provide you with limited usage rights to run certain classic SAP solutions on SAP S/4HANA. However, you must have acquired software usage rights for these solutions, as set forth in your license agreements. More details regarding compatibility packs can be gathered from SAP Note 2269324. Currently, the use of compatibility packs in SAP S/4HANA 1909 is set to expire on December 31, 2025—this includes WM. This will give customers sufficient time to migrate from classic SAP solutions to the new solutions provided with SAP S/4HANA.

If you have an existing integration with decentralized WM, you can continue to work on this integration even after migration to SAP S/4HANA. However, new customers need to play with caution here, as embedded EWM has been and will continue to be the focus area of SAP as its strategic warehousing solution going forward in SAP S/4HANA.

1.4 Deployment Options for EWM in SAP S/4HANA

EWM can be deployed in your landscape through a centralized or decentralized deployment. In general, there are no specific guidelines to help businesses decide which deployment option to use. Businesses can review their existing landscapes and business processes and use that review to decide which deployment option will best fit their strategic warehousing road map. In the following sections, we'll cover the different deployment options for SAP S/4HANA and the key features of each option.

1.4.1 Embedded EWM in SAP S/4HANA

As of SAP S/4HANA 1909, EWM is embedded in the SAP S/4HANA core to provide state-of-the-art warehousing capabilities. This integration doesn't replace the standalone SAP EWM deployment option, but it simply offers you the choice between centralized and decentralized deployments depending on your business and IT requirements. This also enables simplified integration with SAP S/4HANA processes.

The centralized deployment option is usually recommended over decentralized deployment for small- to medium-scale warehouses and distribution centers with reduced complexity and less data throughput. This also saves on the costs required to set up additional infrastructure to support the separate SAP EWM server instance.

Note

We recommended not deploying SAP EWM as an add-on to SAP ERP if you have plans to upgrade to SAP S/4HANA 1909 because currently there's no release of SAP EWM as an add-on for SAP S/4HANA. Hence, this limits any migration option for adopting SAP S/4HANA 1610 or 1709 and leveraging an existing SAP EWM add-on setup.

When choosing among the various deployment options, businesses also need to review other criteria, such as their strategic business road maps, scalability impacts, and hardware and operation costs. For example, if you choose a centralized option, then you can only connect a single SAP S/4HANA system to the embedded EWM application. This SAP S/4HANA system will be the system on which the application is sitting. When assessing the scalability impact, businesses will have to consider the proposed growth of their warehousing operations. Massive increases in volumes and throughput can significantly affect system performance, thus creating operational risks. Operational costs also become a factor because deploying SAP EWM on a separate instance would require separate maintenance of servers and database space, which can be reduced with centralized deployment.

At the end of the day, it's up to each business to review the advantages and disadvantages of each of the deployment options and decide which path to follow for their implementation project. For more details on SAP EWM deployment option best practices, see SAP Note 1606493.

Note

Because embedded EWM is only available in SAP S/4HANA 1909 on-premise, the scope of this book will be limited to discussing embedded EWM features and capabilities in the on-premise environment. Whenever a reference is made to SAP S/4HANA, readers can assume that we're talking about on-premise SAP S/4HANA 1909.

1.4.2 Decentralized EWM on SAP S/4HANA

To enable current customers to use their existing SAP ERP or SAP S/4HANA landscapes, SAP provided a new deployment option known as decentralized EWM on SAP S/4HANA. In all versions of SAP S/4HANA prior to SAP S/4HANA 1809 FSP 01, embedded EWM could only be used with close integration with inventory management (IM) processes within the SAP S/4HANA system. This was disadvantageous for clients who wanted to run their SAP S/4HANA or SAP ERP system on a separate client than that of their embedded EWM application to ensure higher performance levels and warehouse business process continuity in case of any SAP S/4HANA system downtime.

Note

In Chapter 5, we'll discuss the master data integration required for running decentralized EWM on SAP S/4HANA, which provides an overview of the technical setup and objects required for the integration of master data objects between SAP ERP and decentralized EWM.

Until the release of SAP S/4HANA 1809 FSP 00, embedded EWM could only be used with IM in the same SAP S/4HANA client. The capability for any SAP customer, based on their business continuity, system performance, or legal requirement, to implement embedded EWM in a decentralized deployment manner by integrating it with a different client hosting an SAP ERP or SAP S/4HANA system was technically not provided as part of the embedded EWM application.

To cater to the need for embedded EWM in SAP S/4HANA as an application on a separate client, SAP delivered innovations in SAP S/4HANA 1809 FPS02 on-premise version: decentralized EWM on SAP S/4HANA. Using this deployment option, the embedded EWM in SAP S/4HANA application can be integrated with the IM component of a decentralized SAP ERP or SAP S/4HANA system and doesn't have to depend on the IM of SAP S/4HANA.

Tip

A centralized landscape from the point of view of embedded EWM is the one in which embedded EWM in SAP S/4HANA uses the master data and IM component of the same client in which the embedded EWM is installed. You can't link warehouses of such a deployment to any plant and storage location combination outside of the client. All transactional updates are synchronously received from the SAP S/4HANA core in this case and sent back to the SAP S/4HANA core. No data replication is required from the remote system in this case.

For decentralized deployment, EWM in SAP S/4HANA when activated as decentralized, uses the master data and IM component of another client rather than the one in which embedded EWM is installed. You can't link warehouses of such a deployment to any plant and storage location combination inside the client. All transactional updates are asynchronously received from the SAP S/4HANA core in this case and sent back to the SAP S/4HANA core deployed on a separate client.

The deployment option and process flow differences between centralized and decentralized EWM on SAP S/4HANA are shown in Figure 1.5.

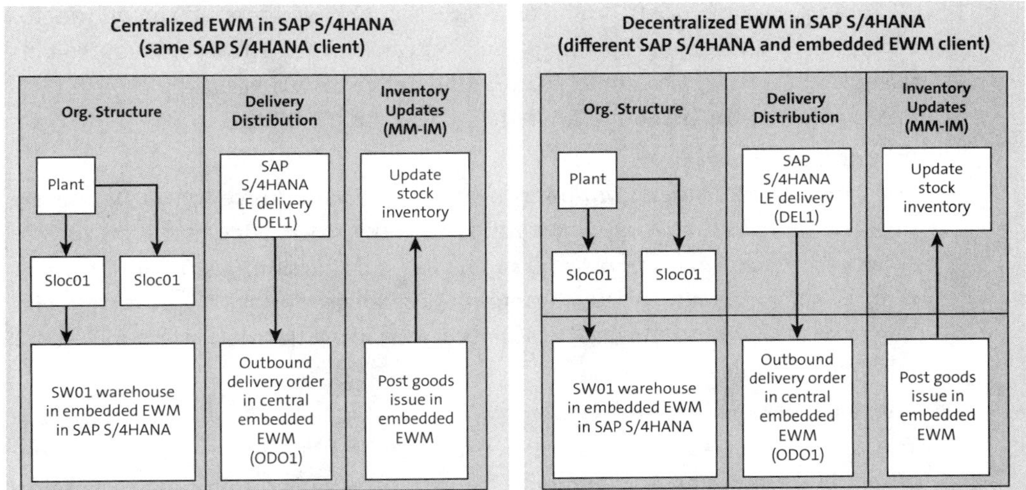

Figure 1.5 Centralized versus Decentralized EWM in SAP S/4HANA

1.4.3 Stock Room Management

A third alternative to embedded EWM or decentralized EWM is stock room management (offered as part of SAP S/4HANA)—a new warehousing landscape for companies with small, low-complexity warehouse operations. It also provides an added incentive to customers who are working with SAP ERP WM to onboard to the SAP S/4HANA application stack without disrupting their warehouse operations due to application upgrade from WM to embedded EWM or decentralized EWM.

Therefore, customers can continue using their existing WM as they onboard to SAP S/4HANA as stock room management but with reduced features so that basic warehousing operations can be executed. The various features of WM in SAP S/4HANA that can be used under stock room management have been combined into various groups, as follows:

- **Inventory management process**
  You can manage stock quantity in different stock categories in the warehouse organization levels, such as storage bin, storage unit, batch, stock status, and stock attributes.
- **Outbound stock movement**
  You can pick the stock from the warehouse bin and move the stock out of the warehouse for business processes such as the following: send to external and internal customers, supply stock to production, return stock to vendors, or supply stock for scrapping or for internal consumption. You can pick the stock from source bins using transfer orders created for outbound deliveries via various picking strategies, such as last in, first out (LIFO); first in, first out (FIFO); and so on.
- **Inbound stock movement**
  You can put away stock from interim staging bins and move the stock into the final warehouse storage bin when you receive the stock using processes such as receive from external vendors, and supply from production, customer returns, or returns from other internal business units. You can use various putaway strategies to put away the stock into final destination bins using transfer orders created for inbound deliveries.
- **Internal stock movement**
  You can pick the stock from source warehouse bins and move the stock to any other physical area of the warehouse using transfer orders. You can use this process for replenishment or reorganization of stock at the end of the day. You can also make use of ad hoc transfer orders to move stock from one place to another based on stock requirements within a warehouse.
- **Physical inventory**
  You can plan, count, and post the physical stock inventory in the bins in the warehouse and compare them with book inventory by using stock room management features. You can post the physical inventory count and correct the book inventory based on regular counting of the stock. The three different ways of counting supported in stock room management are as follows:
  - Annual counting
  - Continuous counting
  - Cycle counting
- **Reports for stock data**
  You can gain information about open and confirmed warehouse transfer orders, stock information in bins, information about the bins attributes and information

about open and closed transfer requirements, and so on by using various reports available in WM.

1.5 Basic and Extended Warehouse Management

In this section, we'll talk briefly about the two levels of warehouse management available within embedded EWM in SAP S/4HANA and how you can adopt them in your deployment.

The two modes in which users can use embedded EWM in SAP S/4HANA are basic warehouse management and advanced warehouse management. Basic warehouse management covers basic warehouse management functionalities for small, low-complexity warehouses. The features available in basic warehouse management in embedded EWM are included in the SAP S/4HANA system by default. Advanced warehouse management, also called extended warehouse management, includes advanced warehouse management functionalities that are ideal for medium- to large warehouses with medium- to high-complexity processes. You'll need an additional license to use the functionalities provided by advanced warehouse management. Table 1.2 highlights some of the key differences between basic and advanced warehouse management.

Basic Warehouse Management	Advanced Warehouse Management
▪ Warehouse structure ▪ Inventory management ▪ Inbound processing ▪ Outbound processing ▪ Internal warehouse movements ▪ Physical inventory ▪ Warehouse management monitor ▪ Resource management ▪ Quality management ▪ Production integration	▪ Inventory management optimization ▪ Inbound process optimization ▪ Outbound process optimization ▪ Material flow control ▪ Yard management ▪ Labor management ▪ Value-added services ▪ Kitting ▪ Cross docking ▪ Warehouse billing ▪ Cartonization planning ▪ SAP Dock Appointment Scheduling ▪ Shipping and receiving ▪ Transit warehousing

Table 1.2 Basic and Advanced Warehouse Management Functions

You can select the warehouse management level from the three available options via IMG path, **SCM Extended Warehouse Management • Extended Warehouse Management • Master Data • Acknowledge Use of Advanced Functions** (see Figure 1.6).

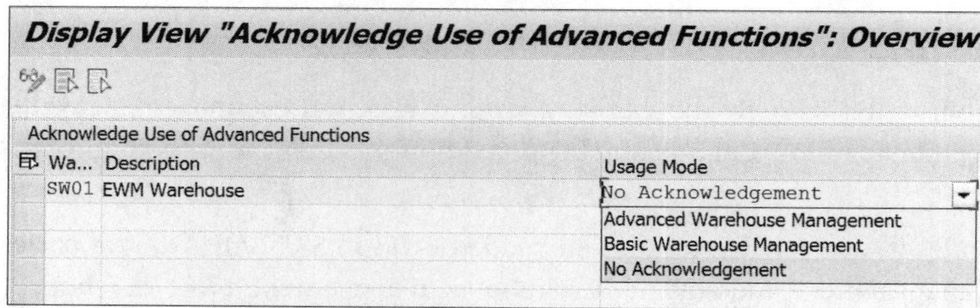

Figure 1.6 Acknowledge Use of Warehouse Functions

You can change the warehouse management level at any point, provided your license agreement fulfills the required criteria.

1.6 Summary

In this chapter, we discussed SAP's supply chain offering in SAP S/4HANA—embedded EWM—as well as warehouse management and the warehousing solutions offered by SAP. As we progressed through the chapter, we discussed the integration features of embedded EWM as an application component in SAP S/4HANA. We discussed the migration scenarios that you might face when trying to adopt embedded EWM in SAP S/4HANA, including new features such as decentralized EWM on S/4HANA and stock room management. Finally, we talked about the basic and advanced warehouse management functionality levels that are available to end users for deployment. In the next chapter, we'll introduce you to organizational structures in embedded EWM.

Chapter 2
Organizational Structures

In this chapter, we'll talk about the organizational structure that forms the foundation for setting up the enterprise and executing warehouse operations. The enterprise structure setup is a one-time activity and, as such, should clearly align with the organizational structure for an accurate mapping of business processes.

An organizational structure gives a hierarchical layout of various entities that create the organization, with each entity having a distinct function and role. The organizational structure for any embedded EWM implementation is always set up in the master system. Such was the case with standalone SAP Extended Warehouse Management (SAP EWM). Because SAP EWM is now integrated within SAP S/4HANA, the organizational structure detailed in this chapter is set up in the SAP S/4HANA system. If you're already familiar with warehouse management (WM) and standalone SAP EWM, you'll notice no difference in the way the organizational structure is set up in SAP S/4HANA.

In this chapter, we'll cover the basic organizational structure that needs to be set up in the system for a warehouse to support purchases, sales, and other business operations for any business implementing SAP S/4HANA. We'll describe the client, company, company code, plant, and storage locations. Section 2.6 describes the steps required for creating a warehouse in embedded EWM and integrating it with the SAP S/4HANA warehouse to carry out warehousing.

A sample organizational structure is shown in Figure 2.1 for a small, fictional company, ABC Ltd., which will be used throughout this book to explain various elements in the organizational structure.

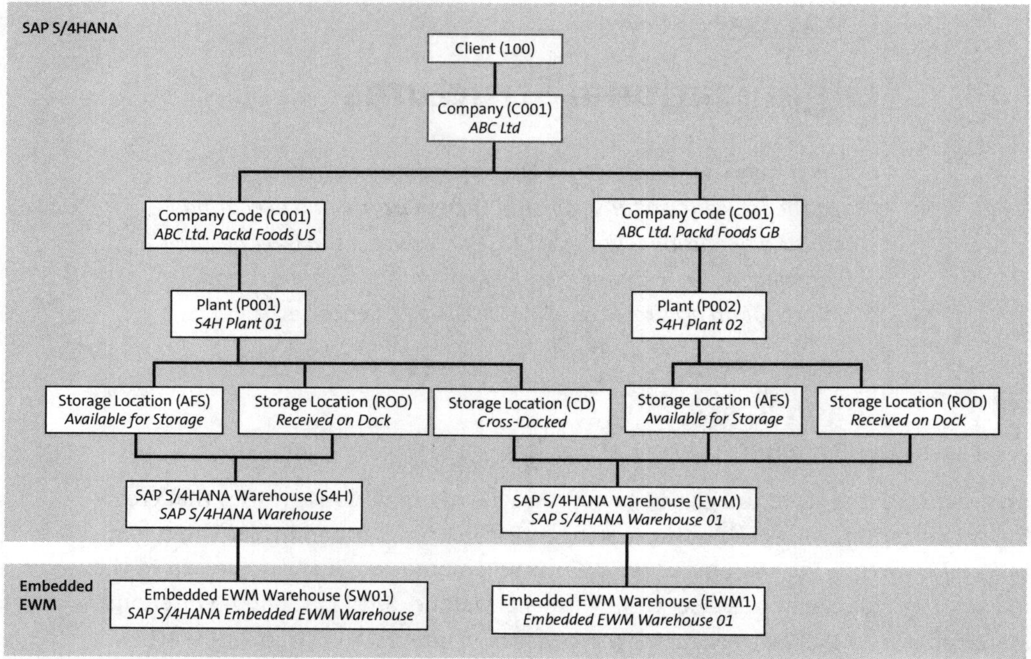

Figure 2.1 Organizational Structure for ABC Ltd. Example Company

2.1 Client

A *client* is a self-contained commercial, organizational, and technical unit within the SAP system. To understand the concept of a client, let's look at an example of a company that has different lines of business, each with its own legal entity, business transactions, reporting structures, and application usage, but tied together under the common objectives for the parent company. The company can be assigned to a client, which will group the different lines of business within the company as separate businesses or legal entities, all aligned with the objectives of the parent company.

A client also can act as a self-contained entity in the SAP system. Businesses can decide to have separate clients for development, testing, and production environments. Choosing how many clients to have from an organizational or technical standpoint should occur at the beginning of the implementation.

Clients can be designed for business units, geographies, or discrete processes. Each client contains its own separate set of tables and authorizations for users to log in. Users belonging to a specific business unit or working on a specific business process log in to a specific client and perform transactions. These transactions are then performed at lower levels, such as company code, purchase organization, plant, or warehouse, but they can be rolled up to the level of the client for legal, administrative, and financial purposes.

As shown in Figure 2.2, when you log in to an SAP system, you can specify which client to log in to.

Figure 2.2 Selecting Login Client in SAP

2.2 Company

A *company* is the next organizational unit in an embedded EWM organizational structure. This optional entity represents a business organization according to the statutory requirements of a country.

In SAP, consolidation of financial transactions and accounting is rolled up at the company level and used for analysis and decision-making. A company can be linked to one or more company codes.

Organizations implementing SAP and creating a company unit should bear the following points in mind:

- Proper design of the organizational structure should be done based on company operations so that companies can be created in SAP based on their lines of business and operational spheres.
- To report financial statements at a company level, company codes can be assigned to the company when the organizational structure is linked in a client.

In our example, company C001 will use client 100 in its organizational structure.

A company can be created via IMG path **Enterprise Structure • Definition • Financial Accounting • Define Company**, as shown in Figure 2.3. Here, you enter the basic information about the company, including name, address, language, and the currency used.

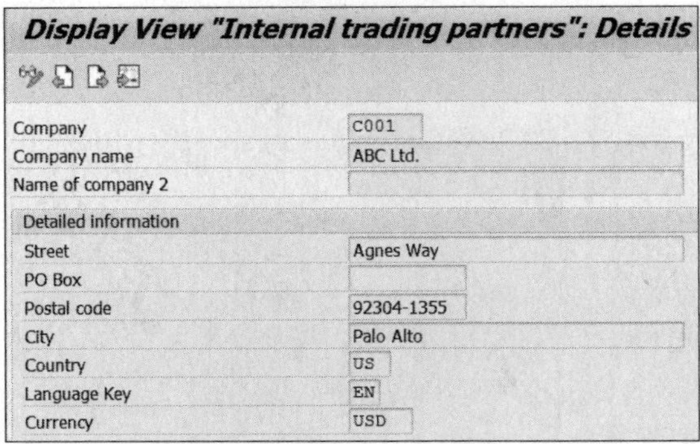

Figure 2.3 Defining the Company

2.3 Company Code

The next element in the organizational structure hierarchy is the *company code*, which is the central organizational unit for external accounting in SAP. The business transactions relevant for a company's financial accounting are entered at the company code level.

A company code in the SAP system represents an independent legal entity; therefore, any financial postings for transactions from lower-level elements of the organizational structures are posted at the company code level.

Choosing how many company codes to create in SAP is based on financial and geographical factors such as currency, country of operations, and so on. Usually, companies in most implementations try to maintain a separate company code for each line of business in a different country because each country has its own financial regulations and documentation to be submitted at the end of each financial year.

In our example, ABC Ltd. has structured its business to have two separate company codes:

- **C001**
  This is the business unit of the company that owns a packaged foods business in the United States.

- C002
  This is the business unit of the company that owns a packaged foods business in the United Kingdom.

Each company code will have its own financial statements, such as balance sheets and profit and loss statements.

Company codes are created in SAP by the financials team based on discussions between business teams from finance, sales, purchasing, and so on, as well as IT. Company codes can be created by navigating to the following IMG path: **Enterprise Structure • Definition • Financial Accounting • Copy, Delete, Check & Edit Company Code**. Then, select **Edit Company Code Data**. Select **New Entries** to create a new company code, and provide the additional data, as shown in Figure 2.4.

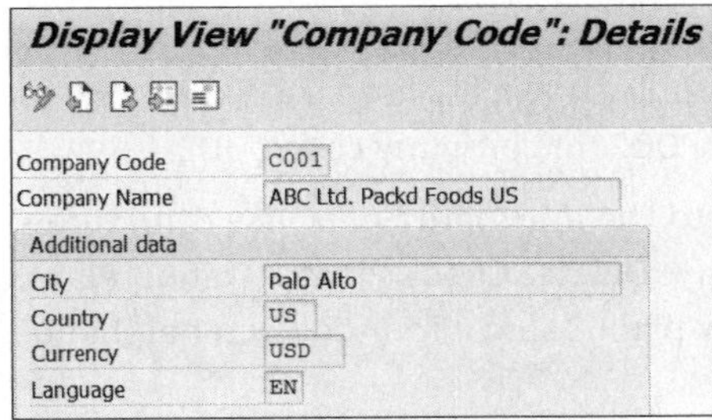

Figure 2.4 Defining the Company Code

In addition to creating a company code from scratch, SAP also provides a way to copy an existing company code. This option copies all the dependent table entries from the source company code to the target company code. To do this, navigate in the IMG to **Enterprise Structure • Definition • Financial Accounting • Copy, Delete, Check & Edit Company Code**, and then select **Copy, Delete, Check Company Code**. Click on and provide the **From** and **To** company codes.

2.4 Plant

A *plant* is the organizational element in SAP under which all planning, procurement, and distribution of goods and services take place within a company code. A plant in SAP can be used to model a manufacturing unit of a company, a distribution center, a warehouse, a contract facility, a third-party warehouse, and so on. While designing its organizational structure, any company must clearly identify the physical entities that have to be defined as plants and whether the stock in each plant is valuated (stock maintained in both quantity and value) or nonvaluated (stock maintained in quantity only).

In SAP, one plant can be linked to only one company code. The inventory stored in a plant can be valued at a plant level. The assignment of a plant to a company code then drives financial accounting based on stock movement into and out of the plant and can be rolled up to the company code level. There are various reasons that a company may decide to create a new plant in SAP: a plant can be created in SAP based on the geographical location of the manufacturing unit, bonded warehouse, or corporate office, for example, or a company might create a different plant for separate financial accounting of goods stored in that plant.

Any stock movement into, out of, or within the plant is captured using a material document. If the plant holds valuated stock, then an accounting document is created along with the material document. In the example shown in Figure 2.1, we've created plant P001 for company code C001 and plant P002 for company code C002.

A plant can be created in SAP by navigating to the IMG path **Enterprise Structure • Definition • Logistics—General • Define, Copy, Delete, Check Plant • Define Plant**. There, click on **New Entries**, and define a new plant using a four-character alphanumeric code, as shown in Figure 2.5.

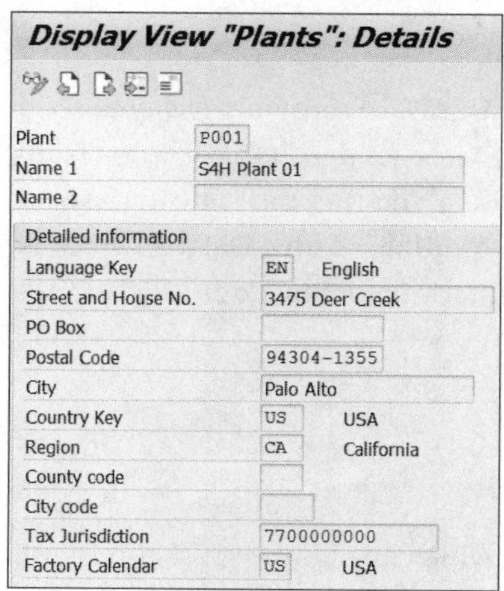

Figure 2.5 Creating the Plant

The plant is then assigned to a company code to roll up the valuation for financial reporting by navigating to **Enterprise Structure • Assignment • Logistics—General •**

Assign Plant to Company Code. Once there, click on **New Entries** and provide the combination of company code (**CoCd**) and plant (**Plnt**) that needs to be mapped, as shown in Figure 2.6.

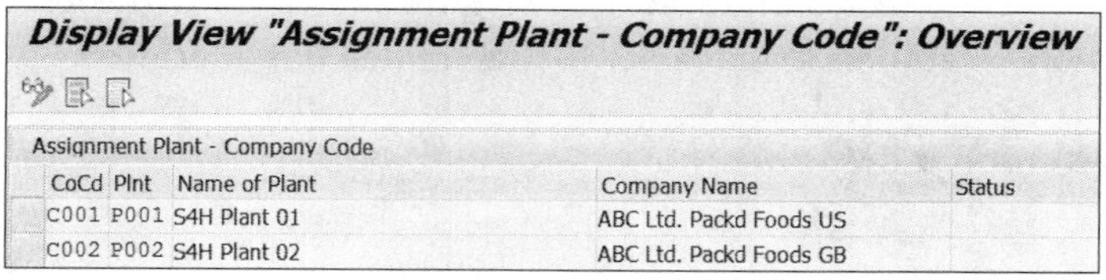

Display View "Assignment Plant - Company Code": Overview

Assignment Plant - Company Code

CoCd	Plnt	Name of Plant	Company Name	Status
C001	P001	S4H Plant 01	ABC Ltd. Packd Foods US	
C002	P002	S4H Plant 02	ABC Ltd. Packd Foods GB	

Figure 2.6 Assigning the Plant to the Company Code

2.5 Storage Location

The next organizational entity after plant in SAP S/4HANA is the *storage location*. Usually, a storage location is a physical place within a plant where material stock is kept, but a storage location can also designate a physical location outside a plant at a certain distance from it, or a plant can have a logical storage location.

Storage locations in materials management/inventory management (MM/IM) refer to the physical locations within a plant where the inventory stock is maintained in quantity, although the valuation of the stock in any storage location is maintained at the plant level. A plant can have many storage locations, but one storage location can only be assigned to one plant. A plant can have various storage locations defined depending on stock ownership, type of stock, and physical location of the storage location.

Which processes the stock undergoes also affects a company's need to create different storage locations. For example, raw materials ready to go into the production process, scrap materials, or stock that requires quality inspections may be required to be stored in a separate storage location.

In interplant stock transfer, stock can move out of a source plant from a storage location and can move into a target plant using a one-step or two-step stock transfer. This can be done for both intracompany stock transfer (quantity posting only) and intercompany stock transfer (both quantity and value posting) using a stock transport order or Transaction MIGO. There are also internal stock movements in which stock moves from one storage location to another within the same plant. Therefore, storage locations play a central role in MM/IM. In our sample organizational structure, we've decided to create two storage locations: ROD for storing goods received on dock, and AFS for storing goods available for sale within plant P001.

In the SAP system, a storage location is defined using a four-character alphanumeric code. To define storage locations in a plant as shown in Figure 2.7, navigate to **Enterprise Structure • Definition • Materials Management • Maintain Storage Location**.

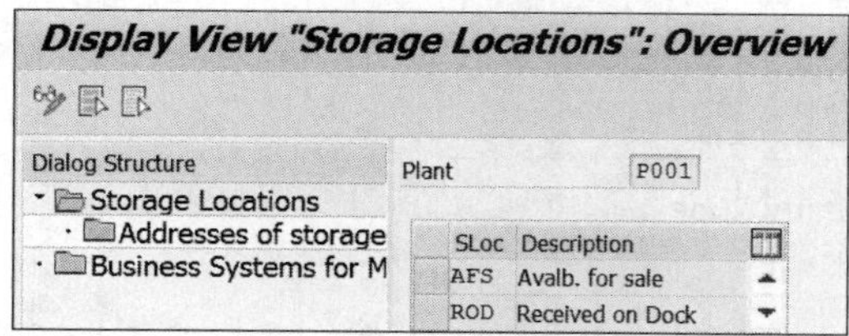

Figure 2.7 Defining Storage Locations for the Plant

While defining the storage location, you must provide the work area or plant for which you want to define the storage location. After the storage location identification code is given, you can also provide an address of the storage location by selecting the storage location and clicking on **Addresses of storage locations** in the **Dialog Structure** on the left side. Because the storage location is defined for a specific plant during creation, no separate assignment to a plant needs to occur.

2.6 Warehouse

A *warehouse* is used for stocking goods to be used later for various supply chain operations. A warehouse is usually a building or closed space used for storage and handling of goods. Warehouses are key organizational elements in the supply chain because goods are continuously moving into and out of them. Depending on business requirements, a warehouse can be private, public, bonded, climate-controlled, and so on. A warehouse can be used to stock any type of good or material, including raw materials from suppliers and finished goods from plants or manufacturers.

In this section, we'll discuss the steps required to create a warehouse in SAP S/4HANA and integrate it with the warehouse in embedded EWM. This will enable users to carry out their warehouse management processes in embedded EWM.

2.6.1 Creating a Warehouse in SAP S/4HANA

The first step in setting up a warehouse for use in embedded EWM in SAP S/4HANA is to set up the warehouse in the SAP S/4HANA system. Each warehouse is assigned to a combination of plant and storage location. We can assign a warehouse to multiple plants, which can also belong to different company codes. As shown earlier in Figure 2.1, we assigned warehouse S4H to plant P001 by mapping the plant and its storage locations to the warehouse.

Define the warehouse in SAP S/4HANA by navigating to **Enterprise • Structure • Definition • Logistics Execution • Define, Copy, Delete, Check Warehouse Number • Define Warehouse Number**, as shown in Figure 2.8. Click on **New Entries**, and define the warehouse in SAP S/4HANA using a three-character alphanumeric code.

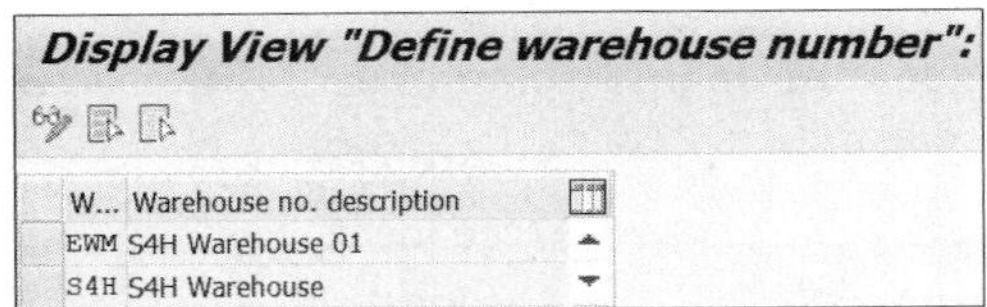

Figure 2.8 Creating the Warehouse in SAP S/4HANA

Next, you assign the warehouse to a plant and storage location by navigating to **Enterprise Structure • Assignment • Logistics Execution • Assign Warehouse Number to Plant/Storage Location**, as shown in Figure 2.9. Click on **New Entries**, and assign the combination of plant and storage location to a warehouse in SAP S/4HANA.

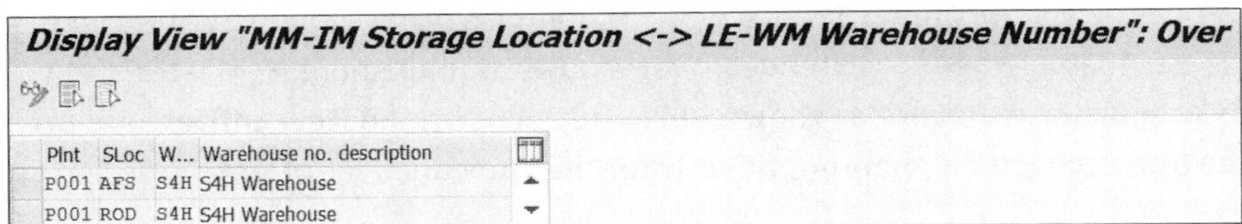

Figure 2.9 Assigning the Plant to the Warehouse

2.6.2 Creating a Warehouse in Embedded EWM

Before we take a deep dive into the configurations required to set up an embedded EWM-specific warehouse, let's discuss the relevance of this warehouse in an embedded EWM implementation:

- The embedded EWM warehouse code represents the highest-level organizational entity in setting up the warehouse structure within embedded EWM. Further elements defining the warehouse structure, such as storage types, storage sections, and bins, are linked to a warehouse code, and most of the configuration and reporting in embedded EWM is done with respect to this warehouse code.
- The stock in an embedded EWM warehouse is logically separated using the concept of a *party entitled to dispose*, which demarcates which part of the stock is owned by which plant in a shared warehouse.
- Any deliveries created in the warehouse are distributed to the embedded EWM application and mapped to the embedded EWM-specific warehouse if the SAP S/4HANA warehouse is marked as **EWM Managed**. From here, all warehouse-specific processes for picking and putaway are handled in EWM.

As shown earlier in Figure 2.1, we've assigned the example warehouse S4H created previously to embedded EWM warehouse SW01.

Shared Warehouses

In earlier versions of WM (before SAP R/3 version 4.0A), there was a restriction by which a single warehouse could be assigned only to a unique combination of plant and storage location. Thus, a warehouse couldn't map stock from different plants. This issue isn't relevant anymore; an embedded EWM warehouse now can be mapped to storage locations assigned to multiple plants.

You can define an embedded EWM-specific warehouse via IMG path **SCM Extended Warehouse Management • Extended Warehouse Management • Master Data • Define Warehouse Numbers**, as shown in Figure 2.10. Click on **New Entries**, and provide the four-character alphanumeric code for the embedded EWM warehouse.

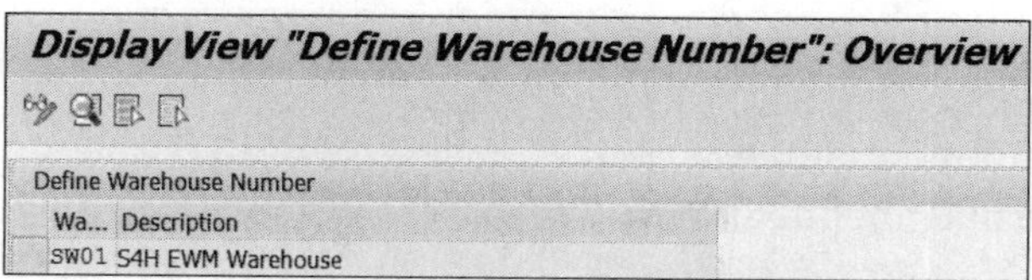

Figure 2.10 Define the Warehouse in Embedded EWM

2.6.3 Linking Embedded EWM and SAP S/4HANA Warehouses

In the next step, you link the EWM warehouse with the warehouse in SAP S/4HANA by clicking on **New Entries** in IMG path **Integration with Other MySAP.com Components • Extended Warehouse Management • Assign Warehouse Number to Warehouse Number of Decentralized SCM System**, as shown in Figure 2.11.

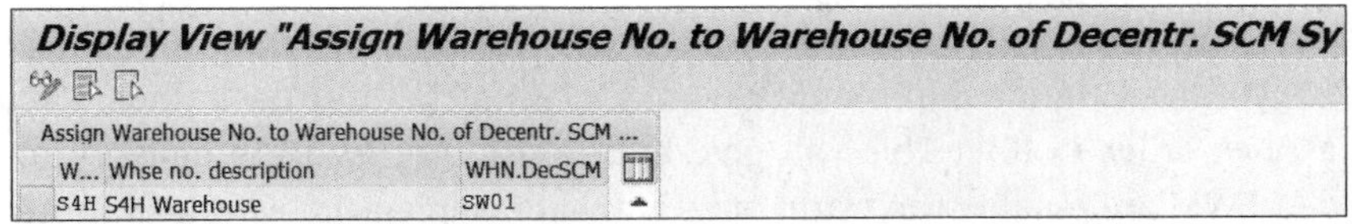

Figure 2.11 Assigning the Warehouse in SAP S/4HANA to the Embedded EWM Warehouse

The next step is to activate the embedded EWM-specific settings for the warehouse in SAP S/4HANA that you previously assigned to the embedded EWM warehouse. You can configure this using IMG path **Logistics Execution • Extended Warehouse Management Integration • Basic Setup of Connectivity • Configure SAP EWM-Specific Parameters**. For the SAP S/4HANA warehouse displayed on the screen, set up the various embedded EWM-specific parameters as shown in Figure 2.12.

Display View "Extended Warehouse Management system": Overview

Extended Warehouse Management system

W...	Whse no. description	Ext. WM	Dist. Mode	UD	BatchDetEW	GR fr. EWM	Comm. WM	Deliv.Chg
S4H	S4H Warehouse	E EWM (Extended Warehouse Management)	Distribution Immediately a	☐	✓	✓	Q Queued and Serialized Asy	☐

Figure 2.12 Configuring the Embedded EWM-Specific Warehouse

The parameters required for this integration are as follows:

- **Warehouse number**
  The mandatory **WhN** indicator is the first entry, and it designates the SAP S/4HANA warehouse that acts as a connection warehouse between SAP S/4HANA and embedded EWM.
- **External warehouse management**
  The **Ext. WM** parameter indicates whether the integration of SAP S/4HANA with respect to warehouse operations is via local WM, a decentralized warehouse management system (WMS), or embedded EWM. To integrate SAP S/4HANA with embedded EWM, this field should be set to **ERP with EWM (Extended Warehouse Management)**.

- **Communication with WM**
  The **Comm. WM** parameter notes how communication should take place between SAP S/4HANA and embedded EWM. For embedded EWM, it should be set to **Queued and Serialized Asynchronous RFC**.
- **Unchecked deliveries**
  The **UD** parameter enables the distribution of unchecked deliveries to embedded EWM from SAP S/4HANA. The unchecked deliveries are created when you create an SAP Customer Relationship Management (SAP CRM) sales order rather than create a sales order in SAP. This will give better visibility into the delivery to embedded EWM and enable the warehouse manager to plan the workload more efficiently.
- **Distribution mode**
  The **Dist. Mode** parameter sets when the deliveries will be distributed to embedded EWM from SAP S/4HANA. If you want deliveries to be distributed to embedded EWM immediately after creation, select the **Distribution Immediately at Document Creation** option. If this setting is set to **Stop Distribution**, then you can manually distribute deliveries from the warehouse monitor using Transaction LL04.
- **Batch determination in embedded EWM**
  The **BatchDetEW** parameter controls whether batch selection is allowed in embedded EWM. After you set this parameter, the batch selection criteria are passed to embedded EWM, where batch selection can be performed.

Note

As a prerequisite for setting this indicator, automatic batch determination should be activated for both sales orders and deliveries in SAP S/4HANA.

- **Goods receipt from embedded EWM only**
  The **GR fr. EWM** parameter controls if an inbound delivery can be created due to a production order or process order in both SAP S/4HANA and embedded EWM. If this parameter isn't set, delivery for process orders and production orders can be created in both systems, resulting in overdelivery of order quantity. If the parameter is set, then the delivery can only be created in embedded EWM.

Note

In addition to using embedded EWM in SAP S/4HANA, you can also manage warehouse stock using a decentralized WMS or standalone SAP EWM (i.e., SAP EWM on an SAP Supply Chain Management [SAP SCM] system). The decentralized WMS can be an SAP system or an external application. You can set up the warehouse with a decentralized WMS using the following IMG path: **Logistics Execution • Decentralized WMS Integration • Central Processing • Application • Activate Decentralized WMS**.

2.6.4 Linking Decentralized EWM on SAP S/4HANA with SAP ERP

Several SAP ERP integration-related settings have been added for decentralized EWM in SAP S/4HANA to integrate it easily with the SAP ERP system:

- **Skip request for messages from SAP ERP**
  In decentralized EWM, if you want to skip creating a warehouse request notification but want to directly create a processing document (e.g., inbound delivery or outbound delivery order) when you replicate a delivery from SAP ERP, you can do so by activating the **Skip** checkbox at the warehouse level. Not only can you skip the warehouse request notification, but this setting also allows you to split the inbound delivery notification into various inbound delivery documents and split outbound delivery requests into outbound delivery orders based on different routes at the line item level. To make this setting, follow SAP IMG path **SCM Extended Warehouse Management • Extended Warehouse Management • ERP Integration • ERP Integration for Decentralized EWM • SCM Extended Warehouse Management • Extended Warehouse Management • Interfaces • ERP Integration • ERP Integration for Decentralized EWM • Set Control Parameters For ERP Version Control**. Click on **New Entries**; enter the document type, category, warehouse, and business system; and then activate the **Skip** checkbox.
- **Set control parameters for SAP ERP version control**
  You can set which features are to be eliminated for decentralized EWM or whose behaviors are to be changed in such a way that their confirmations are in line with the connected SAP ERP. As shown in Figure 2.13, you add this setting by clicking on **New Entries**, entering the SAP ERP **Business System**, **SAP Release**, **Package Name**, and all other parameter settings via SAP IMG path **SCM Extended Warehouse Management • Extended Warehouse Management • Interfaces • ERP Integration •**

ERP Integration for Decentralized EWM • Set Control Parameters for ERP Version Control.

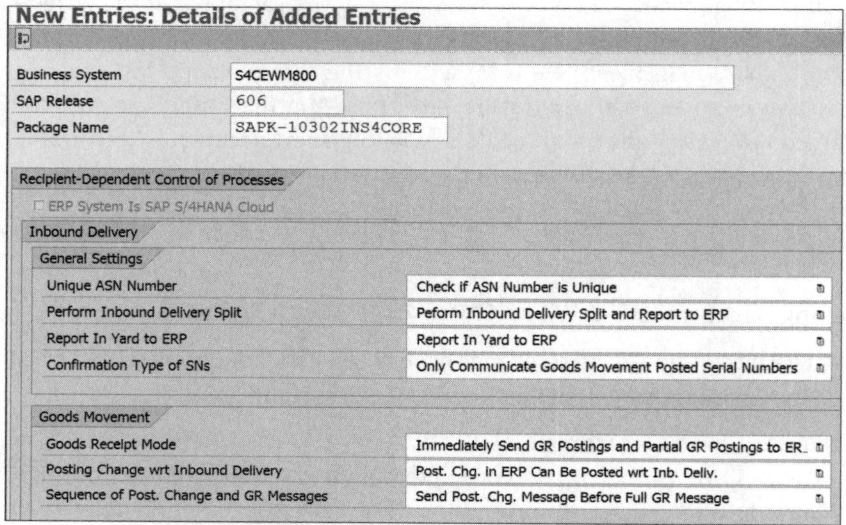

Figure 2.13 Setting Control Parameters for SAP ERP Version Control

- **Goods receipt process for decentralized EWM**
  Embedded EWM doesn't have an expected goods receipt document creation process because the expected goods receipt documents are created entirely in embedded EWM based on purchase or manufacturing orders. However, when decentralized EWM is activated, you can again integrate the purchase order or manufacturing order using an expected goods receipt document and then use that document to create an inbound delivery and a complete putaway process.

  You must complete the following settings to use the expected goods receipt process in decentralized EWM via SAP IMG path **SCM Extended Warehouse Management • Extended Warehouse Management • Goods Receipt Process • Goods Receipt Process for Decentralized EWM • Expected Goods Receipt**:

  - **Define Document Types for Expected Goods Receipt**
    Using this setting, you define the document type to be used for the expected goods receipt process in decentralized EWM. You must click on **New Entries** and enter the document type as well as related parameters for expected goods receipt document types.

- **Define Item Types for Expected Goods Receipt**
  Using this setting, you define the item type to be used for the expected goods receipt process in decentralized EWM. You must click on **New Entries** and enter the item type as well as related parameters for expected goods receipt item types.
- **Define Allowed Item Types for Expected Goods Receipt**
  Using this setting, you define the allowed item type to be used for expected goods receipt for document types in decentralized EWM. You must click on **New Entries** and enter the item type for the expected goods receipt document types.
- **Define Document Type Determination for Expected Goods Receipt**
  Using this setting, you define the document type determination to be used for expected goods receipt for SAP ERP purchase orders or manufacturing orders in decentralized EWM. You must click on **New Entries** and then enter the expected goods receipt document type for the SAP ERP document type and document category.
- **Define Item Type Determination for Expected Goods Receipt**
  Using this setting, you define the item type determination to be used for the expected goods receipt process for ERP purchase orders or manufacturing orders in decentralized EWM. You must click on **New Entries** and enter the expected goods receipt item type for the ERP document type, document category, hierarchy type, item category, and predecessor expected goods receipt item type.

To set up quality management (QM) integration between SAP ERP and decentralized EWM, a basic indexing is set up for the inspection documents. If you search for an inspection document, a sample, or an item based on properties such as a material and a plant, for example, the system uses the defined indexes for the search. You define the indexes via SAP IMG path **SCM Extended Warehouse Management • Extended Warehouse Management • Cross-Process Settings • Quality Management • Quality Management for Decentralized EWM • Basics & Integration • Define Indexes for QIE Objects**. You must click on **New Entries** and then enter the **Index**, **Object Type**, and appropriate **Property** to set up the indexes for the QM process, as shown in Figure 2.14.

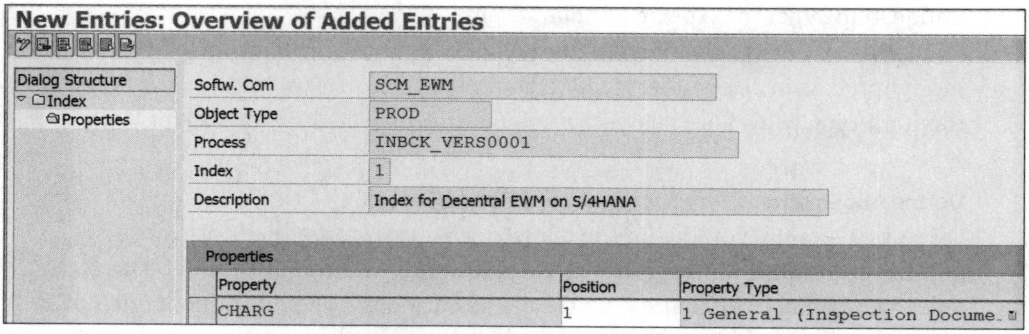

Figure 2.14 Quality Integration Indexes for Decentralized EWM

To set up QM integration between SAP ERP and decentralized EWM, a basic QM planning is set up for the inspection documents. The QM planning process involves various settings such as QM document types, samples, findings, counting, dynamic modifications, and number ranges, which are required to execute the quality inspection successfully. The various QM-related settings to be set up are as follows:

- **Define number ranges for inspection documents**
  You set up the number range for inspection documents to be created in decentralized EWM using SAP IMG path **SCM Extended Warehouse Management • Extended Warehouse Management • Cross-Process Settings • Quality Management • Quality Management for Decentralized EWM • Inspection Planning • Define Number Ranges for Inspection Documents.** You must click on **New Entries (+)** and enter the new number ranges.
- **Dynamic modification**
  You define the properties of the inspection object that are used to form the quality level using dynamic modifications. Using the IMG path, **SCM Extended Warehouse Management • Extended Warehouse Management • Cross-Process Settings • Quality Management • Quality Management for Decentralized EWM • Inspection Planning • Dynamic Modification**, you can define both dynamic modification criteria and rules by clicking on **New Entries** and adding the criteria and rules along with their parameters.
- **Counting**
  You define the quantity and value intervals for counting during the QM process using the IMG path **SCM Extended Warehouse Management • Extended Warehouse Management • Cross-Process Settings • Quality Management • Quality Management for Decentralized EWM • Inspection Planning • Counting**. Click on

New Entries to add and define both quantity and value interval, along with their parameters.

- **Findings**
  You define the settings for findings during the QM process using the IMG path **SCM Extended Warehouse Management • Extended Warehouse Management • Cross-Process Settings • Quality Management • Quality Management for Decentralized EWM • Inspection Planning • Findings**. Click on **New Entries** to add and define finding catalogs, finding types and their number ranges, and their related parameters.
- **Samples and items**
  You define the settings for samples and items using the IMG path **SCM Extended Warehouse Management • Extended Warehouse Management • Cross-Process Settings • Quality Management • Quality Management for Decentralized EWM • Inspection Planning • Samples and Items**. Click on **New Entries** to add and define sample types, item types, and number ranges, along with their parameters.
- **Define document types**
  You can define new document types for document assignment in the inspection rule. You can define the same via SAP IMG path **SCM Extended Warehouse Management • Extended Warehouse Management • Cross-Process Settings • Quality Management • Quality Management for Decentralized EWM • Inspection Planning • Define Document Types**. Click on **New Entries** and add new document types along with the required characteristics and parameters.

To set up QM integration between SAP ERP and decentralized EWM, the QM inspection result is set up so that the inspection results can be assigned to the inspection documents. The QM inspection planning process involves various settings, such as QM decision codes, error codes, and efforts and follow-up actions, which are required to successfully execute the quality inspection and finish it using the inspection results. These settings are set up via SAP IMG path **SCM Extended Warehouse Management • Extended Warehouse Management • Cross-Process Settings • Quality Management • Inspection Results**. Click on **New Entries** to add the relevant objects and their associated parameters and properties.

> **Note**
>
> Decentralized EWM can be connected to a single SAP ERP system that has an implemented and active customer/vendor integration (CVI) done on the SAP HANA database.

The packaging instructions on the enterprise management system (SAP ERP or SAP S/4HANA) can be replicated as packaging specifications on decentralized EWM.

2.6.5 Mapping Warehouses

After the embedded EWM warehouse is defined, the next step is to map it to an SAP S/4HANA warehouse code. This can be configured as shown in Figure 2.15 via IMG path **SCM Extended Warehouse Management • Extended Warehouse Management • Interfaces • ERP Integration • General Settings • Map Warehouse Number from ERP System to EWM**. Click on **New Entries**, and map the combination of business system and SAP S/4HANA warehouse with the warehouse in embedded EWM.

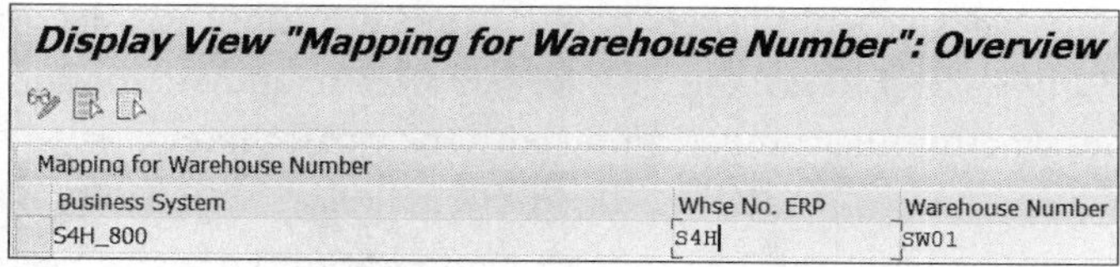

Figure 2.15 Mapping the Warehouse Number in SAP S/4HANA to Embedded EWM

In addition to SAP S/4HANA and embedded EWM warehouses, this setting also applies to other business systems in SAP S/4HANA. This helps to provide a unique combination of business system and SAP S/4HANA warehouse; the same SAP S/4HANA warehouse can be used to map to two different embedded EWM warehouses if it's assigned to different business systems.

2.6.6 Assignment of Business Partners

In this setting, you define the supply chain unit, custodian, default party entitled to dispose, and default ship-to party for the warehouse; this information is used as default data in deliveries created in embedded EWM. First, you need to assign the **Supply Chain Unit**. A supply chain unit is used to map the business characteristics of an organization unit. You can create a supply chain unit for a plant or warehouse and assign it the warehouse business attribute. The **Custodian** is a business partner that maintains physical ownership of stock, but not legal ownership, as in the case of consignment stock. The **Dflt. Pty Entld** setting is used to define the default party entitled to dispose, which is the business partner responsible for planning the movement of goods in and out of the warehouse. This is usually the plant for the embedded EWM warehouse. The **Default Ship-to Party** is used to specify the default customer to which goods are sent in specific business processes, such as direct outbound deliveries. (The concepts of business partners and supply chain units will be explained in more detail in Chapter 5.)

To assign business partners and supply chain units to an embedded EWM warehouse, use Transaction /SCWM/LGNBP, or go to the **SAP Easy Access** menu path: **Logistics • SCM Extended Warehouse Management • Extended Warehouse Management • Settings • Assignments: Warehouse Numbers/Business Partners**. Click on **New Entries**, and assign the supply chain unit and relevant business partners to the embedded EWM warehouse.

> **Note**
> Without this setting established, the system won't be able to perform correct delivery replication and goods movement postings. This setting provides the connection between plant, storage location, and warehouse in embedded EWM.

2.6.7 Delivery Split

The delivery split indicator is used in SAP S/4HANA as a control parameter to ensure that delivery items designated for different warehouses are sent to corresponding warehouses when there are multiple line items in the delivery requiring goods issue from different warehouses. The delivery split is configured both for delivery type and warehouse number, as shown in Figure 2.16.

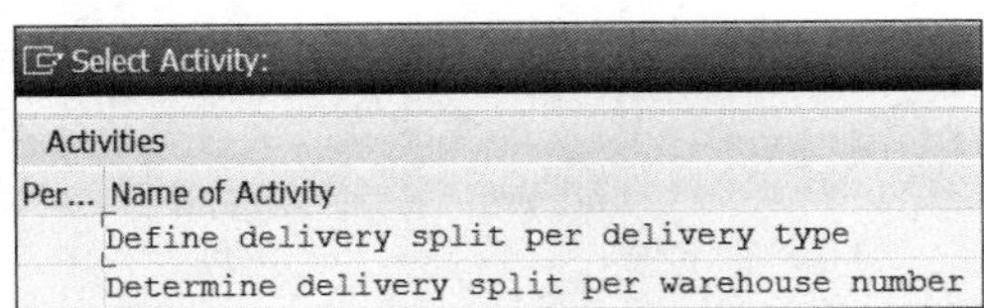

Figure 2.16 Setting the Delivery Split in SAP S/4HANA

You can configure the delivery split from the IMG path **Logistics Execution • Shipping • Deliveries • Define Split Criteria for Deliveries • Delivery Split by Warehouse Number**. Select the **Define Delivery Split per Delivery Type** option, and set the **Delivery Split - WhNo** indicator for the delivery types that are required to be transferred to embedded EWM for the embedded EWM warehouse, as shown in Figure 2.17.

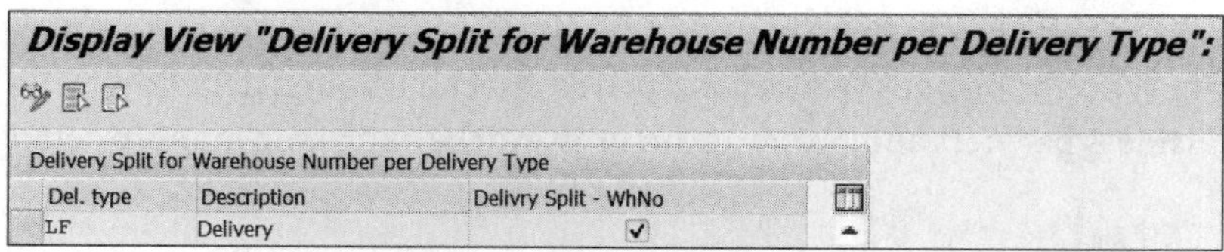

Figure 2.17 Delivery Split for Warehouse Number per Delivery Type

2.7 Summary

In this chapter, we discussed setting up an organizational structure in SAP. The organizational structure includes elements such as client, company, company code, plant, warehouse, and so on. Each entity was explained from a system point of view to enable you to create the required organizational structure for project implementation. We also discussed the settings required to integrate the SAP S/4HANA warehouse and embedded EWM, which will help you replicate deliveries in embedded EWM and post goods movements back to SAP S/4HANA. In the next chapter, we will discuss the basic integration settings that need to be established in embedded EWM and in SAP S/4HANA before the two systems can interact.

3

Chapter 3
First Steps in Implementing Embedded EWM in SAP S/4HANA

Embedded EWM in SAP S/4HANA requires some basic integration settings to be established before the two systems can interact with each other seamlessly. In this chapter, we'll cover the steps for setting up the system integration and data transfer.

SAP S/4HANA 1909 comes with an embedded EWM application component. However, a few integration steps are still required to allow the exchange of master data and transactional data between the two. After installing and configuring SAP S/4HANA, the next step is to set up the queued remote function call (qRFC) connections between the embedded EWM application component and SAP S/4HANA. Setting up these integrations lets you create your warehouse in embedded EWM and integrate it with the enterprise structure of SAP S/4HANA. In the following sections, we'll cover how to set up the warehouse organizational structure, master data, and warehouse processes in embedded EWM.

Note

Although EWM is embedded in SAP S/4HANA 1909, it still acts as an independent application and requires RFC connections to allow it and SAP S/4HANA to exchange transactional data. However, the embedded application benefits from using the same master data for customers, materials, and the like and by avoiding data redundancies, such as direct duplication of deliveries, unlike standalone SAP EWM.

In this chapter, we'll discuss the steps required to set up the integration of SAP S/4HANA and the embedded EWM application component. Section 3.1 covers the basic settings that need to be configured in the SAP S/4HANA system. Next, in Section 3.2, we talk about master data integration in SAP S/4HANA, and we describe the settings required for delivery integration in Section 3.3. In Section 3.4, we cover migration from third-party systems and, in Section 3.5, from warehouse management (WM) to embedded EWM in SAP S/4HANA. In Section 3.6, we cover the details on how to migrate from standalone SAP EWM to decentralized EWM in SAP S/4HANA.

3.1 Basic System Setup

After installing the SAP S/4HANA client, you can either configure the client manually or set up a best practice client and activate the content.

> **Note**
>
> If you're implementing decentralized EWM in SAP S/4HANA, you must enable the **EWM is Decentralized** checkbox using **SAP IMG SCM Extended Warehouse Management • Extended Warehouse Management • Enable Decentralized EWM**.

> **Note**
>
> For more details, refer to the SAP Best Practices content at SAP Service Marketplace (*https://rapid.sap.com/bp*).

In this section, we'll cover the required configuration settings in SAP S/4HANA to set up the integration with embedded EWM. The following steps are usually carried out by the Basis team at your organization:

1. **Define the RFC destination.**
   Communication between the embedded EWM application component and SAP S/4HANA happens via qRFCs. You'll set up RFC destinations for qRFC to help manage communication processes, error handling, and so on.

   The RFC destination can be created in Transaction SM59, which can also be accessed from IMG path **SAP NetWeaver • Application Server • IDoc Interface/ Application Link Enabling (ALE) • Communication • Create RFC Connections**. The name of the RFC destination should match that of the logical system.

2. **Define the logical system.**
   In this step, you define the logical system for SAP S/4HANA. The logical system can be created from Transaction BD54, which can also be accessed from IMG path **SAP**

NetWeaver • Application Server • IDoc Interface/Application Link Enabling (ALE) • Basic Settings • Logical Systems • Define Logical System.

3. **Define the dummy logical system.**
   In this step, you define a dummy logical system for the embedded EWM application. This setting is required for creating the distribution model needed for setting up the qRFC communication. The logical system can be created from Transaction BD54, which can also be accessed from IMG path **SAP NetWeaver • Application Server • IDoc Interface/Application Link Enabling (ALE) • Basic Settings • Logical Systems • Define Logical System**.

> **Note**
> Although EWM is embedded in SAP S/4HANA, a dummy logical system still needs to be created to establish communication between embedded EWM and SAP S/4HANA. Standalone SAP EWM, however, would require you to create an actual logical system for the SAP EWM system.

4. **Assign the logical system to client.**
   In this step, you assign the logical system of SAP S/4HANA to the client. The assignment can be made from IMG path **SAP NetWeaver • Application Server • IDoc Interface/Application Link Enabling (ALE) • Basic Settings • Logical Systems • Assign Logical System to Client**. You can skip this step if the SAP S/4HANA logical system is already assigned to a client.
5. **Determine the RFC destination for the method calls.**
   In this step, you set up the RFC destinations for the method calls in SAP S/4HANA. Enter the RFC destination of the embedded EWM system as the RFC destination in the SAP S/4HANA system. This assignment is made from Transaction BD97, which can also be accessed from IMG path **SAP NetWeaver • Application Server • IDoc Interface/Application Link Enabling (ALE) • Communication • Determine RFC Destinations for Method Calls**.

   You'll also assign the RFC destination for method calls in SAP S/4HANA. This assignment is made from Transaction SE38, which can also be accessed from IMG path **Tools • ABAP Workbench • Development • ABAP Editor**. On the program selection screen, enter "/SCWM/R_ERP_RFC_DEST". In the **RFC Destination** field, enter the RFC destination of the SAP S/4HANA system.
6. **Define the queues.**
   In this step, you define the queues for transfer of data to embedded EWM. You

need to do so because data is sent to embedded EWM using qRFCs. In the **Receiver** field, provide the logical destination of the embedded EWM system. The queues can be defined via IMG path **Logistics Execution • Extended Warehouse Management Integration • Basic Setup of Connectivity • Define Queue for Transfer to SAP EWM**.

7. **Set the QOUT and QIN schedulers.**
   In this step, you set up the scheduler for automated processing of inbound and outbound queues in SAP S/4HANA. Set the QOUT scheduler in Transaction SMQS. While setting the outbound scheduler, set the logical system for the SAP S/4HANA system as the destination because that is where data from qRFCs will be sent. The QIN scheduler is called with Transaction SMQS. For the inbound scheduler, provide the names of inbound queues that need to be registered. If the queues aren't registered, they won't be processed.

The configuration settings that need to be made in the embedded EWM application component to complete the integration with SAP S/4HANA application are as follows:

1. **Define your business system.**
   In this step, you define your own business system. Provide the name of the system where you installed EWM, which, in this case, is the name of the SAP S/4HANA logical system. Figure 3.1 shows how your business system is defined in embedded EWM. Follow IMG path **SCM Extended Warehouse Management • Extended Warehouse Management • Interfaces • ERP Integration • General Settings • Define Business System**.

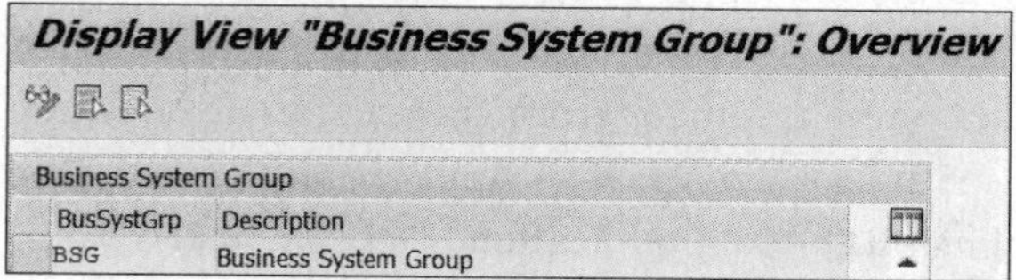

Figure 3.1 Defining Your Own Business System

2. **Define all the systems in the system landscape.**
   In this step, you define the business system and all systems that are part of the system landscape. In this case, provide the name of the SAP S/4HANA logical system. The embedded EWM system uses the business system stored in the warehouse to request documents to identify the logical system of SAP S/4HANA. Figure 3.2 shows how your business system is defined in embedded EWM. Follow IMG path

SCM Extended Warehouse Management • Extended Warehouse Management • Interfaces • ERP Integration • General Settings • Define Business System.

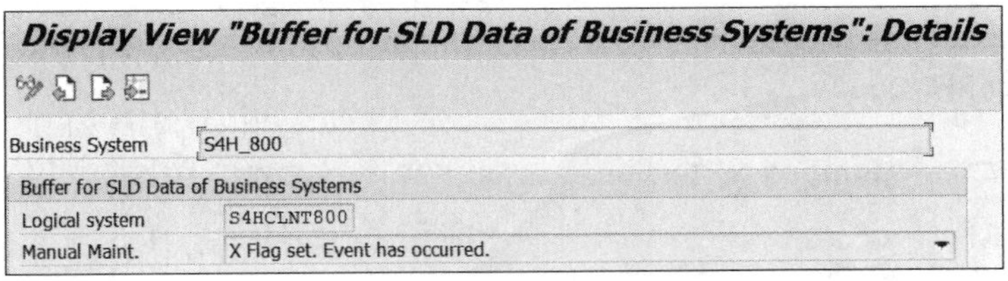

Display View "Buffer for SLD Data of Business Systems": Details

Business System S4H_800

Buffer for SLD Data of Business Systems

Logical system S4HCLNT800

Manual Maint. X Flag set. Event has occurred.

Figure 3.2 Business System Definition

3. **Maintain the business system group.**
   Next, define the business system group as shown in Figure 3.3. Follow IMG path **SCM Extended Warehouse Management • SCM Basis • Integration • Basic Settings for Creating System Landscape • Maintain Business System Group.**

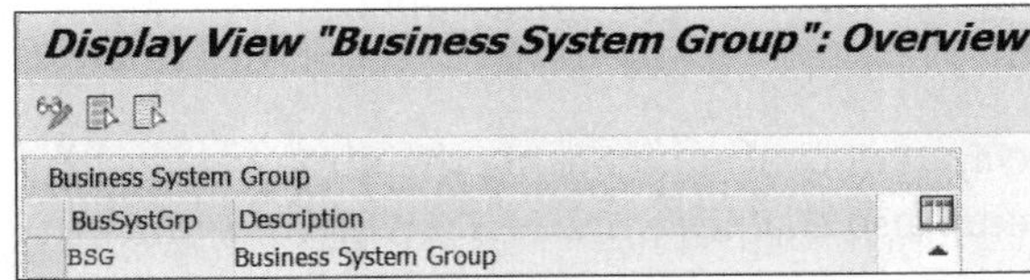

Figure 3.3 Defining the Business System Group

4. **Assign the logical system and queue type.**
   In this step, assign the logical system of SAP S/4HANA and the queue type to the business system group. Figure 3.4 shows the assignment of the business system group to the logical system of the SAP S/4HANA system. Follow IMG path **SCM Extended Warehouse Management • SCM Basis • Integration • Basic Settings for Creating System Landscape • Assign Logical System and Queue Type.**

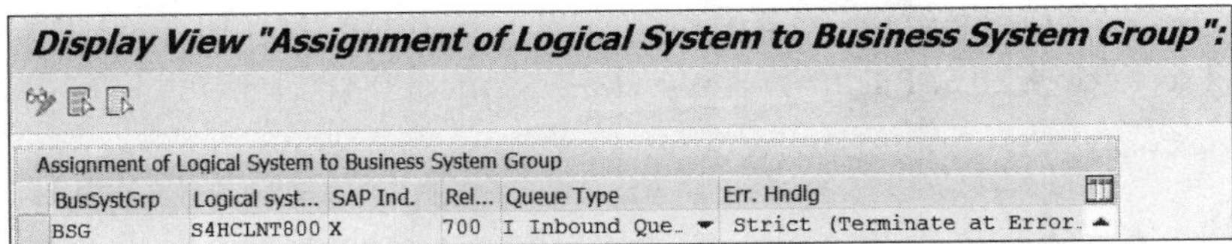

Figure 3.4 Assignment of the Logical System

5. **Define the control settings for the RFC queue.**
   In this step, define the settings for outbound communication from embedded

EWM to SAP S/4HANA. Embedded EWM uses qRFCs to send data related to deliveries and goods movements to SAP S/4HANA. Figure 3.5 shows the control settings required for qRFCs. Follow IMG path **SCM Extended Warehouse Management • Extended Warehouse Management • Interfaces • ERP Integration • General Settings • Control for RFC Queue.**

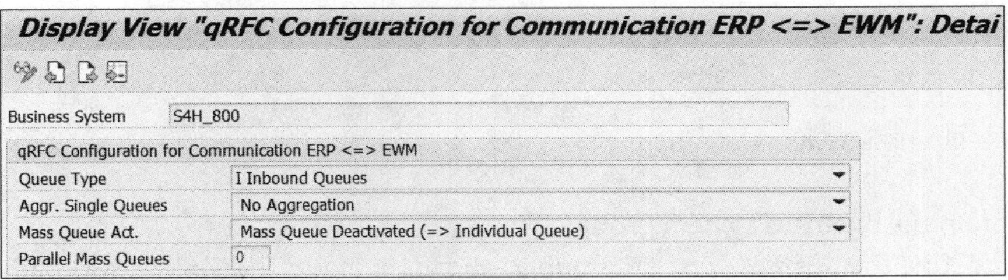

Figure 3.5 Control Settings for the RFC Queue

3.2 Master Data Integration

Embedded EWM leverages the one-system concept by using the same master data that exists in SAP S/4HANA. This setup also enables embedded EWM to use the master data improvements in SAP S/4HANA, such as support for 40-digit material numbers.

Master data objects, such as customers and vendors, are created as *business partners* in SAP S/4HANA and can be reused in embedded EWM. Material masters created in SAP S/4HANA can be used in embedded EWM directly after extending the product master in embedded EWM by providing the embedded EWM warehouse number and the party entitled to dispose. The Core Interface (CIF) is no longer needed with embedded EWM. Embedded EWM uses business partner, material, and batch master data directly, as well as batch classification data created in SAP S/4HANA. The CIF is only needed in embedded EWM for the transfer of customer locations in the transit warehousing scenario with SAP Transportation Management (SAP TM).

Note

Readers familiar with standalone SAP EWM will notice that the CIF is no longer needed to transfer business partner, material, and batch master data in embedded EWM.

The product master can be extended in embedded EWM from Transaction /SCWM/MAT1, which can also be accessed from **SAP Easy Access** path: **Logistics • SCM Extended Warehouse Management • Extended Warehouse Management • Master Data • Product • Maintain Warehouse Product**. (The setup of product master data in embedded EWM will be discussed in detail in Chapter 5, Section 5.3.)

> **Tip**
>
> Materials and batches that were created in SAP S/4HANA releases prior to 1610 must be enabled for use in embedded EWM. To do so, run report PRD_SCM_GUID_CONVERSION for materials and report RVB_BATCH_GUID_GENERATOR for batches.

3.3 Delivery Settings and Integration

When a delivery is created in SAP S/4HANA, the system checks for the plant and storage location and confirms whether the warehouse maintained against that plant and storage location is managed by embedded EWM. If it is, the deliveries in SAP S/4HANA are distributed to embedded EWM via qRFCs. The overall creation of inbound deliveries in embedded EWM requires setting up two important interface configurations.

In the following sections, we explain how to create a distribution model in SAP S/4HANA that will distribute the deliveries to embedded EWM and map the deliveries in embedded EWM with the deliveries in SAP S/4HANA so that the correct embedded EWM delivery type is used. We also explain how to map the plant and storage location in SAP S/4HANA to the warehouse in embedded EWM.

3.3.1 Distribution Model

Deliveries are sent from SAP S/4HANA to embedded EWM via qRFCs. These can be inbound deliveries, outbound deliveries, or posting change requests initiated in SAP S/4HANA. A distribution model decides which objects are transferred from SAP S/4HANA to embedded EWM via qRFC.

The distribution model in SAP S/4HANA is created via IMG path **Logistics Execution • Extended Warehouse Management Integration • Basic Setup of Connectivity • Generate Distribution Model from S/4HANA to SAP EWM**, as shown in Figure 3.6. You provide the name of the warehouse in SAP S/4HANA (**Warehouse Number**), the logical system for embedded EWM (**Logical System of SAP EWM**), and a name for the view of the distribution model for which you need to create entries (**Distribution Model View**); then, click . The delivery model creation tells the system which function module will be called at the time of delivery creation changes or for creation of production material requests in embedded EWM on the basis of manufacturing orders in SAP S/4HANA.

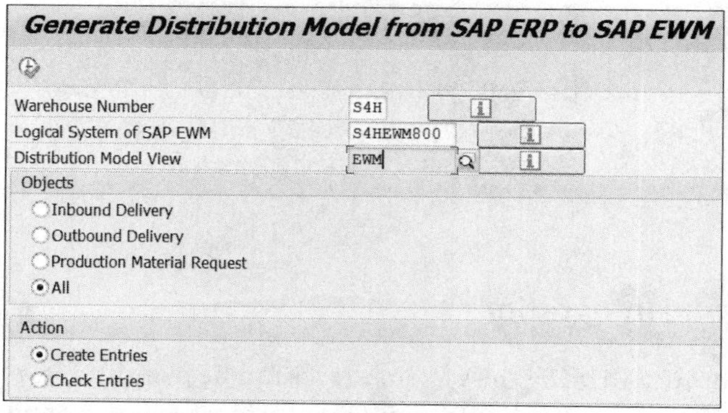

Figure 3.6 Generating the Distribution Model

You don't need a distribution model for transferring the deliveries back to SAP S/4HANA. The embedded EWM system triggers the Post Processing Framework (PPF) action in deliveries and uses the logical system in the reference document to find the corresponding SAP S/4HANA system in which the delivery needs to be updated for delivery changes, splits, or confirmation of goods receipt or issue.

3.3.2 Delivery Mapping in Embedded Extended Warehouse Management

In this section, we'll cover the basic configuration settings for delivery document integration and processing. The following mappings are necessary for the seamless flow of transactional data from SAP S/4HANA to embedded EWM:

1. **Define the number range for SAP S/4HANA documents.**
   Set up the number range for delivery documents created in embedded EWM and sent to SAP S/4HANA. You can create delivery documents directly in embedded EWM either manually or automatically upon delivery split. The number range should be an internal number range and should not overlap with the number range defined for deliveries in SAP S/4HANA. The setting can be made from IMG

path **SCM Extended Warehouse Management • Extended Warehouse Management • Interfaces • ERP Integration • Delivery Processing • Define Number Range for ERP Documents**. Click on [Intervals] to create a new number range.

2. **Map document types from the SAP S/4HANA system to embedded EWM.**
   Multiple documents from SAP S/4HANA can be mapped to the document types in embedded EWM. Similarly, multiple document types from embedded EWM can be mapped to one document type in the SAP S/4HANA system.

   The setting can be made from IMG path **SCM Extended Warehouse Management • Extended Warehouse Management • Interfaces • ERP Integration • Delivery Processing • Map Document Types from ERP System to EWM**. Once there, click on **New Entries** to map the document type in the SAP S/4HANA system to the document type in the embedded EWM system.

3. **Map item types from the SAP S/4HANA system to embedded EWM.**
   Multiple item types from SAP S/4HANA can be mapped to the item types in embedded EWM. Similarly, multiple item types from embedded EWM can be mapped to one item type in the SAP S/4HANA system. The setting can be made from IMG path **SCM Extended Warehouse Management • Extended Warehouse Management • Interfaces • ERP Integration • Delivery Processing • Map Item Types from ERP System to EWM**. Once there, click on **New Entries** to map the item type in the SAP S/4HANA system to the item type in the embedded EWM system.

4. **Map data types from the SAP S/4HANA system to embedded EWM.**
   In this setting, you map the date/item type in the SAP S/4HANA system to the date/types in embedded EWM. The system considers the planned and actual start and end dates/times. The start and end dates/times are recorded in the warehouse request as planned start and end dates/times. If you choose to send confirmation of the start or end date/time or both, the system sends the actual goods received or goods issue time to the SAP S/4HANA system, which is updated in the delivery. The setting can be made from IMG path **SCM Extended Warehouse Management • Extended Warehouse Management • Interfaces • ERP Integration • Delivery Processing • Map Data Types from ERP System to EWM**. Once there, click on **New Entries**, and map the date/item type in the SAP S/4HANA system with the **Start Date** and **End Date** in the warehouse request in embedded EWM.

   Figure 3.7 shows how the start and end date/time types are mapped from SAP S/4HANA to embedded EWM.

Display View "Mapping ERP Date/Time Types": Overview of Selected Set

Mapping ERP Date/Time Types

Business System	DType ERP	Doc. Type	Item Type	Start Date	End Date	Conf.D/T
	WSHDRKODAT	OUTB	ODLV	SPICK	EPICK	E Confirm End Date
	WSHDRLDDAT	OUTB	ODLV	SLOAD	ELOAD	E Confirm End Date
	WSHDRWADAT	OUTB	ODLV	SGOODSISSUE	EGOODSISSUE	Do Not Confirm Date/Time
	WSHDRWADTI	OUTB	ODLV		EGOODSISSUE	E Confirm End Date

Figure 3.7 Mapping Date/Item Types

5. **Map partner roles from the SAP S/4HANA system to embedded EWM.**
   In this setting, you map the partner roles from the SAP S/4HANA system to the partner roles in embedded EWM. The setting can be made from IMG path **SCM Extended Warehouse Management • Extended Warehouse Management • Interfaces • ERP Integration • Delivery Processing • Map Partner Roles from ERP System to EWM**. Once there, click on **New Entries**, and map the partner role and document type in SAP S/4HANA with the corresponding partner role in embedded EWM.
6. **Control message processing that is dependent on the recipient.**
   In this setting, you set the control for sending data from embedded EWM to the SAP S/4HANA system. You can make the settings for both the embedded EWM document type and the SAP S/4HANA document type. The setting can be made via IMG path **SCM Extended Warehouse Management • Extended Warehouse Management • Interfaces • ERP Integration • Delivery Processing • Control Message Processing Dependent on Recipient**. Once there, click on **New Entries**, and set the control parameters for the document type in embedded EWM, as shown in Figure 3.8.

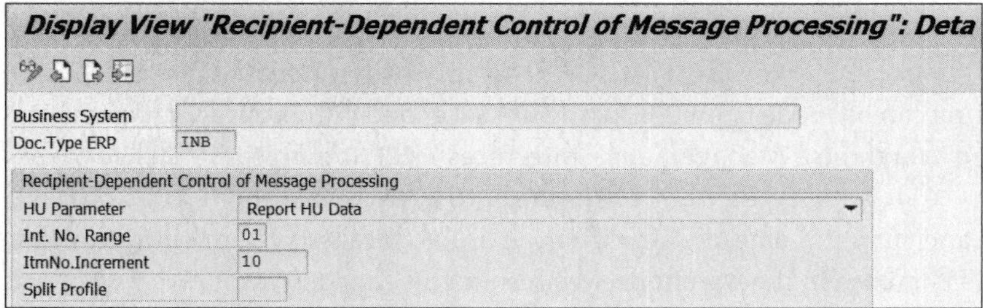

Figure 3.8 Recipient-Dependent Control of Message Processing

3.3.3 Mapping Plant and Storage Location in Embedded EWM

In embedded EWM, you map the plant and storage location for a source SAP S/4HANA logical system to an embedded EWM warehouse. Figure 3.9 shows how the logical system, plant, and storage location are mapped to the embedded EWM warehouse. The setting can be accessed from IMG path **SCM Extended Warehouse Management • Extended Warehouse Management • Interfaces • ERP Integration • Goods Movement • Map Storage Locations from ERP system to EWM**. (We'll discuss availability groups in detail in Chapter 7, Section 7.2.4.)

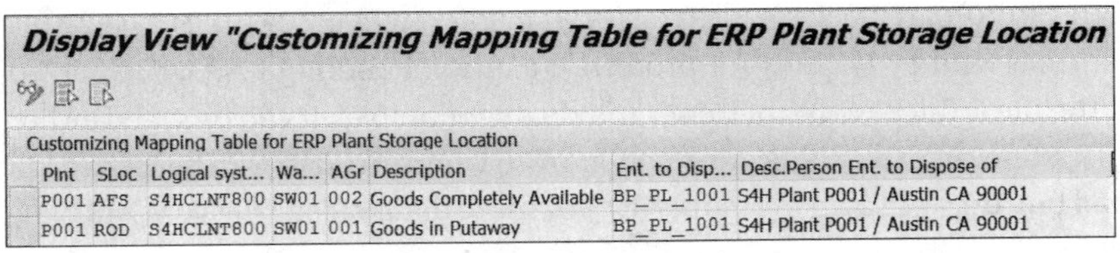

Display View "Customizing Mapping Table for ERP Plant Storage Location

Customizing Mapping Table for ERP Plant Storage Location

Plnt	SLoc	Logical syst...	Wa...	AGr	Description	Ent. to Disp...	Desc.Person Ent. to Dispose of
P001	AFS	S4HCLNT800	SW01	002	Goods Completely Available	BP_PL_1001	S4H Plant P001 / Austin CA 90001
P001	ROD	S4HCLNT800	SW01	001	Goods in Putaway	BP_PL_1001	S4H Plant P001 / Austin CA 90001

Figure 3.9 Mapping Storage Locations in Embedded EWM

3.4 Migration from Third-Party Systems

The overall warehouse landscape of any organization may be built on other third-party applications, such as Manhattan, Oracle Warehouse Management, and so on. In addition, a section of an organization's business might have some warehouses that are managed by embedded EWM and others that are managed by third-party applications.

Whenever enterprises migrate from completely non-SAP applications to embedded EWM in SAP S/4HANA, they also need to migrate their stock, packing details, and storage bin data from the legacy system to embedded EWM so that the right inventory is reflected at the bin level in embedded EWM. This initial data upload from the legacy system is part of the cutover activity in any implementation and has a set of planning and execution steps.

To upload initial data from other legacy systems to embedded EWM, certain initial configurations (e.g., warehouse organization structure) and master data (e.g., bins and product master) must be created successfully. The data can be uploaded using standard SAP tools that require filled comma-separated value (CSV) files in a specific format. The master data to be uploaded using the tools discussed ahead usually comes as an extract from the third-party systems or is created manually. It might need some changes or rearrangements to align with the expected upload file template that can be processed by embedded EWM.

The data upload tools for migrating stock and bin data from third-party systems to embedded EWM are available via **SAP Easy Access** path **Logistics • SCM Extended Warehouse Management • Extended Warehouse Management • Interfaces • Data Upload**.

The objects that can be migrated using these tools are as follows:

- **Initial stock data transfer (Transaction /SCWM/ISU)**
  Stock from a third-party system is extracted and entered in upload files based on a specific format with provisions for product, quantity, handling unit (HU), and so on. After the file is filled with stock data and ready for upload, it can be saved either on a local system or on an application server from where the data can be loaded via the **Upload** button, as shown in Figure 3.10. For more details, see SAP Note 2483936.

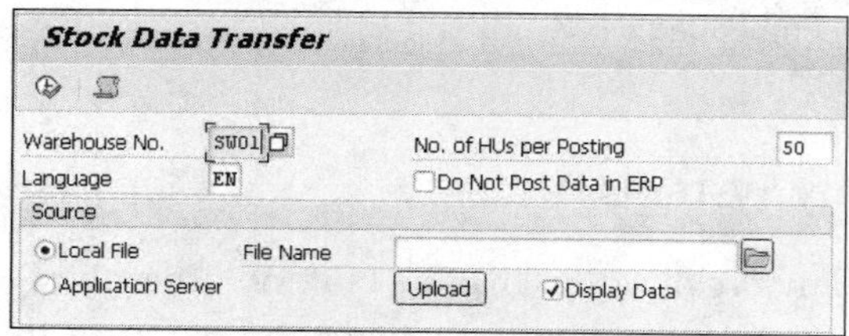

Figure 3.10 Initial Stock Data Transfer

- **Initial data transfer for packaging specification (Transaction /SCWM/IPU)**
  Packaging data from a third-party system is extracted and entered in upload files based on the packaging needs of the organization. A packaging specification report uses the function module `/SCWM/API_PACKSPEC_CREATE` to load the packaging specification. The columns in the CSV file should correspond to the components of structure `/SCWM/S_PS_DL_PS_CSV`. After the file is filled with packaging data and ready for upload, it can be saved either on the local system or on an application server from where the data can be loaded via the **Upload** button, as shown in Figure 3.11.

- **Initial load of storage bins (Transaction /SCWM/SBUP)**
  Storage bins can be uploaded using the same process as for master data. For storage bins, the CSV upload file has the format required for creating bin-specific data, including details for warehouse, storage type, and so on. After the file is filled with bin data and ready for upload, it can be saved either on the local system or on an

application server from where the data can be loaded via the **Upload** button, as shown in Figure 3.12.

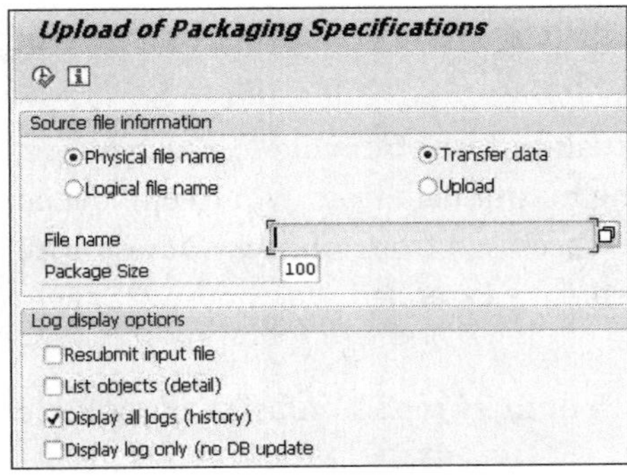

Figure 3.11 Packaging Specification Upload

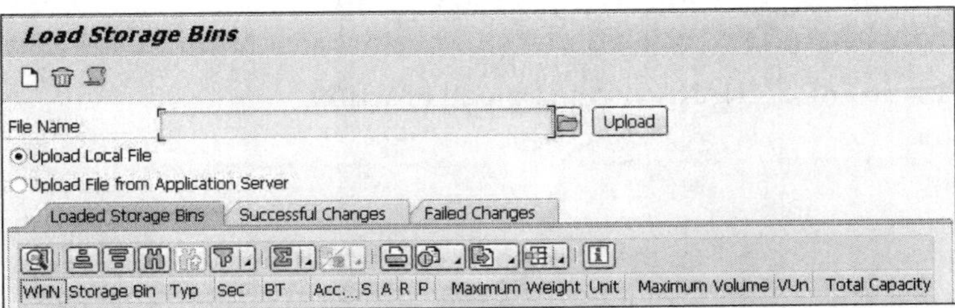

Figure 3.12 Storage Bins Upload

- **Initial load of storage bin sorting (Transaction /SCWM/SRTUP)**
  Storage bin sorting can be uploaded using the same process as for master data. After the file is filled with storage bin data and ready for upload, it can be saved either on the local system or on an application server from where the data can be loaded via the **Upload** button, as shown in Figure 3.13.

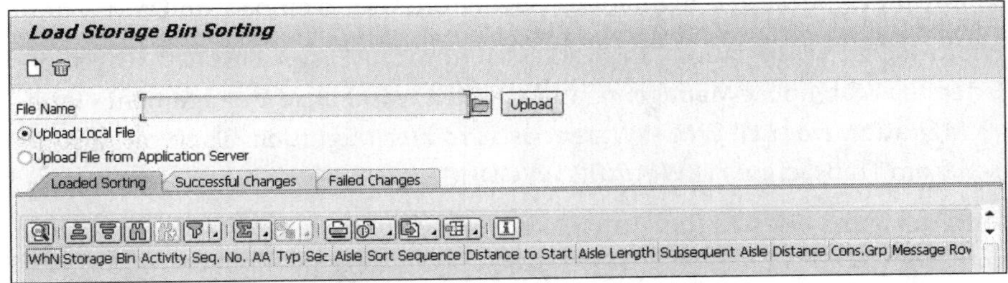

Figure 3.13 Storage Bin Sorting Upload

3.5 Migration from WM to Embedded EWM

Organizations requiring migration to SAP S/4HANA should first decide if they want to use standalone SAP EWM or embedded EWM. In this section, we'll discuss tools for migration from WM to embedded EWM in SAP S/4HANA.

To help organizations with successful master data cutover from old to new systems, SAP has provided standard tools for migrating master data from WM to embedded EWM. The reports for such a migration can be accessed from **SAP Easy Access** path **Logistics • SCM Extended Warehouse Management • Extended Warehouse Management • Interfaces • Migration from LE-WM**.

The usual process for data migration from each of these reports consists of multiple steps:

1. Download data from the source WM warehouse in SAP ERP to a CSV file.
2. After the data is downloaded from the source system in a CSV file, the data is checked for data consistency and validation by the business data team.
3. Upload the CSV file to SAP S/4HANA via the **Upload** function.

> **Warning**
>
> For the migration tool to work, ensure that the source warehouse in SAP S/4HANA is mapped to the target embedded EWM warehouse; otherwise, the report will error out.

3.5.1 Migration of Warehouse Product Data

The warehouse product migration report is used to migrate not only warehouse-specific product data but also data such as fixed bin assignments, palletization, and more. This is the most important data migration report as it helps business teams migrate the most crucial and high-volume data from WM to embedded EWM.

The reports for such a migration can be accessed from **SAP Easy Access** path: **Logistics • SCM Extended Warehouse Management • Extended Warehouse Management • Interfaces • Migration from LE-WM • Warehouse Product Migration**. They can also be accessed from Transaction /SCWM/MIG_PRODUCT.

As shown in Figure 3.14, this tool provides a two-step process to migrate warehouse products from WM to embedded EWM in SAP S/4HANA. In the first step, data is downloaded in a CSV file from various material tables, such as tables `MLGN`, `MLGT`, `MARA`, and so on, from the SAP S/4HANA system on either the local desktop or on the application server. The same template is then used to upload data from the local desktop or application server to SAP S/4HANA from the same transaction screen but by using the **Upload** option.

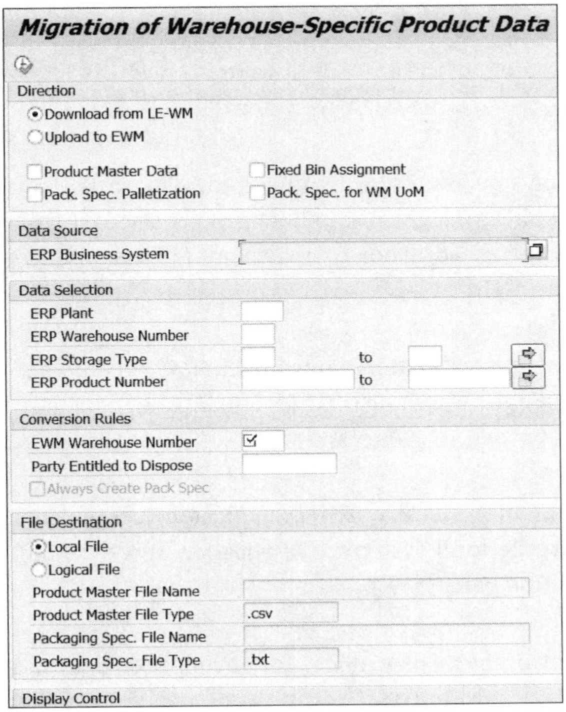

Migration of Warehouse-Specific Product Data

Direction
Download from LE-WM
Upload to EWM
Product Master Data
Fixed Bin Assignment
Pack. Spec. Palletization
Pack. Spec. for WM UoM

Data Source
ERP Business System

Data Selection
ERP Plant
ERP Warehouse Number
ERP Storage Type to
ERP Product Number to

Conversion Rules
EWM Warehouse Number
Party Entitled to Dispose
Always Create Pack Spec

File Destination
Local File
Logical File
Product Master File Name
Product Master File Type .csv
Packaging Spec. File Name
Packaging Spec. File Type .txt

Display Control

Figure 3.14 Product Migration Tool

The process is a bit different if we want to download the packaging and unit of measure (UoM) data. In this case, the data is downloaded from WM to a TXT file, and then this data is uploaded to embedded EWM using report /SCWM/IPU. The process to update data in embedded EWM from the source WM system is the same as for all the other objects. In each case, different source structures and fields are read from WM, and different fields in embedded EWM are populated as target fields based on how the objects are created in embedded EWM.

Now, let's look at some important sections and fields required to understand the workings of this tool:

- **Direction**
  This section contains filters for whether you want to download data from WM or upload to embedded EWM. You can download product master data, fixed bin assignments, palletization, and WM UoM from WM. This data can then be updated to the embedded EWM application based on selections made in this setting.
- **Data Source**
  This field contains the business system of the SAP ERP system from which data is to be pulled into a CSV file for the target SAP S/4HANA system.
- **Data Selection**
  This section contains the selection screen for bins that need to be extracted into the source file. You can select all bins for a given warehouse or for select storage types at the warehouse level. You can also drill down to the names of the products that need to be extracted.
- **Conversion Rules**
  This section contains the name of the destination embedded EWM-specific warehouse that has been created to map the warehouse in SAP S/4HANA to which the data is to be uploaded.
- **File Destination**
  The source file can be downloaded on the local system or application server from WM, or it can be uploaded from the local system or application server to SAP S/4HANA depending on the selection here.
- **Display Control**
  The selections in this section control the display of logs for downloaded data and errors if needed.

3.5.2 Storage Bin Migration

The next data object that can be migrated from WM to embedded EWM is storage bin data. As shown in Figure 3.15, storage bins can be downloaded from a source SAP ERP system along with bin master and/or sortation data in a CSV file; as a second step, they can be uploaded to the embedded EWM system.

The reports for such a migration can be accessed from **SAP Easy Access** path **Logistics • SCM Extended Warehouse Management • Extended Warehouse Management • Interfaces • Migration from LE-WM • Storage Bin Migration**; they also can be accessed from Transaction /SCWM/MIG_BIN.

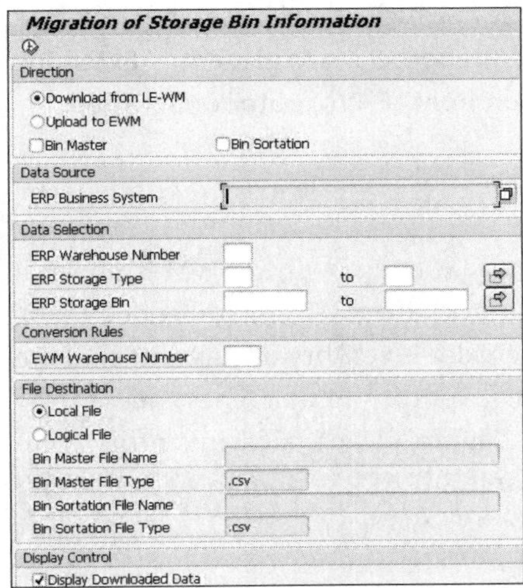

Figure 3.15 Bin Migration Tool

3.5.3 Stock Migration

The next data object that can be migrated from WM to embedded EWM is stock data. As shown in Figure 3.16, stock data can be downloaded from the source SAP ERP system in a CSV file and then can be uploaded to the SAP S/4HANA system.

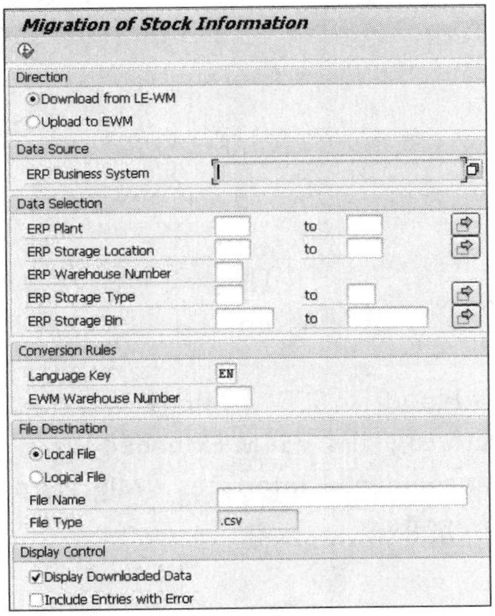

Figure 3.16 Stock Migration Tool

The stock migration report is /SCWM/MIG_STOCK, which can be accessed from **SAP Easy Access** path **Logistics • SCM Extended Warehouse Management • Extended Warehouse Management • Interfaces • Migration from LE-WM • Stock Migration**.

3.5.4 Physical Inventory Completeness

The next data object that can be migrated from WM to embedded EWM is physical inventory completeness. When you migrate the stock from WM to embedded EWM, although the stock of a product is migrated, there are inventory documents that are created but not completed. As such, the physical inventory completeness needs to be migrated to SAP S/4HANA as well. As shown in Figure 3.17, physical inventory completeness data can be downloaded from the source SAP ERP system in a CSV file and then uploaded in the embedded EWM system.

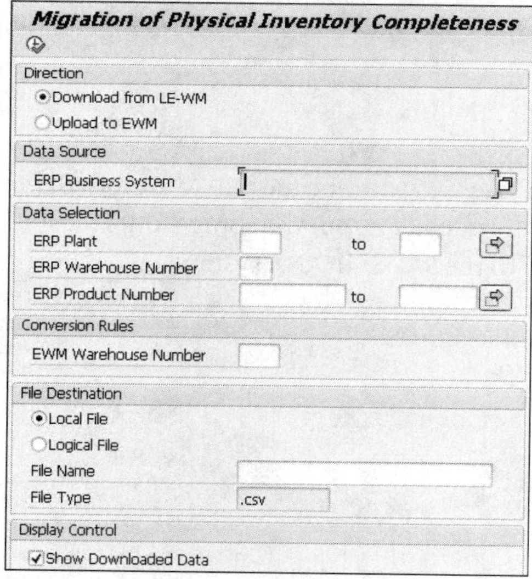

Figure 3.17 Physical Inventory Migration Tool

The migrating physical inventory completeness report is /SCWM/MIG_PI_COMPL, which can be accessed from **SAP Easy Access** path **Logistics • SCM Extended Warehouse Management • Extended Warehouse Management • Interfaces • Migration from LE-WM • Physical Inventory Completeness Migration**.

There are certain prerequisites you must ensure are in place in embedded EWM before physical inventory completeness data is migrated:

- The physical inventory area is defined.
- Activity areas are defined.
- The physical inventory area is mapped to the activity area.
- In the physical inventory settings in the embedded EWM warehouse, physical inventory is set to always occur at the complete warehouse level rather than at a single activity area level.

The details of setting up and executing physical inventory in embedded EWM will be discussed in Chapter 10.

3.6 Migration of Objects from SAP EWM to Decentralized EWM in SAP S/4HANA

SAP has provided a set of data objects that can be migrated from SAP EWM to decentralized EWM in SAP S/4HANA using the SAP S/4HANA migration cockpit.

The migration cockpit is a tool that enables you to migrate various objects from the SAP ERP system to the SAP S/4HANA system. It extracts data from SAP ERP source structures and maps it to in SAP S/4HANA destination structures using standard fields and conversion rules on source data to make it compatible for target structure fields. The technical working of such a migration involves creating an RFC connection to connect the SAP S/4HANA migration cockpit to the SAP ERP system. It selects the data from the source SAP ERP system using specific selection criteria based on the type of migration scenario being used.

After the migration cockpit is set up between the SAP EWM and decentralized EWM in SAP S/4HANA clients, using the standard data objects and filtering criteria, the following business objects can now be migrated: warehouse stock, warehouse product, storage bin, storage bin sorting, and fixed bin assignment.

This will help you migrate the essential master data from SAP EWM to decentralized EWM so that migration can be completed between the two landscapes with faster time to value and reduce total cost of ownership.

3.7 Summary

In this chapter, we discussed important concepts around integration of embedded EWM, data load, and migration tools to be used during cutover when moving from WM to embedded EWM. We also saw that no CIF process is required for transfer of master data from SAP S/4HANA to embedded EWM. In the next chapter, we'll discuss the warehouse structure of the warehouse created in embedded EWM.

Chapter 4
Warehouse Structures

In this chapter, we'll discuss warehouse structures, which map the physical layout of warehouses in embedded EWM and define their characteristics based on their purpose and other attributes. Together with master data, the warehouse structure forms the foundation on which all warehouse processes are mapped.

Warehouse structures map different areas of warehouses into the system based on their purpose and other characteristics. These include storage types, storage sections, and activity areas, to name a few. Businesses with physical warehouses, usually buildings or covered areas, try to map different areas of the warehouse into the system based on how products are stored, areas where different activities are carried out, frequency of goods moving in and out, and so on. However, if the physical warehouse hasn't been set up yet, you can plan your warehouse setup from scratch based on your business requirements.

In both cases, businesses can either map their warehousing structures and processes to use the standard functionalities offered by embedded EWM or customize structures and processes in embedded EWM to align the system with the actual way of working in the warehouse. In large, complex warehouses, businesses typically prefer the latter option because their warehousing operations have evolved over years of operation, so they prefer to streamline their embedded EWM solutions with their actual business requirements.

Each warehouse is unique; even within a business organization, each warehouse will have its own distinct features. For example, a warehouse can be a distribution center, manufacturing facility, or third-party logistics warehouse. There can be variations in the products stored (raw materials, finished goods), storage conditions (multitemperature storage), and handling mechanisms (pallets, cases). Even while performing the operation of storing, for example, finished goods, a warehouse structure can vary based on the industry. For instance, a warehouse to stock clothing and accessories for a retail company can look significantly different from a warehouse stocking beverages for a consumer goods company.

Before laying out a warehouse structure, you need to understand the following parameters, each of which plays a key role in influencing the warehouse design:

- **Goods movement**
  You first need to know how goods move in the warehouse, including stock putaway, removal, and internal stock movement. The warehouse needs to be set up in such a way that stock can move seamlessly and optimally. Packing areas and other work centers should be easily accessible so that relevant actions can be taken on a product while it's moving through the warehouse.
- **Accessibility**
  Products in the warehouse not only should be easily accessible but also prioritized for accessibility. For example, fast-moving products such as umbrellas during the rainy season should be stocked near the warehouse door so they can be directly loaded onto a truck, which saves time and improves efficiency. Products can also be stocked based on shelf-life expiration. It's therefore also important to ensure that warehouse workers can access HUs with closer shelf-life expirations easily.
- **Area**
  Another important parameter to consider is to make the most efficient use of warehouse space. Most warehouses are big-box structures with clearly distinguished storage spaces and work centers. The intention is to use the most space for storage and the remaining space for work centers, conveyors, offices, and so on.
- **Stocking**
  The last and most important parameter in deciding on your warehouse structure is how products will be stocked in the warehouse. Products can be stocked on racks, on floors, in carousels, and so on. A product can also be stocked into multiple stock-keeping units (SKUs), such as pallets and cases, and often it's important to track each SKU's shelf-life or best-before date, as in the case of pharmaceutical or perishable products.

In the previous chapter, you created the four-character warehouse number in embedded EWM that maps the embedded EWM-specific warehouse to the logical warehouse in SAP S/4HANA. Figure 4.1 shows the various elements in the warehouse structure. Within each warehouse, there are storage types that are divided into storage sections, which hold products with unique attributes, such as fast-moving and slow-moving goods. Each storage type and storage section consists of storage bins, which are used to manage stock of the product.

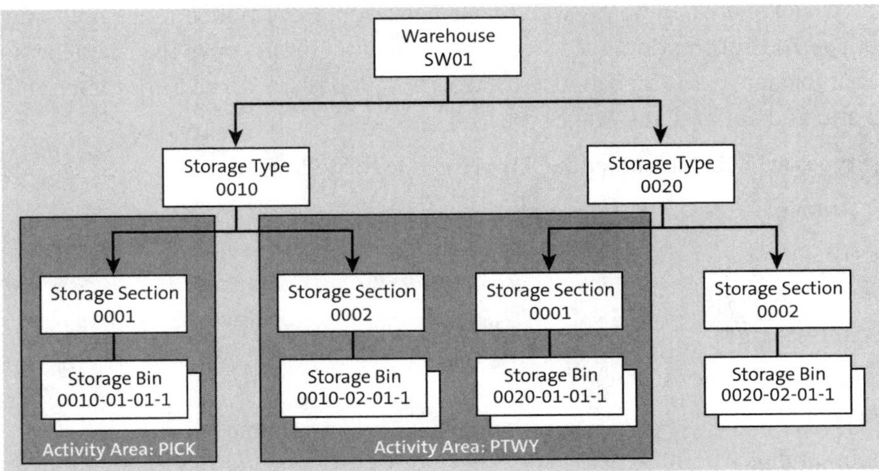

Figure 4.1 Warehouse Structural Elements

In this chapter, you'll see how different warehouse elements, such as storage types, work centers, doors, and so on, can be set up in embedded EWM and how you can use the different configuration options in each one to map to actual warehouse properties. Section 4.1 describes storage types in embedded EWM and how to use Customizing to set their spatial and organizational settings. In Section 4.2, we'll talk about storage sections, which are subdivisions of storage types. Section 4.3 describes storage bins, which are used to store products in the warehouse. Section 4.4 covers the concept of staging areas and warehouse doors, through which goods move in and out of the warehouse. Section 4.5 describes activity areas, which are logical groupings of storage bins for particular activities, such as picking or putaway. Finally, Section 4.6 describes work centers, which are used to carry out specific activities on products before they're moved out of the warehouse.

4.1 Storage Type

A *storage type* is a distinct physical area in the warehouse. A warehouse is distributed into storage types based on the nature of the storage, type of storage, spatial layout, and so on. A warehouse can have many different storage types, which can be used for different purposes: stocking products, providing work centers for packaging, serving as staging areas for loading, and so on.

Storage types are created at the warehouse level. A storage type doesn't hold any product-specific information. Each storage type is configured to map the characteristics of that storage type, which in turn controls how goods are placed into storage and moved into and out of that storage type.

Storage types available in embedded EWM include the following:

- Rack storage
- Bulk storage
- General storage area
- Fixed bin storage
- Hazardous substance storage
- Work center
- ID point and pick point
- Yard storage

Each storage type maps a physical location in the warehouse where a product is placed for storage. Storage types can be used for final putaway of goods, as in the cases of rack storage and bulk storage. They can also be used as work centers for carrying out activities such as packing or labeling or as intermediate storage locations where goods are placed before they're moved to the next location in the warehouse, for example, ID points and pick points. The use of a storage type within a warehouse is indicated by the storage type role, which we'll discuss when we talk about customization settings ahead. You can configure a storage type from IMG path **SCM Extended Warehouse Management • Extended Warehouse Management • Master Data • Define Storage Type**. Click on **New Entries** to define a new storage type and define its unique attributes.

In the following sections, we'll review the various customization settings that describe the technical, spatial, and organizational structure of a physical storage type. These are categorized into sections for specific settings: **General**, **Putaway Control**, **Stock Removal Control**, **Goods Movement Control**, and **Replenishment**.

4.1.1 General Settings

The **General** settings hold configurations that aren't relevant to specific warehouse movements (e.g., putaway, stock removal, and replenishment). These are general warehouse attributes such as the purpose of a storage type, how the quantities need to be managed in the storage types, control settings for fixed bins, and so on.

Figure 4.2 shows the general settings that need to be maintained for any storage type. We'll discuss these in detail ahead.

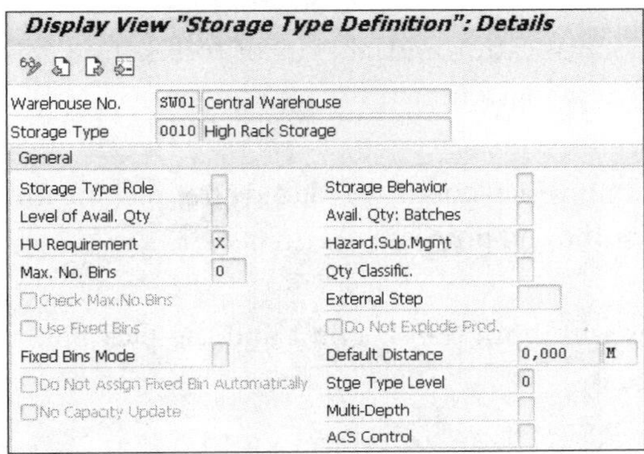

Figure 4.2 General Settings for the Storage Type

Storage Type Role

Storage Type Role is used to classify storage types based on the nature of the storage. SAP provides the storage type roles shown in Figure 4.3. A storage type must be assigned to any one of these roles.

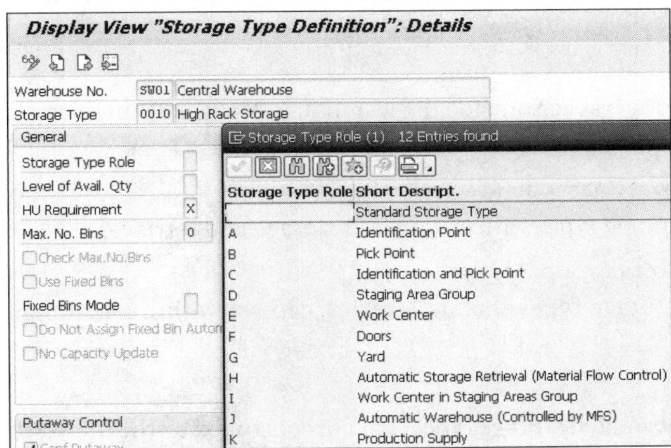

Figure 4.3 Storage Type Roles in Embedded EWM

The storage type roles in embedded EWM are as follows:

- **Standard Storage Type**
  This role is for storage types used for final putaway of products in the warehouse.

These storage types are characterized by their spatial and material handling characteristics.

- **Identification Point**
  This role is for storage types used for identification and labeling of goods. It's commonly used in automated storage/retrieval systems.
- **Pick Point**
  This role is assigned to storage types into which goods are placed after picking for inspection, packing, and labeling for outbound processes.
- **Identification and Pick Point**
  This role is assigned to storage types with both the ID point and the pick point roles.
- **Staging Area Group**
  This role is assigned to storage types in which goods are staged right before they're brought into or out of the warehouse.
- **Work Center**
  This role is assigned to storage types used to carry out specific activities such as packing, deconsolidation, inspection, and so on.
- **Doors**
  This role is assigned to storage types that act as a door of the warehouse from which goods move into and out of the warehouse.
- **Yard**
  This role is assigned to storage space outside the warehouse. It's usually used as an incoming and outgoing area for vehicles and transportation units (TUs).
- **Automatic Storage Retrieval (Material flow control)**
  This role is assigned to storage types with automated storage and retrieval.
- **Work Center in Staging Areas Group**
  This role is assigned to storage types that act as work centers within a material staging area.
- **Automatic Warehouse**
  This role is assigned to automated storage types that are controlled by the material flow system.
- **Production Supply**
  This role is assigned to a warehouse used to store products that are ready to be issued for production.

Level of Available Quantity

The **Level of Avail. Qty** field is used to set the level at which the stock is visible for stock removal. There are two possible values:

- **Storage Bin**
  This checkbox helps set visibility for stock removal at the storage bin level. If this checkbox is selected, the warehouse task created for stock removal has no source HU selected. A warehouse operator can select the HU by choice. As an example, this option can be selected for final storage types such as bulk storage so that the operator has the flexibility to select the most easily available HU rather than an HU at an inaccessible location.
- **Highest-Level HU**
  If this option is selected, the warehouse task is created with a source HU. A warehouse operator will go to the bin where this HU is physically stored and scan the HU, pick it, and confirm the warehouse task. As an example, this option can be selected for storage types such as work centers for which a specific HU needs to be specified in the warehouse task.

Handling Unit Requirement

The **HU Requirement** option helps control whether stock is placed in the storage type with or without HUs. The selection options available for this field are as follows:

- **HU Allowed but Not a Requirement**
- **HU Requirement**
- **HU Not Allowed**

If the first value is selected, then you can stock both products and HUs in the storage type. Unlike standard warehouse management (WM), embedded EWM allows users to stock HUs and products within the same storage types and storage bins.

Maximum Number of Bins

The **Max. No. Bins** field is used to set the maximum number of fixed bins per product in the storage type. The purpose of this field is to avoid one product overfilling one storage type. If the maximum bin capacity is reached, the product is directed to another storage type. The value in this field is only considered if the **Check Max.No.Bins** indicator is selected in the storage type setting.

The warehouse product master also has a similar field in the **Storage Type Data** view to limit the maximum number of fixed bins in a storage type for that product. If this value is set in the product master, it's given preference over the value set at the storage type level. As in the previous case, this checkbox is only selected if **Check Max.No.Bins** is selected for the corresponding storage type in the storage type settings.

Check Maximum Number of Bins

If the **Check Max.No.Bins** indicator is set, the system looks for the value in **Max. No. Bins** at the storage type and product master levels, as discussed previously.

Use Fixed Bins

The value in this field is set if you want to store a product only in fixed bins allocated to that product. A storage type can use either fixed bins or dynamically allocated bins. If this checkbox is selected, then the system checks during putaway whether the identified bin in the storage type is a fixed bin. If it isn't, then the system throws an error.

Fixed Bins Mode

The value in this field is checked if the **Use Fixed Bins** checkbox is selected at the storage type level. The value in this field determines how the system will identify the fixed bins in the storage type during putaway. This setting is used if you use slotting to determine optimal fixed bins for products—that is, if the product is stored in the ideal fixed bin or if there is a better bin available. If the system does find a better optimized fixed bin for the product, it sets the bin as **Improvable** in the fixed bin assignment table. There are two selection options in this field:

- **Putaway to Optimum Fixed Storage Bins Only**
- **Putaway to Optimum Fixed Storage Bins Preferred**

If you use the first option, the system looks only for fixed bins assigned to the product without the **Not Improvable** value set. If you choose the second option, the system tries to put away the product into the optimal fixed bins first; if no bin is available, then it moves to bins that are improvable.

Do Not Assign Fixed Bins Automatically

The value of this indicator is checked if the **Use Fixed Bins** checkbox is selected at the storage type level. Select **Use Fixed Bins** if you don't want the system to assign a bin as a fixed bin automatically for a product during putaway. Thus, putaway will only be allowed in bins that are preallocated fixed bins for a product. You can maintain a fixed bin for a product from Transaction /SCWM/BINMAT, which can also be accessed from **SAP Easy Access** path **Logistics • SCM Extended Warehouse Management • Extended Warehouse Management • Master Data • Storage Bin • Maintain Fixed Storage Bin**.

No Capacity Update

The **No Capacity Update** checkbox is selected if you don't want to update the bin capacity at the same time as the warehouse task confirmation. If this checkbox isn't set, then the bin capacity is updated along with the warehouse task confirmation, which increases the processing time. This checkbox can be set based on warehousing requirements and storage type settings. For example, you might not need capacity data (e.g., the number of HUs) for an automated storage type such as a conveyor system; therefore, the checkbox can be set. On the other hand, for a storage type for final putaway, such as the rack storage type with the putaway rule set to **Empty Bin**, you'll need to know the number of empty bins available for bin determination, so the checkbox shouldn't be set.

Storage Behavior

This field defines the general nature of a storage type. Storage types can be categorized as follows:

- **Standard warehouse**
  The bins in these storage types don't have any special attributes and are used for general storage in the warehouse. A standard storage type, work center, or production supply area will have the storage behavior set to **Standard Warehouse**.
- **Pallet storage**
  This storage behavior is set for storage types used to store pallets by giving specific characteristics to the bins. Pallets of a particular HU type are put into a bin, which creates bin subsections upon first putaway. The subsections are later used for putaway of pallets of the same HU type. Depending on the HU type, the system creates identical subsections to stack the HUs together.

- **Bulk storage**
  This storage behavior is set for storage types to stack goods in large volumes. A storage space, such as a floor, is divided into rows, and each row represents a storage bin. The pallets are stacked on top of one another and grouped into blocks.

Available Quantity in Batches

The **Avail. Qty: Batches** field is set based on the requirements for batch management in the warehouse. The settings in this field determine whether the available quantities in the warehouse are saved with or without a batch reference. There are two selection options available in this setting:

- **Available Quantity: Batch-Specific**
- **Available Quantity: Batch-Neutral**

If the available quantity is batch-specific, you can track the available quantity for each bin or HU at the batch level. Thus, if a warehouse task is created for a specific batch, the system can automatically determine the required stock for that batch. If a warehouse task is created when the available quantity is batch-neutral, the system won't be able to determine the required batch automatically. If you don't want to create a warehouse request with a specified batch, set the level to batch-neutral. You can give the batch later, during warehouse task confirmation.

Hazardous Substance Management

The settings in the **Hazard.Sub.Mgmt** field determine the level at which a hazardous substance should be managed. You can set it to one of the following depending on the warehouse requirements:

- **No Hazardous Substance Check**
- **Hazardous Substance Check at Storage Type Level**
- **Hazardous Substance Check at Storage Type and Storage Section Level**

Quantity Classification

Qty Classific. describes the different packaging units in which a product is stored in the warehouse. The different packaging units can be eaches, cases, pallets, and so on. The value set in this field is used during storage type determination in stock removal to identify the right storage type that stocks the products in the required unit. For example, if you pack 12 EA in a case, then you map that quantity to a quantity classification of **Case**. When a task is created to pick 12 EA from the storage type, the system gets the quantity classification from the packaging specification level that maps 12 EA to a case. This quantity classification is then used in the stock removal search sequence to determine the storage type that holds the right SKU.

In addition, quantity classification helps identify the operative unit of measure (UoM) from the packaging specification level. This operative UoM is also the alternative AUoM in the warehouse task. The allowed values for quantity classification are maintained via IMG path **SCM Extended Warehouse Management • Extended Warehouse Management • Cross-Process Settings • Warehouse Task • Define Quantity Classifications,** by clicking on **New Entries**.

External Step

In the **External Step** field, define the external process step that needs to be assigned to the HU when it reaches a storage type but hasn't yet achieved the required step from the routing profile in process-oriented storage control. The last completed external step in the HU is overwritten by the external step maintained in the storage type. The external step is mapped to an internal process step that defines the nature of the warehouse process. You'll learn more about external steps when we discuss process-oriented storage control in Chapter 6, Section 6.5.4.

Do Not Explode Product

The **Do Not Explode Prod.** indicator is set if you don't want to track movements of products contained within an HU during HU task confirmation. For a warehouse storage type for which inventory management is a sensitive business process, don't set this indicator, which enables you to monitor the movement at a product level within the HU rather than at the HU level. The product movements can be tracked from the embedded EWM warehouse monitor by choosing **Documents • All Movements of Products • Display All Movements of a Product**.

Tracking the movement of products within an HU also adds to the system overhead during HU task confirmation and should only be set for storage types that require such a detailed level of tracking. If this checkbox is selected, any HU movement can only be tracked at the HU level, and no separate product-specific tracking is possible.

Default Distance

The **Default Distance** field holds the default distance to reach the first bin in the storage type for travel distance calculations. The default distance can be specified in any

UoM of length allowed in the warehouse. The value in this field is used if labor management is active in the warehouse and is used for planning purposes. The default distance is required because the last known location of the warehouse worker isn't known at the time of planning or during a paper-driven warehouse order-execution process. In such a case, the system takes this default distance as the distance a worker must travel to reach the first bin in the warehouse order. For warehouse order confirmations using radio frequency (RF), the last position of the resource is known, so the field isn't used.

Storage Type level

The **Storage Type Level** setting is used to map the actual levels in the physical warehouse where the storage types can be located. The value in this field is used by the graphical warehouse layout to select the level at which the warehouse view needs to be seen. The system then only shows the storage types present at the given level. If the field is left blank for all storage types in the warehouse, the system assumes that all storage types in the warehouse are at the same level.

4.1.2 Putaway Control

These settings control the putaway of stock into the storage type. The putaway can be the final putaway into the storage type after goods receipt or the putaway during bin-to-bin stock transfer. Therefore, these settings control any stock movement for which stock is being placed into a bin in the storage type. Figure 4.4 shows the different settings that control putaway in a storage type in embedded EWM. We'll discuss each setting in detail ahead.

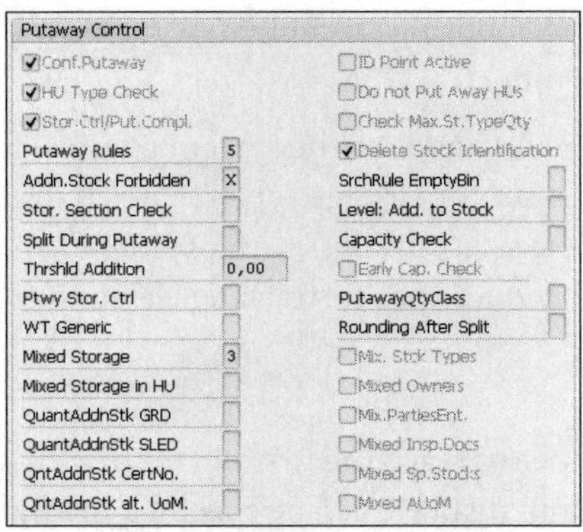

Figure 4.4 Storage Type Settings for Putaway Control

Confirm Putaway

The **Conf.Putaway** checkbox is selected if putaway of stock into that storage type requires confirmation of a warehouse task. This means that the warehouse task needs to be fully confirmed for the stock putaway to happen and the available quantity in the bin to increase. (We'll cover a similar checkbox for confirmation of stock removal in this chapter.) If the checkbox isn't set for both confirmation of putaway and stock removal, then the warehouse task doesn't need to be confirmed to reflect a change in available stock. Stock in the destination bin will increase as soon as the putaway warehouse task is created.

Handling Unit Type Check

If the **HU Type Check** indicator is set, the system checks whether the HU being put away is allowed in the destination storage type. The system performs two checks if this indicator is set in the storage type settings:

- HU allowed in the storage type
- HU allowed in storage bin type

Storage Control/Putaway Completed

The **Stor.Ctrl/Put.Compl.** indicator applies when you use process-oriented storage control in the putaway process. The indicator is set for a storage type if it's a final putaway storage type and marks the end of process-oriented storage control during the putaway process. For example, you can set this indicator for bulk or rack storage types that are final storage types for putaway. Don't set this indicator for interim storage types such as work centers, pick points, and so on. The warehouse request is marked as complete after the stock putaway is completed for storage types with this indicator set.

Putaway Rules

The value in the **Putaway Rules** field plays a key role in how stock is placed in the bins in a storage type. These rules help in the optimum placement of goods in the storage type depending on business requirements. The putaway rules available for a storage type are as follows:

- **Empty bin**
  In this rule, the system puts stock in the next available empty bin. This strategy is used for storage types with no clearly defined requirements for bin allocation for

putaway. You can use this strategy for a storage type that has clearly defined sections for products, such as a rack storage type. You can use bin sorting to determine the sequence in which the system looks for the next empty bin. You'll learn more about bin sorting when we discuss bin master data in Section 4.3.7.

- **Addition to existing stock/empty bin**
  In this rule, the system adds stock to a bin that already holds stock. The maximum stock quantity in the bin can be controlled by activating the capacity check in the storage type settings. The system puts stock in the next empty bin if there's no bin holding the required product or if the bin is full.
- **Consolidation group**
  This rule is used to group HUs based on consolidation groups. The consolidation group is created when the first HU is put away into the storage type. The follow-up HUs with the same consolidation group (based on the ship-to party) are put in the same bins. This rule is mostly used for packaging work centers to group HUs that need to be shipped together.
- **General storage area**
  As the name suggests, this rule allows additions to stock in a bin without any restriction on HU type, product, and so on. The entire storage type consists of one bin that stocks all the products.
- **Transit warehouse: staging area for door**
  This rule is used in transit warehousing scenarios. If the HU being moved during transit warehousing belongs to a delivery for which the TU is already at the door, the system suggests the corresponding door bin.

Additional Stock Forbidden

The value in this field determines whether additional stock is permitted in an existing bin in a storage type. The selection options available in this setting are as follows:

- **Addition to Existing Stock Permitted**
- **Addition to Existing Stock Generally Not Permitted**
- **Product Putaway Profile Decides**

If you don't want to continue to add similar stock in a bin after the first putaway, set the rule to the second option. If you select the third option, the value set in the product putaway profile determines whether additional putaway will be allowed. The product putaway profile can be defined from IMG path **SCM Extended Warehouse**

Management • Extended Warehouse Management • Goods Receipt Process • Strategies • Define Product Putaway Profile, by clicking on **New Entries** and defining the putaway profile for the putaway control indicator (**PutawayControlInd**) and **Storage Type**, as shown in Figure 4.5.

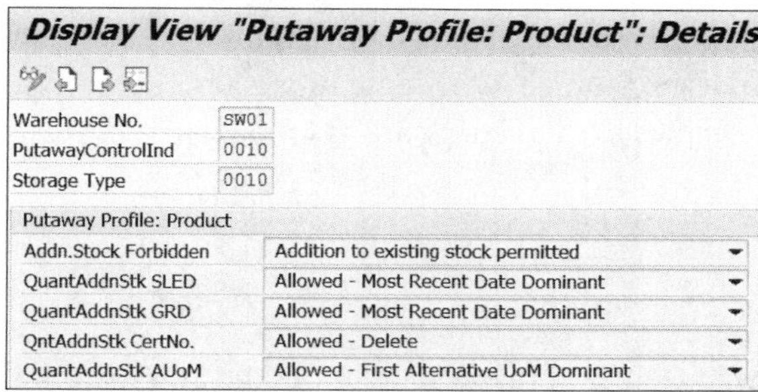

Figure 4.5 Product Putaway Profile

The product putaway profile can be used to control additions to existing stock at the product level through the putaway control indicator assigned to the product master. The combination of putaway control indicator and storage type can influence the settings discussed ahead if the storage type is set to **Product Putaway Profile Decides**.

Storage Section Check

The value in **Stor. Section Check** determines whether storage section determination or checks will be carried out during putaway. The three allowed values are as follows:

- **No Storage Section Determination and Check**
- **Storage Section Determination and Check**
- **Storage Section Determination; No Check**

The system performs storage section determination during automatic bin determination and checks whether it can select a bin in a given storage section. It performs a check when the destination storage section or bin is given manually. For a storage type, you can select whether you want one, both, or neither to happen during putaway.

Split During Putaway

The **Split During Putaway** field controls whether the product can be split into multiple bins if the putaway quantity exceeds the total available bin capacity. The system first checks the maximum storage type quantity if the **Check Max.St.TypeQty** indicator is set for the storage type. It also checks the weight, volume, and capacity key figures based on the settings for capacity check at the storage type level. If the available space in the bin is less than the quantity being put away, then the system looks for the value in this field to determine whether a split is required. If set to **Do Not Split During Putaway**, then the system looks for the next bin with the required space in the storage type or another bin in another storage type, depending on the search sequence for putaway. The available values in this setting are as follows:

- **Do Not Split During Putaway**
- **Split During Putaway**
- **Product Master Decides**

In the last setting, the value in the **Split During Putaway** field under the **St. Type Data** tab in the product master determines whether the split should happen. This helps control the split at the product level rather than the storage type level. The check for the split happens only for product warehouse tasks, not HU warehouse tasks.

Threshold Addition

The **Threshold Addition** indicator is set if the **Split During Putaway** indicator discussed previously is set to split the product during putaway. The value holds a percentage of the actual bin capacity. When deciding whether a split should occur, the system checks if the available quantity in the bin is greater than the threshold and only then allows the split to happen. This is required for operational efficiency so that the system doesn't split the product disproportionately into very small units, thereby increasing the putaway time.

Putaway Storage Control

The **Ptwy. Stor. Ctrl** indicator defines which type of warehouse task should be created for putaway of a HU with process-oriented storage control. The value in this field is considered only if you're using process-oriented storage control. Otherwise, the type of task is determined from the **Select HU w/o Storage Process** indicator at the warehouse process type level. We'll discuss this setting further when we discuss warehouse process types in Chapter 6, Section 6.3.2.

The allowed values in this field are as follows:

- **Storage Control: Dynamically Evaluated**
  The system determines the creation of a product or HU warehouse task based on

the value of the **Prod/HU WT** field while assigning storage process steps to the storage process definition in process-oriented storage control.

- **Storage Control: Putaway with HU WT**
  If this value is selected, the system createhs an HU warehouse task.
- **Storage Control: Putaway with Product WT**
  If this value is selected, the system creates a product warehouse task.

Warehouse Task Generic

This field determines which destination data is determined when a putaway task is created. A storage destination is determined by storage type, section, and bin. This setting controls the level up to which the system should do the storage destination determination before stopping while creating the task.

The values in this field are as follows:

- **Not Generic**
- **Storage Type and Section**
- **Only Storage Type**

If **Only Storage Type** is selected, then the system only determines the destination storage type during task creation and leaves the **Storage Section** and **Storage Bin** fields blank. These fields are populated at the time of warehouse task confirmation. For example, you can maintain this setting for packing stations for which you want the bin to be selected at the time of putaway.

Mixed Storage

The **Mixed Storage** field controls whether multiple HUs and products are allowed in a storage type. The allowed options in this field are as follows:

- **Mixed Storage without Limitations**
  The system allows multiple products and multiple HUs in the storage bin.
- **Several Non-Mixed HUs with the Same Product/Batch**
  The system allows multiple HUs with the same product or allows the same product with the same batch (if the product is batch-managed) in a storage bin.
- **Several HUs with Different Batches of the Same Product**
  The system allows multiple HUs in the storage bin of the same product and multiple HUs with different batches of the same product if the product is batch-managed.

- **One HU Allowed per Bin**
  The system allows only one HU per bin.

These settings aren't limited to putaway of HUs. If you want to putaway unpacked goods, then each bin acts like a HU, making the **Mixed Storage in HU** field that we discuss next relevant.

Mixed Storage in Handling Unit

The value in the **Mixed Storage in HU** field controls whether multiple quants can be stored in an HU. The different quants can include products with different attributes, such as batches and shelf-life date, or multiple products.

The options available in this field are as follows:

- **Mixed Storage Not Allowed**
  The system doesn't allow different quants in an HU.
- **Several Batches of the Same Product per HU**
  The system allows multiple batches of the same product in an HU.
- **Mixed Storage without Limitations in HU**
  The system allows multiple batches of the same product or multiple products in an HU.

Quant Addition to Stock Goods Receipt Date

The **QuantAddnStck GRD** setting allows you to receive quants with a different goods receipt date in the same bin or HU if you allow additions to existing stock in the storage type. The goods receipt date on the quant is populated when the goods receipt is confirmed for that item in a warehouse request. The value in this field is used to set the correct goods receipt date if the addition of stocks with different goods receipt dates is allowed in the bins in the storage type. The available options for this field are as follows:

- **Allowed—Most Recent Date Dominant**
  The system allows putaway of stock and updates the goods receipt date on stock that was originally present in the bin or HU.
- **Allowed—Earliest Date Dominant**
  The system allows putaway of stock and updates the goods receipt date on new stock being put away to the oldest goods receipt date on the stock that was originally present in the bin or HU.

- **Not Allowed**
  The system doesn't allow putaway into a bin or HU if the current stock and new stock have different goods receipt dates.
- **Product Putaway Profile Decides**
  The addition of stock is determined by the product putaway profile.

Quant Addition to Stock Shelf-Life Expiration Date

The **QuantAddnStck SLED** setting allows you to receive quants with a different shelf-life expiration date in the same bin or HU if you allow additions to existing stock in the storage type. The value in this field is used to set the correct shelf-life expiration date if addition of stock with different goods receipt dates is allowed in the bins in the storage type.

There are four possible values for this field:

- **Allowed—Most Recent Date Dominant**
  The system allows putaway of stock and updates the shelf-life expiration date on stock that was originally present in the bin or HU.
- **Allowed—Earliest Date Dominant**
  The system allows putaway of stock and updates the shelf-life expiration date on new stock being put away to the oldest shelf-life expiration date on the stock that was originally present in the bin or HU.
- **Not Allowed**
  The system doesn't allow putaway into a bin or HU if the current stock and new stock have different shelf-life expiration dates.
- **Product Putaway Profile Decides**
  The addition of stock is determined by the settings maintained in the product putaway profile.

Quant Addition to Stock Certificate Number

The **QuantAddnStck CertNo.** setting allows you to receive quants with a different stock certificate number in the same bin or HU if you allow additions to existing stock in the storage type. The value in this field is used to set the correct stock certificate number if stocks with different stock certificate numbers are allowed to be added in the bins in the storage type.

The options available are as follows:

- **Allowed—Most Recent Date Dominant**
  The system allows putaway of stock and updates the certificate number on stock that was originally present in the bin or HU.
- **Allowed—Earliest Date Dominant**
  The system allows putaway of stock and updates the certificate number on new stock being put away to the oldest certificate number on the stock that was originally present in the bin or HU.
- **Not Allowed**
  The system doesn't allow putaway into a bin or HU if the current stock and new stock have different certificate numbers.
- **Product Putaway Profile Decides**
  The addition of stock to already existing stock with any change in certificate number is determined by the settings maintained in the product putaway profile.

Quant Addition to Stock Alternative Unit of Measure

The **QuantAddnStck alt. UoM** setting allows you to receive quants with an AUoM in the same bin or HU if you allow additions to existing stock in the storage type. The value in this field is used to set the correct UoM if the addition of stocks with different bases and AUoMs is allowed in the bins in the storage type.

The options available are as follows:

- **Allowed—First Alternative UoM Dominant**
  The system allows putaway of stock and updates the first AUoM on the stock.
- **Allowed—Manage Stock in BUoM Only**
  The system allows putaway of stock but continues to keep the stock in the base UoM (BUoM) only.
- **Not Allowed**
  The system doesn't allow putaway into a bin or HU if the current stock has a different UoM than the BUoM.
- **Product Putaway Profile Decides**
  The addition of stock to already-existing stock with any change in the UoM is determined by the settings maintained in the product putaway profile.
- **Partly Allowed—Manage Stock in AUoM**
  The addition of stock to already existing stock is partly allowed.

Identification Point Active

An identification point (ID point) is an intermediate storage space in the warehouse where a product is kept for identification and labeling before it's put away. If the **ID Point Active** checkbox is selected, then an ID point is set for the given storage type. The stock is then routed through the ID point before it moves to the final putaway location. The settings for this are controlled through layout-oriented storage control. You'll learn more about layout-oriented storage control when we discuss storage control in Chapter 6, Section 6.5.

Do Not Putaway Handling Units

Select the **Do Not Put Away HUs** indicator if you don't want to put away HUs in the storage type. If an HU is to be put away, then a product warehouse task is created to move stock from the HU into the product, which is then moved into the final storage bin.

Check Maximum Storage Type Quantity

Set the **Check Max.ST.TypeQty** checkbox if you want the system to check the maximum quantity for the product in the storage type before putaway. If the quantity to be put away exceeds the maximum storage type capacity for that product, then putaway bin determination moves to the next storage type in the storage type search sequence. This checkbox is required if you want to limit the quantity of products stored in a storage type.

Delete Stock Identification

This checkbox is used if you want to delete stock identification after a product is put away into the storage type. Stock identification identifies a stock or product with all its unique attributes, such as quantity, batch, or stock type. This indicator must be set for all final putaway storage types. If this indicator isn't set for final putaway storage types, then you'll get an error while saving the storage type settings.

Search Rule Empty Bin

The **SrchRule EmptyBin** indicator is set if the system needs to put stock in empty bins. It helps determine how the system looks for the next empty bin in the storage type. There are three options available in this setting:

- **Sorting According to Definition**
  The bins are sorted according to the value specified in the **Sort** field in the bin master data. We'll discuss bin master data further in Section 4.3.7.
- **Near to Fixed Bin**
  The bins are sorted based on their nearness to fixed bins for the product.
- **Product Decides**
  If this field is selected, the sort sequence is determined based on the value in the **Emp. Storbin Sch** field in the **St. Type Data** tab of the product master.

Level: Addition to Stock

The **Level: Add. To Stock** field controls at which level stock is added during warehouse task creation for putaway. The value in this field is considered if you allow additions to existing stock in a bin. The options available for this setting are as follows:

- **Addition to Stock at Bin Level**
  This value allows you to add stock at the bin level. Thus, when a warehouse task is created, the **Destination HU** field remains blank and you can select the HU of your choice in which to put the stock during putaway. This setting grants the flexibility to choose the destination HU in which to add stock based on accessibility and proximity.
- **Addition to Stock at Highest HU Level**
  In this setting, the system proposes the destination HU at the time of warehouse task creation. The warehouse operator will go over to the storage type, identify the HU, and put stock in that HU to complete putaway. This value is selected if the HUs can be easily accessed, and you can let the system choose the HU into which stock will go.

Capacity Check

This indicator is used to control how much stock is stored in a storage type. A bin's capacity may be limited due to its size, shape, and volume. Therefore, it's important to factor in bin capacity while determining a destination bin in a warehouse task, especially when additions to existing stock are allowed or when performing putaway into fixed bins. You can check bin capacity based on weight, volume, or capacity key figure.

A capacity key figure in embedded EWM means a dimensionless capacity that is maintained in embedded EWM in the product master. This figure is compared with the maximum bin capacity, which is maintained at the bin master or bin type level, to check if maximum capacity has been reached.

There are four options available for this setting:

- **No Check According to Key Figure**
  Select this value when you don't want the system to check capacity based on any key figure. However, the system still performs a capacity check based on maximum weight and maximum volume maintained at the storage bin or bin type level.
- **Check According to Key Figure Product**
  If this value is selected, the system checks the capacity consumption of the product based on the capacity maintained in the **Units of Meas.** tab in the product master. This is then compared against the maximum capacity maintained at the storage bin or bin type level to check whether maximum capacity is being reached.
- **Check According to Key Figure Packaging Material**
  If this value is set, the system checks the capacity consumption based on the HU being put away. The capacity consumption of the HU is calculated based on the value set in the **Units of Meas.** tab of the product master for the packaging material.
- **No Check against Key Figure, Weight, and Volume**
  Select this value when you don't want any check based on capacity key figures at the bin level. The system still performs a check based on maximum weight and volume if they're specified at the bin master or bin type level. This setting is ideal for work centers or staging areas.

Early Capacity Check

If the **Early Cap. Check** indicator is set, then the system checks the maximum capacity of the bin type before looking for the capacity of individual bins in the bin type. The system rules out bin types for which maximum capacity is less than the capacity of the product or HU being put away.

Putaway Quantity Classification

PutawayQtyClass describes the packaging unit in which a product is stored in the warehouse.

Rounding after Split

The settings in this field determine how split quantity is rounded off if the storage type settings allow split during putaway. The system checks the bin capacity before finalizing the split quantities to ensure that the additional rounded off quantities can be included in the bin.

The options available for this setting are as follows:

- **No Rounding**
  With this setting, the split quantities aren't rounded off. Thus, the entire rounded quantity is added to the storage bin as is.
- **Round Down WT Quantity to a Multiple of a Unit**
  If this setting is selected, the system rounds down the warehouse task quantity based on the putaway quantity classification.

The system checks the value maintained in the **PutawayQtyClass** field to ensure that only allowed units are put away in the storage bin. Thus, for a storage type, if the putaway quantity classification is maintained at the case level, the system rounds off the warehouse task quantity to a few cases, and then the cases are moved to different bins.

Mixed Stock Type

The **Mix. Stck Types** indicator controls whether quants with different stock types can be placed into a storage bin/HU. Stock types in embedded EWM distinguish stocks that are unrestricted, blocked, need quality inspection, and so on. If this indicator is selected, then only products and batches with similar stock types can be stored in the bin or HU.

Mixed Owners

The **Mixed Owners** indicator controls whether similar stock with different owners are allowed in the storage bin or HU. An *owner* in a warehouse is the person or body that owns the warehouse stock. If this indicator isn't set, then the system allows addition of stock to a bin or HU for which the owner is different from the owner of the existing quant in the storage bin or HU. If this indicator is selected, then only products and batches with the same owners can be stored in the bin or HU.

Mixed Parties Entitled

The **Mix. Partiesent.** indicator allows new stock to be added in a bin if the parties entitled to dispose are different than on the quants already in the bin or HU. The *party entitled to dispose* is the person or body responsible for disposing of the stock. If this indicator isn't set, then the system allows the same product and same batch with different parties entitled to dispose in the storage bin or HU. If this indicator is selected, then only products and batches with the same parties entitled to dispose can be stored in the bin or HU.

Mixed Inspection Documents

The **Mixed Insp.Docs** indicator decides whether stock allocated to different inspection documents can be put away in the same bin. Addition of stock with different inspection documents into a bin or an HU will cause a new quant to be created. If this indicator isn't selected, then the system allows stock with different inspection documents in the storage bin or HU; otherwise, it will only allow single inspection stock.

Mixed Special Stock

The **Mixed Sp. Stocks** indicator allows stock with different special stock indicators in the storage type. Special stock includes stock reserved for special purposes, such as project stock or sales order stock. If this indicator isn't set, the system allows materials with different special stock indicators in the same storage bin or HU. Addition of stock with a different special stock indicator or special stock reference number will cause a new quant to be created. If this indicator is selected, then the system will only allow groups of materials assigned to the same special stock indicator.

Mixed Alternative Units of Measure for the Same Product

The **Mix.AUoMStocks** indicator controls whether a product or batch can exist in a bin or HU with different AUoMs. If this indicator isn't set, then the system allows the same product and same batch with different AUoMs in the storage bin or HU. If this indicator is selected, then only products and batches with the same AUoMs can be stored in the bin or HU.

4.1.3 Stock Removal Control

This section in the storage type settings controls the stock removal process from storage bins in the storage type. Stock removal can include picking for sales orders, stock transfer orders, consumption orders, or bin-to-bin transfers. You can also create picking strategies that determine the order in which bins will be selected for picking in the storage type. We'll discuss stock removal strategies further in Chapter 8, Section 8.4.3.

Figure 4.6 shows the configurations available in this section of the storage type settings. We'll discuss each one in detail in the following sections.

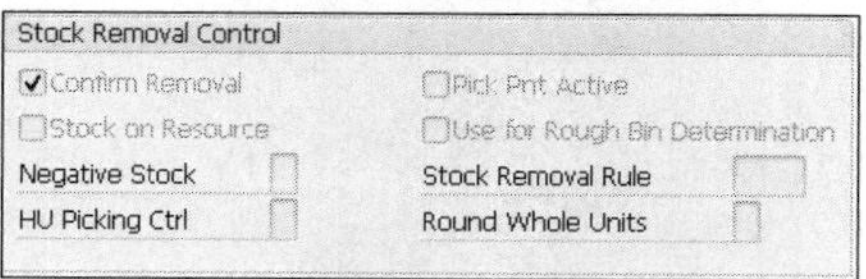

Figure 4.6 Stock Removal Control Settings in Storage Type

Confirm Removal

If the **Confirm Removal** indicator is selected, then stock removal requires confirmation of the warehouse task before stock is reduced from the storage bin. If this indicator isn't set, and the **Confirm Putaway** indicator (discussed in the previous section) isn't set, then the stock is removed from the storage type as soon as the warehouse task is created. You don't need to confirm the warehouse task in this case to reflect the reduced quantity in the storage bin.

Stock on Resource

If this indicator is set, the system looks for stock on a resource in the storage type. A *resource* can be a forklift or dolly used to pick stock and move it to the required destination. This helps the system keep track of the stock that might have already been picked and is halfway through the process. For example, the system can account for stock on a pallet picked from bulk storage that's en route to the pick point or deconsolidation center.

Negative Stock

This setting controls if negative stock is allowed in the storage type when picking warehouse tasks are created. Negative stock is stock below the available quantity.

The options available for this setting are as follows:

- **Negative Stocks Not Allowed**
  Negative stock isn't allowed in the storage type during task creation. Thus, if the

available quantity in the storage bin is less than the picked quantity, task creation will throw an error for the storage bin.

- **Negative Available Quantity Allowed**
  The system allows a negative quantity in the storage bin; however, in this case, the system considers both the available quantity and the quantity scheduled for putaway. This includes quantities in open putaway warehouse tasks with destination bins set as the bin from which stock removal is being planned. If the picking quantity is more than the available quantity but less than the available and planned putaway quantity combined, then the stock removal task will be created. The task can only be confirmed when the available quantity exceeds the stock removal quantity.
- **Negative Stocks Allowed**
  Stock removal tasks are created from the storage bin even if the available quantity is less than the picking quantity. However, the picking task can only be confirmed when the available quantity exceeds the picking quantity.

Handling Unit Picking Control

The **HU Picking Ctrl** indicator controls how a full pallet being picked should be affected if it matches the required pick quantity.

The options available are as follows:

- **Adopt Source HU with Lower-Level HUs into Pick HU**
  The source HU is selected as the lower-level HU into the pick HU when the picking task is confirmed.
- **Propose Source HU as Destination HU**
  The source HU becomes the destination HU upon picking warehouse task confirmation.
- **Warehouse Process Type Controls Proposal for Destination HU**
  How the source HU will be affected when picked is determined by the value of the **Control for HU Pick** setting in the warehouse process type. The settings for the warehouse process type can be accessed from IMG path **SCM Extended Warehouse Management • Extended Warehouse Management • Cross Process Settings • Warehouse Tasks • Define Warehouse Process Type**. We'll discuss the warehouse process type in detail in Chapter 6, Section 6.3.2.
- **Only Adopt Contents (Prod. and Lower-Level HUs) into Pick-HUs**
  Only the products in the source HUs and any lower-level HUs are included in the

pick HU. This option is used only if the product or lower-level HUs are to be picked from the issuing HU.

Pick Point Active

The **Pick Pnt Active** indicator is used for storage types for which a pick point is active. A *pick point* is an intermediate location in the warehouse where HUs are placed for picking, packing, or inspection. The picked quantity is moved to a pick HU (if pick HUs are used), while the rest of the pallet is moved back.

Use for Rough Bin Determination

This indicator is used to determine the source storage type for picking and is populated in the warehouse request line item as soon as it's created. The storage type is selected based on stock removal strategies and even if no available stock is present in the storage type. This setting is used in combination with *order-related replenishment*, in which the replenishment quantity is calculated based on the rough bins determined in open orders. The replenishment then can be run to make the required stock available in the required bins, and the warehouse picking request can be completed.

Stock Removal Rule

The **Stock Removal Use** setting is used to control the order in which quants will be selected for picking in the required storage type. There are various stock removal rules available in embedded EWM that allow the system to sort quants in order of preference for picking. The stock removal rules can be maintained from IMG path **SCM Extended Warehouse Management • Extended Warehouse Management • Goods Issue Process • Strategies • Specify Stock Removal Rule**. The stock removal rules are also set at the storage type search sequence level and storage type group level. The system only looks for stock removal rules at the storage type level if they're not maintained at either of these two places. We'll discuss stock removal rules in outbound processing further in Chapter 8, Section 8.4.3.

Round Whole Units

The settings in this field control how the quantity being picked will be rounded off. Stock can be picked from storage types in full pallets, cases, or eaches, depending on the storage type. Use this field if you need to pick only whole units from the storage types. The following options are available:

- **No Rounding**
  Picked quantities from the storage type aren't rounded off.
- **Round Down WT Quantity to Single Unit**
  Quantities in a warehouse task are rounded off to a single unit. For example, for multiple full pallet picks, the system creates a separate warehouse task for full pallets.
- **Round Down WT Quantity to a Multiple of a Unit**
  Quantities in a warehouse task are rounded off to a multiple of a unit. For example, the entire pick quantity is rounded off to multiples of cases or pallets, and the remaining quantity is moved to a different warehouse task for picking from a different storage type.
- **Round Up WT Quantity to a Multiple of a Unit**
  Quantities in a warehouse task are rounded up to a multiple of a unit. The remaining quantity can be moved back to storage or moved to a different storage area created for storing loose cases.

4.1.4 Goods Movement Control

The **Goods Movement Control** section in the **Storage Type** settings controls how goods movement happens in the storage type. Figure 4.7 shows the different settings available in this section.

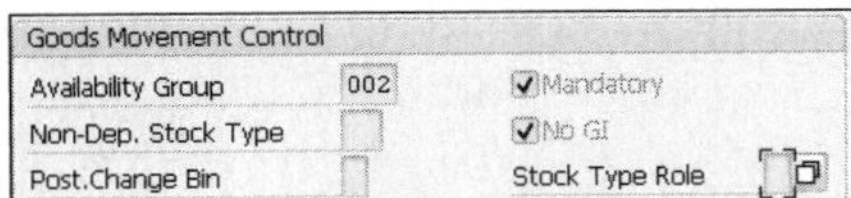

Figure 4.7 Goods Movement Control Settings

We'll discuss each setting in detail in the following sections.

Availability Group

The **Availability Group** setting controls the availability of stock in the storage type. The availability group is used to map SAP S/4HANA plants and storage types in embedded EWM via IMG path **SCM Extended Warehouse Management • Extended Warehouse Management • Interfaces • ERP Integration • Goods Movement • Map Storage Locations from ERP System to EWM**. When stock is placed into a storage bin for the storage type, the stock type for the product is changed based on the settings for the availability group in the storage type. We'll discuss availability groups further in Chapter 7, Section 7.2.4.

Nondependent Stock Type

The **Non-Dep. Stock Type** field is used if you want the storage type to stock only goods belonging to a certain nondependent stock type. The nondependent stock type indicates the quality status of the stock: unrestricted stock, blocked stock, quality inspection, or returns blocked stock.

Posting Change Bin

The **Post.Change Bin** field controls whether a quant will be moved to another bin if a posting change is made to the quant. This is required if you want the system to adhere to the mixed storage settings discussed in earlier sections. The options available are as follows:

- **Posting Change Always in Storage Bin**
  Posting changes will be performed in the storage bin, and stock won't move out of the bin. If putaway settings don't allow mixed stock types in the same bin, this setting will gain preference, and the system will allow bins to have stock with different stock types even if a posting change only occurs for partial stock in the bin.
- **Posting Change According to Mixed Storage Setting**
  Posting changes will happen in the storage bin, and if the storage type setting doesn't allow multiple stock types in the storage bin, then a warehouse task is created to move stock to another storage bin.
- **Posting Change Never in Storage Bin**
  The system will always create a warehouse task to move stock to another bin if a posting change is happening in the storage type.

Mandatory

If the **Mandatory** indicator is selected, then the system only allows stocks with allowed availability groups in the storage type. If you try to move stock into a storage type for which the availability group is different than the availability group mentioned in the storage type setting, then the system posts the stock to the availability group of the storage type. The corresponding change in storage location or stock qualification is reflected in inventory management (IM) in SAP S/4HANA.

No Goods Issue

If the **No GI** indicator is set, the system doesn't allow goods issue from bins in the storage type. This indicator is usually set for final putaway storage types such as rack storage and bulk storage.

Stock Type Role

The settings in this field are used if you want to store only a particular stock type in the storage type. If stock of a different stock type is moved into the bins in the storage type, then the stock type is changed to the stock type defined in this setting. The stock type roles that may be assigned are as follows:

- Custom block stock
- Scrapping stock
- Normal stock

You can use this setting for storage types reserved for scrapping. The stock type role can be set to scrapping stock, and any stock then moved to this storage type will be moved as scrapped stock.

4.1.5 Replenishment Control

The **Replenishment** section includes storage type settings for controlling replenishment. Replenishment is used to fill stock in a picking area so that it reaches a minimum required threshold level and can be used for direct picking. We'll discuss replenishment further in Chapter 9, Section 9.1. Figure 4.8 shows replenishment control settings made at the storage type level. We'll discuss each setting in the following sections.

Figure 4.8 Replenishment Settings in the Storage Type

Replenishment Level

The **Repl. Level** indicator determines the level in the storage type from which the stock levels will be read when replenishment tasks are being created to fill stock in the storage type.

The options available in this setting are as follows:

- **Storage Bin Level for Fixed Bins**
  Stock levels for replenishment are calculated at bin levels for fixed bins allocated to a product. Based on these, the replenishment tasks are created to pick stock from reserve storage types and reach the required threshold level.
- **Storage Type Level**
  Stock levels for replenishment are calculated at the storage type level. Thus, current stock quantities will be calculated for all the bins in the storage type; based on that, replenishment tasks will be created to move required quantities from reserve storage types.

Tolerance

Tolerance is a numeric field that holds a percentage figure. The value of this field defines the percentage of the requested replenishment quantity that would make the replenishment complete if delivered. Thus, if the replenished quantity is less than the quantity for which the replenishment request is created but is more than the tolerance level, the replenishment warehouse request will be marked as **Complete**, and no further replenishment tasks are created.

4.2 Storage Section

A storage type is divided into storage sections based on bins with the same attributes. These attributes vary based on the products that need to be put away into the storage section. You can create sections in a storage type for attributes such as temperature, load-bearing capacity, and so on. For example, a storage type can be divided into separate sections for fast-moving or slow-moving goods. If you use rack storage, you can use the lower levels of the rack to store fast-moving goods so that they're easily and quickly accessible and use the higher levels for slow-moving goods.

Figure 4.9 shows how a storage type can be divided into multiple storage sections.

Storage sections can be created in embedded EWM by navigating to IMG path **SCM Extended Warehouse Management • Extended Warehouse Management • Master Data • Define Storage Section.** Click on **New Entries**, and provide a four-character alphanumeric value for a new storage section for your storage type.

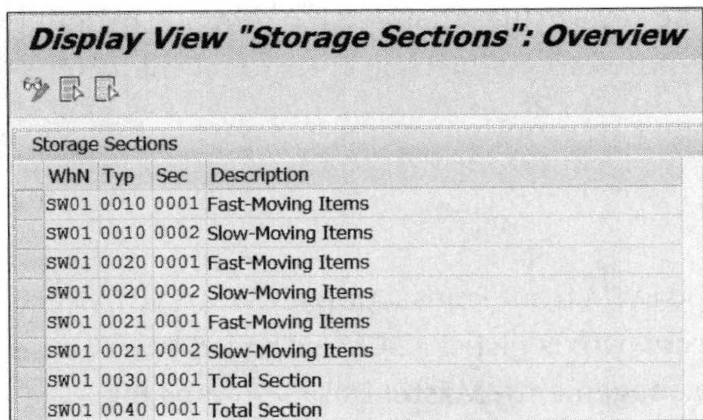

WhN	Typ	Sec	Description
SW01	0010	0001	Fast-Moving Items
SW01	0010	0002	Slow-Moving Items
SW01	0020	0001	Fast-Moving Items
SW01	0020	0002	Slow-Moving Items
SW01	0021	0001	Fast-Moving Items
SW01	0021	0002	Slow-Moving Items
SW01	0030	0001	Total Section
SW01	0040	0001	Total Section

Figure 4.9 Storage Sections in the Warehouse

It isn't always necessary to create storage sections for a storage type in embedded EWM. A storage section only needs to be created if it's used in storage section determination and checks. This is controlled by the **Stor. Section Check** indicator in the **Putaway Control** section for storage type settings that we discussed in Section 4.1.2. Unlike SAP ERP WM, storage bins can be created in WM in SAP S/4HANA without storage sections. Each business should decide the number of storage sections that might be needed for a storage type.

4.3 Storage Bins

A storage type is a collection of multiple storage spaces called *storage bins*, the smallest spatial units used to store a product in the warehouse. There are multiple storage types in embedded EWM representing various entities, such as work centers, doors, yards, and so on, but each one must be linked to a storage bin in the warehouse.

Thus, a storage bin represents an exact position in a warehouse where a product can be stored or located. When you define a storage bin in a warehouse, you can also assign unique geographical coordinates to it so the storage bin can be located by a resource. This identification is made easier by setting the bin names based on their physical locations in the warehouse. For example, you can name a bin in a rack storage type in aisle 01, stack 02, and level 03 as 01-02-03, which helps a warehouse user identify the bin location. Bins can also be named based on the process areas where they're located, such as goods receipt or goods issue zones.

The standard bin structure in embedded EWM uses an 18-digit alphanumeric code. Choosing a naming convention for your bins is an important decision that must be finalized before the bins are created and used in the system.

In the following sections, we'll look at the key settings that need to be made to define storage bins and the configurations required to define their functional characteristics in the system.

4.3.1 Storage Bin Master

Storage bins can be created in embedded EWM from Transaction /SCWM/LS01, which can also be accessed from **SAP Easy Access** path **Logistics • SCM Extended Warehouse Management • Extended Warehouse Management • Master Data • Storage Bin • Create Storage Bin**. A storage bin can be uniquely created for a warehouse number, as shown in Figure 4.10.

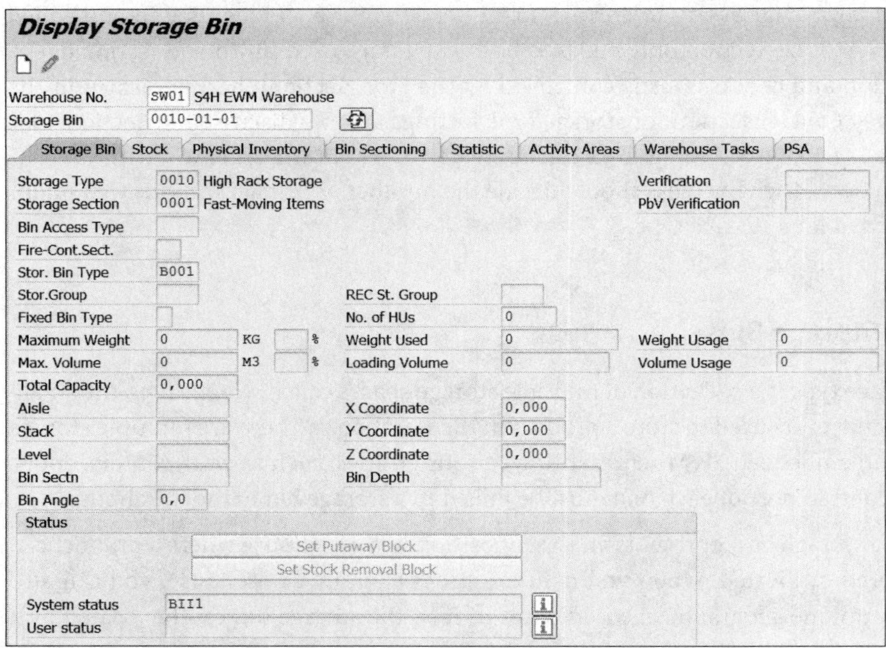

Figure 4.10 Storage Bin in Embedded EWM

The following are some of the key pieces of data used while creating storage bins in embedded EWM:

- **Storage Type**
  This mandatory field stores the storage type in which the storage bin is created.

- **Storage Section**
  This represents a storage section within a storage type to which the storage bin belongs. It's specially populated for operations in which the storage section check is made mandatory for a storage type during putaway.
- **Bin Access Type**
  This field is used to constrain a resource of a resource type to access a bin based on the bin access type assigned to both the resource and storage bin. We'll discuss this further in Section 4.3.3.
- **Fire-Cont.Sect.**
  This field is used to designate a bin for a fire containment section in a warehouse and is used in connection with hazardous substances. It appears in a report the fire department can execute to find hazardous substances in fire containment sections in a warehouse.
- **Stor. Bin Type**
  This field is used to subdivide bins based on the physical capacity of the bins, such as weight, volume, length, width, height, and so on. This enables the system to enhance performance via early bin filters based on capacity. See Section 4.3.2 for more information.
- **Stor.Group**
  This field is used to combine multiple bins of a storage type based on logical or spatial criteria for usage in layout-oriented storage control. You can create a storage group from IMG path **SCM Extended Warehouse Management • Extended Warehouse Management • Cross-Process Settings • Warehouse Task • Define Storage Group For Layout-Oriented Storage Control**. The storage groups created here are then assigned to storage bins. We'll discuss layout-oriented storage control further in Chapter 6, Section 6.5.5.

> **Example**
> While setting up storage groups for layout-oriented storage control, we recommend assigning storage bins in proximity to one another—for example, in the same aisle—to the same storage group. In this way, stock from all bins in the same aisle can be picked together and brought to an intermediate area for further processing.

- **Rec St. Group**
  This field is used to group storage bins into resource execution constraint storage groups for which you want to introduce resource execution constraint. *Resource*

execution constraint is used to limit the number of resources of different resource types that can be used to execute work in an area of a warehouse at one point in time to avoid congestion and increase resource efficiency. The resource execution constraint storage group is used to group bins for the resource execution constraint check. We'll discuss resource execution constraint further in Chapter 11, Section 11.6.

Example

A warehouse supervisor activates the resource execution constraint for storage type ST01. He also creates two storage groups for the storage type—SG01 and SG02—for two different aisles. For each storage group, resources of different resource types can be assigned to optimize the number of resources that can work with the bins in the storage group.

- **Maximum Weight/Max. Volume**
  These parameters control the maximum weight and volume that can be stored in the storage bin. They also display the percentage utilization of weight and volume at any point in time.
- **Total Capacity**
  This parameter represents unitless capacity, based on which maximum stock quantity added in the bin can be constrained. This capacity is checked against the total capacity maintained for the product or HU in the **Unit of Measure** tab of the product master.
- **Aisle**, **Stack**, **Level**, **Bin Sectn**, **Bin Depth**, and **Bin Angle**
  These parameters are used to represent the spatial characteristics of bins in a warehouse. They help warehouse workers identify the location of the bin in the warehouse. The values in these parameters are also used in the graphical warehouse layout.
- **X Coordinate**, **Y Coordinate**, **Z Coordinate**
  These fields are used to represent the geographical coordinates of the bin in a warehouse. The spatial location of the bin in a warehouse complex is available based on these parameters. These parameters are also used to calculate the distance and duration for a resource to move between the bins, which are used to estimate planned workload in labor management in embedded EWM.

- **System status**
  This field provides information about system status codes assigned to the bin, for example, putaway block or stock removal block.
- **User status**
  This field provides information about user status codes assigned to the bin. The user status is used to complement the system status assigned to a given object. The user status should be assigned to a status profile and to the corresponding status objects. You can define a user status profile from IMG path **SCM Extended Warehouse Management • Extended Warehouse Management • Master Data • Storage Bins • Define User Status Profiles**. If you define a status profile after creating bins, you can manually assign the status codes to the bins from SAP Easy Access path **Logistics • SCM Extended Warehouse Management • Extended Warehouse Management • Master Data • Storage Bins • Add User Status for Storage Bins**. You can manually set and reset the user status assigned to the storage bins. For example, you can use the system status to define various reasons for blocking a storage bin.
- **Verification**
  This field is used to set a verification code that can be used to verify the storage bin based on mobile data entry using RF. The entry in this field should match the bar code physically located on the bin. This field is used as an alternative way for a user to identify a storage bin rather than identifying it physically. For simplicity, most warehouses usually name the verification field in the bin by picking up the first or last few characters of the bin name so that they can be easily related.
- **PbV Verification** can set a verification code that can be used to verify the storage bin while using pick-by-voice. After a pick-by-voice verification code is assigned in the storage bin, a resource can easily confirm a warehouse task by speaking the verification code for the storage bin.

4.3.2 Storage Bin Types

Storage bin types are used to group bins with the same physical attributes: weight, volume, dimensions, and so on. Bin types include large bins, small bins, and so on. To create storage bin types, follow IMG path **SCM Extended Warehouse Management • Extended Warehouse Management • Master Data • Storage Bins • Define Storage Bin Types**. As shown in Figure 4.11, you can divide storage bins into bin types based on their physical attributes (size and height) and then create bins for those bin types.

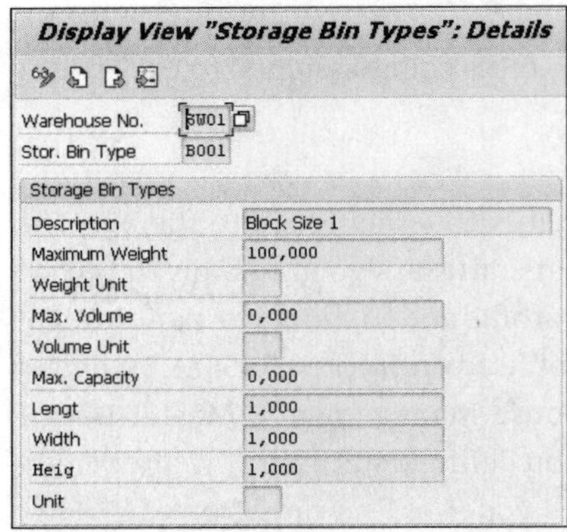

Figure 4.11 Defining Storage Bin Types

As discussed in the previous section, if you've activated early capacity checks at the storage type level, the system will consider the bin type capacity to exclude all bins of a bin type for which the putaway quantity is greater than the available quantity, which increases system performance.

Note

The **Stor. Bin Type** field is optional, but it becomes mandatory if the **HU Type Check** setting is activated at the storage type level.

4.3.3 Bin Access Type

The bin access type controls if stock in a bin can be accessed by a resource of a resource type. Define bin access types via IMG path **SCM Extended Warehouse Management • Extended Warehouse Management • Cross-Process Settings • Resource Management • Define Bin Access Types**. Click on **New Entries**, and define new access types for the embedded EWM warehouse.

The defined bin access type is then assigned to the resource type via IMG path **SCM Extended Warehouse Management • Extended Warehouse Management • Cross-Process Settings • Resource Management • Define Resource Types**. Select a resource type, and click on **Assign Bin Access Types** in the left-hand menu, as shown in Figure 4.12. This configuration allows resources of a resource type to only access bins with the same bin access types, thus limiting unrestricted access of a bin by any other resource.

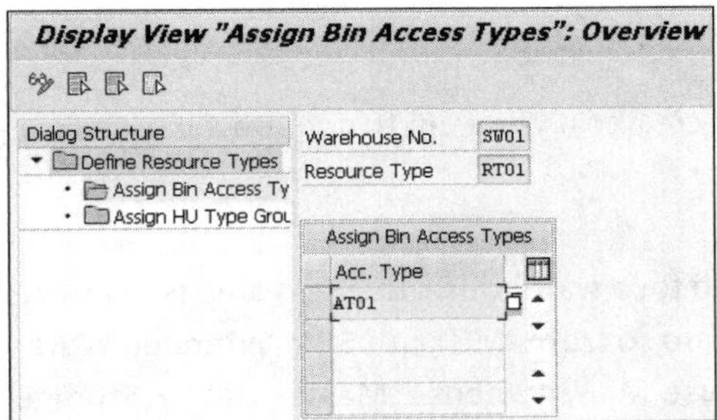

Figure 4.12 Assigning the Resource Type to the Bin Access Type

4.3.4 Storage Bin Structure

The storage bin structure is used to create a structure for bin nomenclature for bins with the same physical attributes. It serves as a template based on which the bins for various storage types can be created automatically using a mass-creation transaction. The first step in creating the storage bin structure is to define the storage bin identifiers. These help identify parts of the bin structure related to the aisle, stack, level, bin subdivision, and bin depth. The storage bin identifiers are created by navigating to IMG path **SCM Extended Warehouse Management • Extended Warehouse Management • Master Data • Storage Bins • Define Storage Bin Identifiers for Storage Bin Structures**. As shown in Figure 4.13, the storage bin identifiers are created at the warehouse level by clicking on **New Entries** for the warehouse and are used to map aisles, stacks and levels, bin subdivisions, and bin depths in the physical warehouse. These parameters make it easier to identify a bin in the storage type.

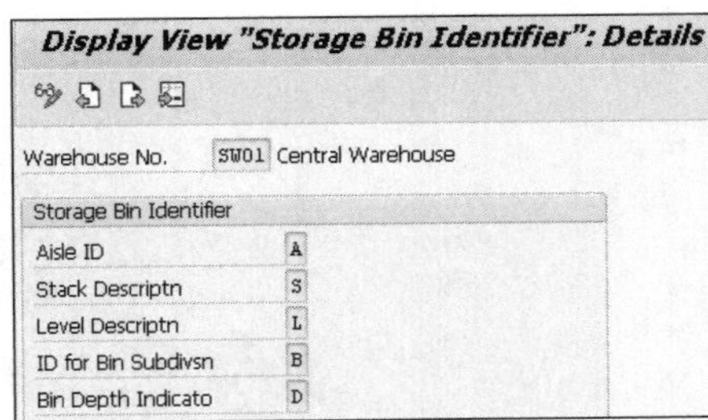

Figure 4.13 Defining the Storage Bin Identifier

> **Note**
>
> The storage bin identifiers also need to be created if you want to define activity areas independent of the storage types.

After the storage bin identifiers are created for a warehouse, the next step is to create a bin structure for a storage type. You can do so from IMG path **SCM Extended Warehouse Management • Extended Warehouse Management • Master Data • Storage Bins • Define Storage Bin Structure.** Click on **New Entries**, and define a new bin structure for the next sequence, as shown in Figure 4.14.

For a warehouse and sequence number, the storage bin structure comprises three main sections: **Bin Definition**, **XYZ - Coordinates**, and **Additional Data**. We'll summarize each section briefly ahead.

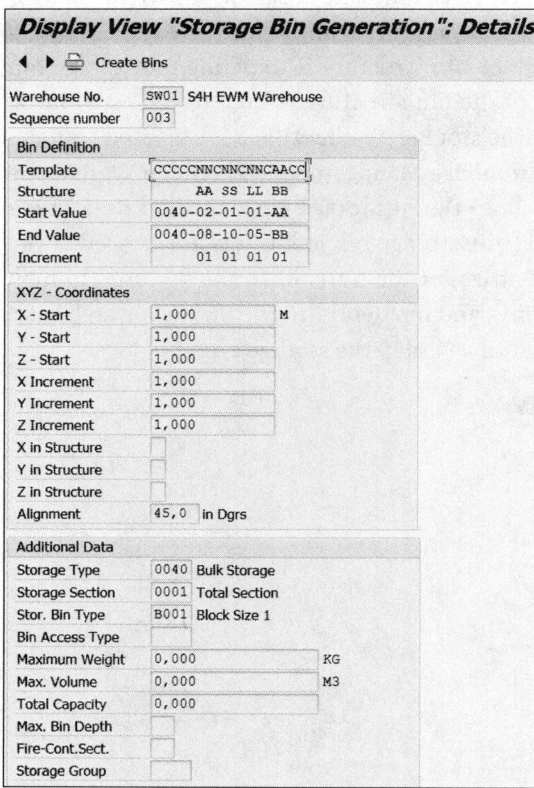

Figure 4.14 Creating the Storage Bin Structure

Bin Definition

The bin definition lays down the rules of how the bins can be named using bin identifiers. The **Bin Definition** section includes the following data:

- **Template**
  This describes the basic nomenclature for the naming of bins. Embedded EWM supports 18-character bin names, so the length of this field is also 18 characters. The template is defined with a combination of three characters: C, A, and N:
  - C defines a constant that won't change value during bin creation.
  - N defines a numeric digit and is variable.
  - A defines a letter and is variable.

> **Example**
>
> To create a bin structure for storage bins ranging from 0040-01-01-01-AA to 0040-08-10-05-BB, specify the template as CCCCCNNCNNCNNCAACC. Any empty characters at the end of a bin name should be filled with C because they're constant. Any incrementing letters in the bin name should be defined by A, and any incrementing numbers by N. Any character or symbol that remains constant should be defined by C.

- **Structure**
  This field is used to define the bin structure for a group of bins based on spatial characteristics such as aisle, stack, bin subdivision, and bin depth. Use the predefined bin identifiers for this purpose. The position of each identifier should align with the respective character in the template so that the system knows which group of characters is for the aisle, stack, bin subdivision, and bin depth.

> **Example**
>
> For storage bins ranging from 0040-01-01-01-AA to 0040-08-10-05-BB, as in the previous example, specify the structure as AA SS LL BB, where AA denotes aisle 01 to 08, SS denotes stack 01 to 10, LL denotes level 01 to 05, and BB denotes bin depth from AA to BB. The rest of the fields are denoted by spaces.

- **Start Value**, **End Value**, and **Increment**
  The **Start Value** defines the name of the first bin in the sequence, the **End Value** denotes the last name of the bin, and the **Increment** defines the increment that will be added to create the name of the next bin in the sequence. You should only

define increments for those variables in the template that will increase in value. An increment can be defined for each identifier of the bin, such as A, S, L, B, and D, based on the bin template being used.

> **Example**
>
> For storage bins ranging from 0040-01-01-01-AA to 0040-08-10-05-BB, specify the increments as 01 01 01 01. The system will create the first bin as 0040-01-01-01-AA, followed by 0040-01-01-01-BB, then 0040-01-01-02-AA, and so on.

XYZ - Coordinates

The various fields in the **XYZ - Coordinates** section are used to map each bin to its geographical coordinates. These coordinates are used to define the geographic location of bins in a physical warehouse structure. Define X, Y, and Z coordinates for the first bin in the storage structure, and then set appropriate increments for the subsequent bins. This allows the unique geographical coordinates of each bin in the storage structure to be identified.

Additional Data

The various fields in the **Additional Data** section are used to define additional attributes for the storage bin structure. The **Storage Type** field is mandatory so that the system knows for which storage type the bin structure is being created. You can set other parameters, such as **Stor. Bin Type**, **Bin Access Type**, **Maximum Weight**, and so on. These parameters are used during the process of putaway and picking to filter out the bins at runtime so that only a small number of bins can be used from a process perspective.

4.3.5 Creating Storage Bins

After the storage types, sections, and bin types have been defined, they can be used to create storage bins. Storage bins can be created in embedded EWM in three ways:

- **Manual creation**
  To create storage bins manually, navigate to **SAP Easy Access** path **Logistics • SCM Extended Warehouse Management • Extended Warehouse Management • Master Data • Storage Bin • Create Storage Bin**, or use Transaction /SCWM/LS01. Click on [icon].

Transaction /SCWM/LS02 is used to modify existing bins, and Transaction /SCWM/LS03 is used to display existing bins.

- **Mass creation**
  You can also generate a group of storage bins using the bin structure created in the previous section. The bins can be created from **SAP Easy Access** path **Logistics • SCM Extended Warehouse Management • Extended Warehouse Management • Master Data • Storage Bin • Generate Storage Bins**, which can also be accessed from Transaction /SCWM/LS10. As shown in Figure 4.15, select the sequence of bins you want to create, and click on the **Create Bins** button. The system creates a group of storage bins based on the values provided for the **Template**, **Start Value**, **End Value**, and **Increments** in the bin structure.

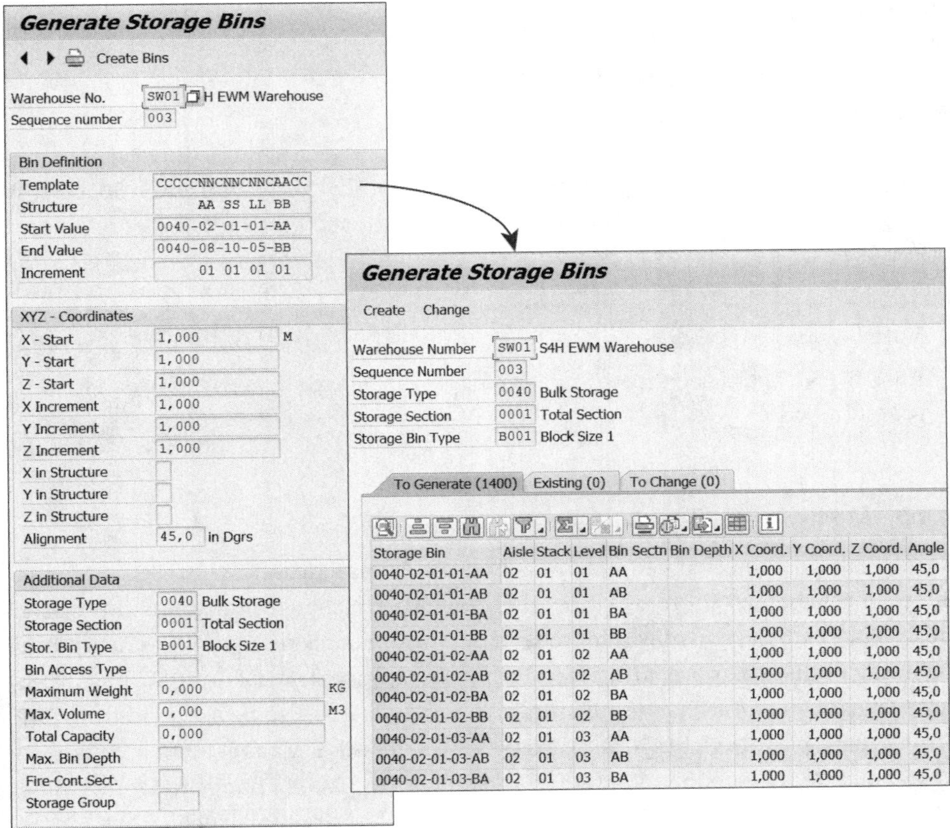

Figure 4.15 Mass Creation of Storage Bins

- **Storage bin upload**
  As explained in Chapter 3, you may also need to load storage bins from a third-party system or from your SAP system. Use Transaction /SCWM/SBUP to upload bins using a CSV file. You can also access this option from **SAP Easy Access** path **Logistics • SCM Extended Warehouse Management • Extended Warehouse Management • Master Data • Storage Bin • Load Storage Bins**, as shown in Figure 4.16.

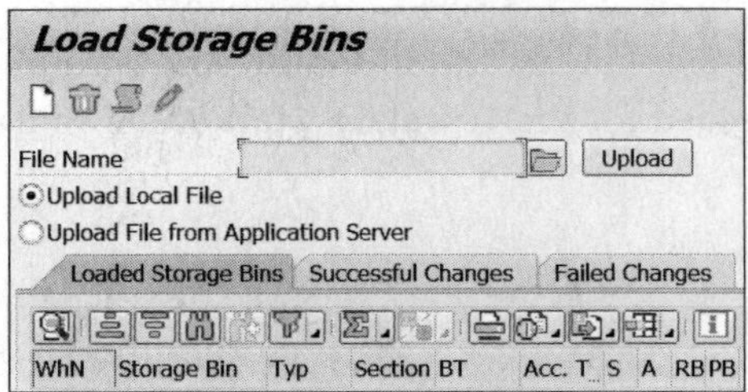

Figure 4.16 Storage Bin Upload

Upon successful upload, bins are created automatically. You can use the **Successful Changes** and **Failed Changes** tabs to view reports for success and failure on bin creation.

> **Note**
> The SAP Fiori app called Create Storage Bins is available to create bin master data in your warehouse.

4.3.6 Modifying Storage Bins

Storage bins can be changed individually using Transaction /SCWM/LS02. SAP also allows mass changes to storage bins when you want to change many bins simultaneously. For example, you may want to set a putaway or stock removal block on a group of storage bins when preparing for physical inventory. Transaction /SCWM/LS11 is used to execute mass changes to storage bins, which can also be accessed from **SAP Easy Access** path **Logistics • SCM Extended Warehouse Management • Extended Warehouse Management • Master Data • Storage Bin • Mass Change to Storage Bins.** The selection screen is used to provide criteria for bin selection, such as bin names, storage type, or section. The next screen lists all the storage bins based on the selection criteria. You can select some or all bins and click on **Change Storage Bins.** A popup screen appears so you can select the fields to be changed, as shown in Figure 4.17. The storage bins mass change is complete after you save your selections.

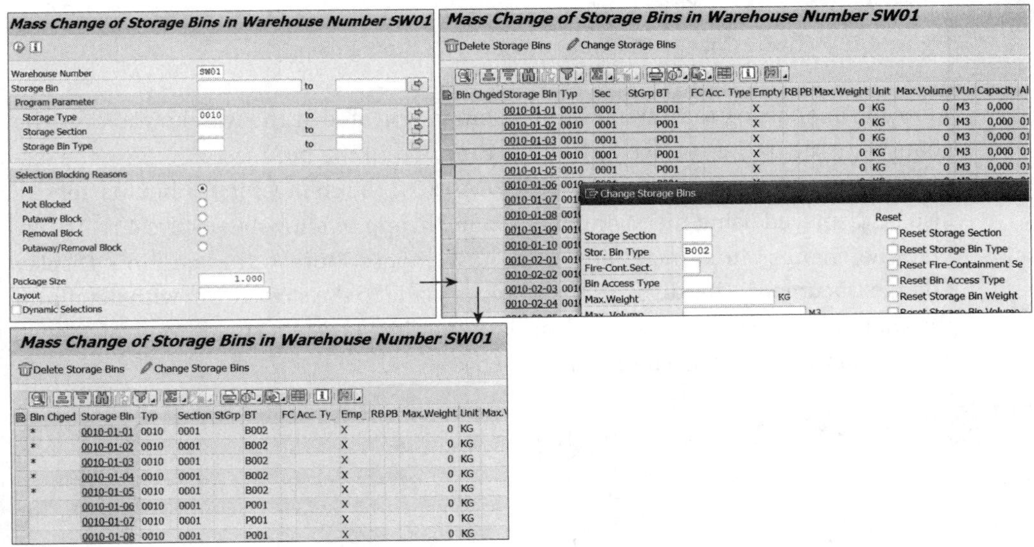

Figure 4.17 Mass Change to Storage Bins

4.3.7 Change Documents for Storage Bins

The storage bin is one of the most important master data objects in embedded EWM operations, and it's important to have a view of any changes made in the storage bin master and know who made the changes. This helps users track the changes made and revert them. It also helps maintain accountability of the changes by knowing who made the changes and when were they made. The embedded EWM system creates a log document where it records all changes made to storage bins, and the log is made available to users for reporting purposes.

As shown in Figure 4.18, the change logs for bin master data can be captured in embedded EWM system by activating the **Storage Bins** checkbox via IMG path **SCM Extended Warehouse Management • Extended Warehouse Management • Master Data • Storage Bins • Activate Change Documents.**

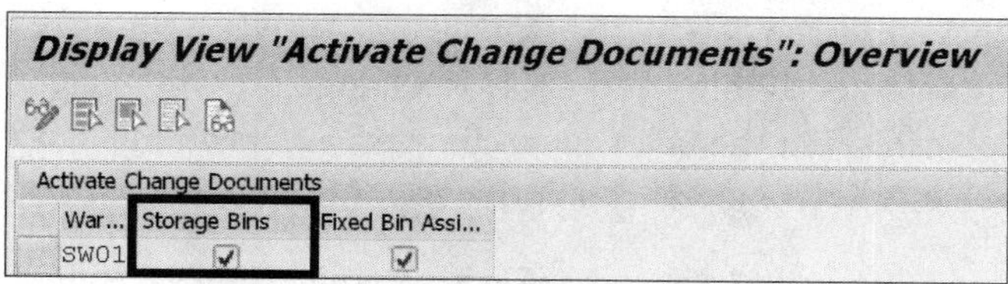

Figure 4.18 Activate Change Documents Screen for Storage Bins

After the change log for the master data bin is activated at the warehouse level, the changes made to the storage bin will be captured in the bin master and can be displayed to the user using Transaction /SCWM/LS03. The changes in the bin master can also be displayed using the Maintain Storage Bin app, as shown in Figure 4.19. To display the changes in storage bins, you must choose **More • Storage Bin • Display Change Document**. This displays the changes made to the storage bin with details on the changes made by the user, such as date and time change is made, type of change made, and transaction used to make the change.

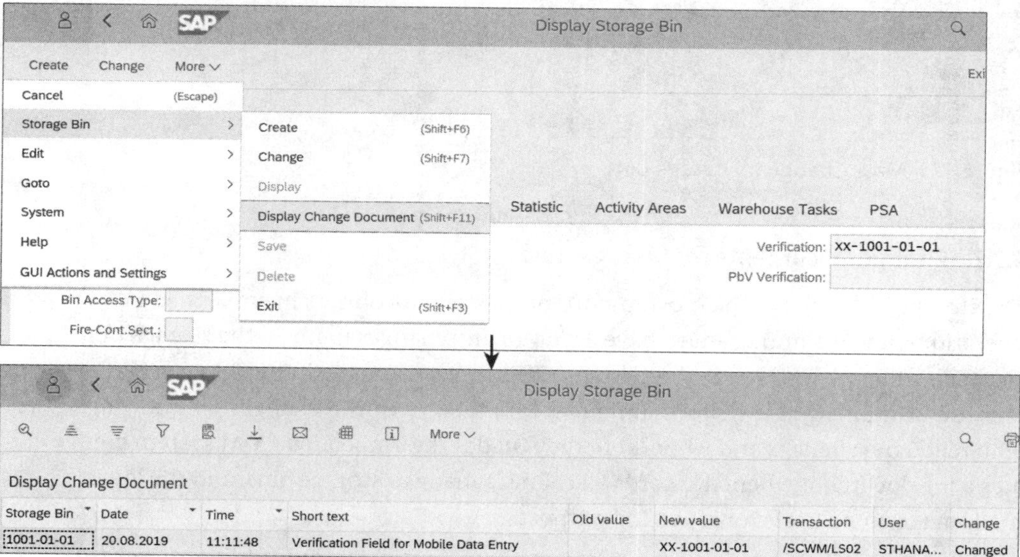

Figure 4.19 Display Change Logs in Bin Master Showing Changes

> **Note**
>
> The following SAP Fiori apps are available to maintain bin master data:
>
> - **Change Storage Bins**
>   This app allows you to edit and change storage bin master data for the warehouse.
> - **Display Storage Bins**
>   This app allows you to display storage bin master data in the warehouse.

4.3.8 Executing Storage Bin Sorting

Storage bin sorting is needed to work with activity areas in embedded EWM. This allows warehouse tasks to be sorted, which is needed during warehouse order creation. Bins are sorted based on the sort sequence defined for activity areas via IMG path **SCM Extended Warehouse Management • Extended Warehouse Management • Master Data • Activity Area • Define Sort Sequence For Activity Area**. Use Transaction /SCWM/SBST or navigate to **SAP Easy Access** path **Logistics • SCM Extended Warehouse Management • Extended Warehouse Management • Master Data • Storage Bin • Sort Storage Bins**, to execute bin sorting, as shown in Figure 4.20. You can perform bin sorting based on the **Activity Area** and **Activity**, or you can leave these fields blank and click on . If you leave these fields blank, the system will determine all possible combinations of activity areas and activities and then execute bin sorting.

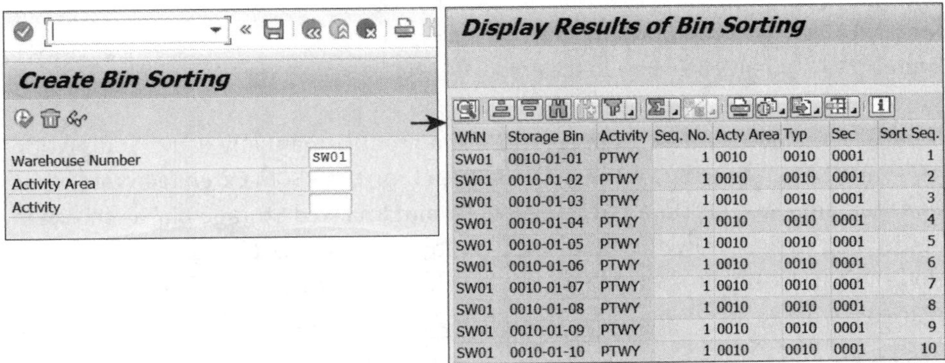

WhN	Storage Bin	Activity	Seq. No.	Acty Area	Typ	Sec	Sort Seq.
SW01	0010-01-01	PTWY	1	0010	0010	0001	1
SW01	0010-01-02	PTWY	1	0010	0010	0001	2
SW01	0010-01-03	PTWY	1	0010	0010	0001	3
SW01	0010-01-04	PTWY	1	0010	0010	0001	4
SW01	0010-01-05	PTWY	1	0010	0010	0001	5
SW01	0010-01-06	PTWY	1	0010	0010	0001	6
SW01	0010-01-07	PTWY	1	0010	0010	0001	7
SW01	0010-01-08	PTWY	1	0010	0010	0001	8
SW01	0010-01-09	PTWY	1	0010	0010	0001	9
SW01	0010-01-10	PTWY	1	0010	0010	0001	10

Figure 4.20 Storage Bin Sorting

4.3.9 Assignment of Fixed Bins to Product

You can assign fixed bins to products in embedded EWM when you want products to go into a predefined fixed bin. Putaway and stock removal of a product also originate from the same bin. You can use fixed bin storage for products that are temperature controlled, inflammable, oversized, or have high value. Fixed bin assignment also ensures that a product doesn't spill over to other bins that may be required to store other products. After the bin master data is created in embedded EWM, some bins of a storage type can be assigned to a product as fixed bins using Transaction /SCWM/FBINASN or using **SAP Easy Access path Logistics • SCM Extended Warehouse Management • Master Data • Storage Bin • Assign Fixed Storage Bins to Products**, as shown in Figure 4.21. After providing the mandatory input data for **Product**, **Warehouse Number**, **Storage Type**, and **No. of Storage Bins** that need to be assigned for the product, click on . The system will assign the required number of fixed bins in the storage type to the product.

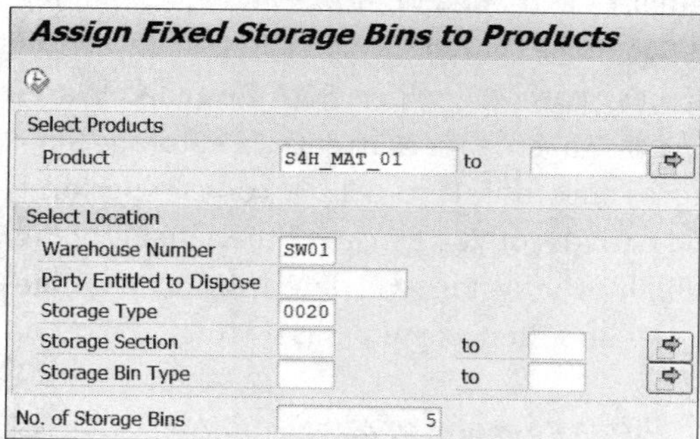

Figure 4.21 Assigning Fixed Bins to the Product

You can also maintain fixed storage bins for a product manually using Transaction /SCWM/BINMAT or using **SAP Easy Access** path **Logistics • SCM Extended Warehouse Management • Master Data • Storage Bin • Maintain Fixed Storage Bin**, as shown in Figure 4.22. Assign a product to a fixed bin by opening the transaction in change mode and selecting the execute icon, which will lead to a new row being created.

You can delete fixed bin assignments using Transaction /SCWM/FBINDEL, which can also be accessed from **SAP Easy Access** path **Logistics • SCM Extended Warehouse Management • Master Data • Storage Bin • Delete Fixed Storage Bin Assignment**. Provide the product and required bin search criteria, and click on the icon. The system will delete all fixed bins assigned to this product in the warehouse.

Warehouse Number SW01: Maintain Fixed Storage Bin

WhN	Ent.toDisp	Storage Bin	Typ	Product	StBinImp	Changed On	Max.Qty	Display UoM	Min. Qty	Display UoM	Fixed
SW01	BP_PL_1001	0020-01-01-A	0020	S4H_MAT_01		14.12.2017	0,000		0,000		☐
SW01	BP_PL_1001	0020-01-01-B	0020	S4H_MAT_01		14.12.2017	0,000		0,000		☐
SW01	BP_PL_1001	0020-01-01-C	0020	S4H_MAT_01		14.12.2017	0,000		0,000		☐
SW01	BP_PL_1001	0020-01-01-D	0020	S4H_MAT_01		14.12.2017	0,000		0,000		☐
SW01	BP_PL_1001	0020-01-01-E	0020	S4H_MAT_01		14.12.2017	0,000		0,000		☐
SW01	BP_PL_1001	0020-01-01-F	0020	S4H_MAT_01			0,000		0,000		☑

Figure 4.22 Fixed Bin Assignment

4.3.10 Change Log for Fixed Storage Bin Assignments

Along with assigning fixed bins to products to cap the number of bins in a storage area that a product can occupy, you can also access the logs of changes made for any data related to such fixed bin assignments. These change logs are recorded in the system when there are any changes, creations, or deletions of data to the fixed bin assignment with products.

As shown in Figure 4.23, the change logs for fixed bin assignment master data can be captured in the embedded EWM system by selecting the **Fixed Bin Assi.** checkbox via IMG path **SCM Extended Warehouse Management • Extended Warehouse Management • Master Data • Storage Bins • Activate Change Documents**.

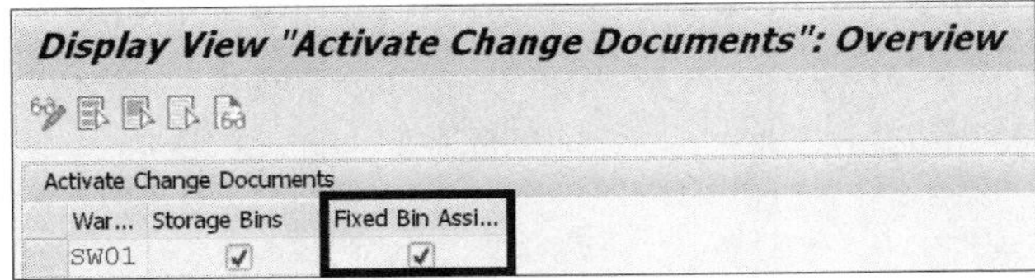

Figure 4.23 Activating Change Documents for Fixed Bin Assignment

After the change log for fixed bin assignment master data is activated at the warehouse level, the changes made to the fixed bin assignment will be captured in the bin master and can be displayed to the user using Transaction /SCWM/BINMAT, as shown in Figure 4.24. To display the changes in storage bins, you must choose **Fixed Storage Bin • Display Change Documents**. This displays the changes made to the fixed storage bin assignment with details on the changes made by the user, such as date and time change is made, type of change made, and transaction used to make the change.

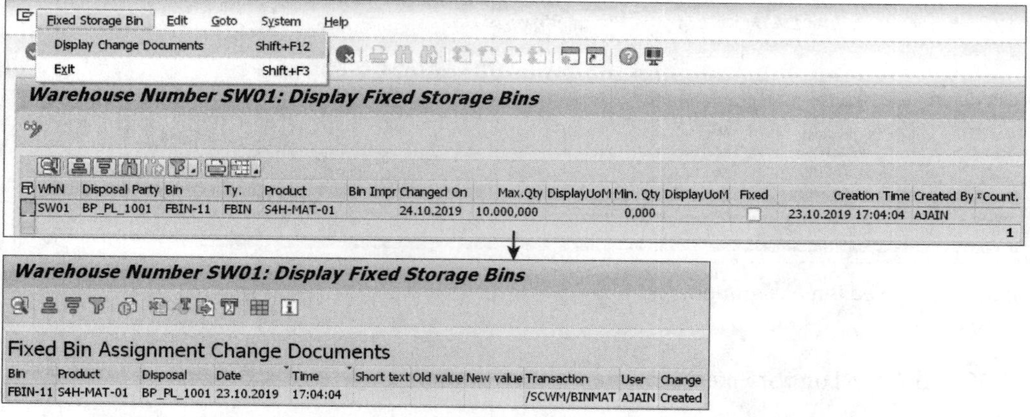

Figure 4.24 Displaying Change Documents for Fixed Bin Assignment

Users can also display the changes via the warehouse monitor by choosing **Stock and Bin • Storage Bin • Fixed Bin Assignment**. The change logs for fixed bin assignment can be displayed using warehouse monitor path of node: **Stock and Bin • Fixed Bin Overview • Fixed Bins • Fixed Bin Assignment**. The change logs for fixed bin assignment can also be displayed by choosing **Product Master Data • Warehouse Attribute** in the warehouse monitor.

> **Note**
>
> The Assign Fixed Bins app in SAP Fiori allows you to assign fixed bins to products so that a particular product can't swamp a large area of warehouse.

4.3.11 Bin Verification Field

Embedded EWM provides a report to create bin verification fields for storage bins automatically in the background. With this report, you can create bin verification fields for the created bins and update them to the bins simultaneously. Set up bin verification fields from **SAP Easy Access** path **Logistics • SCM Extended Warehouse Management • Extended Warehouse Management • Master Data • Storage Bin • Maintain Verification Field**, which can also be accessed from Transaction /SCWM/LX45. Use this transaction to update both bin verification fields and pick-by-voice bin verification fields. After providing the input criteria in the selection screen to maintain the verification field, click on [icon]. The system provides the proposed verification field value for each storage bin. You can accept the proposed values by clicking on the **Update** button, after which the system updates the values in the **Verification** field in the bin master, which can be seen using Transaction /SCWM/LS03, as shown in Figure 4.25.

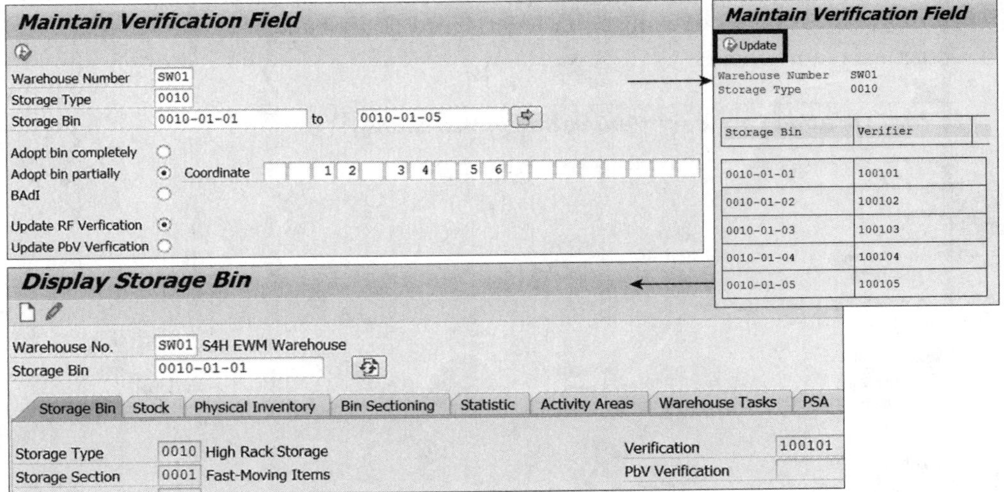

Figure 4.25 Maintaining the Bin Verification Field

SAP provides three options to create verification fields:

- **Adopt bin completely**
  Using this option, the bin name is completely adopted as the bin verification code.
- **Adopt bin partially**
  Using this option, you can choose which characters of the bin name can be used to create the bin verification code. You can remove any prefix, suffix, or hyphen from the bin name. You can also realign the characters from the 18-character bin name for this purpose.
- **BAdI**
  Using a business add-in (BAdI), you can define your own sequence for creating bin verification.

4.3.12 Printing Storage Bin Labels

A bin label holds the bin number of the storage bin and the verification code based on screen selection and is used to identify a storage bin in a warehouse. You can print bin labels in SAP using Transaction /SCWM/PRBIN, which can also be accessed from **SAP Easy Access** path **Logistics • SCM Extended Warehouse Management • Extended Warehouse Management • Master Data • Storage Bin • Print Storage Bin Label**. Provide the bin details and print parameters as shown in Figure 4.26, and click on . The standard smart form /SCWM/BIN_LABEL is used to print the labels. You can create a custom smart form in SAP using Transaction SMARTFORM and assign it here per your business requirements.

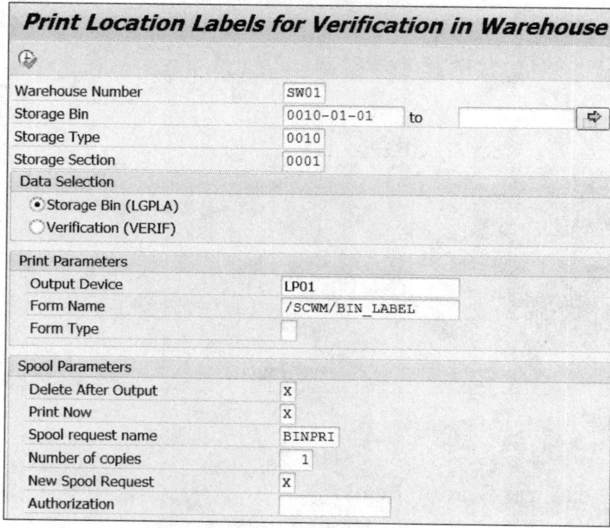

Figure 4.26 Printing Storage Bin Labels

SAP also provides an option to print labels for fixed bins. These labels include the product identification on the bin label as well. You can print bin labels using Transaction /SCWM/FIXBIN_LABEL,, which can also be accessed from **SAP Easy Access** path **Logistics • SCM Extended Warehouse Management • Extended Warehouse Management • Master Data • Storage Bin • Print Fixed Bin Label**. Provide the bin details and print parameters, and click on . Embedded EWM uses a standard Post Processing Framework (PPF) process to issue the bin label to the label printer connected to SAP.

> **Note**
>
> The Print Storage Bins Labels app allows you to print storage bin master labels that can be stuck on physical bins for bin identification.

4.4 Staging Area and Warehouse Door

A staging area is an area in the warehouse where goods are temporarily staged before they're put away in the warehouse or sent outside the warehouse. Warehouse doors are areas in the warehouse through which goods come into and out of the warehouse. We'll now discuss both of these organizational elements in detail.

4.4.1 Staging Area

Staging areas are defined in SAP from IMG path **SCM Extended Warehouse Management • Extended Warehouse Management • Master Data • Staging Areas • Define Staging Areas**, by clicking on **New Entries**, as shown in Figure 4.27.

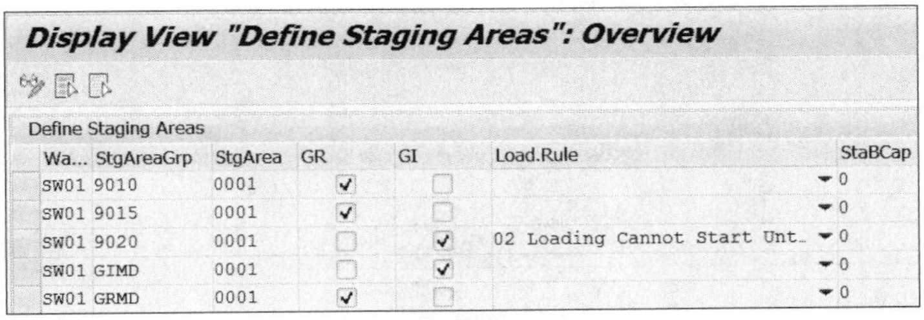

Display View "Define Staging Areas": Overview

Define Staging Areas

Wa...	StgAreaGrp	StgArea	GR	GI	Load.Rule	StaBCap
SW01	9010	0001	✓	☐		0
SW01	9015	0001	✓	☐		0
SW01	9020	0001	☐	✓	02 Loading Cannot Start Unt…	0
SW01	GIMD	0001	☐	✓		0
SW01	GRMD	0001	✓	☐		0

Figure 4.27 Staging Area in Embedded EWM

Before defining staging areas in embedded EWM, you must first define staging area groups. A staging area group corresponds to a storage type with storage type role D. Next, the staging area is defined in embedded EWM as a storage section used specifically for staging. Using the **GR/GI** checkboxes, you can restrict the direction of goods movement in the staging area to inbound, outbound, or both. The **Load.Rule** setting is used to define the loading rule for the staging area. These rules determine when loading of goods to a vehicle or TU should start after they reach the staging area. The options available are as follows:

- Loading can start when the first HU has arrived.
- Loading can't start until staging has been completed.
- Loading can't start until 24 hours wait time has passed.

In the next step, you define the staging area and door determination group via IMG path **SCM Extended Warehouse Management • Extended Warehouse Management • Master Data • Staging Area • Define Staging Area and Door Determination Groups**, by clicking on **New Entries**. Assign the staging area/door determination group in the

StagArea/DoorDet.Grp field in the **Whse Data** tab of the product master if you want specific products to use specific staging areas for loading and unloading.

4.4.2 Warehouse Door

Doors are organizational units in embedded EWM from which goods move into and out of the warehouse. If you use TUs and vehicles, then they arrive at the warehouse door from which all loading and unloading of goods happens. You can define doors in SAP from IMG path **SCM Extended Warehouse Management • Extended Warehouse Management • Master Data • Warehouse Door • Define Warehouse Door**, by clicking on **New Entries**, as shown in Figure 4.28.

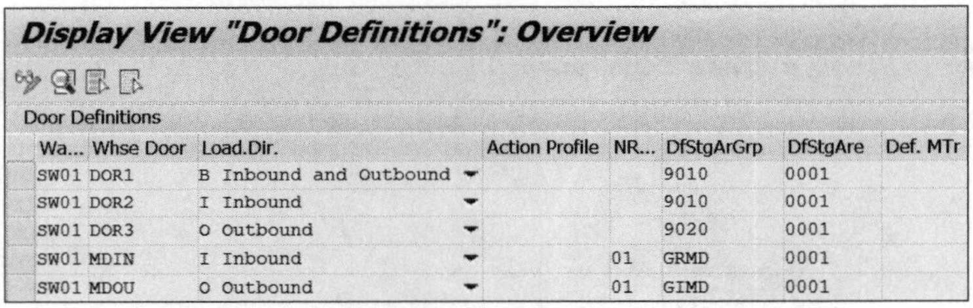

Display View "Door Definitions": Overview

Door Definitions

Wa...	Whse Door	Load.Dir.	Action Profile	NR...	DfStgArGrp	DfStgAre	Def. MTr
SW01	DOR1	B Inbound and Outbound			9010	0001	
SW01	DOR2	I Inbound			9010	0001	
SW01	DOR3	O Outbound			9020	0001	
SW01	MDIN	I Inbound		01	GRMD	0001	
SW01	MDOU	O Outbound		01	GIMD	0001	

Figure 4.28 Defining the Warehouse Door

The **Load.Dir.** field represents the *loading direction*, that is, the direction in which goods flow in the warehouse. A door can be used only for incoming goods, only for outgoing goods, or for both. **Action Profile** is used to give the PPF information for printing. **DfStgArGrp** and **DfStgAre** represent the default staging area group and default staging area, respectively, that will be mapped to the door if the system can't find a direct assignment of a warehouse door to a staging area. **Def. MTr** represents the default means of transport that will be used for creation of vehicles and TUs.

4.4.3 Assigning the Staging Area to the Door

In the next step, assign the staging area/door determination group to warehouse doors. In this way, you can segregate loading of different types of goods, for example, bulk materials versus palleted goods. This is done from IMG path **SCM Extended Warehouse Management • Extended Warehouse Management • Master Data • Warehouse Door • Assign Staging Area/Door Determination Group to Door**, by clicking on **New Entries** and creating the mapping for the embedded EWM warehouse.

You also assign the staging area to a warehouse door from IMG path **SCM Extended Warehouse Management • Extended Warehouse Management • Master Data • Warehouse Door • Assign Staging Area to Warehouse Door**. Click on **New Entries**, and map the staging area to door in the warehouse, as shown in Figure 4.29. This assignment is used to update the staging area in the delivery based on the door assignment. The loading and unloading of goods will happen from this staging area.

Display View "Assignment of Staging Area to Warehouse Door": Overview

Assignment of Staging Area to Warehouse Door

Wa...	Whse Door	StgAreaGrp	StgArea
SW01	DOR2	9010	0001
SW01	DOR2	9015	0001
SW01	DOR3	9020	0001

Figure 4.29 Assigning the Staging Area to the Warehouse Door

4.5 Activity Area

An activity area group's storage bins are based on the activities performed in the warehouse, such as picking, putaway, replenishment, physical inventory, and so on. You can perform multiple activities in an activity area. An activity area also can include bins from multiple storage types.

As an example, consider Figure 4.30. The figure shows two storage types, A and B, and both have bins used to stock fast-moving goods. You can combine bins from both storage types to create an activity area for picking fast-moving goods.

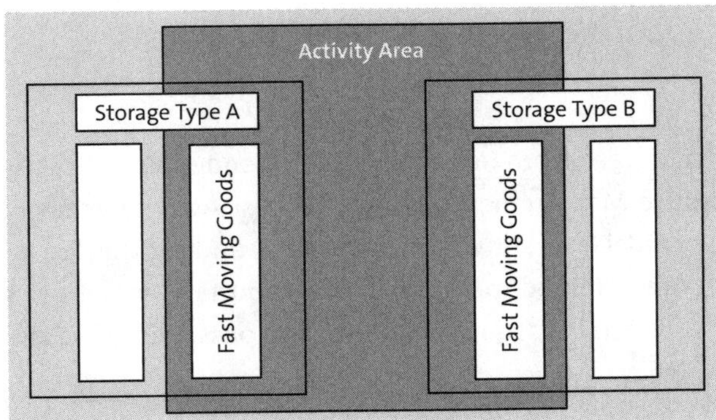

Figure 4.30 Activity Area in Embedded EWM

The activity area concept doesn't exist in WM in SAP ERP; it's specific to embedded EWM in SAP S/4HANA. An activity area is used to group warehouse tasks into warehouse orders, which are then assigned to resources. Activity areas are also used for bin sorting based on activity area and activity.

The prerequisite to setting up activity areas in a warehouse is to define the activities. You can define an activity in embedded EWM from IMG path **SCM Extended Warehouse Management • Extended Warehouse Management • Master Data • Activity Area • Activities • Define Activities**. Click on **New Entries**. Each activity should be assigned to a warehouse process category, which describes the different types of goods movement in the warehouse, as shown in Figure 4.31. There are six fundamental warehouse process categories:

- **Putaway**
- **Stock Removal**
- **Internal Warehouse Movement**
- **Physical Inventory**
- **Posting Change**
- **Cross-Line Stock Putaway**

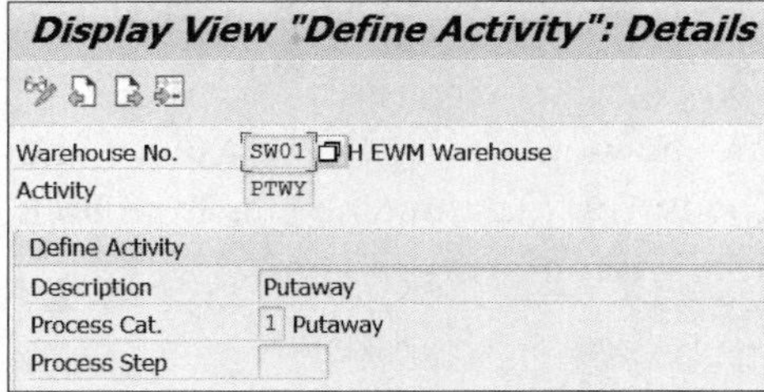

Figure 4.31 Define Activity

In the next step, you define activity areas from IMG path **SCM Extended Warehouse Management • Extended Warehouse Management • Master Data • Activity Areas • Define Activity Area**. Click on **New Entries** as shown in Figure 4.32, and set the **Areas Joined** indicator if required. The **Areas Joined** indicator is used to mark an activity area as a higher-level activity area, which is used in pick, pack, and pass. We'll discuss this further in Chapter 11, Section 11.5.

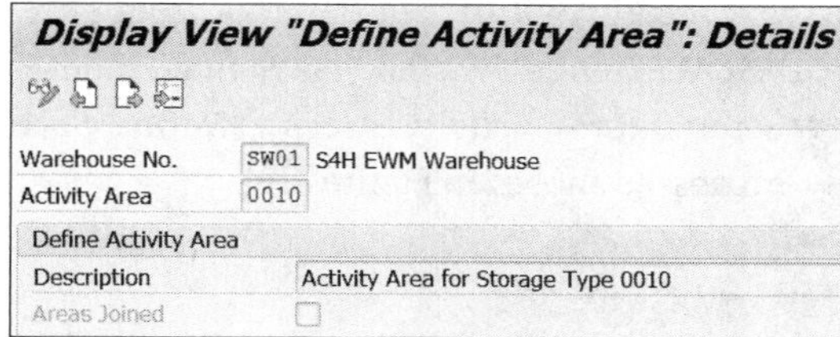

Display View "Define Activity Area": Details

Warehouse No.	SW01	S4H EWM Warehouse
Activity Area	0010	

Define Activity Area

Description	Activity Area for Storage Type 0010
Areas Joined	☐

Figure 4.32 Defining an Activity Area

Next, assign the storage bins to activity areas, as shown in Figure 4.33, via IMG path **SCM Extended Warehouse Management • Extended Warehouse Management • Master Data • Activity Areas • Assign Storage Bins to Activity Areas**, and click on **New Entries**.

Display View "Activity Area": Details

Warehouse No.	SW01	S4H EWM Warehouse
Activity Area	0020	Activity Area for Storage Type 0020
Sequence No.	1	

Activity Area

Storage Type	0020	Rack Storage
Aisle Start		
Aisle End		
Stack Start		
Stack End		
Level Start		
Level End		
Bin Section Start		
Bin Section End		
Cons.Grp	0001000002	
Int. Storage Type		
Interm. Stor. Sec.		
Intermediate Bin		

Figure 4.33 Assigning Storage Bins to Activity Areas

An activity area can include bins from more than one storage type. When you map the activity area to the storage type; the list of bins to be included in that activity area is defined by bin attributes such as aisle, stack, level, bin subdivision, and so on. You can also assign consolidation groups to your entry to determine if products in HUs should go through deconsolidation if they belong to different consolidation groups.

After the storage bins are assigned to activity areas, you can create the sort sequence for the bins in an activity area via IMG path **SCM Extended Warehouse Management • Extended Warehouse Management • Master Data • Activity Areas • Define Sort Sequence for Activity Area**. Click on **New Entries**, as shown in Figure 4.34.

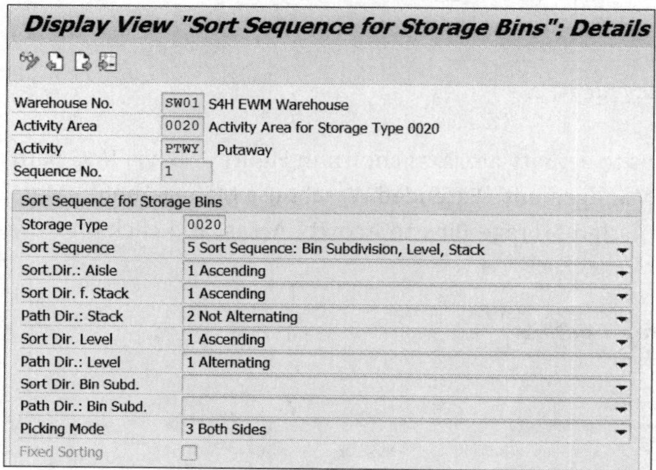

Figure 4.34 Defining the Sort Sequence for the Activity Area

The bins in an activity area are sorted for all the activities that need to be performed in that activity area. You need to create a sort sequence because this order is used for sequencing warehouse tasks in a warehouse order and also controls the path and distance that need to be traveled by a warehouse operator while carrying out warehouse processes in embedded EWM.

4.6 Work Center

A *work center* is a physical location in the warehouse used for specific activities such as deconsolidation, packing, value-added services (VAS), and so on. SAP provides customizable user interfaces (UIs) for different types of work centers based on work center layouts. Figure 4.35 shows a work center used for packaging in embedded EWM.

In the following sections, we'll discuss work center layouts and defining work centers in embedded EWM in detail.

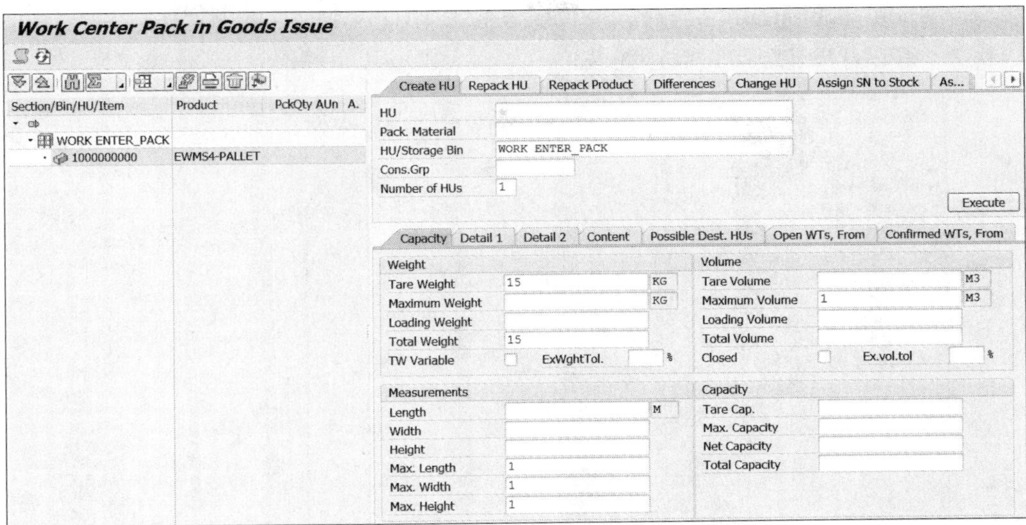

Figure 4.35 Work Center in Embedded EWM

4.6.1 Work Center Layout

A *work center layout* controls the features and functionalities available in a work center. The work center is created for a specific work center layout. Work center layouts can be created via IMG path **SCM Extended Warehouse Management • Extended Warehouse Management • Master Data • Work Center • Specify Work Center Layout**. Click on **New Entries**, which opens a new empty layout screen. Figure 4.36 shows a sample work center layout that can be used to create a work center for packaging.

There are three main sections in the settings for work center layouts:

- **Tab Pages in Scanner Area**
  The selections made in this section appear in the top-right section of the work center. For a packaging work center, you can include tabs for creating HUs, repacking HUs and products, and so on.

- **Tab Pages in Detail Area**
  The selections made in this section appear in the lower-right section of the work center. This section displays details of HUs or storage bins selected in the tree control in the work center.

- **Tree Control**
  The selections made in this section appear in the left screen of the work center. If

you click on any of the objects—such as HUs or bins—in the tree, the details appear in the tab pages detail area.

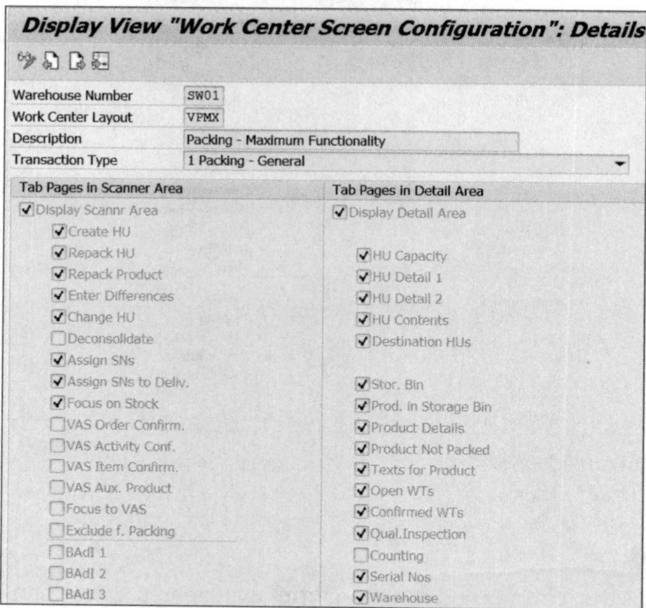

Figure 4.36 Work Center Layout

4.6.2 Define Work Center

In this setting, you define a work center based on work center layouts created previously. Create the work center via IMG path **SCM Extended Warehouse Management • Extended Warehouse Management • Master Data • Work Center • Define Work Center**. Click on **New Entries**, and define the new work center and its attributes for the embedded EWM warehouse. Figure 4.37 shows a sample work center used for packaging.

Some of the key settings that need to be defined to set up a work center in embedded EWM are as follows:

- **External step**
  The **External Step** field is used to specify external process steps assigned to the work center. When an HU is moved to a work center, the system checks the external process step assigned to the HU. It assigns the external step assigned to the work center to the HU if this step is later in the storage process control sequence than the external step assigned to the HU.

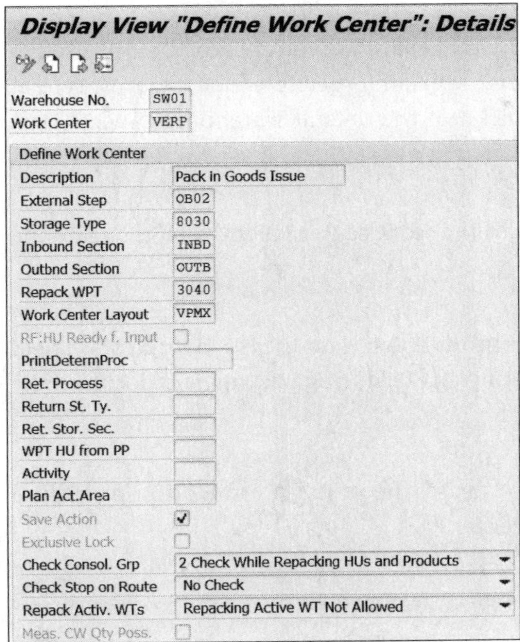

Figure 4.37 Defining the Work Center

- **Storage type**
  The **Storage Type** field is used to provide the storage type of the work center. You can only use the storage type for work centers if it has any of the following storage type roles:
  - **Work Center (E)**
  - **Pick Point (B)**
  - **Work Center in Staging Area Group (I)**
  - **Identification and Pick Point (C)**
- **Inbound section**
  The **Inbound Section** field is used to specify the storage section in the work center where stock will be stored before it's processed in the work center.
- **Outbound section**
  The **Outbnd Section** field is used to specify the storage section in the work center where stock will be stored after it's been processed at the work center.

- **Repack warehouse process type**
  The **Repack WPT** field is used to specify the repack warehouse process type used to create a repack task in the work center. If you don't specify a repack process type at the work center level, the system picks up the default warehouse process type maintained at the warehouse control level.
- **Work Center Layout**
  The **Work Center Layout** field specifies the work center layout used to create the work center.
- **RF: HU Ready for Input**
  The **RF: HU Ready f. Input** indicator controls if you want the **HU Identification** field to appear in an RF screen while creating an HU during packing and deconsolidation with RF.
- **Print Determination Procedure**
  The **PrntDetermProc** field is used to specify the print determination procedure used for printing labels in the work center.
- **Return Process**
  The **Ret. Process** field is used to provide a warehouse process type to create warehouse tasks to move unused goods from the pick point back to the return storage type when the work center is the pick point.
- **Return Storage Type**
  The **Return. St. Ty.** field is used to specify the return storage type where the remaining contents of the source HU should be moved after picking.
- **Return Storage Section**
  The **Return. Stor. Sec.** is used to specify the return storage type where the remaining contents of the source HU should be moved after picking.
- **Warehouse process type HU from pick point**
  The **WPT HU from PP** field is used to provide the warehouse process type to create the HU warehouse task to move the source HU from the pick point back to the return storage type when the work center is a pick point.
- **Activity**
  The **Activity** field is used to provide the name of the activity for which text is displayed in the work center.
- **Plan activity area**
  The **Plan Act.Area** field is used to provide the planning activity area if labor management is active and is used in creating the planned workload.

- **Save action**
  If the **Save Action** indicator is set, it saves any activity performed in the work center immediately.
- **Exclusive lock**
  The **Exclusive Lock** indicator is set if you want to set an exclusive lock on the HU when it's being unpacked. You may want to repack an HU either to unpack it or move the product in the HU to another HU. You should set this indicator if you don't want multiple users to unpack an HU simultaneously.
- **Check consolidation group**
  Check Consol. Grp controls how the system checks for a consolidation group while repacking an HU. By default, the system always checks to see if the consolidation group of the product being packed matches the consolidation group of the destination HU. With this setting, you can control any additional checks that need to be done. The options available for this setting are as follows:
  - **No Check**
    No checks other than the default described previously are performed.
  - **Check while Repacking Products**
    The system not only compares the consolidation group of the product with the destination HU but also, if the destination HU is in a higher-level HU, the system ensures that its consolidation group is the same.
  - **Check while Repacking HUs and Products**
    The system performs the default check and the check described previously not only while repacking products but also while repacking HUs.
- **Check stop on route**
  The **Check Stop on Route** setting controls whether a stop on the route is to be considered while repacking products or HUs in the work center. The options available for this setting are as follows:
  - **No Check**
  - **Check while Repacking Products**
  - **Check while Repacking HUs and Products**
- **Repack active warehouse tasks**
  The **Repack Activ. WTs** setting helps control if you can repack products or HUs in active warehouse tasks. There are two options available in this setting:
  - **Repacking Active WT Not Allowed**
  - **Repacking Active WT Allowed**

- **Measuring catch weight quantity in work center possible**
  The **Meas. CW Qty Poss.** indicator controls whether you can capture the catch weight quantity of a product in the work center. If this indicator isn't set, the system doesn't capture the catch weight of products. We'll discuss catch weight management further in Chapter 6, section 6.9.

Each work center should be assigned to a storage type and bin to manage the stock in a work center. You assign the storage bin to a work center via **SAP Easy Access** path **Logistics • SCM Extended Warehouse Management • Extended Warehouse Management • Master Data • Work Center • Define Master Data Attributes.** The transaction screen displays the preexisting work centers in embedded EWM to which you can assign the storage bin.

4.6.3 Optimizing Work Center Determination

These settings help optimize work center determination by specifying the sequence in which the system should look for the presence of key fields in the determination process. Work center determination is set up using Transaction /SCWM/PACKSTDT, which can also be set up from **SAP Easy Access** path **Logistics • SCM Extended Warehouse Management • Extended Warehouse Management • Master Data • Work Center • Determine Work Center in Goods Issue.** Figure 4.38 shows how a work center is determined in embedded EWM based on route, activity area, and consolidation group.

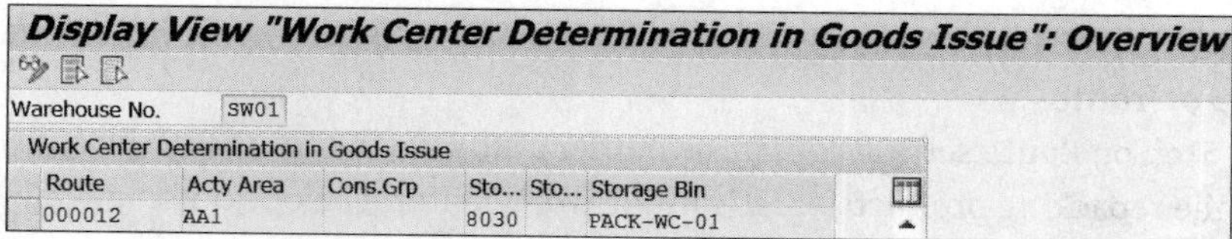
Display View "Work Center Determination in Goods Issue": Overview

Warehouse No. SW01

Work Center Determination in Goods Issue

Route	Acty Area	Cons.Grp	Sto...	Sto...	Storage Bin
000012	AA1		8030		PACK-WC-01

Figure 4.38 Work Center Determination

Numerous combinations of selection fields are possible for the system to determine the correct work center. You can use work center optimization to define a sequence based on which the system looks for entries in the determination table. Figure 4.39 shows how the optimization sequence is set up in embedded EWM for work center determination for activities such as packing during stock removal.

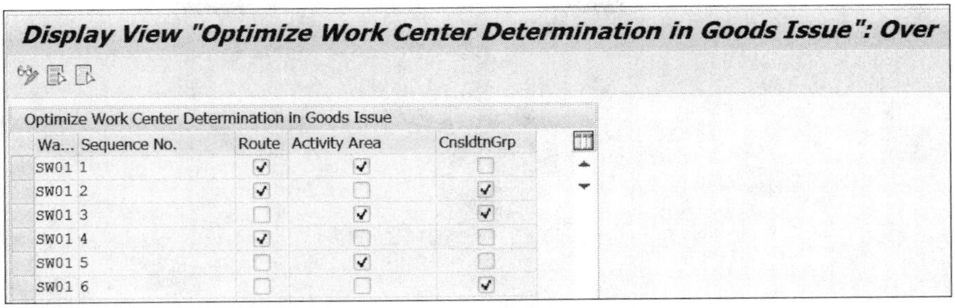

Display View "Optimize Work Center Determination in Goods Issue": Over

Optimize Work Center Determination in Goods Issue

Wa...	Sequence No.	Route	Activity Area	CnsldtnGrp
SW01	1	✓	✓	☐
SW01	2	✓	☐	✓
SW01	3	☐	✓	✓
SW01	4	✓	☐	☐
SW01	5	☐	✓	☐
SW01	6	☐	☐	✓

Figure 4.39 Optimize Work Center Determination in Goods Issue

For example, the system first looks for a row in the work center determination table with all fields for route, activity area, and consolidation group populated and then selects the work center maintained for them, which is also called a *qualified entry*. If no such row is found, the system looks in the optimization sequence and gives preference to only those fields that are given preference in the optimization table and are also maintained in the determination table. All other fields are ignored. Based on the given sequence, the system stops looking as soon as it finds a row that matches the required criteria.

4.7 Summary

In this chapter, we discussed how to set up a warehouse structure in embedded EWM. We discussed storage types, storage sections, staging areas, doors, activity areas, and work centers. We explained that a warehouse structure is a key element in setting up a warehouse in embedded EWM and that therefore you should try to capture all requirements for each of these elements clearly during the blueprinting phase so that the scope of rework is reduced. Each of these elements maps the physical warehouse with the warehouse in embedded EWM and lays down the framework for the next step, which is setting up master data. We'll discuss this step in the next chapter.

Chapter 5
Master Data

Warehouse master data comprises products, business partners, storage bins, packaging specifications, and more data used to carry out warehouse processes in embedded EWM. This data can be maintained directly in the system and is usually owned by the master data team. In this chapter, we'll cover master data in embedded EWM and discuss how it's set up.

Warehouse master data forms the basis for creating transactional documents in embedded EWM. We covered bin master data in Chapter 4, and, in this chapter, we'll discuss the remaining master data in embedded EWM. Depending on project requirements, you can either create or upload master data from scratch, as in new implementations, or use existing master data in the system, as in migration from SAP ERP Warehouse Management (WM) to embedded EWM in SAP S/4HANA. Embedded EWM provides direct usage of master data, such as business partners (customers, vendors, etc.) and materials, by leveraging the one-system concept.

In this chapter, we'll cover the different types of master data, their significance, and important steps in master data setup. In Section 5.1, we start with the supply chain unit, which is used to model an organization's supply chain functions. In Section 5.2, we cover business partners—customers, vendors, carriers, and so on—used in delivery creation. Section 5.3 covers product masters. Material masters created in SAP S/4HANA become product masters in embedded EWM after they're extended to specific embedded EWM warehouses. Section 5.4 covers packaging materials, which are used to create HUs in the warehouse. Section 5.5 covers packaging specifications, which hold packaging instructions for products in embedded EWM. Section 5.6 covers the concept of routes.

> **Note**
>
> Readers familiar with standalone SAP Extended Warehouse Management (SAP EWM) will remember that master data is created in SAP ERP and sent to SAP EWM

using the Core Interface (CIF) from SAP Advanced Planning and Optimization (SAP APO). The CIF is no longer needed to transfer master data to embedded EWM, which uses business partner, material, and batch master data, as well as batch classification data, created in SAP S/4HANA. The CIF is only needed in embedded EWM for the transfer of customer locations in the transit warehousing scenario with SAP Transportation Management (SAP TM).

5.1 Supply Chain Unit

The supply chain unit is used to model the supply chain of an organization. It represents physical locations or organizational elements, such as shipping points or warehouses in embedded EWM. A supply chain unit in embedded EWM contains data about its geographical location, address, time zone, and so on. You can create a supply chain unit using Transaction /SCMB/SCUMAIN, which can also be accessed from path **Logistics • SCM Extended Warehouse Management • Extended Warehouse Management • Master Data • Maintain Supply Chain Unit**. On the transaction screen, provide the supply chain unit and type, and click on **Create**. Each supply chain unit is assigned to one or more business attributes, such as warehouse, shipping office, goods receipt office, and so on, which describe its purpose and role.

For example, you can create a supply chain unit for a plant and assign it to the business attributes of **WAREHOUSE**, **SHIPPING OFFICE**, and **GOODS RECEIPT OFFICE**, as shown in Figure 5.1. The supply chain unit is assigned to the warehouse in embedded EWM, as discussed in Chapter 2.

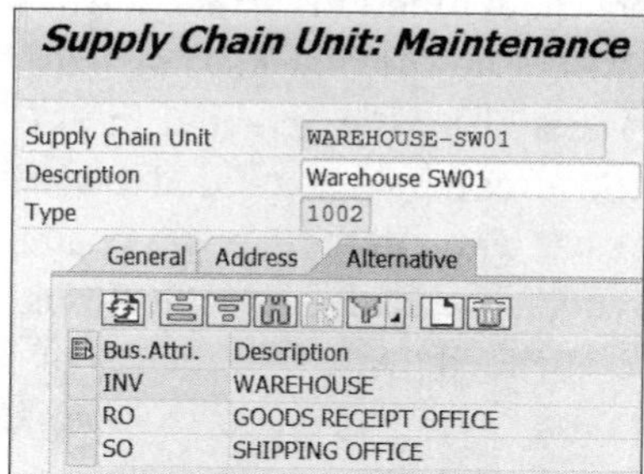

Figure 5.1 Maintaining the Supply Chain Unit

5.2 Business Partners

Business partners are external and internal parties with which you do business and that play a key role in the execution of business processes in embedded EWM. Transaction BP is used to create a business partner; it can also be accessed from path **SCM Extended Warehouse Management • Extended Warehouse Management • Master Data • Maintain Business Partner**. This transaction is a single point of entry to create, change, and display business partners (e.g., customers and vendors) in SAP S/4HANA. Following are some of the business partners used in embedded EWM:

- Customer
- Supplier
- Contact person
- Carriers

Figure 5.2 shows the screen layout for Transaction BP. Near the upper-left corner of the screen is the **Find** option.

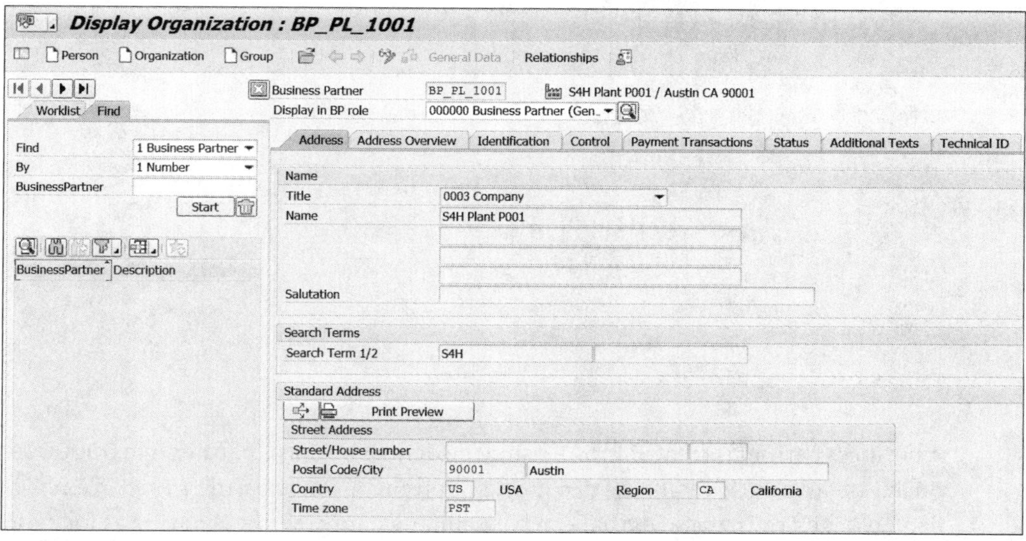

Figure 5.2 Business Partner

Various search options are available to look for a specific business partner or group of business partners. Some of these options include searching by number, address, name, and search term. After providing search criteria, click on **Start**; the system will display a list of business partners. You can double-click on any business partner to see its details on the right-hand side of the transaction screen. At the top of the screen, there is an option to select the business partner's role via the **Display in BP role** dropdown, which displays the data maintained in the business partner for the role selected.

You can create business partners in embedded EWM for a **Person**, **Organization**, or **Group** (see the menu bar). A business partner can have multiple roles depending on business requirements. For example, the same business partner can act as a customer and supplier. The number of data tabs presented in the business partner details screen varies depending on the role selected. You can extend business partner roles for a business partner by opening the business partner in change mode and selecting the appropriate role from the **Display in BP role** dropdown.

There are various business roles available in SAP S/4HANA depending on business requirements. Some of these roles are shown in Table 5.1.

Business Partner Role	Description
000000	Business Partner (General)
FLCU01	Customer
FLCU00	Customer (Fin. Accounting)
CRM010	Carrier
FLVN01	Supplier
FLVN00	Supplier (Fin. Accounting)
LM0001	Processor

Table 5.1 Business Partner Roles

A business partner is created in SAP using the default business partner role 000000 – Business Partner (General). The two most important business partners used in embedded EWM and the data fields that can be maintained for creating them are as follows:

- **Customer**
  Customers are created in SAP S/4HANA from Transaction BP with business role FLCU01 – Customer. You can also extend or create customers for other business partner roles, such as TR0818 – Cust. Bill-to Party, FLCU00 – Customer (Fin.

Accounting), and so on. There are three views available for creating customer business partners:

- **General:** This view holds general customer-specific data, such as address information, tax information, legal data, tax data, and text fields.
- **Sales and Distribution**: This view holds data specific to sales areas, including shipping, billing, partner functions, and status.
- **ETM Data**: This view is used for storing industry-specific data for customers.

- **Supplier**
  Supplier business partners are created with partner role FLVN01 – Supplier. The two views available for a supplier are as follows:
  - **General Data**: This tab holds general data about the vendor, such as address, identification, control, payment transactions, status, legal data, vendor general data, and vendor tax data.
  - **Purchasing**: This tab holds data specific to the purchasing organization regarding the vendor, such as purchasing data, partner functions, additional purchasing data, and so on.

You can delete a business partner by first marking the business partner for deletion using Transaction BUPA_PRE_DA, then selecting the business partner to be deleted, and finally clicking on , as shown in Figure 5.3.

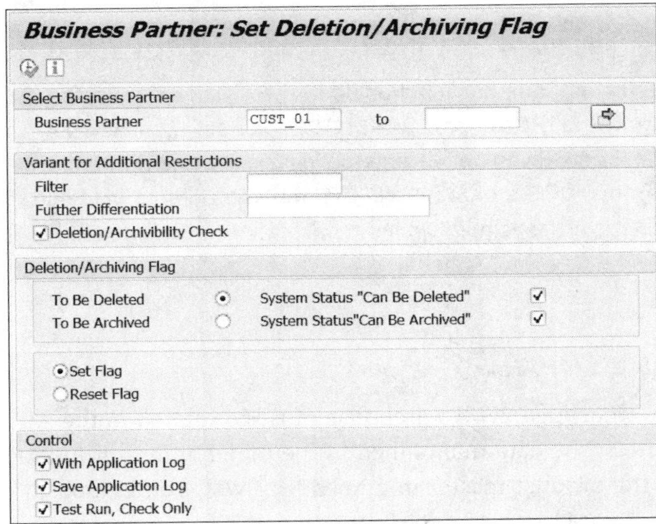

Figure 5.3 Business Partner: Marked for Deletion

After the business partner is marked for deletion, you can delete it using Transaction BUPA_DEL. Click on after entering the business partner, as shown in Figure 5.4.

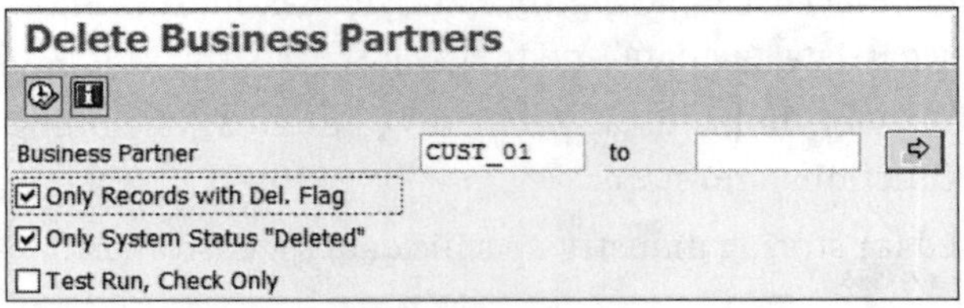

Delete Business Partners

Business Partner CUST_01 to

☑ Only Records with Del. Flag

☑ Only System Status "Deleted"

☐ Test Run, Check Only

Figure 5.4 Business Partner Deletion

5.3 Product Master

The warehouse product master is one of the most important types of master data in embedded EWM. The material master data created in SAP S/4HANA is extended in embedded EWM with some additional views created, and it becomes product master data in embedded EWM. Transaction /SCWM/MAT1 is used to create, change, and display product master data. You use the warehouse number and party entitled to dispose to create the product master in embedded EWM.

Note

Because embedded EWM uses the same master data as SAP S/4HANA, you can leverage the functionalities of SAP S/4HANA to support a material master code with 40 characters. The extended material number functionality is switched off by default when you switch from traditional SAP ERP to SAP S/4HANA or set up a new SAP S/4HANA system, but it can be switched on. Automated logic is in place that is executed when you convert from SAP ERP to SAP S/4HANA, but you need to give due consideration to any custom code that might need modification to accommodate 40-character code.

5.3.1 Material Master in SAP S/4HANA

A material managed in the embedded EWM warehouse must be created in the SAP S/4HANA system first. Some of the data maintained in the material master in SAP S/4HANA also appears on the product master in embedded EWM. You extend the product master in embedded EWM for the warehouse and supply chain unit and then add data specific to embedded EWM.

The material creation is handled via Transaction MM01, which can be accessed from **SAP Easy Access** path **Logistics • Materials Management • Material Master • Material • Display • Display Current**. You need to extend materials at the plant and storage location levels for goods movement posting in SAP S/4HANA. As discussed, embedded EWM product masters use some of the data maintained in the following four views in the material master in SAP S/4HANA (e.g., general data properties, units of measure [UoMs], packaging data, etc.):

- **Basic Data**
- **Unit of Measure**
- **Sales: General/Plant**
- **Plant Data/Storage 1**

We'll discuss these common fields in the SAP S/4HANA material master in detail in the next section when we discuss product masters in embedded EWM. You also need to maintain data at the warehouse level in the following two material master views in SAP S/4HANA, which are used especially for embedded EWM purposes:

- **WM Execution**
- **WM Packaging**

Warehouse Management Execution

The **WM Execution** view requires data specifically for embedded EWM. Figure 5.5 shows the **WM Execution** view for the material master in SAP S/4HANA.

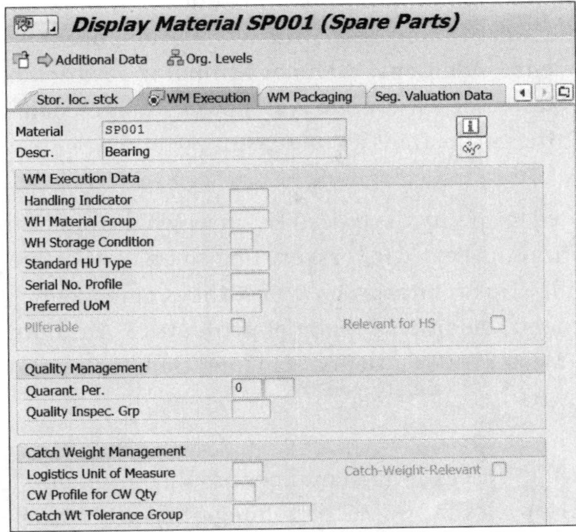

Figure 5.5 WM Execution View

The data in this view is divided into three broad sections: **WM Execution Data**, **Quality Management**, and **Catch Weight Management**.

The data maintained on the **WM Execution** tab is as follows:

- **Handling indicator**
  The **Handling Indicator** field is used to specify how material will be handled in the warehouse (e.g., fragile materials that require handling with care). This indicator is for information purposes only. You define handling indicators in IMG path **Integration with Other Components • Extended Warehouse Management • Additional Material Attributes • Attribute Values for Additional Material Master Fields • Define Handling Indicator**; once there, click on **New Entries** in the transaction screen.
- **Warehouse material group**
  The **WH Material Group** field is used to group materials based on certain processes in the warehouse. You create material groups by navigating to IMG path **Integration with Other Components • Extended Warehouse Management • Additional Material Attributes • Attribute Values for Additional Material Master Fields • Define Warehouse Material Group**; once there, click on **New Entries** in the transaction screen.
- **Warehouse storage condition**
  The **Wh Storage Condition** field is used to classify products based on conditions for storage (e.g., materials requiring temperature-controlled conditions). You define storage conditions from the IMG path **Integration with Other Components • Extended Warehouse Management • Additional Material Attributes • Attribute Values for Additional Material Master Fields • Define Warehouse Storage Condition**; once there, click on **New Entries** in the transaction screen.
- **Standard HU type**
  The **Standard HU Type** field is used to specify the type of HU in which the product can be packed, for example, cartons, pallets, wire baskets, and so on. You define handling unit (HU) types from IMG path **Integration with Other Components • Extended Warehouse Management • Additional Material Attributes • Attribute Values for Additional Material Master Fields • Define Handling Unit Type**; once there, click on **New Entries** in the transaction screen.
- **Serial number profile**
  The **Serial No. Profile** field is used to specify a serial number profile for serialized parts. You define serial number profiles from IMG path **Integration with Other Components • Extended Warehouse Management • Additional Material Attributes •**

Attribute Values for Additional Material Master Fields • Define Serial Number Profile; once there, click on **New Entries** in the transaction screen.

- **Pilferable**
  The **Pilferable** indicator is specified only for products that are theft-prone. This indicator is for information purposes only and helps warehouse users know that the material needs to be handled carefully.
- **Relevant for HS**
  The **Relevant For HS** indicator is set for hazardous materials in the warehouse and lets the system know that it should read the hazardous substance data for additional information about storing this product.
- **Quarantine period**
  The **Quarant. Per.** field is used to specify the amount of time a material should spend in the warehouse before it's shipped to a customer.
- **Quality inspection group**
  The **Quality Inspec. Grp** field is used to group materials for quality management (QM). You can assign products requiring the same inspection rules to the same quality inspection group, which can be defined from IMG path **Integration with Other Components • Extended Warehouse Management • Additional Material Attributes • Attribute Values for Additional Material Master Fields • Define Quality Inspection Group**; once there, click on **New Entries** in the transaction screen.
- **Catch-weight relevant**
  The **Catch-Weight-Relevant** indicator is used to confirm that a material is catch-weight-relevant in embedded EWM. In such a case, the material inventory is managed in embedded EWM in two types of UoMs: parallel UoMs (PUoMs) and base UoMs (BUoMs). Parallel inventory management happens in embedded EWM only; SAP S/4HANA continues to manage the stock in the BUoM only.
- **Logistics unit of measure**
  The **Logistics Unit of Measure** is used to move catch-weight-relevant products in the warehouse. It's different from the BUoM in which stock valuation is performed. A UoM is marked as a logistics UoM (LUoM) by the system if it's marked as a PUoM in the **Additional Data** screen **Units of Measure** tab in the material master.
- **Catch weight profile for catch weight quantity**
  The **CW Profile for CW Qty** is used to control the input of catch weight quantities for catch weight material in embedded EWM at the process level, for example, at the work center level or during good receipt and goods issue. You define these profiles from IMG path **Integration with Other Components • Extended Warehouse**

Management • Additional Material Attributes • Attribute Values for Additional Material Master Fields • Define Catch Weight Input Control; once there, click on **New Entries** in the transaction screen.

- **Catch weight tolerance group**
  The **Catch Wt Tolerance Group** (catch weight tolerance group) is used to perform a plausibility check for the quantities entered in a logistics process for a catch weight material. You can set a tolerance above the planned conversion factor for converting the BUoM and PUoM; if the tolerance is exceeded, then the system will throw an error or warning. You define tolerance groups from the IMG path **Integration with Other Components • Extended Warehouse Management • Additional Material Attributes • Attribute Values for Additional Material Master Fields • Define Catch Weight Tolerance Groups**; once there, click on **New Entries** in the transaction screen.

Warehouse Management Packaging

The **WM Packaging** view contains packaging-specific data for materials used as packaging materials, as shown in Figure 5.6. Data in this tab is divided into two main sections: **General Packaging** and **Maximum Packaging**.

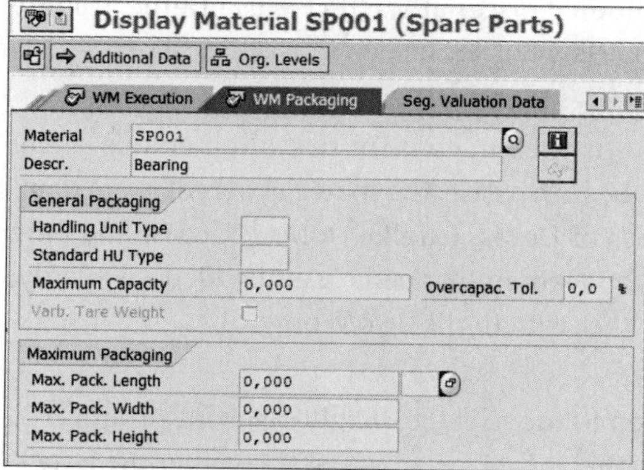

Figure 5.6 WM Packaging View

The data maintained on the **WM Packaging** tab is as follows:

- **HU type**
  The **Handling Unit Type** field is used to specify the HU type for packaging material. You define HU types from IMG path **Integration with Other Components • Extended Warehouse Management • Additional Material Attributes • Attribute Values for**

Additional Material Master Fields • Define Handling Unit Type; once there, click on **New Entries** in the transaction screen.

- **Standard HU type**
  The **Standard HU Type** field is used to specify the standard HU type for mixed HUs.
- **Maximum capacity**
  The **Maximum Capacity** field is used to confirm the maximum capacity of packaging material.
- **Overcapacity tolerance**
  The **Overcapac. Tol.** field is used to specify capacity tolerance for packaging material over the maximum capacity tolerance.
- **Variable tare weight**
  Tare weight or unladen weight is the weight of an empty HU. The **Varb. Tare Weight** checkbox is set if the empty weight of packaging materials of this packaging material type isn't accurately known.
- **Maximum packaging length/width/height**
  The **Max. Pack. Length/Width/Height** fields are used to specify dimensions of the packaging material.

5.3.2 Product Master in Embedded EWM

The materials and packaging materials created in SAP S/4HANA are created in embedded EWM as warehouse products. Transaction /SCWM/MAT1 is used for this purpose and also can be accessed from **SAP Easy Access** path **Logistics • SCM Extended Warehouse Management • Extended Warehouse Management • Master Data • Product • Maintain Warehouse Product**. As shown in Figure 5.7, on the transaction screen to display/change/create a warehouse product, you can enter the **Warehouse No.** and the **Party Entitled to Dispose**, and the product master screen will open. The party entitled to dispose is defined at the warehouse level and refers to the business partner who is entitled to dispose of the stock. In most cases, this is the plant that owns the stock.

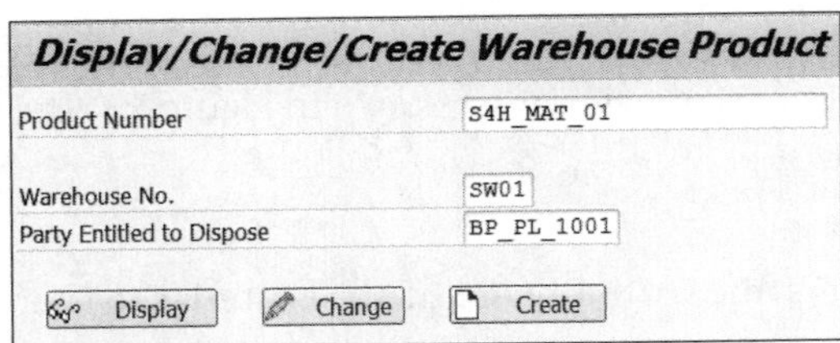

Figure 5.7 Product Master Maintenance

If this is the first time you're creating the product master in embedded EWM, click on **Create**, and the warehouse product master creation view opens. There are nine views available in the standard product master screen:

- **Properties**
- **Unit of Measure**
- **Additional GTINs/EANs**
- **Classification**
- **Packaging Data**
- **Storage Data**
- **Warehouse Data**
- **Slotting**
- **Storage Type Data**

The first six views are populated by default from the material master data fields when the material is created in SAP S/4HANA. These fields are grayed out in this transaction to maintain data consistency between the material master data in SAP S/4HANA and the product master data in embedded EWM. These views hold global data for the material, which remains the same across warehouses.

The **Whse. Data**, **Slotting**, and **St. Type Data** tabs are specific to embedded EWM. You need to maintain data in these tabs to be able to use the material in embedded EWM.

> **Warning**
>
> The material should be created in SAP S/4HANA first; only then will you be able to create the product master in embedded EWM.

In the following sections, we'll discuss each of the views available in the product master and their significance.

Properties

The **Properties** tab holds general data about the material, as shown in Figure 5.8. The data maintained on this page is as follows:

- **External product number**
  The **External Product Number** is the same as the name of the material master record created in SAP S/4HANA.

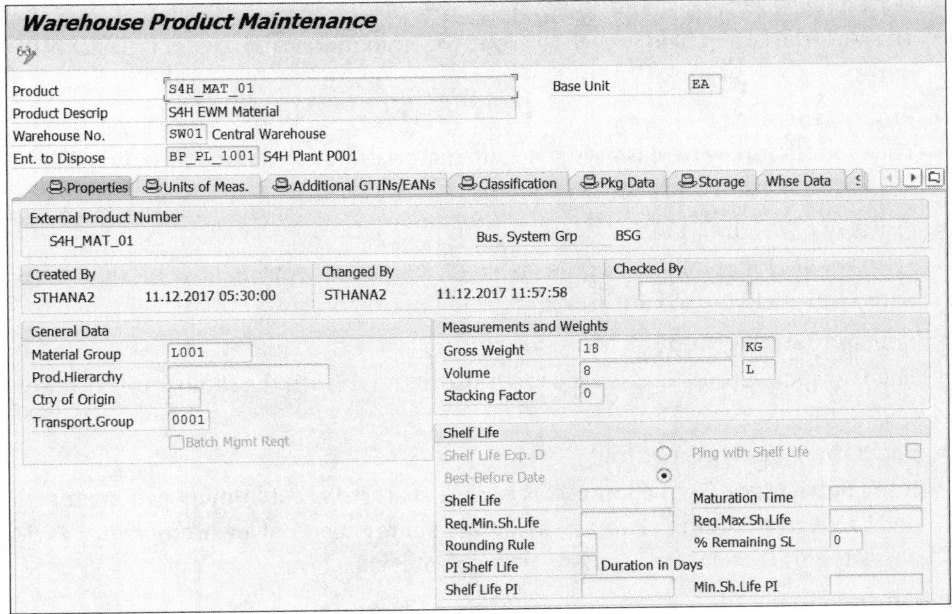

Figure 5.8 Properties Tab in the Product Master

- **Business system group**
  The **Bus. System Grp** field holds the name of the business system group that was created to group the logical system of SAP S/4HANA and the logical system of embedded EWM.
- **Created by**
  The **Created By** field contains the name of the person who created the material master in SAP S/4HANA.
- **Changed by**
  The **Changed By** field contains date and time stamps of when the product was last modified.
- **Checked by**
  The **Checked By** field contains the details of the person who last checked the product. The value in this field is populated with the user name and current system time stamp if you activate the **Set To Checked** indicator next to the field. The value in this field is set if the product needs to be reviewed by a material master expert before it's used in the production environment.

- **Material group**
  The **Material Group** field is used to group together materials based on similar attributes.
- **Product hierarchy**
  The **Prod.Hierarchy** field is used to group materials by combining different characteristics using alphanumeric characters.
- **Country of origin**
  The **Ctry of Origin** field is used to specify the country in which the product originated. This field is used during export and import control.
- **Transportation group**
  The **Transport.Group** field is used to group materials with the same transportation requirements.
- **Batch management required**
  If the **Batch Mgmt Reqt** checkbox is set, the material is batch-managed in embedded EWM. In addition to batch management at the material level, embedded EWM also supports batch management at the plant level.
- **Gross weight**
  The **Gross Weight** field confirms the gross weight of the product or HU. If the material is a packaging material, then the gross weight signifies the tare weight or unladed weight of the HU.
- **Volume**
  Volume indicates the volume of the product or of the HU if the material is a packaging material.
- **Stacking factor**
  Stacking Factor indicates whether pallets of this product can be stacked on top of one another. An empty value in this field or a value of **1** indicates that pallets can't be stacked. Any other value indicates the number of pallets that can be stacked.
- **Shelf life expiration date**
  The **Shelf Life Exp. D** radio button is selected for products for which you want to track the ability to use or sell the product based on its shelf life. Alternatively, use the **Best-Before Date** radio button when you want to express shelf-life expiration as the earliest date when a material might not be acceptable for use.
- **Planning with shelf life**
  If you set the **Plng with Shelf Life** indicator, the system includes product maturity,

shelf life of product receipts, and shelf-life requirements while performing product planning.

- **Shelf life**
  The value in the **Shelf Life** field indicates the total duration for which a product can be sold.
- **Maturation time**
  The value in the **Maturation Time** field suggests the minimum duration for which the product should be kept in the warehouse before it's sold. Maturation time is part of the shelf life of the product and is only considered if the **Plng with Shelf Life** indicator is set in the product master.
- **Required minimum shelf life**
  The **Req.Min.Sh.Life** field indicates the minimum shelf life remaining for a product before it can be used for planning in the warehouse. The value in this field is only considered if the **Plng with Shelf Life** indicator is set in the product master.
- **Required maximum shelf life**
  The **Req.Max.Sh.Life** indicator indicates the maximum shelf life remaining for a product before it can be used for planning in the warehouse. The value in this field is only considered if the **Plng with Shelf Life** indicator is set in the product master.
- **Percentage of remaining shelf life**
  The **% Remaining SL** field is used to define the percentage of total shelf life that should be remaining on the product for intersite stock transfers.
- **Rounding rule**
  The **Rounding Rule** is used for calculation of shelf-life expiration dates in combination with the period indicator for shelf-life expiration set in the material master in SAP S/4HANA. The rounding rule can be used to round off shelf-life expiration dates to the first or last day of the week, month, or year, depending on the value selected.

The data in this tab is copied from various material master views in SAP S/4HANA and is grayed out to avoid any changes to general product master data. We've summarized these data mappings in Table 5.2.

Embedded EWM Product Master View	Embedded EWM Product Master Field	SAP S/4HANA Material Master View	SAP S/4HANA Material Master Field
Properties	Material Group	Basic Data	Material Group
	Product Hierarchy	Basic Data	Product Hierarchy
	Transportation Group	Sales: General/ Plant	Transportation Group
	Batch Management Required	Plant Data/ Storage 1	Batch Management
	Shelf Life		Shelf Life
	Required Minimum Shelf Life		Required Minimum Shelf Life
	Rounding Rule		Rounding Rule
	% Remaining Shelf Life		% Remaining Shelf Life
	Maturation Time		Maturation Time
	Required Maximum Shelf Life		Required Maximum Shelf Life

Table 5.2 Mapping of Fields in Properties Tab from SAP S/4HANA to Embedded EWM

Units of Measure

The **Units of Meas.** tab contains data for the conversion of a BUoM to an alternative UoM (AUoM), as shown in Figure 5.9.

The most important data in this tab is as follows:

- **Denominator/AUoM/numerator/BUoM**
  The **Denom.** field represents the denominator used to convert a BUoM to an AUoM. **Num.** represents the numerator used to convert the base unit to the alternative unit. The **BUn** field signifies the BUoM used for inventory valuation. The **AUn**. field is used to store UoMs that can be used instead of BUoM. The ratio of numerator to denominator is called the *quotient*, and when multiplied by the BUoM, it should give the quantity in the BUoM that's equal to a single quantity in AUoM.

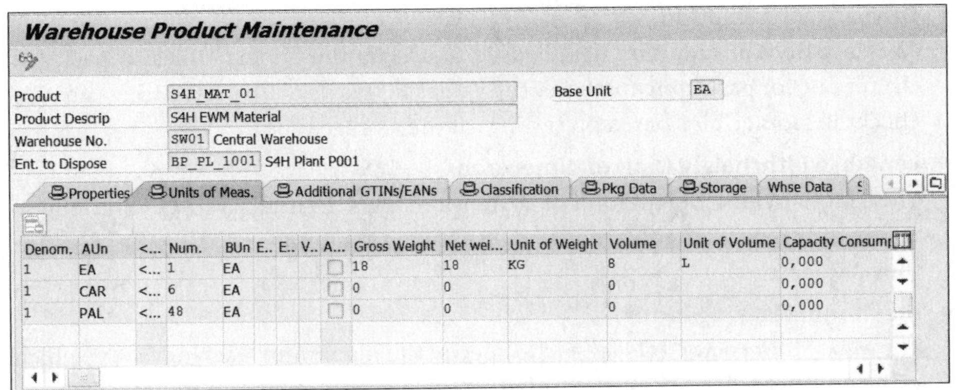

Figure 5.9 Units of Meas. Tab in the Embedded EWM Product Master

- **EAN/UPC**
  The **EAN/UPC** field holds the EAN (also known as the International Article Number), which was originally known as the Universal Product Code (UPC).
- **EAN category**
  The **EAN Category** field holds the number category for the EAN/UPC. This lets you maintain EAN attributes such as number range information, check digits, and so on.
- **Additional GTINs/EANs exist**
  The **Additional GTINs/EANs Exist** indicator is used to specify that other Global Trade Item Numbers (GTINs), including EANs and UPCs, exist for the product and are assigned to the product in the chosen UoM.
- **Variant GTIN**
  The **Variant GTIN** field specifies the GTIN and is used to make distinctions between minor variants of a product within a company.
- **Gross weight/net weight/unit of weight**
  The **Gross Weight/Net weight/Unit of Weight** fields are used to specify the gross weight, net weight, and unit of weight for a product. If the material is a packaging material, these fields specify the tare weight of the container or HU and its unit of weight.
- **Volume/unit of volume**
  The **Volume/Unit of Volume** fields are used to specify the volume and unit of volume for a product. If the material is a packaging material, they specify the tare volume of the container or HU and its unit of volume.

- **Capacity consumption**
  The **Capacity Consumption** field is used to specify the dimensionless capacity of the product or packaging material. The values in this field are used during capacity checks in storage bins based on settings at the storage type level.
- **Length/width/height/unit of dimension**
  The **Length/Width/Height/Unit of Dimension** fields are used to specify the length, width, and height of the product or packaging material and the unit in which they're measured.
- **Maximum stacking factor**
  The **Max. Stack Factor** field is used to specify the maximum stacking factor, which is the number of HUs or products that can be placed atop one another.
- **Remaining volume after nesting**
  The **Rem. Vol. After Nestg** field is used to specify the remaining volume after *nesting*, or putting one container or product within another. It's specified as a percentage of the total volume of the product without nesting.
- **Unit of measure category**
  The **UoM Category** field is used to specify the category of the UoM as an AUoM or PUoM. The latter is used in catch weight management.

The data in this tab is copied from the **Units of Measure** view in the **Additional Data** tab of the material master in SAP S/4HANA and is grayed out to maintain consistency with central master data. Table 5.3 summarizes the different material master views from which data is derived in the **Units of Measure** product master tab in embedded EWM.

Embedded EWM Product Master View	Embedded EWM Product Master Field	SAP S/4HANA Material Master View	SAP S/4HANA Material Master Field
Units of Measure	Denominator	Units of Measure	Denominator (X)
	Alternate Unit of Measure		Alternate Unit of Measure
	Numerator		Numerator (Y)

Table 5.3 Mapping of Fields in the Units of Measure Tab from SAP S/4HANA to Embedded EWM

Embedded EWM Product Master View	Embedded EWM Product Master Field	SAP S/4HANA Material Master View	SAP S/4HANA Material Master Field
	Base Unit of Measure		Base Unit of Measure
	EAN or UPC		EAN/UPC
	EAN Category		Category
	Additional GTINs/EANs Exist		Additional EANs Exist
	Gross Weight		Gross Weight
	Net Weight		Net Weight
	Unit of Weight		Unit of Weight
	Volume		Volume
	Unit of Volume		Unit of Volume
	Capacity Consumption		Capacity Consumption
	Length		Length
	Width		Width
	Height		Height
	Unit of Dimension		Unit of Dimension
	Maximum Stacking Factor		Maximum Stacking Factor
	Remaining Volume after Nesting		Remaining Volume after Nesting
	UoM Category		Category of Unit of Measure

Table 5.3 Mapping of Fields in the Units of Measure Tab from SAP S/4HANA to Embedded EWM (Cont.)

Additional GTINs/EANs

The **Additional GTINs/EANs** tab holds additional GTINs, EANs, and UPCs, along with their GTIN and EAN categories and the UoMs to which they are assigned, as shown in Figure 5.10. The data in this tab is copied from the **Additional EANs** tab of the **Additional Data** view of the material master in SAP S/4HANA.

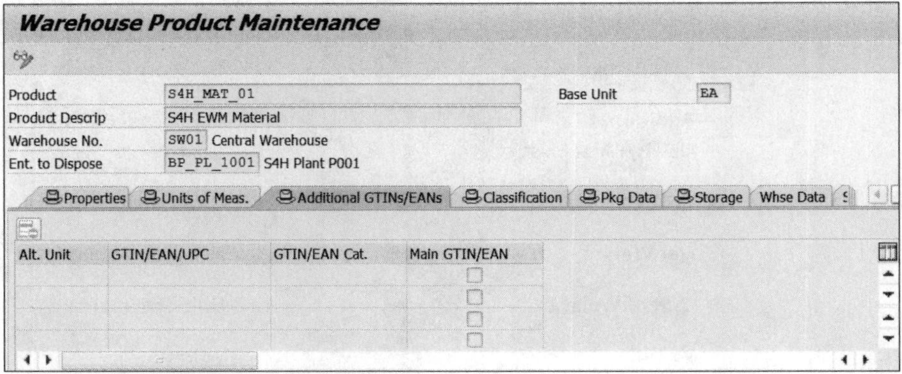

Figure 5.10 Additional GTINs/EANs Tab

If there is more than one EAN or GTIN for each UoM (as specified by setting the **Additional GTINs/EANs Exist** indicator in **Units of Meas.** tab), then you can set the **Main GTIN/EAN** checkbox to specify the primary GTIN/EAN for that UoM.

Classification

The **Classification** tab contains data about the classifications for materials with different characteristics, as shown in Figure 5.11. You use classification types to group together products with distinct attributes.

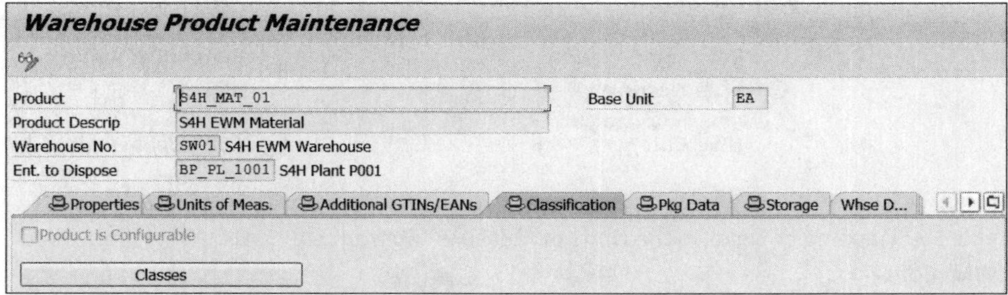

Figure 5.11 Classification Tab in Warehouse Product Master

We'll discuss classification in more detail when we discuss batch management in Chapter 6, Section 6.7.

Packaging Data

As shown in Figure 5.12, the **Pkg Data** tab contains information relevant to packing products into HUs and for the packaging materials themselves.

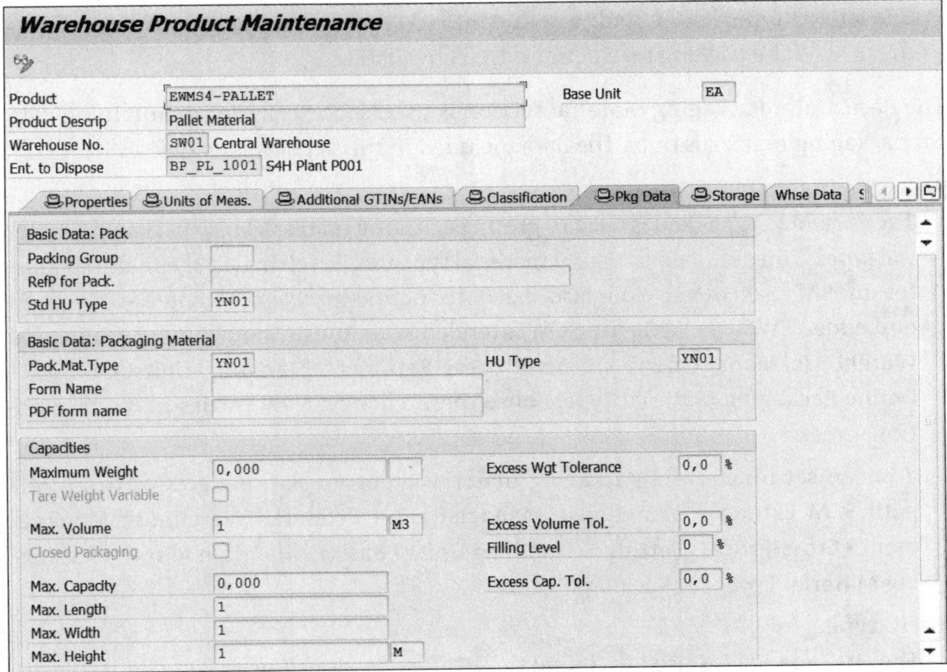

Figure 5.12 Packaging Data View

Data in this tab is divided into three broad sections: **Basic Data: Pack**, **Basic Data: Packaging Material**, and **Capacities**. Let's look at the data contained in each of these sections.

The **Basic Data: Pack** section has fields for materials requiring packing into HUs. The data included in this section is as follows:

- **Packing group**
  Packing Group is used to group products with the same packing requirements.

- **Reference product for packing**
  The **RefP for Pack.** field is used to store reference material for packaging, which aids simplification of packaging specifications by reducing the need to create a separate packaging specification for each product. Thus, you can specify the name of a product with similar packaging specifications in this field, and the system will use its specifications to determine the packaging requirements of the other product.
- **Standard HU type**
  The **Std HU Type** field is used to define the HU type used to pack multiple products in an HU if the packing instructions aren't available.

The **Basic Data: Packaging Material** section is used specifically for maintaining data for packaging materials only. The data included in this section is as follows:

- **Packaging material type**
  The **Pack.Mat.Type** field is used to group packaging materials into packaging material types. You defined packaging material types while setting up the material master in SAP S/4HANA. You also need to define packaging material types in embedded EWM via IMG path **SCM Extended Warehouse Management • Extended Warehouse Management • Cross-Process Settings • Handling Units • Basics • Define Packaging Material Types**; once there, click on **New Entries** in the transaction screen.

  You can set up allowed packaging material types for packing groups from IMG path **SCM Extended Warehouse Management • Extended Warehouse Management • Cross-Process Settings • Handling Units • Basics • Maintain Allowed Packaging Material Types for Packing Group**.
- **HU type**
  The **HU Type** field is used to define the HU types that will be created by the corresponding packaging material.
- **Form name**
  The **Form Name** field is used to designate the smart form name that will be used for printing the HU labels created using this packaging material.
- **PDF form name**
  The **PDF Form Name** field is used to select the PDF smart form used to print the HU label. It's used if a smart form isn't used. The data in this field is only considered if the **Smart Form** field is blank.

The data in the **Capacities** section is used to specify the capacity of the packaging materials used; this data is used only for packaging materials:

- **Maximum weight**
  The data in the **Maximum Weight** field is used to specify the maximum weight that can be loaded in an HU created by this packaging material.
- **Excess weight tolerance**
  The **Excess Wgt Tolerance** field is used to specify the excess weight tolerance allowed over and above the maximum weight. This tolerance is defined as a percentage.
- **Tare weight variable**
  The **Tare Weight Variable** indicator is set if the weight of the unloaded HU is variable.
- **Maximum volume**
  The **Max. Volume** field is used to specify the maximum volume that can be loaded in an HU created by this packaging material.
- **Excess volume tolerance**
  The **Excess Volume Tol.** field specifies the excess volume tolerance allowed over and above the maximum volume. This tolerance is defined as a percentage.
- **Closed packaging**
  The **Closed Packaging** indicator is set if the packaging material is closed packaging, such as a closed box. In this case, the total volume of the HU remains unchanged. For an open pallet, for example, the total volume will vary depending on the tare volume and loaded volume, so this indicator won't be set.
- **Filling level**
  The **Filling Level** setting is used to define the percentage to which an HU should be filled. The data in this field is for information purposes only.
- **Maximum capacity**
  The **Max. Capacity** field is used to specify the maximum capacity allowed for the HU created with the packaging material.
- **Excess capacity tolerance**
  The **Excess Wgt Tolerance** field is used to specify the percentage of the maximum capacity that can be loaded in the HU over and above the allowed maximum capacity.
- **Maximum length/width/height**
  The **Max. Length/Width/Height** fields are used to specify the maximum length, width, and height of the packaging material.

In Table 5.4, we review the fields available in this view and the views in the SAP S/4HANA material master from which they are copied.

Embedded EWM Product Master View	Embedded EWM Product Master Field	SAP S/4HANA Material Master View	SAP S/4HANA Material Master Field
Packaging Data	Packing Group	Sales: General/Plant	Material Group Packaging Materials
	Reference Product for Packaging		Reference Material for Packaging
	Packaging Material Type		Packaging Material Type
	Maximum Weight		Allowed Package Weight
	Excess Weight Tolerance		Excess Weight Tolerance
	Maximum Volume		Allowed Package Volume
	Excess Volume Tolerance		Excess Volume Tolerance
	Filling Level		Maximum Level
	Closed Packaging		Closed
	Standard HU Type	WM Packaging	Standard HU Type
	HU Type		HU Type
	Maximum Capacity		Maximum Capacity
	Tare Weight Variable		Variable Tare Weight
	Maximum Length		Maximum Packaging Length

Table 5.4 Mapping of Fields in Packaging Data Tab from SAP S/4HANA to Embedded EWM

Embedded EWM Product Master View	Embedded EWM Product Master Field	SAP S/4HANA Material Master View	SAP S/4HANA Material Master Field
	Maximum Width		Maximum Packaging Width
	Maximum Height		Maximum Packaging Height
	Excess Capacity Tolerance		Overcapacity Tolerance

Table 5.4 Mapping of Fields in Packaging Data Tab from SAP S/4HANA to Embedded EWM (Cont.)

> **Tip**
> Unlike standalone SAP EWM, embedded EWM doesn't require that you define the packaging material type, packing groups for products, and HU types in the Transaction SPRO node for customization. The system picks these values from SAP S/4HANA's logistics customization settings.

Storage

This tab is used to store data related to storage-specific settings for the product. The data in this section is divided into three sections: **Basic Data**, **Catch Weight Data**, and **Hazard/Danger Data** (see Figure 5.13).

The data contained in these three sections is as follows:

- **Warehouse product group**
  The **Whse Product Group** field is used to group together products from a warehouse point of view. The warehouse product group is used to determine the packaging specifications and to determine the deletion indicator for fixed bin assignments.
- **Warehouse storage condition**
  The **Whse. Storage Cond.** field is used to define the various storage conditions under which a product can be stored in the warehouse. These can include temperature, handling, or other requirements.

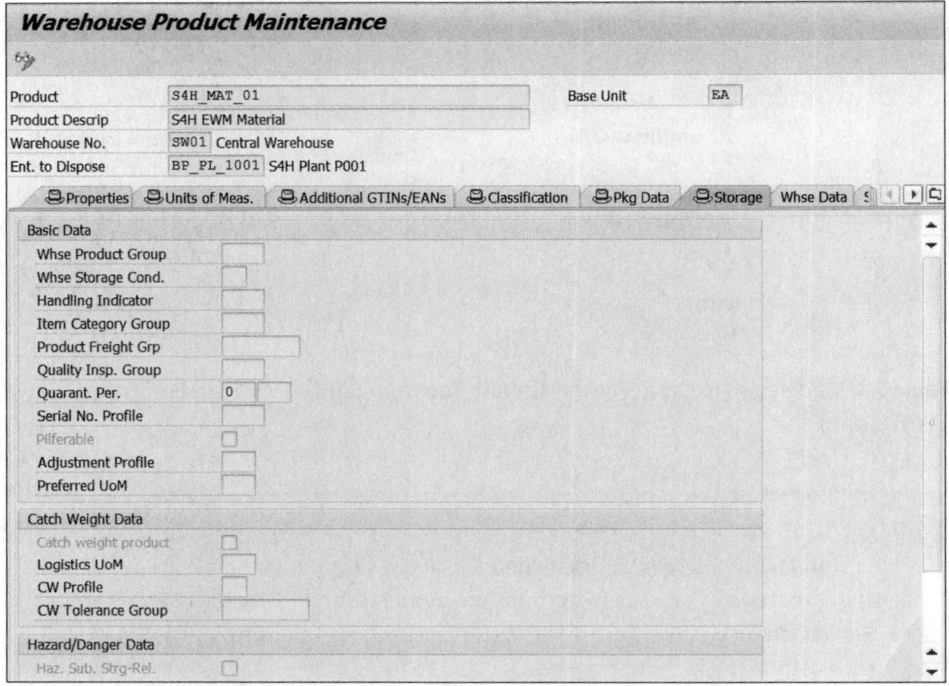

Figure 5.13 Storage Tab

- **Handling indicator**
  The **Handling Indicator** field is used to specify handling options—for example, fragile—available for products in the warehouse.
- **Item category group**
  The **Item Category Group** field is used in the determination of the item category in embedded EWM.
- **Product freight group**
  The **Product Freight Grp** field is used to group products with similar freight requirements and to determine the freight code and freight classes. It's used by transportation service providers for transportation services.
- **Quality inspection group**
  The **Quality Insp. Group** field is used to group products with similar quality inspection requirements. You can define a quality inspection group under IMG path **Integration with Other SAP Components • Extended Warehouse Management •**

Additional Material Attributes • Attribute Values for Additional Material Master Fields • Define Quality Inspection Group; once there, click on **New Entries** in the transaction screen.

- Quarantine period
  The **Quarant. Per.** field is used to specify the time for which the product should stay in the warehouse before it's shipped to customers. The data in this field is only for information purposes in embedded EWM.
- Serial number profile
  The **Serial No. Profile** field is used to specify how serial numbers are managed in the warehouse. The data in this field is copied from the **Serial No. Profile** field in the **WM Execution** tab of the material master in SAP S/4HANA.
- Pilferable
  The **Pilferable** indicator is used for materials with a high probability of theft. This indicator can be used in custom enhancements to determine specific storage bins for safe storage in the warehouse.
- Adjustment profile
  Adjustment Profile is used in the merchandise distribution flow through cross-docking. It's used to determine the way in which inbound delivery quantities are divided among outbound deliveries if there's a deviation in the quantity received in the inbound delivery.
- Preferred unit of measure
  The **Preferred UoM** field is used to define the preferred UoM for storing the product in the warehouse. The preferred unit can be used in inbound and outbound processes to allow the option to pick or put away stock in the preferred unit first.
- Catch weight product
  The **Catch Weight Product** indicator is set for products that are catch-weight-relevant.
- Logistics unit of measure
  The **Logistics UoM** field is used to store the LUoM for a catch weight-relevant product.
- CW profile
  The **CW Profile** field is used to store the catch weight profile relevant for this product. These profiles are used for entering the catch weight for catch weight-relevant products.

- **CW tolerance group**
  The **CW Tolerance Group** field is used to store the catch weight tolerance group for a catch weight product.
- **Hazardous substance storage-related**
  The **Haz. Sub. Strg-Rel.** indicator is used to notify users that hazardous substance data exists for this material that must be read to ensure proper storage.
- **Environmentally relevant**
  The **Environmentally Rlvt.** indicator is used for products that are relevant to the environment.
- **DG indicator profile**
  The **DG Indicator Prof.** field is used to set the dangerous goods indicator profile to control the application of dangerous goods.

Note

It's no longer required to replicate dangerous goods and hazardous substances in embedded EWM. Embedded EWM directly accesses this data from product safety and stewardship services in SAP S/4HANA.

In Table 5.5, we've summarized the fields discussed in this section and the views from which they're derived from the material master in SAP S/4HANA. For more details on each field and how it's defined, Section 5.3.1.

Embedded EWM Product Master View	Embedded EWM Product Master Field	SAP S/4HANA Material Master View	SAP S/4HANA Material Master Field
Storage	Warehouse Product Group	WM Execution	WH Material Group
	Warehouse Storage Condition		WH Storage Condition
	Handling Indicator		Handling Indicator
	Item Category Group	Basic Data	General Item Category Group

Table 5.5 Mapping of Fields in Storage Tab from SAP S/4HANA to Embedded EWM

Embedded EWM Product Master View	Embedded EWM Product Master Field	SAP S/4HANA Material Master View	SAP S/4HANA Material Master Field
	Product Freight Group	Material Freight Group	Sales: General/Plant
	Quality Inspection Group	WM Execution	Quality Inspection Group
	Quarantine Period	WM Execution	Quarantine Period
	Pilferable	WM Execution	Pilferable
	Preferred UoM	WM Execution	Preferred UoM
	Catch Weight Product	WM Execution	Catch Weight Relevant
	Logistics UoM	WM Execution	Logistics Unit of Measure
	CW Profile	WM Execution	CW Profile for CW Quantity
	CW Tolerance Group	WM Execution	Catch Weight Tolerance Group
	Hazardous Substance Storage Related	WM Execution	Relevant for HS

Table 5.5 Mapping of Fields in Storage Tab from SAP S/4HANA to Embedded EWM (Cont.)

Warehouse Data

The next three sections that we'll cover hold embedded EWM-specific data and are directly maintained in embedded EWM: warehouse data, slotting data, and storage type data. We'll begin our discussion with the **Whse Data** view, which holds general settings required for following embedded EWM-specific processes such as putaway, stock removal, and quality inspection. The data in this view is divided into four sections. The first is **General Data,** shown in Figure 5.14.

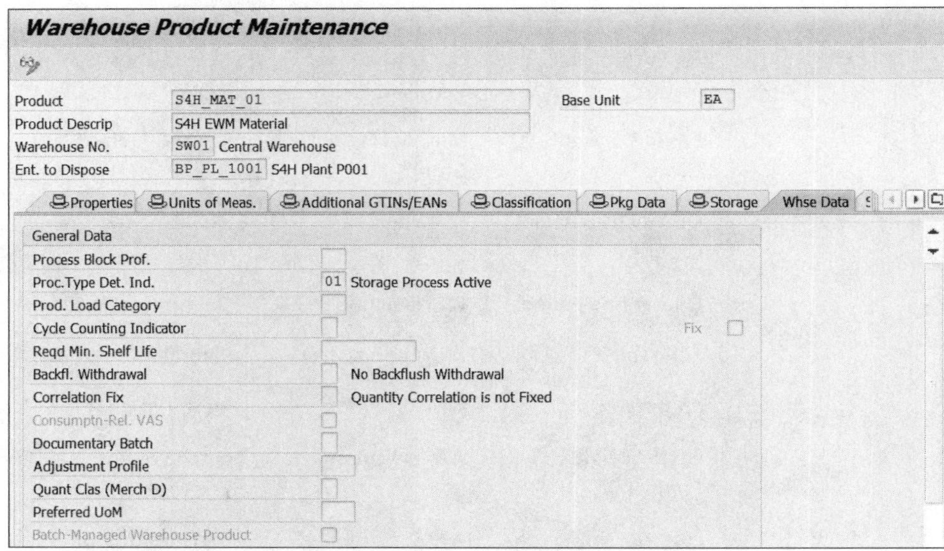

Figure 5.14 Warehouse Data: General Data

The most important data fields contained in this section are as follows:

- **Process block profile**
  The **Process Block Prof.** field allows you to issue a warning or error message when certain specific processes are carried out for a product in the warehouse. Examples of such processes include creation or confirmation of warehouse tasks, posting of goods receipt/goods issue, and so on. You can define block profiles from IMG path **SCM Extended Warehouse Management • Extended Warehouse Management • Master Data • Product • Define Process Block Profile**; once there, click on **New Entries** in the transaction screen.
- **Process type determination indicator**
  Proc. Type Det. Ind. is used to set indicators that influence warehouse process type determination. To create these entries, follow IMG path **SCM Extended Warehouse Management • Extended Warehouse Management • Cross-Process Settings • Warehouse Tasks • Define Control Indicators for Determining Warehouse Process Types**; once there, click on **New Entries** in the transaction screen. It's not mandatory to use these entries in warehouse process type determination.
- **Product load category**
  The value in the **Prod. Load Category** field is used to classify products that are similar in their workload and handling. The value in this field is used in workload

calculation in labor management. To create these entries, follow IMG path **SCM Extended Warehouse Management • Extended Warehouse Management • Cross-process Settings • Warehouse Task • Define Extract Time Determination**. Once there, select the **Define Product Load Categories** activity, and click on **New Entries** in the transaction screen.

- **Cycle counting indicator**
  Cycle Counting Indicator is used to group materials into various cycle counting categories. This helps determine the time period during which cycle counting will be carried out for this product. You can define this indicator from IMG path **SCM Extended Warehouse Management • Extended Warehouse Management • Internal Warehouse Processes • Physical Inventory • Warehouse Number Specific Setting • Configure Cycle Counting**.
- **Required minimum shelf life**
  The **Reqd. Min Shelf Life** field is used to specify the required minimum shelf life during goods receipt if you don't want to specify a global value for required minimum shelf life but instead want to limit it to a warehouse and party entitled to dispose.
- **Backflush withdrawal**
  The **Backfl. Withdrawal** field is used in kit-to-stock processes to determine at which stage components are backflushed when a kit issue is posted.
- **Correlation fix**
  The **Correlation Fix** indicator is used to specify whether kit components have a fixed correlation with the kit header material. If you specify fixed correlation, then the kit components are automatically adjusted if the kit header is changed; otherwise, they're left unchanged.
- **Consumption-relevant VAS**
  The **Consumptn-Rel. VAS** indicator is set for auxiliary products if you want to enable consumption posting for value-added services (VAS).
- **Documentary batch**
  The **Documentary Batch** setting is used to define a product as documentary batch-relevant. Documentary batches aren't relevant to inventory posting but are used to ensure traceability.
- **Adjustment profile**
  The **Adjustment Profile** field is used in merchandise distribution processes to define how inbound delivery item quantities will be distributed to outbound

delivery order item quantities in the flow-through scenario. To define the adjustment profile, navigate to IMG path **SCM Extended Warehouse Management • Extended Warehouse Management • Cross-Process Settings • Cross-Docking (CD) • Planned Cross-Docking • Merchandise Distribution • Define Adjustment Profile**; once there, click on **New Entries** on the transaction screen.

- **Quantity classification (merchandise distribution)**
  The **Quant Clas (Merch D)** field is used to specify quantity classifications in merchandise distribution quantity adjustments.
- **Preferred unit of measure**
  The **Preferred UoM** field is used to specify the preferred UoM at the warehouse level. If this value isn't specified, the system picks up the preferred UoM maintained at a global level in the **Storage** tab of the product master.
- **Batch-managed warehouse product**
  Set the **Batch-Managed Warehouse Product** indicator if you want to use batch management at the plant level. For batch management at all other levels, use the **Batch Mgmt Reqt** field in the **Properties** tab of the material master. You can set batch management at the plant level in SAP S/4HANA from IMG path **Logistics-General • Batch Management • Specify Batch Level and Activate Status Management**.

Next, we'll review the remaining three sections in the **Whse Data** view in embedded EWM: **Quality Inspection**, **Putaway**, and **Stock Removal** (see Figure 5.15).

The most important data in these three sections is as follows:

- **Inspection interval**
  The **Inspection Interval** field is used to specify the inspection interval in days for a QM active material.
- **Goods receipt block**
  The **Goods Receipt Block** field is used to specify a good receipt block on a product for quality reasons. The default setting is to allow good receipt.
- **Quality inspection group**
  The **Quality Insp. Group** field is used to group together products for quality inspection. Products in the same quality inspection group are governed by the same quality inspection rules.

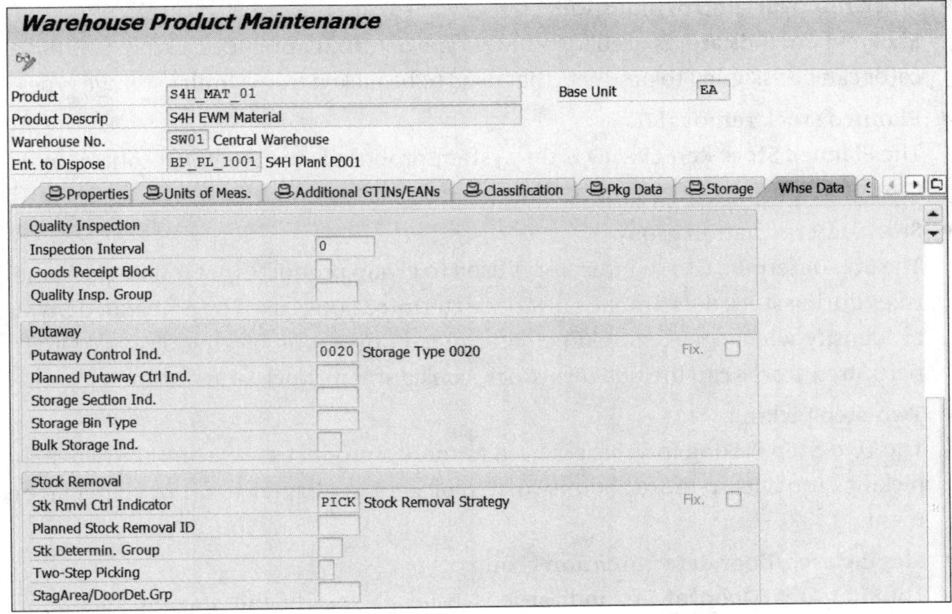

Figure 5.15 Warehouse Data: Quality Inspection, Putaway, and Stock Removal

- **Putaway control indicator**
  The **Putaway Control Ind.** field is used for storage type determination for putaway. This indicator can be assigned to products that need to be putaway to similar storage types.
- **Planned putaway control indicator**
  The **Planned Putaway Ctrl Ind.** is the system-proposed putaway control indicator determined during slotting for optimal product placement.
- **Storage section indicator**
  The **Storage Section Ind.** field is used in storage section determination for putaway into a specific storage section.
- **Storage bin type**
  Storage Bin Type is used to group bins with similar attributes. Here, you specify the bin type in which product will be put away. We discussed bin types in Chapter 4.
- **Bulk storage indicator**
  The **Bulk Storage Ind.** is used to classify products based on how they're stored in a bulk storage area. This indicator is used to structure the number of stacks and stack height for stacking products in a bulk storage area.

- **Stock removal control indicator**
  Stk Rmvl Ctrl Indicator is used for storage type determination for picking. This indicator can be assigned to products that need to be picked from similar storage types.
- **Planned stock removal ID**
  The **Planned Stock Removal ID** is the system-proposed stock removal control indicator used during slotting for optimal product placement.
- **Stock determination group**
  The **Stk. Determin. Group** indicator is used to group products that follow the same rules during stock determination. Stock determination is used by embedded EWM to identify which stock should be determined during the picking process. Other permitted stocks can include own stock, consignment stock, and more.
- **Two-step picking**
  The **Two-Step Picking** indicator is used to mark a product as relevant for two-step picking. You'll learn more about two-step picking in Chapter 16 on wave management.
- **Staging area/door determination group**
  The **StagArea/DoorDet.Grp** indicator is used to specify the staging area/door determination group. The value assigned here helps determine the door from which loading and unloading activities will be carried out for a specific product.

Slotting

The data in the **Slotting** tab is used specifically for slotting processes in embedded EWM. Slotting in embedded EWM is the process of automatic determination of a storage concept for a product for optimal putaway and picking. The data in this tab is divided into three main sections: **General Data**, **Requirement/Demand Data**, and **Dimension Data** (see Figure 5.16).

The most important fields in this tab are as follows:

- **Status slotting**
  The data in the **Status Slotting** field controls the status of material slotting. The status is updated after every slotting run. Four slotting statuses are available in embedded EWM:
  - **Product Not Yet Slotted/Slotting Allowed**
  - **Product Not Yet Slotted/Slotting Not Allowed**
  - **Product Already Slotted/Re-Slotting Allowed**
  - **Product Already Slotted/Re-Slotting Not Allowed**

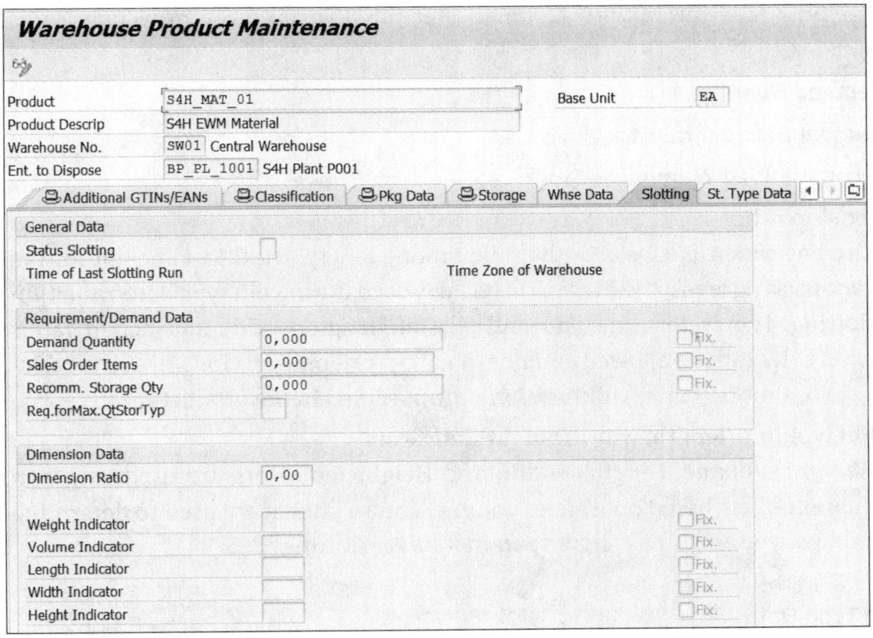

Figure 5.16 Slotting Tab

- **Time of last slotting run**
  The **Time of Last Slotting Run** is updated with the date and time when the slotting run is performed for this product.
- **Demand quantity**
  The **Demand Quantity** field is used during slotting to calculate the open demand for a product in the warehouse.
- **Sales order items**
  The **Sales Order Items** field is used to specify the total number of sales order items to be shipped for this product from the warehouse.
- **Recommended storage quantity**
  The **Recomm. Storage Qty** field is used to specify the recommended storage quantity for a product in the warehouse.
- **Requirements for calculation of maximum quantity**
  The **Req.ForMax.QtStorTyp** field is used to specify which of the three parameters described earlier are used to calculate the maximum quantity for the storage type. The outcome of this exercise is stored in the **Planned Maximum Qty** field in the

storage type data view of the material master. Possible options for this field are as follows:
  - **Demand Quantity**
  - **Number of Order Items**
  - **Recommended Warehouse Stock**
- **Dimension ratio**
  The **Dimension Ratio** considers the ratio among length, width, and height for the relevant packing level. The data in this field is used during bin type determination for slotting. The system calculates all possible length, width, and height ratios based on orientations allowed and doesn't allow orientations for which the calculated ratio is more than the dimension ratio specified in the product master.
- **Weight/volume/length/width/height indicators**
  The **Weight**, **Volume**, **Length**, **Width**, and **Height Indicators** are used to group together products based on weight, volume, and so on and are used to determine the storage type and bin type rule parameters for slotting.

Storage Type Data

This tab holds storage type-specific data for products in the warehouse. You can extend the data in this view for multiple storage types by clicking on the **Adopt Data** button shown in Figure 5.17.

The data fields in this tab are as follows:

- **Storage type**
  The **Storage Type** field is used to specify the storage type for which the remaining settings in the view are being populated. Storage types for which this view has been created appear as a list on the left-hand side of the screen.
- **Storage section indicator**
  The **StorSect.Indic.** indicator is used in storage section determination for putaway into a specific storage section. Set this indicator here to limit the storage sections the product will go into.
- **Planned storage section indicator**
  The **Pl.Stor.Sect.Ind.** field is used to specify the storage section indicator proposed by the slotting run.
- **Storage bin type**
  The **Stor. Bin Type** field is used to specify the allowed storage bin types for this product in the warehouse.

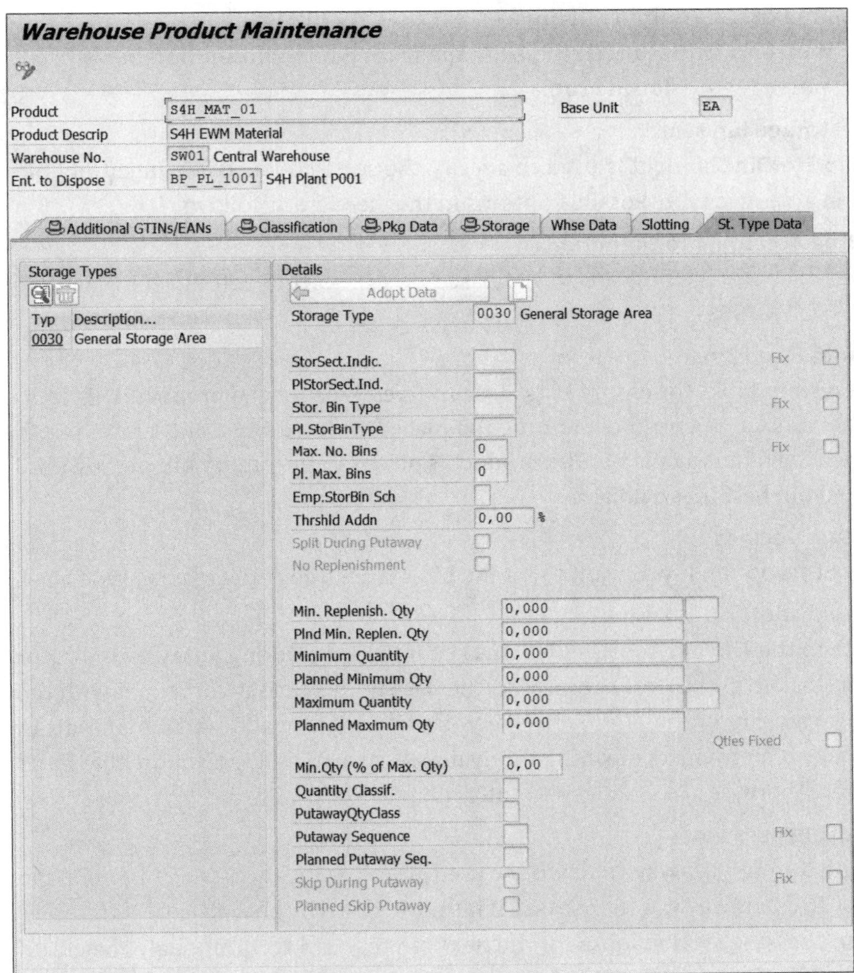

Figure 5.17 Storage Type Data Tab

- **Planned storage bin type**
  The **Pl.StorBinType** field is used to specify the planned storage bin type proposed by the slotting run.
- **Maximum number of bins**
  The **Max. No. Bins** field is used to specify the maximum number of fixed bins for this product in the warehouse.

- **Planned maximum number of bins**
  The **Pl. Max. Bins** field is used to specify the planned maximum number of fixed bins proposed by the slotting run.
- **Empty storage bin search**
  The **Emp.StorBin Sch** field is used to specify the sort sequence for the empty bin search in a storage type. Possible options in this field are as follows:
  - **Sorting According to Definition**
    The empty storage bins are sorted based on bin sorting definition in Transaction /SCWM/SBST.
  - **Near to Fixed Bins**
    The system looks for empty bins close to fixed bins for the product. This technique is used when products must be placed in fixed bins, and there are no empty fixed bins available. The product is placed in the empty bin nearby until a fixed bin becomes available.
  - **Product Decides**
    Select this option if you want to set the bin search rule at the storage type level.
- **Threshold addition**
  The data in the **Thrshld Addn** field is checked if the **Split During Putaway** indicator is set in this tab in the product master. The data in this field is compared with the available capacity of the bin to check if you can put away additional materials in the storage bin provided, meaning the available capacity is less than the threshold addition; otherwise, the putaway quantity is split.
- **Split during putaway**
  The **Split During Putaway** indicator is used if you want the system to split the quantity in a putaway warehouse task if it's more than the bin capacity. If this indicator isn't set, the system looks for the next bin that can accommodate the entire quantity.
- **No replenishment**
  The **No Replenishment** indicator is used to specify products not relevant for replenishment. You'll learn more about replenishment in Chapter 9.
- **Minimum replenishment quantity/minimum quantity/maximum quantity**
  The **Min. Replenish. Qty** field is used to specify the minimum quantity that must be picked during the replenishment process. You can set it to a whole number to

avoid warehouse users having to break a pallet or case to pick the system-proposed replenishment quantity. The **Minimum Quantity** field is used to specify the minimum quantity that should be stored in a storage type. Similarly, the **Maximum Quantity** field is used to specify the maximum quantity that should be stored in a storage type. The data in both these fields is used in planned replenishment.

- **Planned minimum replenishment quantity/planned minimum quantity/planned maximum quantity**
  Plnd. Min. Replen. Qty is used to specify the proposed minimum replenishment quantity based on the slotting run. **Planned Minimum Qty** and **Planned Maximum qty** are used to specify the proposed minimum and maximum replenishment quantity based on the slotting run. After the slotting run is activated, the data in the planned fields is moved to the actual quantity fields.
- **Minimum quantity as percentage of maximum quantity**
  The data in **Min.Qty (% of Max. Qty)** field is used as an alternate way to specify minimum quantity for a storage type. The minimum quantity is proposed as a percentage of maximum quantity.
- **Quantity classification**
  The data in the **Quantity Classif.** field is used to determine the operative UoM for the packaging specification and is used during picking if the quantity classification isn't stored at the storage type level.
- **Putaway quantity classification**
  The **PutawayQtyClass** field is checked if the putaway quantity classification isn't stored.
- **Putaway sequence**
  The **Putaway Sequence** is used to sort storage types within a storage type group for putaway bin determination.
- **Planned putaway sequence**
  The **Planned Putaway Seq.** value holds the planned putaway sequence determined during slotting.
- **Skip during putaway**
  The **Skip During Putaway** indicator is set automatically during slotting. If this indicator is set, the storage type isn't picked for bin determination during putaway.

- **Planned skip putaway**
  The **Planned Skip Putaway** indicator is set during slotting so that the storage type isn't picked for bin determination during putaway.

5.4 Packaging Material

Packaging materials such as cartons, pallets, crates, and wire baskets are used to pack products in the warehouse. Packaging materials in SAP S/4HANA usually are of standard material type VERP. If such a packaging material type doesn't exist, you can create it from IMG path **Logistics—General • Material Master • Basic Settings • Material Types • Define Attributes of Material Types**. When a product is packed with a packaging material, it becomes an HU. Products are usually stored in the warehouse in HUs. You can also create an empty HU in embedded EWM and use it to pack goods at the work center. Before creating a material master for packaging materials in SAP S/4HANA and using it in embedded EWM, you need to complete the following steps:

1. **Define the HU type.**
   You can create HU types for pallets, cartons, and more. HU types are used to classify HUs with the same physical properties. You can define HU types from IMG path **Integration with Other SAP Components • Extended Warehouse Management • Additional Material Attributes • Attribute Values for Additional Material Master Fields • Define Handling Unit Type**.
2. **Define the packaging material type.**
   The packaging material type is used to group packaging materials. The SAP transaction to create packaging material types is Transaction VHAR, which also can be accessed from IMG path **Logistics—General • Handling Unit Management • Basics • Define Packaging Material Types**. You can also define packaging material types for serial shipping container code (SSCC) pallets.
3. **Define the packaging material types in embedded EWM.**
   In addition to creating packaging material types in SAP S/4HANA, you also create the packaging material types in embedded EWM from IMG path **SCM Extended Warehouse Management • Extended Warehouse Management • Cross-Process Settings • Handling Units • Basics • Define Packaging Material Types**. Once there, click on **New Entries** in the transaction screen (see Figure 5.18).

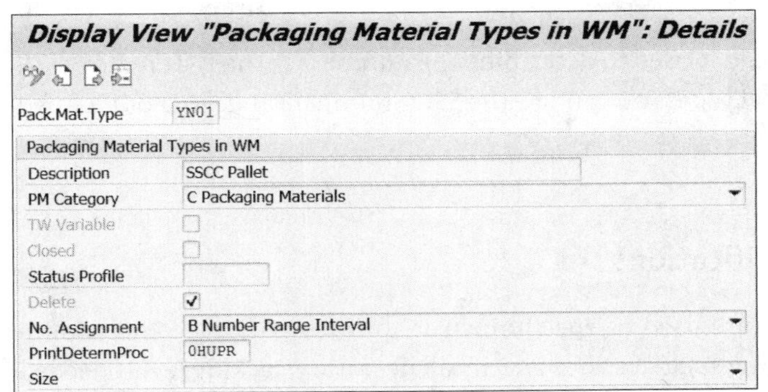

Figure 5.18 Packaging Material Type in Embedded EWM

The packaging material type holds some important settings for specific characteristics of the packaging material:

- **Packaging material category**
  The **PM Category** field is used to specify the nature of the packaging material. If the packaging material is a truck, specify the category as **Means of Transports**. If the packaging material is used for packing along with the main packaging material, such as bubble wrap or shrink wrap, specify the category as **Auxiliary Packaging Material**. Auxiliary packaging materials can't be used to create HUs.

- **Variable tare weight**
  The **TW Variable** indicator is used for packaging material types for which the weight of empty HUs varies. An example is a randomly created container with no predefined standards.

- **Closed**
  The **Closed** indicator field is set if the volume of the HU created with that packaging material doesn't vary after it's packed. For example, a container with a lid will have this indicator, but an open pallet won't.

- **Status profile**
  The **Status Profile** field is used for status management.

- **Delete**
  The **Delete** indicator is set if you want the system to delete an HU after it's been unpacked. This will help avoid leaving unpacked, emptied HUs in the system. You can still create empty HUs in the system even if this checkbox is set.

- **Number assignment**
  The **No. Assignment** field is used to determine the number for the HU created with this packaging material type. You can use the SSCC number range or a predefined number range interval.

5.5 Packaging Specifications

Packaging specifications are used to specify instructions for packing a material in embedded EWM. Packaging specifications specify all necessary packing levels needed to store a product in the warehouse or to transport it. Include the product quantities that need to be packed at various levels and the packaging materials required to pack them. For example, a product may require eight pieces to be packed in one carton, and then 12 such cartons to be packed into one pallet.

Next, we'll explain the general structure and elements of packaging specifications (Section 5.5.1), creating and determining packaging specifications in embedded EWM and decentralized EWM (Section 5.5.2 and Section 5.5.3, respectively), and distributing packaging specifications from SAP ERP to decentralized EWM (Section 5.5.4).

5.5.1 Packaging Specification Structure

A packaging specification holds a set of instructions for packaging a product in the warehouse. Because a product can be packed into several layers, packaging specifications are structured into levels, with each level having details for packing the product at that level. Figure 5.19 shows the structure of a packaging specification in embedded EWM.

The elements of the packing specification structure are as follows:

- **Header**
  The header contains administrative data details such as the name of the packaging specification, status, description, and so on.
- **Contents**
  This section is used to specify the name of the material being packed. Use it to specify one or more products or another packaging specification.

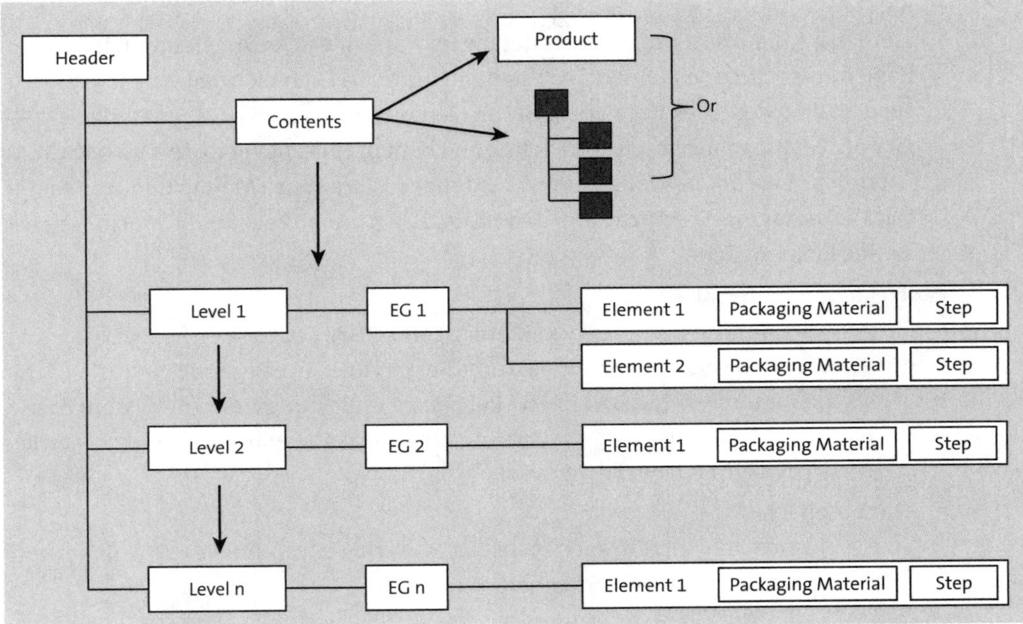

Figure 5.19 Packaging Specification Structure

- **Level**
  You can create more than one level in the packaging specification. Each level contains the level type, minimum quantity, and quantity per layer, which is used to specify how many quantities from the previous level can be packed at this level, and total quantity. The level type can be used to hold generic data for a level and is created via IMG path **SCM Extended Warehouse Management • Extended Warehouse Management • Master Data • Packaging Specification • Maintain Structure of Packaging Specification • Define Level Type**; once there, click on **New Entries.**

- **Element group**
  The element group is used to group details such as packaging material, quantity, and so on required at each level. To group these details, create an element in the element group that holds all the packaging-specific details. The element group is a reusable component and can be used in other packaging specifications too. When an element group is assigned to a packaging specification, all details in the associated element are copied by default.

- **Elements**
  Elements hold packaging-specific details for a specific level. An element group can have more than one element, as the name implies. Each element has an element type, which identifies the nature of the element (main packaging material, auxiliary packaging material, etc.). To define an element type, navigate to IMG path **SCM Extended Warehouse Management • Extended Warehouse Management • Master Data • Packaging Specification • Maintain Structure of Packaging Specification • Define Element Type**.
- **Packaging material**
  Element details also include **Pack. Material** and **Quantity** to specify the packaging material used to pack the materials from the previous level and the quantity of the packaging material required. The **HU-Relevance** indicator guides the system to use the packaging material being used in HU creation as the main packaging material, auxiliary packaging material, or other.
- **Work step**
  You can also include text to specify instructions that a warehouse user might need to keep in mind in the **Work Step** field.

Figure 5.20 highlights all the elements discussed for the packaging specifications in SAP S/4HANA.

Here, you'll see the **Packaging Specification** section containing the status, name, and so on ❶; the **Content** folder (product name and quantity) ❷; and the **Level** section ❸ (each level is characterized by a **Level Type** ❹). In this example, we defined the level type as **Main** to signify that this is the main level of packaging. The **Total Quantity** of 48 means we'll pack 48 units of the product at this level. The level is assigned to an **Elem. Group** ❺, which in this case is **100000010**. The element group is made of a single element with a single quantity of packaging material, **EWMS4-PALLET** ❻, used to pack the main product. The **Work Step** field ❼ can be used to hold long text for specifying packing instructions.

The level type and element type are defined to a **Level Set**. A level set outlines the number of levels and details such as the default condition technique for packaging specification determination. To create a level set, navigate to the IMG path **SCM Extended Warehouse Management • Extended Warehouse Management • Master Data • Packaging Specification • Maintain Structure of Packaging Specification • Define Level Set**.

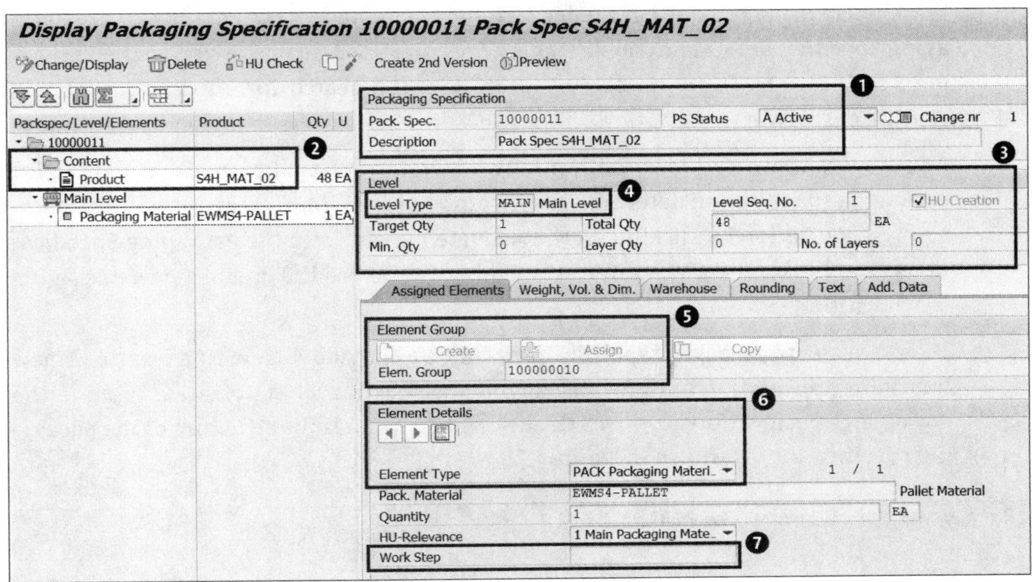

Figure 5.20 Packaging Specifications Example

You also define the **Packaging Specification Group**, which is used to store high-level data needed for creation of packaging specifications. It holds details such as the number range assignment for creating new packaging specifications, level set for identifying levels in the packaging specification structure, and indicator for using condition techniques in determining packaging specifications. To define a packaging specification group, navigate to IMG path **SCM Extended Warehouse Management • Extended Warehouse Management • Master Data • Packaging Specification • Define Packaging Specification Group**.

To define a number range for creating packaging specifications in SAP and assigning them to a packaging specification group, navigate to IMG path **SCM Extended Warehouse Management • Extended Warehouse Management • Master Data • Packaging Specification • Define Number Ranges for Packaging Specification**.

5.5.2 Creation of Packaging Specification

As shown in Figure 5.21, a packaging specification is created via Transaction /SCWM/PACKSPEC, which can also be accessed from IMG path **Logistics • SCM Extended**

Warehouse Management • Extended Warehouse Management • Master Data • Packaging Specification • Maintain Packaging Specification. This takes you to the **Packaging Specifications Overview** screen where you can search for, modify, or delete a specific packaging specification.

A packaging specification should be activated in the system before it can be used for packaging specification determination in embedded EWM. You can activate the packaging specification by clicking on the **Activate** button from the **Packaging Specifications Overview** screen. The same screen also can be used to create a new packaging specification.

To create a new packaging specification, click on the **Add A New Line** button. A new line item appears for the new packaging specification being created. Provide the packaging specification group (**PS Group**), which outlines the structure of the packaging specification, as shown in Figure 5.21.

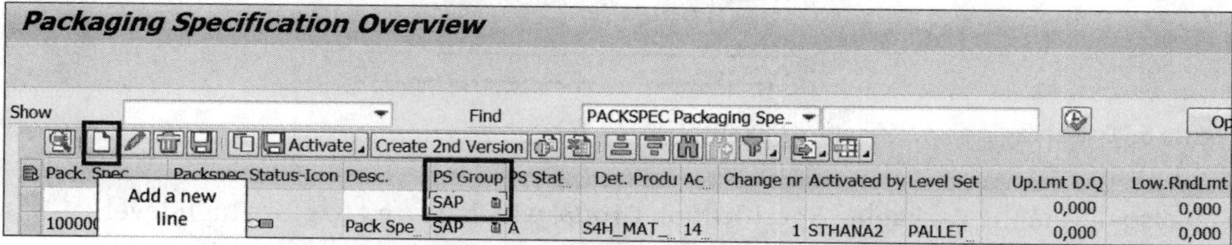

Figure 5.21 Packaging Specification Overview Screen

In the next step, select the packaging specification, and click on the **Change** button, which takes you to the detail screen. Here, provide administrative details, such as **Description**, in the **Packaging Specification** section. The product to be packed is entered in the **Content** area.

Example

Consider a product for which we need to pack six units in one carton and eight such cartons to a pallet. The total product quantity on a full pallet will be 48 units. You can create a packaging specification with two levels in this case. For the first level, you'll pack six units of the product into one carton. For the next level, you'll pack eight cartons into one pallet.

In Figure 5.22, we've specified packing instructions for first-level packing. The **Total Qty** specifies the total product quantity packed at this level. In our example, we pack six units in one carton using packaging material **EWMS4_PALLET**.

In this example, you're packing eight cartons to form a pallet. On the next level, enter the **Target Qty** as "8" because you want to pack level 1 eight times into the main packaging material for level 2. In other words, eight cartons are packed on one pallet. You can also specify the **Min. Qty** and **Layer Qty** to specify a minimum number of quantities of the previous level to be packed together at this layer to form a layer. In the example, we've created two such layers, which will be stacked on top of one another, as shown in Figure 5.23. This will save packing space and prevent the package from breaking.

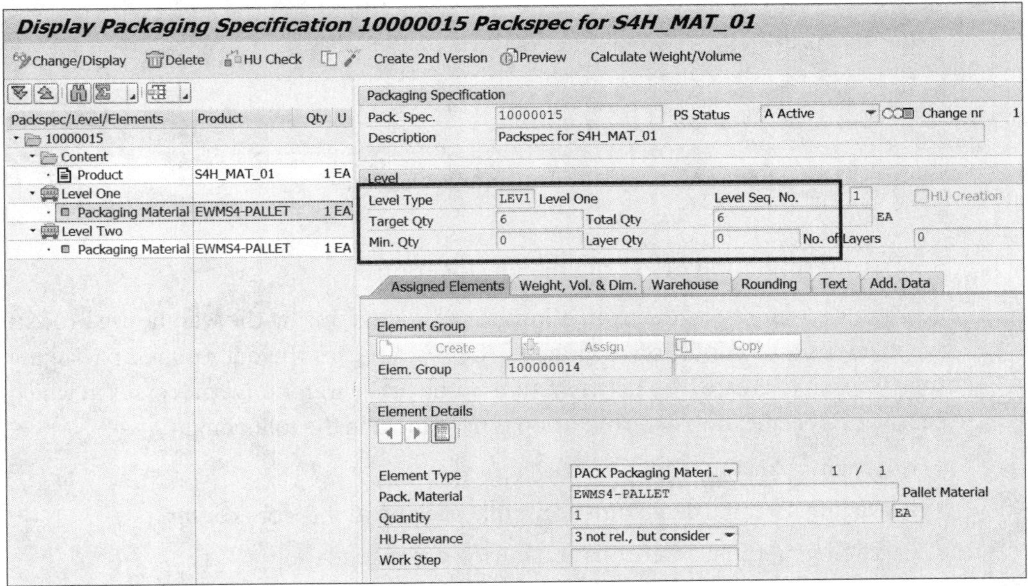

Figure 5.22 Creation of Packaging Specification

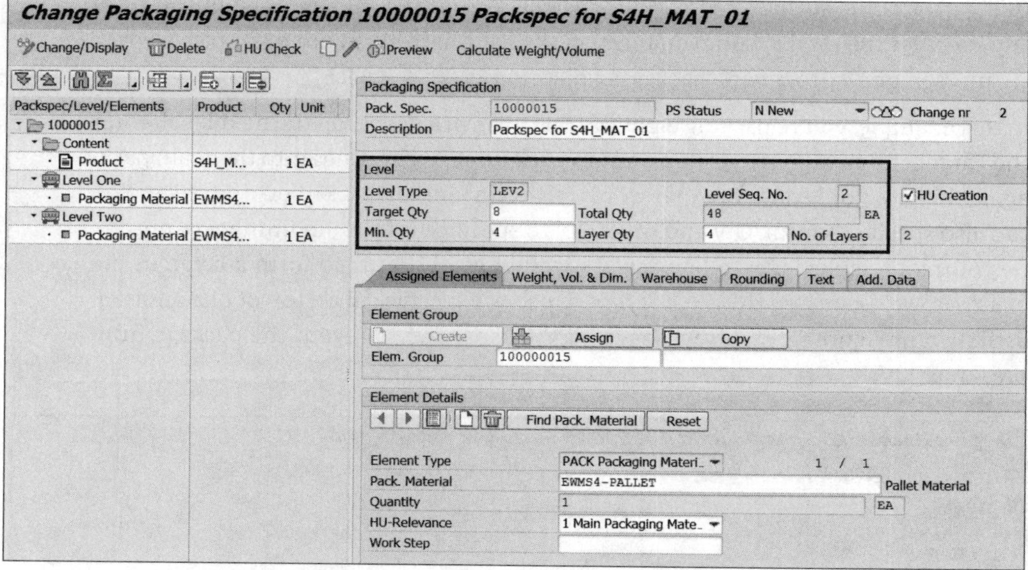

Figure 5.23 Creation of Multilevel Packaging Specification

5.5.3 Determination of Packaging Specification

Packaging specification determinations for a product during the warehouse process are made using a condition technique. The system uses the determined packaging specification to create HUs in the system. Some of the warehouse processes in which packaging specification determination is used include the following:

- Automatic packing in inbound delivery
- Packaging material determination while packing in the work center
- Packaging material determination during deconsolidation

To make Customizing settings for packaging specification determination, navigate to IMG path **SCM Extended Warehouse Management • Extended Warehouse Management • Master Data • Packaging Specification • Determination of Packaging Specification**. Create the following for packaging specification determination:

- Condition table
- Access sequence
- Condition type
- Determination procedure

You can define the determination procedures for separate business processes and assign them at the warehouse number control level in IMG path **SCM Extended Warehouse Management • Master Data • Define Warehouse Number Control**.

After you've set controls for packaging specification determination, define the condition records for condition types. You can maintain condition records in the header data of the packaging specification, as shown in Figure 5.24.

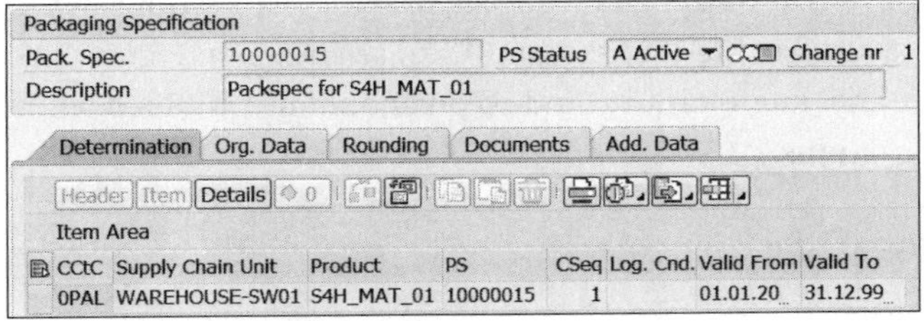

Figure 5.24 Condition Record Maintenance

You can also do this via Transaction /SCWM/PSCT6 or from IMG path **SCM Extended Warehouse Management • Extended Warehouse Management • Master Data • Packaging Specification • Condition Maintenance**.

You can specify the determination procedure at the document type level for automatic determination of packaging materials for creation of HUs. For example, you can assign the determination procedure at the document type level for inbound processes in IMG path **SCM Extended Warehouse Management • Extended Warehouse Management • Goods Receipt Process • Inbound Delivery • Manual Settings • Define Document Types for Inbound Delivery Process**. If you set the **No Automatic Packing** indicator, then the system doesn't pack the items in the inbound delivery immediately upon creation, and you can perform manual packing of inbound delivery items by navigating to the packing work center. The system will propose the packaging material and quantity based on packaging specification determination.

5.5.4 Distribution of Packing Instructions as Packaging Specifications

If you're using decentralized EWM and want to use the packing instructions from another enterprise management system (e.g., a remote SAP ERP or SAP S/4HANA system), you can distribute the packing instructions created in the remote system connected with decentralized EWM in the SAP S/4HANA system. Based on these distributed packing instructions, packing specifications are created in decentralized

EWM and then used by the warehouse workers to pack products in decentralized EWM, thus creating HUs.

To distribute the packing instructions from an enterprise management system, the following activities must be completed in the enterprise management system:

- **Create packing instructions in the remote enterprise management system.**
  To distribute the packing instructions from a remote enterprise management system to decentralized EWM, you need to first create the packing instructions in the enterprise management system using Transaction POP1, as shown in Figure 5.25. The material, packing material and quantity, and so on should be provided while creating the packing instructions.

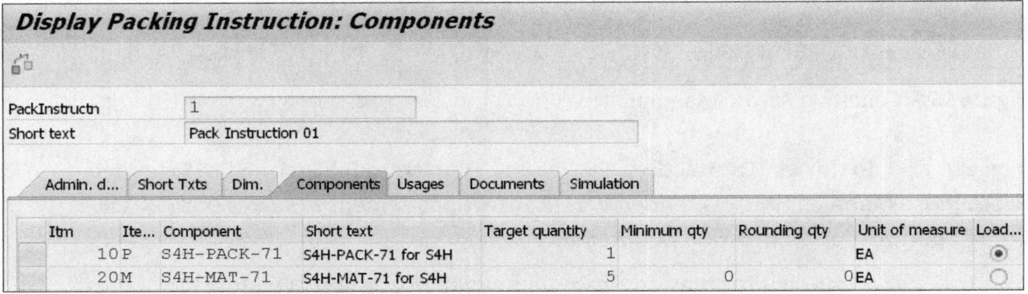

Figure 5.25 Define Packing Instruction: Components Screen

- **Distribute the packing instructions from the remote enterprise management system.**
  To distribute the created packing instructions from the previous step, you need to create a distribution model using Transaction CFM1, as shown in Figure 5.26. Enter the **Model Name**, **Logical System** of decentralized EWM and **APO Application**, and the **Material** for which the packing instruction has been created, and select the **Packaging Specification in Integration Model** checkbox. After entering all the data, you must click on **Execute** in turn to generate the integration model.

  As a next step using Transaction CFM2, enter the **Model Name** and **Logical System** of decentralized EWM and **APO Application** used in the previous step. Execute the model for data distribution after activating the model instance.

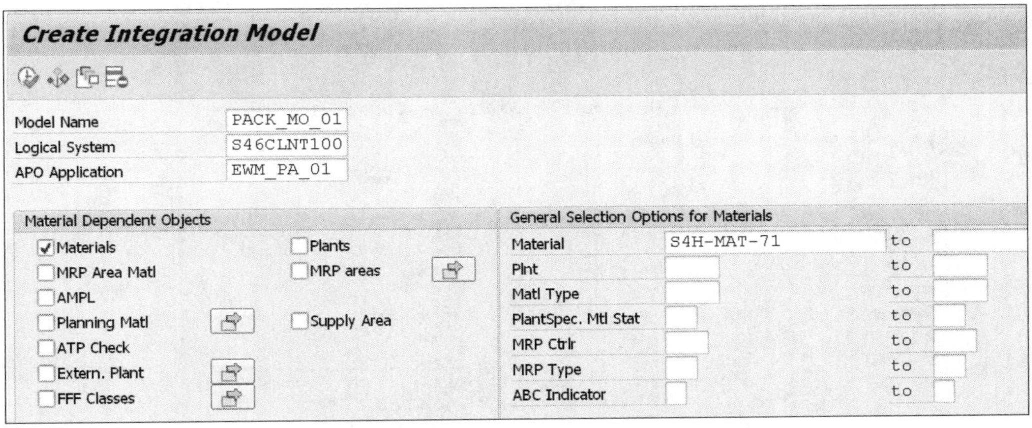

Figure 5.26 Create Integration Model

- **Validate the packing instructions.**
  After the distribution model displays the logs of successful packing instructions distribution from the enterprise management system to decentralized EWM, you can validate the packing instruction by entering the packing instruction name in the **Packing Specification** field using Transaction /SCWM/PACKSPEC.

> **Note**
>
> It's important to note that the number ranges of packing instructions in the enterprise management system and the packing specification in decentralized SAP EWM should be synched by taking the same number range between the two systems while making the same number ranges external in a decentralized EWM system.

5.6 Routes

Routes are used to determine the itinerary, means of transport, and so on in a sales order. Route scheduling is used to set schedules of deliveries to customers from the same shipping points on the same routes. Route schedules are set at the header level for the delivery in the SAP S/4HANA system.

A route in embedded EWM is copied from the **Route** field in the delivery that was created in SAP S/4HANA. Thus, sales and distribution (SD) routes are copied to the delivery in embedded EWM, as shown in Figure 5.27. You can't perform a new route determination and scheduling in embedded EWM because SAP Supply Chain Management (SAP SCM) routes are no longer supported.

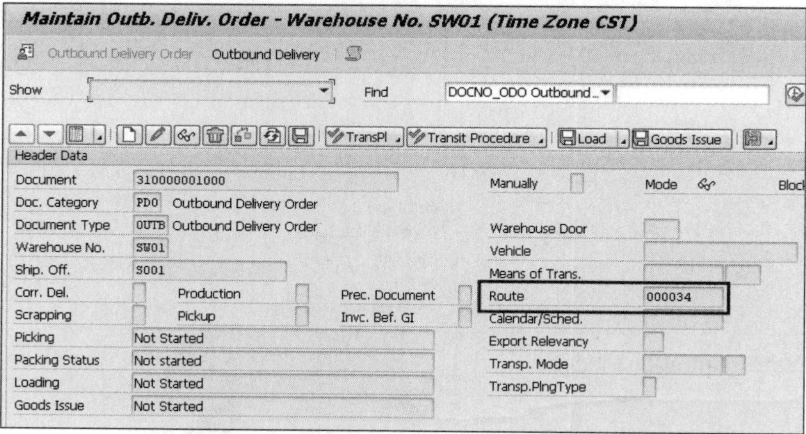

Figure 5.27 Route in Embedded EWM

You can set up scheduling with a route schedule for sales document types on the following three levels in SAP S/4HANA:

- Sales document type
- Delivery type
- Shipping point

Tip

Embedded EWM in SAP S/4HANA 1909 doesn't use SAP SCM routes. Only SD routes determined in the delivery in SAP S/4HANA are carried forwarded to the distributed delivery in embedded EWM. Thus, transactions such as Transaction /SCTM/RGINT for route determination simulation and Transaction /SCWM/ROUTE for route creation are obsolete in embedded EWM in SAP S/4HANA 1909. Routes in SAP S/4HANA can only be used for decentralized EWM.

Note

If you're using decentralized EWM, you can use SAP SCM routes, but they first have to be mapped. You'll then have to complete the route determination settings and make all the route scheduling settings.

5.7 Summary

In this chapter, we discussed the master data needed in embedded EWM to carry out warehousing operations. We discussed the product master in embedded EWM, which is created after the material master is created in SAP S/4HANA. We discussed important fields in the product master and how they're determined from the material master in SAP S/4HANA. We also discussed other important master data in embedded EWM such as packaging materials, packaging specifications, and so on. You should now understand the master data required to support your business processes and be able to set up master data for your embedded EWM implementation projects. In the next chapter, we'll discuss the cross-process settings for embedded EWM.

Chapter 6
Cross-Process Settings

Cross-process settings are independent configurations used across processes in warehouse management. In this chapter, we'll discuss how they supply the basic elements in embedded EWM based on which inbound, outbound, and internal warehouse processes are carried out.

In this chapter, we'll discuss the business relevance of and configuration settings required for cross-process definitions in embedded EWM. Because these functionalities cut across multiple embedded EWM processes, we need to discuss them before we dive into business processes in detail in later chapters. This chapter covers the following topics:

- Warehouse requests
- Handling units (HUs)
- Warehouse tasks
- Warehouse orders
- Storage control
- Exception handling
- Batch management
- Stock identification
- Catch weight management
- Post Processing Framework (PPF)
- Travel distance calculations
- Serial number management
- Quality management (QM)

Let's begin with the general configuration tasks you need to perform for warehouse operations.

6.1 Warehouse Requests

SAP S/4HANA delivery or posting change requests become warehouse requests in embedded EWM. A warehouse request is the planning document for all internal movements in embedded EWM and is used only in embedded EWM. A warehouse request is made up of a document header and document type. The document header contains general data relevant to the entire request and the entire document; the document item contains data specific to each item in the delivery document, with the option to create follow-up documents and take follow-up actions for each item, independent of the delivery document header.

You define a number range for documents created in embedded EWM, such as outbound deliveries, inbound deliveries, outbound delivery orders, and production material requests. To create a number range, navigate to IMG path **SCM Extended Warehouse Management • Extended Warehouse Management • Cross-Process Settings • Delivery-Warehouse Requests • Number Ranges,** and click on **Intervals**.

Note

Embedded EWM can access existing SAP S/4HANA Customizing directly for the following:

- Catch weight tolerance group and catch weight profile for catch weight quantities
- Delivery priority
- Handling indicator and HU type
- Incoterms
- Packing group and quality inspection group
- Serial number profile
- Shipping conditions and transportation group
- Warehouse product group and warehouse storage condition

Service profiles are used in embedded EWM to define how documents are processed and to define the business features of the documents. These profiles are associated with the document type and item type in embedded EWM and control their features and behavior. There are two types of service profiles in embedded EWM:

- **System profile**
  System profiles are included in the scope of the standard embedded EWM system and can't be modified. Internally, system profiles are linked to both document category profiles related to header settings and to item categories for item profile settings.
- **Customer profile**
  Customer profiles are required to manage individual business processes and can be modified based on business requirements. SAP has provided a set of predefined customer profiles, each of which is linked to a corresponding system profile. The customer profiles are assigned to document types and item types based on the specific business process for which they are used.

The various service profiles available in embedded EWM are explained in the following sections. First, however, let's take a brief look at what warehouse requests are and how they work.

6.1.1 What Are Warehouse Requests?

Warehouse requests are planned documents for warehouse stock movements within and outside the warehouse. They form the basis for creation of warehouse tasks, which are assigned to warehouse workers for stock movement completion. Some of the warehouse requests that can be created in embedded EWM are outbound delivery orders, inbound delivery orders, posting change documents, and so on. In the following sections, we explain the business context in which the physical inventory process can be used in real-world scenarios and how to carry these processes out in the system.

Business Process

American company Alpha Medicals receives an order from one of its customers based in Mexico. The order sent by the customer requires Alpha Medicals to provide the products in time and packed in cases and pallets for delivery. Stock that will be delivered to the customer is to be picked from source bins of the supplying warehouse by the warehouse workers, packed in the required packaging material, and staged in the goods issue area. As a regular Alpha Medicals practice, the warehousing activities performed by the warehouse workers are planned and created as warehouse requests in embedded EWM that will be executed as stock movements by warehouse workers. To ensure that all such activities of warehouse workers are planned and assigned to customers for execution in the embedded EWM system, the company has implemented embedded EWM.

System Process

The following list describes the basic system flow, including the documents and data required to process warehouse requests (e.g., outbound delivery orders) in embedded EWM and decentralized EWM:

1. An outbound delivery order is created as a warehouse request in embedded EWM and contains information about the products Alpha Medicals will deliver to the external customer.
2. Initial picking warehouse tasks are created based on the warehouse request and assigned to the warehouse workers. This request directs the warehouse workers to carry out the product movement from source bin to staging area.
3. The warehouse orders allocated to the warehouse workers are executed by the workers in the order in which they are created.
4. All the activities related to warehouse requests are captured in the embedded EWM system and are used for analysis and follow-on decision-making by the warehouse administrator.

6.1.2 Process Code Profile

Process codes are used in warehouse requests to perform quantity adjustments at the item level. A process code profile determines which process codes are available for use in a warehouse request and is assigned at the item type level. SAP provides predefined process code profiles that are assigned to the corresponding system profiles. If you want to use different process codes for a business process, you can create a new process code profile and assign it to the system profile. You can also create new process codes for a business process via IMG path **SCM Extended Warehouse Management • Extended Warehouse Management • Cross-Process Settings • Delivery-Warehouse Requests • Process Codes • Define Process Codes**, as shown in Figure 6.1, by clicking on **New Entries**.

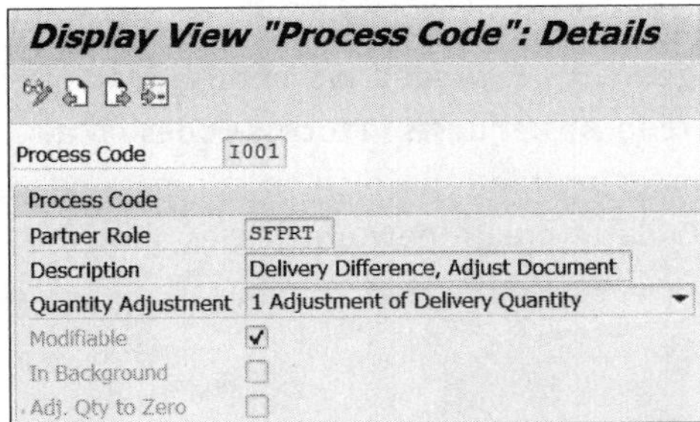

Figure 6.1 Defining Process Codes

You can define process codes with the following parameters:

- **Partner role**
  The **Partner Role** field is used to specify the role that causes the quantity difference to happen. For example, if a quantity difference happens because of goods received from a source, you set the **Partner Role** as **SFPRT** (ship-from party or vendor).
- **Quantity adjustment**
  The **Quantity Adjustment** setting is used to control if and how the delivered quantity is adjusted in embedded EWM. Choose one of three options:
  - Only apply the process code in embedded EWM, with no change in delivered quantity.
  - Adjust delivered quantity only in embedded EWM.
  - Adjust delivered quantity both in embedded EWM and SAP S/4HANA. This causes a delivery split and a new delivery is distributed to embedded EWM.
- **Modifiable**
  The **Modifiable** indicator is used to control if a process code is modifiable.
- **Background**
  The **In Background** indicator is used to control if a process code is relevant for background processing.
- **Adjust quantity to zero**
  The **Adj. Qty. to Zero** indicator is used if you want to adjust the delivery quantity to 0. If this indicator is set, you can't adjust the delivered quantity to any other number than zero.

To create a new process code profile or make changes to an existing one, navigate to IMG path **SCM Extended Warehouse Management • Extended Warehouse Management • Cross-Process Settings • Delivery-Warehouse Requests • Process Codes • Maintain Process Code Profiles**. Select the customer profile for which the process code needs to be created, and click on **Process Code** to create new entries, as shown in Figure 6.2.

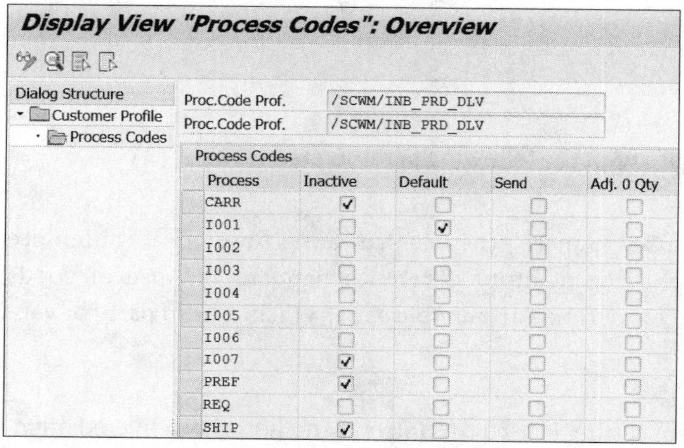

Display View "Process Codes": Overview

Dialog Structure
- Customer Profile
  - Process Codes

Proc.Code Prof. /SCWM/INB_PRD_DLV
Proc.Code Prof. /SCWM/INB_PRD_DLV

Process Codes

Process	Inactive	Default	Send	Adj. 0 Qty
CARR	✓			
I001		✓		
I002				
I003				
I004				
I005				
I006				
I007	✓			
PREF	✓			
REQ				
SHIP	✓			

Figure 6.2 Process Code Profile

6.1.3 Status Profile

A status profile is used to control the status of a warehouse request to allow or prohibit processing from certain business transactions. You can use status management to set a status in a document for information purposes only or to change a document status after transaction execution. To define a status profile, navigate to IMG path **SCM Extended Warehouse Management • Extended Warehouse Management • Cross-Process Settings • Delivery-Warehouse Requests • Process Codes • Define Status Profiles**. Select the **Status Profile**, and click on **Status Types** to create new entries.

Figure 6.3 shows different status types set for **Status Profile /SCDL/INB_PRD_STANDARD**, which is assigned to a document type for the inbound delivery process. You can see various inbound-relevant statuses such as goods receipt, planning, putaway, and so on, reflecting different document-processing statuses.

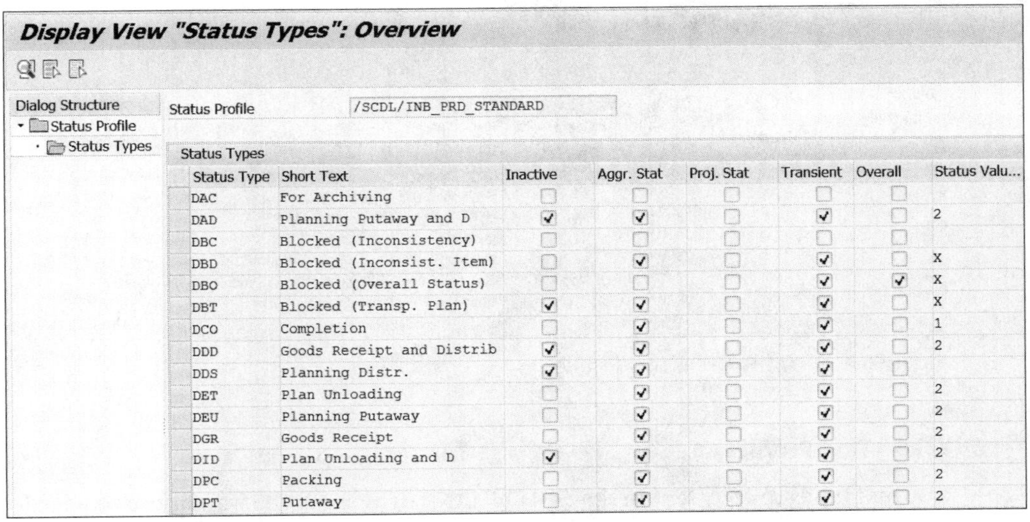

Display View "Status Types": Overview

Dialog Structure
- Status Profile
  - Status Types

Status Profile: /SCDL/INB_PRD_STANDARD

Status Types

Status Type	Short Text	Inactive	Aggr. Stat	Proj. Stat	Transient	Overall	Status Valu...
DAC	For Archiving	☐	☐	☐	☐	☐	
DAD	Planning Putaway and D	☑	☑	☐	☑	☐	2
DBC	Blocked (Inconsistency)	☐	☐	☐	☐	☐	
DBD	Blocked (Inconsist. Item)	☐	☑	☐	☑	☐	X
DBO	Blocked (Overall Status)	☐	☐	☐	☑	☑	X
DBT	Blocked (Transp. Plan)	☑	☑	☐	☑	☐	X
DCO	Completion	☐	☑	☐	☑	☐	1
DDD	Goods Receipt and Distrib	☑	☑	☐	☑	☐	2
DDS	Planning Distr.	☑	☑	☐	☑	☐	
DET	Plan Unloading	☐	☑	☐	☑	☐	2
DEU	Planning Putaway	☐	☑	☐	☑	☐	2
DGR	Goods Receipt	☐	☑	☐	☑	☐	2
DID	Plan Unloading and D	☑	☑	☐	☑	☐	2
DPC	Packing	☐	☑	☐	☑	☐	2
DPT	Putaway	☐	☑	☐	☑	☐	2

Figure 6.3 Status Profile

6.1.4 Quantity Offsetting Profile

A quantity offsetting profile is used for performing calculations for relevant delivery quantities, such as open quantity, requested quantity, reduced quantity, and so on. Define the quantity offsetting profile via IMG path **SCM Extended Warehouse Management • Extended Warehouse Management • Cross-Process Settings • Delivery-Warehouse Requests • Quantity Offsetting • Define Quantity Offsetting Profiles**. Click on **New Entries**, as shown in Figure 6.4.

The quantity roles and quantity categories are used for defining the algorithms for quantity determination quantity offsets. To assign a quantity role, click on **Assignment of Quantity Roles** in the left-hand menu, and then click on **New Entries**. The quantity role is assigned to quantity categories and, if required, a determination rule and offset rule by selecting the required quantity role and clicking on **New Entries**. The quantity determination rule is used for calculation of a reduced quantity. The offsetting rule is used to calculate the open quantity for a document. The quantity offsetting profile is assigned to delivery types and item types in embedded EWM.

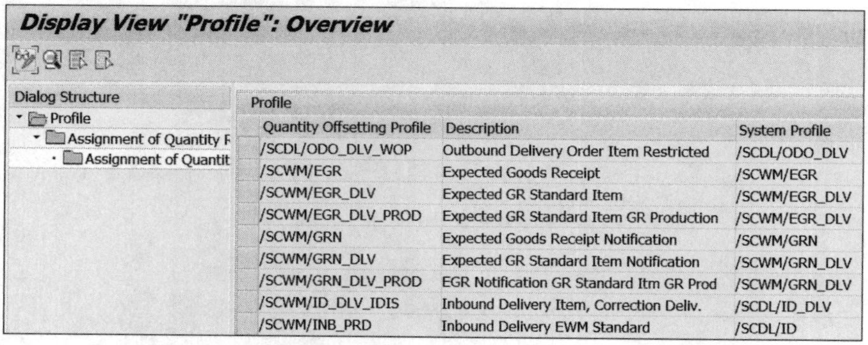

Display View "Profile": Overview

Dialog Structure: Profile · Assignment of Quantity F · Assignment of Quantit

Profile

Quantity Offsetting Profile	Description	System Profile
/SCDL/ODO_DLV_WOP	Outbound Delivery Order Item Restricted	/SCDL/ODO_DLV
/SCWM/EGR	Expected Goods Receipt	/SCWM/EGR
/SCWM/EGR_DLV	Expected GR Standard Item	/SCWM/EGR_DLV
/SCWM/EGR_DLV_PROD	Expected GR Standard Item GR Production	/SCWM/EGR_DLV
/SCWM/GRN	Expected Goods Receipt Notification	/SCWM/GRN
/SCWM/GRN_DLV	Expected GR Standard Item Notification	/SCWM/GRN_DLV
/SCWM/GRN_DLV_PROD	EGR Notification GR Standard Itm GR Prod	/SCWM/GRN_DLV
/SCWM/ID_DLV_IDIS	Inbound Delivery Item, Correction Deliv.	/SCDL/ID_DLV
/SCWM/INB_PRD	Inbound Delivery EWM Standard	/SCDL/ID

Figure 6.4 Quantity Offsetting Profile

6.1.5 Text Profile

Use text types to copy text in the SAP S/4HANA delivery to the warehouse request in embedded EWM. You can also use text types to add text directly to the embedded EWM delivery. A text profile is used to group together text types for a delivery header or item. You can create text types for the delivery header and delivery item levels. Text types at the delivery header level include shipping instructions, bills of lading, and so on.

As shown in Figure 6.5, define the text profiles for delivery documents via IMG path **SCM Extended Warehouse Management • Extended Warehouse Management • Cross-Process Settings • Delivery-Warehouse Requests • Text Management • Define Text Profiles with Access Sequence**. Click on **Define Text Profiles** in the left-hand menu, and then click on **New Entries**. The text profiles for the delivery header text are assigned to document types, and text profiles for the delivery item text are assigned to item types.

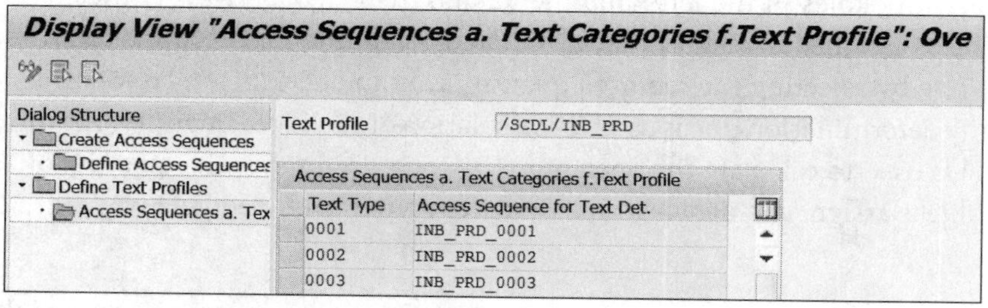

Display View "Access Sequences a. Text Categories f.Text Profile": Ove

Dialog Structure: Create Access Sequences · Define Access Sequences · Define Text Profiles · Access Sequences a. Tex

Text Profile: /SCDL/INB_PRD

Access Sequences a. Text Categories f.Text Profile

Text Type	Access Sequence for Text Det.
0001	INB_PRD_0001
0002	INB_PRD_0002
0003	INB_PRD_0003

Figure 6.5 Text Management Profile

6.1.6 Field Control Profile

A field control is used to determine which fields are displayed as display-only or modifiable fields during delivery processing. A field control profile contains all allowed fields and their attributes for a document or item type. As shown in Figure 6.6, you can define a field control profile via IMG path **SCM Extended Warehouse Management • Extended Warehouse Management • Cross-Process Settings • Delivery-Warehouse Requests • Field Control • Define Field Control Profiles**. Click on **Field Control Profile** in the left-hand menu, and then click on **New Entries**. This setting controls the fields displayed at both the delivery header and item levels. A field control profile for the document header is assigned to a document type, and a field control profile for a delivery item is assigned to an item type. A field control becomes active in the following scenarios in embedded EWM:

- Creating a new document or line item
- Saving a change in the document
- Switching between display and change mode

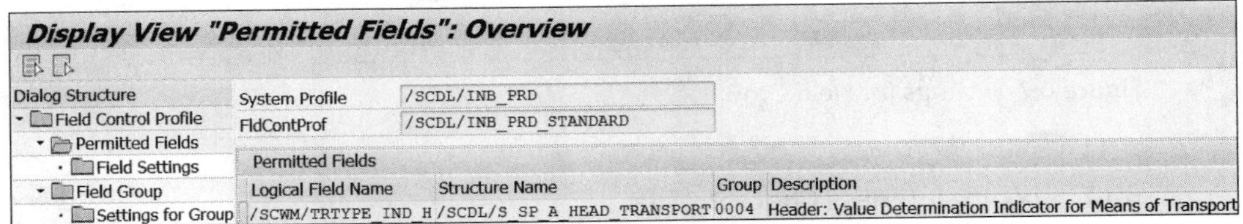

Figure 6.6 Field Status Profile

Within embedded EWM, you define all fields in a delivery as components of structures, and each element in the structure is uniquely identified by a logical field name. The combination of logical field name and structure is assigned to a field group by selecting the required **FldContProf** (field control profile) and creating new entries for **Permitted Fields**. To define a field group, double-click on **Field Group**, and then click on **New Entries**. Next, assign different status types and the values associated with them to field groups along with the settings to classify them as display-only fields (**DspField**) and system-entry (**Sys. Entry**) fields, as shown in Figure 6.7.

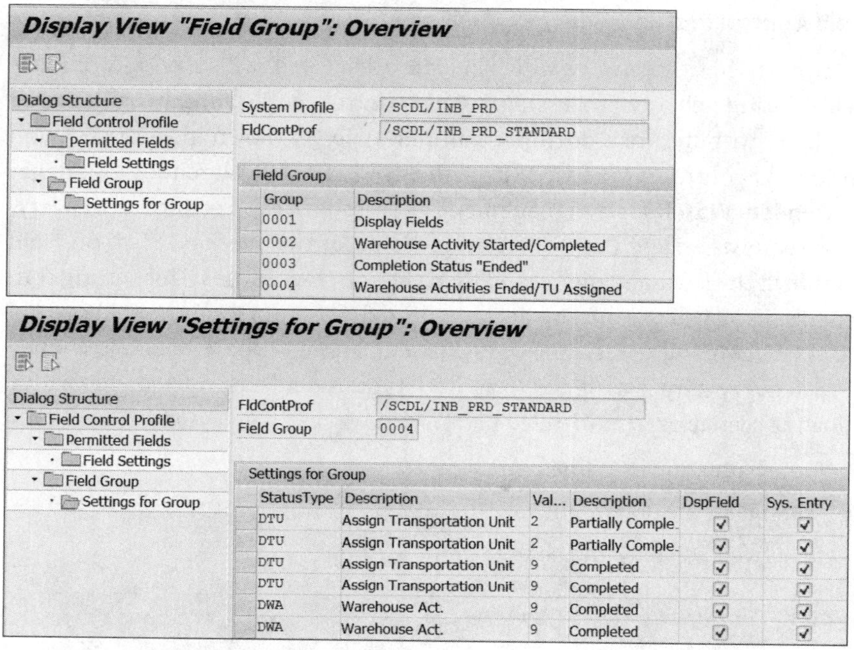

Display View "Field Group": Overview

Dialog Structure
- Field Control Profile
  - Permitted Fields
    - Field Settings
  - Field Group
    - Settings for Group

System Profile: /SCDL/INB_PRD
FldContProf: /SCDL/INB_PRD_STANDARD

Field Group

Group	Description
0001	Display Fields
0002	Warehouse Activity Started/Completed
0003	Completion Status "Ended"
0004	Warehouse Activities Ended/TU Assigned

Display View "Settings for Group": Overview

Dialog Structure
- Field Control Profile
  - Permitted Fields
    - Field Settings
  - Field Group
    - Settings for Group

FldContProf: /SCDL/INB_PRD_STANDARD
Field Group: 0004

Settings for Group

StatusType	Description	Val...	Description	DspField	Sys. Entry
DTU	Assign Transportation Unit	2	Partially Comple.	✓	✓
DTU	Assign Transportation Unit	2	Partially Comple.	✓	✓
DTU	Assign Transportation Unit	9	Completed	✓	✓
DTU	Assign Transportation Unit	9	Completed	✓	✓
DWA	Warehouse Act.	9	Completed	✓	✓
DWA	Warehouse Act.	9	Completed	✓	✓

Figure 6.7 Settings for Field Group

6.1.7 Incompleteness Check Profile

Embedded EWM allows the system to perform an incompleteness check on a document to ensure that all required fields are filled before a document can be processed. These mandatory field names are mapped to a logical field name and contained in an incompleteness profile, which is assigned to a delivery document type for header fields and a delivery item type for item-related fields. The incompleteness profiles can be defined via IMG path **SCM Extended Warehouse Management • Extended Warehouse Management • Cross-Process Settings • Delivery-Warehouse Requests • Incompleteness Check • Define Incompleteness Profile**, by clicking on **New Entries**.

As shown in Figure 6.8, you can bind logical fields in the delivery document with appropriate actions. For example, logical field **ENTITLED_I** is assigned to action **20 - Save Document**, which means the system should throw an error if the **Party Entitled to Dispose** is empty in the delivery line item. If specific checks are required for the logical field for an action, then a custom class with appropriate logic can also be assigned to the logical field name and action combination.

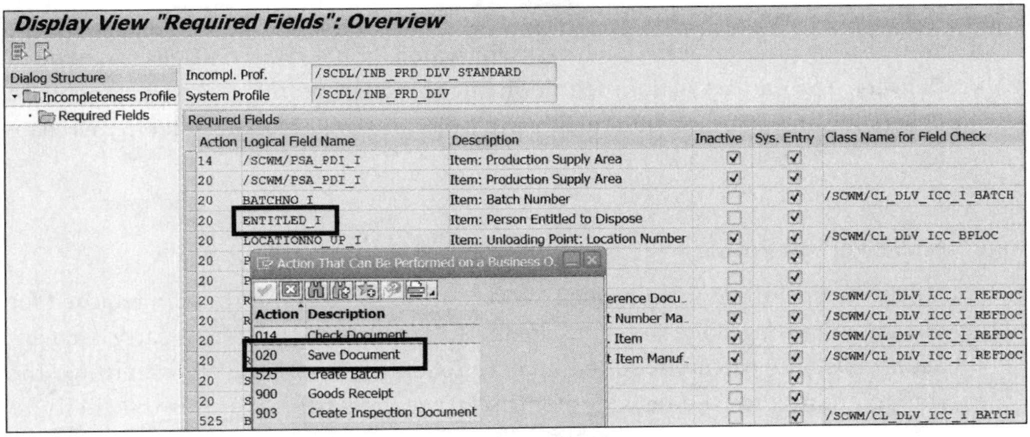

Figure 6.8 Incompleteness Profile

6.1.8 Action Profile

Embedded EWM uses the PPF for message/output control in delivery processing. All actions in a warehouse request document are generated by the framework based on action definitions and processed by the system. These actions can be print commands, email alerts, and so on. The actions are stored in an action profile assigned to a document type in EWM. Set up a PPF action profile via IMG path **SCM Extended Warehouse Management • Extended Warehouse Management • Cross-Process Settings • Delivery-Warehouse Requests • Actions • Change Actions and Conditions • Define Action Profiles and Actions.**

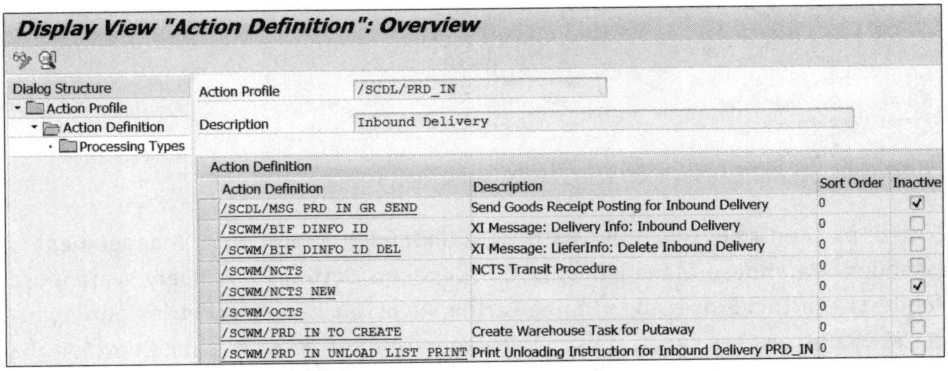

Figure 6.9 Action Profile and Action Definition

In Figure 6.9, we've defined various actions such as printing unloading instructions and creating putaway warehouse tasks for **Action Profile /SCDL/PRD_IN** for **Inbound Delivery**. You can set action definitions in an action profile as **Active** or **Inactive** depending on business requirements. We'll discuss the PPF further later in this chapter.

6.1.9 Partner Profile

A delivery document in embedded EWM contains partner information required for further processing of the warehouse request. For example, the ship-to party is a mandatory business partner required in an outbound delivery order to determine the ship-to address for the delivery items. Partner processing provides the ability to maintain partner information at the delivery header or item level. As shown in Figure 6.10, all business partners are defined with specific business partner roles in embedded EWM, and each business partner role has a specific business partner category assigned to it. Some examples of business partner roles available in embedded EWM are carrier, supplier, ship-to party, and ship-from party.

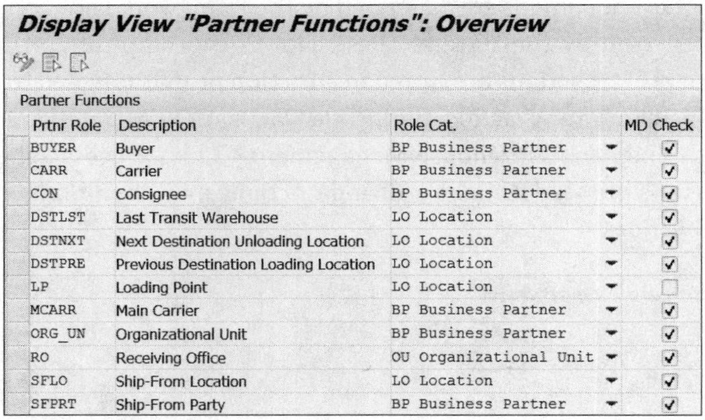

Display View "Partner Functions": Overview

Partner Functions

Prtnr Role	Description	Role Cat.	MD Check
BUYER	Buyer	BP Business Partner	✓
CARR	Carrier	BP Business Partner	✓
CON	Consignee	BP Business Partner	✓
DSTLST	Last Transit Warehouse	LO Location	✓
DSTNXT	Next Destination Unloading Location	LO Location	✓
DSTPRE	Previous Destination Loading Location	LO Location	✓
LP	Loading Point	LO Location	
MCARR	Main Carrier	BP Business Partner	✓
ORG_UN	Organizational Unit	BP Business Partner	✓
RO	Receiving Office	OU Organizational Unit	✓
SFLO	Ship-From Location	LO Location	✓
SFPRT	Ship-From Party	BP Business Partner	✓

Figure 6.10 Business Partner Role

Define partner roles via IMG path **SCM Extended Warehouse Management • Extended Warehouse Management • Cross-Process Settings • Delivery-Warehouse Requests • Partner Processing • Define Partner Roles**. Click on **New Entries**, enter partner role controls, and save. A business partner category sets a business partner of a given business partner role as **Business Partner**, **Location**, or **Organizational Unit**. If required, you can also configure the system to perform a master data check for the business partner role in embedded EWM during creation of the warehouse request by setting the **MD Check** indicator.

Partner profiles are used to group partner roles and are assigned at the document type and item type levels. As shown in Figure 6.11, you can create or change customer partner profiles via IMG path **SCM Extended Warehouse Management • Extended Warehouse Management • Cross-Process Settings • Delivery-Warehouse Requests • Partner Processing • Define Partner Profiles**. Double-click on **Partner Roles** for a customer profile, and then click on **New Entries**. Set the **Multiple** dropdown to **Yes** if multiple business partners are required for a specific partner role in the delivery.

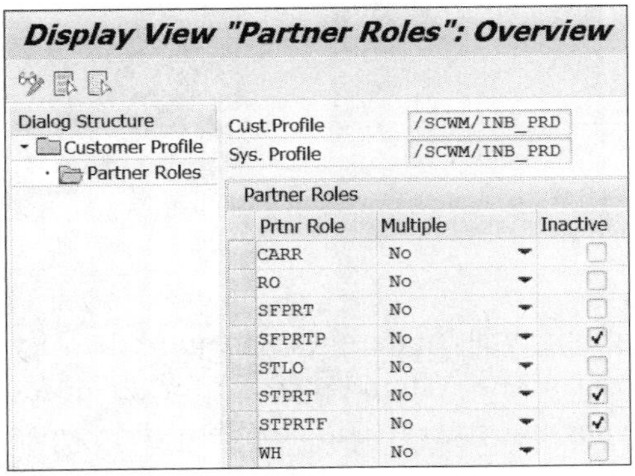

Display View "Partner Roles": Overview

Dialog Structure
- Customer Profile
  - Partner Roles

Cust.Profile /SCWM/INB_PRD
Sys. Profile /SCWM/INB_PRD

Partner Roles

Prtnr Role	Multiple	Inactive
CARR	No	☐
RO	No	☐
SFPRT	No	☐
SFPRTP	No	☑
STLO	No	☐
STPRT	No	☑
STPRTF	No	☑
WH	No	☐

Figure 6.11 Partner Profiles in Embedded EWM

6.1.10 Reference Document Profile

A reference document profile allows you to add one or more preceding document references in embedded EWM. Each document is categorized using a reference document category code, as shown in Figure 6.12. To do this, navigate to IMG path **SCM Extended Warehouse Management • Extended Warehouse Management • Cross-Process Settings • Delivery-Warehouse Requests • Reference Documents • Define Reference Document Categories**, and click on **New Entries**.

After the reference document categories are defined, they can be assigned to a reference document profile via IMG path **SCM Extended Warehouse Management • Extended Warehouse Management • Cross-Process Settings • Delivery-Warehouse Requests • Reference Documents • Define Reference Document Types Profiles**. Double-click on **Reference Document Categories** for a customer profile, and then click on **New Entries**. Figure 6.12 shows the preconfigured reference document customer and system profile provided by SAP for standard delivery processing. After these profiles are assigned to a delivery header or item, the reference document number can be added to the document in embedded EWM.

Display View "Reference Document Categories": Overview

Dialog Structure
- Customer Profile
  - Reference Document Cat

Cust.Profile /SCWM/INB_PRD
Sys. Profile /SCWM/INB_PRD

Reference Document Categories

Doc. Cat.	Inactive
ASN	☐
BOL	☐
ERO	☐
ERP	☐
FRD	☑
PRO	☑
Q01	☐
TCD	☑

Figure 6.12 Reference Document Profile

6.1.11 Date Profile

In embedded EWM, it's possible to add new date types in warehouse request delivery documents to capture the date and time of various system processes for the document. SAP has provided predefined date types, but you can add new date/time types via IMG path **SCM Extended Warehouse Management • Extended Warehouse Management • Cross-Process Settings • Delivery-Warehouse Requests • Date/Times • Define Date Types**, as shown in Figure 6.13. Click on **New Entries**. The time of day is automatically added to the date using system-provided settings. Date types include delivery date, goods issue date, and others.

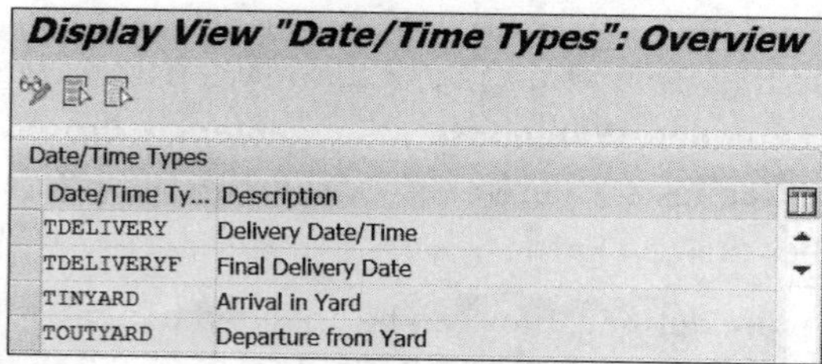

Display View "Date/Time Types": Overview

Date/Time Types

Date/Time Ty...	Description
TDELIVERY	Delivery Date/Time
TDELIVERYF	Final Delivery Date
TINYARD	Arrival in Yard
TOUTYARD	Departure from Yard

Figure 6.13 Date Types in Embedded EWM

After the new date/time types are defined, they can be bundled into date profiles via IMG path **SCM Extended Warehouse Management • Extended Warehouse Management • Cross-Process Settings • Delivery-Warehouse Requests • Reference Documents • Define Date Profiles**. Double-click on **Date/Time Types** for a customer profile, and then click on **New Entries**, as shown in Figure 6.14. Assign the profile to the delivery document type and item type. By doing so, you allow the system to capture a specific set of dates and times at the delivery header and item levels based on delivery processing in embedded EWM.

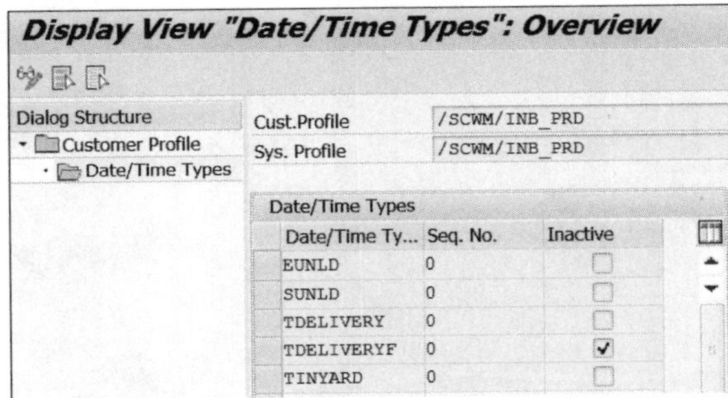

Figure 6.14 Date/Time Profile

6.1.12 Process Profile

Embedded EWM uses process profiles for delivery headers and items, which control the processes allowed in a delivery document. Embedded EWM supports separate process profiles for delivery headers and items. As shown in Figure 6.15, define a process profile for a delivery header via IMG path **SCM Extended Warehouse Management • Extended Warehouse Management • Cross-Process Settings • Delivery-Warehouse Requests • Process Profile • Define Process Profile for Delivery Header**. Click on **New Entries**, add a process profile control for the header, and save. Some of the process indicators set for the process profile at the header level are as follows:

- **Create Manually**
  This field determines whether a document can be created manually in embedded EWM.
- **Del. with Follow-Up**
  This field determines whether you can delete a warehouse request after creation and cancellation of a successor document.

- **Prec. Document**
  This field allows reference to a preceding document.

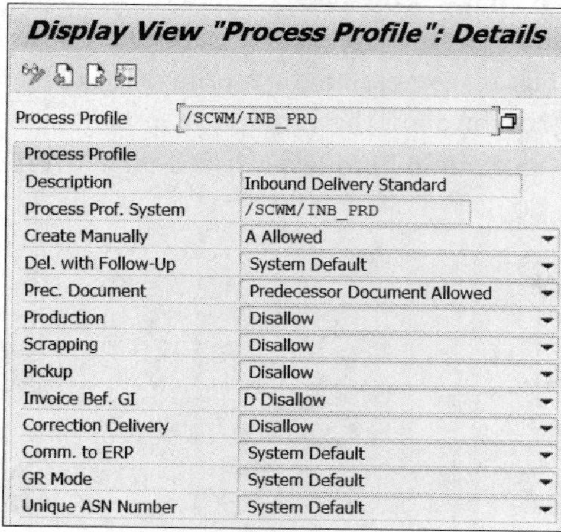

Figure 6.15 Process Profile

Similarly, you can create process profiles for a document item via IMG path **SCM Extended Warehouse Management • Extended Warehouse Management • Cross-Process Settings • Delivery-Warehouse Requests • Process Profile • Define Process Profile for Delivery Item**. Click on **New Entries**, add a process profile control for the header, and save. The process indicators that can be set at the item level are as follows:

- **Create Manually**
  This field allows manual creation of a new delivery line item.
- **Invoice Bef. GI**
  This field allows invoicing of a delivery before goods issue is posted.

6.2 Handling Units

Handling units (HUs) are defined as physical units with products inside or on a packaging material. HUs are represented in SAP with unique identification numbers that are used when stock is moved in and out of the warehouse, thus providing ease of handling for the material and tracking of its whereabouts. It's an industry-standard practice to receive and pick products in to or out of the warehouse using packing materials, which makes HU creation and setup an essential component while modeling business processes in embedded EWM.

The following sections explain various configurations and processes related to HUs in embedded EWM. We explain the basic concept of HUs, including the structure of an HU object (Section 6.2.1); the configuration settings required to create HUs with desired characteristics in embedded EWM (Section 6.2.2); and the configuration for and process of printing HUs so that printed sheets can be used in other warehouse processes (Section 6.2.3).

> **Note**
>
> The SAP Fiori app called Pack Warehouse Stock allows you to pack products at dedicated work centers with or without favorite packing products and create HUs for storage or shipment.

6.2.1 What Are Handling Units?

HUs in a warehouse can be in the form of pallets, wire baskets, containers, trucks, and so on. An HU in embedded EWM can be simple or nested. Products packed inside a single layer of packaging material is a simple HU. You can pack multiple simple HUs inside another packaging material to create a new HU, called a nested HU. Figure 6.16 shows an example of simple and nested HUs.

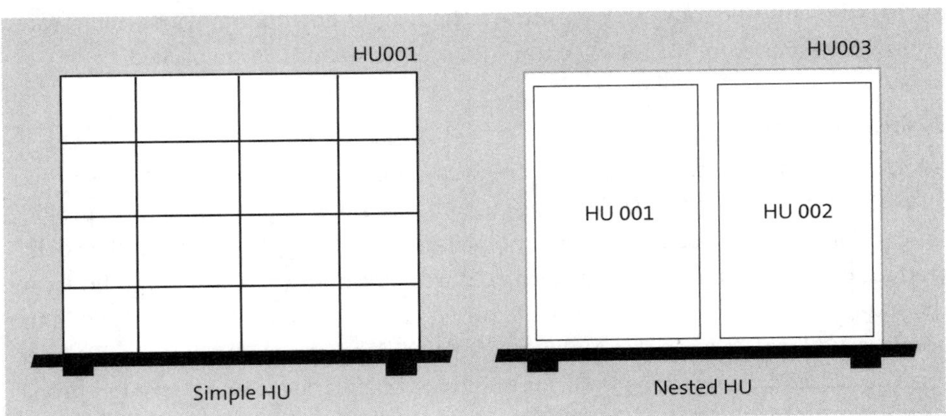

Figure 6.16 Simple and Nested HUs in Embedded EWM

A nested HU can have several layers of packed goods inside it. Consider Figure 6.17, which shows a truck carrying products from a distribution center to a customer store with products packed in multiple boxes. Each box in this case can be created as a separate HU in embedded EWM. In the figure, products are packed in two separate boxes and labeled as HU 310 and HU 320. A set of these boxes can be packed in a third box using the same or different packaging material, thereby creating a new HU.

In Figure 6.17, HU 310 and HU 320 are packed into Box 3, thereby creating HU 300. That is, HU 310 and HU 320 are nested within HU 300. In the final step, nested HU 300 is loaded onto a truck, thereby creating another HU for the truck—HU 400.

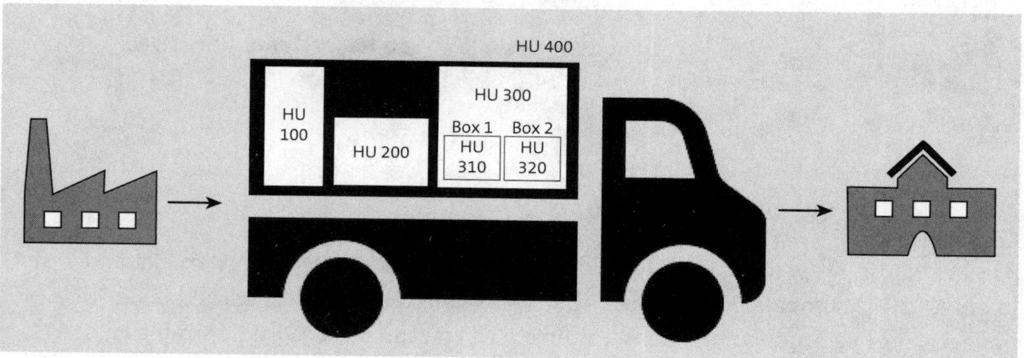

Figure 6.17 Example of Nested HUs

In the following sections, we explain the HU-related documents with which warehouse request documents are executed and products and HUs are packed.

Business Process

American company Alpha Medicals receives an order from one of its customers based in Mexico. The order sent by the customer requires Alpha Medicals to provide the products in time packed in cases and pallets for delivery. Stock that will be delivered to the customer is to be picked from source bins of the supplying warehouse by the warehouse workers, packed in the required packaging material, and staged in the goods issue area. As a regular Alpha Medicals practice, the warehouse workers perform activities on packed materials or materials that are loose and packed in proper packaging material, creating a HU. To ensure that all stock movement activities of warehouse workers are performed using products packed in a proper manner, the company uses HUs in embedded EWM.

System Process

The following covers basic system flow, including the documents and data required to execute an outbound business process using HUs in embedded EWM and decentralized EWM:

1. An outbound delivery order is created as a warehouse request in embedded EWM and contains information about the products Alpha Medicals will deliver to the external customer.
2. Initial picking warehouse tasks are created based on the warehouse request and assigned to the warehouse workers. This request directs the warehouse workers to carry the product from source bin to staging area.
3. The warehouse orders are allocated to the warehouse workers. After picking the product from the source bin, the products are taken to a work center and packed in packaging materials to create HUs.
4. The HUs are then assembled together to create a carton of HUs and staged onto the staging area from where the pallets are loaded onto the truck docked to the door.

Note

We've explained the system process using the outbound process only. It's equally applicable to inbound and internal stock movement processes.

An HU in embedded EWM consists of a header and an item. Figure 6.18 shows an HU in a work center with header and item level sections highlighted.

The header data of the HU includes the following:

- Weight/volume and other capacity-related data
- General data such as created by, changed by, packaging material, packaging material type, HU type, and so on
- Storage data applicable to all the products packed in the HU

The HU item includes the following data:

- Product data, such as product name, batch, stock type, quantity, goods receipt date, and so on
- Serial number data
- Text data for delivery text and hazardous substances

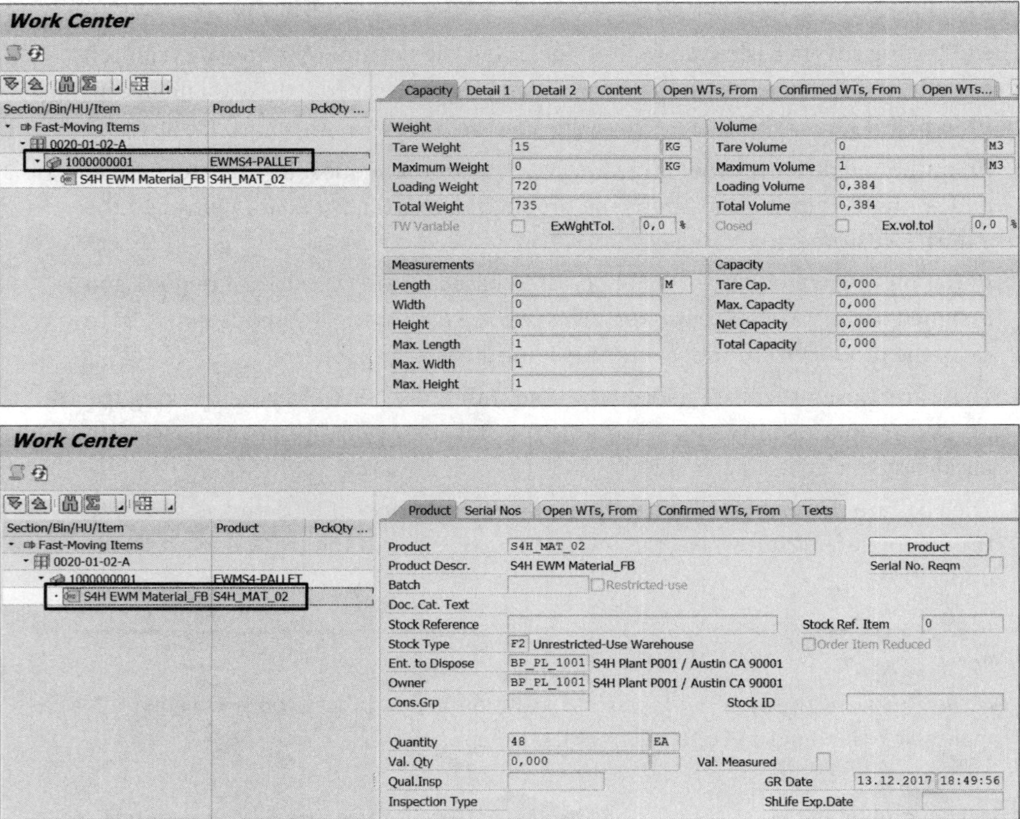

Figure 6.18 HU Header and Item

You define a packaging specification in embedded EWM to specify packaging instructions for packing a product into an HU. A packaging specification is created as master data in embedded EWM and is used to provide specific details such as the packaging material that should be used to create the HU and the quantity of the packaging material required. Create and maintain packaging specifications using Transaction /SCWM/PACKSPEC. You can also use packaging specifications to create nested HUs in embedded EWM by selecting the **Create HU** checkbox on the transaction screen. For more details about packaging specifications in embedded EWM, see Chapter 5, Section 5.5.

6.2.2 Configuring Handling Units

The configuration settings required for setting up HUs in embedded EWM are as follows:

1. Packaging material types are used in embedded EWM to group multiple packaging materials based on their characteristics and usage. Define the packaging material types via IMG path **SCM Extended Warehouse Management • Extended Warehouse Management • Cross-Process Settings • Handling Units • Basics • Define Packaging Material Types**. Click on **New Entries**, and select the packaging material categories (**PMCat**). Some examples of packaging material types in embedded EWM are pallets, cartons, and means of transport, as shown in Figure 6.19.

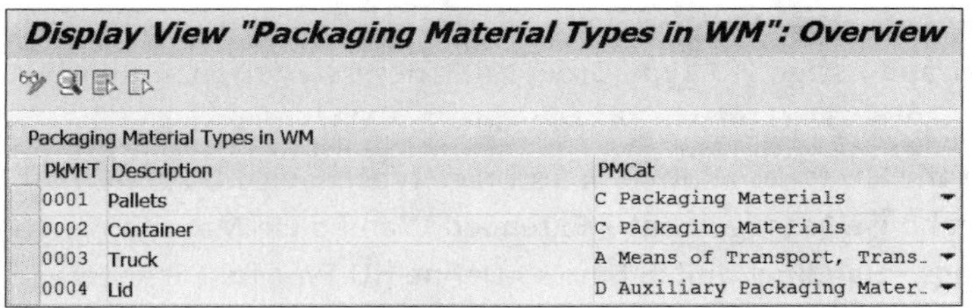

Display View "Packaging Material Types in WM": Overview

Packaging Material Types in WM

PkMtT	Description	PMCat
0001	Pallets	C Packaging Materials
0002	Container	C Packaging Materials
0003	Truck	A Means of Transport, Trans…
0004	Lid	D Auxiliary Packaging Mater…

Figure 6.19 Packaging Material Types in Embedded EWM

> **Note**
>
> Embedded EWM can access existing SAP S/4HANA Customizing directly for the following objects:
>
> - **HU type**
>   HU types are used to group together HUs with the same physical characteristics. Define HUs via IMG path **Integration with Other SAP Components • Extended Warehouse Management • Additional Material Attributes • Attribute Values for Additional Material Master Fields • Define Handling Unit Types.**
> - **Packing group**
>   Packing groups are used to group products with the same packaging requirements. Define packaging groups in SAP S/4HANA via IMG path **Logistics Execution • Shipping • Packing • Define Material Group for Packaging Material.**

2. Assign the packaging material types to a packaging group for products with the same packaging requirements by navigating to IMG path **SCM Extended Warehouse Management • Extended Warehouse Management • Cross-Process Settings •**

Handling Units • Basics • Maintain Allowed Packaging Material Types for Packing Group. Click on **New Entries**, and map the allowed packaging material types for each packing group based on the unit of measure (UoM) of the product in the HU. This mapping is used by the system during HU creation to check if the packaging material of a given packaging material type can be used to pack the product or not.

3. Define the HU type groups for the warehouse by navigating to IMG path **SCM Extended Warehouse Management • Extended Warehouse Management • Cross-Process Settings • Handling Units • Basics • Define HU Type Groups**. The HU type groups are used to group HU types with similar physical attributes.
4. Assign the HU type group to HU types for the warehouse by navigating to IMG path **SCM Extended Warehouse Management • Extended Warehouse Management • Cross-Process Settings • Handling Units • Basics • Define HU Types for Each Warehouse Number and Assign HU Type Groups**. It's necessary to maintain this setting if you want to use an HU type in an embedded EWM warehouse.
5. If you want to limit the HU types allowed in a storage type, navigate to IMG path **SCM Extended Warehouse Management • Extended Warehouse Management • Cross-Process Settings • Handling Units • Basics • Define HU Type for Each Storage Type**. This setting is only relevant if the **HU Type** checkbox is enabled at the storage type level, as discussed in Chapter 4.
6. Set up a number range for managing HUs by navigating to IMG path **SCM Extended Warehouse Management • Extended Warehouse Management • Cross-Process Settings • Handling Units • External Identification • Define Number Range for HU Identification**.

Tip

When using embedded EWM, you must use the same number range for HUs in both SAP S/4HANA and embedded EWM. In addition, the HU number range in SAP S/4HANA should be defined as external in embedded EWM to avoid any conflict with system-generated HUs in embedded EWM.

7. Set the number range defined for the packaging material types in which the products are packed by navigating to IMG path **SCM Extended Warehouse Management • Extended Warehouse Management • Cross-Process Settings • Handling Units • External Identification • Assign Number Range Interval to Packaging Material Type**.

8. The HU number assigned to a packaging material type in embedded EWM is a unique number within the warehouse, but it loses its significance after the HU has left the warehouse. The HU travels from the warehouse using multiple carriers before it finally reaches the end users, and often companies require the ability to track the HU throughout the supply chain process. Embedded EWM leverages the serial shipping container code (SSCC) to create unique HU numbers that can be tracked globally. Choose to use the internal number range or the SSCC number range by selecting the required option in the **No. Assignment** field while defining packaging material types in embedded EWM (Figure 6.20).

Display View "Packaging Material Types in WM": Details

Pack.Mat.Type: YN01

Packaging Material Types in WM

Description	SSCC Pallet
PM Category	C Packaging Materials
TW Variable	☐
Closed	☐
Status Profile	
Delete	☑
No. Assignment	A SSCC
PrintDetermProc	0HUPR
Size	

Figure 6.20 Assigning the SSCC Number Range Type to the Packaging Material Type

9. To use SSCCs for HU creation in embedded EWM, define and maintain the SSCC number range for the warehouse by navigating to IMG path **SCM Extended Warehouse Management • Extended Warehouse Management • Cross-Process Settings • Handling Units • External Identification • SSCC Generation Acc. to EAN128 • Maintain SSCC Generation for Each Warehouse Number**, as shown in Figure 6.21. Click on **New Entries**, and set the number range for number range object (**NumberRngeObj**) as **/SCWM/SSCC**.

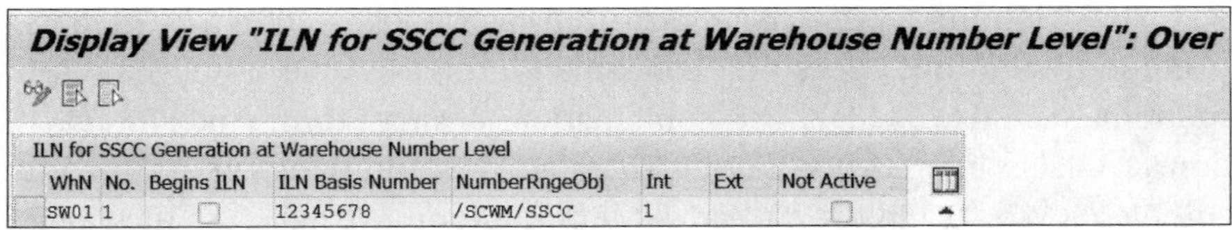

Display View "ILN for SSCC Generation at Warehouse Number Level": Over

ILN for SSCC Generation at Warehouse Number Level

WhN	No.	Begins ILN	ILN Basis Number	NumberRngeObj	Int	Ext	Not Active
SW01	1	☐	12345678	/SCWM/SSCC	1		☐

Figure 6.21 Defining the Warehouse-Specific SSCC Number Range

The SSCC number has a total of 18 characters and consists of the International Location Number (ILN) and a check digit from a sequential number, the area of which you can define. The ILN, which is the basic number of the SSCC, usually has 7 characters and uses up the second through eighth characters. With the check digit, there are 10 remaining characters that you must specify for your company.

6.2.3 Printing Handling Units

HUs are identified in embedded EWM using the labels printed on them. An HU label contains basic details such as product number, quantity, batch number, weight, volume, serial number, dangerous goods information, and so on. Usually, HUs are labeled when they're sent by the vendor. However, if required, the receiving warehouse can create another label and put it on the HU along with the vendor label. HU labels also need to be printed if you're receiving unpacked goods in the warehouse, and packing and labeling is done before such goods are put away in embedded EWM. Embedded EWM uses the PPF for scheduling and execution of HU label printing. In addition, embedded EWM uses the condition technique in the schedule condition for the PPF to determine the printer, form type, and spool parameters.

You can trigger prints based on the desired step in the storage process. Your business must decide at which stage of HU movement in the warehouse it wants to print the label. For example, you may want to print HU labels as soon as goods receipt is posted for the delivery, right when the HUs physically arrive in the warehouse, so that HUs can be labeled immediately after goods receipt. Some other processes for which companies might want to trigger HU label printing include the following:

- Creating HUs in work centers
- Repacking HUs in work centers
- Creating shipping labels for HUs before loading

SAP provides various standard smart forms to print HU labels, which are assigned to appropriate PPF action definitions based on their business significance. It's often required to include company-specific information such as logos, addresses, headers, footers, and so on, and you can customize the smart forms available to suit your business requirements. Table 6.1 highlights combinations of smart forms and PPF action definitions available in embedded EWM. These action definitions are assigned to action profile /SCWM/HU in the /SCWM/WME application. We'll discuss the PPF in detail in Section 6.10.

Smart Forms	Description	Action Definition
/SCWM/HU_HAZARD	**Print Dangerous Goods Label**	HU_HAZARD
/SCWM/HU_SERIAL	**Print HU Label with Serial Number**	HU_SERIAL
/SCWM/HU_EXPRESS	**Print Express Shipping Label**	HU_EXPRESS
/SCWM/HU_TO	**Print HU Warehouse Task**	HU_TO
/SCWM/HU_CONTENT	**Print HU Content with serial number**	HU_CONTENT
/SCWM/HU_SHLABEL	**Print Shipping Label**	HU_SHLABEL
/SCWM/HU_LABEL	**Print HU Label**	HU_LABEL

Table 6.1 HU Labels in Embedded EWM

6.3 Warehouse Tasks

This section explains warehouse tasks in embedded EWM (Section 6.3.1), the uses and configuration of a warehouse process type used to create a warehouse task (Section 6.3.2), the configuration and business usage of product warehouse tasks (Section 6.3.3), and the HU warehouse task, including the processes in which it's used and the different ways it can be generated (Section 6.3.4).

Note

The following SAP Fiori apps are available to process warehouse tasks for stock movements in warehouse:

- **Create Warehouse Tasks**
  This app allows you to create warehouse tasks with or without reference to warehouse requests to complete stock movement processes.
- **Display Warehouse Tasks**
  This app allows you to display warehouse tasks created with or without reference to warehouse requests.
- **Confirm Warehouse Tasks**
  This app allows you to confirm warehouse tasks created with or without reference to warehouse requests.

6.3.1 What Are Warehouse Tasks?

Each goods movement in embedded EWM is done with the help of a document known as a *warehouse task*. Warehouse tasks can be created with or without reference to a warehouse request in embedded EWM. Any warehouse task always contains information such as the following:

- Which product or HU is being moved?
- What is the quantity of the product or HU being moved?
- What are the source bin and destination bin for the move?

Warehouse tasks for posting changes contain information about the change in stock, such as the change in stock type. Warehouse tasks are created in embedded EWM for all movements, such as the following:

- *Picking* warehouse tasks are used to move a quantity of the product from a source bin to destination bin.
- *Putaway* warehouse tasks are used to move a quantity of the product from a source bin to destination bin.
- *Internal goods movement* warehouse tasks are created to move stock from one bin to another within the warehouse. Examples of internal warehouse movements include replenishment, ad hoc movements, and so on.
- *Posting change* warehouse tasks are created when there's a change in an embedded EWM stock type or stock category. Examples of posting changes include changing a stock category from unrestricted to blocked.
- *Goods receipt posting* warehouse tasks are created to post receipt of goods in the warehouse back to SAP S/4HANA.
- *Goods issue posting* warehouse tasks are created to post goods issue in the warehouse back to SAP S/4HANA.

A warehouse task can have the following statuses from the time of its creation until confirmation:

- **Open**
  The warehouse task is waiting to be processed.
- **Confirmed**
  The warehouse task has been confirmed, and goods movement or posting change is complete.

- **Waiting**
  The warehouse task has reserved the stock and capacity on the final bin and is waiting to be processed.
- **Canceled**
  The warehouse task has been canceled.

6.3.2 Warehouse Process Type

A warehouse process type is used to determine the nature of goods movement happening in the warehouse. This movement can be a physical movement or posting change. The warehouse process type is initially determined at the item level in a warehouse request. If you're using multistep putaway, such as in process-oriented storage control or layout-oriented storage control, then the system will create a separate warehouse task for each of the process steps, and each warehouse task will have a unique warehouse process type to determine the nature of the movement.

As shown in Figure 6.22, you can define warehouse process types in embedded EWM via IMG path **SCM Extended Warehouse Management • Extended Warehouse Management • Cross-Process Settings • Warehouse Task • Define Warehouse Process Type**. Click on **New Entries**, and define a new warehouse process type and its controls.

The settings for a warehouse process are divided into three broad sections, as follows:

- **General Settings**
  These settings are used to control the general behavior of a warehouse process type. The functional use of the general settings of the warehouse process type are as follows:
  - **Whse Proc. Cat.**
    Whse Proc. Cat. determines the nature of warehouse movement. Each warehouse process type is assigned to an appropriate warehouse process category and activity, which define the unique nature of the process type. For example, if the warehouse task is to be created for picking, then the process category is assigned in **2-Stock Removal** with the **Activity** set to **Pick**.
  - **Manual WT Forbidden**
    If this checkbox is set, the system doesn't allow manual creation of a warehouse task for the warehouse process type.
  - **Propose Confirmation**
    If this checkbox is set, the system shows a popup message if the task should be confirmed immediately.

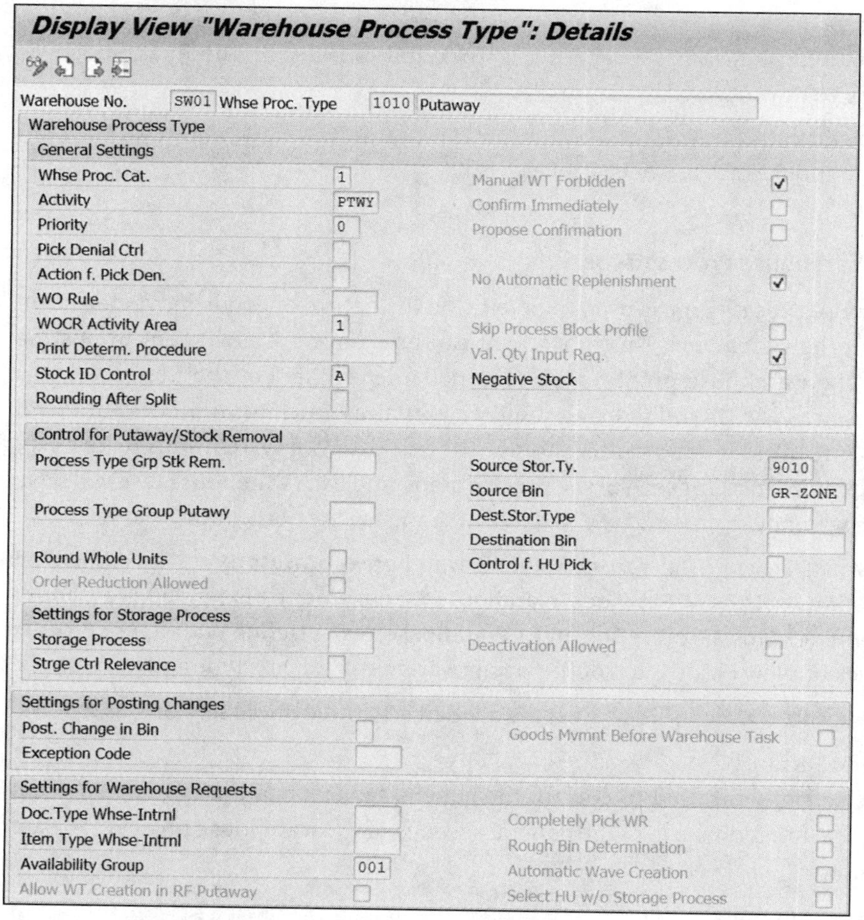

Display View "Warehouse Process Type": Details

Warehouse No. SW01 Whse Proc. Type 1010 Putaway

Warehouse Process Type

General Settings

Whse Proc. Cat. 1 — Manual WT Forbidden ☑
Activity PTWY — Confirm Immediately ☐
Priority 0 — Propose Confirmation ☐
Pick Denial Ctrl ☐
Action f. Pick Den. ☐ — No Automatic Replenishment ☑
WO Rule
WOCR Activity Area 1 — Skip Process Block Profile ☐
Print Determ. Procedure — Val. Qty Input Req. ☑
Stock ID Control A — Negative Stock ☐
Rounding After Split ☐

Control for Putaway/Stock Removal

Process Type Grp Stk Rem. — Source Stor.Ty. 9010
Source Bin GR-ZONE
Process Type Group Putawy — Dest.Stor.Type
Destination Bin
Round Whole Units ☐ — Control f. HU Pick ☐
Order Reduction Allowed ☐

Settings for Storage Process

Storage Process — Deactivation Allowed ☐
Strge Ctrl Relevance ☐

Settings for Posting Changes

Post. Change in Bin ☐ — Goods Mvmnt Before Warehouse Task ☐
Exception Code

Settings for Warehouse Requests

Doc.Type Whse-Intrnl — Completely Pick WR ☐
Item Type Whse-Intrnl — Rough Bin Determination ☐
Availability Group 001 — Automatic Wave Creation ☐
Allow WT Creation in RF Putaway ☐ — Select HU w/o Storage Process ☐

Figure 6.22 Warehouse Process Type in Embedded EWM

- **Confirm Immediately**
  If this checkbox is set, the system confirms the warehouse task immediately after creation.

- **WOCR Activity Area**
  Warehouse order creation rules are determined based on activity area and activity. The activity area can be picked from the source or destination storage bin defined in the warehouse task. Using this setting, the system determines which activity area must be considered to determine the warehouse order creation rule.

- **No Automatic Replenishment**
  If this indicator is set, the system doesn't allow creation of replenishment warehouse tasks using this warehouse process type. For example, this indicator can be set for scrapping warehouse process types.
- **Negative Stock**
  This indicator allows creation of warehouse tasks for negative available quantities in the storage type. Only task creation is allowed, not task confirmation.
- **Print Determ. Procedure**
  This procedure is used to print warehouse orders assigned to warehouse workers if they aren't using radio frequency (RF). You confirm the warehouse orders and enter the confirmation manually in SAP GUI.

- **Control for Putaway/Stock Removal**
  These settings control the behavior of warehouse tasks while carrying out stock removal and putaway in embedded EWM. The functional use of the putaway/stock removal settings for warehouse process types are as follows:
  - **Round Whole Units**
    This setting is used to control how warehouse tasks should be rounded. You can also set this control at the storage type level.
  - **Source Stor. Ty./Source Bin**
    The **Source Stor. Ty.** and **Source Bin** fields are used to provide the default source storage type and source bin during picking, and the **Dest. Stor.Type** and **Destination Bin** fields are used to provide the default destination storage type and bin during putaway.
  - **Control f. HU Pick**
    Using this setting, you can control how the system should proceed when confirming a complete stock pick of a homogeneous HU.
  - **Process Type Group Putawy/Process Type Grp Stk Rem.**
    The process type groups for putaway or removal fields allow you to group warehouse process types to use the groups to simplify Customizing in the putaway/picking strategy.
- **Settings for Storage Process**
  These configurations are used to control complex stock movements in the warehouse using storage control. The functional relevance of the storage process settings for warehouse process types is as follows:

- **Storage Process**
  This field is used to assign a storage process to the warehouse process type. Storage processes help carry out complex stock movements in the warehouse using process-oriented storage control.
- **Strge Ctrl Relevance**
  This field lets you control whether layout-oriented storage control or process-oriented storage control is relevant for tasks created with this process type.
- **Deactivation allowed**
  This setting allows you to deactivate the storage process while confirming a warehouse task if the warehouse process type is relevant for storage control.

- **Settings for Posting Changes**
  These settings are used to set controls for carrying out posting changes using the warehouse process type. The functional relevance of the posting change settings for warehouse process types is as follows:
  - **Post. Change in Bin**
    This setting controls whether a posting change is done in the bin by creation and confirmation of a warehouse task, or if stock is moved to another bin with a warehouse request or directly using a warehouse task.
  - **Exception Code**
    This field contains the exception code applied during confirmation of a posting change warehouse task.
  - **Goods Mvmnt Before Warehouse Task**
    Using this indicator, the system creates a warehouse request to move the stock to another bin before a posting change can be done.
- **Settings for Warehouse Requests**
  These settings enable the system to create a warehouse request document when performing internal warehouse processes. The functional use of the warehouse request settings for warehouse process types is as follows:
  - **Doc.Type Whse-Intrnl/Item Type Whse-Intrnl**
    By assigning the document and item type at the process type level to these fields, you enable the system to create a warehouse request document for internal warehouse processes, for example, posting changes, stock transfers, and replenishment.
  - **Availability Group**
    The availability group maps the stock type in embedded EWM with the plant

and storage location in the delivery in SAP S/4HANA. The availability group also can be assigned at the storage type level. When confirming the warehouse task, the system gives preference to the availability group assigned at the process type level.

- **Allow WT Creation in RF Putaway**
  This indicator controls whether the system creates warehouse tasks for HUs referring to inbound deliveries by scanning the HUs in RF transactions **Putaway by HU** or **Putaway by HU (Clustered)** if the warehouse tasks have not yet been created.
- **Completely Pick WR**
  This indicator controls whether the requested quantity in the warehouse request should be picked in full or if partial picking is allowed.
- **Rough Bin Determination**
  If this indicator is set, the system determines the storage type for items in the warehouse request at the time of warehouse request creation.
- **Automatic Wave Creation**
  If this checkbox is set, the system creates waves automatically for warehouse request items with this process type.
- **Select HU w/o Storage Process**
  If this checkbox is set, the system creates HU warehouse tasks for putaway to a destination bin when working without a storage process, instead of creating a product warehouse task.

6.3.3 Product Warehouse Task

A product warehouse task contains all the information required to transfer products inside, outside, or within the warehouse. A product warehouse task contains the following details:

- Product to be moved
- Quantity to be moved
- Source and destination storage bins

If the actual quantity confirmed is less than the planned quantity, the difference quantity is posted to a difference interface by embedded EWM. Product warehouse tasks can be created via Transaction /SCWM/ADPROD, which also can be accessed via **SAP Easy Access** menu path **Logistics • SCM Extended Warehouse Management • SCM**

Extended Warehouse Management • Work Scheduling • Create Warehouse Task without Reference • Move Product. Click [icon]; enter the product, quantity, source bin, destination bin, and stock parameters; and save.

> **Note**
>
> A product warehouse task reserves the quantities so that they're no longer available for other product warehouse tasks.

6.3.4 Handling Unit Warehouse Task

An HU warehouse task contains all the information required to execute the transfer of HUs inside, outside of, or within the warehouse. Unlike product warehouse tasks, HU warehouse tasks can also be used for loading and unloading purposes. An HU warehouse task contains the following information:

- HU number that needs to be moved
- Source and destination storage bin

Unlike a product warehouse task, an HU warehouse task does not reserve any quantity. You can create an HU warehouse task using Transaction /SCWM/ADHU, which also can be accessed from **SAP Easy Access** path **Logistics • SCM Extended Warehouse Management • SCM Extended Warehouse Management • Work Scheduling • Create Warehouse Task without Reference • Move Handling Unit**. Search for HUs using different search parameters. Select the HU; click on **Create**; enter the source bin, destination bin, and stock parameters; and save.

6.4 Warehouse Order

A warehouse order combines multiple warehouse tasks in embedded EWM using a set of rules to create an executable work package for the warehouse worker. Using resource management in embedded EWM, warehouse orders are assigned to appropriate resources who will complete the assigned work packages for picking, putaway, consolidation, deconsolidation, physical inventory, value-added services (VAS), and so on. This grouping of tasks into warehouse orders and their assignment to resources also helps in optimal use of resources in the warehouse. Based on the activity area assigned to the warehouse task, the system determines the appropriate warehouse order creation rule.

A warehouse task must always be assigned to a warehouse order. The system ensures this by determining a warehouse order creation rule in embedded EWM. If the system can't determine a warehouse order creation rule for a warehouse task, it assigns the warehouse task to a default warehouse order creation rule.

In the following sections, we'll discuss various customization settings required for setting up and determining warehouse order creation rules in embedded EWM. We'll also discuss the concepts of rules, limits, filters, and profiles. Profiles are determined in embedded EWM based on warehouse order creation rule determination.

Note

The Create Warehouse Orders app allows you to create and process warehouse orders for stock movement with or without reference to warehouse request for processes such as outbound, inbound, or internal stock movements.

6.4.1 What Are Warehouse Orders?

Warehouse orders are bundles of warehouse tasks for warehouse workers. In the following sections, we explain the processes carried out in the system as well as the warehouse, and order-related documents with which the warehouse request documents are executed and posted.

Business Process

American company Alpha Medicals receives an order from one of its customers based in Mexico. The order sent by the customer requires Alpha Medicals to provide the products in time and packed in cases and pallets for delivery. Stock that will be delivered to the customer is to be picked from source bins of the supplying warehouse by the warehouse workers, packed in the required packaging material, and staged in the goods issue area. The activities of picking, packing, staging, and so on are treated as individual activities that are bundled together for optimizing the time and resource constraints of the warehouse worker. To ensure that all stock movement activities of warehouse workers are performed in an optimized manner using maximum capacity and minimizing idol time, the company uses embedded EWM.

System Process

The concept of warehouse orders comes into play after warehouse tasks are created in embedded EWM. Figure 6.23 shows the end-to-end process for creation of warehouse orders in embedded EWM.

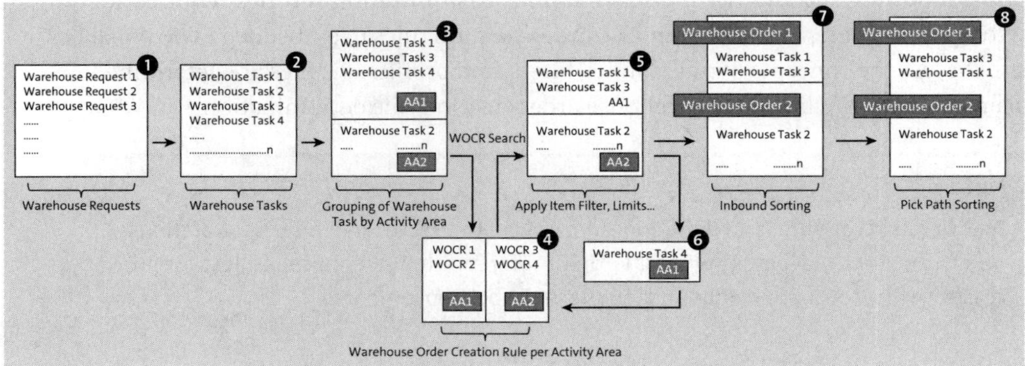

Figure 6.23 Warehouse Order Creation in Embedded EWM

The highlighted steps are as follows:

❶ Warehouse requests for inbound, outbound, posting changes, and so on are created in embedded EWM.

❷ Warehouse tasks are created for open warehouse requests. You can create these tasks manually or do so automatically using the PPF. These tasks represent various activities, such as picking, putaway, and so on, that a resource must perform in the warehouse to process a warehouse request.

❸ Warehouse tasks are grouped together based on activity area and queue. Embedded EWM determines the activity area of a warehouse task based on the activity area of either the source or destination storage bin and activity. You can set the determination of the activity area based on the source or destination bin of the warehouse task by setting the value in **WOCR Activity Area** in the warehouse process type customization to either **Source** or **Destination**.

❹ In the next step, embedded EWM looks for possible warehouse order creation rules assigned to an activity area. You can assign multiple warehouse order creation rules for a combination of activity area and activity and then assign them to a sequence for determination. Embedded EWM assigns all open warehouse tasks to the first warehouse order creation rule in the sequence. It then looks through the next steps for sorting and filtering to decide if warehouse tasks need to be assigned to another warehouse order in the sequence.

Note

If no warehouse order creation rule is set up in embedded EWM, it assigns all warehouse orders to default rule **DEF**.

❺ In this step, embedded EWM sorts the warehouse tasks in the order defined by the sorting profile. It then applies item filters and subtotal filters to the warehouse task to see if it can be processed by a given warehouse order creation rule. Any open warehouse tasks that don't meet the filtering criteria are assigned to the next warehouse order creation rule in the sequence for that activity area.

❻ As discussed in Step 5, in this step, embedded EWM assigns the warehouse task to the next warehouse order creation rule in the sequence. It applies the item filter and subtotal filter on the tasks assigned to the next warehouse order creation rule until it finds a valid warehouse order creation rule for all the open warehouse tasks.

Note

If there are no more warehouse order creation rules left in the sequence for a warehouse order, the system assigns them to default rule **UNDE**.

❼ In this step, embedded EWM sorts the warehouse tasks based on defined sorting criteria. This is called *inbound sorting*. We'll discuss setting up sort profiles in the next section. Embedded EWM then uses the sorted warehouse tasks to check the warehouse order limit. Often, you need to set a limit on a warehouse order based on the carrying capacity of the resource. For example, if the carrying capacity of a forklift is no more than 80 kg, you need to set a maximum weight limit of 80 kg on the warehouse order. If the total size of the warehouse tasks assigned to the warehouse order exceeds 80 kg, the system then creates a new warehouse order with the same warehouse order creation rule.

❽ In this step, the system creates the required number of empty HUs using the capacity of the warehouse order and the capacity of the packaging material determined by the packaging profile. The packing profile is used for creation of pick HUs for packing the picked goods and is assigned to the warehouse order. Finally, the system carries out warehouse order sorting for sorting the warehouse tasks assigned to the warehouse order for execution. For example, you can create a sort rule to sort warehouse tasks based on the pick path sequence.

You can also use warehouse orders together with wave management. Waves are used to group warehouse requests to allow the creation of multiple warehouse tasks at the same time. You can schedule the release of waves for task creation to enable efficient task management in the warehouse. These tasks can then be grouped into warehouse orders for further assignment to resources. We'll discuss wave management in detail in Chapter 16.

6.4.2 Configuring Warehouse Orders

In this section, we'll discuss the configuration settings required for filters, limits, packing profiles, and the like. These settings help set up an executable work package for the warehouse resource. The resource can complete multiple open tasks in an activity area together, thus reducing travel into and out of the warehouse for each task execution. The settings used for creation of a warehouse order are as follows:

- **Sort rules for warehouse task**
  Sort rules are used to sort warehouse tasks in a warehouse order. To create sort rules, navigate to IMG path **SCM Extended Warehouse Management • Extended Warehouse Management • Cross-Process Settings • Warehouse Order • Define Sort Rules for Warehouse Tasks**, as shown in Figure 6.24. Use this setting to define the sort rules and assign them to one or more sort fields. Click on **New Entries**, and, for each sort rule, define the fields in the warehouse tasks that can be used for sorting and whether they need to be sorted in ascending or descending order.

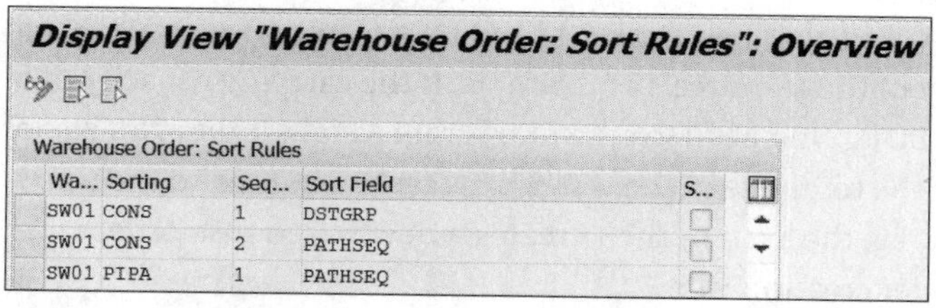

Display View "Warehouse Order: Sort Rules": Overview

Warehouse Order: Sort Rules

Wa...	Sorting	Seq...	Sort Field	S...
SW01	CONS	1	DSTGRP	☐
SW01	CONS	2	PATHSEQ	☐
SW01	PIPA	1	PATHSEQ	☐

Figure 6.24 Sort Rule in the Warehouse Order Creation Rule

- **Filters for warehouse order creation rule**
  Filters are used to set rules for processing a warehouse task. Embedded EWM

applies filters on warehouse tasks that have not been assigned to any warehouse order to check if they can be processed by a warehouse order creation rule.

To create filters, navigate to IMG path **SCM Extended Warehouse Management • Extended Warehouse Management • Cross-Process Settings • Warehouse Order • Define Filters for Warehouse Order Creation Rules**, as shown in Figure 6.25. Click on **New Entries** to define a new filter and set the filter controls.

Display View "Warehouse Order: Filter for Rules": Details

Warehouse No.	SW01
WOCRule Filter	HE01

Warehouse Order: Filter for Rules

Description	Heavy Items
Filter Type	Warehouse Task
Filter Type	I Filter at Item Level
Minimum Volume	0
Max. Volume	0
Volume unit	M3
Minimum Weight	20
Maximum Weight	0
Weight unit	KG
Min. Proc. Time	0
Max. Extr. Time	0
Time Unit	MIN
Min.Itm per STI	0
Max.Itm per STI	0
Alternatve Unit	
Whse Proc. Type	
Priority	0
Reason f. Mvmt	
Route	
Wave Category	
Complete HU	No Restrictions
No Putaway	✓
No Stock Removal	☐
No Int. Stk Transfer	✓
No Phys. Inv.	✓

Figure 6.25 Filter for the Warehouse Order Creation Rule

There are two types of filters that can be used in warehouse order creation based on the value set in **Filter Type**:

- **Item filter**
  Item filters are used to check individual warehouse tasks for a warehouse order and are defined by setting **Filter Type** to **I Filter at Item Level**. The system checks to see if the warehouse task is within the min/max volume, weight, and processing limits of the item filter. It also checks whether the warehouse task has been created using a specific warehouse process type, route, wave category, and reason for movement. If a warehouse task doesn't meet the filtering criteria, the

system checks to see if it can use the next warehouse order creation rule in the sequence to process the warehouse task.

- **Subtotal filter**
  Embedded EWM uses subtotal filters to compare several warehouse tasks against a subtotal; they're defined by setting **Filter Type** to **S Filter at Subtotal Level**. To use subtotal filters, it's important to sort warehouse tasks using sorting rules with a sort field consolidation group.

- **Limit value for size of warehouse order**
  As discussed earlier, embedded EWM passes the warehouse tasks that successfully passed through the item filter through a limit value to determine the size of the warehouse order. Define a limit value via IMG path **SAP Extended Warehouse Management • Extended Warehouse Management • Cross-Process Settings • Warehouse Order • Define Limit Values for the Size of a Warehouse Order**. Click on **New Entries**, enter a limit name, and set the limit control values.

  The limit value is assigned to each warehouse order creation rule. Warehouse tasks assigned to a warehouse order creation rule are assessed for limit values, which are used to set a limit on the size of the warehouse order. As soon as the warehouse task exceeds any of the limit filter criteria, it's taken out of the existing warehouse order and assigned to a new warehouse order using the same warehouse order creation rule. The system again applies a limit filter to the warehouse tasks assigned to the new warehouse order. A limit filter can be used to set limits for maximum/minimum warehouse tasks in a warehouse order, maximum/minimum weight, volume, processing time, and so on.

  In Figure 6.26, we've created a maximum weight limit of 25 kg for a warehouse order by setting the value in the **Maximum Weight** field to "25" and the **Weight unit** to "KG". You can set a limit value type (**Limit Val. Type**) of **Physical Inventory** if warehouse tasks included in the warehouse order are for physical inventory.

- **Packing profile**
  Packing profiles are used to create pick HUs during the creation of warehouse orders for outbound/picking processes. Using a packing profile, the system determines a packaging specification and HU type using the packaging material master data for the pick HU. The system uses data such as weight, volume, capacity, and so on from the assigned warehouse order when determining the appropriate number of pick HUs in the embedded EWM system. For example, if the assigned warehouse tasks don't fit into one HU, then the system creates another pick HU using a predefined packaging material.

Create a packing profile via IMG path **SCM Extended Warehouse Management • Extended Warehouse Management • Cross-Process Settings • Warehouse Order • Define Packing Profile for Warehouse Order Creation**, as shown in Figure 6.27.

Display View "Warehouse Order: Limits for Rules": Details

Warehouse No.	SW01
Limit	LI01

Warehouse Order: Limits for Rules

Description	Maximum 25 kg Total Weight
Limit Val. Type	Warehouse Task
Min.Items/WO	0
Max. Itm per WO	0
Minimum Volume	0
Max. Volume	0
Volume unit	M3
Minimum Weight	0
Maximum Weight	25
Weight unit	KG
Min. Proc. Time	0
Max. Extr. Time	0
Time Unit	MIN
Max. CGr per WO	0
Max.CGrp per HU	0
Max. No. of HUs	0
Min. WTs per HU	0
Max. WTs per HU	0

Figure 6.26 Limit Value of Warehouse Order

Display View "Packing Profile for Warehouse Order Creation": Details

Warehouse No.	SW01
Packing Profile	YP02

Packing Profile for Warehouse Order Creation

Description	Picking onto Pallet
Pack. Mode	A Simple Algorithm
Sorting	
Create HUs	☐
Assn WTs to HUs	☑
Split WT	Do Not Split
Split WT based on AUoM	☐
Skip WT	☐
Check LWH	☐

Figure 6.27 Define Packing Profile

There are multiple parameters that control the creation of pick HUs. These parameters and their relevance are as follows:

- **Pack. Mode**
  A packing mode is used to determine the number of packaging materials, which can be used for pick HU creation. Three different packing modes are available for creating pick HUs:
  - **Simple:** Using this algorithm, the system uses one packaging material for packing a product in pick HUs. For this case, one packaging material is defined per product in a packaging specification.
  - **Complex:** Using this algorithm, the system uses multiple packaging materials to decide on an optimal packaging material for packing a product in pick HUs, and a number of pick HUs are required for the same. For this case, multiple packaging materials are defined per product in a packaging specification.
  - **Business add-in (BAdI):** Using a BAdI, you can bypass the standard system process for determining optimal packaging material for packing a product in pick HUs and use customer-specific logic for the same.
- **Sorting**
  The sort rule is used to sort warehouse tasks in a particular sequence before the creation of pick HUs.
- **Create HUs**
  This checkbox is used to create pick HUs for warehouse tasks automatically. If this indicator isn't set, you can create the pick HU manually.
- **Assn WTs to HUs**
  This indicator is used to assign warehouse tasks to pick HUs.
- **Split WT**
  This setting provides the option to split a warehouse task for optimal packing in a pick HU if required.
- **Split WT Based on AUoM**
  If this indicator is set, the system only causes a warehouse task to split if it can determine a whole number for a quantity in an alternative UoM (AUoM). Thus, if a product has a pallet as an AUoM, then the system won't cause a warehouse task to split in a way that requires the picker to open the HU.
- **Skip WT**
  This indicator is set if you want a warehouse task to skip a warehouse order creation rule if it doesn't fit a pick HU.

- **Check LWH**
  This indicator is set if you want the system to check the dimensions of the product while creating pick HUs.
- **Warehouse order creation rule**
  The filters, profiles, and limits described previously are used to create a container in the form of a warehouse order creation rule that creates warehouse orders for open warehouse tasks. Define warehouse order creation rules via IMG path **SCM Extended Warehouse Management • Extended Warehouse Management • Cross-Process Settings • Warehouse Order • Define Creation Rules for Warehouse Orders**. Click on **New Entries** to define a new warehouse order creation rule, and assign it to filters, profiles, and other controls, as shown in Figure 6.28.

6

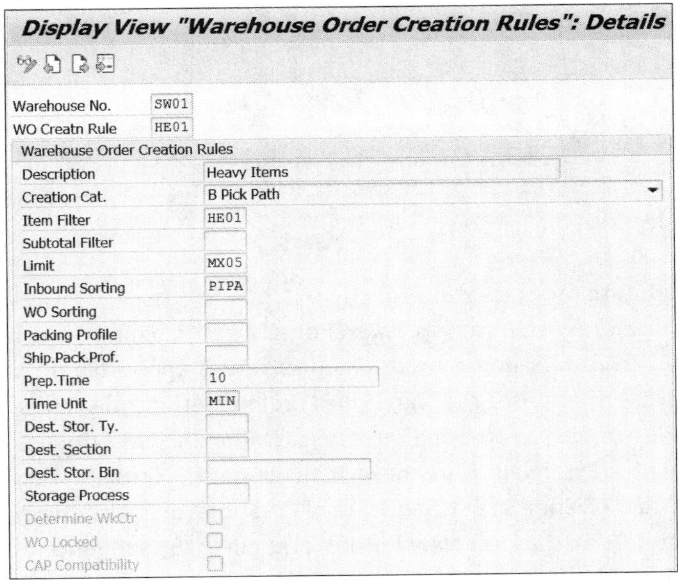

Display View "Warehouse Order Creation Rules": Details

Warehouse No.	SW01
WO Creatn Rule	HE01

Warehouse Order Creation Rules

Description	Heavy Items
Creation Cat.	B Pick Path
Item Filter	HE01
Subtotal Filter	
Limit	MX05
Inbound Sorting	PIPA
WO Sorting	
Packing Profile	
Ship.Pack.Prof.	
Prep.Time	10
Time Unit	MIN
Dest. Stor. Ty.	
Dest. Section	
Dest. Stor. Bin	
Storage Process	
Determine WkCtr	☐
WO Locked	☐
CAP Compatibility	☐

Figure 6.28 Defining the Warehouse Order Creation Rule

The warehouse order creation rule also contains the time required for the worker to complete the warehouse order. This may include any time required for preparing paperwork, for example. It's also possible to assign a specific destination bin of a work center to the warehouse order creation rule so that the product is sent directly to a work center once picked. In an outbound process, if the product is to follow complex movement, then a storage process can be assigned to the warehouse order creation rule. Set the **Determine WkCtr** indicator if you want the system to determine a specific work center using a warehouse order creation rule. This indicator is only relevant if you haven't defined a storage process in the warehouse order creation rule.

You can review the created warehouse order creation rules by navigating to IMG path **SCM Extended Warehouse Management • Extended Warehouse Management • Cross-Process Settings • Warehouse Order • Overview of Creation Rules for Warehouse Orders**, as shown in Figure 6.29. Select the warehouse order creation rule from the **WO Cr. Rle** column, and click on the required filters and profiles in the left-hand side menu to view them in detail.

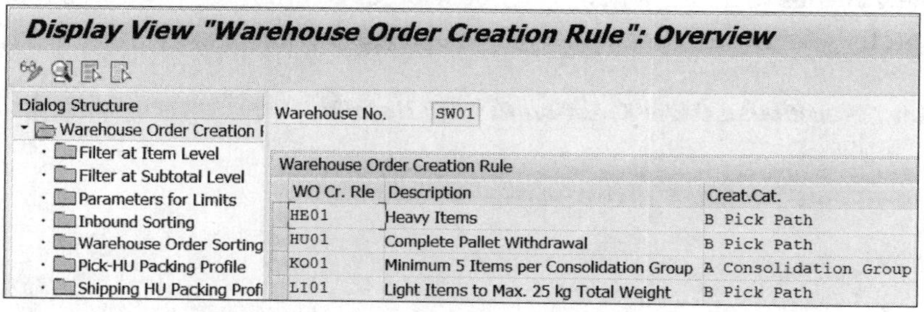

Display View "Warehouse Order Creation Rule": Overview

Dialog Structure
- Warehouse Order Creation I
  - Filter at Item Level
  - Filter at Subtotal Level
  - Parameters for Limits
  - Inbound Sorting
  - Warehouse Order Sorting
  - Pick-HU Packing Profile
  - Shipping HU Packing Profi

Warehouse No. SW01

Warehouse Order Creation Rule

WO Cr. Rle	Description	Creat.Cat.
HE01	Heavy Items	B Pick Path
HU01	Complete Pallet Withdrawal	B Pick Path
KO01	Minimum 5 Items per Consolidation Group	A Consolidation Group
LI01	Light Items to Max. 25 kg Total Weight	B Pick Path

Figure 6.29 Warehouse Order Creation Rule Overview

- **Determination of warehouse order creation rule**
  Warehouse orders are used to group multiple warehouse tasks in a single work package. To determine which warehouse order creation rule is applicable for a warehouse task, a search sequence for the warehouse order creation rule can be assigned to a combination of activity area and activity via IMG path **SCM Extended Warehouse Management • Extended Warehouse Management • Cross-Process Settings • Warehouse Order • Define Search Sequence of Creation Rules for Activity Areas**, as shown in Figure 6.30. Click on **New Entries**, and enter the sequence of warehouse order creation rules for an activity area and activity.

Display View "Warehouse Order: Search Sequence for Rules per Activity"

Warehouse Order: Search Sequence for Rules per Activity Area

Wa...	Acty Area	Activity	Sequence No.	WO Cr. Rle	Description
SW01	0010	PICK	1	HU01	Complete Pallet Withdrawal
SW01	0010	PICK	2	KO01	Minimum 5 Items per Consolidatioı
SW01	0020	PTWY	1	PU01	Putaway
SW01	0050		1	PU01	Putaway

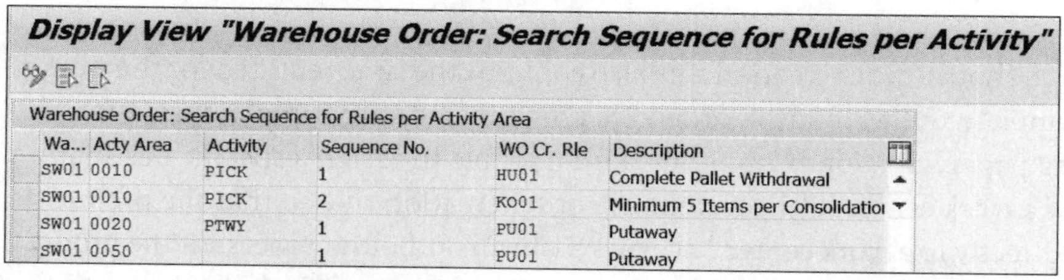

Figure 6.30 Determination of Warehouse Order Creation Rule

You can define more than one warehouse order creation rule for an activity area and activity. This way, the system searches for a warehouse order creation rule based on the defined search sequence and picks the first warehouse order creation rule that fits the required filtering criteria. For warehouse order creation rule determination, it's mandatory to sort the storage bins for activity area and activity.

6.4.3 Printing Warehouse Orders

Embedded EWM allows automatic printing of warehouse orders during their creation using smart forms or SAPscript. The warehouse order printing activity also can be carried out from the warehouse monitor. The printing is carried out via the PPF, along with the use of a condition technique. Embedded EWM supports action definitions in the /SCWM/WME application in action profile /SCWM/HU. Each action definition has a smart form associated with it, as shown in Table 6.2.

Action Definition	Description	SAP Smart Forms
WO_MULTIPLE	Print list for warehouse order with serial numbers	/SCWM/WO_MULTIPLE
WO_SINGLE	Print single document for warehouse order with serial numbers	/SCWM/WO_SINGLE
WO_HUSHIP	Print shipping label	/SCWM/WO_HUSHIP
WO_LOAD	Print loading instructions with warehouse tasks	/SCWM/WO_LOAD
WO_UNLOAD	Print unloading instructions with warehouse tasks	/SCWM/WO_UNLOAD

Table 6.2 Warehouse Order Print Smart Forms

A simple run of a warehouse order print consists of the following steps:

1. Embedded EWM determines the print determination procedure assigned to the warehouse process type. To do this, navigate to IMG path **SCM Extended Warehouse Management • Extended Warehouse Management • Warehouse Order • Print • Assign Determination Procedure**.
2. The PPF calls the /SCWM/WME application with action profile /SCWM/WO and checks for the condition record for the print action definition.

3. On successfully finding both the schedule and trigger condition, the system triggers the function module to print the SAP Smart Form.
4. The PPF saves the action executed and issues print logs.

6.4.4 Manual Assembly of Warehouse Orders

This function is used in the goods receipt process to delete warehouse tasks of different HUs from an existing warehouse order and group them in a new warehouse order using both SAP GUI and RF. To do so, navigate to **SAP Easy Access** path **Logistics • SCM Extended Warehouse Management • Extended Warehouse Management • Execution • Manually Assemble Warehouse Orders**, as shown in Figure 6.31. Select the warehouse task to be deleted, and click on .

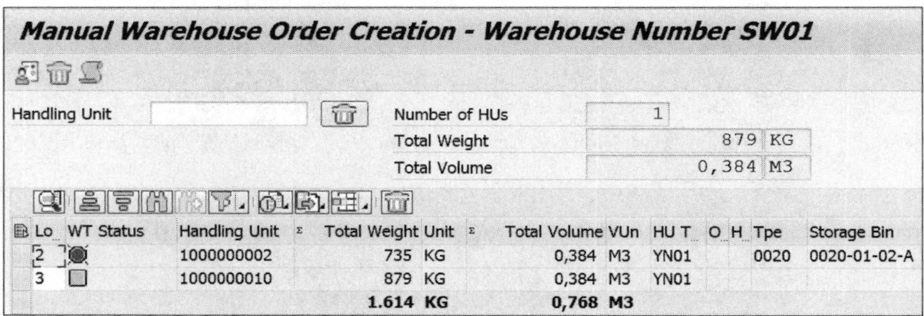

Figure 6.31 Manual Assembly of Warehouse Orders

The HUs are shown here with traffic light indicators in the **WT Status** column. The HUs are entered one by one, and they fall into two categories, represented by two different colors:

- **Green**
  If the entered HU has warehouse tasks created for each product inside it, it shows a green traffic light.
- **Red**
  If the entered HU doesn't have warehouse tasks created for at least one product inside it, it shows a red traffic light.

After adding the HUs in the list, click on **Save**. This deletes all existing warehouse tasks from the warehouse orders of the HUs in green and creates a new warehouse order to collect all the warehouse tasks for the selected HUs. If embedded EWM can successfully do so, it displays a message with the warehouse task/order number if it generated a single warehouse order. If it generates multiple warehouse orders, then it shows a message about the number of warehouse orders it's generated. The system generates a single warehouse order if all tasks belong to the same source and destination activity area and activity. Automatic printing of these warehouse orders also can be carried out if the condition records for printing are set in embedded EWM. Alternatively, they can be printed manually using the warehouse monitor.

6.5 Storage Control

In warehouses, the movement of goods is often guided by multistep movements for inbound, outbound, and internal warehouse processes. To configure complex movements of products in the warehouse, embedded EWM uses a process known as *storage control*. The process step, which can be movement of stock in the warehouse or an activity, is defined as a work step and is determined automatically as part of warehouse process flow.

Any business process, such as inbound, outbound, or internal warehouse movements of goods, often consists of multiple operations. For example, in the case of an outbound process, a product can move through multiple stages such as picking, packing, staging, and loading. The same is true for inbound and internal product movement in an embedded EWM warehouse. These warehouse process steps are mapped in embedded EWM using process-oriented storage control.

Products also may have to be moved to destination bins through intermediate locations such as conveyor belts or elevators due to the physical layout of the warehouse. This scenario is mapped in embedded EWM using layout-oriented storage control. You can combine process-oriented storage control with layout-oriented storage control, in which case, embedded EWM always executes process-oriented storage control first. While the process steps defined in process-oriented storage control are carried out, embedded EWM checks whether any of the process steps need to be combined with layout-oriented storage control based on the physical layout of the warehouse.

Note

For process-oriented storage control to work, the stock must be contained in an HU. This is because the current process step for the HU is contained in the HU itself, which helps track the storage process steps completed.

In the following sections, we'll explain the configurations and master data settings to configure storage processes in embedded EWM.

6.5.1 What Is Storage Control?

Storage control is a concept in embedded EWM that guides complex movements of products inside the warehouse. It may often happen that a certain product, from the time it's picked to the time it's staged, requires some extra processes to be carried out such as wrapping, cleaning, and so on. In the following sections, we explain the processes carried out in the system and documents related to complex goods movement (storage process) with which product/HUs can be moved.

Business Process

American company Alpha Medicals receives an order from one of its customers based in Mexico. The order sent by the customer requires Alpha Medicals to provide the products in time, in proper packing, and with additional activities for delivery. Stock that will be delivered to the customer is to be picked from source bins of the warehouse by the warehouse workers, packed in the required packaging material, and moved to different activity work centers before staging in the goods issue area. As a regular Alpha Medicals practice, additional warehouse workers perform warehousing activities various physical locations on products packed in packaging material before the product is moved from the source bin to the destination bin. To ensure that all stock movement activities of warehouse workers are performed on products packed in the proper manner at different physical areas, the company uses storage control in embedded EWM.

System Process

The following explains the basic system flow, including the documents and data required to execute process-oriented storage control in the outbound business process for stock in embedded EWM and decentralized EWM:

1. An outbound delivery order is created as a warehouse request in embedded EWM and contains information about the products Alpha Medicals will deliver to the external customer.
2. Initial picking warehouse tasks are created based on the warehouse request and assigned to the warehouse worker. The warehouse request directs the warehouse workers to carry out the product movement from source bin to staging area.

3. The warehouse orders are allocated to a warehouse worker. After picking the product from the source bin, the products are taken to a work center as the next step of storage control, packed in packaging materials and moved on to the next physical location in the warehouse.
4. The products move on to different physical areas in the warehouse before being placed in the destination bin of the warehouse.

6.5.2 Storage Control in the Outbound Process

During stock removal, you may need to carry the product through multiple stock locations (bins) based on business processes or layout requirements before loading it onto transportation units (TUs)/vehicles for dispatch. In this section, we'll cover both process-oriented storage control and layout-oriented storage control. The first scenario covers a storage process using only process-oriented storage control, and the second scenario covers stock removal in an outbound process using both process-oriented storage control and layout-oriented storage control:

- **Scenario 1: Using only process-oriented storage control**
  Figure 6.32 shows an outbound process with multiple process steps before loading the goods onto a truck. You can use process-oriented storage control to map such a process in embedded EWM.

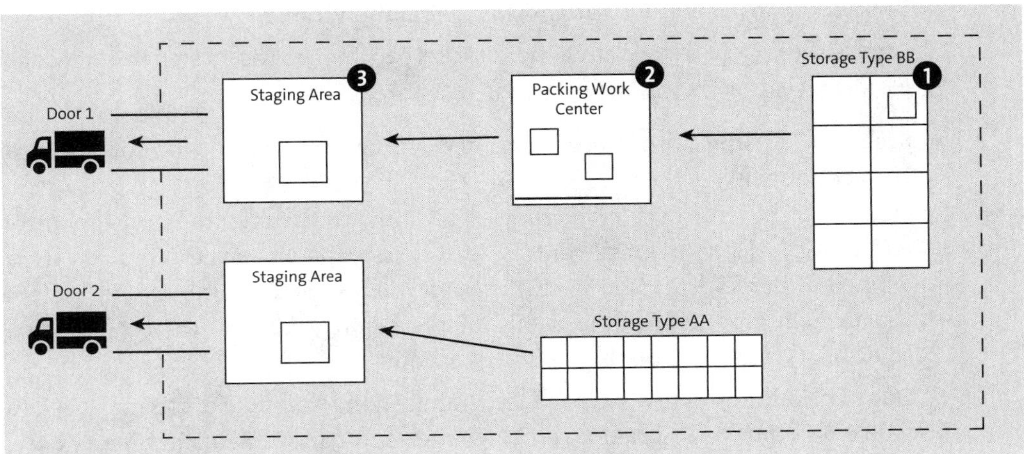

Figure 6.32 Process-Oriented Storage Control in Outbound Process

The steps required to execute process-oriented storage control for an outbound process in embedded EWM can be summarized as follows:

- **Picking**
  Pick warehouse tasks are created for outbound delivery order items. For all open warehouse tasks, a warehouse order creation rule is determined to create warehouse orders in embedded EWM. After the picking task is confirmed, products are sent for further packing at the packing work center.
- **Packing**
  At the packing work center, products are repacked from pick HUs to shipping HUs. Alternatively, if picking warehouse tasks are bundled by pick path, then the picked stock is consolidated and packed at the packing work center. You can also print shipping labels at the packing work center. The process step for packing is completed manually.
- **Staging**
  After packing is complete, embedded EWM creates a new warehouse task for moving the HUs to the staging area. A warehouse worker confirms these tasks as and when the HUs are moved to the staging area.
- **Loading**
  In the last step, the warehouse worker loads the HUs from the staging area to a door bin. If a TU is docked at the door, then the destination of the warehouse task is changed to the TU after task confirmation from RF.

Each of these steps in the warehouse process becomes a process step in embedded EWM, and each is executed by creation of a warehouse task.

- **Scenario 2: Using both process-oriented storage control and layout-oriented storage control**
  Figure 6.33 shows an outbound process with both process-oriented storage control and layout-oriented storage control. As discussed previously, the process steps defined by process-oriented storage control will take precedence, and the system will include process steps in layout-oriented storage control to accommodate additional steps based on the warehouse layout.

  Due to physical structure or space constraints in the warehouse, you may need to perform both process-oriented and layout-oriented movements in a warehouse. The various steps required to execute the same in an outbound process in embedded EWM can be summarized as follows:

- Full pallet picking is done from the source bin in full pallet storage. Embedded EWM determines that the source bin is pick point active and creates a warehouse task to move an HU to the pick point.
- After goods are packed in a pick HU at the pick point, they're moved to a packing work center, where groups of HUs are packed together to create a shipping HU. You can also print shipping labels at this work center.
- Embedded EWM determines the next step as staging and creates another warehouse task to move the HU from the packing work center to the staging area after the previous warehouse task is confirmed.
- After the HU is moved to the staging area, the HU warehouse task is completed. Embedded EWM determines loading as the next task per warehouse processes. This task can be created manually or via the PPF after a truck arrives at the warehouse door. The loading step is completed after goods are loaded on the truck.

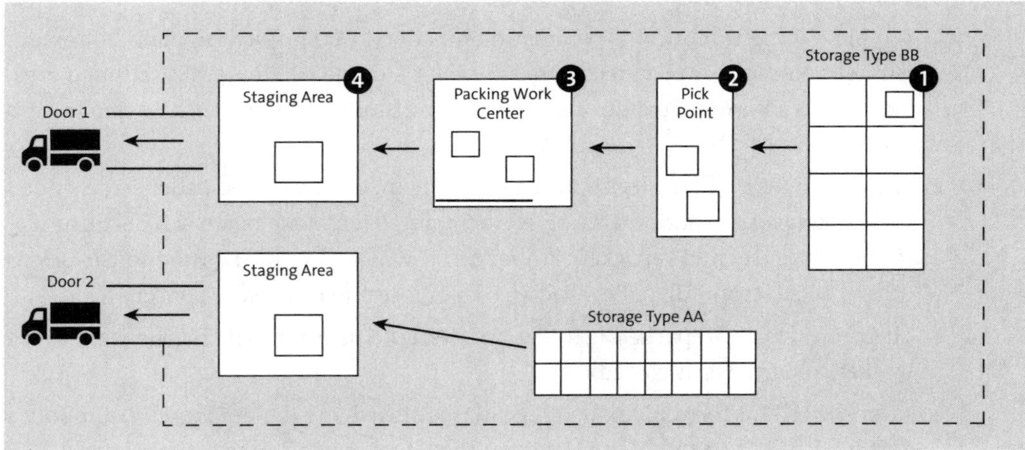

Figure 6.33 Process-Oriented Storage Control and Layout-Oriented Storage Control in Outbound Process

6.5.3 Storage Control in Internal Process

During internal warehouse movements, such as replenishment, embedded EWM can be configured to take the product from the source to destination bin via multiple process steps. Figure 6.34 shows an example of moving a product from a source to destination bin using storage control.

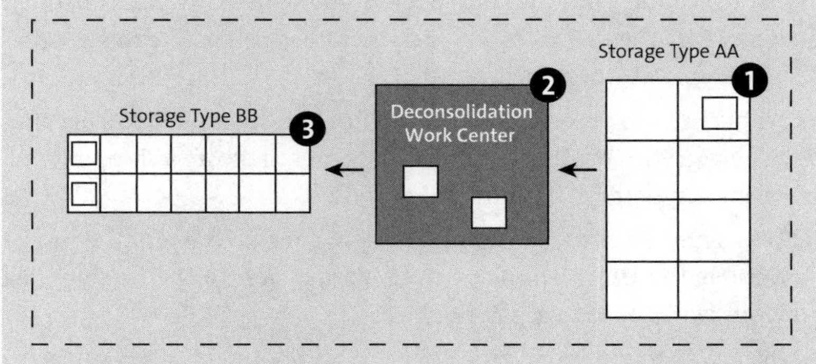

Figure 6.34 Process-Oriented Storage Control in the Internal Process for Replenishment

The various steps required to execute process-oriented storage control for an internal stock movement process in embedded EWM can be summarized as follows:

1. A replenishment request is created in embedded EWM based on planned replenishment to move a product from full pallet storage to a case pick storage area. Embedded EWM creates an inactive replenishment product task to move HUs from pallet storage.
2. Embedded EWM recognizes that the products inside the mixed pallet are assigned to different consolidation groups; as such, the HU must be taken to a deconsolidation work center and repacked. Embedded EWM creates an HU warehouse task to move the HU from full pallet storage to a deconsolidation work center.
3. The products are repacked into a separate replenishment HU by the warehouse worker, and the HU is closed.
4. After the HU for the replenished products is closed, the replenishment warehouse task is activated to move the HU from the deconsolidation work center to a case pick area.

6.5.4 Process-Oriented Storage Control

In this section, we'll discuss how warehouse processes can be mapped as process steps in EWM. These process steps are defined in a sequence to map them with the actual order in which they're carried out in the warehouse. We can also automate the creation of subsequent warehouse tasks after the previous tasks have been confirmed.

To make settings for process-oriented storage control, navigate to the IMG path **SCM Extended Warehouse Management • Extended Warehouse Management • Cross-Process Settings • Warehouse Task • Define Process-Oriented Storage Control**. The following configurations are maintained on this screen:

- **Define external process step**
  Each warehouse-specific business process step is mapped as an external storage process step in embedded EWM. Each external process step is mapped to an internal process step, as shown in Figure 6.35. The internal process steps are predefined in SAP and can't be changed. Examples of available internal process steps include putaway, packing, deconsolidation, and VAS. Each of these internal process steps provides a way of specifying in which directions movement can be allowed for the newly defined external process step by selecting the correct value in the **Direction** field.

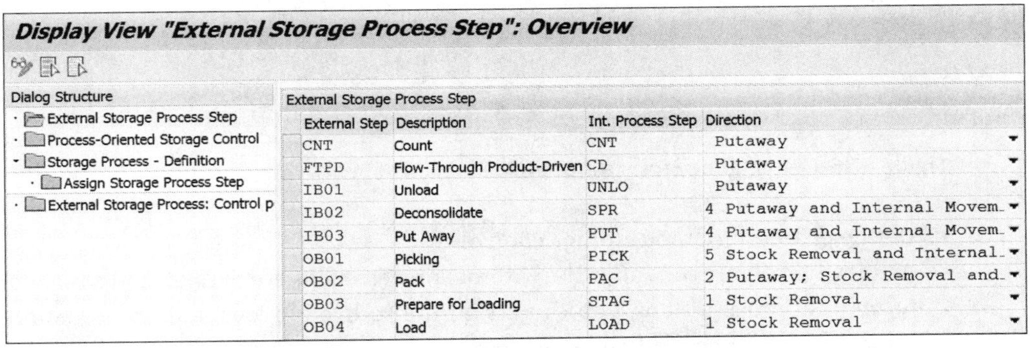

Display View "External Storage Process Step": Overview

Dialog Structure
- External Storage Process Step
- Process-Oriented Storage Control
- Storage Process - Definition
  - Assign Storage Process Step
- External Storage Process: Control p

External Storage Process Step

External Step	Description	Int. Process Step	Direction
CNT	Count	CNT	Putaway
FTPD	Flow-Through Product-Driven	CD	Putaway
IB01	Unload	UNLO	Putaway
IB02	Deconsolidate	SPR	4 Putaway and Internal Movem...
IB03	Put Away	PUT	4 Putaway and Internal Movem...
OB01	Picking	PICK	5 Stock Removal and Internal...
OB02	Pack	PAC	2 Putaway; Stock Removal and...
OB03	Prepare for Loading	STAG	1 Stock Removal
OB04	Load	LOAD	1 Stock Removal

Figure 6.35 Defining the External Process Step

- **Storage process definition**
  The storage process is used to sum up the end-to-end process steps an HU must go through during process-oriented storage control. A sequence of external process steps is assigned to a storage process by selecting the storage process and clicking on **Assign Storage Process Step** in the left-hand menu. The storage process governs the way in which goods are moved into and out of the warehouse.

  As shown in Figure 6.36, example **Storage Process INB1** consists of five external process steps: unload, count, oil, deconsolidate, and putaway. Each of these steps can be assigned additional configurations to control the type of actions being carried out in each step. The controls that can be assigned to each external step in the storage process are as follows:

- **Auto. WT**
  If this checkbox is selected, embedded EWM automatically creates subsequent HU warehouse tasks.
- **Prod/HU WT**
  This checkbox is used to signify during which external storage process step level the final putaway warehouse task (product/HU) is created. The warehouse task is created in **Inactive** status, and only becomes active when all the previous tasks in the process steps have been confirmed.

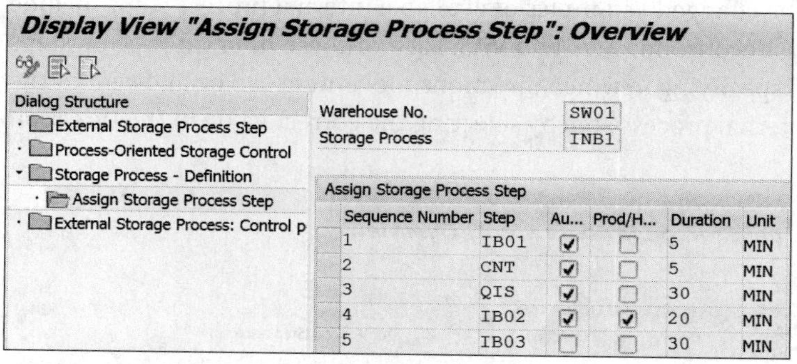

Display View "Assign Storage Process Step": Overview

Dialog Structure
- External Storage Process Step
- Process-Oriented Storage Control
- Storage Process - Definition
  - Assign Storage Process Step
- External Storage Process: Control p

Warehouse No. SW01
Storage Process INB1

Assign Storage Process Step

Sequence Number	Step	Au...	Prod/H...	Duration	Unit
1	IB01	[x]	[ ]	5	MIN
2	CNT	[x]	[ ]	5	MIN
3	QIS	[x]	[ ]	30	MIN
4	IB02	[x]	[x]	20	MIN
5	IB03	[ ]	[ ]	30	MIN

Figure 6.36 Defining the Storage Process in Embedded EWM

- **Define process-oriented storage control**
  As shown in Figure 6.37, after the external process steps are defined and assigned to internal process steps, you can assign the source bin, destination bin, warehouse process type, and stock movement rule to each of the external process steps.

Display View "Process-Oriented Storage Control": Overview

Dialog Structure
- External Storage Process Step
- Process-Oriented Storage Control
- Storage Process - Definition
  - Assign Storage Process Step
- External Storage Process: Control p

Process-Oriented Storage Control

War...	External Step	Sour...	HUTGr	Whse Proc. Type	Dest...	Dest...	Dest. Stor. Bin
SW01	IB01	9030	0001	3065			
SW01	IB01	DRMD		3065			
SW01	IB02			3060			
SW01	OB02			3070			
SW01	OB03			3070			
SW01	OB04			3070			
SW01	QIS			3060			
SW01	VS01			3060	8050	0001	WVI1
SW01	VS02	8050		3060	8050	0001	WVI2

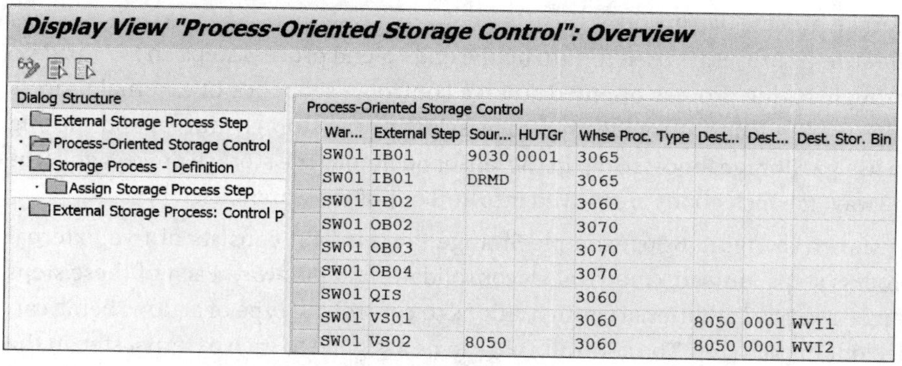

Figure 6.37 Process-Oriented Storage Control

The warehouse process type defined here is used to create the warehouse task to move a product/HU from a source to destination bin as defined in the storage process. As for the source bin for the external step of a storage process, it takes the destination bin of the previous external step in the storage process.

The storage process is assigned to the warehouse process type or warehouse order creation based on the nature of the warehouse process, as follows:

- In inbound processes, the storage process for process-oriented storage control is assigned to the warehouse process type in the **Storage Process** field.
- In outbound processes, the storage process for process-oriented storage control is assigned to the warehouse order creation rule in the **Storage Process** field.
- For internal warehouse movements, the storage process determination depends on the process being performed. For example, for replenishment, the storage process is assigned to the warehouse order creation rule, whereas for pick cancelation, the storage process is determined using the warehouse process type.

6.5.5 Layout-Oriented Storage Control

Layout-oriented storage control is a storage process used to carry out movement of goods through multiple points in the warehouse due to restrictions in the physical layout of the warehouse. For example, a product might need to be moved to the first floor in the warehouse to reach a final putaway bin via an elevator or contour checking zone.

In Figure 6.38, a full pallet is picked from the storage type BB. However, due to space constraints, it isn't possible to pack the products in a pick HU at the source storage bin.

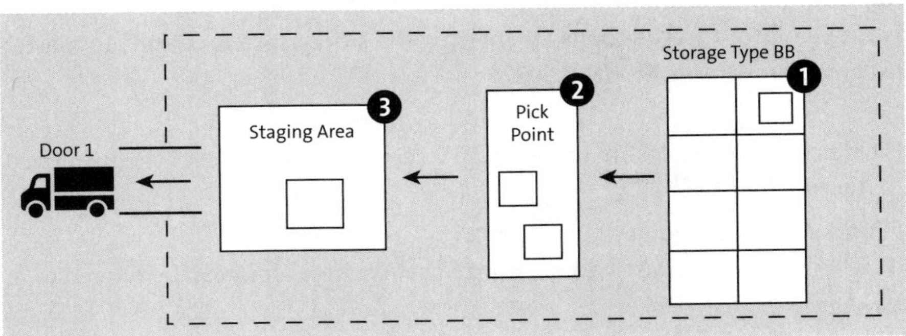

Figure 6.38 Layout-Oriented Storage Process

A pick point is created in embedded EWM, which identifies a place near the source storage bin where the warehouse worker unpacks the HUs and packs them in pick HUs, as shown in Step 2. From here, the goods are taken to the staging area. Embedded EWM creates an inactive warehouse task from the source bin (source type BB) to a staging area and an active warehouse task from the source bin (source type BB) to a pick point area. After the warehouse worker moves the HU from the source bin to the pick point and confirms the warehouse task, embedded EWM changes the source bin of the inactive HU warehouse task to the pick point and activates it. This is later confirmed by the warehouse worker on physical movement of the HU from the pick point to the staging area.

Configure layout-oriented storage control via IMG path **SCM Extended Warehouse Management • Extended Warehouse Management • Cross-Process Settings • Warehouse Task • Define Layout-Oriented Storage Control**. Click on **New Entries**, and define the following parameters for the storage control process:

- **Warehouse Number**
  This field contains the embedded EWM warehouse number for which the layout-oriented storage control is being configured.
- **Source Storage Type**
  This field contains the source storage type from which the product is being picked in the warehouse.
- **Source Storage Group**
  Storage bins in a storage type can be logically grouped together in a storage group, which is assigned in this field. To define a storage group, navigate to IMG path **SCM Extended Warehouse Management • Extended Warehouse Management • Cross-Process Settings • Warehouse Task • Define Storage Groups for Layout-Oriented Storage Control**. Click on **New Entries** to define new storage groups. Storage bins are grouped into storage groups by entering the storage group in the bin master data using Transaction /SCWM/LS02.
- **Type**
  This field contains the destination storage type where the product is being moved to in the warehouse.
- **Destination Storage Group**
  This field contains the destination storage group where stock can be moved to in the warehouse.

- **Whole HU**
  Using this setting, you can control how you want to withdraw stock using warehouse tasks from the source HU. Embedded EWM provides the following options:
  - **Not Relevant**
  - **Partial Removal—Product Warehouse Task**
  - **Empty Handling Unit—HU Warehouse Task**
  - **Complete Stock Pick—Product Warehouse Task**
  - **Movement of a Handling Unit (Not Empty)—HU Warehouse Task**
- **Int. Storage Type/Interm. Stor. Sec./Intermediate Bin**
  These fields contain the intermediate storage type, section, or storage bin where the HU is brought before it's moved to the destination bin.
- **HUTGr**
  This field contains the HU type group, which groups together HU types with similar stock movement requirements based on which intermediate bin in layout-oriented storage control is determined.
- **Whse Proc. Type**
  The movement of the HU from a source to an intermediate bin is done by the system using the warehouse process type assigned in this field.
- **ID Point**
  This field specifies that the current intermediate bin is used as an identification point during the receipt process or stock movement to an automated warehouse.
- **Pick Point**
  This field specifies that the current intermediate bin is used as a pick point during the stock removal process.
- **Segment**
  This field contains the conveyer segment of the material flow system for moving HUs using layout-oriented storage control.

6.6 Exception Handling

Exception handling is used to handle exceptions occurring in planned and actual warehousing operations—for example, differences between the planned quantity in the inbound delivery and the actual stock received in the warehouse. If such inconsistencies aren't corrected as soon as they are detected, they can lead to adverse situations.

For example, say a plant is running with multiple production lines, and each production line is being replenished with stock at regular intervals based on the replenishment strategy set for the consumption bin. To fulfill replenishment, a warehouse worker uses a forklift to pick product from a bulk area and move stock to production lines. The worker may not find enough stock in the desired storage bin to fulfill the replenishment request. In this case, the warehouse worker needs to confirm the replenishment warehouse task with the actual quantity available in the storage bin.

This process can be handled by embedded EWM using exception handling. You can confirm the warehouse task by entering an exception code, either by using SAP GUI or RF on a mobile device. This allows task confirmation with a quantity that is different from the original quantity in the warehouse task. Based on the type of action configured for exception code handling, the system can trigger replenishment, create a physical inventory document, block the bin, or direct a picker to another bin.

SAP has provided a set of predefined exception codes that can be used directly in embedded EWM. Alternatively, you can create new exception codes in the system based on business requirements. Any new exception code must be assigned with a specific action and business context. Exceptions can be applied in almost any stock movement in embedded EWM. In the following sections, we'll explain the basic configurations required to set up exception handling in embedded EWM and provide examples of how exception codes can be used in handling business scenarios.

6.6.1 What Is Exception Handling?

Exception handling is the process in which the planned warehouse workload, such as inbound, outbound, and internal stock movement in the warehouse, is confirmed with actual stock quantity in the source or destination bin. Because the actual stock quantity in the source or destination bin isn't equal to the planned quantity, the workload is confirmed using exception handling. In the following sections, we explain the processes carried out in the system and confirmation of warehouse tasks using exception codes. The sections also explain how warehouse tasks are confirmed using exception codes.

Business Process

American company Alpha Medicals receives an order from one of its customers based in Mexico. The order sent by the customer requires Alpha Medicals to provide the products in time, in proper packing, and with additional activities for delivery.

Stock that will be delivered to the customer is to be picked from source bins of the warehouse by the warehouse workers, packed in required packaging material, and moved to different activity work centers before staging in the goods issue area. As a regular Alpha Medicals practice, if the products being picked from the source bin aren't equal to what is demanded as part of the outbound delivery warehouse task, the company confirms the warehouse task with a difference quantity and stock shortfall reason using exception handling. To ensure that all stock movement activities of warehouse workers are captured against original stock quantity, the company uses exception handling in embedded EWM.

System Process

The following explains the basic system flow, including the documents required to process the outbound delivery document using an exception code for stock differences in embedded EWM and decentralized EWM:

1. An outbound delivery order is created as a warehouse request in embedded EWM that contains information about the products to be delivered to the external customer by Alpha Medicals.
2. Initial picking warehouse tasks are created based on the warehouse request and assigned to the warehouse worker. This warehouse request directs the warehouse worker to carry out the product movement from source bin to staging area.
3. The warehouse orders are allocated to the warehouse worker. During picking of the product from the source bin, the warehouse worker tries to pick up the stock quantity as displayed in the warehouse task. Because the stock available in the source bin is in shortage, the warehouse worker uses exception handling to capture this difference.

> **Note**
>
> We've explained the system process using the outbound process only. It's equally applicable to inbound and internal stock movement processes.

6.6.2 Configuration Elements of Exception Codes

Exception codes guide embedded EWM to take follow-up actions after an exception code is inserted and saved in the system. Any follow-up system action, such as creation of a physical inventory document or a replenishment request, is triggered based on settings for the exception handling performed in the system. Before we dive into the application of exception codes, let's go over the basic building blocks in exception handling:

- **Internal process codes**
  Internal process codes are used to define how embedded EWM should react after the exception code is assigned to a warehouse task. You can define an external exception code with any name, but you must assign an internal process code to it for embedded EWM to perform relevant follow-up actions. Internal process codes are predefined by SAP. Table 6.3 shows some commonly used internal process codes in embedded EWM.

Internal Process Code	Description
BIDU	Stock Removal Denial
CHHU	Change Handling Unit
HUMI	No Handling Unit Exists
LIST	Display of Valid Exceptions
DIFF	Post with Difference

Table 6.3 Internal Process Codes in Embedded EWM

- **Internal exception code**
  Internal exception codes are also predefined by SAP and are automatically triggered when an exception is triggered in the warehouse. You can assign internal exception codes to user-defined exception codes to handle exceptions more flexibly. To assign internal exception codes to external codes, navigate to IMG path **SAP Extended Warehouse Management • Extended Warehouse Management • Cross-Process Settings • Exception Handling • Assign Internal Exception Codes to Exception Codes**. Click on **New Entries**, enter the external exception codes, and assign them to the internal exception codes.

- **Business context and execution step**
  A business context represents a business process for which the exception code can be applied. Business contexts include processes in embedded EWM such as confirming warehouse tasks (putaway), wave creation, indirect labor tasks, and so on. Assign a user-defined exception code to a business context and execution step via

IMG path **SAP Extended Warehouse Management • Extended Warehouse Management • Cross-Process Settings • Exception Handling • Maintain Business Context for Exception Codes**. Click on **New Entries**, and enter the business context along with the associated execution steps.

An execution step is used to designate the way in which process execution is handled for a business context when an exception code is inserted. For example, in Figure 6.39, we've assigned **Business Context TPT** for confirmation of a warehouse task for putaway to execution **Step 01** for execution via desktop and **Step 03** for execution via RF.

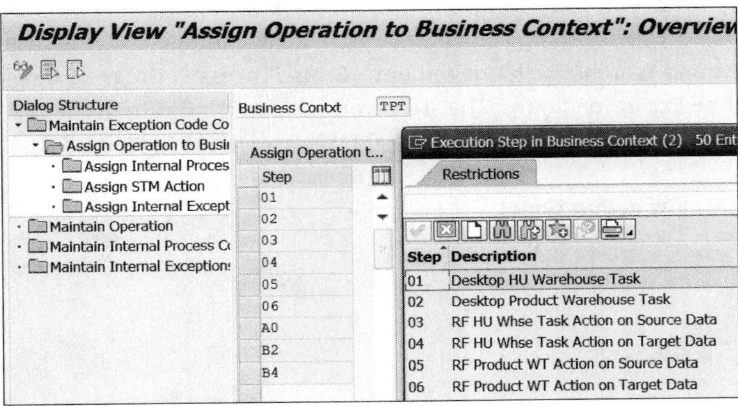

Figure 6.39 Assignment of Operation to Business Context

- **Exception code profile**
  Exception code profiles are used to restrict authorization for usage of exception codes to select users. This may be required if you want certain exceptions and follow-up actions to be allowed for employees with specific roles in the warehouse. You can assign exception code profiles to users via Transaction /SCWM/EXCUSERID or from **SAP Easy Access** path **Logistics • SCM Extended Warehouse Management • Extended Warehouse Management • Settings • Assign Users to Exception Code Profile**, as shown in Figure 6.40. Click on **New Entries**, enter the external exception code profile (**Excp.Code Prof.**), and save. Next, select the defined exception code profile, and click on the **Assign Users** node to assign users to the exception code profile.

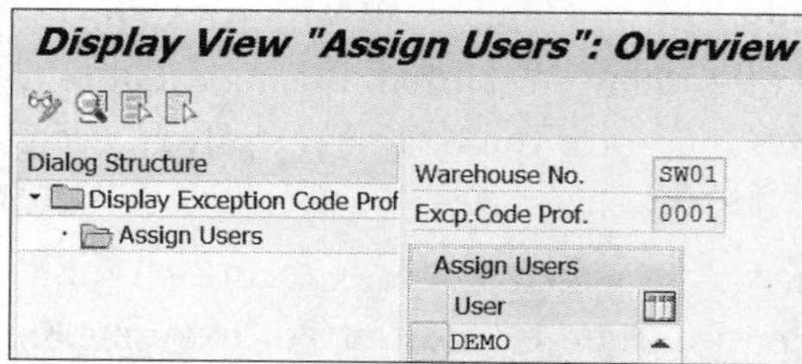

Figure 6.40 Defining the Exception Code Profile

6.6.3 Define New Exception Code

A new exception code can be defined via IMG path **SCM Extended Warehouse Management • Extended Warehouse Management • Cross-Process Settings • Exception Handling • Define Exception Codes**. The steps you need to configure in the system for setting up exception handling in embedded EWM are shown in Figure 6.41.

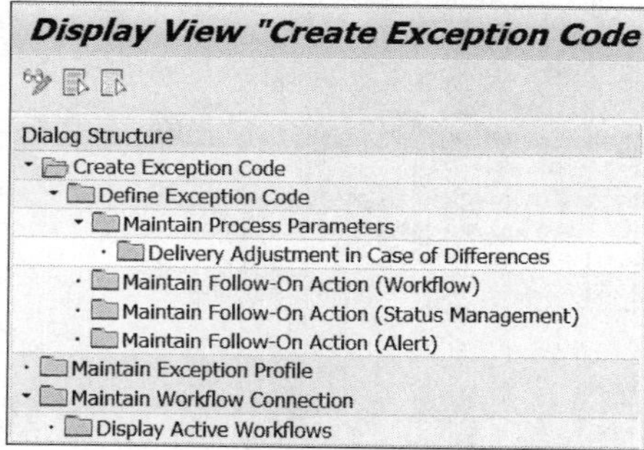

Figure 6.41 Exception Handling in Embedded EWM

The following steps create a new exception code, INBT, for an incorrect batch received in the warehouse from a vendor in the warehouse request. This exception code will be entered when a warehouse user is unloading HUs from a truck into the warehouse. Follow these steps:

1. To define an exception code for the warehouse, select **Create Exception Code**, as shown in Figure 6.42. Enter a **Description**. You can keep a history of the object, in context of which the exception code is used, by selecting the **With Hist**. indicator. If the exception is to be blocked for the warehouse for which it's defined, select the **Block**. In this case, the exception code disappears from the dropdown list of exceptions available when trying to execute exceptions for a business context.

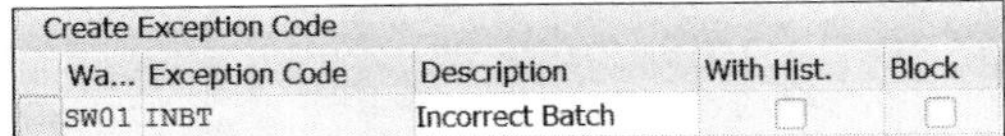

Figure 6.42 Creating the Exception Code

2. After the exception code is defined, select the exception code, and click on **Define Exception Code**. In this node, assign the business context and execution steps to the exception code. To restrict the usage of an exception code to certain business contexts and execution steps by a certain set of users, assign the code to the exception code profile, as shown in Figure 6.43.

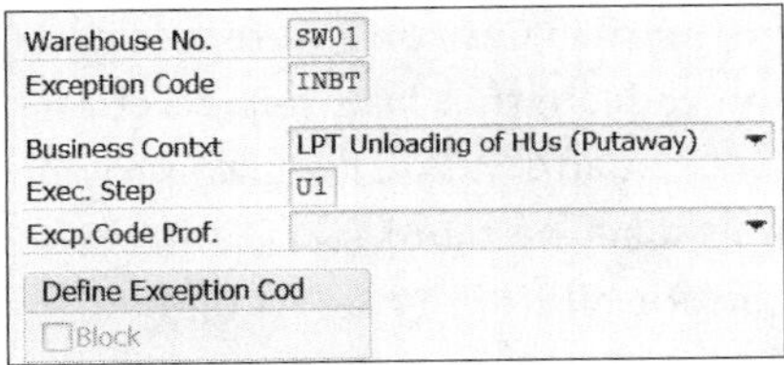

Figure 6.43 Defining the Exception Code

If a certain follow-up action for the exception code isn't working, and the exception code is to be deactivated, this can be done by setting the **Block** control. In this case, you want to set this exception code during the unloading process, so set the business context LPT for unloading of HUs during putaway, and assign it to execution **Step U1** (for HU selection during unloading via RF) so that you can enter the exception code while executing unloading from RF. You can assign multiple execution steps to a business context.

3. Assign the combination of business context and execution step to an internal process code by selecting **Maintain Process Parameters** from the left-hand side of the screen. This activity tells the system how to react when the exception code is entered. In this case, assign the internal process code (**Int. Proc.Code**) **HUMI** because the expected HU of the given batch doesn't exist, as shown in Figure 6.44. In addition, maintain the **Diff. Cat.** as **3** because you want to update the quantity received in the inbound delivery.

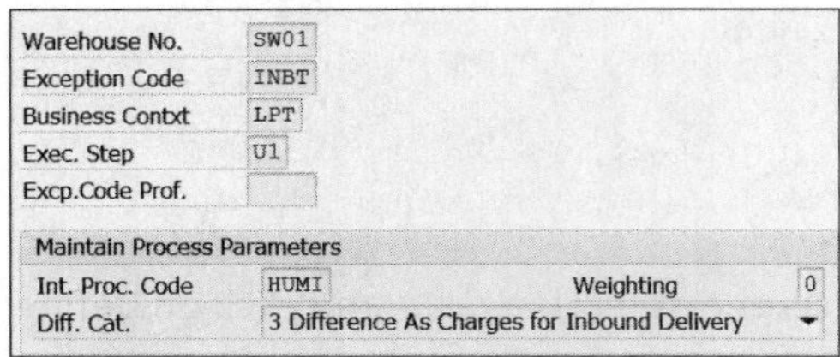

Figure 6.44 Maintaining Process Parameters

As shown in Figure 6.45, if you want the system to update the difference quantity in the inbound delivery, provide the process code and required adjustment in the delivery quantity by selecting the **Delivery Adjustment in Case of Differences** node in the left-hand menu for the defined exception code. In this case, select option **1** to adjust the delivery quantity with the difference quantity. You can also provide the item type for which you want the system to take the required action. If you want the system to take the appropriate action for all item types in embedded EWM, set **Item Type** to ****.

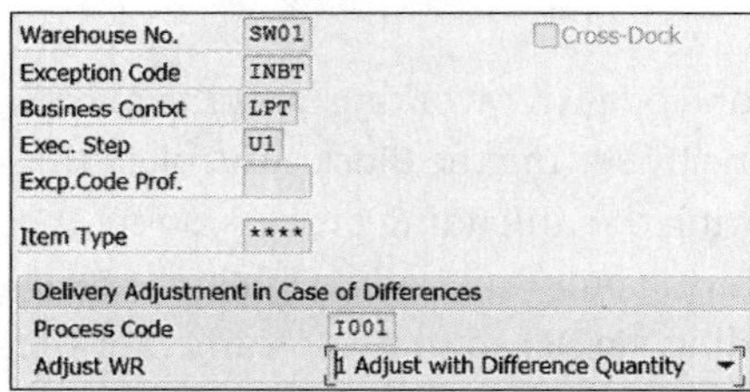

Figure 6.45 Defining the Delivery Adjustment Follow-Up Action

These settings are sufficient to use exception codes in embedded EWM. However, you can also assign additional follow-up actions such as workflow, alerts, and status management for further exception handling.

6.6.4 Exception Code Usage

In the preceding example, after the exception code is defined, you can use it during pick task confirmation. While confirming the unloading warehouse task using Transaction /SCWM/TODLV, assign the exception code if the required batches in HUs weren't found. The unloading warehouse task is confirmed with the modified quantity by providing exception code INBT defined previously, which will also update the quantity in the inbound delivery.

Exception handling also can be used while executing transactions using RF. SAP offers many predefined exceptions in embedded EWM that can be applied while executing various transactions using RF such as picking, putaway, loading, unloading, and so on. These allow you to continue working from the location in the warehouse where the exception has occurred without having to see a supervisor to take corrective measures.

The exception code field is available in all RF screens while executing a business process for which an exception code can be entered. Depending on the configurations for exception handling defined for a particular exception code as discussed earlier, you can stay on the same screen after applying an exception code, or you can move to a new screen to take corrective measures after applying the exception code. For example, while applying exception code DIFF for a missing quantity, you're taken to a new screen to enter the difference quantity.

Note

The Maintain User Settings app allows you to assign an exception code profile to warehouse users so that specific exception codes can be available during warehouse tasks confirmation.

6.7 Batch Management

Batch management is used to capture important details about certain products that are perishable in nature or have a certain shelf life after which they must be recycled or returned for disposal. A batch in SAP contains characteristics of a product that affect how the product is handled in the warehouse. Batch characteristics describe different identifiable properties of a product. It's therefore important to have products of a perishable nature batch-managed so that after their shelf life ends, they can be either scrapped or returned to the supplier for appropriate action.

Embedded EWM provides an extensive solution to execute batch management in the warehouse. You can create and maintain batches for products during putaway in the warehouse. Embedded EWM also provides ways to search for products in a specific batch from the warehouse to fulfill demand for outbound requests.

Note

In embedded EWM, you don't have to send the batches, classes, and characteristics of products from SAP S/4HANA to embedded EWM using the Core Interface (CIF). Batches are centrally maintained in SAP S/4HANA.

Batch creation in SAP S/4HANA is dependent on classes and characteristics, so it's important to ensure that all required classes and characteristics are created in SAP S/4HANA so that they can be used in embedded EWM. Embedded EWM can create batches dynamically for deliveries if the material is batch-managed and batch creation is allowed. Batches can be created in SAP S/4HANA using Transaction MSC1N; in embedded EWM, they can be created manually from **SAP Easy Access** path **Logistics • SCM Extended Warehouse Management • Extended Warehouse Management • Master Data • Product • Maintain Batches for Product**, or by using Transaction /SCWM/WM_BATCH_MAINT.

In the next few sections, we'll talk about the basic configuration and master data used for batch management in embedded EWM and the processes in which batches are used.

6.7.1 What Is Batch Management?

Batch management is how stock of the same product, but with different characteristics, is managed in the warehouses. Characteristics of the products can be country of origin, best before date, color, and so on. These diverse product stocks are stored, managed within the warehouse, and supplied out of the warehouse. In the following sections, we explain confirmation of warehouse requests using materials that are batch managed. The sections also explain how warehouse tasks are confirmed for batch-managed products.

Business Process

American company Alpha Medicals receives an order from one of its customers based in Mexico. The order sent by the customer requires Alpha Medicals to provide the products in time, in proper packing, and with Germany as the country of origin. Stock that will be delivered to the customer is to be picked from source bins of the warehouse by the warehouse workers, packed in the required packaging material, and move to the staging area for goods issue. It's a regular Alpha Medicals practice that the products are stored in the warehouse with different product characteristics in the same as well as different bins. For example, Product P with country of origin Mexico and country of origin Germany is stored in the warehouse, even in the same bin. To ensure that the embedded EWM system proposes the stock to be picked based on desired product characteristics that are ordered (in this case, country of origin as Germany), the company uses batch management in embedded EWM.

System Process

The following explains the basic system flow, including the documents required to pick batch-managed products from source bins in embedded EWM and decentralized EWM:

1. An outbound delivery order is created as a warehouse request in embedded EWM and contains information about the products to be delivered to an external customer by Alpha Medicals.
2. Picking warehouse tasks are created based on the warehouse request and assigned to the warehouse worker. The warehouse request directs the warehouse worker to move the products from the source bin to the staging area.
3. The warehouse orders are allocated to the warehouse worker. During picking of the product from the source bin, the warehouse worker picks up the stock quantity as displayed in the warehouse task.
4. The warehouse task is created by the system so that it picks up the product stock with Germany as the country of origin.
5. After the worker picks the stock from the source bin and completes intermediate stock movements, the stock is finally staged at the goods issue area.

> **Note**
> We've explained the system process using the outbound process only. It's equally applicable to inbound and internal stock movement processes.

6.7.2 Configuring Batch Management

In this section, we'll discuss the configurations required to create and use batches in embedded EWM. Some of the base configurations for batch management are as follows:

- **Batch level**
  The batch level specifies the level at which the batch is unique in the system. The batch level can be set per business needs via IMG path **Logistics—General • Batch Management • Specify Batch Level and Activate Status Management • Batch Level.** The batch can be set to be unique at the level of the client, plant, or material by selecting the appropriate radio button and saving the setting. Embedded EWM supports batch management at both the plant and material levels.
- **Define classes and characteristics**
  As shown in Figure 6.46, you can define classes via Transaction CL02, which can also be accessed via IMG path **Cross-Application Components • Classification System • Master Data • Classes**. Click on , and enter the **Class** name, **Class type**, validity, and characteristics for the class. To use batches in embedded EWM, create a class of class type 023.

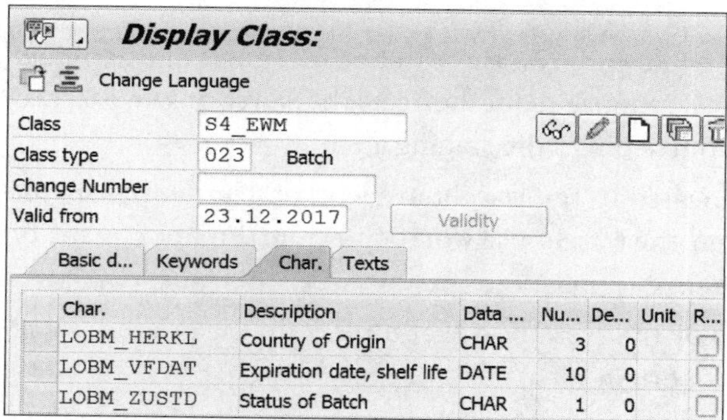

Figure 6.46 Defining Classes in SAP S/4HANA

- **Batch determination in embedded EWM**
  As discussed previously, when you set up integration between SAP S/4HANA and embedded EWM, you can set up transfer of batch selection criteria to embedded EWM for automatic batch determination in outbound deliveries. To do so, navigate to IMG path **Logistics Execution • Extended Warehouse Management Integration • Basic Setup of EWM Connectivity • Maintain Extended WM-Specific Parameters**. The **BatchDetEW** checkbox ensures that batch selection criteria are sent to embedded EWM and that automatic batch determination is triggered in the embedded EWM system (see Figure 6.47).

Display View "Extended Warehouse Management system": Overview

Extended Warehouse Management system

WhN	Whse no. description	Ext. WM	Dist. Mode	UD	BatchDetEW
S4H	S4H Warehouse	E EWM (Extended Warehouse Management)	Distribution Immediately at...	☐	☑

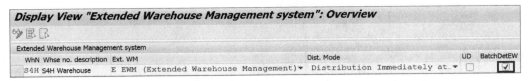

Figure 6.47 Batch Determination in Embedded EWM

> **Note**
>
> For this configuration to work, it's important that automatic batch determination is set up in SAP S/4HANA at both the sales order item and delivery item levels via IMG path **Logistics General • Batch Management • Batch Determination and Batch Check • Activate Automatic Batch Determination in SD**.

You also need to configure batch settings per delivery category in embedded EWM. Warehouse-request-specific settings are made in embedded EWM via IMG path **SCM Extended Warehouse Management • Extended Warehouse Management • Cross-Process Settings • Batch Management • Define Settings for Delivery—Warehouse Request**.

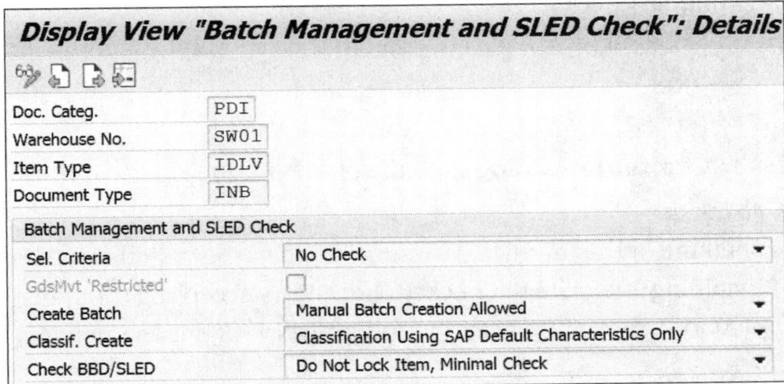

Figure 6.48 Batch Settings in Embedded EWM

Click on **New Entries**, and select the batch-specific parameters described as follows for the embedded EWM warehouse, document category, document, and item type (see Figure 6.48):

- **Selection criteria**
  By setting the value for **Sel. Criteria** to **Check** or **No Check**, you can set whether the

batch entered will be checked against the selection characteristics of the delivery item.

- **Goods movement restricted**
  If the **Gdsmvt 'Restricted'** checkbox is selected, you can restrict goods issue or goods receipt of blocked batches in embedded EWM.
- **Create batch**
  The settings in the **Create Batch** dropdown control whether manual batch creation is allowed or not for the document type for inbound delivery. By assigning the option to create batches in the inbound delivery automatically, you can also allow batch creation with either an external or internal number range only.
- **Batch classification during creation**
  By setting the value of **Classif. Create**, you can set the system to valuate new batches created during delivery processing using either the SAP default characteristics or customer-specific characteristics.
- **Check best before date**
  You can assign one of the following values to the **Check BBD/SLED** setting to guide how the embedded EWM system should react to the shortfall of remaining shelf life in the inbound delivery process:
  - **Do Not Lock Item, Minimal Check**
    The system pops up a message noting a shortfall in the remaining shelf life of the product.
  - **No Check**
    The system doesn't check the remaining shelf life of the product.
  - **Lock Item, Manual Release Allowed**
    If the remaining shelf life of the product is in shortfall, then the system sets the status of **Check Remaining Shelf Life** to **Checked, Not OK**. By accepting the shortfall, you can allow goods receipt, reject inbound delivery, or set the delivery quantity to zero.
  - **Lock Item, Manual Release Not Allowed**
    This is the same as the previous option, except that if you set this status, you can't reject the shortfall.
- **Goods movement for restricted batches**
  It's possible to allow goods movement and warehouse task creation for restricted batches created in embedded EWM by navigating to IMG path **SCM Extended Warehouse Management • Extended Warehouse Management • Cross-Process**

Settings • Batch Management • Batch Status Management • Define Setting for Delivery - Warehouse Request, and setting the for **GdsMvt 'Restricted'** checkbox, as shown in Figure 6.49.

Display View "Batch Management in the Delivery: Batch Status": Details

Doc. Categ.	PDI
Warehouse No.	SW01
Item Type	IDLV
Document Type	INB

Batch Management in the Delivery: Batch Status

GdsMvt 'Restricted' ☑

Figure 6.49 Batch Management in Delivery

As shown in Figure 6.50, you can also allow the creation of warehouse tasks with restricted batches by setting the **Sts Restr.** indicator in IMG path **SCM Extended Warehouse Management • Extended Warehouse Management • Cross-Process Settings • Batch Management • Batch Status Management • Define Setting for Warehouse Task Creation**.

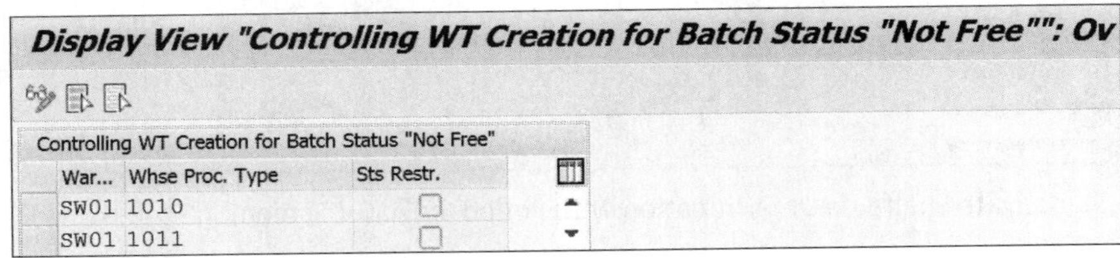

Figure 6.50 Batch Management at the Warehouse Task Level

- **Number ranges for batches**
  For the batch management process to work between SAP ERP and decentralized EWM, you must configure the number range as explained in Table 6.4 using IMG path **SCM Extended Warehouse Management • Extended Warehouse Management • Cross-Process Settings • Batch Management • Batch Management for Decentralized EWM • Define Number Ranges for Batches**. Click on the **+** button, and add the relevant internal and external number ranges for batch management.

Batch Master Origin	SAP ERP or SAP S/4HANA	Decentralized EWM in SAP S/4HANA
SAP ERP	Internal number range	External number range
Decentralized EWM	External number range	Internal number range

Table 6.4 Number Range Alignment between SAP ERP and Decentralized EWM in SAP S/4HANA for Batch Management

- **Activate shelf-life determination with period indicator**
  If you want to activate the warehouse level shelf-life indicator to calculate shelf-life expiration and latest delivery date in decentralized EWM, navigate to IMG path **SCM Extended Warehouse Management • Extended Warehouse Management • Cross-Process Settings • Batch Management • Batch Management for Decentralized EWM • Activate Shelf Life Determination with Period Indicator,** as shown in Figure 6.51. Click on **New Entries**, and select the **Use Period Ind.** checkbox for the warehouse.

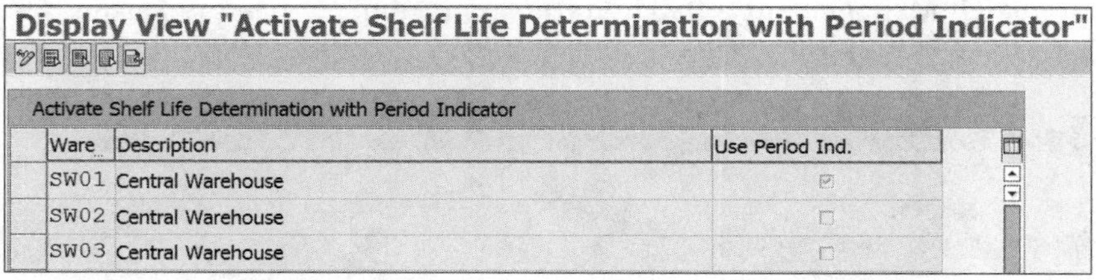

Figure 6.51 Activate Shelf-Life Determination with Period Indicator Screen

The shelf-life period indicator is defined in the material master in the SAP ERP system and sent over to the product master in decentralized EWM. When you define the period indicator and assign it in the material master, the system calculates shelf-life expiration and latest delivery date using the unit of time defined in the period indicator. As an example, when the shelf-life period indicator is activated at the warehouse level, if a product is produced on June 10th, and **Period Ind. for SLED** "D" and **Total Shelf Life** "2" has been set up, as shown in Figure 6.52, the shelf life expiration date (SLED) will be calculated by the system as August 10th.

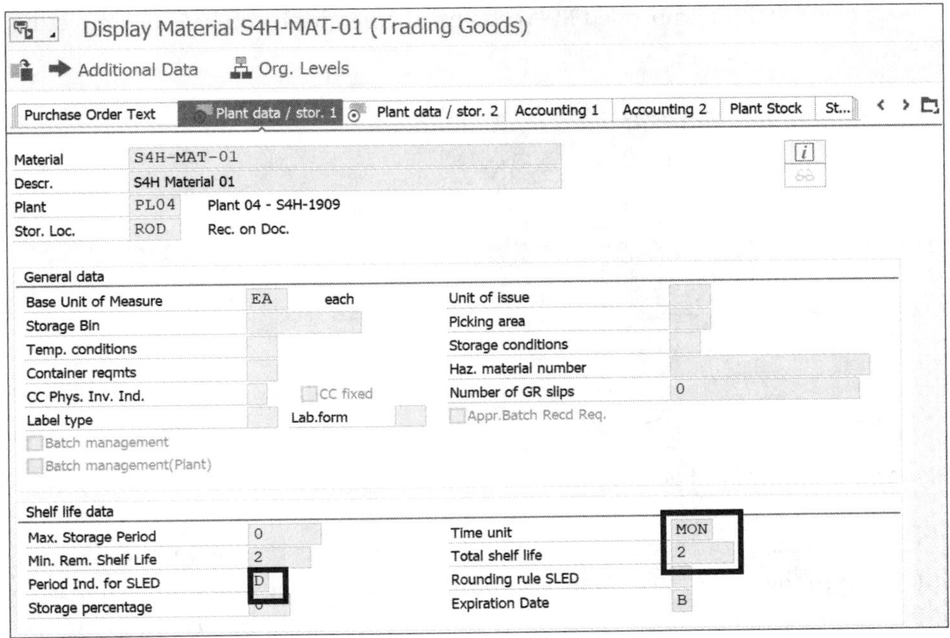

Figure 6.52 Shelf-Life Setting in Material Master Data

6.7.3 Batches in Goods Movement

Batches can be used in both the goods receipt and goods issue processes in embedded EWM. This involves creation or transfer of batches via inbound or outbound delivery from SAP S/4HANA to embedded EWM or determination of the correct batch in outbound delivery in embedded EWM for the products. Each of these scenarios works as follows:

- **Goods receipt process**
  An inbound delivery is created in embedded EWM in various scenarios, such as goods receipt from a vendor, production receipt, customer returns, stock transfer from another plant, and so on.

  If you're receiving goods from a production line, you can create new batches in embedded EWM via the **Batches** button, as shown in Figure 6.53. If you're receiving multiple batches of a product, you can create batch subitems and specify the quantity and batch of products received. If you're receiving products from a vendor, the inbound delivery can come with a vendor-specified batch. The vendor-specified batch is listed in the **Vendor Batch** field in the inbound delivery. You can create your own batch in embedded EWM against the vendor batch before completing putaway.

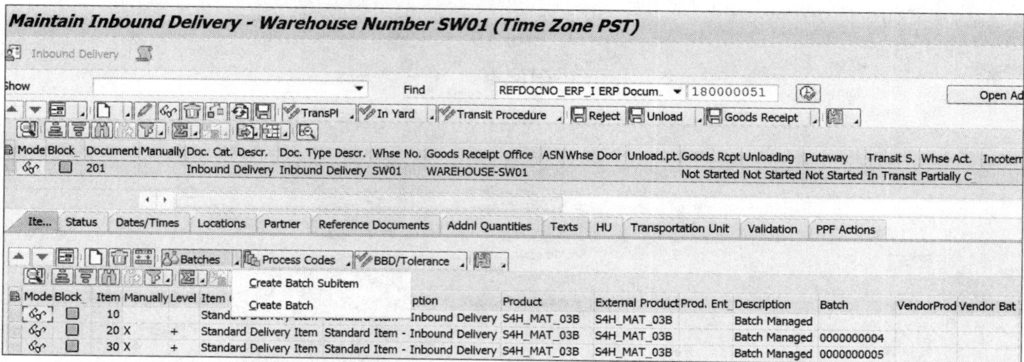

Figure 6.53 Batches in Inbound Delivery

It's also possible for an inbound delivery to have batches specified at the line item level, as in the case of stock transfer from another warehouse. If the batch master data is present in the system, then it's used for inbound delivery, putaway, and goods receipt; however, if the batch master isn't present, then embedded EWM can create a new batch either in the foreground or automatically in the background. Embedded EWM takes the values of characteristics such as country of origin, expiration date, SLED, production date, and so on, defined in the batch class, to create the batch in embedded EWM.

- **Goods issue process**
  It's possible to display the selection criteria for each delivery item in the outbound delivery after the delivery is distributed to embedded EWM for picking. The system selects the batches that match the selection criteria when creating the picking warehouse task. When the system creates a picking warehouse task, embedded EWM picks the stock per the selection criteria in the outbound delivery item.

  It may also be possible for the system to pick multiple batches to fulfill the demand of the outbound delivery order. In that case, you may need to perform a delivery item split, which can be done by selecting the item of the delivery and clicking on the **Batch Split** button.

Note

You can define selection classes in embedded EWM via IMG path **Logistics—General • Batch Management • Batch Determination and Batch Check • Define Selection Classes**, or via Transaction CL01.

You can create your own batch search strategy in SAP S/4HANA using Transaction VCH1 or by navigating to IMG path **Logistics • Sales and Distribution • Master Data • Products • Batch Search Strategy • Create**. For example, you can define customer-specific search strategies based on characteristics of a product such as color, country of origin, and so on. The system determines the batch in embedded EWM based on the predefined batch search strategies.

6.7.4 Documentary Batch

In the warehouse, you may need to track batches without maintaining the actual stock in the warehouse inventory in batches. This is done in embedded EWM using documentary batches. In the inbound process, embedded EWM creates a documentary batch before goods receipt in the inbound delivery. In an outbound delivery order, the documentary batch can be assigned to the delivery before creation of the picking task. The following configurations need to be completed to configure documentary batches in embedded EWM:

1. As shown in Figure 6.54, documentary batches are activated via IMG path **Logistics—General • Batch Management • Documentary Batches • Activate Documentary Batch**, by selecting the **Active** radio button.
2. The material type to be managed using documentary batches is defined in SAP S/4HANA via IMG path **Logistics—General • Batch Management • Documentary Batches • Define Entry per Material Type**. Click on **New Entries**, and enter a material type and control for using documentary batches. You can also set up whether the automatic creation of a batch in the background is allowed for the documentary batch via this configuration.

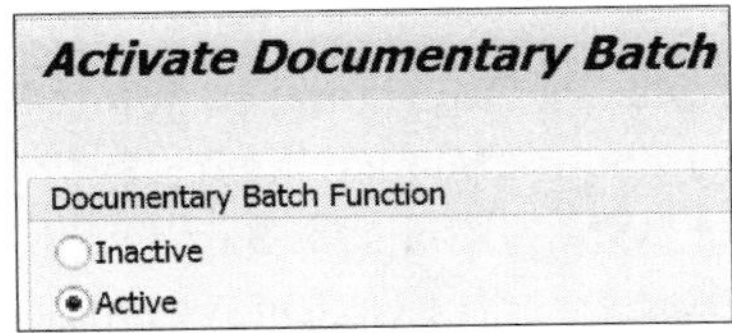

Figure 6.54 Activate Documentary Batch

3. Define the process step for which the documentary batch is applicable via IMG path **Logistics—General • Batch Management • Documentary Batches • Define Entry for Manual Process Step**. Click on **New Entries**, enter the documentary batch process and controls, and then save. This setting also restricts the maximum number of documentary batches that can be created for a process step in the system.
4. You also need to activate the documentary batch functionality for a combination of item type and document category for the delivery via IMG path **SCM Extended Warehouse Management • Extended Warehouse Management • Cross-Process Settings • Batch Management • Set Documentary Batch**, as shown in Figure 6.55. Set the **Doc. Batch** indicator for the **Item Type** and document category (**Doc. Cat.**). This setting activates the creation of a documentary batch in embedded EWM.

Display View "Item Types: Delivery: Add-On Data": Overview

Item Types: Delivery: Add-On Data

Item Type	Doc. Cat.	Description	Doc. Batch
IDLV	PDI	Standard Item - Inbound Delivery	☑
IDPD	PDI	Lean InbDeliv GR Production	☐
IDPP	PDI	Inbound Delivery Std. Item GR Production	☐
ODLV	PDO	Standard Item - Outbound Delivery	☐

Figure 6.55 Documentary Batch Setting in Embedded EWM

6.7.5 Plant-Specific Batch Handling

Embedded EWM provides further enhancements where the products can be batch managed at the plant level. For example, in the process industry, this feature helps users classify homogenous partial quantities of a material or product at the plant level throughout the logistics chain. Users can use the batch characteristics or batch number to select the right stock in the warehouse management monitor.

To activate plant-level batch handling in embedded EWM, you need to perform the following configurations:

1. Ensure that the following business functions are activated: `LOG_SCM_MEAN_INT` and `LOG_SCM_EWM_INT`.
2. Select activation of plant-level batch management via SAP IMG menu path **Integration with Other SAP Components • Extended Warehouse Management • Basic Settings for Data Transfer • Specify Destination SAP EWM Systems for Batches on Plant**, as shown in Figure 6.56. You click on **New Entries**, enter the **Logical system** of

embedded EWM, and select the checkbox for plant-level batch activation, that is, **EWM Only**.

Display View "Specify Destination SAP EWM Systems for Batches on Plant

Specify Destination SAP EWM Systems for Batches on Plant

Logical system	EWM Only
S46CLNT100	☑

Figure 6.56 Activating Plant-Level Batch Handling

In our example using the process industry, after the batches at the plant level are activated for embedded EWM, whenever you create a material master, a product master is automatically created, and batches at the plant level are activated in the **WHSE DATA** view of product master. The plant-level batch handling can be verified using Transaction /SCWM/MAT1, as shown in Figure 6.57.

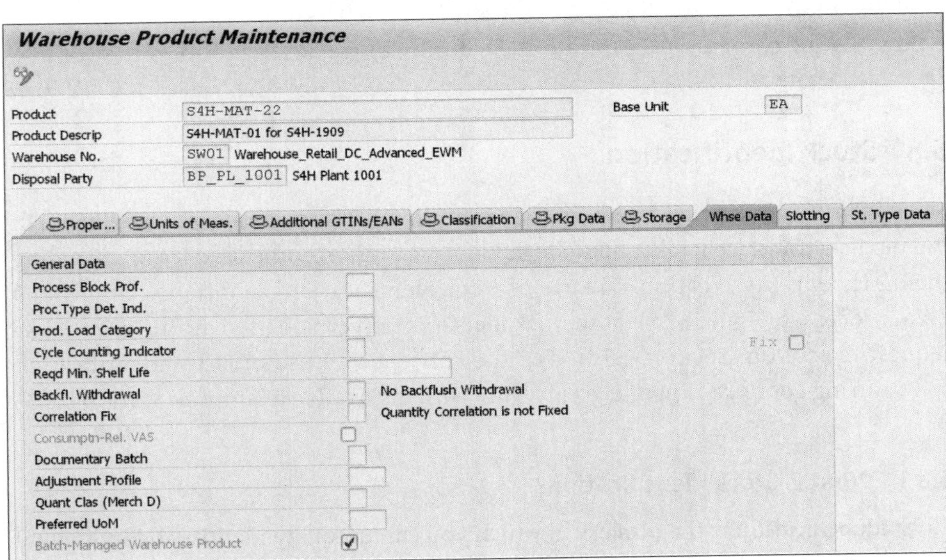

Figure 6.57 Displaying Plant-Level Batch Activation in Warehouse Product Master

6.7.6 Product Genealogy for Batch-Managed Materials

In SAP Global Batch Traceability (SAP GBT), you can trace all batches and HUs that are based on batch-managed materials in embedded and decentralized EWM. With this feature embedded EWM and decentralized EWM can send data to SAP GBT, which helps to trace HUs. For integration, a web service interface is used that requires some prerequisites such as setting up SAP GBT and the inbound web service in SAP GBT, and activating the integration for certain warehouses, among others. All the relevant configuration and customizations of SAP EWM integration with global batch management must be completed using the instructions found here: *http://s-prs.co/v500500*.

When the EWM system is integrated with SAP GBT, you can perform the following processes:

- Trace the different process steps of an HU, such as goods issue, good receipt, packing, unpacking, and so on.
- Trace HUs from production to purchase and from purchase to sales process in the global supply chain.
- Trace the HUs, sites, or customer to identify any bad HUs.
- Identify any HU containing a specific batch or batch number.
- Identify the content of HUs to aid users during the repacking process.

6.8 Stock Identification

Stock identification provides a way to identify stock items uniquely in a delivery. In the next sections, we'll talk about stock identification in embedded EWM, including the basic concepts, creation, and use of stock identifications in different embedded EWM processes (Figure 6.58); how stock identification can be used during warehouse request execution (Section 6.8.2); and the concept and use of stock identification splits during goods receipt and goods issue with illustrative examples (Section 6.8.3).

6.8.1 What Is Stock Identification?

Stock identification is the process in which you can uniquely identify the individual product pieces inside the warehouse for all warehouse processes. In the following sections, we explain confirmation of warehouse tasks using stock identification. The sections also explain how warehouse tasks are confirmed using stock identification.

Business Process

American company Alpha Medicals receives an order from one of its vendors based in Mexico. The order sent by the vendor requires Alpha Medicals to put away its vendor products in the proper area of the warehouse in such a way that each piece of the stock can be identified in the warehouse. Stock that will be delivered from the vendor is picked from the source goods receipt bin of the warehouse by the warehouse workers, unpacked in individual pieces, and moved to the destination bin using a unique identifier generated by the system for easy handling. It's a regular Alpha Medicals practice that individual product pieces are stored in the warehouse as well as verified and moved across the warehouse using unique identifiers. For example, individual pieces of Product ABC can be stored and moved across the warehouse using unique alphanumerical identifiers. To ensure that the embedded EWM system proposes the stock to be picked and moved around with ease, the company uses stock identification in embedded EWM.

System Process

The following explains the basic system flow, including the documents and data required to process the outbound stock picking process using stock identification for individual stock pieces in embedded EWM and decentralized EWM:

1. An outbound delivery order is created as a warehouse request in embedded EWM and contains information about the products that are to be delivered to the external customer by Alpha Medicals.
2. Picking warehouse tasks are created based on the warehouse request and assigned to the warehouse worker. The warehouse request directs the warehouse worker to move the products from the source bin to the staging area.
3. The warehouse orders are allocated to the warehouse worker. During picking of the product from the source bin, the warehouse worker picks up the stock quantity as displayed in the warehouse task.
4. The warehouse task is created by the system so that it proposes to pick and move around the product's individual pieces using stock identification.
5. After the worker picks the stock from the source bin and completes the intermediate stock movements, the stock is finally staged at the goods issue area.

> **Note**
> We've explained the system process using the outbound process only. It's equally applicable to inbound and internal stock movement processes.

It's often required to identify stock items when goods are moved into or out of the warehouse. This is achieved by configuring stock identification at the warehouse process type level by navigating to IMG path **SCM Extended Warehouse Management • Extended Warehouse Management • Cross-Process Settings • Warehouse Task • Define Warehouse Process Type**, as shown in Figure 6.58. Select the warehouse process type, click on , and enter the stock identification control value in the **Stock ID Control** field.

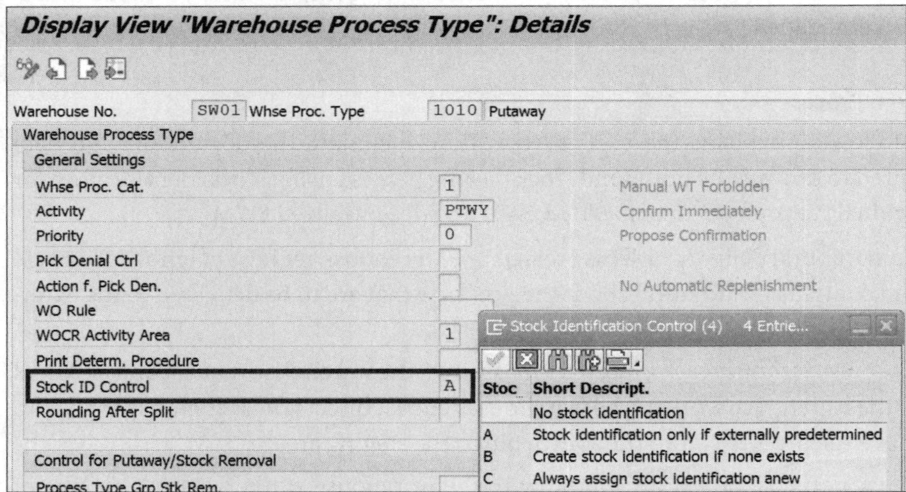

Figure 6.58 Warehouse Process Type Setting for Stock Identification

The **Stock ID Control** field has four options:

- [Blank]: **No stock identification**
  If the handling of the stock doesn't require unique identification during the goods receipt and goods issue process, make this setting blank.
- **A: Stock identification only if externally predetermined**
  If this option is selected, stock identification will only be assigned to the stock in a warehouse task if it already exists. If there's no existing stock identification, then the system creates a warehouse task with the stock identification blank.

- **B: Create stock identification if none exists**
  If this option is selected, a new stock identification will be created by embedded EWM if one doesn't exist for that stock item. If the stock already has a stock identification, it will be copied into the new warehouse task created.
- **C: Always assign stock identification anew**
  If this option is selected, a new stock identification will be created by embedded EWM even if the stock already has a stock identification assigned.

A stock identification is a unique 16-digit number that is created as a combination of the embedded EWM warehouse number and the warehouse task number. Rather than using system logic for generating stock identification numbers, you can use the `/SCWM/EX_CORE_CR_STOCK_ID` BAdI to create your own stock identification numbering.

The advantage of generating a unique stock ID in embedded EWM is that even if the stock is moved to different places in the warehouse using warehouse tasks, the stock ID remains unchanged. Thus, stock items can be uniquely identified in the warehouse during goods receipt or goods issue because the stock ID is at the stock level in embedded EWM. This number also helps keep track of the stock as it moves from one warehouse to another. The stock identification can also be printed as a barcode label for the shipping HU.

6.8.2 Using Stock Identification

Stock identifications can be used in the warehouse monitor to look for warehouse tasks and stocks. You also can work with stock identification in a work center rather than working with warehouse tasks by searching for the warehouse task based on the stock identification to move goods into and out of the work center.

When an HU is to be deconsolidated during goods receipt using Transaction /SCWM/DCONS, the warehouse task for individual products can be selected based on the stock ID. Scan the source HU, and specify the stock ID of the contained product in the **Deconsolidation** tab. Embedded EWM finds the warehouse task for the products in the HU that belong to different consolidation groups.

The same process can be used during packing in the work center using Transaction /SCWM/PACK. Select the product to be repacked using stock identification, and then the system creates warehouse tasks to move the product to another HU based on the stock ID. Similarly, while entering quality inspection results, such as usage decisions and findings, you can find the stock for which a decision is to be made using stock identifications. The stock search using stock identifications for the processes described earlier can be performed by using both SAP GUI and RF devices.

6.8.3 Using Stock Identification for Splitting Stock

If a warehouse task split occurs during the putaway and picking process, then a new stock identification is created for the split quantity, and the original warehouse task retains the original stock ID. The effect of warehouse task splits on stock identifications for both goods receipt and goods issue processes are as follows:

- **Splitting stock in goods receipt**
  As discussed in the previous section, it's possible to confirm putaway warehouse tasks for partial quantities based on stock identification. In this case, new warehouse tasks are created with new stock IDs but retain references to the original stock identification as well. Let's discuss this via a deconsolidation example, as shown in Figure 6.59.

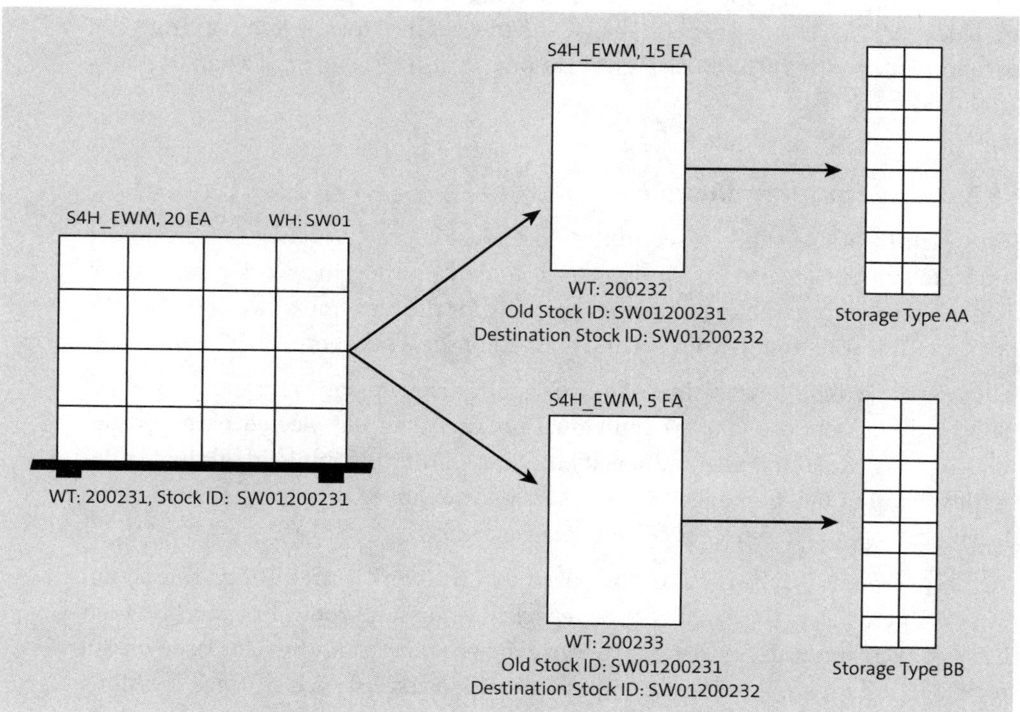

Figure 6.59 Stock Split in Goods Receipt

The warehouse receives a mixed pallet (HU) from another warehouse with 20 EA and gets stock ID SW01200231. Based on the different destinations of the products in the inbound HU, embedded EWM creates two different warehouse tasks: 4511 with six EA and 4512 with four EA. If the warehouse tasks aren't immediately confirmed, they acquire the parent HU stock ID SW01248458, as well as new destination stock IDs SW01200232 and SW01200233. As soon as the warehouse tasks are confirmed, embedded EWM transfers the target stock identification to the stock confirmed using each warehouse task.

- **Splitting stock in goods issue**
  It's also possible to split stock and create new stock identifications during the packing of stock in goods issue. In this case, new warehouse tasks are created with new stock IDs and can be used for further stock movements in the warehouse. Let's look at a repacking example, as shown in Figure 6.60.

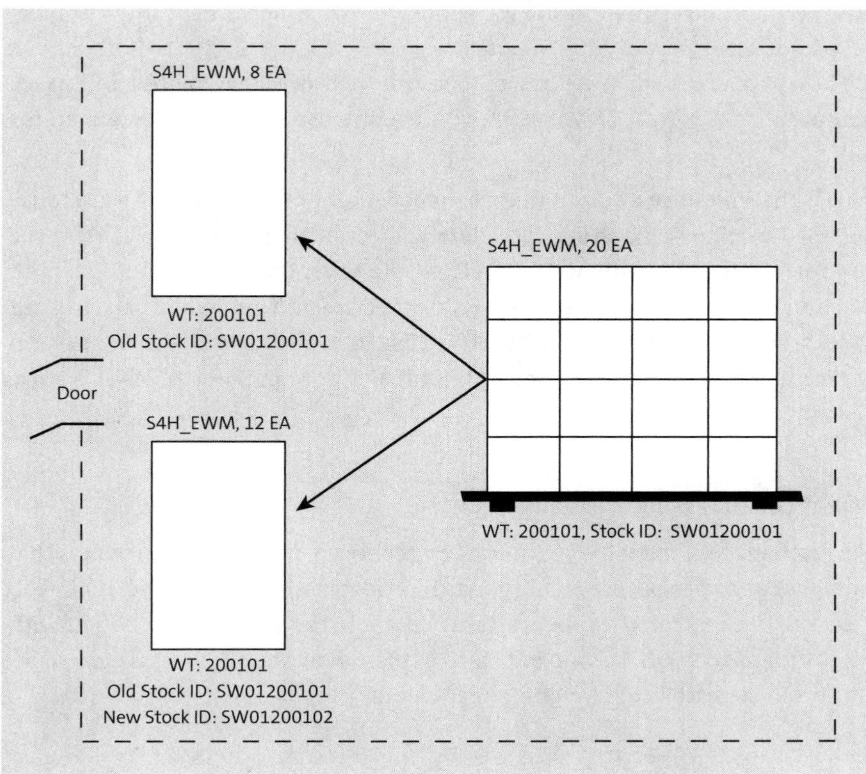

Figure 6.60 Stock Split in Goods Issue

In this example, when packing products in a work center, you need to pack 20 EA (stock ID SW01200101) of the product in an HU, but only 8 EA can be packed in it due to capacity issues. In this case, a stock split is carried out. The original warehouse task is confirmed with the quantity in the warehouse task reduced from 20 EA to 8 EA, with the original stock identification SW01200101. Due to this partial packing, a repack warehouse task is created for the remaining quantity of 12 EA and assigned to a new stock identification, SW01200102.

6.9 Catch Weight Management

Catch weight is used in the warehouse for products that change their weight due to changes in their physical characteristics with the passage of time. These products include products in the food and dairy industry such as meat, cheese, and so on. These products are thus stored in the warehouse in two independent units of measure: a *logistics UoM (LUoM)* and a *catch weight UoM*. For logistics purposes in embedded EWM, you usually use units of measure such as eaches, pieces, and so on. For valuation purposes in SAP S/4HANA, you usually use UoMs such as kilograms and pounds.

We'll discuss the influence of catch weight management on some of the warehouse processes in the following sections. Readers will recall that in SAP S/4HANA, the inventory-managed UoM is the valuation UoM. However, in embedded EWM, both the LUoM and the valuation UoM are inventory-managed. Thus, while carrying out warehouse processes such as quantity offsetting in embedded EWM, the system delivery area relates to the LUoM. For this reason, the UoM in SAP S/4HANA is automatically converted in embedded EWM.

6.9.1 What Is Catch Weight Management?

Catch weight management helps you manage warehouse processes for products that change weight over a period, especially goods that are perishable in nature. In the following sections, we explain the processes carried out in the system for products with catch weight management. The sections also explain how warehouse tasks are confirmed for products with catch weight management.

Business Process

American company Alpha Medicals receives an order from one of its customers based in Mexico. The order sent by the customer requires Alpha Medicals to provide the products in time and within proper weight limits. Stock that will be delivered to the customer is to be picked from source bins of the warehouse by the warehouse workers, packed in the required packaging material, and moved to the staging area for goods issue. As a regular Alpha Medicals practice, products are stored in the warehouse as well as verified and moved across the warehouse using not only base UoMs (BUoMs) but also AUoMs, which depict the valuations unit for the product. For example, Product ABC can be stored as well as moved across the warehouse using both BUoM and LUoM. To ensure that the embedded EWM system proposes the stock to be picked and moved around with ease, the company uses catch weight management in embedded EWM.

System Process

The following explains the basic system flow, including the documents and the data required to process outbound deliveries having catch weight products in embedded EWM and decentralized EWM:

1. An outbound delivery order is created as a warehouse request in embedded EWM that contains information about the products to be delivered to the external customer by Alpha Medicals.
2. Picking warehouse tasks are created based on the warehouse request and assigned to the warehouse worker. This warehouse request directs the warehouse worker to move the products from the source bin to the staging area but also allow the warehouse to pick the products based on LUoM.
3. The warehouse orders are allocated to the warehouse worker. During picking of the product from the source bin, the warehouse worker picks up the stock quantity as displayed in the warehouse task.
4. The warehouse task is created by the system so that it proposes to pick and move the product pieces around using LUoM.
5. After the worker picks the stock from the source bin and completes intermediate stock movements, the stock is finally staged at the goods issue area.

> **Note**
>
> We've explained the system process using the outbound process only. It's equally applicable to inbound and internal stock movement processes.

6.9.2 Master Data Changes for Catch Weight

To create a material as catch weight-relevant in embedded EWM, it's managed using two PUoMs. The two UoMs don't have a fixed conversion factor between them. When a new material is created in SAP S/4HANA, you assign it to a BUoM. As soon as a parallel PUoM is added for a product in SAP S/4HANA, it becomes catch weight-relevant. You can decide whether the BUoM or the PUoM is the valuation UoM. The LUoM is the BUoM.

A product can be made catch weight-relevant by setting the **Category of Unit of Measure** to **EWM Parallel Unit of Measure**, as shown in Figure 6.61.

Display Material S4H_MAT_03CW (Trading Goods)

Main Data

Descriptio... | Units of measure | Additional EANs | Document data | Basic data text | Inspection

Material: S4H_MAT_03CW
Descr.: S4H EWM Material

Units of measure/EANs/dimensions

X	AUn	Measure...	<=>	Y	BUn	Measure...	Category of Unit of Measure
1	EA	each	<=>	1	EA	each	Alternative Unit ...
1	KG	kg	<=>	12	EA	each	B EWM Parallel Unit
1	PAL	Pallet	<=>	48	EA	each	

Alternative Unit of Measure
B EWM Parallel Unit of Measure
C Alternative Parallel Unit of Measure

Figure 6.61 Creating Catch Weight-Managed Material in SAP S/4HANA

After a material becomes catch weight-relevant, the **Catch weight product** indicator is set in the storage type data view of the product master in embedded EWM, as shown in Figure 6.62.

You may need to restrict users from making overvalue or undervalue entries for catch weight products in logistics and parallel quantities. This can be controlled using tolerance groups, which are defined via IMG path **Integration with Other SAP Components • Extended Warehouse Management • Additional Material Attributes • Attribute Values for Additional Material Master Fields • Define Catch Weight Tolerance Groups**.

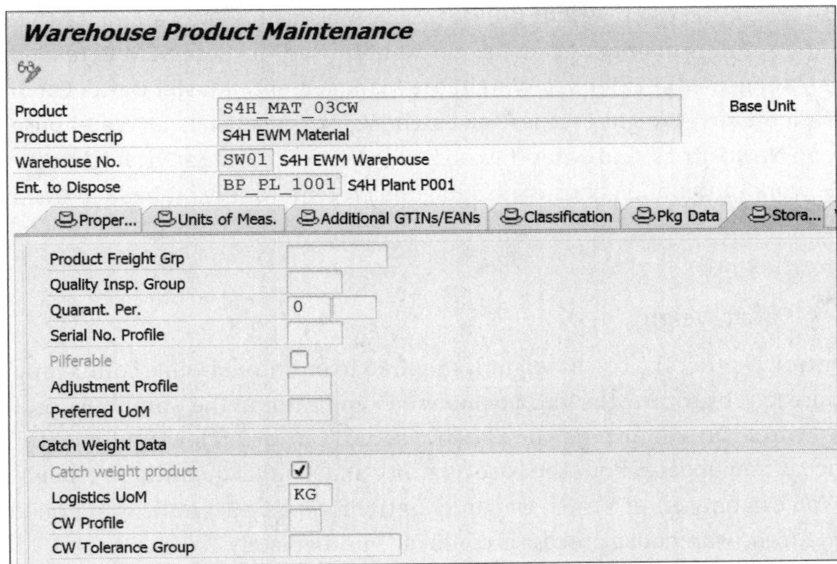

Figure 6.62 Catch Weight-Managed Product in Embedded EWM

Click on **New Entries**, enter a tolerance group, and define upper and lower tolerance values for the tolerance group. After defining the tolerance groups, you can assign them to specific products to keep a check on the quantity entered for the UoMs in the **CW Tolerance Group** field in the storage type data view of the product master.

You can also use the created tolerance groups for product levels and assign them to a warehouse number. This enables the system to choose the specified product tolerance group in the assigned warehouse. To do so, navigate to IMG path **SCM Extended Warehouse Management • Extended Warehouse Management • Master Data • Product • Catch Weight • Define Catch Weight Tolerance Groups at Warehouse Level**. Click on **New Entries**, and enter a tolerance group and lower and upper tolerance limit values for the tolerance group for the embedded EWM warehouse.

To require the system to enter a catch weight for the products during goods receipt and goods issue, as well as for work centers using a catch weight profile, navigate to IMG path **Integration with Other SAP Components • Extended Warehouse Management • Additional Material Attributes • Attribute Values for Additional Material Master Fields • Define Catch Weight Input Control**. Click on **New Entries**, enter a catch weight profile, and select the catch weight controls for the work center and goods issue and goods receipt.

You can also assign the catch weight profile to an embedded EWM warehouse that overwrites the settings maintained at the global level via IMG path **SCM Extended Warehouse Management • Extended Warehouse Management • Master Data • Catch Weight • Define Catch Weight Profiles for Catch Weight Quantities at Warehouse Level**. Click on **New Entries**, and enter the catch weight profile and catch weight controls for the work center and goods issue and goods receipt for the embedded EWM warehouse.

6.9.3 Using Catch Weight

You can control whether the catch weight is required to be entered while confirming the warehouse task by setting the **Val. Qty Input Req.** indicator in the warehouse process type settings. On confirming the warehouse task for a catch-weight-enabled product, the system updates both the base quantity and parallel quantity in embedded EWM. You can only enter a catch weight quantity for a product if the warehouse task created for the warehouse process is confirmed immediately.

Let's go over the use of catch weight in deliveries and physical inventory in embedded EWM:

- **Catch weight in delivery**
  When an inbound delivery is created in embedded EWM, it contains a delivery item with its catch weight active either in packed or unpacked form. When the goods receipt for the inbound delivery request is posted using the warehouse task, the catch weight is entered in the warehouse task during confirmation and is updated in the inbound delivery. You also can manually update the catch weight in the inbound delivery item so that the updated weight is passed to SAP S/4HANA for valuation purposes. Any differences in the catch weight are manually posted in the delivery and interfaced to the SAP S/4HANA system.

  When an outbound delivery order is being picked in embedded EWM and contains a delivery item with its catch weight active, the system adds the catch weight in the delivery based on the product master. This catch weight can vary if there is a difference in the actual quantity picked. When the goods are weighed in the work center, the actual catch weight quantity is updated in the outbound delivery order and is updated in SAP S/4HANA.
- **Catch weight in physical inventory**
  Embedded EWM supports catch weight management for catch-weight-relevant products while performing physical inventory. To execute catch-weight-based

physical inventory, it's important to define and assign physical inventory tolerance groups for difference analyzer, posting differences, and recounting in embedded EWM.

Catch weight comes into effect during processing of physical inventory documents while entering the count. When entering the count results, both the logistics quantity and catch weight quantity are entered, and both parameters can be viewed for catch weight-relevant products in the stock inventory in embedded EWM. The count for catch weight in embedded EWM can be entered using SAP GUI and RF.

It's possible to deactivate the separate entry of catch weight in embedded EWM manually while entering the count by selecting the **Entering Catch Weight Quantity Is Not Allowed** checkbox at IMG path **SCM Extended Warehouse Management • Extended Warehouse Management • Internal Warehouse Processes • Physical Inventory • Warehouse-Number-Specific Settings • Reason and Priority • Define Reason for Physical Inventory**. Set the **No CW Qty** indicator for the correct **Reason**, as shown in Figure 6.63. In such a case, the system automatically calculates the catch weight quantity by using the conversion logic between the LUoM and catch weight UoM.

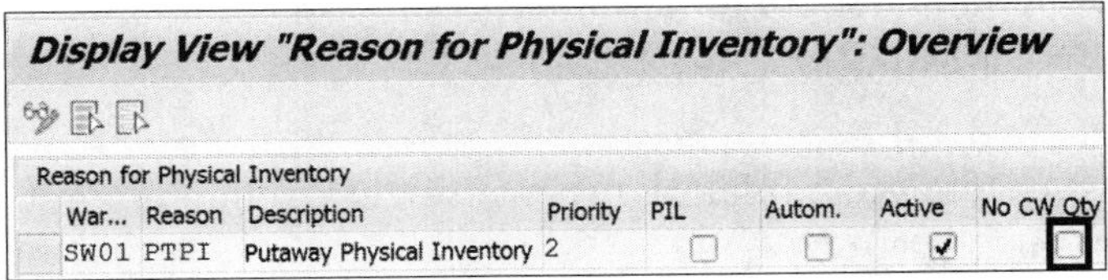

Figure 6.63 Catch Weight in Physical Inventory

When preparing to post differences, embedded EWM displays the price of the catch weight product related to the catch weight UoM, rather than the LUoM. In the difference analyzer, embedded EWM displays both LUoMs and catch weight UoMs and uses both when you post differences in stock inventory in embedded EWM.

6.10 Postprocessing Framework

Embedded EWM uses the PPF to issue outputs of documents in varying forms, such as email, print, and faxes. It can also be used to trigger follow-up actions, such as creating a new document, to trigger a BAdI, or in workflows that are event-driven. The framework can be leveraged for scheduling, triggering, and monitoring of actions based on conditions that enable asynchronous action execution. PPF can trigger various output actions in embedded EWM, such as printing, workflows, BAdIs, faxes, emails, and even method calls. These actions are triggered when specific conditions are met in the background.

The framework is used in various applications in embedded EWM, including delivery processing, shipping and receiving, HU management, physical inventory, and others. The PPF provides the flexibility to customize action scheduling and execution depending on business requirements, as follows:

- **Printing**
  The framework can be used to print embedded EWM–specific documents required for completion of warehousing operations. These include warehouse orders, physical inventory documents, bills of lading, and so on. The printing can be triggered after completion of an event, for example, printing a delivery note after goods issue is posted.
- **Interface messages**
  The PPF helps send interface messages to other SAP applications, such as SAP Transportation Management (SAP TM), SAP Global Trade Services (SAP GTS), SAP Event Management (SAP EM), and so on, as well as third-party applications using an intermediate system such as SAP Process Integration (SAP PI).
- **Workflows**
  The framework can be used to trigger workflows in processes that require approval for processing a document.
- **BAdI call**
  You may need to trigger custom functionality, such as a follow-up action, through standard embedded EWM objects. The PPF can call BAdIs and trigger the custom logic for the embedded EWM process, which enables embedded EWM to create other documents, such as waves, warehouse tasks, goods receipt/goods issue postings, and so on.

The following sections explain the PPF in embedded EWM. Section 6.10.1 explains various configurations that are crucial for the output process in embedded EWM and how embedded EWM objects can use the framework to trigger output in embedded EWM. Section 6.10.2 then walks through a sample case to demonstrate how the framework works and what it looks like in an embedded EWM object.

6.10.1 Configuring the Postprocessing Framework

Embedded EWM triggers a PPF action if scheduling conditions are met. The action can be processed immediately or scheduled for processing at a later time based on customization settings. If the action is scheduled for processing, it's executed in a background process when scheduling conditions are met. The SAP transaction to set up PPF Customizing for all applications is Transaction SPPFCADM. Some of the important settings that help trigger PPF actions across various application objects are as follows:

- **Application**
  As shown in Figure 6.64, embedded EWM provides three application areas from which PPF actions can be scheduled:
  - /SCDL/DELIVERY
    This application area defines action profiles and definitions for warehouse request documents.
  - /SCWM/WME
    This application area defines action profiles and definitions for warehouse management engines.
  - /SCWM/SHP_RCV
    This application area defines action profiles and definitions for shipping and receiving in embedded EWM.

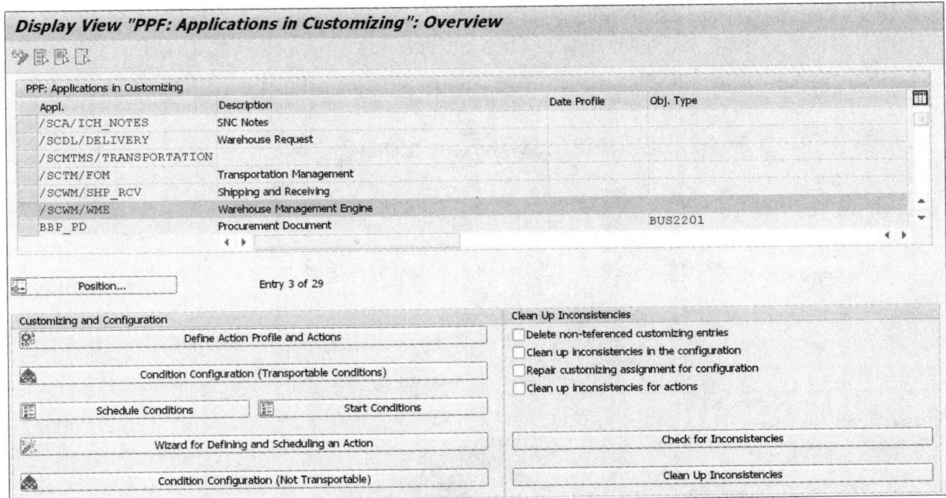

Figure 6.64 Define Applications for PPF

The PPF allows these applications to trigger actions such as generating printing, starting a workflow, sending emails, and so on. The decision about whether the action is to be triggered can be made using ABAP logic or condition logic.

- **Action profile**
  Each application object in embedded EWM is mapped to an application profile. PPF action profiles are containers that hold various action definitions and settings for the action profiles. An action profile is linked to various application objects that define all the actions that can be executed for that object. For example, for deliveries, the action profile is assigned at the document type level. The actions in an application object are only executed when appropriate conditions for them are put in place. You can use a standard profile for an object, or a new profile can be created based on business requirements.

  Action profiles for business objects in embedded EWM can be configured using Transaction SPPFCADM. It's also possible to configure the action profile for individual application objects by navigating to the respective customization paths in Transaction SPRO. For deliveries, follow IMG path **SCM Extended Warehouse Management • Extended Warehouse Management • Cross-Process Settings • Delivery-Warehouse Request • Actions • Change Actions and Conditions • Define Action Profiles and Actions.** You can set an action profile as a composite profile by selecting the **Composite Profile** indicator, or you can work on the action definitions contained in the action profile.

  Figure 6.65 shows a sample action profile, /SCWM/VASORDER, for a VAS order in application object /SCWM/WME. This object has an action definition /SCWM/PRINT_VAS to manage printing of the VAS order in embedded EWM.

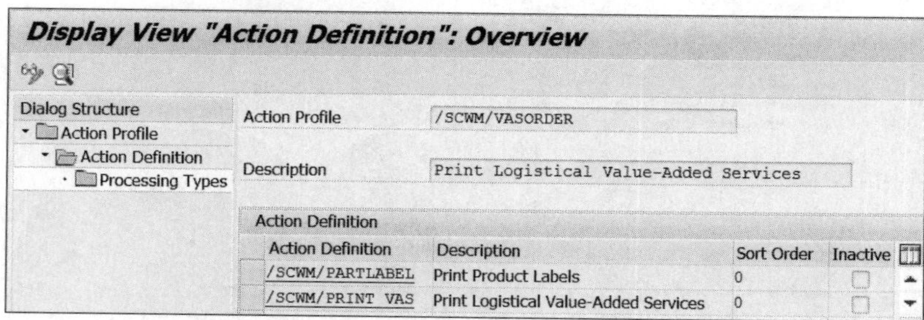

Figure 6.65 Defining the Action Profile

- **Action definition**
  Each application profile in embedded EWM has various action definitions that

contain the details of the actions that can be taken for a document when a business process is executed. The following settings control the execution of the action, as shown in Figure 6.66:

– **Processed At**
  This setting controls the time when an action is processed. The three options available in this setting are as follows:
  - **Immediate processing**
  - **Processing when saving the document**
  - **Processing using selection report**

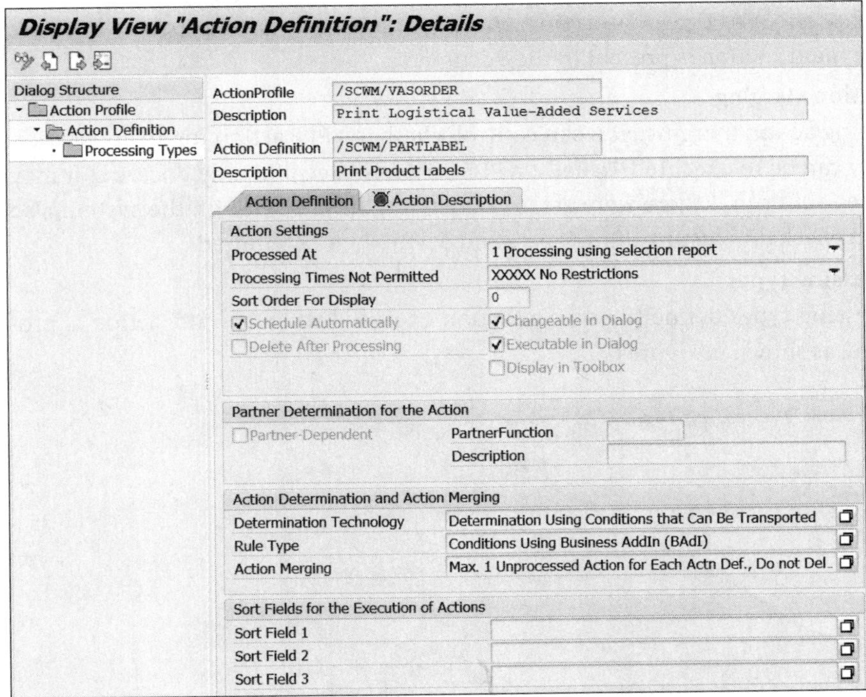

Figure 6.66 PPF Action Definition

The first setting is used only if the action needs to be executed immediately after execution of a business process; it has a direct impact on the runtime behavior of the main process. Use this option for scenarios such as printing labels after unloading so that the labels are generated immediately without any delay. The last two options trigger asynchronous execution of the PPF action. If the last option is selected, then the action is executed using a batch job with a variant created via report RSPPFPROCESS.

- **Processing Times Not Permitted**
  This option specifies when the processing of the action can be triggered, for example, whether the framework action should be executed immediately using a selection report or while saving a document.
- **Schedule Automatically**
  This indicator should always be set for an action definition; otherwise, the PPF must be triggered manually.
- **Partner-Dependent/PartnerFunction**
  It's possible to trigger an action only when a partner with a specific business partner function is present in the document.
- **Action Merging**
  Using action merging, you can control whether a PPF action for an application key can be re-executed. Usually, a PPF action is executed only once, but it may need to rerun if there were errors. Depending on the settings, the system also can check for existing PPF triggers and delete them if required.

- **Processing types**
  Processing types define the type of action executed when the PPF action is processed, as shown in Figure 6.67.

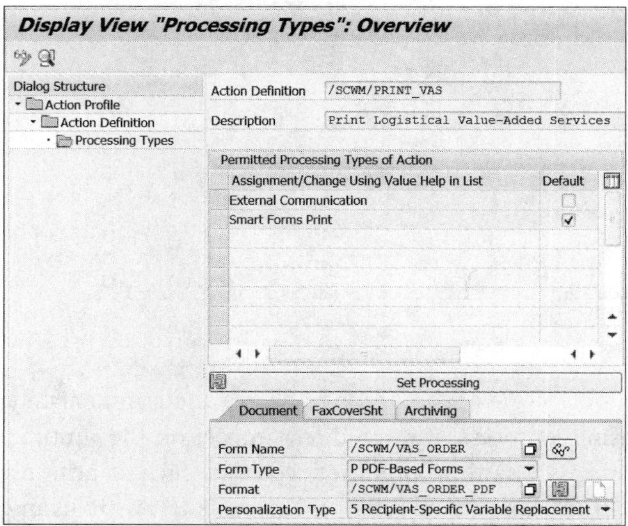

Figure 6.67 Defining the Processing Type for Action Definition

Standard processing types available in the framework include printing, emails, method calls, alerts, workflows, and so on. For method calls, corresponding methods must be assigned to the processing type, and for printing documents, the appropriate smart forms must be assigned.

- **Schedule and start conditions**
  The schedule condition and start condition are used for scheduling the execution of action definitions in embedded EWM objects. These conditions can be configured for embedded EWM objects using Transaction SPPFCADM. You also can configure the conditions for individual objects by navigating to the respective paths in Customizing. For example, for deliveries, you can define the conditions via IMG path **SCM Extended Warehouse Management • Extended Warehouse Management • Cross-Process Settings • Delivery-Warehouse Request • Actions • Define Conditions**, as shown in Figure 6.68. Click on the required **Action Definition**, and then define the **Schedule Condition** and **Start Condition**. We'll discuss these in detail next.

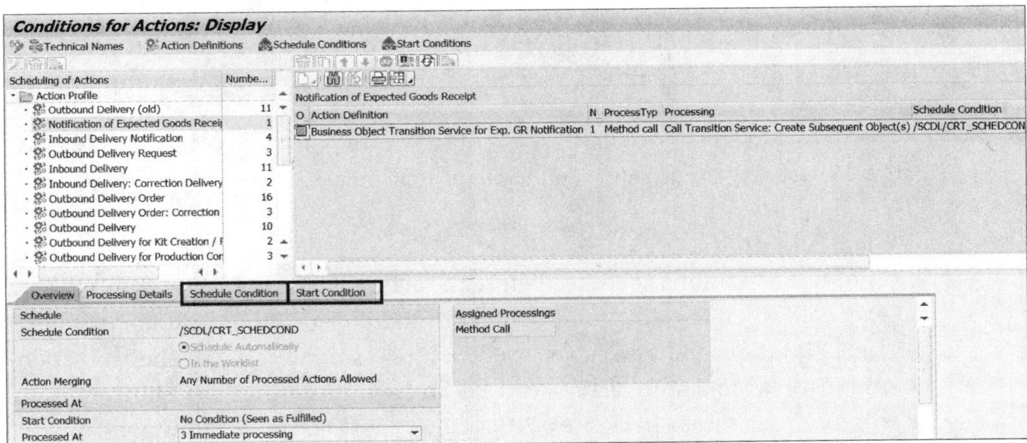

Figure 6.68 Defining Conditions for Actions

Using the schedule and start conditions, the following controls can be configured for processing actions assigned to embedded EWM objects such as deliveries, VAS orders, TUs, and so on. The conditions are as follows:

- **Schedule condition**
  The schedule condition determines whether an action should be scheduled for processing. An action is only generated if the schedule condition is met. Either a standard embedded EWM schedule condition can be used for scheduling an action in the action definition or a new schedule action can be created by editing the standard schedule condition, as shown in Figure 6.69. It's also possible to define condition parameters and values for the parameters.

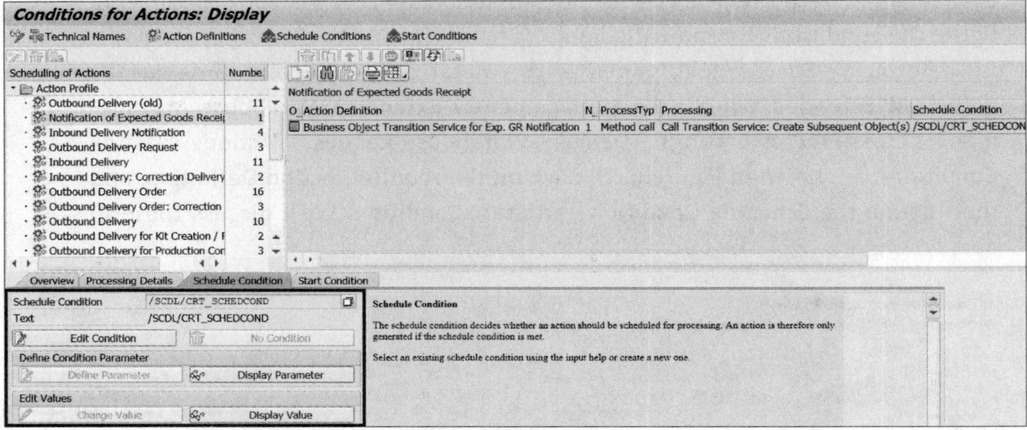

Figure 6.69 Defining the Schedule Condition for an Action

- **Start condition**
  The start condition is checked before the action is executed. The action is only executed when the start condition has been fulfilled. Either a standard embedded EWM start condition can be used for processing an action in the action definition or a new start action can be created by editing the standard start condition, as shown in Figure 6.70.

> **Note**
> If the **Schedule Automatically** checkbox is set in the action definition with the schedule condition, then the action is automatically triggered, for example, printing a warehouse order.

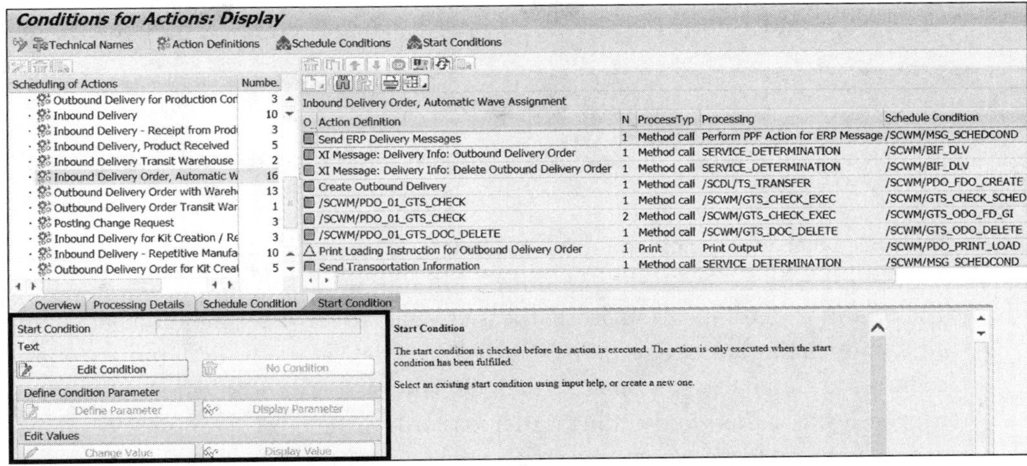

Figure 6.70 Defining Trigger Conditions for PPF Actions

- **Condition technique to schedule action definition**
  After the action profiles, definitions, and schedule/start conditions are configured for PPF output, a condition technique for activating PPF actions is configured. This is done individually for each object (e.g., delivery, HU, etc.) using PPF output. For example, you can set up a condition technique for determining action execution via IMG path **SCM Extended Warehouse Management • Extended Warehouse Management • Cross-Process Settings • Delivery—Warehouse Request • Actions • Configure Action Scheduling**. The objects listed in Table 6.5 are configured for setting up condition techniques for PPF processing.

Object	Usage
Field and field catalog	Attributes of business objects in embedded EWM used for runtime determination of conditions
Condition table	Contains field combinations used for determining a valid condition record
Access sequence	A sequence of condition tables used for determining a valid condition record
Condition type	A container containing access sequences used for determining a valid condition record

Table 6.5 Objects for Condition Technique

Object	Usage
Determination procedure	A container containing condition types used for determining a valid condition record
Condition maintenance group	Bundles condition tables and types for condition maintenance

Table 6.5 Objects for Condition Technique (Cont.)

The condition determination procedure is assigned to the determination parameter and action definition, as shown in Figure 6.71. For deliveries, the determination procedure is assigned to a combination of document category and document types. For triggering PPF actions for printing warehouse orders, the print determination procedure is assigned to the warehouse process type.

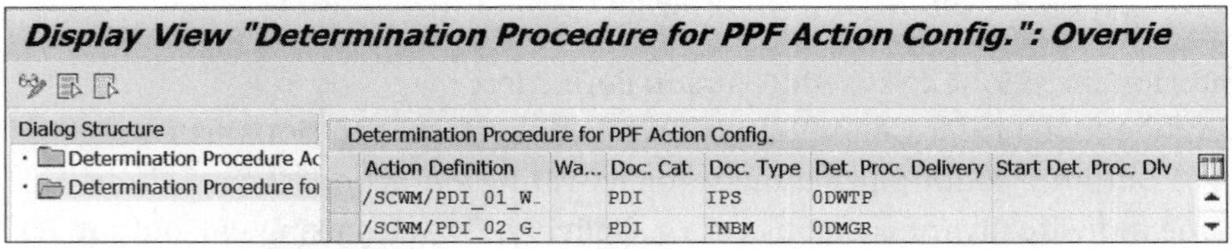

Display View "Determination Procedure for PPF Action Config.": Overvie

Dialog Structure
- Determination Procedure Ac
- Determination Procedure foi

Determination Procedure for PPF Action Config.

Action Definition	Wa...	Doc. Cat.	Doc. Type	Det. Proc. Delivery	Start Det. Proc. Dlv
/SCWM/PDI_01_W_		PDI	IPS	0DWTP	
/SCWM/PDI_02_G_		PDI	INBM	0DMGR	

Figure 6.71 Assigning the Determination Procedure to Business Object and PPF Action

> **Note**
> We've explained the PPF output configuration for embedded EWM delivery objects, but note that similar configuration can be done for other objects, such as HUs, TUs, VAS orders, and so on.

6.10.2 Postprocessing Framework Execution

When a business process is executed in embedded EWM, the system checks for all activated action definitions in an action profile and the schedule condition. If the schedule condition is met, the system checks the start condition. If the start condition is met, the PPF action is triggered, unless the **Processed At** field in the action definition is set to **Processing Using Selection Report**.

To clarify how to use the PPF in embedded EWM, let's look at an example of a PPF action triggered automatically during wave creation. As shown in Figure 6.72, as soon as the outbound delivery order is created for an outbound delivery in SAP S/4HANA, embedded EWM determines the wave relevance, valid condition record, schedule, and start condition; it then assigns a wave to the order using a PPF action. We'll discuss wave management further in Chapter 16.

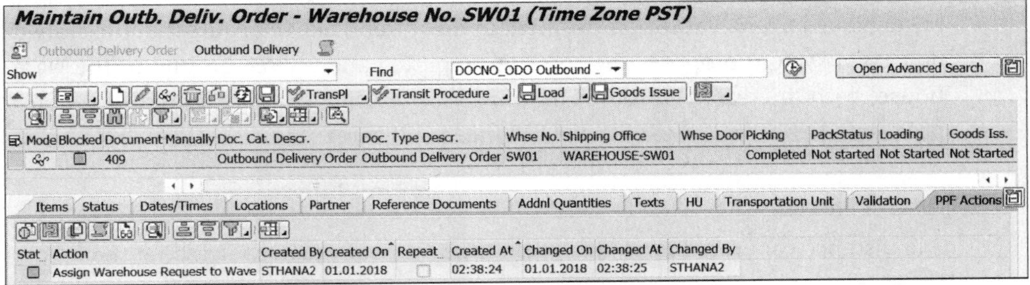

Figure 6.72 Automatic Wave Creation Using PPF for the Outbound Delivery Order

6.11 Travel Distance Calculation

A warehouse is a huge layout in which storage bins, work centers, doors, and so on can be far away from one another. A warehouse worker might have to cover some distance in the warehouse before the execution can be completed. To calculate the distance a worker in the warehouse must travel on a forklift, tugger train, or manually to complete a warehouse order, you can use travel distance calculation.

6.11.1 What Is Travel Distance Management?

Travel distance management is the process in which the distance to be traveled by warehouse resources—workers, robots, forklifts, and so on—is optimized to increase resource productivity during completion of warehouse processes. In the following sections, we explain the processes carried out in the system for travel distance calculation for work allocation. The sections also explain how travel distance management is calculated for warehouse resources and is then used for planning and warehouse order allocation to warehouse workers.

Business Process

American company Alpha Medicals receives an order from one of its customers based in Mexico. The order sent by the customer requires Alpha Medicals to provide the products in time and in proper packaging. Stock that will be delivered to the customer is to be picked from the source bins of the warehouse by the warehouse workers, packed in the required packaging material, and moved to the staging area for goods issue. As a regular Alpha Medicals practice, products are picked not only by warehouse workers manually but also using dollies, forklifts, and so on. Even robots are deployed to enable stock movement in the warehouse. To ensure that the embedded EWM system proposes the stock to be picked and moved around in the warehouse with increased resource productivity during completion of warehouse processes, the company uses travel distance management in embedded EWM.

System Process

The distance calculated is used in various business processes, including the following:

- Calculation of a planned estimate required to execute the warehouse order to plan the number of warehouse workers are required in the warehouse
- Calculating Engineered Labor Standards (ELS)
- Calculating the latest start time of a warehouse order

Because the travel distance signifies the distance in a warehouse the warehouse worker needs to travel to execute a warehouse order, it includes the time taken to go to the bin, execute the activity, and come back. The travel distance calculation involves both planning and capture of actual travel distance, as follows:

- **Planning**
  In this case, the system estimates the distance the resource must travel using the following data during creation of the warehouse order:
  - The speed of the slowest resource.
  - The default distance required to reach a storage type. This distance is defined in the **Default Distance** field in the storage type customization settings. The UoM for distance is picked from the default measures defined for the warehouse.
  - The travel network created for the warehouse, which shows all possible routes and resource type restrictions.
- **Evaluation**
  This is the actual distance traveled by a resource executing the warehouse order, which helps determine the actual values for the following parameters:
  - The speed of the resource that actually executed the warehouse order

- The distance traveled to reach the target storage bin, as calculated by the system using the last known position of the resource
- The travel network allowed for the resource

The following two methods are used for calculating travel distance for resources in embedded EWM:

- **Direct distance**
  Embedded EWM calculates travel distance based on Euclidean (point-to-point distance calculation) or Manhattan (distance calculation after following a grid-like path from source to destination bins) metrics. In the top part of Figure 6.73, the solid line represents the Euclidean method, whereas the dotted line represents the Manhattan method.
- **Distance based on network**
  If there are available networks for possible routes in the warehouse, then the system can calculate the travel distance based on the networks. (Networks are explained next.) The lower half of the screen in Figure 6.73 represents the distance calculation based on network.

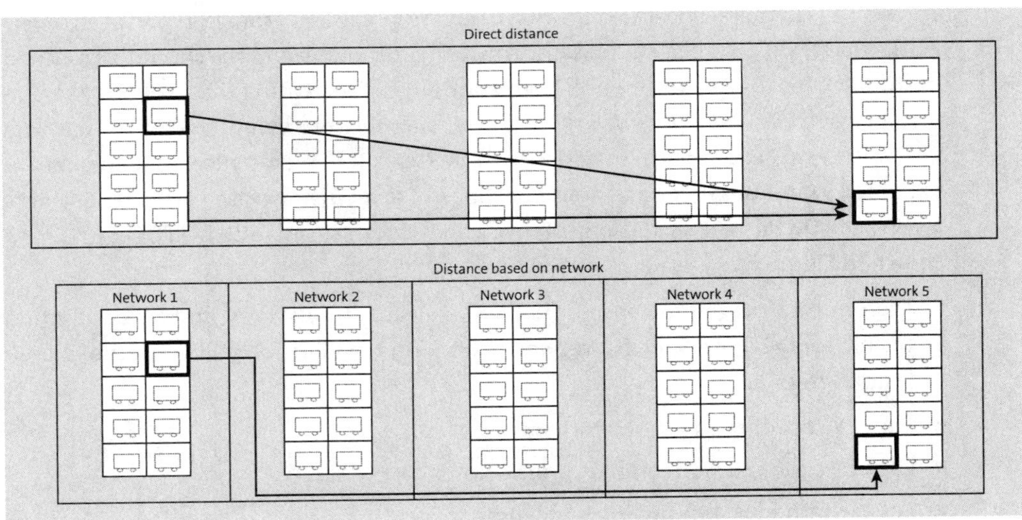

Figure 6.73 Distance Calculation Types in Travel Distance Calculation

Networks represent routes in the warehouse that a resource can take to execute warehouse processes. They provide the basic data that is used to calculate travel distances in embedded EWM. Networks consist of edges (routes) and nodes (crossings) in the warehouse. To optimize the travel distance for the worker, two types of networks are defined:

- **Storage type-specific networks**
  These networks are created specifically for each storage type based on the spatial arrangement of bins in the storage type. Storage type networks consist of edges mapping individual aisles and are also used for connecting aisles to one another. Each storage bin should be assigned to one of the following:
  - An edge if the bins are located in the same aisle and an edge exists for the aisle
  - A node that matches the geometric coordinates of the storage bin and is close to a node if isn't assigned to an edge
- **Global networks**
  Global networks are created by connecting multiple storage-type-specific networks with each other. While traversing from one bin to another, if no storage type-specific network exists, then the global network connects the bins directly.

6.11.2 Settings for Travel Distance Calculation

The settings in this section are required to create global and storage-type-specific networks for travel distance calculation. The XYZ coordinates of bins should be defined in storage bins for the warehouse. Define the edges for creating the network, average distance between storage type and resource, and network validity per resource type via **SAP Easy Access** path **Logistics • SCM Extended Warehouse Management • Extended Warehouse Management • Settings • Travel Distance Calculation • Settings for Travel Distance Calculation,** or by using Transaction /SCWM/TDC_SETUP, as shown in Figure 6.74.

For defining a storage-type-specific network, select a storage type, and click on **Define Edges in Storage-Type-Specific Networks**. Click on **New Entries**, and enter the following parameters:

- X and Y coordinates for network start and end
- Edge direction (unidirectional, bidirectional)
- Edge length in warehouse unit of length
- Any resource type excluded for the edge

For defining global networks, select a storage type, and click on **Define Edges in Global Network**. Click on **New Entries**, and enter the following parameters:

- X and Y coordinates for edge start and end
- Edge direction (unidirectional, bidirectional)
- Edge length in warehouse unit of length
- Any resource type excluded for the edge

Display View "Average Distance of Resource to Storage Type": Overview

Dialog Structure
- Average Distance of Resource to Storage Type
  - Define Edges in Storage-Type-Specific Networks
    - Excluded Resource Types per Edge
- Define Edges in Global Network
  - Excluded Resource Types per Edge
- Network Validity per Resource Type

Average Distance of Resource to Storage Type

Wa...	Sto...	Default Distance	Unit
SW01	0010	0,000	M
SW01	0020	0,000	M
SW01	0021	0,000	M
SW01	0030	0,000	M
SW01	0040	0,000	M
SW01	0050	0,000	M

Figure 6.74 Defining Network Settings for Travel Distance Calculation

Embedded EWM also allows generation of the storage-type-specific network using a report via **SAP Easy Access** path **Logistics • SCM Extended Warehouse Management • Extended Warehouse Management • Settings • Travel Distance Calculation • Generate Network**. Enter the warehouse number and storage type for which the network is to be created, and click on [Execute].

As shown in Figure 6.75, for a warehouse and storage type, the system can generate the network by executing the report. Two scenarios are possible:

- **Generate network with aisles only**
  If the **Aisles Edges Only** checkbox is selected, then embedded EWM creates a network with aisles only.
- **Generate complete network**
  If the **Aisles Edges Only** checkbox isn't selected, then embedded EWM creates a complete network by creating the aisle and connecting edges.

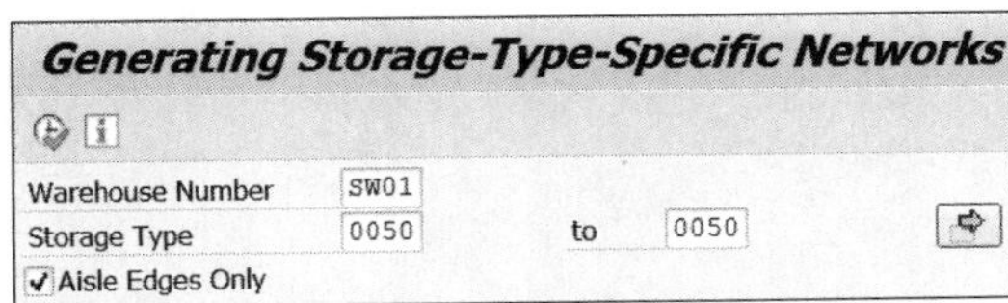
Generating Storage-Type-Specific Networks

Warehouse Number: SW01
Storage Type: 0050 to 0050
☑ Aisle Edges Only

Figure 6.75 Generating the Network by Executing the Report

6.11.3 Travel Distance Calculation

Travel distance is determined in embedded EWM for a group of storage bins. The group of storage bins is determined from the warehouse order creation rule, which also provides the sequence in which the bins are processed.

You can calculate both the horizontal and vertical distance traveled to access a bin. It's assumed that the resource travels the horizontal distance first and then the vertical distance. The total distance calculated is the sum of horizontal and vertical distances traveled. The total vertical distance traveled is twice the distance required to reach the Z coordinate of the bin to incorporate the distance traveled by the resource to reach the bin and come back. The horizontal distance is the total horizontal distance traveled in the warehouse and is influenced by the following factors:

- **Direct distance between bins**
  Calculate the distance between the bins within the storage types or the distance between bins in an aisle. It can also be the distance between bins in different storage types if no storage-type-specific network exists.
- **Distance between bin and network node**
  Calculate the distance between a storage bin and the nearest node by using either of the two cases to identify the node for the storage bin. Use the nearest node of the storage-type-specific network or the global network if the former doesn't exist and if no edge has been assigned to the storage bin. Use the node of an edge if the storage bin is in an aisle and an edge exists for the aisle.
- **Distance within a network**
  Calculate the distance traveled between storage bins in different aisles in a storage-type-specific network or in different storage types with valid global networks.

In Figure 6.76, a resource requires picking from three storage bins—A, B, and C—in a storage type. Four options are available to calculate the total distance required to be traveled to complete the picking. The system uses Option 1 because it requires the least time to complete the picking.

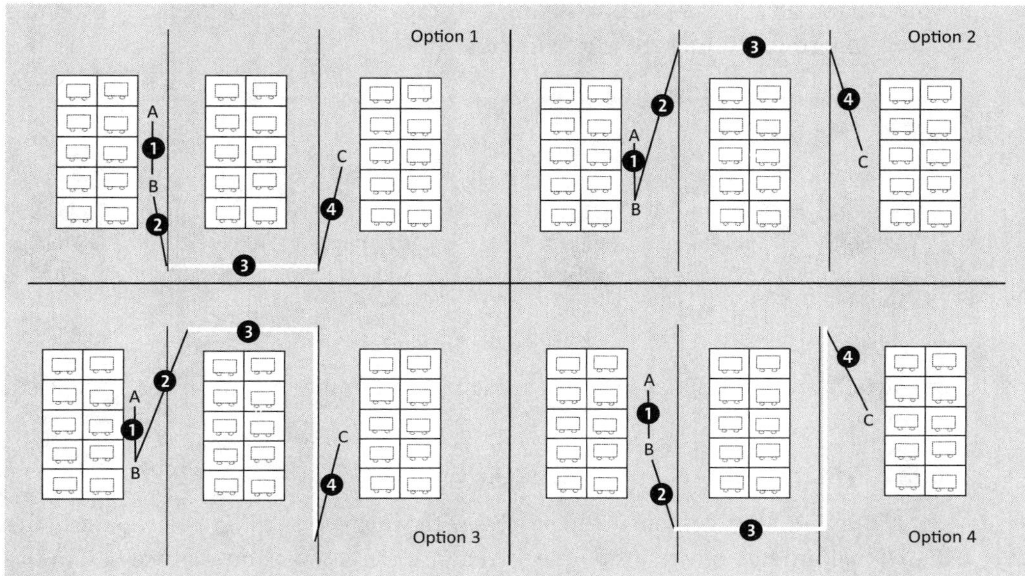

Figure 6.76 Travel Distance Calculations

6.12 Serial Number Management

Serial numbers are unique numbers assigned to materials in the warehouse to differentiate different units of the same material. Serial numbers help track parts in and out of the warehouse. An organization can use serial numbers on parts being used to assemble an end product to keep a track of which parts have gone into the assembly of which end product, for example, a compressor in a refrigerator or a fan blade in an engine. If serial numbers are managed at the inventory management (IM) level in the warehouse, then serial numbers can stand for the product in the storage bin and can be used to track products in a storage bin. Serial numbers may be required and used in following cases:

- If a logistics service provider damages a pallet during transportation, embedded EWM can track the part in the pallet using the serial number on the part packed in that pallet.
- The location of a part in the warehouse can be tracked using its serial number.
- During a customer return, the serial number can be used to verify if the same product was supplied to the customer.

- For manufacturing defects, serial numbers can be used to track the faulty products and identify customers to whom it was sold.

Tip

Embedded EWM allows users to use serial numbers with a maximum of 30 characters, but the maximum length of serial numbers in SAP S/4HANA is 18 characters. Therefore, if it's a business requirement to perform mapping between SAP S/4HANA and embedded EWM serial numbers, you can do so with BAdI `/SCWM/EX_ERP_SN` (Converting Serial Numbers ERP–EWM).

In the following sections, we'll walk through serial number management.

6.12.1 What Is Serial Number Management?

Serial number management is the process with which you can uniquely identify the individual product pieces inside the warehouse for all warehouse processes. In the following sections, we explain the processes carried out in systems for products using serial number management for identification of individual pieces. The sections also explain how warehouse tasks are confirmed for products using serial number management for identification of individual pieces.

Business Process

American company Alpha Medicals receives an order from one of its vendors based in Mexico. The order sent by the vendor requires Alpha Medicals to put away its vendor products in the proper area of the warehouse in such a way that each piece of the stock can be identified in the warehouse. Stock that will be delivered from the vendor is picked from the source goods receipt bin of the warehouse by the warehouse workers, unpacked in individual pieces, and moved to the destination bin using unique serial numbers generated by the system for easy handling. As a regular Alpha Medicals practice, individual product pieces are stored in the warehouse, verified, and moved across the warehouse using unique identifiers. For example, individual pieces of Product XYZ can be stored and moved across the warehouse using unique serial numbers. To ensure that the embedded EWM system proposes the stock to be picked and moved around with ease, the company uses serial number management in embedded EWM.

System Process

The following points explain the basic system flow, including the documents and data required to process the outbound stock picking process using serial numbers for individual stock pieces:

1. An outbound delivery order is created as a warehouse request in embedded EWM and contains information about the product that will be delivered to the external customer by Alpha Medicals.
2. Picking warehouse tasks are created based on the warehouse request and assigned to the warehouse worker. The warehouse request directs the warehouse worker to move the products from the source bin to the staging area.
3. The warehouse orders are allocated to the warehouse worker. During picking of the product from the source bin, the warehouse worker picks up the stock quantity as displayed in the warehouse task.
4. The warehouse task is created by the system so that it proposes to pick and move the product's individual pieces around using serial numbers.
5. After the worker picks the stock from the source bin and completes the intermediate stock movements, the stock is finally staged at the goods issue area.

Note

We've explained the system process using outbound process only. It's equally applicable to inbound and internal stock movement processes.

6.12.2 Serial Number Profile

A serial number profile is a four-digit identifier that determines the controls based on which serial numbers are allocated to each unit of the product. After the serial number profile is defined, it's assigned to the material master data in SAP S/4HANA. The serial number profile assigned to the material master in SAP S/4HANA is a warehouse-independent serial number profile, and the same appears in the **Storage** tab view of the product master in embedded EWM. As shown in Figure 6.77, warehouse-independent serial number profiles are defined via IMG path **Integration with Other SAP Components • Extended Warehouse Management • Additional Material Attributes • Attribute Values for Additional Material Master Fields • Define Serial Number Profile**. Click on **New Entries**, enter the serial number profile identifier and serial number control parameters, and save.

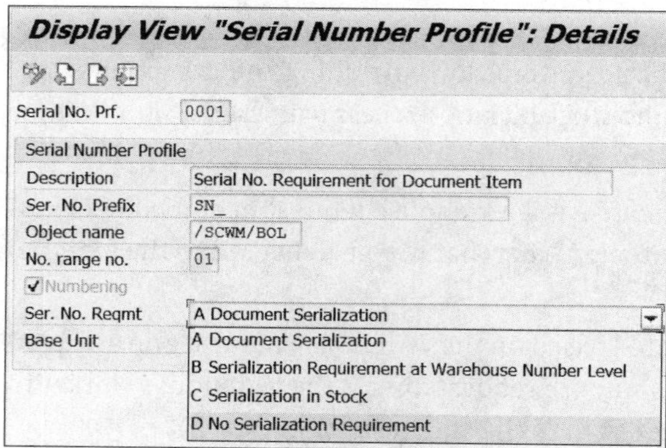

Figure 6.77 Defining the Warehouse-Independent Serial Number Profile

You can also define a warehouse-dependent serial number profile in embedded EWM. The system first looks for a warehouse-dependent serial number profile, and if it doesn't find one, it assigns the warehouse-independent serial number profile in the product master. Warehouse-dependent serial number profiles are defined via IMG path **SCM Extended Warehouse Management • Extended Warehouse Management • Master Data • Product • Define Serial Number Profiles • Define Warehouse-Number Dependent Serial Number Profiles**, as shown in Figure 6.78.

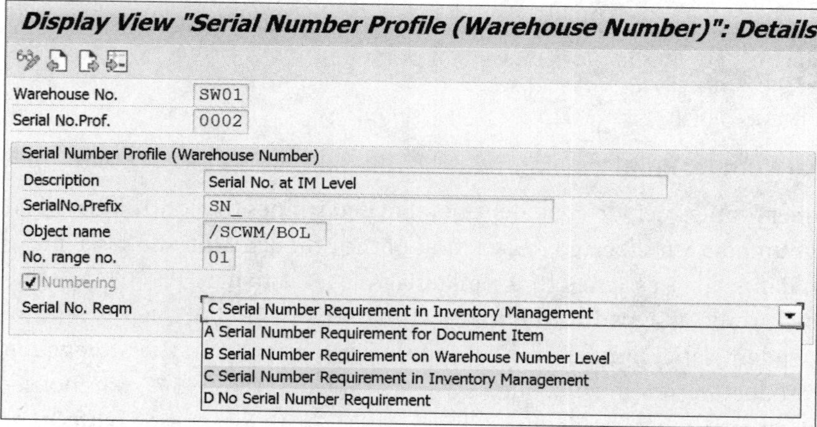

Figure 6.78 Defining the Warehouse-Dependent Serial Number Profile

Example

In Figure 6.77 and Figure 6.78, we've created warehouse-independent serial number profile 0001. The same is assigned to the material master in SAP S/4HANA. However, if we assign warehouse-dependent serial number profile 0002 for warehouse SW01, the same serial number profile will appear in the product master in embedded EWM.

The following customization settings are available while defining warehouse-dependent serial number profiles:

- **Description**
  This placeholder contains the description of the serial number profile being defined at this node.
- **SerialNo. Prefix**
  The setting is used to add a predefined prefix to serial numbers created in embedded EWM.

Example

The number range interval 01 for serial numbers is defined from 2000 to 3000, and a company wants to add SN_ as a prefix, as shown in Figure 6.78. Embedded EWM will create serial numbers SN_2000, SN_2001, and so on.

- **Object name/No. range no.**
  Embedded EWM allows you to use the number range defined for another object for allocating the serial numbers to serialized material.
- **Numbering**
  By setting this checkbox, you allow automatic numbering if embedded EWM is to continue counting from the last allocated serial number.
- **Ser. No. Reqmt**
  A warehouse can have different requirements for the level to which serial number creation and tracking is required. The serial number requirement can be set up at three levels, depending on the usage of the serial number: document item, warehouse, and IM levels. We'll discuss these in detail in the next section.

> **Note**
>
> To define warehouse-dependent serial numbers in embedded EWM, you must define a warehouse-independent serial number profile. After the warehouse-independent serial number profile is defined, it can be extended with warehouse-specific features for the required warehouse to create the warehouse-dependent serial number profile.

6.12.3 Serial Number Requirements

After the serial number profile is defined based on the requirements of the serial numbers of the product items in the warehouse, the following serial number requirements are set up:

- **Serial numbers at the document item level**
  You may need to use serial numbers in certain business processes only. For example, it may be required to document serial numbers in customer returns. By ensuring serial numbers at the document item level, embedded EWM can check if the piece being received into the warehouse through a return delivery is the same piece that was delivered to the customer.

  While processing the inbound/outbound delivery in embedded EWM, the system determines the serial number profile and deduces that serial numbers are required at the document item level. For inbound delivery, either the serial numbers are received as part of an advanced shipping notification (ASN), or they can be entered manually or through RF scanning during warehouse task confirmation or at a work center, after which goods receipt is posted for the delivery.

  As shown in Figure 6.79, serial numbers for inbound delivery items can be displayed in the **Serial Numbers** tab of the inbound delivery. In the outbound process, before goods issue, serial numbers are entered manually or through RF scanning for the picked parts during warehouse task confirmation or at the work center, and then goods issue is posted. The serial numbers are then communicated to the delivery in SAP S/4HANA as well. After goods receipt or goods issue is completed, you can work on the product in the warehouse as if it's nonserialized.

  In Customizing, you can specify whether serial numbers are optional or mandatory for delivery item types for document-level serialization via IMG paths, **SCM Extended Warehouse Management • Extended Warehouse Management • Goods**

Receipt Process • Inbound Delivery • Define Item Types for Inbound Delivery Process and **SCM Extended Warehouse Management • Extended Warehouse Management • Goods Issue Process • Outbound Delivery • Define Item Types for Outbound Delivery Process**. Select the outbound delivery item type, click on , and then set the indicator for **Serialization**.

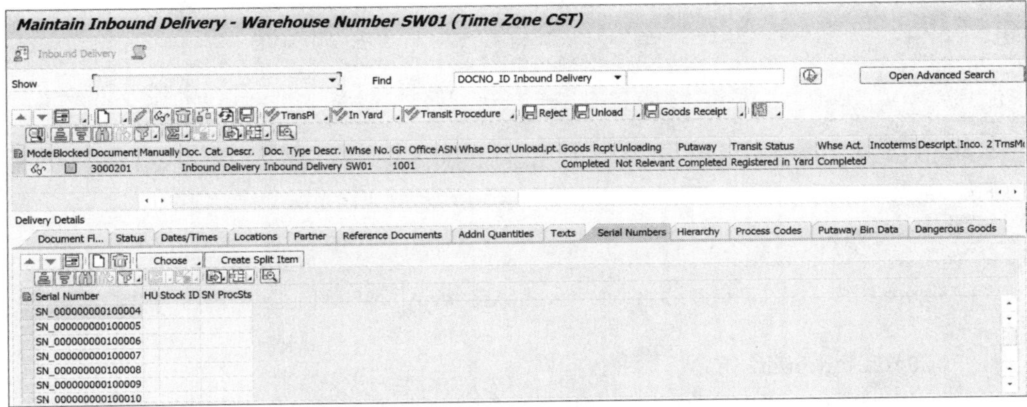

Figure 6.79 Serial Numbers at the Document Item Level

- **Serial numbers at the warehouse number level**
  You may also need to use serial numbers for tracking parts in the warehouse during goods receipt and goods issue. The serial numbers in this case aren't stored at the bin level but only at the warehouse level. The serial numbers at the warehouse level can be viewed in the embedded EWM warehouse monitor via node **Stock and Bin • Serial Number On Whse Level**, as shown in Figure 6.80.

  You'll need to enter a serial number while processing a goods receipt/goods issue. While processing an inbound/outbound delivery in embedded EWM, the system determines the serial number profile and deduces that the serial numbers are required at the warehouse level. The serial numbers are entered while confirming the warehouse task or at the work center. If you're working with provisional serial numbers, they should be replaced with actual serial numbers before goods receipt or goods issue can be completed. The system doesn't ask for serial numbers during internal warehouse processes if the serial number requirement type is set at the warehouse level.

Warehouse Management Monitor SAP - Warehouse Number SW01

Show Hidden Nodes

- Receiving Overview
- Processes
- Physical Inventory
  - Count Overview
  - Difference Overview
  - Physical Inventory Documents
  - Physical Inventory Progress
- Documents
- Stock and Bin
  - Storage Bin
  - Fixed Bin Overview
  - Physical Stock
  - Available Stock
  - Stock Overview
  - BBD/SLED Overview
  - Stock Not In Pref. UoM
  - Resource
  - Handling Unit
  - Transport Unit (Stock View)
  - Serial Number On Whse Level

Serial Number On Whse Level

Product	Serial Number	Del.Assgmt	Cat	Doc. No.	Item	HU	Created By	Created On	Created At	Counter
S4H_MAT_SN3	SN_000000000100014	A	PDI	3000203	10		DEMO	07.01.2018	12:17:22	
S4H_MAT_SN3	SN_000000000100015	A	PDI	3000203	10		DEMO	07.01.2018	12:17:22	
S4H_MAT_SN3	SN_000000000100016	A	PDI	3000203	10		DEMO	07.01.2018	12:17:22	
S4H_MAT_SN3	SN_000000000100017	A	PDI	3000203	10		DEMO	07.01.2018	12:17:22	
S4H_MAT_SN3	SN_000000000100018	A	PDI	3000203	10		DEMO	07.01.2018	12:17:22	
S4H_MAT_SN3	SN_000000000100019	A	PDI	3000203	10		DEMO	07.01.2018	12:17:22	
S4H_MAT_SN3	SN_000000000100020	A	PDI	3000203	10		DEMO	07.01.2018	12:17:22	
S4H_MAT_SN3	SN_000000000100021	A	PDI	3000203	10		DEMO	07.01.2018	12:17:22	
S4H_MAT_SN3	SN_000000000100022	A	PDI	3000203	10		DEMO	07.01.2018	12:17:22	
S4H_MAT_SN3	SN_000000000100023	A	PDI	3000203	10		DEMO	07.01.2018	12:17:22	
										10

Figure 6.80 Serial Numbers at the Warehouse Level in Warehouse Monitor

- **Serial numbers in IM**
  To use serial numbers for tracking parts in the warehouse at the bin level, set the serial number requirement at the IM level in Customizing for the serial number profile. The serial numbers at the IM level can be viewed in the embedded EWM warehouse monitor in the **Stock and Bin • Serial Number On Whse Level** node hierarchy, as shown in Figure 6.81.

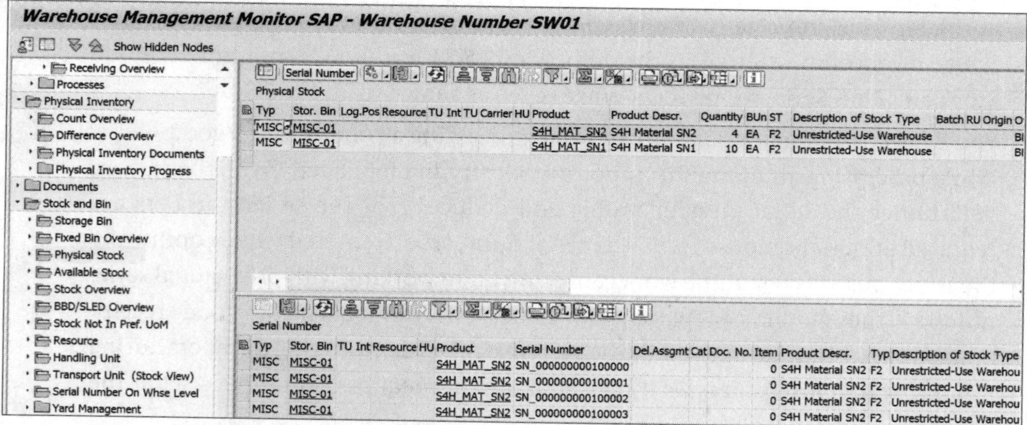

Figure 6.81 Serial Numbers at IM Level in Warehouse Monitor

While processing the inbound/outbound or internal warehouse movements in embedded EWM, the system determines the serial number profile and deduces that the serial numbers are required at the IM level. The serial numbers are entered while confirming the warehouse task or at the work center. If you're working with provisional serial numbers, they should be replaced with actual serial numbers before goods receipt or goods issue can be completed. While executing physical inventory documents, the serial numbers are entered while entering the count in the system.

6.12.4 Provisional Serial Numbers

Provisional serial numbers are 30-character strings that begin with a dollar sign ($). They're automatically assigned by the system to products requiring serial numbers in embedded EWM. The system expects the presence of serial numbers before goods receipt or goods issue posting if the serialization level is set at the warehouse or IM level. You replace these provisional numbers with actual serial numbers upon completion of putaway in embedded EWM. Provisional serial numbers can be activated for the warehouse via IMG path **SCM Extended Warehouse Management • Extended Warehouse Management • Master Data • Product • Define Serial Number Profiles • Serial Numbers: Settings for Warehouse Number,** by setting the **Prov. SNs** indicator.

Example

It may be required to unload and post goods receipt for a truckload of deliveries without specifying serial numbers because the goods are packed in an HU, and the actual serial numbers are known only when the pallet is opened. This can be done using provisional serial numbers despite the serialization requirement set at the warehouse or IM level. The actual serial numbers are provided later in the goods receipt process, either during repacking or deconsolidation.

6.12.5 Using Serial Numbers

Serial numbers can be provided directly in deliveries created in embedded EWM, at the time of warehouse task confirmation, or in the work center, depending on business process requirements. The various ways in which serial numbers are added in the deliveries and warehouse tasks and monitored in embedded EWM are as follows:

- **In deliveries**
  Embedded EWM assigns the serial numbers to the delivery items of the delivery document. If serial numbers are specified in the inbound or outbound delivery created in SAP S/4HANA, the same are copied into the warehouse request document created in embedded EWM. If serial numbers are provided during packing of the delivery items in an HU in a work center, these serial numbers become available at the item-level-detail in the inbound delivery. The serial numbers can be printed along with the delivery note. If no serial numbers are assigned to the distributed delivery in embedded EWM, provide the serial numbers manually depending on the serial number profile settings. In the inbound process, embedded EWM copies the serial number in inbound deliveries created in the SAP S/4HANA system. Any duplicate serial numbers are ignored. The serial numbers can be changed in the inbound delivery for both products and HUs before goods receipt is posted.

  In the outbound process, embedded EWM lets you capture the serial numbers in the outbound delivery order created in SAP S/4HANA in multiple ways. If no serial numbers are sent from the delivery in SAP S/4HANA, you can enter the serial numbers during manual or RF-based warehouse task confirmation. Alternatively, you can enter serial numbers directly in the outbound delivery order if no warehouse task exists as soon as the goods movement bin is determined in the outbound delivery order.

- **In warehouse tasks**
  A serial number is entered either while creating or confirming the warehouse task for inbound, outbound, or internal warehouse processes, depending on the requirement type set in the serial number profile. This also helps identify the missing serial numbers during picking, packing, and putaway; apply appropriate exception codes; and take follow-up actions.

  As shown in Figure 6.82, serial numbers for the warehouse task are entered in the **Serial Number** tab in the warehouse task confirmation screen. Quantity differences and corresponding serial numbers for missing items can be listed in the same screen. While confirming the putaway warehouse tasks, provisional serial numbers are replaced with valid serial numbers. For picking, serial numbers for the picking warehouse task must be entered either manually or using RF scanners. If task confirmation is done in the background, the system automatically populates the serial numbers, provided it can identify them.

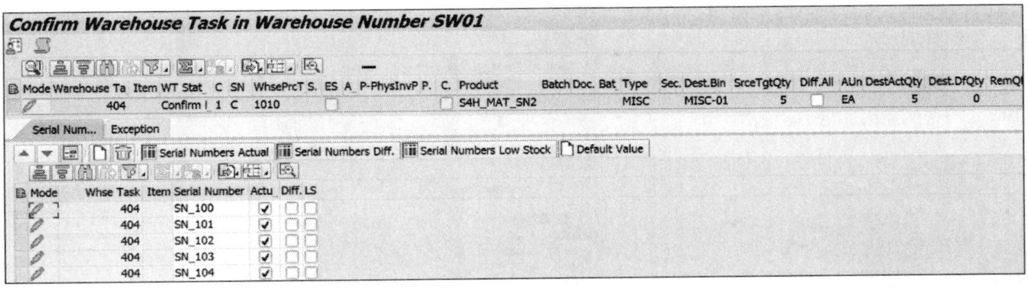

Figure 6.82 Inserting Serial Numbers during Warehouse Task Confirmation

- **Predetermined serial numbers**
  In embedded EWM, it's possible to work with predetermined serial numbers in an outbound delivery order replicated to embedded EWM when the outbound delivery is sent from SAP S/4HANA. For inbound delivery, predetermined serial numbers can be replicated to embedded EWM as part of an ASN sent to embedded EWM, which can be confirmed by the system during the putaway task confirmation.

  For the inbound process, predetermined serial numbers can be overridden in embedded EWM; no change is allowed in the outbound process. If the EWM system can't find serial numbers for the outbound delivery, it triggers pick denial for the unavailable serial numbers and flags unconfirmed serial numbers as invalid. No picking task is created for these invalid serial numbers in embedded EWM. When you check the outbound delivery orders in Transaction /SCWM/PRDO, the serial numbers that couldn't be picked can be seen marked as **Invalid**.

  Embedded EWM splits the warehouse tasks for an outbound delivery order if the requested quantity exceeds the capacity of the warehouse order creation rule. The system creates a second task for the excess amount and reassigns the predetermined serial numbers in accordance with the split of the outbound delivery quantity.

- **In work centers**
  As shown in Figure 6.83, serial numbers can be assigned at a work center for HU items either manually or using RF. For example, if the external vendor didn't send serial numbers for the items in the HU received in the warehouse, then goods receipt can be posted for a complete HU, and serial numbers can be assigned to items in the HU while unpacking it in the work center.

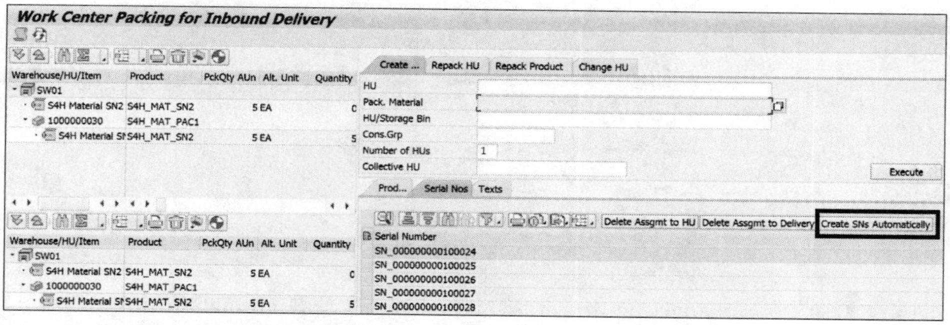

Figure 6.83 Assigning Serial Numbers to Products in the Work Center

To enable the assignment of serial numbers in the work center, set the **Assign SNs** and **Assign SNs to Deliv.** indicators in the scanner area view of the work center layout and the **Serial Nos** indicator in the detail area view of the work center layout via IMG path **SCM Extended Warehouse Management • Extended Warehouse Management • Master Data • Work Center • Define Work Center Layout.**

- **In warehouse monitor**
  Serial numbers can be displayed in the embedded EWM warehouse monitor using Transaction /SCWM/MON if the serialization level for the product is set at the warehouse level or the IM level. For the products with serialization at the IM level, relevant information about serial numbers can be accessed from the **Stock and Bin • Physical Stock on EWM Monitor** node. After the physical stock is displayed, you can select the stock row and double-click to display the serial numbers at the bottom screen area. This is because serial numbers are stored at the quant level in the storage bin. For the products with serialization at the warehouse level, relevant information about serial numbers can be accessed from the **Stock and Bin • Serial Number On Whse Level** node.

  The **Serial Number** tab for the serialized stock in the embedded EWM warehouse monitor shows information such as serial number movements, current location/HU of a specified serial number, serial number query, and display of serial numbers for confirmed warehouse tasks (for RF).

- **In RF**
  Embedded EWM supports serial numbers in RF for the following processes:
  - Deconsolidation
  - Putaway
  - Picking
  - Packing

After a serial number requirement is added to a product, embedded EWM displays the placeholder to enter the serial numbers in the RF screen when the **SNum** button is clicked. Serial numbers can be added manually or through a barcode scan. Serial numbers added for the product either can be overridden using a rescan of a barcode or deleted by clicking the **Del** button.

For predetermined serial numbers, after the delivery is selected in the RF environment, embedded EWM displays the predetermined serial numbers in the warehouse tasks. For outbound delivery, these are presented in a nonchangeable format. They can be confirmed either for complete or partial quantities of the outbound delivery order. If the quantity being confirmed in the outbound delivery is different from the requested quantity by applying exception code DIFW, then you can enter the required number of serial numbers after quantity adjustment in RF. After the serial numbers are adjusted, embedded EWM makes a posting change for these selected serial numbers in embedded EWM and updates the delivery in SAP S/4HANA.

6.12.6 Item Unique Identification (US Department of Defense)

To facilitate unique identification of each piece of equipment in a warehouse for different warehouse operations, SAP provides a feature in which item unique identification (IUID) can be assigned to each piece of equipment being received in a warehouse. It's particularly important for the US Department of Defense for equipment identification.

To ensure IUID can be activated and consumed for equipment identification in embedded EWM, the following configurations must be made in the system:

1. As shown in Figure 6.84, IUID can be selected for equipment identification by activating it for the serial number profile in SAP S/4HANA via IMG path **Integration with Other SAP Components • Extended Warehouse Management • Additional Material Attributes • Attribute Values for Additional Material Master Fields • Define Serial Number Profile**. Select the **IUID Active** checkbox.
2. With this selected, it becomes mandatory for users to enter IUID for serialized materials in all warehouse processes. If you want to make it optional, you can use the `/SCWM/EX_UII_OPTIONAL` (Set IUID Optional) BAdI with the `CHANGE_IUID_ACTIVE` method.

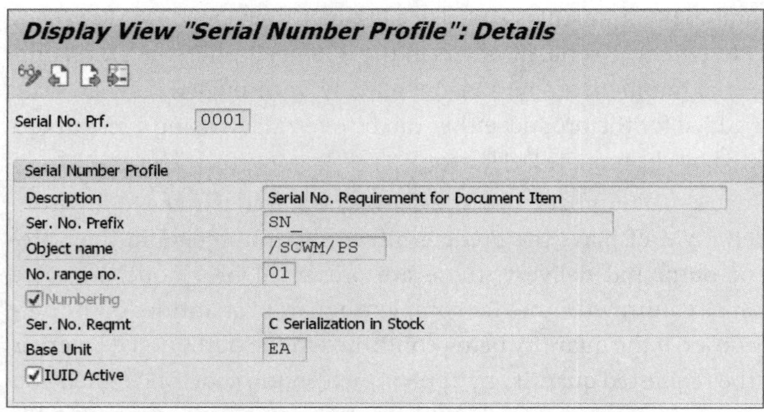

Figure 6.84 Activating IUID in the Serial Number Profile

3. After the product is delivered that has the IUID active serial number profile assigned, the embedded EWM system requires the user to fill in both the serial number and IUID data per equipment item during warehouse task confirmation, as shown in Figure 6.85.

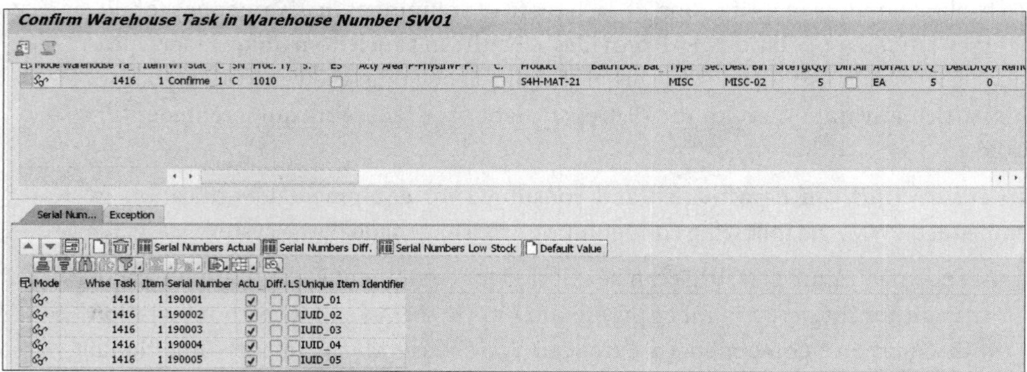

Figure 6.85 Confirming the Warehouse Task with the IUID Number

4. After the warehouse task for the warehouse request and the IUID for the equipment of the product are confirmed, the same are saved along with the serial number data. They can be displayed using the warehouse monitor via Transaction /SCWM/MON, as shown in Figure 6.86.

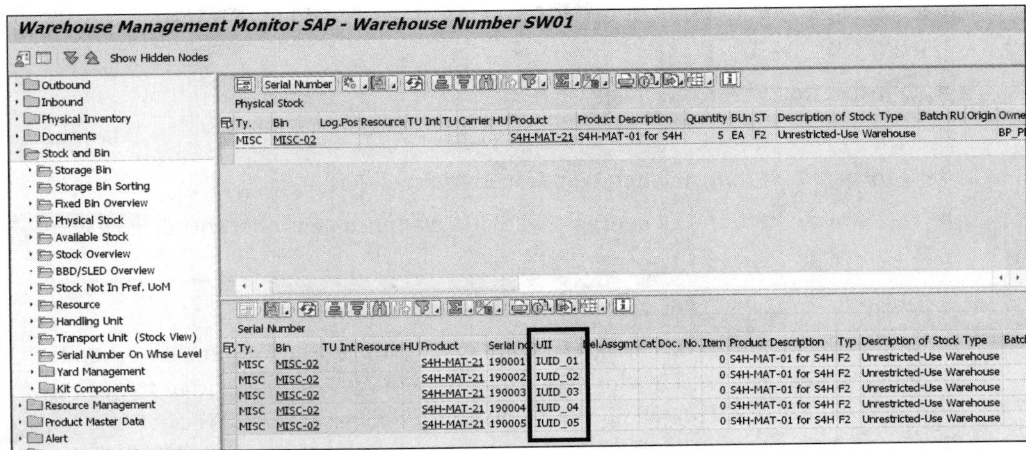

Figure 6.86 Displaying the IUID in the Warehouse Monitor

6.13 Quality Management

The warehouse process in an organization usually requires a check of the product quality before receiving it or issuing it to a customer. This helps eliminate situations in which faulty or damaged material sits in the warehouse and is shipped to customers or production plants, causing significant issues in regular manufacturing processes or costly returns of material that lead to sales losses.

To eradicate such problems and avoid products that are defective, damaged, or nonconforming to quality standards being received in the warehouse, embedded EWM uses QM. This leads to a reduction in customer or interplant returns of products, resulting in financial savings. Embedded EWM delivers the means to perform a quality check of the material for good receipt, returns, goods received from production, and inspections triggered using exception codes. Each of these inspections is explained in detail later. First, we'll consider the basic configuration, master data, and processes used in QM in embedded EWM.

Embedded EWM supplies an inspection object type data element, which defines software components, processes, and objects for which the inspection is to be carried out. Standard inspection object types are provided by SAP and are activated with versions in embedded EWM. Inspection documents are created for the related inspection object type if a corresponding inspection rule for the same is determined by embedded EWM. Additional quality specifications, procedures, and properties are defined as part of inspection rules in embedded EWM. SAP has provided four inspection object types:

- Q-Inspection Returns Delivery (IOT 3)
- Q-Inspection Product/Batch Inbound Delivery (IOT 4)
- Q-Inspection Product/Batch Warehouse-Internal (IOT 5)
- Q-Counting Inbound Deliveries (IOT 2) (only applicable for decentralized EWM)

Tip

QM in embedded EWM is integrated with QM in SAP S/4HANA using inspection lot origin 17. Readers familiar with decentralized SAP EWM will notice that the quality document isn't created in embedded EWM; only the inspection lot is created in SAP S/4HANA. A decision code is applied to the inspection lot either in SAP S/4HANA or an embedded EWM work center, which updates both embedded EWM and SAP S/4HANA stock.

6.13.1 What Are Quality Inspections?

Quality inspection is the process in which product quality inspections and checks take place during stock movement in the warehouse. Based on the quality inspection of stock, stock is made available for further warehouse processing or can be returned to vendors or putaway to the quarantine zone before being finally scrapped or sold. In the following sections, we explain the processes carried out in the system for products using QM. The sections also explain how quality inspection lots are created, inspected, and posted to scrap or normal stock.

Business Process

American company Alpha Medicals orders a few products from one of its vendors based in Mexico. The order sent by the vendor requires Alpha Medicals to make sufficient quality checks and inspections before finally putting the stock away in the destination bin or quarantine bin, or returning them to vendors. Stock that will be received from the vendor is to be received at the goods receipt area of the warehouse where the quality inspection is completed by the warehouse quality managers, and then the stock is moved into the quarantine area or returned the vendor. As a regular Alpha Medicals practice, individual product's pieces are quality inspected using inspection lots and before being stored in the warehouse and later used in the warehouse. For example, inbound delivery line item with Product ABC creates an inspection lot, which is, in turn, quality inspected by the quality department of the company. After the quality decision, the stock is either posted to quarantine stock or put away as final usable product. To ensure that the embedded EWM system proposes quality inspection for stock to be put away in the destination bin with ease, the company uses quality inspection in embedded EWM.

System Process

The following explains the basic system flow, including the documents and data required, to process quality lots for the inbound process and post to quality or unrestricted stock in embedded EWM and decentralized EWM:

1. An inbound delivery is created and a warehouse request is created in embedded EWM that contains information about the product be delivered by the external customer to Alpha Medicals.
2. Quality inspection lots are created per line item of the inbound delivery, which riggers the process for QM and mandates the quality inspection manager to make a quality inspection decision on the stock.
3. The quality inspection manager inspects the lot and supplies a quality inspection decision for the inspection lot.
4. If the inspection is successful, putaway warehouse tasks are created against the warehouse request and assigned to the warehouse worker. The warehouse request directs the warehouse worker to move the products from the staging area to the destination bin. The warehouse worker does so and confirms the warehouse task.
5. If the inspection isn't successful and the lot fails the quality inspection, then the stock is posted to the quarantine area or returned to the vendor directly.

Note

We've explained the system process using the inbound process only. It's equally applicable to outbound and internal stock movement processes.

6.13.2 Configuring Quality Management

To set up QM processes in embedded EWM, follow these steps:

1. **Generate an inspection object type version.**
   The inspection object type specifies the software component, process, and object for which the inspection lot is to be created in SAP S/4HANA. As shown in Figure 6.87, a new version of the inspection object type is generated via IMG path **SCM Extended Warehouse Management • Extended Warehouse Management • Cross-Process Settings • Quality Management • Basics • Generate Inspection Object Types Versions**. Select the required inspection object type, and click on **Generate New Version**.

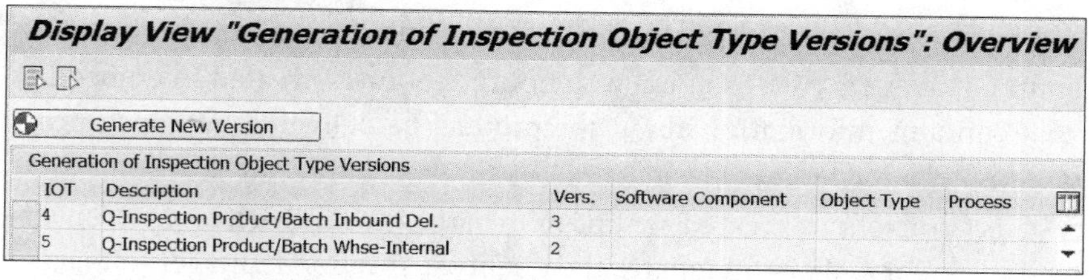

Display View "Generation of Inspection Object Type Versions": Overview

Generate New Version

Generation of Inspection Object Type Versions

IOT	Description	Vers.	Software Component	Object Type	Process
4	Q-Inspection Product/Batch Inbound Del.	3			
5	Q-Inspection Product/Batch Whse-Internal	2			

Figure 6.87 Defining the Inspection Object Type Version

2. **Activate the generated inspection object type version.**
   As shown in Figure 6.88, activate the inspection object type version generated in the previous step via IMG path **SCM Extended Warehouse Management • Extended Warehouse Management • Cross-Process Settings • Quality Management • Basics • Maintain Inspection Object Type Version**. Click on **New Entries**, create a new version of **Insp. Object Type**, and activate it. In addition to activating the inspection object type, properties for the inspection object type can also be maintained by clicking on the **Maintain Properties** node.

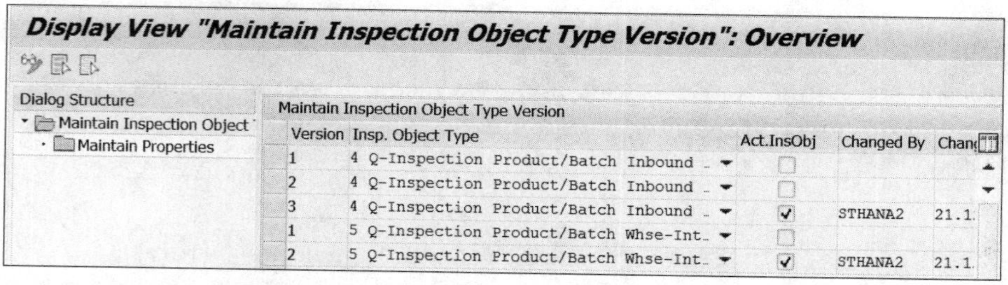

Display View "Maintain Inspection Object Type Version": Overview

Dialog Structure
- Maintain Inspection Object
  - Maintain Properties

Maintain Inspection Object Type Version

Version	Insp. Object Type		Act.InsObj	Changed By	Chan
1	4	Q-Inspection Product/Batch Inbound …	☐		
2	4	Q-Inspection Product/Batch Inbound …	☐		
3	4	Q-Inspection Product/Batch Inbound …	☑	STHANA2	21.1
1	5	Q-Inspection Product/Batch Whse-Int…	☐		
2	5	Q-Inspection Product/Batch Whse-Int…	☑	STHANA2	21.1

Figure 6.88 Activating the Inspection Object Type for QM in Embedded EWM

3. **Activate the inspection object type at the warehouse level.**
   As shown in Figure 6.89, the inspection object type activated at the client level using the previous configuration is activated at the warehouse level. This can be done via IMG path **SCM Extended Warehouse Management • Extended Warehouse Management • Cross-Process Settings • Quality Management • Basics • Warehouse-Dependent Activation of Inspection Object Type**. Click on **New Entries**, and activate quality processes for the inspection object type for the embedded EWM warehouse.

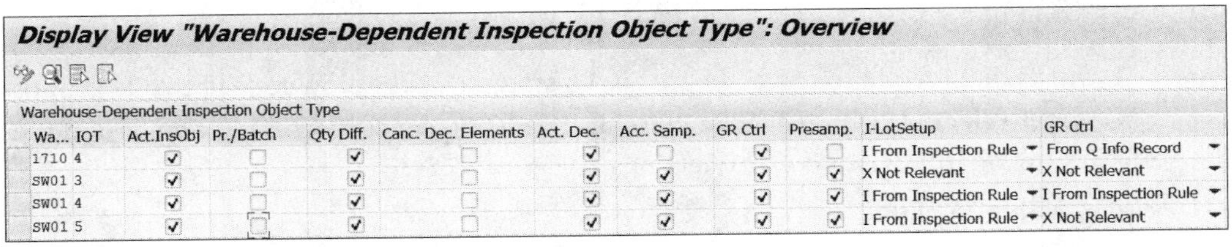

6

Display View "Warehouse-Dependent Inspection Object Type": Overview

Warehouse-Dependent Inspection Object Type

Wa...	IOT	Act.InsObj	Pr./Batch	Qty Diff.	Canc. Dec. Elements	Act. Dec.	Acc. Samp.	GR Ctrl	Presamp.	I-LotSetup	GR Ctrl
1710	4	✓	☐	✓	☐	✓	☐	✓	☐	I From Inspection Rule	From Q Info Record
SW01	3	✓	☐	✓	☐	✓	✓	✓	✓	X Not Relevant	X Not Relevant
SW01	4	✓	☐	✓	☐	✓	✓	✓	✓	I From Inspection Rule	I From Inspection Rule
SW01	5	✓	☐	✓	☐	✓	✓	✓	✓	I From Inspection Rule	X Not Relevant

Figure 6.89 Activating the Inspection Object Type at the Warehouse Level in Embedded EWM

4. **Maintain the usage decision codes.**
   Because embedded EWM is integrated with the SAP S/4HANA QM functionality, a usage decision for the inspection lot is created via IMG path **Quality Management • Quality Inspection • Inspection Lot Completion • Edit Code Groups and Codes for Usage Decisions**, as shown in Figure 6.90. Click on **New Entries**, and enter a code group—in this example, **01—UD for Goods Received from External Delivery**. Multiple decision codes can be assigned to it by selecting the code group and double-clicking on **Codes for Usage Decision**. These decision codes will guide the follow-up action the system takes for the created inspection lot in SAP S/4HANA.

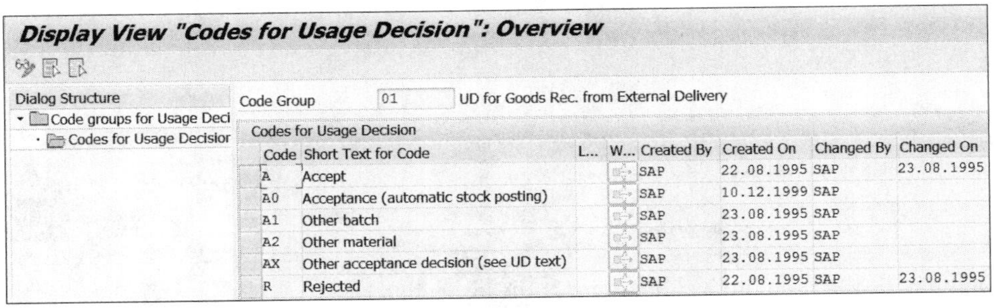

Display View "Codes for Usage Decision": Overview

Dialog Structure
- Code groups for Usage Deci
  - Codes for Usage Decisior

Code Group: 01 UD for Goods Rec. from External Delivery

Codes for Usage Decision

Code	Short Text for Code	L...	W...	Created By	Created On	Changed By	Changed On
A	Accept			SAP	22.08.1995	SAP	23.08.1995
A0	Acceptance (automatic stock posting)			SAP	10.12.1999	SAP	
A1	Other batch			SAP	23.08.1995	SAP	
A2	Other material			SAP	23.08.1995	SAP	
AX	Other acceptance decision (see UD text)			SAP	23.08.1995	SAP	
R	Rejected			SAP	22.08.1995	SAP	23.08.1995

Figure 6.90 Maintaining Usage Decision Codes

5. **Maintain the code sets for the inspection lot.**
   Code sets for the inspection lots are maintained for making a usage decision for both full and partial quantities in an inspection lot via IMG path **Quality Management • Quality Inspection • Inspection Lot Completion • Edit Selected Sets for Usage Decisions**. Click on **New Entries**, and enter a plant, selection set, and quality parameters. Next, select the selection set, click on **Selected Set Code for Usage Decision**, click on **New Entries**, and then enter the usage decision, code groups, and quality parameters. In Figure 6.91, we have a code set for a plant, in this case, the plant for which the storage location is mapped with an embedded EWM warehouse. Using the standard QM controls assigned to the selection set, you'll assign the decision code to the code group. To assign the decision codes to code groups under selected sets, select the plant and decision set combination and assign the following important control settings:
   - **Valuation Code**
     The valuation code specifies if the inspection lot is selected or rejected by applying the decision code.
   - **Quality Score**
     The decision code also applies a quality score to the inspection lot, which is used for vendor evaluation and vendor selection processes.
   - **Posting in UD**
     Using this setting, the system sets to which stock category it must post the stock. For example, the stock can be posted to unrestricted, blocked, scrap, sample, and so on.
   - **FollowUp**
     Using this setting (not shown), the system triggers a follow-up action for a decision code assigned to the inspection lot.

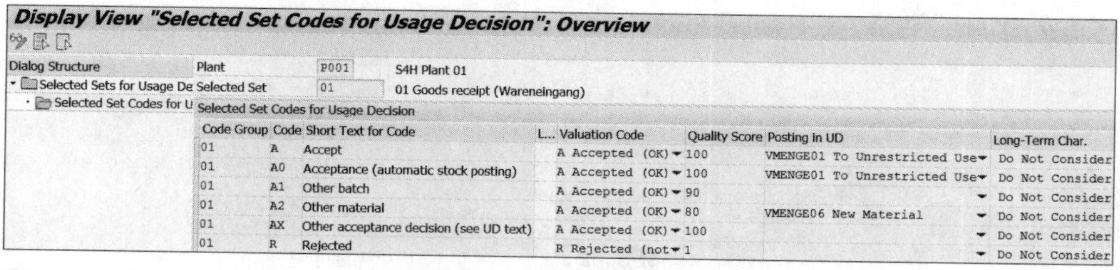

Display View "Selected Set Codes for Usage Decision": Overview

Dialog Structure
- Selected Sets for Usage De
  - Selected Set Codes for U

Plant: P001 S4H Plant 01
Selected Set: 01 01 Goods receipt (Wareneingang)

Selected Set Codes for Usage Decision

Code Group	Code	Short Text for Code	L...	Valuation Code	Quality Score	Posting in UD	Long-Term Char.
01	A	Accept		A Accepted (OK)	100	VMENGE01 To Unrestricted Use	Do Not Consider
01	A0	Acceptance (automatic stock posting)		A Accepted (OK)	100	VMENGE01 To Unrestricted Use	Do Not Consider
01	A1	Other batch		A Accepted (OK)	90		Do Not Consider
01	A2	Other material		A Accepted (OK)	80	VMENGE06 New Material	Do Not Consider
01	AX	Other acceptance decision (see UD text)		A Accepted (OK)	100		Do Not Consider
01	R	Rejected		R Rejected (not	1		Do Not Consider

Figure 6.91 Maintaining the Code Sets for the Inspection Lot

6. **Assign the set codes to the plant.**
   After the decision codes and set codes are defined in QM, set codes are assigned to the plant, as shown in Figure 6.92. This configuration can be done via IMG path **Quality Management • Basic Settings • Maintain Settings at Plant Level**. Click on **New Entries**, enter the plant, click on [icon], and enter the quality parameters.

   Next, select the plant, click on the **Inspection Type-Specific Settings for Plant** node, click on **New Entries**, and enter inspection type "17" along with the selection set for quality codes for full, partial, and return quantities. SAP S/4HANA also can assign the usage decision automatically to the inspection lot as soon as it's created in the system for both full and partial lots.

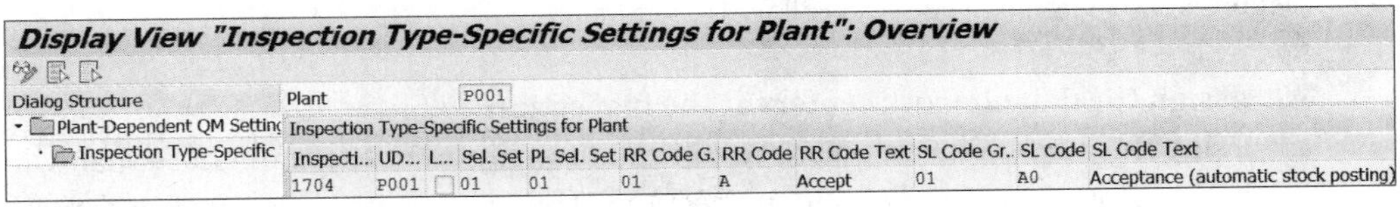

Display View "Inspection Type-Specific Settings for Plant": Overview

Dialog Structure
- Plant-Dependent QM Settin(
  - Inspection Type-Specific

Plant P001

Inspection Type-Specific Settings for Plant

Inspecti...	UD...	L...	Sel. Set	PL Sel. Set	RR Code G.	RR Code	RR Code Text	SL Code Gr..	SL Code	SL Code Text
1704	P001	☐	01	01	01	A	Accept	01	A0	Acceptance (automatic stock posting)

Figure 6.92 Assigning Code Sets to the Plant

7. **Maintain the follow-up actions for the usage decisions.**
   After the decision codes, set codes, and code groups are defined in embedded EWM, follow-up actions are defined so that they can be used to trigger the follow-up stock postings for full or partial lots created for embedded EWM–specific inbound deliveries. Follow-up actions for usage decisions can be defined via IMG path **SCM Extended Warehouse Management • Extended Warehouse Management • Cross-Process Settings • Quality Management • Result • Maintain Follow-Up Actions**. Click on **New Entries**, enter a follow-up action code, and save. There are four predefined follow-up actions with SAP S/4HANA:
   - **For a full inspection lot:**
     - **EWM_A: Putaway to Final Storage Bin**
     - **EWM_R: Putaway to Blocked Stock Area**
   - **For a partial inspection lot:**
     - **EWM_AP: Putaway to Final Storage Bin (Partial Quantity)**
     - **EWM_RP: Putaway to Blocked Stock Area (Partial Quantity)**

   As shown in Figure 6.93, select one predefined follow-up action, and click on the **Assign Logistical Follow-up Actions** node, which will take you to the screen where you can assign internal actions to be triggered in embedded EWM. These actions will be triggered for the stock for which a decision is being made, that is, the stock type to which the stock is to be posted in embedded EWM and the warehouse process type to be used for the posting change of the stock. The system automatically creates and confirms the posting change warehouse task from the quality inspection stock type to the unrestricted or blocked stock type.

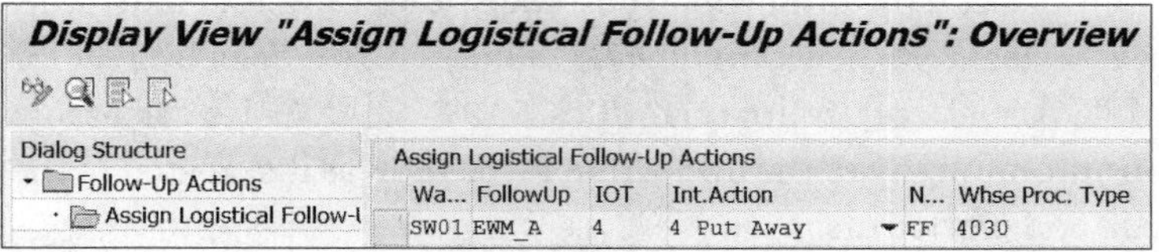

Figure 6.93 Assigning Logistical Follow-Up Actions

8. **Assign the default work center for the inspection.**
   Using this node, a default work center can be assigned to the warehouse that will be used for stock-based quality inspections. This work center supports functionality for quality inspections such as closing HUs and printing HU labels during quality inspection. The default work center for inspection is assigned to the warehouse via IMG path **SCM Extended Warehouse Management • Extended Warehouse Management • Cross-Process Settings • Quality Management • Result • Assign Default Work Center for Inspection**, as shown in Figure 6.94. Click on **New Entries**, and enter a work center for the embedded EWM warehouse.

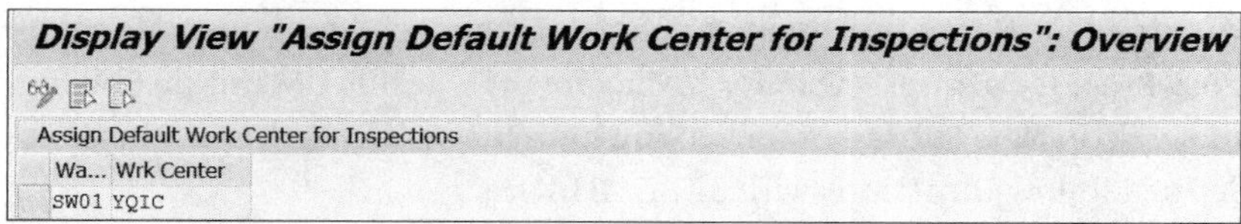

Figure 6.94 Assigning the Default Work Center for Quality Inspection

Note

The Maintain Follow-Up Actions app allows you to define follow-up actions for stock movements in the warehouse so that stock can be posted to quality stock, scrapped, put in unrestricted stock, or incur some follow-up actions based on the decision code used in the quality inspections.

6.13.3 Master Data in Quality Management

In the following sections, we explain the various master data settings required to be completed as a prerequisite to completing the quality inspection process. We also discuss the master data objects, such as inspection rules, and changes in material master data required in embedded/decentralized EWM.

Master Data for Inspection Rules

After the basic configuration used for quality inspection in embedded EWM is set up, the master data for activating deliveries in embedded EWM for quality inspection is created using inspection rules. The following master data is created for the quality inspection process:

- **Material master**
  As shown in Figure 6.95, inspection types and their attributes can be maintained in the **Quality management** tab in the material master in SAP S/4HANA via the **Ins. Setup** button. Assign an inspection type for the inspection rule, specify inspection attributes, and activate it to create an inspection lot for the material.

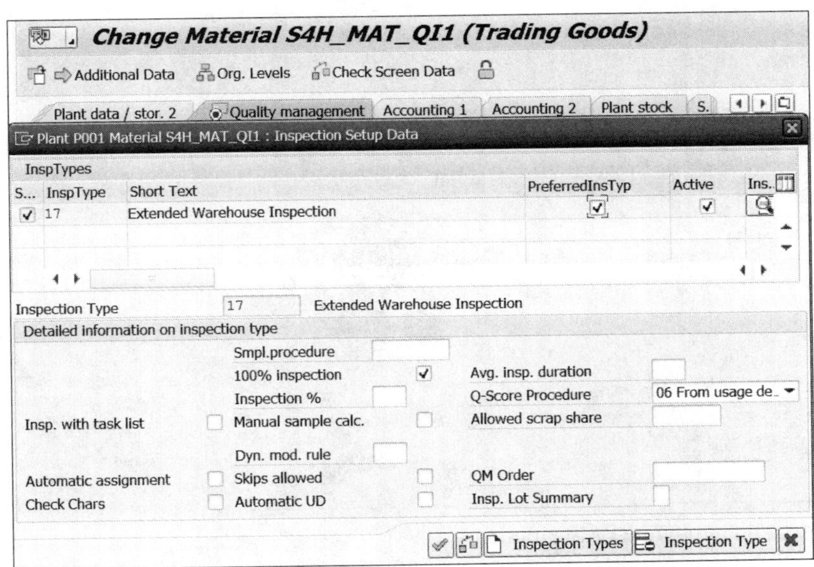

Figure 6.95 Material Master Setup for Creating the Inspection Lot

- **Defining inspection rule**
  An inspection rule is used to determine whether a delivery item or stock item in

embedded EWM is relevant to quality. An inspection rule consists of multiple properties that help determine inspection relevance and the type of inspection. In this case, it's not required to maintain the inspection setup in the material master in SAP S/4HANA. As shown in Figure 6.96, the inspection rule is maintained via **SAP Easy Access** path **Logistics • SCM Extended Warehouse Management • Extended Warehouse Management • Master Data • Quality Management • Maintain Inspection Rule**, or by using Transaction /SCWM/QRSETUP.

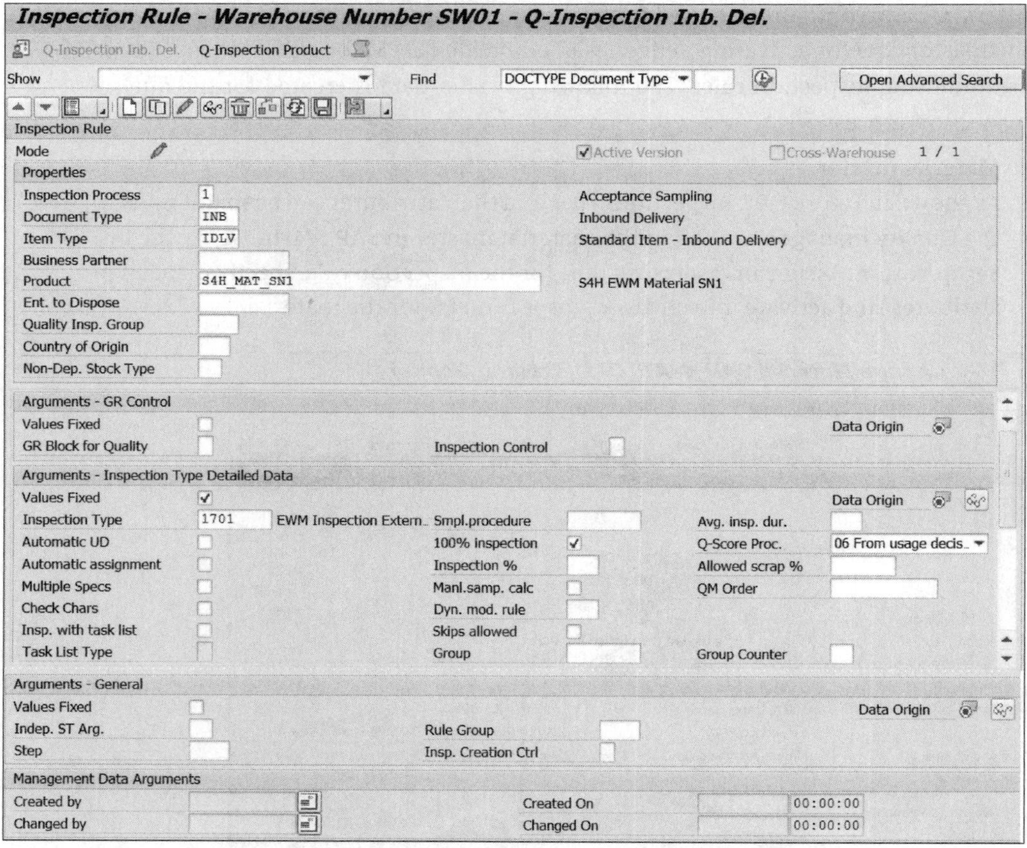

Figure 6.96 Inspection Rule for QM in Embedded EWM

Click on , and enter filter values such as document type, item type, product, and so on. In addition, enter quality parameters and controls for the product, and then save the inspection rule. The inspection rule can be created either for quality inspection of stock in a delivery or quality inspection of the product already in the warehouse, with each one having its own set of settings and controls.

- **Change documents for inspection rule**
  The inspection rule is one of the most important master data objects in the embedded EWM quality inspection process, and it's important to have a view of any changes made in the inspection rule master and by whom the changes are made. This helps users track the changes made and revert them. It also helps maintain accountability of the changes by knowing who made the changes and when were they made. The embedded EWM system creates a log document where it records all changes made to storage bins, and the log is made available to users for reporting purposes. The change logs are activated by default in the SAP S/4HANA system, so any changes made to the inspection rule are captured as part of change documents and can be displayed.

  After the change log for the master data bin is activated at the warehouse level, the changes made to the inspection rule will be captured and can be displayed to the user using Transaction /SCWM/QRSETUP.

  To display the changes in the inspection rule, you must highlight the inspection rule and follow the **Change Documents** option path using the [icon] icon. This displays the details about the changes made to the inspection rule by the user, such as date and time the change is made, type of change made, and transaction used to make the change, as shown in Figure 6.97.

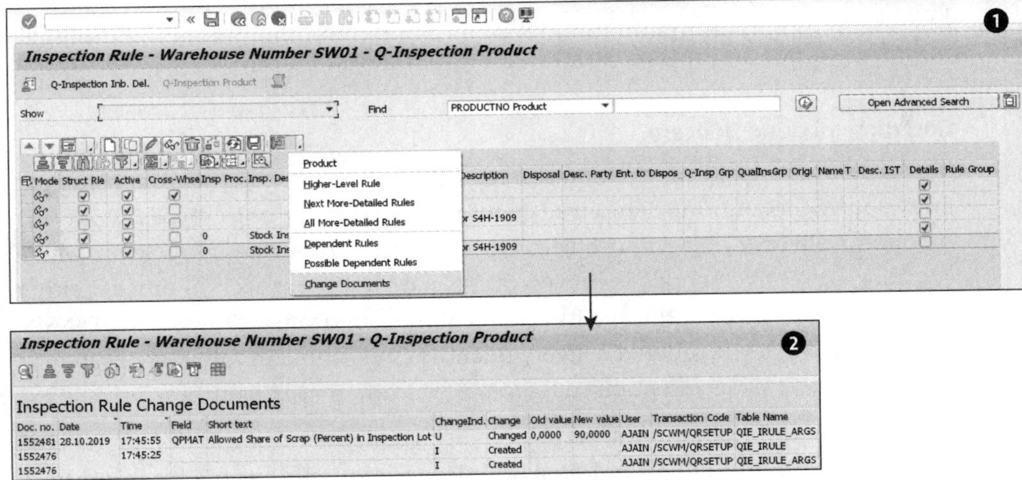

Figure 6.97 Displaying Change Logs for the Inspection Rule

- **Setting up inspection rule determination**
  To see if properties of the inspection rule have been maintained properly, check the inspection rule determination and simulation for an inbound delivery item and verify the resulting arguments of the inspection rule determination. This can be done via Transaction /SCWM/QRSETUP. Choose **More • Inspection Rule • Determination**. If the inspection rule determination needs to be tested for inbound delivery items, this can be done using Transaction /SCWM/PRDI. Select the inbound delivery and inbound delivery item, choose the details, and select **Disp. Insp. Rule Simulation**.

Master Data Synchronization to Control Quality Management Processes

You also can create inspection rules for QM in decentralized EWM, based on the connected external enterprise management systems (SAP S/4HANA or SAP ERP system).

The synchronization of QM data can be done by following these process steps:

1. Set up Application Link and Enabling (ALE) distribution of inspection setup data from the external enterprise management system to decentralized EWM.
2. Connect decentralized EWM with the external enterprise management system (SAP S/4HANA or SAP ERP).
3. Enter inspection setup data in the QM view on material master in the external enterprise management system.

The system then creates, updates, or deleted the inspection rules in decentralized EWM based on the QM inspection setup data maintained manually in the material master as part of the previous step.

Counting Inbound Delivery

You can determine the destination storage bin when unpacked stocks are being put away during the counting of received goods using inspection object type 2 (Counting Inbound Delivery). Inspection object type 2 is used in business processes where counting of received goods is carried out as part of the inspection process either using the RF screen or in the quality work center (using Transaction /SCWM/QINSP_S4) to ensure that the ordered delivery quantity is delivered in full. Any differences are noted down using exception codes to post the difference quantities.

To set up that the destination storage bin is determined using inspection object type 2, you assign an external process step to the inspection rule created for this inspection object type, as shown in Figure 6.98.

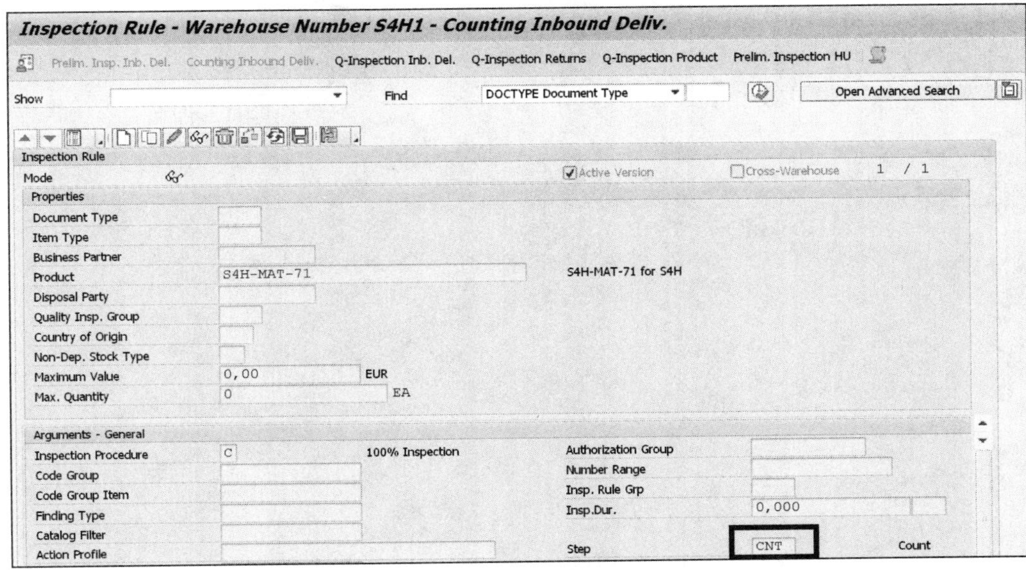

Figure 6.98 Assigning an External Process Step to the Inspection Rule

6.13.4 Quality Inspection Process

The quality inspection process in embedded EWM consists of the following steps:

1. **Request the document.**
   The quality inspection process starts with the creation of a request document (e.g., inbound delivery) in embedded EWM for which the line item and inspection object types have been activated and the inspection rule master data has been defined.

2. **Create the inspection lot.**
   After embedded EWM determines the quality-relevant inspection object type and inspection rule for the delivery line item, an inspection lot is created in SAP S/4HANA, as shown in Figure 6.99.

3. **Enter the usage decision.**
   A usage decision is assigned to either a full or partial quantity in the inspection lot in embedded EWM. The usage decision indicates what should happen with the inspected stock items, that is, whether they should be accepted or rejected during inspection. Decisions about inspection lots can be made either in SAP S/4HANA or in the embedded EWM quality work center.

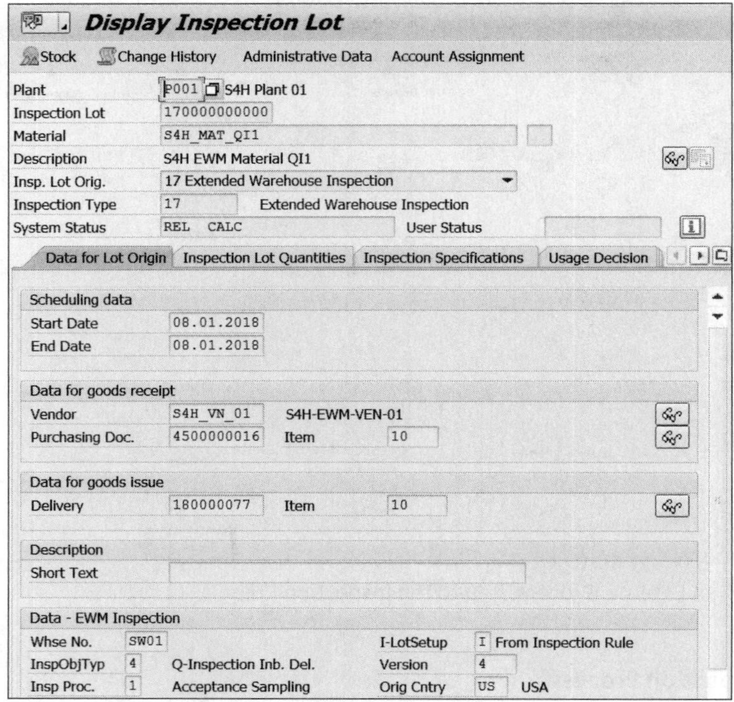

Figure 6.99 Inspection Lot for Inbound Delivery in Embedded EWM

> **Tip**
>
> It's important to ensure that the inspection lot created is released; that is, make sure that no decision blocks are assigned to the inspection lot. If a decision block is assigned to the inspection lot, the system won't allow you to enter a usage decision in the inspection lot. If any additional inspection characteristics are configured, results are noted for all of them (e.g., results, defects, etc.).

A usage decision can be assigned to the generated inspection lot either in SAP S/4HANA or in the embedded EWM quality work center:

- **Usage decision in SAP S/4HANA**
  As shown in Figure 6.100, a usage decision in QM can be recorded by following **SAP Easy Access** path **Quality Management • Quality Inspection • Inspection Lot • Usage Decision • Record**, or by using Transaction QA32. Enter any of the selection criteria

for the inspection lot, and click on [icon]. After the inspection lots are displayed, select the inspection lot, and click on **Usage Decision**. Next, enter the usage code for either a full lot or partial quantity.

- **Usage decision in embedded EWM**
  A usage decision in a quality work center of embedded EWM can be made via **SAP Easy Access** path **Logistics • SCM Extended Warehouse Management • Extended Warehouse Management • Execution • Quality Workload Overview**. The stock for inspection can be selected using the following selection criteria: warehouse number, quality work center, HU, or inspection lot. On the **Stock Item to Be Inspected** screen, the inspection lot is selected in edit mode, and the quantities of the inspection lot, usage decision, follow-up action, and HU number are entered in the **Qual.Inspection** tab, as shown in Figure 6.101. It's also possible to mass inspect the inspection lot documents using the **Mass Inspection for Selected Items** button.

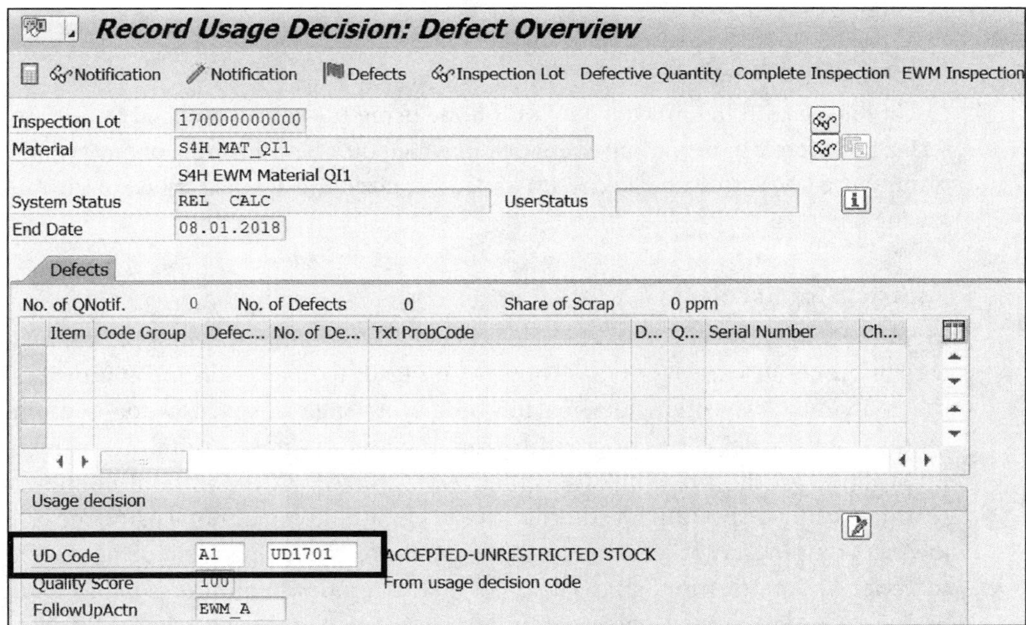

Figure 6.100 Assigning the Decision Code to the Inspection Lot in SAP S/4HANA

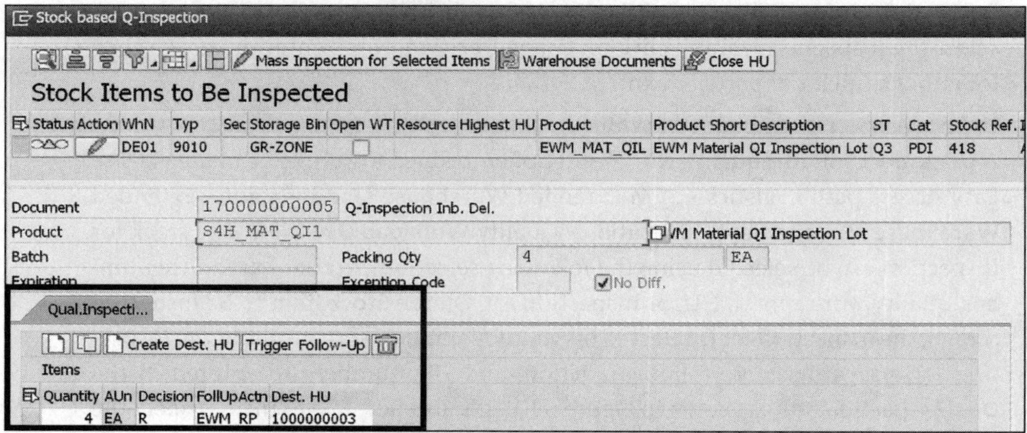

Figure 6.101 Assigning the Usage Decision to the Inspection Lot in Embedded EWM

6.13.5 Quality Inspection Scenarios

Quality inspection in embedded EWM is done using the steps described in Section 6.13.4, but there can be various scenarios in which different business organizations want to use QM with embedded EWM or decentralized EWM, as described in the following sections.

Inspection Lot Summaries

In SAP S/4HANA, a new inspection lot is created for delivery quantities created with reference to sales or purchase orders. This leads to inspection and approval of the individual inspection lots for the orders. A single inspection lot is often required for the deliveries originating from a sales or purchase order. Embedded EWM allows for the grouping of such deliveries created with or without reference to orders using inspection lot summaries. This grouping can be done using the following grouping criteria: delivery item, purchase order, manufacturing order, material, and batch number. It's also possible to group the products using BAdI `QPLEXT_LOT_SUMMARY` (Insp. Lot Summary for Extended Warehouse Insp.).

To set the inspection lot summaries, settings are made at one of two places:

- **Inspection setup using the material master**
  As shown in Figure 6.102, to set up inspection lot summaries using a material master in SAP S/4HANA, enter how you want to group the material using the **Insp. Lot Summary** field on the **Quality Management** tab.

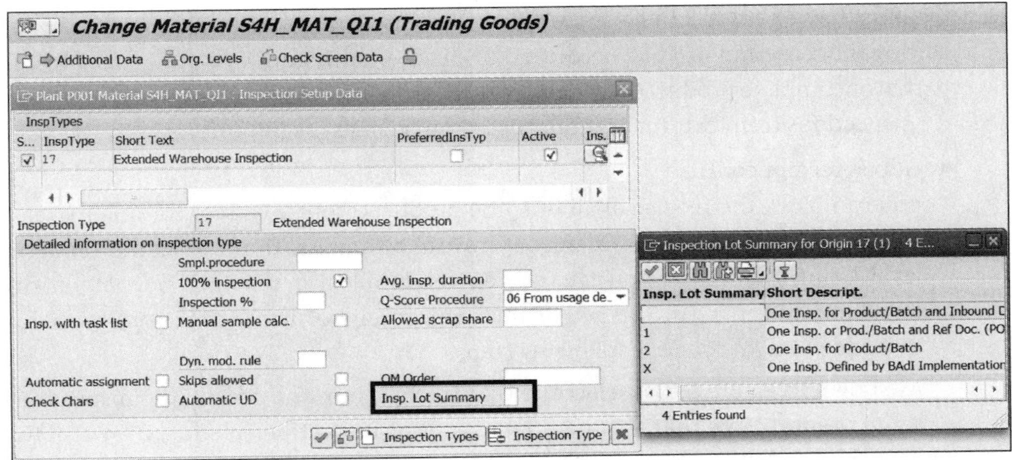

Figure 6.102 Setting Up the Inspection Lot Summary in the Material Master

- **Inspection setup using an inspection rule**
  As shown in Figure 6.103, if the inspection setup is done in the embedded EWM inspection rule, add grouping data using the **Insp. Creation Ctrl** field directly.

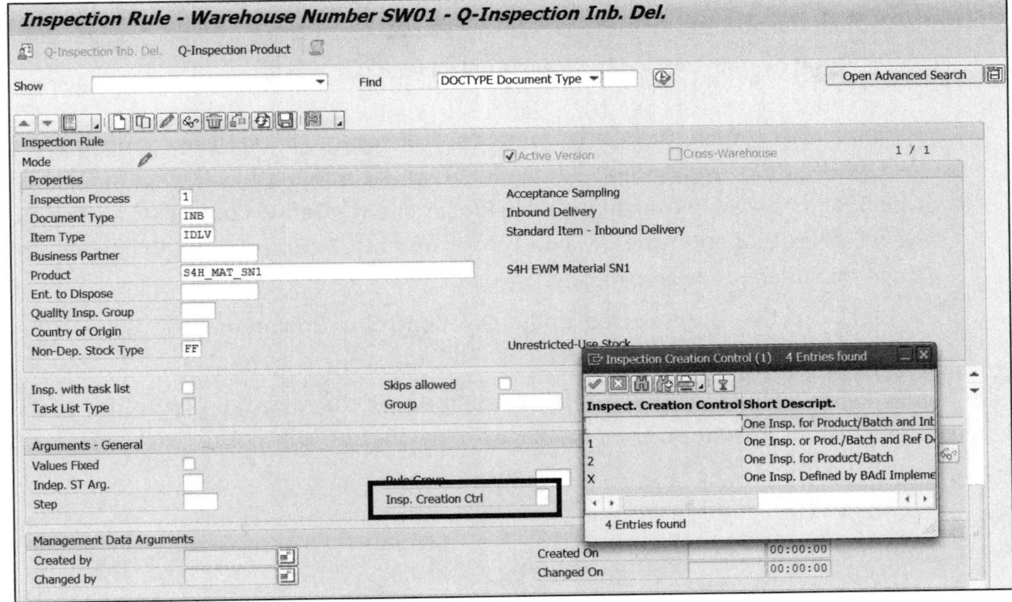

Figure 6.103 Setting Up the Inspection Lot Summary in the Inspection Rule

Inspection of Externally Procured Goods

During the receipt of products procured from external vendors, you may need to do partial or complete product/pallet quality checks. There are multiple variants of quality inspections from external vendors based on business requirements:

- **Goods receipt control**

  You can block the receipt of all or some products from a vendor for quality reasons. The setting for goods receipt control can be made at the product master data level. Using this setting, you can ignore a vendor block or display a warning/error for a blocked vendor in SAP S/4HANA. Goods receipt control can be configured in embedded EWM using the following steps:

  As shown in Figure 6.104, select the **GR Ctrl** checkbox and specify the inspection setup origin 17 in either the material master or inspection rule for **IOT 4** at IMG path **SCM Extended Warehouse Management • Extended Warehouse Management • Cross-Process Settings • Quality Management • Basics • Warehouse-Dependent Activation of Inspection Object Type**.

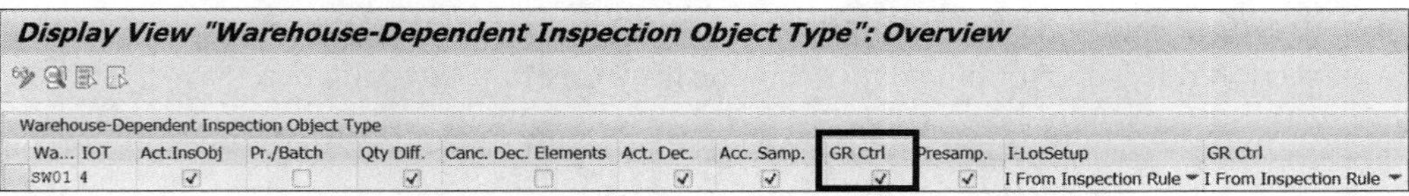

Display View "Warehouse-Dependent Inspection Object Type": Overview

Warehouse-Dependent Inspection Object Type

Wa...	IOT	Act.InsObj	Pr./Batch	Qty Diff.	Canc. Dec. Elements	Act. Dec.	Acc. Samp.	GR Ctrl	Presamp.	I-LotSetup	GR Ctrl
SW01	4	✓	☐	✓	☐	✓	✓	✓	✓	I From Inspection Rule	I From Inspection Rule

Figure 6.104 Activating the Goods Receipt Control for IOT 4

  As shown in Figure 6.105, configure the control key for giving the error during the receipt of goods from a blocked vendor. This is configured at IMG path **Quality Management • QM in Logistics • QM in Procurement • Define Control Keys**. Click on **New Entries**, and enter the QM control key and block controls. The following settings are added to the control key:

  - **Block Inactive** is deselected under **QM Control in Procurement** to disable the blocking of the vendor master.
  - The **Message Mode** is set to **W Warning** under the **Message Control for Locks** section to activate an error message for products to be blocked for the vendor.

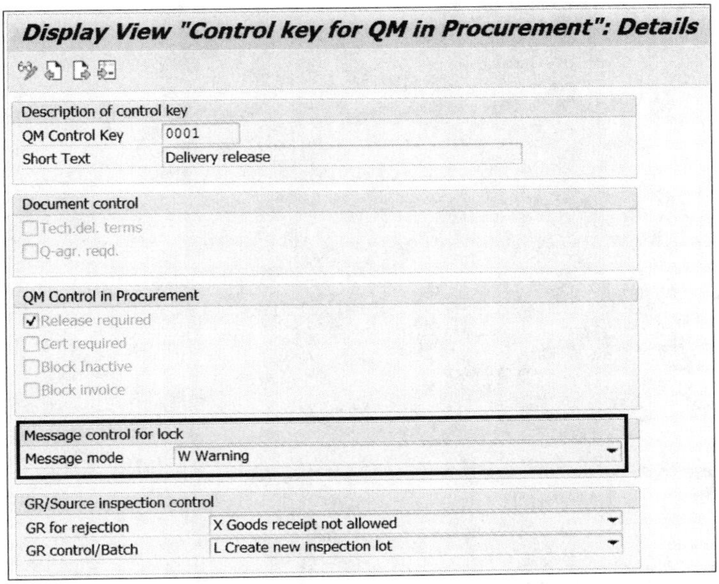

Display View "Control key for QM in Procurement": Details

Description of control key
QM Control Key 0001
Short Text Delivery release

Document control
Tech.del. terms
Q-agr. reqd.

QM Control in Procurement
Release required
Cert required
Block Inactive
Block invoice

Message control for lock
Message mode W Warning

GR/Source inspection control
GR for rejection X Goods receipt not allowed
GR control/Batch L Create new inspection lot

Figure 6.105 Configuring the Control Key for Quality Management

Next, create or edit the master data to perform the goods receipt control process in embedded EWM:

- In the SAP S/4HANA material master **Quality Management** tab, activate the **QM Proc. Active** control under the **Procurement data** section, and assign the QM control key that issues a warning/error message while performing goods receipt for materials during inspection execution, as shown in Figure 6.106.
- The goods receipt block is set either at the vendor master level or in the quality info record. The receipt block can also be set in the embedded EWM inspection rule via **SAP Easy Access** path **Logistics • SCM Extended Warehouse Management • Extended Warehouse Management • Master Data • Quality Management • Maintain Inspection Rule**, as shown in Figure 6.107. Create an inspection rule by clicking on [icon] and entering determination data (e.g., product, document type, item type, etc.) and a block control value for the **GR Block for Quality** field.

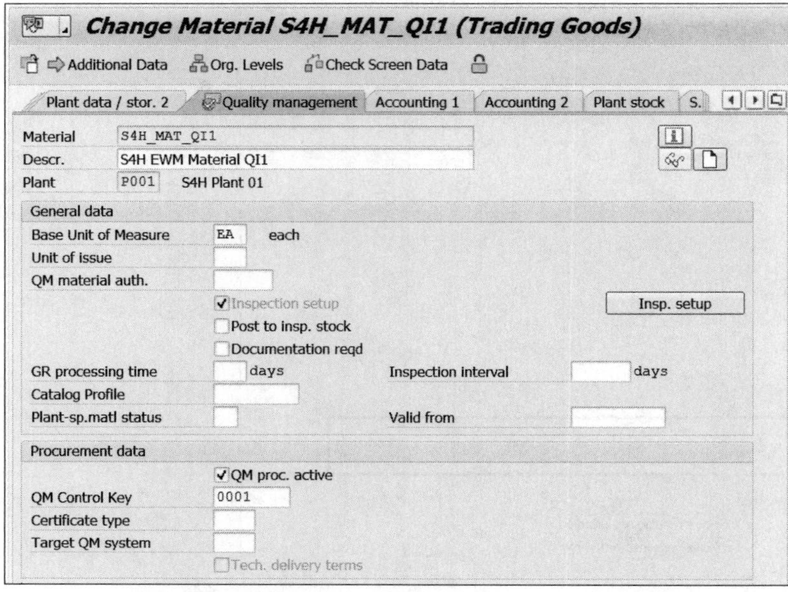

Figure 6.106 Assigning the Control Key in the Material Master

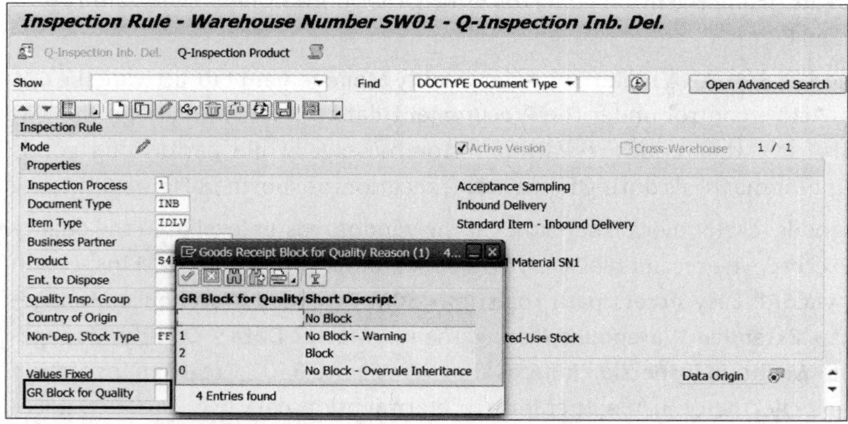

Figure 6.107 Setting the Goods Receipt Block in the Inspection Rule

- **Acceptance sampling**
  When externally procured goods are received, it's possible to block and allow goods receipt. If restricted receipt is allowed, the stock category to which the

receipt is to be made can be configured in the follow-up action using the usage decision.

Acceptance sampling can be configured by selecting the **Acceptance Sampling** checkbox for inspection object type **4 Q-Inspection Product/Batch Inbound Del.** at IMG path **SCM Extended Warehouse Management • Extended Warehouse Management • Cross-Process Settings • Quality Management • Basics • Warehouse-Dependent Activation of Inspection Object Type**, as shown in Figure 6.108. Click on **New Entries**, enter "4" for **IOT**, and select the **Acc. Samp.** checkbox.

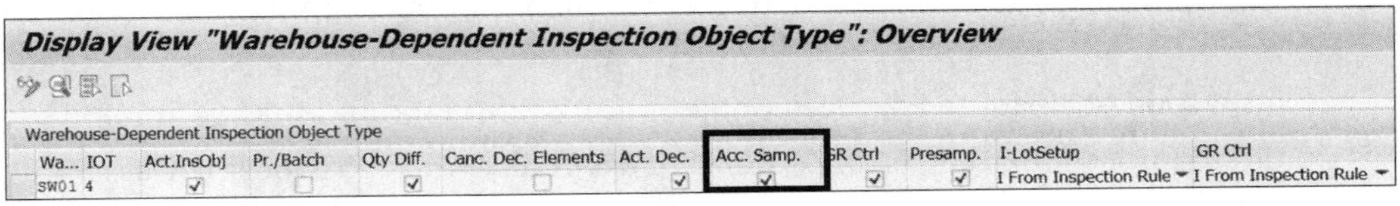

Display View "Warehouse-Dependent Inspection Object Type": Overview

Warehouse-Dependent Inspection Object Type

Wa...	IOT	Act.InsObj	Pr./Batch	Qty Diff.	Canc. Dec. Elements	Act. Dec.	Acc. Samp.	R Ctrl	Presamp.	I-LotSetup	GR Ctrl
SW01	4	☑	☐	☑	☐	☑	☑	☑	☑	I From Inspection Rule	I From Inspection Rule

Figure 6.108 Activating the Acceptance Sampling for IOT 4

Inspection after Goods Receipt

In many cases, it's also required to quality inspect the goods after they're received in the warehouse; in effect, the goods receipt posting in embedded EWM isn't delayed. While executing the process, embedded EWM determines the inspection relevance for an inbound delivery item when the goods receipt is posted. If the product in the delivery item is inspection relevant, the system creates an inspection lot based on the inspection rule setup. While performing the product quality inspection, you can record the inspection result and assign a usage decision for full/partial inspection lots in SAP S/4HANA or the embedded EWM quality work center. If the usage decision assigned to the delivery is mapped to follow-up actions, the system performs the same: putaway, scrapping, and so on.

> **Note**
>
> In a variant of this process, the system determines if the product is relevant for quality inspection during warehouse task creation and creates an inspection lot. Based on the quality decision of the inspection lot, goods receipt is posted if the stock is posted as an unrestricted stock type and put away to a destination bin as a follow-up action.

To enable inbound delivery for inspection after goods receipt, you must ensure that inspection object type (**IOT**) **4 Q-Inspection Product/Batch Inbound Del.** is activated for the warehouse and that an inspection rule for the product is created for it. Assign function module QFOA_EWM_LOG_FOLLOW_UP_S4 and a stock type to these follow-up actions.

In addition, it's important to assign either a putaway or scrap follow-up action or specify customer-specific follow-up actions using BAdI /SCWM/EX_QFU_STOCK_ACTION (Influence Stock Action after Decision). The BAdI can be configured via IMG path **SCM Extended Warehouse Management • Extended Warehouse Management Business Add-Ins (BAdIs) for Extended Warehouse Management • Cross-Process Settings • Quality Management • Follow-Up Actions • BAdI: Influence Stock Action After Decision**. Click on [icon], create a new implementation for the BAdI, and activate it.

Inspection of In-House-Produced Goods

Just as inspection of goods can be done for externally procured goods, it's possible to perform inspection of goods produced in house by the organization. The different variants of quality inspection for goods receipt from production in the warehouse are as follows:

- **Presampling in production**
  For the goods manufactured internally by an organization, it's often necessary to quality inspect the goods before receiving them in inventory. This allows an organization to separate the bad lot of manufactured goods and reduce the work of moving the bad product lot from the warehouse inventory to the scrap area. This is achieved in embedded EWM using a presampling process.

  In this process, a manufacturing order (process order/production order) is created and released in SAP S/4HANA for the plant. The inspection lot is created in SAP S/4HANA after the manufacturing order is released and is available to both the embedded EWM quality work center and SAP S/4HANA. The inspection result is captured for the inspection lot, and a usage decision is assigned to the lot. Based on the usage decision, after the inbound delivery is created in embedded EWM, the stock is posted to an appropriate stock type in embedded EWM, and a material document is created in SAP S/4HANA. The usage decision assigned to the inspection lot drives which stock category (e.g., blocked stock or unrestricted stock) the product is posted to during goods receipt.

  To enable the production process for presampling, configure QM in embedded EWM with these settings:

  - A new version of inspection object type 4 (**Q-Inspection Product/Batch Inbound Del.**) is created and activated in embedded EWM.

- As shown in Figure 6.109, the **Presamp.** checkbox for **IOT 4** (generated previously) is checked via IMG path **SCM Extended Warehouse Management • Extended Warehouse Management • Cross-Process Settings • Quality Management • Basics • Warehouse-Dependent Activation of Inspection Object Type**.

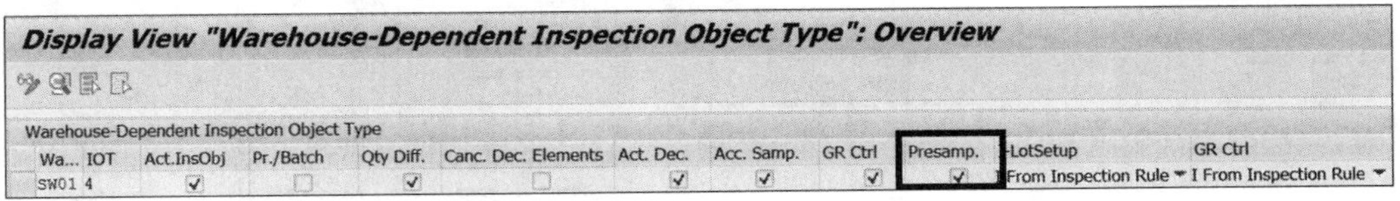

Figure 6.109 Activating Presampling for IOT 4

- **Inspection after goods receipt**
  In this case, inspection can be done for the products in the inbound delivery created for the production order after goods receipt. This process follows the same steps for the internally produced goods as explained for inspection after goods receipt of externally procured materials. The only difference is that the inbound delivery created in this case is based on the production order, that is, internally produced goods.

Warehouse Internal Inspection

Internal inspections are performed if a company decides to perform an ad hoc inspection of the products in its warehouse that aren't related to any inbound or outbound movement from the warehouse.

> **Tip**
> Use inspection type **EWM: Stock Transfer Inspection (1708)** for internal inspections.

The following methods can be used to create inspection lots for internal inspections:

- **Manually for stock items**
  The internal inspection document is created manually using the embedded EWM monitor. Go to the monitor using Transaction /SCWM/MON, and then select the **Stock and Bin • Physical Stock** node. On the selection screen, enter the selection criteria for determining the products for which the inspection document is to be created. Next, the stock for which the inspection is to be done is selected. As shown in Figure 6.110, from the menu options, click on [icon], and select **More Methods • Create InspDoc (IOT5)**. A popup appears with the default value of exception code CRID.

Click on the green checkmark, and the system creates an inspection lot with the CRID exception code.

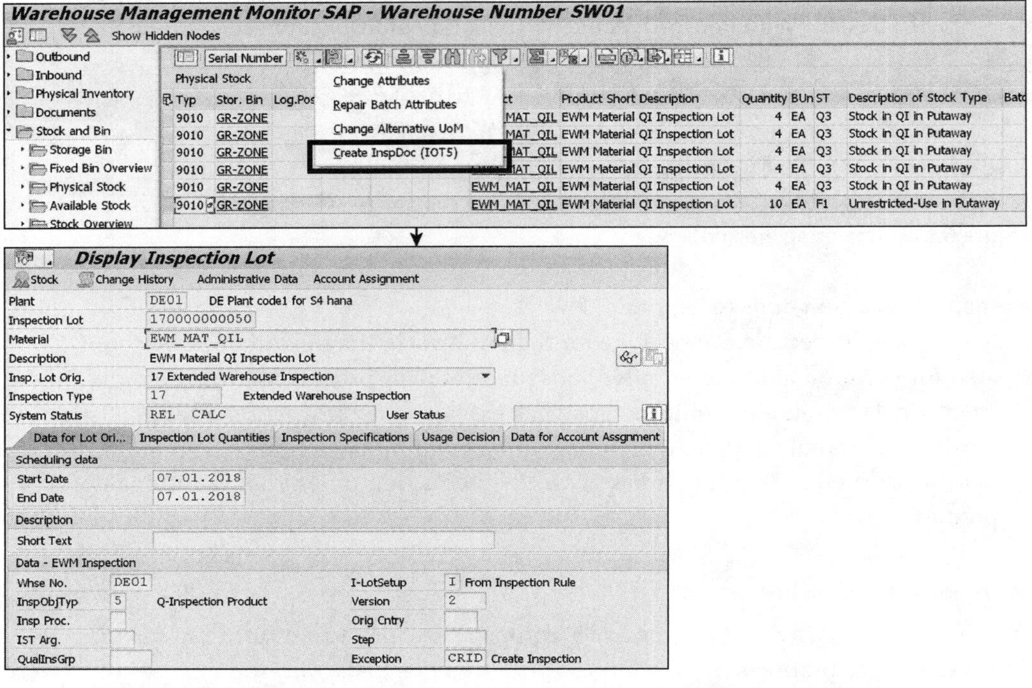

Figure 6.110 Creating the Inspection Lot for IOT 5 from the Warehouse Monitor

- **Automatically by the system**
  To create an inspection lot automatically for the stock items, run report /SCWM/R_STOCK_TYPE_CHANGE (Change Stock Type) using Transaction SE38. In the **Mode** field, select **2 Create Inspection and Post Stock to QM S**. The report offers various selection criteria to identify the stock for creating the inspection lot. The product for which you want to create an inspection lot is entered in the selection report.
- **Using RF scanners**
  To create an inspection lot using RF for the stock items, log on to the RF menu on a mobile device using Transaction /SCWM/RFUI. In the RF menu, choose **05 Internal Process • 04 Quality Management • 03 Product Inspection**. An inspection lot is created by scanning either the HU or the storage bin and adding the exception code CRID (Create Inspection) to create an internal inspection.

To enable the process for internal inspection, it's important to configure the quality component in embedded EWM with the following settings:

- Inspection object type **(IOT) 5 Q-Inspection Product/Batch Whse-Internal** must be activated in embedded EWM.
- An inspection rule is created under the **Q-Inspection Product** tab for the product for which the inspection lot is to be created.

Recurring Inspection

To inspect the batch-managed products at regular periods in embedded EWM, use the recurring inspection process. The system assigns the next inspection date to the batch characteristic `LOBM_QNDAT` when a new batch is created for the product. The calculation of recurring intervals follows set logic:

- The next inspection date equals the production date plus the inspection interval if the production date is available.
- The next inspection date equals the batch creation date plus the inspection interval if the production date isn't available.

After the inspection date is set for the product, report /SCWM/R_STOCK_TYPE_CHANGE (Change Stock Type) is executed at a regular frequency to retrieve the stock with the next inspection date in the past and post it to quality stock. After the inspection lot is created, a usage decision is assigned to the inspection lot. If the lot is accepted, the next inspection date is set as the accepted date plus the inspection interval. If it's rejected, then the inspection date isn't recalculated.

To enable the process for recurring inspection, it's important to configure the quality component in embedded EWM with the following settings:

- Inspection object type **5 Q-Inspection Product/Batch Whse-Internal** must be created and activated in embedded EWM.
- A valuation class containing characteristic `LOBM_QNDAT` must be assigned to the product batch.
- As shown in Figure 6.111, an inspection interval must be assigned in the QM view in the material master.
- An inspection rule must be set up for the product under the **Q-Inspection Product** section in embedded EWM.

- Background report /SCWM/R_STOCK_TYPE_CHANGE (Change Stock Type) must be scheduled for periodic inspection. The report automatically creates inspection lots and calculates the next inspection date for the batch-enabled product.

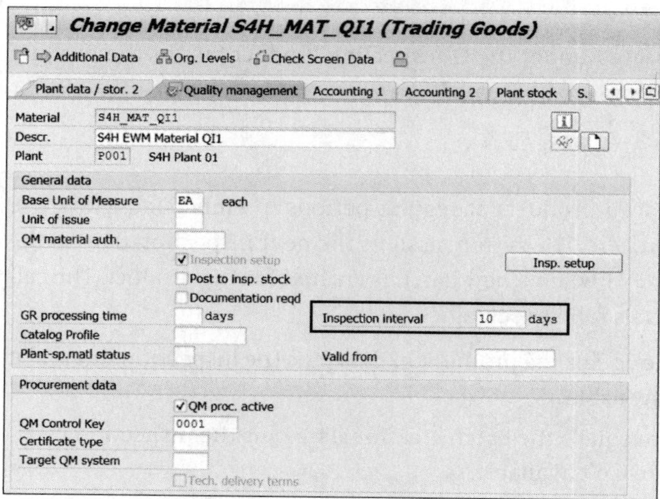

Figure 6.111 Assigning the Inspection Interval to the Material Master

Returns Inspection

A returns inspection inspects customer or supplier returns to the warehouse. Goods receipt is posted for the goods when they're returned to the embedded EWM system with reference to the sales order. If there are no inspection results in the orders, an inspection lot is created automatically. If there's an inspection result with a decision code, a follow-up action is carried out by the system.

To perform returns-based quality inspection, it's important to configure the settings for advanced returns management via IMG path **Logistics General • Advanced Returns Management**. To speed up the process in embedded EWM for advanced returns, apply BC set `/SCWM/DLV_ADVANCED_RETURNS` using Transaction SCPR20.

In embedded EWM, release and activate inspection object type **3 Q-Inspection Returns Delivery** for your warehouse. There are four warehouse scenarios used in the returns inspection process in embedded EWM:

- Returns delivery process
- Posting change for valuation posting

- Posting change with warehouse order for putaway
- Posting change with warehouse order for scrapping

Quality inspection in the returns process creates a return document (a returns order). An inbound delivery is created in SAP S/4HANA for the returns document, which creates a warehouse request in embedded EWM. Goods receipt is posted in embedded EWM for the inbound delivery when the goods physically arrive in the warehouse and the inspection lot is created. In SAP S/4HANA, inspection results are assigned to the inspection lot, and follow-up actions are triggered by the embedded EWM system. This is done via **SAP Easy Access** path **Logistics • Central Functions • Advanced Returns Management • Material Inspection • Enter Material Inspection in Warehouse**. Enter selection values for selecting the inspection lot for the returns process, click on [icon], open the inspection lot in edit mode, and enter a decision code.

After goods are returned from a customer, it's also possible to assign an inspection result to a partial quantity of returned goods. To make an inspection decision on a partial quantity of returned goods, returns inbound delivery is selected using Transaction /SCWM/PRDI, and the inbound delivery items for which partial inspection is to be executed is selected. Click on [icon], and select **Display Quality Inspection (Item)**; this opens the **Quality Inspection WorkLoad** screen. On this screen, the quantity for which the inspection is to be carried out is selected and a decision code is assigned. Based on the decision code, the system executes the follow-up action on the selected partial stock.

Quality Inspection without Inspection Rules

You can perform quality inspections and decision processes without the use of inspection rules for warehouse-dependent inspection object types 4 and 5. As QM is a central feature of SAP S/4HANA, it's required to eliminate the creation of inspection rules in embedded EWM so that QM settings using the material master can be used for creation of inspection lots. Using the quality inspection without inspection rules, you can make quality acceptance decision for acceptance sampling, inspections after good receipt, presampling in production, stock inspections, and recurring inspections processes. In embedded EWM, inspection types 01 (Goods Receipt Insp. for Purchase Order), 04 (Goods Receipt Inspection from Production), 08 (Stock Transfer Inspection), and 09 (Recurring Inspection of Batches) are supported.

There are some changes that must be configured if you want to run quality inspection processes without inspection rules. You must ensure that the embedded EWM logistical follow-up action is triggered for embedded EWM inspections when recording a usage decision. Various changes required for this process are summarized here:

- You must assign a follow-up action to selected set codes for a usage decision that contains function module QFOA_EWM_LOG_FOLLOW_UP_S4. For partial lots, you should assign a decision code to function module QTFA_EWM_LOG_FOLLOW_UP_S4 via IMG menu, **Quality Management • Quality Inspection • Inspection Lot Completion • Edit Selected Sets for Usage Decisions**.
- The follow-up actions should be marked as EWM-relevant follow-up actions via IMG menu, **SCM Extended Warehouse Management • Extended Warehouse Management • Cross-Process Settings • Quality Management • Inspection Results • Maintain Follow-Up Actions • Define Follow-Up Actions**, as shown in Figure 6.112. Enter a follow-up action and follow-up function as the **Usage Decision for Inspection Lot**, and then select **EWMFolUpAct**.

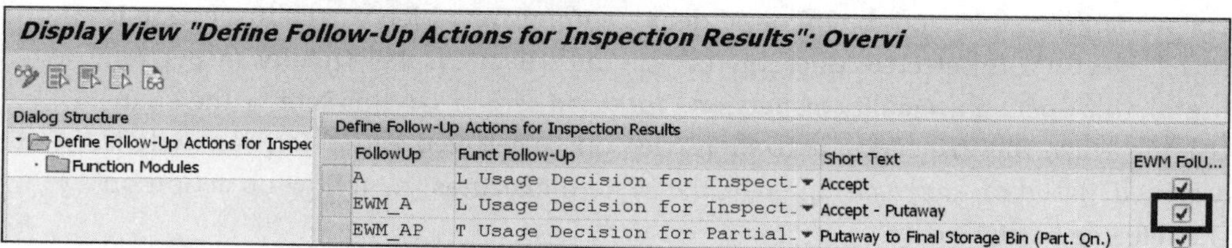

Figure 6.112 Marking Usage Design as Relevant to Embedded EWM

- You must assign follow-up actions to logistical follow-up actions via IMG menu, **SCM Extended Warehouse Management • Extended Warehouse Management • Cross-Process Settings • Quality Management • Inspection Results • Maintain Follow-Up Actions • Assign Logistical Follow-Up Actions.** Enter the follow-up action, select it, and enter the logistical action per warehouse.

Quality Inspection Engine Integration to Multiple ERP Systems

It's possible to connect decentralized EWM to more than one enterprise management system; that is, the connection can be made to multiple SAP ERP or SAP S/4HANA systems. These enterprise management systems act as external QM systems for the quality inspection engine of decentralized EWM.

After the goods receipt or quality-related stock transaction occurs in the SAP S/4HANA system, decentralized EWM is able to determine the external QM system based on the warehouse and party entitled to dispose present in the business transaction.

6.14 Summary

This chapter introduced cross-process settings used across the warehouse while carrying out inbound, outbound, and internal warehouse processes. This chapter explained some key topics such as process profiles, warehouse orders, the PPF, travel distance, serial numbers, and QM in embedded EWM and decentralized EWM. Configuration and use of these features in embedded EWM were explained in detail.

As you go through the next chapters, you'll see how these settings can be used for carrying out warehouse processes in basic warehousing and complex processes in advanced warehouse management. You should now be able to set up these cross-process definitions and objects and use them in your warehouse per your business requirements. In the next chapter, we'll discuss inbound processing.

Chapter 7
Inbound Processing

Goods receipt in embedded EWM refers to movement of goods into the warehouse. Embedded EWM offers a wide array of functionalities for managing goods receipt and putaway in the warehouse, as we'll discuss in detail in this chapter.

Inbound processing is one of the key processes in warehouse management. You can receive goods in the warehouse via a purchase order if you're getting stock from a vendor, a stock transfer order if you're receiving stock from another facility, through production receipts, or from customer returns.

The process starts with the arrival of a transportation unit (TU) or vehicle in the warehouse, unloading of goods, and carrying out a set of activities on the received goods, such as counting, quality inspection, unpacking, or deconsolidation, before goods are finally put away in the warehouse. The nature of activities that need to be performed on a product before they're stocked depends on a wide array of factors, including the nature of the product, where it must be stocked, storage conditions, and so on. You also need to make sure that goods move optimally in the warehouse during putaway to ensure maximum utilization of warehouse resources and storage space. Embedded EWM offers a wide range of functionalities for goods receipt in the warehouse to handle both simple and complex inbound processes.

In this chapter, we'll cover goods receipt in embedded EWM for inbound deliveries created in the SAP S/4HANA system. We'll discuss the basic inbound process (Section 7.1), the configuration settings required to set up goods receipt (Section 7.2), and the delivery document created in embedded EWM after the inbound delivery is distributed to the system (Section 7.3). Next, we'll discuss how TUs are checked in for inbound warehouse requests (Section 7.4), unloading and goods receipt (Section 7.5), and, finally, putaway and putaway strategies for optimizing warehouse capacity and material flow (Section 7.6).

Note

The delivery created in SAP S/4HANA is now called logistics execution delivery in embedded EWM.

7.1 What Happens During Inbound Processing?

You can perform goods receipt for external procurement, production receipt, internal stock transfer, and customer returns. In this section, we'll discuss goods receipt from external procurement and production receipt, both from a business process and system process point of view.

7.1.1 Business Process

If you're receiving goods from an external vendor, the goods receipt process may vary depending on whether you're using an advanced shipping notice (ASN). Whether you require an ASN from the vendor is controlled by setting the confirmation control key at the purchase order item level. If the confirmation control key is set, then you need to create an inbound delivery to complete goods receipts in embedded EWM.

Based on the material requirements planning (MRP) run, you decide to go ahead with the creation of a planned order or purchase requisition. You can create the purchase order manually or convert the purchase requisition to form a purchase order. The purchase order is sent to the supplier, and the supplier can either physically send the goods or send an ASN to confirm when the goods will arrive in the warehouse. The receipt of an ASN creates the inbound delivery in SAP S/4HANA.

If you're working with ASNs, the inbound process in embedded EWM begins with the receipt of an ASN sent from the vendor and the creation of an inbound delivery in SAP. The SAP S/4HANA system is the leading system for creation of purchase orders and inbound deliveries. The complete process of goods receipt and putaway is then carried out in embedded EWM. You can post the goods receipt when the goods physically arrive in the warehouse.

When an ASN is created, the system checks for the plant and storage location in the ASN and validates whether the corresponding warehouse for that plant and storage location is managed by embedded EWM. If it is, then the system distributes the inbound delivery to embedded EWM and creates the inbound delivery by calling function module enabled by a queued remote function call (qRFC). This document becomes the warehouse request in embedded EWM for goods receipt management and putaway.

Figure 7.1 summarizes how the inbound delivery document is created in embedded EWM using an ASN in SAP S/4HANA.

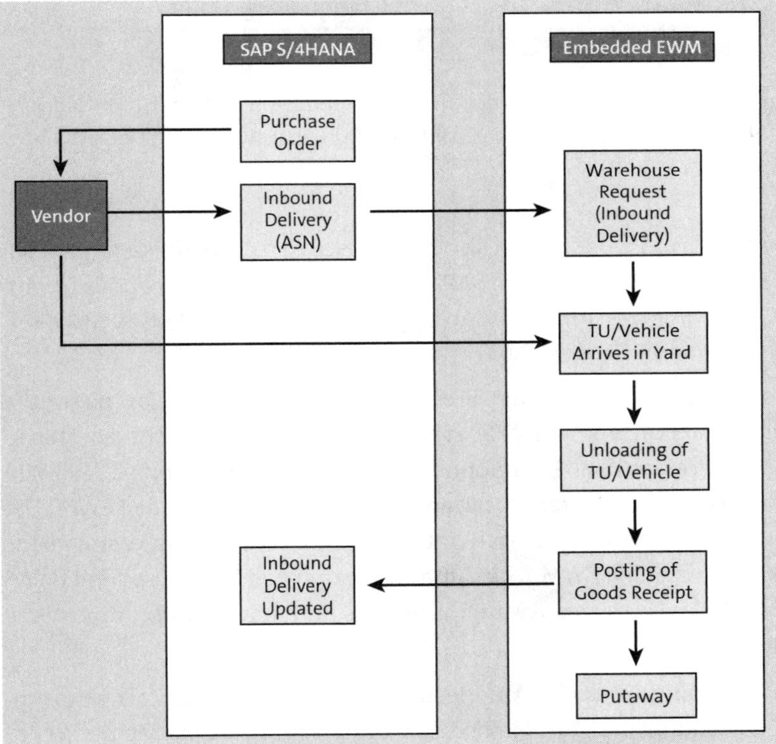

Figure 7.1 Goods Receipt in Embedded EWM Based on the Advanced Shipping Notice

Note

Users with prior experience working with decentralized EWM will notice that an inbound delivery notification is no longer created in SAP S/4HANA. This is one of the simplification strategies in embedded EWM.

After the inbound delivery is created, you can progress to the next steps in the inbound process, which may include the following:

- Arrival of vehicle or TU in the yard
- Unloading of TU for delivery
- Posting of goods receipt
- Putaway of products/handling units (HUs)

Note

Creation of an expected goods receipt document for goods receipt isn't required in embedded EWM. The inbound delivery gets information directly from the purchase/manufacturing order in SAP S/4HANA.

The inbound process in embedded EWM also can be used to receive finished goods in the warehouse. Depending on settings in SAP S/4HANA, you can trigger goods receipt posting directly from SAP S/4HANA or from embedded EWM. We'll discuss these settings in detail in Chapter 13, Section 13.6.

You can trigger goods receipt posting directly from SAP S/4HANA by using the inbound delivery created in SAP S/4HANA as soon as you've executed the last step in the production or process order. The inbound delivery is created in embedded EWM only if the receiving plant and storage location are managed by embedded EWM. The finished products are moved into the warehouse from the assembly line, and goods receipt is posted in embedded EWM. The same is also updated in the inbound delivery in SAP S/4HANA. You then create warehouse tasks for putaway and complete the putaway in embedded EWM.

To continue our running example, American company Alpha Medicals sends an order to one of its vendors based in Mexico. The order sent by Alpha Medicals contains various pharmaceutical products that are to be delivered to them in a timely manner. An Alpha purchase representative keys in the order in SAP S/4HANA and, based on material requirements, creates an inbound delivery in SAP S/4HANA that contains the products to be supplied as part of a single delivery.

As shown in Figure 7.2, after the inbound delivery is saved in SAP S/4HANA, it flows through to embedded EWM and is saved as an inbound delivery order. After the goods are received in the goods receipt area of the warehouse, goods receipt is posted in the staging area of the warehouse. Goods may also be flagged for quality inspection if quality management (QM) is activated for the product. After the checks and any ongoing packaging requirements, the goods are put away by the warehouse worker in the final putaway area based on the destination bin that the embedded EWM system proposes. The warehouse workers usually get putaway warehouse tasks on their Process Warehouse Tasks – Putaway app or the RF device they use to work in the warehouse.

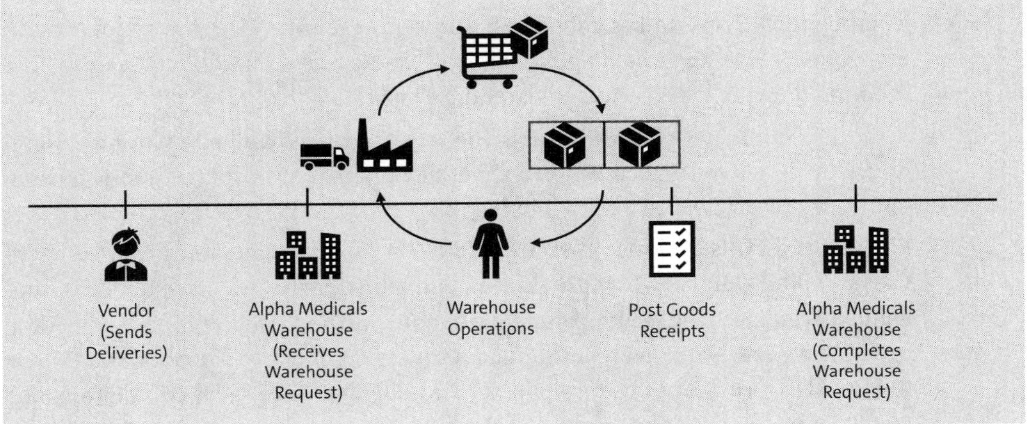

Figure 7.2 Business Flow for Inbound Processing

7.1.2 System Process

The following explains the basic system flow, including the documents and the data required to execute putaway of stock from the inbound door to the destination bin in embedded EWM and decentralized EWM. Briefly, each step in the inbound process is as follows:

1. The inbound process starts with the creation of an inbound delivery in SAP S/4HANA. The inbound delivery can be created from various business processes:
   - Purchase: A purchase order is created in SAP S/4HANA that requires putaway of goods from an embedded EWM–managed warehouse.
   - Customer returns: A customer returns order can be created in SAP S/4HANA that requires putaway of goods to an embedded EWM–managed plant for the goods returning from the customer location.
   - Production staging: A manufacturing order is created for receiving finished materials for production in the production staging area. These goods are put away to a destination bin based on the product putaway characteristics.

2. An inbound delivery is created in SAP S/4HANA for putaway to the embedded EWM warehouse. The inbound delivery can be created for any of the scenarios described in the previous step. The inbound delivery contains all the relevant data required for stock putaway: product, quantity, batch, and so on.
3. The inbound delivery is replicated to embedded EWM, and an inbound delivery is created in embedded EWM. This document serves as the requirements document in embedded EWM and is called the warehouse request. Further processing in embedded EWM such as staging, packing, and putaway is done based on the inbound delivery via creation of warehouse tasks.
4. After the warehouse worker finishes the stock putaway, and all associated warehouse tasks are confirmed, the embedded EWM system posts the goods receipt. The goods receipt is also updated in the inbound delivery in SAP S/4HANA.
5. The use of a TU is optional in embedded EWM. However, organizations can activate shipping and receiving functions in embedded EWM and make use of TU and vehicle activities to execute carrying of goods in the warehouse and unloading them. The stock is moved to a staging area after TU docks to the door and then is unloaded from a TU. Goods receipt can be posted after putaway is complete, which results in posting of goods receipt in the outbound delivery in SAP S/4HANA.

Storage control is used in a complex putaway process, in which a product must move through various process steps based on warehouse processes or the physical layout of the warehouse before it's moved to the destination storage bin. As you've read about in previous chapters, there are two types of storage control in embedded EWM: process-oriented storage control and layout-oriented storage control.

As discussed in Chapter 6, Section 6.5.4, process-oriented storage control is used for executing process steps based on warehouse processes. Some of the warehouse processes include quality inspection, value-added services (VAS), deconsolidation, and kitting. Layout-oriented storage control is used to execute warehouse processes based on the warehouse layout. For example, a product might need to be moved to the first floor in the warehouse to reach the final putaway bin via an elevator. In this case, the putaway storage process will have two process steps. The first step will move the product from the staging area to the elevator, and the second process step will move the product from the elevator to the door. The purpose of this storage control is to have stock visibility at all times in the warehouse. If a product must undergo both process-oriented and layout-oriented storage control, embedded EWM gives preference to process-oriented storage control.

Figure 7.3 shows complex movement in the inbound process using only process-oriented storage control.

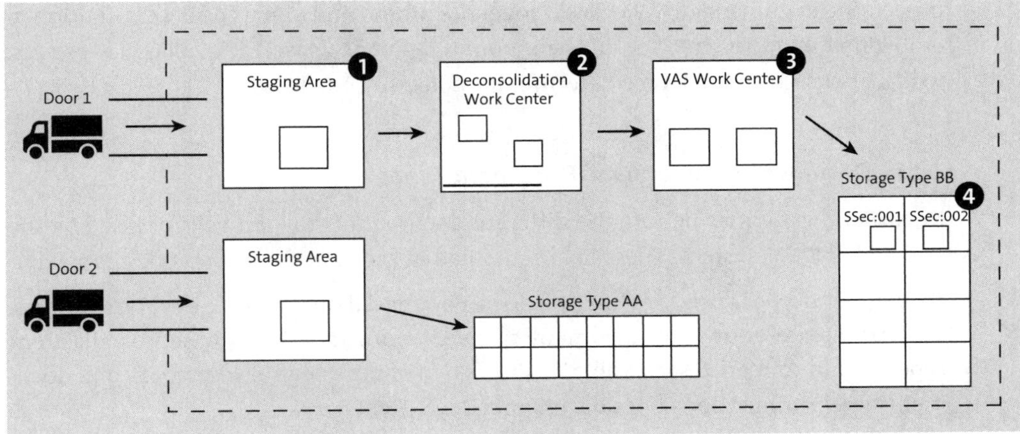

Figure 7.3 Storage Control in Inbound Processing

The primary steps involved in complex putaway are as follows, but note that they can include further steps (counting, quality inspection, etc.):

1. **Unloading**
   After the truck docks at the warehouse door, it's unloaded using an HU warehouse task.
2. **Deconsolidation**
   The pallets are taken to a deconsolidation work center where they're broken down to move individual products to their destination.
3. **Value additions**
   Based on relevance for VAS, embedded EWM creates an HU warehouse task to move the product to a VAS work center. VAS activities performed at the VAS work center include painting, oiling, packaging, and so on.
4. **Putaway**
   A final putaway HU warehouse task is now created or activated to move the product from the VAS work center to the destination storage bins. You can confirm the warehouse task from SAP GUI or by using an RF device.

7.2 Configuring Inbound Delivery Processing

In this section, we'll discuss system configurations required for inbound delivery processing in embedded EWM. We'll cover document and item type determination in embedded EWM for creation of the inbound delivery, as well as availability groups, which are used for stock type determination in embedded EWM.

7.2.1 Document Category and Document Types

Document categories denote the different documents that can be processed by the embedded EWM system. These are predefined in the system and can't be changed.

A document type is used to classify a document based on a specific business process. You can create your own document types in embedded EWM based on different types of inbound processes. Table 7.1 shows two of the document category and document type combinations possible in embedded EWM.

Document Category	Document Type	Document Type Description
PDI	INB	Inbound delivery
PDI	INBI	Inbound delivery, production

Table 7.1 Document Category and Document Types for Inbound Processing

Together, the document category and document type uniquely define the delivery document header in embedded EWM and uniquely define a business process. Define document types via IMG path **SCM Extended Warehouse Management • Extended Warehouse Management • Goods Receipt • Define Document Type**. Click on **New Entries**, and enter the document type code, description, and control parameters. A document type is used to define several key settings, including settings specific to the purpose for which it's being set up. It contains settings for document types, profiles, packing, and process controlling. Some of the key settings defined here are as follows:

- Internal number range for a document type
- Retention period in the system before the document is archived
- Profiles assignments such as action profile, status profile, text profile, and so on
- Indicator for automatic packing during inbound delivery creation

- Setting document relevance for warehousing processes such as production, scrapping, and so on

7.2.2 Item Category and Item Types

Item categories are used to group items based on their use for packing, returns, and so on. Item category codes are predefined in SAP and can't be changed. Item types define the business characteristics of an item in a delivery document. Table 7.2 shows two of the document category and document type combinations possible in embedded EWM.

Item Category	Item Type	Item Type Description
DLV	IDLV	Standard item, inbound delivery
DLV	IDPP	Inbound delivery standard item goods receipt production

Table 7.2 Item Category and Item Types in Embedded EWM

You can create item types via IMG path **SCM Extended Warehouse Management • Extended Warehouse Management • Goods Receipt Process • Inbound Delivery • Manual Settings • Define Item Types for Inbound Delivery Process**. Click on **New Entries**, and enter the item type code, description, and control parameters. Item types hold some key settings relevant to profiles and process management and control:

- Profile assignments such as status profile, incompletion profile, and process profile (note that action profiles aren't defined here, but at the document type level)
- Manual creation of line items in delivery
- Permission to allow invoice before goods issue
- Flag an item as relevant for document-related serialization, documentary batches, and so on

7.2.3 Mapping the Inbound Delivery

The deliveries created in SAP S/4HANA are distributed to embedded EWM and create deliveries in embedded EWM that are called *warehouse requests* and become the principle documents for carrying out embedded EWM-specific business processes such as creation of putaway warehouse tasks. It's important to map the delivery document type from SAP S/4HANA with the corresponding document type of the warehouse request, as shown in Figure 7.4. This helps the system know which embedded EWM document type to create based on the document type in the SAP S/4HANA system.

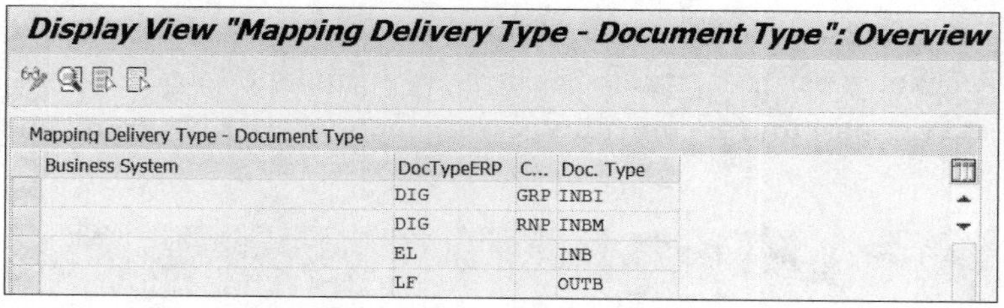

Display View "Mapping Delivery Type - Document Type": Overview

Mapping Delivery Type - Document Type

Business System	DocTypeERP	C...	Doc. Type
	DIG	GRP	INBI
	DIG	RNP	INBM
	EL		INB
	LF		OUTB

Figure 7.4 Mapping Delivery Type to Document Type

Document type mapping is done in embedded EWM from IMG path **SCM Extended Warehouse Management • Extended Warehouse Management • Interfaces • ERP Integration • Delivery Processing • Map Document Types from ERP system to EWM**. Click on **New Entries**, and enter the document type in embedded EWM for a combination of document types in SAP S/4HANA and the business system.

The **Business System** is the business system of the source SAP S/4HANA system. You can map multiple document types in SAP S/4HANA to multiple item types in embedded EWM based on the settings in the **Cde Init.Com** (code for initiator of a communication chain) field (shown in Figure 7.4). This field is used to segregate business processes based on discrete attributes such as splitting up goods receipt from production into two subprocesses for discrete manufacturing and repetitive manufacturing. This allows you to have more control over carrying out business processes in embedded EWM. Similarly, you can map multiple document types in SAP S/4HANA to one document type in embedded EWM.

Next, map item types for deliveries in SAP S/4HANA with the item types in warehouse requests in embedded EWM, as shown in Figure 7.5. To do so, navigate to IMG path **SCM Extended Warehouse Management • Extended Warehouse Management • Interfaces • ERP Integration • Delivery Processing • Map Item Types from ERP System to EWM**. Click on **New Entries**, and map the embedded EWM item type with a combination of the SAP S/4HANA business system, document type, and item type in SAP S/4HANA, and the embedded EWM item type.

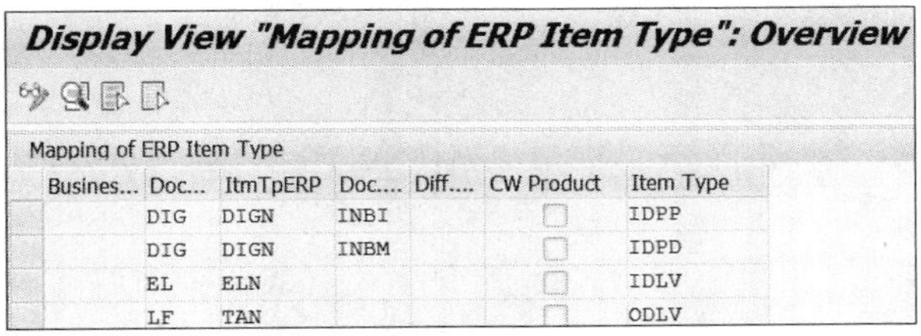

Display View "Mapping of ERP Item Type": Overview

Mapping of ERP Item Type

Busines...	Doc...	ItmTpERP	Doc....	Diff....	CW Product	Item Type
	DIG	DIGN	INBI		☐	IDPP
	DIG	DIGN	INBM		☐	IDPD
	EL	ELN			☐	IDLV
	LF	TAN			☐	ODLV

Figure 7.5 Mapping of Item Types in SAP S/4HANA with Item Types in Embedded EWM

You can map one document type in SAP S/4HANA to multiple item types in embedded EWM based on differentiation attributes. This allows you to have more control over carrying out business processes in embedded EWM. For this, you need to map the profile for the differentiation attribute used to the SAP S/4HANA document type via IMG path **SCM Extended Warehouse Management • Extended Warehouse Management • Interfaces • ERP Integration • Delivery Processing • Define ERP Document Types for Differentiation Attributes**. Click on **New Entries**, and enter a combination of SAP S/4HANA business system, document type, and profile. Similarly, you can map multiple document types in SAP S/4HANA to one document type in embedded EWM.

7.2.4 Stock Type Determination in Inbound Delivery

SAP S/4HANA tracks stock based on plant, storage location, and stock category. The stock type in embedded EWM is traced using the concept of *availability groups*. An availability group is used to control which stock is available for a storage type.

You can set up availability groups in embedded EWM from IMG path **SCM Extended Warehouse Management • Extended Warehouse Management • Goods Receipt Process • Configure Availability Group for Putaway**. The following settings are made here:

- **Define availability group**
  In this step, define the availability group for use in your warehouse. In standard embedded EWM, you use two main availability groups: 001 for goods in putaway and 002 for goods available for sale (Figure 7.6). You can create more availability groups per your business requirements.

Display View "Customizing Table - Availability Groups": Overview

Customizing Table - Availability Groups

Wa...	AGr	Description	DType ERP
SW01	001	Goods in Putaway	
SW01	002	Goods Completely Available	
SW01	003	Stock in Production	
SW01	CD	Cross-Docking	

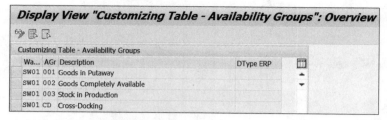

Figure 7.6 Defining Availability Groups

- **Define non-location-specific stock type**
  In this step, define the non-location-specific stock type for the warehouse. These are stock types that group stock based on their attributes and are independent of stock location in the warehouse. SAP has provided some non-location-specific stock types by default, as shown in Figure 7.7, but you can create more per your business requirements, for example, for quarantined stock.

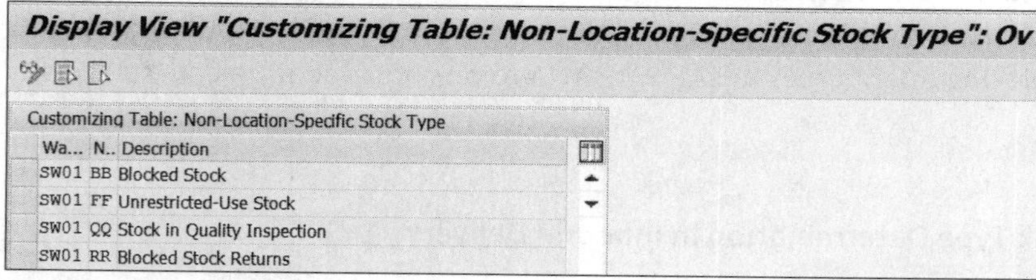

Display View "Customizing Table: Non-Location-Specific Stock Type": Ov

Customizing Table: Non-Location-Specific Stock Type

Wa...	N..	Description
SW01	BB	Blocked Stock
SW01	FF	Unrestricted-Use Stock
SW01	QQ	Stock in Quality Inspection
SW01	RR	Blocked Stock Returns

Figure 7.7 Defining Non-Location-Specific Stock Types

- **Configure stock type**
  In this activity, map the availability group and non-location-specific stock type with the stock type in embedded EWM for a specific warehouse, as shown in Figure 7.8.

The availability group described is also assigned to the plant and storage location of the embedded EWM warehouse in SAP S/4HANA, as shown in Figure 7.9. This is done via IMG path **SCM Extended Warehouse Management • Extended Warehouse Management • Interfaces • ERP Integration • Goods Movement • Map Storage Locations from ERP System to EWM**. Click on **New Entries**; enter a combination of embedded EWM warehouse, embedded EWM stock type, availability group, location-independent stock type, and stock type role; and click on **Save**. In this way, the stock type in embedded EWM is tracked using a combination of plant and storage location (using the availability group) and non-location-specific stock type (e.g., unrestricted stock, blocked stock, etc.).

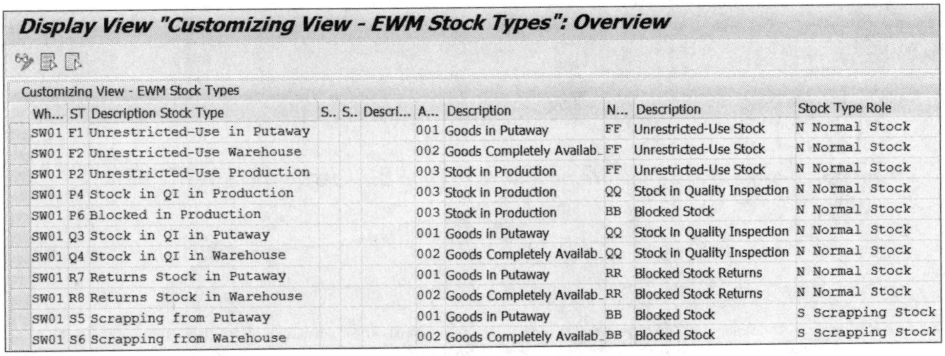

Display View "Customizing View - EWM Stock Types": Overview

Customizing View - EWM Stock Types

Wh...	ST	Description Stock Type	S..	S..	Descri...	A...	Description	N...	Description	Stock Type Role
SW01	F1	Unrestricted-Use in Putaway				001	Goods in Putaway	FF	Unrestricted-Use Stock	N Normal Stock
SW01	F2	Unrestricted-Use Warehouse				002	Goods Completely Availab...	FF	Unrestricted-Use Stock	N Normal Stock
SW01	P2	Unrestricted-Use Production				003	Stock in Production	FF	Unrestricted-Use Stock	N Normal Stock
SW01	P4	Stock in QI in Production				003	Stock in Production	QQ	Stock in Quality Inspection	N Normal Stock
SW01	P6	Blocked in Production				003	Stock in Production	BB	Blocked Stock	N Normal Stock
SW01	Q3	Stock in QI in Putaway				001	Goods in Putaway	QQ	Stock in Quality Inspection	N Normal Stock
SW01	Q4	Stock in QI in Warehouse				002	Goods Completely Availab...	QQ	Stock in Quality Inspection	N Normal Stock
SW01	R7	Returns Stock in Putaway				001	Goods in Putaway	RR	Blocked Stock Returns	N Normal Stock
SW01	R8	Returns Stock in Warehouse				002	Goods Completely Availab...	RR	Blocked Stock Returns	N Normal Stock
SW01	S5	Scrapping from Putaway				001	Goods in Putaway	BB	Blocked Stock	S Scrapping Stock
SW01	S6	Scrapping from Warehouse				002	Goods Completely Availab...	BB	Blocked Stock	S Scrapping Stock

Figure 7.8 Mapping the Embedded EWM Stock Type

Based on the availability group, you can set up different stock types for the inbound and outbound processes. For example, in Figure 7.9, we mapped availability group 001 (linked to storage location ROD, which marks the location for stock received on the docks) to embedded EWM stock type F1, and availability group 002 (linked to storage location AFS for storing goods available for sale) to embedded EWM stock type F2.

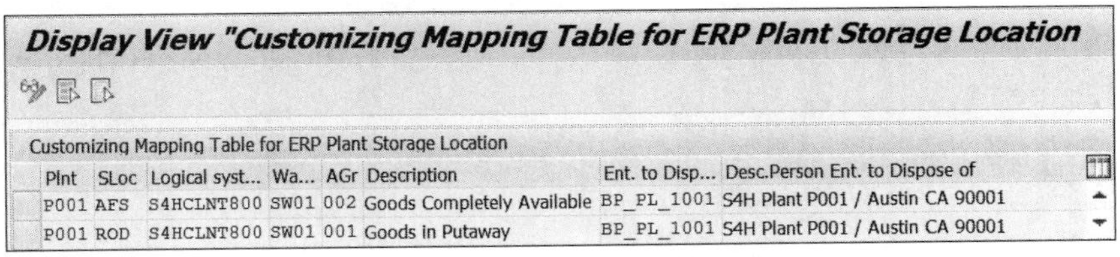

Display View "Customizing Mapping Table for ERP Plant Storage Location

Customizing Mapping Table for ERP Plant Storage Location

Plnt	SLoc	Logical syst...	Wa...	AGr	Description	Ent. to Disp...	Desc.Person Ent. to Dispose of
P001	AFS	S4HCLNT800	SW01	002	Goods Completely Available	BP_PL_1001	S4H Plant P001 / Austin CA 90001
P001	ROD	S4HCLNT800	SW01	001	Goods in Putaway	BP_PL_1001	S4H Plant P001 / Austin CA 90001

Figure 7.9 Mapping Storage Locations from SAP S/4HANA to Embedded EWM

When an inbound delivery is created in embedded EWM, the system checks the plant and storage location for the delivery in SAP S/4HANA and determines the availability group for that plant and storage location combination. Next, it determines the embedded EWM stock type by looking at the mapping of the availability group and non-location-specific stock type based on the stock category for the delivery in SAP S/4HANA and determines the embedded EWM stock type. This stock type is populated in the inbound delivery created in embedded EWM, as shown in Figure 7.10.

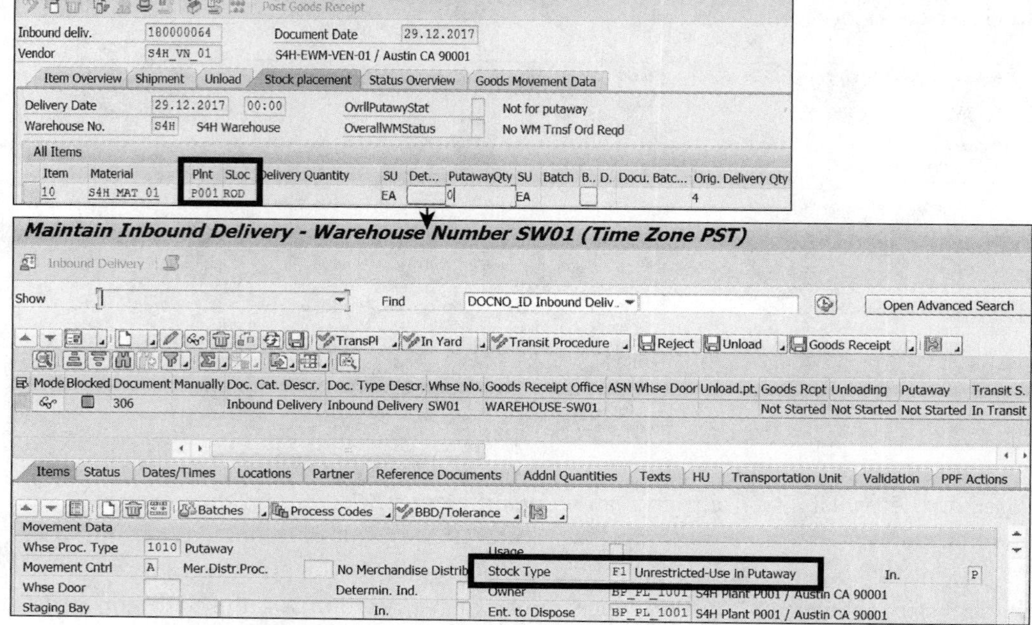

Figure 7.10 Stock Type in the Inbound Delivery from SAP S/4HANA to Embedded EWM

You can also assign an availability group to storage types in storage type settings, as shown in Figure 7.11.

Goods Movement Control

Availability Group	002	Mandatory	✓
Non-Dep. Stock Type		No GI	✓
Post.Change Bin		Stock Type Role	

Figure 7.11 Assigning the Availability Group to the Storage Type

If the availability group of stock being put away into a storage bin for the storage type is different from the availability group set in the storage type, then the system does a posting change for the stock. For example, if stock in the delivery with stock type F1, as shown in Figure 7.11, is put away in a storage type with availability group 002, then based on the settings discussed previously—availability group 002 mapped to stock type F2—the system will perform a posting change on stock being put away and change it to type F2, which is unrestricted stock available for sale.

Note

We discussed in Chapter 6, Section 6.3.2, that an availability group is also set at the warehouse process type level. The system always gives preference to the availability group set at the storage type level; if it doesn't find one, it looks for an availability group set at the process type level. If no availability group is set at either of these levels, then the embedded EWM stock type remains unchanged.

7.2.5 Stock Type Enhancement

You can define the stock type description at the warehouse level, so that plant/storage location descriptions can be saved in a warehouse-dependent manner via IMG path **SCM Extended Warehouse Management • Extended Warehouse Management • Goods Receipt Process • Configure Availability Group for Putaway • Configure Stock Type**.

Note

Prior to SAP S/4HANA 1809, the description of the stock types could only be defined in a warehouse-independent manner. Using this text description of the stock type, you can mention the plant and storage location when referring to a stock type, which helps users easily identify the plant and stock type combination linked to a stock type. You can, for example, describe stock type F1 for the SW01 sample warehouse as "Unrestricted stock in PL04/AFS."

This feature allows you to display a description for warehouse stock types and availability groups, which makes mapping plants, storage locations, stock types, and availability groups transparent.

7.3 Inbound Delivery

The inbound delivery document is created in embedded EWM after the inbound delivery or a returns delivery in SAP S/4HANA is successfully distributed to embedded EWM. The inbound delivery also can be created directly in embedded EWM while carrying out goods receipt from production. This document contains all the data required for carrying out goods receipt and putaway in embedded EWM. The TU or vehicle is registered in the yard based on the delivery it's carrying. The warehouse tasks for unloading and putaway are created for warehouse requests. You can adjust the quantity in the inbound delivery in embedded EWM based on the goods receipt quantity, and the same is updated in the delivery in SAP S/4HANA. If the settings for the item type permit, you can also create new items in the delivery. The inbound delivery in embedded EWM has two levels: document header and document item.

The document header is defined by the document category and document type, and it contains important data such as the following:

- Goods receiving office
- ASN number
- Processing statuses
- Transportation details

The document item is defined by the item category and item type, and it holds item-specific data for items in the inbound delivery, such as the following:

- Warehouse process type
- Item-level status
- Product-specific data, such as product number, batch, and so on
- Line item quantity

Figure 7.12 shows an inbound delivery in embedded EWM with the document header and **Item** section highlighted.

Note

The following SAP Fiori apps are available to create and process inbound deliveries:

- **Create Inbound Deliveries**
  This app allows you to create inbound deliveries for purchase orders that are then used for stock putaway in the warehouse.
- **Change Inbound Deliveries**
  This app allows you to change inbound deliveries created for purchase orders that are then used for stock putaway in the warehouse.
- **Maintain Inbound Deliveries**
  This app allows you to change the inbound delivery warehouse request in embedded EWM/decentralized EWM warehouses.

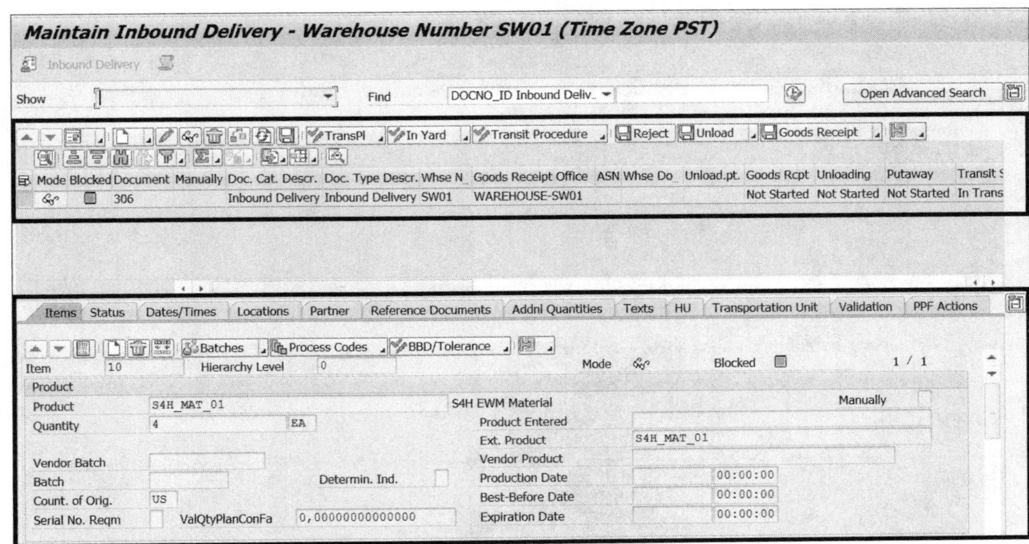

Figure 7.12 Inbound Delivery Header and Item Section in Display Mode

7.4 Check-In

The next step after creation of an inbound delivery in embedded EWM is physical receipt of goods in the warehouse. Goods arrive in the warehouse in vehicles or TUs. Use yard management in embedded EWM to manage vehicles coming into the yard (as discussed in detail in Chapter 18).

The *yard* is the space outside the warehouse used for managing incoming and outgoing vehicles. It's typically made up of checkpoints, parking, and doors. The first step in managing inbound vehicles is to acknowledge their entry past the entry checkpoint and into the warehouse premises. This is done by the shipping office, which validates the deliveries in the TU and relevant paperwork, such as the delivery note.

This process is called *check-in* in embedded EWM and is done via Transaction /SCWM/CICO, which also can be accessed from **SAP Easy Access** path **Logistics • SCM Extended Warehouse Management • Extended Warehouse Management • Shipping and Receiving • Yard Management • Arrival at/Departure from Checkpoint**, as shown in Figure 7.13. Enter the TU search criteria, and search for the TU. Select the **TU**, click on **Arrive at Checkpoint**, and then **Save** to set the TU as checked-in at the warehouse.

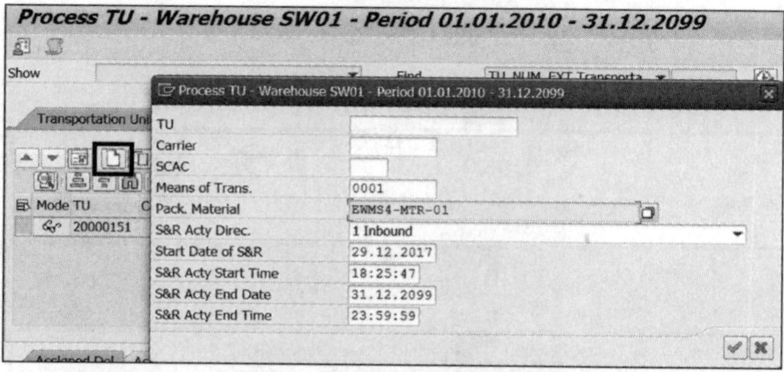

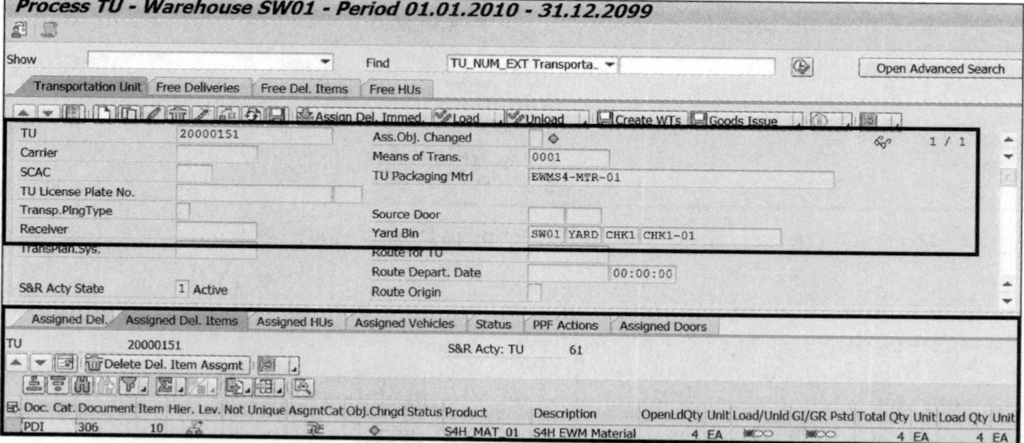

Figure 7.13 Transportation Unit Containing the Inbound Delivery

> **Note**
>
> Yard management is available as a component of shipping and receiving in advanced warehouse management in embedded EWM. Using yard management in the inbound process in embedded EWM is optional.

If a vendor has already sent an ASN, then the inbound delivery will already exist in the warehouse. If there is no ASN, then you can create the inbound delivery in embedded EWM directly by getting required information from the purchase order or manufacturing order. This delivery in embedded EWM creates the inbound delivery in SAP S/4HANA.

Assign the delivery to a TU using Transaction /SCWM/TU. Click on the **Assign. Del. Immed.** button, and select the delivery to be assigned. The TU can then be assigned to a vehicle using Transaction /SCWM/VEH by selecting the vehicle and clicking on the **TU Assignment** button on transaction screen. You can't assign a delivery directly to a vehicle. The vehicle information—license plate number, driver, carrier, and so on—is updated for the vehicle/TU. After the TU is checked-in, the status of the TU is updated to **Arrived at Checkpoint**.

If there is no empty warehouse door available, then the vehicle is moved to a parking lot, where it waits for one of the doors to become available. After a door becomes available, the TU is moved to a warehouse door, where the unloading process begins. Do this via Transaction /SCWM/YMOVE, which also can be accessed from **SAP Easy Access** path **Logistics • SCM Extended Warehouse Management • Extended Warehouse Management • Shipping and Receiving • Yard Management • Create Warehouse Task in Yard**. Click on the **Create + Save for TUs** button. This creates a warehouse task to move an HU with the name of the TU. The warehouse task has the source bin as the current location of the HU for the TU. The destination bin for the warehouse door can be determined using process-oriented storage control or can be entered manually. (We'll discuss yard management further in Chapter 18.)

Note

Advanced/extended warehouse management in embedded EWM in SAP S/4HANA offers the added advantage of inbound process optimization. In this way, you can group multiple deliveries in a single TU or vehicle and complete the inbound process for those deliveries together.

7.5 Unloading and Goods Receipt

Unloading and goods receipt begin after the inbound delivery has been verified at the checkpoint and the TU/vehicle is docked at the door. You can verify the inbound delivery using Transaction /SCWM/PRDI, which can also be accessed from **SAP Easy Access** path **Logistics • SCM Extended Warehouse Management • Extended Warehouse Management • Delivery Processing • Inbound Delivery • Maintain Inbound Delivery**.

You can review the TU to which the delivery is assigned by navigating to the **Transportation** tab in the **Delivery Item** section. The inbound deliveries can be viewed in the warehouse monitor using Transaction /SCWM/MON, which can be accessed from **SAP Easy Access** path **Logistics • SCM Extended Warehouse Management • Extended Warehouse Management • Monitoring • Warehouse Management Monitor**. In the navigation tree, navigate to **Inbound • Documents • Inbound Delivery**; in the search criteria, provide details for the inbound delivery. You'll see results like those shown in Figure 7.14.

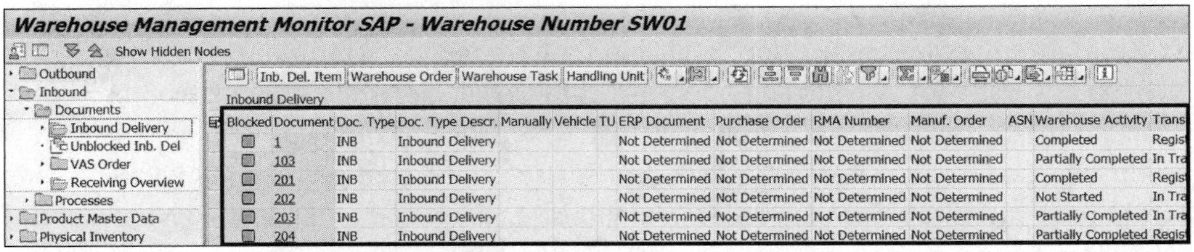

Warehouse Management Monitor SAP - Warehouse Number SW01

Show Hidden Nodes

- Outbound
- Inbound
  - Documents
    - Inbound Delivery
    - Unblocked Inb. Del
    - VAS Order
    - Receiving Overview
  - Processes
- Product Master Data
- Physical Inventory

Inb. Del. Item | Warehouse Order | Warehouse Task | Handling Unit

Inbound Delivery

Blocked	Document	Doc. Type	Doc. Type Descr.	Manually	Vehicle	TU	ERP Document	Purchase Order	RMA Number	Manuf. Order	ASN	Warehouse Activity	Trans
	1	INB	Inbound Delivery				Not Determined	Not Determined	Not Determined	Not Determined		Completed	Regis
	103	INB	Inbound Delivery				Not Determined	Not Determined	Not Determined	Not Determined		Partially Completed	In Tra
	201	INB	Inbound Delivery				Not Determined	Not Determined	Not Determined	Not Determined		Completed	Regis
	202	INB	Inbound Delivery				Not Determined	Not Determined	Not Determined	Not Determined		Not Started	In Tra
	203	INB	Inbound Delivery				Not Determined	Not Determined	Not Determined	Not Determined		Partially Completed	In Tra
	204	INB	Inbound Delivery				Not Determined	Not Determined	Not Determined	Not Determined		Partially Completed	Regis

Figure 7.14 Inbound Delivery in the Warehouse Monitor

The goods are unloaded from the TU/vehicle and moved to a staging area for goods receipt. In the following sections, we'll cover the unloading and goods receipt processes in detail.

7.5.1 Unloading

Unloading is the process of moving goods from the TU/vehicle and bringing them to the staging area assigned to a door in the warehouse. The SAP transaction for unloading is Transaction /SCWM/UNLOAD, which can also be accessed from **SAP Easy Access** path **Logistics • SCM Extended Warehouse Management • Extended Warehouse Management • Delivery Processing • Inbound Delivery • Unload**. The delivery to be unloaded can be searched for and unloaded using the **Unload** button.

Embedded EWM supports two types of unloading: *simple unloading* and *complex unloading*. Simple unloading is used to update the unload status of the delivery in the TU manually without creating an unloading warehouse task. If goods receipt is performed directly in the staging area, then unloading isn't required or can be done using simple unloading. You can do simple unloading by selecting the **Unload** button, as shown in Figure 7.15. You can also perform unloading directly for the inbound delivery using Transaction /SCWM/PRDI or for the TU using Transaction /SCWM/TU. After unloading is complete, the unloading status of HUs and the status of delivery items are updated to **Unloading Complete**.

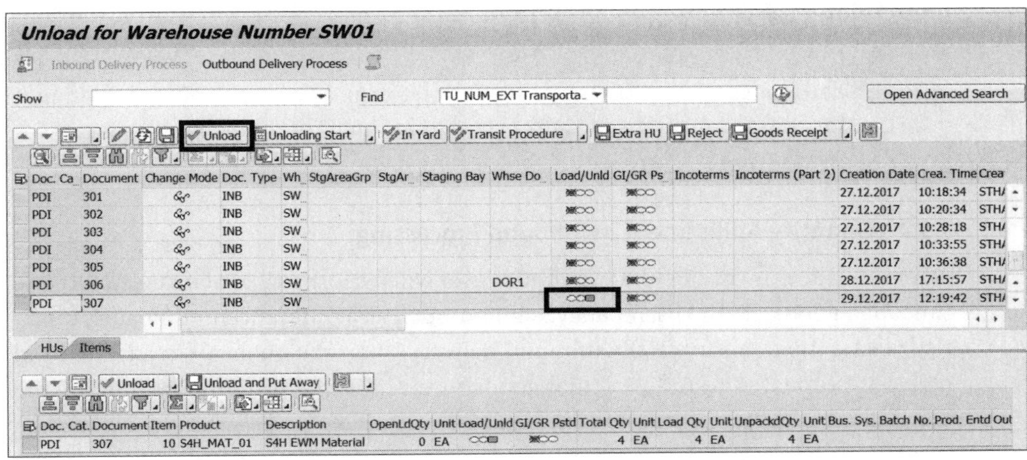

Figure 7.15 Simple Unloading of the Inbound Delivery

Complex unloading, on the other hand, requires creation and confirmation of warehouse tasks to complete the unloading process. Complex unloading is used when the receipt of delivery items is posted to TU or the door bin and can be done with or without process-oriented storage control. The destination bin for the unloading warehouse task is the staging bay for inbound deliveries. The unloading warehouse tasks can be confirmed either from SAP GUI or from the RF interface.

While executing unloading of inbound delivery without a storage process, the warehouse task created for the process type in the inbound delivery line item performs both unloading and putaway upon task confirmation. You can change the destination bin in the warehouse task manually and unload the HU to the staging bin of the delivery item. For unloading with process-oriented storage control, the unloading warehouse task is created from the goods receipt location to the staging area of the inbound delivery. The unloading warehouse tasks can be grouped together into warehouse orders by using the **Load/Unload** creation category in the warehouse order creation rule.

You can maintain a staging area and door determination for the inbound process via Transaction /SCWM/STADET_IN or via **SAP Easy Access** path **Logistics • SCM Extended Warehouse Management • Extended Warehouse Management • Settings • Shipping and Receiving • Staging Area and Door Determination (Inbound)**. Click on **New Entries**, and enter a combination of warehouse process type and staging area door determination group.

> **Note**
>
> The Unload Transportation Units app allows you to unload an inbound delivery from a TU onto the warehouse staging area using either simple or complex unloading.

7.5.2 Quantity Adjustment in Inbound Processing

After unloading is complete, a warehouse user will perform a visual inspection of the unloaded goods. If any discrepancy is noted, such as a difference in unloaded quantity versus the quantity in the inbound delivery, then the quantity in the inbound delivery is updated to reflect actual goods received in the warehouse. This is done using process codes, as shown in Figure 7.16.

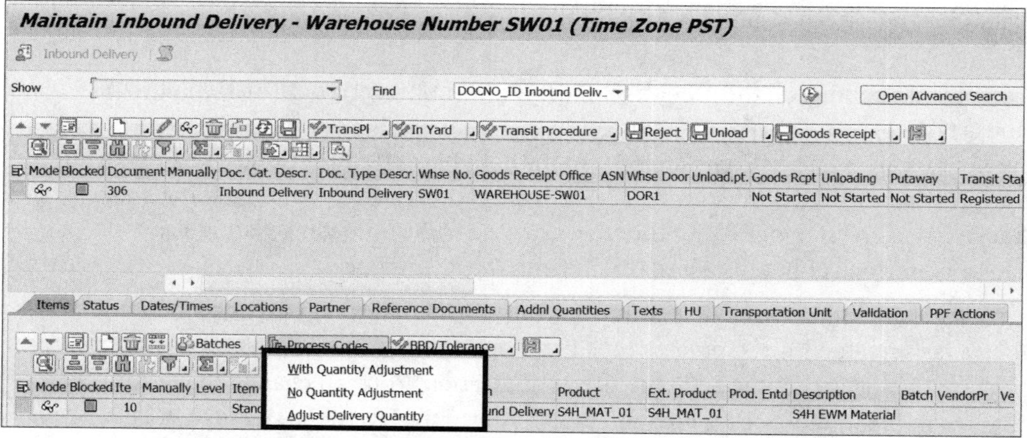

Figure 7.16 Using Process Codes for Quantity Difference

If the delivery quantity is changed manually, the system determines the default process code based on settings that can be viewed in the **Process Codes** tab in the inbound delivery at the item level in embedded EWM. If there is a difference between the quantity in the inbound delivery and the quantity for which warehouse tasks have been created, then you can select the **Adjust Delivery Quantity** option, as shown in Figure 7.16. This automatically updates the delivery quantity to the quantity specified in the warehouse tasks.

Some of the process codes available in embedded EWM to manage quantity adjustments for deliveries are as follows:

- **1001 Delivery Difference, Adjust Document**
  In this case, the delivery quantity is adjusted in embedded EWM, and the process code is saved in the delivery, but the transferred delivery quantity isn't adjusted in SAP S/4HANA.
- **1002 Delivery Difference, Adjust Document + Quantity**
  In this case, embedded EWM updates both the delivery quantity in embedded EWM and the transferred delivery quantity. This results in a delivery split, wherein the adjusted quantity remains in the original delivery and the remaining quantity is moved to a new delivery in embedded EWM.
- **1003 Delivery Difference, No Adjustment**
  No change is made to the delivery quantity. The process code is updated in the delivery for documentation purposes.
- **1004 Reject Inbound Delivery**
  This process code is used to set the quantity in the inbound delivery to 0. For example, if an inbound delivery is created for 10 pieces, you can reject the inbound delivery by setting a quantity of 10-, which will set the total quantity in the warehouse request to 0.

> **Note**
> Process codes should be applied before goods receipt is completed in embedded EWM.

7.5.3 Goods Receipt

After unloading is complete, you can post goods receipt for the inbound delivery in embedded EWM. You can perform complete and partial goods receipt in embedded EWM using inbound delivery or warehouse tasks, as follows:

- **Complete goods receipt using inbound delivery or warehouse tasks**
  Complete goods receipt using inbound delivery can be done from Transaction /SCWM/GR. You can search for and select the inbound delivery by entering search criteria such as TU, inbound delivery, door, SAP S/4HANA document, and so on. To execute goods receipt, click on the **GR** button, or enter Transaction /SCWM/PRDI, and click on the **Goods Receipt** button. If you need to perform goods receipt after putaway, you can wait for the system to set the goods receipt to **Complete** automatically after all putaway warehouse tasks are confirmed. This will also update the goods receipt status for the inbound delivery in SAP S/4HANA.

- **Partial goods receipt using warehouse tasks**
  If an inbound delivery has more than one putaway warehouse task, the status of the goods receipt in the inbound delivery remains set to **Partially Complete** until all tasks are confirmed. The system updates the goods receipt status in the inbound delivery in SAP S/4HANA using the Post Processing Framework (PPF).
- **Goods receipt reversal using returns delivery**
  Goods often need to be returned to the vendor or other warehouses after they've physically arrived in the warehouse and have been put away. To perform stock returns using deliveries, the following actions need to be performed:
  - The inbound delivery for which the putaway is completed and goods receipt status is set as **Complete** is searched for and selected using Transaction /SCWM/PRDI.
  - Follow the **Inbound Delivery • Follow-on Function • Return to Vendor** path in the menu of the selected inbound delivery. This takes you to the SAP S/4HANA core in the Transaction VL60 screen.
  - On the **Returns Delivery** screen, select **Quantity Differences • Return Quantities**, enter the quantity to be returned to the vendor from the warehouse, and save. This creates a return delivery in SAP S/4HANA and distributes it to embedded EWM, creating an outbound delivery order.
  - Stock to be returned to the vendor is then picked based on the outbound delivery order, issued out of the warehouse, and then sent to the original vendor as part of the return process.

Note

The following SAP Fiori apps are available to perform goods receipt in embedded EWM warehouse:

- **Display Workload**
  This app allows you to search for inbound deliveries for putaway based on various filtering criteria such as overdue purchase orders or a subset of timelines (e.g., a few days, hours, etc.).
- **Process Goods Receipt**
  This app allows you to display, edit, change, batch, scan, pack, and edit TUs, as well as perform goods receipt for inbound deliveries selected based on search criteria such as purchase order, vendors, and so on.

7.6 Putaway

After unloading is complete, the next step in processing the inbound delivery in embedded EWM is putaway. This means moving products from the staging area to final putaway storage bins in the warehouse. However, putaway in embedded EWM isn't always direct putaway into destination bins. Usually, a product moves through one or more intermediate steps, such as labeling, deconsolidation, or quality inspection, before it becomes ready for final putaway. In such cases, the product moves through several intermediate bins before it reaches the destination storage bin. This is called *complex putaway*, as opposed to *simple putaway*, in which products received in the staging area in the warehouse are directly moved to the final bin.

In the following sections, we'll cover various processes involved in putaway in the warehouse. We'll also discuss putaway strategies in embedded EWM that are used for determination of the final storage bin in the warehouse.

7.6.1 Deconsolidation

Deconsolidation is the process of breaking an HU into multiple HUs based on products that belong to different consolidation groups. Consolidation groups are used to group products based on similar attributes. Deconsolidation allows you to perform distributed putaway in embedded EWM. For example, when the goods receipt process is started in the inbound delivery, the system checks the destination activity area and consolidation groups of the products contained within the HU. If it finds that an HU has products that belong to different consolidation groups, it sets the original putaway task to **Inactive** and creates a new warehouse task to move the HU to the deconsolidation work center. In the outbound process, you create consolidation groups for products with the same shipping requirements, such as route, ship-to party, and so on.

During the putaway process, embedded EWM determines an HU as relevant for deconsolidation if it meets one of the following criteria:

- The activity areas for the products within an HU are different.
- The activity areas for the products within an HU are the same, but the consolidation groups are different.
- The activity areas and consolidation groups for the products within an HU are the same, but the maximum number of warehouse tasks for the HU has been exceeded.

The following configuration settings are required for setting up deconsolidation in embedded EWM:

- **Assign number range interval**
  Assign the number range interval created for consolidation groups to the warehouse via IMG path **SCM Extended Warehouse Management • Extended Warehouse Management • Goods Receipt Process • Deconsolidation • Assign Number Range Interval to Consolidation Groups**, as shown in Figure 7.17. Click on **New Entries**, and add a combination of embedded EWM warehouse, number range type, and number range interval.

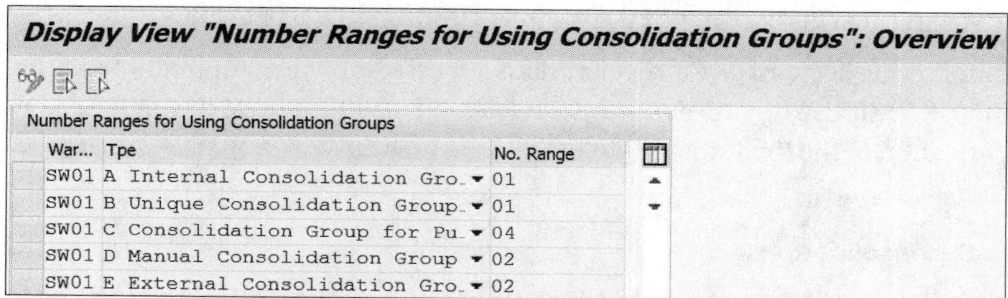

Display View "Number Ranges for Using Consolidation Groups": Overview

Number Ranges for Using Consolidation Groups

War...	Tpe	No. Range
SW01	A Internal Consolidation Gro...	01
SW01	B Unique Consolidation Group...	01
SW01	C Consolidation Group for Pu...	04
SW01	D Manual Consolidation Group	02
SW01	E External Consolidation Gro...	02

Figure 7.17 Assigning the Number Range Interval to the Consolidation Group

- **Define deconsolidation attributes**
  If you want to use deconsolidation in process-oriented storage control, you also need to define deconsolidation attributes for each activity area. The attributes are required in the process step for deconsolidation in embedded EWM. The value in the **MaxP** field is used to define the maximum number of warehouse tasks in the putaway HU. The value in the **MaxD** field is used to define the maximum number of warehouse tasks in the deconsolidation HU (Figure 7.18). If the actual number of warehouse tasks exceeds the maximum number of permitted warehouse tasks, then the HU is moved to the deconsolidation work center.

Display View "Deconsolidation HU: Determination Procedure and No. of I

Deconsolidation HU: Determination Procedure and No. of Items

War...	Acty Area	Activity	MaxP	MaxD
SW01	0010	PTWY	5	7
SW01	0020	PTWY	5	7

Figure 7.18 Assigning Attributes to the Activity Area

> **Example**
>
> You receive a deconsolidation HU with 10 putaway warehouse tasks. The system moves the HU to the deconsolidation work center because the maximum number of tasks allowed in a deconsolidation HU is only seven. Here, the system creates another putaway HU with five warehouse tasks. The HU is then closed, and a putaway warehouse task is created because the maximum number of putaway warehouse tasks in an HU can't be more than five, as shown in Figure 7.18. The system then creates another HU with the remaining products.

- **Define deconsolidation station**
  You also need to define the deconsolidation station where the HU will be deconsolidated. To do this, assign the deconsolidation work center or storage type, section, and bin details to the combination of warehouse, source storage bin, HU type group, and destination storage area. The source storage type can be a staging area or door at which the TU is docked. The system determines the warehouse process type to create warehouse tasks to move the HU to a deconsolidation work center based on settings maintained in process-oriented storage control.

  You can define the determination of the deconsolidation work center via IMG path **SCM Extended Warehouse Management • Extended Warehouse Management • Goods Receipt Process • Deconsolidation • Specify Deconsolidation Station**, as shown in Figure 7.19. Click on **New Entries**, and provide either the deconsolidation work center or storage type, section, and bin for the deconsolidation work center.

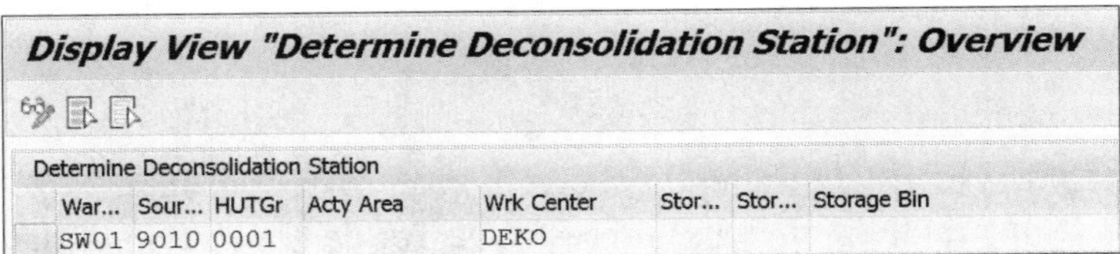

Display View "Determine Deconsolidation Station": Overview

Determine Deconsolidation Station

War...	Sour...	HUTGr	Acty Area	Wrk Center	Stor...	Stor...	Storage Bin
SW01	9010	0001		DEKO			

Figure 7.19 Determination of Deconsolidation Work Center

To view the HUs in a deconsolidation work center via Transaction /SCWM/DCONS, which can also be accessed via **SAP Easy Access** path **Logistics • SCM Extended Warehouse Management • Extended Warehouse Management • Execution • Deconsolidation in Goods Receipt**, provide the deconsolidation work center for your embedded EWM warehouse. Upon execution, the left-hand side of the screen, or the tree control, shows the HUs available in the deconsolidation work center. The upper-right area shows various tabs that can be used to execute actions in packing.

7.6.2 Putaway in Embedded EWM

The goods receipt process ends after putaway of the product in the destination storage type. This is done by confirming the final putaway warehouse tasks. You can schedule the automatic creation of putaway warehouse tasks by setting up the PPF action `/SCWM/PDI_01_WT_CREATE` for action profile `/SCWM/PDI_01` after goods receipt has been processed. If required, you can also create the warehouse tasks manually. To do so, navigate to **SAP Easy Access** path **Logistics • SCM Extended Warehouse Management • Extended Warehouse Management • Work Scheduling • Create Warehouse Task for Warehouse Request • Putaway for Inbound Delivery**. The system combines the putaway tasks into warehouse orders that are assigned to resources in the warehouse.

You can review the status of warehouse task creation by viewing the value of the **Putaway Planning** status in the warehouse request. The system sets the **Putaway Planning** to **Partially Completed** if you've created warehouse tasks for some of the quantities in the inbound delivery. The system sets the **Putaway Planning** status to **Completed** if it's created warehouse tasks for the entire quantity in the warehouse request.

The putaway bin determination is done beginning with determination of storage type, section, and bin. We'll discuss how the system determines the destination storage bin for putaway in the following sections.

Storage Type Determination

In simple putaway, the system determines the source storage type based on the storage type and bin defined in the warehouse process type. For determination of the putaway storage bin, the system first starts by determining the storage type by obtaining information from the inbound delivery document, warehouse product master, packaging specification, and hazardous substance master data (if the product is hazardous) to determine the storage type search sequence. The following data is determined based on the information provided in the inbound delivery (also shown in Figure 7.20):

- Based on the product in the inbound delivery, the system determines the process type indicator and putaway control indicator.

- The system checks if the product is hazardous and determines the hazard rating from the hazardous substance master.
- The system also determines the packaging specifications of the product and assigned warehouse to determine the quantity classification.

The putaway control indicator is used to control putaway for products into similar storage types. The putaway indicator is created via IMG path **SCM Extended Warehouse Management • Extended Warehouse Management • Goods Receipt Process • Strategies • Storage Type Search • Define Putaway Control Indicator**. Click on **New Entries**, and define a new putaway control indicator for the warehouse, which is then assigned to the warehouse product master in the **Storage Data** tab using Transaction /SCWM/MAT1.

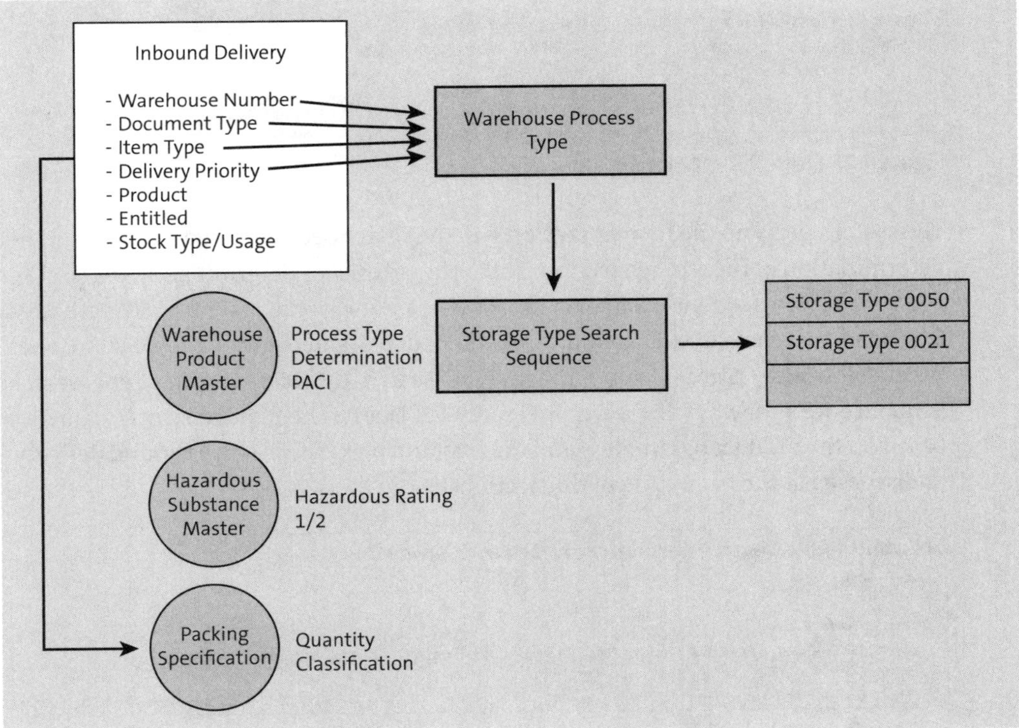

Figure 7.20 Storage Type Determination

To define a storage type search sequence, navigate to IMG path **SCM Extended Warehouse Management • Extended Warehouse Management • Goods Receipt Process •**

Strategies • Storage Type Search • Define Storage Type Search Sequence for Putaway. Click on **New Entries**, and define a new storage type search sequence for the embedded EWM warehouse.

The storage type search sequence is used to group together storage types in a sequence. To group together storage types, navigate to IMG path **SCM Extended Warehouse Management • Extended Warehouse Management • Goods Receipt Process • Strategies • Storage Type Search • Assign Storage Types to Storage Type Search Sequence**, as shown in Figure 7.21. Click on **New Entries**, and add a sequence of storage types to the search sequence.

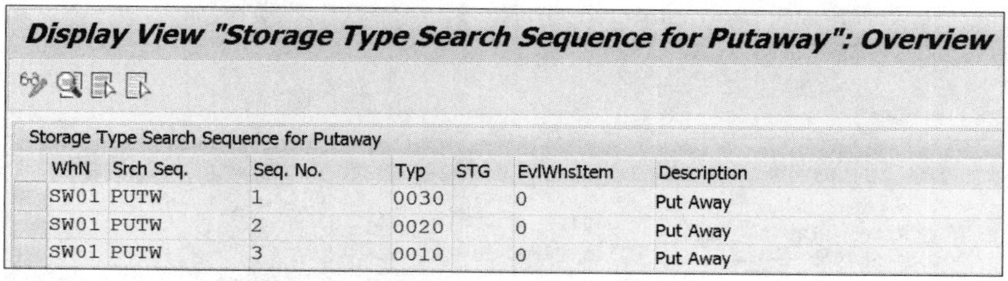

Display View "Storage Type Search Sequence for Putaway": Overview

Storage Type Search Sequence for Putaway

WhN	Srch Seq.	Seq. No.	Typ	STG	EvlWhsItem	Description
SW01	PUTW	1	0030		0	Put Away
SW01	PUTW	2	0020		0	Put Away
SW01	PUTW	3	0010		0	Put Away

Figure 7.21 Storage Type Search Sequence

The system picks up the first storage type in the search sequence and begins with the determination of the storage section. To set the criteria for determination of the storage type search sequence for a product during putaway, navigate to IMG path **SCM Extended Warehouse Management • Extended Warehouse Management • Goods Receipt Process • Strategies • Storage Type Search • Specify Storage Type Search Sequence for Putaway**, as shown in Figure 7.22. Define the storage search sequence based on the product parameters and information picked from the inbound delivery, as discussed at the beginning of this section.

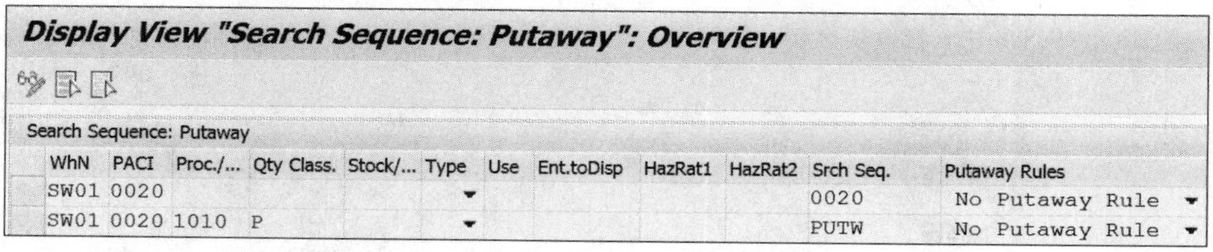

Display View "Search Sequence: Putaway": Overview

Search Sequence: Putaway

WhN	PACI	Proc./...	Qty Class.	Stock/...	Type	Use	Ent.toDisp	HazRat1	HazRat2	Srch Seq.	Putaway Rules
SW01	0020									0020	No Putaway Rule
SW01	0020	1010	P							PUTW	No Putaway Rule

Figure 7.22 Determination of the Storage Type Search Sequence

As shown in Figure 7.22, thousands of combinations are possible in the system for determining the right storage type search sequence for a combination of input criteria. We used optimization of the access sequence for optimizing the access strategy for storage type searches during putaway. The system first looks for a fully qualified entry, that is, an entry in the determination table with all values set. If the system doesn't find a fully qualified entry, then it looks at the access sequence maintained in the optimization table.

As shown in Figure 7.23, based on sequence number 0, the system first looks for an entry in the determination table for which both the putaway control indicator and the process type are specified and picks the storage type search sequence maintained for that entry.

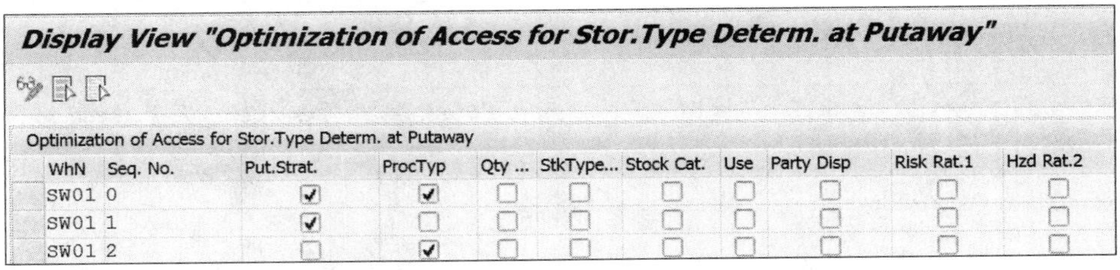

Display View "Optimization of Access for Stor.Type Determ. at Putaway"

Optimization of Access for Stor.Type Determ. at Putaway

WhN	Seq. No.	Put.Strat.	ProcTyp	Qty ...	StkType...	Stock Cat.	Use	Party Disp	Risk Rat.1	Hzd Rat.2
SW01	0	☑	☑	☐	☐	☐	☐	☐	☐	☐
SW01	1	☑	☐	☐	☐	☐	☐	☐	☐	☐
SW01	2	☐	☑	☐	☐	☐	☐	☐	☐	☐

Figure 7.23 Optimization of the Access Sequence

Storage Section Determination

In the next step, the system begins the storage section determination if the storage type contains more than one storage section. The storage section indicator is used to group products that are to be stored in the same storage section during putaway. The section indicator also is assigned to the product master in the **Storage Section Ind.** field of the **Storage Data** tab. To define a storage section indicator, navigate to IMG path **SCM Extended Warehouse Management • Goods Receipt Process • Strategies • Storage Section Search • Create Storage Section Indicators**. Click on **New Entries**, and define the section indicators for your embedded EWM warehouse.

The system determines the storage section based on the storage type determined previously, the storage section indicator determined from the product master, and the hazardous rating determined from the hazardous substance master, as shown in Figure 7.24.

Display View "Storage Section Search": Overview

Storage Section Search

WhN	Typ	HazRat1	HazRat2	SecIn	Sequence No.	Sec	EvlWhsItem
SW01	0010			0001	1	0001	0
SW01	0010			0002	1	0002	0

Figure 7.24 Defining the Storage Section Determination

The storage section search is only triggered based on the settings for storage section determination and the check set via IMG path **SCM Extended Warehouse Management • Goods Receipt Process • Strategies • Storage Section Search • Storage Section Check**, as shown in Figure 7.25. Click on **New Entries**, and set the section check control for the embedded EWM warehouse number and storage type.

Display View "Storage Section Check and Haz. Subst. Mgmt per Storage T

Storage Section Check and Haz. Subst. Mgmt per Storage Type

WhN	Typ	St	HS
SW01	0010	No storage section determination or check	No hazardous substance check
SW01	0020	No storage section determination or check	No hazardous substance check
SW01	0021	X Storage section determination and check	No hazardous substance check
SW01	0030	Y Storage section determination; no check	No hazardous substance check

Figure 7.25 Storage Section Check

You can set the following three values for storage section check:

- **Storage section determination or check**
  If storage section determination is active, the system performs putaway of goods only in those storage sections defined in the storage section search sequence. If the storage section check is active, the system checks the storage section specified in the putaway warehouse task against the predefined search sequence.
- **Storage section determination; no check**
  The system performs putaway of goods only in those storage sections defined in the storage section search sequence. However, the system performs no check for predefined storage sections in the warehouse tasks, which means that putaway is allowed in a storage section specified in the warehouse task even if it isn't present in the storage section search sequence.
- **No storage section determination or check**
  The system performs no storage section determination or check.

Storage Bin Search

After storage section determination, the system looks for storage bins in the determined storage type and storage section. The storage bin is determined based on the settings for storage bin type, bin capacity, and putaway rules as defined in the storage type search strategy. The following data is determined based on the information provided in the product and storage type determination settings:

- **Storage bin type**
  This is determined based on storage type.
- **HU type**
  This is determined from packaging specifications of the product.
- **Maximum number of bins**
  This is determined from the product master in embedded EWM.

The system also looks for the maximum number of fixed bins, capacity check settings, and putaway rules defined at the storage type level to identify the right storage bin for putaway, as shown in Figure 7.26.

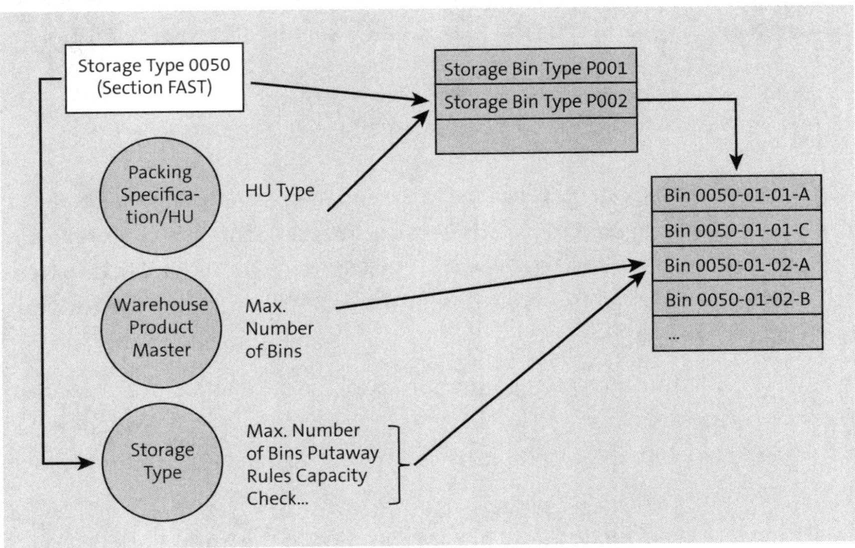

Figure 7.26 Storage Bin Type Determination

The storage bin type is used to group bins with the same physical attributes: dimension, capacity, and so on. Assign the storage bin types to storage types; the system only allows putaway into bins of a bin type assigned to that storage type. You can assign bin types to storage types via IMG path **SCM Extended Warehouse Management • Goods Receipt Process • Strategies • Storage Bin Determination • Assign Storage Bin Types to Storage Types**, as shown in Figure 7.27. Click on **New Entries**; add a combination of embedded EWM warehouse, storage type, and storage bin type; and click on **Save**.

The system only performs a bin type check if you've activated the **HU Type** check at the storage type level. In this case, the system also checks the allowed HU types for a storage type and bin type in which putaway can be done for the warehouse product. Assign HU types to storage types via IMG path **SCM Extended Warehouse Management • Extended Warehouse Management • Goods Receipt Process • Strategies • Storage Bin Determination • HU Types • Define HU Types for each Storage Type**. Click on **New Entries**, and define the allowed HU types in a storage type for your embedded EWM warehouse.

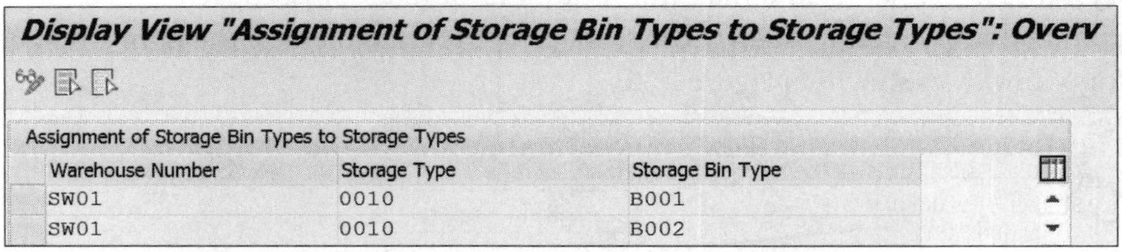

Display View "Assignment of Storage Bin Types to Storage Types": Overv

Assignment of Storage Bin Types to Storage Types

Warehouse Number	Storage Type	Storage Bin Type
SW01	0010	B001
SW01	0010	B002

Figure 7.27 Assignment of Storage Bin Types to Storage Types

Assign HU types to bin types via IMG path **SCM Extended Warehouse Management • Extended Warehouse Management • Goods Receipt Process • Strategies • Storage Bin Determination • HU Types • Define HU Types for each Storage Bin Types**. Click on **New Entries**, and define the allowed bin types for an HU type in a storage type for your embedded EWM warehouse.

If the system is unable to find a storage bin for a storage type and storage section, then it looks for the next storage section in the storage section search sequence. If it still can't find a storage bin, it looks for bins in the next storage type in the storage type search sequence.

After the right storage type, section, and bin are specified in the warehouse task, you can confirm the warehouse orders using RF or print the open warehouse orders for putaway and confirm them in the system after putaway is complete. You can confirm a warehouse order in the system using Transaction /SCWM/TO_CONF or by navigating to **SAP Easy Access** path **Logistics • SCM Extended Warehouse Management • Extended Warehouse Management • Execution • Confirm Path**.

To confirm warehouse orders in RF, navigate to RF menu **Inbound Processes • Putaway • Putaway by Warehouse Orders**. After you enter the warehouse order, the system displays the first warehouse task in the warehouse order. You can confirm the source bin, product/HU, quantity, and destination bin to confirm the warehouse task, which automatically confirms the warehouse order if there's only one task in the warehouse order.

Embedded EWM also allows you to correct warehouse tasks that have already been confirmed by using status profiles. After a putaway task is confirmed, embedded EWM sets the **Warehouse Activity (DWA)** status type to **Completed**. You can set up a delay in embedded EWM customization so that embedded EWM waits for a defined period before setting the status type **Completion Flag (DWM)** to **Completed** after task confirmation. This allows you to go back into the warehouse task and confirm the warehouse task with a revised quantity. When the system sets the DWM status to **Completed**, it also sets the **Completion (DCO)** status to **Completed** by scheduling a background job that marks the completion of goods receipt in embedded EWM; this is also sent back to SAP S/4HANA.

To define a delay in the completion of the inbound delivery, navigate to IMG path **SCM Extended Warehouse Management • Extended Warehouse Management • Goods Receipt Process • Inbound Delivery • Define Delay in Completing Inbound Deliveries**.

You can define the confirmation delay in seconds for a combination of warehouse, document type, and item type, as shown in Figure 7.28. If you want to process the completion of several items simultaneously, you can define a **Tolerance** in seconds. During this time, the system collects all the items for which embedded EWM has set the DWA status to **Completed** and sets the DWM status to **Completed**. The background job to set the DWM status to **Completed** is executed using report /SCWM/R_PRDI_SET_DWM, which is run by default every 120 seconds if the job can't set the status to **Completed** on the previous try. This may happen because of a document lock.

Display View "Delay in Completing Inbound Deliveries": Overview

Delay in Completing Inbound Deliveries

War...	Doc. Ty...	Item Ty...	StatusRel.	Completion De...	Tolerance...	Delay in Job Resched...
SW01	INB	IDLV	I Relevance at Item Leve...	300	0	0

Figure 7.28 Setting for Delay in Inbound Delivery

You can also specify your own custom value to reschedule the execution of this job in the **Delay in Job Reschedule** field.

> **Note**
> You can only use confirmation correction with a document type and item profile mapped to a status profile for which the DWM status is **Active**.

Process Warehouse Tasks – Putaway App

The Process Warehouse Tasks - Putaway app from SAP Fiori enables you to perform stock putaway operations by confirming the putaway warehouse task. In the overview screen, as shown in Figure 7.29, you can display all information relevant to the putaway warehouse tasks, which enables you to choose a warehouse task to process. From the list, you can either confirm or cancel multiple putaway warehouse tasks at once, as well as print putaway lists for the open putaway warehouse tasks. You can also perform putaway warehouse task processing using exception codes for exception handling in the picking warehouse task.

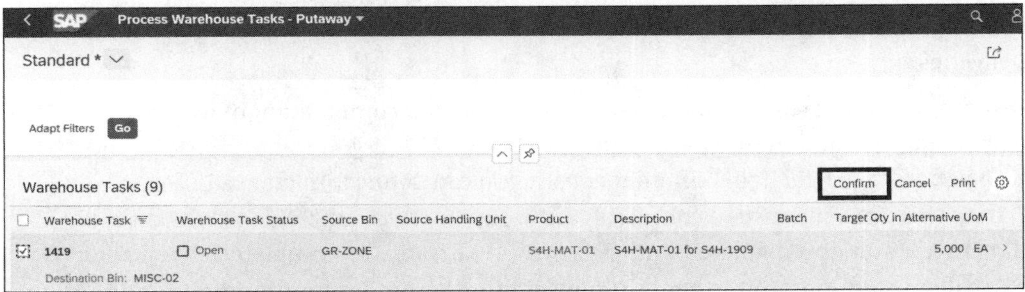

Figure 7.29 SAP Fiori App: Process Warehouse Tasks - Putaway

You can also display and check warehouse task source bins, confirm and cancel the warehouse task, and print the task list, as shown in Figure 7.30. In addition, you can perform filtering based on different filtering criteria as well as navigate to manage product master data for displaying additional information about the product for which the warehouse task is created.

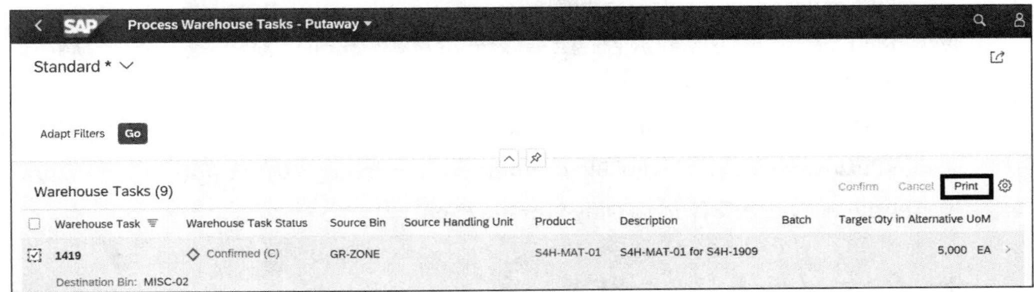

Figure 7.30 Printing the Warehouse Task List Using the Process Warehouse Tasks – Putaway App

7.6.3 Putaway Strategies

Putaway rules and strategies that help in determining the destination bin during putaway are predefined in embedded EWM. The putaway strategies available in embedded EWM are as follows:

- Manual entry
- Fixed storage bin
- General storage
- Addition to existing stock
- Empty storage bin
- Near fixed picking bin
- Pallet storage (by HU type)
- Bulk storage

We'll discuss each of these putaway strategies in detail in the following sections, including the business reason for using each putaway strategy and the settings required in the system to carry it out.

Manual Entry

In this strategy, the storage bin is manually entered in the warehouse task by the warehouse worker at the time of warehouse task creation or confirmation. This strategy is used if the putaway is performed manually by a warehouse worker by scanning the destination bin available. It's usually used in storage types with the staging area group role.

Make the following configurations in the settings for storage type via IMG path **SCM Extended Warehouse Management • Extended Warehouse Management • Master Data • Define Storage Type**:

- Set **Storage Behavior** to **Standard Warehouse**.
- Set **Putaway Rules** to **Empty Bin** or **Addition to Existing Stock/Empty Bin**.
- Set the **WT Generic** field to **Only Storage Type**.

Fixed Storage Bin

This strategy is used for putaway into fixed storage bins. You can predefine the fixed bins for a product or, if you've defined the fixed storage bin strategy for a storage type, the system determines a suitable storage bin for the product and assigns it a fixed storage bin. This strategy is used if you want to put away products only in specific storage bins. It's mostly used for products that are prone to pilfering. The picking is usually done manually from this storage type.

Make the following configurations in the storage type settings via IMG path **SCM Extended Warehouse Management • Extended Warehouse Management • Master Data • Define Storage Type**:

- Set **Storage Behavior** to **Standard Warehouse**.
- Set **Putaway Rules** to **Empty Bin** or **Addition to Existing Stock/Empty Bin**.
- Select the **Fixed Bins Allowed** indicator.
- Define the maximum number of fixed storage bins in the storage type in the **Max. Fixed Bins** field. Alternatively, define the maximum fixed bins for the product in the storage type in the **Max. No. Bin** field in the storage type data view of the product master.
- Set the **Addition to Existing Stock Permitted** value in the **Addn.Stock Forbidden** field.
- Set a method of **Capacity Check** so that the bin won't be overfilled with a product.

General Storage

As the name suggests, this putaway strategy is used to put away products in the general storage area. A general storage type usually has a single bin per storage section. You can store multiple products in a general storage area. This strategy is used if you want to put away products that are low in volume and can be combined with other products in the warehouse.

Make the following configurations in the storage type settings via IMG path **SCM Extended Warehouse Management • Extended Warehouse Management • Master Data • Define Storage Type**:

- Set **Storage Behavior** to **Standard Warehouse**.
- Set **Putaway Rules** to **General Storage Area**.
- Set the **Mixed Storage** field to **Mixed Storage without Limitations**.

Addition to Existing Stock

This strategy is used if you want to put away stock in a storage bin that already holds similar products. A form of capacity check should be activated at the storage type level so that the bin capacity isn't exceeded. If the system doesn't find a bin with the required bin capacity, it moves the product to an available empty bin. This strategy violates the FIFO rule, so it should be used only when there is insufficient space in the warehouse.

Make the following configurations in the storage type settings via IMG path **SCM Extended Warehouse Management • Extended Warehouse Management • Master Data • Define Storage Type**:

- Set **Storage Behavior** to **Standard Warehouse**.
- Set **Putaway Rules** to **General Storage Area**.
- Choose **Addition to Existing Stock Is Allowed** in the **Addn. Stock Forbidden** field, and set **Product Putaway Profile Decides** in the product master. If the latter is selected, then addition to existing stock should be allowed in product master setting.
- Activate a form of capacity check in the storage type settings.
- Set **Mixed Storage** to **One HU Allowed per Bin** so that one bin holds only a single type of product.

Empty Storage Bin

This putaway strategy is used to put away product in the next empty storage bin available in the storage type and is used in warehouses organized randomly in which products are stored in individual storage sections. Such a storage strategy is most suited for high-rack storage and shelf storage.

Make the following configurations in the storage type settings:

- Set **Storage Behavior** to **Standard Warehouse**.
- Set **Putaway Rules** to **Empty Bin**.
- If required, define relevant settings in **Srchrule Emptybin** to determine the sequence in which the system sorts empty bins.

Near Fixed Picking Bin

This strategy is used to stock products in a reserve storage area near fixed bins assigned for the warehouse product. You can configure the system to first check if a fixed bin is available in the fixed bin storage type (also called the reference storage type). If the system doesn't find a fixed bin, it looks in empty bins near the fixed bins. The stock is put away into the reserve storage bins until one of the fixed bins becomes empty, at which point the warehouse worker manually moves the stock to the fixed bins. Although both fixed bins and near fixed bins are in proximity, they're defined as separate storage types.

This strategy is used to put away stock in reserve storage bins in close proximity to fixed bins. It can only be used for products assigned to fixed bin storage.

Make the following configurations in the storage type settings:

- Set **Storage Behavior** to **Standard Warehouse**.
- Set **Putaway Rules** to **Empty Bin** or **Addition to Existing Stock/Empty Bin**.
- Set **Srchrule Emptybin** to **Near to Fixed Bin** so that the system will search for empty bins near the fixed bins.

As shown in Figure 7.31, you can assign a fixed bin storage type to a reserve storage type and define sorting rules for the near to picking bin putaway strategy via IMG path **SCM Extended Warehouse Management • Extended Warehouse Management • Goods Receipt Process • Strategies • Putaway Rules • Sorting Near To Picking Bin • Storage Type Control: Near to Picking Fixed Bin**. Click on **New Entries**, and define a reference storage type and its attributes for the fixed bin storage type.

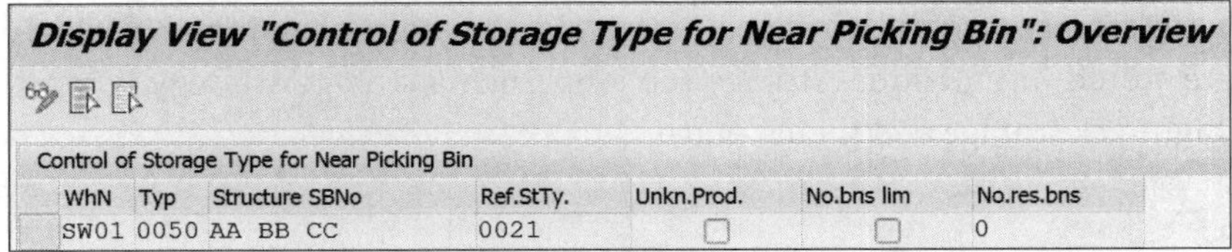

WhN	Typ	Structure SBNo	Ref.StTy.	Unkn.Prod.	No.bns lim	No.res.bns
SW01	0050	AA BB CC	0021	☐	☐	0

Figure 7.31 Settings for Near Fixed Picking Bin

You should also define the search scopethat the system uses to look for reserve bins based on the reference fixed bins. To do this, navigate to IMG path **SCM Extended Warehouse Management • Extended Warehouse Management • Goods Receipt Process • Strategies • Putaway Rules • Sorting Near To Picking Bin • Define Search Scope for Each Level**. Click on **New Entries**, and add a combination of storage type, level, and search width for your embedded EWM warehouse.

As a rule, the system always looks for empty bins in the same stack, begins its search from the bottom level, and moves to the top before moving to a neighboring stack. If the system is unable to determine an empty bin, then it moves to the next aisle. If the system is still unable to find a reserve bin based on the defined search scope, it moves to a different bin in the next storage type defined in the search sequence. In Figure 7.32, for bins in fixed storage type 0050 at level A, the system looks for reserve storage bins up to a maximum of two stacks in either direction for all the levels in the reserve storage type.

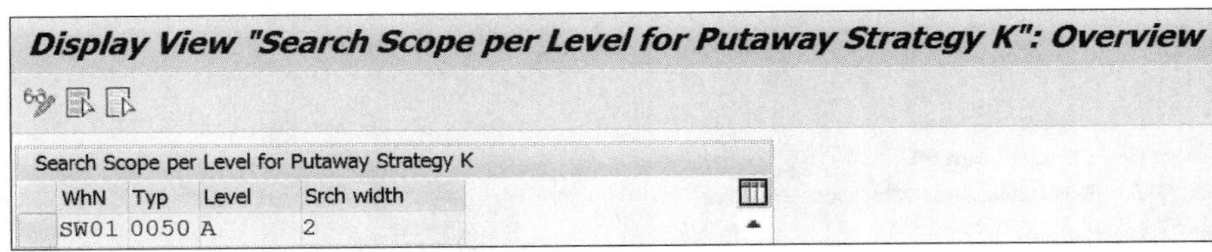

Figure 7.32 Defining the Search Scope for Each Level

Pallet Storage

This putaway strategy is used for storing pallets of different HU types in the warehouse. A storage type is assigned to different bin sections, and only HUs belonging to the same HU types can be stocked in the bin section. The storage bin sections are created upon first putaway in the storage type. These sections are automatically deleted when the last HU is removed from the storage bin. The system also determines the maximum number of HUs that can be stored in the storage bin. Pallet storage also provides easy access to product for conducting physical inventory and cycle counts.

This strategy is mostly used in high-rack storage for stacking HUs of different HU types. Dynamic creation of bin sections provides adaptability for change in warehousing and storage needs.

Make the following configurations in the storage type settings:

- Set **Storage Behavior** to **Pallet Storage**.
- Set **Putaway Rules** to **Empty Bin**.
- Activate **HU Type Check** at the storage type level.
- Set **Mixed Storage** to **Mixed Storage without Limitation**.

As shown in Figure 7.33, you can define how many storage bin sections can be created in the storage bin. These sections help control the number of HUs that can be contained in a storage bin. To define bin sections, navigate to IMG path **SCM Extended Warehouse Management • SCM Extended Warehouse Management • Management • Goods Receipt Process • Strategies • Putaway Rules • Storage Behavior: Pallets • Define Bin Sections**. Click on **New Entries**, and define the number of HUs that can be stored in the bin, section keys, and positioning for defining the naming convention of the bin section.

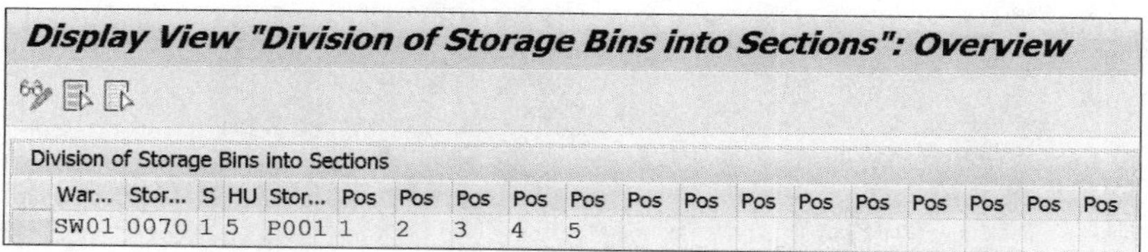
Display View "Division of Storage Bins into Sections": Overview

Division of Storage Bins into Sections

War...	Stor...	S	HU	Stor...	Pos	Pos	Pos	Pos	Pos	Pos	Pos	Pos	Pos	Pos	Pos	Pos	Pos	Pos
SW01	0070	1	5	P001	1	2	3	4	5									

Figure 7.33 Defining Bin Sections

Section Key is used to describe the sections in a storage bin. You can specify the number of sections that need to be created for a bin in a storage type and the naming convention that can be used to create the storage bin section. The created storage bin section is added as a suffix to the storage bin name. For example, based on the settings defined earlier, the system creates five storage bin sections for a storage bin. If the bin name is 05-10-01, then the storage bins sections are created from 05-10-01/1 to 05-10-01/5.

The created section keys are also assigned to storage types, bin types, and HU types. To do so, navigate to IMG path **SCM Extended Warehouse Management • SCM Extended Warehouse Management • Goods Receipt Process • Strategies • Putaway Rules • Storage Behavior: Pallets • Perform Bin Sectioning for Bin Type and HU Type**. Click on **New Entries**; add a combination of embedded EWM warehouse, storage type, bin type, and HU type; and click on **Save**. As shown in Figure 7.34, the system creates five storage sections when HU type E1 is put into a storage bin for a storage type.

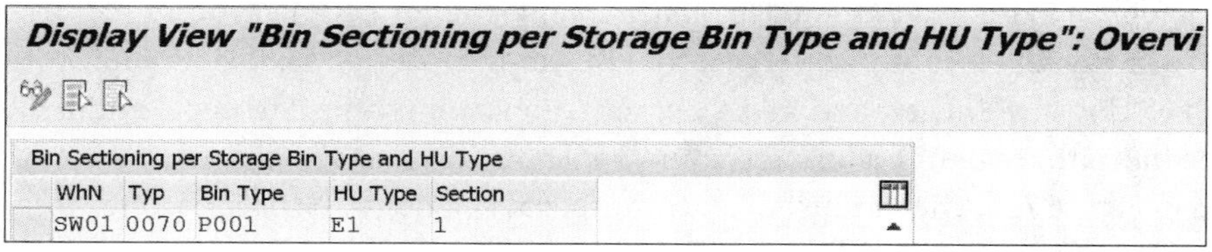

Display View "Bin Sectioning per Storage Bin Type and HU Type": Overvi

Bin Sectioning per Storage Bin Type and HU Type

WhN	Typ	Bin Type	HU Type	Section
SW01	0070	P001	E1	1

Figure 7.34 Perform Bin Sectioning for Bin Type and HU Type

Bulk Storage

Bulk storage is used to store products requiring a large amount of storage space. The advantages of bulk storage are as follows:

- Reduced need for physical bins
- Faster access to bins
- Clear structuring of the warehouse into blocks and rows

Bulk storage is mostly used to store containerized goods. It's an economical form of storage because it doesn't require setting up racks and other infrastructure. Putaway can be done directly on the warehouse floor. The pallets or containers are usually stackable and can be stored on top of one another. Putaway and retrieval is mostly done using a forklift.

Make the following configurations in the storage type settings:

- Set **Storage Behavior** to **Bulk Storage**.
- Set **Putaway Rules** to **Addition to Existing Stock/Empty Bin**.
- Set **Addn. Stock Forbidden** to **Addition to Existing Stock Permitted**.
- Do not activate **HU Type Check** and **Capacity Check**.

You can store different HU types in bulk storage. However, each bulk bin can have only a single HU type. Bulk storage is created by dividing the warehouse floor into rows. Each row is classified as a storage bin based on the storage bin type. The pallets can be stacked on top of one another, which should also take the warehouse height into account. To define the capacity of a bulk bin, define a bulk structure using a bulk storage indicator.

The bulk storage indicator is used to classify products according to their stacking requirements. The bulk structure is created via IMG path **SCM Extended Warehouse**

Management • Extended Warehouse Management • Goods Receipt Process • Strategies • Putaway Rules • Storage Behavior: Bulk Storage • Define Bulk Storage Indicators. Click on **New Entries**, and add a combination of bin type, HU type, and bulk storage indicator to define a bulk structure for a bulk storage type in a warehouse, as shown in Figure 7.35. The product of stack and stack height can be used to determine the number of HUs contained in a bulk bin.

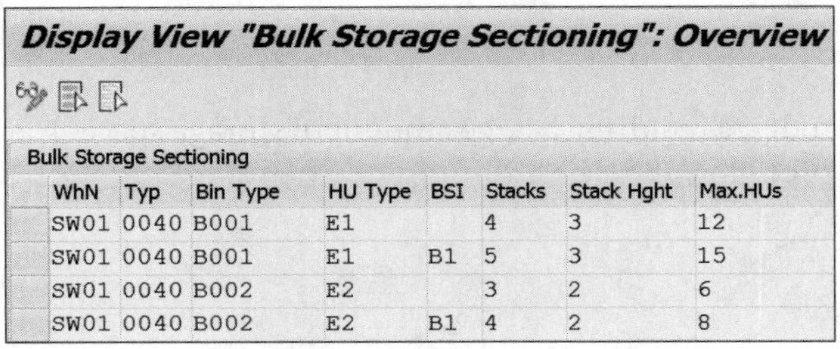

Display View "Bulk Storage Sectioning": Overview

Bulk Storage Sectioning

WhN	Typ	Bin Type	HU Type	BSI	Stacks	Stack Hght	Max.HUs
SW01	0040	B001	E1		4	3	12
SW01	0040	B001	E1	B1	5	3	15
SW01	0040	B002	E2		3	2	6
SW01	0040	B002	E2	B1	4	2	8

Figure 7.35 Defining the Bulk Structure

The number of HUs in a bulk bin and maximum number of allowed HUs can be seen in the **Bin Sectioning** tab of the bin master in Transaction /SCWM/LS03. Bulk storage directly violates the FIFO principle due to the stacking of products. You can control it via settings available at **SCM Extended Warehouse Management • Extended Warehouse Management • Goods Receipt Process • Strategies • Putaway Rules • Storage Behavior: Bulk Storage • Storage Type Control for Bulk Storage**, as shown in Figure 7.36.

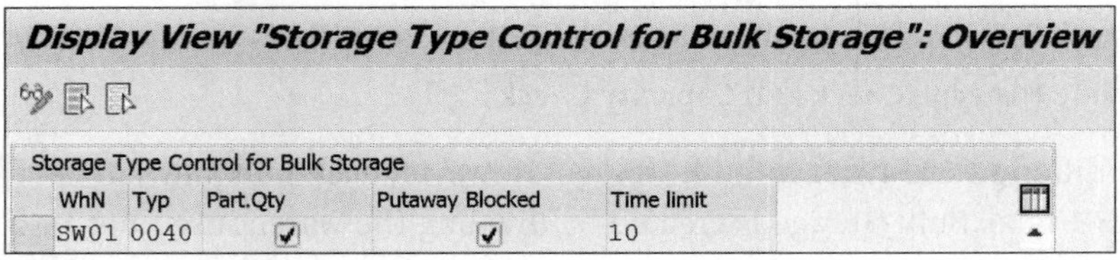

Display View "Storage Type Control for Bulk Storage": Overview

Storage Type Control for Bulk Storage

WhN	Typ	Part.Qty	Putaway Blocked	Time limit
SW01	0040	☑	☑	10

Figure 7.36 Control for Bulk Storage

The **Putaway Blocked** indicator is used to block putaway in bulk bins after the first stock removal has taken place. This prevents a product from being left in the bulk bin for a significantly long time due to continuous putaway. The **Time limit** field is used to specify the amount of time in days for which putaway is allowed in the bulk bin. Because the stock in the bulk bin takes the goods receipt date of the first goods receipt in the bin, it's a good idea to block putaway after a certain number of days so that FIFO principles aren't violated. Bulk storage only allows full pallets in the warehouse. You can set the indicator for **Part.Qty** if you want to store partial pallets in bulk bins.

7.7 Summary

In this chapter, we covered the goods receipt process in embedded EWM. We discussed the concept of warehouse requests and the document- and item-level settings required to map deliveries from SAP S/4HANA in embedded EWM. We also discussed various processes that occur in the warehouse during inbound processing, such as unloading, storage process control, yard management, and so on. Finally, we discussed various putaway strategies and how the destination storage bin for putaway is determined in embedded EWM. In the next chapter, we will move on to outbound processing in embedded EWM.

Chapter 8
Outbound Processing

The outbound process in embedded EWM caters to various processes of stock removal from the warehouse, including activities such as picking, staging, and loading goods into transportation units or vehicles. We'll discuss these activities in detail in this chapter.

With embedded EWM in SAP S/4HANA, organizations can make use of the integrated landscape provided by SAP to manage their outbound warehousing operations to issue stock to customers or to other locations. The outbound operations can be simple or complex: In a *simple outbound process*, the goods are picked from storage bins and moved to a goods issue area, and goods issue is completed. In a *complex outbound process*, the goods move through various stages such as picking, packing, staging, and loading before goods issue can be initiated. This involves integration with process-oriented storage control and layout-oriented storage control, which we discussed in the previous chapter.

An outbound operation initiates with the creation of a *logistics execution delivery* in SAP S/4HANA, which creates an outbound warehouse request in embedded EWM. This delivery can be created for a customer sales order, stock transport order, or posting change in SAP S/4HANA. The process can work with or without integration with other application modules, such as SAP Advanced Planning and Optimization (SAP APO) for availability checks. You can also create a direct warehouse request without a delivery in SAP S/4HANA by creating a direct outbound delivery in embedded EWM. Direct goods issue can be posted for processes such as scrapping and unplanned goods issue from embedded EWM. You can create warehouse tasks for each warehouse request to complete the outbound process or schedule the creation of multiple warehouse requests simultaneously using waves to optimize the picking process further. We'll talk more about waves in Chapter 16.

This chapter explains the outbound process flow in embedded EWM (Section 8.1); the configuration settings for the outbound process in embedded EWM (Section 8.2); outbound delivery (Section 8.3); stock removal process (Section 8.4), picking, packing, and handling exceptions (Section 8.5); the loading process (Section 8.6); and, finally, goods issue posting and partial goods issue (Section 8.7).

8.1 What Happens during Outbound Processing?

Outbound process includes all the subprocesses that a product undergoes in a warehouse starting from being picked from a physical location in a warehouse to being shipped out of the warehouse in a transportation unit (TU). In the following sections, we've explained the business and system aspects of outbound processing of products in embedded EWM using a business case.

Note

In our example, we're explaining a single business variant of outbound processes; the same outbound process flow can be used for most outbound process variants.

8.1.1 Business Process

American company Alpha Medicals receives an order from one of its customers, Medimax Corporation Limited, based in Mexico. The order sent by Medimax contains various pharmaceutical products that are to be delivered to them in a timely manner. An Alpha sales representative keys in the order in SAP S/4HANA and, based on material availability, creates an outbound delivery in SAP S/4HANA that contains the products to be supplied as part of a single delivery.

As shown in Figure 8.1, after the outbound delivery is saved in the SAP S/4HANA system, it flows through to the embedded EWM system and is saved as an outbound delivery order. Because Alpha Medicals has deployed wave management for picking, the outbound delivery order is assigned to a suitable picking wave in embedded EWM based on the picking times. When the time for wave release is reached, the wave is released by the system, which creates warehouse tasks for picking the product based on the picking strategy used for each product. Because Alpha Medicals also has resource and queue management deployed in its landscape, the embedded EWM system assigns the created picking warehouse tasks to appropriate queues so that the warehouse tasks can be accessed by warehouse workers. The warehouse workers get these picking warehouse tasks on their SAP Fiori app in the sequence they are assigned to the picking queues.

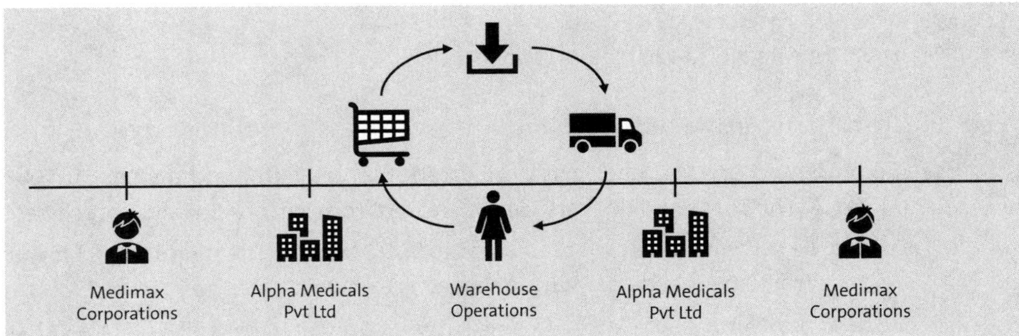

Figure 8.1 Business Flow for Outbound Processing

The warehouse worker then picks up the products and sends them to the packing area. Some of the products also require additional process execution, such as sterilization, which is performed in the work center as a value-added activity by warehouse workers. After the packing process for the product (with or without value-added services [VAS]) is completed, based on the next warehouse task, the warehouse worker stages packed products in the form of handling units (HUs) at dedicated staging lanes close to dispatch gates. After the staging of the products is completed, the HUs are loaded onto the truck docked at the goods issue door using the next warehouse task. After completion of the HU loading process, the truck departs from the door toward the gate in the yard and finally leaves for its destination in Mexico by checking out of the yard. This in turn sets the status of all the deliveries assigned to the TUs as **GI Completed**.

8.1.2 System Process

Figure 8.2 shows the sequence of document creation in embedded EWM during the outbound process.

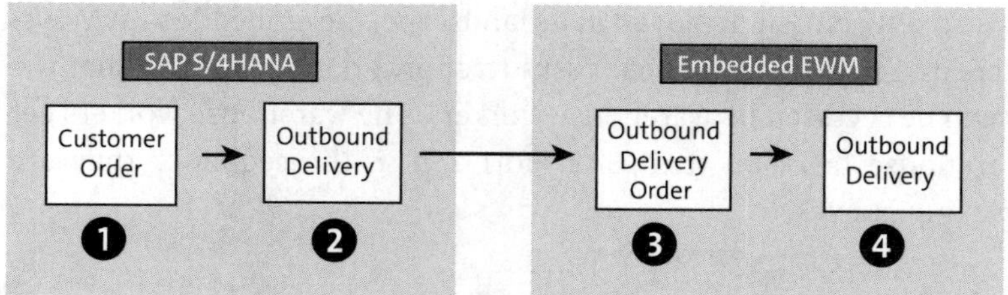

Figure 8.2 Document Flow in the Outbound Process

Briefly, each step in the outbound process is as follows:

❶ The outbound process starts with the creation of an outbound delivery in SAP S/4HANA. The outbound delivery can be created from various business processes:

- Sales: A customer sales order is created in SAP S/4HANA that requires picking of goods from an embedded EWM-managed warehouse.
- Stock transfers: A stock transfer order can be created in SAP S/4HANA that requires picking of goods from an embedded EWM-managed source plant to be sent to another location.
- Production staging: A manufacturing order is created for staging of raw materials for production in the production staging area. These goods are consumed based on requirements in the manufacturing order, and the goods issue is posted.

❷ An outbound delivery is created in SAP S/4HANA for picking from the embedded EWM warehouse. The outbound delivery can be created for any of the scenarios described in the previous step. The outbound delivery contains all relevant data required for stock picking: product, quantity, batch, and so on.

❸ The outbound delivery is replicated to embedded EWM, and an outbound delivery order is created in embedded EWM. This document—the warehouse request—serves as the requirement document in embedded EWM. Further processing in embedded EWM, such as picking, packing, and staging, is done based on the outbound delivery order via creation of warehouse tasks.

❹ After the picking and staging of stock is completed by the warehouse worker, and all associated warehouse tasks are confirmed, the warehouse operator posts the goods issue in embedded EWM, resulting in creation of an outbound delivery in embedded EWM. The goods issue is also updated in the outbound delivery in SAP S/4HANA.

The use of a TU is optional in embedded EWM. However, organizations can activate shipping and receiving functions in embedded EWM and make use of TU and vehicle activities to execute loading of goods and carrying them out of the warehouse. The stock is moved to a staging area after picking and loaded on a TU. Goods issue can be posted after loading is complete, which results in posting of goods issue in the outbound delivery in SAP S/4HANA.

The outbound process can include either simple or complex movement of the stock from the source to destination bin. In complex movements, product is moved using multiple steps, which includes picking, packing, staging, and loading, before it reaches the destination bin. A detailed explanation of the configuration and usage of the storage process using process-oriented storage control and layout-oriented storage control was provided in Chapter 6.

Note

Readers familiar with standalone SAP EWM will notice that an outbound delivery request is no longer created in embedded EWM. The system directly creates an outbound delivery order in embedded EWM based on the outbound delivery in SAP S/4HANA. This reflects a simplification strategy in SAP S/4HANA.

Figure 8.3 shows a complex movement scenario in an outbound process using only process-oriented storage control. Each of these steps is configured as a process step and provided in a sequence to let the system know the next step that needs to be executed after the previous step is completed. Each step is mapped with logic to identify the source and destination so that the system will know where to pick the step from and move it to after the required process step is completed. Storage control consists of the following steps:

❶ **Picking**
A picking warehouse task is created to move product from the source bin to the packing work center. You confirm the warehouse task, and, depending on settings in process-oriented storage control, the next warehouse task can be created automatically or manually. For more about the steps required to set up process-oriented storage control, see Chapter 6.

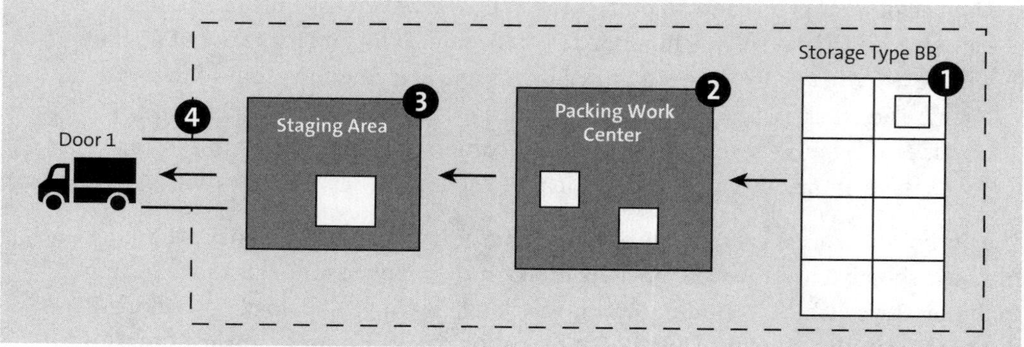

Figure 8.3 Storage Control in the Outbound Process

- ❷ **Packing**
  The products are packed or repacked in the packing work center. A warehouse task is created to move pallets to the staging area.
- ❸ **Staging**
  Products are taken to the staging area, where they wait for the transportation vehicle to arrive. The staging warehouse task is confirmed.
- ❹ **Loading**
  After the truck docks at the warehouse door, HU warehouse tasks are created for loading the goods onto the vehicle. The tasks are confirmed when loading is complete.

The picking process can also involve a combination of process-oriented storage control and layout-oriented storage control to execute specific processes based on the warehouse layout. For example, pallets picked from the source storage bin might need to be moved to a pick point, where required goods will be packed into a pick HU. This is done by activating the pick point for the source storage type. The pick HU can then be moved for other outbound operations, such as packing, staging and loading.

8.2 Configuring Outbound Delivery Processing

To carry out warehouse activities for outbound processing in embedded EWM, it's important to perform some initial settings in both SAP S/4HANA and embedded EWM so that the delivery documents are sent to embedded EWM along with all attributes, such as stock type, serial number, batch requirements, and so on. We'll cover each of these basic settings in this section.

8.2.1 Document Type and Item Type in the Outbound Process

We discussed document categories, item categories, document types, and item types in the previous chapter. Some of the document types available in embedded EWM for the outbound process are shown in Table 8.1.

Document Category	Document Type	Document Type Description
PDO	OUTB	Outbound delivery order
PMR	PWR	Production material request
FDO	OUTB	Outbound delivery

Table 8.1 Document Types for the Outbound Process

New document types are created manually via IMG path **SCM Extended Warehouse Management • Extended Warehouse Management • Goods Issue Process • Outbound Delivery • Use the Wizard to Define Document Types for Outbound Delivery Process.** They also can be created manually without wizard assistance via IMG path **SCM Extended Warehouse Management • Extended Warehouse Management • Goods Issue Process • Outbound Delivery • Manual Settings • Define Document Types for Outbound Delivery Process.**

Click on **New Entries**, and add a **Document Type** with its **Doc. Categ.** (document category), **Int.No.RngeInt.**, and control profiles, as shown in Figure 8.4.

The item types available in embedded EWM for the outbound process are shown in Table 8.2.

Item Category	Item Type	Item Type Description
DLV	ODLV	Standard item—outbound delivery
DLV	ODPS	Item production supply (outbound)

Table 8.2 Item Types in Embedded EWM for the Outbound Process

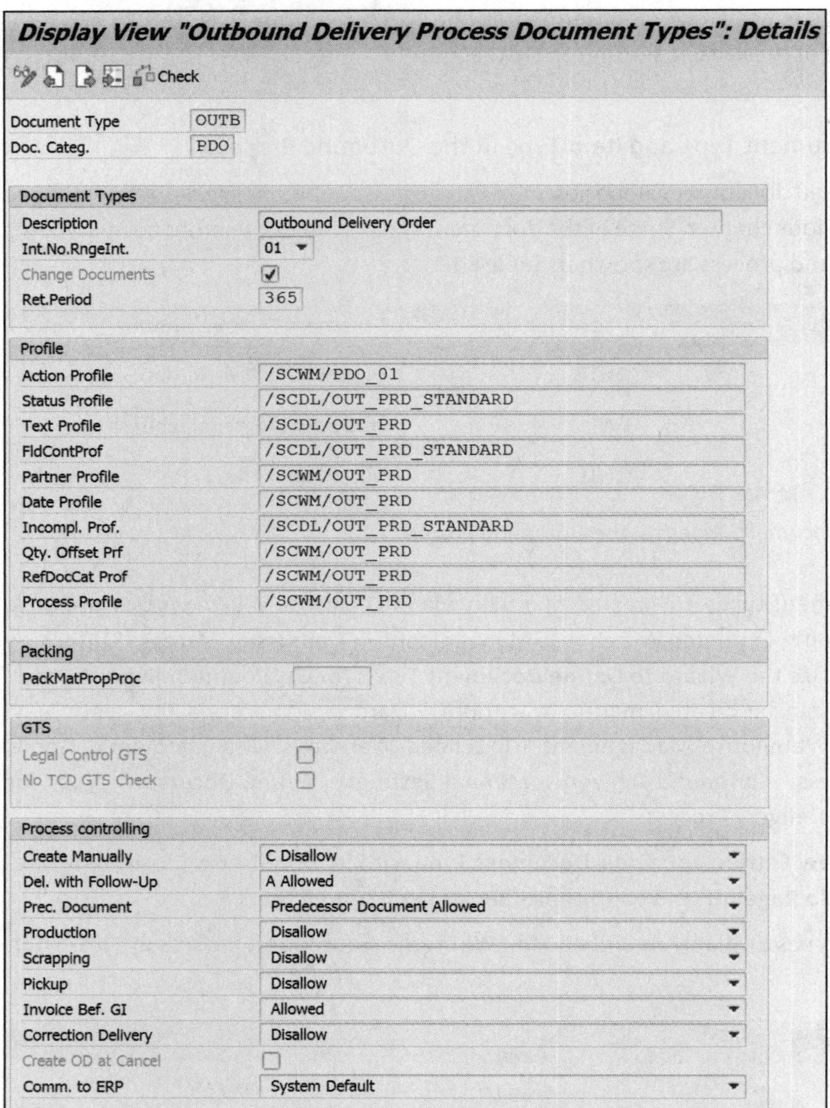

Figure 8.4 Defining the Document Type for the Outbound Process

You create item types using a wizard via IMG path **SCM Extended Warehouse Management • Extended Warehouse Management • Goods Issue Process • Outbound Delivery • Use the Wizard to Define Item Types for Outbound Delivery Process** or manually via IMG path **SCM Extended Warehouse Management • Extended Warehouse Management • Goods Issue Process • Outbound Delivery • Manual Settings • Define Item Types for Outbound Delivery Process**, as shown in Figure 8.5.

Click on **New Entries**, add the **Item Type** and **Item Category**, and define control profiles and other process management controls.

Display View "Outbound Delivery Process Item Types": Details

Check

Item Type	ODLV
Doc. Categ.	PDO Outbound Delivery Order

Outbound Delivery Process Item Types

Item Category	DLV Standard Delivery Item
Description	Standard Item - Outbound Delivery

Profile

Status Profile	/SCDL/OUT_PRD_DLV_STANDARD
Qty. Offset Prf	/SCWM/OUT_PRD_DLV
FldContProf	/SCDL/OUT_PRD_DLV_STANDARD
Incompl. Prof.	/SCDL/OUT_PRD_DLV_STANDARD
Text Profile	/SCDL/OUT_PRD_DLV
RefDocCat Prof	/SCWM/OUT_PRD_DLV
Partner Profile	/SCWM/OUT_PRD_DLV
Date Profile	/SCWM/OUT_PRD_DLV
Proc.Code Prof.	/SCWM/OUT_PRD_DLV
Process Profile	/SCWM/OUT_PRD_DLV

Process Management and Control

Create Manually	C Disallow
Invoice Bef. GI	D Allowed
Serialization	☐
Create Kit Item Automatically	☐
Documentation Batch Required	☐
Item Split Allowed	☐
Apply ERP AUoM as SUoM	☐
Update Delivery Item SUoM	☐

Figure 8.5 Defining the Item Type for the Outbound Process

8.2.2 Mapping Outbound Deliveries

It's important to map the delivery document type from SAP S/4HANA with the corresponding document type of the warehouse request because this helps the system know which embedded EWM document type to create based on the document type of the SAP S/4HANA system. Document type mapping is done in embedded EWM from IMG path **SCM Extended Warehouse Management • Extended Warehouse Management • Interfaces • ERP Integration • Delivery Processing • Map Document Types from ERP System to EWM**. Click on **New Entries**, and map the document type in SAP S/4HANA and the target embedded EWM document type.

Similarly, you also need to map item types in the deliveries in SAP S/4HANA with the item types in warehouse requests in embedded EWM. To do so, navigate to IMG path **SCM Extended Warehouse Management • Extended Warehouse Management • Interfaces • ERP Integration • Delivery Processing • Map Item Types from ERP System to EWM.** Click on **New Entries**, and map the SAP S/4HANA document and item type and the embedded EWM document type with the item type in embedded EWM.

8.2.3 Assigning Item Types to Document Types

The item types defined previously are assigned to document types to restrict the allowed item types for a delivery type for the outbound process. The assignment of item types to delivery types is done via IMG path **SCM Extended Warehouse Management • Extended Warehouse Management • Goods Issue Process • Outbound Delivery • Manual Settings • Define Allowed Item Types for in Outbound Delivery Process**, as shown in Figure 8.6. Click on **New Entries**, and add document types and item types. A document type may have more than one item type.

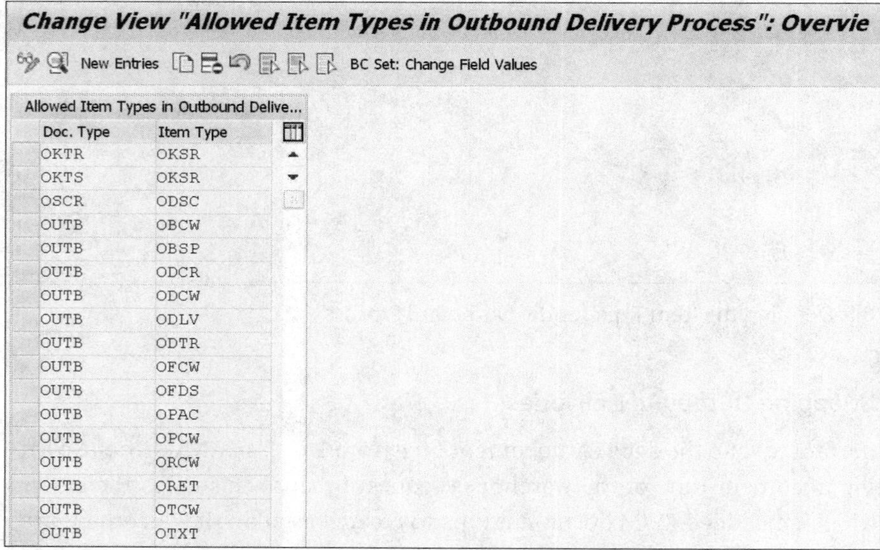

Doc. Type	Item Type
OKTR	OKSR
OKTS	OKSR
OSCR	ODSC
OUTB	OBCW
OUTB	OBSP
OUTB	ODCR
OUTB	ODCW
OUTB	ODLV
OUTB	ODTR
OUTB	OFCW
OUTB	OFDS
OUTB	OPAC
OUTB	OPCW
OUTB	ORCW
OUTB	ORET
OUTB	OTCW
OUTB	OTXT

Figure 8.6 Assigning Item Types to Document Types for the Outbound Process

8.2.4 Configuring and Using Consolidation Groups

Consolidation groups are used to identify the outbound delivery items that can be picked or packed together in an HU. Consolidation groups are used if the **Packing Consolidation** checkbox is selected for an outbound delivery item.

To consolidate delivery items with similar requirements for picking or packing, consolidation groups are assigned to the delivery items either manually or automatically by embedded EWM. To ensure a consolidation group is assigned to the delivery item, you'll make the following settings:

- **Define Consolidation Group**
  In this setting, define the delivery values by which the consolidation group is assigned to the delivery item via IMG path **SCM Extended Warehouse Management • Extended Warehouse Management • Goods Issue Process • Define Consolidation Group**. Select checkboxes for parameters used for determination of the consolidation group, as shown in Figure 8.7.

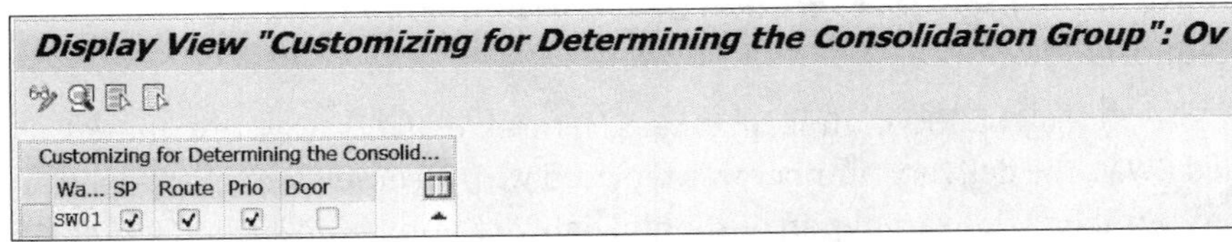

Figure 8.7 Defining the Consolidation Group for Grouping Delivery Items

- **Assign Number Range Intervals to Consolidation Group**
  In this setting, define warehouse-dependent settings for the consolidation group assignment to a delivery item via IMG path **SCM Extended Warehouse Management • Extended Warehouse Management • Goods Issue Process • Assign Number Range Intervals to Consolidation Group**. Click on **New Entries**, and provide the consolidation group number range identifier and type. As shown in Figure 8.8, you can configure automatic or manual consolidation group assignment for the stock removal and putaway process. You can also direct the system to always assign a unique consolidation group to a delivery item if products must never be consolidated in an HU.

Note

A consolidation group can be added manually in a delivery item. Manually added consolidation groups must have the external number range assigned to warehouse.

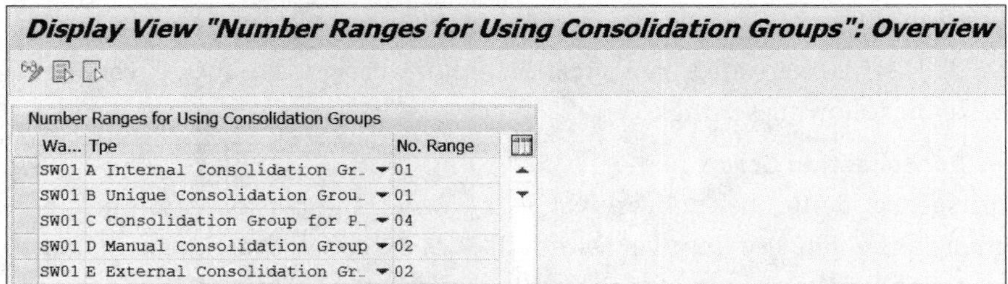

Figure 8.8 Assigning the Consolidation Group Number Range to the Warehouse

8.2.5 Reuse of the Logistics Execution Delivery Number in Warehouse Requests

Prior to SAP S/4HANA 1809, after an SAP S/4HANA delivery was distributed to embedded EWM, the delivery number was replaced with an embedded EWM-specific document number. For example, an outbound delivery numbered such as 45678965 in SAP S/4HANA created an outbound delivery order with number 99867632683 in embedded EWM and retained a reference to the outbound delivery of 45678965. This made it difficult for business users to identify the deliveries in embedded EWM in inbound, outbound, and posting change processes.

SAP S/4HANA 1809 introduced a new functionality in which you can choose to use the same delivery number throughout, if required (in embedded EWM, it's called the warehouse request number, but the number itself is the same). Using the same number for embedded EWM delivery leads to easy identification and filtering of the delivery documents in embedded EWM during processing of such deliveries, as well as better monitoring of deliveries using the embedded EWM monitor.

This feature can be activated by document type for the document categories of inbound deliveries, outbound deliveries, outbound delivery orders, and posting changes. To ensure the same number deliveries are created in embedded EWM as that of SAP S/4HANA deliveries, you need to make the following settings:

1. **Activate the ERP Ref No is Doc No checkbox.**
   To activate the embedded EWM deliveries/warehouse request numbers to have the same number as SAP S/4HANA deliveries for inbound/outbound/posting change processes, follow SAP IMG menu path **SCM Extended Warehouse Management • Extended Warehouse Management • Goods Issue Process • Outbound Delivery • Manual Settings • Define Document Types for Outbound Delivery Process**. Once there, select the **ERP Ref No is Doc No** checkbox at the delivery document type level, as shown in Figure 8.9.

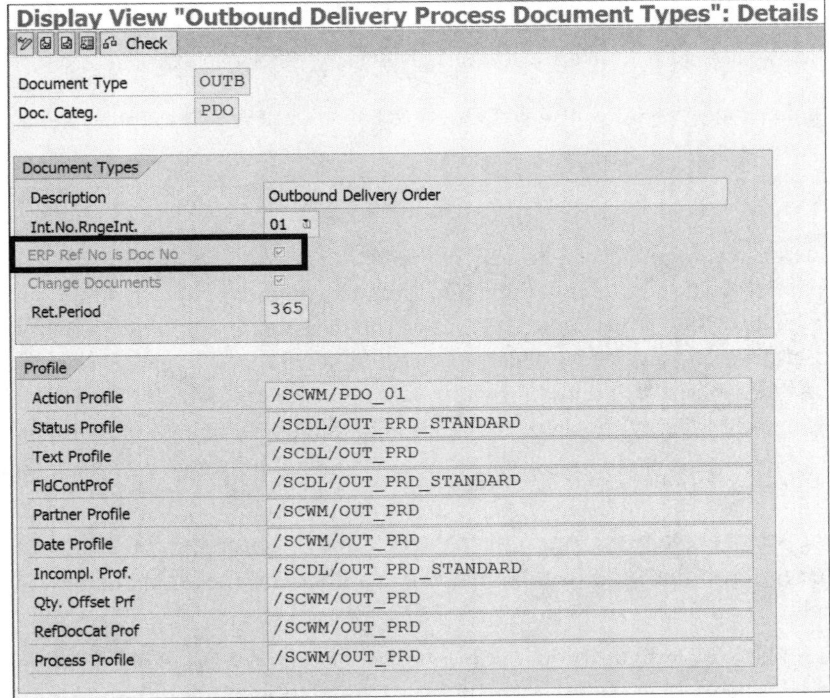

Figure 8.9 Activating the Same Number for SAP S/HANA Delivery as for EWM Delivery

2. **Set up number ranges in SAP S/4HANA and embedded EWM.**
   To use the same SAP S/4HANA number for deliveries in embedded EWM, set the SAP S/4HANA delivery internal number range as the external number range for deliveries in embedded EWM, as shown in Table 8.3. Set the number ranges for SAP S/4HANA and embedded EWM delivery types via the following IMG paths:

- SAP S/4HANA: **Logistics Execution • Shipping • Deliveries • Define Number Ranges for Deliveries**
- Embedded EWM: **SCM Extended Warehouse Management • Extended Warehouse Management • Cross-Process Settings • Delivery - Warehouse Request • Number Ranges • Define No. Range Intervals for Inbound Deliveries and Outbound Del. Orders**

Delivery Type	Internal Range	External Range
LE Delivery	280000000–289999999	
Embedded EWM Delivery	480000000–489999999	280000000–289999999

Table 8.3 Number Range for SAP S/4HANA Delivery to Embedded EWM Delivery Mapping

Note

SAP S/4HANA (logistics execution) delivery numbers can contain a maximum of 10 characters as part of their standard number range, whereas the maximum number range in embedded EWM is 20 characters. Thus, it's important to ensure that there is no conflict of number ranges in embedded EWM and SAP S/4HANA delivery numbers. This can be achieved by ensuring that the number range used by SAP S/4HANA deliveries is marked as an external number range in case of embedded EWM deliveries.

The following steps explain the reuse of delivery numbers process, depicting the same number for both the SAP S/4HANA delivery number and the embedded EWM outbound delivery number:

1. After you make the configuration and number ranges changes as explained previously, the delivery document is created, and the document is saved in SAP S/4HANA, it will be replicated to embedded EWM with the same number and can be easily identified in embedded EWM.
2. The outbound delivery created in the SAP S/4HANA system can be seen in the embedded EWM application using Transaction /SCWM/PRDO with the same delivery number, as shown in Figure 8.10.

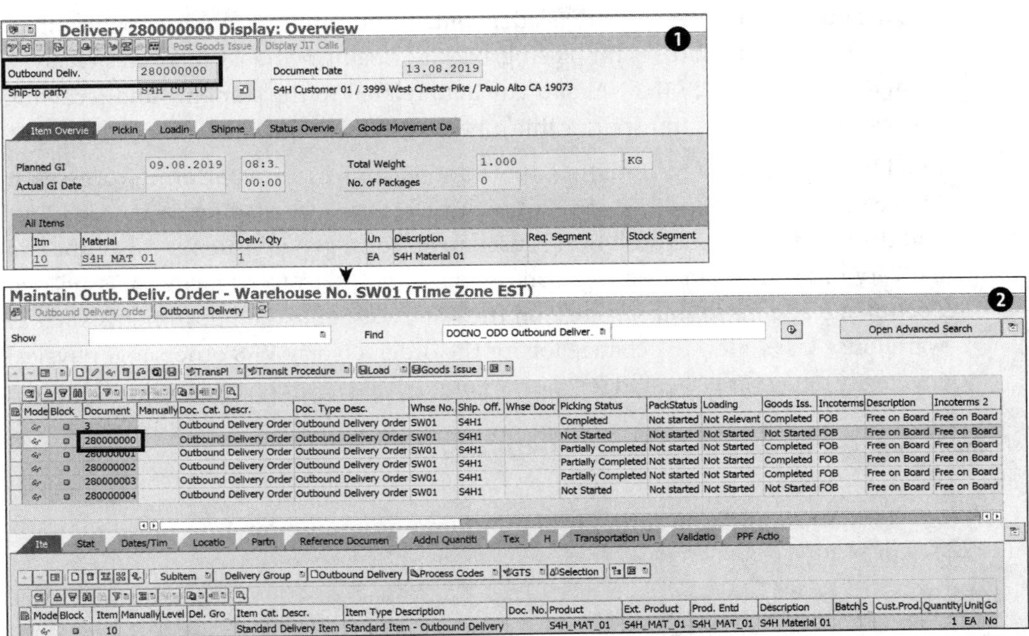

Figure 8.10 Example Showing the Same SAP S/4HANA and Embedded EWM Delivery Number

8.3 Outbound Delivery

In this section, we'll explain the structure and some important features of outbound delivery orders and outbound delivery documents used in the outbound process in embedded EWM. We'll explain the outbound process from the perspective of the order-to-cash cycle, but the same warehouse processes also can be performed for other business processes that involve issuing stock out of the warehouse, such as stock transfer orders or goods issue to production orders.

8.3.1 Outbound Delivery Order

As discussed in Section 8.1, the outbound delivery order is the warehouse request in embedded EWM, based on which the picking process is carried out. The outbound delivery order consists of a header section and an item section. As shown in Figure

8.11, the outbound delivery order header contains general information such as shipping office; various statuses for picking, packing, loading, and issue; routes received from delivery in SAP S/4HANA; and any data related to the shipping and receiving process (e.g., means of transport, vehicle, etc.).

In addition to general information, there are buttons used to perform processes at the header level, such as the **Load** button, which is used for loading/reverse loading, and the **Goods Issue** button, which is used to perform goods issue for the outbound delivery order. The order header also provides an option to navigate to associated documents and data. You can click on the icon and open documents such as warehouse tasks, view the change log for the order, display VAS orders and physical inventory documents created for the outbound delivery order, and more.

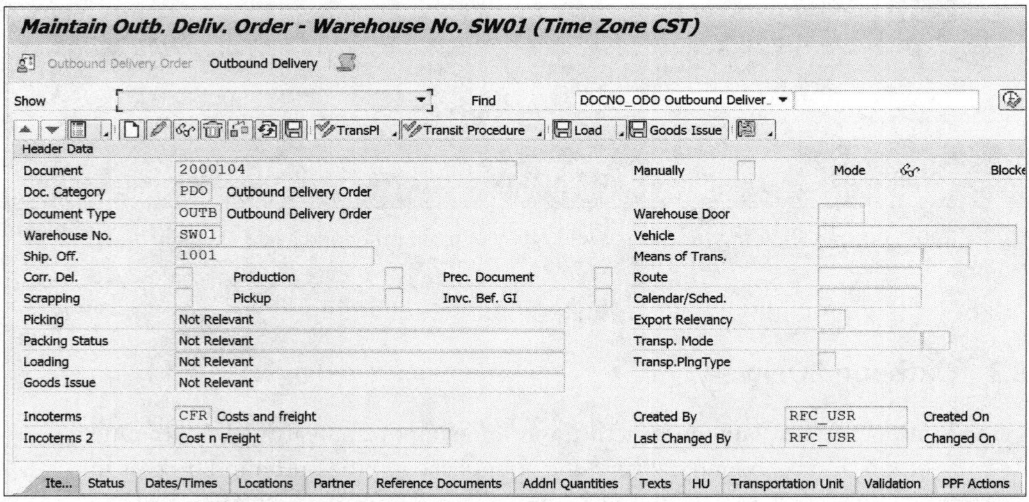

Figure 8.11 Outbound Delivery Order Header

The outbound delivery order document also contains the following tabs that contain more data about the order and its processing status at the header level:

- **Status**
  This tab contains all applicable statuses for the outbound delivery order document at the header level. The statuses come from the status profile assigned to the combination of document category and document type for the outbound delivery

order. For example, after an operation such as picking is completed for all outbound delivery order items, the relevant status value is set from **Not Started** to **Complete** for status type **DPI** for picking.

- **Dates/Times**
  This tab contains all applicable statuses for the outbound delivery order document at the header level. The dates/times come from the date/time profile assigned to the combination of document category and document type for the outbound delivery order. After an operation such as goods issue is completed for all items in the outbound delivery order, the actual date and time values are set for the **EGOODSISSUE** date/time type. Planned and actual values for new dates and time can be manually added in this tab for an outbound delivery order.
- **Locations**
  This tab contains all applicable locations for the outbound delivery order document, such as a warehouse number. New locations can also be manually added in this node.
- **Partner**
  This tab contains all applicable business partners for the outbound delivery order header. The business partner roles come from the partner profile assigned to the combination of document category and document type for the outbound delivery order header. New business partners with applicable business partner roles can be manually added in this tab.
- **Reference Documents**
  This tab contains all reference documents for the outbound delivery order. The applicable reference document categories come from the reference document profile assigned to the combination of document category and document type for the outbound delivery order. Reference documents can include the number of the logistics execution delivery in SAP S/4HANA, VAS orders, and more. A new reference document for the applicable reference document category can be added manually in this node.
- **Addnl Quantities**
  The additional quantities tab contains all quantities and their units of measure applicable to the outbound delivery order document.

- **Texts**
  This tab contains all text types applicable to the outbound delivery order document header. The applicable text types come from the text profile assigned to the combination of document category and document type for an outbound delivery order. New text for a text type can be added manually in this node.
- **HU**
  This tab contains details of any HUs created for the outbound delivery order items after packing goods in the order. You also can create new HUs for an item type manually in this node. The delivery can be split with a selected HU, which can be used to create an outbound delivery or to post goods issue directly.
- **Transportation Unit**
  This tab contains details of the TU assigned to the outbound delivery order. The TU represents the vehicle on which stock is loaded during the outbound process.
- **PPF Actions**
  This tab contains details of any Post Processing Framework (PPF) action being carried out in the outbound delivery order to create any follow-up documents or execute an action. For example, you can schedule a PPF action for creation of warehouse tasks for picking or creation of a wave for the warehouse request. You can also execute an unprocessed PPF action from this tab or manually retrigger a PPF action.

As shown in Figure 8.12, the **Item** tab in the outbound delivery order contains general information, such as product number, quantity, batch, country of origin, and expiration date, defined by the item category and item type. This level also contains important information that guides the movement of the product inside the embedded EWM warehouse. Some of these include warehouse process type, stock type, staging bay, door, goods movement bin, and consolidation group.

Various processes can be performed from this screen using different buttons, for example, creation of batch subitems using the **Subitem** button. A delivery group also can be added to the item manually, which adds a text item to the main product using the **Delivery Group** button. If selection criteria for the batch have been passed on to embedded EWM, then batches can be selected using the **Selection** button. If required, the delivery quantity can be adjusted using appropriate process codes, and the same information is relayed back to SAP S/4HANA for updating the outbound delivery.

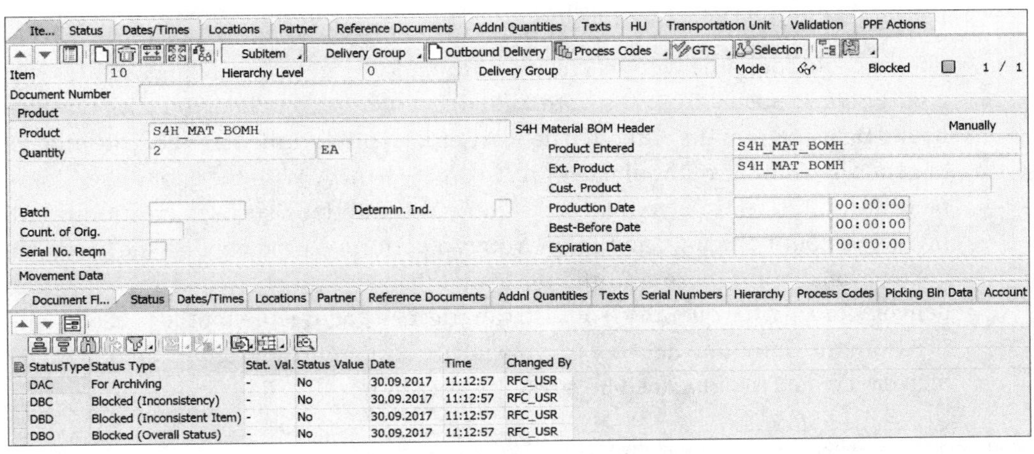

Figure 8.12 Outbound Delivery Order Item

The outbound delivery order item contains a detailed item-level view with various tabs to show the processing status of the individual document items. Some of these tabs at the item level are similar to the tabs available for the outbound delivery order at the header level. The data in tabs at the item level is determined based on the profiles assigned to the combination of item categories and item types. Some tabs are applicable only to outbound delivery order items, such as the following:

- **Serial Numbers**
  This tab is used to provide the serial numbers for the items picked in the outbound delivery if the item is relevant for serialization.
- **Process Codes**
  This tab contains information about all process codes applied on the outbound delivery order item. This node also contains information about the delivery quantity, which is adjusted by applying process codes.
- **Account Assignments**
  This tab shows whether an item transferred to embedded EWM from SAP S/4HANA has an account assignment linked to it, such as a cost center, work breakdown structure (WBS) element, or order. This data acts as a filter in the embedded EWM warehouse monitor to filter out the delivery for a specific account assignment.
- **Dangerous Goods**
  This tab shows dangerous goods indicator if the product in the line item of the outbound delivery order is a dangerous good. All information, such as the dangerous goods class, hazard ID, and so on, is captured in this node.

8.3.2 Outbound Delivery Creation

The final outbound delivery is created automatically in embedded EWM after the goods issue is posted from the outbound delivery order or when you click on **Outbound Delivery** from the outbound delivery order. This document triggers the update of goods issue in the outbound delivery in SAP S/4HANA. With the goods issue complete in SAP S/4HANA, you can take subsequent actions such as creation of an invoice, account postings, and so on. You can perform partial goods issue based on goods available for picking in the outbound delivery, which creates an outbound delivery for a partial quantity. You also can trigger a goods issue for the partial quantity from the outbound delivery in embedded EWM. Figure 8.13 shows an outbound delivery created in embedded EWM.

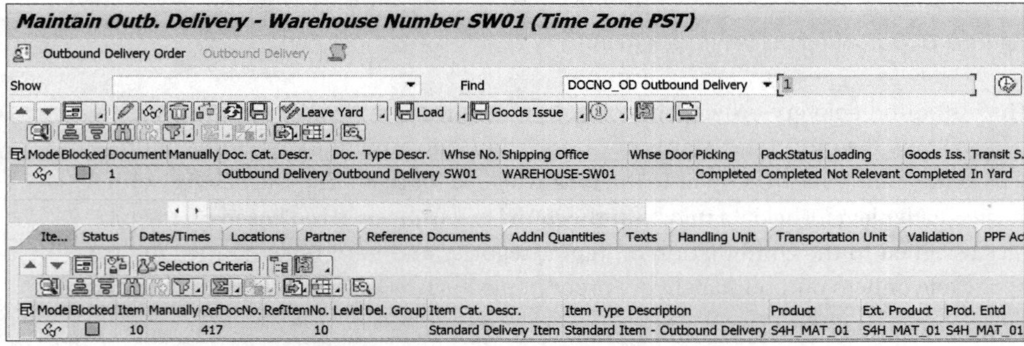

Figure 8.13 Outbound Delivery in Embedded EWM

The outbound delivery is used as the basis to print delivery documents such as delivery notifications, bills of lading, and so on. Some of the functions available in the outbound delivery are as follows:

- Setting and resetting yard status
- Setting and resetting loading status
- Posting and canceling a goods movement
- Requesting and canceling an invoice if the document supports invoicing before goods issue

8.3.3 Delivery Creation Using References

The order-to-cash process starts with a sales order being created after the customer inquiry is converted into a quotation. Usually, organizations have an active availability check to find out if they have sufficient stock in their inventory. After the sales order schedule line is confirmed, a delivery is created per the delivery schedule line and distributed to embedded EWM for carrying out warehouse activities.

After the delivery is replicated to embedded EWM, a warehouse request or an outbound delivery order document is created. The outbound delivery order forms the basis for all warehousing activities in embedded EWM. As explained in Section 8.4.1, picking warehouse tasks are created and grouped into warehouse orders to be assigned to a resource for execution. The resource completes picking, packing, staging, and loading for the available stock and posts goods issue for the outbound delivery order. If the shipping and receiving function is activated in the warehouse, then goods issue can also be posted from TU display Transaction /SCWM/TU, thus creating an outbound delivery in embedded EWM. As a follow-up step, goods issue is posted in the outbound delivery in SAP S/4HANA. After this process, the billing and financial posting is carried out in SAP S/4HANA by relevant departments.

The outbound delivery also can be created without reference to a sales order, such as during issue of stock to a network order using movement type 281. This creates an outbound delivery in SAP S/4HANA that is replicated to embedded EWM and processed in the same way as explained for the order-to-cash process. In effect, you can say embedded EWM isn't concerned about whether the delivery is created with or without reference to an order as long as the right delivery document determination configuration is maintained as mentioned in Section 8.2.

8.3.4 Direct Outbound Delivery Process

An outbound delivery order also can be created directly in embedded EWM, which in turn creates an outbound delivery in SAP S/4HANA. Many business scenarios require the outbound delivery to be created directly in embedded EWM, such as the following:

- Some extra space is left in the truck after loading all customer deliveries, and you want to push some additional products (e.g., perishable items) to the customer.
- A customer makes an urgent request from to send over products that weren't included in the original delivery.

- Returnable packaging material (e.g., reusable empties, containers) is sent back to a supplier or another location that needs it urgently.
- A sale is made to an internal customer, such as a project system team, for internal consumption. In this case, the internal customers may pick up the products from the warehouse, and the stock is posted to the cost center of the account assignment category during goods issue.
- After the scrapping stock is placed in the scrapping work center and the scrapping process is completed, goods issue is posted using the direct outbound delivery order for the quantity to be scrapped.

SAP Global Trade Services (SAP GTS) and the global available-to-promise (GATP) system may be required to check the global inventory availability or carry out customs and clearance checks. The availability check in embedded EWM is configured per business requirements made in embedded EWM, SAP APO, or SAP S/4HANA. If the delivery is designated for product exports, an integration with SAP GTS is performed for custom and compliance checks.

After all the mandatory and optional steps are performed for the delivery, the outbound delivery order created in embedded EWM is replicated to SAP S/4HANA. The warehouse activities are performed in the same way as for the outbound delivery order created from sales orders. For direct outbound delivery orders, invoicing before goods issue can also be done. After the goods issue is posted for the outbound delivery order in embedded EWM, it's replicated to the outbound delivery in SAP S/4HANA to facilitate delivery-related billing.

To enable creation of an outbound delivery in SAP S/4HANA for a direct outbound delivery order created in embedded EWM, map a delivery type from embedded EWM to a delivery type in SAP S/4HANA. You can optionally assign the embedded EWM delivery type to a cross-company delivery type in SAP S/4HANA if the direct outbound delivery in embedded EWM is for a stock transfer order. To do so, navigate to IMG path **Logistics Execution • EWM Integration • Outbound Process • Direct Outbound Deliveries • Determine Document Types for Direct Outbound Deliveries**. Click on **New Entries**, and enter the SAP S/4HANA outbound delivery type to be determined for the direct outbound delivery type created in embedded EWM, as shown in Figure 8.14.

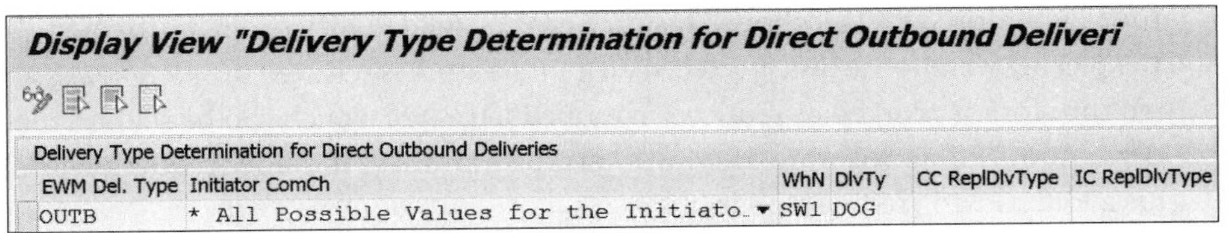

Display View "Delivery Type Determination for Direct Outbound Deliveri

Delivery Type Determination for Direct Outbound Deliveries

EWM Del. Type	Initiator ComCh	WhN	DlvTy	CC ReplDlvType	IC ReplDlvType
OUTB	* All Possible Values for the Initiato…	SW1	DOG		

Figure 8.14 Mapping the SAP S/4HANA Delivery Type

In a similar way, map the SAP S/4HANA delivery item type with the embedded EWM document type, item category of SAP S/4HANA, and item type of the embedded EWM outbound delivery order via IMG path **Logistics Execution • EWM Integration • Outbound Process • Direct Outbound Deliveries • Determine Item Categories for Direct Outbound Deliveries**. Click on **New Entries**, and enter the SAP S/4HANA outbound delivery item type to be determined by the embedded EWM direct outbound delivery item type.

8.3.5 Changing Order Quantity

SAP has provided a functionality in embedded EWM by which order quantity changes in a sales order are communicated to embedded EWM and automatically updated in the outbound delivery order. Quantity changes in a sales order are communicated to embedded EWM by selecting the for **Deliv.Chg** checkbox at IMG path **Logistics Execution • Extended Warehouse Management • Basic Setup of Connectivity • Configure EWM Specific Parameters**, as shown in Figure 8.15.

Display View "Extended Warehouse Management system": Overview

Extended Warehouse Management system

W...	Whse no. description	Ext. WM	Dist. Mode	UD	BatchDetEW	GR fr. EWM	Comm. WM	Deliv.Chg
S4H	S4H Warehouse	E EWM (Extended Warehouse Management)	Distribution Immediately a	☐	☑	☑	Q Queued and Serialized Asy	☑

Figure 8.15 Order Reduction

Embedded EWM performs these follow-up actions in the warehouse request after the quantity is changed:

- **Order reduction with warehouse task for outbound delivery order created but not confirmed**
  The warehouse task for the outbound delivery order item is canceled, and the new warehouse task is created, which is confirmed by the warehouse worker.

- **Order reduction with warehouse task for outbound delivery order confirmed**
If the picking warehouse task is confirmed and the stock is reduced in SAP S/4HANA, then the stock is marked as reduced in embedded EWM, which can be seen in the work center. This allows warehouse workers to be aware of the stock reduction and thus avoid packing reduced quantities.

8.4 Stock Removal

In this section, we'll explain the independent objects and configurations required for the stock removal process in the warehouse. First, we'll explain the process for creating warehouse tasks for different outbound processes such as picking, packing, loading, and so on. Then, we'll talk about the process of source storage type determination during the stock removal process to identify the source bin for the requested stock. Finally, we'll explain standard stock removal strategies that can be used during the stock removal process and explain the process if a custom stock removal strategy needs to be configured.

Before we jump into those topics, however, consider the following:

- **Waves for the outbound process**
In embedded EWM, warehouse requests for outbound and internal warehouse processes can be grouped into waves to further optimize stock picking. Waves are created for products that share similarities such as being picked from the same source area or picked together because they need to be shipped at the same time. Items within the wave are processed together, and picking warehouse tasks are created for all assigned warehouse requests at a scheduled time. This enables completion of multiple picking requests from the warehouse simultaneously, which reduces the number of round trips in the warehouse. A detailed explanation of waves is provided in Chapter 16.
- **Warehouse order creation for outbound requests**
In embedded EWM, warehouse orders are created mandatorily whenever warehouse tasks are created. Warehouse orders are containers that hold warehouse tasks, which are grouped together using warehouse order creation rules to create executable work packages assigned to a worker via resource management. A warehouse operator prints the warehouse order and confirms the tasks assigned to it.

Alternatively, if an operator is using radio frequency (RF), then the system displays the warehouse tasks assigned to the warehouse order in a sequence on RF screens. The warehouse order is confirmed when the last task assigned to the warehouse order is confirmed, and its status is changed to **Complete**. These work packages are created based on settings configured in the warehouse order creation rule, such as how many items can be in one warehouse order, maximum weight/volume, and so on. A detailed explanation of the warehouse order creation process is provided in Chapter 6, Section 6.4.

8.4.1 Warehouse Tasks

We'll pick up the flow from where we left off. You've created a warehouse request in embedded EWM to work with in the form of an outbound delivery order. When the outbound delivery order is created, certain determinations take place in the delivery, such as warehouse process type, consolidation group determination, dates, partner, batch, and so on.

The next step in processing the outbound delivery order is creation of warehouse tasks for stock removal. You can create warehouse tasks for individual warehouse requests or group them into waves to allow simultaneous creation of warehouse tasks for multiple warehouse requests. To create a warehouse task for the outbound delivery order, access the outbound delivery order from the embedded EWM warehouse monitor using Transaction /SCWM/MON. Expand the **Outbound • Document • Outbound Delivery Order** nodes, as shown in Figure 8.16. Select the outbound delivery order displayed after providing selection criteria, click on , and select the **Create WT in Background** option.

You can also access the outbound delivery order for maintenance via **SAP Easy Access** path **Logistics • SCM Extended Warehouse Management • Extended Warehouse Management • Delivery Processing • Outbound Delivery • Maintain Outbound Delivery Order** or via Transaction /SCWM/PRDO.

As shown in Figure 8.17, after the outbound delivery order is opened, choose **Outbound Delivery Order • Follow-On Functions • Warehouse Task**, and click on the **Create + Save** button to create the warehouse task directly from the delivery.

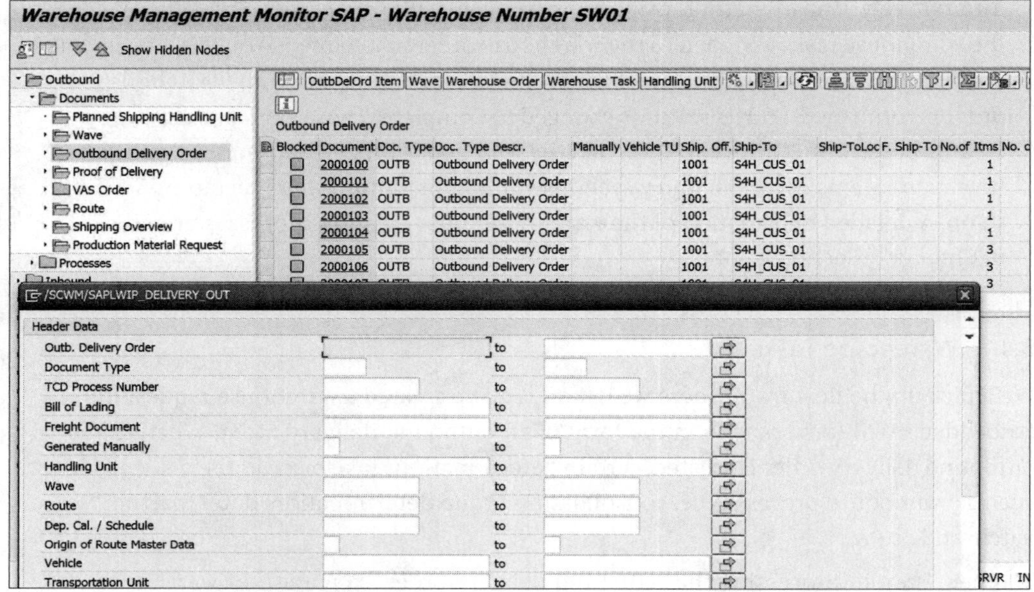

Figure 8.16 Warehouse Monitor to Search Outbound Delivery Order

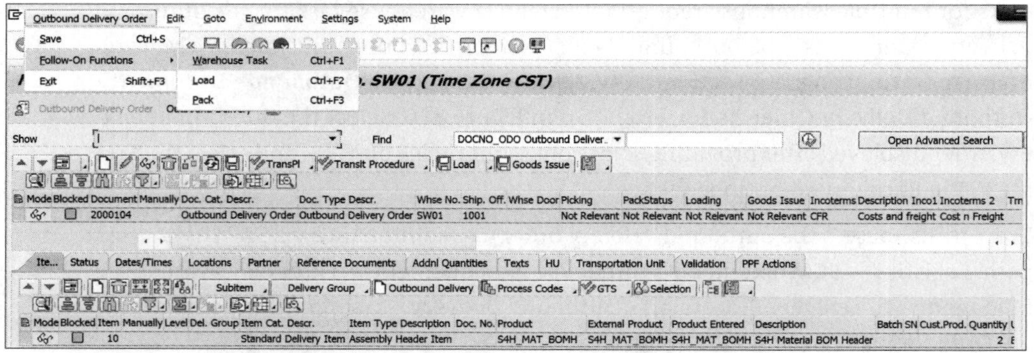

Figure 8.17 Creating the Warehouse Task for the Outbound Delivery Order

You can also create the warehouse task for an outbound delivery order via **SAP Easy Access** path **Logistics • SCM Extended Warehouse Management • EWM Work Scheduling • Create Warehouse Task for Warehouse Request • Stock Removal for Outbound Delivery Order** or via Transaction /SCWM/TODLV_O. Select the **Stock Removal** option. Embedded EWM finds the source bin for the stock to be picked. It considers the storage type search sequence and stock removal strategy to determine the source bin.

After warehouse tasks are created, the system determines the warehouse order creation rule for creating a warehouse order and assigns the warehouse order to a queue from which it will be picked up by a resource. We'll discuss resource management further in Chapter 11.

Note

To create a warehouse task for stock removal for the outbound delivery order, embedded EWM requires a warehouse process type, which enables it to create warehouse tasks that guide warehouse workers about the source bin of the stock, what operations are to be performed, and other parameters that affect stock placements in embedded EWM.

The warehouse process type is determined at the item level of the outbound delivery order and is then used in the creation of warehouse tasks for stock removal. As a follow-up document, the warehouse order is created as a container consolidating one or more warehouse tasks. Because the warehouse order contains warehouse tasks, the system uses the warehouse process type to determine the queues to allocate work to the warehouse workers. The details of how the warehouse process type is determined in delivery items are explained in Chapter 6, Section 6.3.2.

8.4.2 Storage Type Determination

The first step in execution of the outbound process is the identification of source bins for creation of warehouse tasks for picking. The system won't create a picking warehouse task if it can't find a source storage bin. The system uses the storage type determination process to determine the picking bins.

The storage types determined in embedded EWM begins with the determination of the storage type. Storage types are grouped together into a storage type search sequence. The system looks for products in the storage types in the sequence in which they're added in the storage type search sequence. The storage type search sequence is defined via IMG path **SCM Extended Warehouse Management • Extended Warehouse Management • Goods Issue Process • Strategies • Specify Storage Type Search Sequence**, as shown in Figure 8.18. Click on **New Entries**, and enter the storage type search sequence for the embedded EWM warehouse. Select the search sequence, click on **Assign Storage Types to Storage Type Search Sequence**, and enter the storage types the system should search.

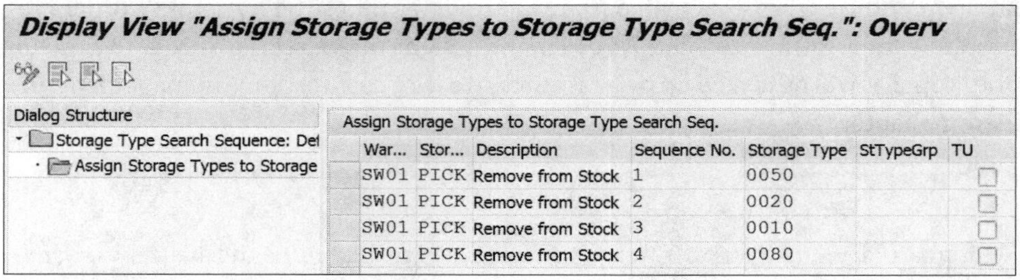

Display View "Assign Storage Types to Storage Type Search Seq.": Overv

Dialog Structure
- Storage Type Search Sequence: Def
  - Assign Storage Types to Storage

Assign Storage Types to Storage Type Search Seq.

War...	Stor...	Description	Sequence No.	Storage Type	StTypeGrp	TU
SW01	PICK	Remove from Stock	1	0050		☐
SW01	PICK	Remove from Stock	2	0020		☐
SW01	PICK	Remove from Stock	3	0010		☐
SW01	PICK	Remove from Stock	4	0080		☐

Figure 8.18 Defining the Outbound Search Strategy in Embedded EWM

In the next step, you define the criteria to determine the storage type search sequence via IMG path **SCM Extended Warehouse Management • Extended Warehouse Management • Goods Issue Process • Strategies • Define Storage Type Search Sequence for Stock Removal**. Click on **New Entries**, define a stock removal control indicator for the embedded EWM warehouse, and save.

After the search sequence determination identifier is defined, configure the setting used by the system to determine the source storage type while creating the stock removal warehouse task. This is configured via IMG path **SCM Extended Warehouse Management • Extended Warehouse Management • Goods Issue Process • Strategies • Determine Storage Type Search Sequence For Stock Removal**, as shown in Figure 8.19. Click on **New Entries**, and set the determination of the search sequence based on the following parameters for your embedded EWM warehouse:

- **SRCI**
  The stock removal control indicator is assigned to the **Warehouse Data** tab in the product master and is used to group products that can be picked from bins in the same storage type search sequence.
- **HazRat1/HazRat2**
  These options are used if the material is hazardous.
- **Quantity Classif.**
  This contains the quantity classification and is determined from the packaging specification. It's used to determine the storage type for a product stored in cases, pallets, and so on.

- **Whse Process Type**
  This is for the warehouse process type determined at the outbound delivery order item level.
- **Tpe/Use**
  These options are used for classifying stocks based on special stock and usage, respectively.

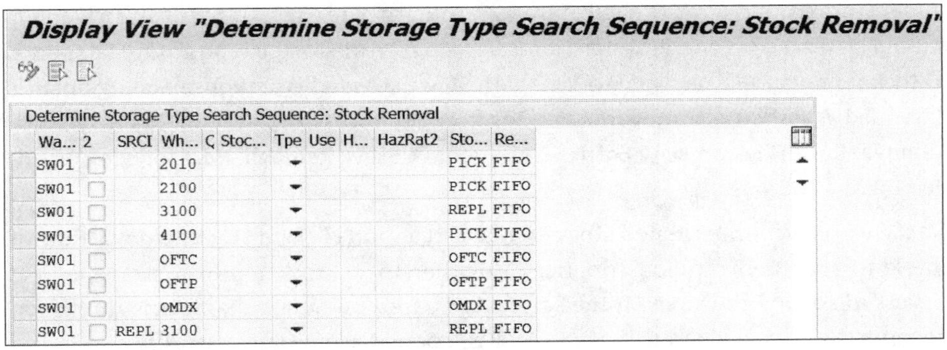

Display View "Determine Storage Type Search Sequence: Stock Removal"

Determine Storage Type Search Sequence: Stock Removal

Wa...	2	SRCI	Wh...	Q	Stoc...	Tpe	Use	H...	HazRat2	Sto...	Re...
SW01	☐		2010							PICK	FIFO
SW01	☐		2100							PICK	FIFO
SW01	☐		3100							REPL	FIFO
SW01	☐		4100							PICK	FIFO
SW01	☐		OFTC							OFTC	FIFO
SW01	☐		OFTP							OFTP	FIFO
SW01	☐		OMDX							OMDX	FIFO
SW01	☐	REPL	3100							REPL	FIFO

Figure 8.19 Settings to Determine the Storage Type Search Sequence

After the storage type determination is configured, you can provide an access sequence optimization, based on which the system determines the storage type search sequence using the set parameters. The access sequence is set via IMG path **SCM Extended Warehouse Management • Extended Warehouse Management • Goods Issue Process • Strategies • Optimization of Access Strategies for Storage Type Determination in Stock Removal**, as shown in Figure 8.20. Click on **New Entries**, select the parameters for determining the storage type search sequence in the descending sequence, and save.

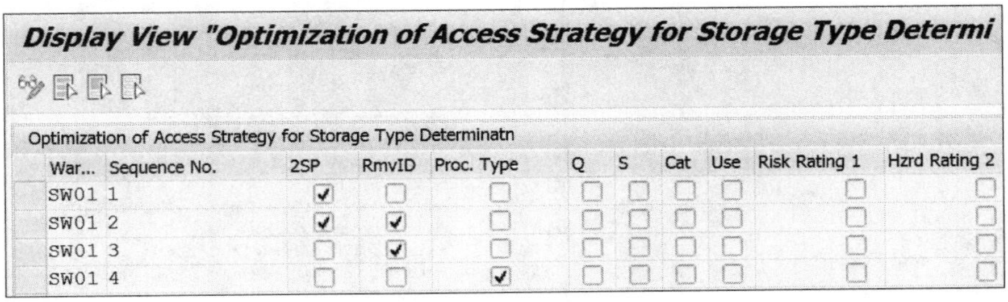

Display View "Optimization of Access Strategy for Storage Type Determi

Optimization of Access Strategy for Storage Type Determinatn

War...	Sequence No.	2SP	RmvID	Proc. Type	Q	S	Cat	Use	Risk Rating 1	Hzrd Rating 2
SW01	1	☑	☐	☐	☐	☐	☐	☐	☐	☐
SW01	2	☑	☑	☐	☐	☐	☐	☐	☐	☐
SW01	3	☐	☑	☐	☐	☐	☐	☐	☐	☐
SW01	4	☐	☐	☑	☐	☐	☐	☐	☐	☐

Figure 8.20 Settings to Optimize the Stock Removal Search Sequence

8.4.3 Stock Removal Strategies

Stock removal strategies are used by the system to determine the bin in the storage type from which picking will be carried out. These strategies can be used to identify which stock the system must pick up based on goods receipt date, shelf-life expiration date, and so on.

Stock removal strategies are assigned to a storage type search sequence determination under **Storage Rule**, as shown in Figure 8.21. Thus, they're used to identify which quant should be picked up by the system for a storage type or storage type group. To specify a stock removal rule, navigate to IMG path **SCM Extended Warehouse Management • Extended Warehouse Management • Goods Issue Process • Strategies • Specify Stock Removal Rule**. Click on **New Entries**, and define a **Stock Removal Rule** for the embedded EWM warehouse.

Next, select the newly created **Stock Removal Rule**, and click on **Stock Removal Rule** in the left-hand menu to add sort fields for the stock. Stock removal strategies are means of sorting the stock in the source bin based on quant characteristics (which become the sort fields in this case), such as goods receipt date, shelf-life expiration date, and so on, either in ascending or descending order. As shown in Figure 8.21, one or more sort fields can be assigned to a stock removal rule via a predefined list of fields available in standard embedded EWM that can be used in defining the sort rule.

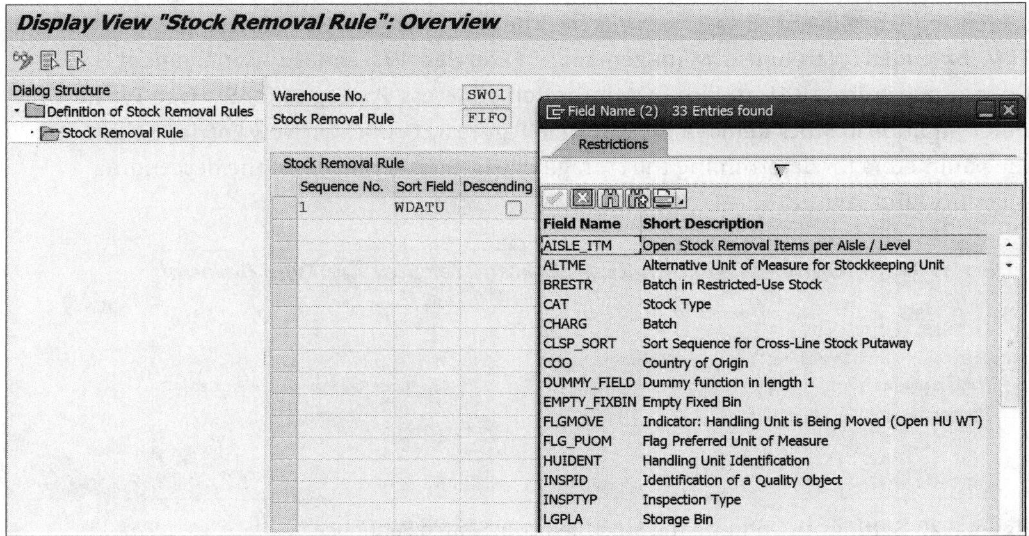

Figure 8.21 Assigning Sort Field to the Stock Removal Rule

Some of the stock removal strategies that can be defined in the system and used for stock removal are as follows:

- **First in, first out (FIFO)**
  FIFO is the stock removal strategy in which the goods receipt date is used as the sort field, and quants are sorted in ascending order of goods receipt date. Thus, based on this strategy, the quant with the earliest goods receipt date is proposed for picking from a storage type. This strategy is mostly used for products that are perishable in nature.
- **Stringent FIFO**
  Stringent FIFO is a removal strategy in which the oldest quant is picked not from a single storage type, but from a group of storage types. This strategy is useful if you want the system to look for quants with the oldest goods receipt dates across multiple storage types in the warehouse. Storage type groups are defined via **SAP Easy Access** path **SCM Extended Warehouse Management • Extended Warehouse Management • Master Data • Define Storage Type Groups**, as shown in Figure 8.22. Click on **New Entries**, and set the stock removal rule (**RemR**) as **FIFO** while defining the storage type group.

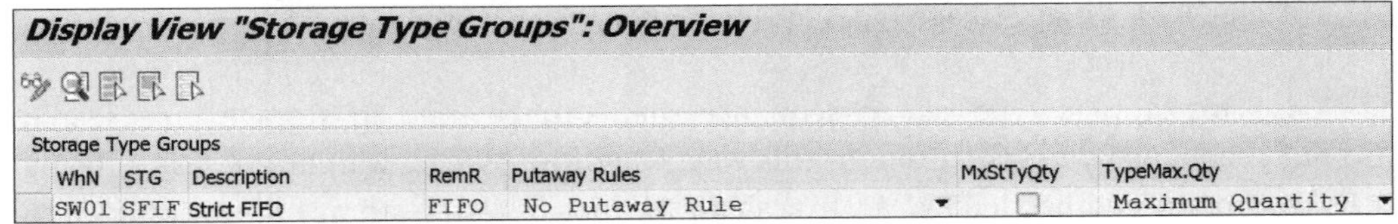

Figure 8.22 Defining the Storage Type Group

After defining the storage type group, storage types to be assigned to the storage type group are assigned via IMG path **SCM Extended Warehouse Management • Extended Warehouse Management • Master Data • Assign Storage Type to Storage Type Group**, as shown in Figure 8.23. Click on **New Entries**, enter the storage type group, and assign it to a sequence of storage types.

While configuring the search strategy for product removal in a warehouse, apply the stock removal rule to all the storage types assigned to the storage group. This is done by assigning the storage type group search sequence to a storage group in the **StTypeGrp** field rather than to individual storage types via IMG path **SCM Extended Warehouse Management • Extended Warehouse Management • Goods Issue Process • Strategies • Specify Storage Type Search Sequence**, as shown in Figure 8.24.

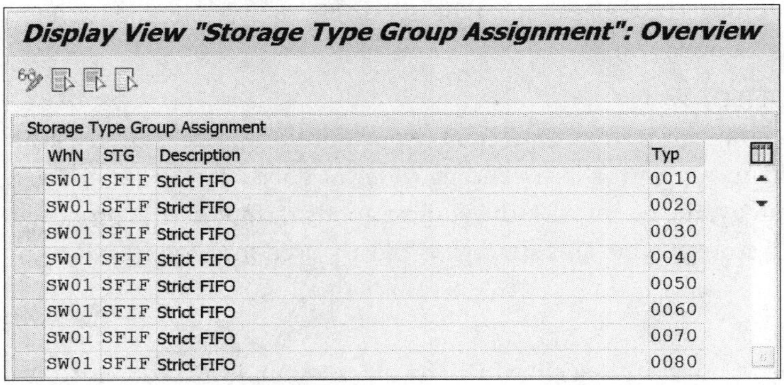

Display View "Storage Type Group Assignment": Overview

Storage Type Group Assignment

WhN	STG	Description	Typ
SW01	SFIF	Strict FIFO	0010
SW01	SFIF	Strict FIFO	0020
SW01	SFIF	Strict FIFO	0030
SW01	SFIF	Strict FIFO	0040
SW01	SFIF	Strict FIFO	0050
SW01	SFIF	Strict FIFO	0060
SW01	SFIF	Strict FIFO	0070
SW01	SFIF	Strict FIFO	0080

Figure 8.23 Assigning Storage Types to the Storage Type Group

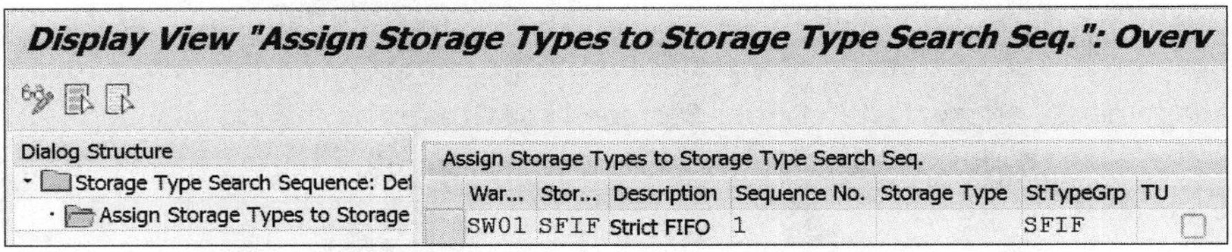

Display View "Assign Storage Types to Storage Type Search Seq.": Overv

Dialog Structure
- Storage Type Search Sequence: Def
  - Assign Storage Types to Storage

Assign Storage Types to Storage Type Search Seq.

War...	Stor...	Description	Sequence No.	Storage Type	StTypeGrp	TU
SW01	SFIF	Strict FIFO	1		SFIF	

Figure 8.24 Assign Storage Types to Storage Types Search Sequence

This storage type search sequence then can be used in storage type search sequence determination. In this way, when the picking warehouse task is being created, embedded EWM will scan all the bins in all the storage types assigned to the storage type search sequence and choose the source bin that holds the stock with the oldest goods receipt date.

- **Last in, first out (LIFO)**
  In the LIFO search strategy, the stock removal rule is defined with the goods receipt date being used as sorting criteria for the stock in the storage type, but in descending order. Thus, embedded EWM always picks up the quant last placed in stock. This strategy is specifically used in processes in which products don't have shelf lives, for example, pallets of mobile phone boxes. In these cases, rather than removing all the stock from the top and then removing the one at the bottom, the warehouse operator picks the stock placed at the top, which is the quant last received in stock in embedded EWM.
- **Partial quantities first**
  Partial quantities first is the stock removal strategy in which the system overrides

FIFO principles for stock removal and optimizes the number of HUs in the warehouse. This strategy aims to keep the number of partial HUs in the warehouse as low as possible. As discussed in the previous chapter, during putaway, the stock for products are stored in the following:

- Full pallets as specified in the packaging specification
- Partial pallets in which the quantity is less than that of a standard HU

While setting up this strategy, two stock removal rules are defined, one for ascending quantity (pieces) and the other for descending quantity (full HUs). A packaging specification is defined with two levels: one with the quantity classification as a pallet and other with pieces, for example. Next, the stock removal rules are assigned to the storage type search sequence so that stock is picked up based on the quantity classification as a filtering parameter.

During the search for the source bin to remove the stock, the system proceeds as follows:

- If the quantity of the warehouse request is the same or greater than that of the standard HU, the system sorts the pallets in descending order and removes full pallets from the source bin.
- If the quantity of the warehouse request is less than that of the standard HU, the system sorts the pieces in ascending order and picks up one or more partial pallets that equal the picking quantity.

- **Large/small quantities**
This strategy is used if stock picking will be done based on quantity. For example, when small quantities (cartons) are requested, the system can search for them in one storage type in which cartons are stocked; when large quantities (pallets) are requested, the system can search the stock in another storage type used for stocking pallets. This strategy is implemented using quantity classification. Alternatively, rather than using packaging specifications, a stock-specific unit of measure (UoM) can be used. Alternative UoMs (AUoMs) must be defined in the product master and should be assigned to the quantity classification in embedded EWM.

Example

Two quantity classifications are defined: C for carton and P for pallet. Now, a packaging specification is defined for the products to be picked, and the picking relevance is set in packaging specifications using the quantity classification. The packaging specification contains two levels, one level with quantity classification P, containing the full quantity for a pallet (e.g., 140 EA), and the other for quantity classification C, containing the full quantity for carton (e.g., 70 EA). The pallets are stored in storage type A, and cartons are stored in storage type B. While configuring the search strategy for quantity classification P, the search sequence with storage type A will be determined by the system; for quantity classification C, the search sequence for storage type B will be determined.

- **Fixed bins**
  Using a fixed bin strategy, embedded EWM picks stock from fixed bins assigned to the product master. If a fixed bin strategy is used for picking, then the system allows the determination of empty storage bins for picking that don't contain any stock and creates picking warehouse tasks even when no stock exists in the bin. This scenario triggers the replenishment process for the source bins. This can also be handled using pick denial and picker-based replenishment. We'll cover picker-based replenishment in Chapter 9.
- **Shelf-life expiration date**
  This strategy is implemented by using a stock removal rule that contains the shelf-life date as the sorting field, sorted in ascending order. This strategy sorts all the quants in the source storage type in ascending order of shelf-life expiration date (sort field **VFDAT**) and proposes the bin containing stock with the oldest such date.
- **Customer-specific strategy**
  If the standard characteristics fields of a quant don't provide an effective way of sorting and selecting the quant from a source bin, organizations can implement their own stock removal rules to identify a storage bin for picking. They can do so by implementing a business add-in (BAdI) via IMG path **SCM Extended Warehouse Management • Extended Warehouse Management • Goods Issue Process • Strategies • Stock Removal • Strategies • BAdI: Deletion of Quant Buffer and BADI: Filtering and/or Sorting of Quants**. A new implementation code for the BAdI method is written and activated for the system to follow the custom stock removal process.

8.5 Picking and Packing

The picking process is performed manually based on a printed warehouse order that contains picking-related information or via RF. The warehouse operator confirms the picking task after physically carrying the stock from the source bin to the destination bin. This can involve moving the stock directly to the goods issue area or moving it via multiple intermediate locations, as shown in Figure 8.25, using process-oriented storage control.

After the stock picking is confirmed using process-oriented storage control, a new warehouse task is created manually or automatically for packing the product in a packing station. Stock picking can also use a pick HU if it's configured in the warehouse order creation rule settings. If the pick HU needs further packing, it can be moved to a packing work center by creating a separate process step to move the pick HU to the packing work center. Packing is done in a packing work center in the goods issue process using desktop Transaction /SCWM/PACK (if there's access to a desktop in the work center) or using RF (for smaller work centers equipped with RF devices).

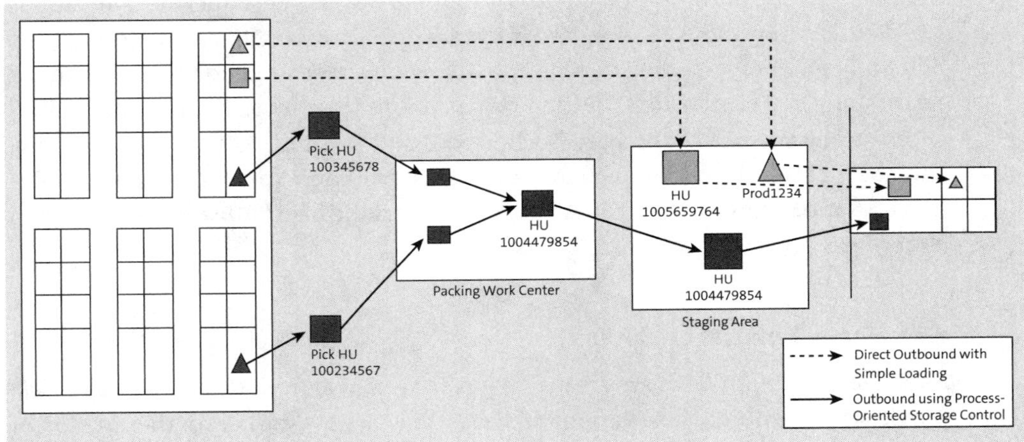

Figure 8.25 Picking Process in Embedded EWM

After completing the packing step, the HU is closed using the [icon] icon, which creates a new warehouse task for staging the stock and moving the stock from the packing station to the staging bin. In addition, ad hoc warehouse tasks also can be created manually to move the stock from a packing station to a staging bin if you're not using the PPF for automatic creation of follow-up warehouse tasks in process-oriented storage control. After the warehouse task is created, the stock is physically moved to the staging area by the worker, and the warehouse task is confirmed. After the stock is moved to the staging area, a new warehouse task is created for loading the stock on the truck. A loading task can be created manually or automatically using the PPF when the truck arrives at the loading door and the product is ready for loading. A loading warehouse task is needed if you're performing complex loading. For simple loading, the loading status can be set to **Complete** manually from the outbound delivery order by clicking on the **Load** button.

After the loading is completed, the outbound delivery is created, and goods issue is performed for the outbound delivery order or for the complete TU in one go for all outbound delivery orders assigned to the TU. As soon as goods issue is performed for the outbound delivery order, an outbound delivery is created in embedded EWM. This in turn sends the goods issue message to SAP S/4HANA and posts the goods issue in the outbound delivery in the same. After you trigger billing for the issued delivery, a financial document is posted.

The following sections discuss the different actions that can be performed on the warehouse stock during picking and packing processes. These include the various ways stock removal can be executed, such as paper-based or RF-based picking (Section 8.5.1); pick denial during picking and follow-up actions (Section 8.5.2); canceling successfully picked products, putting them back in their bins, and handling differences during the picking process (Section 8.5.3 and Section 8.5.4); standard packing and using pick HUs for packing stock during the outbound process execution (Section 8.5.5 and Section 8.5.6); and using advanced packing in the Advanced Packing app (Section 8.5.7).

8.5.1 Stock Removal Execution

After the warehouse tasks are created, the stock removal from the source bin of the warehouse is performed via various methods. The process starts with the creation of warehouse tasks and warehouse orders; then, warehouse workers can perform picking using a manual pick list, mobile data entry, or SAP Fiori apps. Let's discuss each of these execution methods in detail:

- **Pick-list-based execution**
  In this method, the picking in the warehouse is performed via a pick list. The pick list is printed from the warehouse orders created for the outbound delivery order. This process is executed as follows:
  - Warehouse orders are created for the outbound delivery order.
  - These orders are printed to create a pick list for the warehouse operator.
  - The warehouse worker executes physical picking and updates the results in the picking sheet.

- The worker confirms the warehouse order using SAP GUI at a workstation.
- In case of exceptions, appropriate exception codes are applied in SAP to trigger follow-up actions, such as replenishment.

Printing warehouse orders in embedded EWM is done using the PPF and condition techniques. Warehouse orders can be printed manually from the embedded EWM warehouse monitor or by scheduling the printing action execution. The warehouse orders are printed on SAPscript texts or smart forms as templates. Users can customize the form layout depending on business requirements. SAP provides various action definitions for printing warehouse orders via the PPF in the /SCWM/WME application and the /SCWM/WO action profile. The action definitions and corresponding smart forms for printing single and multiple warehouse orders are given in Table 8.4. You can print both if required simultaneously.

Action Definition	Description	SAP Smart Form
WO_MULTIPLE	Print list for warehouse order with serial numbers	/SCWM/WO_MULTIPLE
WO_SINGLE	Print single document for warehouse order with serial numbers	/SCWM/WO_SINGLE

Table 8.4 PPF Actions Definitions and Smart Forms

After the physical stock picking is completed by the warehouse worker based on the provided pick list, the worker must confirm the warehouse order in SAP GUI to complete the picking process in embedded EWM. This is done via **SAP Easy Access** path **Logistics • SCM Extended Warehouse Management • Extended Warehouse Management • Execution • Confirm Warehouse Task** or via Transaction /SCWM/TO_CONF, as shown in Figure 8.26.

To confirm all the items in the warehouse task, click on the **Confirm + Save** button in the header. Alternatively, to confirm the individual warehouse tasks, click on the **Confirm** button after selecting individual warehouse tasks at the item level. A warehouse order is set to **Confirmed** only when all the warehouse tasks in the order are confirmed.

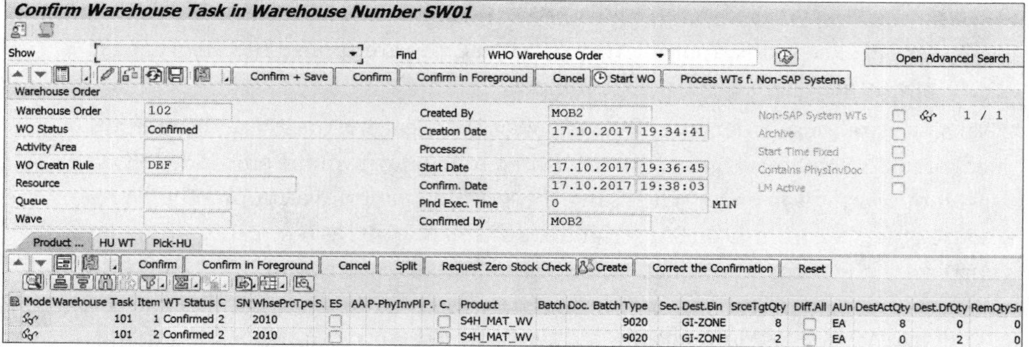

Figure 8.26 Confirming Warehouse Tasks for Picking

- **RF-based execution**
  Warehouse orders created for the outbound delivery order can also be confirmed from mobile devices via RF, which is used extensively in organizations. This provides an easy and paper-free way of confirming stock removal and movement from source to destination. Any exceptions encountered during the picking process can be directly handled from RF and updated in SAP. You can also trigger follow-up actions based on the exception triggered.

  To confirm warehouse orders using RF, log on to RF via **SAP Easy Access** path **Logistics • SCM Extended Warehouse Management • Extended Warehouse Management • Execution • Log on to RF Environment** or use Transaction /SCWM/RFUI.

  You can manually select the warehouse order, HU, or warehouse request that needs to be picked, or you can let the system determine the next warehouse order for picking if system-guided processing is active. There are two options available in the system-guided process:

  - **System-guided picking:** With this option, the system assigns the warehouse order based on the queue assigned to the resource group to which the resource belongs. The user is already logged on to a resource and picks the warehouse order assigned to the resource. This is a fully automated option.
  - **System-guided by queue:** With this option, you can choose a queue, and the system will display the details for the first open warehouse order in that queue.

    When a warehouse order is selected for confirmation using RF, the system displays the warehouse tasks in the warehouse order in the sequence in which they're assigned to the warehouse order. You confirm the first warehouse task, and the system will automatically display the next warehouse task included in the warehouse order. The warehouse order is only confirmed in the system after all warehouse tasks included in the warehouse order are confirmed.

> **Note**
>
> We'll discuss using RF for completing warehouse processes in Chapter 14.

- **SAP Fiori-based execution**

  In SAP S/4HANA, SAP offers the option to use SAP Fiori apps to confirm warehouse tasks using mobile devices. The apps provide an easy way for you to scan a product using barcodes to confirm which product is being picked for the outbound delivery order. The SAP Fiori app available for picking is called Outbound Delivery Orders (Pickup). If you need to pick multiple outbound delivery orders in a single cart trip across the warehouse, you can use the Pick by Cart app. In the Pick by Cart app, the pick step allows you to pick multiple HUs from the same bin in one step in the cart, and HUs can be taken to a destination bin using a single warehouse task.

  SAP has also provided the Process Warehouse Tasks – Picking app, which enables you to perform stock picking operation by confirming picking warehouse tasks. In the overview screen, as shown in Figure 8.27, you can display all information relevant to the picking warehouse tasks.

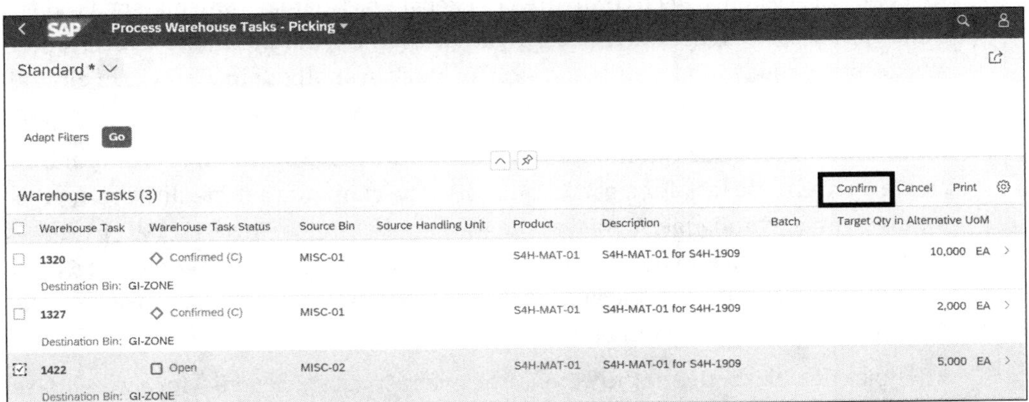

Figure 8.27 Confirming Picking Warehouse Tasks Using the Process Warehouse Tasks – Picking App

This enables you to choose a warehouse task that you want to process. From the list of warehouse tasks, you can either confirm or cancel multiple picking warehouse tasks at once. It's also possible to print pick lists for the open picking warehouse tasks using this mobile app. You can also perform picking warehouse task processing using exception codes for exception handling in the picking warehouse task.

8.5.2 Handling Denials during Picking

During the creation of a warehouse task for picking stock for an outbound delivery order, it may happen that sufficient stock isn't found in the bin, thus leading to a short pick or complete pick denial. Pick denials can occur for multiple reasons, such as issues with the inventory product counting in a storage bin or misplaced stock may in the warehouse. In addition, due to physical inventory in progress, the goods issue from the bin may be blocked or there may have been physical damage in the bin.

Pick denial can happen at various points in the outbound process. For example, there may not be enough stock of a product in the warehouse, and picking warehouse tasks might not be created. It's also possible that picking warehouse tasks are created, but there's no stock in the source bin when a warehouse worker goes to the bin to execute picking. Embedded EWM offers a way to execute pick denial in both cases. In the first case, the system can be configured to execute pick denial immediately if there's a shortage of stock in the warehouse. In the latter case, a warehouse worker can enter an exception code for bin denial and look for stock in another bin. If stock isn't found in any other bin in the warehouse, the system executes a pick denial.

Pick denial occurs if the system can't create the warehouse task at all or is only able to create a warehouse task for a partial quantity. The configuration required to set this up involves activating pick denial at the warehouse number level via IMG path **SAP Extended Warehouse Management • Extended Warehouse Management • Goods Issue Process • Pick Denial • Activate Pick Denial at Warehouse Number Level**. Set the **ActPickDen** indicator for your embedded EWM warehouse.

After pick denial is active at the warehouse level, activate pick denial for a warehouse process type via IMG path **SAP Extended Warehouse Management • Extended Warehouse Management • Goods Issue Process • Pick Denial • Activate Pick Denial at Warehouse Process Type Level**. Click on **New Entries**, and assign the pick denial control and action for the warehouse process type. Here, you can also configure what should happen in a pick denial scenario in terms of passing information to the user and what action the system should take to adjust the warehouse request quantity. For example, as shown in Figure 8.28, as part of pick denial control, the system can issue a warning to the user and trigger an automatic follow-up action in the background that both adjusts the quantity in the outbound delivery order to the available quantity in the warehouse and updates the delivery quantity in SAP S/4HANA.

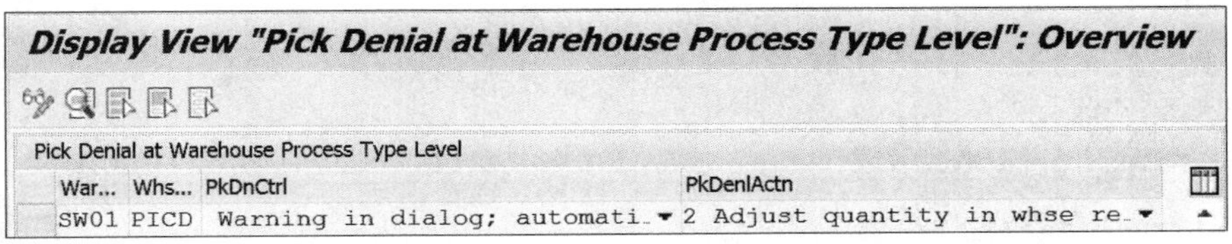

Display View "Pick Denial at Warehouse Process Type Level": Overview

Pick Denial at Warehouse Process Type Level

War...	Whs...	PkDnCtrl	PkDenlActn
SW01	PICD	Warning in dialog; automati...	2 Adjust quantity in whse re...

Figure 8.28 Setting the Pick Denial Control and Action for the Warehouse

To enable execution of a follow-up action, define the workflow that is triggered when the exception code is entered. The settings for managing exception codes are made via IMG path **SAP Extended Warehouse Management • Extended Warehouse Management • Goods Issue Process • Pick Denial • Assign Internal Exception Codes to Exception Codes**. Click on **New Entries**, and map the user-defined exception code to an internal exception code, as shown in Figure 8.29. The standard exception code is PD02. We covered exception handling in detail in Chapter 6, Section 6.6.

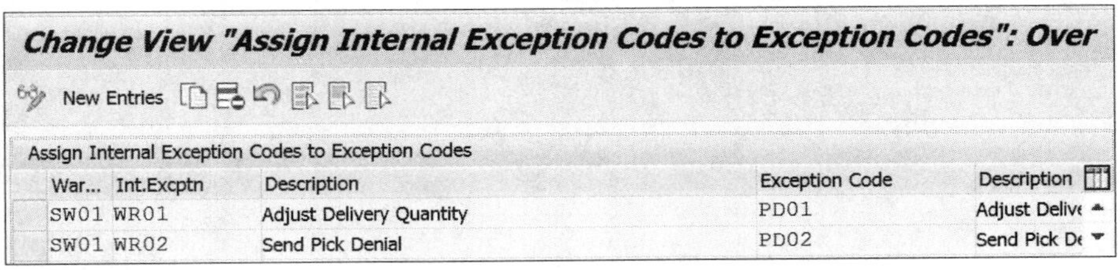

Change View "Assign Internal Exception Codes to Exception Codes": Over

New Entries

Assign Internal Exception Codes to Exception Codes

War...	Int.Excptn	Description	Exception Code	Description
SW01	WR01	Adjust Delivery Quantity	PD01	Adjust Delive
SW01	WR02	Send Pick Denial	PD02	Send Pick De

Figure 8.29 Assigning the External Exception Code to the Internal Exception Code

Using the exception code configuration, the workflow for activating pick denial using an exception code is configured via IMG path **SAP Extended Warehouse Management • Extended Warehouse Management • Cross-Process Setting • Exception Handling • Define Exception Code**, as shown in Figure 8.30. Select **Maintain Follow-On Action (Workflow)**, and assign the exception code with a workflow ID (**WF Start ID**). This workflow is triggered when a pick denial scenario occurs in the warehouse.

For example, in Figure 8.31, an outbound delivery order is created with a requested quantity of 10 EA. However, at the time of the picking warehouse task creation, only 5 EA is available in the warehouse. This triggers a pick denial in embedded EWM, which triggers the workflow to adjust the quantity in the outbound delivery order and send the revised quantity to the outbound delivery in SAP S/4HANA.

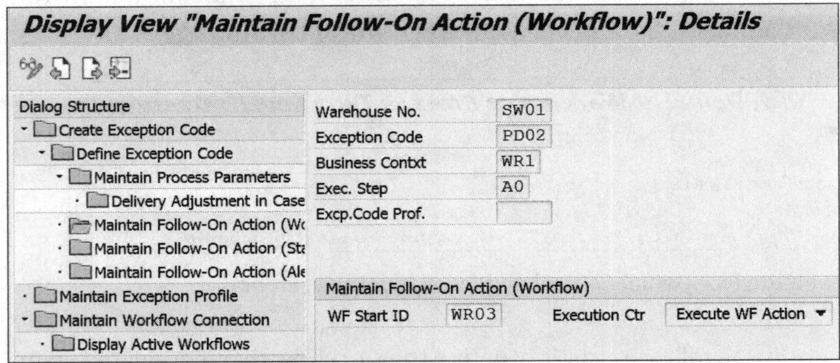

Figure 8.30 Assigning the Workflow to the Pick Denial Exception Code

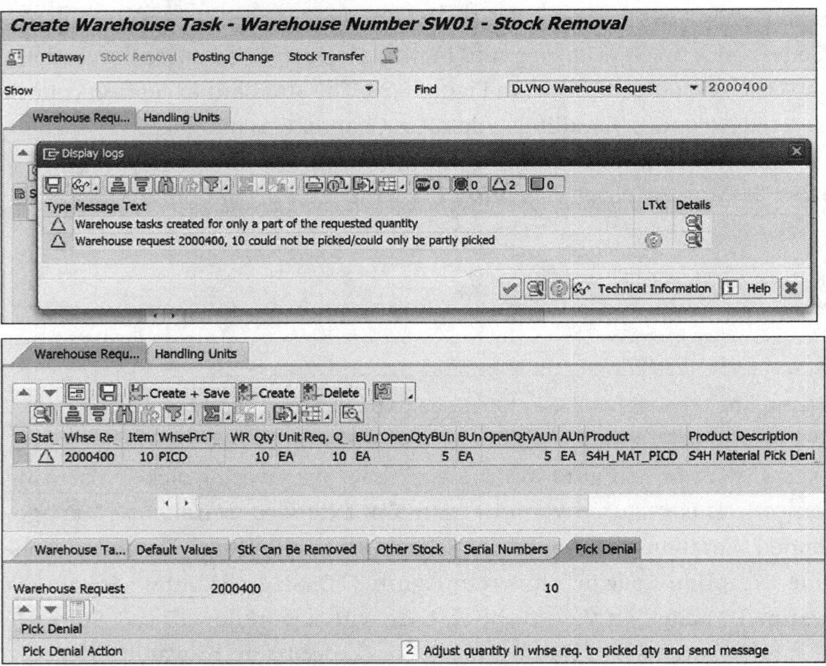

Figure 8.31 Pick Denial in the Outbound Delivery Order

8.5.3 Picking Cancellations

During the outbound process in embedded EWM, it's often necessary to cancel the picked quantity and send it to suitable storage bins. This may be the case if more than the required quantity has been picked or the stock needs to be made available for another urgent outbound delivery. Embedded EWM provides a process to enable such cancellations and send the picked stock back to suitable bins. The picking cancellation happens for warehouse request items, HUs, and reserved stock of warehouse tasks. Embedded EWM releases the stock assigned to the warehouse request item, HU, or warehouse task and makes it available to be used again. For stock in HUs, stock is made available at the highest-level HU. Embedded EWM can only release stock for a complete HU.

As explained earlier, stock can be both released and put away in suitable bins by creating a transfer warehouse task. The system follows a set series of steps:

1. Embedded EWM releases the stock.
2. If the stock isn't packed in HUs, the system calls the screen for moving the products. If the stock is packed, the system calls the screen for moving the HU.
3. You supply the destination bin where the stock is to be put away, and the system creates a transfer warehouse task.

There are two important settings to be made for canceling picks in embedded EWM. First, define the warehouse process type to be used for transferring the stock back after picking in embedded EWM via IMG path **SAP Extended Warehouse Management • Extended Warehouse Management • Goods Issue Process • Cancel Picking • Define Warehouse Process Type for Put-Back**. Click on **New Entries** to define a new return warehouse process type. This warehouse process type has the warehouse process category of **3 Internal Warehouse Movement**. SAP provides warehouse process type 3030 for transferring the stock from the source bin (where the stock is released) to the destination bin. You also need to configure the warehouse number control for pick cancellation; you can assign the warehouse process type defined previously to the warehouse and allow the system to create a stock ID for the stock quantities to be put away. This is configured via IMG path **SAP Extended Warehouse Management • Extended Warehouse Management • Goods Issue Process • Cancel Picking • Define Warehouse Number Control for Put-Back**, as shown in Figure 8.32. Click on **New Entries**, enter the put-back warehouse process type (**WPT Putbk**), and set the control for stock ID cancellation (**Sk ID Canc**) if required for the embedded EWM warehouse.

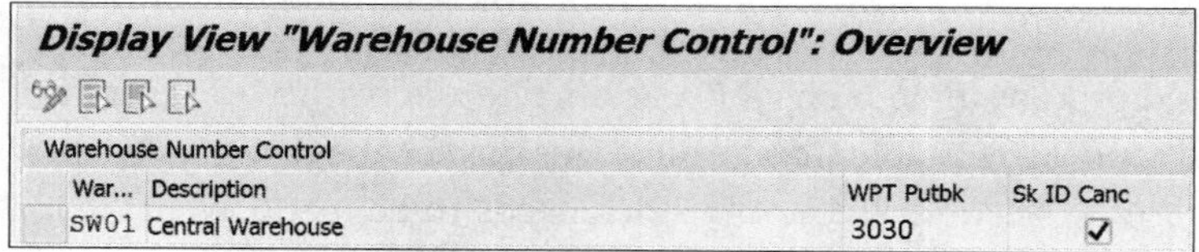

Figure 8.32 Setting Up Picking Cancellation

Note

Stock ID creation is allowed during picking cancellation because it allows the quants of split picks for a delivery item not to be mixed up when they're being put away to a destination bin; the reference to the original delivery item is lost during pick cancellation.

For example, suppose a delivery of product A requires 15 EA to be picked. The warehouse worker picks 1 carton (10 EA) from storage bin A and 1 carton (5 EA) from storage bin B. A split pick is done based on available quants picked from different bins, and two split line items, 20 and 30, are created in the delivery for each AUoM, for example, C10 and C05. Each of these quants have references to the delivery items. During pick cancellation, this reference to the delivery is lost. If the **Stock ID** checkbox is set in configuration, the system creates stock identification for the two AUoMs as follows: 10 EA with AUoM C10, stock ID 1234; and 5 EA with AUoM C05, stock ID 5467.

The following processes can be carried out in the warehouse to execute pick cancellation in embedded EWM:

- **Releasing stock for warehouse request items**

  After the picking task for an outbound delivery order item has been confirmed by the warehouse worker, the picking can be canceled via **SAP Easy Access** path **Logistics • SCM Extended Warehouse Management • Extended Warehouse Management • Execution • Cancel Picking** or via Transaction /SCWM/CANCPICK. From this screen, search for the outbound delivery order item for which picking has to be canceled, as shown in Figure 8.33.

  You can release the complete picked delivery quantity for a warehouse request item by selecting the warehouse request item on the **Warehouse Request Item** tab and clicking on **Release Stock**.

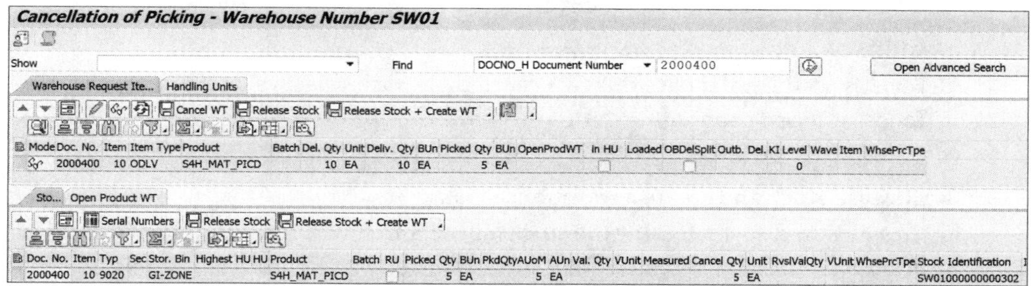

Figure 8.33 Canceling Picking for the Outbound Delivery Order

8

Partial stock for picked warehouse request items can also be released by selecting the warehouse request item as described previously and going to the **Stock** tab, entering the quantity to be released, and then clicking on **Release Stock**.

- **Releasing stock for HUs**

  If instead of canceling items by selecting a warehouse request you want to cancel picking of HUs, go to the **Handling Units** tab on the transaction screen for pick cancellation. On this screen, search for HUs for which cancellation must be executed, and take one of the following actions based on your requirements:

  - Release the completely picked delivery quantity for an HU by selecting the HU and clicking on **Release Stock**.
  - Cancel picking for a partial HU, and repack the HU by selecting the HU on the transaction screen and clicking on **Re-Pack HU**.

- **Cancel reserved stock in warehouse task**

  You can cancel stock reserved for warehouse tasks for an outbound delivery order or HU. In this case, the same process is followed as for stock release, but rather than using the **Release Stock** button, use the **Cancel WT** button for canceling the warehouse tasks for a warehouse request item or HU.

  If partial cancellation is being made for select warehouse tasks for a warehouse request, select the warehouse request item in the pick cancellation screen, and go to the **Product WT** tab at the bottom. In this tab, select the warehouse task to be canceled, and click on **Cancel WT** to complete the process.

Note

For HUs, all the warehouse tasks are canceled; as such, selective pick warehouse task cancellation isn't applicable for HUs in embedded EWM.

- **Release stock and create a warehouse task**
  In addition to just releasing the stock for the warehouse request item or for an HU, the system also lets you create a stock transfer warehouse task. To release stock and create warehouse tasks simultaneously, click on the **Release Stock + Create WT** button in the transaction screen. This can be done in both the foreground and background.

8.5.4 Handling Differences while Picking

After stock picking is carried out for an outbound warehouse request, it's confirmed in the system by confirmation of a warehouse task. While confirming the warehouse task in the system, you can get a difference between the requested and available quantity. If the picked quantity is smaller than the requested quantity in the warehouse task, then the following steps can be taken:

- The difference is recorded in the warehouse task by entering the actual picked quantity in the warehouse task.
- A warehouse task with the difference is confirmed.
- You can either repick the remaining amount in the warehouse request document by creating a warehouse task for the difference quantity, or you can choose not to pick the difference quantity by using the **Adjust Delivery Quantity** option in the **Process Codes** button at the item level in the outbound delivery order to equate the delivery quantity with the picked quantity. This changes the status of picking from **Partially Completed** to **Completed** and allows you to post goods issue for the outbound delivery order. This process is shown in Figure 8.34.

Example

An outbound warehouse request is created to pick 50 EA from a bin, but only 45 EA are available; the worker will confirm the warehouse task with a difference of 5 EA.

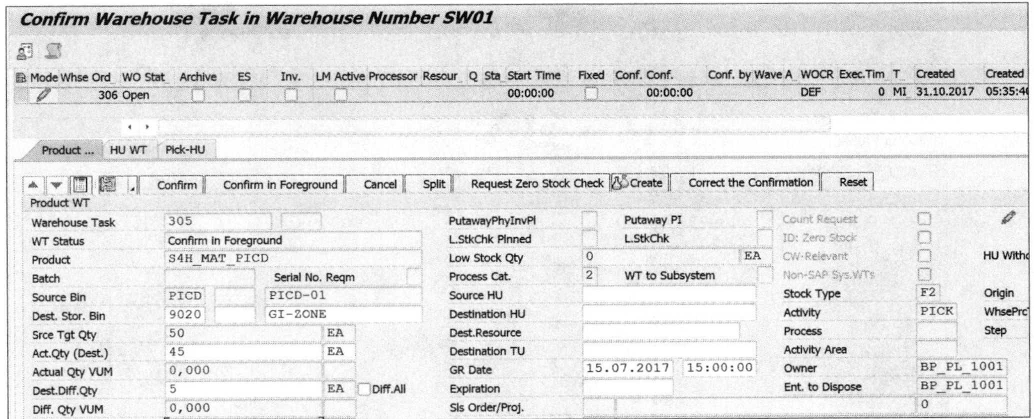

Figure 8.34 Confirming the Outbound Delivery Order with Differences

8.5.5 Use of Pick Handling Units in Picking

If you're picking a partial quantity from a pallet or picking multiple products, you can create pick HUs to carry out the picking process. The pick HU can then be packed and labeled in a packing work center. The pick HU can be created manually while picking the product. Alternatively, you can have the pick HUs created automatically at the time of warehouse order creation. The system-generated pick HUs can be seen in the **HU** tab of the outbound delivery order. If you don't define a packing profile, the system doesn't propose a pick HU. However, you can still create a pick HU manually and assign it to a warehouse task for picking.

To create a pick HU, a packing profile needs to be defined and assigned to the warehouse order creation rule. The packing profile is configured via IMG path **SAP Extended Warehouse Management • Extended Warehouse Management • Cross-Process Settings • Warehouse Order • Define Packing Profile**, as shown in Figure 8.35. Click on **New Entries** to define a packing profile for the warehouse, and set the control parameters as described next.

If you select the **Create HUs** indicator, the pick HU is created automatically by embedded EWM. If the **Assn WTs to HUs** indicator is set, the pick HU is automatically assigned to the warehouse task. When you're confirming the warehouse task, you can manually change the pick HU and its assignment to a warehouse task. Figure 8.36 shows a pick HU created for an outbound delivery and assigned to the warehouse task.

Display View "Packing Profile for Warehouse Order Creation": Details

Warehouse No.	SW01
Packing Profile	PAC1

Packing Profile for Warehouse Order Creation

Description	Packing profile for Pick-HU
Pack. Mode	A Simple Algorithm
Sorting	
☑ Create HUs	
☑ Assn WTs to HUs	
Split WT	Do Not Split
☐ Split WT based on AUoM	
☐ Skip WT	
☐ Check LWH	

Figure 8.35 Define the Packing Profile for the Warehouse Order

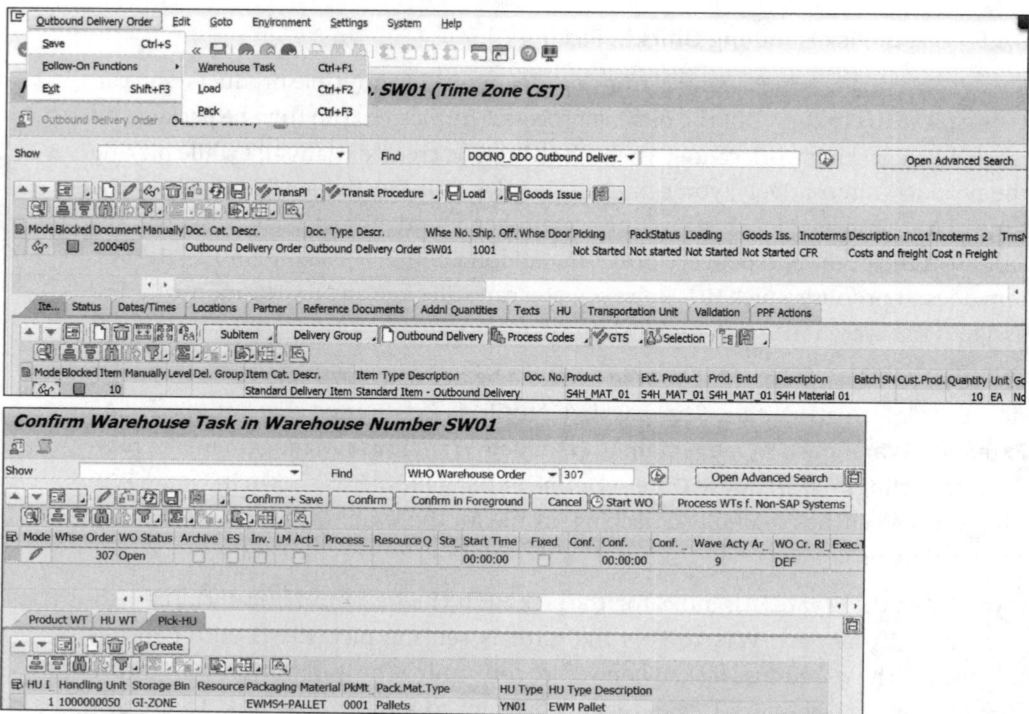

Figure 8.36 Creating the Pick HU for Picking Outbound Delivery Order Products

If you haven't selected **Create HUs** and **Assn WTs to HUs** settings in the packing profile definition, the system only proposes the packaging material and number of pick HUs required for the task at the time of warehouse order creation. You can create the pick HUs by confirming the proposal of the packaging material at the time of warehouse task confirmation. The value in the **Split WT** field controls whether the warehouse task should be split if the pick HU is too small to pack the entire quantity in the warehouse task.

8.5.6 Packing in the Outbound Process

Embedded EWM offers detailed sets of packing-related functionalities that can be carried out at a packing work center after stock has been moved to the packing work center for packing. The first step for executing packing in the outbound process in embedded EWM is to set up the packing work center and its determination. The packing work center determination is made from settings in the warehouse order creation rule. While defining a warehouse order creation rule for picking via IMG path **SAP Extended Warehouse Management • Extended Warehouse Management • Cross-Process Settings • Warehouse Order • Define Creation Rule for Warehouse Order**, select the **Determine WkCtr** checkbox, which will enable embedded EWM to determine the packing work center. This is the case if you're not using process-oriented storage control.

As shown in Figure 8.37, embedded EWM uses the route, activity area, and consolidation group as filters to determine the work center in the goods issue via **Logistics • SCM Extended Warehouse Management • Extended Warehouse Management • Master Data • Work Center • Determine Work Center in Goods Issue** or via Transaction /SCWM/PACKSTDT. Click on **New Entries**, and enter a combination of route, activity area, and consolidation group that may be used to determine the corresponding work center storage type, section, and bin for your embedded EWM warehouse. You can optimize work center determination in goods issue via IMG path **SAP Extended Warehouse Management • Extended Warehouse Management • Master Data • Work Center • Optimize Work Center Determination in Goods Issue**. In the transaction screen, create the access sequence that the system can use to determine the work center based on the filter values determined from the warehouse task.

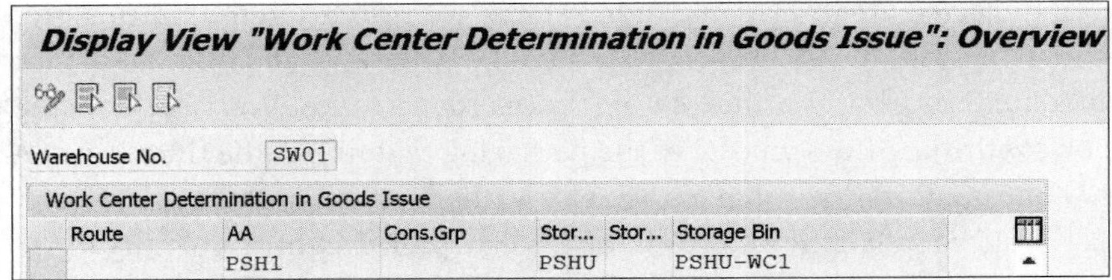

Figure 8.37 Determination of the Work Center in Goods Issue

If you're using process-oriented storage control, then the packing work center is defined in the storage process step for packing. For more details on setting up process-oriented storage control, see Chapter 6.

The packing work center for the goods issue process can be accessed using Transaction /SCWM/PACK or via **SAP Easy Access** path **Logistics • SCM Extended Warehouse Management • Extended Warehouse Management • Execution • Packing—General or Deconsolidation in Goods Receipt**. Provide the embedded EWM warehouse number and packing work center, and click on **Execute**. The next screen displays the packing work center, as shown in Figure 8.38.

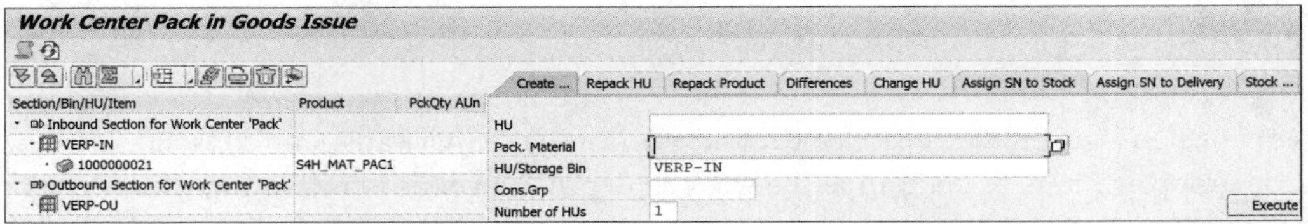

Figure 8.38 Packing Products during the Outbound Process

A packing work center can be used for performing the following tasks:

- Creating HUs
- Repacking HUs
- Repacking products
- Posting differences
- Changing HUs
- Assigning serial numbers to stock
- Displaying stock details

If the order reduction functionality (refer to Section 8.3.5) is activated for the product being packed, the system issues a message that the product is excluded from outbound processes. In addition to basic configuration for the work center (discussed in Chapter 4, Section 4.6), perform settings for assigning a work center to the terminal so the system always identifies the correct warehouse number and work center. You can also assign scales connected to the work center to transmit the exact weight to the SAP system, as well as a local printer to print HU labels. This is done via **SAP Easy Access** path **Logistics • SCM Extended Warehouse Management • Extended Warehouse Management • Master Data • Work Center • Define Master Data Attributes**. Click on **New Entries**, and enter the work center storage bin, work center terminal, and scales for the packing work center.

Note

SAP has provided the new SAP Fiori app called Pack Warehouse Stock for packing stock from one HU or storage bin into another HU. This app can also be used for internal movement of stock in the warehouse. This SAP Fiori app will be explained in detail in Section 8.5.7.

8.5.7 Advanced Packing for Outbound Deliveries

Quick packing refers to the process of packing stock faster using mobile solutions to improve efficiency and reduce packing errors, especially in peak sales season or in fast-moving-goods industries. To address this issue, SAP introduced the Pack Outbound Deliveries app, in which a user can pack goods either using the basic packing process or advanced packing process for serialized and batch-managed products. The user can also use his favorite packing material, synchronous packing process, and access codes to improve packing process efficiency.

The advantage of the advanced packing process using the Pack Outbound Deliveries app is that you have a list of packing material catalog available on the mobile app, and you don't have to search it each time you pack a product or a group of products. To enable the configuration for advanced packing, the following settings must be made:

- **Adding favorite packaging material for a work center**
  You can define up to six favorite packaging materials for a work center via **SAP Easy Access** path **Logistics • SCM Extended Warehouse Management • Extended Warehouse Management • Master Data • Work Centre • Define Favorite Packaging Materials**, as shown in Figure 8.39. Click on **New Entries**; enter the warehouse, work

center, and packaging materials; and save. You can add a maximum of six packaging materials as favorites for a work center.

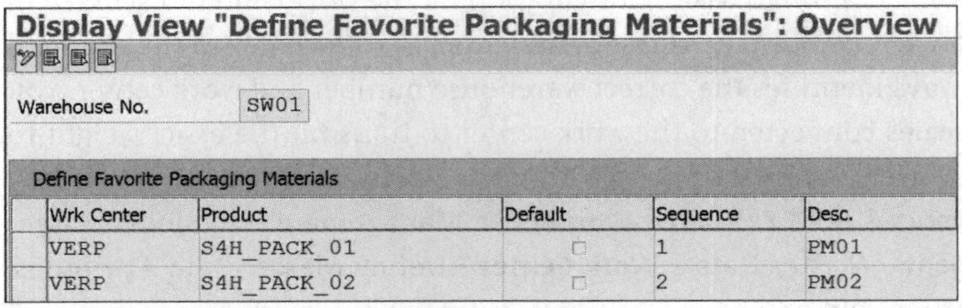

Display View "Define Favorite Packaging Materials": Overview

Warehouse No. SW01

Define Favorite Packaging Materials

Wrk Center	Product	Default	Sequence	Desc.
VERP	S4H_PACK_01	☐	1	PM01
VERP	S4H_PACK_02	☐	2	PM02

Figure 8.39 Assigning Favorite Packaging Materials to the Work Center

- **Activate asynchronous packing (optional)**
  You can optionally activate asynchronous packing via **SAP Easy Access** path **Logistics • SCM Extended Warehouse Management • Extended Warehouse Management • Settings • Performance Settings • Activate Asynchronous Packing**. By doing so, you can pack the next item in the delivery list before having completed the packing of the previous item, thus improving the packing speed of worker.
- **Verify product using URL (optional)**
  You can also verify the product by using the URL where the stock picture is hosted, so that a visual verification of the packing product and packaging material can be carried out. This can be achieved by using BAdI /SCWM/EX_POD_MAT_PIC (Retrieval of Product Picture URLs), which is accessible via IMG path **SCM Extended Warehouse Management • Extended Warehouse Management • Business Add-Ins (BAdI) for Extended Warehouse Management • Master Data • Product.**

Note

After these configurations are completed, the role for the Pack Outbound Deliveries app must be added to the SAP user ID of the person trying to perform advanced packing.

The advanced packing of products in embedded EWM can be achieved using the Pack Outbound Deliveries app. As shown in Figure 8.40, the app displays all packable items of a selected HU. The app user interface also displays the favorite packaging materials, so that you don't have to search the packaging material explicitly while packing the product. Using the mobile application, you can pack a single product or all products, print the packed products list, and enter the gross weight of the packed products. You can pack the items in an HU using a packaging material by giving the HU number in the **Reference Number** field, and create the shipping HU. You can also create empty shipping HUs, print the labels, stick them on shipping HUs, and keep them ready so that you can pack the items in readily created HUs and send them to the staging area. Also in Figure 8.40, products have been packed, and the packed shipping HUs are displayed on the app. The packed products show the number of products contained in each packing and can be printed while sending it over to the customer via this mobile app.

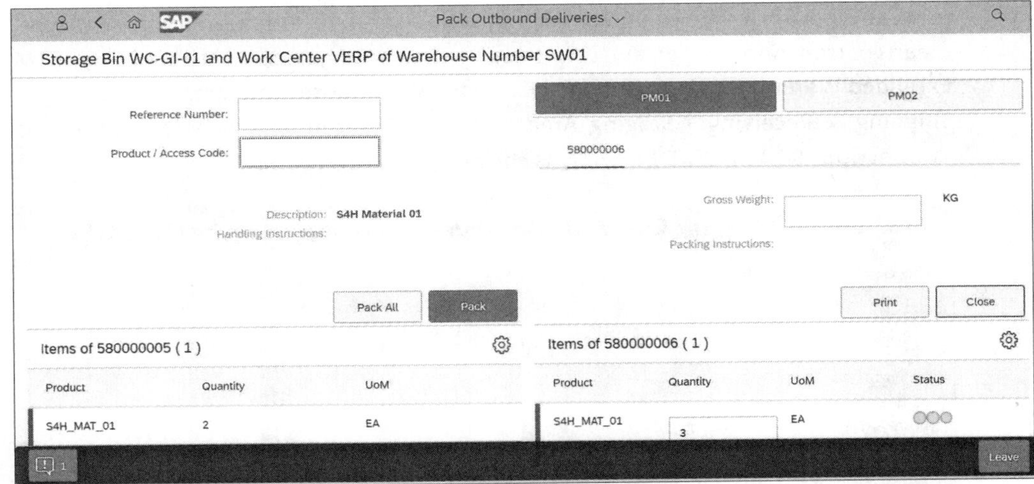

Figure 8.40 Pack Outbound Delivers SAP Fiori App Showing Advanced Packing for Outbound Deliveries

8.6 Loading

In this section, we'll explain the loading subprocess for completing the outbound process in embedded EWM. Section 8.6.1 talks about the configuration and usage of doors and staging area determination in embedded EWM for outbound deliveries. Then, Section 8.6.2 builds on these topics and explains the different actions and movements of TUs in the yard, which can support the loading subprocess to complete the overall outbound process.

8.6.1 Door and Staging Area Determination

After the materials are packed, the next set of processes are staging and shipping of products. If storage control is active for the end-to-end outbound process, a warehouse task is created automatically or manually to move the HU to a staging area when the HU is closed in the packing work center. After defining a door, staging area, and staging area door determination group, assign a staging area to the door via IMG path **SAP Extended Warehouse Management • Extended Warehouse Management • Master Data • Assign Staging Area/Door Determination Group to Door** and **Assign Staging Area to Warehouse Door**.

You can enable the system to determine the staging area based on route, warehouse process type, departure calendar, staging area/door determination group, HU type, means of transport, carrier, and ship-to party via **SAP Easy Access** path **Logistics • SCM Extended Warehouse Management • Extended Warehouse Management • Settings • Shipping & Receiving • Staging Area and Door Determination (Outbound)** or via Transaction /SCWM/STADET_OUT, as shown in Figure 8.41.

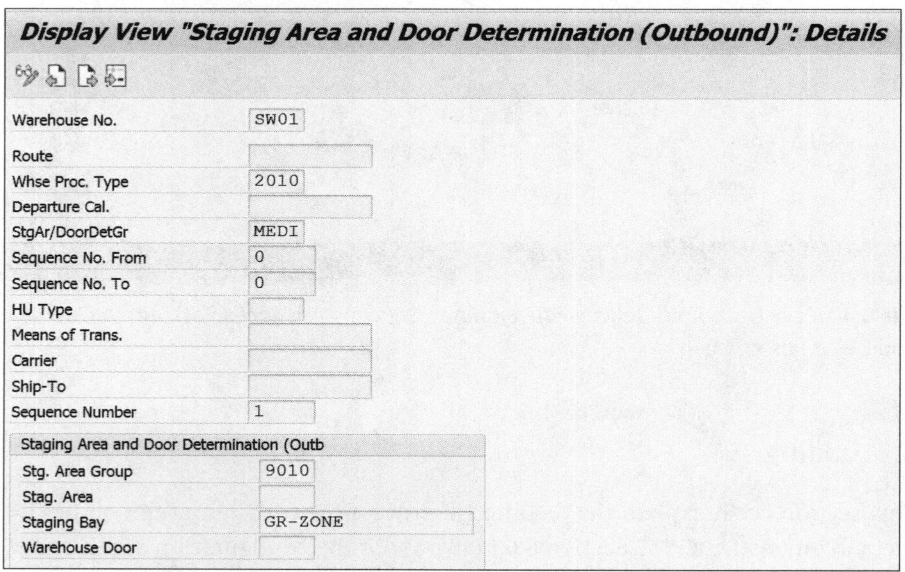

Figure 8.41 Staging Area and Door Determination in the Outbound Delivery Order

Click on **New Entries**, and enter the values for the route, warehouse process type, staging area/door determination group, means of transport, carrier, and ship-to party that will be used for determination of the destination staging area.

To limit the table size and improve system performance, specify an access sequence for determining the staging area and door via **SAP Easy Access** path **Logistics • SCM Extended Warehouse Management • Extended Warehouse Management • Settings • Shipping & Receiving • Access Sequence to Staging Area and Door Determination**.

When these settings are complete, the staging area determination is executed during the creation of the outbound delivery, and the system populates the staging area at the item level, with the value determined from these settings. The corresponding door is also assigned at the outbound delivery order header level.

8.6.2 Integration with Yard Management

It's possible to activate shipping and receiving in the embedded EWM warehouse to enable the use of vehicles and TUs for managing transports in the warehouse, carry out loading and unloading activities from the warehouse door, and integrate with yard management. Organizations often use a vehicle to load multiple deliveries for a customer or for multiple customers on a single route. The process starts with creation of a TU in embedded EWM and a planned shipping and receiving activity. A TU in embedded EWM represents a truck, trailer, container, or other such element used for carrying items from the warehouse to the customer. They're created via **SAP Easy Access** path **Logistics • SCM Extended Warehouse Management • Extended Warehouse Management • Shipping & Receiving • Create Transportation Unit** or via Transaction /SCWM/TU. For more details on the shipping and receiving process, see Chapter 18. Organizations often print a loading list that displays the deliveries to be loaded onto the TU. A TU is used for displaying the deliveries to be loaded on the truck/trailers and shows the shipping and receiving activities that represent TU movements in the warehouse.

After the picking and packing process is complete, goods are moved to a staging area in the warehouse. When a TU arrives in the warehouse, click on the **Activate** button in the TU transaction screen, which changes the status of the shipping and receiving activity from **Planned** to **Active**. The TU is assigned to a door. If you're using yard management, then a yard warehouse task is created to move the TU to the door. Otherwise, the user can execute the **Arrival at Door** action by choosing **Action • Door • Arrival** at the door from the vehicle or TU transaction by selecting the relevant vehicle or TU. Because the staging area is assigned to a unique door, after the TU is docked to the door, goods staged in the staging area are loaded in the TU. Loading is done using a simple or complex loading process. Simple loading doesn't involve actual movement of goods from the staging bay to the TU but only a change of loading status after the **Load** button is clicked for the TU or outbound delivery order. Alternatively, you can also perform loading via **SAP Easy Access** path **Logistics • SCM Extended Warehouse Management • Extended Warehouse Management • Shipping & Receiving • Load** or via Transaction /SCWM/LOAD by selecting the TU and clicking on the **Load** button.

Perform complex loading to track the loading process for each pallet on the TU using warehouse tasks. In this process, warehouse tasks are created for loading, and after loading is completed, the warehouse tasks are confirmed. You can configure goods issue posting from a TU when it's checked out from the yard by selecting the **Post Goods Issue at Departure** checkbox via IMG path **SCM Extended Warehouse Management • Extended Warehouse Management • Cross-Process Settings • Shipping and Receiving • General Settings for Shipping and Receiving**, as shown in Figure 8.42.

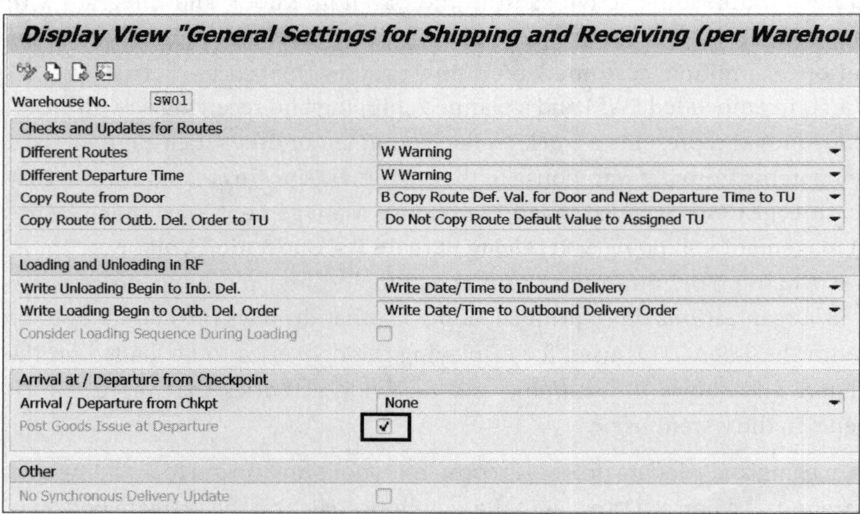

Figure 8.42 Activating Goods Issue during Check Out

8.7 Goods Issue Posting and Partial Goods Issue Using Delivery Splits

Performing goods issue is required for full delivery quantity and partially picked and shipped quantities both in embedded EWM/decentralized EWM and in SAP S/4HANA outbound delivery. In the following sections, we explain how this can be achieved using the standard goods issue process or using exception handling in embedded EWM and decentralized EWM.

8.7.1 Goods Issue Posting

The goods issue posting confirms the physical departure of products from the warehouse. After goods issue is complete, a notification can be sent to customers to let them know of the upcoming arrival of goods, and the billing process can be initiated in SAP S/4HANA. Goods issue for the outbound delivery order is posted using various options in embedded EWM.

8

Goods issue can be posted manually at the header level in the outbound delivery order using Transaction /SCWM/PRDO, as shown in Figure 8.43. Click on the **Goods Issue** button to post the goods issue for the selected outbound delivery order.

If you're using integration with shipping and receiving, it can also be posted from the TU via Transaction /SCWM/TU. In addition to complete goods issue, partial issue can also be posted. This is done only for stock loaded on the TU or items picked in an outbound delivery order. On posting the goods issue for select warehouse request items, the information for goods issue is replicated for the deliveries in SAP S/4HANA, and the partial goods issue is posted in the deliveries in SAP S/4HANA.

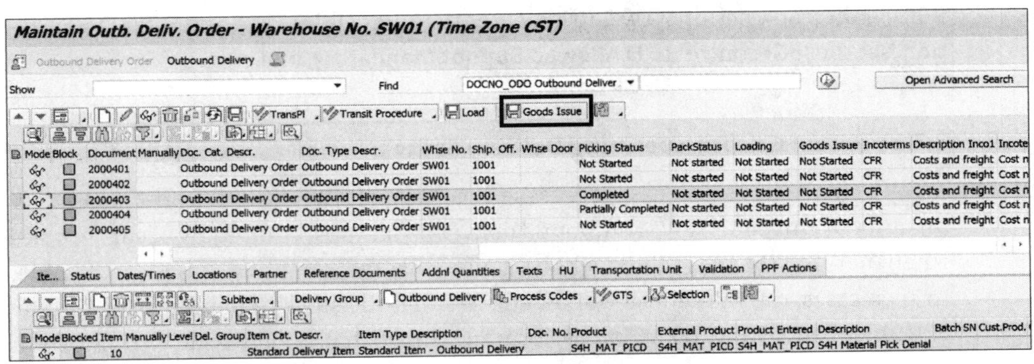

Figure 8.43 Posting Goods Issue for the Outbound Delivery Order

If required, you can reverse goods issue posted for items in a delivery or on a TU by choosing the **Reverse Goods Issue** option from the **Goods Issue** button, as shown in Figure 8.44.

In a normal outbound process, the invoice is created and printed after the goods issue in SAP S/4HANA. However, you may require the invoice to be created before you post the goods issue, as is often the case for international shipments and the direct outbound delivery process. An invoice can be printed for outbound deliveries created in embedded EWM using Transaction /SCWM/FD or Transaction /SCWM/TU. You select the outbound delivery or TU containing the outbound delivery requests, click on [icon], and select **Request Invoice**.

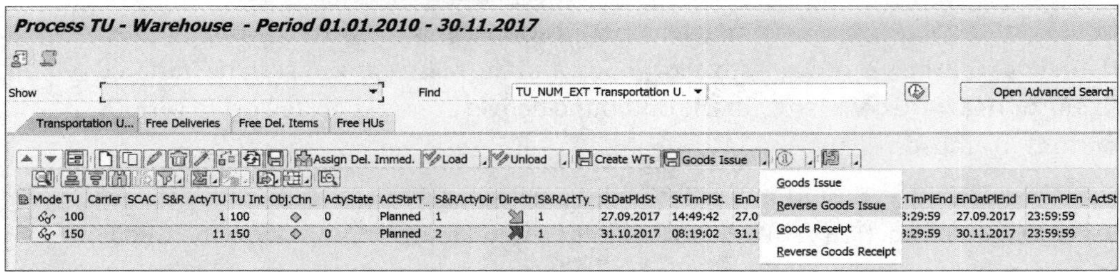

Figure 8.44 Reversing Goods Issue for the Outbound Delivery Order

To enable this functionality, activate the invoice before goods issue for the process profile assigned to the document type and the item type for the outbound delivery. You have to maintain the **IBGI** indicator for both the sales order types and sales organization in SAP S/4HANA via IMG path **Logistics Execution • Extended Warehouse Management Integration • Billing Settings • Determine Invoicing Before Goods Issue (IBGI) Indicator**. Click on **New Entries**, enter the **Sales Order Type** and **Sales Organization**, set the **IBGI** control to **D Allowed But not Mandatory**, and save.

8.7.2 Partial Goods Issue Using Delivery Splits

Many organizations need to goods issue a partial quantity of stock from the delivery quantity of embedded EWM outbound delivery. This most commonly occurs in cases when there is a change in the stock availability that the warehouse has to goods issue. In such cases, the warehouse worker ensures that the stock in hand is issued to the customer/requesting plant by performing the partial goods issue process from embedded EWM.

> **Note**
>
> SAP doesn't allow partial goods issue of stock in SAP S/4HANA (logistics execution) deliveries because the goods issue status is set at header level when all the line items of the SAP S/4HANA outbound delivery are issued.

Therefore, embedded EWM achieves this process of partial goods issue using a process called delivery splits.

Using the delivery split functionality, the line item of outbound delivery order is split to create a subitem (child item) of the split line item. It can be seen as a new line item in the outbound delivery order, having a reference to the parent line item with a "+" sign.

Figure 8.45 summarizes the split of an outbound delivery in embedded EWM. After the line item of the delivery is split, it creates a subitem in the existing outbound delivery order and relays the message to SAP S/4HANA. After SAP S/4HANA receives this information, it creates a new outbound delivery for the split quantity. This new outbound delivery contains the reference of the old SAP S/4HANA outbound delivery and points to the same outbound delivery order in the embedded EWM system.

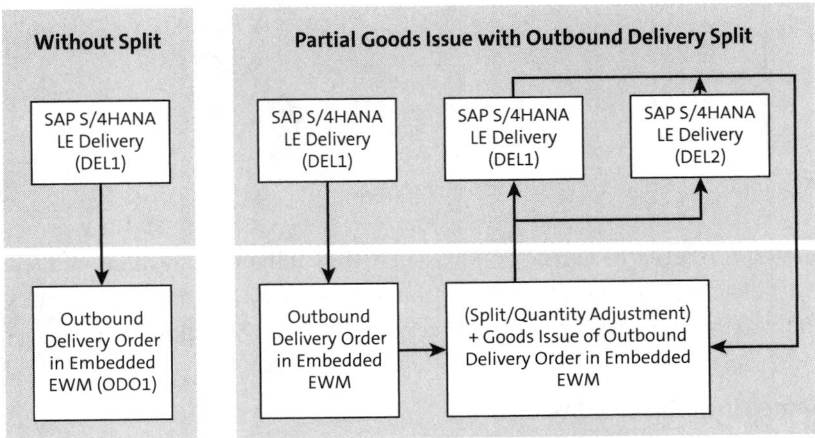

Figure 8.45 Partial Goods Issue in the Outbound Delivery Using Splits

You can configure partial goods issue in the embedded EWM system using the following settings:

- **Define process codes to adjust and transfer delivery quantity**
  You must define process codes that not only adjust the delivery quantity in the delivery line item but also transfer the same to the SAP S/4HANA system. You can do this via IMG path **SAP Extended Warehouse Management • Extended Warehouse Management • Cross-Process Settings • Delivery Processing • Process Codes • Define Process Codes.** Once there, choose value **2 Adjustment of Delivery Quantity and Del. Quant. Transferred for quantity Adjustment** in process codes.

- **Define process code profiles for process codes**
  You define a new process code profile for the process code for assignment to the delivery item type via IMG path **SAP Extended Warehouse Management • Extended Warehouse Management • Cross-Process Settings • Delivery Processing • Process Code • Maintain Process Code Profiles.**
- **Define and assign delivery split profile to delivery type**
  You define a split profile and assign it to the outbound delivery types via IMG path **Logistics Execution • Shipping • Deliveries • Subsequent Delivery Split**, as shown in Figure 8.46.

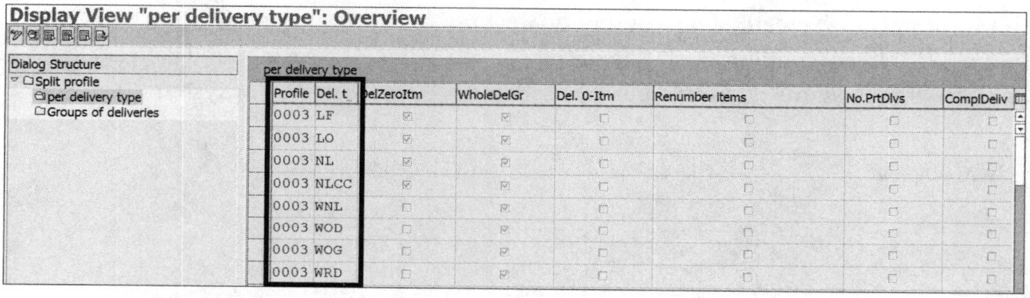

Display View "per delivery type": Overview

Dialog Structure
- Split profile
  - per delivery type
  - Groups of deliveries

per delivery type

Profile	Del. t	DelZeroItm	WholeDelGr	Del. 0-Itm	Renumber Items	No.PrtDlvs	ComplDeliv
0003	LF	☑	☑	☐	☐	☐	☐
0003	LO	☑	☑	☐	☐	☐	☐
0003	NL	☑	☑	☐	☐	☐	☐
0003	NLCC	☑	☑	☐	☐	☐	☐
0003	WNL	☐	☑	☐	☐	☐	☐
0003	WOD	☐	☑	☐	☐	☐	☐
0003	WOG	☐	☑	☐	☐	☐	☐
0003	WRD	☐	☑	☐	☐	☐	☐

Figure 8.46 Assigning the Split Profile to the Delivery Type

While completing the setup of partial goods issue using delivery split in embedded EWM, you must ensure that you set up the number range of SAP S/4HANA (logistics execution) delivery to be created by this delivery split using the following IMG settings:

- **Number Range in embedded EWM**
  The number range for the SAP S/4HANA delivery should be set up via IMG path **SCM Extended Warehouse Management • Extended Warehouse Management • Interfaces • ERP Integration • Delivery Processing • Define Number Ranges for ERP Deliveries.**
- **Assign number range to embedded EWM delivery type**
  You must assign the number range defined in the previous item to the embedded EWM delivery type via IMG path **SCM Extended Warehouse Management • Extended Warehouse Management • Interfaces • ERP Integration • Delivery Processing • Control Message Processing Dependent on Recipient.**

- **Number range in SAP S/4HANA**
  The number range for the SAP S/4HANA delivery should be set up via IMG path **Logistics Execution • Shipping • Deliveries • Define Number Ranges for Deliveries**.
- **Assign number range to embedded EWM delivery type**
  You must assign the number range defined in the preceding item to a combination of SAP S/4HANA delivery type and embedded EWM to enable SAP S/4HANA warehouses via IMG path **Logistics Execution • Decentralized WMS Integration • Local Operations • Applications • Subsequent Outbound-Delivery Split • Set Number Assignment for Deliveries That Have Been Split**.

> **Tip**
>
> You must ensure that the number range set up as the internal number range in embedded EWM is set up as the first number range and is uniquely available in the settings node. In addition, you must ensure that the same number range is marked as the external number range for the SAP S/4HANA delivery number.

Let's look at an example in the SAP S/4HANA system (Figure 8.47) where we've split the delivery line item after partially completed the picking. In this example, an outbound delivery was created with 10 EA line item quantity and distributed to embedded EWM. After the outbound delivery is successfully distributed to embedded EWM, it creates an outbound delivery order in the system.

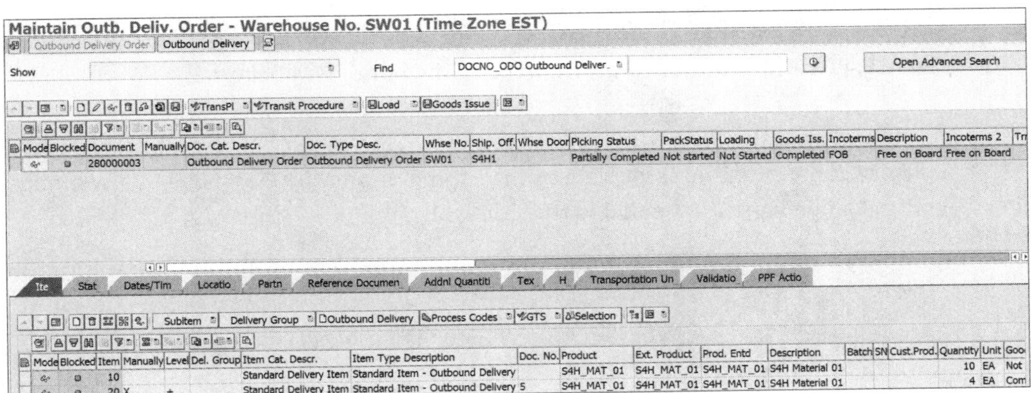

Figure 8.47 Outbound Delivery Order Showing the Delivery Split

Partial picking (4 EA) was carried out for the outbound delivery order, out of a total 10 EA quantity. After the partial picking is confirmed for the outbound delivery order, you can split the delivery by clicking on the **Subitem** button and then choosing **Create Subitem for Outbound Delivery Split** from the dropdown. This will result in the creation of a new SAP S/4HANA outbound delivery for the split quantity of the line item. As shown in Figure 8.47, the split quantity for the line item will be shown just below the original line item with a **+** sign.

As shown in Figure 8.48, both the new and old SAP S/4HANA outbound deliveries refer to the same direct outbound delivery in embedded EWM, thus leading to ease of reporting and searching outbound delivery orders for split deliveries in embedded EWM. You can search and display both the original and the new split delivery in the document flow of the base document (sales order, in our case). It's also worth noting that the original SAP S/4HANA delivery quantity is reduced by the split delivery quantity value.

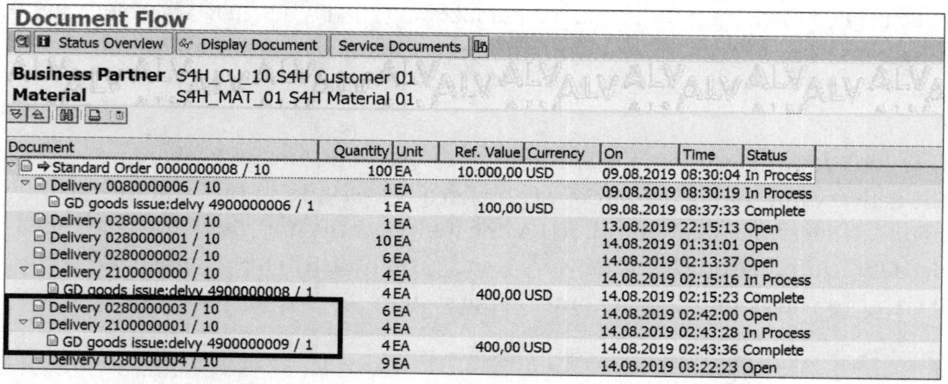

Document Flow

Status Overview | Display Document | Service Documents

Business Partner S4H_CU_10 S4H Customer 01
Material S4H_MAT_01 S4H Material 01

Document	Quantity	Unit	Ref. Value	Currency	On	Time	Status
Standard Order 0000000008 / 10	100	EA	10.000,00	USD	09.08.2019	08:30:04	In Process
Delivery 0080000006 / 10	1	EA			09.08.2019	08:30:19	In Process
GD goods issue:delvy 4900000006 / 1	1	EA	100,00	USD	09.08.2019	08:37:33	Complete
Delivery 0280000000 / 10	1	EA			13.08.2019	22:15:13	Open
Delivery 0280000001 / 10	10	EA			14.08.2019	01:31:01	Open
Delivery 0280000002 / 10	6	EA			14.08.2019	02:13:37	Open
Delivery 2100000000 / 10	4	EA			14.08.2019	02:15:16	In Process
GD goods issue:delvy 4900000008 / 1	4	EA	400,00	USD	14.08.2019	02:15:23	Complete
Delivery 0280000003 / 10	6	EA			14.08.2019	02:42:00	Open
Delivery 2100000001 / 10	4	EA			14.08.2019	02:43:28	In Process
GD goods issue:delvy 4900000009 / 1	4	EA	400,00	USD	14.08.2019	02:43:36	Complete
Delivery 0280000004 / 10	9	EA			14.08.2019	03:22:23	Open

Figure 8.48 SAP S/4HANA Delivery Referencing the Same EWM Deliveries

As shown in Figure 8.49, the new split SAP S/4HANA delivery is a replica outbound delivery containing the same data as that of the original SAP S/4HANA delivery but with a changed quantity (equal to the split quantity).

Note

It's important to note here that the new outbound delivery created in SAP S/4HANA will be fully picked and issued, while the leftover quantity of the item stays in the SAP S/4HANA delivery to be picked and issued later.

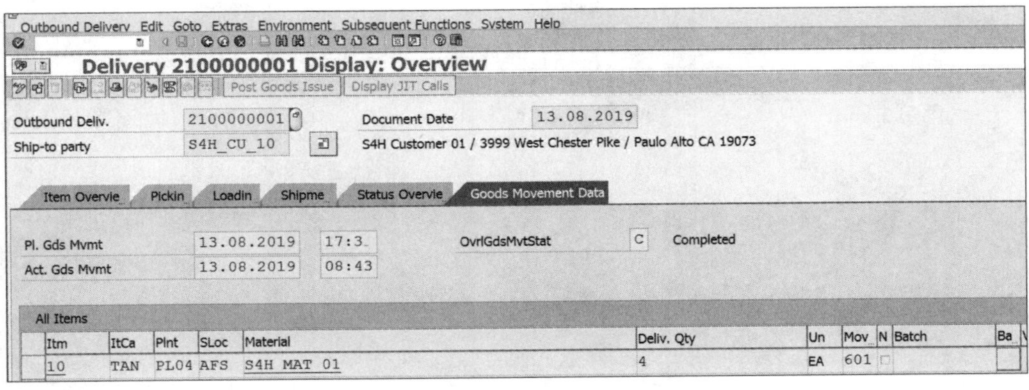

Figure 8.49 SAP S/4HANA Delivery with Split Quantity

8.8 Summary

This chapter introduced outbound processes and documents supporting outbound processes in embedded EWM. We discussed the settings required to distribute outbound deliveries from SAP S/4HANA to embedded EWM. We covered the warehouse request created to execute the picking process in embedded EWM. We reviewed all subprocesses used in outbound operations, such as picking cancellation, pick denial, and handling differences to manage exceptional scenarios in the warehouse. We also discussed how packing is carried out using pick HUs and in work centers.

We discussed how the same SAP S/4HANA delivery number can be used as the outbound delivery order number. We explained the use of the Pack Outbound Deliveries app for advanced packing and Process Warehouse Tasks – Picking app for processing picking warehouse tasks. Toward the end of the chapter, we discussed the integration of yard management with outbound processes in embedded EWM using trailers and trucks. We also discussed goods issue and partial goods issue posting for outbound delivery documents in embedded EWM and the use of invoice creation before goods issue in embedded EWM. In the next chapter, we will cover internal warehouse processes.

Chapter 9
Internal Warehouse Processes

Stock movements within the warehouse are internal movements. Stock movements can be changes in the physical location of the stock or changes in quant characteristics. This chapter will introduce the different types of stock movement in embedded EWM and the configuration settings required to carry them out.

9

Stock is moved within the warehouse for various reasons; for example, stock may need to be moved based on an open stock transfer requirement, or you may want to move stock from one bin to another if it's not in the right place. The internal warehouse movements allowed in basic warehouse management are as follows:

- Replenishment
- Ad hoc movements
- Posting change
- Stock transfer

We'll discuss each of these internal warehouse movements in detail in this chapter. Section 9.1 covers replenishment, which is used to replenish stock in a storage type from a reserve storage type. We'll discuss various replenishment strategies available in embedded EWM. Section 9.2 covers ad hoc movements and stock consolidation. These movements are created to move stock in the warehouse on an ad hoc basis or due to space optimization in warehouse bins. Section 9.3 covers the business application and configuration required for implementation of stock consolidation for warehouse bin space optimization. In Section 9.4, we discuss the posting change process and the configurations required for using embedded EWM. Finally, Section 9.5 covers the process and configuration with which stock can be moved from a source bin to a target bin in a warehouse with or without reference to the warehouse request in embedded EWM.

9.1 Replenishment

Replenishment is used when you want to move stock from a reserve stock bin to a picking bin that's closer to the staging area to ease the picking process. For example, you can use replenishment to move stock from a reserve storage type to the required picking bins from which picking should happen. Replenishment allows you to stock only the planned number of handling units (HUs) or products in the picking area. In this way, a warehouse worker doesn't have to go into the warehouse to fulfill every open warehouse request. Based on the amount of stock moved from the picking area, the stock can be replenished again later.

Five types of replenishment strategies are available in embedded EWM:

- Planned replenishment
- Automatic replenishment
- Order-related replenishment
- Direct replenishment
- Crate part replenishment

In the following sections, we'll discuss different replenishment strategies at both the storage bin level and product level. This will provide you with a fundamental understanding of replenishment settings in embedded EWM. We'll start with an overview of replenishment as a concept.

> **Note**
>
> The Replenish Stock app allows you to replenish stock from source to destination bin based on the replenishment strategy chosen by the warehouse administrator.

9.1.1 What Is Replenishment?

Replenishment is the process with which you can refill the bins in the warehouse based on various planning parameters with products required based on historical transactions and future stock requirements. In the following sections, we explain the business context in which internal warehouse stock movement can be used in real-world scenarios. We also explain the processes carried out in the system and internal warehouse movement-related documents used for processing ad hoc or internal stock movements in embedded EWM and decentralized EWM.

Business Process

American company Alpha Medicals replenishes the warehouse bins of its warehouse on a nightly basis. The bins are replenished based on historical stock velocity and future stock requirements in the warehouse. As a regular practice, products are replenished in a planned manner so that planned replenishment requests are created and assigned to warehouse workers. For example, Product ABC can be replenished in the assigned fixed bins based on the replenishment quantities assigned to the product as master data. To ensure that the embedded EWM system proposes the stock replenishment in destination storage bins with ease, the company uses stock replenishment in embedded EWM.

System Process

The following explains the basic system flow, including the documents and data required to execute replenishment of stock from high-rack storage to picking areas in embedded EWM and decentralized EWM:

1. A warehouse request is created in embedded EWM that contains information about the products to be replenished in the destination storage bins and the quantity based on which the replenishment is to be done.
2. Replenishment warehouse tasks are created based on the warehouse request and assigned to the warehouse worker. The warehouse request directs the warehouse worker to move the products from the source bin to the destination storage bin (replenishment area).
3. The warehouse orders are allocated to the warehouse worker. During picking of the product from the source bin, the warehouse worker picks up the stock quantity as displayed in the warehouse task.
4. The warehouse task is created by the system so that it proposes to pick and move around the product to the destination storage bin (replenishment area).
5. After the worker picks the stock from the source bin and completes intermediate stock movements, the stock is finally moved to the destination storage bin (replenishment area).

You use a separate warehouse process type for replenishment, which is part of the internal stock transfer category. Based on configuration settings for replenishment, you can control if you want the system to create a warehouse request for replenishment before creation of warehouse tasks.

You also can use waves to execute replenishment in embedded EWM. Thus, you can plan several replenishments together by releasing waves, leading to simultaneous warehouse task creation for multiple replenishment warehouse requests. We'll discuss wave management further in Chapter 16.

Replenishment can be either planned replenishment or unplanned replenishment. The crate part replenishment and order-related replenishment strategies fall under the umbrella of warehouse stock replenishments. Planned replenishments can be scheduled in the system as background jobs, which will create the warehouse tasks to move the stock. You can execute planned replenishments in embedded EWM using Transaction /SCWM/REPL, which also can be accessed from **SAP Easy Access** path **Logistics • SCM Extended Warehouse Management • Extended Warehouse Management • Work Scheduling • Schedule Replenishment**, as shown in Figure 9.1.

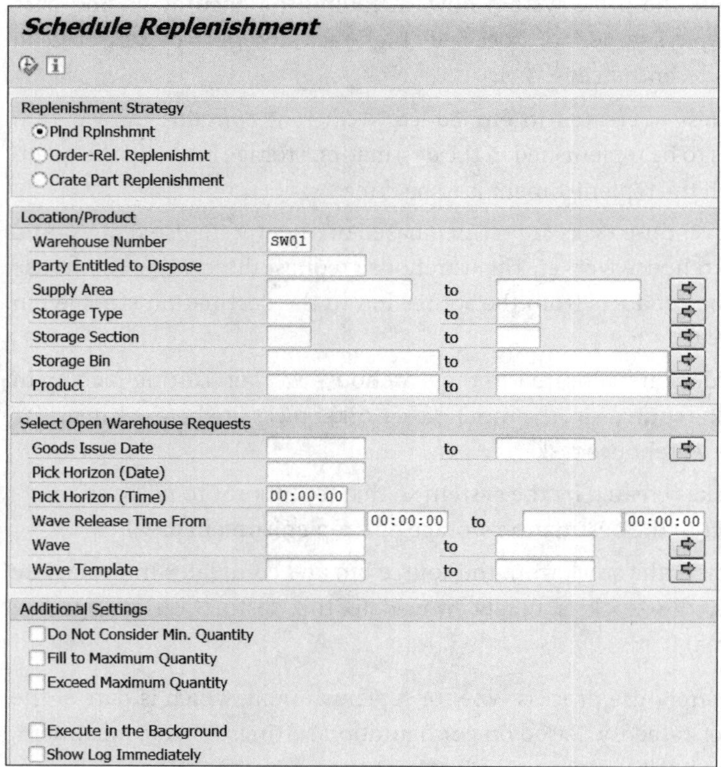

Figure 9.1 Replenishment in Embedded EWM

You also can save a program variant based on selection screen inputs and schedule it to run as a background job in embedded EWM. To select products for replenishment using this report, various selection criteria can be used: replenishment strategy; storage bin/product attributes such as storage type, product, and bin; and warehouse request selections such as goods issue date, picking horizon, and wave selection criteria.

Direct replenishment and automatic replenishment are unplanned replenishments. Unplanned replenishment is triggered on an ad hoc basis upon execution of another transaction. For example, you can trigger direct replenishment when a picker is directed to a fixed bin, and the bin doesn't have sufficient stock. Unplanned replenishment can't be run in batch mode.

9.1.2 Basic Settings

Figure 9.2 shows a standard scenario for setting up replenishment in embedded EWM. The picking area has storage bins from storage type 0050, which is close to the staging area. Based on warehouse requirements, the picking area can have multiple products in picking bins, which enables multiple picks from a single area in the warehouse. In this case, the picking area contains product S4H_MAT_02, which is replenished from a reserve storage type per open requirements.

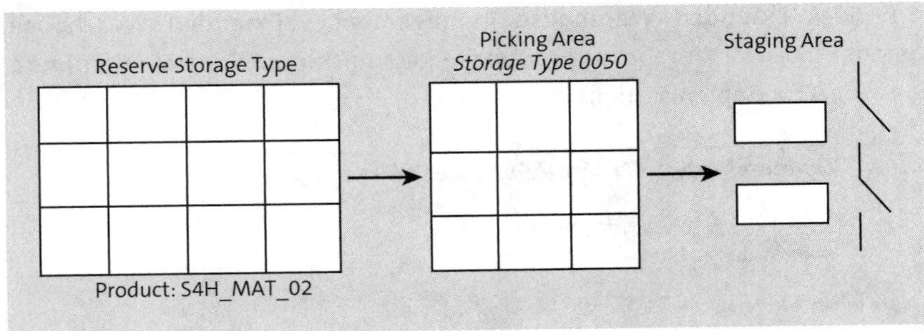

Figure 9.2 Replenishment in the Warehouse

Now, let's walk through the configurations required for setting the minimum/maximum replenishment levels for replenishment, as well as configurations required for creating replenishment requests in embedded EWM.

Activate Replenishment Strategies for Storage Types

For each storage type, you can select more than one mode of replenishment, depending on business requirements. This setting will determine the replenishment strategies that can be used to replenish stock in the storage bins in this storage type. Navigate to IMG path **SCM Extended Warehouse Management • Extended Warehouse Management • Internal Warehouse Processes • Replenishment Control • Activate Replenishment Strategies in Storage Types**. The following configuration settings need to be maintained at the storage type level to activate replenishment for the storage type, as shown in Figure 9.3:

- **Warehouse process type**
  Whse Proc. Type is the warehouse process type used to create warehouse tasks for replenishment. This process type is of the internal stock transfer warehouse process category.
- **Quantity type used**
  The **Qty Type Used** setting controls whether the system should use **Physical Quantity** or **Available Quantity** to calculate current stock in the storage type.
- **Indicator for execution time**
  The **Ind. Exec. Time** indicator is used to determine the replenishment planning time, which is used to calculate the total planned completion time to finish the replenishment. Set the indicator for execution time at the warehouse level via IMG path **SCM Extended Warehouse Management • Extended Warehouse Management • Internal Warehouse Processes • Replenishment Control • Configure Execution Times for Replenishment**.

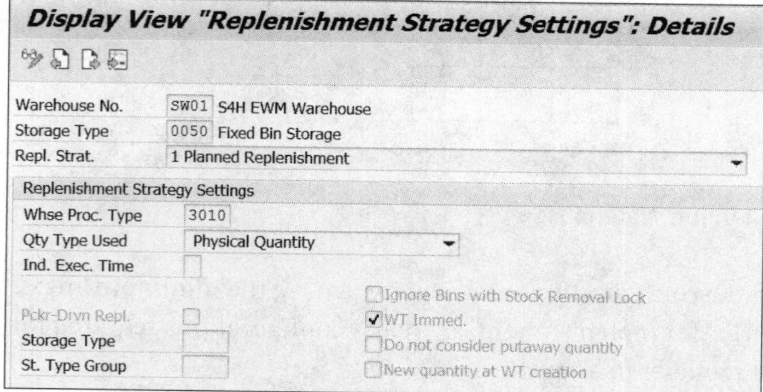

Figure 9.3 Activating the Replenishment Strategy at the Storage Type Level

- **Picker-driven replenishment**
  The **Pckr-Drvn Repl.** indicator controls whether picker-driven replenishment is allowed while performing direct replenishment in the storage type. We'll discuss picker-driven replenishment in Section 9.1.6.
- **Storage type**
  The **Storage Type** field is only used if you allow picker-driven replenishment in the storage type. This field is used to specify the storage type from which replenishment can be done if picker-driven replenishment is active.
- **Storage type group**
  The **St. Type Group** field is only used if you allow picker-driven replenishment in the storage type. If the **Pckr-Drvn Repl.** indicator is set, the system allows replenishment only from storage types maintained in the storage type group.
- **Warehouse task immediately**
  The **WT Immed.** indicator is used to control the immediate creation of a warehouse task after replenishment execution. If this indicator isn't set, the system creates a warehouse request first.
- **New quantity at warehouse task creation**
  The **New quantity at WT creation** indicator is set if you want the system to update the replenishment quantity during warehouse task creation, if warehouse tasks are created after warehouse requests are created.

Replenishment Setting at the Storage Type Level

You also need to set up replenishment levels for the storage type. These settings are made at the storage type level for bins being replenished. The replenishment levels available are as follows:

- Storage bin levels for fixed bins
- Storage type level

Setting Up Minimum and Maximum Quantities

As discussed previously, you set replenishment at the storage type level in the storage type setting. Enter the warehouse product master using Transaction /SCWM/MAT1, and click on the **Storage Type** tab. Then, define the minimum and maximum quantities for the product master in embedded EWM, as shown in Figure 9.4.

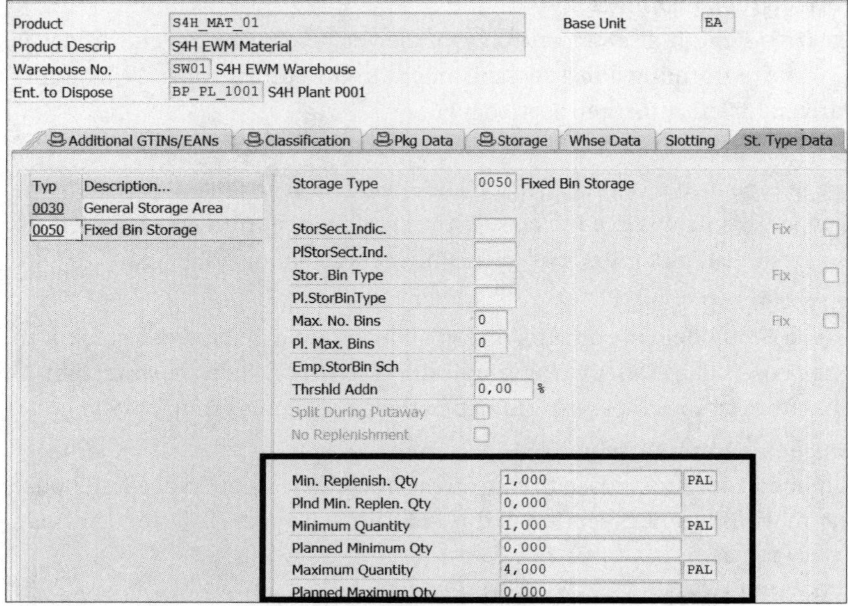

Figure 9.4 Minimum and Maximum Quantities at the Storage Type Level

If you decide to replenish only fixed bins, set the replenishment level (**Repl. Level**) in the storage type settings to **Storage Bin Levels for Fixed Bins**. In this case, define the minimum and maximum quantities in the fixed bin assignment to a product via Transaction /SCWM/BINMAT, as shown in Figure 9.5. Provide the selection criteria for assigning a fixed bin to the product master, and click on . In Figure 9.5, you'll see the assignment of a fixed bin to the product. Here, you can perform a mass change of assignment parameters such as maximum quantity.

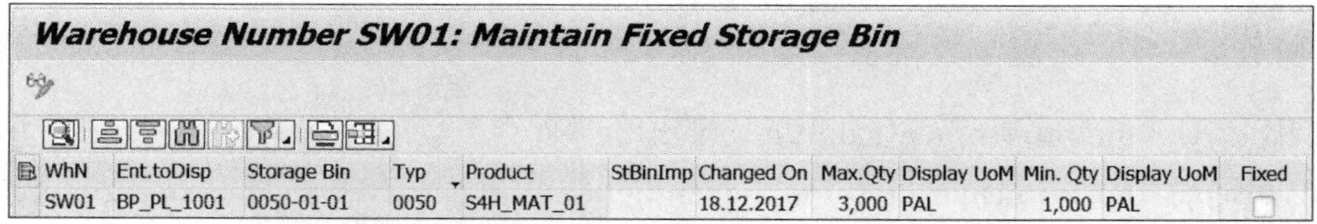
Warehouse Number SW01: Maintain Fixed Storage Bin

WhN	Ent.toDisp	Storage Bin	Typ	Product	StBinImp	Changed On	Max.Qty	Display UoM	Min. Qty	Display UoM	Fixed
SW01	BP_PL_1001	0050-01-01	0050	S4H_MAT_01		18.12.2017	3,000	PAL	1,000	PAL	

Figure 9.5 Minimum and Maximum Quantities at the Fixed Bin Level

Setting Up a Warehouse Request for Replenishment

To set up a warehouse request for replenishment, navigate to IMG path **SCM Extended Warehouse Management • Extended Warehouse Management • Internal**

Warehouse Processes • Replenishment Control • Maintain Document/Item Categories for Replenishment Warehouse Request, as shown in Figure 9.6. Assign the document type and item type for creating warehouse requests during replenishment for the given warehouse process type in the **Document Type** and **Item Type** columns. You can set up creation of warehouse requests for replenishment in embedded EWM if you want to manage task creation from warehouse requests via waves.

Display View "Document and Item Type for Replenishment Warehouse Reque

Document and Item Type for Replenishment Warehouse Request

Wa...	Wh...	Description	Documen...	Item Type
SW01	3010	Replenishment	SRPL	SRPL

Figure 9.6 Assigning Document Type and Item Type for Replenishment

While executing, the replenishment system looks for products in reserve storage types. You can create a storage type search sequence to help the system determine the reserve storage types via the IMG path **SCM Extended Warehouse Management • Extended Warehouse Management • Goods Receipt Process • Strategies • Storage Type Search • Define Storage Type Search Sequence**. Click on **New Entries**, and assign a storage type search sequence to the embedded EWM warehouse.

You can then assign the warehouse process type to the storage type search sequence. If you want the system to execute replenishment for different products from different reserve storage types, then you can define a new stock removal control indicator in embedded EWM and assign it to a product master. These indicators are used in the determination sequence to identify storage bins for picking from reserve storage, as shown in Figure 9.7.

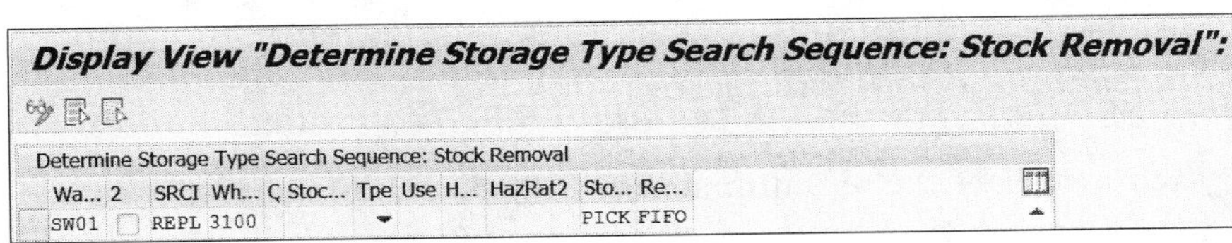

Display View "Determine Storage Type Search Sequence: Stock Removal":

Determine Storage Type Search Sequence: Stock Removal

Wa...	2	SRCI	Wh...	Ç	Stoc...	Tpe	Use	H...	HazRat2	Sto...	Re...
SW01	☐	REPL	3100							PICK	FIFO

Figure 9.7 Storage Type Search for Replenishment

9.1.3 Planned Replenishment

Planned replenishment is done when stock falls below a certain defined threshold, and you trigger replenishment to refill the stock to a certain maximum value. To execute planned replenishment, use Transaction /SCWM/REPL. In the selection screen, give the storage type, product, bin, and so on for which replenishment needs to be carried out. Planned replenishment can be done in the foreground or in the background as a batch job by saving a variant for program /SCWM/REPLENISHMENT and scheduling it for execution. As shown in Figure 9.8, the following steps summarize how planned replenishment is executed in embedded EWM:

1. The minimum and maximum quantities are defined at the storage type or fixed bin level based on storage type settings. In Figure 9.9, we've maintained the minimum quantity as 48 EA and the maximum quantity as 96 EA.

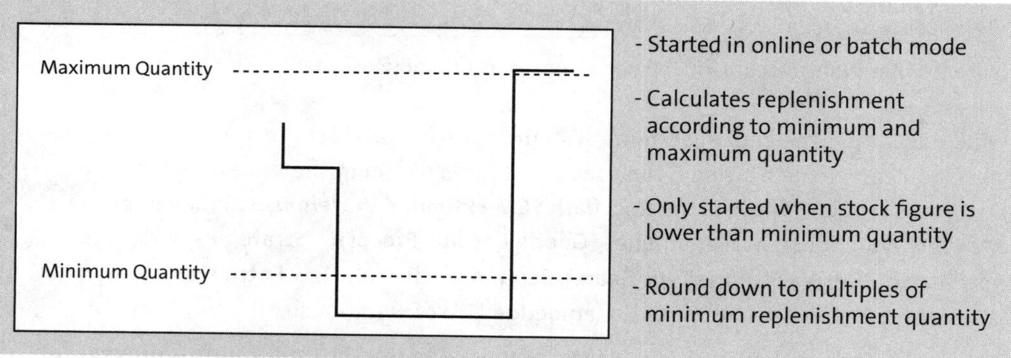

Figure 9.8 Planned Replenishment

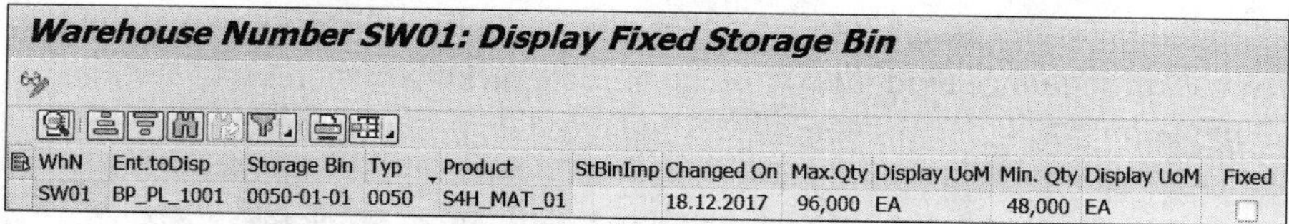

Warehouse Number SW01: Display Fixed Storage Bin

WhN	Ent.toDisp	Storage Bin	Typ	Product	StBinImp	Changed On	Max.Qty	Display UoM	Min. Qty	Display UoM	Fixed
SW01	BP_PL_1001	0050-01-01	0050	S4H_MAT_01		18.12.2017	96,000	EA	48,000	EA	

Figure 9.9 Setting Minimum and Maximum Quantities

2. The system calculates the replenishment quantity based on the minimum and maximum quantities.
3. Planned replenishment is only triggered when the quantity in the storage type is less than the minimum quantity in the storage type. In this case, the fixed bin 0050-01-01 is empty, so the system calculates the replenishment quantity as the maximum quantity in the storage bin, as shown in Figure 9.10.

Figure 9.10 Planned Replenishment Items

4. The system rounds down the replenishment quantity to a multiple of the minimum replenishment quantity.
5. After you select the planned replenishment item and click on **Execute**, the system creates the warehouse task for replenishment. You can confirm the warehouse task, which will move stock from the reserve storage type to a fixed bin in the picking area.

9.1.4 Order-Related Replenishment

In order-related replenishment, the system calculates the replenishment quantity based on the quantity of open outbound delivery orders. To set up order-related replenishment, set the replenishment strategy (**Repl. Strat.**) at the storage type level to **Order-Related Replenishment**, as shown in Figure 9.11.

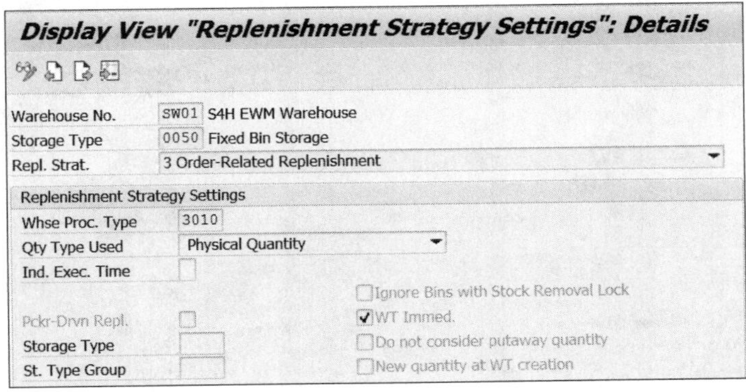

Figure 9.11 Storage Type Setting for Order-Related Replenishment

Next, set up **Rough Bin Determination** for the warehouse process type used in your outbound delivery order items, as shown in Figure 9.12.

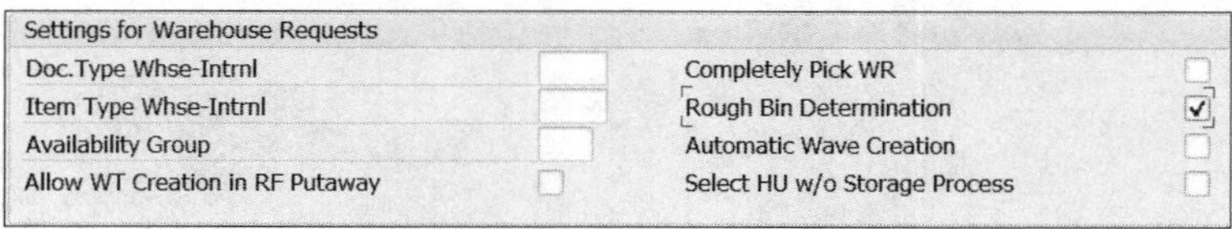

Figure 9.12 Settings in the Warehouse Process Type

If the **Rough Bin Determination** checkbox is set, the system populates the source bin in the outbound delivery orders from which picking is done. If there are multiple source bins, they're updated in table /SCWM/DB_ITEMSPL.

The following steps summarize how planned replenishment is executed in embedded EWM:

1. The minimum and maximum quantities are defined at the storage type or fixed bin level based on storage type settings. If you refer to Figure 9.9, you'll see we've maintained the minimum quantity as 48 EA and the maximum quantity as 96 EA.
2. The system calculates the sum of quantities in all open deliveries for the warehouse product, as shown in Figure 9.13.

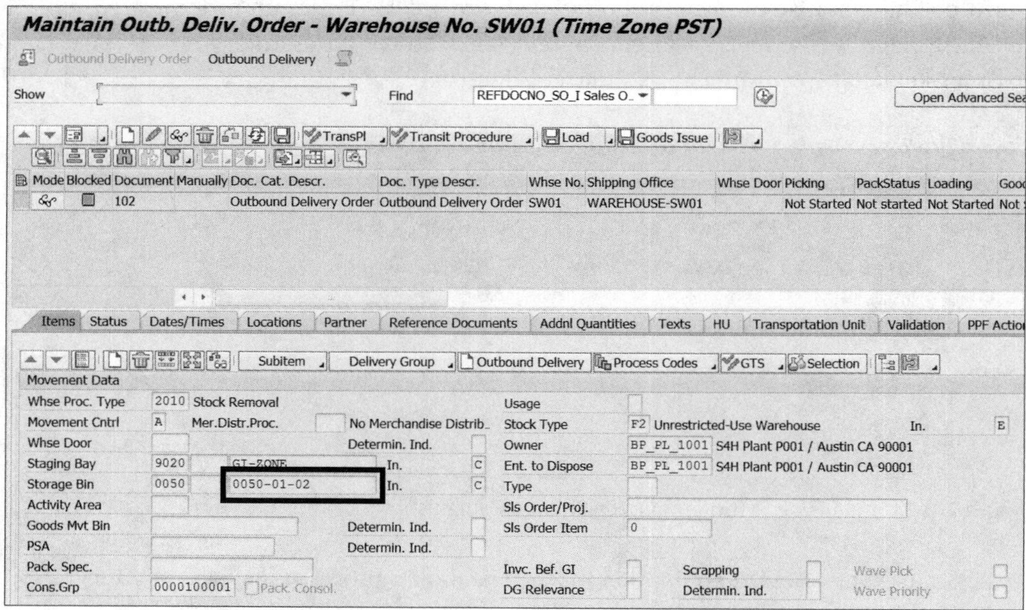

Figure 9.13 Rough Bin Determination in Delivery

The system triggers order-related replenishment if the total stock is less than the open warehouse request quantity. In this example, we've created an open delivery request with a quantity of 49 EA.

3. The system calculates the replenishment quantity by rounding up the order quantity to a multiple of the minimum replenishment quantity. This ensures that total open quantities of a given product are always replenished.

   In the example in Figure 9.14, because the total quantity in the open warehouse request is 49 EA, the system calculates the replenishment quantity by rounding up the order quantity to a multiple of the minimum replenishment quantity (48 EA), which comes out to be 96 EA.

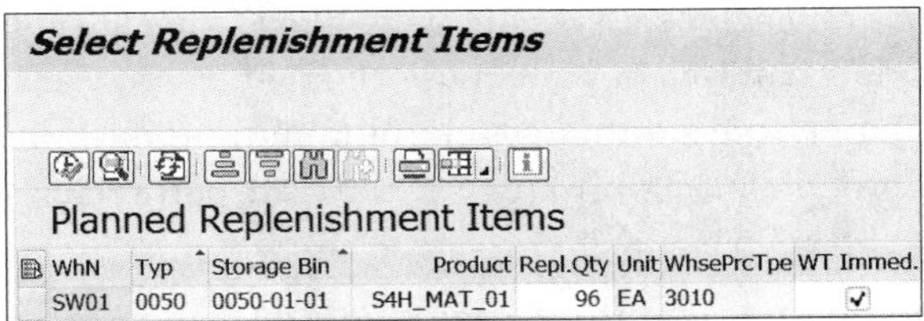

Figure 9.14 Planned Replenishment Item

4. You can set the indicator to exceed the maximum quantity in the replenishment screen if you want to allow the replenished quantity to exceed the maximum quantity allowed in the storage type by selecting the **Check Max.St.TypeQty** control. However, the system still performs a check for bin capacity to ensure that the same isn't exceeded.

9.1.5 Crate Part Replenishment

This replenishment strategy is used to trigger material staging if stock in the production supply area falls below the minimum stock specified for the product. The prerequisite for setting up crate part replenishment is that a production supply area should be created in the system. To create such an area, use Transaction /SCWM/PSA or navigate to **SAP Easy Access** path **Logistics • Extended Warehouse Management • Extended Warehouse Management • Master Data • Production Supply Area (PSA) • Define PSA**, as shown in Figure 9.15.

Display View "Define Production Supply Area": Details

Warehouse No.	SW01
Supply Area	PSA_EWM

Define Production Supply Area

PSA Description	PSA EWM
Trigger GI at PSA	☐

Figure 9.15 Defining the Production Supply Area

You also need to assign a storage bin to the production supply area via Transaction /SCWM/PSASTAGE or via **SAP Easy Access** path **Logistics • Extended Warehouse Management • Extended Warehouse Management • Master Data • Production Supply Area (PSA) • Assign Bin to PSA/Product/Entitled in Warehouse Number**. If you want to use crate part replenishment, you also need to assign a minimum production quantity (**Min.Prd.Qty PSA**) in the production supply area and the crate part replenishment quantity (**Replmt Qty**), as shown in Figure 9.16.

You also need to set the replenishment strategy at the storage type level for crate part replenishment, as shown in Figure 9.17.

Display View "PSA Assignment to Bin by Entitled/Product": Details

Warehouse No.	SW01
Ent. to Dispose	BP_PL_1001 S4H Plant P001 / Austin CA 90001
Supply Area	PSA_EWM PSA EWM
Product Group	
Product	S4H_MAT_02
	S4H EWM Material_FB

PSA Assignment to Bin by Entitled/Product

Storage Bin	PSA_BIN
Stag. Det. Outb.	☐
Staging Method	1 Crate Part Replenishment
Qty Calc. Type	2 Quantity-Based Calculation
Qty Classific.	
No. Containers	0
Min. No. Cont.	0
Replmt Qty	48
Min.Prd.Qty PSA	96
Unit	EA
Staging WPT	
Clear PSA WPT	

Figure 9.16 Assign Storage Bin to Production Supply Area

Display View "Replenishment Strategy Settings": Details

Warehouse No.	SW01	S4H EWM Warehouse
Storage Type	1000	Production Supply
Repl. Strat.	5 Crate Part Replenishment	

Replenishment Strategy Settings

Whse Proc. Type	3100	
Qty Type Used	Physical Quantity	
Ind. Exec. Time	☐	
		☐ Ignore Bins with Stock Removal Lock
Pckr-Drvn Repl.	☐	☑ WT Immed.
Storage Type		☐ Do not consider putaway quantity
St. Type Group		☐ New quantity at WT creation

Figure 9.17 Replenishment Settings for the Storage Type

Execute crate part replenishment by selecting the corresponding radio button in the transaction screen for replenishment execution. Figure 9.18 shows the result of executing crate part replenishment in embedded EWM. The system proposes a replenishment quantity of 96 EA because the crate part replenishment quantity is 48 EA, and the minimum product quantity in the production supply area is 96 EA. Therefore, the system proposes two crates of the product for replenishment, making the total quantity 96 EA.

Select Replenishment Items

Planned Replenishment Items

WhN	Typ	PSA	Stor. Bin	Product	Repl.Qty	Unit	WhsePrcTpe	WT Immed.
SW01	1000	PSA_EWM	PSA_BIN	S4H_MAT_02	96	EA	3100	☑

Figure 9.18 Crate Part Replenishment

9.1.6 Direct Replenishment

Direct replenishment is only triggered during picking from fixed storage bins. It's started during bin denial when a warehouse worker is unable to find sufficient stock in the designated picking storage bin. For direct replenishment to trigger, the exception code entered during bin denial should point to the internal process code **Replenishment**. You also need to set the replenishment strategy (**Repl. Strat.**) at the storage type level to **Direct Replenishment**, as shown in Figure 9.19.

Display View "Replenishment Strategy Settings": Details

Warehouse No.	SW01	S4H EWM Warehouse
Storage Type	0050	Fixed Bin Storage
Repl. Strat.	4 Direct Replenishment	

Replenishment Strategy Settings

Whse Proc. Type	3010	
Qty Type Used	Physical Quantity	
Ind. Exec. Time	☐	
		☐ Ignore Bins with Stock Removal Lock
Pckr-Drvn Repl.	☐	☑ WT Immed.
Storage Type		☐ Do not consider putaway quantity
St. Type Group		☐ New quantity at WT creation

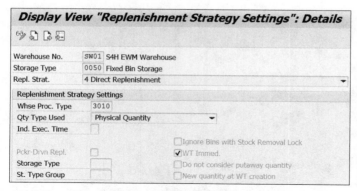

Figure 9.19 Storage Type Settings for Direct Replenishment

As shown in Figure 9.20, the following steps summarize how planned replenishment is executed in embedded EWM:

1. The minimum and maximum quantities are defined at the storage type or fixed bin level based on storage type settings. We've maintained the minimum quantity as 48 EA and the maximum quantity as 96 EA.

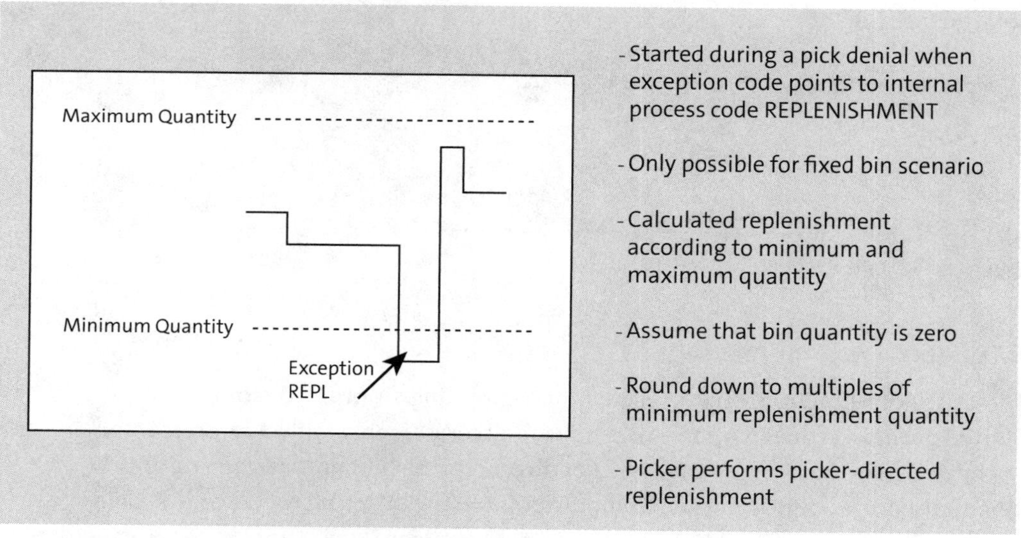

Maximum Quantity
Minimum Quantity
Exception
REPL
- Started during a pick denial when exception code points to internal process code REPLENISHMENT
- Only possible for fixed bin scenario
- Calculated replenishment according to minimum and maximum quantity
- Assume that bin quantity is zero
- Round down to multiples of minimum replenishment quantity
- Picker performs picker-directed replenishment

Figure 9.20 Direct Replenishment

2. Direct replenishment is triggered during bin denial when an exception code refers to internal process code **Replenishment**, as shown in Figure 9.21.

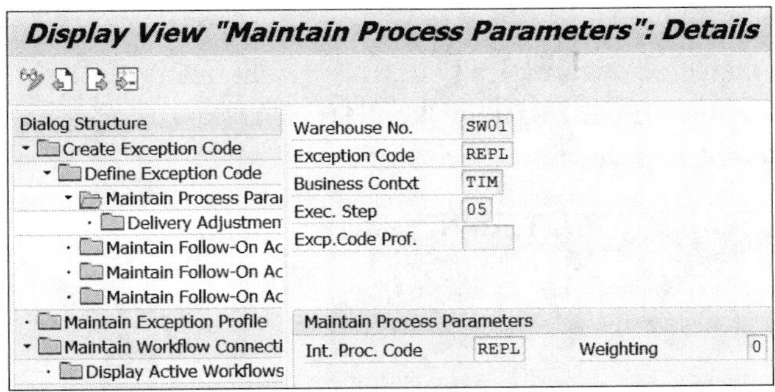

Figure 9.21 Exception Code for Pick Denial

3. The system calculates the replenishment quantity by rounding up the order quantity to a multiple of the minimum replenishment quantity. The system assumes that the quantity in the storage bin is zero.
4. Direct replenishment can be done in two ways:
   - The system creates a replenishment warehouse task that is assigned to another resource in the warehouse to move stock from the reserve storage type to the picking bin.
   - The picker can execute the replenishment himself. In this case, it's important that the indicator for picker-driven replenishment is set in the settings for replenishment strategies for the storage type, as shown in Figure 9.22. You can also set the storage type and storage type group to provide the source storage bin from which the picker can pick stock for replenishment. Picker-driven replenishment can only be done via radio frequency (RF).

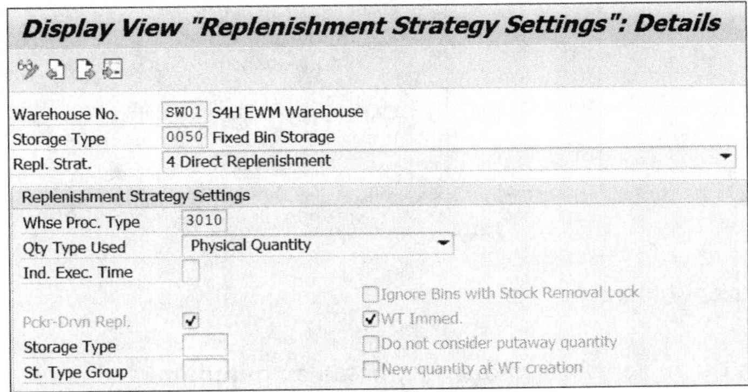

Figure 9.22 Settings for Picker-Driven Replenishment

9.1.7 Automatic Replenishment

Automatic replenishment is triggered automatically during warehouse task execution. You also need to set the replenishment strategy (**Repl. Strat.**) at the storage type level to **Automatic Replenishment**, as shown in Figure 9.23.

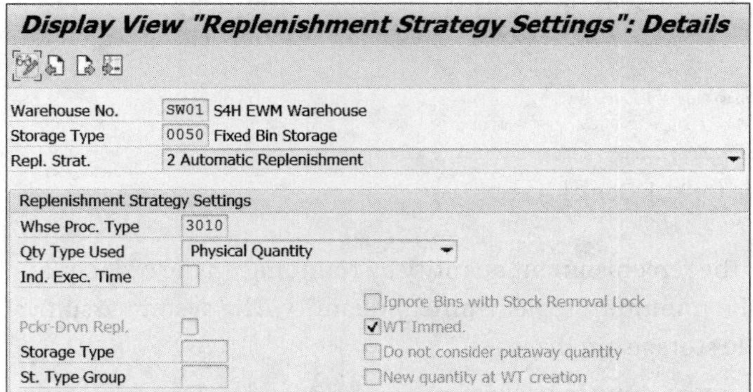

Figure 9.23 Setting Automatic Replenishment for the Storage Type

As shown in Figure 9.24, the following steps summarize how automatic replenishment is executed in embedded EWM:

1. The minimum and maximum quantities are defined at the storage type or fixed bin level based on storage type settings.

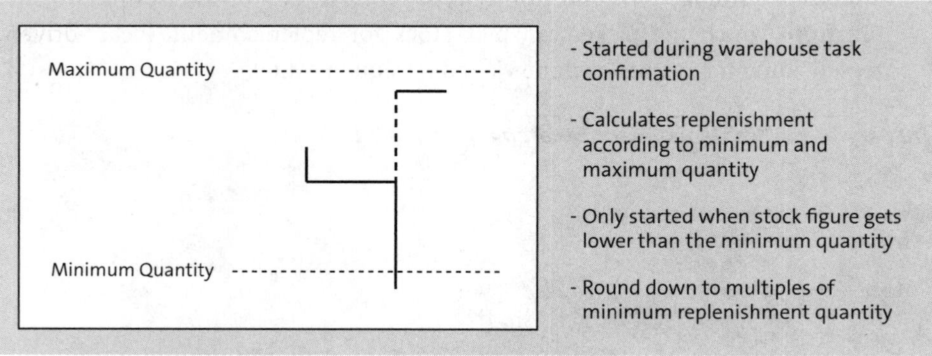

Figure 9.24 Automatic Replenishment

2. The system calculates the replenishment quantity based on minimum and maximum quantities.

3. The system triggers replenishment when stock is less than the minimum quantity.
4. The system rounds down the replenishment quantity to a multiple of the minimum replenishment quantity.

9.2 Ad Hoc Warehouse Movement

Ad hoc movements are unplanned movements in the warehouse and are done without reference to any warehouse document. There are various reasons for moving stock within the warehouse on an ad hoc basis: incorrect stock placements, damaged or expired products, and so on. In this section, we'll cover ad hoc stock transfers based on the creation of warehouse tasks. Two types of ad hoc movements can be made in the warehouse:

- Product movement
- HU movement

The transactions to create ad hoc warehouse tasks can be accessed via **SAP Easy Access** path **Logistics • SCM Extended Warehouse Management • Extended Warehouse Management • Work Scheduling • Create Warehouse Task without Reference**.

You create an HU warehouse task when you want to move an HU from one bin to another. You can do so via Transaction /SCWM/ADHU. Provide the following information while creating an HU warehouse task:

- HU that needs to be moved
- Source and destination storage bins

A product task is created when you want to move product from one bin to another. The product can also be contained in an HU. You can create a product warehouse task via Transaction /SCWM/ADPROD.

The following information is required when creating a product warehouse task:

- Product that needs to be moved
- Quantity of the product that needs to be moved
- Source and destination storage bins

Figure 9.25 shows how an HU warehouse task is created in embedded EWM. You can search for an HU by specifying the HU number, product, storage bin, and so on. In the next step, select the HU line item, and enter the warehouse process type (**WhseP**) (e.g., "9999") and destination storage bin (**Dest.Bin**).

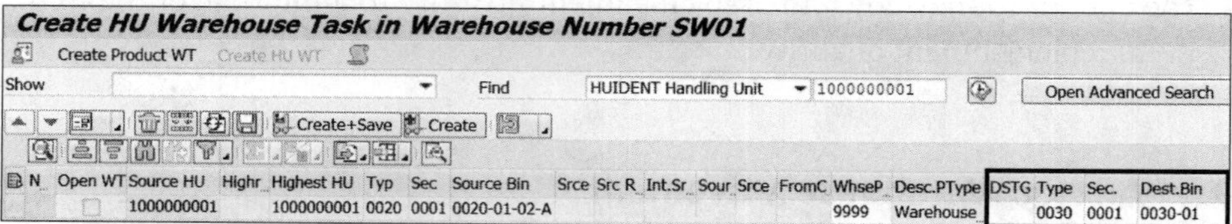

Figure 9.25 Creating an HU Warehouse Task

You can confirm the HU warehouse task (see Figure 9.26) from the same screen by choose **Warehouse Task • Confirm**. The next screen will show the warehouse task and the warehouse order created for the warehouse task. You can confirm the warehouse task overall by selecting **Confirm** for the warehouse task or for the warehouse order.

Alternatively, you can confirm a warehouse task from the warehouse monitor by selecting the warehouse task and navigating to **Documents • Warehouse Task**.

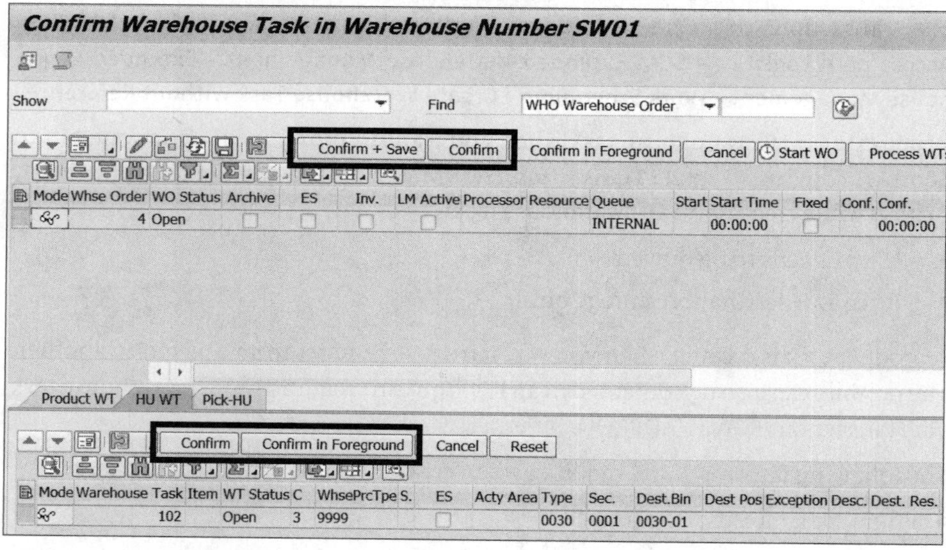

Figure 9.26 Confirming the Warehouse Task

9.3 Stock Consolidation

Space-constrained warehouses are often required to optimize the stock placement in bins to make the most of limited and costly physical warehouse space via stock consolidation by unplanned goods movement. SAP has provided four new strategies to achieve this optimization:

- **Consolidation to reach full quantity**
  In fast-moving warehouses, stock with the same attributes are often placed in bins in a suboptimal manner in which partial stock is placed in different bins leading to multiple partially filled bins. This wastes a lot of physical space that could be occupied with other products and denies the opportunity to create full pallets wherever they can be created for the material to be used in the future in the warehouse, as shown in Figure 9.27.

9

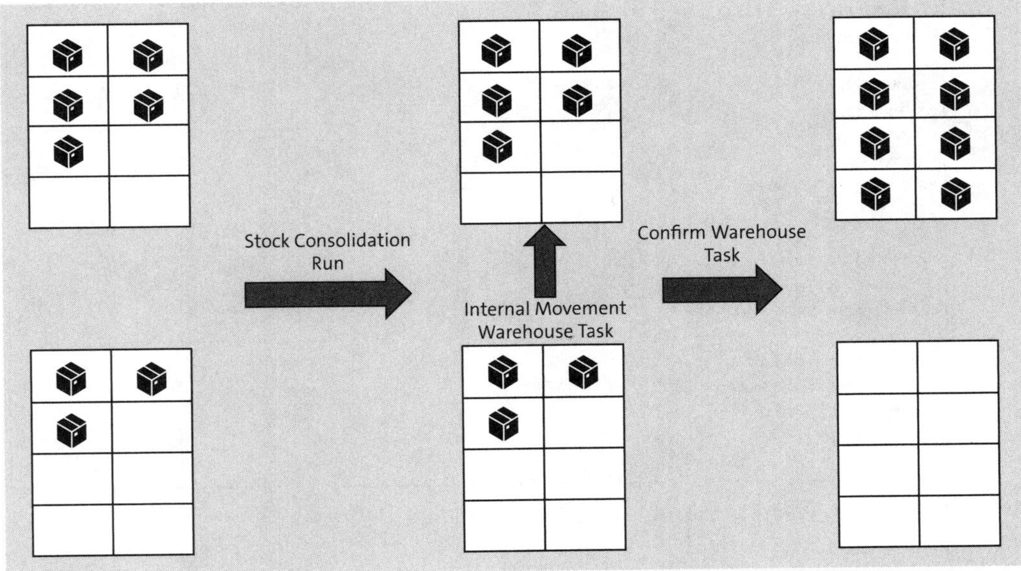

Figure 9.27 Stock Consolidation to Optimize Storage Space

You can start the stock consolidation process via **SAP Easy Access** path **Logistics • SCM Extended Warehouse Management • Extended Warehouse Management • Work Scheduling • Consolidate Stock**. Enter the stock consolidation criteria such as product and batch, owner, stock consolidation criteria, stock usage, sales order and item number, and so on, as shown in Figure 9.28.

You can also make additional processing parameters, such as unit of measure (UoM), to use for stock consolidation quantity, the number of physical moves that stock can undergo for consolidation, decision to move partial quantities to make full pallets, and minimum percentage of a full quantity to help create a full pallet via consolidation. After the report is executed, the system picks up unpacked partial quantities or packed partial HUs and creates an ad hoc warehouse task so that stock consolidation can be done to prepare a complete HU.

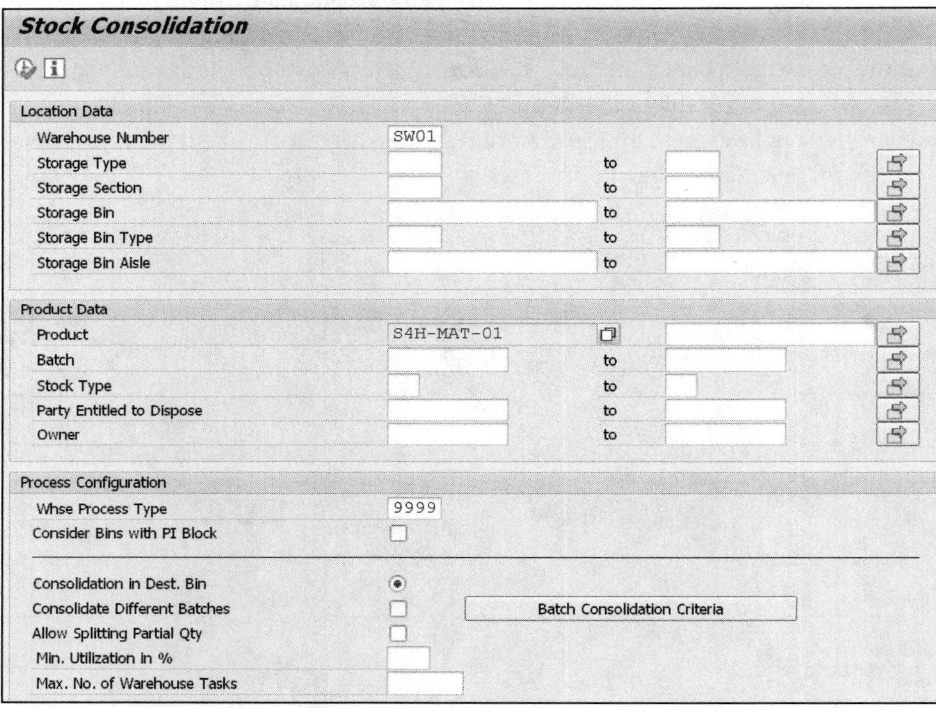

Figure 9.28 Report to Execute Stock Consolidation

- **Consolidation to reach full quantity using mixed batches**
  It's also possible to consolidate partial packed or unpacked stock of goods with different batch characteristics for the material with the rest of the attributes remaining the same, thus leading to storing stock with different batches in the same bin. The batch characteristics that can be used for this consolidation are country of origin, vendor batch, expiration date, and so on.

To consolidate the stock with different batches in the same destination bin, you must start the consolidation report via **SAP Easy Access** path **Logistics • SCM Extended Warehouse Management • Extended Warehouse Management • Work Scheduling • Consolidate Stock**, enter the required selection criteria for material as explained in the previous section, and then select the **Consolidate Different Batches** checkbox. In this case, the system consolidates all the batches of the stock for consolidation and space optimization. If you want to consolidate the stock in the destination bin for selected batches, you must select the **Consolidate Different Batches** checkbox and any of the selection criteria, such as **Expiration Date**, **Country of Origin**, **Supplier Batch**, **Date of Manufacture**, **Next Inspection Date**, or **Status of Batch**, as shown in Figure 9.29. You enter the warehouse location data, product data, warehouse process type, and batch attributes after selecting the **Consolidate Different Batches** checkbox.

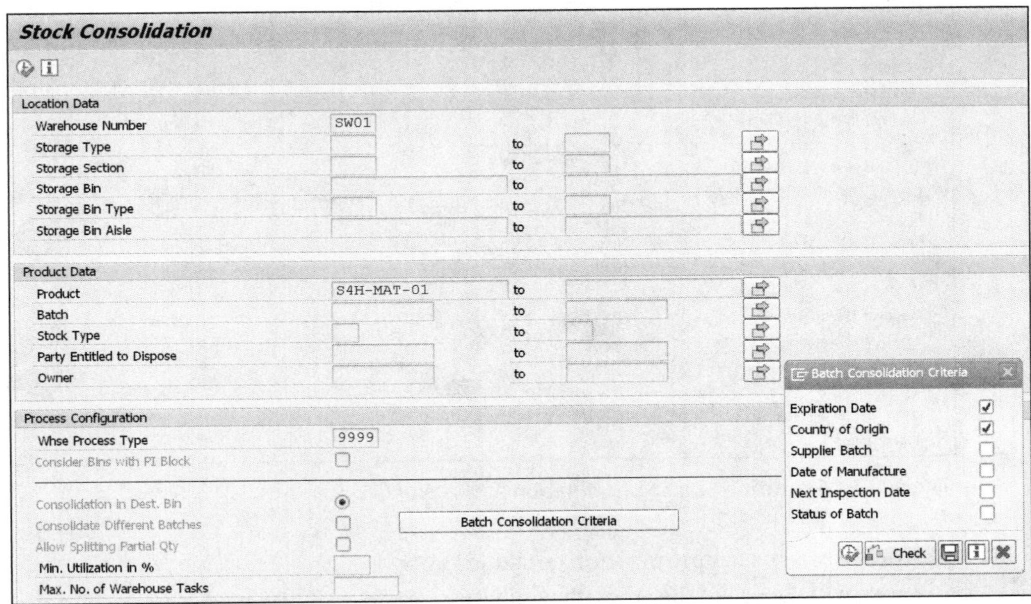

Figure 9.29 Batch Criteria for Stock Consolidation

- **Work center-based consolidation**
  You can also use the report via **SAP Easy Access** path **Logistics • SCM Extended Warehouse Management • Extended Warehouse Management • Work Scheduling • Consolidate Stock** to consolidate the stock in the final destination bin. However,

this option will first shift the stock to the work center where processes such as repacking, labeling, sorting, and so on, can be carried out and then putaway to the final destination bin can be carried out to create fully filled destination bins and to reduce partially filled destination bins. You must enter the warehouse, storage location data, product data, and warehouse process type; select the **Consolidation on Work Center** radio button; and enter the **Work Center**, as shown in Figure 9.30.

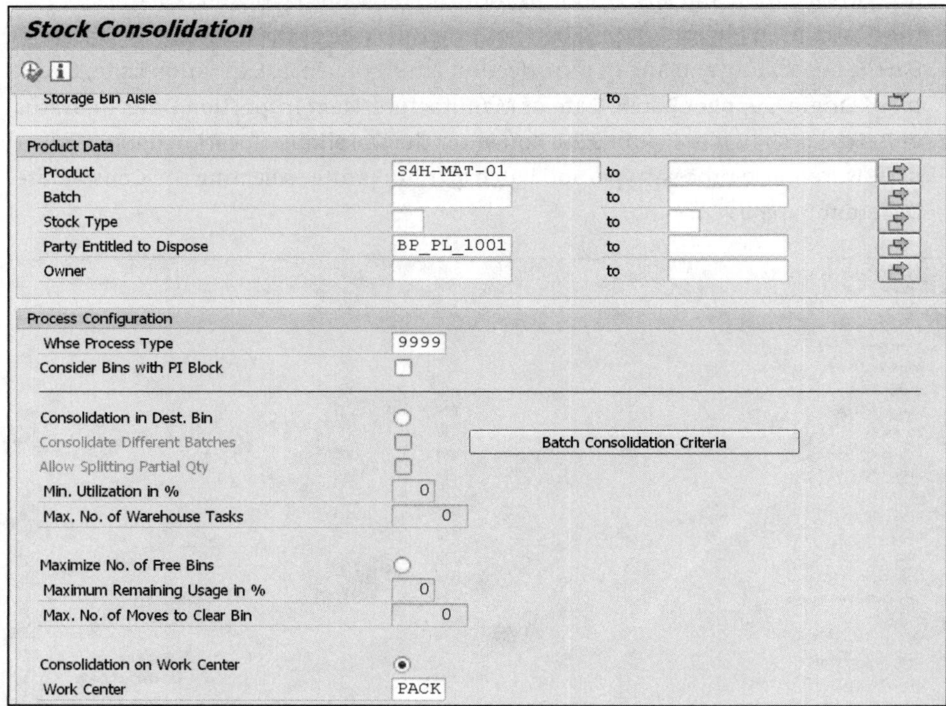

Figure 9.30 Executing Stock Consolidation at the Work Center

- **Storage bin space optimization consolidation**
  You can make use of the stock consolidation report via **SAP Easy Access** path **Logistics • SCM Extended Warehouse Management • Extended Warehouse Management • Work Scheduling • Consolidate Stock** to consolidate the stock from partially filled bins by maximizing utilized weight, volume, or the number of HUs of the storage bins. You can limit the number of warehouse tasks to clear the source storage bins. If you enter the **Maximum Remaining Usage in %** in the source bin, the

bin can only be emptied with the chosen percentage of remaining utilized weight, volume, or number of HUs, as shown in Figure 9.31.

Stock Consolidation

Storage Section		to	
Storage Bin		to	
Storage Bin Type		to	
Storage Bin Aisle		to	
Product Data			
Product	S4H-MAT-01	to	
Batch		to	
Stock Type		to	
Party Entitled to Dispose	BP_PL_1001	to	
Owner		to	
Process Configuration			
Whse Process Type	9999		
Consider Bins with PI Block	☐		
Consolidation in Dest. Bin	○		
Consolidate Different Batches	☐	Batch Consolidation Criteria	
Allow Splitting Partial Qty	☐		
Min. Utilization in %	0		
Max. No. of Warehouse Tasks	0		
Maximize No. of Free Bins	◉		
Maximum Remaining Usage in %	10		
Max. No. of Moves to Clear Bin	1		

Figure 9.31 Stock Consolidation by Setting the Remaining Usage Percentage for Bin

After you execute the report, the system performs the following process steps:

- The system starts searching the storage bins with a lower level of utilization and accumulates data about the material stored in the bin.
- The system then searches storage bins for the products with the same storage type, section, and bin types as the aforementioned bin to find the bins with a high storage percentage. Based on the way the stock should be moved to maximize the bin utilization, the system proposes the creation of ad hoc warehouse tasks from a low utilization source bin to a high utilization target bin.

Note

You must ensure that you've maintained different UoMs for products in material master and defined appropriate warehouse process types for ad hoc warehouse task creation and stock movement from the source to the target storage bin.

The Consolidate Stock app allows you to consolidate stock from the source to the destination bin based in the space optimization strategy so that storage bin space utilization can be maximized.

9.4 Posting Change

A posting change is a change in the quant characteristic and doesn't necessarily involve physical movement of the stock. A posting change can be a change of stock category, batch number, stock type, or other characteristic.

A posting change can be triggered from SAP S/4HANA or embedded EWM as follows:

- **Posting change in SAP S/4HANA**

  A posting change can be triggered in SAP S/4HANA via Transactions MIGO, MB1B, or VL_MOVE, which generate an outbound delivery for posting change. This delivery is distributed to embedded EWM and creates a posting change warehouse request.

  Based on settings at the warehouse process type level, you can control whether the posting change can be performed directly by warehouse task creation in embedded EWM or a warehouse request needs to be created for the posting change. The settings also control the order in which the posting change is made and the warehouse task is created and confirmed.

- **Posting change in embedded EWM**

  A posting change can be performed in embedded EWM by directly triggering a posting change request. Use Transaction /SCWM/POST, which also can be accessed via **SAP Easy Access** path **Logistics • SCM Extended Warehouse Management • Extended Warehouse Management • Work Scheduling • Make Posting Change for Product**. The rest of the process in embedded EWM remains the same as when the posting change is created from SAP S/4HANA.

  Based on the settings at the warehouse process type level, you can control whether the posting change can be made directly in the bin or by creation of a warehouse request if the destination bin needs to be changed simultaneously. It's always possible to create a warehouse request to trigger a posting change in embedded EWM. When the posting change is complete in embedded EWM, it's sent to SAP S/4HANA via queued remote function call (qRFC). In SAP S/4HANA, the posting change is carried out for the stock, and the material document is created.

In the following sections, we'll discuss the configuration settings required in the system to support these two types of posting change, as well as the posting change process itself.

9.4.1 What Is Posting Change?

Posting change is the process with which you can change the product characteristics within or by moving to another bin in the warehouse requests raised from SAP S/4HANA or embedded EWM. In the following sections, we explain the business context in which posting change can be used in a real-world scenario and the processes carried out in system.

Business Process

American company Alpha Medicals often change product characteristics or do product conversions in warehouse bins. Posting change is done based on warehouse requests raised from SAP S/4HANA and interfaced to embedded EWM or based on warehouse requests raised within embedded EWM. As a regular practice, posting change is done for products in a planned manner based on warehouse requests or unplanned requests based on a quality inspection process. To execute these processes, warehouse tasks are created and assigned to warehouse workers. For example, Product ABC's stock owner can be changed from the current plant to a vendor if the subcontracting process or stock type can be changed to quality or scrap stock. To ensure that the embedded EWM system completes stock characteristic changes with ease, the company uses posting change in embedded EWM.

System Process

The following explains the basic system flow, including the documents and data required to execute posting change:

1. A warehouse request is created in embedded EWM that contains information about the product characteristics which must be changed and the quantity for which such change is to be done.

2. Posting change warehouse tasks are created based on the warehouse request and assigned to the warehouse worker. The warehouse request directs the warehouse worker to convert the products within the storage bin or in a different storage bin.
3. The warehouse orders are allocated to the warehouse worker. During characteristics changing of the product in the storage bin, the warehouse worker changes the stock's physical attribute or location as displayed in the warehouse task.
4. After the posting change warehouse task is confirmed by the warehouse worker, the stock characteristics change in embedded EWM and in inventory management (IM) in SAP S/4HANA.

9.4.2 Basic Settings

The standard SAP warehouse process type for a posting change is 4010, but you can create your own variant of a warehouse process type for posting changes. The process type has the posting change warehouse process category.

Figure 9.32 Setting for Posting Change in the Warehouse Process Type

As shown in Figure 9.32, the **Post. Change in Bin** field controls whether the system needs to create a warehouse request when performing the posting change. The options available are as follows:

- **[Blank]**
  Posting change is always in the same bin.
- **Posting change according to storage type settings**
  In this case, the storage type setting determines how the posting change is to be done: always in the same bin, never in the same bin, or follow the mixed stock settings of the storage type.
- **Posting change never in storage bin**
  If a posting change is never carried out in the same bin—that is, the destination bin is different from the source bin—then a warehouse request is created for stock movement.

If you need to move the stock to some other bin before performing a posting change in embedded EWM, then the **Goods Mvmnt Before Warehouse Task** checkbox should be selected.

The **Exception Code** field allows the system to start follow-up actions after the warehouse task is confirmed. This is used in cases in which a certain follow-up action is to be mandatorily executed upon task confirmation, for example, if labeling of products is required during a posting change. You can change the exception code during task confirmation in the foreground.

The following settings are required to perform posting changes using warehouse requests:

- The warehouse request document type needed to perform a posting change is defined via IMG path **SCM Extended Warehouse Management • Extended Warehouse Management • Internal Warehouse Processes • Delivery Processing • Posting Change • Define Document Type for Posting Change Process**. TWPR is the standard document type used for the posting change process. Click on **New Entries**, enter a document type and its profiles for the embedded EWM warehouse, and save.
- The warehouse request item type needed to perform a posting change is defined via IMG path **SCM Extended Warehouse Management • Extended Warehouse Management • Internal Warehouse Processes • Delivery Processing • Posting Change • Define Item Type for Posting Change Process**. TWPR is the standard item type used for the posting change process. Click on **New Entries**, enter the item type and its profiles for the embedded EWM warehouse, and save.
- The item types allowed for posting changes are assigned to the posting change document type via IMG path **SCM Extended Warehouse Management • Extended Warehouse Management • Internal Warehouse Processes • Delivery Processing • Posting Change • Define Allowed Item Types for Posting Change Process**. Click on **New Entries**, enter the document and item type for the embedded EWM warehouse, and save.
- The warehouse request documents and item types are assigned to the warehouse process type via IMG path **SCM Extended Warehouse Management • Extended Warehouse Management • Cross Process Settings • Warehouse Task • Define Warehouse Process Type**. In the **Settings for Warehouse Requests** section, as shown in Figure 9.33, select the warehouse process type, enter the document type for **Doc.Type Whse-Intrnl** and the item type for **Item Type Whse-Intrnl**, and save.

Settings for Warehouse Requests			
Doc.Type Whse-Intrnl	TWPR	Completely Pick WR	☐
Item Type Whse-Intrnl	TWPR	Rough Bin Determination	☐
Availability Group		Automatic Wave Creation	☐
Allow WT Creation in RF Putaway	☐	Select HU w/o Storage Process	☐

Figure 9.33 Assigning the Warehouse Request Document to the Warehouse Process Type

9.4.3 Posting Change Process

As shown in Figure 9.34, a posting change initiated by embedded EWM can be done using Transaction /SCWM/POST. A product for posting change can be searched by **Product ID**, **Handling Unit**, **Storage Bin**, **Resource**, **Transportation Unit**, **Party Entitled**, and **Owner** in the **Search** field of the screen for posting change. After the product is displayed, the product line for the posting change is selected and displayed in a form view.

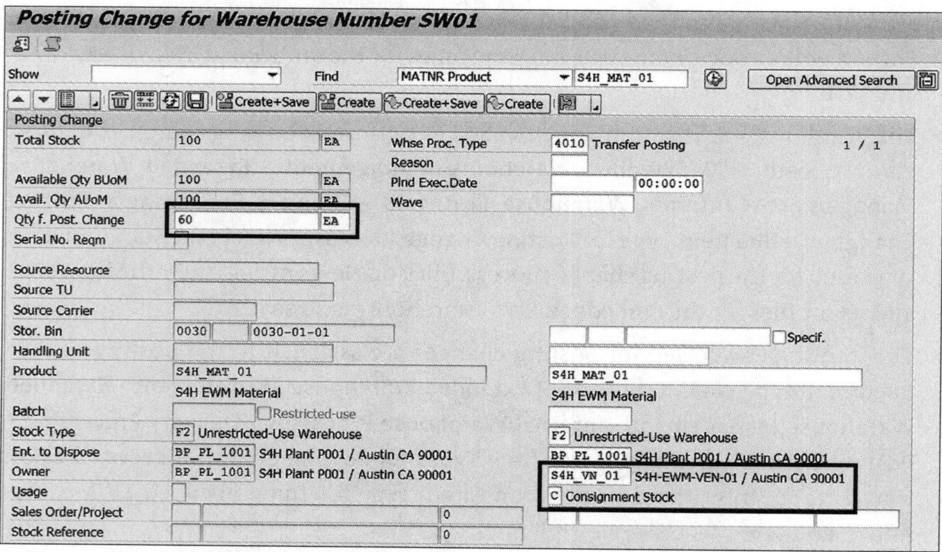

Figure 9.34 Posting Change Screen

You can enter the following input values for posting change: quantity for posting change, wave, posting change reason, storage bin, HU, product, batch, stock type, party entitled, owner, usage, and consumption order details. In Figure 9.34, we changed the stock usage for 10 EA of our product and converted the stock to consignment stock. This requires entering the vendor for whom the stock is being converted to consignment stock.

A posting change can be made using either of the following options:

- **Posting change without warehouse request**
  After the details for a posting change are entered on the screen, as shown in Figure 9.34, the posting change is triggered by clicking the **Create + Save** button. If the posting change in the bin is set as blank, embedded EWM automatically creates and confirms the posting change warehouse task. If the posting change in the bin is set as **2**, the system creates a warehouse order that can be confirmed using SAP GUI or an RF device by a warehouse employee.
- **Posting change with warehouse request**
  After the details for the posting change are entered in the screen as shown in Figure 9.34, a posting change request is created and saved by clicking the **Create + Save** button. The warehouse request can be accessed in the warehouse monitor (Transaction /SCWM/MON) using the **Documents • Posting Change** node path. If the posting change in the bin is set as blank, embedded EWM automatically creates and confirms the posting change warehouse task for the warehouse request, and the status of the warehouse request is set as **Completed**, as shown in Figure 9.35.

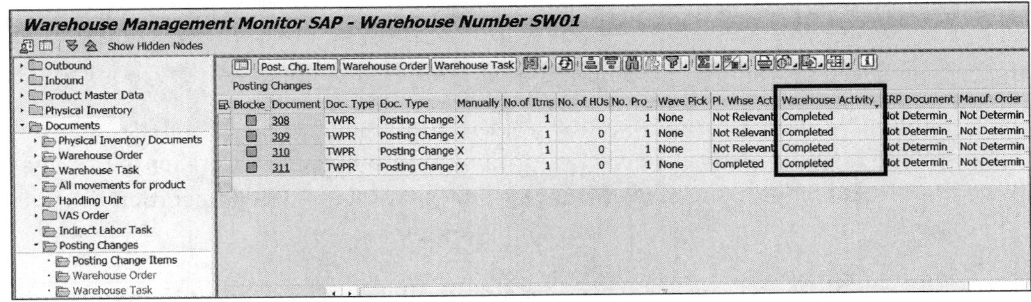

Figure 9.35 Posting Change Request in the Warehouse Monitor

If the posting change in the bin is set as **2**, the system expects the user to create and confirm a warehouse task for the posting change request. Thus, open the warehouse request document, and create and confirm the warehouse task via the **Posting Changes • Follow-On Functions • Warehouse Tasks** path from the top-left menu. After confirming the warehouse task, the posting change is exehcuted in embedded EWM and communicated to SAP S/4HANA.

9.4.4 Synchronous Goods Movement

You can create a synchronous goods movement posting from embedded EWM to IM in SAP S/4HANA on successful warehouse processing of the stock in embedded EWM. For example, after the stock posting for posting change is initiated from embedded EWM, if the material is locked in SAP S/4HANA, the failed queue used gets stuck in SAP S/4HANA despite embedded EWM showing transaction success. In SAP S/4HANA 1909, warehouse stock movement does a synchronous stock posting to SAP S/4HANA IM. This allows users to save time on transaction processing in there are errors because any errors occurring on the IM side are displayed immediately on the user interface of embedded EWM and can be corrected before actual goods movement posting in SAP S/4HANA.

The synchronous updates as well as real-time capture of IM posting errors avoids open, failed queues and reduces stock mismatches between IM and embedded EWM. The following operations in embedded EWM are aligned with synchronous stock posting:

- Unplanned goods issue
- Analyze differences
- Stock upload
- Posting changes
- Change stock type report /SCWM/R_STOCK_TYPE_CHANGE
- Methods for posting changes or goods movements in the warehouse monitor

As shown in Figure 9.36, synchronous goods movement can be activated in embedded EWM at the warehouse level via IMG path **SCM Extended Warehouse Management • Extended Warehouse Management • Interfaces • ERP Integration • Goods Movements • Activate Synchronous Goods Movement Posting**.

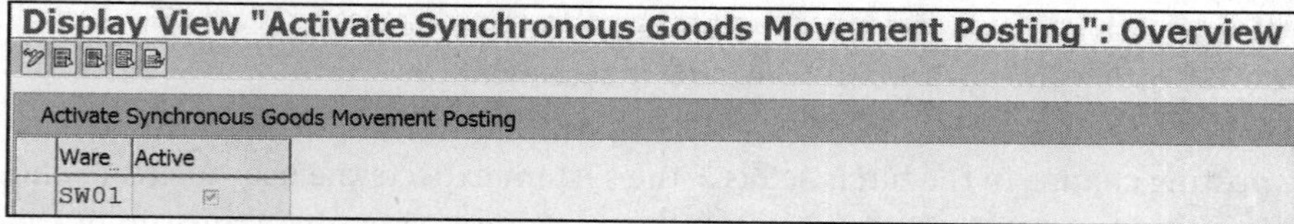

Figure 9.36 Activating Synchronous Goods Movement Posting

As shown in Figure 9.37, after the posting change process for a stock type that doesn't exist in IM is initiated, the system errors out with relevant logs without creating a posting change warehouse task or warehouse request. This will enable you to make appropriate corrections in IM and restart the posting change process. In our example, the storage location linked to stock type P2 wasn't created in the SAP S/4HANA system before posting change was triggered. After the posting change was triggered, this leads to synchronous communication between embedded EWM and SAP S/4HANA, which in turn displays the popup window containing the information about the error encountered in the SAP S/4HANA system.

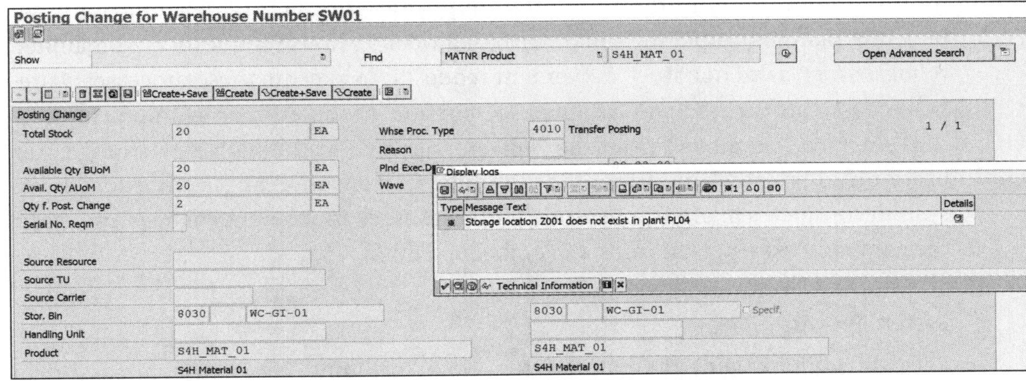

Figure 9.37 System Message during Synchronous Goods Movement Posting

9.5 Stock Transfer

The stock transfer process in embedded EWM is used for the internal transfer of stock for warehouse processes such as production supply and replenishment. The internal stock transfer document contains all information required for planning internal stock transfers in embedded EWM. Because this document is used only in the warehouse, you don't need a delivery-based predecessor document in the SAP S/4HANA system. You execute and confirm the internal stock movement in embedded EWM, and the goods movement is updated in the SAP S/4HANA system simultaneously.

In the following sections, we'll explain the process of stock transfer by creation of either a warehouse request or a warehouse task in embedded EWM.

9.5.1 What Is Stock Transfer?

Stock transfer is the process with which you can transfer the product from source bins to destination bins with or without warehouse requests in an embedded EWM system. In the following sections, we explain the business context in which stock transfer can be used in a real-world scenario and how the processes are carried out in the system.

Business Process

American company Alpha Medicals often moves product on an ad hoc basis from the source to destination bin; such movements are also done using a planned manner for completing rearrangement. As a regular practice, stock transfer is done for products in a planned/unplanned manner based on warehouse requests or unplanned requests such as ad hoc stock movement requests. To execute these processes, warehouse tasks are created and assigned to warehouse workers. For example, product ABC stock can be moved from the bulk storage area to the high-rack storage area based on ad hoc stock movement requirements. To ensure that the embedded EWM system completes planned/unplanned internal stock movement changes with ease, the company uses stock transfers in embedded EWM.

System Process

The following explains the basic system flow, including the documents and data required to execute stock transfer:

1. A warehouse request is created in embedded EWM that contains information about the product along with the quantity to be moved from the source to destination bin.
2. Stock transfer warehouse tasks are created based on the warehouse request and assigned to the warehouse worker. The warehouse request directs the warehouse worker to move the products from the source to destination storage bin.
3. The warehouse orders are allocated to the warehouse worker. During stock transfer of the product from the source storage bin to the destination storage bin, the warehouse worker completes this process and confirms its warehouse task.

9.5.2 Warehouse Request for Stock Transfer

The first step in setting up an internal stock transfer is the creation of a warehouse request. A warehouse request is made up of a document type and item type in embedded EWM. Define the document type by navigating to IMG path **SCM Extended Warehouse Management • Extended Warehouse Management • Internal Warehouse**

Processes • Delivery Processing • Stock Transfers • Define Document Types for the Stock Transfer Process and Define Item Types for the Stock Transfer Process.

In the next step, set up the determination of warehouse requests by navigating to IMG path **SCM Extended Warehouse Management • Extended Warehouse Management • Internal Warehouse Processes • Delivery Processing • Stock Transfers • Define Document Type Determination for the Stock Transfer Process and Define Item Type Determination for the Stock Transfer Process.** Delivery document determination is required when you create an embedded EWM delivery document as a successor document or manually without reference to a document. For document type determination, the system looks for the document category and document type of the source document. It uses these settings to determine the document category and document type of the destination document. You only have to specify the document category of the source document if you want the destination document to be created as a successor of the source document. Item type determination is used for providing the settings for determination of the item type based on the document category, item type group, hierarchy type, and corresponding item type.

9.5.3 Internal Stock Transfer Process

Internal stock transfers are created via Transaction /SCWM/IM_ST or by navigating to **SAP Easy Access** path **Logistics • SCM Extended Warehouse Management • Extended Warehouse Management • Work Scheduling • Maintain Internal Stock Transfer**.

Click on the **Create** button, and select the document type and item type for creating the stock transfer warehouse request. In addition, provide the product, quantity, stock type source, and destination storage bin, and then click on **Save**, which creates the stock transfer order in embedded EWM (see Figure 9.38).

After the stock transfer document is created, create the warehouse tasks either automatically through the Post Processing Framework (PPF) or manually from the document by choosing **Internal Stock Transfer • Follow-On Functions • Warehouse Task.** After the warehouse task is confirmed, the goods movement is also updated in SAP S/4HANA.

You can also use wave management to manage creation of warehouse tasks for multiple stock transfer requests. You can group multiple stock transfer requests and create warehouse tasks for stock transfer simultaneously. We'll talk more about wave management in Chapter 16.

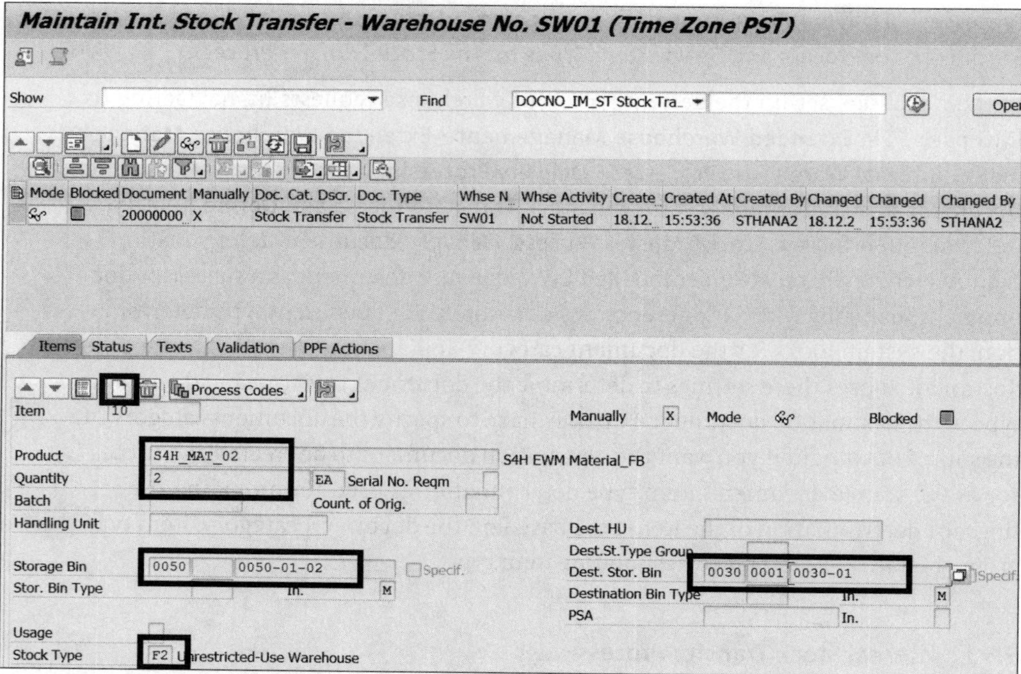

Figure 9.38 Internal Stock Transfer

9.6 Summary

In this chapter, we discussed various internal warehouse movements in embedded EWM. We discussed configurations for internal warehouse processes for replenishment, posting change, internal stock transfer, and ad hoc warehouse movements. We explained each process with the help of an example to walk through the process in detail. You should now be able to set up these internal warehouse processes in your warehouse based on your business requirements. In the next chapter, we will cover the physical inventory process.

Chapter 10
Physical Inventory

Physical inventory is a key warehouse process to keep count of physical stock in the warehouse. Physical inventory helps maintain stock balance in the warehouse and manage balance sheets correctly. In this chapter, we'll cover physical inventory in embedded EWM and how stock quantities in inventory management in SAP S/4HANA are kept in sync with the stock count in embedded EWM.

In organizations, it's a pressing requirement to keep a count of the products and packages in the warehouses for stock quantity and valuation consistency between system stock and physical stock in the warehouse. Stock is maintained in storage bins in embedded EWM. You can count the stock in individual bins or for a specific product in the warehouse. Although EWM is embedded in SAP S/4HANA, you still need to send the updated results to the SAP S/4HANA system so that the inventory count is updated at the storage location level within a plant. The process of counting the products or handling units (HUs) in the warehouse and posting it back to SAP S/4HANA is an integral component of warehouse management, and this process is called *physical inventory*. In this chapter, we'll talk about the physical inventory process in embedded EWM in detail, including the concept of physical inventory in warehousing (Section 10.1); the different physical inventory procedures in embedded EWM (Section 10.2); basic settings required for completing the physical inventory process (Section 10.3); documents created for counting, stock comparison, and posting differences from embedded EWM to SAP S/4HANA (Section 10.4); managing physical inventory using a paper-driven process (Section 10.5); and, finally, the use of RF for completing physical inventory processes (Section 1.6).

10.1 What Is Physical Inventory?

Warehouse operations are complex, and there are various reasons that stock situations change continuously, which requires regular monitoring. For example, while undergoing transfer to different places in the warehouse, a product can get lost, stolen, broken, or spoiled. Sometimes, due to lack of time or unavailability of stock in the required bin, a warehouse user can pick stock from another storage bin. This may not be immediately updated in the system, thus causing a discrepancy in the physical and system stock count, which further leads to interruptions in fulfilling demand. An accurate view of inventory also helps improve material requirements planning (MRP) and accurate availability checks. Thus, counting of physical stock is an important activity for organizations not only for meeting reporting and statutory requirements but also for maintaining operational efficiency in the warehouse.

Counting of stock isn't only important from the perspective of tracking stock and aligning it with the book value of stock in the system as it's often required for audit purposes and can be asked for by external or internal auditors. Stock count also enables organizations to trigger important processes such as stock replenishment if the actual stock count falls below a certain limit. Thus, it's important to always have a clear picture of the inventory in the warehouse to avoid stock out or inaccurate stock count in the warehouse.

Physical inventory in embedded EWM can be divided into three main subprocesses that together complete the physical inventory process in the warehouse. Each of these steps (planning, execution, and reconciliation) is key for setting up an end-to-end physical inventory process in the warehouse. They are as follows:

- **Planning physical inventory**
  This step involves the overall planning of physical inventory for stock in the warehouse, including the frequency at which physical inventory is to be done, who will be doing it, and what process will be used for doing physical inventory. Depending on the type of physical inventory process chosen, the blocking/freezing of bins, creation of physical inventory documents, and other activities are carried out. This also involves planning the security roles and authorizations required for carrying out the count, managing actual and system stock differences, and posting the final stock count from embedded EWM to SAP S/4HANA.
- **Physical inventory execution**
  The physical inventory execution process includes activities involving carrying out the actual count, saving count results in embedded EWM, recording differences between actual and system stock counts, and initiating a recount.

- **Physical inventory posting and reconciliation**
  After the stock is physically counted by the warehouse worker, a difference analysis is performed by the warehouse supervisor in the difference analyzer to review the reasons for differences between booked and actual stock. Based on tolerances defined and assigned to specific roles, the physical inventory document is posted in both the embedded EWM and SAP S/4HANA systems to bring both systems in sync with respect to inventory counts.

In embedded EWM, you can perform a physical inventory at both the bin level and product level:

- **Storage bin-specific physical inventory**
  Storage bin-specific physical inventory is used to count products or HUs at the storage bin level. The stock can be counted for a set of bins that belong to a storage section or storage type.
- **Product-specific physical inventory**
  Product-specific physical inventory is done for a specific product in one or more storage bins or HUs.

In the following sections, we explain the business context in which the physical inventory process can be used and how the processes are carried out in the system.

10.1.1 Business Process

American company Alpha Medicals wants to ensure that its stock inventory is reflected correctly in embedded EWM. The warehouse stock department manager of Alpha Medical plans the physical inventory process based on the company's physical inventory strategy. Based on the physical inventory plan, the physical inventory process is executed using the following highlighted processes shown in Figure 10.1:

1. Using the Create Physical Inventory – Documents app, the warehouse stock manager creates a physical inventory document for a specific bin (0010-01-01) and activates it based on the physical inventory strategy of the company.
2. After the physical inventory document is activated, it's assigned to the warehouse worker using queue management by embedded EWM. The warehouse worker gets the physical inventory warehouse task on his Physical Inventory app in the sequence it's assigned to the physical inventory queues.

3. The warehouse worker then starts counting the products in the storage bin by scanning the barcodes/entering the counts against the products in the Process Physical Inventory app. After counting the bin stocks, the warehouse worker saves the count using the same app.
4. As a next process step, the stock inventory manager gets the result of the counted stocks and checks it for counting correctness based on count tolerances configured by Alpha Medicals. If the stock manager deems the counting incorrect or out of stock tolerances, the physical inventory document is sent back to the warehouse worker. In this case, the warehouse worker recounts the stock in the bin and resaves it for approval. If the stock counting is within the posting range, the posting is completed by the stock manager.
5. After successful posting of stock using the physical inventory document, the stock reconciliation manager runs difference analysis, and differences are posted to inventory management (IM) in SAP S/4HANA to bring the stock count both IM and embedded EWM in sync.

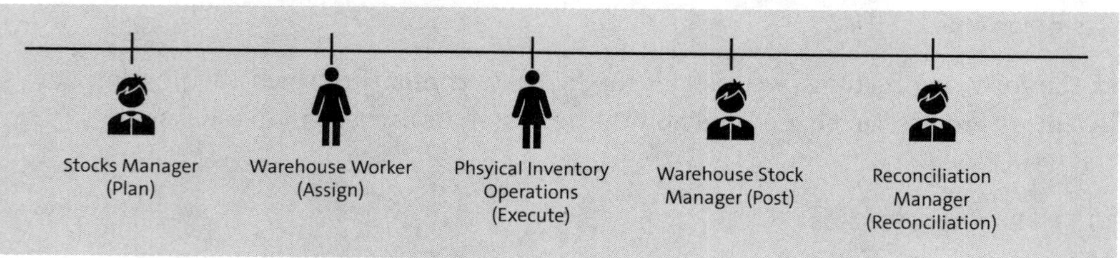

Figure 10.1 Business Flow for Physical Inventory Processing

> **Note**
>
> In our example, we explained a single business variant of physical inventory processes, but the same process flow can be used for most physical inventory process variants.

10.1.2 System Process

Figure 10.2 shows the sequence of process steps in embedded EWM during the physical inventory process.

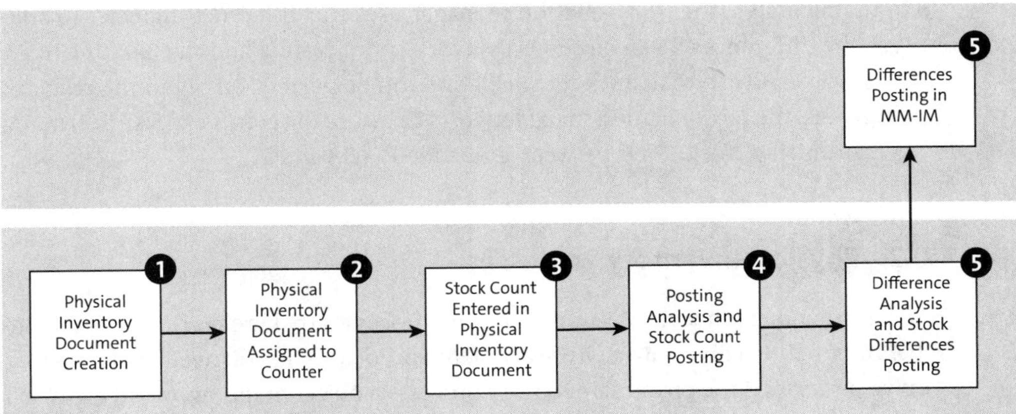

Figure 10.2 Process Steps in the Physical Inventory Process

Briefly, each step in the physical inventory process is as follows:

❶ The physical inventory process starts with creation of a physical inventory document in embedded EWM and setting the physical inventory document status as **Active**. The physical inventory document can be created by the Alpha Medical employee (with the appropriate role) either from SAP GUI or via the Create Physical Inventory – Documents app.

❷ The physical inventory document contains all relevant data required for stock counting: product, bin, batch, workers required to perform counting, and so on. The warehouse worker opens the physical inventory document assigned to his queue and available in his mobile app and starts counting the stock per the physical inventory document.

❸ After the worker finishes the counting, the results for the document are saved; this changes the status of the physical inventory document to **Counted**.

❹ The successful counting of the stock triggers a workflow to the warehouse stock manager to approve or disapprove the counting results. If the stock manager deems the count results to be wrong, he sets the physical inventory document to be recounted and sets the physical inventory document status to **Recount**. In such a scenario, the warehouse worker recounts the stock and resends the results for approval to the stock manager. If the count results are accepted by the stock manager, he posts the count results in the document, which sets the status of the physical inventory document as **Posted**.

❺ In the next step, the reconciliation manager uses the difference analyzer to analyze the differences between the EWM stock count results and the SAP S/4HANA IM stock results so that stock reconciliation can be posted. On obtaining relevant approvals, the reconciliation manager posts the stock differences to SAP S/4HANA, synchronizing stock levels between embedded EWM and IM.

10.2 Physical Inventory Processes

SAP has provided multiple physical inventory processes that are product- or bin-specific. Thus, before you create a physical inventory document, you need to ensure that you've performed the physical inventory process to object mapping, based on which a physical inventory document is created in embedded EWM. Because physical inventory is done for a specific area of a warehouse, the following parameters become important before starting the physical inventory process in embedded EWM:

- Embedded EWM warehouse
- Physical inventory procedure

Table 10.1 shows various physical inventory procedures available in embedded EWM.

Procedure Code	Applicable To	Physical Inventory Procedure
AL	Storage bin-specific	Annual physical inventory procedure
AS	Product-specific	
CC	Product-specific	Cyclic physical inventory procedure
HL	Storage bin-specific	Ad hoc physical inventory procedure
HS	Product-specific	
ML	Storage bin-specific	Storage bin check physical inventory procedure
NL	Storage bin-specific	Low stock check physical inventory procedure
PL	Storage bin-specific	Putaway physical inventory procedure

Table 10.1 Physical Inventory Procedures

In the following sections, the usage and applicability of each procedure is explained in detail.

10.2.1 Periodic Physical Inventory

Many companies require a physical inventory at least once a year. Many organizations need to perform a physical inventory process, but not on a continuous basis and only periodically. The inventory counting can be done on a specific day or during a small window anytime of the year to account for all the stock in the warehouse at once. Periodic physical inventory can be done at the bin level or product level. One type of periodic physical inventory available in embedded EWM is an annual physical inventory.

In this procedure, stock counting is done in the warehouse on a certain day or at a short interval of time during which stock movement is prohibited. This is done to get an exact stock count in the warehouse by avoiding any incoming or outgoing products. This inventory procedure is usually carried out near the end of a fiscal year to get a clear stock count and prepare for the next year.

10.2.2 Continuous Physical Inventory

In continuous physical inventory, the inventory is done over time. This is considered a better way to perform physical inventory as the cost and effort to perform a physical inventory isn't concentrated into one day of the year but distributed throughout the year. Continuous physical inventory saves costs and increases the accuracy of the stock situation. It also prevents any impact to regular warehouse processes, as the inventory for the entire warehouse isn't focused on a particular period.

Following are the continuous physical inventory procedures available in embedded EWM.

- **Ad hoc physical inventory**
  An ad hoc physical inventory procedure can be performed at any time during the fiscal year at both the storage bin level and product level. As the name suggests, it's done on an ad hoc basis when, for example, there's been product damage or a theft, which requires an immediate stock assessment for the product in the warehouse.
- **Low-stock check**
  A low-stock check is a continuous physical inventory procedure that can only be done at the storage bin level. This physical inventory procedure is triggered while confirming the stock removal warehouse task. A low-stock check requires that after removal of stock only a small quantity will be left in the bin for a product,

which is also the threshold value based on which physical inventory can be triggered.

Define this threshold as a limit value based on an operative unit of measure (UoM) for a product at IMG path **SCM Extended Warehouse Management • Extended Warehouse Management • Internal Warehouse Processes • Physical Inventory • Physical-Inventory-Area-Specific-Settings • Define Physical Inventory Area**, as shown in Figure 10.3. Click on **New Entries**, and enter the threshold quantity (**Qty**) for the **Physical Inventory Area**.

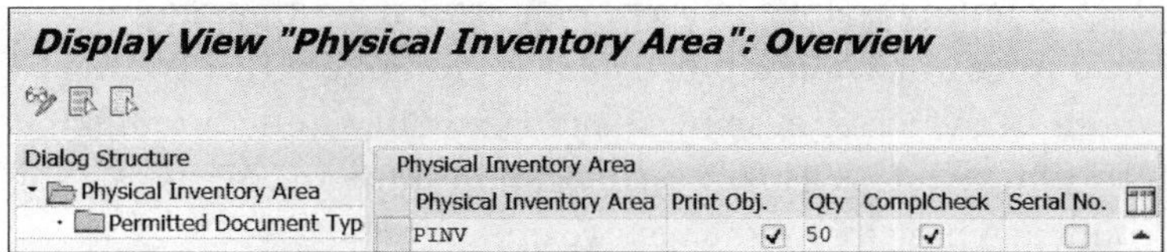

Figure 10.3 Threshold Quantity for Low-Stock Check Procedure

The steps involved in a low-stock check are as follows:

- If the actual stock in the storage bin falls below the limit value, the picker enters the counted stock during warehouse task confirmation, and a physical inventory document for a low-stock check is created.
- The counter performs the physical inventory process and posts the correct inventory quantity for the product. The inventory count is posted to embedded EWM and SAP S/4HANA either with or without a difference.

- **Zero-stock check**
  A zero-stock check physical inventory is a variant of a low-stock physical inventory procedure; however, in this case, the threshold limit is set to zero. This triggers a low-stock check if during the picking warehouse task creation, the available stock in the storage bin becomes zero.
- **Putaway physical inventory**
  The putaway physical inventory procedure is a continuous procedure at the storage bin level. In this procedure, stock counting is done during the first putaway of product in the empty storage bin in the fiscal year. No other physical inventory is done in the bin after that until the end of the fiscal year, even if the stock situation

in the bin keeps changing. The steps involved in the putaway physical inventory are as follows:

- A warehouse task is created for stock putaway.
- The system checks for prerequisites for destination bins in the storage type such as checking bin history to see if it's the first putaway in the current fiscal year, if the storage bin is empty, and if mixed storage isn't permitted.
- If these conditions are met, the picker enters the stock being put away in the storage bin during warehouse task confirmation, and a physical inventory document is created.
- If the storage bin isn't empty, the picker rejects the physical inventory and no physical inventory document is created.

10.2.3 Cycle Counting

Cycle counting is the process of physical inventory in which the physical inventory is done at regular intervals within a fiscal year. The physical inventory intervals (cycles) are determined based on business decisions about how many days each product requires physical inventory to be done. In any organization, each product doesn't hold a similar financial value as other products. Therefore, it makes business sense for organizations to perform physical inventory at regular intervals for fast-moving products or those of more financial value.

As shown in Figure 10.4, using this setting, you can set up the indicators used in the cycle counting process. In addition, you can add the intervals on which the cycle counting physical inventory document is to be created. Cycle counting groups products based on value or rate of movement in the warehouse using a cycle counting indicator, which is assigned to the product master. Thus, a warehouse can decide to perform a physical inventory of fast-moving goods at more frequent intervals than for slow-moving goods.

To create a cycle counting indicator, navigate to IMG path **SCM Extended Warehouse Management • Extended Warehouse Management • Internal Warehouse Processes • Physical Inventory • Warehouse-Number-Specific-Settings • Configure Cycle Counting**. Click on **New Entries**, and enter the cycle counting indicator (**CC Ind.**) with the time interval for physical inventory and buffer time.

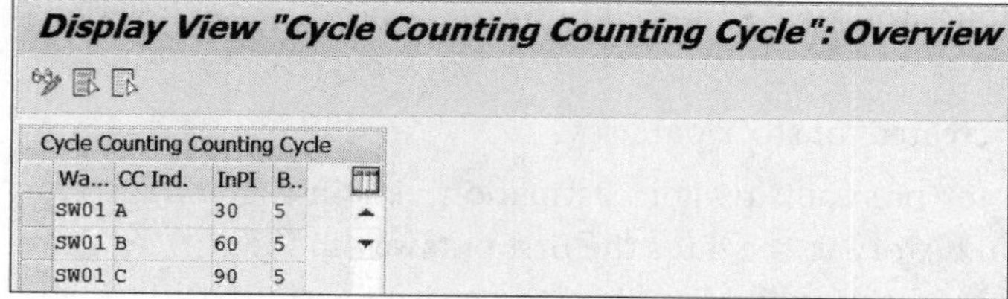

Figure 10.4 Configuring Cycle Counting Intervals

The parameters are defined in the following settings:

- **Cycle counting indicator**
  CC Ind. is the base indicator assigned to the product master, based on which the physical inventory interval is determined.
- **Interval of physical inventory**
  InPI is the interval in days on which physical inventory is to be done for a product. Based on this interval, a new physical inventory document is created from the last successful physical inventory for the product.
- **Buffer interval**
  The **BT** field is the interval in days the cycle counting considers as buffer time for considering a physical inventory document for completion.

The cycle counting indicator created earlier is assigned to products in the **Cycle Counting Indicator** field in the **Warehouse Data** tab of the product master.

10.2.4 Sample-Based Inventory

The sample-based physical inventory procedure is used to provide an interface with third-party systems that either provide or take data from the same for physical inventory purposes. A report is used to download the stock situation based on the physical inventory process in embedded EWM at both the product level (by using inventory procedure **ES External Procedure (Product Specific)**) and storage bin level (by using inventory procedure **EL External Procedure (Storage-Bin-Specific)**). Let's walk through how to perform sample-based physical inventory in embedded EWM in SAP S/4HANA:

1. **Download the sample from embedded EWM.**
   This process is used if you want to download the stock situation in embedded EWM for a physical inventory area and provide it to a third-party system to perform stock reconciliation on their end. To download the stock situation in comma-separated values (CSV) format, go to **SAP Easy Access** path **Logistics • SCM Extended Warehouse Management • Extended Warehouse Management • Physical Inventory • Interfaces for Sample-Based Physical Inventory • Download Stock Population**, and download the stock situation using the following filtering criteria:
   - **Warehouse Number** (mandatory)
   - **Activity Area**
   - **Owner**
   - **Party Entitled to Dispose**
   - **Stock Type**

   Enter the physical inventory sampling ID and expiration date, based on which the report pulls out the data in SAP List Viewer (ALV) format. The data can then be downloaded and provided to the third-party system, which can then enter the data per its physical inventory count.
2. **Upload the sample from embedded EWM to create the physical inventory document.**
   After the third-party system has filled in the data for the correct count of stock in the data dictionary (DDIC) structure /SCWM/S_UPLOAD_CREATE, it can be loaded back into the system using **SAP Easy Access** path **Logistics SCM Extended Warehouse Management • Extended Warehouse Management • Physical Inventory • Interfaces for Sample-Based Physical Inventory • Upload Sample to Create Physical Inventory Document**. In the report to upload the sample data, enter the warehouse number and sample ID. You can also provide the state in which the physical inventory documents will be created and the file from which data must be uploaded in the system. After the data is successfully loaded in the system, the physical inventory document is created.
3. **Download the results.**
   After you've downloaded the stock count from embedded EWM and uploaded it back to create the physical inventory document, the stock situation from the physical inventory documents is downloaded to match it with third-party systems

as well. Access this report via **SAP Easy Access** path **Logistics • SCM Extended Warehouse Management • Extended Warehouse Management • Physical Inventory • Interfaces for Sample-Based Physical Inventory • Download Results or Stock Population**. Provide the selection criteria for the warehouse and the sample ID.

10.3 Configuring Physical Inventory

The settings described in this section need to be set up to plan, execute, and reconcile the physical inventory process using physical inventory documents in embedded EWM.

10.3.1 Settings Specific to the Physical Inventory Area

The settings in this section are defined for the physical inventory area, which is the level at which physical inventory is carried out in the embedded EWM warehouse.

The first step in setting up the physical inventory process is to define the physical inventory area. All the bins for which physical inventory is to be done are grouped together in a logical grouping that you define as a physical inventory area. The physical inventory area is defined via IMG path **SCM Extended Warehouse Management • Extended Warehouse Management • Internal Warehouse Processes • Physical Inventory • Physical-Inventory-Area-Specific Setting • Define Physical Inventory Area**. Click on **New Entries**, enter the physical inventory area, and set the following indicators if required, as shown in Figure 10.5:

- **Putaway PI**
  This indicator checks whether putaway physical inventory is allowed.
- **LSPI**
  This indicator checks whether low-stock or zero-stock physical inventory is allowed.
- **LS Check**
  This indicator checks whether the low-stock/zero-stock check is done during the warehouse task confirmation.
- **PstgAfterCount**
  This indicator checks whether automatic posting is done after count completion if within the user-defined threshold.

- **Dsp. Qty**
  This enables the display of book quantity at the time of count while executing counting in the system or using an inventory document printout.
- **Dsp. Obj.**
  This enables the display of products and HUs contained in the storage bin at the time of counting so that rather than adding the information manually, it can be loaded automatically.
- **HU Complete**
  This enables setting the top-level HU count as **Complete** without needing to count the items or HUs inside the HU.
- **HU Count**
  This sets whether the count at the HU level is good enough or if items inside the HU also should be counted.
- **Print Obj.**
  This enables whether the items/HU hierarchy within a bin should be printed out for a counter in a bin-specific physical inventory process.
- **Qty**
  This is the threshold quantity that exists in a bin to enable creation of a physical inventory document using low-stock check or zero-stock check (if the quantity is 0).
- **ComplCheck**
  This sets the completion check indicator to process a completion check for the physical inventory area only in offline mode rather than in online mode to help avoid performance problems.
- **Serial No.**
  This allows you to activate the display of serial numbers during the physical inventory process.

10

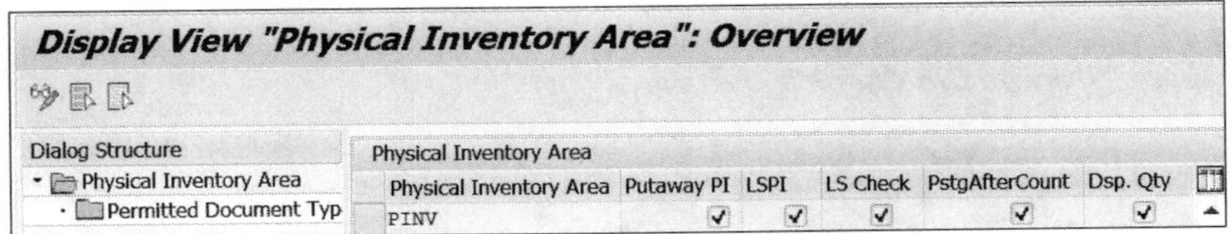

Figure 10.5 Physical Inventory Area Definition

After the general settings for the physical inventory area are completed, you can define which physical inventory procedures are applicable to the physical inventory area, as shown in Figure 10.6. On the same screen, select the defined **Physical Inventory Area**, and click on the **Permitted Document Types** node. Next, click on **New Entries**, and enter the physical inventory procedures that need to be activated.

Display View "Permitted Document Types": Overview

Dialog Structure
- Physical Inventory Area
  - Permitted Document Typ

Permitted Document Types

Physical Inventory Area	Procedure
PINV	AL Annual Ph...
PINV	AS Annual Ph...
PINV	CC Cycle Cou...
PINV	EL External ...
PINV	ES External ...
PINV	HL Ad-hoc Ph...
PINV	HS Ad-hoc Ph...
PINV	ML Storage B...
PINV	NL Low Stock...
PINV	PL Putaway P...

Figure 10.6 Assigning Physical Inventory Procedures to the Physical Inventory Area

You also have to set the physical inventory interval and buffer in the number of days in the storage bin check. This interval provides the time interval within which stock for a physical activity area must be physically inventoried to ensure completion of physical inventory. It's configured via IMG path **SCM Extended Warehouse Management • Extended Warehouse Management • Internal Warehouse Processes • Physical Inventory • Physical-Inventory-Area-Specific Setting • Periodicity of Storage Bin Check**, as shown in Figure 10.7. Click on **New Entries**, and enter the time interval and buffer for the physical inventory area (**Acty Area**). When you display a physical inventory progress situation in the warehouse monitor, the system considers the buffer time while calculating physical inventory count completeness. Products aren't shown as physical inventory completed until the buffer time in days has elapsed.

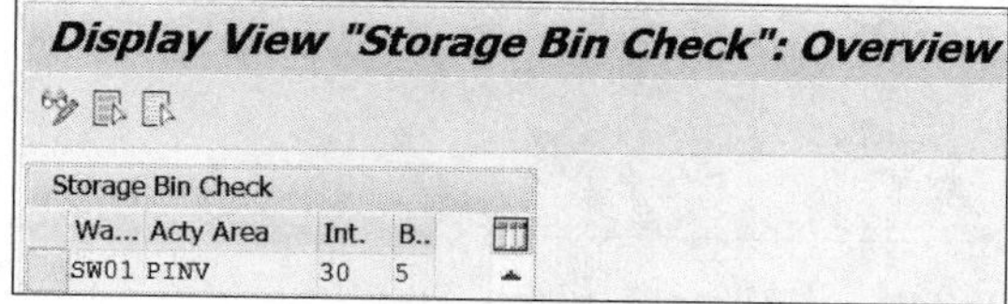

Figure 10.7 Setting the Time Interval for Physical Inventory of the Activity Area

10.3.2 Settings Specific to the Warehouse Number

The next step in setting up the physical inventory process is to establish the physical inventory settings at the specific warehouse level as follows:

- **Assign the physical inventory area to the activity area.**
An activity area is assigned to the defined physical inventory area created earlier so that the bins of the assigned activity area become eligible for the physical inventory process. The configuration is done via IMG path **SCM Extended Warehouse Management • Extended Warehouse Management • Internal Warehouse Processes • Physical Inventory • Warehouse-Number-Specific-Settings • Assign Physical Inventory Area to Activity Area**. Click on **New Entries**, and enter the physical inventory area against the activity area of the warehouse.

- **Define the number ranges for the physical inventory document.**
A suitable number range can be defined for physical inventory documents via IMG path **SCM Extended Warehouse Management • Extended Warehouse Management • Internal Warehouse Processes • Physical Inventory • Warehouse-Number-Specific-Settings • Define Number Range for Physical Inventory Documents**. Enter the embedded EWM warehouse against object "/SCWM/PIDO", and click on **Intervals** to define the number range and fiscal year for which the number range is valid.

- **Specify the physical-inventory-specific settings in the warehouse.**
As shown in Figure 10.8, there are some important physical inventory settings specific to the warehouse that help control the key parameters that influence counting. These settings can be accessed via IMG path **SCM Extended Warehouse Management • Extended Warehouse Management • Internal Warehouse Processes • Physical Inventory • Warehouse-Number-Specific-Settings • Specify Physical Inventory Specific Settings in the Warehouse.** Click on **New Entries**, and enter control settings for the embedded EWM warehouse.

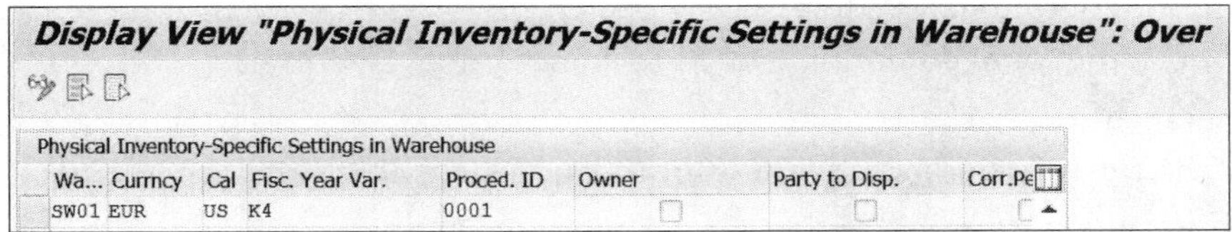
Display View "Physical Inventory-Specific Settings in Warehouse": Over

Physical Inventory-Specific Settings in Warehouse

Wa...	Currncy	Cal	Fisc. Year Var.	Proced. ID	Owner	Party to Disp.	Corr.Pe
SW01	EUR	US	K4	0001	☐	☐	☐

Figure 10.8 Physical-Inventory-Specific Settings for the Embedded EWM Warehouse

The control settings are as follows:

- **Currency**
  The value in the **Currncy** field denotes the currency in which the stock is valuated. The stock value in SAP S/4HANA directly accesses embedded EWM. Every time the stock valuation changes in SAP S/4HANA, the updated value is made accessible to embedded EWM.
- **Factory calendar**
  The factory calendar (**Cal**) is used to keep a count of working days in a calendar year. The count of working days is required to schedule the dates for inventory counting for period inventory processes such as cycle counting.
- **Fiscal year variant**
  The **Fisc. Year Var.** field helps in posting financial and material documents in accordance with the fiscal year of the country in which the warehouse operates.
- **Procedure**
  The **Proced. ID** field refers to the procedure to print inventory documents such as counting sheets. This procedure needs to be set up if you're not using RF for stock counting.
- **Owner/party entitled to dispose**
  The **Owner** and **Party to Disp.** checkboxes are selected if you want the owner and party entitled to dispose to appear as defaults on the physical inventory document based on the warehouse defaults.
- **Correction permitted**
  If the **Corr.Perm.** checkbox is selected, you can change the count value for a physical inventory document in the difference analyzer before posting the difference to SAP S/4HANA.
- **Allow percentage**
  The **Allowed Percent. Diff. in Counting** field gives the percentage variation that's allowed. You need to have a tolerance check so you can get a warning if there's a variation in the count entered above the tolerance value.
- **No tolerance**
  Select the **No Tol.** checkbox if you want to completely deactivate the tolerance check.
- **Number range of physical inventory document**
  The **NRI PI Document** setting is used to assign the number range of the physical inventory document to the warehouse number in embedded EWM.

- **Cycle counting completeness at the warehouse level**
  The **Compl. WhN** indicator is used in the cycle counting process to indicate that physical inventory is complete for all the physical inventory areas for a product if the physical inventory for it is complete. If it isn't checked, then the physical inventory completeness check is marked as complete for each physical inventory area of the product individually.

10.3.3 Define Tolerance Group

Tolerance is the positive or negative variance in the actual versus booked inventory count. The stock difference is posted after the physical inventory process is completed. To ensure that no abnormal variance is posted by the counter, assign a tolerance group to a user who has specialized in judging and posting the allowed physical inventory variances.

Tolerances are defined in the form of multiple settings combined into a tolerance group, which is assigned to users in embedded EWM. Three different types of tolerance group settings are used in the physical inventory process:

- **Tolerance group for the difference analyzer**
  The tolerance group for the difference analyzer is used to block difference values outside the tolerance limits when differences are being analyzed in the difference analyzer tool. This setting is accessed via IMG path **SCM Extended Warehouse Management • Extended Warehouse Management • Internal Warehouse Processes • Physical Inventory • Warehouse-Number-Specific-Settings • Define Tolerance Groups • Define Tolerance Group for Difference Analyzer**. Click on **New Entries** to create a new tolerance group, and assign the following values:
  - **Value-Based Tolerance**
    This is the maximum allowed to be posted from the difference analyzer cockpit.
  - **No Tol.**
    This indicator is used if no tolerance is applicable for the user in the difference analyzer.
  - **Wait Time**
    This is the time (in days) after which the physical inventory would be posted automatically from embedded EWM to SAP S/4HANA.
- **Tolerance group for posting differences**
  The tolerance group for posting differences is used to block values outside of the tolerance limit based on differences analyzed in the difference analyzer tool. This

setting is accessed via IMG path **SCM Extended Warehouse Management • Extended Warehouse Management • Internal Warehouse Processes • Physical Inventory • Warehouse-Number-Specific-Settings • Define Tolerance Groups • Define Tolerance Group For Posting Differences**. Click on **New Entries**, and assign the following values for the tolerance group for posting differences:

- **Allowed Percentage Tol.**
  This is the maximum absolute value tolerance allowed for a user to be posted.
- **Value-Based Tolerance**
  This is the maximum allowed tolerance value between book and actual stock allowed for a user to be posted.
- **No Tol.**
  Set this indicator if no tolerance is applicable for the user to post stock differences.
- **Alert**
  An alert can be sent by the system in case there's a tolerance breach by the user in the counting process.

- **Tolerance group for recounting**
  The tolerance group for recounting is used to define allowed tolerance values based on which the recount is to be issued. This setting is accessed via IMG path **SCM Extended Warehouse Management • Extended Warehouse Management • Internal Warehouse Processes • Physical Inventory • Warehouse-Number-Specific-Settings • Define Tolerance Groups • Define Tolerance Group for Recounting**. Click on **New Entries**, and define the following values for the defined tolerance group:
  - **Allowed Percentage Tol.**
    This is the maximum absolute value tolerance allowed for a user to issue a recount.
  - **Value-Based Tolerance**
    This is the maximum percentage value tolerance between booked and actual stock allowed for a user to issue a recount.
  - **No Tol.**
    Set this indicator if no tolerance can allow the user to issue a recount.

After the tolerance groups have been defined, they must be assigned to individual users. To do so, navigate to **SAP Easy Access** path **Logistics • SCM Extended Warehouse Management • Extended Warehouse Management • Settings • Physical Inventory •**

Assign User to Tolerance Group for Difference Analyzer. Click on **New Entries**, and enter a user for the tolerance group for the difference analyzer.

Similarly, the tolerance group created for posting change and recounting is assigned to a user via **SAP Easy Access** path **SCM Extended Warehouse Management • Extended Warehouse Management • Settings • Physical Inventory • Assign User to Tolerance Group for Recount/Clearing** by clicking on **New Entries** and entering a user for the recount/clearing tolerance group.

> **Note**
>
> Embedded EWM can access product valuation data directly from SAP S/4HANA. It's no longer required to replicate product valuation in embedded EWM using Transaction /SCWM/VALUATION_SET for tolerance checks.

10.3.4 Define Reasons and Priority

Reasons and priorities are supporting controls that are used in the physical inventory process. They can help prioritize documents or trace why a certain decision was made in the physical inventory process.

Priorities are defined for a warehouse in embedded EWM and are used to signify the urgency of a physical inventory document. A maximum of nine priorities can be defined and assigned to the warehouse. To define priorities, navigate to IMG path **SCM Extended Warehouse Management • Extended Warehouse Management • Internal Warehouse Processes • Physical Inventory • Warehouse-Number-Specific-Settings • Reasons & Priority • Define Priorities**. Click on **New Entries**, and define a priority and its description for your embedded EWM warehouse.

Next, define reason codes in embedded EWM. These reason codes are applied for various purposes throughout the physical inventory process. Let's discuss the settings for creating different types of reason codes:

- **Define reasons for physical inventory**
  In this step, define reasons for physical inventory. Reasons also provide additional functionality at the physical inventory document level assigned to the reason code. The settings can be accessed via IMG path **SCM Extended Warehouse Management • Extended Warehouse Management • Internal Warehouse Processes • Physical Inventory • Warehouse-Number-Specific-Settings • Reasons & Priority • Define Reason for Physical Inventory**. Click on **New Entries**, and enter a

reason and its controls (described as follows) for your embedded EWM warehouse (see Figure 10.9):

- **Priority**
  The **Priority** field is used to assign the priority code discussed previously to the reason code to make a physical inventory document more urgent than other documents.
- **Product in location**
  If the **PIL** indicator is set, you can mark a physical inventory document as **Complete** without inserting the actual count. The PRIL exception code allows you to mark the physical inventory document as **Complete** at any stage of the physical inventory process and enables you to activate a workflow assigned to the exception code.
- **No automatic posting in embedded EWM system**
  The **Autom.** setting disables automatic posting of physical inventory quantities to SAP S/4HANA if the post after count setting is activated for the physical inventory area.
- **Active physical inventory document**
  If the **Active** setting is set in the reason code, then the physical inventory document created with this reason code has the **Active** status; otherwise, it's created with the **Inactive** status.
- **No catch weight quantity allowed**
  The **No CW Qty** setting is made to ensure that the catch weight quantity value isn't allowed for catch-weight-relevant products during the physical inventory process.

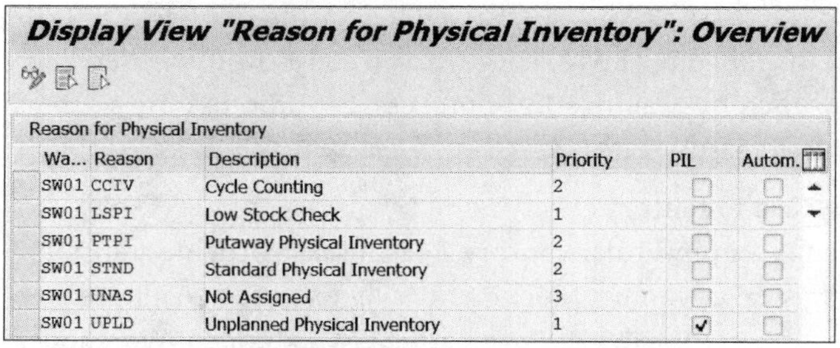

Display View "Reason for Physical Inventory": Overview

Reason for Physical Inventory

Wa...	Reason	Description	Priority	PIL	Autom.
SW01	CCIV	Cycle Counting	2	☐	☐
SW01	LSPI	Low Stock Check	1	☐	☐
SW01	PTPI	Putaway Physical Inventory	2	☐	☐
SW01	STND	Standard Physical Inventory	2	☐	☐
SW01	UNAS	Not Assigned	3	☐	☐
SW01	UPLD	Unplanned Physical Inventory	1	☑	☐

Figure 10.9 Defining Reason Codes for Physical Inventory

- **Define reasons for differences**
  The reasons for differences are used while processing differences in the difference analyzer. The reason codes are assigned to predefined processes that indicate the cause of the difference in the actual count. These settings can be accessed via IMG path **SCM Extended Warehouse Management • Extended Warehouse Management • Internal Warehouse Processes • Physical Inventory • Warehouse-Number-Specific-Settings • Reasons & Priority • Define Reason for Differences**. Click on **New Entries**, and enter a reason for a chosen process for the embedded EWM warehouse.

  As shown in Figure 10.10, the following five standard processes are defined in SAP and can be assigned to user-defined reason codes:
  - **CO Pending Claim from Sales**
  - **COR Correction of a Difference**
  - **QI Inspection Document**
  - **STO Pending Claim from Stock Transfer**
  - **WT Warehouse Task**

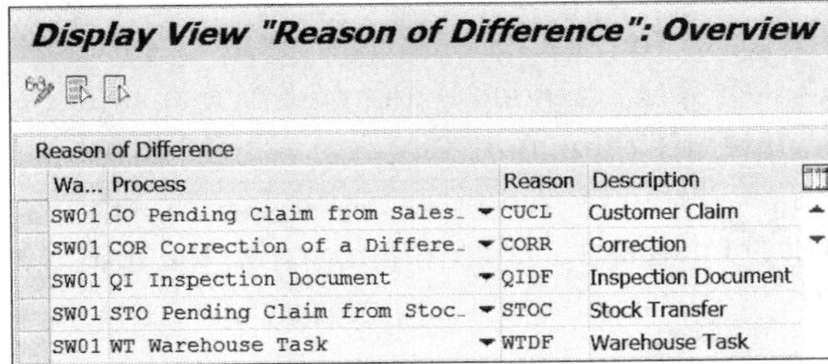
Display View "Reason of Difference": Overview

Reason of Difference

Wa...	Process	Reason	Description
SW01	CO Pending Claim from Sales_	CUCL	Customer Claim
SW01	COR Correction of a Differe_	CORR	Correction
SW01	QI Inspection Document	QIDF	Inspection Document
SW01	STO Pending Claim from Stoc_	STOC	Stock Transfer
SW01	WT Warehouse Task	WTDF	Warehouse Task

Figure 10.10 Defining Difference Analyzer Reason Codes

- **Define reason per physical inventory procedure**
  In this process, define a default reason code per each physical inventory procedure for the embedded EWM warehouse. As shown in Figure 10.11, these settings can be accessed via IMG path **SCM Extended Warehouse Management • Extended Warehouse Management • Internal Warehouse Processes • Physical Inventory • Warehouse-Number-Specific-Settings • Reasons & Priority • Define Standard Reason for Each Physical Inventory Procedure**. Click on **New Entries**, and enter a **Reason** for a physical inventory **Procedure** for the embedded EWM warehouse.

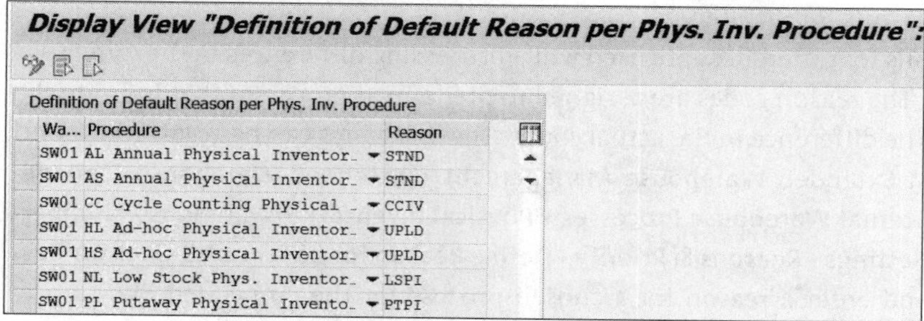

Figure 10.11 Defining Physical Inventory Procedure-Specific Reason Codes

10.3.5 Printing for the Physical Inventory Process

Printing physical inventory documents is required in warehouses that don't use RF for count execution. In this case, the counter is provided a printout of the physical inventory document, on which the counter updates the counting results. The count results are then updated by the counter at workstations directly into SAP. You also can make settings for printing physical inventory documents as PDFs or in other formats. To set up the trigger and printer determination for printing physical inventory documents, a condition technique is used. The configuration for printing physical inventory documents is set via IMG path **SCM Extended Warehouse Management • Extended Warehouse Management • Internal Warehouse Processes • Physical Inventory • Print**. The steps for setting up a condition technique using the Post Processing Framework (PPF) were discussed in detail in Chapter 6. We'll summarize the settings here in the context of this topic:

- **Specify field catalog**
  The field catalog contains the fields that can be used to create condition tables to activate an output action for printing physical inventory documents.
- **Condition table**
  Define a condition table by selecting fields from the field catalog, which are used in determination of print output.
- **Access sequence**
  The access sequence is used to assign condition tables to an action sequence. The system looks through condition tables in an access sequence until it finds a valid condition record.

- **Condition type**
  The condition table defined earlier is assigned to a condition type. You can create a condition type for printer determination to print physical inventory documents.
- **Determination procedure**
  The condition type defined earlier is assigned to a determination procedure. The determination procedure defined here is assigned to the **Proced. ID** field while specifying physical-inventory-specific settings in the warehouse as discussed earlier.
- **Condition maintenance group**
  The condition maintenance group defines acts as a link between the condition type and context and is used to activate an output action for printing physical inventory documents.
- **PPF action profile**
  As shown in Figure 10.12, action profiles are used to define a container holding action definitions that are loaded for a physical inventory object. In standard SAP, the action profile /SCWM/PI_COUNT and action definition PI_COUNT can be used to print physical inventory documents.

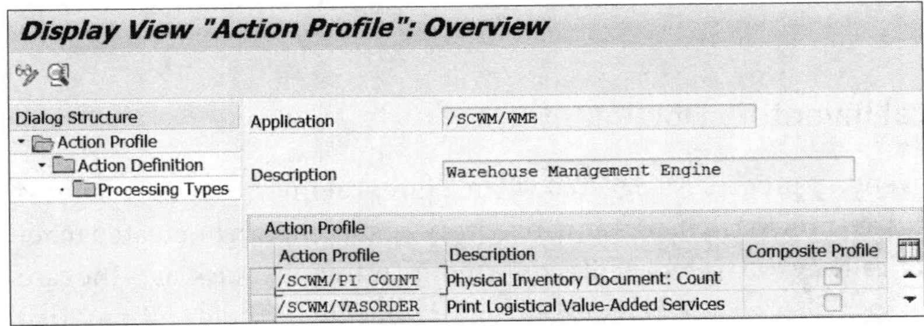

Figure 10.12 Action Profile for Printing Physical Inventory Documents

- **PPF action conditions**
  As shown in Figure 10.13, action conditions are used to define a filter mechanism to select an action definition for activation of output for physical inventory documents. You can define both the schedule condition and start condition in this node.

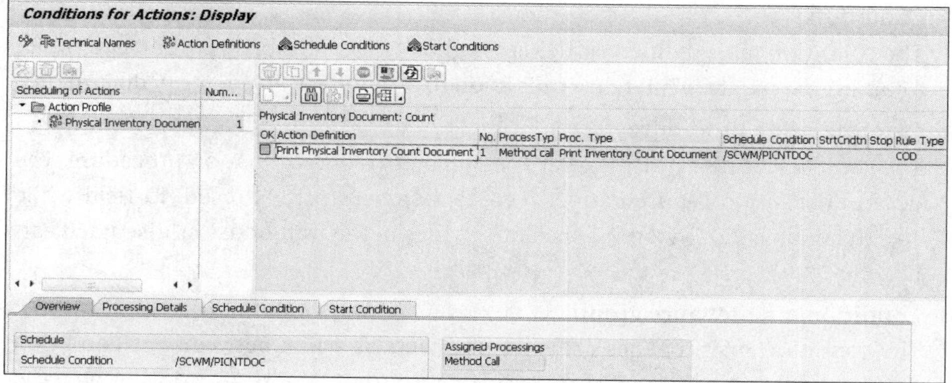

Figure 10.13 PPF Condition Definition for Physical Inventory Document Printing

> **Note**
>
> The SAP Fiori app Print Physical Inventory Documents allows you to print physical inventory documents for handing the counting sheets to warehouse workers for initiation and completion of stock counting.

10.4 Physical Inventory Documents

The physical inventory process is triggered when a physical inventory document is created. As discussed previously, a physical inventory document can be created manually or automatically by the system while confirming a warehouse task, as is the case with low-/zero-stock checks. The physical inventory document holds all required information for executing the count, such as the counter, type of physical inventory process, planned count date, reasons, priority, and so on. As shown in Figure 10.14, the general flow of the physical inventory process is as follows:

1. The physical inventory document is created in **Inactive** status.
2. The document is set to an active state to make it ready for counting.
3. The count result is entered in the physical inventory document manually or using an RF device.
4. If the count result doesn't meet expectations, a recount is initiated, leading to creation of another physical inventory document in **Active** status.

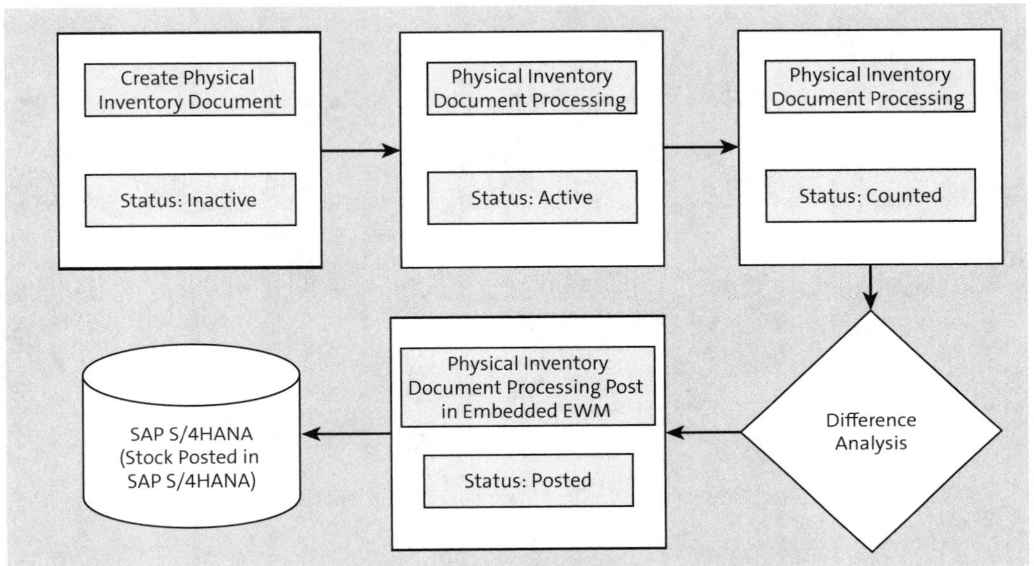

Figure 10.14 General Flow of Physical Inventory Process

5. The count is completed in the recount document.
6. The physical inventory document is posted to post the correct inventory level in the bins in the embedded EWM warehouse.
7. The stock difference is analyzed in the difference analyzer in embedded EWM.
8. After the differences are posted in embedded EWM, the stock count is updated in SAP S/4HANA at the storage location level.

Any physical inventory document goes through multiple statuses before moving to the complete status, as shown in Figure 10.15. The document is first created in **Inactive** status and becomes available for counting after it moves to **Active** status.

In the following sections, we'll discuss the execution process for physical inventory in embedded EWM. We'll discuss the creation of a physical inventory document, executing the count, and processing the stock differences before the actual count is posted in SAP S/4HANA.

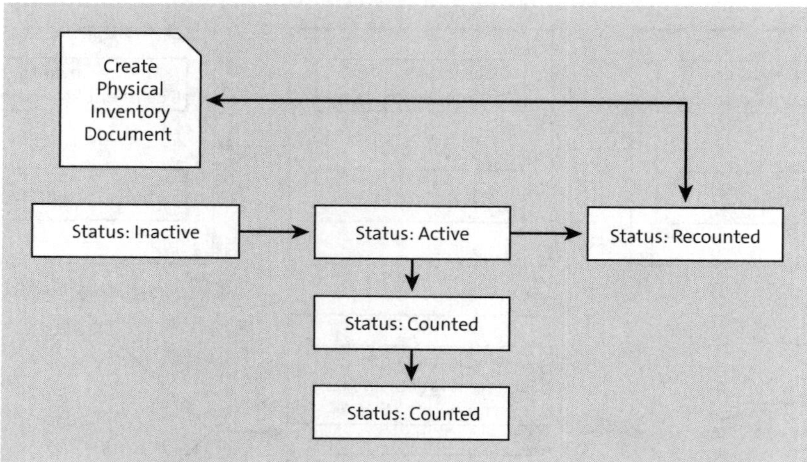

Figure 10.15 Status Flow of the Physical Inventory Document

10.4.1 Create a Physical Inventory Document

This is the first step in the physical inventory process, in which the physical inventory document is created either manually or automatically. This base document is where all the processes of the physical inventory are handled and data is captured. Using the count result from this document, the differences between booked value and actual value or quantity is analyzed and posted to both embedded EWM and SAP S/4HANA.

To create a physical inventory document, navigate to **SAP Easy Access** path **Logistics • SCM Extended Warehouse Management • Extended Warehouse Management • Physical Inventory • Create Physical Inventory Document** or use Transaction /SCWM/PI_CREATE, and click on [icon]. As shown in Figure 10.16, the system asks you to add the embedded EWM warehouse (**Warehouse No.**), physical inventory procedure (**Phys. Inv. Procedure**), and one of the following indicators as an optional control indicator:

- **Propose Ind.**
  This indicator is set if you want the system to propose creation of a physical inventory document for all items determined for counting based on the inventory process.
- **Blocking Indicator**
  This indicator is used to block the storage bin if a physical inventory document is created for bin-specific physical inventory or to block product movement for

product-specific physical inventory. Ensure that there are no open warehouse tasks before you set this indicator for a physical inventory process.

- **Freeze Book Inv.**
  The indicator is used to freeze the book inventory in the physical inventory process so that further goods movement can take place in the physical inventory area, but the difference analysis for the actual stock count can be performed against the book inventory set at the start of the physical inventory process.

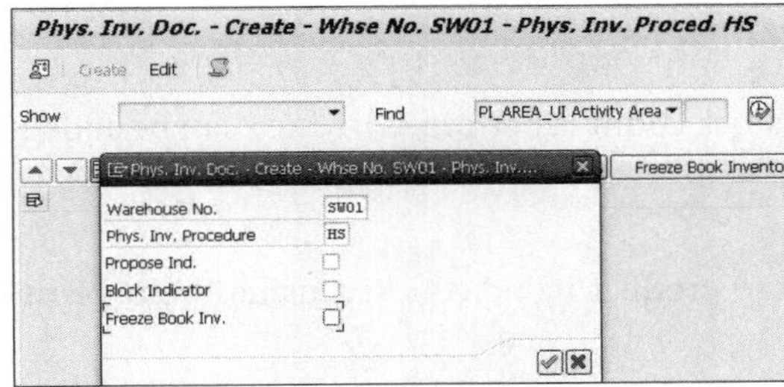

Figure 10.16 Create Physical Inventory Document: Initial Screen

Not only can you set the block and freeze indicators manually, but you can also select these indicators as default for a user either by clicking on the **Default Values** button or pressing F5 in Transaction /SCWM/PI_CREATE.

Figure 10.17 shows a product-specific physical inventory document. Some important fields and values in the physical inventory document are as follows:

- **Inventory Item Data**
  - **Procedure**
    This is the physical inventory procedure based on which the present physical inventory document is created.
- **Physical Inventory Data**
  - **Freeze Book Inv./Blocking Indicat**
    These are freeze and block indicators for the bins/stock count in the bins, which can be set before the stock count.
  - **Plnd Count Date**
    This is the planned count date on which the physical inventory count should start. It's a planned date based on which the physical inventory document should be created.

- **Reason**
  This is the reason code that guides various control factors in the physical inventory process, such as exception code, automatic posting, and so on.

- **Location Data**
  - **Storage Bin**
    This field becomes mandatory during a storage-bin-specific physical inventory procedure.
- **Product Data**
  - **Product**
    This is the product for which the stock count is performed, which can be added by a counter during stock count.
  - **Batch**
    This field contains the batch of the product being counted using the present physical inventory document.
  - **Stock Type**
    This field contains the stock type of the product being counted using the present physical inventory document.
  - **Ent. to Dispose**
    This field contains the party entitled to dispose for the warehouse.
  - **Usage**
    This field contains the usage (special stock, e.g., consignment, subcontractor, returnable packing, etc.) of the product.
  - **Owner**
    This field contains the owner (plant, vendor, etc.) of the product being counted using the present physical inventory document.
  - **Sls Order/Proj.**
    This field contains the sales order/project number for which the product is reserved if you're working with special stock.

Note

The Create Physical Inventory Documents app allows you to create physical inventory documents for execution and completion of the physical inventory process.

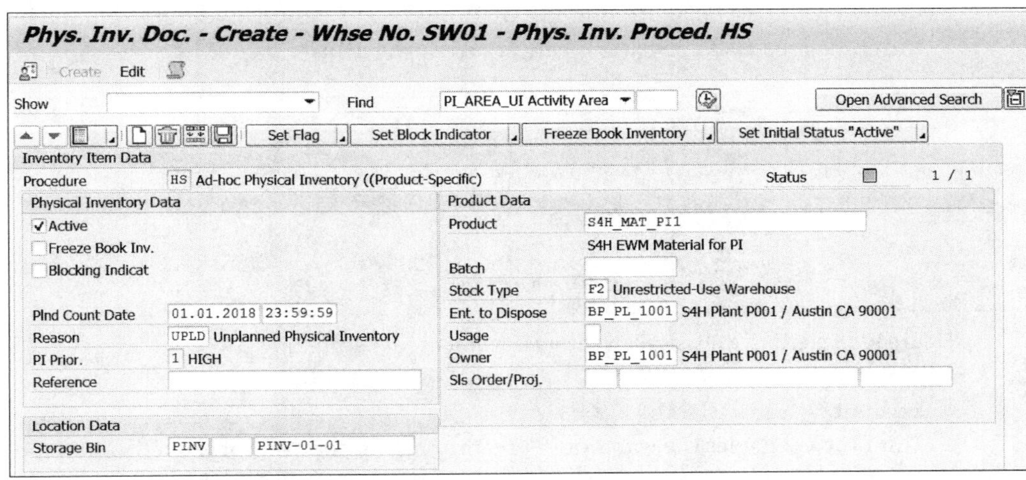

Figure 10.17 Structure of the Physical Inventory Document

10.4.2 Process a Physical Inventory Document

This is the second step in the physical inventory process, in which the physical inventory document created in the previous step is processed. You access the physical inventory document using the search field with reference to a physical inventory document number, reference request number, or warehouse order. You can process a physical inventory document via **SAP Easy Access** path **Logistics • SCM Extended Warehouse Management • Extended Warehouse Management • Physical Inventory • Process Physical Inventory Document**. As shown in Figure 10.18, change the inventory document status by clicking on the following buttons, which execute the required action:

- **Activate**
  This button sets the physical document status to **Active**.
- **Count**
  This button sets the physical document status to **Counted**. If required, you can also set the document status to **Recounted** by selecting the **Recount** option.
- **Change Count**
  This button enables the warehouse worker to change the inventory quantity on the physical inventory document for which the physical inventory process of count is done and the document is saved. It's specifically used in cases where the warehouse workers realize they made a mistake in the initial count. The **Change**

Count feature is available in the SAP GUI, the Count Physical Inventory app, and in the embedded EWM physical inventory counting RF user menu.

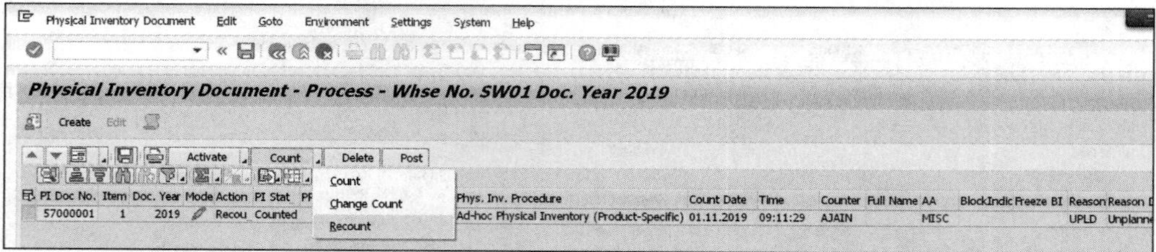

Figure 10.18 Setting a Physical Inventory Document for Recounting

- **Recount**
  This button enables the warehouse inventory manager to enforce a recount of the inventory quantity on the physical inventory document for which the physical inventory process of count is done and the document is saved. It's specifically used in cases where the count done by a warehouse worker is found to be above or below a tolerance limit of the inventory book quantity, and it's assumed that the worker made a mistake in the initial count. By using the **Recount** option as shown in Figure 10.18, a new version of the already counted physical inventory document is created and assigned to a warehouse worker. The new recount feature is available in SAP GUI, the Process Physical Inventory app, and the embedded EWM physical inventory RF user menu.

  The following explains the configuration and settings required to enable the assignment of a recounting physical inventory document to a warehouse worker different from the original counter:

  - **Avoid recount assigned to original counter**
    Until the latest version of embedded EWM, when working in the RF option of the physical inventory recount, the new physical inventory document created for recounting was assigned automatically to the original counter, and the same worker had to perform the count. With the latest version of embedded EWM, it's possible to assign the new physical inventory document created for recounting to another warehouse worker using the recounting queue. You can enable queue-based assignment of recount documents to a different warehouse worker by adding the queue in the **Queue for Recounting** field via IMG path **SCM Extended Warehouse Management • Extended Warehouse Management • Cross-Process Settings • Resource Management • Define Queues**, as shown in Figure 10.19.

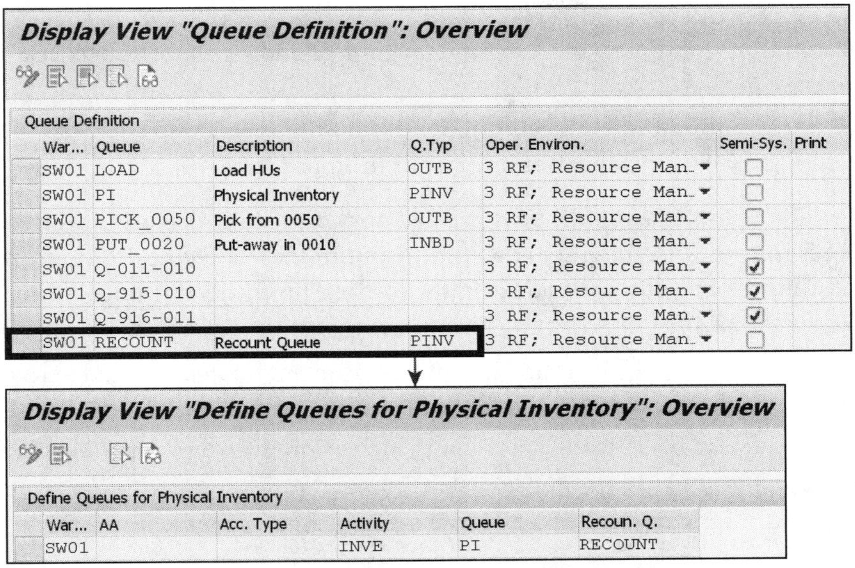

Display View "Queue Definition": Overview

Queue Definition

War...	Queue	Description	Q.Typ	Oper. Environ.	Semi-Sys.	Print
SW01	LOAD	Load HUs	OUTB	3 RF; Resource Man...	☐	
SW01	PI	Physical Inventory	PINV	3 RF; Resource Man...	☐	
SW01	PICK_0050	Pick from 0050	OUTB	3 RF; Resource Man...	☐	
SW01	PUT_0020	Put-away in 0010	INBD	3 RF; Resource Man...	☐	
SW01	Q-011-010			3 RF; Resource Man...	☑	
SW01	Q-915-010			3 RF; Resource Man...	☑	
SW01	Q-916-011			3 RF; Resource Man...	☑	
SW01	RECOUNT	Recount Queue	PINV	3 RF; Resource Man...	☐	

Display View "Define Queues for Physical Inventory": Overview

Define Queues for Physical Inventory

War...	AA	Acc. Type	Activity	Queue	Recoun. Q.
SW01			INVE	PI	RECOUNT

Figure 10.19 Defining and Assigning the Queue for Recounting during Physical Inventory

– **Activate recount queue to different warehouse worker**
  To ensure that a different warehouse worker is assigned to the recount physical inventory document based on the queue defined previously, you need to select the **Diff. User** checkbox in the physical-inventory-specific settings via IMG path **SCM Extended Warehouse Management • Extended Warehouse Management • Internal Warehouse Processes • Physical Inventory • Warehouse-Number-Specific Settings • Specify Physical-Inventory-Specific Settings in the Warehouse**, as shown in Figure 10.20.

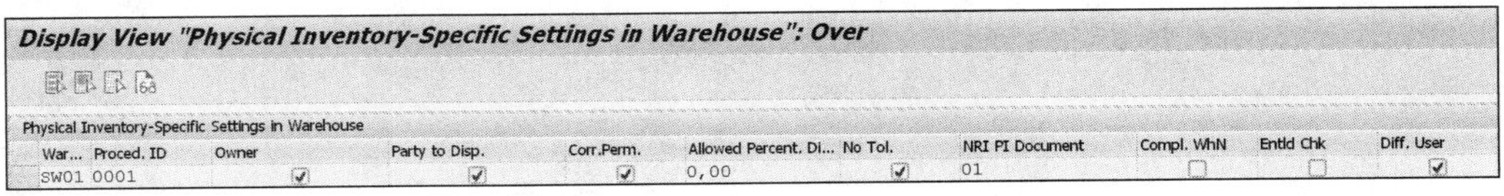

Display View "Physical Inventory-Specific Settings in Warehouse": Over

Physical Inventory-Specific Settings in Warehouse

War...	Proced. ID	Owner	Party to Disp.	Corr.Perm.	Allowed Percent. Di...	No Tol.	NRI PI Document	Compl. WhN	Entld Chk	Diff. User
SW01	0001	☑	☑	☑	0,00	☑	01	☐	☐	☑

Figure 10.20 Activating the Different User Queue Assignment for Recounting

These settings will ensure that the newly created recount physical inventory document will be assigned to a different warehouse worker to achieve correct count of the stock in the inventory.

- **Delete**
  This button is used to delete the inventory document and set the status to **Deletion Indicator Set**.
- **Post**
  This button is used to post the counting results in embedded EWM.

Based on tolerance limits set for the physical inventory procedure for a user, an error or warning is thrown when the user enters the count result in a physical inventory document. The count result can be added in the physical inventory document using the following methods:

- Count data can be added in a physical inventory document for line items added by the system for a product or an HU based on book inventory in embedded EWM.
- Count data can also be added for new items such as product stock or HU stock, which may not be proposed by embedded EWM.

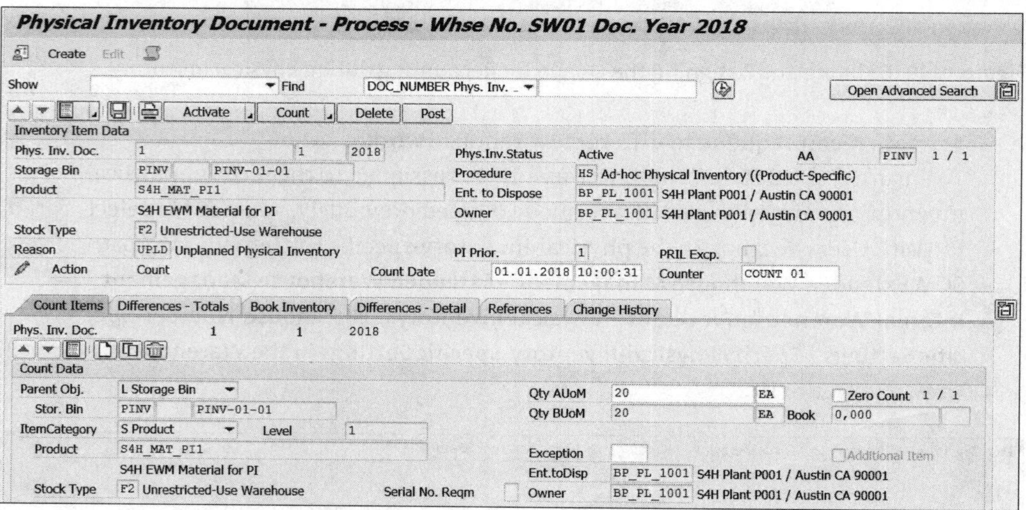

Figure 10.21 Processing the Physical Inventory Document

After the count results are captured in the physical inventory document, the document status changes from **Action** (as seen in Figure 10.21) to **Post Differences**, and the physical inventory status changes to **Counted**. As shown in Figure 10.22, if you click on the **Differences - Total** and **Differences - Detail** tabs, you can see the stock and HU difference count details. The **References** tab shows the warehouse order linked to the physical inventory document, and the **Change History** tab displays the sequence of actions taken on the physical inventory document.

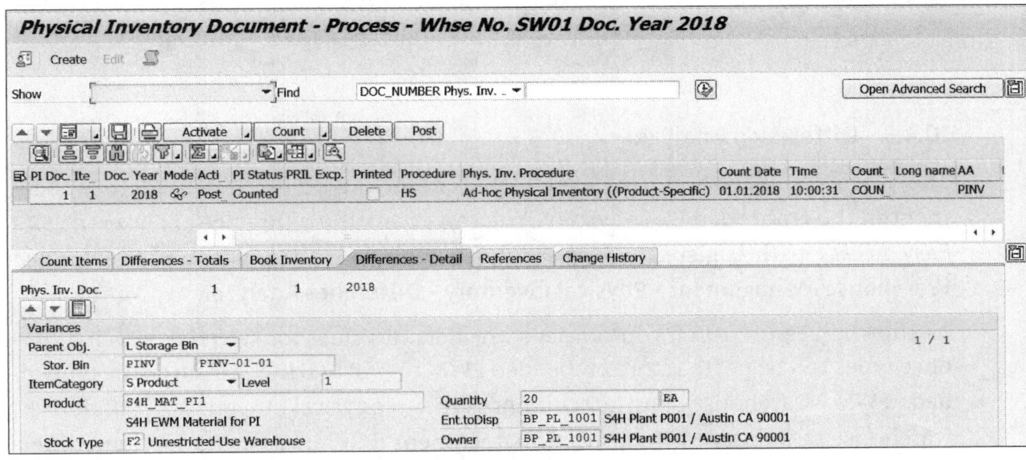

Figure 10.22 Difference Detail Tab after Entering and Saving Count Results

After capturing the count data in the physical inventory document, differences should be posted using the **Post** button. After posting the document, its status changes to **Posted**, and the action status changes to **blank**. The differences posted in this transaction clear the differences in the embedded EWM system only.

As shown in Figure 10.23, navigate to **SAP Easy Access** path **Logistics • SCM Extended Warehouse Management • Extended Warehouse Management • Physical Inventory • Create Phys. Inventory Count in the List**. Enter the number of either the physical inventory document or warehouse order, and click on [icon]. For the selected physical inventory document, enter the count result for all items or HUs of the physical inventory document in one screen.

Enter Count Results for Physical Inventory

Document Data
Warehouse No. SW01 LM Active
Document Year 2018
Phys. Inv. Doc. 2
Warehouse Order

Count Data
Counter STHANA2
Count Date 01.01.2018
Time 10:13:04

Phys. Inventory Doc. Item

PI Doc.	Item	Typ	Sec	Storage Bin	SBin Empty	HU	Product	Product Description	Qty	AUoM	AUn	AltVal Qty	AltVal UoM	Zero Count	ProdExists	ST	Exception
2	1	PINV		PINV-01-01	☐		S4H_MAT_PI1	S4H EWM Material for PI	35		EA			☐	☐	F2	

Figure 10.23 Entering the Count Result Using the Count List

> **Note**
>
> The Process Physical Inventory Documents app allows you to process physical inventory documents for execution and completion of the physical inventory process.

10.4.3 Difference Analyzer

The difference analyzer is used to get details of the posted physical inventory document in the embedded EWM system. You can access the difference analyzer via **SAP Easy Access** path **Logistics • SCM Extended Warehouse Management • Extended Warehouse Management • Physical Inventory • Difference Analyzer**.

As shown in Figure 10.24, you can set some default values for selecting which difference types can be posted from embedded EWM to SAP S/4HANA, such as the embedded EWM warehouse and document types (physical inventory differences, warehouse task differences, inspection document differences, pending claim differences, differences in VMware Update Manager [VUM], etc.).

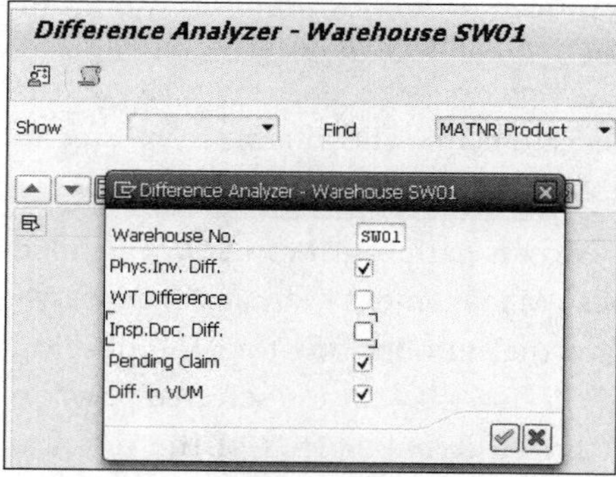

Figure 10.24 Selecting Default Settings for the Difference Analyzer

You can search the posted physical inventory documents using selection criteria such as product or priority. The difference analyzer, as shown in Figure 10.25, shows the difference between the counted quantity value and book quantity value as posted using the physical inventory document. You can **Add Notes** at the header and item levels in the difference analyzer program. You also can **Block** or **Release** the physical inventory document differences from posting to SAP S/4HANA. In addition, you can post the differences from the difference analyzer using the **Post** button.

The posted differences can be corrected from the difference analyzer tool, and stock types also can be changed. You also can post the individual items from the difference analyzer from embedded EWM to SAP S/4HANA. After you post the document, a material document is created in SAP S/4HANA. All the goods movement postings can be accessed in the SAP S/4HANA core using Transaction MB51 or **SAP Easy Access** path **Logistics • Materials Management • Physical Inventory • Environment • Material Document for Material**. Enter any of the item or header selection criteria, and click on [icon].

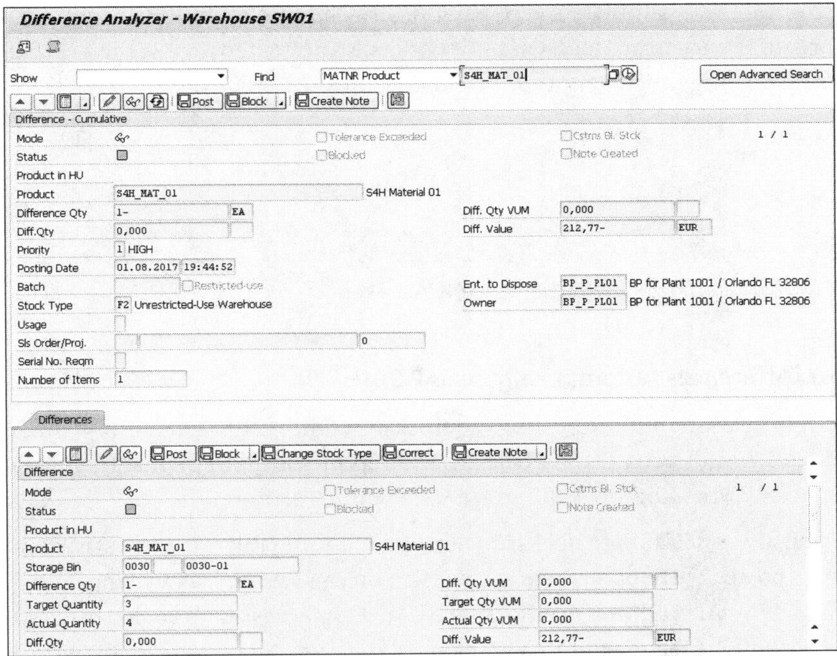

Figure 10.25 Difference Analyzer to Post Stock Difference to SAP S/4HANA

> **Note**
>
> The Analyze Differences app allows you to analyze differences between the counted and book inventory for further posting of stock in embedded EWM and SAP S/4HANA.

10.4.4 Stock Comparison with SAP S/4HANA

Embedded EWM provides a standard report to compare and post the differences between the stock situation in SAP S/4HANA and embedded EWM. It enables you to clear the differences from a single tool. SAP S/4HANA stock can be compared with embedded EWM stock and cleared using Transaction **/SCWM/ERP_STOCKCHECK**. It can also be accessed from **SAP Easy Access** path **Extended Warehouse Management • Physical Inventory • Periodic Processing • Stock Comparison ERP**.

As shown in Figure 10.26, you can see the stock quantity in SAP S/4HANA and embedded EWM. You can even simulate the posting via the **Simulation** button. When you post the stock difference from this UI, warehouse tasks are created to post the *+ve* and *-ve* differences, posting movement types 711 and 712 in SAP S/4HANA.

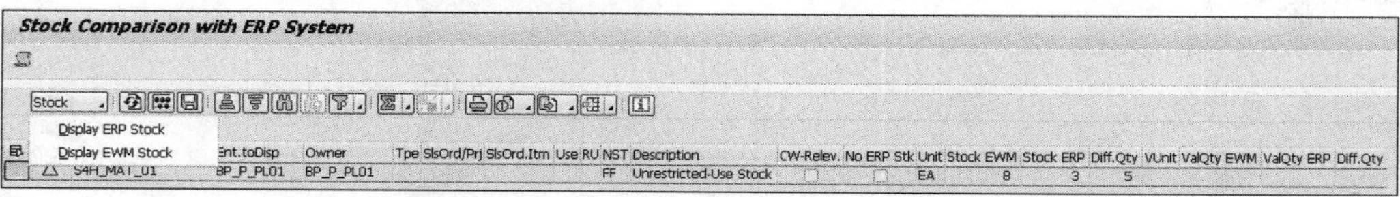

Figure 10.26 Stock Comparison with the SAP S/4HANA Report

10.4.5 Post Differences Automatically to SAP S/4HANA

Many business situations require posting the stock differences between SAP S/4HANA and embedded EWM directly from a background report without any manual intervention, especially when the stock differences are within tolerances.

It requires a business decision to determine up to what value tolerance the stock difference can be posted without any manual check. You can set this value using Transaction /SCWM/WM_ADJUST or by navigating to **SAP Easy Access** path **Logistics • SCM Extended Warehouse Management • Extended Warehouse Management • Physical Inventory • Periodic Processing • Post Differences to ERP System**. You can use filters such as warehouse, product, party entitled, owner, priority, reason, and physical inventory procedure. You also can choose which differences you want to clear. After entering the selection criteria, click on . To reduce any manual intervention, this report can be saved as a variant and run as a part of a background job.

Note

The Post Differences app allows you to post differences between the counted and book inventory for further posting of stock in embedded EWM.

10.5 Physical Inventory Using Paper-Driven Counting

The new SAP Fiori app in embedded EWM called Count Physical Inventory facilitates the physical inventory process, specifically where paper-driven counting is involved. The Count Physical Inventory app streamlines the physical inventory process for warehouse workers by enabling quick counting of products and HUs in the warehouse, filtering physical inventory documents based on storage type, activating/deactivating physical inventory documents, entering counted results, and printing physical inventory documents when needed.

Figure 10.27 shows the layout of the printouts of physical inventory documents, which can be used for printing physical inventory documents using both the SAP Fiori app and SAP GUI. You can configure this layout via IMG path **SCM EWM • Extended Warehouse Management • Internal Warehouse Processes • Physical Inventory • Print • Define Print Form For Physical Inventory Documents**.

Display View "Define Print Form for Physical Inventory Documents": Ove

Define Print Form for Physical Inventory Documents

Ware	Physical Inventory Area	PI Item	Stor. Bin	Bin Empty	HU	HU Comple.	HU Emp.	HU Missing	Nest. HU	Ne. HU Co.	Ne. HU Em.	Ne. HU M
SW01	SW01_1001	☑	☑	☑	☑	☐	☐	☐	☐	☐	☐	☐

Figure 10.27 Defining the Print Form for Physical Inventory Documents

As shown in Figure 10.28, you can choose whether to display the inventory quantity in the system at the time of count entry and determine this for each physical inventory area. You can also configure whether to ignore the setting for default stock type that is set on the warehouse level via IMG path **SCM EWM • Extended Warehouse Management • Internal Warehouse Processes • Physical Inventory • Physical-Inventory-Area-Specific Settings • Define Physical Inventory Area**.

Display View "Physical Inventory Area": Overview

Dialog Structure
- Physical Inventory Area
  - Permitted Document Types

Physical Inventory Area

Physical Inventory Area	Putaway PI	LSPI	LS Check	PstgAfterCount	Dsp. Qty	Prop. Qty	Dsp. Obj.
SW01_0001	☐	☑	☐	☐	☑	☐	☐
SW01_1001	☑	☑	☑	☑	☑	☑	☑

Figure 10.28 Enabling Book Quantity Display in Physical Inventory Documents

As shown in Figure 10.29, you can choose whether to display the default stock type during physical inventory counting for each warehouse via IMG path **SCM EWM • Extended Warehouse Management • Master Data • Define Warehouse Number Control**.

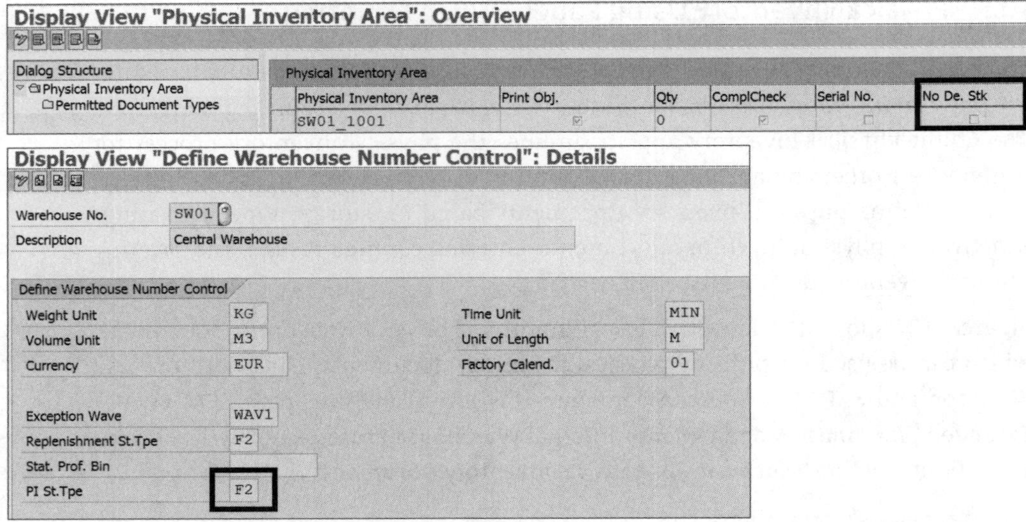

Figure 10.29 Defining Default Stock Type at the Physical Inventory Area

As mentioned earlier, paper-driven counting of stock in the warehouse can done using the Count Physical Inventory app. As shown in Figure 10.30, the initial screen of the app is used for filtering the physical inventory documents using various filtering criteria such as storage type, storage bin, physical inventory procedure, physical inventory reason, physical inventory document status, and so on. From the same screen, various other operations can be performed such as physical inventory document activation, deactivation, printing, and counting, among others.

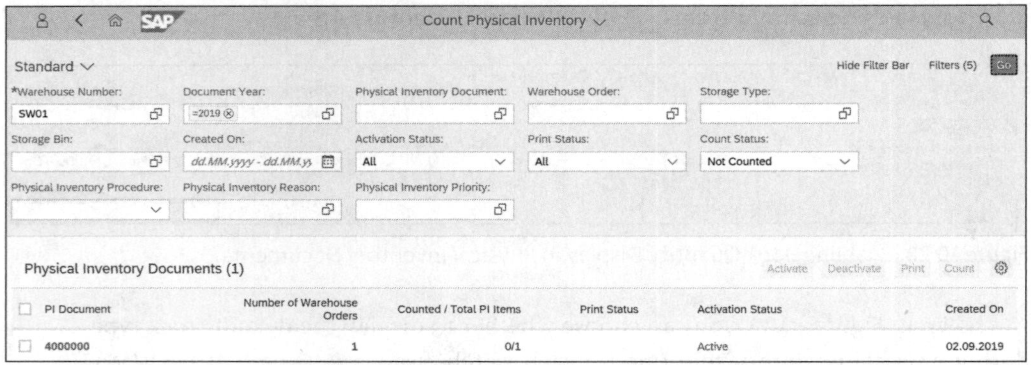

Figure 10.30 Physical Inventory Document Filtering Criteria in the Paper-Based Count Physical Inventory App

Because it's a paper-driven counting process, by clicking on the **Print** button shown in Figure 10.31, you can print the physical inventory document and use it to record product/HU counts.

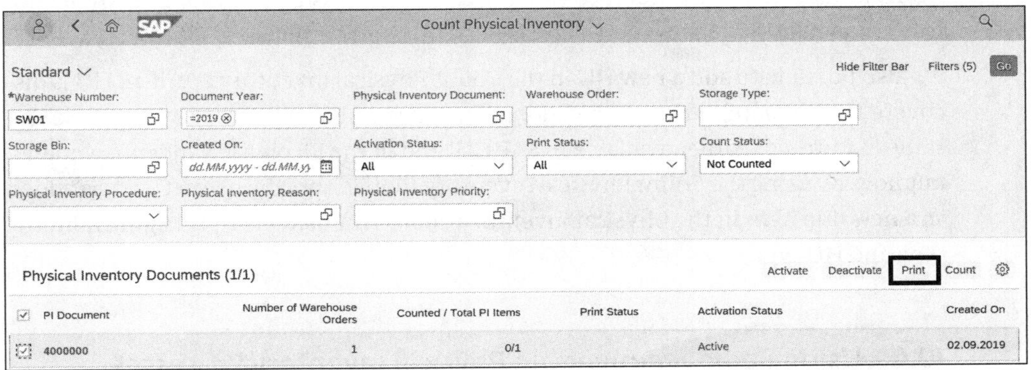

Figure 10.31 Printing the Physical Inventory Document Using the Paper-Based Count Physical Inventory App

The product/HU count, if required, can again be added to the physical inventory document in the system for posting by manually entering it in **Quantity** field in edit mode, as shown in Figure 10.32.

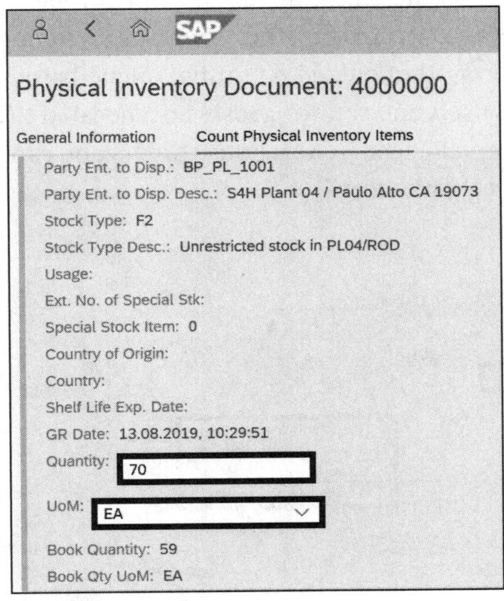

Figure 10.32 Entering Stock Quantity Using the Paper-Based Count Physical Inventory App

After the count results are added in the system using this app, further processing of stock difference analysis and posting can be done using the Analyze Differences app of embedded EWM. After the posting of difference analysis is successfully performed from embedded EWM, difference clearing can be done as part of the standard inventory reconciliation process between SAP S/4HANA and embedded EWM.

It's also possible to add a new HU in the Count Physical Inventory app if an HU is discovered in the warehouse bin that didn't exist in the book inventory of the stock. The same feature was earlier available in SAP GUI and in the RF physical inventory menu, but now, by using the Count Physical Inventory mobile app, the new HU can be added as a new line item in the physical inventory document using the packaging material type and HU type.

10.6 Using Radio Frequency in Physical Inventory Processes

Physical inventory counting can also be carried out using the RF framework along with manual processes. The RF UI for physical inventory can be accessed using Transaction /SCWM/RFUI or via the RF menu at **SAP Easy Access** path **Logistics • SCM Extended Warehouse Management • Extended Warehouse Management • Execution • Log On to RF Environment**.

As shown in Figure 10.33, the RF framework provides counting options for completing the stock/HU count. The RF UI provides two options for stock counting: system-guided counting and manual counting. For system-guided counting, queue-based warehouse order assignment to resources is used, and counting tasks are allocated to counters. For manual counting, you can manually feed in warehouse orders and can perform standard product-/bin-based physical inventory.

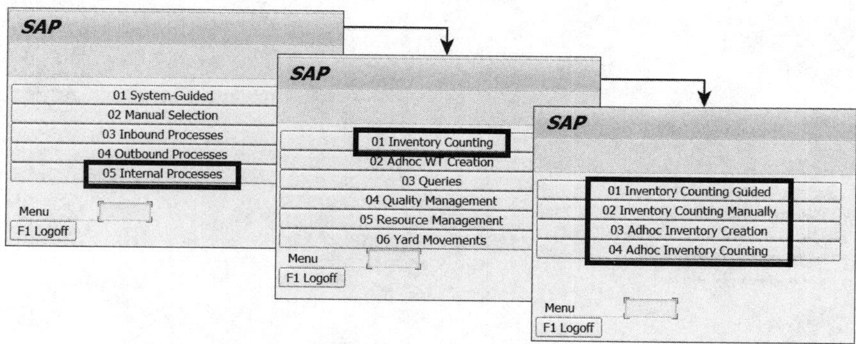

Figure 10.33 Physical Inventory Using the RF UI

There are three distinct scenarios available for RF-based physical inventory:

- **Standard counting**
  Use a physical inventory document to perform counting using a manual or system-guided process in the RF device. The device automatically records the counter, date, and count result in the system.
- **Ad hoc counting**
  Perform physical inventory counting without using a physical inventory document. Start by adding a storage bin in which you want to perform counting. The system automatically creates a physical inventory document and records the time and counter.
- **Collective counting**
  If the storage bin is HU-managed, then you can perform a physical inventory using collective counting using RF devices. You may encounter two scenarios here:
  - **Verifying the number of HUs:** You can enter the number of HUs in the bin; if the number matches the number of HUs in the system, then you'll see a message indicating the process is **Complete**.
  - **Verifying content of HUs:** You can enter the number of products in the bin in full and partial HUs; if the count matches with the product count in the system, then the physical inventory for all the HUs will be marked as **Complete**.

10.7 Summary

This chapter introduced basic concepts of physical inventory and the process of physical inventory in embedded EWM. We explained the basic settings for physical inventory in embedded EWM as well. Documents created as part of the physical inventory process and the status of the documents during and after the process were explained with the help of examples. You should now be able to perform simple and cycle counting physical inventory processes in embedded EWM and use RF for physical inventory processes. You should also be able to work on physical inventory reports and use them in tracking various data points in the physical inventory process. By using the SAP Fiori Count Physical Inventory app for paper-driven counting, you now also know how to enter unknown or misplaced HUs directly in physical inventory documents during counting. In the next chapter, we will discuss resource management.

Chapter 11
Resource Management

In this chapter, we'll discuss warehouse resources, which can refer to people or equipment. Resource management is used in embedded EWM for optimizing the allocation of work to these resources.

Because warehouse workers and equipment are the resources that move stock in the warehouse, utilizing and tracking them in the warehouse is an important part of warehouse management. This is done using resource management in embedded EWM. Both workers and equipment are mapped as resource master data in embedded EWM, and executable workloads, in the form of warehouse orders, are assigned to the resources using queues. Embedded EWM uses queues as master data; they act as an assignment link between the workload—that is, warehouse orders—and resources in embedded EWM. Warehouse orders are assigned to resources either automatically or manually by warehouse supervisors. Resource management can be further integrated with radio frequency (RF) to simplify execution of warehouse processes even more.

In this chapter, we explain configuration settings, master data, and processes in resource management in embedded EWM. Section 11.1 explains configuration settings and master data for resources and queues, including assignment of queues to resources, which enables the workload to be assigned to the resources. Section 11.2 explains how resource management is executed in embedded EWM and walks through a sample process to show how the workload is assigned to resources. Section 11.3 details using RF and system- and semi-system-guided processing in resource management. Section 11.4 explains task interleaving, which is used to optimize resource movement in the warehouse. Section 11.5 explains pick, pack, and pass, which enables a single pick handling unit (pick HU) to complete multiple warehouse pick orders. This helps to optimize the picking process further. Finally, Section 11.6 explains the resource execution constraint with which you can control the number of resources in any area of the warehouse at one point in time.

11.1 What Is Resource Management?

Workers and equipment performing warehouse tasks are referred to as *resources* in embedded EWM. Because optimized use of resources is essential for warehouse productivity, assigning warehouse orders to the right resource at the correct time is crucial for an efficient warehouse. This is where resource management comes into play. Resource management is critical in a warehouse for the following reasons:

- Providing effective utilization of warehouse resources
- Managing the number of warehouse operators required in the warehouse
- Minimizing the amount of *deadheading* in the warehouse—the time during which the resource travels empty
- Helping overcome resource capacity constraints, thus improving warehouse efficiency

Resource management in embedded EWM helps ensure effective utilization of resources by dividing work packages in the form of warehouse orders into queues. The assigned work can be executed by the resource in both RF- and non-RF-based environments. The embedded EWM warehouse monitor provides a single interface to monitor and control resources and workloads in the warehouse, which makes it easier for the warehouse supervisor to manage and distribute the workload. In the following sections, we explain the business context in which resource management can be used and the processes carried out in the system.

11.1.1 Business Process

American company Alpha Medicals optimizes its product placement and picking process using various mechanical as well as human resources. The warehouse of Alpha Medicals uses robots, dollies, and other mechanical and automatic product-handling resources that the warehouse workers can use to move the stock in the warehouse in a planned manner. To ensure that such movement of warehouse stock is executed, planned, and captured for reporting using handling and human resources in an optimized manner in the embedded EWM system, the company has implemented resource management in embedded EWM.

Figure 11.1 shows a scenario in which stock movement is carried out using resource management in embedded EWM. The warehouse worker receives a warehouse request to complete the stock movement from source to destination bin. The material handling equipment planned and used in embedded EWM is selected by the system and assigned to the warehouse worker in an optimized manner by taking the master data of resource and resource-related constraints into consideration.

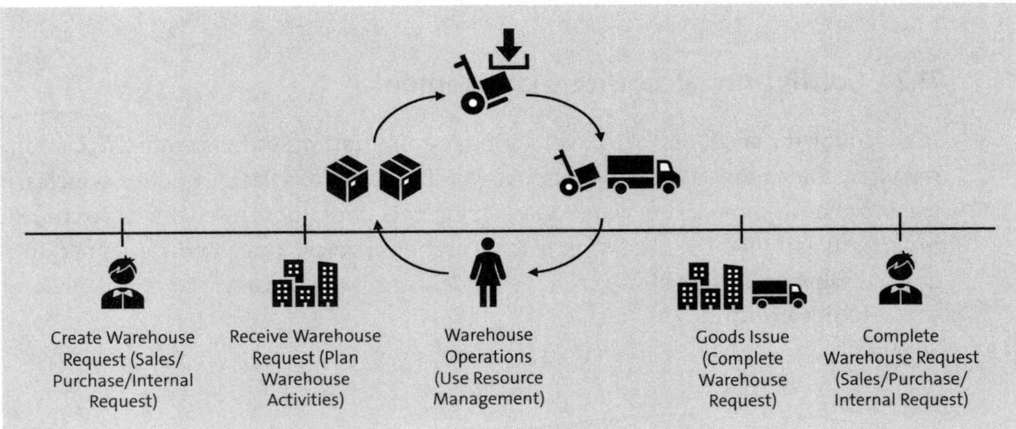

Figure 11.1 Business Flow Using Resource Management

11.1.2 System Process

Many master data and transactional documents are used for resource management planning and execution in embedded EWM and are fed as parameters for resource management execution. The following explains the steps to be performed in the system to execute resource management:

1. Based on demand, stock movement tasks, and resource parameters, the warehouse tasks are created for stock movement within the warehouse for warehouse workers and warehouse resources.
2. Warehouse workers use the resources in the warehouse and move the stock from the source bin to the destination bin.
3. All the data regarding the planned and actual execution details of warehouse tasks using resources is captured in embedded EWM.
4. The captured data as part of previous steps is analyzed by the warehouse administrator to change the resource optimization strategy and attributes for the next day's pick.

> **Note**
>
> We've explained the system process using the outbound process only. It's equally applicable to inbound and internal stock movement processes.

11.2 Configuring Resource Management

In the following sections, we'll cover various configuration settings required to set up resource management in the warehouse. We'll begin by discussing queues, which are used to allocate work in the warehouse. Queues are containers into which warehouse orders are assigned for execution. Each warehouse resource group is assigned to a queue sequence, from which warehouse orders are assigned to resources that belong to a resource group.

11.2.1 Define Queue Types

In this setting, we assign the queue to queue types. Various types of queues are created in embedded EWM for inbound, outbound, and internal warehouse processes to execute processes more efficiently. Queue types are used when you configure interleaving in an RF environment, which we'll discuss later in this chapter. You define queue types from IMG path **SCM Extended Warehouse Management • Extended Warehouse Management • Cross-Process Settings • Resource Management • Define Queue Types**. Once there, click on **New Entries**, and define queue types for the embedded EWM warehouse, as shown in Figure 11.2.

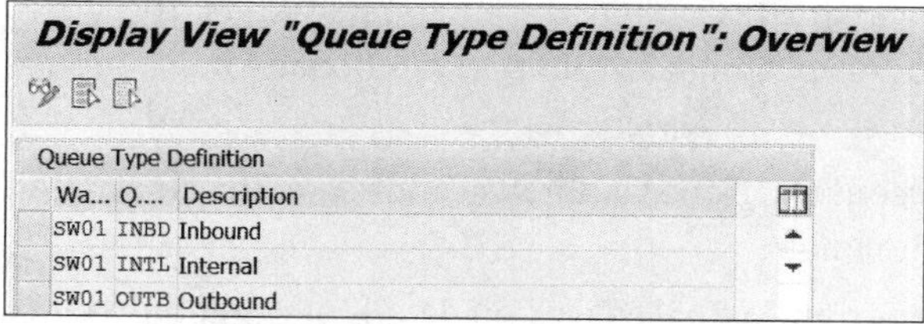

Wa...	Q....	Description
SW01	INBD	Inbound
SW01	INTL	Internal
SW01	OUTB	Outbound

Figure 11.2 Defining Queue Types

11.2.2 Define Queues

A queue defines a logical container to which warehouse orders are assigned. Resources are assigned to resource groups, which are assigned to queue sequences. A resource can only work with the warehouse orders assigned to the queue to which the resource is assigned, unless the warehouse order is manually assigned. The settings to define queues in embedded EWM can be accessed from IMG path **SCM Extended Warehouse Management • Extended Warehouse Management • Cross-Process Settings • Resource Management • Define Queues**. Three configuration settings need to be maintained within this node:

- **Queue Definition**
  In this setting, you define the queues that need to be set up in the warehouse. The warehouse order is assigned to a queue, which is then assigned to a resource. The queue can also determine the nature of warehouse orders assigned to a resource. Click on **Define Queues**, and then click on **New Entries** to define new queues for a queue type. Select the operative environment for the queue by selecting a value from **Oper. Environ.**, as shown in Figure 11.3.

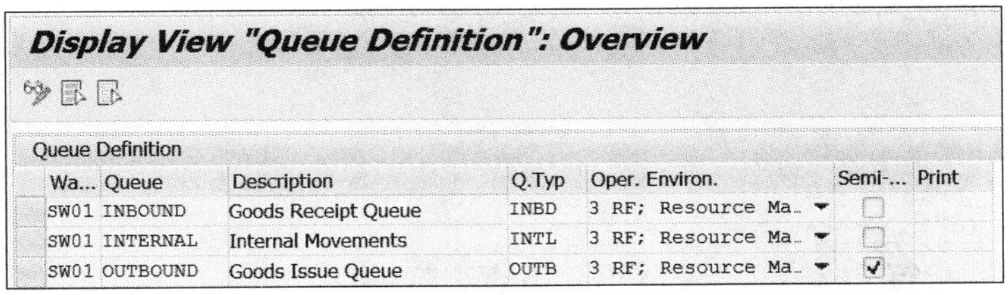

Display View "Queue Definition": Overview

Queue Definition

Wa...	Queue	Description	Q.Typ	Oper. Environ.	Semi-...	Print
SW01	INBOUND	Goods Receipt Queue	INBD	3 RF; Resource Ma...	☐	
SW01	INTERNAL	Internal Movements	INTL	3 RF; Resource Ma...	☐	
SW01	OUTBOUND	Goods Issue Queue	OUTB	3 RF; Resource Ma...	☑	

Figure 11.3 Defining Queues for Resource Management

  The operating environment defines whether the queue is part of RF, the material flow system, or paper-based resource management processing. A resource working with an operating environment can only execute warehouse orders belonging to a queue in the same operating environment. You can also specify if the queue can be used for semi-system-guided processing.

Example

There are various reasons for creating different types of queues in embedded EWM. For example, queues can be created based on the nature of warehouse processes, so you could have queues named *inbound*, *outbound*, and *internal*. Any warehouse order for putaway can be configured to always be assigned to the inbound queue;

similarly, any warehouse order for internal stock movement, such as physical inventory or replenishment, can always be assigned to the internal queue.

Another logical way to create queues is based on the geographical layout of the warehouse. For example, if a large warehouse complex has doors in the northern and southern parts of the warehouse, then you might have north-inbound and south-inbound queues. Thus, only warehouse orders for putaway from the north gate are assigned to the north-inbound queues. This helps avoid unnecessary movement of resources throughout the warehouse.

- **Access Queue Determination Criteria**
  In this section, you define the criteria for determination of the queue for a warehouse task. When a warehouse order is created, the system looks for the following criteria to determine the queue for the warehouse order. Select **Queue Determination Criteria**, and assign the queue to a combination of input criteria (see Figure 11.4):
  - Source activity area
  - Destination activity area
  - Bin access type
  - Warehouse process type
  - Activity

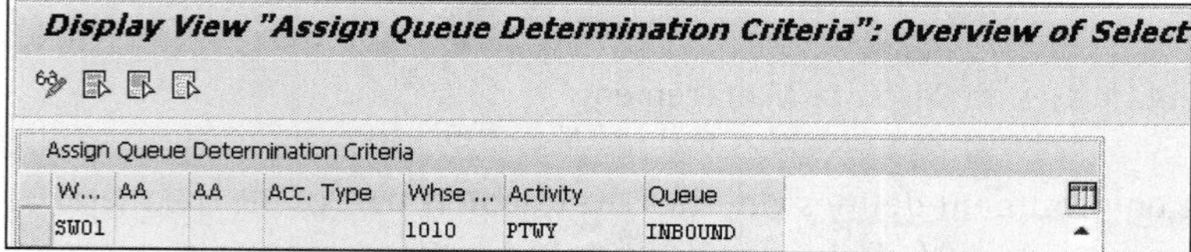

Figure 11.4 Defining the Queue Determination Criteria

- **Queue Access Sequence**
  Because various combinations are possible for determination of the queue, you can use the queue access sequence to help the system perform an optimized search based on a preferred access sequence. Select **Define Queue Access Sequences**, and define a new sequence number in **Seq. No.**, which lists preferences for the determination criteria, as shown in Figure 11.5. The system first looks for all fields in the warehouse task that match the first line in the access sequence; if it

doesn't find any of the fields, then it moves on to the next line in the access sequence.

Display View "Queue Access Sequence": Overview of Selected Set

Queue Access Sequence

W...	Seq. No.	Srce Area	Dest. Area	Stor. Bin	Proc. Type	Activity
SW01	1	☐	☐	☐	☑	☐
SW01	2	☑	☐	☐	☐	☐
SW01	3	☐	☑	☐	☐	☐

Figure 11.5 Defining the Queue Access Sequence

11.2.3 Define Resource Types

Resource types are used to group resources with similar technical or physical qualifications. You can define resources from IMG path **SCM Extended Warehouse Management • Extended Warehouse Management • Cross-Process Settings • Resource Management • Define Resource Type**; once there, click on **New Entries**, and define a new resource type with the following fields, as shown in Figure 11.6:

- **No Interleaving**
  This setting deactivates task interleaving for resources created using this resource type.
- **ResTypeVel**
  This represents the horizontal velocity of the resource and is used to determine the latest start date of a warehouse order.
- **Velocity Z**
  This represents the vertical velocity of the resource.
- **UoM**
  This field stores the unit of measurement (UoM) in which the velocity is specified.

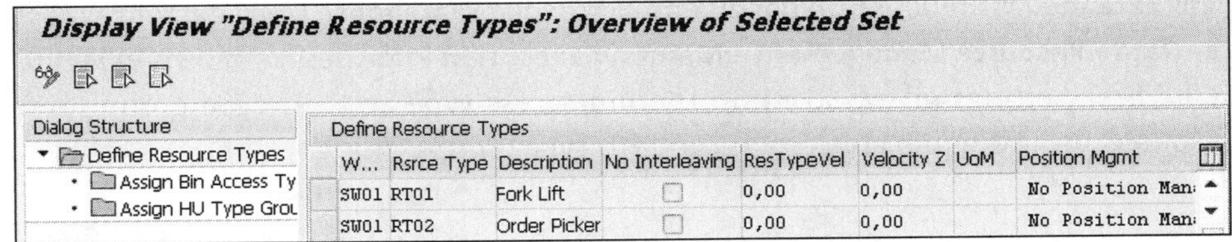

Display View "Define Resource Types": Overview of Selected Set

Dialog Structure
- Define Resource Types
  - Assign Bin Access Ty
  - Assign HU Type Grou

Define Resource Types

W...	Rsrce Type	Description	No Interleaving	ResTypeVel	Velocity Z	UoM	Position Mgmt
SW01	RT01	Fork Lift	☐	0,00	0,00		No Position Man:
SW01	RT02	Order Picker	☐	0,00	0,00		No Position Man:

Figure 11.6 Defining the Resource Type

- **Position Mgmt**
  This specifies whether position management is used. Position management helps an RF user find HUs by their position numbers rather than HU labels. This is useful when the HUs are stacked on top of one another.

As shown in Figure 11.7, within the same setting, you can assign a resource type to a bin access type by selecting **Assign Bin Access Types**; this limits the bins the resource has access to. You can also assign the resource type to an HU type group by selecting **Assign HU Type Groups**; this limits the types of HUs the resource has access to.

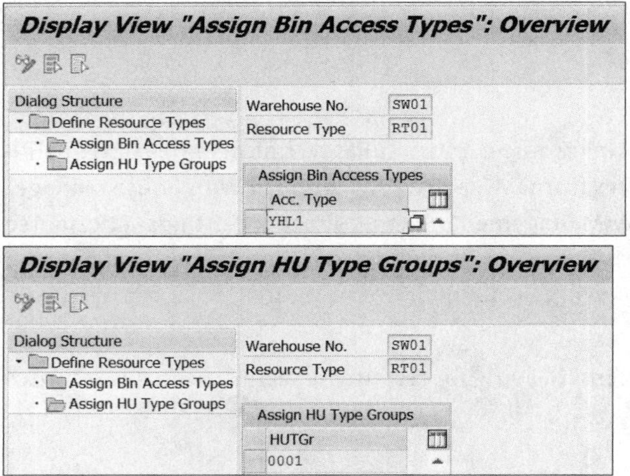

Figure 11.7 Assigning Bin Access Type and HU Type Group to the Resource Type

11.2.4 Maintain Execution Priorities for Resource Types

Execution priorities can be assigned to bin access types and HU type groups that are assigned to resource types by selecting the options **Maintain Bin Access Type Priority Value** and **Maintain HU Type Grp Priority Value** via **SAP Easy Access** path **Logistics • SCM Extended Warehouse Management • Extended Warehouse Management • Master Data • Resource Management • Maintain Execution Priorities,** as shown in Figure 11.8. These settings give priority to the bin access type and HU type group for a resource over other bin access types and HU type groups.

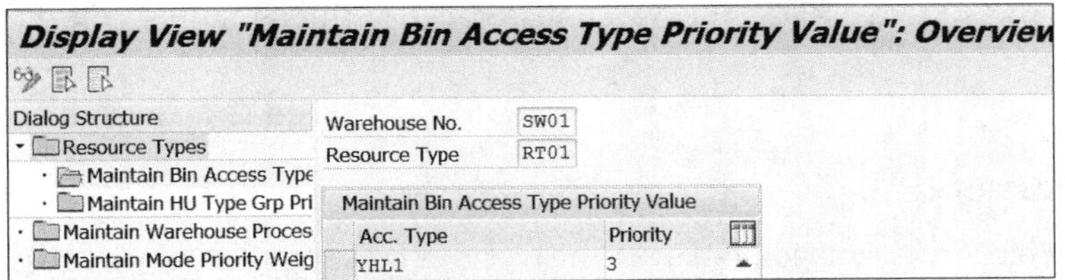

Figure 11.8 Assigning Priorities for the Resource Type

11.2.5 Define the Resource Group

A resource group is used to group resources together, and these groups are then used for queue sequence assignment. This assignment is used for system-guided processing. From Transaction /SCWM/RGRP, which can also be accessed from **SAP Easy Access** path **Logistics • SCM Extended Warehouse Management • Extended Warehouse Management • Master Data • Resource Management • Maintain Resource Group**, click on **New Entries** to define a new resource group.

As shown in Figure 11.9, the queues are assigned to a resource group in the proper sequence to use system-guided processing. To do this, navigate to **SAP Easy Access** path **Logistics • SCM Extended Warehouse Management • Extended Warehouse Management • Master Data • Resource Management • Maintain Queue Sequence for Resource Group** or use Transaction /SCWM/QSEQ, click on **New Entries**, and then map queues to resource groups to form a sequence.

Display View "Queue Sequence Per Resource Group": Overview

Warehouse No. SW01

Queue Sequence Per Resource Group

Rsrce Grp	Sequence No.	Queue	No Interleaving
RG01	1	INBOUND	☐
RG01	2	OUTBOUND	☐
RG01	3	INTERNAL	☐

Figure 11.9 Assigning the Queue Sequence to the Resource Group

The warehouse tasks and warehouse orders are assigned to the queues based on the queue determination criteria discussed earlier. When a resource logs on to the system, that resource can pick up the next open warehouse order assigned to the queue in the queue sequence. If there are no warehouse orders in the first queue in the queue sequence, the system assigns the warehouse order in the next queue in the queue sequence.

11.2.6 Define Resource

After configuring resource management, it's time to move on to setting up resources in embedded EWM. As shown in Figure 11.10, you can create a resource from Transaction /SCWM/RSRC, which can also be accessed from **SAP Easy Access** path **Logistics • SCM Extended Warehouse Management • Extended Warehouse Management • Master Data • Define Resource**.

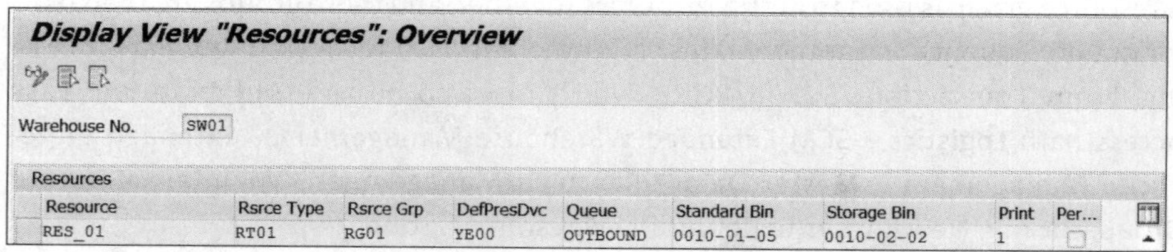

Figure 11.10 Defining Resources

Using this setting, assign the following control parameters to the resource:

- **Rsrce Type**
  The resource type constrains the access type of bins for a resource and the HU types that the resource can access.
- **Rsrce Grp**
  The resource group groups together resources with the same attributes.
- **DefPresDvc**
  The default presentation device for RF allows you to log on to a presentation screen as soon as a resource logs on to an RF device.
- **Queue**
  The queue is used to assign warehouse orders to a resource.
- **Standard Bin**
  This field assigns a default storage bin as the current bin of the resource if the resource isn't assigned to a current storage bin.
- **Storage Bin**
  This field is used to set the current storage bin of a resource and to calculate travel distance for the resource from the current bin to the source bin in the warehouse order.

- **Print**
  This setting is used to control the printing (on/off) of the warehouse order assigned to the queues.
- **Perf. Meas.**
  The RF performance measurement setting allows for performance measurement of RF transactions.

Assign a resource directly to a queue from Transaction /SCWM/RSRC or from the warehouse monitor. Figure 11.11 shows how to assign a queue to a resource via the warehouse monitor.

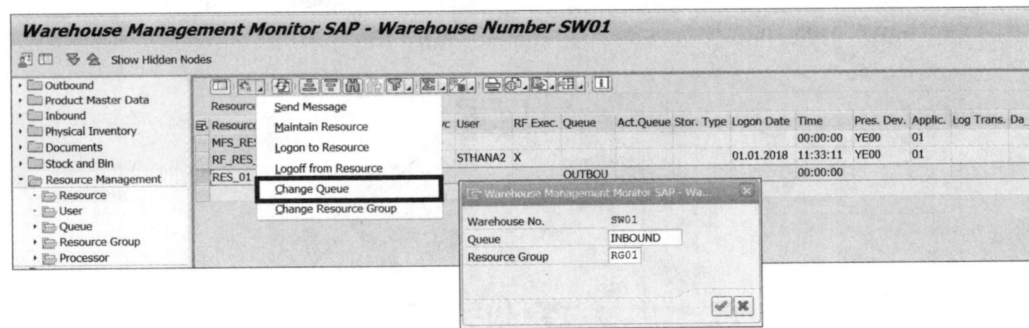

Figure 11.11 Assigning the Queue to the Resource in the Warehouse Monitor

You also can assign a queue sequence to a resource group. This is done from Transaction /SCWM/QSEQ, which also can be accessed from **SAP Easy Access** path **Logistics • SCM Extended Warehouse Management • Extended Warehouse Management • Master Data • Resource Management • Maintain Queue Sequence for Resource Group**. Click on **New Entries**, and assign a sequence of queues to a resource group, as shown in Figure 11.12.

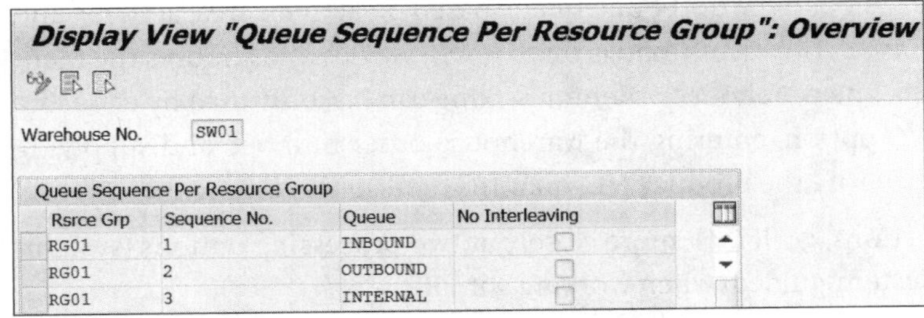

Display View "Queue Sequence Per Resource Group": Overview

Warehouse No. SW01

Queue Sequence Per Resource Group

Rsrce Grp	Sequence No.	Queue	No Interleaving
RG01	1	INBOUND	☐
RG01	2	OUTBOUND	☐
RG01	3	INTERNAL	☐

Figure 11.12 Assigning Resource Groups to Queues

11.3 Radio Frequency

Resource management executes processes using both RF and non-RF environments. As shown in Figure 11.13, resource management execution involves assignment of warehouse orders to resources manually or automatically. For manual assignments, both RF and non-RF environments are used. A resource can select the next warehouse order for processing manually or can pick up a warehouse order that is assigned by the warehouse supervisor. The warehouse supervisor can print the warehouse order and hand it over to the resource for manual execution. Automatic assignment of a warehouse order to a resource can only be done using queues and RF environments. The warehouse order should be assigned to a queue in which a resource is allowed to work.

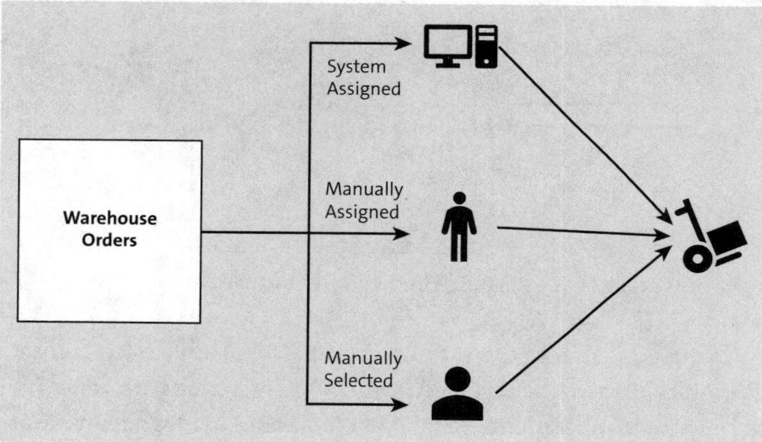

Figure 11.13 Executing Warehouse Orders Using Resource Management

In the example shown in Figure 11.14, the warehouse order for picking the outbound delivery order is assigned to the outbound queue based on activity area, activity, and warehouse process type. The resource logs on to the RF device and chooses the **Manual Selection** option. The warehouse order for picking can be confirmed by choosing the **Selection by WO** option, entering the warehouse order number, and supplying the data required to verify the product/HU, quantity, and source bin.

In the following sections, we'll look more closely at two processing options (system-guided and semi-system-guided) when working with RF.

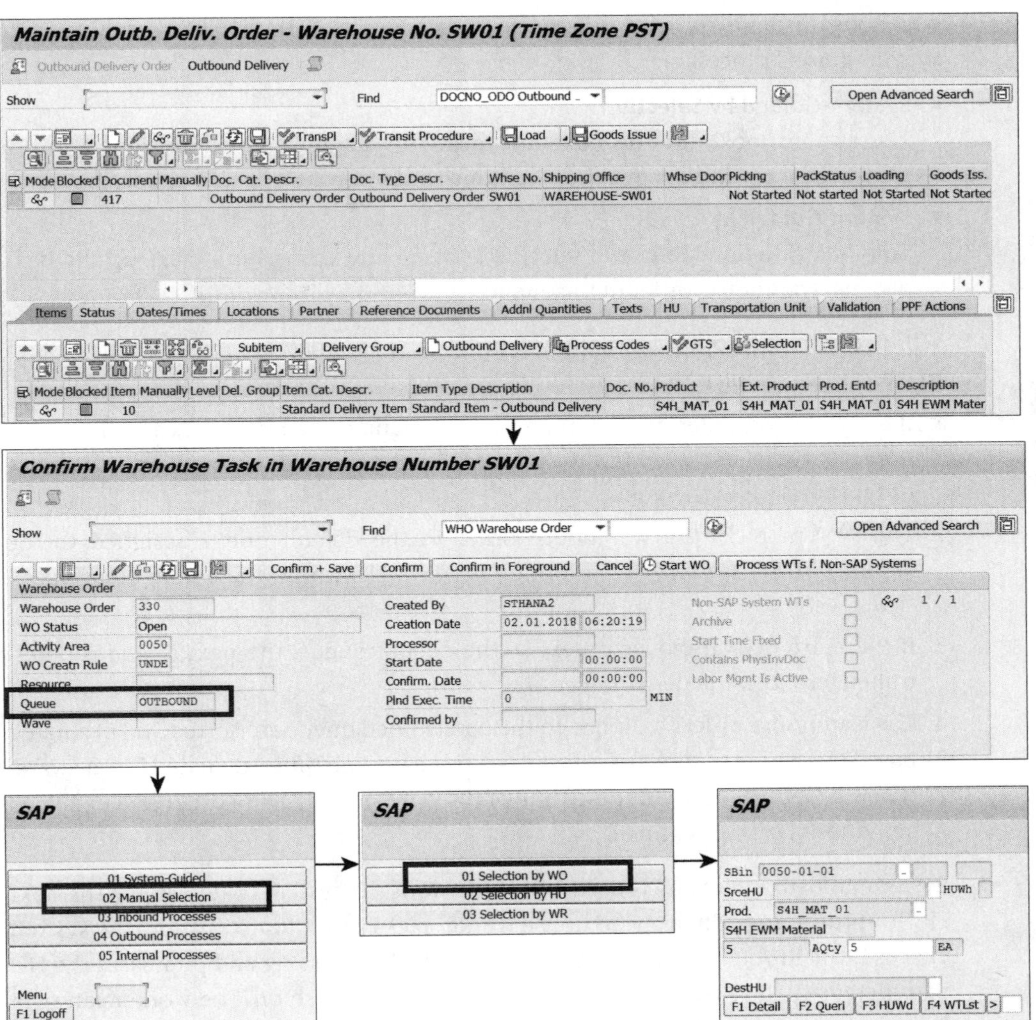

Figure 11.14 Confirming Warehouse Tasks Using Manual Selection

11.3.1 System-Guided Processing

System-guided processing is used when you want the system to determine the next warehouse order to be allocated to a resource. This is determined based on the queue types assigned to the resource groups and the queue determination criteria discussed in Section 11.2.2. Use system-guided processing when you use RF to confirm warehouse orders. You can select one of two menu options when working with system-guided processing:

- **System-Guided by Selection**
  The system looks for the next queue in the queue sequence assigned to the resource group and assigns the warehouse order for the selected queue.
- **System-Guided by Queue**
  You assign the queue in the selection screen, and the system picks up the next optimal warehouse order in the queue.

While selecting the optimal warehouse order to be assigned to a resource, the system makes the following checks:

1. If a warehouse order has been manually assigned to a resource, then this warehouse order is displayed in the system-guided process if there are no warehouse orders before it in the queue.
2. The system picks the warehouse order in the default queue assigned to the resource if the system-guided option is selected without the queue being specified.
3. If there are no warehouse orders in the default queue, the next queue is determined based on queue sequence.
4. The warehouse orders assigned to the determined queue are sorted and evaluated based on criteria such as priority, latest start date, and time calculated for the warehouse order from the shipping time of the outbound delivery order and expected activities of storage control.

System-guided processing is used when you want the system to determine the next HU for processing. When a warehouse worker picks a task for execution, the system checks if the RF execution is set to system-guided processing and populates the HU with details such as HU number, product, quantity, and so on. The worker can scan the required HU from the storage bin and confirm the warehouse task.

To return to the example from the start of this section, for system-guided execution, a resource logs on to the RF device and chooses the **01 System-Guided** option. The warehouse order for picking task can be confirmed by choosing one of the following options:

- **1 System-Guided Selection**
- **2 System-Guided by Queue**

If option **1** is selected, the system picks the first warehouse order assigned to the queue in the queue sequence, as shown in Figure 11.15. If you select option **2**, you can choose a queue, for example, the outbound queue. The system displays the first warehouse order assigned to the queue, and you can confirm the warehouse order by supplying the data required to verify the product/HU, quantity, and source bin.

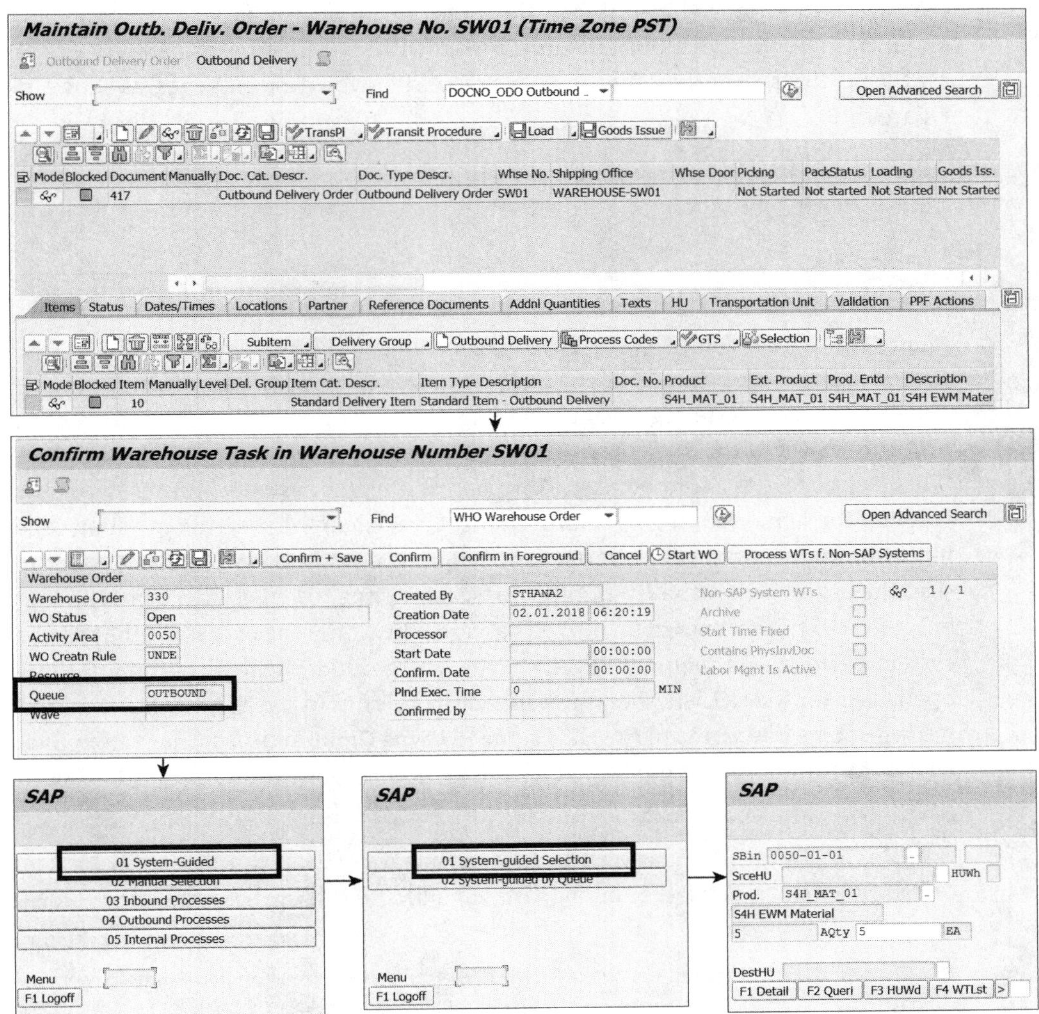

Figure 11.15 System-Guided Warehouse Task Confirmation

11.3.2 Semi-System-Guided Processing

Semi-system-guided processing is used within the system-guided mode. If you have more than one HU in a storage bin, system-guided processing can be time-consuming and tedious; it means that warehouse workers will have to spend time looking for specific HUs. Use semi-system-guided processing when you want the system to guide the user to the storage bin and then allow the user to pick any HU that is accessible and meets all selection requirements. To work with semi-system-guided processing, set the **Semi-sys.** checkbox for the queue type when you define queues, as shown in Figure 11.16.

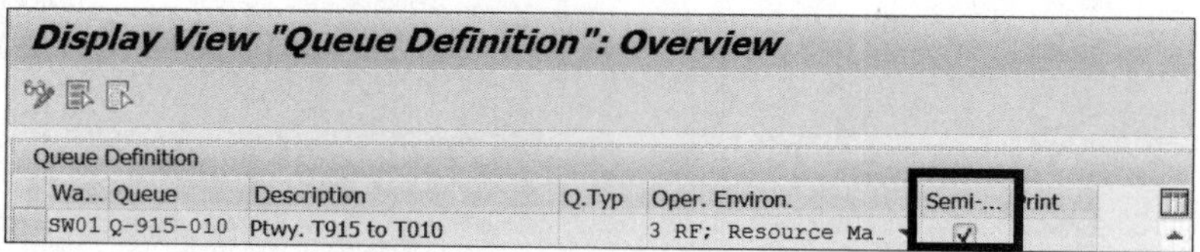

Figure 11.16 Activating the Semi-System-Guided Warehouse Task Execution

You can use semi-system-guided processing when you store one HU per storage bin or for picking from work centers from which you want to work with specific HUs. When a user selects a warehouse task for processing, the system checks if the queue is set up for semi-system-guided processing. If yes, then the system only shows the bin name and scans the field for bin verification. The **HU** field is left blank. A user can scan the bin and enter the HU number by scanning the HU label. This helps the user enter the HU number based on the HU's accessibility. After the user scans the HU, the system performs all required checks in the background, such as checking for any open tasks for the HU, whether the scanned HU belongs to the right storage bin, and if the resource has access to the HU via the **HU Type Group** settings. The system then allows the warehouse task to be confirmed.

> **Note**
>
> The warehouse task is locked during system-guided processing.

> **Note**
>
> The Maintain Resources app allows you to assign RF devices to resources.

11.4 Task Interleaving

Task interleaving is used to avoid deadheading within the warehouse. For example, when a resource is assigned to the inbound queue for putaway, it's a waste of time for the resource to come back to the door empty-handed every time a putaway is complete. You therefore can set up a queue type sequence in task interleaving and inbound, internal, and outbound sequence queue types, as shown in Figure 11.17. Thus, when a resource has completed putaway, it can complete a warehouse task for picking if an open warehouse order exists in the picking queue in the queue sequence. This optimizes the reduction of empty resource runs from the putaway area to the staging area by ensuring available resource capacity after a putaway task is used by picking HUs on the resource from the storage bin and bringing them to the staging area.

Set up task interleaving from Transaction /SCWM/QTSQ, which can also be accessed from **SAP Easy Access** path **Logistics • SCM Extended Warehouse Management • Extended Warehouse Management • Master Data • Resource Management • Maintain Queue Type Sequence.** Click on **New Entries**, and define a sequence of queue types for a resource group.

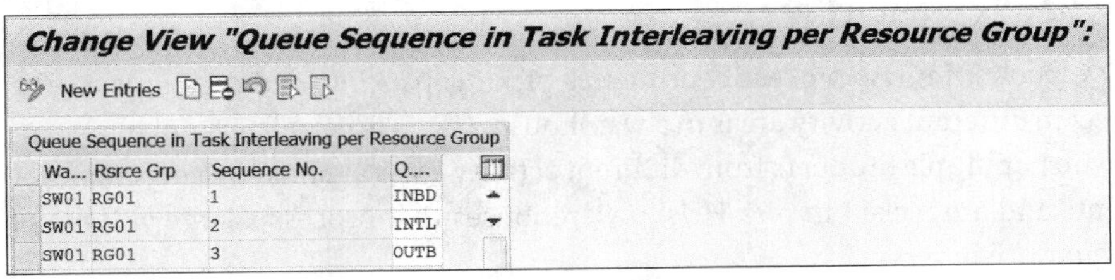

Change View "Queue Sequence in Task Interleaving per Resource Group":

New Entries

Queue Sequence in Task Interleaving per Resource Group

Wa...	Rsrce Grp	Sequence No.	Q....
SW01	RG01	1	INBD
SW01	RG01	2	INTL
SW01	RG01	3	OUTB

Figure 11.17 Queue Type Sequence for Interleaving

As shown in Figure 11.18, without task interleaving, a warehouse resource assigned to the inbound queue would complete the first putaway and then be assigned to the next warehouse task for putaway. This would mean the empty resource would come to the staging area to pick products after every task confirmation. Task interleaving helps reduce the distance a resource travels in the warehouse. Thus, after completing the warehouse tasks for putaway, the system determines a picking warehouse task to pick goods located near the resource. The system determines the distance between bins to choose the task that is closest to the resource.

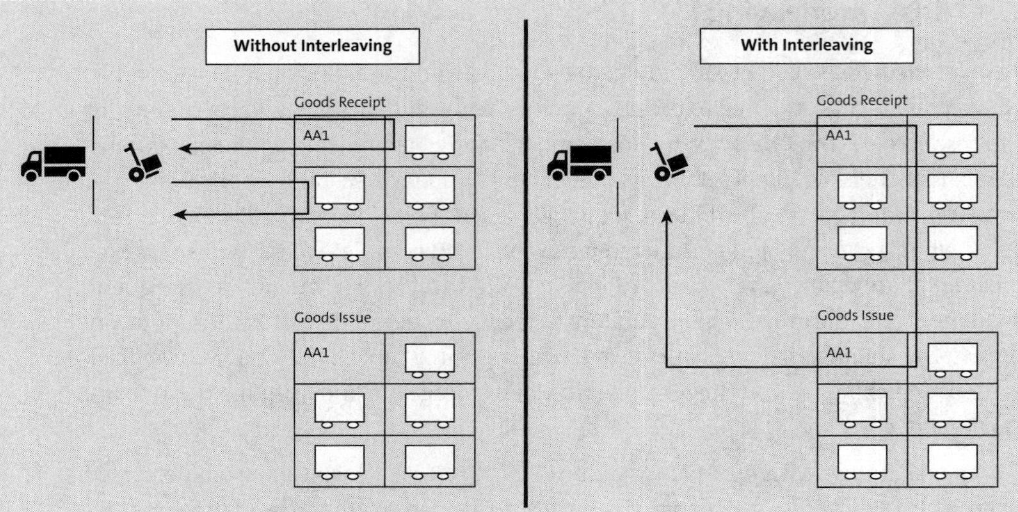

Figure 11.18 Task Interleaving

11.5 Pick, Pack, and Pass

The *pick, pack, and pass* process coordinates picking, packing, and passing over the products in different activity areas in a warehouse. This is especially useful in scenarios in which multiple products from different activity areas are linked using conveyer segments and are picked in pick HUs in warehouses that process a large volume of small-quantity orders.

Consider a scenario in which a warehouse operator picks goods from two different picking areas into a pick HU. The warehouse operator picks the goods in a pick HU. In the system, embedded EWM creates two warehouse orders, one for picking from each activity area and a higher-level warehouse order to group together the two picking warehouse orders. The picking HU is assigned to the top-level warehouse order. After picking the product, the worker passes the HU to the next activity area, until all the products are picked in the HU. Pick, pack, and pass can only be used in RF environments.

There are two types of pick, pack, and pass processes:

- **System-controlled**
  With this option, the system specifies the pick HUs and warehouse orders

sequence (based on the sequence of activity areas in Customizing). The system creates a higher-level warehouse order that contains all lower-level warehouse orders. Only the lower-level warehouse orders are assigned to the resource. The first order in the sequence is active; others are inactive. After the warehouse orders tagged as active are picked, the next inactive order is activated until all the warehouse orders are confirmed, and the pick HU is moved to the goods issue (GI) area.

- **User-controlled**
  In this process, the system creates pick HUs for all warehouse orders to be picked and a higher-level warehouse order that contains all lower-level warehouse orders. All warehouse orders in the sequence are active. A user picks warehouse orders relevant to the area he's in and confirms them in a desired order.

In the following sections, we'll discuss the configurations required to set up pick, pack, and pass in embedded EWM and its execution in the warehouse.

11.5.1 Configuration

The following settings are required to configure the pick, pack, and pass process:

1. **Create the activity area.**
   The activity area for each distinct work area is defined as explained in Chapter 4, Section 4.5. While defining the activity area for each picking area, define a higher-level activity area by setting the **Joined** indicator, as shown in Figure 11.19.

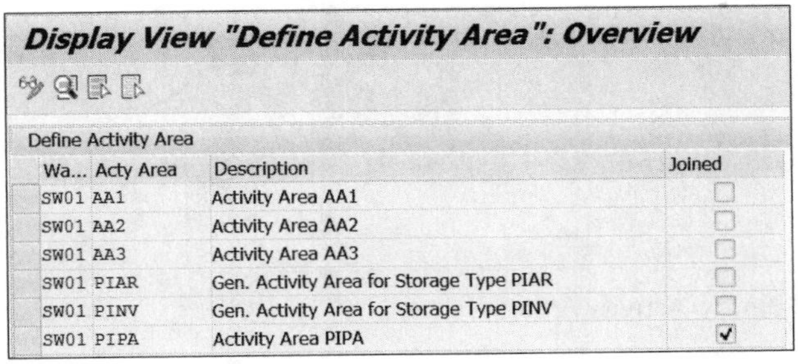

Display View "Define Activity Area": Overview

Define Activity Area

Wa...	Acty Area	Description	Joined
SW01	AA1	Activity Area AA1	☐
SW01	AA2	Activity Area AA2	☐
SW01	AA3	Activity Area AA3	☐
SW01	PIAR	Gen. Activity Area for Storage Type PIAR	☐
SW01	PINV	Gen. Activity Area for Storage Type PINV	☐
SW01	PIPA	Activity Area PIPA	☑

Figure 11.19 Defining the Activity Area for Pick, Pack, and Pass

2. **Assign bins, activities, and sort sequence to the activity area.**
   After the lower-level activity areas are defined, assign them to relevant bins and activities created for picking, and create the sort sequence for picking, as explained in Chapter 4, Section 4.3.8.

3. **Join the activity area.**
   After the higher-level and lower-level activity areas are created, they're joined using the setting defined via IMG path **SCM Extended Warehouse Management • Extended Warehouse Management • Cross-Process Settings • Warehouse Order • Join Activity Area Together**. Click on **New Entries**, and provide a sequence of activity areas for the high-level activity area, as shown in Figure 11.20.

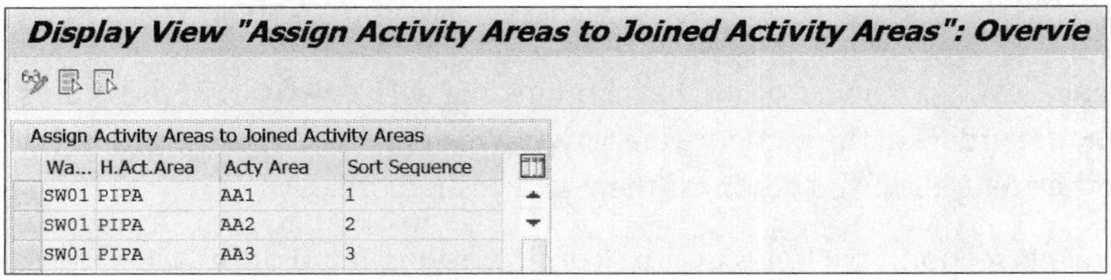

Display View "Assign Activity Areas to Joined Activity Areas": Overvie

Assign Activity Areas to Joined Activity Areas

Wa...	H.Act.Area	Acty Area	Sort Sequence
SW01	PIPA	AA1	1
SW01	PIPA	AA2	2
SW01	PIPA	AA3	3

Figure 11.20 Join Activity Area for Pick, Pack, and Pass

4. **Assign start/end bins to the activity area.**
   After the lower-level activity areas are defined, assign start and end bins to the activity area via **SAP Easy Access** path **Logistics • SCM Extended Warehouse Management • Extended Warehouse Management • Master Data • Storage Bin • Assign Start/End Storage Bins For Activity Area**. Click on **New Entries**, and enter the bins in the **Starting Point** and **End Point** fields for the **Acty Area** and **Activity**, as shown in Figure 11.21.

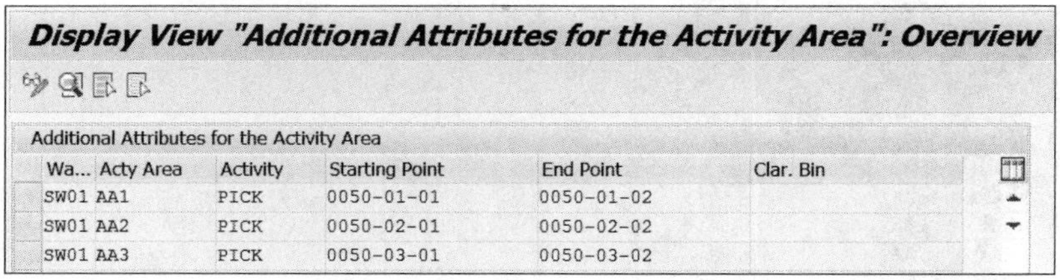

Display View "Additional Attributes for the Activity Area": Overview

Additional Attributes for the Activity Area

Wa...	Acty Area	Activity	Starting Point	End Point	Clar. Bin
SW01	AA1	PICK	0050-01-01	0050-01-02	
SW01	AA2	PICK	0050-02-01	0050-02-02	
SW01	AA3	PICK	0050-03-01	0050-03-02	

Figure 11.21 Assigning Start/End Bins to Activity Areas

5. **Define and determine the warehouse order creation rule.**
   A warehouse order creation rule is defined for the higher-level activity area to create pick HUs for warehouse tasks in the warehouse orders. The creation category for the warehouse order creation rule is set as **Pick, Pack, and Pass: System-Driven** in the Customizing settings for the warehouse order creation rule (see Figure 11.22). (For more details on warehouse order creation rules, see Chapter 6, Section 6.4.)

Display View "Warehouse Order Creation Rules": Details

Warehouse No.	SW01
WO Creatn Rule	PPHL

Warehouse Order Creation Rules

Description	Pick, Pack, Pass
Creation Cat.	C Pick, Pack, and Pass: System-Driven
Item Filter	
Subtotal Filter	
Limit	CONS
Inbound Sorting	PIPA
WO Sorting	
Packing Profile	YP02
Ship.Pack.Prof.	
Prep.Time	0
Time Unit	MIN
Dest. Stor. Ty.	
Dest. Section	
Dest. Stor. Bin	
Storage Process	
Determine WkCtr	☐
WO Locked	☐
CAP Compatibility	☐

Figure 11.22 Warehouse Order Creation Rule

After the warehouse order creation rule is defined, the determination of the warehouse order creation rule is set up for the higher-level activity area with which the pick, pack, and pass process is carried out. To do this, navigate to IMG path **SCM Extended Warehouse Management • Extended Warehouse Management • Cross-Process Settings • Warehouse Order • Define Search Sequence of Creation Rules for Activity Areas**, and assign the warehouse order creation rule defined previously to the higher-level activity area in **Acty Area**, as shown in Figure 11.23.

Display View "Warehouse Order: Search Sequence for Rules per Activity"

Warehouse Order: Search Sequence for Rules per Activity Area

War...	Acty Area	Activity	Sequence No.	WO Cr. Rle	Description
SW01	PIPA	PICK	1	PPHL	Pick, Pack, Pass

Figure 11.23 Determination Rule for the Warehouse Order

11.5.2 Warehouse Order Processing

As shown in Figure 11.24, when you use pick, pack, and pass, the system creates a higher-level warehouse order. This warehouse order contains pick HUs for all warehouse tasks created for picking from the lower-level activity areas. The steps carried out by the system for pick, pack, and pass are as follows:

1. The system creates a higher-level warehouse order for warehouse tasks in the three-activity area (AA1, AA2, AA3) and determines pick HUs for the same.
2. After the picking tasks are assigned to the warehouse, the first worker takes pick HUs from the source bin. The worker picks the product and passes the HU to the destination storage bin of the activity area.
3. The HU moves from the destination bin of the previous activity area to the source bin of the next activity area, and the process as defined in the previous step is repeated.
4. After the last warehouse order is executed, the worker puts the pick HU in the destination bin, such as the GI zone.

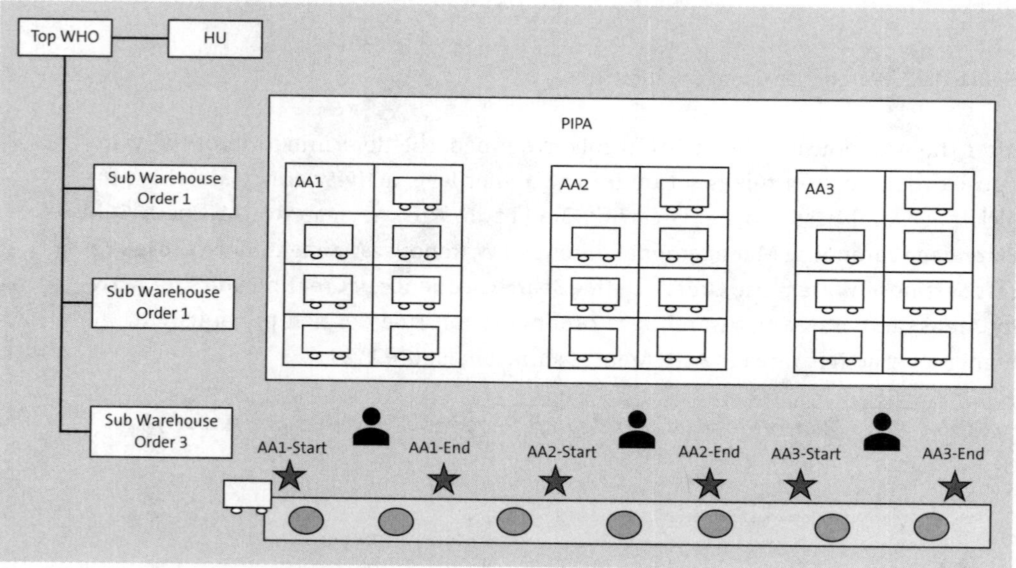

Figure 11.24 Pick, Pack, and Pass Process

11.6 Resource Execution Constraint

When performing warehousing operations, it isn't feasible to have all resources concentrated within a single part of the warehouse. Therefore, the concept of *resource execution constraint* controls the number of resources in any area of the warehouse at one point in time. You do this by assigning a resource execution constraint storage group of bins in the storage type and setting the maximum number of permitted resources for each resource execution constraint group. The bins assigned to a resource execution constraint group can be based on storage type, section, aisle, and so on. In the following sections, we'll discuss the configurations required to complete execution based on the resource execution constraint in embedded EWM, as well as the steps for carrying out the resource execution constraint in the warehouse.

11.6.1 Configuration

The following settings need to be made to work with resource execution constraints:

1. **Define the resource execution constraint.**
   Define resource execution constraints by grouping resource types into groups to specify the combination of allowed resource types in a resource execution constraint storage group. You should also specify the maximum number of allowed resources for each resource type within a storage type group. Define resource execution constraints from the IMG path **SCM Extended Warehouse Management • Extended Warehouse Management • Cross-Process Settings • Resource Management • Control Data • Define Resource Execution Constraints (REC)**, as shown in Figure 11.25.

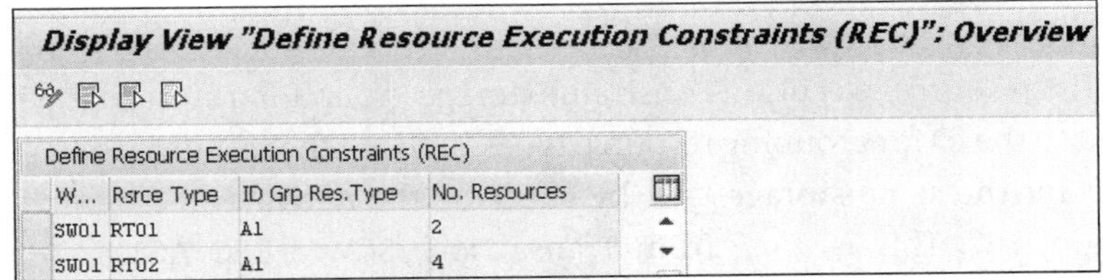

Display View "Define Resource Execution Constraints (REC)": Overview

Define Resource Execution Constraints (REC)

W...	Rsrce Type	ID Grp Res.Type	No. Resources
SW01	RT01	A1	2
SW01	RT02	A1	4

Figure 11.25 Defining Resource Execution Constraints

The **ID Grp Res. Type** field is used to group together resource types that are allowed together in the resource execution constraint storage group. You can assign the same ID to multiple resource execution constraint groups. The **No. Resources** field is used to specify the maximum number of resources allowed per resource type in a resource execution constraint storage group.

2. **Assign the resource execution constraints to the resource execution constraint storage group.**
   Assign the resource execution constraints to a resource execution constraint storage group. Use IMG path **SCM Extended Warehouse Management • Extended Warehouse Management • Cross-Process Settings • Resource Management • Control Data • Assign Resource Execution Constraints to REC Storage Group**, as shown in Figure 11.26.

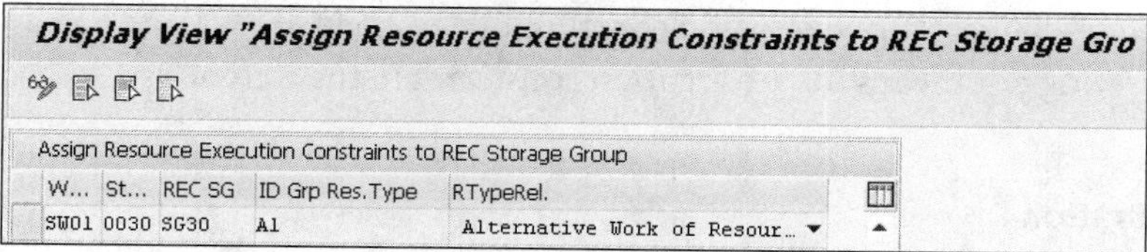

Figure 11.26 Assigning Resource Execution Constraints to the Resource Execution Constraint Storage Group

   You can assign the same ID to different resource execution constraint storage groups. The **RTypeRel.** field can use either an **OR** or an **AND** option. Select the **Alternative Work of Resources from Different Resource Types** value when you want to allow resources from a single resource type at a time in a resource execution constraint storage group. Select the **Additional Resource Can Work from Other Resource Type** value when you want multiple resources from multiple resource types in the resource execution constraint storage group, for example, a forklift and a warehouse worker.

3. **Activate resource execution constraint**
   After creating the resource execution constraint storage group for a storage type and assigning it to the ID for grouping resource types, activate the resource execution constraint for the same storage type by checking the **Activate REC** box, as shown in Figure 11.27. This is done from Transaction /SCWM/REC_ACTIVATE, which can also be accessed from **SAP Easy Access** path **Logistics • SCM Extended Warehouse Management • Extended Warehouse Management • Master Data • Resource Management • Activate Resource Execution Control for Storage Groups**.

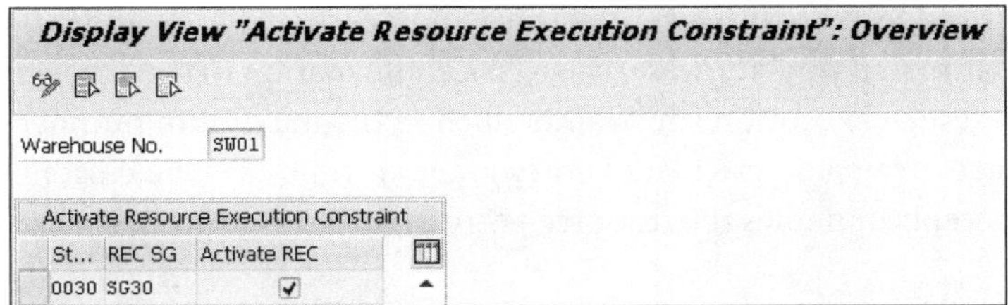

Figure 11.27 Activating the Resource Execution Constraint

4. **Assign the resource execution constraint storage group to storage bins.**
   After configuring the resource execution constraint for a storage type, the final step is to set the resource execution constraint storage group in the **REC ST. GROUP** field in the bin master data. You can populate this field for select bins in a storage type for which you want to activate the resource execution constraint based on aisle, stack, storage section, or any other grouping as needed.

11.6.2 Task Execution

The resource execution constraint control is based on calculated times. Each time a resource enters a constraint-activated storage group, the system calculates the estimated exit time for the resource as a sum of the following three parameters:

- Time to move from the current location to the entry point of the resource execution constraint storage group
- Working time in the resource execution constraint storage group
- Exit time of the resource to move from the last completed warehouse order bin to the resource execution constraint storage group exit bin

When a resource wants to enter the resource execution constraint storage group, the system calculates the estimated exit time and entry time for the resource and checks the maximum resources allowed for the storage group. The exit time is calculated based on the time the resource takes to move from the current position to the entry point in the resource execution constraint group, the time taken to complete the warehouse process, and the time taken by the resource to move from the current bin to the exit point in the resource execution constraint group. The system calculates the optimal routes for the resource using travel distance calculations.

If labor management is active, then the system uses the Engineering Labor Standards (ELS) to calculate the estimated time for warehouse task confirmation in the storage group. Based on the resource execution constraints, such as the maximum number of resources in a storage group and calculated entry and exit times for the current resource, the system accepts or denies the resource entry in the storage group.

11.7 Summary

In this chapter, we explained the basic configuration and master data settings for resource management in embedded EWM. We explained both automated and manual warehouse order assignment to resources using queues. We talked about system-guided and semi-system-guided process in embedded EWM, as well as task interleaving to optimize warehouse worker runs and to reduce empty returns from putaway areas. We explained the pick, pack, and pass process to optimize the sequential picking process in embedded EWM.

Finally, we discussed the use and setting of resource execution constraints to decongest various aisles and areas of the warehouse. With the knowledge gained in this chapter, you should now be able to configure and use resource management in warehouses. In the next chapter, we'll discuss warehouse monitoring and reporting.

Chapter 12
Warehouse Monitoring and Reporting

Monitoring day-to-day warehouse operations against set key performance indicators (KPIs) is an important process for any organization. In this chapter, we discuss how monitoring and reporting warehouse activities are handled in embedded EWM.

Warehouse monitoring is a key requirement for any warehouse supervisor to know the status of warehouse activities. This includes monitoring the stock situation, monitoring warehouse requests, identifying bottlenecks in process execution, and more. Embedded EWM provides a central tool for monitoring warehouse activities and the execution of actions: the warehouse management monitor (also known as the warehouse monitor).

This chapter will focus on the monitoring and reporting tools available in embedded EWM. In Section 12.1, we'll cover the concept of warehouse monitoring and reporting in SAP EWM. Then, in Section 12.2, we'll walk you through the warehouse monitor itself and discuss the graphical warehouse layout, which provides a graphical view of stock positions in the warehouse. For each topic, we'll cover the configuration details required to set up the related tools and customize them based on user requirements. Next, we'll cover the measurement services used in embedded EWM in Section 12.4, followed by exploring the SAP Fiori app Warehouse KPIs – Operations in Section 12.5. Finally, Section 12.6 summarizes a few important core data services (CDS) views available for embedded EWM.

12.1 What Is Warehouse Monitoring and Reporting?

The warehouse monitor offers a single interface for monitoring the status of warehouse processes and understanding the stock situation in the warehouse. It also provides an interface called the alert monitor to set up alerts when there are any bottlenecks that need to be resolved. These tools keep warehouse supervisors updated about the current warehouse situation and help them make timely decisions in case of emergencies. For example, a warehouse supervisor can know the number of open inbound and outbound deliveries; open warehouse orders for picking, putaway, or internal stock movements; open physical inventory documents; and more. The supervisor can also take required actions based on information from the monitor, such as confirming warehouse tasks or assigning warehouse orders to resources. In the following sections, we'll use a business case to explain the business as well as system aspect of using warehouse monitor in embedded EWM in SAP S/4HANA.

> **Note**
> In our example, we're explaining a single business variant of warehouse monitor usage; however, there are multiple reporting and execution processes that can be done using warehouse monitor in embedded EWM in SAP S/4HANA.

12.1.1 Business Process

American company Alpha Medicals wants to have a common cockpit that can view, consolidate, slice, and dice the warehouse requests for inbound, outbound, and internal warehouse processes. The warehouse monitor provides a common cockpit that not only helps in reporting but also helps in executing transactions. This sort of reporting will help the operational managers in the warehouse check on the stock load waiting for warehouse process execution. The operational managers can allocate warehouse requests to warehouse workers and keep an eye on the resource execution efficiency of the warehouse workers.

Apart from normal reporting features, warehouse power users can decongest the stock traffic in the warehouse by releasing waves for tasks using the warehouse monitor. They can also create and confirm warehouse tasks from a single user interface (UI) using two interactive SAP Fiori apps: the Process Warehouse Tasks – Picking app and the Process Warehouse Tasks – Putaway app.

The shipping and receiving clerk can perform all shipping and receiving operations, such as transportation unit (TU) check-in, TU yard movements, product stock loading/unloading, and TU check-out using a common cockpit interface.

The Alpha Medicals power users want to have a view of all the waves due to be released in two days to plan picking and avoid stock congestion. The user logs on to the embedded EWM cockpit, gets a list of all the picking waves, and views the waves that are due to be released for picking.

The user finds one of the waves required to be released on an emergency basis. After getting the appropriate approvals, the user releases the emergency wave for the products to be picked and prioritizes it for loading and GI.

12.1.2 System Process

To access the warehouse monitor in embedded EWM, use Transaction /SCWM/MON or navigate to SAP Easy Access path **SCM Extended Warehouse Management • Extended Warehouse Management • Monitoring • Warehouse Management Monitor**. Upon execution, a selection screen opens as shown in Figure 12.1.

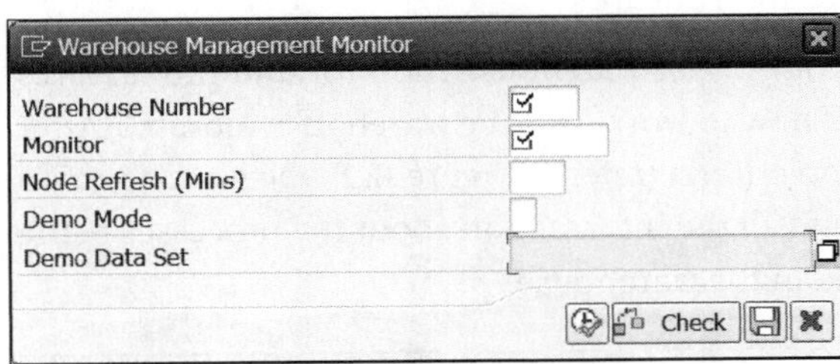

Figure 12.1 Warehouse Management Monitor Entry Screen

The following fields must be completed on this screen:

- **Warehouse Number**
  This is the warehouse number of the embedded EWM warehouse for which you need to access the warehouse monitor.
- **Monitor**
  This is the name of the warehouse monitor and can be customized based on business requirements. Standard SAP provides a default monitor, **SAP**.
- **Node Refresh (Mins)**
  This option is used to provide the default refresh interval for all the nodes displayed in the warehouse.
- **Demo Mode**
  You can upload demo data in the system and view the demo data in demo mode. The SAP default is to execute the monitor in productive mode.

- **Demo Data Set**
  Demo data sets are used to work with demo data in the warehouse instead of real-time data. If this field is left blank, the system displays the real-time data in the warehouse by default in the monitor.

12.2 Warehouse Monitor

In the following sections, we'll walk through the structure of the warehouse monitor and its features. We'll also discuss how you can personalize the warehouse monitor layout per your business requirements.

12.2.1 Warehouse Monitor Layout and Features

In this section, we'll discuss the layout of the warehouse monitor and the features that it offers to help you understand how to work with the warehouse monitor. After you've entered the required selection criteria (refer to Figure 12.1), the screen shown in Figure 12.2 opens. This screen shows all the information about the processes being carried out and stocks being handled in the warehouse.

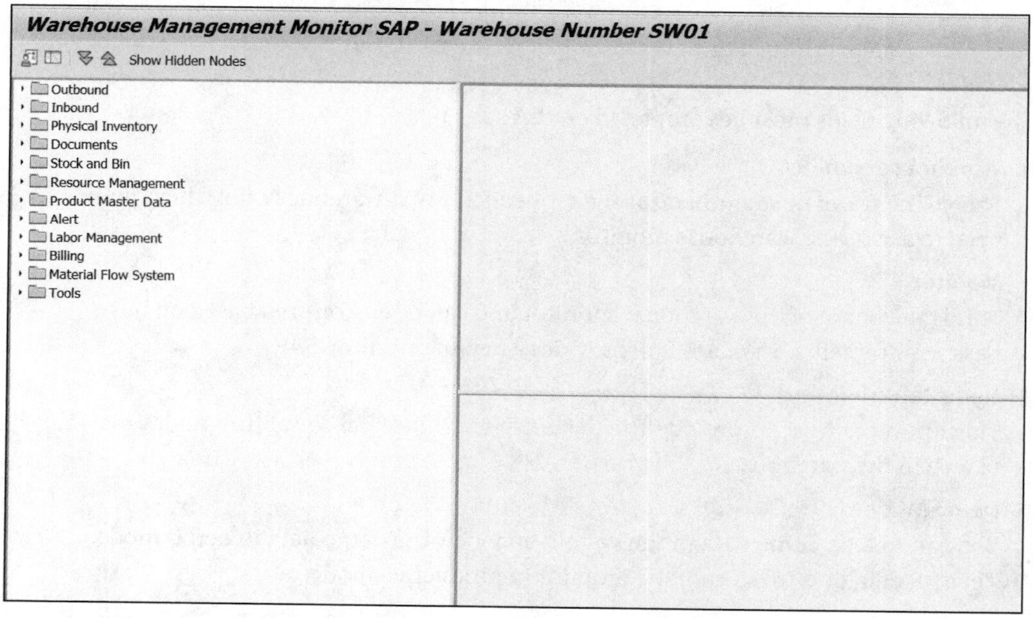

Figure 12.2 Warehouse Monitor Layout

The UI of the warehouse monitor is based on the SAP List Viewer (ALV) grid controls and is divided into three views. Each of these views can be aligned flexibly with respect to size. The left-hand side of the warehouse monitor shows the *node hierarchy tree*, which consists of two types of nodes:

- **Category nodes**
  These nodes are represented as folders in the warehouse monitor and contain other category nodes and/or profile nodes. The category nodes into which the monitor nodes are divided are as follows:
  - **Outbound**
  - **Inbound**
  - **Physical Inventory**
  - **Documents**
  - **Stock and Bin**
  - **Resource Management**
  - **Product Master Data**
  - **Alert**
  - **Labor Management**
  - **Billing**
  - **Material Flow System**
  - **Tools**
- **Profile nodes**
  The profile nodes contain data for specific object classes. Each profile node is assigned to a node profile in configuration that controls the data displayed for the profile node and its logical hierarchy. These object classes can be one of the following:
  - Documents, such as inbound or outbound deliveries
  - Processes, such as stock and bin, resource management, and so on
  - Alerts, such as overdue inbound, outbound deliveries, warehouse tasks, and so on

The node hierarchy tree is used for navigation purposes and helps you navigate to data contained in these object classes via various search criteria. The search criteria are presented after double-clicking on the required node.

The right side of the monitor is divided into two sections. The upper section is called the *upper view* area and holds the parent data for the data that appears based on node selection. The lower-right side of the screen, called the *lower view* area, is used to display child data. The child data that is available to view for a given parent row appears as pushbuttons on the warehouse monitor screen. You can select any of these buttons to view the corresponding child data for parent data. For example, in Figure 12.3, we've selected an outbound delivery and selected the **Warehouse Task** button, which displays the warehouse tasks created for the delivery in the lower view area.

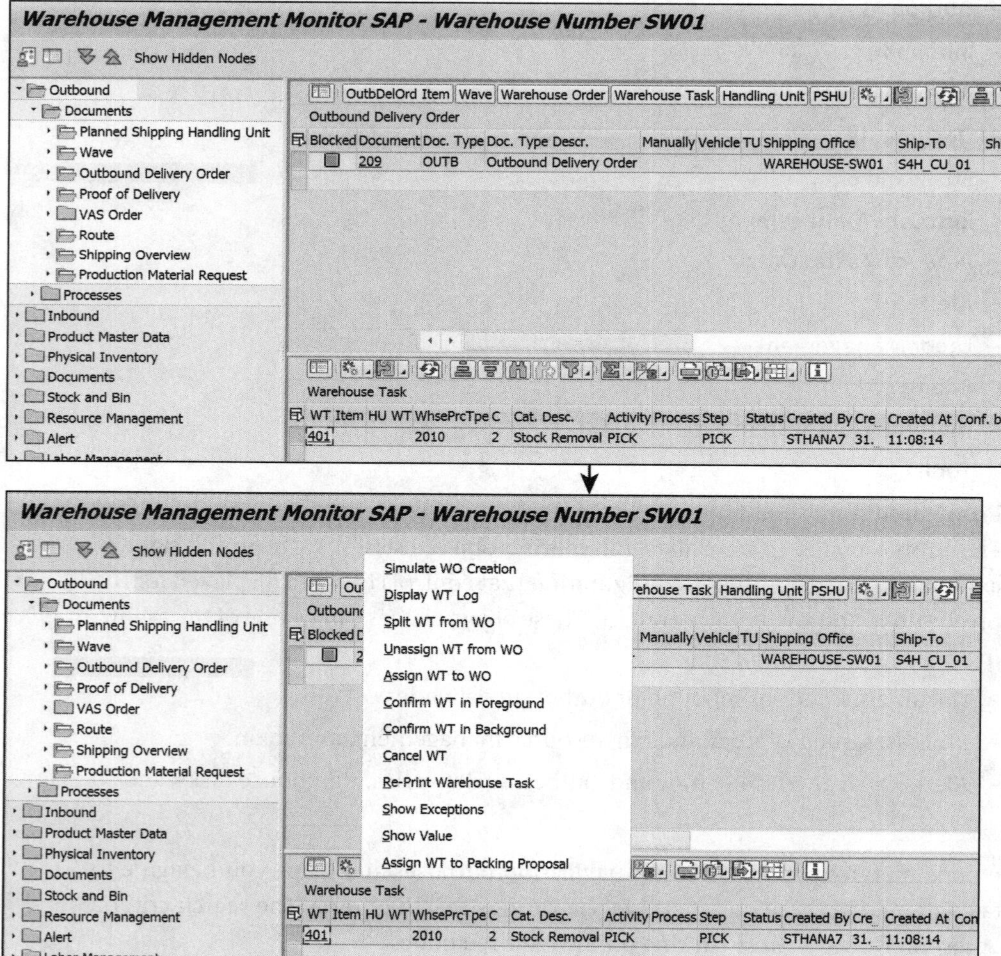

Figure 12.3 Parent and Child Data in the Warehouse Monitor

You can access more options by clicking the [icon] icon available in the child view in which the warehouse task is displayed. You can confirm the warehouse task in either the foreground or background using the **Confirm WT in Foreground** or **Confirm WT in Background** options.

The data in both the parent and child views can be seen in both ALV and form view. By default, all the data is displayed in ALV view. There are several other functionalities offered by the warehouse monitor, as follows:

- Methods to execute actions on selected objects
- Ability to navigate directly to a transaction to display selected data in the warehouse monitor
- Use of all standard functionalities offered by the ALV view, such as sorting, filtering, and printing
- Direct access to documents by clicking on the document hotspot, represented by underlined text
- View of alerts and queues and their execution statuses

You also can create a custom monitor based on business requirements. SAP provides a graphical tool with which you can drag and drop categories and object nodes from the default SAP monitor and create a new monitor. To access this tool, navigate to IMG path **SCM Extended Warehouse Management • Extended Warehouse Management • Monitoring • Warehouse Management Monitor • Customize Monitor Tree**. The transaction screen displays a UI with all monitor nodes displayed on the left and an empty canvas on the right to create a custom monitor in embedded EWM. You can choose to create either a warehouse-dependent monitor or a warehouse-independent monitor.

12.2.2 Personalizing the Warehouse Monitor

You can enhance or personalize the warehouse monitor in embedded EWM to fit your needs. You can add, delete, and modify nodes and create custom methods for action execution. You have the flexibility to create a completely new monitor or enhance the standard warehouse monitor. Changes can be localized for specific users or can be made available for all users. Various methods of personalizing the warehouse monitor are discussed in the following sections.

Hiding Irrelevant Nodes and Branches

You can hide a node or branch in the warehouse monitor by right-clicking on a node or branch and selecting the **Hide Node** option, as shown in Figure 12.4. To reveal the hidden nodes, click on the **Show Hidden Nodes** button in the warehouse monitor. The hidden nodes are invisible to the user who hides them, but they remain visible to all other users.

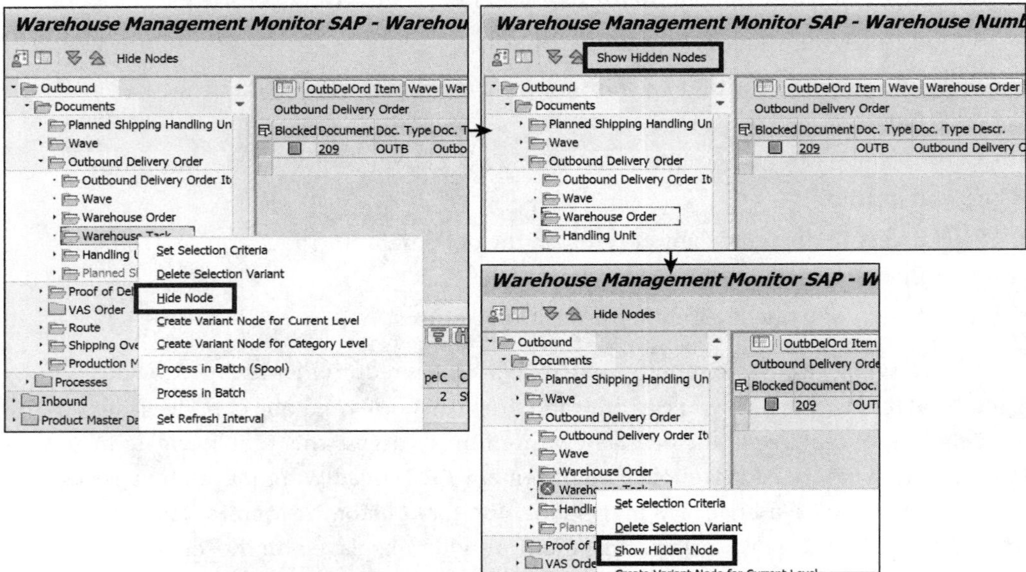

Figure 12.4 Hiding Nodes in the Warehouse Monitor

Creating Selection Criteria for Standard Nodes

Often, you'll want to display only a specific set of transactional objects in the warehouse monitor. This can reduce the overhead involved in inputting data in the selection screen of the warehouse monitor every time it's used. You can enter the selection criteria in the search screen of the monitor and create a variant to display data based on predefined selection criteria. To create a selection criteria variant for nodes, right-click on the node, and select **Set Selection Criteria**.

As shown in Figure 12.5 and Figure 12.6, the input value is specified in the selection box. In this example, we want the monitor to display only open picking tasks. To do this, select the indicator for open warehouse tasks (**Open WTs**) and the warehouse process category 2 (**Whse Proc. Cat. 2**) for picking. Next, click on **Save** to save the selection variant with a **Variant Name** and **Description**. The variant can be selected in the warehouse monitor via the **Get Variant** button at the bottom of the screen.

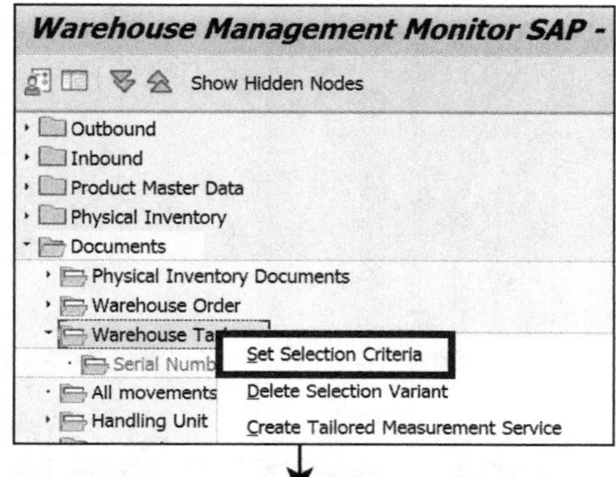

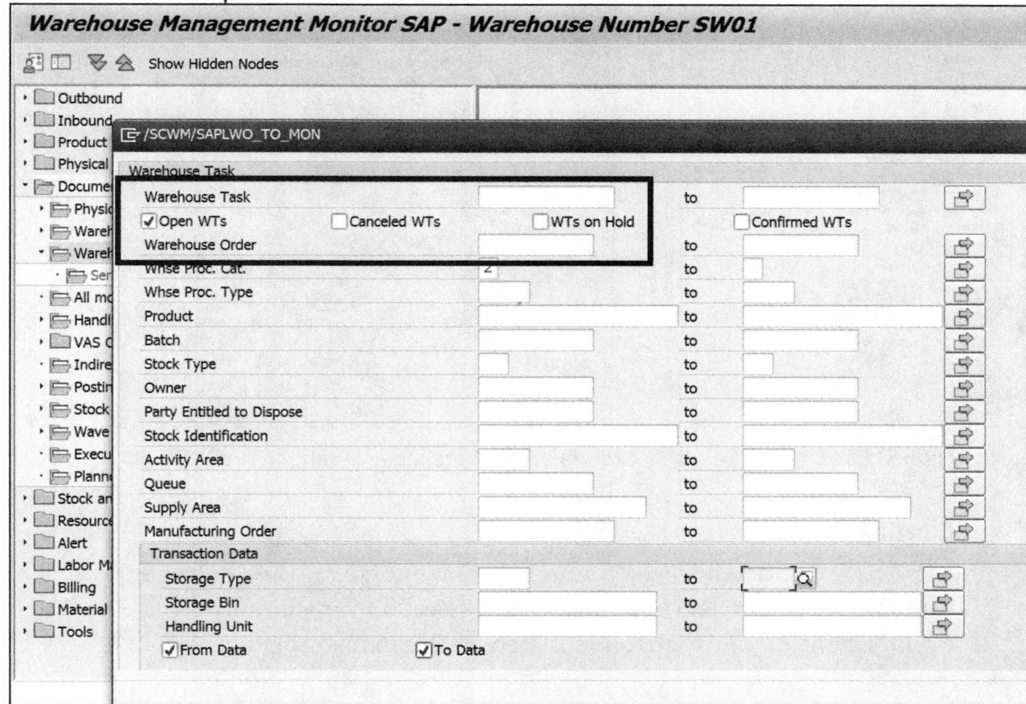

Figure 12.5 Creating Selection Criteria in the Warehouse Monitor (Part 1)

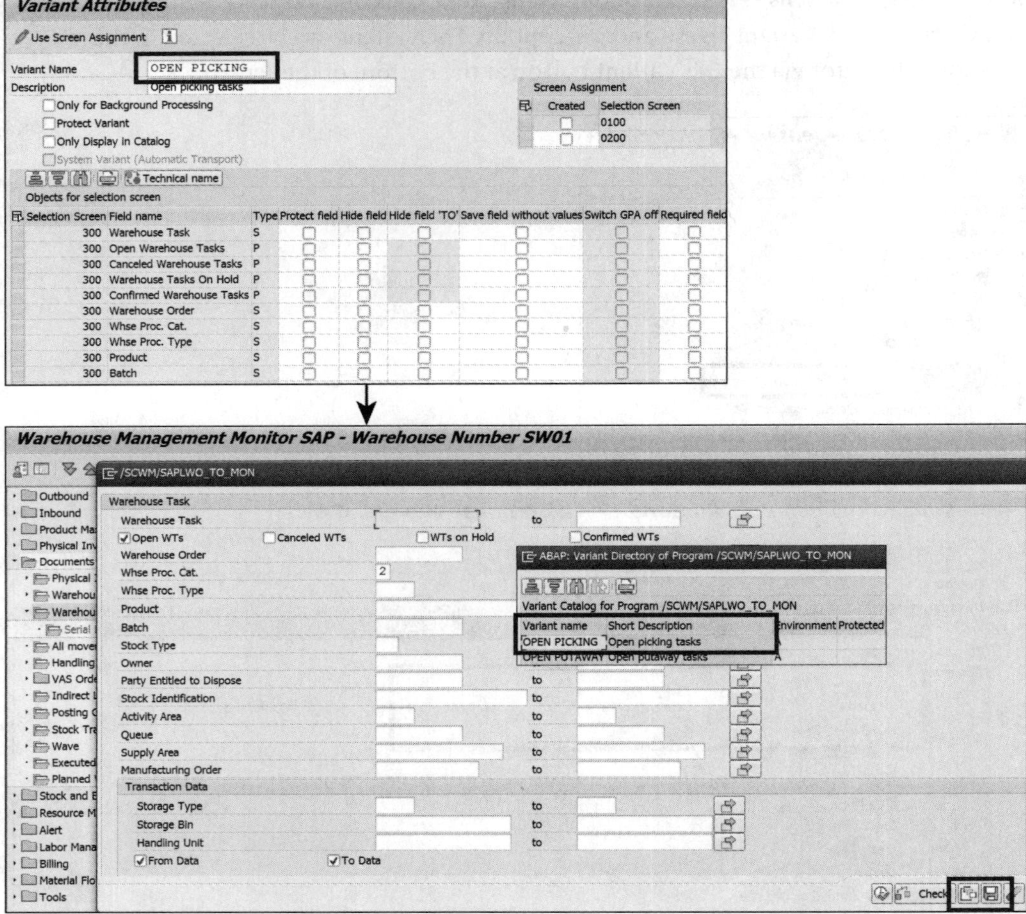

Figure 12.6 Creating Selection Criteria in the Warehouse Monitor (Part 2)

Creating Variant Node in Hierarchy Tree

You can create a new node in the warehouse monitor to call the result of the selection variant. This is especially required when a selection variant must be displayed frequently in the monitor. Two options are available in this category:

- **Create Variant Node for Current Level**
  In this case, the variant node is created below the original node.
- **Create Variant Node for Category Level**
  In this case, the variant node is created below the original node but on the same level as the node's category.

To create a new node, right-click on the node, and select **Create Variant Node** either for the current level or category level (see Figure 12.7). The following execution buttons are available while creating the variant node:

- **Execute**
  Clicking this button creates only the variant node based on the source node.
- **Execute with Sub-Tree**
  Clicking this button creates the variant node, as well as the same lower-level nodes that are contained in the source node.

You can create a new selection variant or assign an existing selection variant to the new variant node.

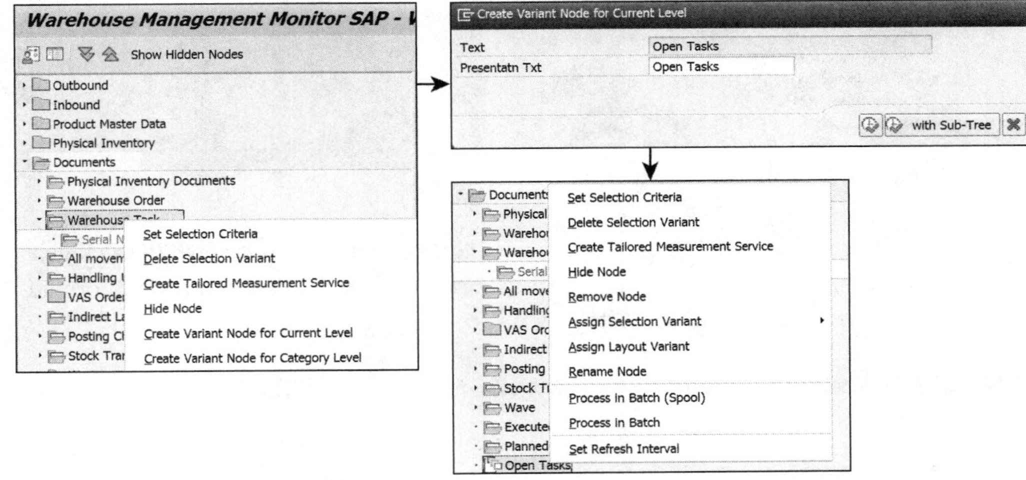

Figure 12.7 Creating Variant Nodes in the Hierarchy

Creating New Nodes for the Warehouse Monitor

You also can create new nodes in the warehouse monitor rather than create a variant of a standard node. This enables you to have additional filter criteria and display data in the warehouse monitor. After the new node is created, you can adjust the assigned function module, selection criteria, display data, and so on.

The following example creates a new node, **S4H1**, on the first level of the hierarchy and a subnode based on the **Inbound Delivery** standard node. New nodes can be created via IMG path **SCM Extended Warehouse Management • Extended Warehouse Management • Monitoring • Warehouse Management Monitor • Define Nodes**. To begin, follow these steps:

1. Define an object class to categorize objects for management and control purposes. As shown in Figure 12.8, use the standard object class **WHRI** in this example, rather than creating a new object class. Search for WHRI by clicking on **Position** and entering "WHRI" as the search value.

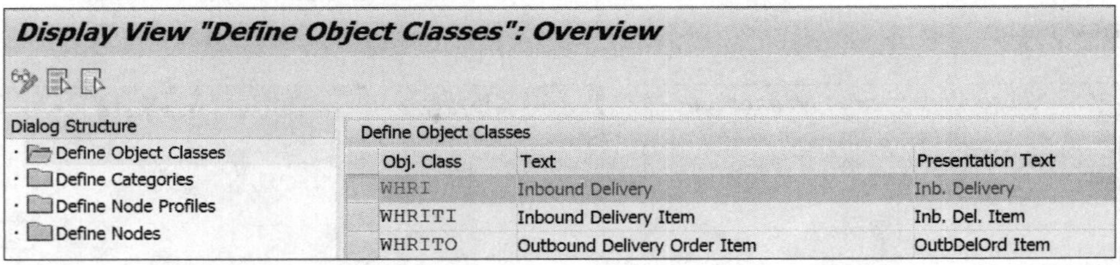

Display View "Define Object Classes": Overview

Dialog Structure
- Define Object Classes
- Define Categories
- Define Node Profiles
- Define Nodes

Define Object Classes

Obj. Class	Text	Presentation Text
WHRI	Inbound Delivery	Inb. Delivery
WHRITI	Inbound Delivery Item	Inb. Del. Item
WHRITO	Outbound Delivery Order Item	OutbDelOrd Item

Figure 12.8 Defining the Object Class

2. As shown in Figure 12.9, define a new object category, **S4H1**, to enable the logical grouping of nodes by clicking on the **New Entries** option in the menu and providing the name of the object category.

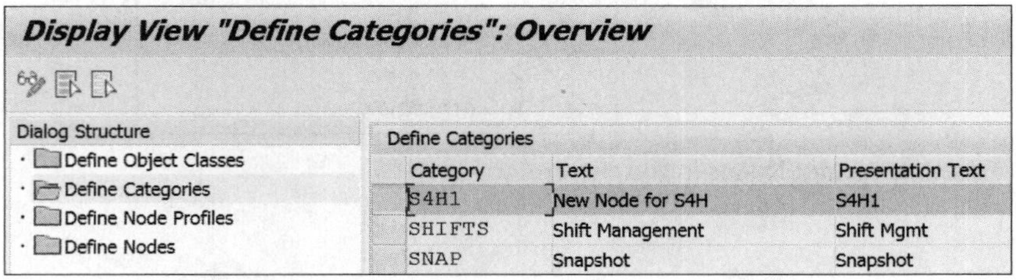

Display View "Define Categories": Overview

Dialog Structure
- Define Object Classes
- Define Categories
- Define Node Profiles
- Define Nodes

Define Categories

Category	Text	Presentation Text
S4H1	New Node for S4H	S4H1
SHIFTS	Shift Management	Shift Mgmt
SNAP	Snapshot	Snapshot

Figure 12.9 Defining the Object Category

3. Create a node profile to define node characteristics such as class association, function modules, form/list view, and so on. This profile is required only if you need a new structure, content for list, and form views. Select the standard node profile using the search process by clicking on **Position** and entering "P0000085" as the search value (see Figure 12.10).

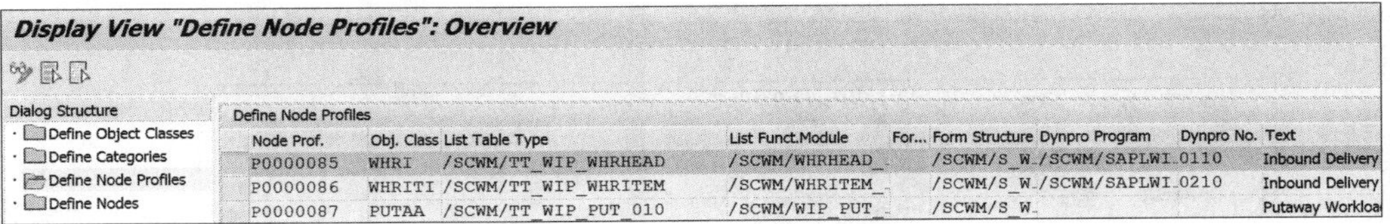

Figure 12.10 Defining the Node Profile

4. Define the node, which appears as a folder in the monitor hierarchy tree. Create a new node, **ZS4H1**, and assign it to node profile **P0000085** for inbound delivery by clicking on the **New Entries** option from the menu, as shown in Figure 12.11.

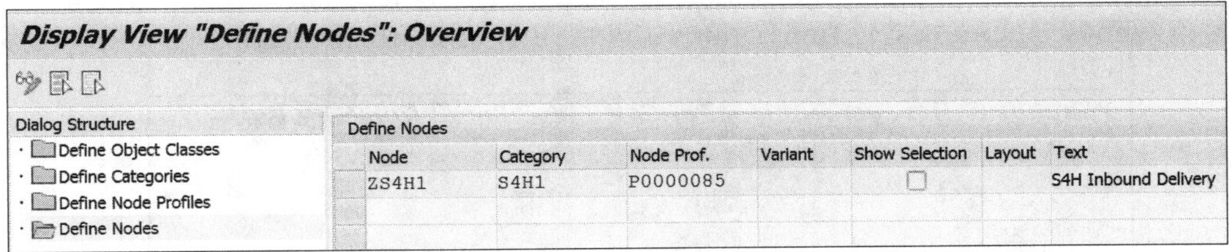

Figure 12.11 Defining the Node

5. The new node and node profile can be assigned to a custom monitor or to the default SAP warehouse monitor by navigating to IMG path **SCM Extended Warehouse Management • Extended Warehouse Management • Monitoring • Warehouse Management Monitor • Define Monitors**. As shown in Figure 12.12, click on **New Entries** from the menu, select the EWM **Warehouse No.** and **Monitor** combination, click on the **Define Node Hierarchy** node, and assign a higher-level (**Higher-Node**) and lower-level (**Lower Node**) monitor node to custom monitor S4H.

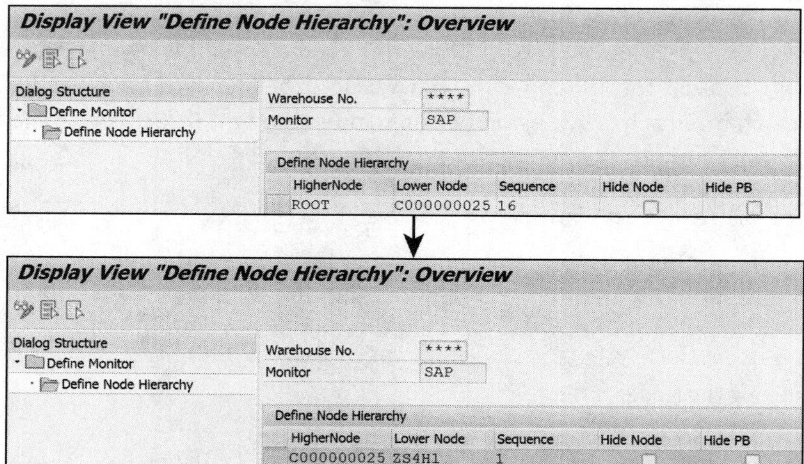

Figure 12.12 Adding a New Node to the Monitor

After this configuration is complete, the new custom node can be seen in the warehouse monitor using Transaction /SCWM/MON, as shown in Figure 12.13.

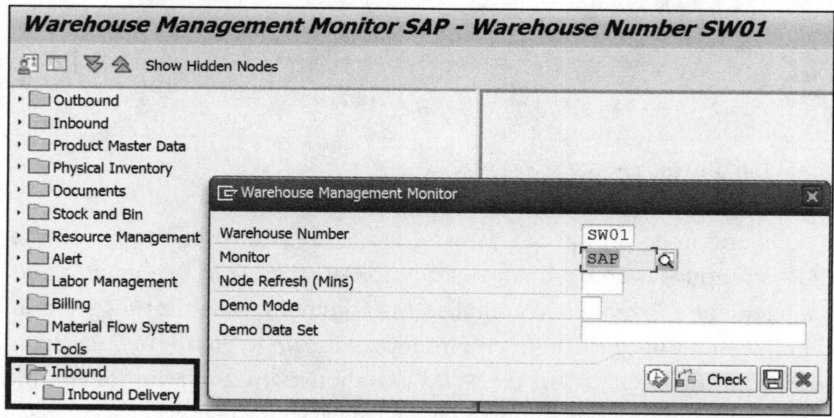

Figure 12.13 New Node in the Warehouse Monitor

Creating New Methods

Embedded EWM provides methods that are assigned to each object class in Customizing. These methods contain specific logic that can be executed using a specific object class in the warehouse monitor.

You can add new methods to a process object class in the warehouse monitor, in addition to using the standard methods provided by SAP, to increase the processing capability of the warehouse monitor. After the methods are defined, they can be assigned to the relevant object class via IMG path **SCM Extended Warehouse Management • Extended Warehouse Management • Monitoring • Warehouse Management Monitor • Define Object Class Methods**. Once there, select **Define Methods Presentation** on the left-hand side of the screen, and assign the method to the required object class.

12.2.3 Message Queue Monitoring

The embedded EWM warehouse monitor also offers a **Message Queue** node to monitor the status of queued remote function call (qRFC) messages in message queues in embedded EWM, as shown in Figure 12.14.

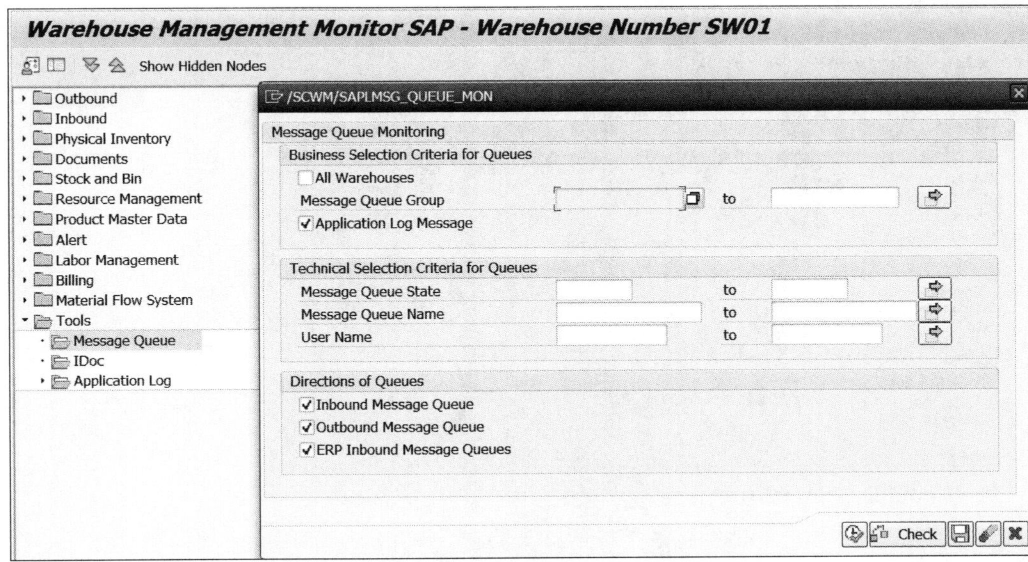

Figure 12.14 Message Queue in the Warehouse Monitor

The selection screen can be used to select queues based on business criteria and technical criteria. You can provide the selection criteria, such as message queue group, message queue state, message queue name, and so on, to view queues for only the current warehouse or for all warehouses.

In embedded EWM, a message queue group is used to group together queue definitions that shouldn't appear in the selection screen for a message queue group for a user. Each queue-monitoring definition refers to a business object such as delivery, warehouse task, warehouse request, and so on. To define a message queue group in embedded EWM, navigate to IMG path **SCM Extended Warehouse Management • Extended Warehouse Management • Monitoring • Message Queue Monitoring • Define Message Queue Definitions.** Click on **New Entries** to define a new **Queue-Group**, and assign it to one or more message queue definitions by selecting the **Message Queue Definitions** option. The message queue groups can be used to group together one or more queue definitions.

After you execute the **Message Queue** node in the warehouse monitor by providing selection criteria and clicking on [icon], the next screen displays the queues between SAP S/4HANA and embedded EWM and their processing statuses, as shown in Figure 12.15.

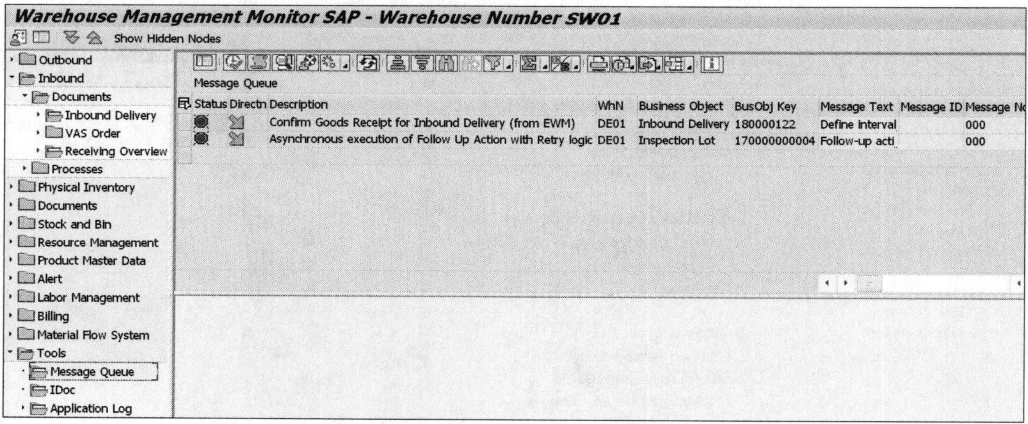

Figure 12.15 Message Queue

This node offers a more user-friendly interface to manage queues in embedded EWM. Rather than having to reply in Transactions SMQ1 and SMQ2, you can directly monitor unprocessed queues from this screen and execute appropriate methods to reprocess them. Some of the methods available on the monitor screen are as follows:

- **Execute**
  This command will restart queue processing. Select a queue to be processed, and click on [icon].

- **Reject**
  This command will reset the status of the queue. Select a queue to be rejected, and click on [icon].
- **qRFC Monitor**
  This command directly navigates to the qRFC monitor. This can be directly accessed via Transaction SMQ1 for outbound queues and Transaction SMQ2 for inbound queues. Select a queue to be processed, click on [icon], and select **qRFC Monitor**.
- **Reset Status**
  This command is used to reset the queue status. Select a queue to be processed, click on [icon], and select **Reset Status**.
- **Raise Alert**
  This command is used to raise an alert to pertinent users. Select a queue to be processed, click on [icon], and select **Raise Alert**.

12.2.4 Process Execution via the Warehouse Monitor

With the new releases of embedded EWM, SAP had been making many improvements so that users can use the warehouse monitor not only for reporting processes but also for warehouse tasks and stock-related actions.

Enabling the warehouse monitor with such features allows the warehouse monitor to be used by power users and operational users who want to make transactional decisions and feed them to the system at the warehouse task and stock levels.

However, after the warehouse monitor is fully operational in the client landscape, the client business users often expect more features, such as closing the warehouse tasks using exception codes, handling units (HUs) processing, or internal warehouse processes execution from a single point in the embedded EWM system. In all such cases, the standard warehouse monitor of embedded EWM will provide a major process improvement as it can be used both for operational and transactional purposes.

> **Tip**
>
> No specific configuration is required to perform either of the transactional processes. The changes work with the warehouse monitor provided with SAP S/4HANA using Transaction /SCWM/MON.

We'll explain the changes to different warehouse processes that can be performed using the warehouse monitor in the following sections. It's worth noting that you can perform multiple subprocesses within each category of process addition using different nodes of the warehouse monitor. Each of these nodes is explained in detail as well.

Warehouse Tasks Confirmation Using Exception Codes

As shown in Figure 12.16, you can confirm open product warehouse tasks with commonly used exceptions. You can access the execution criteria by clicking on [icon] and selecting **Confirm WT with Exception**.

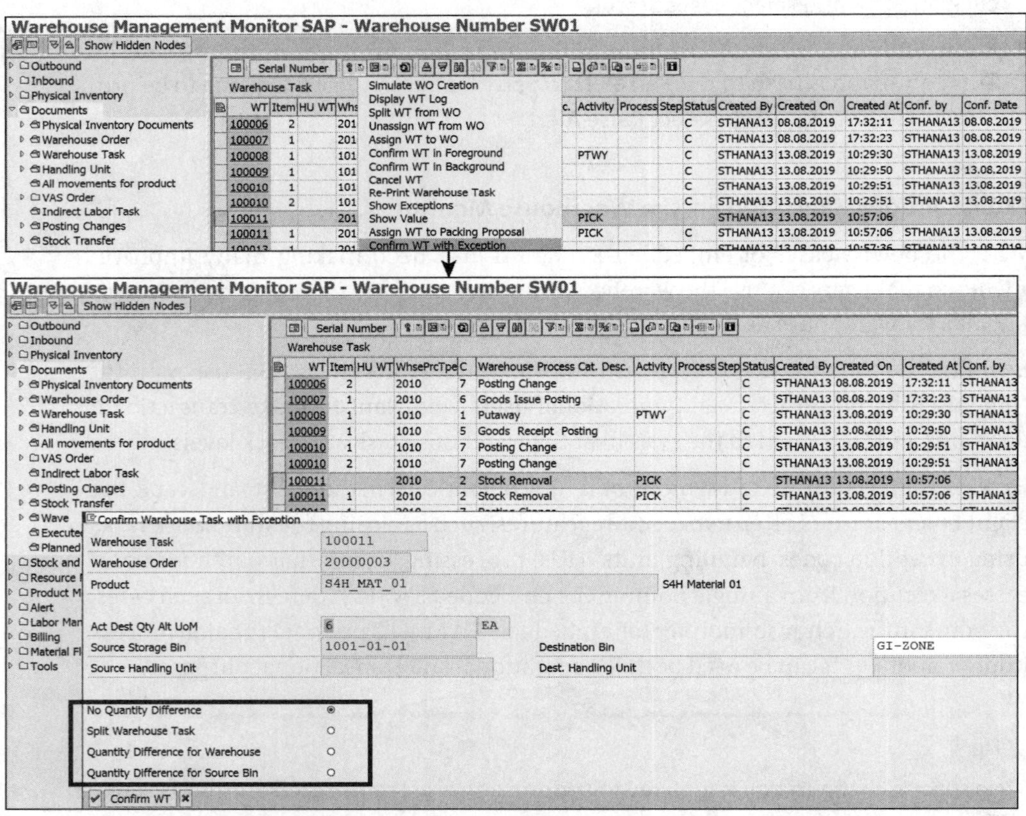

Figure 12.16 Confirming Product WT Using Exception Codes

You can perform the following processes using one of the following options based on your business requirements:

- **No Quantity Difference**
- **Split Warehouse Task**
- **Quantity Difference for Warehouse**
- **Quantity Difference for Source Bin**

Confirm Handling Unit Tasks

You can confirm HU tasks using the warehouse monitor. In this case, you enter the destination bin for the HU and confirm the task, as shown in Figure 12.17. You can access the execution criteria by selecting the HU, clicking on [icon], and selecting **Confirm WT with Exception**.

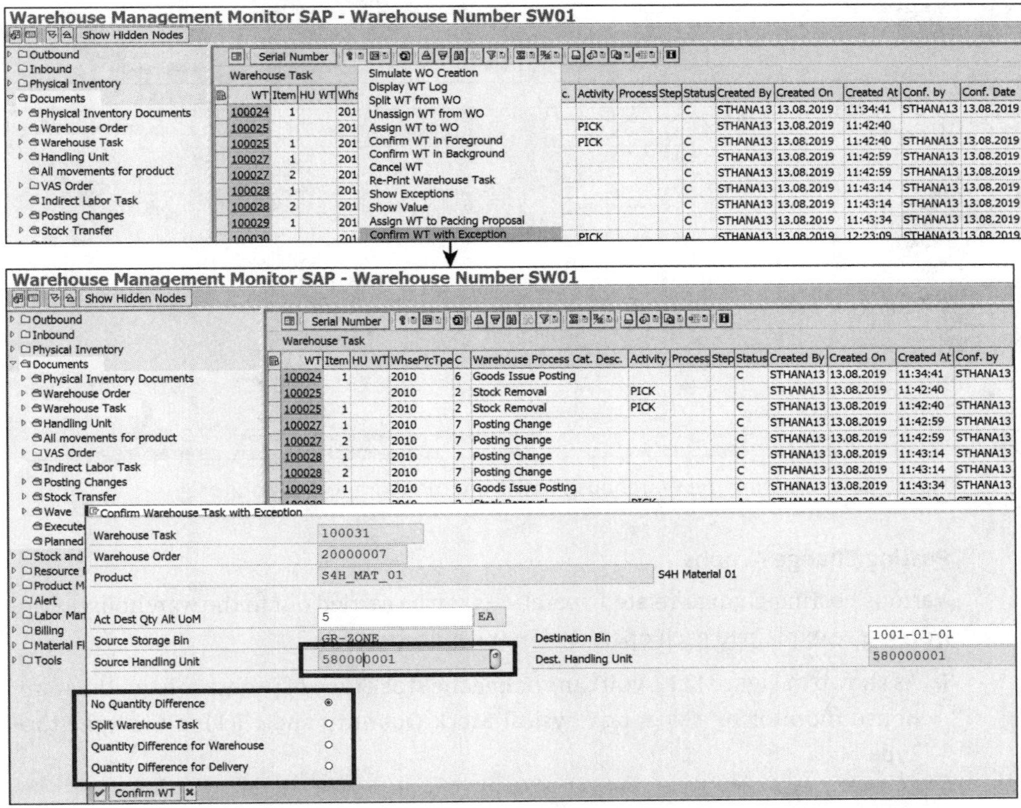

Figure 12.17 Confirming HU Warehouse Tasks Using Exception Codes

Warehouse Task Creation Actions

Using the warehouse monitor, you can create product warehouse tasks for available stock items, as shown in Figure 12.18. This enables power users to create such tasks from the warehouse monitor without hovering between the transactions of various processes, such as outbound, inbound, and internal operations. You can also create HU warehouse tasks for the warehouse monitor using the same process as for product warehouse task creation. You can access the execution criteria by selecting the HU, clicking on [icon], and selecting **Confirm WT In Background**.

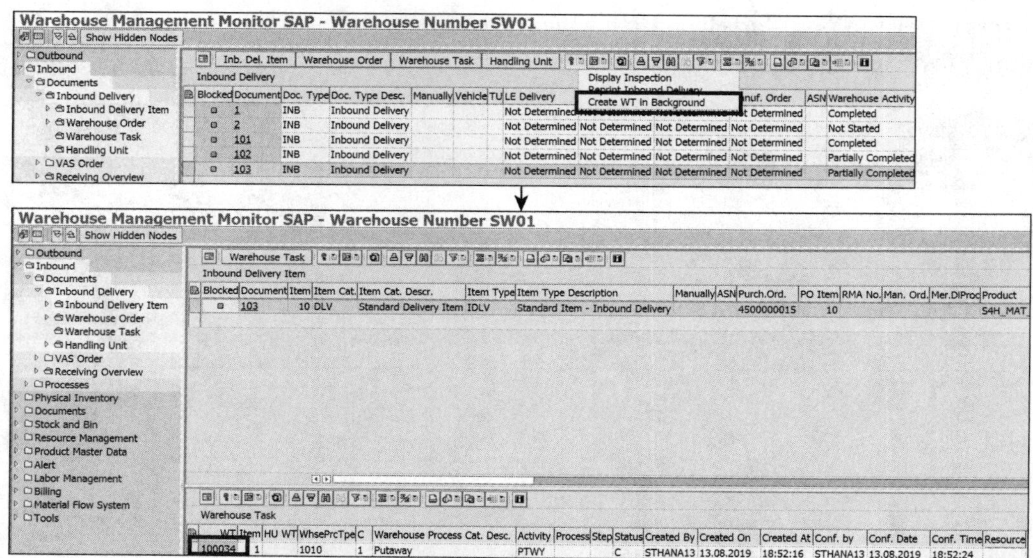

Figure 12.18 Creating the Warehouse Task from the Warehouse Monitor

Posting Change Actions

Various posting-change-related operations can be carried out in the warehouse monitor. We've explained each operation in the following:

1. As shown in Figure 12.19, you can change the stock type of products from the warehouse monitor by selecting **Physical Stock Quantity** and clicking **Change Stock Type**.

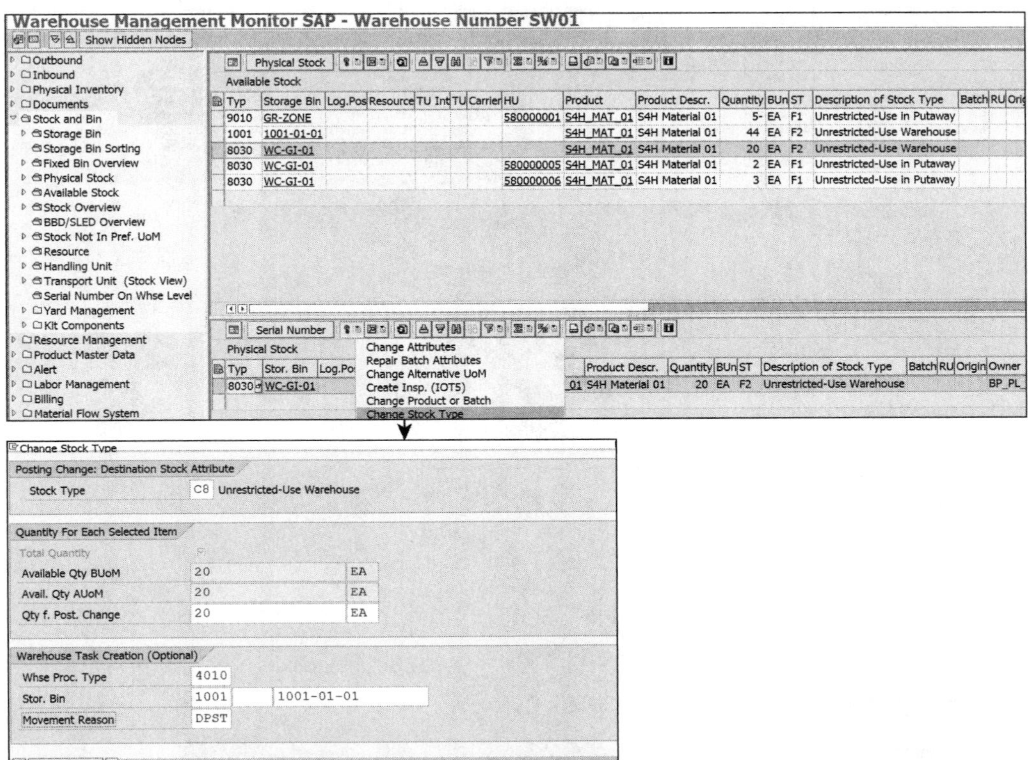

Figure 12.19 Stock Type Change from the Warehouse Monitor

2. As shown in Figure 12.20, you can change the sales order or project of the products from the warehouse monitor by selecting **Physical Stock Quantity** and clicking **Change Sales Order or Project**.

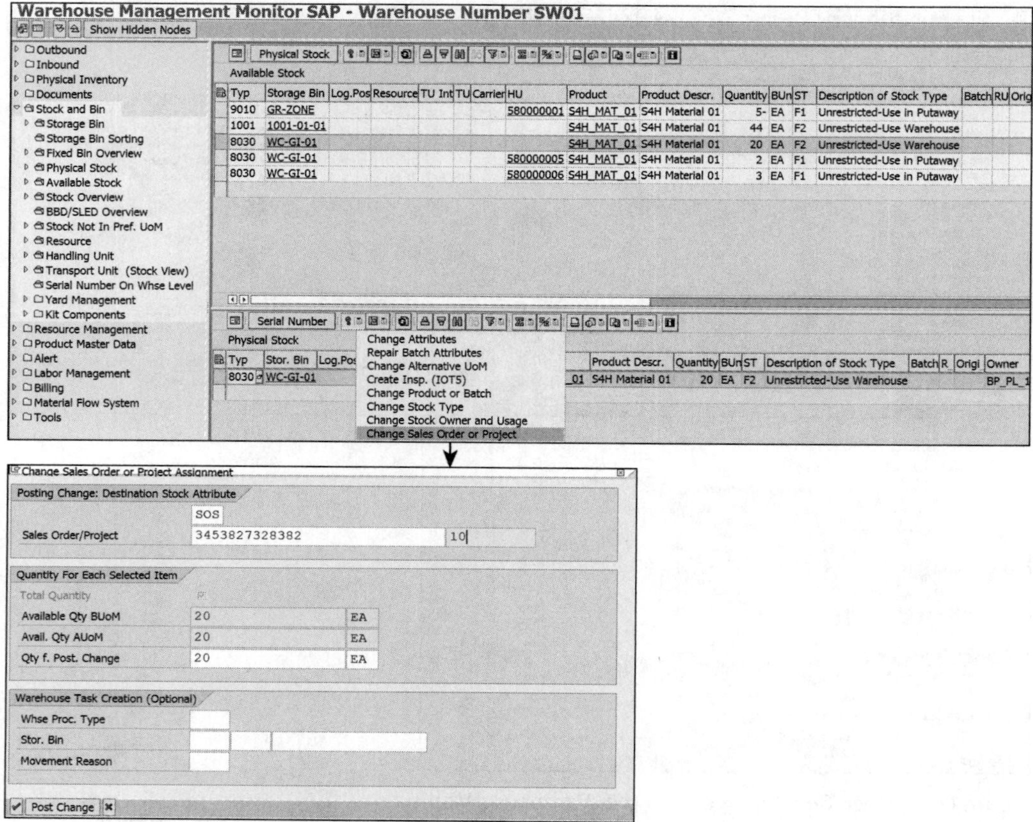

Figure 12.20 Sales Order/Project Change from the Warehouse Monitor

3. As shown in Figure 12.21, you can change the stock usage and owner of the products from the warehouse monitor by selecting **Physical Stock Quantity** and clicking **Change Stock Owner or Usage.**

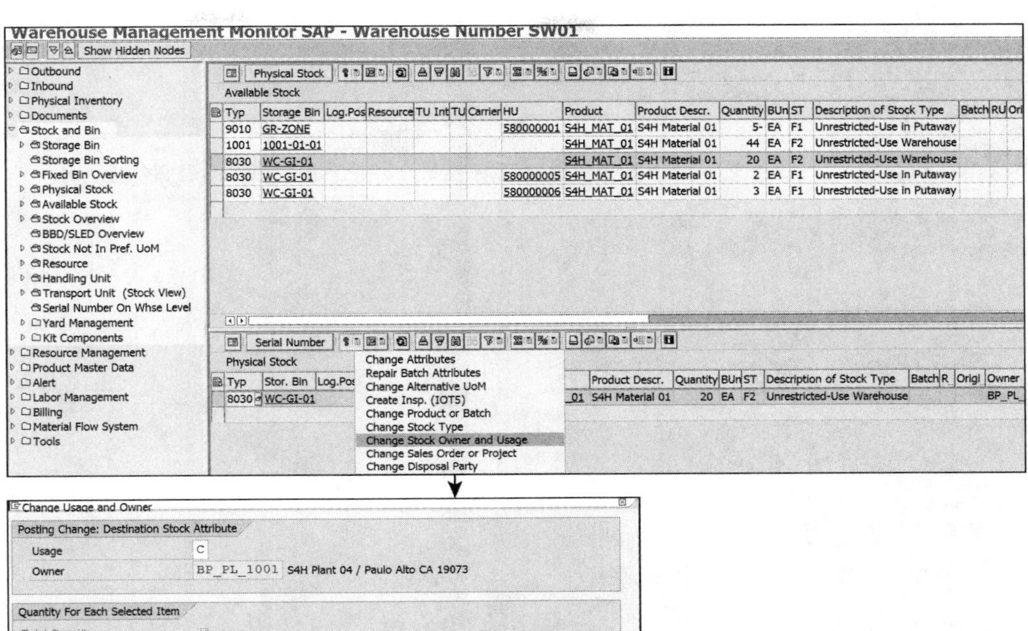

Figure 12.21 Stock Owner/Usage Change

4. As shown in Figure 12.22, you can change the product or batch of the products from the warehouse monitor by selecting **Physical Stock Quantity** and clicking **Change Product or Batch.**

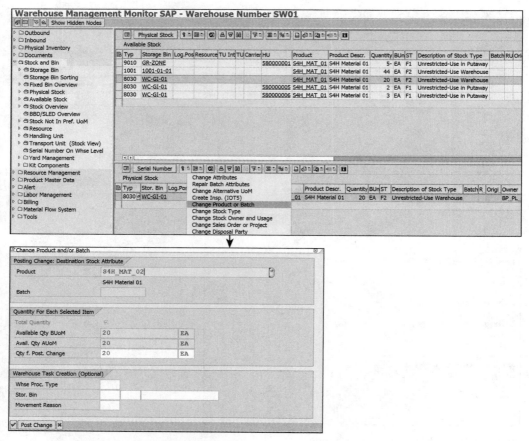

Figure 12.22 Product or Batch Change

5. As shown in Figure 12.23, you can display bin sorting using the warehouse monitor by selecting the **Storage Bin Sorting** node.

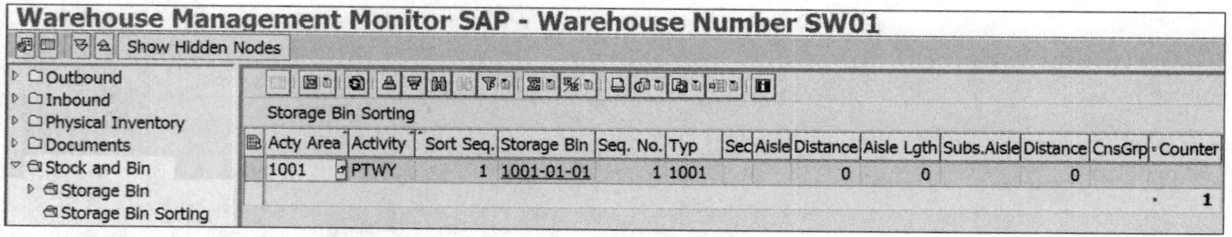

Figure 12.23 Displaying Bin Sorting

> **Note**
>
> This provides the user with just bin sorting report; you can't perform sorting from this node by using the displayed data.

6. As shown in Figure 12.24, you can create warehouse tasks for posting change items from the warehouse monitor by selecting **Posting Change Warehouse Request** and clicking **Create WT in Foreground.** You enter the target quantity, stock type, and other posting change characteristics, and then click the **Create WT** button.

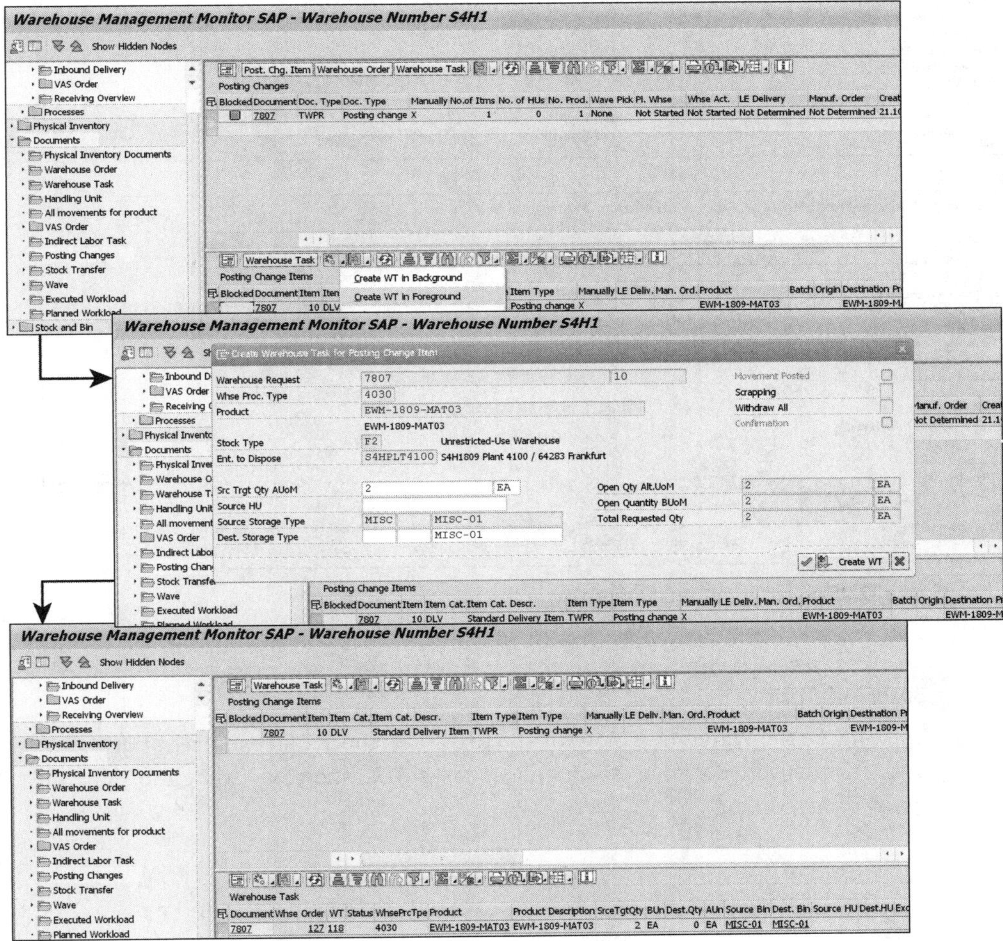

Figure 12.24 Creating the Warehouse Task for Posting Change in the Foreground

7. As shown in Figure 12.25, you can adjust quantities and create warehouse tasks for open posting changes from the warehouse monitor by selecting **Posting Change Warehouse Request** and clicking **Adjust Quantity.**

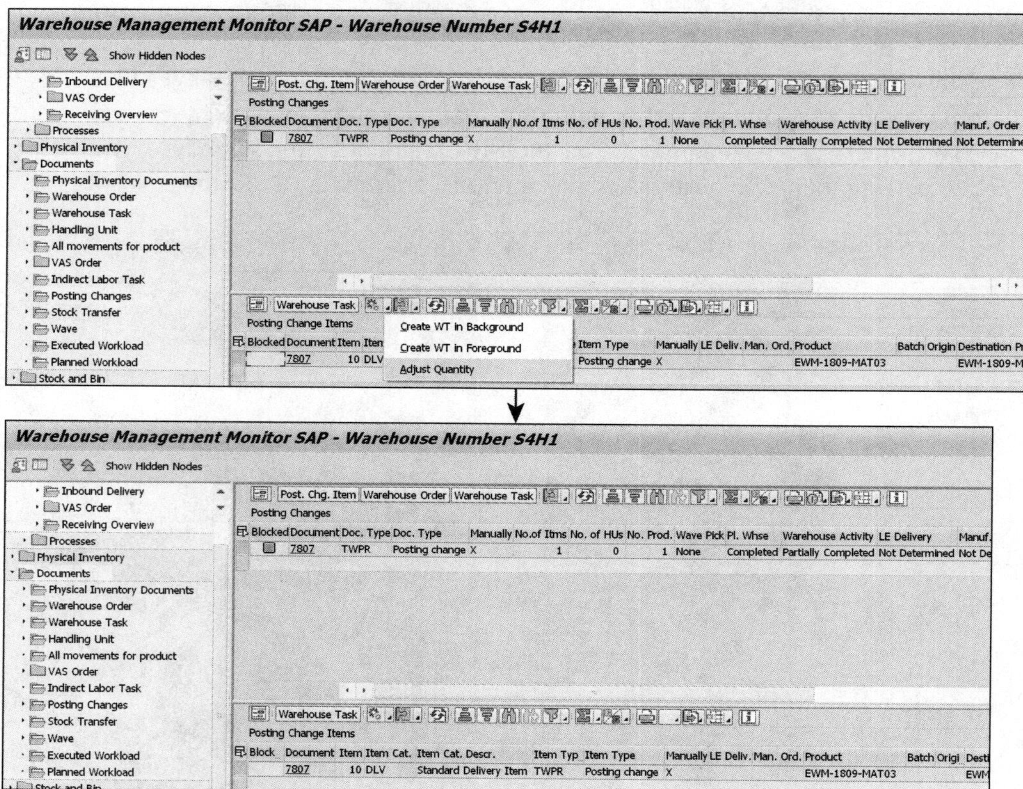

Figure 12.25 Selecting Adjust Quantity

> **SAP Fiori Apps**
>
> You can use the Warehouse Monitor app to display, check, and execute various operations on delivery documents, warehouse tasks, TUs, and so on using the standard warehouse monitor.

Physical Stock for Inspection lot

You can access the physical stock information for which an inspection lot is created without an inspection decision using the warehouse monitor. You can access the **Physical Stock** node in the warehouse monitor by going to **Documents • Inspection** node. This will enable you to search inspection lots based on the filter criteria, as shown in Figure 12.26. The warehouse monitor will display the inspection lots and take appropriate inspection decisions for the inspection lots.

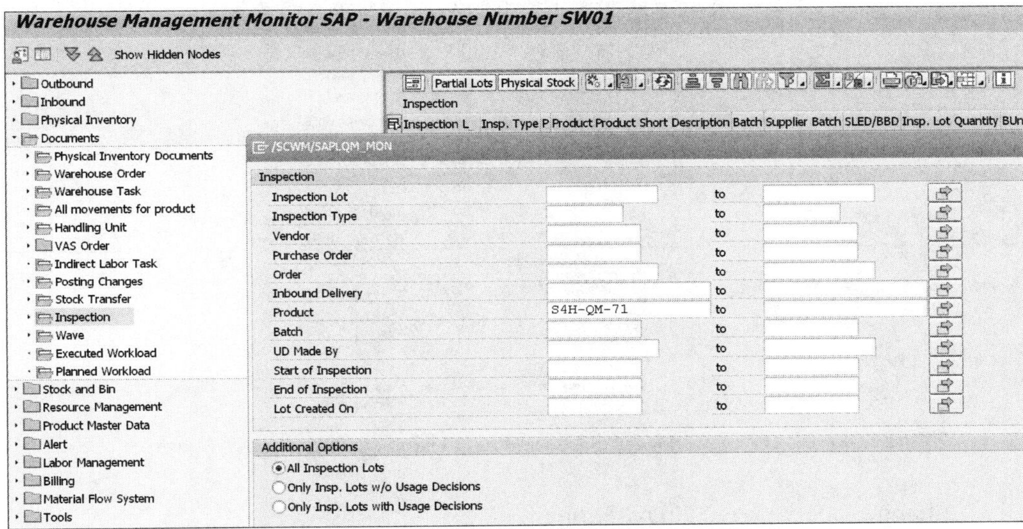

Figure 12.26 Quality Inspection Using the Warehouse Monitor

Storage Bin Change Logs

The storage bin change logs allow you to see any changes made in the storage bin master and by whom. This helps you track the changes made and revert them, if necessary. It also helps maintain accountability of the changes by knowing who made the changes and when were they made. The embedded EWM system creates a log document in which all changes made to storage bins are recorded; the log is made available to users for reporting purposes.

You can display the storage bin change logs via node path **Stock and Bin • Storage Bin** in the warehouse monitor. Using appropriate filter criteria, you click on the **Execute** button to see the bins for which you want to display the change logs. Select one of the storage bins, and click on **Display Bin Change Docs**, as shown in Figure 12.27. This displays the change logs with appropriate data for the storage bin master data.

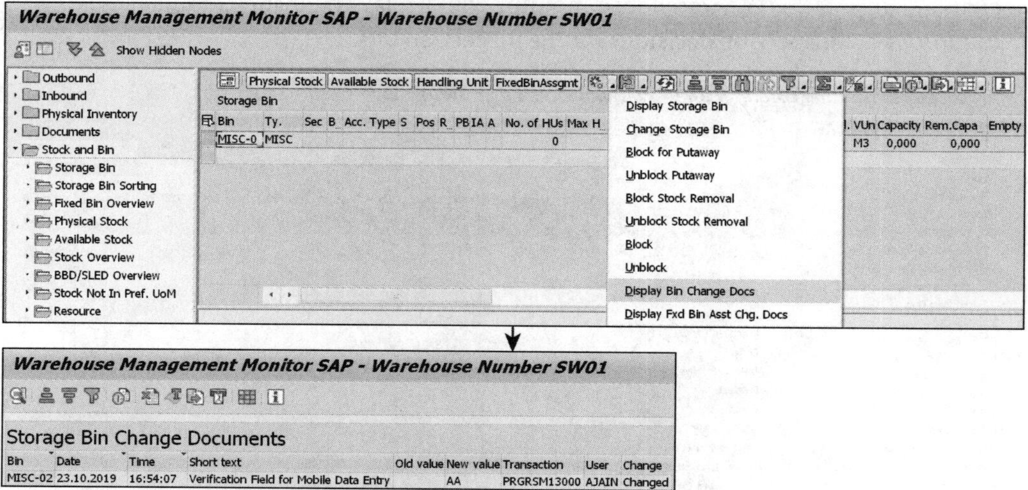

Figure 12.27 Displaying Bin Master Change Logs Using the Warehouse Monitor

Change Logs for Fixed Bin Assignment

Not only can you assign fixed bins to products to cap the number of bins in a storage area that a product can occupy, but you can also get the logs of changes made to any data in such a fixed bin assignment. These change logs are recorded in the system when any data is changed, created, or deleted in the fixed bin assignment with products.

You can display the change logs for fixed bin assignment by via node path **Stock and Bin • Storage Bin • Fixed Bin Assignment** in the warehouse monitor. Using appropriate filter criteria, click on the **Execute** button to display the bins for which you want to display the change logs. Select one of the fixed bin assignments with a product, and click on **Display Fixd Bin Change Asst Chg. Docs**, as shown in Figure 12.28. This displays the change logs with appropriate data for the selected fixed bin assignment.

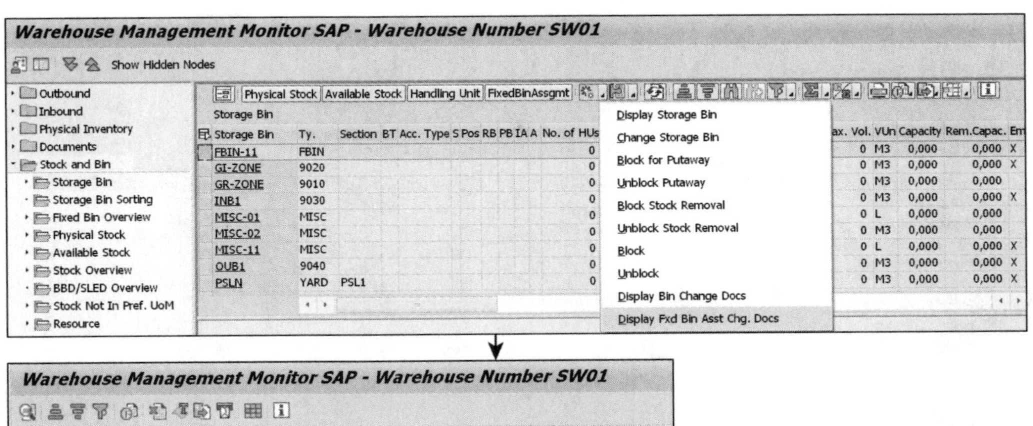

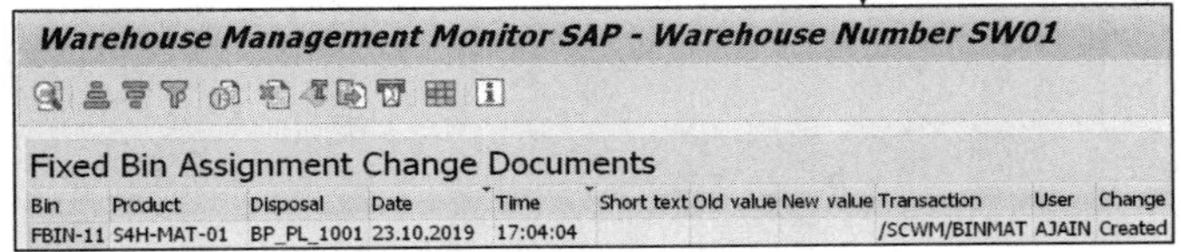

Figure 12.28 Displaying Fixed Bin Assignment Change Logs Using the Warehouse Monitor

> **Tip**
>
> The detail configuration with which the change logs for storage bins and fixed bin assignments can be captured and displayed is covered in Chapter 4, Section 4.3.7 and Section 4.3.9, respectively.

Warehouse Tasks Using a Kanban Container

You can search warehouse tasks in a warehouse with different statuses using a Kanban container ID for production order integration with embedded EWM and decentralized EWM by using repetitive manufacturing. You can display the warehouse tasks in the warehouse monitor via node path **Documents • Warehouse Tasks**. As shown in Figure 12.29, the warehouse monitor allows you to enter the Kanban container IDs so that appropriate warehouse tasks can be displayed in the warehouse monitor and appropriate action can be taken.

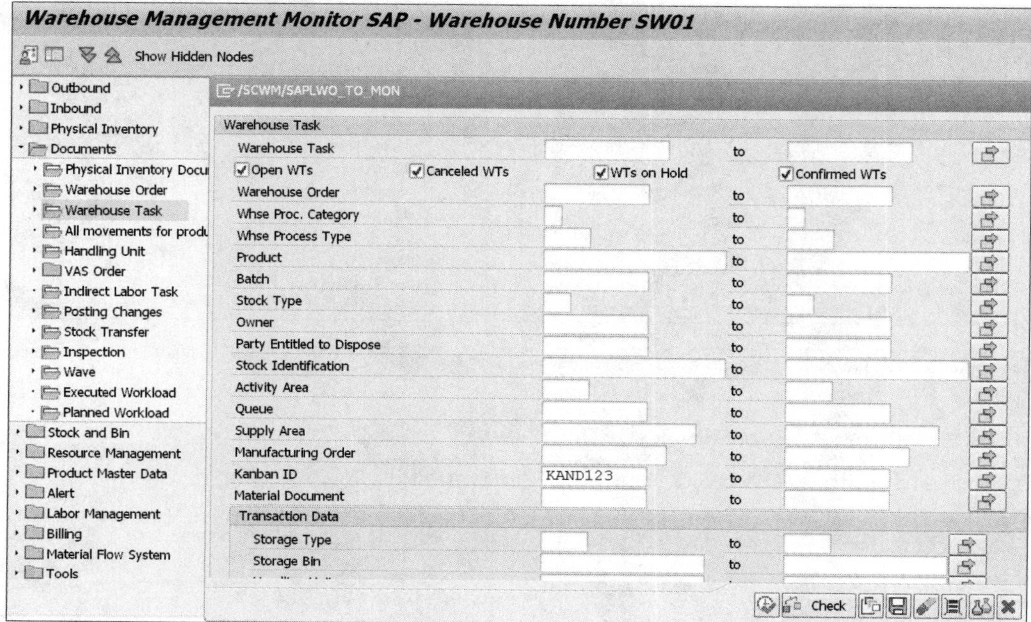

Figure 12.29 Filtering Warehouse Tasks Using the Kankan Container ID

Warehouse Tasks via the Material Document

In the repetitive manufacturing process, it's possible for you to search for warehouse tasks associated with the receipt of finished goods or issue of consumed products in the standard warehouse monitor. Using the **Warehouse Tasks** node under **Documents**, you can also display the material document, material document item, and document posting year, as shown in Figure 12.30.

> **Note**
>
> The Print Inventory List (For Fire Department) app allows you to print a stock inventory list for fire departments.

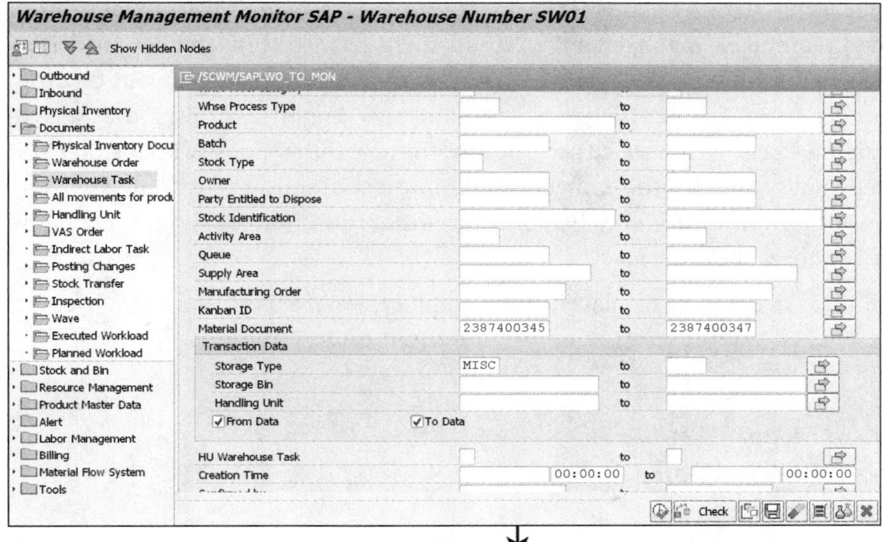

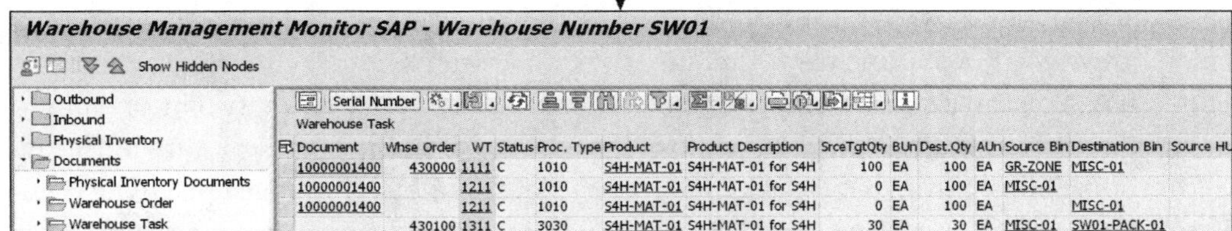

Figure 12.30 Filtering Warehouse Tasks Based on the Material Document

12.3 Graphical Warehouse Layout

You can view the embedded EWM warehouse's structure as a two-dimensional graphic. This graphical view provides an overview of the location of storage bins, stock, and resources in the warehouse. The graphical warehouse layout provides a simple interface that helps warehouse users analyze the current stock situation and bin utilization in the warehouse. For example, warehouse supervisors often need a rough estimate of the area of the warehouse that is suitably empty to hold certain stock for a small period. Using the graphical warehouse layout, a supervisor can see an overview of the current warehouse situation and make an appropriate stock-placement decision.

A graphical view for a warehouse is available via **SAP Easy Access** path **Logistics • SCM Extended Warehouse Management • Extended Warehouse Management • Monitoring • Graphical Warehouse Layout • Display Graphical Warehouse Layout** or using Transaction /SCWM/GWL. The graphical warehouse layout is displayed as a two-dimensional screen that's scaled according to the actual warehouse dimensions. You can set default values for the embedded EWM warehouse, storage type, and level by clicking on . If no level is specified, the system assumes that all storage types in the warehouse are at the same level.

The following data can be displayed in the graphical warehouse layout:

- Storage bins with or without labels
- HUs on conveyors
- Conveyor status
- Edges of the bin network
- Resources

The graphical warehouse layout displays the bins defined in bulk as consolidated areas; if a bin-specific view is required, it can be seen by setting the **Bin Level** checkbox. You can also view empty or blocked bins by selecting the **Empty Bins** or **Blocked Bins** radio button. The dimensions of bins displayed in the graphical warehouse layout are taken from bin type definitions. The locations of the storage bins in the warehouse are derived from the X, Y, and Z coordinates of the bins as defined in the bin master.

A warehouse can be crowded, and you may be required to focus on a certain section of the warehouse to view it in detail, for example, the goods receipt (GR) area. You zoom in by clicking on **Zoom In** or zoom out by clicking on **Zoom Out** to view bins, resources, and so on closely. You also can navigate in all four directions from the current view by entering a percentage value on the transaction screen and clicking on the **Up, Down, Left**, or **Right** buttons.

In addition to the standard objects displayed in the graphical warehouse layout, you can also define custom warehouse objects, such as walls, offices, conveyor segments, and the like, and display those as well in the graphical warehouse layout. To define custom objects, navigate to IMG path **SCM Extended Warehouse Management • Extended Warehouse Management • Monitoring • Graphical Warehouse Layout • Define GWL Object Category**. Click on **New Entries**, and define a new graphical warehouse layout object category in the customer-defined namespace. Note that you can't change the standard graphical warehouse layout object categories provided by SAP.

Next, assign the custom-defined graphical warehouse layout object category to a graphical warehouse layout object by navigating to IMG path **SCM Extended Warehouse Management • Extended Warehouse Management • Monitoring • Graphical Warehouse Layout • Define GWL Object.** Click on **New Entries**, and provide an **Identifier** for the new graphical warehouse layout object category and its dimensions in the warehouse.

Often, you'll need to display more master data objects in the graphical view of the warehouse, such as the conveyer network of the material flow system. This can be done by implementing the `/SCWM/EX_GWLDISPLAY` BAdI (Change Display of GWL). Not only can you add new objects, but you can also perform certain actions or follow-up functions for the existing and new objects in the warehouse graphical layout using the `/SCWM/EX_GWLCM` BAdI (Extend Context Menu).

12.4 Measurement Services

Measurement services are key figures that can be displayed in the warehouse cockpit. Key figures can be created using basic measurement services and tailored measurement services. Examples of key figures in the warehouse include the following:

- Deliveries that left or arrived in the warehouse
- Number of HUs
- Number of open/closed warehouse tasks or orders

You can define key figures in the form of three measurement services in embedded EWM, as follows:

- **Basic measurement services**
  Basic measurement services are key figures that also can be displayed using the warehouse monitor. These measurement services can include lists of inbound deliveries and the total number of inbound deliveries in the warehouse. The standard warehouse monitor provides various actions linked to function modules that can be used to calculate basic measurement services. SAP also allows for the creation of new basic measurement services if required, based on specific warehouse requirements (refer to SAP Note 1178089 for more details). Basic measurement services can be defined via IMG path **SCM Extended Warehouse Management •**

Extended Warehouse Management • Monitoring • Measurement Services • Define Basic Measurement Service. Click on **New Entries**, enter the **Basic Measurement Service ID** and controls (function module, report ID, etc.), and save.

- **Tailored measurement services**
  You can create tailored measurement services by adding selection variants to the basic measurement services to select a subset of basic measurement services. For example, if you need to select only completed warehouse tasks, then a filter for the **Complete** status can be added to the basic measurement services warehouse task in embedded EWM. Embedded EWM provides a wizard to create tailored measurement services via IMG path **SCM Extended Warehouse Management • Extended Warehouse Management • Monitoring • Measurement Services • Define Tailored Measurement Service**. Click on **Create**, and select the basic measurement service for which the new measurement service needs to be created.
- **Calculated measurement services**
  Multiple tailored measurement services can be connected mathematically to create calculated measurement services. These measurement services are used to calculate warehouse KPIs, employee performance in the warehouse, and so on. They can be defined via IMG path **SCM Extended Warehouse Management • Extended Warehouse Management • Monitoring • Measurement Services • Define Calculated Measurement Services with Wizard**. Click on **Create**, and select the tailored measurement services for which the new measurement service needs to be created.

12.5 Warehouse Key Performance Indicators

You can display the KPIs of warehouse transactional operations so that appropriate corrective actions can be taken by the warehouse administrator if the warehouse transactions differ from the established warehouse transaction processing standards of the organization.

As shown in Figure 12.31, you can see different types of KPI cards on the overview screen. A few of the KPIs that are covered using the Warehouse KPIs – Operations app are as follows:

- The number of overdue outbound delivery order items without goods issue by ship-to party/planned goods issue time
- The number of blocked outbound delivery order items by planned goods issue time

- The number of outbound delivery order items without goods issue by ship-to party/planned goods issue time
- The number of outbound delivery order items with incomplete wave assignments by planned goods issue time
- The number of confirmed warehouse orders by queue
- The number of open warehouse orders by queue
- The number of open pick warehouse tasks by activity area
- The number of open putaway warehouse tasks by activity area
- The number of open warehouse tasks by activity area, overdue time in hours, warehouse process category, and warehouse process type

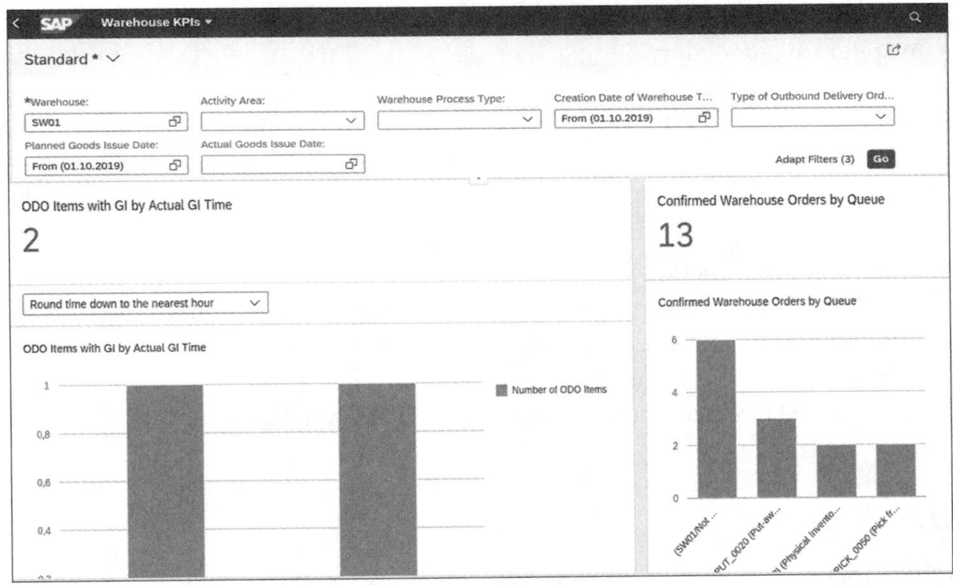

Figure 12.31 SAP Fiori App: Warehouse KPIs – Operations

12.6 Core Data Services Views for Warehouse Processes

As part of innovations in data models creation and consumption within the database layer in SAP HANA, SAP introduced a new data modeling method known as core data services (CDS). CDS also provides features such as conceptual modeling and relationship definition. Given that SAP has implemented this as part of the ABAP application service, development teams can make use of CDS to push the code execution to the database layer. This helps save the valuable execution resources of the hardware and increases the speed of process execution in SAP S/4HANA.

As part of out-of-the-box CDS views for other applications, SAP has also provided multiple standard CDS views for embedded EWM in SAP S/4HANA so that development teams and functional teams can make use of these ready-made data models. Users can then create and consume data using the following data models based on specific input parameters required by a specific data model:

- **Outbound delivery order query with specific dates**
  This CDS view (`C_EWM_OutbDelivOrdQ`) can be used for outbound process analysis by displaying the number of outbound delivery orders and outbound delivery order quantities, weights, and volumes.
- **Warehouse order query**
  This CDS view (`C_EWM_WarehouseOrderQ`) can be used for warehouse order count analysis by displaying the number of warehouse orders in the warehouse in different statuses. This will enable you to determine the amount of stock traffic movement in the warehouse, enabling you to allocate movement resources accordingly in the warehouse.
- **Warehouse task query**
  This CDS view (`C_EWM_WarehouseTaskQ`) is used for answering questions such as number of warehouse tasks, number of warehouse task items, total weight and volume of warehouse task items, actual product quantity, difference product quantity and target product quantity totaled due to warehouse task item.

12.7 Summary

In this chapter, we discussed the various monitoring tools available in embedded EWM. These tools provide an efficient way to monitor activities going on in warehouses and take corrective measures if required. We discussed the warehouse monitor, which can be used for execution of warehouse processes, alert handling, and so on, in addition to its monitoring capabilities. We discussed how the warehouse monitor can be used for displaying inspection lot, change logs for bin master and fixed bin assignment, displaying warehouse tasks and material documents.

We also discussed the graphical warehouse layout of the embedded EWM warehouse, via which the essential master data and structure of the warehouse can be viewed in a two-dimensional graphical format. Measurement services in embedded EWM, which are used to represent key figures used and collected, were explained in detail. We discussed and explained in detail the use of the Warehouse KPIs – Operations app for warehouse KPIs that can be used for decision-making by power users for warehouse administration. In the next chapter, we will discuss advanced production integration.

Chapter 13
Advanced Production Integration

In any organization's production process, it's of prime importance that raw materials are supplied uninterrupted to production lines and that finished goods used either for external or internal consumption are received in the warehouse. In this chapter, we'll discuss using embedded EWM to streamline this process.

The production process for any organization consists of taking raw material from a staging area and using it for production of semifinished or finished goods that are stored in the warehouse. Embedded EWM uses advanced production integration to integrate the supply of raw materials for production and the receipt of finished goods from the embedded EWM-managed warehouse.

This chapter covers the advanced production integration process. We begin by introducing the production process in embedded EWM in Section 13.1. Section 13.2 covers the steps required to set up production integration in the warehouse. Section 13.3 introduces the production material request, which acts as a warehouse request in embedded EWM to execute product staging. Section 13.4 covers setting up the production supply area for staging of raw materials, and we discuss the staging and consumption of raw materials for production in Section 13.5. Section 13.6 covers the receipt of finished products from production, and Section 13.7 covers replenishment strategy using the Kanban container ID and quantities. In Section 13.8, we explain how synchronous posting can be done between embedded EWM and inventory management (IM) in SAP S/4HANA.

13.1 What Is Advanced Production Integration?

Advanced production integration helps streamline the manufacturing process for both production orders and process orders created in SAP S/4HANA. Production integration in embedded EWM enables staging of raw materials for manufacturing orders in the production supply area and receiving of finished goods against the order. You can use the following production processes for advanced production integration in embedded EWM:

- Production order
- Process order
- Repetitive manufacturing
- Kanban

Advanced production integration allows for consolidated staging of products for production, which prompts optimal utilization of space in a production supply area. Packed products can be received manually or using radio frequency-based (RF-based) terminals after production is complete. The inventory for raw materials and finished goods is kept in separate storage locations in the warehouse, thereby improving inventory visibility in both embedded EWM and SAP S/4HANA. Along with the issue and receipt of materials for production processes, you can also integrate the production process with quality inspections for products being received in the warehouse. In Section 13.1.1, we explain the business context in which advanced production integration can be used in real-world scenarios. In Section 13.1.2, we explain the processes carried out in the system and documents related to advanced production integration.

13.1.1 Business Process

American company Beta Beverages regularly manufactures multiple drinks that require its plants to supply raw materials to the nearly connected plants and receive finished and packed products from the plants via automated belts. This is initiated in SAP S/4HANA using a planned production order created as part of production planning (PP). The production order contains the information about required raw materials and finished products to be received from the plant to the warehouse. The raw material is to be picked from source bins by warehouse workers and moved to staging bins so that it can be sent to the plants via goods issue. Similarly, the finished products need to be received in the production bins and moved on to the destination bin in embedded EWM. As shown in Figure 13.1, advanced production integration involves the following steps:

1. The warehouse receives a warehouse request for planned production supply delivery to supply the requested products to the Beta Beverages plant after performing any additional work on the products.

2. The warehouse-request-related warehouse task is assigned to a warehouse worker so that the worker can pick, pack, and stage the stock at the production supply area. Because stock handling based on advanced production integration is active in embedded EWM, the warehouse worker picks the stock required for production based on quantities calculated using the production supply control cycle settings in embedded EWM. The raw material is sent to plant via goods issue out of the production supply area bin.
3. After the final product is created in the Beta Beverages plant using the raw material sent to the plant in the previous step, the finished product is sent to the warehouse to store it in the appropriate storage area.
4. Warehouse workers again get warehouse tasks allocated to them in the handheld device, which they confirm by executing the finished stock movement from the production supply area bin to the final storage area.

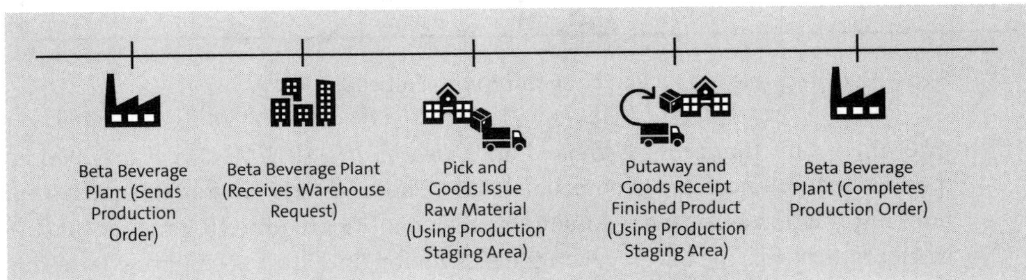

Figure 13.1 Business Flow for Advanced Production Integration

13.1.2 System Process

Figure 13.2 shows an end-to-end flow for the production process in embedded EWM. The production process in embedded EWM can be split into two parts. The first step is *staging and consumption*, which entails staging raw materials in the production supply area and posting their consumption after they're used in the production process. The next step is *receiving*, in which finished goods are received for storage in the warehouse.

For example, a beverage-manufacturing company will stage multiple raw materials, such as sugar syrup, concentrate, and so on, in the production staging area near the production line from where the products will be consumed for production. Based on the production schedule of the beverage, PP in SAP S/4HANA creates a production order to demand components at the production line.

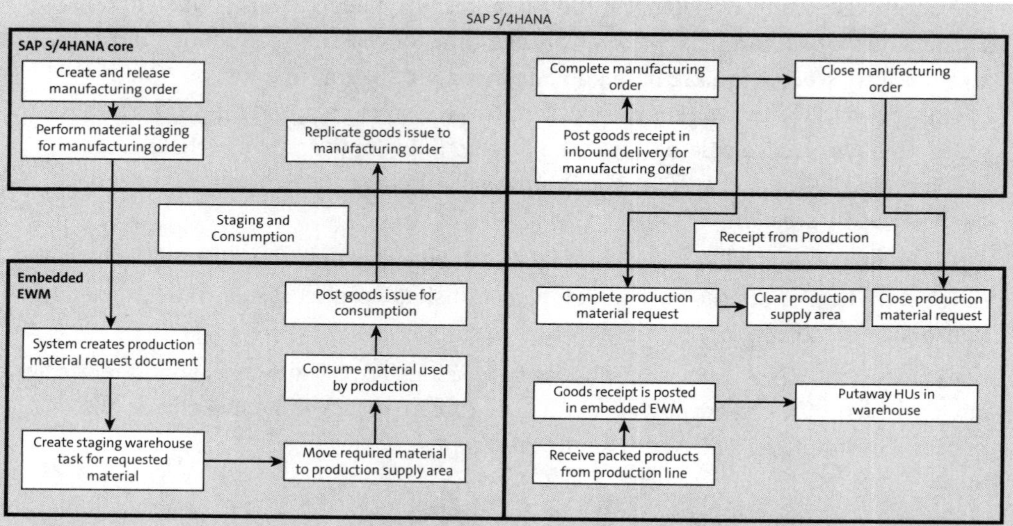

Figure 13.2 Advanced Production Integration with Embedded EWM

After the production order is created and released in SAP S/4HANA, a production material request is created in embedded EWM. The production material request contains information about the raw materials and quantities required to produce the finished product (e.g., the beverage) on the production line. Staging components at the production supply area can be planned over a period based on the time required to supply the components to the production line. Based on requirements, the components are moved to the staging area using staging warehouse tasks, which are confirmed after staging is completed. After components are consumed by the production process, a goods issue is posted for the components, which updates both the production material request in embedded EWM and the production order in SAP S/4HANA.

The finished products from the assembly line usually are packed in pallets (in HUs) before they are stored in the warehouse. Thus, when the beverage bottles are received in the warehouse, they're packed in pallets, labels are printed and scanned, and a goods receipt is posted for the products in embedded EWM. Warehouse tasks for putaway are created and confirmed. The goods receipt is communicated to SAP S/4HANA, in which the inventory of finished goods is increased. The status of the manufacturing order in SAP S/4HANA is set to **Technically Complete**. This sets the production material request in embedded EWM to the **Complete** status. The production supply area is cleared, and unused materials are moved back into the warehouse. The manufacturing order in SAP S/4HANA is set to **Closed**, which sends an update to embedded EWM and closes the production material request as well.

> **Tip**
>
> Any updates made in the production order in SAP S/4HANA are communicated to embedded EWM, and the production material request is updated synchronously. When the status of the production order is set to **Technically Complete**, staging of components can no longer be done, but consumption, reverse consumption, and production supply area clearing off can be achieved. When the status is set to **Complete**, no further action on the production material request can be performed.

13.2 Configuring Advanced Production Integration

The following steps are required to set up advanced production integration in embedded EWM:

1. Activate business function `LOG_PP_EWM_MAN_2` in embedded EWM using Transaction SFW5.
2. Maintain the delivery type determination for the manufacturing order in SAP S/4HANA. The delivery type and movement type are assigned for the plant/storage location via IMG path **Logistics Execution • Extended Warehouse Management Integration • Production Planning and Control • Define Delivery Type Determination**. Once there, click on **New Entries**, and define the movement types for the plant and storage locations, as shown in Figure 13.3.

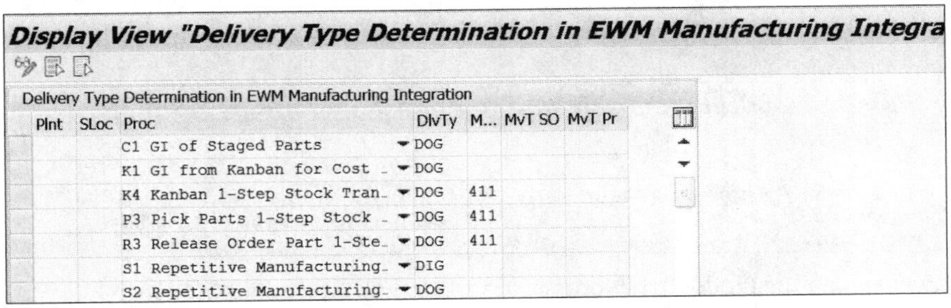

Display View "Delivery Type Determination in EWM Manufacturing Integra

Delivery Type Determination in EWM Manufacturing Integration

Plnt	SLoc	Proc	DlvTy	M...	MvT SO	MvT Pr
		C1 GI of Staged Parts	DOG			
		K1 GI from Kanban for Cost ...	DOG			
		K4 Kanban 1-Step Stock Tran...	DOG	411		
		P3 Pick Parts 1-Step Stock ...	DOG	411		
		R3 Release Order Part 1-Ste...	DOG	411		
		S1 Repetitive Manufacturing...	DIG			
		S2 Repetitive Manufacturing...	DOG			

Figure 13.3 Delivery Type Determination in Production Integration

3. The production staging area is created as a storage type in embedded EWM; from it, staging and consumption of raw materials is posted. The storage type for the production staging area is created via IMG path **SCM Extended Warehouse Management • Extended Warehouse Management • Master Data • Define Storage Type**. Once there, click on **New Entries**, and check that the value in **Storage Type Role** is set to **K-Production Supply**.

4. Configure the availability group to separate production supply stock from stock in the warehouse, from stock in production. We discussed the steps to configure the availability group in detail in Chapter 7, Section 7.2.4. Configuring new stock types for the production staging area enables settings for posting changes of stock from the IM location to the production supply area via IMG path **SCM Extended Warehouse Management • Extended Warehouse Management • Goods Receipt Process • Configure Availability Group for Putaway • Configure Stock Type**. Click on **New Entries**, and define a new stock type for production, as shown in Figure 13.4.

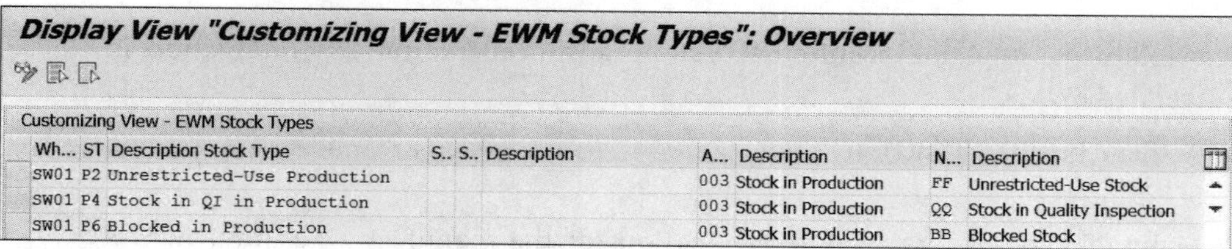
Display View "Customizing View - EWM Stock Types": Overview

Customizing View - EWM Stock Types

Wh...	ST	Description Stock Type	S..	S..	Description	A...	Description	N...	Description
SW01	P2	Unrestricted-Use Production				003	Stock in Production	FF	Unrestricted-Use Stock
SW01	P4	Stock in QI in Production				003	Stock in Production	QQ	Stock in Quality Inspection
SW01	P6	Blocked in Production				003	Stock in Production	BB	Blocked Stock

Figure 13.4 Defining Stock Types for Production Integration

5. Assign an availability group to the production storage location in SAP S/4HANA via IMG path **SCM Extended Warehouse Management • Extended Warehouse Management • Interfaces • ERP Integration • Goods Movement • Map Storage Location from ERP System to EWM**. Click on **New Entries**, and assign the availability group to the storage location where goods will be placed, as shown in Figure 13.5.

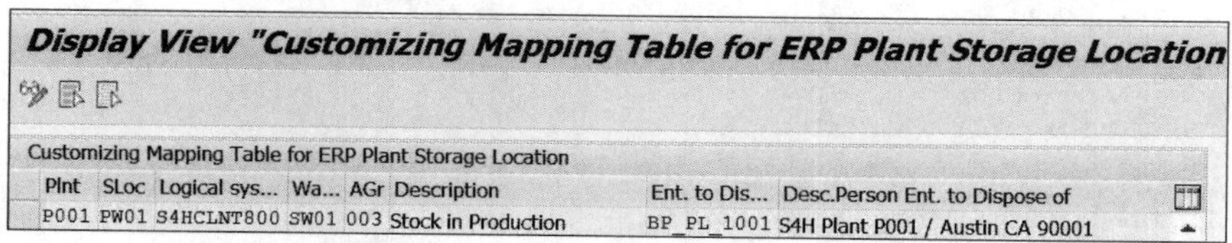
Display View "Customizing Mapping Table for ERP Plant Storage Location

Customizing Mapping Table for ERP Plant Storage Location

Plnt	SLoc	Logical sys...	Wa...	AGr	Description	Ent. to Dis...	Desc.Person Ent. to Dispose of
P001	PW01	S4HCLNT800	SW01	003	Stock in Production	BP_PL_1001	S4H Plant P001 / Austin CA 90001

Figure 13.5 Mapping the Production Storage Location to the Availability Group

6. If automatic goods issue posting is required from the production supply area, it's set via IMG path **SCM Extended Warehouse Management • Extended Warehouse Management • Goods Issue Process • Outbound Delivery • Production Supply • Maintain Settings for Auto. Goods Issue for Production Supply**. Set the **GI from PSA** value to allow background processing for the chosen **Warehouse No.** and **Document Type**, as shown in Figure 13.6.

   The background program can also post goods issue for a partial quantity in embedded EWM if the product staged in the production supply area and issued represents a partial quantity of an outbound delivery order. In that case, the embedded EWM system splits the outbound delivery order and posts a goods issue for a partial quantity. This can be controlled by activating the **OutbDel Spl All** or **Item Split All** checkbox.

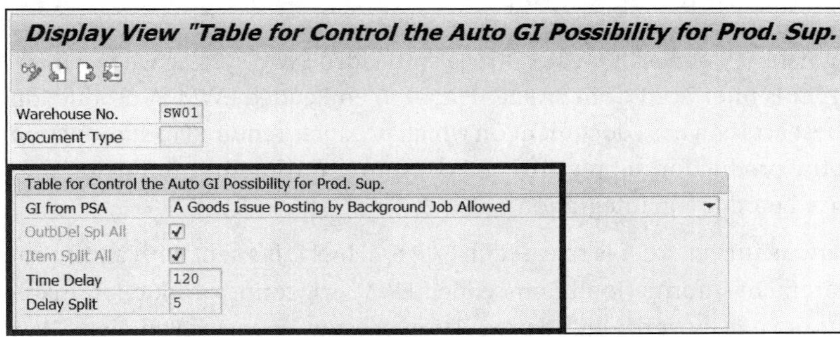

Figure 13.6 Control Setting for Automatic Goods Issue for Production Supply

7. Configure goods issue for consumption posting as shown in Figure 13.7 via IMG path **SCM Extended Warehouse Management • Extended Warehouse Management • Outbound Delivery • Production Supply • Post Goods Issue for Consumption Posting**. Set the controls for goods issue for a **Warehouse No.** and **Document Type**. By setting the **Auto GI for CP Deliv** indicator, you can activate the consumption posting delivery for automatic goods issue.

To activate this delivery type for automatic goods issue, the **/SCWM/PRD_OUT_POST_GI_PP** Post Processing Framework (PPF) profile is assigned to the delivery document type. You can allow partial goods issue for raw materials by setting the **Post Part. GI** indicator. The **Adjust Qty** indicator allows the system to update the quantity in the outbound delivery order in case of a failed goods issue.

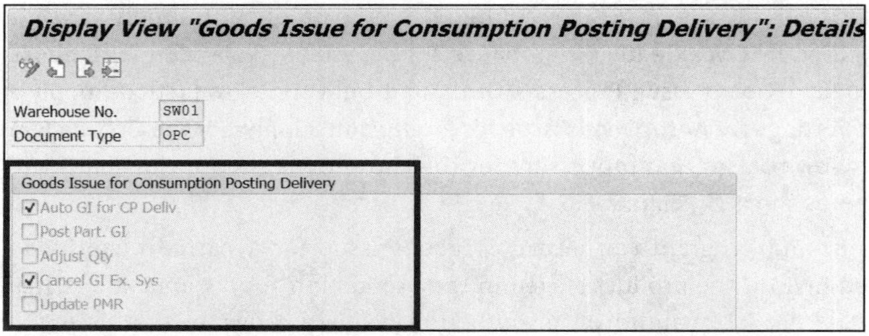

Figure 13.7 Settings for Posting Goods Issue for Consumption Posting

13.3 Production Material Request

A production material request is created in the embedded EWM system when a manufacturing order is interfaced from SAP S/4HANA to embedded EWM. A production material request acts as a base document on which products required for production are staged at the production supply area and consumed during the production process in advanced production integration.

When the manufacturing order is released in SAP S/4HANA, it's sent with all its production requirement information to embedded EWM, triggering production material staging automatically or through a production order by choosing **Function • WM Material Staging • Execute** or by clicking the **WM Material Staging** button in Transaction CO02. A production material request document consists of a document header and document item. The document item contains item-level details such as product number, quantity, production supply area, staging method, consumed quantity, and so on. The production material request can be displayed in embedded EWM via **SAP Easy Access** path **Logistics • SCM Extended Warehouse Management • Extended Warehouse Management • Work Scheduling • Staging for Production • Maintain Production Material Request** or via Transaction /SCWM/PMR.

The following steps are required for creating and displaying a production material request in embedded EWM:

1. Define a document type for the production material request via IMG path **SCM Extended Warehouse Management • Extended Warehouse Management • Goods Issue Process • Production Material Request • Define Document Types for Production**.

2. Define an item type for the production material request via IMG path **SCM Extended Warehouse Management • Extended Warehouse Management • Goods Issue Process • Production Material Request • Define Item Types for Production**.
3. Define the combination of allowed document types and item types in the production material request via IMG path **SCM Extended Warehouse Management • Extended Warehouse Management • Goods Issue Process • Production Material Request • Define Allowed Item Types for Production**.

Note

Additional details about document types and item types can be found in Chapter 7, Section 7.2.

13.4 Production Supply Area

The *production supply area* is the area on the shop floor where the products are staged and withdrawn. To fulfill the requirements for production orders, the embedded EWM system should know where to stage the products. This information is contained in the production supply area and is dependent on the production supply area, the product, and the party entitled to dispose. A production supply area is assigned to one or more storage bins where the products can be staged for a production order. The embedded EWM system uses production supply area information for determination of storage bins for the following:

- Staging to the production supply area
- Consumption of products from the production supply area
- Physical inventory in the production supply area
- Controlling staging of crate parts

In the following sections, we'll discuss the possible layouts of production supply areas in a warehouse and the settings required to set up the production supply area in embedded EWM. We'll also explain how change documents can be captured and displayed for the control cycle of the production supply area. Automatic replication of the production supply area from SAP S/4HANA to embedded EWM is also covered.

13.4.1 Managing Production Supply Area Stock in a Warehouse

Different organization models can be used for organizing production supply area stock, that is, raw materials ready to be used for production and other stock in the warehouse. The organization of stock in the warehouse affects how goods movement will happen in embedded EWM and the SAP S/4HANA system. There are four main options:

- **Two embedded EWM-based storage locations in a warehouse**
  In this case, the stock in the production supply area and other stock are two separate EWM-managed storage locations. When stock is staged in the production supply area, embedded EWM performs a posting change by changing the stock type in embedded EWM. This reflects a stock transfer from one storage location to another in SAP S/4HANA.
- **One embedded EWM-based storage location**
  In this case, the stock required for production and the stock at the production staging area are both kept in the same embedded EWM-managed storage location. When stock is staged at the production supply area, no posting change is executed by embedded EWM.
- **One materials management (MM)/IM-based and one embedded EWM-based storage location in a warehouse**
  In this case, only the raw material stock is kept in a storage location managed by embedded EWM. The stock is staged at the production supply area in a MM/IM storage location. When the stock is staged at the production supply area, it's issued out of embedded EWM using an outbound delivery order, which triggers a posting change to the inventory-managed storage location in SAP S/4HANA.
- **Two embedded EWM-based storage locations in two warehouses**
  In this case, the production supply area stock is managed in one embedded EWM warehouse, and the raw material stock is managed in a different embedded EWM warehouse. Staging stock involves issuing out of stock using outbound delivery in one embedded EWM warehouse and receipt in the receiving embedded EWM warehouse using inbound delivery.

13.4.2 Define the Production Supply Area

Production supply areas can either be defined manually in embedded EWM or replicated from SAP S/4HANA. The production supply area can be manually defined via **SAP Easy Access** path **Logistics • SCM Extended Warehouse Management • Extended**

Warehouse Management • Master Data • Production Supply Area (PSA) • Define PSA. Once there, select **New Entries**, and define the new production supply area for the warehouse. On this screen, set the **Trigger GI** indicator if you want to post goods issue for stock in the production supply area immediately to make it available in SAP S/4HANA.

If the production supply area is created manually in embedded EWM, it's assigned to a production supply area in SAP S/4HANA via **SAP Easy Access** path **SCM Extended Warehouse Management • Extended Warehouse Management • Interfaces • ERP Integration • Map Production Supply Area (PSA)**. Once there, assign the production supply area created in embedded EWM in the **Supply Area** field, as shown in Figure 13.8.

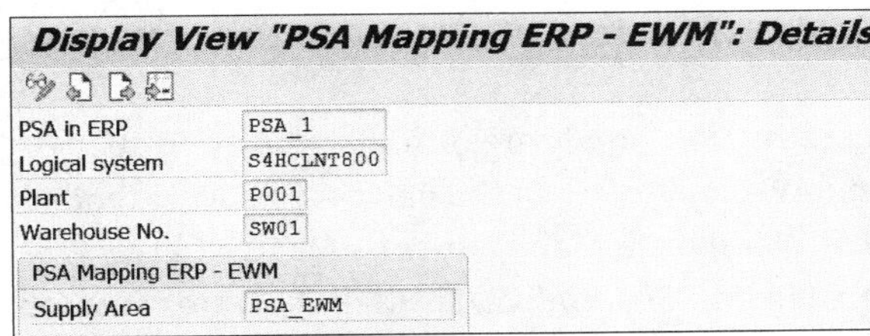

Figure 13.8 Mapping Production Supply Area Created Manually in Embedded EWM

To create a production supply area in SAP S/4HANA, navigate to IMG path **Logistics • Logistics Execution • Master Data • Warehouse • Production Supply • Production Supply Area • Create/Change**, or enter Transaction PK05. You can replicate the production supply area created in SAP S/4HANA to embedded EWM via **SAP Easy Access** path **SCM Extended Warehouse Management • Extended Warehouse Management • Interfaces • ERP Integration • Replicate Production Supply Area (PSA)**. Once there, provide the supply area created in SAP S/4HANA in the **PSA in ERP** field for the embedded EWM warehouse, and click on the icon, as shown in Figure 13.9.

After the production supply area is created, assign the storage bins to the production supply area to hold the stock to be issued for production. You can assign storage bins at multiple levels for each production supply area:

- Default storage bin for each party entitled to dispose
- Storage bin for each party entitled to dispose and product group
- Storage bin for each party entitled to dispose and product

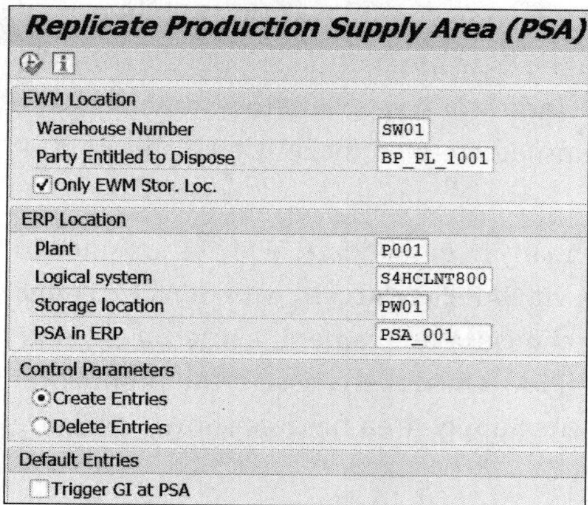

Figure 13.9 Replicating the Production Supply Area from SAP S/4HANA to Embedded EWM

To assign a bin to a combination of production supply area/product/party entitled or product/party entitled, navigate to **SAP Easy Access** path **Logistics • SCM Extended Warehouse Management • Extended Warehouse Management • Master Data • Production Supply Area (PSA) • Assign Bin to PSA/Product/Entitled in Warehouse** or **Assign Bin to Product/Party Entitled to Dispose in PSA**. As shown in Figure 13.10, assign the storage bin for a production staging area in the **Storage Bin** field.

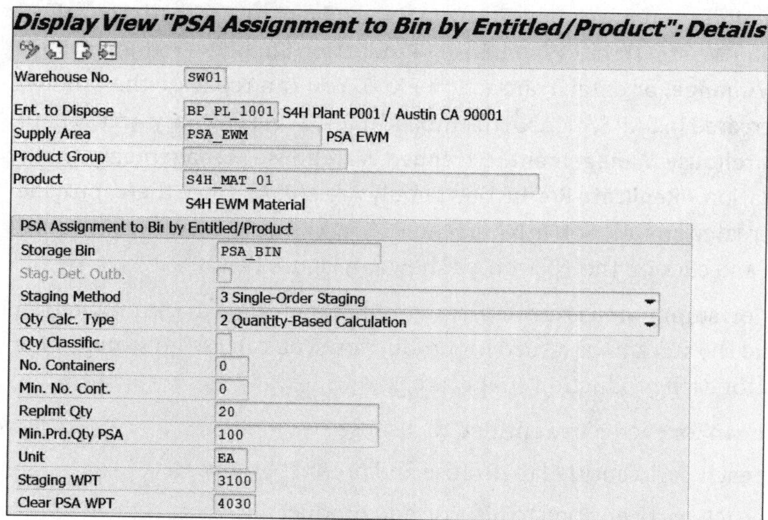

Figure 13.10 Defining the Production Supply Area Setting in Embedded EWM

13.4.3 Change Documents for the Control Cycle

Along with assigning bins to the production supply areas defined in Section 13.4.2, which are used to supply and receive stock for production purposes using Transaction /SCWM/PSASTAGE or Transaction /SCWM/PSASTAGE2, you can also get the logs of changes made to any data regarding this bin assignment to the production supply area. These change logs are recorded in the system when any data is changed, created, or deleted regarding this bin assignment to the production supply area.

After the changes are made to the bin assignment to the production supply area, the changes are captured in the change log and can be displayed to the user using bin assignment Transaction /SCWM/PSASTAGE or Transaction /SCWM/PSASTAGE2. To display the changes in bin assignment to the production supply area, you must select any of the bin assignment production supply areas and click on the **Display Change Documents** button. This displays the changes made to the various parameters of the bin assignment to the production supply area with details on the changes made by the user, such as date and time the change is made, type of change made, and transaction used to make the change.

13.4.4 Automatic Replication of a Production Supply Area

Whenever the production supply area is created in PP using IMG path **Logistics Execution • Warehouse Management • Interfaces • Define Production • Production Supply Area (Maint.)**, or it uses the control cycles supplied by embedded EWM, it's automatically replicated to embedded EWM, as shown in Figure 13.11. You enter the SAP S/4HANA **Plant** ID and press Enter to display the screen to maintain a production supply area in SAP S/4HANA. To create a production supply area, you click on **New Entries**, enter the **Supply Area**, **Storage location**, **Factory Calendar (Consumer)**, and so on, and click **Save**.

Thus, whenever you maintain a control cycle in PP in SAP S/4HANA using Transaction LPK1, you can also go to the dependent control cycle of embedded EWM by clicking the button, as shown in Figure 13.12. The control cycle for this production supply area can then be maintained using the standard control cycle maintenance, as explained in Section 13.4.2.

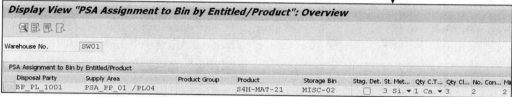

Display View "Production Supply Area": Details

Plant	PL04	Plant 04 - S4H-1909
Supply Area	PSA_PP_01	Production Supply Area
Storage location	AFS	Avail. for Sale
Responsible		
(Auto) Unloading Point		
Unloading Point		
Factory Calendar (Consumer)	US	
Shift Grouping (Consumer)		
Shift Sequence (Consumer)		
Pull Interval [Days]	0	
Pull Interval [h:min]		

Display View "PSA Assignment to Bin by Entitled/Product": Overview

Warehouse No. SW01

PSA Assignment to Bin by Entitled/Product

Disposal Party	Supply Area	Product Group	Product	Storage Bin	Stag. Det.	St. Met...	Qty C.T...	Qty Cl...	No. Con...	Mi
BP_PL_1001	PSA_PP_01 /PL04		S4H-MAT-21	MISC-02	☐	3 Si...	1 Ca...	3	2	2

Figure 13.11 Creating and Replicating the Production Supply Area in Embedded EWM

Display View "PSA Assignment to Bin by Entitled/Product": Details

Warehouse No.	SW01	
Disposal Party	BP_PL_1001	S4H Plant 1001 / Chicago IL 60699
Supply Area	PSA_PP_01 /PL04	Production Supply Area
Product Group		
Product	S4H-MAT-21	
	S4H-MAT-01 for S4H	

PSA Assignment to Bin by Entitled/Product

Storage Bin	MISC-02
Stag. Det. Outb.	☐
Staging Method	3 Single-Order Staging
Qty Calc. Type	1 Calculation Based on Packaging Specification
Qty Classific.	3
No. Containers	2
Min. No. Cont.	2
Replmt Qty	0,000
Min.Prd.Qty PSA	0,000
Unit	
Staging WPT	
Clear PSA WPT	

Figure 13.12 Creating the Control Cycle for Replicating the Production Supply Area in Embedded EWM

Note

As mentioned earlier, automatic replication of the production supply area from PP in the SAP S/4HANA core to production integration in embedded EWM is available in embedded EWM only.

13.5 Staging and Consumption

Staging is the process of moving the stock from the warehouse to the production supply area bin, which may or may not be based on the production material request quantity. The stock quantity to be moved depends on the type of control cycle assigned to the combination of the production supply area and product. You can define the minimum quantity of the product at a production supply area by setting a quantity in **MinPrd.Qty PSA** while assigning a storage bin to a production supply area. If the sum of the quantity of the product at the production supply area and the open warehouse task quantity is lower than the minimum quantity required at the production supply area, then the system creates a warehouse task to replenish the product from the warehouse to the production supply area.

In the following sections, we'll explain the production supply area replenishment process as well as how physical distribution equipment can be configured, simulated, and used in embedded EWM for staging stock at the production supply area.

13.5.1 Process Execution

Embedded EWM provides the flexibility to stage goods depending on business requirements. Thus, goods can be staged all at once or can be moved to the production supply area at regular intervals based on the space available in the production supply area, depending on the frequency of utilization of goods in the production process.

Three different types of staging methods can be configured:

- **Pick parts**
  This staging method is used to fulfill batch-specific requirements in the production process. Embedded EWM creates a warehouse task to move products to the production supply area for each production material request item individually.

Each task references a single production material request item. After task confirmation, stock in the production supply area contains a reference to a production material request item. Thus, the stock can be used for the same production material request for production supply. If the quantity in the production supply area falls below the minimum required level, then replenishment is executed at the individual production material request level.

- **Release order parts**
  Embedded EWM stages products for one or more production material request items by grouping them together. The staging warehouse task and the staged product don't contain references to any production material request in this case. Hence, any production material request can consume the staged product that meets its requirements. If the quantity in the production supply area falls below the minimum required level, then the system proposes a quantity for staging for each component that is required in the production supply area.

Example

If four different production lines require products for manufacturing, the requirements from all four production lines can be staged in a pallet. Any production line can then consume the products from the pallet based on the requirements.

- **Crate parts**
  In this method, products are stored in crates or other containers. This is a case of regular replenishment of products from warehouse to staging area if the required minimum quantity is reached. This method is independent of production material requests.

You can execute the staging of raw materials for open production material requests using Transaction /SCWM/STAGE, which can also be accessed via **SAP Easy Access** path **Logistics • SCM Extended Warehouse Management • Extended Warehouse Management • Work Scheduling • Staging for Production • Schedule Staging for Production**. Here, you'll provide selection screen inputs such as the warehouse number, product, production supply area, and so on, and then execute the report in the foreground or background as a variant in Transaction SM37 (see Figure 13.13). Upon execution, the system creates staging warehouse tasks for open staging requirements within the time period noted in the **Time Period for Requirement Start** section of the report.

Schedule Staging for Production

Staging Report Selections

Warehouse Number	SW01		
Production Supply Area	PSA_001 /P001	to	
Staging Method	3		
Manufacturing Order		to	
Finished Product or Order Text		to	
Product for Staging	S4H_MAT_01	to	S4H_MAT_02

Time Period for Requirement Start

(•) Period ends in hours from now

Number of Hours: 2

( ) Period ends at specific time

Date: 23.12.2017

Time: 04:55:04

Additional Settings

[✓] Test Mode

[✓] Show Log

Figure 13.13 Report to Schedule Staging for Production

After production material request processes are complete, and the status is set to **Technically Completed**, some unused stock may remain at the production supply area that no production material request requires. This stock is cleared so that stock required by another order can be staged at the production supply area. Before moving excess stock from the production supply area back to the warehouse, the reference of the production material request to staged stock must be removed if products have been staged using the single-order staging method. To remove a reference to the production material request from the product staged at the production supply area bin, you must release the assignment manually, after which the unused stock can be put back into the warehouse.

The consumption of raw materials is posted from the production supply area bin in SAP S/4HANA as and when used by the production process. Embedded EWM sends the consumption information to SAP S/4HANA, which in turn updates the manufacturing order for which the product was consumed. You can also reverse the consumption posted against the production material request in embedded EWM.

As discussed in the previous section, the consumption of products can be posted for production material requests if the status of the production material request is **Technically Completed** or **Released.** Consumption can be posted for both packed and unpacked products relevant for staging against a production material request. The consumption posting can be reversed for both partial and complete quantities of the product consumed against a production material request. You can reverse both the product and the HU quantity. For partial HU consumption reversal, the products are returned to the same HU. For complete HU consumption, embedded EWM creates a completely new HU with the same attributes and packaging information.

13.5.2 Distribution Equipment during Staging in a Production Supply Area

As shown in Figure 13.14, it's possible to represent the stock loading onto distribution equipment and then unloading of the same for production supply using distribution equipment in embedded EWM.

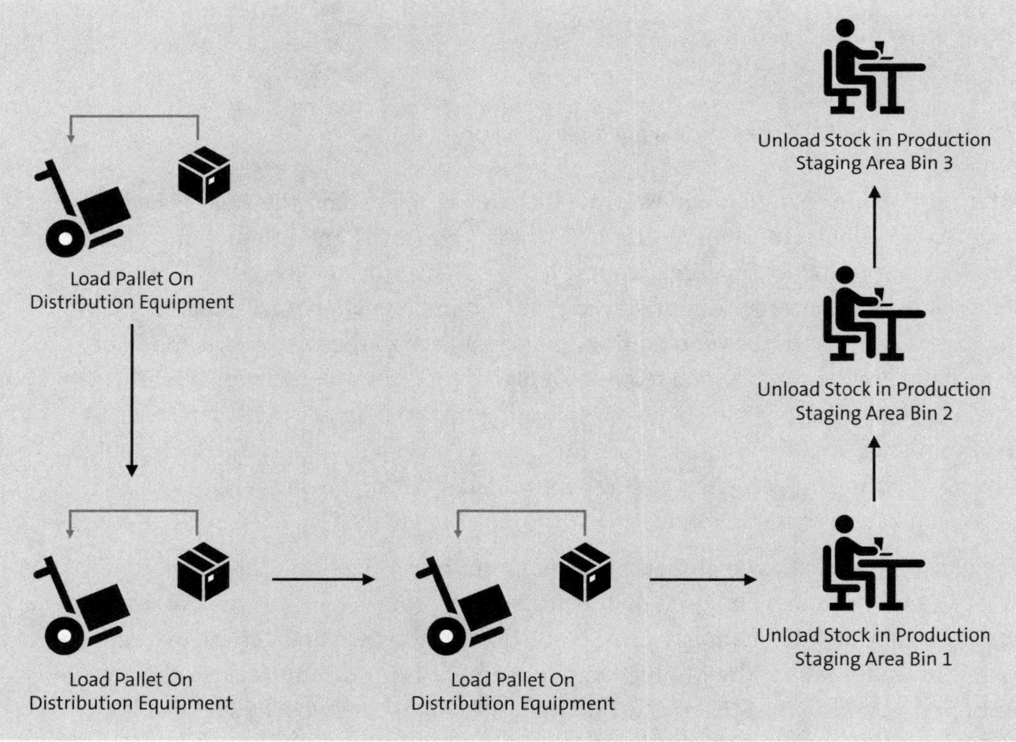

Figure 13.14 Process Flow for the Production Supply Area Stock Staging Using Distribution Equipment

The goods are packed into HUs and are then assigned to the distribution equipment. After the goods are successfully picked and loaded onto the distribution equipment, the goods are moved using the distribution equipment to their respective production supply areas where they are unloaded based on the production requirement. You can also change the loading/unloading details after the goods are loaded onto the distribution equipment.

The process flow for loading and unloading of goods using distribution equipment in embedded EWM is as follows:

1. **Picking**
   The warehouse worker either picks the goods into an empty compartment of an existing handling unit (HU) or picks a complete HU of goods and places it on the distribution equipment using an RF device. When placing the goods on a compartment of an HU, the user can note down the position of the goods in terms of where in the HU they were placed.
2. **Staging for loading**
   After completing the picking process, the warehouse worker moves on to the destination staging bins, which are set up using process-oriented storage control so that they can be staged for loading on distribution equipment.
3. **Loading**
   After the goods are successfully staged onto the staging location for loading, the warehouse worker either picks the goods and places them on to the empty HU compartment on the distribution equipment while noting down the goods location (optional) or picks the complete HU and places it on the distribution equipment.
4. **Change loading and unloading details**
   The warehouse worker can load and unload any goods using the HUs or sub-HU compartments before finally unloading the goods in the production supply areas.
5. **Unloading**
   After the loading step is complete, the warehouse worker moves on to complete the next task for unloading the complete HUs or content of sub-HUs on to the production supply areas from the distribution equipment.

Distribution equipment can be used for the production supply area supply process by performing the following steps:

1. **Create a new warehouse order creation rule.**
   To ensure that the goods are picked up in the HU compartments or complete HUs

are picked in the distribution equipment, a new warehouse order creation rule must be created with **Creation Cat. – I**. Optionally, you can also assign a packing profile to this warehouse order creation rule so that embedded EWM provides a packing proposal with packing material for the goods being picked using a pick HU. A proper determination of the warehouse order creation rule can be set up for the goods movement process or the same can be assigned to the picking warehouse process type.

2. **Create HUs with HU compartments.**
   If your business requires partial or unpacked goods to be picked up in HU compartments, then the HUs with HU compartments should be created via **SAP Easy Access** path **Logistics • SCM Extended Warehouse Management • Extended Warehouse Management • Master Data • Work Center • Create HUs in Compartment Hierarchy.**
3. **Set up packing material for the partial pick goods.**
   If you're picking unpacked goods from the source bin onto the HU compartment, then it's required to be automatically packed to keep track of its position in the HU. You must set this up via **SAP Easy Access** path **Logistics • SCM Extended Warehouse Management • Extended Warehouse Management • Settings • Warehouse Order • Set Up Distribution Equipment**, as shown in Figure 13.15. Click on **New Entries**; enter the packing profile, activity area, packing material, and display settings; and save.

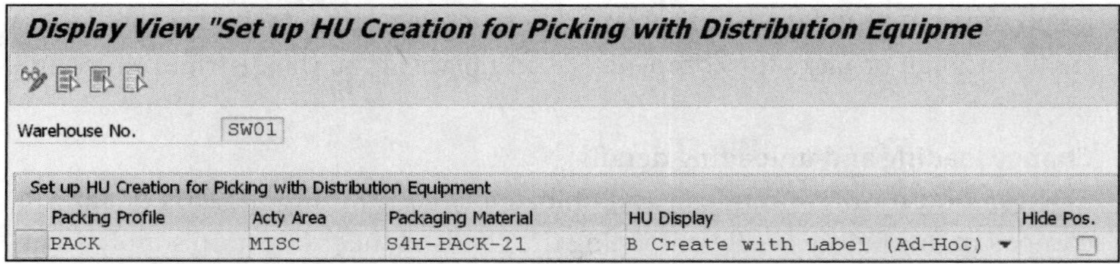

Packing Profile	Acty Area	Packaging Material	HU Display	Hide Pos.
PACK	MISC	S4H-PACK-21	B Create with Label (Ad-Hoc)	☐

Figure 13.15 Setting Up HU Creation Using Distribution Equipment

4. **Define new external process steps for the distribution equipment.**
   You must define new external process steps for three different distribution equipment movements via IMG path **SCM Extended Warehouse Management • Extended Warehouse Management • Cross-Process Settings • Warehouse Task • Define Process-Oriented Storage Control**. Select the **External Storage Process Step**

node, click on **New Entries**, enter the following external process steps, and save (see Figure 13.16):

- "DDLD: Distribution Equipment: Loading"
- "DDST: Distribution Equipment: Staging"
- "DDUL: Distribution Equipment: Unloading"

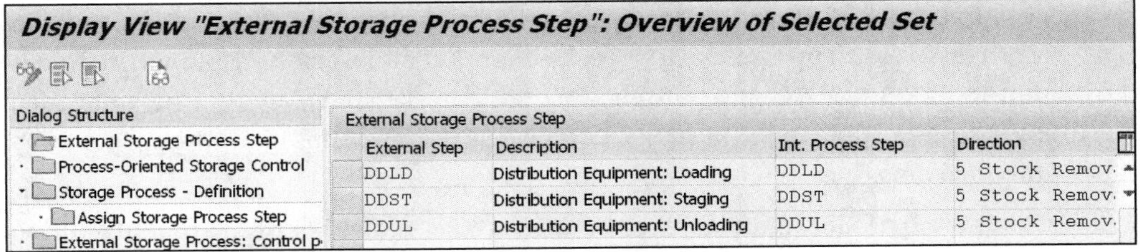

Figure 13.16 Defining the External Process Steps for Distribution Equipment

5. **Assign the new external process steps to storage types.**
   You must now assign the external process steps defined for DDLD and DDST to required storage types and specify automatic creation of warehouse tasks to complete the settings of the process-oriented storage control, as shown in Figure 13.17.

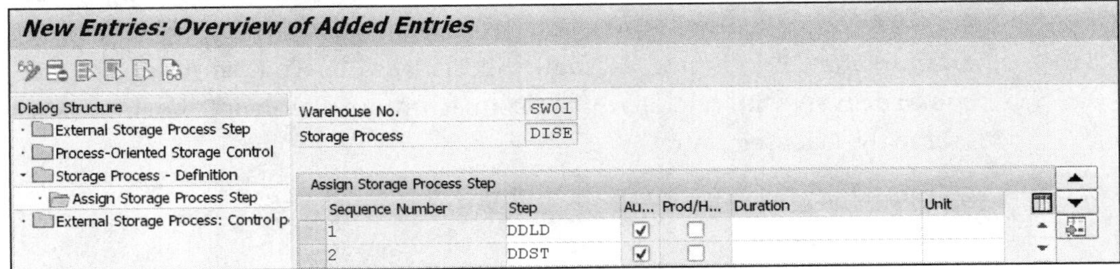

Figure 13.17 Defining the Storage Process for Distribution Equipment-Based Picking

13.6 Receipt from Production

Embedded EWM can be used for receipt of finished and semifinished products from production in the warehouse. You can address production receipt from either SAP GUI or RF. While receiving HUs from production using RF, the HUs are received from production lines for the same manufacturing order in which all HUs have the same material. It's important to set the system to post goods receipt with delivery creation by maintaining the condition record for PPF action /SCWM/PDI_02_GR_POST for condition maintenance group DLVIMFG. You also must set the system to create a warehouse task for putaway after goods receipt posting by maintaining the condition record for PPF action /SCWM/PDI_02_WT_CREATE.

To receive HUs against a manufacturing order using RF, on the **RF** screen, the HU entry screen is reached via path **Inbound Processes • Receiving of Handling Units • Rec. HU by Manufacturing Order**. The first HU is scanned, and the same information is proposed for all upcoming HUs received one after another. Receipt information is sent to SAP S/4HANA, and automatic putaway tasks are created in the embedded EWM system. Next, in the **RF** menu, **Putaway by HU** is selected, and HUs are put away into final bins.

Goods receipt for production processes can be triggered either from a manufacturing order in SAP S/4HANA or from embedded EWM:

- **Goods receipt triggered by SAP S/4HANA**
  Goods receipt for the finished goods of a production order can be initiated in SAP S/4HANA by creating the inbound delivery for receipt of finished goods in SAP S/4HANA, which is distributed to embedded EWM. This is done when the last production step of the manufacturing order is performed. The setting to post goods receipt when the production step is set as **Complete** is made via IMG path **Production • Basic Data • Routing • Operation Data • Define Control Key**. Once there, set the **Automatic GR** indicator, as shown in Figure 13.18. You can also create an inbound delivery with reference to a manufacturing order in SAP S/4HANA after it's set to the **Released** status.

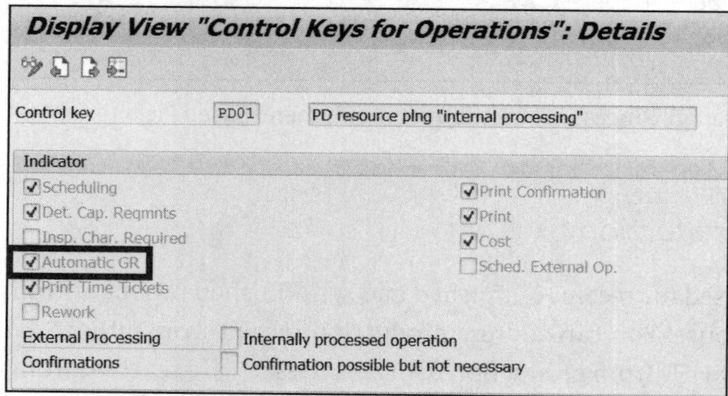

Figure 13.18 Configure Automatic Goods Receipt on Production Order Completion

After the goods physically arrive in the warehouse, goods receipt is posted, and stock is put away into the warehouse. Embedded EWM sends a message to SAP S/4HANA and triggers goods receipt posting for the SAP S/4HANA inbound delivery.

- **Goods receipt triggered by embedded EWM**
  You can trigger goods receipt of finished goods in embedded EWM. In this case, goods movement isn't triggered in SAP S/4HANA until the receipt or putaway for the stock is posted in embedded EWM. After the last production process is completed, the finished quantity is updated in the order, and the production steps are marked as **Completed**. The products that arrive from the production line are received in warehouse inventory using HUs. Embedded EWM creates inbound delivery after all the HUs belonging to a manufacturing order are scanned by using the information contained in the manufacturing order. Goods receipt can be posted for these HUs directly at the goods receipt area or automatically after final putaway.

13.7 Kanban Replenishment Strategy

SAP has provided a new replenishment strategy for stock transfer via Kanban. This replenishment strategy automatically creates replenishment warehouse tasks to replenish a Kanban container after it's emptied of stock or it's set to empty manually in the system. You can confirm the Kanban automatic replenishment task by using either the Process Warehouse Task app or the SAP GUI.

The Kanban production control method is a just-in-time stock replenishment method, where the goods are supplied to the production bins in optimized quantity and in a timely manner so that neither less stock or more stock is kept at the production supply area bin, thus synchronizing the demand and supply of stock in the production supply area. In SAP S/4HANA, usually the demand source bin, supply source bin, and Kanban container quantity are defined in the control cycle of Kankan assigned to a production supply area, as shown in Figure 13.19, using Transaction /SCWM/PSASTAGE2. You enter the warehouse, party entitled, production supply area, stock supply bin, quantity calculation type based on packaging specification, and number of Kanban containers. Based on the type of method set up for Kanban replenishment, either the Kanban containers can be replenished using a constant Kanban container count or event-based Kanban container count can be used such

that when the Kanban container status is set as **Empty**, a new replenishment process is initiated.

Display View "PSA Assignment to Bin by Entitled/Products": Details

Warehouse No.	SW01
Disposal Party	BP_PL_1001 S4H Plant 1001 / Chicago IL 60699
Supply Area	PSA_PP_01 /PL04 Production Supply Area
Product Group	
Product	S4H-MAT-21

PSA Assignment to Bin by Entitled/Products

Storage Bin	MISC-02
Stag. Det. Outb.	☐
Staging Method	3 Single-Order Staging
Qty Calc. Type	1 Calculation Based on Packaging Specification
Qty Classific.	3
No. Containers	2
Min. No. Cont.	2
Replmt Qty	0,000
Min.Prd.Qty PSA	0,000
Unit	
Staging WPT	
Clear PSA WPT	

Figure 13.19 Assigning the Kanban Container Quantity to the Production Supply Area Control Cycle

You can use stock transfer as a replenishment strategy for the embedded EWM-managed storage location, such that the source storage location for replenishment should be managed by embedded EWM. The destination storage location can be either IM-managed or embedded EWM-managed. Using the **0008 Stock Transfer with Warehouse Task** strategy, the system can create and confirm the embedded EWM warehouse task for replenishment automatically after the status of the Kanban container is changed to **Empty**.

Note

The feature to replenish the Kanban container automatically is available only in embedded EWM. The Set Kanban Container Status app is used to manually change the Kanban container status, which can trigger replenishment of the container.

13.8 Synchronous Goods Movements for Repetitive Manufacturing

Prior to SAP S/4HANA 1909, the repetitive manufacturing process was integrated with embedded EWM in an asynchronous manner. With SAP S/4HANA 1909, repetitive manufacturing can be integrated with warehouse management in a synchronous manner so that any goods issue of the components for the repetitive manufacturing process and goods receipt of finished products from the repetitive manufacturing process can be updated both in MM/IM and in embedded EWM warehouses in a synchronous manner. The synchronous postings of inventory reduce manual intervention to complete stock movement transactions, improve control of the warehouse operations, and enable synchronous stock postings in both IM and embedded EWM.

You can also specify whether you want to create automatic warehouse tasks for production-supplied goods to the final bin or do it manually. This helps you manage the putaway process because you can configure automatic warehouse task creation for the goods that you want to directly put away to the final bin without additional processing, such as packing or cleaning. On the other hand, when any additional processing must be done on the goods, you must create the warehouse tasks manually.

To enable automatic warehouse tasks in the synchronous product putaway process, you must configure the following:

1. **Activate synchronous goods receipt**
   Synchronous goods receipt must be activated for repetitive manufacturing in the manufacturing profile via IMG path **Production • Repetitive Manufacturing • Control • Define Repetitive Manufacturing Profiles**. Select the relevant repetitive manufacturing profile, and then select the **Post Synchronously to Bin** checkbox.
2. **Activate automatic warehouse task creation**
   To ensure that after automatic goods receipt posting in repetitive manufacturing a putaway warehouse task can be created automatically, you must activate it via IMG path **SCM Extended Warehouse Management • Extended Warehouse Management • Master Data • Storage Type • Define Storage Type**. Enter the embedded EWM warehouse, storage type, and other characteristics, as well as "1 Active" for **Automatic WT Creation at GR**.
3. **Create entries without document type and item type**
   You must add an entry via IMG path **SCM Extended Warehouse Management • Extended Warehouse Management • Cross-Process Settings • Warehouse Task • Determine Warehouse Process Type** by entering the embedded EWM warehouse

and choosing **Process Ind. 004 Receipt of Unpacked Items (Synchronous Goods Movement)**, but without document type, item type, or delivery priority, as shown in Figure 13.20.

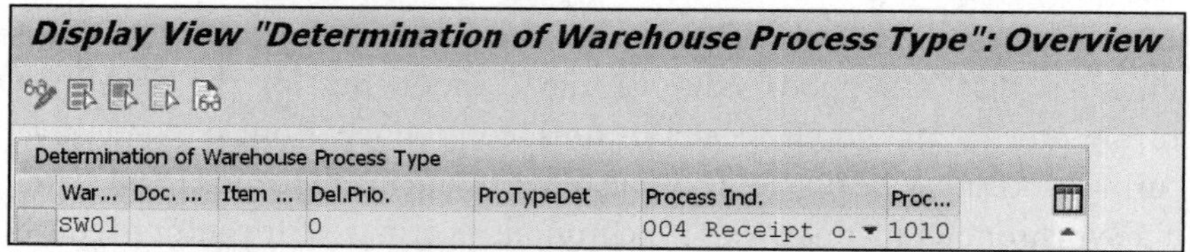

Figure 13.20 Setting Up Synchronous Goods Movement for Repetitive Manufacturing

13.9 Summary

This chapter introduced the production process in embedded EWM and the steps required to set up production integration in the warehouse. It also discussed the production material request, which acts as a warehouse request in embedded EWM to execute product staging. We showed you how to set up the production supply area for staging raw materials, discussed the staging and consumption of raw materials for production, and covered the receipt of finished products from production. In the next chapter, we'll discuss the radio frequency (RF) framework.

Chapter 14
Radio Frequency Framework

Warehouses often use mobile devices to perform stock movements in the warehouse, which not only eases material handling but also improves productivity. In this chapter, we'll review the wide variety of mobile devices supported by SAP and how mobile integration is set up.

Mobile or handheld devices provide warehouse workers with the flexibility of staying connected with the embedded EWM system from any point in the warehouse without needing to stay logged into SAP S/4HANA on an actual computer. Embedded EWM provides a standard solution that uses a radio frequency (RF) framework to display application data on a presentation device via menus and screens. In most cases, businesses use two kinds of RF devices: a handheld device with a small screen and keyboard, and a forklift-mounted device with a bigger screen. Warehouses that have implemented pick by voice can also use a headset with a microphone to execute the picking process. Warehouses usually customize the standard RF screens and include custom RF transactions to align the screen flow and transaction capability with their business processes.

In this chapter, we'll discuss how you can configure the RF framework in embedded EWM to integrate your business operations with handheld devices in the warehouse. We'll begin with an overview of the RF framework (Section 14.1, followed by a discussion of the configurations required to set up the RF framework in the warehouse in In Section 14.2. In Section 14.3, we cover navigation in the RF framework, and, finally, in Section 14.4, we'll discuss some of the warehouse processes that can be carried out using RF.

14.1 What Is the Radio Frequency Framework?

The RF framework supports a wide variety of device types and data entry types. The RF framework provides functionality such as menus for displaying transactional data, which the warehouse operator uses to move stock in the warehouse; backend logic to interpret the actions triggered by workers on RF devices; and follow-up actions and message communication between mobile devices and the embedded EWM application. The framework also supports barcodes for identification and verification of pallets in the warehouse. A few of the processes that can be carried out using the RF framework are as follows:

- Logon, logoff, and recovery
- Triggering of embedded EWM actions such as the following:
  - Putaway and picking
  - Physical inventory
  - Packing and deconsolidation
- Execution of pick by voice for carrying out voice-based picking

In the RF framework, the data presentation can be changed per user preference and device size and type. You can create custom menus and screens, and you can control the logical flow of screens based on actions taken on the RF screen. The mobile data transactions for RF are created in the embedded EWM RF framework, which allows the transactions to leverage embedded EWM functionalities. The functionalities available on the RF screen are limited when compared to working in the embedded EWM application directly by logging on to the system, but there can be an advantage to working with processes in a simplified manner.

The RF framework currently supports GUI and character-based devices as well as browser-based devices. The GUI devices are connected to the SAP system like a client-dependent PC. The screens can be touchscreens using predefined pushbuttons or can be operated using a keyboard. Character-based devices are linked to the system using SAPConsole, which interacts with the RF terminals connected to it. SAPConsole and its required Telnet server run on an additional server. SAPConsole uses the user interface (UI) protocol DIAG to interact with the embedded EWM application in the backend and Telnet to interact with mobile devices. It acts as a relay system, which interprets and converts relay information between embedded EWM and a mobile device so that the mobile device can interpret the data relayed by embedded EWM and display it in text format.

Embedded EWM connects to browser-based devices using a technology called Internet Transaction Server for Mobile (ITS mobile). ITS mobile provides a way for SAP transactions to be used over web browsers. In this browser-based UI technology, the business logic resides in the backend SAP application. It runs in the same embedded

EWM application as a component of SAP NetWeaver. ITS mobile provides a better UI to work with in comparison to the text-based UI using SAPConsole.

Next, in Section 14.1.1, we explain the business context in which the RF framework can be used in real-world scenarios. In Section 14.1.2, we explain the processes carried out in the system as well as RF-framework-related documents.

14.1.1 Business Process

American company Alpha Medicals receives an order from one of its customers based in Mexico. The order sent by the customer requires Alpha Medicals to provide its customer with the products in time and in cases and pallets for delivery. The stock is to be picked up from source bins from warehouse workers and moved to staging bins so that it can be goods issued and sent over to customers. To ensure that products are picked from the correct source storage bins without paper-based picking in embedded EWM, the company has implemented RF-based picking in embedded EWM. To ensure the workers pick the products using RF technology, each warehouse worker has been provided with a handheld device that displays the standard RF menu from embedded EWM and provides the warehouse tasks to warehouse workers based on which picking must be done. As shown in Figure 14.1, RF-based stock handling for outbound sales to customers in embedded EWM involves multiple steps, as follows:

1. The warehouse receives a warehouse request for customer delivery to supply the requested products after performing any additional work on the products.
2. The warehouse-request-related warehouse task is assigned to a warehouse worker so that the worker can pick, pack, and stage the stock at the staging bay. Because RF-based stock handling is active in embedded EWM, the warehouse worker logs on to the handheld device and completes stock picking, staging, and loading.

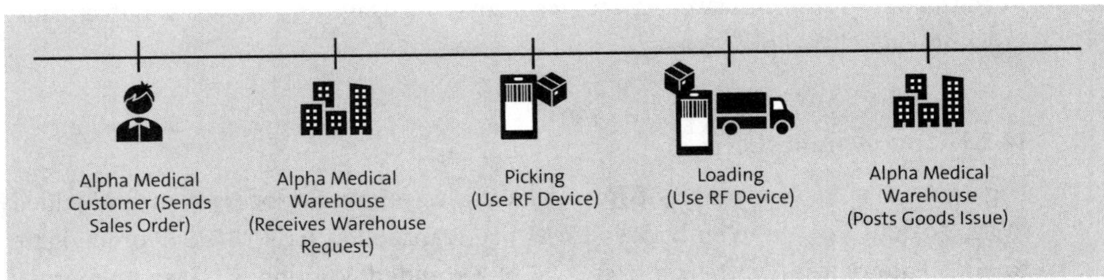

Figure 14.1 Picking Process Using the RF Device

14.1.2 System Process

You can use the RF framework to complete the outbound process in embedded EWM, as follows:

1. An outbound delivery order is created in embedded EWM that contains information about the products to be delivered by Alpha Medicals to the external customer.
2. Picking warehouse tasks are created and assigned to the warehouse worker that direct the warehouse worker to pick the products directly from source bins and move them to the goods issue area, optionally going through a work center for packing or other activities.
3. The warehouse worker logs on to the handheld device so that the next set of tasks are made available to the warehouse worker for execution.
4. The warehouse tasks are made visible to the warehouse worker on the handheld device. The worker moves to the source bin, picks the stock, and takes up other stock movement activities that are typically executed by workers using handheld devices.

Note

We've explained the system process using the outbound process only. It's equally applicable to inbound stock movement processes also.

14.2 Configuring the Radio Frequency Framework

The following sections cover the configuration required in embedded EWM to set up RF in the warehouse. In later sections, we'll cover its usage and application in executing embedded EWM processes.

14.2.1 Logon and Logoff

Log on to the RF environment for executing warehouse processes in embedded EWM. To define a user in embedded EWM, use Transaction /SCWM/USER or navigate to **SAP Easy Access** path **Logistics • SCM Extended Warehouse Management • Extended Warehouse Management • Master Data • Resource Management • Maintain User**. Click on **New Entries**, and provide the **SAP User ID** and **Data Entry Type**. The data entry type can be general or voice-based. Each unique combination of user and data entry type can only be assigned to one warehouse, and you can select the **Auto Logon** checkbox if you need to be logged in to RF automatically.

You can log on to multiple resources in embedded EWM, but only if the **Auto Logon** checkbox isn't set. When logging on to RF, the system needs to know the resource for which you're logging in. Based on assigned resources, the warehouse orders assigned to the resources are made available to you in RF. (For more details, see Chapter 11 on resource management.) The RF framework supports both automatic login and manual login. Automatic login can be triggered in one of two ways:

- **By presentation device**
  This is the case if the presentation device can identify itself in the background based on the IP address or other information. The resource is then determined based on the default resource assigned to the user logging in.
- **By user**
  This is the case when the user is assigned to a default resource, warehouse, and presentation device. The user can be logged in automatically or manually depending on the configuration settings maintained while defining the user.

The RF menu can be started manually in embedded EWM using Transaction /SCWM/RFUI. In Figure 14.2, a resource logs on to a mobile deviceg and provides input for the presentation device, warehouse, and warehouse number.

To define a presentation device, use Transaction /SCWM/PRDVC or navigate to **SAP Easy Access** path **Logistics • SCM Extended Warehouse Management • Extended Warehouse Management • Master Data • Maintain Presentation Devices**. Click on **New Entries** to define a new presentation device; add device attributes such as display profile, device type, function key quantity, and key controls; and then click on **Save**.

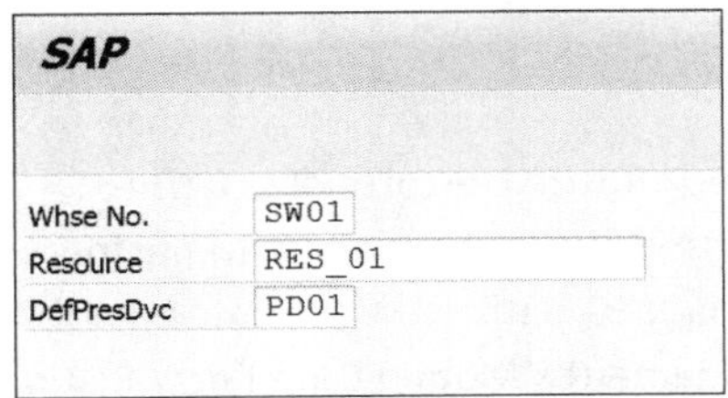

Figure 14.2 RF UI Login Screen

> **Note**
>
> The Maintain User Settings (Radio Frequency) app allows you to assign RF device and logging settings to warehouse workers.

To define a resource and assign presentation devices to the resource, use Transaction /SCWM/RSRC or navigate to **SAP Easy Access** path **Logistics • SCM Extended Warehouse Management • Extended Warehouse Management • Master Data • Maintain Resource**, as shown in Figure 14.3. Click on **New Entries** to create a new resource, and click on **Save.** The resource can be assigned other attributes, such as resource type, resource group, default presentation device, and default queue and bin.

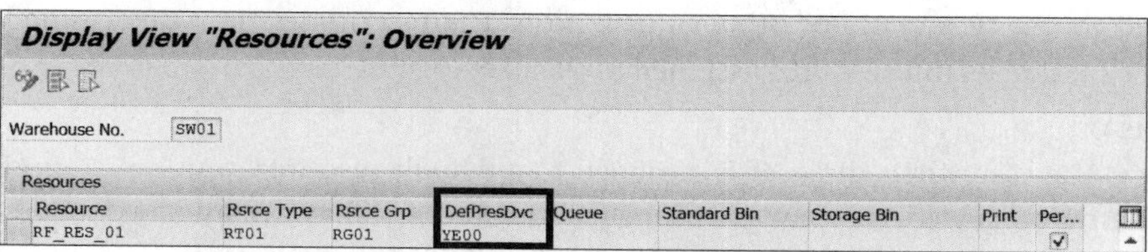

Figure 14.3 Assigning the Presentation Device to the Resource

> **Note**
>
> The Maintain Resources app allows you to assign RF devices to resources.

To log a resource off from RF, press F1 or select the **F1 Logoff** button on the RF screen. Enter a reason code for logoff from RF and press **F1 Save**. Depending on the reason code, the warehouse orders either remain assigned to the resource or are unassigned.

14.2.2 Menu Manager

Any end-to-end process in embedded EWM is represented in the form of a menu hierarchy. You can create, change, or delete a menu for specific embedded EWM business processes. The menu for RF can be maintained via IMG path **SCM Extended Warehouse Management • Extended Warehouse Management • Mobile Data Entry Radio Frequency (RF) Framework • RF Menu Manager**. This takes you to the **Menu Manager** screen, shown in Figure 14.4. To create a menu, enter the **Application**, **Presentation Profile**, and **Personal. Profile**, and then click on .

Figure 14.4 RF Menu Manager

Any existing menu hierarchy can be copied, and you can create your own menu hierarchy with custom presentation text and menu items by creating a new personalization profile for a presentation profile. You must assign a presentation profile to a warehouse. SAP provides the standard presentation profile ****, but you can also define custom presentation profiles and assign them to the warehouse via IMG path **SCM Extended Warehouse Management • Extended Warehouse Management • Mobile Data Entry • Assign Presentation Profile to Warehouse**. The personalization profile used to create different menu layouts as discussed earlier for a presentation profile is assigned at a user level using Transaction /SCWM/USER.

As shown in Figure 14.5, the left side of the **Menu Manager** screen shows all possible menu options and logical transactions available in the system. The right side contains a tree structure that displays the menu structure. You can create a custom menu path by selecting the menu objects and assigning each path to one or more logical transactions to define executable actions that can be taken from that node. The parent node for the menu hierarchy is selected via the **Main Menu** checkbox on the left side of the screen.

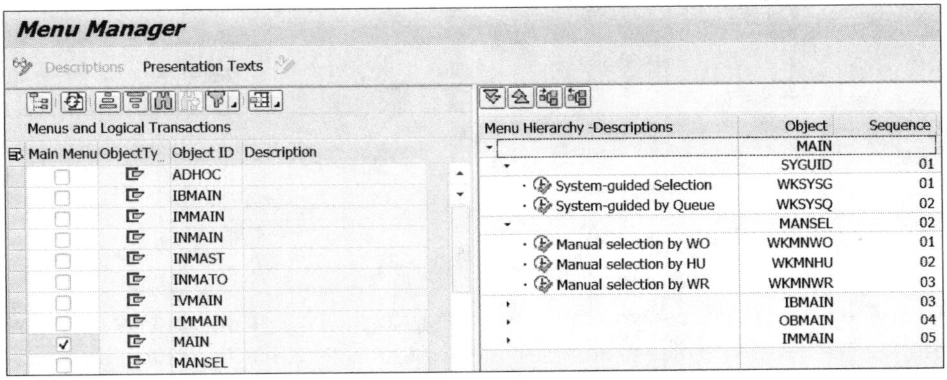

Figure 14.5 Defining and Maintaining RF Menus

14.2.3 Screen Manager

The RF screen manager enables you to change the screen layout of the RF presentation screen. The first step in working with screen manager is to create a display profile. The display profile helps adjust the screen size based on the RF device. A new display profile can be configured via IMG path **SCM Extended Warehouse Management • Extended Warehouse Management • Mobile Data Entry Radio Frequency (RF) Framework • RF Screen Manager**, as shown in Figure 14.6. Provide the name for the **Display Profile**, and click on [icon].

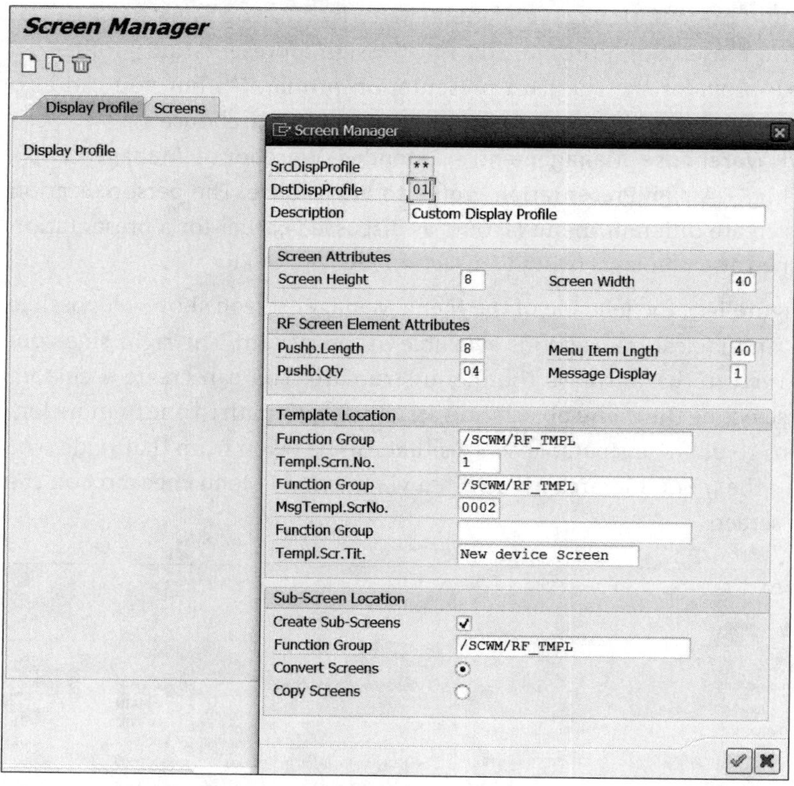

Figure 14.6 Defining the Display Profile

To define new screen sizes, you can copy an existing display profile and create a new profile. The default display profile provided by SAP is ** with a size of 8 × 40, which means 8 lines and 40 columns and indicates the size of the device's screen. This screen size is usually found on RF devices mounted on forklifts. The **Screen Height** and **Screen Width** can be adjusted as required. Based on these changes, the **Menu Item Length** may also require changing so that it doesn't exceed the screen width. The system will create the new screen and calculate the new position of all elements on that screen. You can create custom function groups for the new template screens created by the system by copying the standard RF template screens. It's advisable to select the **Create Sub-Screens** indicator so that the system will copy all subscreens available in standard RF and create them in the required screen size. These include screens for logon, logoff, main menu, and so on.

The next screen displays the screen manager customization UI. Using this UI, you can define or change screen attributes such as screen size, text length, radio buttons, pushbuttons, screen programs, text fields, and so on, as shown in Figure 14.7. The green traffic lights indicate that all subscreens were created successfully. Any further changes to the screen layout can be made in the screen painter by using Transaction SE51.

Screen Manager

Display / Change | Screen

Templates

Displ.Prof	ScrnHeight	ScrnWidth	SScrHeight	SScrWidth	PB Length	Pushb.Qty	MenuLength	MsgDisplay	Templ.Screen Program	Temp.Scr.N	MsgTemplProgram	MsgTmplNo.	Description
**	8	40	7	40	8	04	40	1	/SCWM/SAPLRF_TMPL	1	/SCWM/SAPLRF_TMPL	0002	Standard display profi
*1	25	40	7	40	40	16	40	0	/SCWM/SAPLRF_TMPL	11	/SCWM/SAPLRF_TMPL	0002	Pick-by-Voice

Screen

Sub-Screens

Exception	Applic.	Displ.Prof	Pres. Prof	Prsn. Prof	Log Trans.	Step	State	Sequence	Screen Program	Screen No.	SkipShrtct	LineDefic.	Col.Defic.	Pushb.Qty	FKeyQty	Simulated
	01	**	****	**	******	CWDIFF	******	01	/SCWM/SAPLRF_GENERAL_EN	310	☐					
	01	**	****	**	******	CWFUNC	******	01	/SCWM/SAPLRF_GENERAL_EN	300	☐					
	01	**	****	**	******	CWFUNC	DIFF	01	/SCWM/SAPLRF_GENERAL_EN	310	☐					
	01	**	****	**	******	DIFLST	******	01	/SCWM/SAPLRF_SSCR	3	☐					
	01	**	****	**	******	LGLIST	******	01	/SCWM/SAPLRF_SSCR	3	☐					
	01	**	****	**	******	RFLIST	******	01	/SCWM/SAPLRF_SSCR	3	☐					

Figure 14.7 Creating and Maintaining RF Screens

The newly created display profile is then assigned to a presentation device using Transaction /SCWM/PRDVC, as shown in Figure 14.8. If the display profile is for a new RF device, such as a forklift or handheld, then a new presentation device type is created and assigned to the display profile. Thus, it's possible to run the same RF transactions on different devices using the same transaction flow but with different screen layouts based on screen sizes.

Figure 14.8 Assigning the Display Profile to the Presentation Device

14.2.4 Modifying Radio Frequency Transactions

Embedded EWM provides the flexibility to create or modify transactions in RF to carry out a specific business process. Using this functionality, you can trigger your own follow-up actions, open new screens, and provide new features on screens to carry out a specific process step. Each action you take triggers a logical transaction, and a function module is executed for each action taken by a warehouse worker. You can define logical transactions via IMG path **SCM Extended Warehouse Management • Extended Warehouse Management • Mobile Data Entry Radio Frequency (RF) Framework • Define Steps in Logical Transactions**, as shown in Figure 14.9. Click on **New Entries** to create a new logical transaction, and click on **Save**. The custom logical transactions are usually created with the namespace Z*. The logical transactions can't be executed in standalone mode, unlike standard embedded EWM transactions. These are always executed in the RF environment.

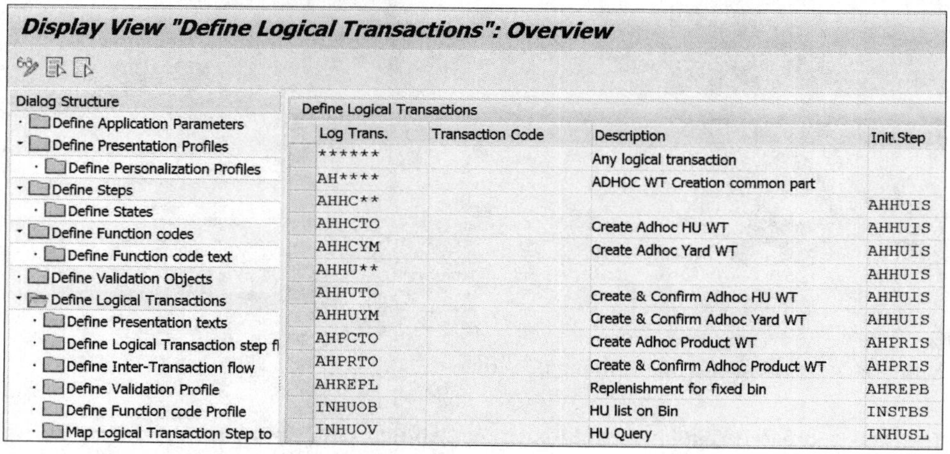

Display View "Define Logical Transactions": Overview

Dialog Structure
- Define Application Parameters
- Define Presentation Profiles
  - Define Personalization Profiles
- Define Steps
  - Define States
- Define Function codes
  - Define Function code text
- Define Validation Objects
- Define Logical Transactions
  - Define Presentation texts
  - Define Logical Transaction step fl
  - Define Inter-Transaction flow
  - Define Validation Profile
  - Define Function code Profile
  - Map Logical Transaction Step to

Define Logical Transactions

Log Trans.	Transaction Code	Description	Init.Step
******		Any logical transaction	
AH****		ADHOC WT Creation common part	
AHHC**			AHHUIS
AHHCTO		Create Adhoc HU WT	AHHUIS
AHHCYM		Create Adhoc Yard WT	AHHUIS
AHHU**			AHHUIS
AHHUTO		Create & Confirm Adhoc HU WT	AHHUIS
AHHUYM		Create & Confirm Adhoc Yard WT	AHHUIS
AHPCTO		Create Adhoc Product WT	AHPRIS
AHPRTO		Create & Confirm Adhoc Product WT	AHPRIS
AHREPL		Replenishment for fixed bin	AHREPB
INHUOB		HU list on Bin	INSTBS
INHUOV		HU Query	INHUSL

Figure 14.9 Defining Logical Transactions

The following list covers the parameters defined in this transaction and how they're assigned to process steps to create a logical transaction flow in embedded EWM:

- **Define Application Parameters**
  Application parameters are used to assign the application data containers to corresponding structures/tables. Application data containers are responsible for transmitting data between the steps and from the program to the screen.
- **Define Presentation Profiles**
  The presentation profile is used to specify the warehouse-specific layout and logic

in embedded EWM. Embedded EWM provides the standard presentation profile ****. Each warehouse should be assigned to a presentation profile. The presentation profile and its associated personalization profile support different menu structures for different users in the warehouse. This can be required if users with different roles should only have access to limited transactions in RF.

- **Define Steps**
  Steps are defined to perform actions in embedded EWM that use RF to complete a process, such as ad hoc product movement. Steps can be executed in the foreground or the background in embedded EWM. In foreground execution, based on the menu and button a warehouse worker clicks on the RF UI, a corresponding step is executed. For background execution, multiple steps can be combined to create an activity that can be executed by the system. When you define a logical transaction, you assign it to a flow of steps that must be carried out to complete an end-to-end warehouse process. Each logical transaction should have at least one step.
- **Define Function Codes**
  To execute various actions using embedded EWM, RF devices have pushbuttons in menu screens. These buttons are mapped with logical transactions such as **Back**, **Upload**, **Enter**, **Save**, and so on. A function code can be up to six characters in length. The function code and button also can be assigned to a function key. When the button is pressed, the function code is executed, and the system takes appropriate action.
- **Define Validation Objects**
  Validation objects are representations of application objects, such as handling units (HUs), products, bins, stacks of products, and so on, which can be validated using RF transactions. This reduces the probability of incorrect processing of the objects. The basic elements described previously are used to define logical transactions in RF. As discussed earlier, a logical transaction covers an entire business process or action from beginning to end. A logical transaction can be assigned to an initial step, SAP transaction, or recovery step (to define a step that is processed during recovery). The default logical transaction called when you execute Transaction /SCWM/RFUI is **RFMAIN** and has the initial step **MENU**. Next, we'll cover the steps required to create a logical transaction in RF.
- **Define Presentation Texts**
  Each logical transaction is assigned to a presentation text to define the text that appears for that transaction or menu item. The texts provide an explanation of the functional use of the logical transaction. They're also used to assign presentation

text in different languages to the screen objects. The length of the text field is defined in the display profile.

- **Define Logical Transaction step flow**
  Each logical transaction triggered in the embedded EWM system is guided by the steps assigned to it, based on which screens for process execution are displayed on RF mobile devices. As shown in Figure 14.10, a logical transaction step is assigned to a step sequence and function code to tell the user the next step that the transaction should go to if a particular function code has been applied. You can display the next step in the foreground or background, as defined in Customizing. The function module is used to define the action executed with the previous step before the next step is executed.

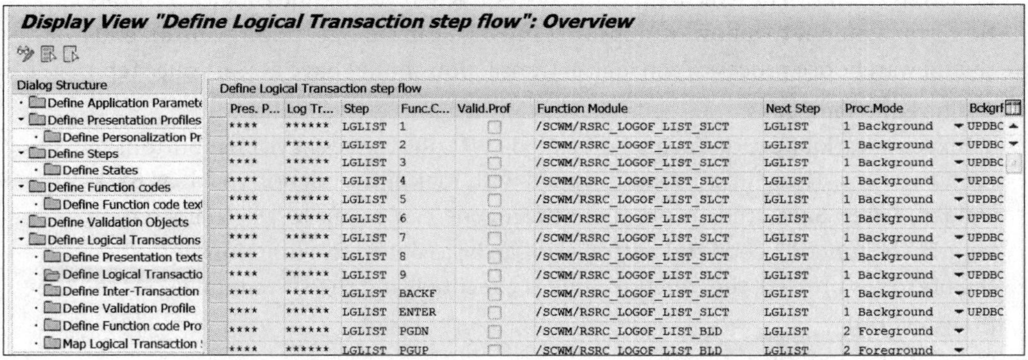

Display View "Define Logical Transaction step flow": Overview

Dialog Structure
- Define Application Paramete
- Define Presentation Profiles
  - Define Personalization Pr
- Define Steps
  - Define States
- Define Function codes
  - Define Function code text
- Define Validation Objects
- Define Logical Transactions
  - Define Presentation texts
  - Define Logical Transactio
  - Define Inter-Transaction
  - Define Validation Profile
  - Define Function code Pro
  - Map Logical Transaction !

Define Logical Transaction step flow

Pres. P...	Log Tr...	Step	Func.C...	Valid.Prof	Function Module	Next Step	Proc.Mode	Bckgrf
****	******	LGLIST	1		/SCWM/RSRC_LOGOF_LIST_SLCT	LGLIST	1 Background	UPDBC
****	******	LGLIST	2		/SCWM/RSRC_LOGOF_LIST_SLCT	LGLIST	1 Background	UPDBC
****	******	LGLIST	3		/SCWM/RSRC_LOGOF_LIST_SLCT	LGLIST	1 Background	UPDBC
****	******	LGLIST	4		/SCWM/RSRC_LOGOF_LIST_SLCT	LGLIST	1 Background	UPDBC
****	******	LGLIST	5		/SCWM/RSRC_LOGOF_LIST_SLCT	LGLIST	1 Background	UPDBC
****	******	LGLIST	6		/SCWM/RSRC_LOGOF_LIST_SLCT	LGLIST	1 Background	UPDBC
****	******	LGLIST	7		/SCWM/RSRC_LOGOF_LIST_SLCT	LGLIST	1 Background	UPDBC
****	******	LGLIST	8		/SCWM/RSRC_LOGOF_LIST_SLCT	LGLIST	1 Background	UPDBC
****	******	LGLIST	9		/SCWM/RSRC_LOGOF_LIST_SLCT	LGLIST	1 Background	UPDBC
****	******	LGLIST	BACKF		/SCWM/RSRC_LOGOF_LIST_SLCT	LGLIST	1 Background	UPDBC
****	******	LGLIST	ENTER		/SCWM/RSRC_LOGOF_LIST_SLCT	LGLIST	1 Background	UPDBC
****	******	LGLIST	PGDN		/SCWM/RSRC_LOGOF_LIST_BLD	LGLIST	2 Foreground	
****	******	LGLIST	PGUP		/SCWM/RSRC_LOGOF_LIST_BLD	LGLIST	2 Foreground	

Figure 14.10 Defining the Logical Transaction Step Flow

- **Define Inter-Transaction flow**
  Inter-transaction flow helps the system navigate to another view on completion of the logical transaction by setting one of the following values in the **DEF. NAVIG.** column:
  - **User Choice**
  - **Main Menu**
  - **Last Menu**
  - **Same Transaction**
  - **Log Off RF User from SAP System**
- **Define Validation Profile**
  A validation profile is used to list fields for a step when it's required to validate those fields. For example, you can set up validation fields for a storage bin to

ensure that the RF user is accessing the right storage bin. These are called *validation objects* in RF.

- **Define Function code Profile**
  A function code profile is used to define function keys and pushbuttons created for a screen or step, as shown in Figure 14.11. You can display a function only as a function key or pushbutton by specifying either the function key or pushbutton. You won't assign standard function codes such as **Back** or **Clear** to buttons. These are only used for nonstandard function codes, such as *HU Create*.

Display View "Define Function code Profile": Overview

Define Function code Profile

Pres. ...	Prsn. ...	Pushb.Qty	FKeyQty	Log Trans.	Step	State	Seq...	FCG...	Func.Code	Pushbutton	Funct...	Short...	Disable	Excep...
****	**	04	**	******	AHREPB	******	01	01	BACK		F7	07		
****	**	04	**	******	AHREPB	******	01	01	CLEAR		F6	06		
****	**	04	**	******	AHREPB	******	01	01	ENTER		ENT		✓	
****	**	04	**	******	AHREPB	******	01	01	FULLMS		F9	09		
****	**	04	**	******	AHREPB	******	01	01	REPLOR	PB2 Pushbutt…	F2			
****	**	04	**	******	AHREPB	******	01	01	REPLPL	PB1 Pushbutt…	F1			
****	**	04	**	******	LGLIST	******	01	01	BACK		F7	07		
****	**	04	**	******	LGLIST	******	01	01	CLEAR		F6	06		
****	**	04	**	******	LGLIST	******	01	01	ENTER		ENT			
****	**	04	**	******	RFLIST	******	01	01	BACK		F7	07		
****	**	04	**	******	RFLIST	******	01	01	CLEAR		F6	06		
****	**	04	**	******	RFLIST	******	01	01	ENTER		ENT			
****	**	04	**	******	RFLIST	******	01	01	FULLMS		F9	09		

Figure 14.11 Defining the Function Code Profile for Logical Transactions

- **Map Logical Transaction Step to Sub-Screen**
  Any step processed in the foreground should have a subscreen and program, as shown in Figure 14.12.

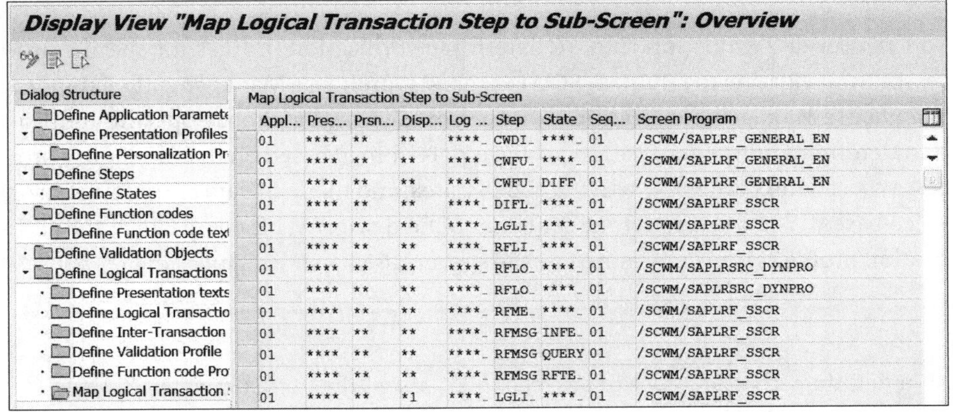

Appl...	Pres...	Prsn...	Disp...	Log ...	Step	State	Seq...	Screen Program
01	****	**	**	****_	CWDI_	****_	01	/SCWM/SAPLRF_GENERAL_EN
01	****	**	**	****_	CWFU_	****_	01	/SCWM/SAPLRF_GENERAL_EN
01	****	**	**	****_	CWFU_	DIFF	01	/SCWM/SAPLRF_GENERAL_EN
01	****	**	**	****_	DIFL_	****_	01	/SCWM/SAPLRF_SSCR
01	****	**	**	****_	LGLI_	****_	01	/SCWM/SAPLRF_SSCR
01	****	**	**	****_	RFLI_	****_	01	/SCWM/SAPLRF_SSCR
01	****	**	**	****_	RFLO_	****_	01	/SCWM/SAPLRSRC_DYNPRO
01	****	**	**	****_	RFLO_	****_	01	/SCWM/SAPLRSRC_DYNPRO
01	****	**	**	****_	RFME_	****_	01	/SCWM/SAPLRF_SSCR
01	****	**	**	****_	RFMSG	INFE_	01	/SCWM/SAPLRF_SSCR
01	****	**	**	****_	RFMSG	QUERY	01	/SCWM/SAPLRF_SSCR
01	****	**	**	****_	RFMSG	RFTE_	01	/SCWM/SAPLRF_SSCR
01	****	**	*1	****_	LGLI_	****_	01	/SCWM/SAPLRF_SSCR

Figure 14.12 Mapping Logical Transactions to Subscreens

14.2.5 Verification Profile

A verification profile is used to configure verification fields to ensure that correct objects are scanned by the operator during warehouse processing. For example, to ensure that the right HU is sent to the correct bin by a warehouse worker during put-away, you can define verification profile YE0001. This verification profile executes the verification using the fields **NLPLA** and **VLENR** for the destination bin and source HU, respectively. The fields appear as single-character fields next to the display field for the object, such as a storage bin or HU, where the user can input the barcode scan data for that object. If the wrong bin is scanned by the worker, the system can generate an alert message on an RF device. Together, the display field and the input field for verification of the object become the validation object. You can define a warehouse-specific verification profile via IMG path **SCM Extended Warehouse Management • Extended Warehouse Management • Verification Control • Define Warehouse-Specific Verification**, as shown in Figure 14.13. Click on **New Entries**, add a combination of embedded EWM warehouse and verification fields, and click on **Save.**

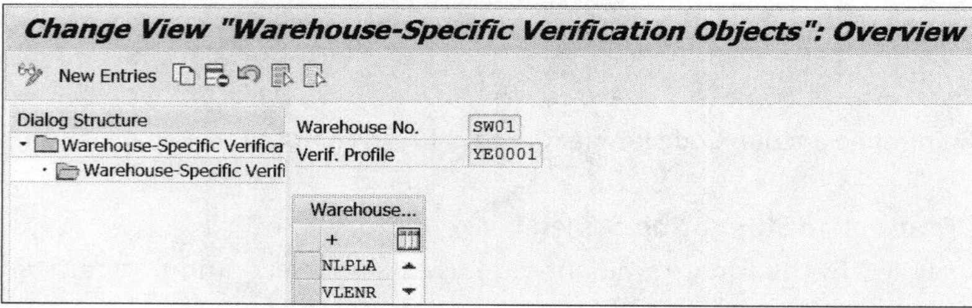

Figure 14.13 Defining the Verification Profile for Objects in RF

You can set determination rules to determine verification profiles for specific processes by navigating to IMG path **SCM Extended Warehouse Management • Extended Warehouse Management • Verification Control • Define Warehouse-Specific Verification Determination**. A verification profile is determined based on the warehouse process type, process category, activity, activity area, and mode of data entry (manual or voice-based). You can also set the sequence of field priority, based on which the verification profile can be determined by the system, as shown in Figure 14.14.

Tip

To find the technical values of a screen in RF, assign the user parameter /SCWM/RF_TECH_TITLE to the RF user.

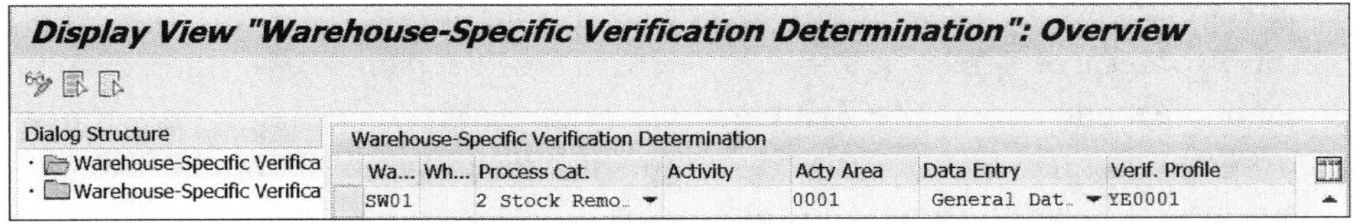

Figure 14.14 Warehouse-Specific Verification Profile Determination

14.3 Navigation in Radio Frequency

After you log in to RF, you can navigate to a transaction using the RF menu path. Each RF menu has its own menu hierarchy, screens, fields, and so on. There are multiple ways to navigate through the menus:

- **Standard navigation**
  Standard navigation allows you to navigate to a logical transaction using a provided menu path. For example, if you want to create an ad hoc warehouse task in RF, you can do so by following the path **Internal Processes • Adhoc WT Creation • Create Adhoc Product WT** (see Figure 14.15).

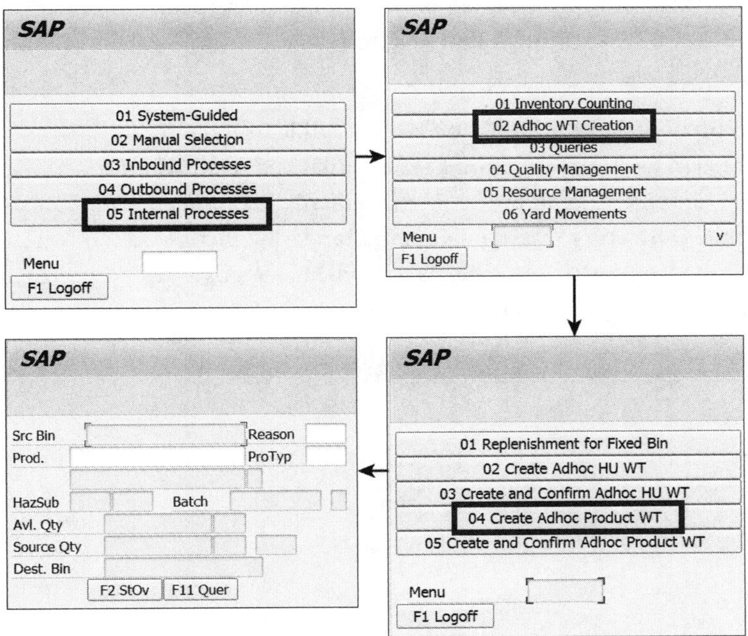

Figure 14.15 Navigating to the Ad Hoc Product WT Creation Screen

- **Direct navigation**
  You also can access the required menu item in the RF screen by entering the number of the menu item in the **Menu** field. For example, if you need to access **Internal Processes** menus, and it's marked as option number **05** on the current screen, you can enter "05" in the **Menu** field and press `Enter` (see Figure 14.16).

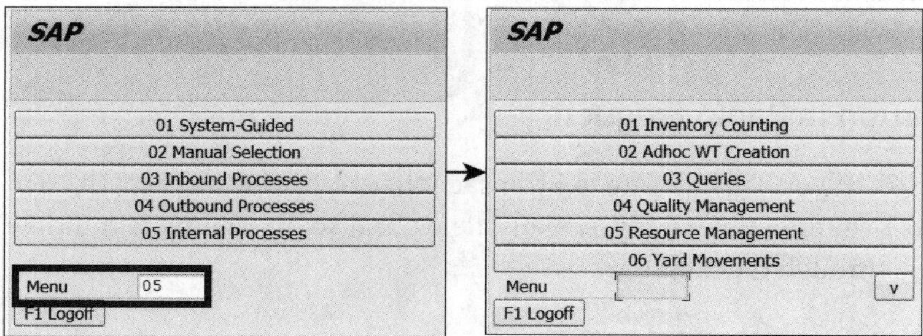

Figure 14.16 Direct Navigation to Internal Processes Menu Items

- **Virtual navigation**
  You can also reach a menu screen directly by entering the screen code for all menu options in the sequence in which they should be navigated in the **Menu** field. For example, you can enter "524" in the **Menu** field to reach the transaction to create an ad hoc warehouse task.

SAP has provided a predefined set of function keys to guide users to move back and forth between screens in RF. These function keys are assigned to standard functions via IMG path **SCM Extended Warehouse Management • Extended Warehouse Management • Mobile Data Entry • Assign FKeys to Standard Functions**, as shown in Figure 14.17. These function keys aren't displayed on RF screens but can be used directly by pressing the corresponding function key.

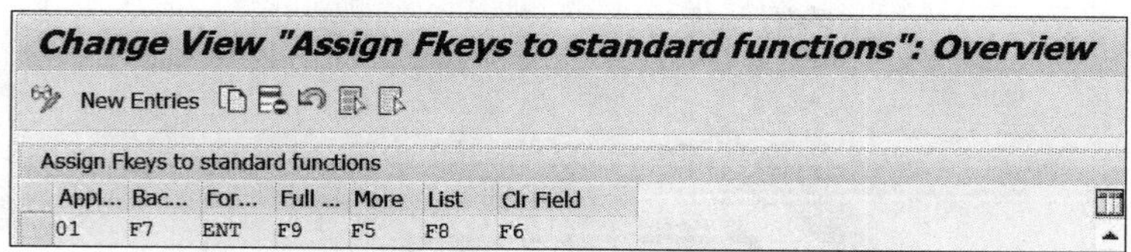

Figure 14.17 Assigning Function Keys to Standard Functions

14.4 Process Execution Using Radio Frequency

RF can be used to carry out various embedded EWM processes from a mobile/handheld device, such as putaway, stock removal, physical inventory, labor management, and so on. After logging on to an RF device using Transaction /SCWM/RFUI, you can navigate to individual transactions via the provided menu options to carry out specific business processes. Figure 14.18 shows the RF screen flow for confirming a warehouse order for picking in embedded EWM, which requires carrying out the following steps:

1. Navigate to the RF menu for **Picking by Warehouse Order**, and enter the warehouse order that needs to be confirmed. A new RF screen opens, showing the details of the warehouse task contained in the warehouse order.
2. Create a pick HU for picking the quantities in the warehouse task, and press `Enter` to navigate to the next screen.

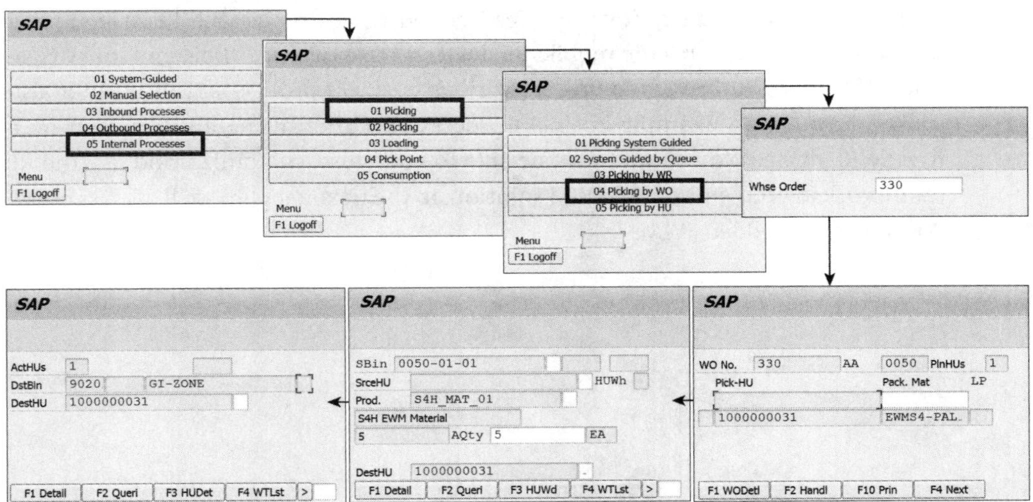

Figure 14.18 Navigating to the Picking Screen in Outbound Processing

3. Complete the picking by providing the source bin, product, and quantity that needs to be picked. As discussed previously, you enter the verification for the displayed object, such as storage bin, source HU, and so on. To do so, you scan the barcode associated with each of these objects in the warehouse. If the input provided is correct, you can move on to providing inputs for the next validation object. If

you scan an incorrect barcode, the system throws an error, and the input field is automatically cleared.

4. In the final step, enter the staging bin where the HU must be staged to complete the picking process on the next RF screen. This confirms the warehouse order for picking for outbound delivery in embedded EWM.

Note

The Test RF Environment app allows you to test if the standard/user-defined RF menu is available and working in an RF environment.

14.5 Summary

This chapter introduced the basic concepts and use of the RF framework in embedded EWM. It explained the various profiles defined to customize the RF screens and menus for customer-specific mobile RF devices. We explained the standard navigation paths using RF menus to process various business processes. This chapter also walked through an example business process execution using an RF screen on a mobile RF device. You should now be able to configure, customize, and use the RF framework in your embedded EWM solution. In the next chapter, we'll discuss cross-docking in embedded EWM.

Chapter 15
Cross-Docking

Cross-docking involves movement of goods through multiple locations, such as manufacturing plants, distribution centers, and warehouses, before they arrive at the destination. In this chapter, we'll cover how cross-docking is handled in embedded EWM.

The process of cross-docking covers the transfer of incoming goods directly to outbound deliveries without the goods entering or being stored in the warehouse. Embedded EWM supports two types of cross-docking: planned cross-docking and opportunistic cross-docking. *Planned cross-docking* is based on predetermination of goods relevant for cross-docking. The requirement to cross-dock incoming products and distribute them among outbound orders is predetermined before the goods reach the warehouse. Embedded EWM supports the following planned cross-docking strategies:

- Merchandise distribution cross-docking
- Merchandise distribution flow-through

Opportunistic cross-docking leverages the availability of just-in-time information about supply and demand. Thus, the incoming goods are directly routed either partially or fully to fulfill a demand for an outbound delivery order. Embedded EWM supports the following opportunistic cross-docking strategies:

- Opportunistic cross-docking
- Push deployment
- Pick from goods receipt

In Section 15.1, we'll introduce you to cross-docking in general before moving on to the two different types of cross-docking. Section 15.2 covers merchandise distribution cross-docking, which is a type of planned cross-docking. We'll also discuss recipient-driven flow-through and product drive flow-through. Section 15.3 covers opportunistic cross-docking and its types.

15.1 What Is Cross-Docking?

Cross-docking helps improve warehousing and lean supply chain management via reduced inventory costs, improved transportation planning, better product handling, and improved order fulfillment. In Section 15.1.1, we'll explain the business context in which cross-docking can be used in real-world scenarios. In Section 15.1.2, we'll explain the processes carried out in the system and discuss cross-docking-related documents.

15.1.1 Business Process

American company Alpha Medicals receives an order from one of its customers based in Mexico. The order sent by the customer requires Alpha Medicals to provide products on time and in cases and pallets for delivery. This product is a high-velocity product and doesn't require storage in the warehouse. As a regular Alpha Medicals practice, the warehousing activities performed by the warehouse workers, such as stock handling, value-added services (VAS), and so on, for these products require the stock to be directly moved on to the staging area without final putaway. To ensure that few high-velocity products are supplied to the goods issue area without much handling, the company has implemented cross-docking in embedded EWM. As shown in Figure 15.1, cross-docking in embedded EWM and its usage involves the following multiple steps:

1. The warehouse receives a warehouse request for customer delivery to supply the requested products to customers after performing any additional work on the products.
2. The warehouse-request-related warehouse task is assigned to a warehouse worker so that the worker can pick, pack, and stage the stock at the staging bay.
3. Because cross-docking is active in embedded EWM, the stock to be supplied to the goods issue is first searched for in the goods receipt area by embedded EWM system.
4. If the stock is found in the goods receipt area, the warehouse worker moves the stock directly from the goods receipt area to the goods issue area so that it can be supplied to the customer.

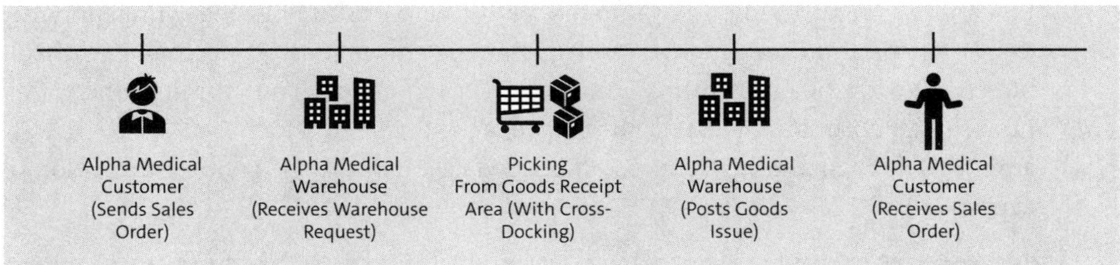

Figure 15.1 Business Flow in the Cross-Docking Process

15.1.2 System Process

The following explains the basic system flow, including the documents and data required to execute cross-docking:

1. An outbound delivery order is created in embedded EWM that contains information about the products to be delivered by Alpha Medicals to the external customer.
2. The embedded EWM system checks the goods receipt area for availability of stock before checking the stock availability in final putaway bins as part of the cross-docking process.
3. Picking warehouse tasks are created and assigned to the warehouse worker, which directs the warehouse worker to pick the products directly from the goods receipt area and move them to the goods issue area, optionally going through a work center for packing or VAS activities.
4. The warehouse orders allocated to the warehouse workers are executed by the workers by bringing the products directly from the goods receipt area to the goods issue area, thus completing the cross-docking process.

15.2 Merchandise Distribution

In this section, we'll introduce the concept of merchandise distribution used in retail and warehouse management. Then, we'll cover the different types of planned cross-docking strategies that can be carried out while executing merchandise distribution.

In planned cross-docking, you equip the system with the intelligence to link inbound deliveries with outbound deliveries to customers automatically. Merchandise distribution allows a business to plan and control the flow of goods through the warehouse in an optimal way. The planning steps are completed in SAP S/4HANA Retail, and the data is then transferred to embedded EWM, where the goods distribution is carried out.

Note

To use embedded EWM with SAP S/4HANA Retail, the following business functions need to be switched on in the SAP S/4HANA system:

- Enterprise business function `ISR_RETAILSYSTEM` is available as of SAP S/4HANA 1610 and needs to be activated to support retail processes across the retail value chain.
- Enterprise business function `ISR_RET_CD/FT_EWM` needs to be activated to link the embedded EWM solution with SAP S/4HANA Retail to carry out cross-docking and the flow-through goods distribution process.

The following settings need to be made to activate merchandise distribution in SAP S/4HANA:

1. Define the quantity adjustment profile and adjustment method to perform quantity adjustment in the inbound and outbound delivery order if the quantity processed is less than the quantity expected. To do this, navigate to IMG path **Integration with Other SAP Components • Extended Warehouse Management • Additional Material Attributes • Attribute Values for Additional Material Master Fields • Define Adjustment Profile** and **Define Adjustment Method**.
2. In IMG path **Logistics—General • Merchandise Distribution • Plant Profiles for Merchandise Distribution**, set the **Inbound Delivery Split by End Customer** indicator.
3. Activate merchandise distribution cross-docking at the warehouse process type level via IMG path **Cross-Process Settings • Cross-Docking (CD) • Planned Cross-Docking • Merchandise Distribution • Basic Settings for Merchandise Distribution**.

In the next sections, we'll discuss the planned cross-docking strategies in detail. We'll start with merchandise distribution cross-docking, in which goods are directly brought in and moved out for goods issue without being stored in the warehouse.

Then, we'll discuss merchandise distribution flow-through, in which goods are taken to a repacking area after goods receipt, after which goods are taken for goods issue.

15.2.1 Merchandise Distribution Cross-Docking

Merchandise distribution cross-docking allows a user to plan for and control the flow of prepacked or unpacked goods from the vendor to the stores through the warehouse or distribution center in an efficient and accurate way. The process begins with a stock transport order or sales order being created to replenish goods from the distribution center to the stores. A collective purchase order is created for a specific vendor, which contains all the items purchased by the distribution center from the vendor. This is a pull-based scenario. In a push-based scenario, the system will create purchase orders and store orders using allocation tables. The inbound and outbound deliveries are created and distributed to embedded EWM. The items on the order are split into handling units (HUs) that need to be delivered to individual stores. Merchandise distribution cross-docking depends on whether goods are arriving in the warehouse as customer-specified prepacked goods or unpacked goods.

If the vendor is sending packed goods in HUs in the inbound delivery, you can use process-oriented storage control and automate the subsequent task creation. The system compares the final ship-to party on the HU in the inbound delivery with the ship-to party on the outbound delivery; if it finds a match, then pick warehouse tasks are created with the destination as the goods issue area. The HUs are then directly picked from the goods receipt area and sent to the goods issue area without being stored in the warehouse. The stock is loaded onto the transportation units (TUs) that will deliver the product stocks to the stores.

If the vendor sends unpacked goods instead of packed goods in the inbound process, the goods receipt is completed in embedded EWM with or without unloading, and the pick warehouse tasks are generated manually to move goods to the goods issue zone. Figure 15.2 summarizes how the merchandise distribution cross-docking works in embedded EWM.

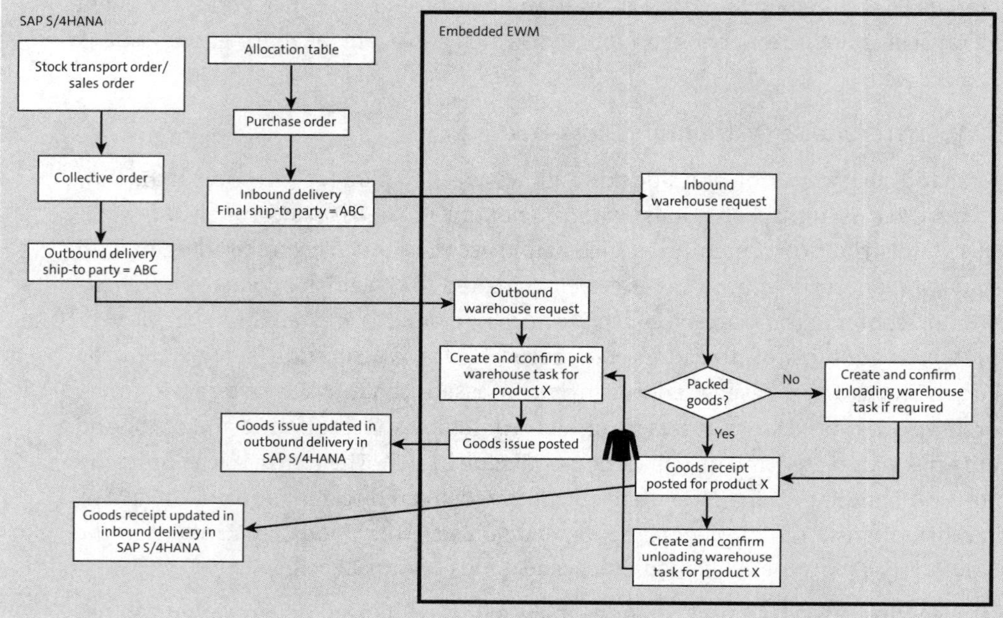

Figure 15.2 Merchandise Distribution Cross-Docking

15.2.2 Merchandise Distribution Flow-Through

In merchandise distribution flow-through, the incoming deliveries are repacked using recipient-driven or article-driven processes. For recipient-driven flow-through, the picking is done for the end recipient from goods received from inbound delivery. For product-driven flow-through, the total quantity of an article received through inbound delivery is distributed to all the recipients. Let's discuss both cross-docking procedures in detail in the following subsections.

Recipient-Driven Flow-Through

The recipient-driven flow-through process also begins with a stock transport order or sales order being created to replenish goods from a distribution center to stores. A collective purchase order is created for a specific vendor, which contains all the items purchased by the distribution center from the vendor. This is a pull-based scenario. In a push-based scenario, the system will create purchase orders and store orders using allocation tables. The inbound and outbound deliveries are created and distributed to embedded EWM.

A recipient-driven flow-through scenario occurs when you aren't able to send the complete goods being received from the vendor to the final ship-to party. In a flow-through process, the goods from the inbound delivery are moved to a special cross-dock area, where the goods are repacked and article-driven picking is done. The picker performs deconsolidation on the delivered HU, and the articles are divided on a per-store basis and packed into a pick HU. In this way, multiple articles are divided into multiple pick HUs per store and moved to the goods issue zone.

In addition to the settings for merchandise distribution described earlier, you define a warehouse order creation rule that groups together warehouse tasks having the same consolidation group. To do this, navigate to IMG path **SCM Extended Warehouse Management • Extended Warehouse Management • Cross-Process Settings • Warehouse Order • Define Creation Rule for Warehouse Orders**, and select **Consolidation Group** for the **Creation** category for the warehouse order creation rule.

Figure 15.3 summarizes how recipient-driven flow-through works in embedded EWM.

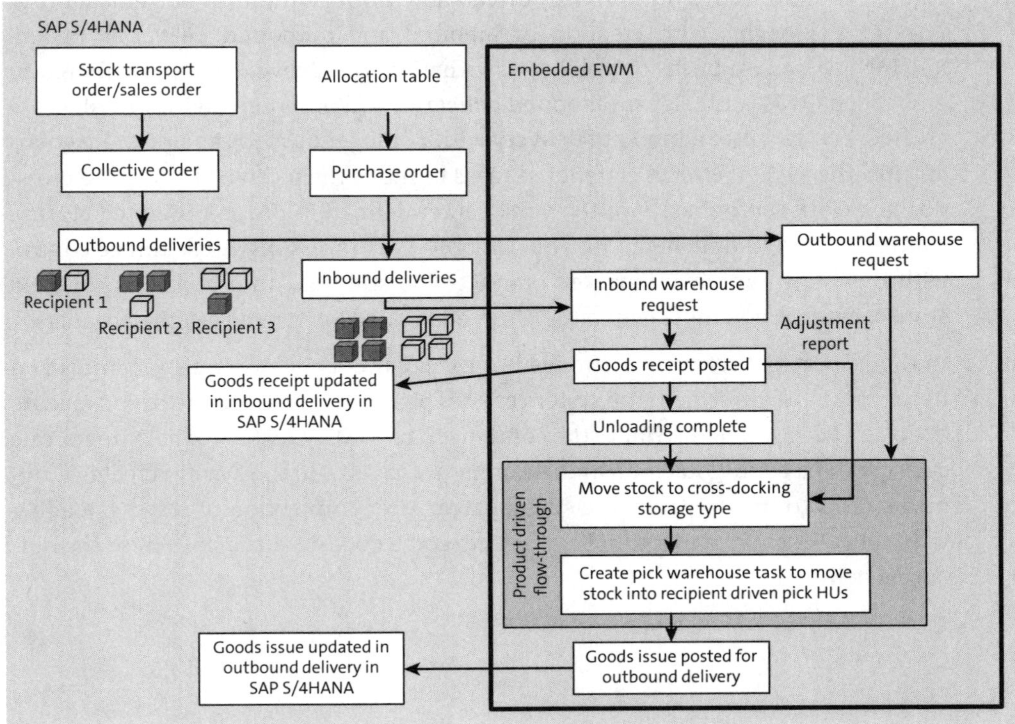

Figure 15.3 Recipient-Driven Flow-Through

Product-Driven Flow-Through

This process begins with receipt of goods in the warehouse. If you're unable to ship the goods to a customer completely, you move the packed or unpacked goods to a cross-dock storage type that's also used as a repacking work center. In product-driven flow-through, you distribute the contents of incoming HUs to customer-specific pick HUs. The picker picks the delivered goods and distributes them into the relevant pick HUs. If the delivered goods are already packed, then the HU is deconsolidated, and contents are repacked into the pick HUs. After the pick HU is ready, it's moved to the goods issue area.

To execute product-driven flow-through, you must define a cross-docking work center via **SAP Easy Access** path **Logistics • SCM Extended Warehouse Management • Extended Warehouse Management • Master Data • Work Center • Determine Work Center in Cross-Docking**. Click on **New Entries**, and define the work center bin for the cross-docking source storage type.

Figure 15.4 summarizes how product-driven flow-through works in embedded EWM. The process begins with creation of inbound and outbound deliveries in SAP S/4HANA based on push- or pull-based scenarios. The deliveries are distributed to embedded EWM, and relevant inbound deliveries and outbound delivery orders are created. You receive an inbound delivery with homogenous HUs and post the goods receipt. The system creates warehouse tasks to move the received HUs to the cross-docking work center based on the work center defined in process-oriented storage control. It's key to note here that you can only use process-oriented storage control with HUs. If you receive unpacked products and still want to use process-oriented storage control, you must generate HUs in embedded EWM and pack the products.

In the next step, the goods are moved to the cross-docking work center, and warehouse tasks are confirmed. The system creates pick warehouse tasks to deconsolidate the received HUs and distribute the contents to pick HUs created for customers, one customer at a time. You confirm the warehouse tasks, and the system creates warehouse tasks to move HUs to the staging area. After completion of staging, loading warehouse tasks are created and confirmed, and a goods issue is posted for the outbound delivery.

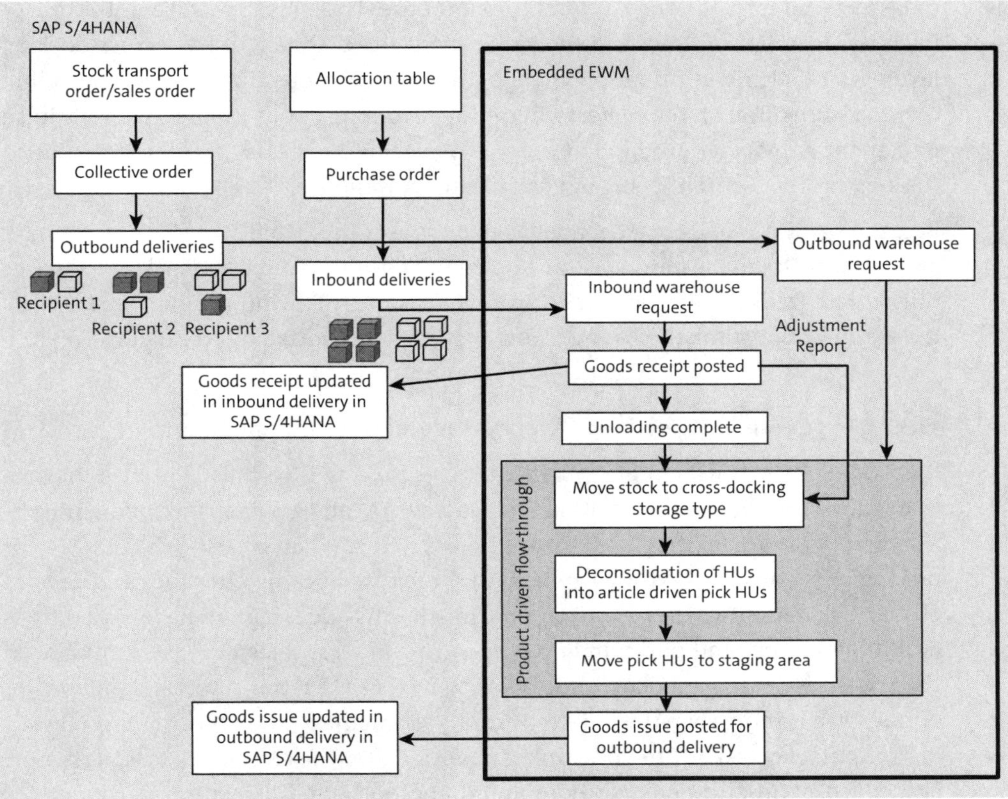

Figure 15.4 Product-Driven Flow-Through

Note

Readers familiar with transportation cross-docking in standalone SAP EWM will notice that it's no longer supported in embedded EWM. This is because transportation cross-docking is based on the SAP Supply Chain Management (SAP SCM) routing guide, which is no longer supported in embedded EWM in SAP S/4HANA 1909.

15.3 Opportunistic Cross-Docking

In opportunistic cross-docking, the inbound and outbound processes are carried out as planned, and cross-docking relevance is determined as soon as the goods are ready to be received into or issued out of the warehouse. This helps improve utilization of logistics, warehouse, and transportation resources. Opportunistic cross-docking leverages real-time information exchanges among various distribution and fulfillment systems. The system determines if the incoming goods can be used to fulfill a demand for an open outbound delivery; if yes, then the goods are directly routed to the staging area without being put away in the warehouse.

Because this form of cross-docking leverages real-time visibility of stock movement and availability, the warehouse must be equipped with radio frequency (RF) devices rather than traditional paper-based processes. In the following sections, we'll review the various opportunistic cross-docking processes supported by embedded EWM.

15.3.1 Triggered in Embedded Extended Warehouse Management

Embedded EWM-triggered opportunistic cross-docking is so called because the process is accomplished entirely within embedded EWM and isn't dependent on integration with other forecasting and distribution systems. When creating the putaway or picking warehouse tasks, the system checks for cross-docking relevance and decides if the stock needs to be rerouted. Opportunistic cross-docking can be initiated from both the inbound and outbound processes. This process doesn't require any break-pallet exercise and is applied only on homogenous HUs. If the quantity being picked or put away is more than the required cross-dock quantity, then the system creates a pick or putaway task for the remaining quantity after the cross-dock task is created. Embedded EWM also determines inbound and outbound delivery order items for opportunistic cross-docking for which warehouse tasks have already been generated. Embedded EWM cancels these warehouse tasks under the following conditions:

- The stock-removal strategy doesn't follow the first in, first out (FIFO) principle.
- Warehouse tasks are processed in the RF environment.
- Embedded EWM hasn't generated the warehouse tasks for the material flow system.

To set up embedded EWM-triggered opportunistic cross-docking, set the relevance for cross-docking at both the warehouse and product levels. The relevance for cross-docking at the warehouse level can be set from IMG path **SCM Extended Warehouse Management • Extended Warehouse Management • Cross Process Settings • Cross-Docking • Opportunistic Cross-Docking • EWM Triggered Opportunistic Cross-Docking • Activate EWM Triggered Opportunistic Cross-Docking**, as shown in Figure

15.5. Click on **New Entries**, and assign the product group type to the embedded EWM warehouse to activate embedded EWM–triggered opportunistic cross-docking for inbound and outbound processes.

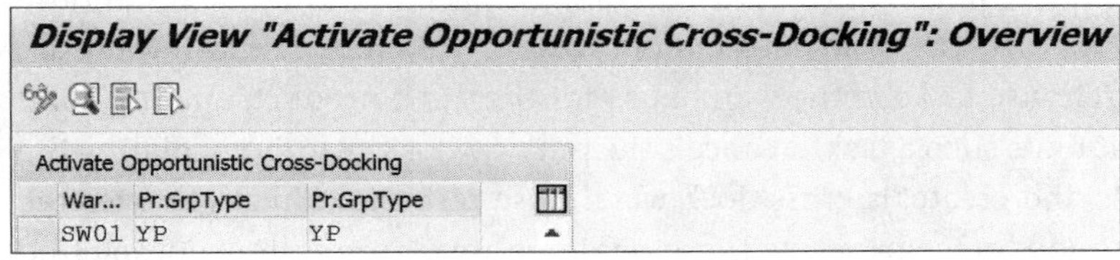

Figure 15.5 Activating Opportunistic Cross-Docking

The relevance for cross-docking is set at the product level by setting the product group type and product group in the global data view of the product master via Transaction /SAPAPO/MAT1.

The following points should be noted while working with embedded EWM–triggered opportunistic cross-docking:

- Embedded EWM only considers inbound delivery items for which goods receipt has been confirmed for embedded EWM-triggered opportunistic cross-docking.
- Embedded EWM doesn't consider inbound delivery items that are relevant for quality inspection.
- If packed quantities in goods receipt are relevant for cross-docking, the product quantity of an HU isn't distributed across different outbound deliveries, meaning the HU isn't split. The product quantity in the HU must be less than or identical to the requested quantity of an outbound delivery.

Following are the details of the inbound- and outbound-driven opportunistic cross-docking processes:

- **Inbound-driven opportunistic cross-docking**
  After the goods receipt is complete and before the goods are put away in the warehouse, the system checks to see if there is an open warehouse task for an outbound delivery for the same product, quantity, and batch characteristics. If the system finds an open warehouse task with matching requirements, it cancels the existing picking task and creates a cross-dock warehouse task for the equivalent quantity without violating the FIFO principle, and then directly moves the goods to the staging area for outbound processing. If the system is unable to find the suitable picking task, it carries on with the inbound process and creates the putaway tasks.

Figure 15.6 summarizes the process of embedded EWM-triggered opportunistic cross-docking in the inbound delivery process.

- **Outbound-driven opportunistic cross-docking**
  Outbound-driven opportunistic cross-docking is triggered during the warehouse task creation for picking in the outbound process. The system checks if there are any open warehouse tasks in the warehouse for the same product, quantity, and batch, and if it finds such a task, it cancels the putaway tasks without violating the FIFO principle and creates a cross-dock warehouse task that directly moves the stock from the goods receipt area to the goods issue area. If the system doesn't find a relevant task for putaway, then it continues with the outbound process and creates the picking tasks.

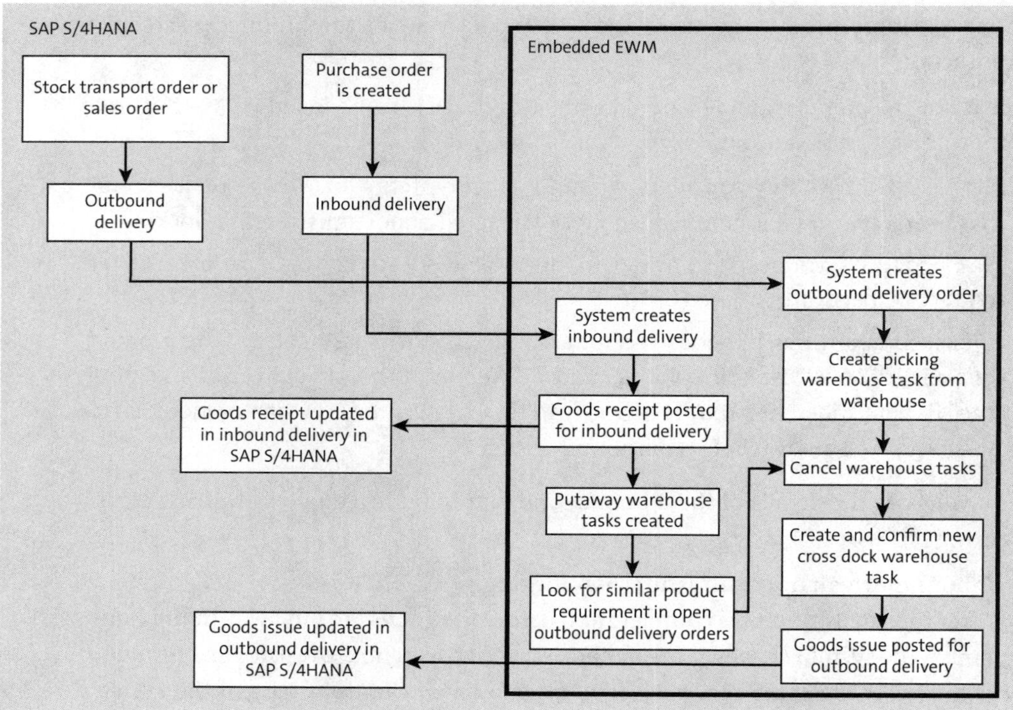

Figure 15.6 Inbound-Driven Opportunistic Cross-Docking

15.3.2 Push Deployment and Pick from Goods Receipt

Push deployment and *pick from goods receipt* are additional forms of opportunistic cross-docking that leverage the integration of SAP S/4HANA with SAP Advanced Planning and Optimization (SAP APO) and SAP Customer Relationship Management (SAP CRM). The process starts with inbound delivery creation for the goods receipt process. The system checks to see if the warehouse process type in the inbound delivery is set for putaway delay. You can set this from IMG path **SCM Extended Warehouse Management • Extended Warehouse Management • Cross-Process Settings • Warehouse Task • Define Putaway Delay** (see Figure 15.7).

If you've set up automatic task creation for putaway after goods receipt is completed, the putaway task creation is delayed by setting a time after the goods receipt is complete. If the stock type and warehouse process type isn't relevant for the inbound delivery, then warehouse tasks are created immediately.

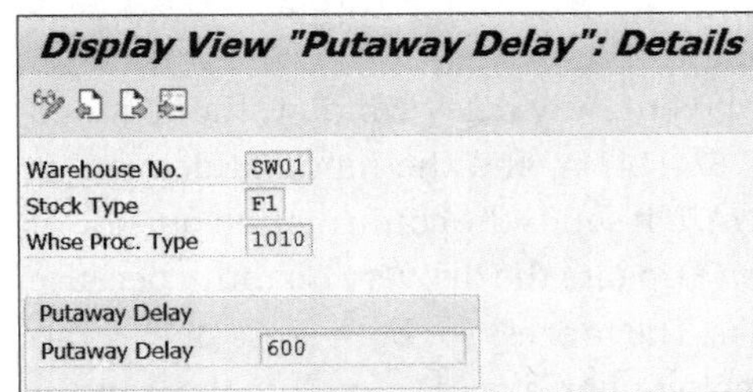

Figure 15.7 Putaway Delay

A list of customization settings required to set up push deployment and pick from goods receipt can be accessed via IMG path **SCM Extended Warehouse Management • Extended Warehouse Management • Cross Process Settings • Cross-Docking • Opportunistic Cross-Docking • Basic Settings for PD and Pick from GR**. This list describes all the customization settings that need to be made in SAP APO to execute push deployment and pick from goods receipt.

If the warehouse process type and stock type aren't relevant for putaway delay, then the system creates the putaway warehouse task immediately; in this case, push deployment or pick from goods receipt isn't triggered.

SAP APO determines whether the inbound delivery is relevant for push deployment or pick from goods receipt via event-driven quantity assignment. The process is as follows: SAP APO informs SAP CRM of the unconfirmed sales orders. SAP CRM then triggers the creation of outbound orders in SAP S/4HANA. The outbound delivery is distributed to embedded EWM, from which the system checks if stock exists in the goods receipt area. If there is stock, it creates warehouse tasks to move the stock from the goods receipt area to the goods issue area. If SAP CRM doesn't require the entire stock of the inbound delivery for picking from goods receipt or no unconfirmed sales order exists, SAP APO checks whether push deployment is required for the remaining stock. If push deployment is necessary, SAP APO generates a stock transport order and sends it to the SAP S/4HANA system. The outbound delivery is distributed to embedded EWM, and the warehouse tasks are created to move stock from the goods receipt area to the goods issue area.

Tip

It's advisable to post a goods receipt before unloading. This allows embedded EWM to consider the stock on a TU while calling for push deployment, which saves on unloading time and helps you make informed decisions for replenishment.

If SAP APO sends the confirmation within the putaway delay window, the required quantity is reserved in the delivery in SAP S/4HANA, and the inbound delivery is updated in embedded EWM and SAP S/4HANA. If it sends the confirmation outside of the putaway delay window, the system doesn't update the delivery quantity because the stock is already assigned to putaway tasks. The process for both cross-dock strategies is the same in embedded EWM. Push deployment is used to execute the transfer of goods from one warehouse to another at short notice without having to put away the goods. Pick from goods receipt is used to confirm a sales order that isn't yet confirmed by the available-to-promise (ATP) check by posting a goods receipt for an inbound delivery.

15.4 Summary

In this chapter, we discussed the concept of cross-docking and how it benefits businesses by optimizing logistics, transportation, and inventory. We covered the two main types of cross-docking: planned and opportunistic cross-docking. We discussed the subtypes of each of these cross-dock processes as well. We also walked through the process the system follows when carrying out each of these cross-docking strategies in the warehouse. You should now have a good feel for each of these processes and the settings required to enable them in your warehouse. In the next chapter, we will discuss wave management.

Chapter 16
Wave Management

In this chapter, we'll discuss wave management, the process by which outbound and posting change warehouse requests in embedded EWM can be grouped based on factors such as customer, product group, and so on. The picking tasks for these requests can be created well before actual loading and goods issue activity starts, resulting in better workforce utilization.

Wave management is the process by which you can combine items or split items from warehouse requests for outbound deliveries into waves, thereby improving picking for multiple deliveries in the warehouse. Warehouse requests generated for outbound delivery orders can be combined into waves based on customer, route, activity area, and so on, and you can plan the creation of warehouse picking tasks for these warehouse requests simultaneously. These tasks are then grouped into warehouse orders that are assigned to resources, which helps optimize the picking process.

In this chapter, we'll discuss wave management in detail (Section 16.1), including the settings required for creating waves in embedded EWM (Section 16.2), creating waves both manually and automatically in the warehouse (Section 16.3), and two-step picking in embedded EWM, which is used to further optimize the picking process (Section 16.4).

16.1 What Is Wave Management?

To understand how wave management works, imagine a scenario in which many deliveries are required to leave the warehouse at 11 a.m., and each one must be picked from a different place in the warehouse. It's cumbersome for a warehouse operator to create a warehouse task for each warehouse request manually and complete the picking. Wave management enables the operator to create warehouse tasks for all selected deliveries simultaneously. These warehouse tasks are then grouped into warehouse orders based on warehouse order creation rules and assigned to resources. Thus, multiple resources can execute simultaneous picking for multiple deliveries in the warehouse from different activity areas.

In Section 16.1.1, we'll explain the business context in which wave management can be used in real-world scenarios. In Section 16.1.2, we'll explain the processes carried out in the system, documents related to wave management, and using wave documents for picking stock.

16.1.1 Business Process

American company Alpha Medicals receives an order from one of its customers, Medimax Corporation Limited, based in Mexico. The order sent by Medimax contains various pharmaceutical products that are to be delivered to the company in a timely manner. Stock that will be delivered to the customer is to be picked from the warehouse of Alpha Medicals in a timely manner by the warehouse workers and placed in the staging area so that it can be picked from the goods issue by the trucks. To ensure that the warehouse worker picks the requested delivery products, packs them in the correct packing materials, performs other functionalities on the products, and still stages the goods in the goods issue area in a timely manner, Alpha Medicals implemented wave management. Wave management ensures that embedded EWM creates waves; using these waves, embedded EWM creates stock picking tasks with an appropriate buffer time that are assigned to the warehouse worker so that after picking, the products can be finally staged in the goods issue area before the truck docks on the warehouse door. As shown in Figure 16.1, the steps involved in the timely staging of products in the goods issue area of the Alpha Medical warehouse involving wave management are as follows:

1. The warehouse receives a warehouse request document for the outbound delivery to supply the requested products to the customer.
2. The warehouse request is assigned to a wave based on delivery times so that the worker can pick, pack, and stage the stock at the staging bay in a timely manner without bay congestion.
3. Using background jobs, the system keeps on releasing the waves for creation of the picking warehouse task. Based on automated warehouse task creation and assignment, the warehouse tasks are assigned to the warehouse workers for execution.

4. The warehouse worker picks the products, packs them in handling units, and stages them so they can be loaded on the transportation unit (TU) docked on the door to take the product to the customers.

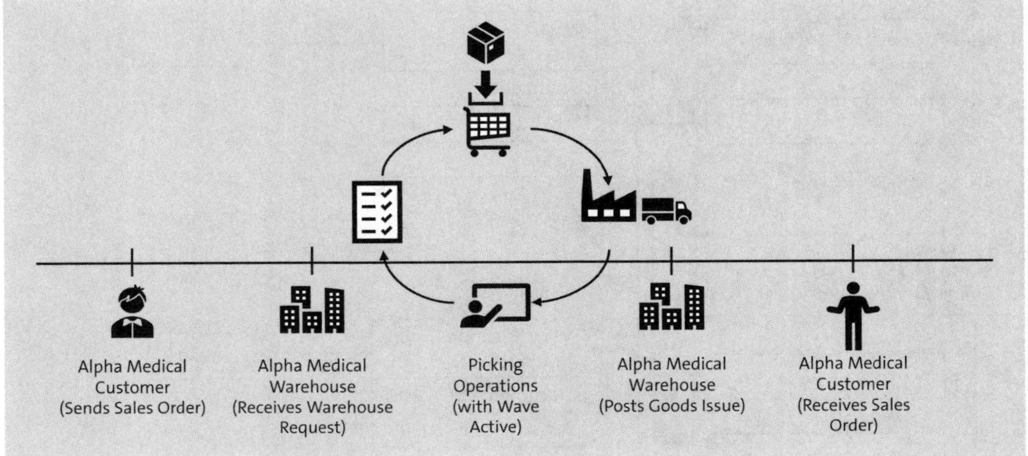

Figure 16.1 Business Flow Using Wave Management

16.1.2 System Process

Waves can be created manually or automatically depending on Customizing settings. You can create waves manually using Transaction /SCWM/WAVE or by navigating to **SAP Easy Access** path **Logistics • SCM Extended Warehouse Management • Extended Warehouse Management • Work Scheduling • Wave Management • Maintain Wave • Create**. Figure 16.2 shows how various warehouse request items belonging to different warehouse requests are grouped together in a wave.

Note that warehouse request items belonging to warehouse requests 1 and 2 are combined in waves 1 and 2 based on the similar attributes of warehouse request items such as activity area, ship-to party, product, and so on. Thus, warehouse tasks can be created in groups for products that share similar attributes for picking and delivery in the warehouse.

Note

Waves can be created in embedded EWM for open warehouse requests created for outbound delivery orders, internal stock transfers, and posting changes.

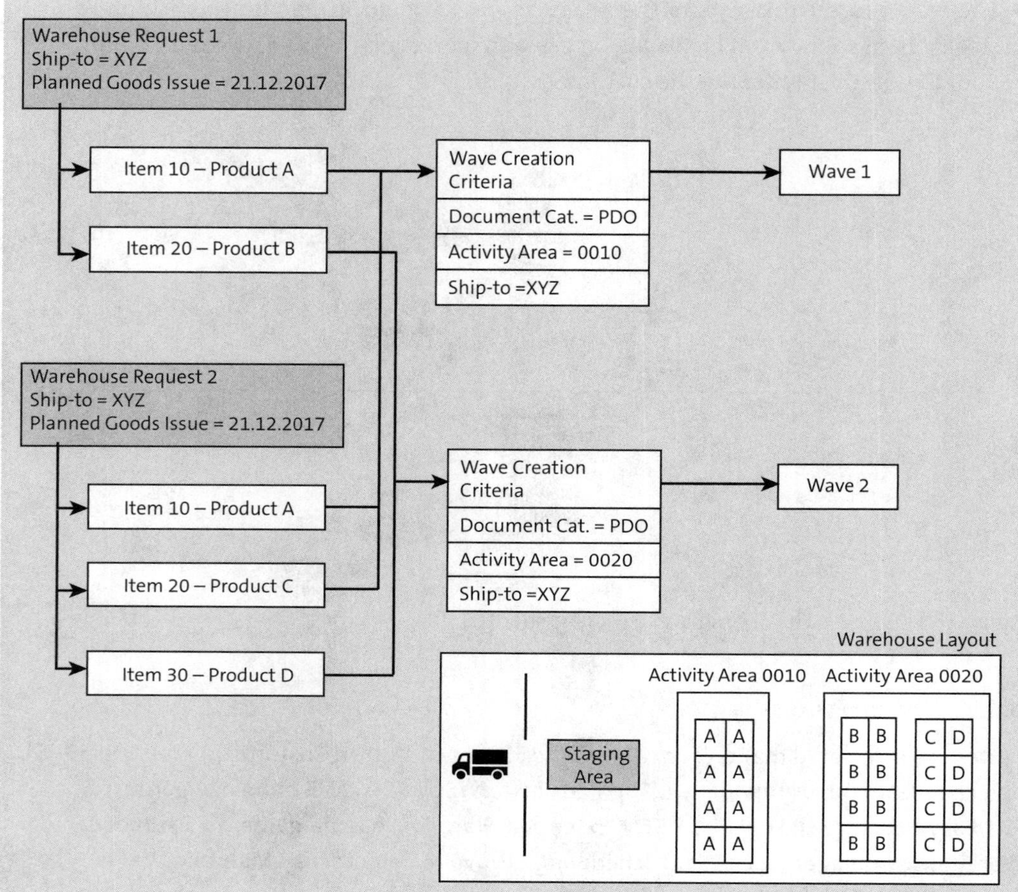

Figure 16.2 Grouping Warehouse Requests in Waves (Picking)

16.2 Configuring Wave Management

Certain basic configurations should be set up for wave management, which we'll discuss in the following sections.

16.2.1 Wave Types

Wave types help identify waves created with special characteristics and behavior. Wave types are primarily used for accessing and filtering waves in the warehouse monitor. Wave types are defined via IMG path **SCM Extended Warehouse Management • Extended Warehouse Management • GI Process • Wave Management • General Settings • Maintain Wave Type**. Click on the **New Entries** button from the menu bar at the top of the screen, and define a four-character alphanumeric **Wave Type** for your warehouse number, as shown in Figure 16.3.

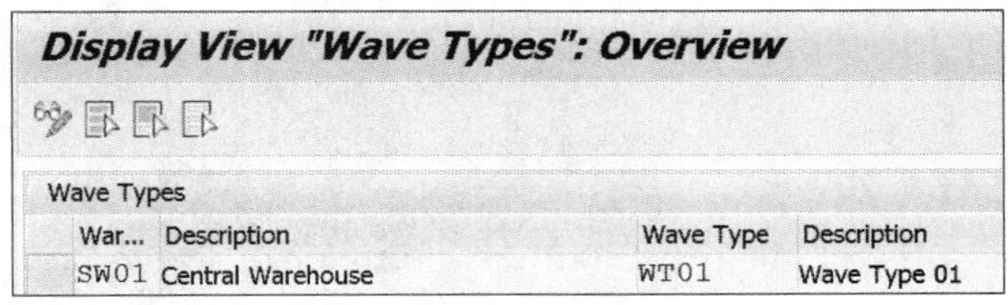

Figure 16.3 Defining the Wave Type

16.2.2 Wave Categories

Wave categories are primarily used as filters for determination and application of warehouse order creation rules. As shown in Figure 16.4, wave categories are defined via IMG path **SCM Extended Warehouse Management • Extended Warehouse Management • GI Process • Wave Management • General Settings • Maintain Wave Categories**. Click on the **New Entries** button, enter a combination of an embedded EWM warehouse number and a two-character alphanumeric wave category, and save.

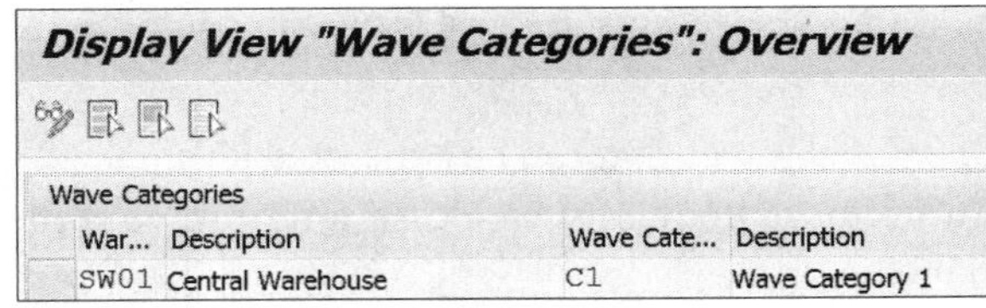

Figure 16.4 Defining the Wave Category

16.2.3 Set Automatic Wave Generation for the Warehouse Process Type

Automatic wave generation enables either the creation of a new wave or assignment of a warehouse request item to an existing wave. Automatic wave generation can be activated via the **AutoWave** indicator for a warehouse process type via IMG path **SCM Extended Warehouse Management • Extended Warehouse Management • GI Process • Wave Management • General Settings • Set Automatic Wave Generation For Warehouse Process Type**, as shown in Figure 16.5.

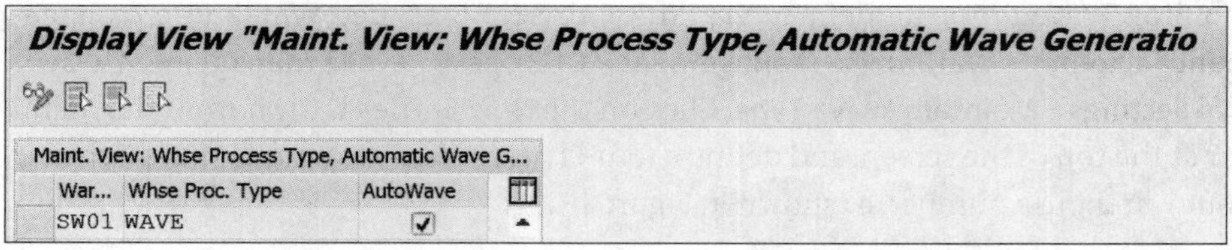

Display View "Maint. View: Whse Process Type, Automatic Wave Generatio

Maint. View: Whse Process Type, Automatic Wave G...

War...	Whse Proc. Type	AutoWave
SW01	WAVE	☑

Figure 16.5 Setting Automatic Wave Creation for the Warehouse Process Type

16.2.4 Maintain Wave Capacity Profile

The wave capacity profile is set up to limit the maximum number of warehouse request items that can be assigned to a wave template option. The number of warehouse requests that can be assigned to the wave template options can be limited by the following elements:

- **Maximum No. Items**
  This is the maximum number of warehouse request items a wave can contain.
- **Maximum Weight**
  This is the maximum weight of warehouse request items a wave can contain.
- **Max. Volume**
  This is the maximum volume of warehouse request items a wave can contain.
- **Max. Capacity**
  This is the maximum capacity of warehouse request items a wave can contain.
- **No. of Waves**
  This is the maximum number of parallel waves that can be generated if the capacity for a wave is exceeded by a warehouse item. In such a case, a new wave with similar characteristics is created by the system.
- **Err AT Cap.Overr.**
  This indicator is used to let the system throw an error if wave capacity has been exceeded and the system shouldn't create any more waves manually. This indicator is only relevant for manual wave creation. The system automatically calculates wave capacity during automatic wave creation.

As shown in Figure 16.6, capacity profile for waves can be configured via IMG path **SCM Extended Warehouse Management • Extended Warehouse Management • GI Process • Wave Management • General Settings • Maintain Wave Capacity Profile**. Click on the **New Entries** button; set the control parameters for capacity, such as **Maximum Weight**, **Max. Volume**, **Max. Capacity**, and so on, for the combination of embedded EWM **Warehouse No.** and capacity profile (**CapacProfil**); and then click **Save**.

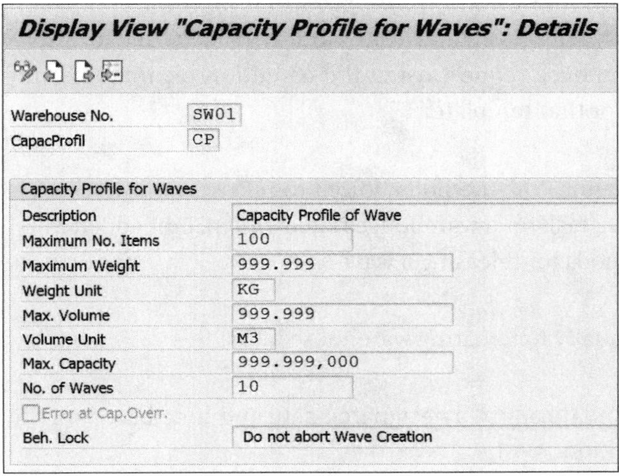

Figure 16.6 Defining the Wave Capacity Profile

16.2.5 Wave Templates

Wave templates are containers for control parameters used to create waves for a warehouse request. Various control parameters shape the features of the wave created for a warehouse request based on the wave template determined using the condition technique. As shown in Figure 16.7, wave templates are defined via **SAP Easy Access** path **Logistics • SCM Extended Warehouse Management • Extended Warehouse Management • Work Scheduling • Wave Management • Maintain Wave Templates** or via Transaction /SCWM/WAVETMP. Click on the **New Entries** button, and then enter a combination of embedded EWM **Warehouse No.** and numeric wave **Template** in the **Define Wave Template** section.

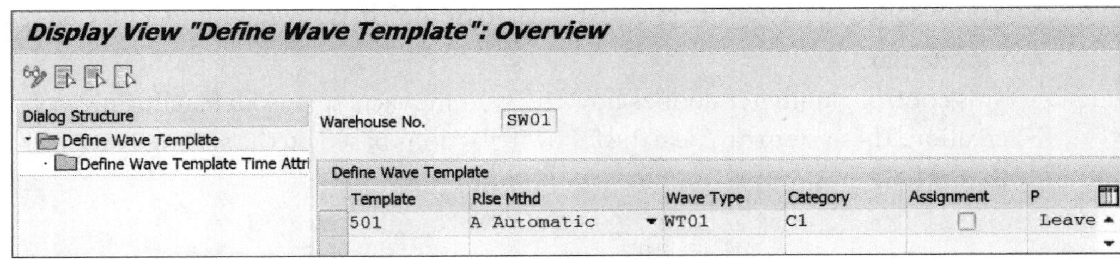

Figure 16.7 Defining the Wave Template

For each wave template, define some key parameters that characterize the template, as follows:

- **Template ID and description**
  Each template is defined with a unique ID and a description that are used for determining the wave for a warehouse request using the condition technique or for manual creation of a wave for that template.
- **Release method**
  The **Rlse Mthd** parameter defines the method allowed to release a wave, which is used to create the warehouse task for a warehouse request item. Embedded EWM provides the following methods for releasing a wave:
  - **Manual**
    The wave is released manually for creating warehouse tasks.
  - **Automatic**
    The wave is released automatically at a designated date and time based on the chosen wave template option.
  - **Immediate**
    The wave is released as soon as it's created by the system.
- **Wave type**
  This parameter is assigned to a wave template to group waves with similar characteristics. For example, you can create waves to stage goods a day in advance or directly at the time of loading.
- **Wave category**
  The wave category is assigned to the wave to filter out warehouse request items based on warehouse order creation rules.
- **Assignment**
  The **Assignment** indicator allows the system to assign warehouse request items to a wave that's already released. This is especially important in scenarios such as cross-docking with immediate release of waves so that new warehouse requests can be added to an already released wave to minimize the total number of waves.
- **Pick denial**
  This control parameter defines how the system reacts to pick denial during wave creation. The system can take the following actions based on the setting in the **Pick Denial** field:

- **Leave item in wave (release later)**
  This setting allows the warehouse request item to be kept in the wave and released after product stock is available in the source bin.
- **Release item from wave (new assignment)**
  This setting allows the warehouse request item to be removed from an existing wave and assigned to a new wave. This wave can be released after product stock becomes available in the source bin.
- **Create warehouse task for alternative source bin immediately**
  If you've set up rough bin determination at the storage type level, then the system assigns the source storage type for picking warehouse request items. This request is assigned to a wave. If the system sees pick denial during warehouse task creation after a wave is released, it creates a new task for the unavailable quantity immediately to pick the product from alternate storage bins.
- **Retry**
  This setting allows for the rerelease of a wave created using the wave template at regular intervals if the wave was released with an error.

Each wave template is assigned to wave template options. Wave template options are time-dependent attributes assigned to a wave template. A wave template can have more than one option. The system compares the requirements in warehouse requests based on the time attributes in each option and selects one to determine wave-dependent attributes such as release time for automatic release and so on. A number of fields need to be defined for a wave template (see Figure 16.8):

- **Option**
  Assign numeric values to wave template options, which provide multiple time windows available for grouping warehouse request items in a wave template.
- **Cutoff time and days**
  Represents the days and time before the wave completion date and time by which the request items can be added to a wave.
- **Release time and days**
  Represents the days and time before the wave completion date and time by which the wave can be released to create warehouse tasks for the request items.
- **Pick start and completion time and days**
  Represents the days and time before the wave completion date and time by which the request items can be picked.

- **Pack start and completion time and days**
  Represents the days and time before the wave completion date and time by which the request items can be packed.
- **Staging start time and days**
  Represents the days and time before the wave completion date and time by which the request items can be staged.
- **Wave completion time**
  Represents the time by which all the processes of the wave are planned to be completed. We'll discuss wave completion time further in the next section.
- **Calendar**
  Contains the calendar based on which the wave completion date, as well as other dates of the wave completion, are calculated.
- **Indicator**
  The special activity indicator is a single-digit numeric indicator assigned to a special activity. It's used to specify that the task created on wave release must be created for a special activity, based on which the picking process must be carried out in a slightly different manner. The special activity assigned to the indicator replaces the actual activity determined during task creation.
- **Staging area group and staging area**
  Represents the staging area at which the picked products using the wave can be staged.
- **Capacity profile**
  Represents the capacity (maximum weight, volume, etc.) that can be added in a single wave.

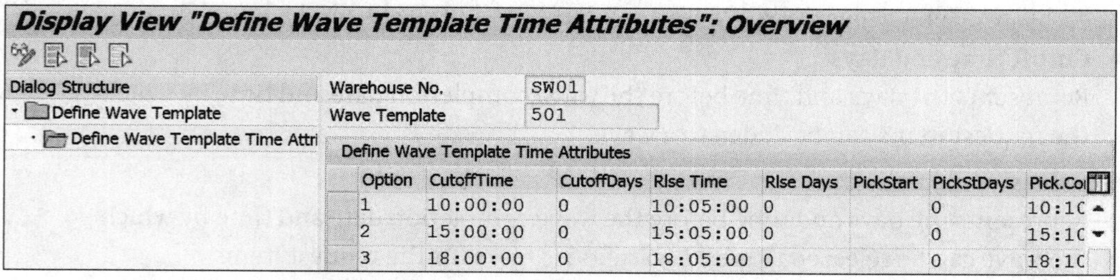

Display View "Define Wave Template Time Attributes": Overview

Dialog Structure
- Define Wave Template
  - Define Wave Template Time Attri

Warehouse No. SW01
Wave Template 501

Define Wave Template Time Attributes

Option	CutoffTime	CutoffDays	Rise Time	Rise Days	PickStart	PickStDays	Pick.Co
1	10:00:00	0	10:05:00	0		0	10:1C
2	15:00:00	0	15:05:00	0		0	15:1C
3	18:00:00	0	18:05:00	0		0	18:1C

Figure 16.8 Defining Wave Template Options

16.2.6 Wave Template Determination

Embedded EWM uses a condition technique to create a wave for a warehouse request item with a warehouse process type that's been activated for automatic wave creation. Wave template determination can be configured via IMG path **SCM Extended Warehouse Management • Extended Warehouse Management • GI Process • Wave Management • General Settings • Maintain Wave Template Determination**. Select the defined wave template, and click on **Define Wave Template Time Attribute**. Now, click on the **New Entries** button, enter a combination of wave template option and cutoff days and time for the options, and save.

Wave template determination is performed in embedded EWM using the Post Processing Framework (PPF). When the warehouse request is created, the system checks to see if the warehouse process type is set for automatic wave creation. If so, the system schedules a PPF action that can be set to process immediately or via a relevant report. Some of the elements that must be configured for setting up automatic wave determination are as follows:

- **Field catalog**
  A field catalog is a collection of fields used for building condition tables. You can select fields of your choice to create a condition table.
- **Condition table**
  Condition tables are used for creating condition records, based on which the system determines wave templates.
- **Access sequence**
  Condition tables are assigned to an access sequence to let the system know the sequence in which it will look at condition tables until it finds a valid condition record.
- **Determination procedures**
  The condition types defined earlier are assigned to a condition determination procedure. The standard system gives two predefined condition determination procedures, 0ODL and 0WHN, as follows:
  - **Assign procedures to document types**
    After the complete condition configuration is defined, it's assigned to the warehouse request document type via IMG path **SCM Extended Warehouse Management • Extended Warehouse Management • GI Process • Wave Management • General Settings • Maintain Wave Template Determination • Assign Procedure to Document Type**, as shown in Figure 16.9. Enter the determination procedure

16

for the embedded EWM warehouse and save. The system uses the assigned condition determination procedure for the document type after the warehouse request is created in embedded EWM.

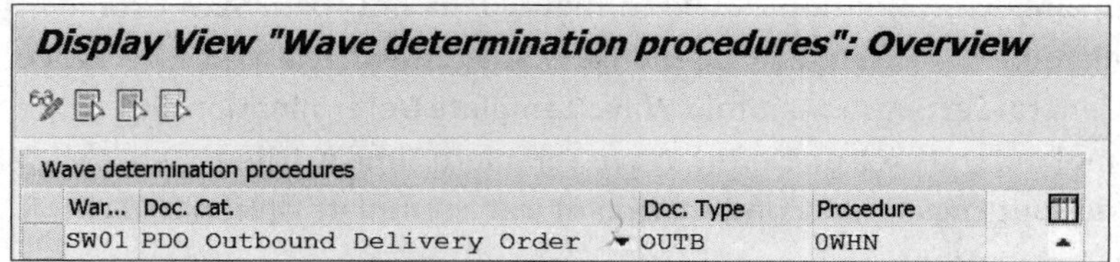

Figure 16.9 Wave Procedure Assignment

- **Create condition records**
  Create condition records for the condition types via **SAP Easy Access** path **Logistics • SCM Extended Warehouse Management • Extended Warehouse Management • Work Scheduling • Wave Management • Maintain Conditions for Determining Wave Templates**, as shown in Figure 16.10. Create condition records for the condition table just created. In the standard system, condition type **0WHN** is used.

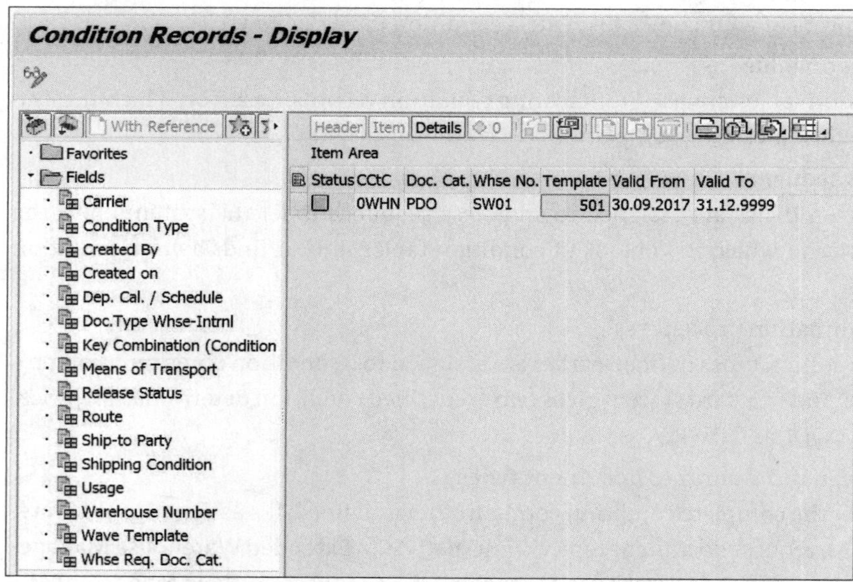

Figure 16.10 Wave Template Determination Conditions

16.3 Wave Creation Process

Automatic wave assignment is performed using condition techniques in embedded EWM, as follows:

1. **Embedded EWM activates the wave PPF.**
   The PPF action for wave creation is activated.
2. **The wave template is determined.**
   Based on the condition records set for wave determination, a valid wave template is determined by the system.
3. **A wave template option is determined.**
   Based on the time attributes and logic explained in the previous section, the wave template options are scanned; based on this, the wave will be created.
4. **Wave times are computed for the wave.**
   Based on the rule set for wave template options, the system calculates planned completion, wave completion, and lock time for the wave. Based on the calculated times, embedded EWM determines the best wave template and wave template option. Embedded EWM determines the planned completion time, wave completion time, and lock time for all warehouse request items before assigning them to waves. Embedded EWM calculates the planned completion date and time of the warehouse request as the yard planned completion date and time.

   If the planned goods issue time from the yard isn't available, then the system uses the goods issue start date from the outbound delivery order. For posting changes or stock transfer processes, the warehouse activity end date and time are used for calculation of the planned completion date and time. The lock time is the time by which the system can add a warehouse request item to a wave. Embedded EWM calculates the lock date, lock time, release date, and release time based on the calculated wave completion date and time.

   Embedded EWM determines the wave completion date and time for each wave template option. The calculation of the wave completion time is dependent on whether the planned completion time of the warehouse request is before or after the wave completion time of the wave template option. Thus, the system uses the following logic to determine the wave completion time for each scenario:

   - **Planned completion before wave completion**
     Figure 16.11 shows how embedded EWM handles the situation in which the planned completion time of the warehouse request item is before the wave completion time of the wave template option.

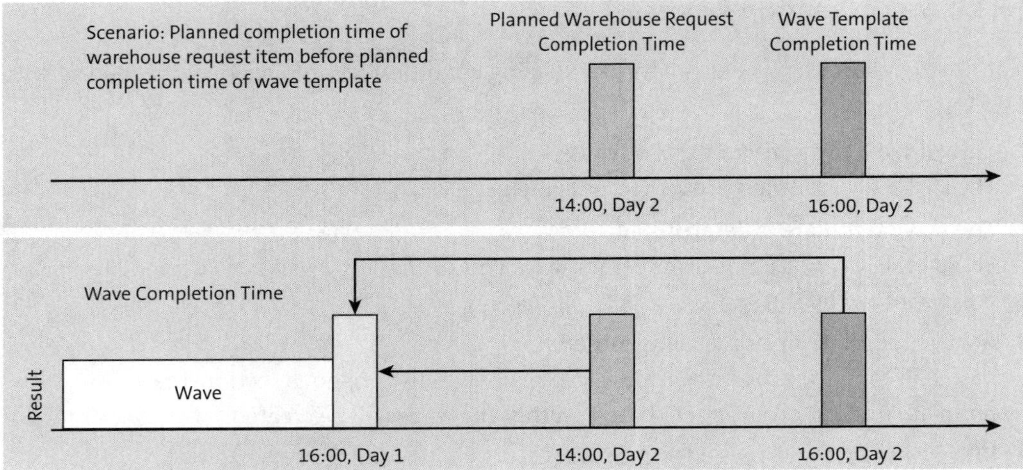

Figure 16.11 Planned Completion before Wave Completion Time

For example, the planned completion time of the warehouse request item is 14:00 on day 2, and the wave completion time in the wave template option is 16:00 on day 2. Because the planned completion time of the request item is before the planned wave completion time, embedded EWM schedules the wave to be created with a wave completion date of the day before the planned completion day of the warehouse request item—that is, 16:00 on day 1.

- **Planned completion after wave completion**

  Figure 16.12 shows how embedded EWM handles the situation in which the planned completion time of the warehouse request item is after the wave completion time of the wave template option.

  The planned completion time of the warehouse request item is 16:00 on day 1, and the wave template completion time is 14:00 on day 1. Because the planned completion time of the request item is after the wave completion time, embedded EWM schedules the wave to be created with a wave completion date on the same day as the planned completion day of the warehouse request item—that is, 14:00 on day 1.

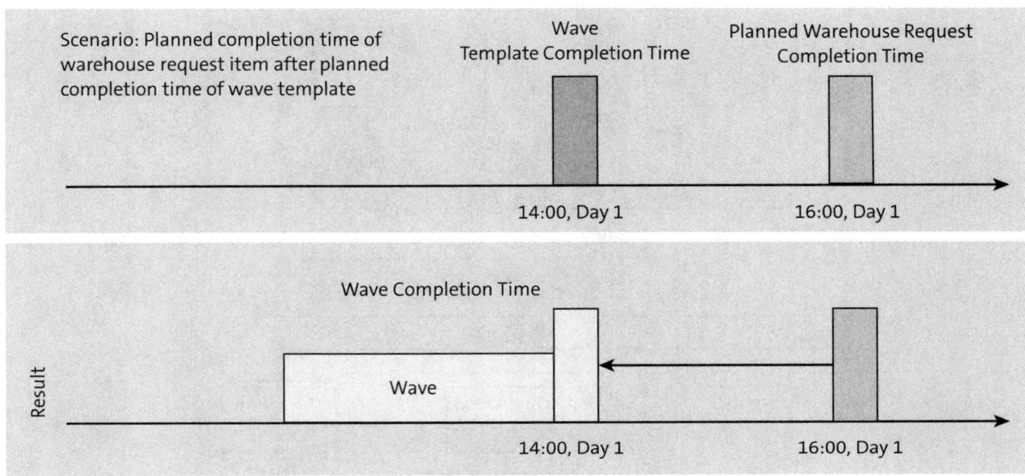

Figure 16.12 Planned Completion after Wave Completion Time

5. **Embedded EWM assigns the wave.**
   After the wave template and option are selected, the system creates a wave for the template and option and tries to assign the warehouse request item to the wave, as shown in Figure 16.13.
   - If a wave with a selected wave template and option is already present, the system tries to assign the warehouse request item to the wave.
   - If the wave capacity was filled during the previous step, and the wave can't accept more request items, a new wave is created with the request item with the same wave template and option.
   - If the wave of the selected wave template and option exists but has been released, then a new wave is created for the selected wave template and option. If settings for assignment after wave release have been selected in the wave template, then the system assigns the request item to the released wave.

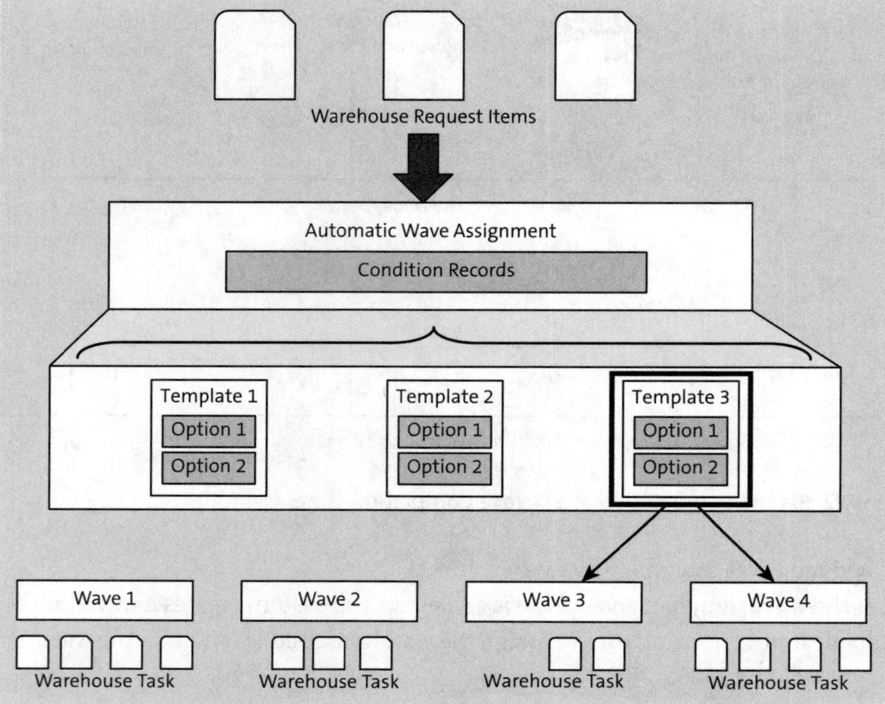

Figure 16.13 Wave Creation Process

Figure 16.14 shows a wave created in embedded EWM for open warehouse requests. The wave screen consists of two main sections: wave header ❶ and wave item ❷. A wave header contains information that embedded EWM determines based on the wave template, wave template options, and delivery requests. The **Items** tab contains the warehouse request items assigned to a wave. Warehouse tasks are created after the wave is released automatically or manually. The **Warehouse Orders** tab ❸ contains information about warehouse orders created for the warehouse request items after the wave is released. The **Warehouse Requests** tab ❹ allows users to search warehouse requests for assignment to waves based on document number, sales order, goods issue date, departure date from yard, or end date of warehouse activities.

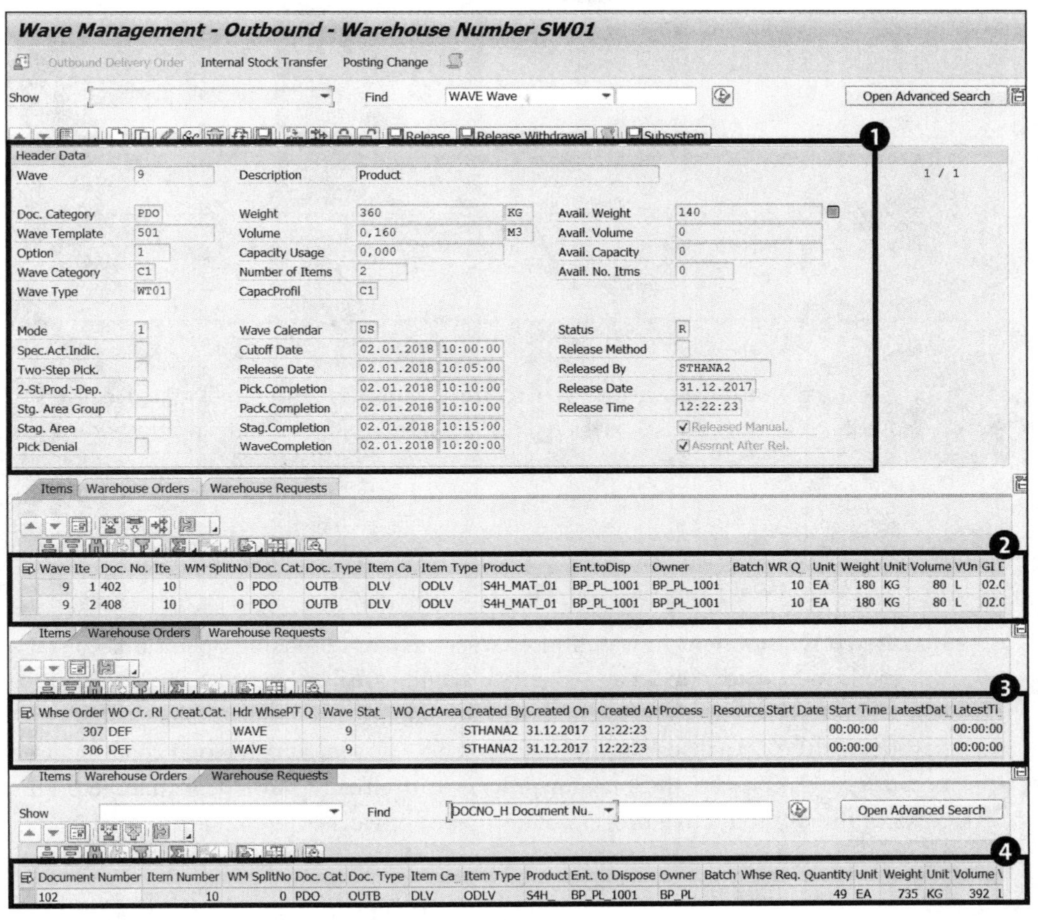

Figure 16.14 Example of a Wave in Embedded EWM

> **Tip**
>
> As shown in Figure 16.15, you can activate logs for wave management via **SAP Easy Access** path **SCM Extended Warehouse Management • Extended Warehouse Management • Settings • Activate Application Log**, and set a value in the **Log Active** column for **Subobject WAVE_REL**. The logs then can be viewed from the transaction screen for wave management, Transaction /SCWM/WAVE.

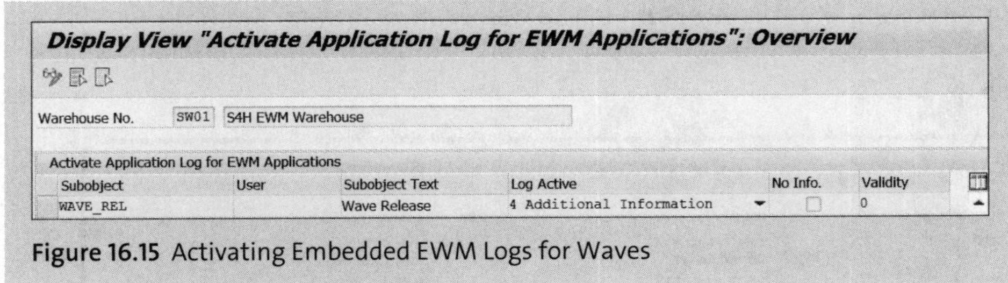

Figure 16.15 Activating Embedded EWM Logs for Waves

Note

The Process Waves app allows you to create and process waves, assign delivery requests to waves, release waves to create warehouse tasks, and perform two-step picking.

16.4 Two-Step Picking

It's often a requirement in warehouses with busy warehousing operations to stage the goods to be loaded in an intermediate staging area and execute the loading process when a TU arrives in the warehouse. The staging process is usually carried out a day before the actual loading is supposed to happen, which saves loading time because any issues in the picking process can already have been handled. This reduces the unproductive process of a warehouse worker fetching the stock from a warehouse source bin for each warehouse request item separately. Instead, the warehouse worker draws the stock for multiple warehouse requests items into an intermediate staging area near the loading bay or goods issue area. This is called the *withdrawal* step in two-step picking. In the next step, the warehouse operator creates warehouse tasks to redistribute the stock to fulfill individual warehouse requests, as shown in Figure 16.16. This step is called the *allocation* step in two-step picking.

In the following sections, we'll look at how to set up and use two-step picking.

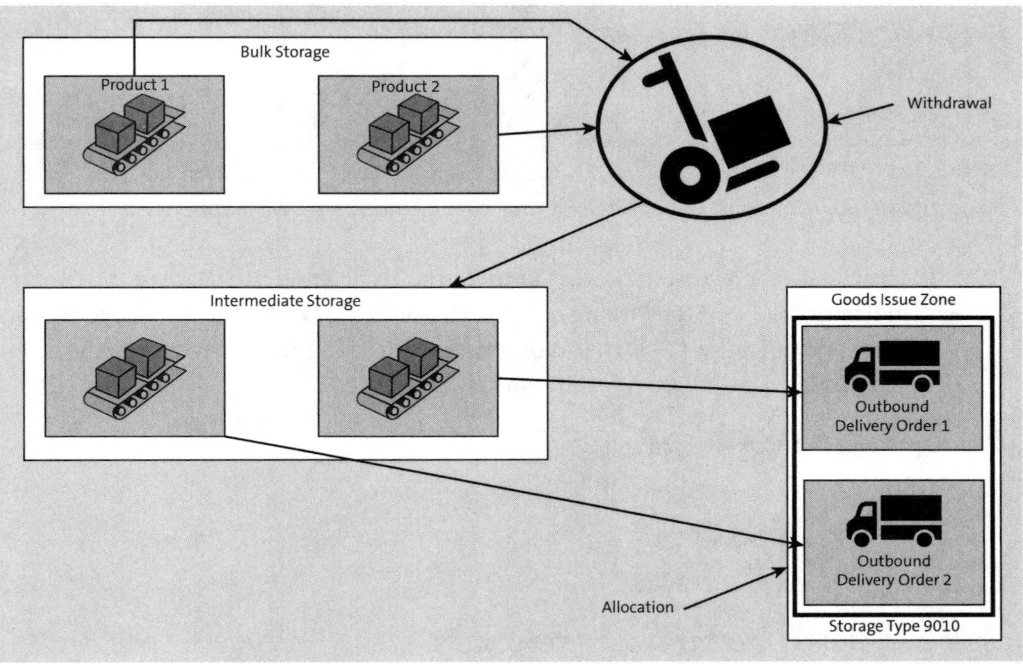

Figure 16.16 Two-Step Picking Process Using Waves

16.4.1 Configuration

There are a couple of important configuration and master data setup entries that need to be made to activate the two-step picking process. Based on the following settings, users can set normal wave picking and wave picking configured as a two-step process in the warehouse:

1. Define a warehouse process type for creating withdrawal warehouse tasks for picking. In the standard system, process type 2020 is defined for picking steps.
2. Set up the relevance for two-step picking at the warehouse level. As shown in Figure 16.17, enter "2" under **Two-Step Pick.** for the warehouse via IMG path **SCM Extended Warehouse Management • Extended Warehouse Management • Goods Issue Process • Wave Management • General Settings • Set Up Two Step Picking.** The warehouse process type used for carrying out the first step in two-step picking is specified in the **Process Type** field. In standard embedded EWM, warehouse process type 2020 is used, but you can create a different warehouse process type.

Display View "Control for Two-Step Picking": Overview

Control for Two-Step Picking

Warehouse Nu...	Description	Two-Step Pick.	2-St.Prod.-Dep.	Process Type	Process Type Description
SW01	Central Warehouse	2	☑	2020	Withdrawal: Two-Step Picking

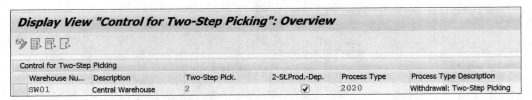

Figure 16.17 Configuring Two-Step Picking for the Embedded EWM Warehouse

3. To activate the two-step process at the product level, set the value of the control indicator for **Two-Step Picking** to "2" in the **Whse Data** tab of the product master, as shown in Figure 16.18. This allows two-step picking to be activated only at the product level, rather than for the entire warehouse.

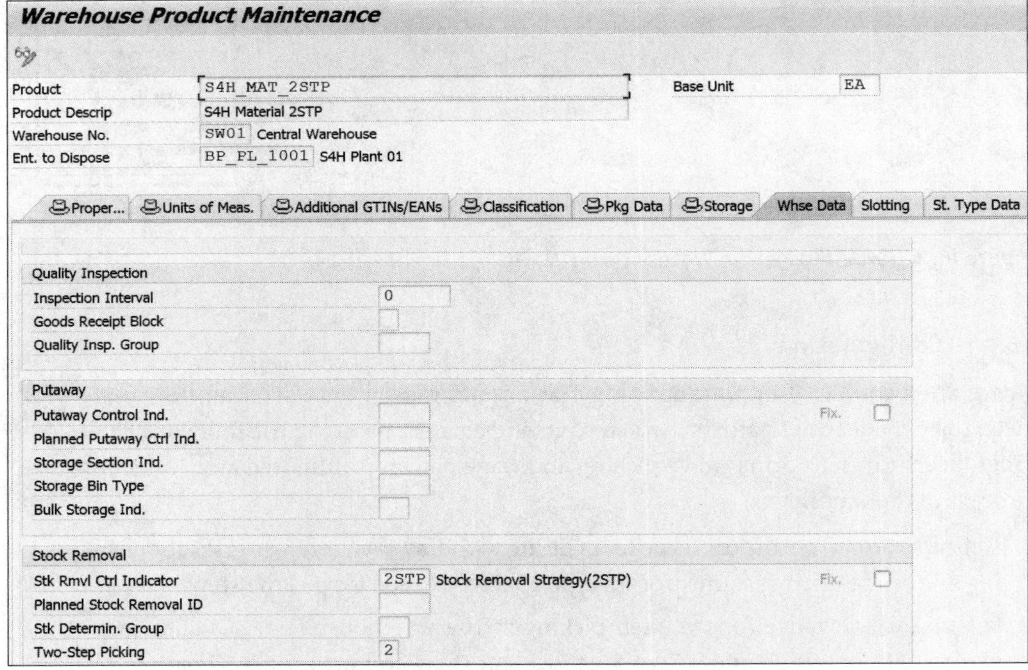

Figure 16.18 Warehouse Product Activation for Two-Step Picking

4. The intermediate storage bin where the stock picked for outbound delivery orders is to be placed is defined in the customization settings for the warehouse process type created in step 1 by providing the destination storage type and bin in the

Dest.Stor.Type and **Destination Bin** fields, respectively. In standard embedded EWM, storage type 2010 is used.

5. In the optimization of the search sequence for picking, as shown in Figure 16.19, set the indicator for two-step picking to sequence 1 to have the system give priority to the two-step picking process.

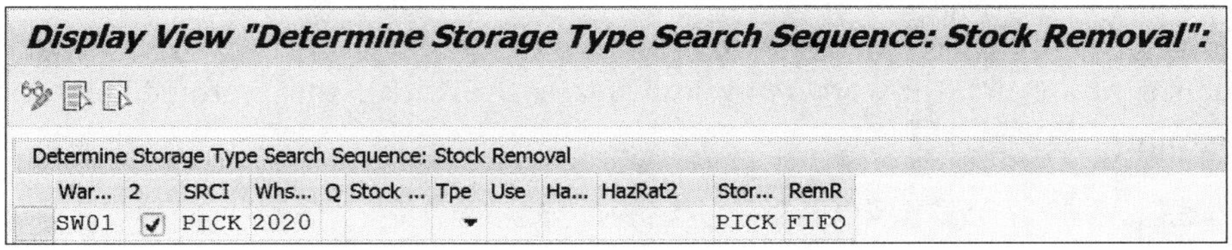

Figure 16.19 Activating Two-Step Picking in the Picking Strategy

6. The stock removal strategy for allocation steps must contain the interim storage type in its search sequence. To do this, specify the intermediate storage type in the storage type search sequence, which is assigned in the determination for warehouse process type 2020, and set the indicator for two-step picking.
7. Ensure that all relevant storage types, sections, and bins are created for an intermediate storage type in which products will be stored after the first picking step.

16.4.2 Execution of Two-Step Picking

Now, let's discuss the two steps for carrying out two-step picking in the warehouse.

Step 1: Withdrawal

This is the step in which stock quantity for multiple outbound delivery orders is withdrawn from the source bin in the warehouse and placed in an intermediate storage area. This step provides optimization by enabling picking for multiple outbound deliveries in one step, thus reducing the number of picking operations that need to be performed by warehouse workers. Stock picking is done from various source storage bins and placed in bins in the intermediate storage. The steps involved in the withdrawal process are as follows:

1. Multiple outbound delivery items are combined into a wave.
2. Embedded EWM determines the relevance of the wave for two-step picking from the configuration and master data of the product, as explained in the previous section. If required, also make a wave relevant for two-step picking by changing the

value of indicator **2StP** to "2" when creating a wave manually using Transaction /SCWM/WAVE.

3. A withdrawal warehouse task is created for the wave using withdrawal steps by clicking on **Release Withdrawal**. This step can also be executed in the embedded EWM warehouse monitor by selecting the required wave and choosing the **Release Withdrawal** option from the **More Methods** button, as shown in Figure 16.20.
4. After the warehouse task for withdrawal is created, it's confirmed by the warehouse worker after the worker physically places the stock in the intermediate storage area.

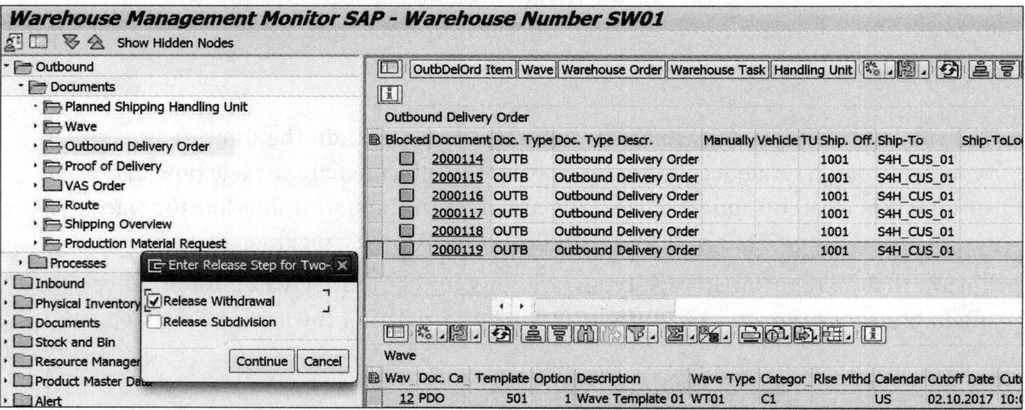

Figure 16.20 Withdrawal Step in Two-Step Picking

Step 2: Allocation

In this step, stock is picked from the intermediate storage bin and distributed to individual outbound delivery orders at the time of loading. The steps involved in the allocation process are as follows:

1. The next set of warehouse tasks is created from the wave maintenance screen using Transaction /SCWM/WAVE, which is then used for assigning the stock from the intermediate storage bin to individual requirement goods issue bins. The allocation warehouse task can also be created in the warehouse monitor using Transaction /SCWM/MON. In the warehouse monitor, the wave for the two-step process is selected, and the **Release Subdivision** option is selected from the **More Methods** button, as shown in Figure 16.21.

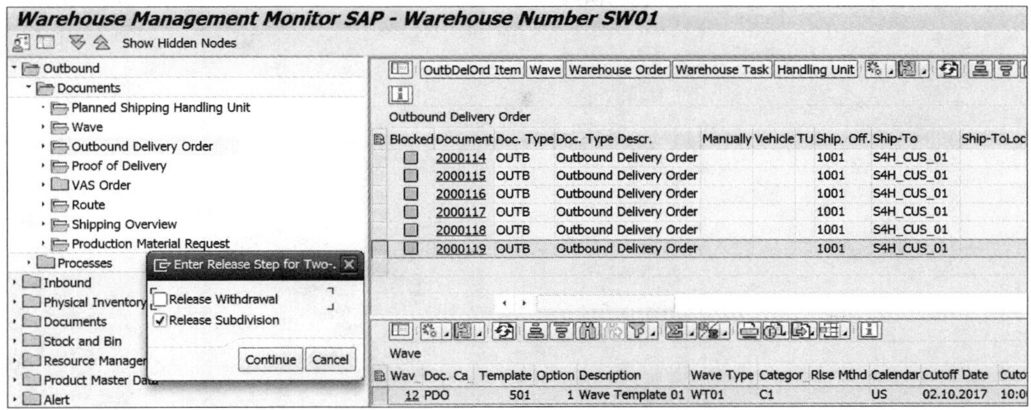

Figure 16.21 Allocation Step in Two-Step Picking

2. A warehouse worker physically moves the stock from the intermediate bin to destination bins for open warehouse requests.
3. After the completion of the physical movement, the warehouse worker confirms the allocation warehouse task created in step 1.

16.5 Summary

This chapter introduced basic concepts of wave management in embedded EWM. You should now understand the business use of waves for outbound delivery orders and posting change warehouse requests. We also explained various building blocks and configuration elements of waves in embedded EWM. We introduced the master data used in the wave process for wave creation, such as wave templates, options, and condition records for determining wave templates. We provided a through explanation of various wave scenarios to explain how delivery times affect the calculation of wave completion and release time.

Finally, we discussed how the picking process can be made more efficient by using two-step picking in the warehouse. The settings required to activate the detailed application log for waves in embedded EWM was also introduced in this chapter. You should now be able to set up wave management for your warehouse, based on your warehouse business requirements. In the next chapter, we will discuss slotting and rearrangement.

Chapter 17
Slotting and Rearrangement

In this chapter, we'll discuss slotting and rearrangement processes used for planning and executing optimized placement of products in a warehouse based on a product and its movement in the warehouse.

Slotting is the process of determining a more efficient storage and picking process in the warehouse. Rearrangement is the process in which the stock is moved from a suboptimal stock area to a physical stocking area based on stock velocity and business requirements of a company. In this chapter, we'll introduce slotting and rearrangement in Section 17.1. We'll then cover the configurations required to set up slotting in embedded EWM in Section 17.2, discuss the execution of slotting in embedded EWM in Section 17.3, explain ABC analysis for stock placement using stock velocity in Section 17.4, and, finally, discuss the process of rearrangement to implement the results of slotting in Section 17.5.

17.1 What Are Slotting and Rearrangement?

Slotting is a process that optimizes placement of a product in a warehouse to optimize the picking process further. Slotting uses relevant warehouse data from the product master, packaging data, demand forecasts, and so on to determine a storage concept for the warehouse. The storage concept is determined in the form of storage parameters stored in the product master. These parameters describe the storage section in which the product is to be stored, properties of the storage bin, and the putaway strategy that is to be used.

Slotting can be run in the foreground or scheduled in the background via a background job. It's mostly carried out in a mature warehouse with a high throughput of data. The slotting process reviews the current product parameters and proposes revised parameters to optimize the picking process. Slotting also forms the basis of rearrangement, which helps rearrange the stock in the warehouse after slotting results have been updated in the product master. The warehouse stock is moved to more optimal bins based on updated indicators set in the product master by slotting.

In the slotting process, storage indicators that signify optimal placement positions in a warehouse are automatically determined for a product based on underlying storage parameters stored in the product and various other master data objects. The master data objects that play a part in determining these storage indicators are product data, requirement data, and packaging data. Using the data from these objects, slotting determines proposed indicators for optimal putaway parameters, such as storage type, section, and bin type. These indicators can be activated at any point in time. Efficient putaway in the warehouse becomes the foundation for more optimized picking, thereby improving the warehouse key performance index. In the following sections, we explain the business context in which slotting and rearrangement can be used in real-world scenarios and discuss how these processes are carried out in the system.

17.1.1 Business Process

American company Alpha Medicals optimizes its product placement at the end of the day by placing the fast-moving goods in the front bins and the slow-moving goods in the back area of the warehouse. At the end of the day, the company places any random lying stock or stock misplaced in the wrong bins on to the correct storage bins. The company performs end-of-day planning daily for such re-placement of the products in optimized storage bins of the warehouse by assigning the warehouse tasks to workers. Warehouse workers move the products to the correct destination bin based on the allocated warehouse tasks and reorganize the product placement in the warehouse so that the next day requirements can be met. To ensure that such reorganization activities of the warehouse are planned and captured in embedded EWM system, the company has implemented slotting and rearrangement in embedded EWM.

Figure 17.1 shows a scenario in which slotting is carried out in embedded EWM. A warehouse stocks umbrellas in storage type 0020. However, as the rainy season starts, the demand for umbrellas increases. To reduce the picking time, you can execute slotting on the warehouse product for umbrellas and have the system determine the new putaway control indicator and other storage parameters, which will help reduce the picking time for the product. We'll discuss slotting execution in the warehouse in detail in Section 17.3.

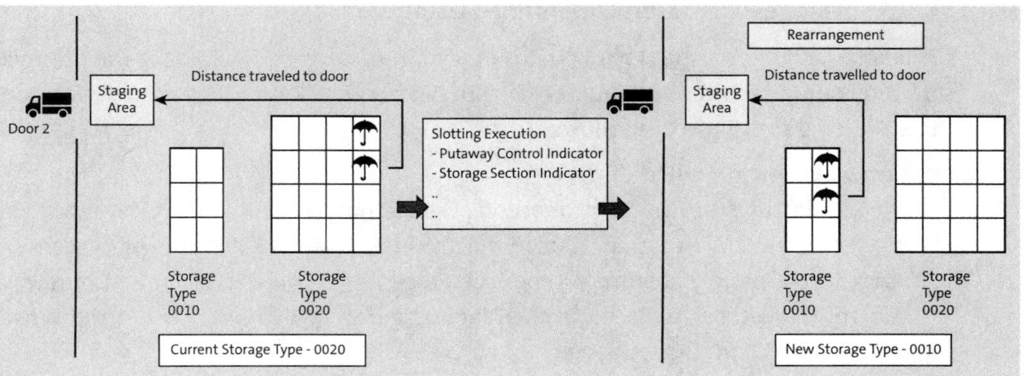

Figure 17.1 Slotting Process in the Warehouse

17.1.2 System Process

The following explains the basic system flow, including the documents and data required to execute slotting and rearrangement:

1. Based on demand, stock movement tasks, and other parameters, regular background jobs are run in embedded EWM, which gives planned values of the storage types, sections, and so on where the products should be moved to from the source bin.
2. The warehouse administrator checks the planned parameters calculated by the embedded EWM system and activates them so that they are permanently stored in the product master to complete slotting process.
3. Using background jobs, embedded EWM system creates warehouse requests, and subsequent warehouse tasks are created for the warehouse requests to move the products from the source bin to the destination bin.
4. Warehouse tasks are assigned to warehouse workers who move the products from source bin to destination bins and complete the rearrangement process.

17.2 Configuring Slotting

In the following sections, we'll discuss how to configure slotting for your warehouse. First, we'll define the storage parameters determined using slotting, and then we'll discuss how parameter determination happens during slotting using a condition technique in embedded EWM.

17.2.1 Storage Parameters Determined Using Slotting

As explained previously, slotting helps determine a storage concept for the product by determining relevant parameters for putaway and picking. The parameters determined using slotting are as follows:

- **Putaway control indicator**
  During slotting, the system proposes a planned putaway control indicator, which, when activated as an actual value in the product master, enables the placement of stock into a preferred storage type or storage type group. The planned putaway control indicator is updated in the **Planned Putaway Ctrl Ind.** field in the **Whse Data** tab of the product master.
- **Storage section indicator**
  Slotting proposes a planned storage section indicator, which when activated as an actual value in the product master, enables the removal of stock from a preferred storage section in a storage type. The planned storage section indicator is updated in the **PlStorSect.Ind.** field in the **St. Type data** view of the product master.
- **Storage bin type**
  During slotting, the system proposes a bin type for bins in which a product can be put away. Bin type determination can be made using the condition technique or a bin type determination rule, depending on business requirements. Select either option via IMG path **SCM Extended Warehouse Management • Extended Warehouse • Goods Receipt Process • Slotting • General Settings • Define Storage Type Parameters for Slotting**, as shown in Figure 17.2.

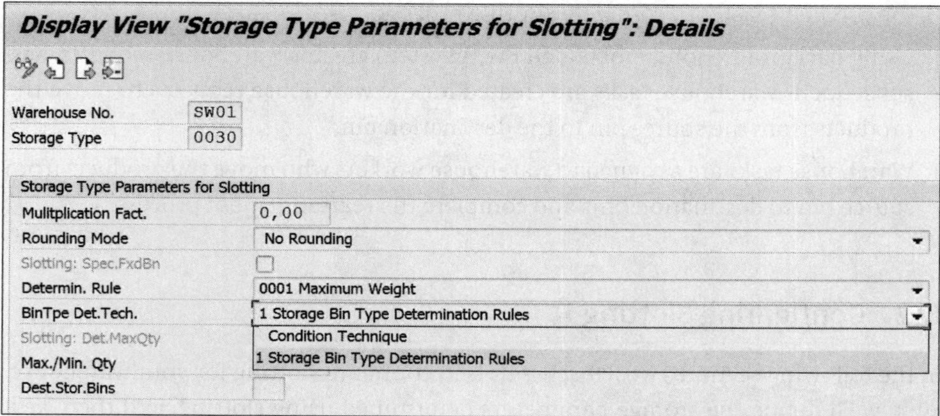

Figure 17.2 Bin Type Determination Rule

If the condition technique is selected, then the storage bin type is determined based on the condition technique (discussed in detail in the next section). If you're determining bin types using the bin type determination rule, then you need to define allowed bin types in a storage type via IMG path **SCM Extended Warehouse Management • Extended Warehouse • Management • Goods Receipt Process • Slotting • General Settings • Define Storage Bin Type List**. Click on **New Entries**, and provide the sequence of allowed bin types for a storage type.

You can also specify a bin type rule for each bin type. SAP provides a list of predefined bin type rules that determine the right bin type for a product using various product and bin characteristics, such as weight, volume, dimension, orientation, and so on. Based on the bin type determination technique set at the storage type level, the system determines the proposed bin type during the slotting run and updates it in the **Pl. StorBin Type** field in the **St. Type Data** tab of the product master.

- **Weight/volume/height/width/length indicator**
  Slotting determines the correct dimension indicator for the product based on the Customizing and master data attributes maintained for the product. These indicators are set via IMG path **SCM Extended Warehouse Management • Extended Warehouse • Management • Goods Receipt Process • Slotting • Influencing Parameter • Intervals • Define Dimension Indicators**. Click on **New Entries**, and define a new dimension indicator for a dimension indicator type such as weight, volume, length, and so on for the embedded EWM warehouse.

  Next, assign intervals to dimension indicators for each indicator type to specify different ranges for that dimension via IMG path **SCM Extended Warehouse Management • Extended Warehouse • Management • Goods Receipt Process • Slotting • Influencing Parameter • Intervals • Assign Intervals to Dimension Indicators**. Based on these intervals, the proposed dimension indicators determined during slotting are updated in the **Dimension Data** section of the **Slotting** tab in the product master.

- **Determine requirement quantity/number of order items/recommended storage quantity**
  Slotting can be used to determine the open demand quantity, sales order items, and recommended storage quantity for a product in the warehouse. These indicators are set via IMG path **SCM Extended Warehouse Management • Extended Warehouse • Management • Goods Receipt Process • Slotting • General Settings • Influencing Parameters • Intervals • Define Requirement Indicators**. Click on **New**

17

Entries, and define new requirement indicators for the embedded EWM warehouse. The optimal values for these parameters are determined during slotting and updated in the **Requirement/Demand Data** section in the **Slotting** tab of the product master.

- **Determine stock removal control indicator**
  During slotting, the system can determine the planned stock removal control indicator, which, when updated as an actual value in the product master, enables the removal of stock from a preferred storage type or storage type groups. After the slotting run, the proposed stock removal control indicator is updated in the **Planned Stock Removal ID** field in the **Whse Data** tab of the product master.
- **Determine maximum/minimum storage type quantity**
  During slotting, the system can propose maximum and minimum storage type quantities based on demand data in the product master and customization settings. The system uses the value maintained in the **Req.For.Max.QtStorTyp** field in the **Slotting** tab of the product master to determine whether demand quantity, number of order items, or recommended storage quantity will be used as the demand quantity to calculate the minimum/maximum storage type quantity.

  The system calculates the minimum/maximum quantity for a storage type if you've activated the setting for determination of maximum quantity in a storage type during slotting. To do this, navigate to IMG path **SCM Extended Warehouse Management • Extended Warehouse • Management • Goods Receipt Process • Slotting • General Settings • Define Storage Type Parameters for Slotting**. There are certain key settings that affect how the storage type quantities are calculated during slotting:

  - **Rounding Mode**: Determines if and how the maximum quantity in the storage type should be rounded.
  - **Slotting: Det.MaxQty**: Controls whether the system is to determine the maximum quantity of a material for the storage type during slotting. The maximum quantity is determined by multiplying the demand quantity by a multiplication factor. The multiplication factor for determining the maximum quantity for a storage type is defined via IMG path **SCM Extended Warehouse Management • Extended Warehouse • Management • Goods Receipt Process • Slotting • General Settings • Define Multiplication Factor for Maximum Quantity in Storage Type**.

- **Max./Min. QTY**: Specifies the minimum quantity in the storage type as a percentage of the maximum quantity. It's mandatory to set this field if you want to calculate the planned minimum quantity in a storage type.

  The proposed minimum and maximum quantities in a storage type are updated in the **Planned Minimum Qty.** and **Planned Maximum Qty.** fields in the **ST. Type Data** tab of the product master.

- **Determine replenishment quantity**
  During slotting, the system can propose a replenishment quantity based on the packaging specification, if one exists for the product. The proposed quantities are updated as **Planned Minimum Qty**, **Planned Maximum Qty**, and **Plnd Min. Replen. Qty** for the product in the **ST. Type Data** tab of the product master.

> **Note**
> The system always determines the putaway control indicator during slotting. All other indicators are optional.

17.2.2 Condition Technique

Slotting is performed in embedded EWM using a condition technique. Condition records are set for various parameters that guide the system in determining the slotting indicators. To set up a condition technique for determining the slotting indicators in the product master, navigate to IMG path **SCM Extended Warehouse Management • Extended Warehouse Management • Goods Receipt Process • Slotting • Condition Technique**.

The following steps walk through an example of how to set up a condition technique for slotting (see Figure 17.3):

1. Create a condition table that contains fields used to determine the storage indicators. The fields used to create condition tables can be selected using a field catalog. Create separate condition tables for determination of putaway control indicator, storage section indicator, and storage bin type depending on the parameters that need to be determined during slotting. You can create more than one condition table for a single parameter determination.
2. Assign the condition table or tables created for each storage parameter to a unique access sequence for that parameter. The access sequence determines the order in which condition tables are accessed by the system.

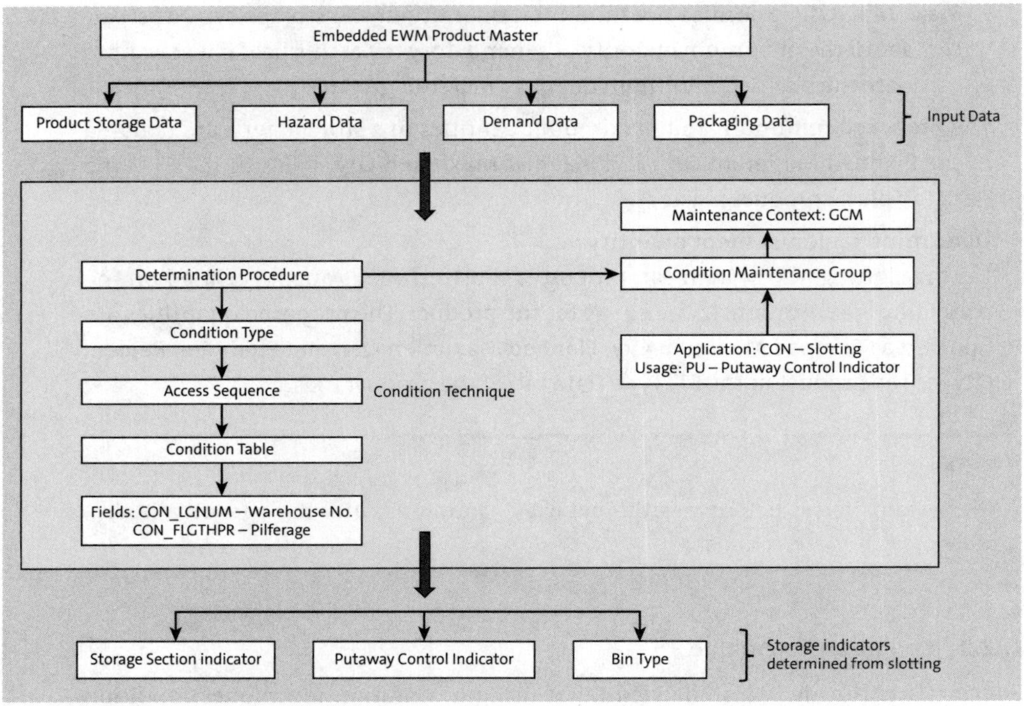

Figure 17.3 Condition Elements in Slotting

3. The newly created access sequence is assigned to a condition type. Thus, you can create a condition type for each storage parameter.
4. Each condition type is linked to a condition determination procedure. The access sequence, condition table, and determination procedure are created for the condition application and usage, which depends on the storage parameter. The usage determines the process for which the condition technique is used in slotting. The following standard values for usage are provided by SAP:
   - **PU**: Determination of putaway control indicator
   - **SC**: Determination of storage section indicator
   - **BT**: Determination of bin type

   The determination procedure defined is determined based on the usage and warehouse number.

5. Create a condition maintenance group. The condition maintenance group is used to group condition tables and condition types for condition maintenance.
6. To register the condition maintenance group, assign it to a condition maintenance context. SAP provides a standard condition maintenance context, defined as GCM, to which the condition maintenance group can be assigned.
7. In the final step, create condition records for slotting using Transaction /SCWM/GCMC, which can also be accessed via **SAP Easy Access** path **Logistics • SCM Extended Warehouse Management • Extended Warehouse Management • Master Data • Slotting • Condition Maintenance for Slotting**. The system determines the storage control parameter if it's able to find a valid condition record for the assigned determination procedure.

Note

The putaway control indicator, storage section indicator, and storage bin types are determined using condition techniques. The storage bin type also can be determined using a storage bin type determination rule.

17.3 Slotting Process Steps

Slotting obtains parameters that help rearrange the placement of products in the warehouse to optimize the picking process. If all the settings defined in the previous section are completed, then slotting can be performed.

In the following sections, we'll discuss the execution of slotting in embedded EWM. We'll start with a discussion of how slotting can be simulated to show slotting results without updating them in the product master. Next, we'll explore the process to perform slotting and save planned values in the product master in embedded EWM. We'll end by discussing how to activate the results of slotting and update the planned storage indicators as actual storage indicators in the product master.

17.3.1 Simulate Slotting

Before starting slotting, you can simulate the process without updating the product master. In this way, slotting results can be analyzed on each run, and you can decide how to optimize the configuration further. When a stage of sufficient optimization is reached during simulation, the result can be adapted by running the slotting program, saving the result, and updating the product master. A slotting simulation can be run using the Transaction /SCWM/SLOTOCC or using **SAP Easy Access** path **Logistics • SCM Extended Warehouse Management • EWM • Master Data • Slotting • Simulate Slotting**, as shown in Figure 17.4. Enter product- and location-specific data in the report, and then click on **Execute**.

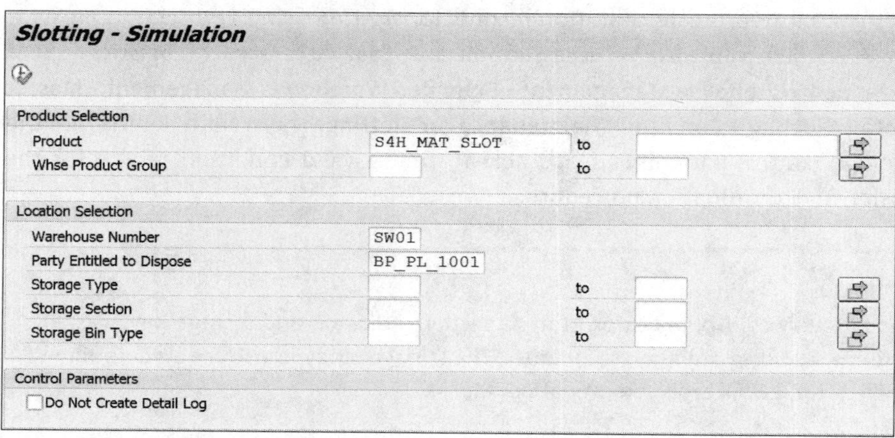

Figure 17.4 Simulate Slotting before Actual Slotting

17.3.2 Perform Slotting

After the basic configuration and master data for the slotting process are completed, the next step is to manually perform slotting or schedule a background job to perform slotting. You can do so by either using Transaction /SCWM/SLOT or using the report via **SAP Easy Access** path **Logistics • SCM Extended Warehouse Management • Extended Warehouse Management • Master Data • Slotting • Slot Products for Warehouse**, as shown in Figure 17.5. The system determines the storage indicators for the product master and stores them as active values or planned values in the product master, as discussed in the previous section.

The product master can be updated based on the traffic light indicator shown by the system after the slotting run. There are three slotting run statuses:

- **Green**
  Slotting was completely successful.
- **Red**
  Slotting was successful with some errors.
- **Yellow**
  Slotting was successful with warnings.

Slotting

Product Selection

Product	S4H_MAT_01		
Whse Product Group		to	
Date of Slotting Run		to	

Location Selection

Warehouse Number	SW01
Party Entitled to Dispose	BP_PL_1001

Select Slotting Steps

- [ ] Determine Weight Indicator
- [ ] Determine Volume Indicator
- [ ] Determine Height Indicator
- [ ] Determine Width Indicator
- [ ] Determine Length Indicator

- [ ] Update Requirement Quantity
- [ ] Update Number of Order Items
- [ ] Update Recommended Storage Qty

- [ ] Determine Req. Quantity Ind.
- [ ] Determine No. Ord. Items Ind.
- [ ] Determine Recom. Stor.Qty Ind.

- [x] Determine Putaway Ctrl Ind.
- [x] Determine Stock Rmvl Ctrl Ind.
- [x] Specify Stor. Sec. Indicator
- [x] Specify Storage Bin Type

- [x] Specify Max. Stor. Type Qty
- [ ] Specify Min. Stor. Type Qty
- [ ] Specify Replenishment Quantity

- [ ] Specify Fixed Storage Bin

Control Parameters

Update Mode:Slotting	Update material master at status green

Control Parameters for Background Run

Save Mode	Do Not Save Results

- [ ] Do Not Create Detail Log
- [ ] Print Overview Log

Package Size	100

Figure 17.5 Slotting Process Screen

As a control parameter, by setting a value in the **Update Mode:Slotting** field, you can choose for which color code you want to update the slotting results in the product master, as shown in Figure 17.5. For example, you can update the slotting results for all products for which the slotting status is green.

The slotting screen also has fields for controlling the behavior of slotting during a background run—for example, for activating the slotting indicators as actual values in the product master—as follows:

- **Save Mode**
  Using this parameter, you can control whether the storage indicators should be stored in the product master or not. If they're to be saved, they can be updated as either planned values or actual values in the product master. There are three options available for save mode:
  - **Do Not Save Results**
  - **Save Results as Planned Value**
  - **Save Results and Activate Values**
- **Do Not Create Detail Log**
  Using this parameter, you can activate or deactivate creation of detailed logs for the slotting run in embedded EWM.
- **Print Overview Log**
  You can issue the slotting run logs to be printed to the system-defined printer.

17.3.3 Activate Planned Values

After slotting is performed, in the foreground or background, the storage indicators may be saved as planned values rather than actual values in the product master. If you're happy with the slotting results, the planned slotting values can be activated using Transaction /SCWM/SLOTACT, which can also be accessed via **SAP Easy Access** path **Logistics • SCM Extended Warehouse Management • Extended Warehouse Management • Master Data • Slotting • Activate Plan Values.** A selection can be made for the product based on **Product ID, Warehouse Product Group**, or **Date of Slotting Run**. Based on the selection criteria chosen, the system displays the last successful slotting run for the product. To update the actual slotting values in the product master, click on [icon], as shown in Figure 17.6. You can also simulate the activation of results by clicking on **Simulation**.

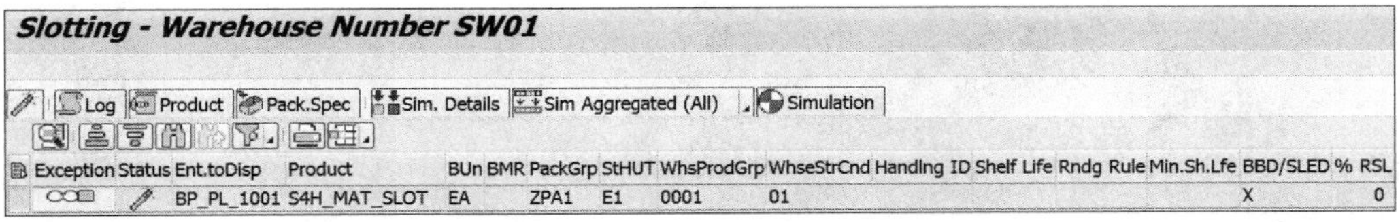

Figure 17.6 Activating Slot Parameters

17.4 ABC Analysis

Companies are often required to optimize the placement of products in the warehouse based on confirmed warehouse tasks, which in turn represents the importance of products in the warehouse. Thus, a product with high movement of stock must be placed in a strategic area so that minimal time is spent in storing, searching for, and picking these products for internal or outbound warehouse processing. The higher the number of confirmed picking tasks with different picking quantities in the warehouse for a product group, the higher the importance is given for product placement.

Table 17.1 showcases an example where storage section indicators, which are used in optimized placement of products for subsequent stock removal, have been set based on the percentage of pick tasks.

ABC Category	Percentage of Pick Tasks	New Storage Section Indicator
A	80	SI1
B	15	SI2
C	5	SI3

Table 17.1 Percent Task Distribution for Section Indicators

Suppose you have four products in the warehouse, and you want to decide on the placement of the product so that the next cycle of picking is optimized. A current snapshot of the confirmed picking tasks is shown in Table 17.2. The warehouse task percentage is found by dividing the task by the total number of tasks. The cumulative percentage is found by dividing the quantity of confirmed tasks by the total quantity of the warehouse tasks based on selection criteria.

	Confirmed Pick Warehouse Task	Cumulated Quantity in the Warehouse Task	Warehouse Task Percentage	Cumulative Percentage	ABC Category
Product A	9	130	52.94	0.5244	A
Product B	5	31	29.41	0.8235	B
Product C	2	52	11.76	0.941176471	B
Product D	1	4	58.82	1	C
Total	17	217			

Table 17.2 System Calculation for Assigning an ABC Category to the Product Master

Note

No special configuration is required to run or execute ABC analysis in embedded EWM system because it's based on the configurations and settings, explained in Section 17.2. The analysis report is run from **SAP Easy Access**, and the results are stored in the product master to complete slotting and prepare material stock for the rearrangement process.

The following explains the report for ABC analysis, execution of ABC analysis, and saving ABC parameters to rearrange the stock for optimal physical space in the warehouse:

- **Report for ABC analysis**
  As shown in Figure 17.7, the **ABC Analysis** screen can be opened using **SAP Easy Access** path **Logistics • SCM Extended Warehouse Management • Extended Warehouse Management • Master Data • Slotting • Perform ABC Analysis**. Using this report, you can select the products to be reorganized using various filtering criteria, such as warehouse, party entitled to dispose, warehouse product group, and so on, as shown in the **Location & Product Selection** section.

  You can also select the relevant analysis strategy, such as confirmed warehouse tasks or quantity moved based on business requirement. It's also important to note that categories can be increased with the appropriate threshold values. You can set threshold values either for the **Basis in %** or **Prod. in %**, and then update the putaway control indicator (**Upd. PACI**), storage section (**Upd.StorSecInd**), or cycle counting indicator (**Upd.CCInd.**). The analysis can be run either in the foreground or in the background based on the data quantity being used in the process.

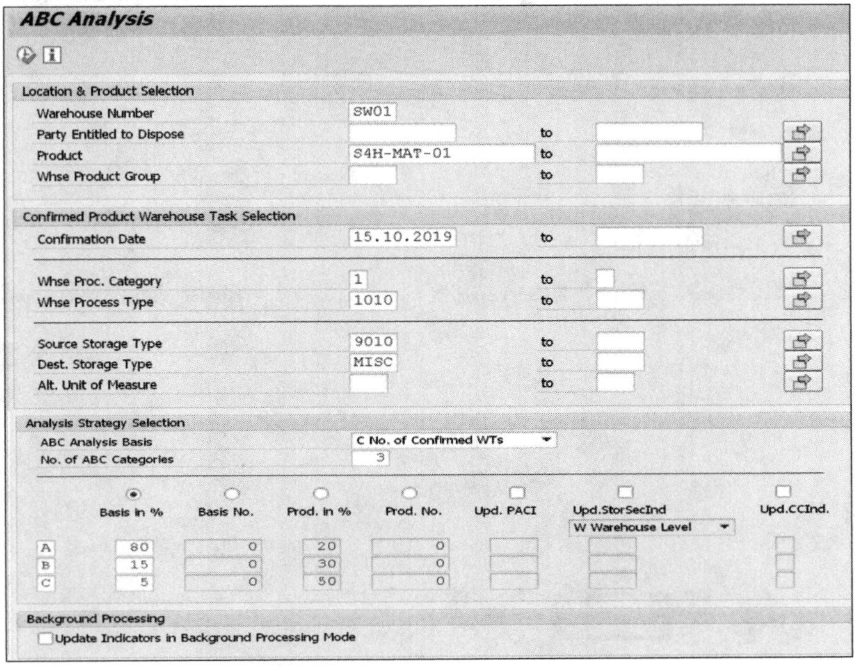

Figure 17.7 ABC Analysis Report

- **Execution report after ABC analysis**
  As shown in Figure 17.8, after performing slotting, the putaway controls to be updated will be displayed as an output report, where the user can update it in the product master by selecting all or a few of the displayed results.

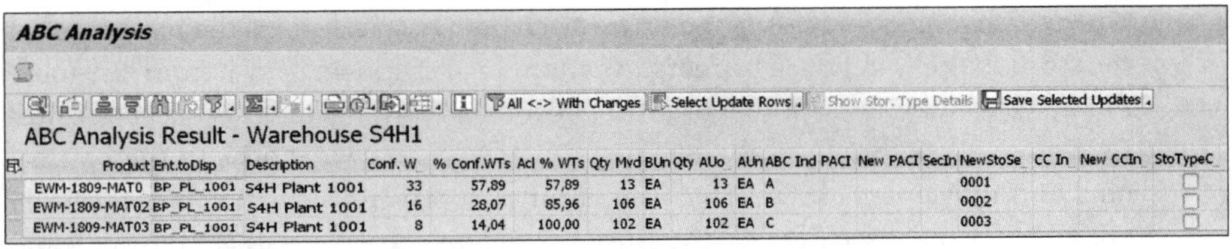

Figure 17.8 Execution Report after ABC Analysis

- **Confirmation of indicator update using ABC analysis**
  To check if the required control indicators are updated in the product master, you can go to Transaction /SCWM/MAT1 and check the values in the **Whse Data** view, as shown in Figure 17.9.

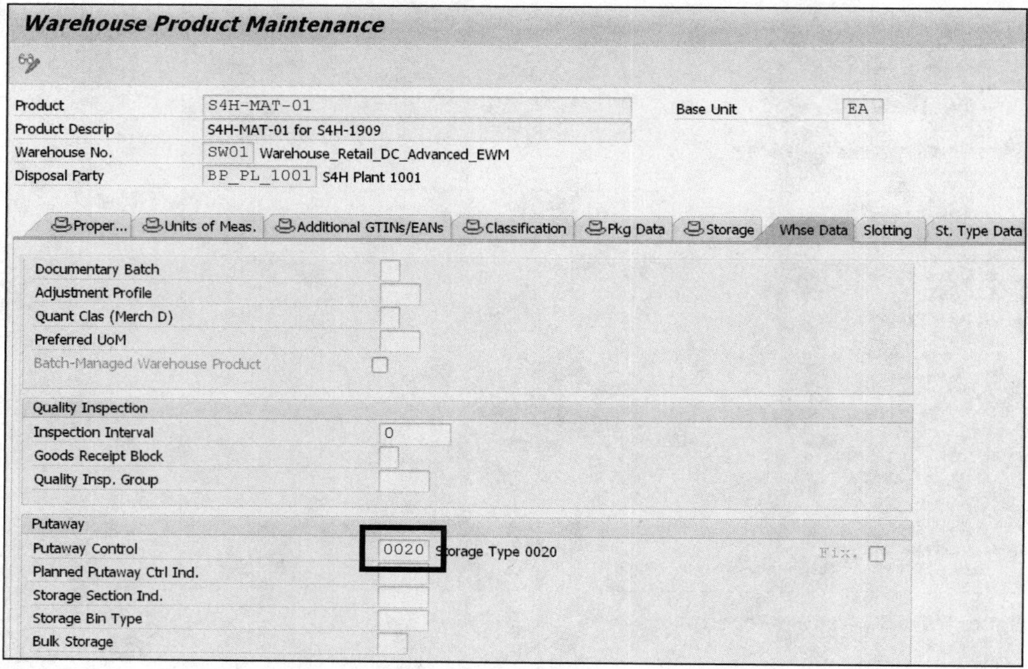

Figure 17.9 Updated Indicator after ABC Analysis

17.5 Rearrangement

The rearrangement process is the way in which you can optimize the placement of the stock in the warehouse by reorganization, such as moving stock from fast-moving items to the most optimal bin. The process of rearrangement is executed after slotting to allow for physical movement of stock in the warehouse to the optimal bins. This movement of stock from source bins to optimal destination bins is carried out either using a warehouse request or by directly creating a stock transfer warehouse task, which is confirmed by the worker when the stock is physically moved to the destination bin.

In the next sections, we'll explain the basic settings for the rearrangement process and execution of the process in embedded EWM.

17.5.1 Configuring Rearrangement

Certain settings must be made before the rearrangement process can be completed in embedded EWM. First, the product stock should exist in embedded EWM, and the default warehouse process type for movement of stock from the source to destination bin must be defined and assigned for the rearrangement process. The warehouse process type assignment must be made via IMG path **SCM Extended Warehouse Management • Extended Warehouse Management • Internal Warehouse Processes • Warehouse Optimization • Specify Default Warehouse Process Type for Rearrangement**. Click on **New Entries**, and define the default warehouse process type for the embedded EWM warehouse, as shown in Figure 17.10.

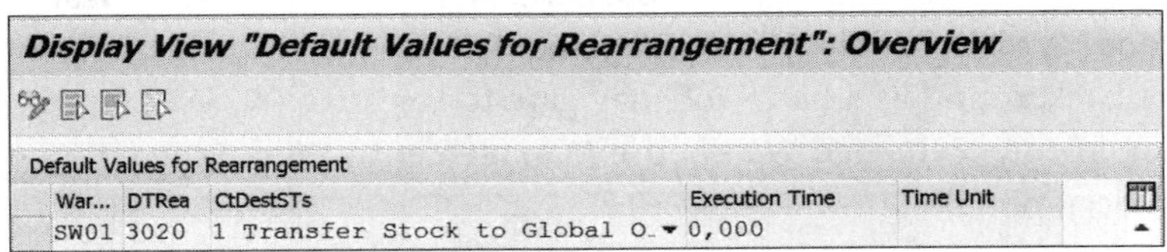

Display View "Default Values for Rearrangement": Overview

Default Values for Rearrangement

War...	DTRea	CtDestSTs	Execution Time	Time Unit
SW01	3020	1 Transfer Stock to Global O...	0,000	

Figure 17.10 Default Warehouse Process Type for Rearrangement

If the rearrangement will be handled via a warehouse request, then the appropriate warehouse request document and item type should be assigned to the warehouse process type. As shown in Figure 17.11, the warehouse request document and item type assignment to a warehouse process type can be made via IMG path **SCM Extended Warehouse Management • EWM • Internal Warehouse Processes • Warehouse Optimization • Document Type And Item Type for Rearrangement**. Click on **New Entries**, and specify the document and item type for the embedded EWM warehouse.

Display View "Document Type and Item Type for Rearrangement": Overview

Document Type and Item Type for Rearrangement

War...	Whs...	Doc.Type	ItemType
W001	3010	SRPL	SRPL
W001	3020	SREA	SREA
W001	3030	SWHI	SWHI

Figure 17.11 Document and Item Type Assignment for Rearrangement

If optimization must be handled using slotting indexes, the required value should be specified in the **EvlWhsItem** field while performing the following configurations in embedded EWM:

- Assigning storage types to the storage type search sequence
- Maintaining the storage section search sequence
- Defining an alternative bin type sequence
- Defining handling unit types for each storage bin type

17.5.2 Rearrangement Process

The process of rearrangement begins with the slotting process, which determines the optimal parameters for putaway. The report for rearrangement can be accessed using Transaction /SCWM/REAR or, for rearrangement in the foreground, via **SAP Easy Access** path **Logistics • SCM Extended Warehouse Management • Extended Warehouse Management • Work Scheduling • Rearrangement**. If you want to execute rearrangement in the background as a batch job, navigate to **Logistics • SCM Extended Warehouse Management • Extended Warehouse Management • Work Scheduling • Rearrangement (Background)**.

In the transaction screen, search for the product to be rearranged using the search field. The required warehouse product is chosen on the report screen, so that it can be rearranged from the source to an optimal storage type, section, and bin type. On execution, the system displays an analysis of current and optimal storage bin types and sections. The next step includes movement of the product stock from the source to the optimized storage bin. After selecting the slotting results and clicking on [icon], the system displays the optimized storage type, section, and bin type for the product in the **Warehouse Task** and **Warehouse Request** tabs. You can create a warehouse request or an internal warehouse task to move the stock to an optimal bin, as shown in Figure 17.12. The process of rearrangement is complete after the warehouse tasks created for rearrangement are confirmed.

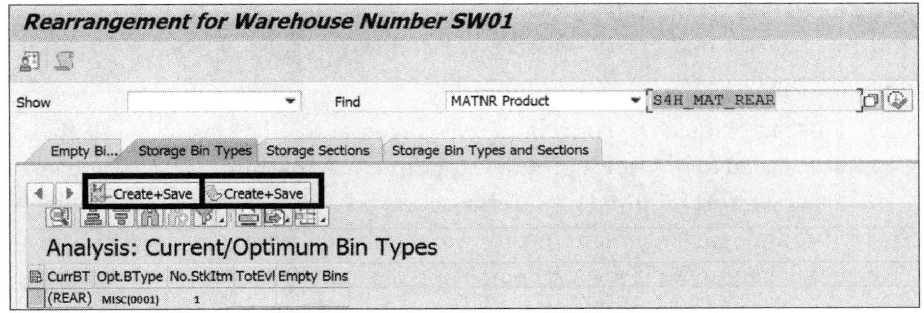

Figure 17.12 Performing Rearrangement Using a Warehouse Task or Warehouse Request

The following logic is used by the system for determining the optimum destination storage bin for putaway:

- When searching for an optimum destination storage bin, the system uses search sequences for storage types, storage sections, and storage bin types. The entries in the search sequences are sorted by the slotting index in descending order.
- You can assign a slotting index for each step in a search sequence in Customizing as discussed in the previous section. The first entry in a search sequence should not have a slotting index; therefore, a storage bin with an optimum storage type, storage section, and storage bin type has a slotting index of zero.
- In the case of rearrangement, the system first tries to propose an optimum storage bin (with a slotting index of zero). If this isn't an option, the system proposes an alternative storage bin with the next-lowest slotting index. The system only proposes an alternative storage bin if its slotting index is lower than that of the current storage bin.

> **Note**
> The Rearrange Stock app allows you to rearrange stock in the warehouse after performing slotting to save storage parameters for optimal stock storage.

17.6 Summary

This chapter introduced the concept of slotting in embedded EWM in SAP S/4HANA. We explained in detail how the slotting process is executed in embedded EWM, various parameters determined as part of slotting, and how a condition technique plays an important role in the slotting process. We provided detailed information about how slotting is performed in embedded EWM and how results can be saved in the warehouse product master.

This chapter also explained the concept of rearrangement and talked in detail about the process steps used to rearrange product stock into optimal bins in a warehouse to reduce the picking effort required of warehouse workers. You should now be able to execute slotting and rearrangement in your warehouse to improve your picking process. In the next chapter, we'll cover shipping and receiving.

Chapter 18
Shipping and Receiving

Shipping and receiving are important processes in a warehouse, especially for those businesses that need to monitor inbound and outbound stock movements. In this chapter, we'll discuss the shipping and receiving process in embedded EWM to facilitate and optimize stock movements in and out of the warehouse using appropriate means of transport.

Organizations use trailers and vehicles to manage stock movements in and out of warehouses. Shipping and receiving functions in embedded EWM provide tools to plan the movement of vehicles and transportation units (TUs) in the warehouse and manage them in an optimized manner. The TU is assigned to delivery documents that help execute inbound or outbound processes in the warehouse.

In this chapter, we'll discuss the concepts of shipping and receiving, as well as yard management, in embedded EWM. Section 18.1 gives an overview of shipping and receiving processes. Section 18.2 covers the settings required to set up shipping and receiving in embedded EWM. We'll also discuss the concepts of TUs and vehicles used to bring stock in and out of the warehouse. Section 18.3 covers the concept of yard management used to manage vehicles and TUs in the yard and reduce their idle time in the warehouse. It also explains the use of the shipping cockpit in embedded EWM yard management, via which yard operations can be planned and executed by yard operators using applications benefitting from the rich SAP Fiori user experience (UX), available out-of-the-box in embedded EWM.

18.1 What Is Shipping and Receiving?

Shipping and receiving can be implemented in embedded EWM with or without using yard management. In the former case, a TU is created, and delivery documents are assigned to it. After TU assignment to the warehouse request is complete, the shipping and receiving activity can be carried out in the warehouse. In the latter case, the deliveries are assigned to the TU, and the TU is checked in to the warehouse and docked to the warehouse door. After the loading or unloading activity is complete, the TU departs from the checkpoint.

Organizations working with high volumes of vehicles and trailers dedicate a specific place in the warehouse called the *yard* to manage incoming and outgoing trailers. To ensure orderly and optimized movement of stock using trailers and trucks from a warehouse yard, it's important that yard operations are properly planned before actual execution of yard movements in the warehouse. Yard management can also be integrated with other logistics applications, such as SAP Transportation Management (SAP TM) and SAP Dock Appointment Scheduling, to handle both the transportation and warehousing for an organization. In the following sections, we'll explain the business context in which shipping and receiving can be used and how these processes are carried out in the system.

18.1.1 Business Process

American company Alpha Medicals receives an order from one of its customers based in Mexico. The order sent by the customer requires Alpha Medicals to provide the products in time inside a container loaded on a truck. To ensure that the products being transported to the customer are loaded on the right truck and the carrying trucks moves in the right areas of the yard of the embedded EWM system, the company has implemented shipping and receiving in embedded EWM. As shown in Figure 18.1, the shipping and receiving process in embedded EWM and its usage involves the following multiple steps:

1. The warehouse receives a warehouse request document for customer delivery to supply the requested products to the customer.
2. The warehouse request-related warehouse task is assigned to the warehouse worker so that the worker can pick, pack, and stage the stock at the staging bay.
3. As shipping and receiving is active in embedded EWM by the company, the truck required to carry the products from the warehouse to the customer checks in the Alpha Medicals warehouse yard via a checkpoint and parks in a specific parking lot.
4. Stock that will be delivered to the customer is picked from the source bins of the supplying warehouse by the warehouse workers, packed in the required packaging material to create finished product cases, and staged in the goods issue area.
5. After the staging of the goods is successfully completed, the truck that needs to pick up the delivery products docks to the door, and the products are loaded on to the truck.

6. After the loading of products on the truck finishes, the truck moves on to the parking lot if the check-out gate is occupied by another truck and finally checks out of the warehouse via the check-out gate.

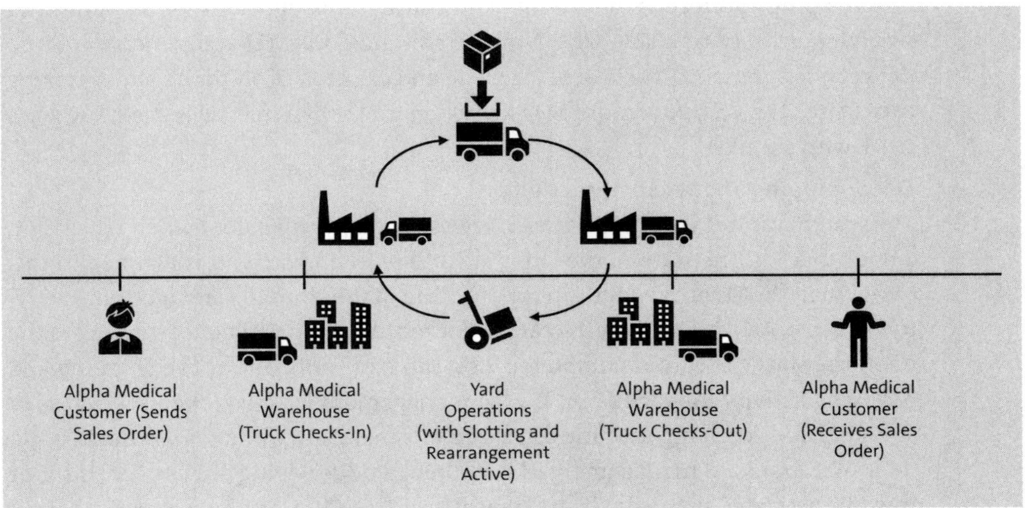

Figure 18.1 Business Flow in Shipping and Receiving

18.1.2 System Process

When you create a TU or vehicle in embedded EWM to manage the movement of multiple inbound and outbound deliveries, the TUs are docked to the warehouse doors from where the loading and unloading process is carried out. With shipping and receiving, you create an activity for each of these warehouse objects: TU, vehicle, and door. The activity is valid for a limited period during which the object is processed. The purpose of each shipping and receiving activity is as follows: 18

- **TU shipping and receiving activity**
  A shipping and receiving activity for TU is created automatically upon creation of the TU. The shipping and receiving activity holds data such as direction (inbound or outbound) or the planned/actual arrival and departure times and is valid only for a specific period. The shipping and receiving activity of the TU holds all the details such as driver, means of transport, seal, and status information. A shipping and receiving activity is created in the **Planned** status. The status of shipping and receiving activity changes to **Active** after the TU arrives at a checkpoint. When the TU leaves the warehouse, the status of the shipping and receiving activity changes

to **Complete**. You can have only one active shipping and receiving activity for each TU in a warehouse.

- **Vehicle shipping and receiving activity**
  The shipping and receiving activity of a vehicle is analogous to the shipping and receiving activity of a TU, except that it contains only TU assignments and no delivery assignments. The use of a vehicle and creation of shipping and receiving activity for the vehicle is more relevant when more than one TU is used, such as a truck with a trailer.
- **Door shipping and receiving activity**
  The system creates the shipping and receiving activity for a door when you assign a door to a TU. The state of the shipping and receiving activity is **Planned** in this case. When the TU arrives at the door, the state of the shipping and receiving activity becomes **Active**. Only one TU can be docked at a door. After departure from the door, the status becomes **Completed**. You can have only one active shipping and receiving activity for each door. If yard management is active, then the status of shipping and receiving activities changes automatically when a TU is docked at a door. Without yard management, the shipping and receiving activity for the door must be activated manually from Transaction /SCWM/TU by selecting the **Arrival at Door** action from the **Action • Door** menu.

Note

We've explained the system process using outbound process only. It's equally applicable to inbound stock movement processes.

18.2 Configuring Shipping and Receiving

Some of the key functionalities that become available by setting up shipping and receiving in the warehouse are as follows:

- Creation of TUs and vehicles
- Assignment of TUs to vehicles
- Assignment of TUs and vehicles to doors
- Assignment of multiple deliveries to TUs

In this section, we'll discuss the settings and master data required for setting up shipping and receiving in the warehouse.

18.2.1 General Settings

The following settings are required to set up shipping and receiving in embedded EWM:

1. **Create number ranges for TUs, vehicles, and shipping and receiving activities in the warehouse.**
   To do this, navigate to IMG path **SCM Extended Warehouse Management • Extended Warehouse Management • Cross-Process Settings • Shipping & Receiving • Number Ranges**, and define the number ranges for TUs, vehicles, and shipping and receiving activities by clicking on the **Insert Line** button.
2. **Setup control parameters for creating TUs and vehicles.**
   To do this, navigate to IMG path **SCM Extended Warehouse Management • Extended Warehouse Management, Cross-Process Settings • Shipping & Receiving • General Settings • Define Control Parameters for Forming Vehicles/Transportation Units**, as shown in Figure 18.2. In this setting, assign the number range created previously for TUs and vehicles, assign Post Processing Framework (PPF) profiles for triggering follow-up actions after the vehicles and TUs are created, and specify the default owner if the TU isn't maintained with a carrier.

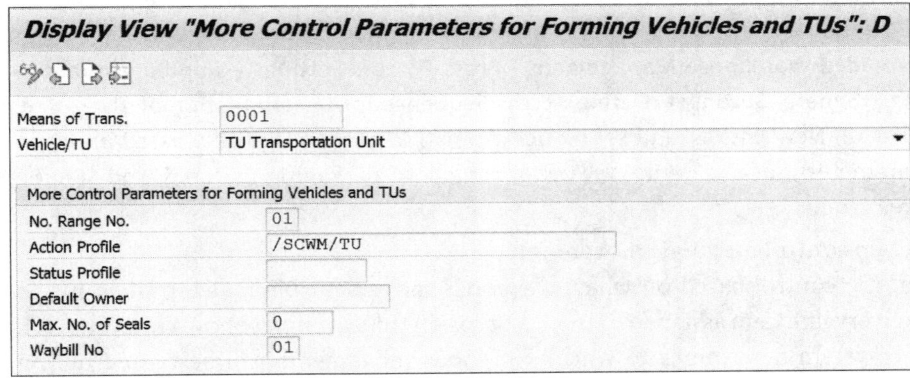

Figure 18.2 Assigning Control Parameters for Vehicles/Transportation Units

3. **Configure the PPF action profiles and conditions for managing the actions executed after TUs, vehicles, and doors are created.**
   To do so, navigate to IMG path **SCM Extended Warehouse Management • Extended Warehouse Management • Cross-Process Settings • Shipping & Receiving • Message Processing.**

4. **Define the TU profile.**
   A TU profile enables users to define the amount of time in hours a TU stays in the yard, at the door, or at a staging bay. The time specified here is used in the shipping cockpit to calculate planned arrival time or in SAP Dock Appointment Scheduling to book appointments based on door block duration or staging area block duration. As shown in Figure 18.3, define a new TU profile for the warehouse by navigating to IMG path **SCM Extended Warehouse Management • Extended Warehouse Management • Cross-Process Settings • Shipping & Receiving • General Settings • Define TU Profile** and clicking on **New Entries**.

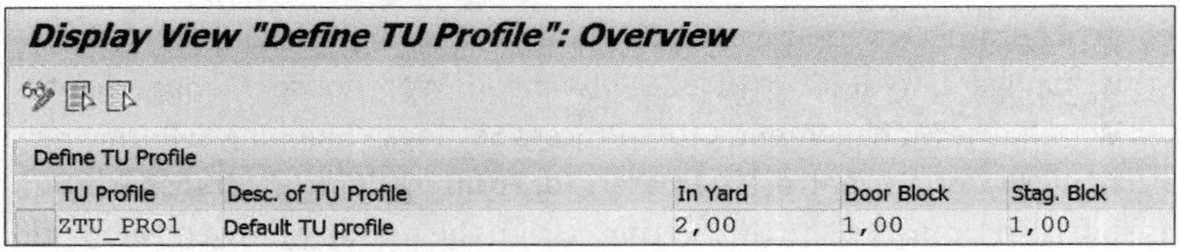

Display View "Define TU Profile": Overview

Define TU Profile

TU Profile	Desc. of TU Profile	In Yard	Door Block	Stag. Blck
ZTU_PRO1	Default TU profile	2,00	1,00	1,00

Figure 18.3 Defining the Transportation Unit Profile

5. **Define the access sequence.**
   The system determines the TU profile while creating a TU based on a predefined access sequence created via IMG path **SCM Extended Warehouse Management • Extended Warehouse Management • Cross-Process Settings • Shipping & Receiving • General Settings • Define Access Sequence for Determination of TU Profile**. Click on **New Entries**, and set up determination of the TU profile based on input parameters such as route, means of transport, packaging material, and staging area group.

6. **Set up control for goods movement.**
   Set the control based on which the goods movement bin is determined in the delivery line item assigned to the TU. Based on this setting, as shown in Figure 18.4, the system determines to which bin goods movements will be posted during delivery creation. This is set up via IMG path **SCM Extended Warehouse Management • Extended Warehouse Management • Cross-Process Settings • Shipping & Receiving • General Settings • Setup Control for Goods Movement**. Click on **New Entries**, and select one of the following options:

   - **1 Goods Movement to Storage Bin Specified in Delivery**
   - **2 Goods Movement to TU**

   In the latter case, if delivery is assigned to a TU, then the goods movement bin in the delivery item is cleared, and the goods movement is posted for the TU. If the goods movement is posted to the TU or door bin, then an unloading warehouse task is required. However, if goods receipt is made in the staging area, then unloading can be performed using simple unloading.

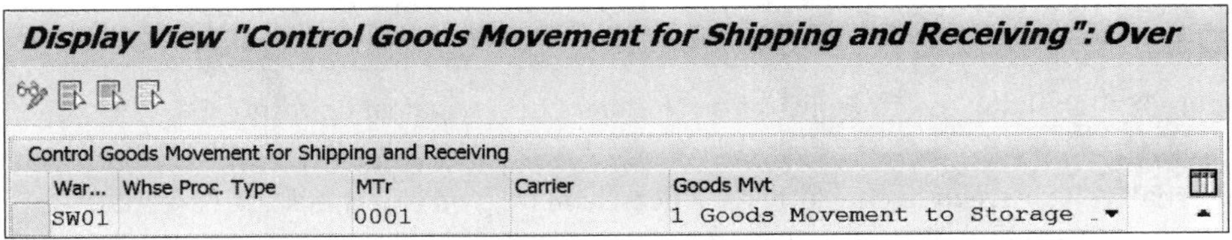

Figure 18.4 Goods Movement Control for Shipping and Receiving

7. **Define compatibility.**
   TUs are created in embedded EWM based on packaging materials and means of transport. You can set up embedded EWM to give a warning if there's a compatibility issue between a means of transport and the goods it carries. This helps you plan transportation of products that are dangerous in nature or have some special requirement for means of transport. Compatibility can be configured via IMG path **SCM Extended Warehouse Management • Extended Warehouse Management • Cross-Process Settings • Shipping & Receiving • General Settings • Define Compatibility of Means of Transport and Transportation Group**. Click on **New Entries**, and map the allowed transportation group to a means of transport, as shown in Figure 18.5.

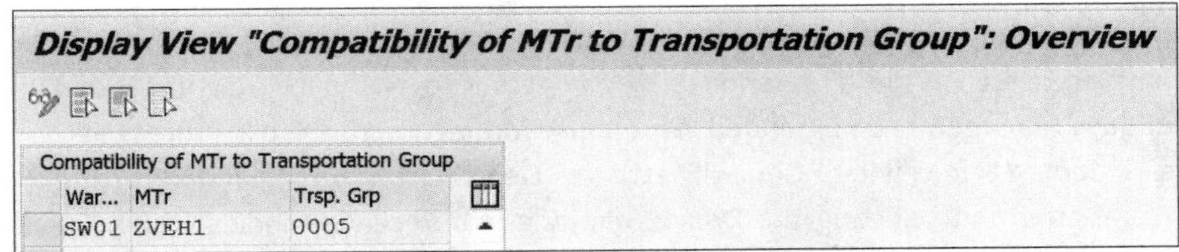

Figure 18.5 Compatibility of Means of Transport and Transportation Group

8. **Configure the license plate check.**
   You can set up a format check for license plates of TUs coming into the warehouse by setting a predefined pattern for a specific country. As shown in Figure 18.6, this is set up via IMG path **SCM Extended Warehouse Management • Extended Warehouse Management • Cross-Process Settings • Shipping & Receiving • General Settings • Check License Plate Number Against Pattern**.

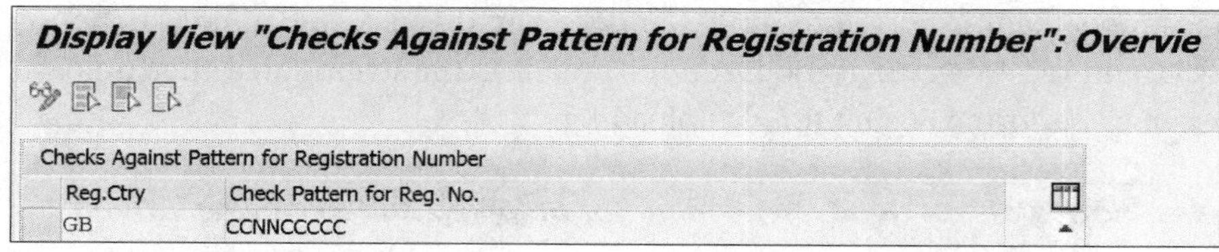

Figure 18.6 Defining the TU Registration Number Checks against Country

Alternatively, instead of checking for a license plate, you can check the external number of a TU against a predefined template. This check can be configured via IMG path **SCM Extended Warehouse Management • Extended Warehouse Management • Cross-Process Settings • Shipping & Receiving • General Settings • Check Number Against Pattern**.

Example

For a UK license plate, for example, you can define the template as two characters, followed by two numbers, followed by four characters (CCNNCCCC). For example, if the license plate number AOW2 HY1 is saved in a TU header during TU processing, the embedded EWM system would produce a warning because a number is expected in the third position, but a character is assigned.

Note

Shipping and receiving are activated by default in a warehouse. You can deactivate shipping and receiving in a warehouse by navigating to IMG path **SCM Extended Warehouse Management • Extended Warehouse Management • Cross-Process Settings • Shipping & Receiving • General Settings • Deactivate Shipping and Receiving for Warehouse** and selecting the **Deact. Shipping and Receiving** indicator for the warehouse.

18.2.2 Transportation Unit and Vehicles

A TU is the smallest possible transportable unit for carrying goods in the warehouse. A vehicle is used to group together TUs. A vehicle may have one or more TUs assigned to it. A TU can be a single, fixed part of a vehicle, as with Vehicle 1 in Figure 18.7, or a vehicle can have multiple TUs, as shown with Vehicle 2.

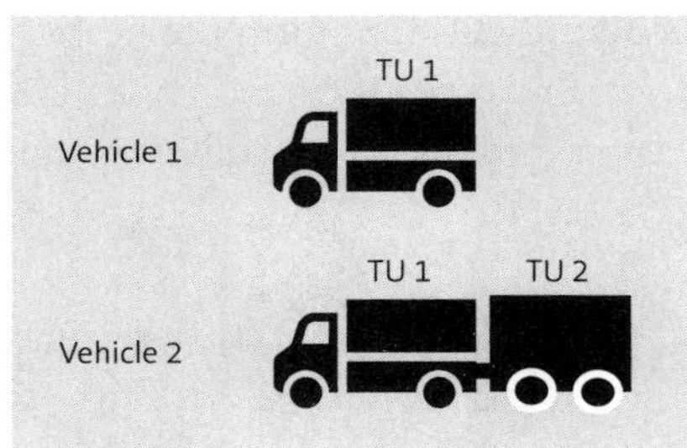

Figure 18.7 Transportation Units and Vehicles

Vehicles and TUs are created as master data in embedded EWM. It's not mandatory to use vehicles in embedded EWM if you can work with only TUs. You can link a packaging material with a means of transport to define a construction rule for a TU by navigating to **SAP Easy Access** path **Logistics • SCM Extended Warehouse Management • Extended Warehouse Management • Settings • Shipping and Receiving • Link between Packaging Material (TU) and Means of Transport**. The carrying capacity of a TU is calculated from the weight and volume defined in the packaging material.

TUs can be created via **SAP Easy Access** path **Logistics • SCM Extended Warehouse Management • Extended Warehouse Management • Shipping and Receiving • Process Transportation Unit** or via Transaction /SCWM/TU by clicking on [icon], as shown in Figure 18.8.

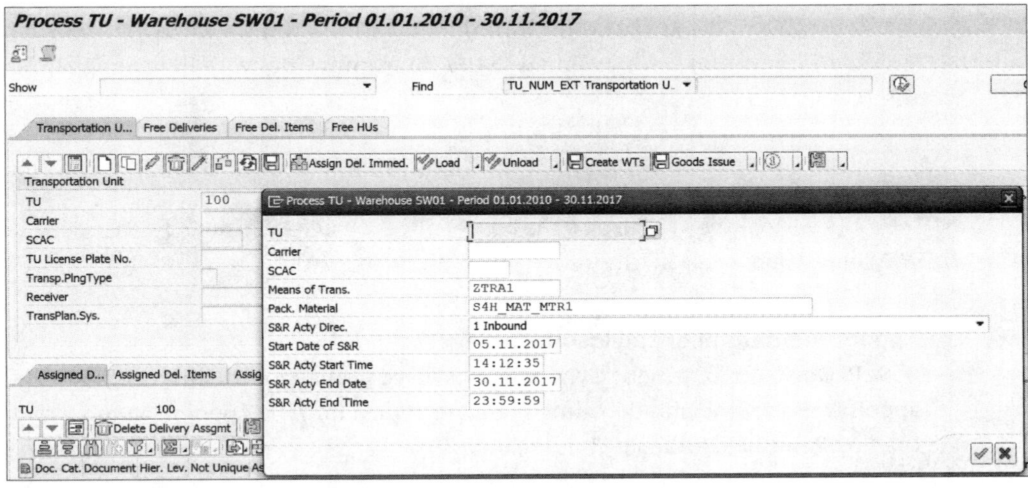

Figure 18.8 Creating Transportation Units

The popup in the TU creation screen displays the input fields that form the header level data for the TU. Some of these input fields are mandatory for creation of a new TU; the rest can be provided later. The following data is provided while defining the attributes for the TU header:

- **Means of transportation**
  The mandatory **Means of Trans.** field refers to the vehicle class representing the TU, such as a truck, trailer, ship, and so on.
- **Packaging material**
  The **Pack. Material** field is used to specify the allowed packaging material for the means of transport.
- **Shipping and receiving activity direction**
  The **S&R Acty Direc.** field is used to assign the direction of the TU movement in the warehouse, such as inbound or outbound.
- **Standard Carrier Alpha Code (SCAC)**
  A TU can be assigned a unique Standard Carrier Alpha Code in the **SCAC** field to identify road transport carriers based on geography.
- **Shipping and receiving activity start and end date/time**
  In the **S&R Acty Start Time/End Time** and **S&R Acty Start Date/End Date** fields, the TU should be assigned a planned shipping and receiving activity date and time against which the actual arrival time of the TU in the warehouse is calculated.
- **Route**
  The **Route** field indicates the transportation route from the source to that destination the TU must take. It's assigned to the TU from the delivery item assigned to the TU.

Note

The route will only be available on the header of TU if you've activated decentralized EWM in your landscape. It isn't available in embedded EWM.

- **Appointment number and loading point**
  If SAP Dock Appointment Scheduling is used for appointment booking, the appointment number and loading point are copied into the **Appoint. Number** and **Loading Point** fields when a TU is created.

In addition, all information regarding security seals put on the TU can be added to the TU header. This information includes seal number, sealing date/time, party role involved in sealing, unsealing date/time, and party role involved in unsealing.

Figure 18.9 shows a sample TU created in embedded EWM. The data in the upper section of the screen forms the TU header, and the lower section contains item-level information for the selected TU.

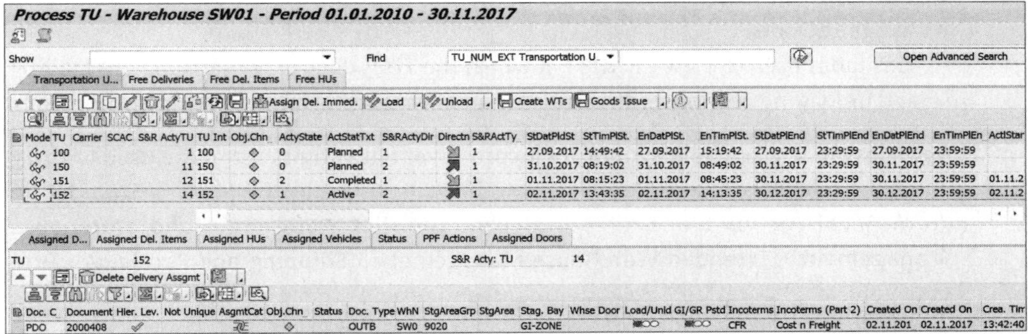

Figure 18.9 Process Transportation Unit

The tabs available at the TU item level are as follows:

- **Assigned Del./Assigned Del. Items**
  These tabs show the deliveries to be loaded in or unloaded from the TU. After the deliveries are assigned to the TU, they're visible in the **Delivery** and **Delivery Item** tabs. These tabs also display the loading and unloading status at the delivery level and delivery line item level. A TU can only depart from the warehouse after all delivery line items assigned to the TU have the status **Loading** or **Unloading Complete**.
- **Assigned HUs**
  The deliveries assigned to TUs may also be packed in handling units (HUs). This tab shows the HUs assigned to deliveries assigned to the TUs. This tab also displays the loading and unloading status at the HU level.
- **Assigned Vehicles**
  This tab is used to display the vehicles assigned to the TU. You can also create a vehicle from this screen by clicking on **Vehicle Assignment**.
- **Status**
  Various statuses can be assigned to TUs, such as **Arrival at Checkpoint**, **Departure**

from Door, **Goods Receipt Posted**, and so on. The status values for these status types are updated as the loading and unloading processes are carried out in the TU. You can also create custom statuses and assign them to the status profile for the TU.

- **PPF Actions**
  Any output, such as waybills or bills of lading, can be created and sent to the intended business partner using the PPF action profiles and actions assigned to the TU.
- **Assigned Doors**
  This tab is used to view the door at which the TU is docked for carrying out loading and unloading of goods. You can also manually assign a door to the TU from this tab.

Vehicles are trucks, trailers, or other locomotives with engines that are used to carry TUs from one place to another. Create a vehicle in embedded EWM using Transaction /SCWM/VEH or via **SAP Easy Access** path **Logistics • SCM Extended Warehouse Management • Extended Warehouse Management • Shipping and Receiving • Process Vehicle**. Click on **Vehicle Assignment**, and provide the means of transport.

Note

You can also post the stock to a TU. This provides stock traceability in TUs and allows for more efficient use of space in the staging areas. You can post goods receipt into a TU in the inbound process. Similarly, you can manage the stock in TUs in the outbound process. If loading is being handled without using TUs, then the stock is posted to a door bin instead of a TU.

Note

The following SAP Fiori apps are available to create and maintain TUs and vehicles, as well as to plan door assignments:

- **Maintain Transportation Units**
  This app allows you to create, edit, and assign delivery to TUs as well as process TUs for yard operations.
- **Maintain Vehicles**
  This app allows you to create, edit, and assign TUs; assign deliveries to vehicles; and process vehicles for yard operations.
- **Plan Doors (Transportation Units)**
  This app allows you to plan and assign doors to TUs for yard operations.

18.2.3 Loading and Unloading

The goods from the delivery are loaded or unloaded from the TU after the TU is docked at the warehouse door if you're using process-oriented storage control; this is done directly if you're not using storage control. The loading and unloading process can be performed from the TU user interface (UI) using simple or complex loading/unloading. After the TU loading or unloading is complete, you can post the goods issue for the TU. There are different ways of executing loading and unloading for a TU, as follows:

- **Simple loading/unloading**
  Simple loading is performed directly for the outbound delivery orders or HUs for outbound delivery orders, which are picked and kept in the goods issue zone. You can load the picked outbound delivery order items or HUs using Transaction /SCWM/LOAD, as shown in Figure 18.10.

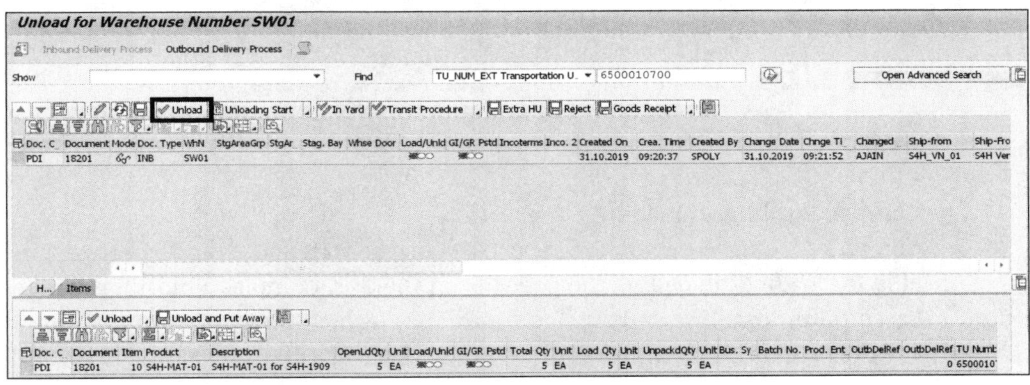

Figure 18.10 Simple Loading of Outbound Delivery Orders

  Set the **Loading Completed** status directly using the **Load** button, or use the **Loading Start** option to set the loading start date and time in the TU. After completing the loading of outbound deliveries or HUs, the loading end date and time can be set using the **Loading End** button.

  Simple unloading is performed for inbound deliveries or HUs assigned to the inbound deliveries. To unload the inbound deliveries or HUs, use Transaction /SCWM/UNLOAD. Set the unload status as **Complete** using the **Unload** button (see highlight in Figure 18.10), or use the **Unloading Start/Unloading End** option to set the start and end time for unloading the delivery.

18

Both simple loading and unloading for deliveries and HUs can be performed using TUs, as shown in Figure 18.11. You can start and end the loading and unloading process, as well as reverse the loading and unloading status for the deliveries.

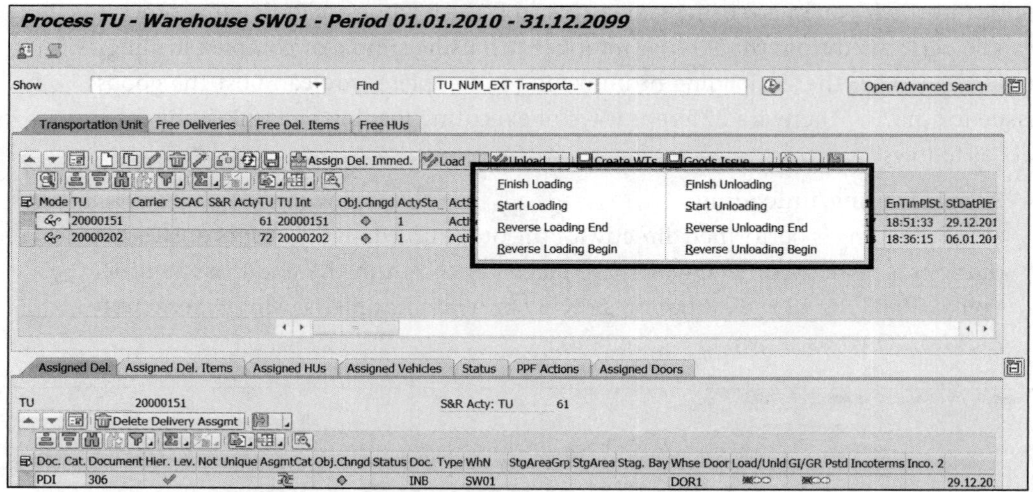

Figure 18.11 Loading/Unloading Using Transportation Units

- **Complex loading/unloading**

  Complex loading and unloading is used when the warehouse tasks are to be created for loading/unloading the goods from the TUs. Complex unloading can be based on process-oriented storage control with which the destination bin for a storage process is determined.

  Loading/unloading warehouse tasks can be created for outbound/inbound deliveries or HUs using Transaction /SCWM/LOAD and Transaction /SCWM/UNLOAD, respectively, as shown in Figure 18.12. The warehouse task for loading can be created manually, or it can be created via PPF when a TU arrives at the door.

> **Note**
>
> When a loading warehouse task is created, the system automatically keeps the door as the destination bin. When the loading warehouse task is confirmed, the system automatically changes the destination storage bin in the task to the TU.

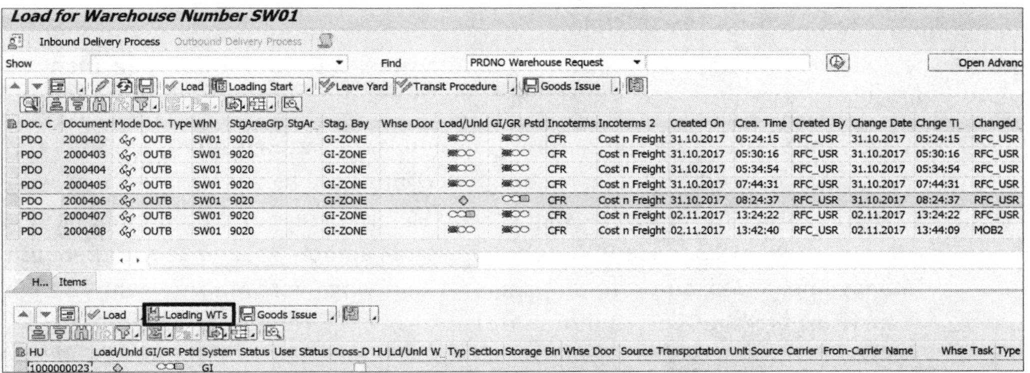

Figure 18.12 Complex Loading for Outbound Delivery Orders

18.3 Yard Management

A yard represents a physical location outside the warehouse that's used for managing vehicles coming into and out of the warehouse. Embedded EWM helps manage yard operations in businesses with the help of yard management. Using yard management, the shipping office can plan the arrival and departure of vehicles in the warehouse. It also helps route the vehicles in the yard before they're docked to the door for loading and unloading goods in the warehouse. Yard management helps reduce the idle time of vehicles in the warehouse, thereby benefitting the carrier and optimizing the goods receipt and goods issue processes for the organization.

In this section, we'll look at the basic building blocks of yard management in embedded EWM and see how it's used to carry out business processes in the warehouse.

You can activate yard management in a warehouse via IMG path **SCM Extended Warehouse Management • Extended Warehouse Management • Cross-Process Settings • Shipping and Receiving • Yard Management • Activate Yard Management for Warehouse**. Select the **YM Active** indicator for the embedded EWM warehouse. Alternatively, activate the /SCWM/YARD_ACTIVATE Business Configuration Set (BC Set) using Transaction SCPR20.

> **Tip**
>
> This book defines a yard as a special storage type with the storage role **Yard**, but a yard can also be modeled as a warehouse if it's used in common among multiple warehouses.

18.3.1 Configuring Yard Management

The following configurations are required for setting up yard management in embedded EWM:

1. Define the yard in a warehouse as a storage type with storage type role **Yard**. After the yard is defined, additional settings to control the behavior of the yard with respect to stock movements using warehouse tasks are set for the warehouse via IMG path **SCM Extended Warehouse Management • Extended Warehouse Management • Master Data • Shipping and Receiving • Yard Management • Define Yard Using Storage Type**, as shown in Figure 18.13.

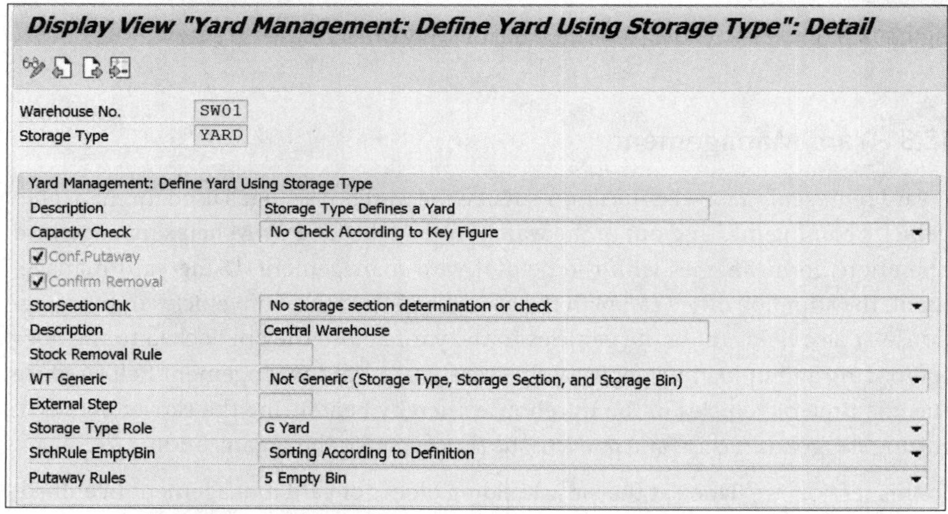

Figure 18.13 Defining Yard Settings for the Yard Storage Type

2. After the yard is created, divide the yard into storage sections to segregate different storage areas for the yard, such as checkpoints, parking areas, and doors. To do this, navigate to IMG path **SCM Extended Warehouse Management • Extended Warehouse Management • Master Data • Shipping and Receiving • Yard Management • Structure Yard Using Storage Areas**, and click on **New Entries** to define parking spaces, checkpoints, and doors as storage sections for the yard storage type, as shown in Figure 18.14. Alternatively, activate the /SCWM/YARD_STRUCTURE BC Set using Transaction SCPR20.

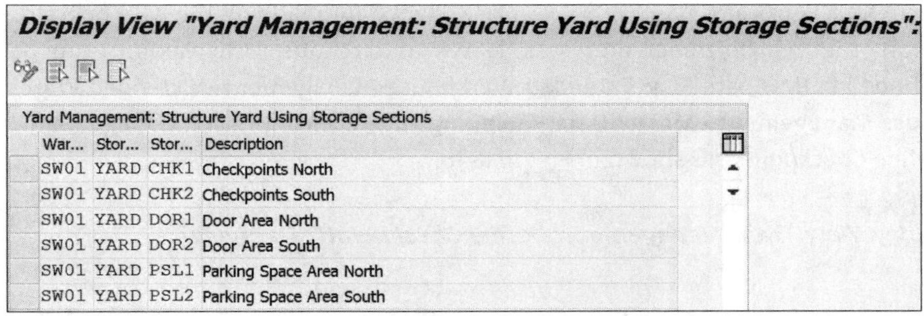

Display View "Yard Management: Structure Yard Using Storage Sections":

Yard Management: Structure Yard Using Storage Sections

War...	Stor...	Stor...	Description
SW01	YARD	CHK1	Checkpoints North
SW01	YARD	CHK2	Checkpoints South
SW01	YARD	DOR1	Door Area North
SW01	YARD	DOR2	Door Area South
SW01	YARD	PSL1	Parking Space Area North
SW01	YARD	PSL2	Parking Space Area South

Figure 18.14 Defining the Yard Structure Using Storage Sections

18.3.2 Yard Structure

A yard is the basic element in yard management in embedded EWM. A yard is made of multiple storage units that help model a physical yard, as shown in Figure 18.15.

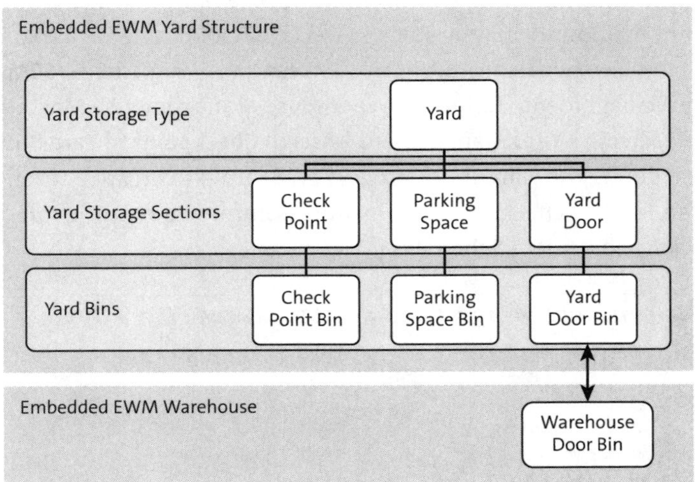

Figure 18.15 Organization Structure in Yard Management

The highest unit in a yard structure is the yard, followed by doors, parking spaces, and checkpoints, as follows:

- **Checkpoints**
  Checkpoints are the entry and exit points of a yard in a warehouse. A warehouse can have more than one checkpoint. They usually serve as a place where shipping

document verification and other security checks are made by the gate operator before the vehicle/trailer enters or leaves a warehouse. Checkpoints can be defined via IMG path **SCM Extended Warehouse Management • Extended Warehouse Management • Master Data • Shipping and Receiving • Yard Management • Define Checkpoints**, as shown in Figure 18.16.

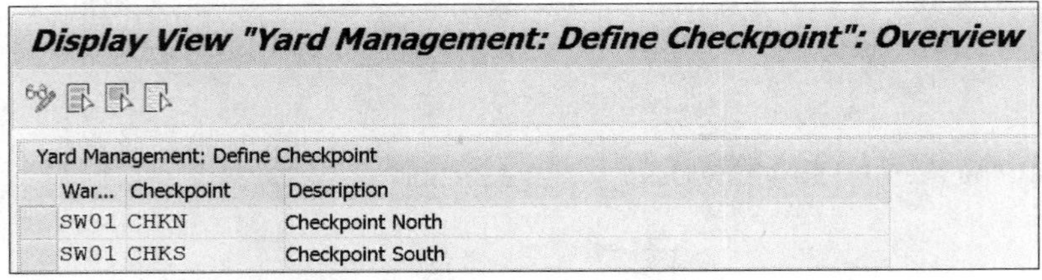

Display View "Yard Management: Define Checkpoint": Overview

Yard Management: Define Checkpoint

War...	Checkpoint	Description
SW01	CHKN	Checkpoint North
SW01	CHKS	Checkpoint South

Figure 18.16 Defining Yard Checkpoints

Each checkpoint should be assigned to a storage bin in a yard storage type to allow tracking of inventory in embedded EWM, as shown in Figure 18.17. You can track the TUs at a checkpoint by monitoring the stock in the checkpoint bins. To assign checkpoints to yard bins, navigate to **SAP Easy Access** path **Logistics • SCM Extended Warehouse Management • Extended Warehouse Management • Master Data • Shipping and Receiving • Yard Management • Assign Checkpoint to Yard Bin and SCU**. You can also define the warehouse process types used to create a warehouse task to move an HU to a checkpoint and loading point if you're using integration with SAP Dock Appointment Scheduling.

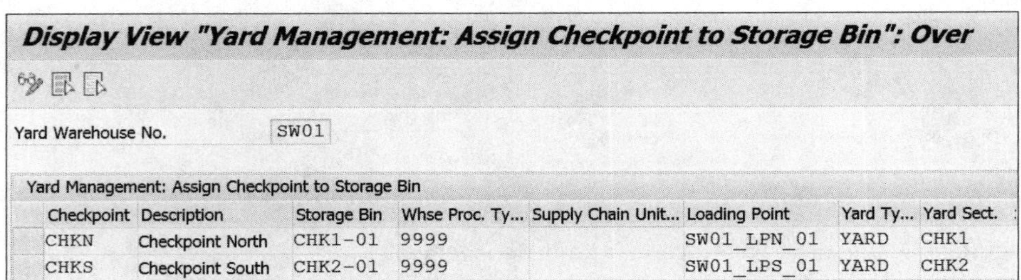

Display View "Yard Management: Assign Checkpoint to Storage Bin": Over

Yard Warehouse No. SW01

Yard Management: Assign Checkpoint to Storage Bin

Checkpoint	Description	Storage Bin	Whse Proc. Ty...	Supply Chain Unit...	Loading Point	Yard Ty...	Yard Sect.
CHKN	Checkpoint North	CHK1-01	9999		SW01_LPN_01	YARD	CHK1
CHKS	Checkpoint South	CHK2-01	9999		SW01_LPS_01	YARD	CHK2

Figure 18.17 Assigning Yard Checkpoint Bins to Yard Checkpoints

- **Parking space**
  A parking space is an area in the yard where the TUs are parked for some time if a free door for loading or unloading isn't available. It's also used for holding TUs when the loading/unloading of the TU is completed, and it's ready to be checked

out of the yard, but the exit checkpoints are occupied. To create yard bins for parking spaces, navigate to **SAP Easy Access** path **Logistics • SCM Extended Warehouse Management • Extended Warehouse Management • Master Data • Shipping and Receiving • Yard Management • Create Storage Bin**.

Note

It's important to create a bin for each of the elements defined for the yard. The bins defined for the yard are then assigned to the organization structures to allow bin-to-bin movement of a TU in the yard, representing physical movement of the vehicle. They also help track the location of a TU in the warehouse monitor.

- **Yard door**

  Doors are the physical places in the warehouse where the TU is docked. Stock is unloaded/loaded from the door to the staging area or vice versa.

  Doors can be defined via IMG path **SCM Extended Warehouse Management • Extended Warehouse Management • Master Data • Warehouse Door • Define Warehouse Door**. Click on **New Entries**, and define the warehouse door and loading direction, as shown in Figure 18.18.

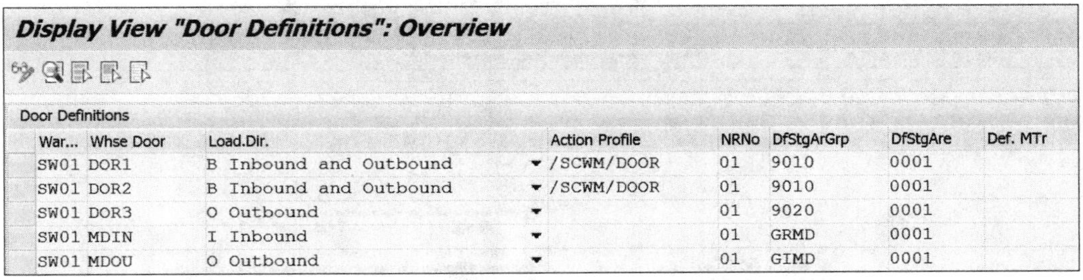

Display View "Door Definitions": Overview

Door Definitions

War...	Whse Door	Load.Dir.	Action Profile	NRNo	DfStgArGrp	DfStgAre	Def. MTr
SW01	DOR1	B Inbound and Outbound	/SCWM/DOOR	01	9010	0001	
SW01	DOR2	B Inbound and Outbound	/SCWM/DOOR	01	9010	0001	
SW01	DOR3	O Outbound		01	9020	0001	
SW01	MDIN	I Inbound		01	GRMD	0001	
SW01	MDOU	O Outbound		01	GIMD	0001	

Figure 18.18 Defining the Yard Doors

After the doors are defined, they're assigned to yard bins created for the yard storage type. This helps you monitor the TU in the warehouse monitor when it's at a door. This assignment is made via **SAP Easy Access** path **Logistics • SCM Extended Warehouse Management • Extended Warehouse Management • Master Data • Shipping and Receiving • Yard Management • Assign Warehouse Door to Yard Bin** or via Transaction /SCWM/YM_DOOR_BIN.

> **Tip**
>
> A yard door is a spatial object that has a direct assignment to another warehouse object: a warehouse door. It acts as a link between the embedded EWM warehouse and yard.

18.3.3 Check-In and Check-Out

The check-in/check-out functionality is used in the yard to manage the arrival and exit of a TU or vehicle to or from the yard checkpoint. To perform check-in/check-out, use Transaction /SCWM/CICO or navigate to **SAP Easy Access** path **Logistics • SCM Extended Warehouse Management • Extended Warehouse Management • Shipping and Receiving • Yard Management • Arrival at/Departure from Checkpoint**. As shown in Figure 18.19, the transaction screen shows two options for arrival and departure from a checkpoint.

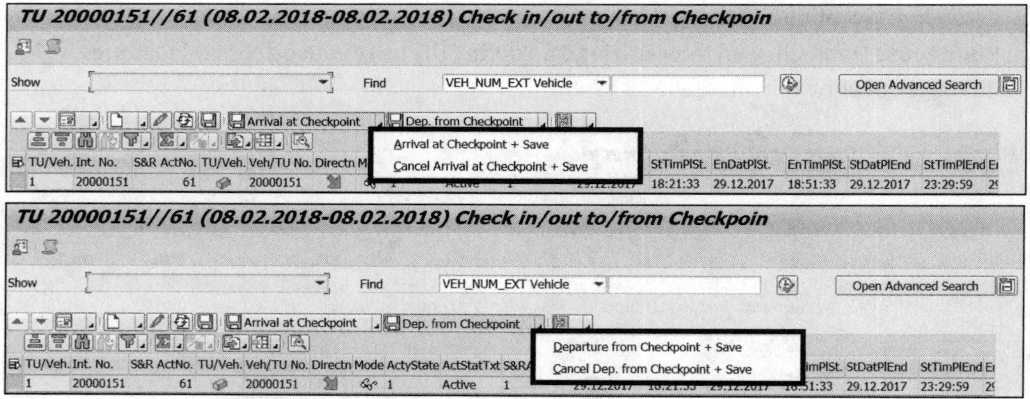

Figure 18.19 Processing the Transportation Unit for Arrival/Departure

To bring a TU into the yard, select the **Arrival at Checkpoint + Save** option. This changes the status of the TU from **Planned** to **Active** and updates the actual start date and time. You can also cancel the arrival at a checkpoint by clicking on the **Cancel Arrival at Checkpoint + Save** option. When the unloading activity is finished, you can move the TU to a checkpoint and select **Departure from Checkpoint + Save** to confirm the TU's departure from the yard.

Tip

You can also check in/out TUs and check in/out vehicles from Transaction /SCWM/TU and Transaction /SCWM/VEH, respectively.

During the check-in/check-out process, you may need to perform additional processes, such as printing certain documents or mailing the documents to certain parties. These additional processes can be performed using the PPF output for the TUs. As explained in the previous section, PPF profiles can be created and assigned to TUs or vehicles with the appropriate trigger and schedule conditions to produce the desired output.

Note

The Arrival and Departure app allows you to check in and check out TUs at warehouse checkpoints.

18.3.4 Internal Yard Movements

The TUs or vehicles checked into the yard can be moved to the parking lot or directly to the door for loading/unloading. At the end of the unloading process, the TU can be moved from the door to either the parking lot or to the checkpoint. These movements of the TU or vehicle in the warehouse are executed with the help of *yard warehouse tasks*. As shown in Figure 18.20, you create and confirm a yard warehouse task by navigating to **SAP Easy Access** path **Logistics • SCM Extended Warehouse Management • Extended Warehouse Management • Shipping and Receiving • Yard Management • Create Warehouse Task in Yard** or using Transaction **/SCWM/YMOVE**. Similar movements can also be made with the help of the shipping cockpit.

As shown in Figure 18.20, in Step ❶, you create the yard warehouse task, warehouse process type, and destination automatically. The source bin is populated automatically based on the current position of the TU in the yard. The destination bin can be a checkpoint, parking area, or door. In Step ❷, you confirm the warehouse task immediately on creation or confirm it later by going to the **Open WTs in Yard** tab and selecting the option to confirm the warehouse task in the foreground or background. You can also use the radio frequency (RF) UI to confirm yard warehouse tasks.

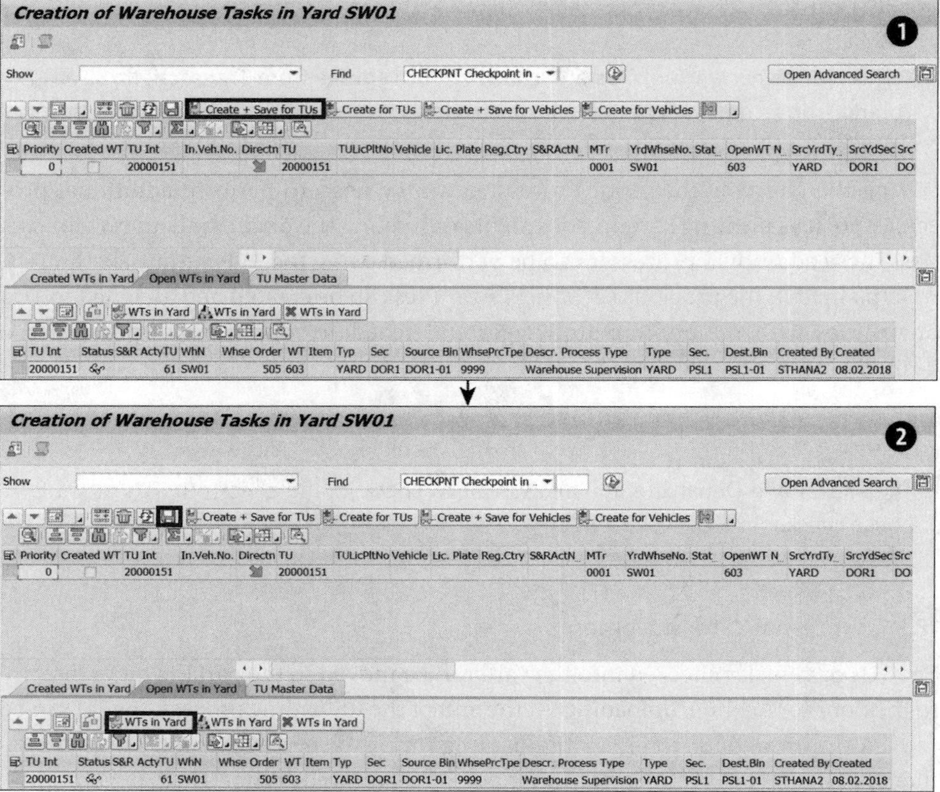

Figure 18.20 Moving Transportation Units Using Yard Warehouse Tasks

18.3.5 Executing Yard Management

So far, we've discussed the concept and structure of yard management in embedded EWM. Now, let's discuss how yard management is combined with goods receipt in embedded EWM. Goods receipt is carried out in embedded EWM for receipt from external vendors, stock transfers, or customer returns. Stock is brought into the warehouse on vehicles/TUs, and the goods receipt process is started. The diagram of goods receipt with yard management is shown in Figure 18.21. As part of inbound receipt using yard management, various steps are executed:

1. An inbound delivery is created in SAP S/4HANA and distributed to embedded EWM, which creates the inbound warehouse request in embedded EWM.

2. TUs or vehicles are manually created in embedded EWM by the yard administrator. The status of the corresponding shipping and receiving activity remains set to **Planned** until the TU physically arrives in the yard.
3. The shipping clerk assigns the deliveries to the TU based on route, ship-to party, and other criteria.
4. The checkpoint guard confirms the arrival of the TU/vehicle in the yard, which sets the TU status to **Arrival at Checkpoint**. This also sets the status of the shipping and receiving activity to **Active** ❶. At this point, the HU of the TU is moved to the checkpoint bin.
5. If the warehouse door isn't available, then the TU is sent to the parking lot by creation of yard warehouse tasks ❷. When the door becomes available, the TU is docked at the warehouse door to carry out unloading of goods ❸.
6. After the TU is docked at the door, the unloading process is carried out. For an outbound process, goods are loaded onto the TU/vehicle from the goods issue area.
7. After the loading or unloading process is complete, the TU or vehicle is moved from the door to the checkpoint or to parking if the checkpoint is occupied. When the checkpoint becomes free, the TU is moved to the checkpoint ❹.
8. The checkpoint clerk checks the required documentation, and the TU/vehicle is checked out ❺.

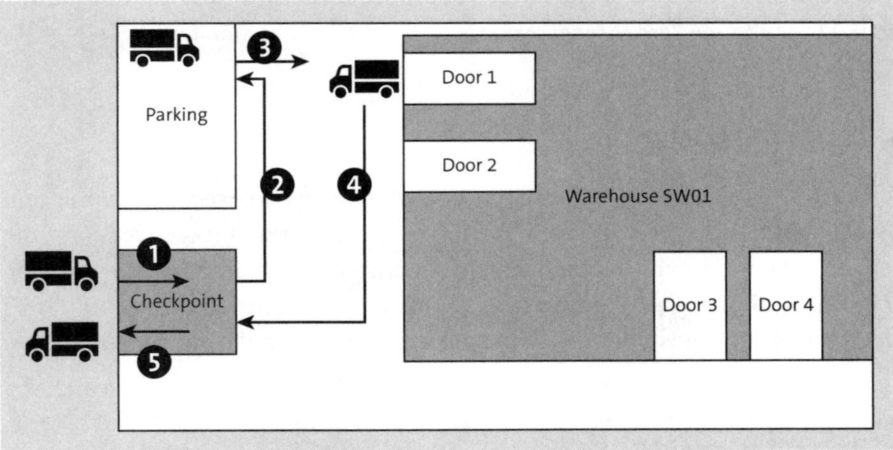

Figure 18.21 Yard Management in Inbound Processing

18.3.6 Monitoring in Yard Management

You can monitor yard activities using the standard embedded EWM monitor. As shown in Figure 18.22, you can provide the yard organizational structure and other yard filters for monitoring stock in the yard. The three nodes available for yard monitoring are **Yard Overview**, **Yard Bins**, and **Yard Doors**. These allow you to monitor stock in the yard, stock in TUs, and availability of yard spaces, such as parking spaces, doors, checkpoints, and so on.

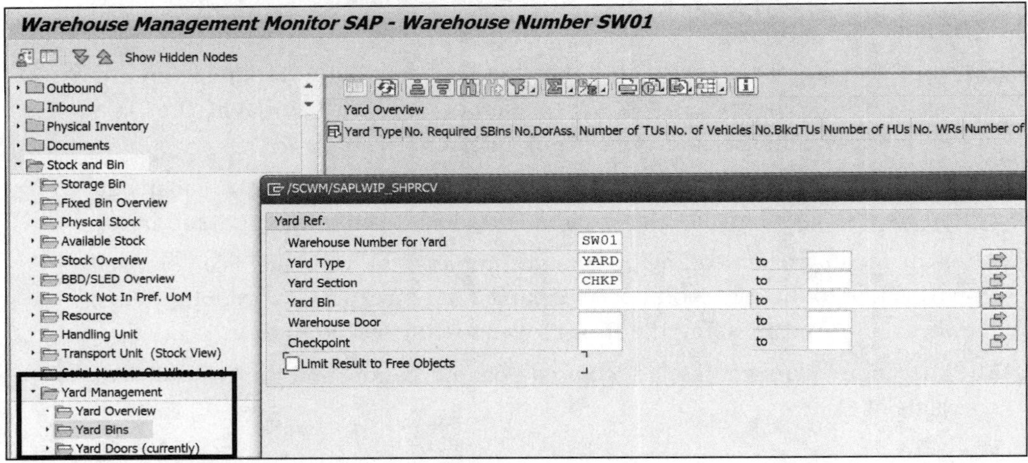

Figure 18.22 Monitoring Yard Management Using the Warehouse Monitor

18.4 Shipping Cockpit

You can use SAP Fiori apps in the shipping cockpit to plan and execute shipping and receiving, as well as yard operations for inbound and outbound deliveries in the embedded EWM warehouse. SAP provides an extensive UI in the form of the shipping cockpit, which allows you to execute various operations detailed in this section. We'll also look briefly at some of the SAP Fiori apps available for yard management.

Using the Shipping Cockpit Planning app, shown in Figure 18.23, you can search the outbound deliveries and TUs present in the warehouse for a certain interval of time. You must have the shipping clerk role assigned to use this application. After the deliveries that need to be planned for the TU are determined, you can either plan them for an existing TU or create a completely new TU by selecting outbound delivery objects and clicking on **Create TU & Assign Delivery**.

You can also perform time scheduling for the TUs, which allows you to set a planned arrival and dispatch time for the TU. Optimization of the TU planned arrival and departure time in a warehouse uses the TU profile. In the **Capacity Overview** tab, you can view the capacity of the loading point in terms of time slots and capacity per time slot to hold a TU if SAP Dock Appointment Scheduling is integrated with embedded EWM (see Chapter 23). The slot for a TU at the loading point can be confirmed by entering the planned arrival/departure time for the TU.

In the **Staging Area Planning** tab, you can view the empty staging areas or bays and assign them to the TU, thus blocking the staging bay by the TU for an interval of time. Assigning staging areas to TUs is often required when optimizing picking for the deliveries for multiple TUs. This is done from the **Transportation Units** tab, where you select TUs and create picking waves for multiple outbound delivery orders assigned to them. This can be automated by setting an automated release for the wave in wave template configuration (see Chapter 16).

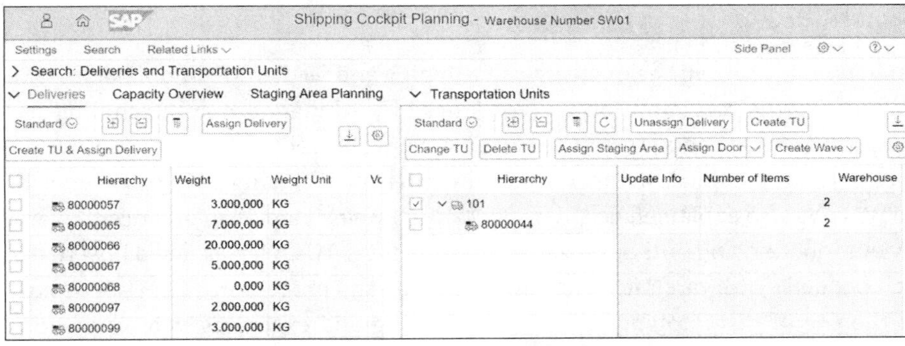

Figure 18.23 Shipping Cockpit for Planning Yard Operations

Using the Shipping Cockpit Execution app, as shown in Figure 18.24, you can search the outbound TUs present in the warehouse for a certain interval of time. You must have the shipping clerk role assigned to use this application. The shipping cockpit provides a rich UI to see both an overview and the hierarchy of the TU. It also allows you to view the completion of various yard operations such as assigning/unassigning deliveries to a TU, arriving/departing from a checkpoint, docking/undocking at a door, loading/unloading start and complete, creating waves for deliveries assigned to a TU, changing a seal, requesting an invoice before goods issue, and posting goods issue for TUs (assigned deliveries).

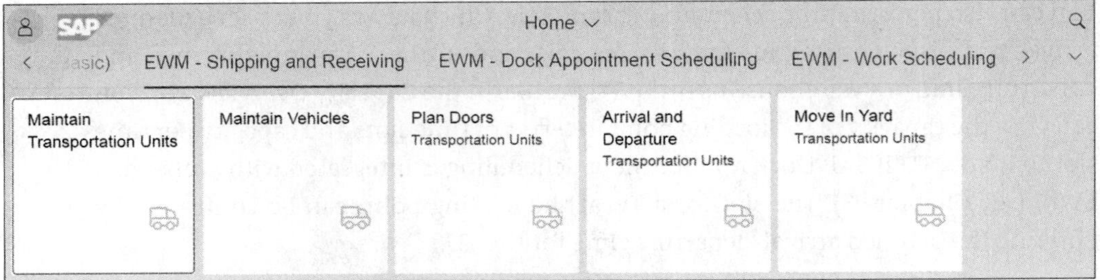

Figure 18.24 Shipping Cockpit for Executing Yard Operations

Because the shipping cockpit provides a common entry point for execution of all TU operations using accessible, mobile SAP Fiori apps, it's used to improve yard operation efficiency in organizations.

18.5 Summary

This chapter introduced basic concepts of shipping and receiving in embedded EWM. We explained the configuration and workings of yard management, including setting up yard storage and assigning storage bins. We introduced the concept of TUs and vehicles and their use in carrying out shipping and receiving activities in embedded EWM. We also explained how to model any complex yard of an organization and carry out inbound and outbound yard movements for TUs. We discussed how to use the embedded EWM warehouse monitor to display and process stock in TUs. We covered the use of the shipping cockpit for planning and executing yard operations involving TUs, and we discussed SAP Fiori apps available for yard management in embedded EWM, via which important yard processes can be executed. In the next chapter, we will cover labor management.

Chapter 19

Labor Management

Labor management is an important aspect of any warehouse, as warehouse employees ensure the operational continuity of warehouse processes. In this chapter, we'll discuss embedded EWM's solution to manage the labor/employee workforce of a warehouse, which can be integrated with HR systems to facilitate performance-based bonus payouts.

The employee workforce is of one of the key elements of any warehouse. It constitutes a majority of the operating cost of any warehouse and ensures operational continuity so that inbound, outbound, and internal warehouse operations continue with minimal downtime.

In this chapter, we'll explain various elements used in embedded EWM labor management, such as master data, labor processes, performance data, and reporting and analytics. Section 19.1 describes the applicability of SAP labor management in business organizations. It lays out the use and advantage of labor management for complex processes in organizations. Section 19.2 describes the setting to activate labor management in embedded EWM. Section 19.3 covers the concept of engineered labor standards used to calculate planned workload. In Section 19.4, we discuss the process for calculating planned workload in the warehouse. Section 19.5 discusses the calculation of executed workload and provides an example of warehouse order confirmation with labor management activated for the warehouse. In Section 19.6, we discuss how results from labor management can be integrated with HR systems to calculate employee bonus payouts.

19.1 What Is Labor Management?

Embedded EWM provides labor management as an out-of-the-box solution to cater to the planning and tracking of employee productivity in a warehouse based on established standards, comparing productive versus unproductive time, and analyzing and transferring employee performance data to an HR system. It involves mapping warehouse employees as business partners for workload planning and capturing the actual executed workload in embedded EWM using shift management, engineered labor standards, and employee performance. By capturing workload data for the employees, the warehouse administrator can improve labor efficiency and performance by changing the workload assignment in the warehouse.

Using labor management in embedded EWM, organizations can optimize performance of warehouse processes by planning and assigning the right amount of workload to the labor in the system. This enables organizations to analyze the results of the executed workload and use them to rate employee efficiency or note a labor bottleneck in a certain business process.

Labor management is used by organizations that have complex warehouse processes and are highly personnel dependent. It's also used by organizations with a fast turnaround time for mission-critical business processes dependent on workers; such organizations need to analyze the execution time of these processes and optimize them.

In Section 19.1.1, we'll explain the business context in which labor management can be used in real-world scenarios. In Section 19.1.2, we'll explain the processes carried out in the system as well as labor management–related documents with which employee performance can be planned, stored, and interfaced to HR systems.

19.1.1 Business Process

American company Alpha Medicals receives an order from one of its customers based in Mexico. The order sent by the customer requires Alpha Medicals to provide the products in time as well as pack them in cases and pallets for delivery. Stock that will be delivered to the customer is to be picked from the source bins of the supplying warehouse by the warehouse workers, packed in the required packaging material to create finished product cases, and staged in the goods issue area. As a regular Alpha Medicals practice, warehousing activities performed by the warehouse workers such as stock handling, value-added services (VAS), and so on, are recorded for reporting and performance handling of the warehouse workers. The company also performs daily planning of warehouse task allocation of workers and equipment to measure planned versus actual performance of assets in their organization. To ensure that all such labor-intensive activities of the warehouse workers are planned and captured in the embedded EWM system, the company has implemented labor management in embedded EWM. As shown in Figure 19.1, a day involving labor management in embedded EWM and its usage involves multiple steps:

1. The warehouse receives a warehouse request document for customer delivery to supply the requested products to the customer after performing any additional work on the products.
2. The warehouse-request-related warehouse task is assigned to the warehouse worker so that the worker can pick, pack, and stage the stock at the staging bay.
3. Because labor management is activated in embedded EWM by the company, each warehouse task is assigned to a processor who is also a warehouse worker. The system provides the warehouse worker a task to move the products to the required areas of the warehouse for additional processes on products, so that finally the products can be staged in the goods issue area.
4. The warehouse worker picks the products, carry them to the interim areas, performs any additional activities, and then stages them in the goods issue area.
5. Each one of these activities is preplanned by the warehousing department administrator using labor management in embedded EWM and is assigned to the processors. After successful completion of the activities, the actual completion data and effort of the activities is captured in labor management in embedded EWM.
6. All the captured data about the labor is analyzed using standard analysis reporting for performance assessment by the company. The data is also provided to the HR department so that working bonuses are linked to the performance shown by the warehouse workers.

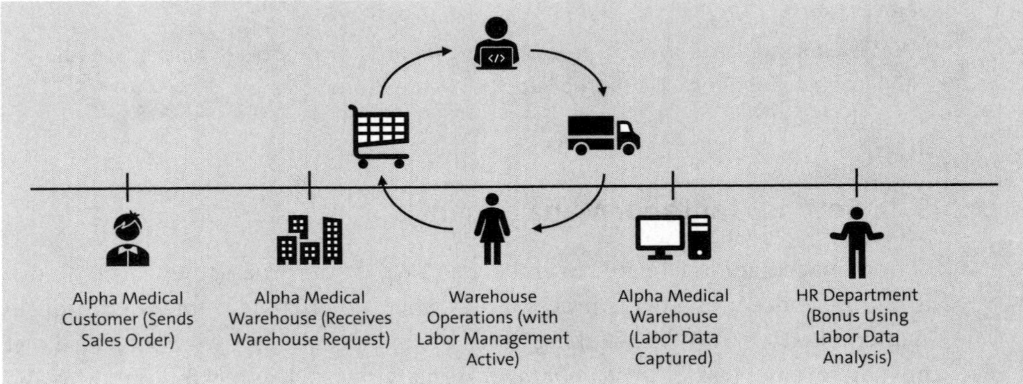

Figure 19.1 Business Flow in Labor Management

19.1.2 System Process

The following explains the basic system flow, including the documents and data required for labor-management-based warehouse workload execution:

1. An outbound delivery order is created in embedded EWM that contains information about the products to be delivered to the external customer by Alpha Medicals.
2. Initial picking warehouse tasks are created and assigned to the warehouse worker to direct the warehouse worker, based on planned workload assignment using labor management, to move the product from source bin to staging area.
3. The warehouse orders allocated to the warehouse workers are executed by the workers in the order in which they are created. During the execution of the warehouse orders, each warehouse order is assigned with the processor master of the warehouse worker who completes the stock movement process. At the end of the activity, the labor management application notes down all the actual execution parameters to use them in labor management reporting and performance analysis.
4. At the end of the day, the warehouse administrator investigates the labor management data for the warehouse and plans adjustments to the workload assignment to warehouse workers based on their efficiency.
5. At the end of the year, the accumulated data from the labor management application in embedded EWM is used to calculate performance bonuses for the warehouse workers.

Note

We've explained the system process using outbound processes only. It's equally applicable to inbound and internal stock movement processes.

19.2 Settings for Labor Management

Labor management is activated in embedded EWM at the process step level. We discussed the concept of storage process steps when we discussed storage controls in Chapter 6, Section 6.5. While working with labor management, you'll work with direct and indirect labor tasks. *Direct labor tasks* are activities such as picking, putaway, and so on, which are related to the execution of warehouse tasks in embedded EWM. An employee may also be involved in various warehouse activities, such as meetings, discussions, and so on, which are recorded as *indirect labor tasks* in embedded EWM.

In this section, we'll review the settings required to activate and start using labor management. We'll then walk through the processor master data created in embedded EWM for warehouse employees, the concept of shifts and formulas, and using the condition editor to map the productive time of employees in their work shifts. These master data elements must be created in embedded EWM before planning and execution of the workload can be carried out in the warehouse using labor management.

19.2.1 Activating Labor Management

Embedded EWM doesn't have labor management activated; therefore, it must be activated for the warehouse if labor management needs to be implemented. Labor management is activated at two different levels: the warehouse level and the internal storage process step level. It can be deactivated selectively for required external process steps that refer to internal process steps in embedded EWM. The activation of labor management at the warehouse level is done via IMG path **SCM Extended Warehouse Management • Extended Warehouse Management • Labor Management • Activate Labor Management**. Select the **LM Is Active** checkbox for the embedded EWM warehouse, as shown in Figure 19.2.

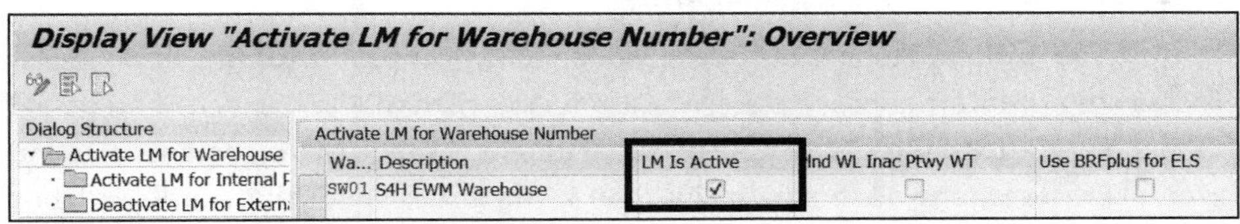

Figure 19.2 Activating Labor Management for the Embedded EWM Warehouse

After activating labor management at the warehouse level, labor management must be activated for internal process steps for the warehouse by clicking on **Activate LM for Internal Process Step** in the left-hand menu and selecting the **LM Is Active** checkbox for the warehouse, as shown in Figure 19.3.

Labor management can be deactivated at the external process step level for the warehouse by clicking on the **Deactivate LM for External Process Step** option for the warehouse and setting the **LM Is Inactive** checkbox, as shown in Figure 19.4. In this way, labor management remains active for the external process step if the internal process step assigned to it is active.

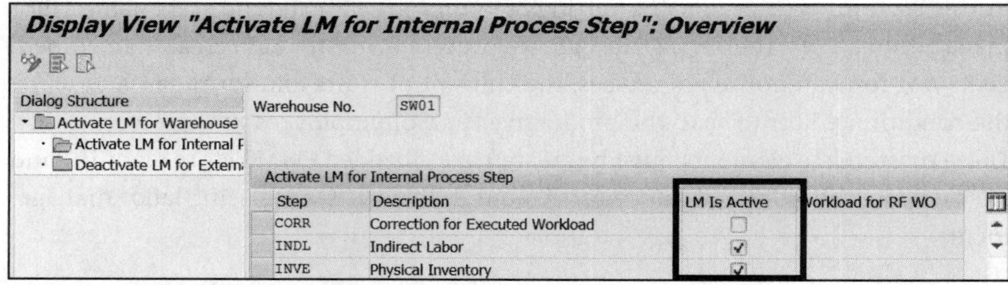

Figure 19.3 Activating Labor Management for Internal Process Steps

Display View "Deactivate LM for External Process Step": Overview

Dialog Structure
Activate LM for Warehouse
Activate LM for Internal F
Deactivate LM for Extern

Warehouse No. SW01

Deactivate LM for External Process Step

Step	Description	LM Is Inactive
NOLM	Movement Without Labor Management	✓

Figure 19.4 Deactivating Labor Management for External Process Steps

19.2.2 Settings for Indirect Labor Tasks

To configure indirect labor tasks in embedded EWM, you need to map an external process step to internal process step **INDL** via IMG path **SCM Extended Warehouse Management • Extended Warehouse Management • Labor Management • Define External Process Steps**, as shown in Figure 19.5. The direction for these indirect labor task external process steps is updated to **Not Relevant for Process-Oriented Storage Control**. These process steps aren't related to warehouse stock operations, so they can be used across the warehouse.

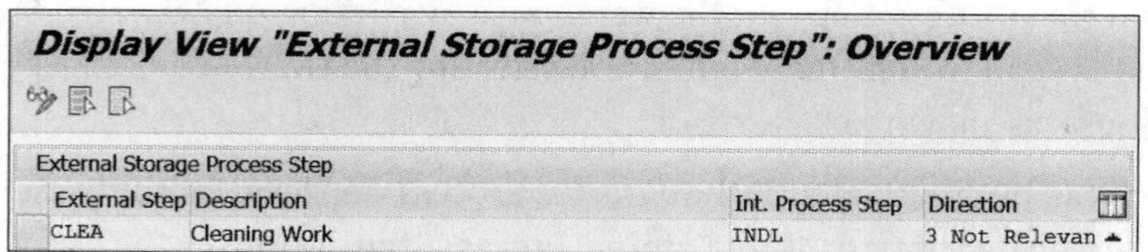

Figure 19.5 Defining the Indirect Labor External Process Step

Indirect labor tasks can be created in embedded EWM via **SAP Easy Access** path **Logistics • SCM Extended Warehouse Management • Extended Warehouse Management • Labor Management • Maintain Indirect Labor Task** by clicking on the [icon] icon and providing the external step previously defined and the processor as input.

> **Note**
>
> The Maintain Indirect Labor Tasks app allows you to maintain and execute indirect labor tasks that are executed without reference to any warehouse requests.

19.2.3 Processor

A warehouse employee is mapped as a processor in embedded EWM to work with labor management. A *processor* is a person who performs various activities in the warehouse based on the assigned workload in the form of warehouse orders. A processor for labor management can be created via **SAP Easy Access** path **Logistics • SCM Extended Warehouse Management • Extended Warehouse Management • Master Data • Resource Management • Processor • Create Processor** or using Transaction /SCMB/PRR1, as shown in Figure 19.6. A processor is a business partner of type **Person** with business partner role of LM0001 (warehouse worker).

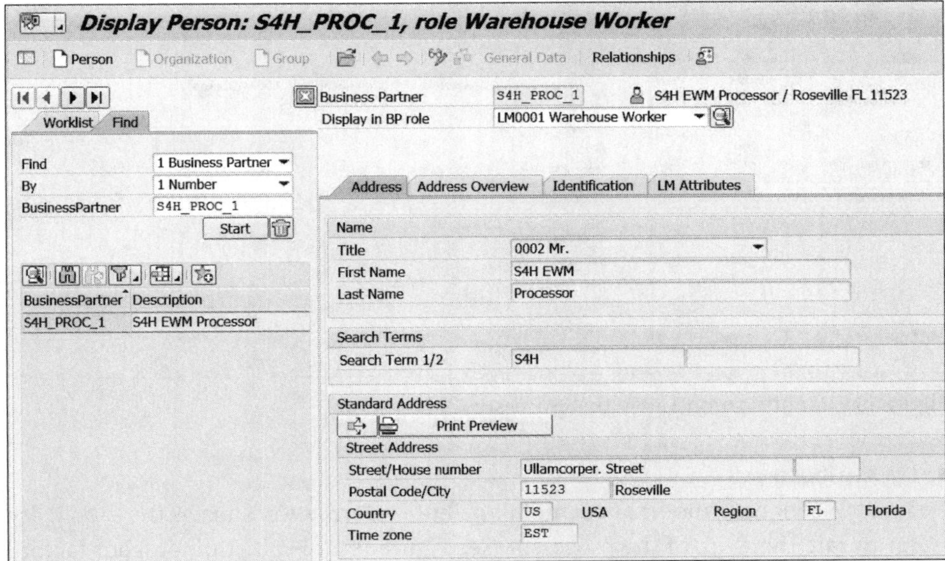

Figure 19.6 Defining Processors for Labor Management

On this screen, click on **Person** and provide the required data. The UI for creation of processors is the same as that for creating a business partner in embedded EWM. Data is assigned to the processor in four different tabs:

- **Address**
  This tab contains general information about the processor, such as name, search time, address, and so on.
- **Address Overview**
  This tab contains concise information about the different addresses for the processor and their purposes.
- **Identification**
  This tab contains information such as the **Personnel number** of the employee and the system **User Name** assigned to the processor, as shown in Figure 19.7. It also contains the **External BP Number**, which signifies a processor maintained in an external or legacy system so that information about the processor can be updated in embedded EWM directly by integrating the third-party/legacy system with embedded EWM if the legacy system acts as the source system for processor data.

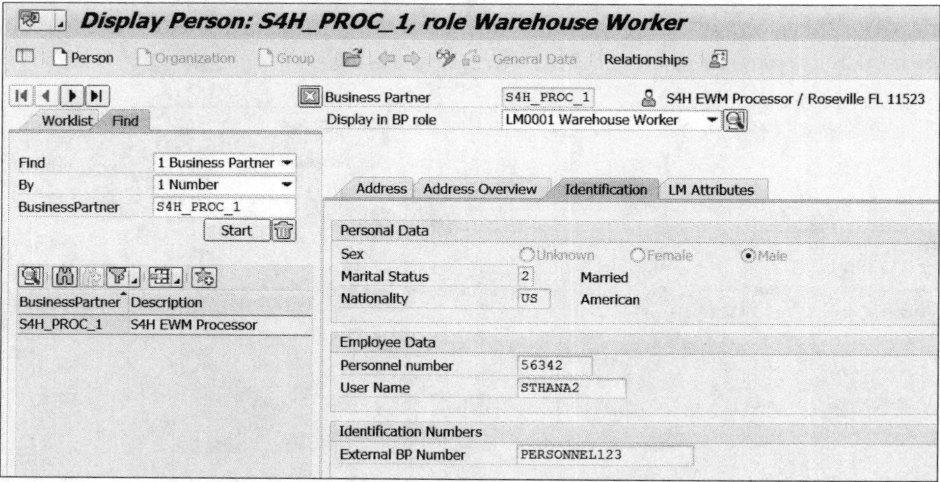

Figure 19.7 Identification Tab in the Processor Master

- **LM Attribute**
  This tab contains labor management attribute information such as the **Labor Factor** to rate the work of the processor (see Figure 19.8). Evaluation of labor factors can be modified by using business add-in (BAdI) /SCWM/EX_LM_BASICS_EPD_AMCALC. A

Supply Chain Unit is assigned to the processor so that the time zone of the supply chain unit is used for evaluating processor work data. If the performance data from the performance document is to be transferred to whichever SAP HR system you use, then HR business system data is assigned to the processor in this tab.

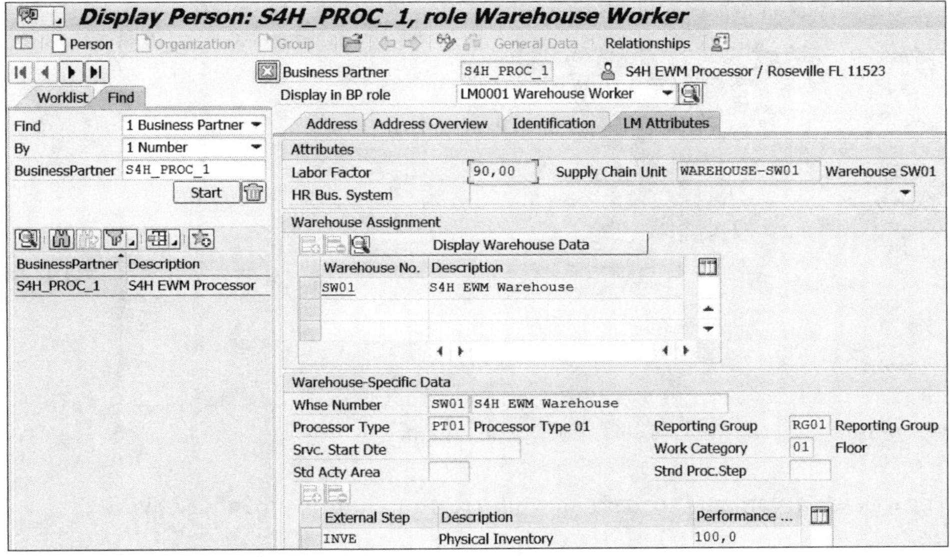

Figure 19.8 LM Attributes Tab in the Processor Master

You can also assign the warehouse where the processor works in this tab, along with some warehouse-specific attributes such as standard activity area (**Std Acty Area**), process step (**Stnd Proc.Step**), and **External Step** for planning purposes. It's also possible to maintain processor attributes in the embedded EWM warehouse monitor using Transaction /SCWM/MON. Navigate to the **Resource Management • Processor** node to select the processor, and click on to select the required action.

19.2.4 Shift Management

Shift management is used to plan employee work schedules in labor management. Shifts are used for defining the work schedule for a warehouse worker in the warehouse. Based on worker productivity, a shift can be used for determining the performance of an employee. If a shift is repeated for a period such as a week or month, it's assigned to a shift sequence.

To create a new shift, navigate to **SAP Easy Access** path **Logistics • SCM Extended Warehouse Management • Extended Warehouse Management • Master Data • Shift Management • Maintain Shifts**, as shown in Figure 19.9. Begin by defining the **Shift Factors**, and then gradually move on to the tabs on the left to define the **Breaks**, **Shifts**, and **Shift Sequences**.

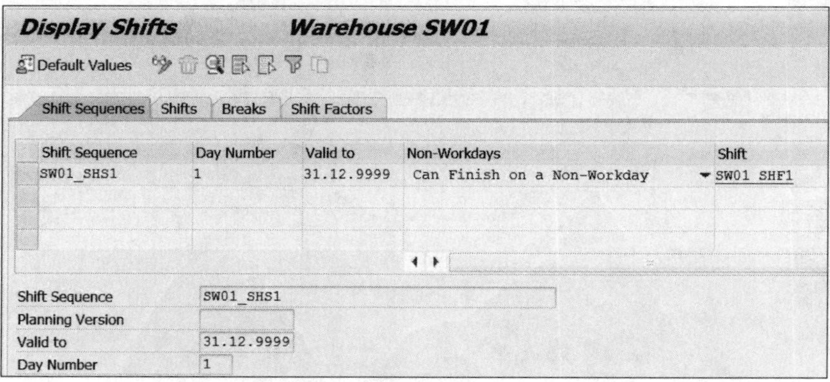

Figure 19.9 Shift Master Data in Labor Management

The following elements are defined while creating shifts in embedded EWM:

- **Shift Factors**
  As shown in Figure 19.10, a shift factor is used to define the utilization rate of a shift for an employee. It signifies actual productive time as a percentage of total working time. The rest is used for nonproductive tasks such as cleaning, sweeping, and so on.

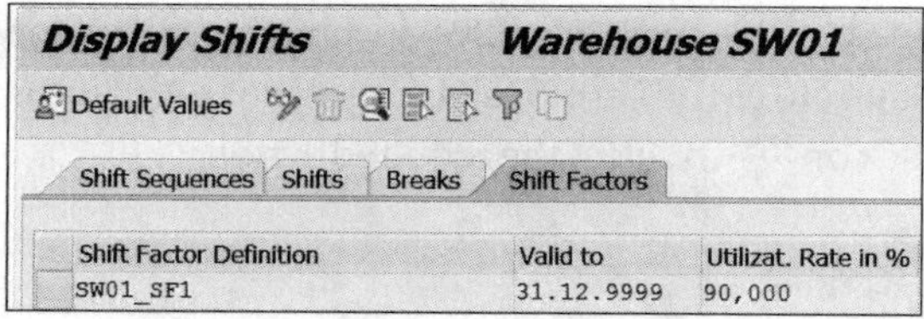

Figure 19.10 Defining Shift Factors for Shifts

- **Breaks**
  In the normal course of working time, it may be required for the warehouse workers to take breaks for lunch and other activities. These are defined for the shift as shown in Figure 19.11.

Display Shifts **Warehouse SW01**

Default Values

Shift Sequences | Shifts | Breaks | Shift Factors

Break Pattern	Break Number	Break St...	Break End	Break After Hours	Break Duration
SW01_BP1	1	12:00:00	12:30:00	00:00:00	00:30:00

Figure 19.11 Defining Breaks in Shift Management

- **Shifts**
  A shift signifies the productive working time defined for a warehouse employee for a single day. It consists of start and end times of normal working hours in combination with breaks and shift factors to determine the nonproductive time of a shift, as shown in Figure 19.12.

Display Shifts **Warehouse SW01**

Default Values

Shift Sequences | Shifts | Breaks | Shift Factors

Shift	Valid to	Start	End	Break Pattern	Break Durati...	Shift Factors
SW01_SHF1	31.12.9999	09:00:00	17:00:00	SW01_BP1	00:30:00	SW01_SF1

Figure 19.12 Defining Shifts for Processors

- **Shift Sequences**
  A shift sequence is a shift that is applicable over a given period, which is recorded in the **Valid to** field in embedded EWM. It also controls whether the shift can start or end on a nonworking day for a processor (**Non-Workdays**), as shown in Figure 19.13.

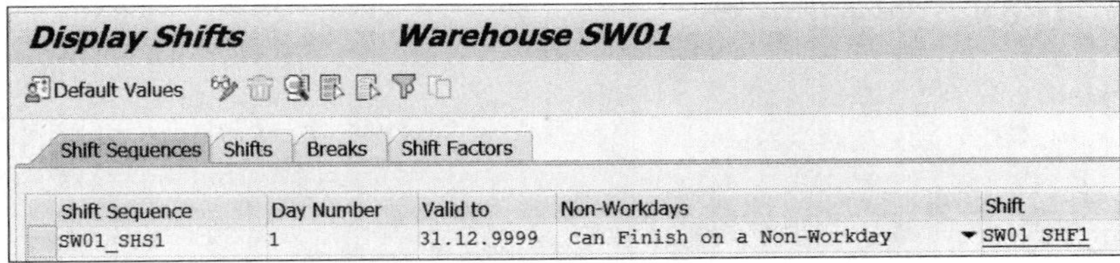

Display Shifts **Warehouse SW01**

Default Values

Shift Sequences | Shifts | Breaks | Shift Factors

Shift Sequence	Day Number	Valid to	Non-Workdays	Shift
SW01_SHS1	1	31.12.9999	Can Finish on a Non-Workday	SW01_SHF1

Figure 19.13 Defining Shift Sequences for Processors

You can manage shifts from the embedded EWM warehouse monitor using Transaction /SCWM/MON. Navigate to the **Labor Management • Shift Management • Shift Sequences by Date** node. Using this node, you can display the shift sequence to which a shift belongs by selecting the shift, clicking on the [button] button, and selecting **Navigate to Shift Sequence**. This takes you directly to the shift screen (see Figure 19.14) we discussed earlier.

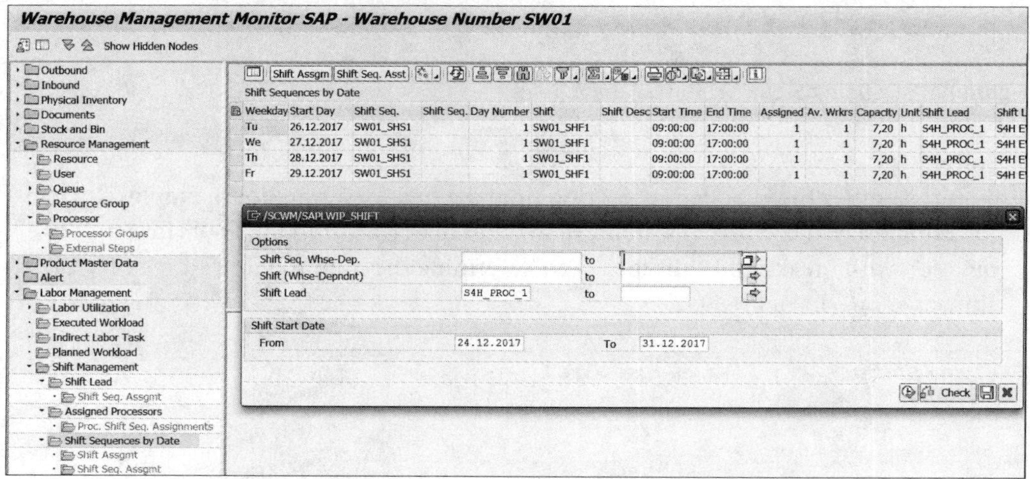

Figure 19.14 Shift Management in Embedded EWM Warehouse Monitor

Embedded EWM uses work schedules to record overtime, absences, and individual breaks for a processor. This data can only be seen for the past 30 and future 360 days for a processor. To define a work schedule, navigate to **SAP Easy Access** path **Logistics • SCM Extended Warehouse Management • Extended Warehouse Management • Master Data • Shift Management • Maintain Work Schedule**, provide the **Warehouse Number** and **Processor**, and click on [button], as shown in Figure 19.15.

Maintain Processor Work Schedule

Warehouse Number	SW01
Processor	S4H_PROC_1
Date From	24.12.2017
Date To	22.06.2018

Figure 19.15 Report to Define Work Schedule for Shift Management

The next screen displays the daily shift data for a processor, as shown in Figure 19.16. Overtime can be recorded by changing the start and end time of the daily shift data of the processor, whereas an absence can be set by setting the day as **Not a Workday**.

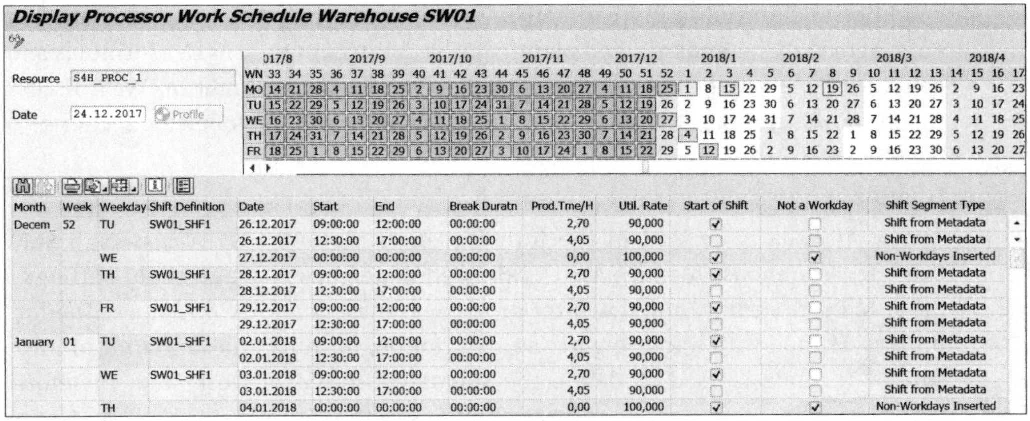

Display Processor Work Schedule Warehouse SW01

Resource S4H_PROC_1

Date 24.12.2017 Profile

017/8 2017/9 2017/10 2017/11 2017/12 2018/1 2018/2 2018/3 2018/4

WN	33	34	35	36	37	38	39	40	41	42	43	44	45	46	47	48	49	50	51	52	1	2	3	4	5	6	7	8	9	10	11	12	13	14	15	16	17
MO	14	21	28	4	11	18	25	2	9	16	23	30	6	13	20	27	4	11	18	25	1	8	15	22	29	5	12	19	26	5	12	19	26	2	9	16	23
TU	15	22	29	5	12	19	26	3	10	17	24	31	7	14	21	28	5	12	19	26	2	9	16	23	30	6	13	20	27	6	13	20	27	3	10	17	24
WE	16	23	30	6	13	20	27	4	11	18	25	1	8	15	22	29	6	13	20	27	3	10	17	24	31	7	14	21	28	7	14	21	28	4	11	18	25
TH	17	24	31	7	14	21	28	5	12	19	26	2	9	16	23	30	7	14	21	28	4	11	18	25	1	8	15	22	1	8	15	22	29	5	12	19	26
FR	18	25	1	8	15	22	29	6	13	20	27	3	10	17	24	1	8	15	22	29	5	12	19	26	2	9	16	23	2	9	16	23	30	6	13	20	27

Month	Week	Weekday	Shift Definition	Date	Start	End	Break Duratn	Prod.Tme/H	Util. Rate	Start of Shift	Not a Workday	Shift Segment Type
Decem	52	TU	SW01_SHF1	26.12.2017	09:00:00	12:00:00	00:00:00	2,70	90,000	✓		Shift from Metadata
				26.12.2017	12:30:00	17:00:00	00:00:00	4,05	90,000			Shift from Metadata
		WE		27.12.2017	00:00:00	00:00:00	00:00:00	0,00	100,000	✓	✓	Non-Workdays Inserted
		TH	SW01_SHF1	28.12.2017	09:00:00	12:00:00	00:00:00	2,70	90,000	✓		Shift from Metadata
				28.12.2017	12:30:00	17:00:00	00:00:00	4,05	90,000			Shift from Metadata
		FR	SW01_SHF1	29.12.2017	09:00:00	12:00:00	00:00:00	2,70	90,000	✓		Shift from Metadata
				29.12.2017	12:30:00	17:00:00	00:00:00	4,05	90,000			Shift from Metadata
January	01	TU	SW01_SHF1	02.01.2018	09:00:00	12:00:00	00:00:00	2,70	90,000	✓		Shift from Metadata
				02.01.2018	12:30:00	17:00:00	00:00:00	4,05	90,000			Shift from Metadata
		WE	SW01_SHF1	03.01.2018	09:00:00	12:00:00	00:00:00	2,70	90,000	✓		Shift from Metadata
				03.01.2018	12:30:00	17:00:00	00:00:00	4,05	90,000			Shift from Metadata
		TH		04.01.2018	00:00:00	00:00:00	00:00:00	0,00	100,000	✓	✓	Non-Workdays Inserted

Figure 19.16 Defining Absence and Overtime for a Processor

When a warehouse employee confirms a warehouse task, embedded EWM determines a shift for the employee and saves it in the executed workload record for future labor performance evaluation. If the system records the activity outside of the assigned shift, then the system determines a shift nearest to the start and end time of the activity within the tolerance limits. If the activity completion appears to be outside the shift, even when using the tolerance limits, then the system doesn't assign any shift to the executed workload for the activity.

19.2.5 Formulas and Conditions

Any activity in a warehouse consists of a set of external work steps performed by the warehouse worker. Every step takes some amount of time to be performed. This time can be either static or dynamic, which is calculated based on conditions and formulas.

Formulas and conditions are used in labor management in embedded EWM for calculation of workload planning and for comparing the actual workload with the planned workload. Formulas and conditions can be used in the following:

- Preprocessing
- Planning and simulation
- Engineered labor standards

A formula or condition is defined with a four-digit alphanumeric code. The formula and condition type details determine the fields that can be used in defining the condition and formula and whether they're relevant for preprocessing, calculation of engineered labor standards, and planning. For the system to consider formulas and conditions, the **Active** indicator must be set in the formula or condition. We'll discuss the formulas and conditions used in labor management in the following sections.

Formula

A new formula is defined in the formula editor via **SAP Easy Access** path **SCM Extended Warehouse Management • Extended Warehouse Management • Settings • Labor Management • Formula Editor** or using Transaction /SCWM/LM_FE. The formula is defined with a four-digit code, description, formula type, and unit of measure. A formula is used to define the standard time for a work step; therefore, variables of the work step are used as operands in the formula. As shown in Figure 19.17, a formula editor has various fields and operations available such as **Addition**, **Multiplication**, and so on to create a formula for the labor management processes. If you need to enter the formula in free text mode, click on the **Expert Mode** button above the editor.

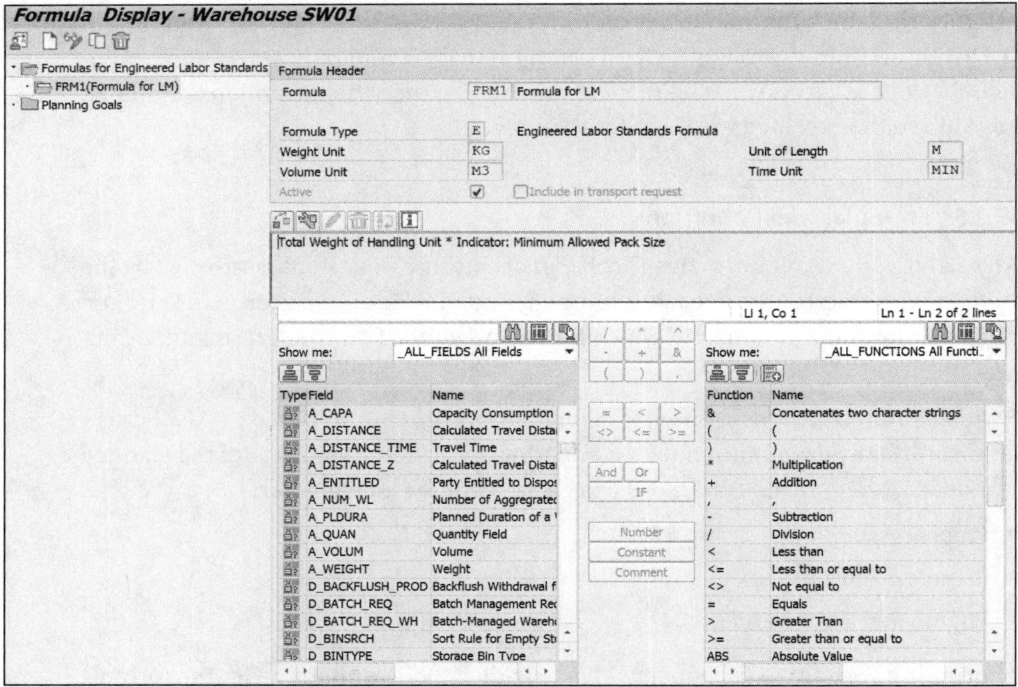

Figure 19.17 Defining Formulas for Engineered Labor Standards

A formula can be saved if it's free of syntax errors by clicking on the **Check** button above the edit area. If you need to transport the formula to a target system, it can be included in a transport request by selecting the **Include in transport request** checkbox in the **Formula Header** section, after which the formula can't be deleted but only set as **Active** or **Inactive**. It's also possible to create a complex formula by using simple formulas as variables. You can also use calculated measurement services in the formula; for example, the average putaway for an area can be used for calculating the expected workload for putaway in an area.

Conditions

Conditions are used in labor management to decide how a process step can be evaluated for calculation of engineered labor standards or preprocessing. Conditions are defined via **SAP Easy Access** path **SCM Extended Warehouse Management • Extended Warehouse Management • Settings • Labor Management • Condition Editor**, as shown in Figure 19.18. Conditions are created in the same manner as formulas and are assigned to condition types. For conditions, there can be conditional operators (>, =, <) within them. If there are no conditional operators, they're always evaluated as *true*. Fields used to build conditions for engineered labor standards come from the product, warehouse order, packaging specification, workload, and other engineered labor standards conditions.

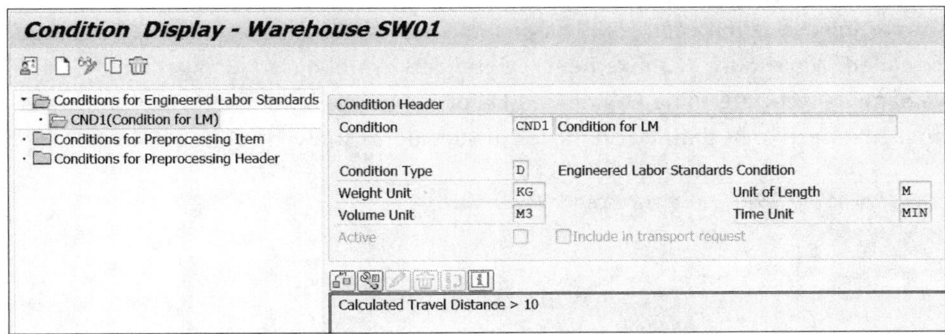

Figure 19.18 Defining Conditions for Engineered Labor Standards

19.3 Engineered Labor Standards

Labor activity constitutes a series of tasks performed in a warehouse. An activity in a warehouse can be a simple activity (e.g., direct picking of goods) or a complex activity (e.g., picking, packing, oiling, dispatching). The completion of any activity consists of multiple steps. For example, a picking step consists of moving a resource to a source bin, scanning the source bin, picking the product, placing the product in a resource, and moving to the next location. Each of these work steps can be done in a fixed or variable amount of time. The time taken by the resource to move to the source bin is fixed, but the time taken to pick the products from the bin depends on the weight of the product. For each labor activity, the following time parameters can be captured:

- **Normal time**
  This is the normal time required to perform a work activity (e.g., picking and packing) under standard operating conditions and methods.
- **Standard time or adjusted planned duration**
  Standard time is the actual time required to execute an activity in the warehouse. It can also be adjusted with allowances (e.g., labor fatigue, equipment breakdown, etc.) and is calculated by multiplying normal time by a personal fatigue and delay factor and adding the related allowance.

The planned duration for completing an activity is updated in the planned workload, and an engineered labor standards document is created. When the activity is completed, the adjusted planned duration is updated in the executed workload, and the document is confirmed. The system uses the standard time to calculate the adjusted planned duration in the warehouse.

The settings to define engineered labor standards can be accessed via IMG path **SCM Extended Warehouse Management • Extended Warehouse Management • Labor Management • Determine Engineered Labor Standards**. The nodes display the settings that need to be defined on the left-hand side, as shown in Figure 19.19.

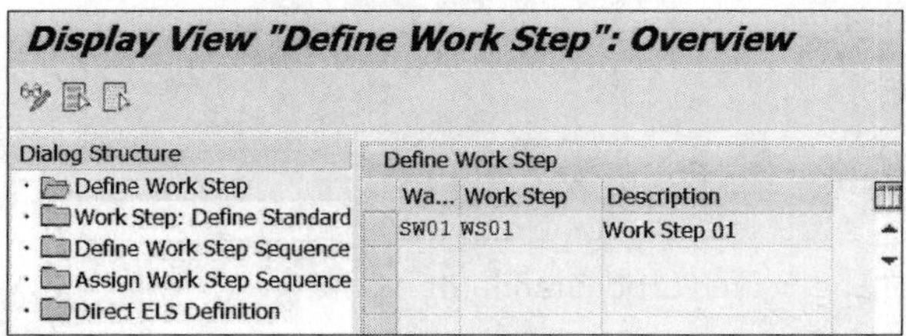

Figure 19.19 Defining Work Steps for Engineered Labor Standards

The following customization settings are required to define engineered labor standards in embedded EWM:

- **Define Work Step**
  This node is used to define a standard work step for which the standard time is calculated.
- **Work Step: Define Standard Time**
  This node is used to define the formula and conditions used to calculate standard time for a work step. As shown in Figure 19.20, you can assign a constant work execution time or a formula for each work step defined for engineered labor standards. If a formula is assigned to the work step, it can be displayed and edited by selecting the line and clicking on the button at the right-hand side of the table. If a condition is assigned to the work step, it can be displayed and edited by selecting the line and clicking on the button at the right-hand side of the table. The work steps required for calculation of time for an activity must be activated.

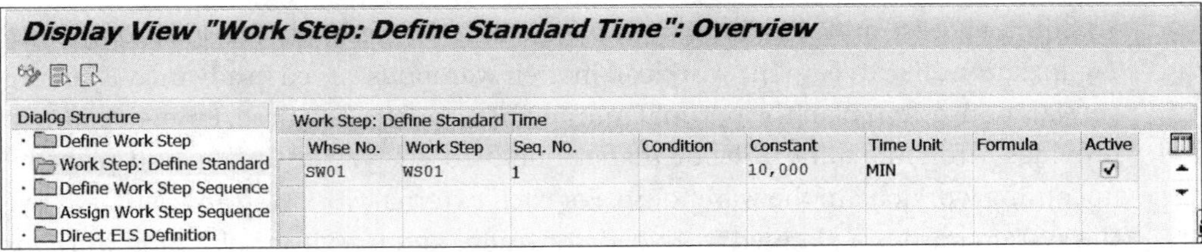

Display View "Work Step: Define Standard Time": Overview

Dialog Structure
- Define Work Step
- Work Step: Define Standard
- Define Work Step Sequence
- Assign Work Step Sequence
- Direct ELS Definition

Work Step: Define Standard Time

Whse No.	Work Step	Seq. No.	Condition	Constant	Time Unit	Formula	Active
SW01	WS01	1		10,000	MIN		✓

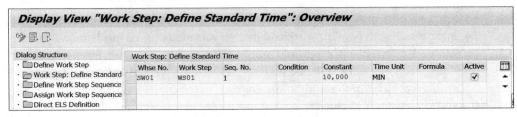

Figure 19.20 Defining Standard Times for Work Steps

- **Assign Work Step Sequence**
  After the work steps are defined, they can be put in a sequence. The planned time for an engineered labor standards activity is the sum of the duration of all the work steps that are part of a work step sequence assigned to the combination of warehouse number, external process step, activity area, and object type, as shown in Figure 19.21.

Display View "Assign Work Step Sequence": Overview

Dialog Structure
- Define Work Step
- Work Step: Define Standard
- Define Work Step Sequence
- Assign Work Step Sequence

Assign Work Step Sequence

Whse No.	Step	Acty Area	Obj.-Typ	Seq. No.	WrkStpSeq.	Active
SW01	INVE	PIAR	I Phys...	1	WS01	☐
SW01	INVE	PIAR	I Phys...	2	0001	✓

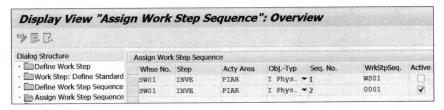

Figure 19.21 Defining and Assigning the Work Step Sequence to the Activity Area

Alternatively, as shown in Figure 19.22, a **Direct ELS Definition** can be made in labor management, which consists of only one external process step and work step. In this case, after the definition is completed and saved, both the work step and work step sequence are created automatically in embedded EWM.

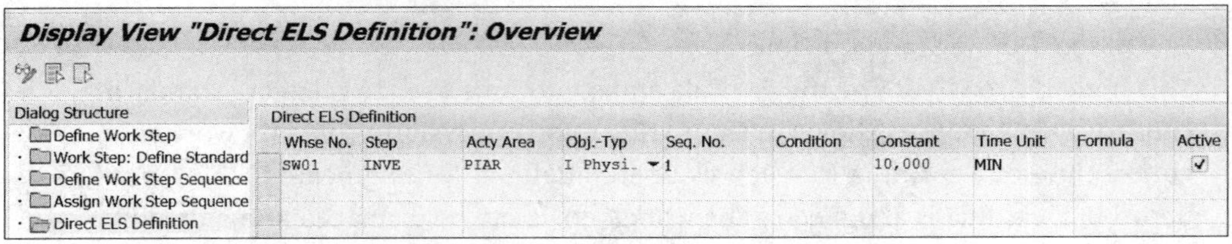

Display View "Direct ELS Definition": Overview

Dialog Structure
- Define Work Step
- Work Step: Define Standard
- Define Work Step Sequence
- Assign Work Step Sequence
- Direct ELS Definition

Direct ELS Definition

Whse No.	Step	Acty Area	Obj.-Typ	Seq. No.	Condition	Constant	Time Unit	Formula	Active
SW01	INVE	PIAR	I Physi...	1		10,000	MIN		☑

Figure 19.22 Direct ELS Definition

19.4 Planning in Labor Management

To eliminate last-minute planning and execution of warehouse workload, mature organizations like to plan the workload in their warehouses well in advance. By doing so, warehouses can plan the optimal number of resources required. Embedded EWM provides a functionality in labor management to analyze, estimate, and plan the upcoming workload in the warehouse. For each external work step and activity area, the system creates a planned workload document and uses it for planning work for warehouse workers. Each task in a warehouse is created with a fixed scope, represented by a warehouse order. Based on the planned workload document, you can make decisions such as the number of warehouse workers to allocate to an activity area at a certain time of the day.

This process requires setting up workload planning by assigning a planning activity area to a storage type, section, or work center, as shown in Figure 19.23, and then calculating workload for these planning activity areas via IMG path **SCM Extended Warehouse Management • Extended Warehouse Management • Labor Management • Assign Planning Activity Areas**.

Display View "Assign Planning Activity Area to Storage Type": Overview

Dialog Structure
- Assign Planning Activity Are
- Assign Planning Activity Are
- Assign Planning Activity Are

Assign Planning Activity Area to Storag...

Wa...	Sto...	Plan Act.Area
SW01	0081	0081
SW01	0082	0082

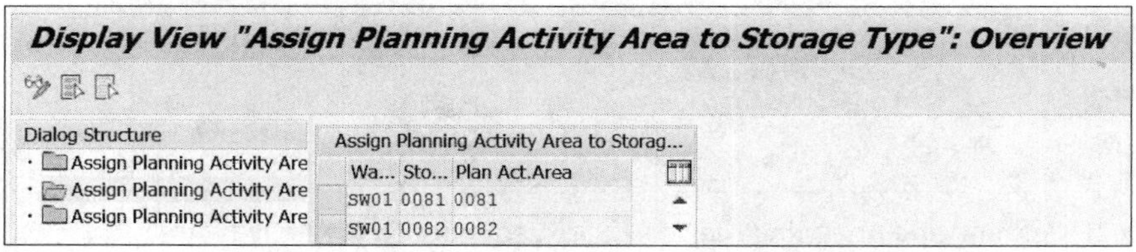

Figure 19.23 Assigning the Planning Activity Area to the Storage Type

The workloads assigned to a warehouse worker using a warehouse order can be planned and simulated before the warehouse order can be assigned to the worker for execution. This is achieved using the different processes explained in the following sections.

19.4.1 Preprocessing

Preprocessing is done if you need an overview of the workload in the warehouse before the actual warehouse tasks and warehouse orders are created. You can execute preprocessing for the following documents in embedded EWM:

- Inbound deliveries
- Outbound deliveries
- Physical inventory documents for cycle counting, only if scheduled and thus relevant for planning

The following settings are required to set up preprocessing in embedded EWM:

1. Assign the document types relevant for preprocessing to a document category and date/time type via IMG path **SCM Extended Warehouse Management • Extended Warehouse Management • Labor Management • Define Delivery Date/Time for Preprocessing**, as shown in Figure 19.24. The date/time types specified here are planned dates/times and not actual date/time types. If you fail to define a date/time, the system always uses the planned delivery date/time for the time calculation.

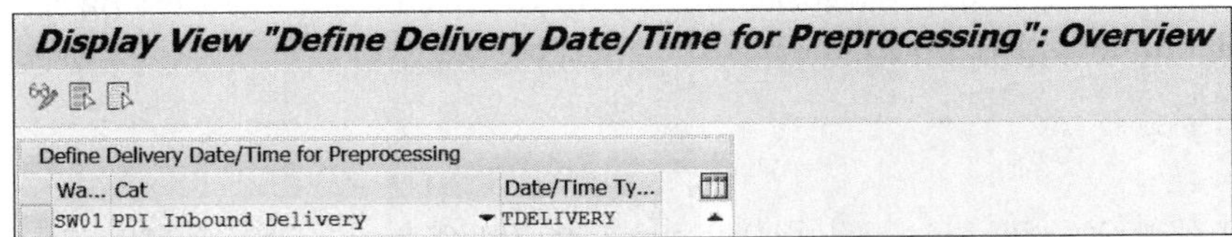

Figure 19.24 Delivery Type for Preprocessing Settings

2. Define preprocessing header settings, as shown in Figure 19.25, via IMG path **SCM Extended Warehouse Management • Extended Warehouse Management • Labor Management • Set Preprocessing**. You can use the activity area, warehouse process type, or both to determine the relevance of a delivery line item for preprocessing.

Select the preprocessing header, and define the item-level details by selecting **Preprocessing**. The duration for a preprocessing item is the duration of the external process step, which can be changed in this setting.

You can also assign a **Percentage** and a **Condition** to a preprocessing item. The percentage designates the percent of deliveries that have already been created in the system. For the missing percentage, the system creates a preprocessing workload for each delivery item's activity area and external process step. The condition is evaluated by the system to determine if the delivery item is relevant for preprocessing by the system.

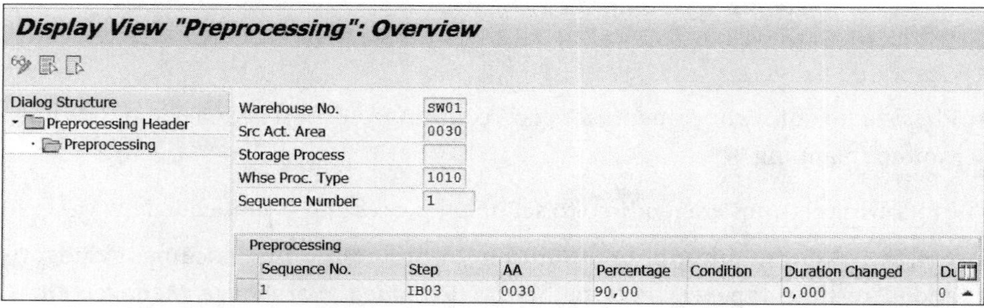

Figure 19.25 Setting Preprocessing for the External Process Step

To execute preprocessing, navigate to **SAP Easy Access** path **Logistics • SCM Extended Warehouse Management • Extended Warehouse Management • Labor Management • Planning • Planning and Simulation**, and select the **Use Preprocessing** checkbox in the **Advanced Search** option of the transaction screen. The results of preprocessing are used for planning purposes only and have no effect on execution.

> **Note**
>
> The Plan Workload app allows you to plan the workload for warehouse workers for an activity area so that workers know what work to perform in a specific quantity and time.

19.4.2 Creating a Planned Workload

Planned workload data can be used in planning and simulation to estimate the work required to be done in an activity area by a processor. The data record for the planned workload contains information about the location of the work, the type, quantity, duration, and capacity. The planned workload document also contains a link to the reference object document for which the planned workload document is created, such as warehouse order, physical inventory document, and so on.

As shown in Figure 19.26, planned workload records can be generated via **SAP Easy Access** path **Logistics • SCM Extended Warehouse Management • Extended Warehouse Management • Labor Management • Planning • Planning and Simulation** or via Transaction /SCWM/PL. You can select the planned workload based on the external process step or activity area or by using advanced search options. After the results for planning are displayed, the formula applicable for the planned workload can be changed. To trigger the planning for the workload, click on **Planning**.

The data contained in the planned workload document includes the activity area, activity (external process step), planned duration calculated using engineered labor standards, planned end date, and so on. After the warehouse tasks are confirmed for the planned work, the system forwards the actual duration to the executed workload and deletes the planned workload.

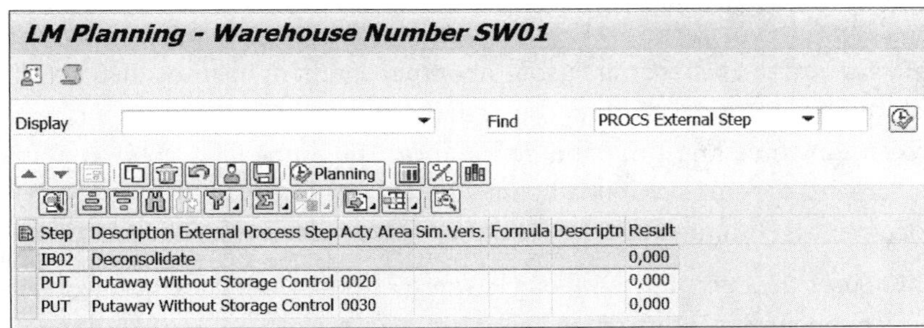

Figure 19.26 Generating the Planned Workload in Labor Management

Note

The following SAP Fiori apps are available for workload maintenance and planning:

- **Load Workload Plan**
  This app allows you to load the workload plan for warehouse workers in the system.
- **Maintain Processor Work Schedule**
  This app allows you to maintain the work schedule for processors for a specific time frame.

19.4.3 Simulation of Planned Workload

Simulation is used to determine how parameter changes in planning parameters (e.g., changes in the number of processors) can affect the planned workload. The result displayed using simulation by the system isn't saved in tables and is discarded by the system as soon as the transaction screen is refreshed. For automatic planning, the system automatically calculates the new result for the planning formula.

The parameters that can be changed to perform workload simulation are as follow:

- Changes in calculated measurement services
- Modifications to the number of processors
- Assignment of a new formula or modification to an existing formula for calculation of planned workload

To execute simulation in the warehouse, navigate to Transaction /SCWM/PL. Select the required process step, make the required changes, and click on [icon].

19.5 Execution in Labor Management

Execution information can be recorded using labor management in embedded EWM. Execution information includes data such as actual duration of a labor task, indirect labor task execution time, and time and attendance. The embedded EWM system automatically creates executed workload data when a warehouse order or physical inventory document is completed.

Embedded EWM uses the executed workload to represent the work done by a worker in the warehouse. It contains information about the time, quantity of work done, and the processor that completed the work. Using an executed workload, the efficiency and utilization of individual employees, groups, or shifts can be calculated and displayed.

If an internal process step for a warehouse task has been activated for labor management, then it becomes mandatory to enter the processor and processing time while confirming the warehouse order for that warehouse task. Let's walk through an example of a putaway warehouse task confirmation, as shown in Figure 19.27. The putaway process step is activated for labor management, so a processor must be assigned to the warehouse order in embedded EWM during warehouse order confirmation. After the processor starts processing the warehouse order in the foreground, click the **Start WO** button to input the start date and time. The **Confirm. Date** is entered in the warehouse order header as soon as the order is confirmed.

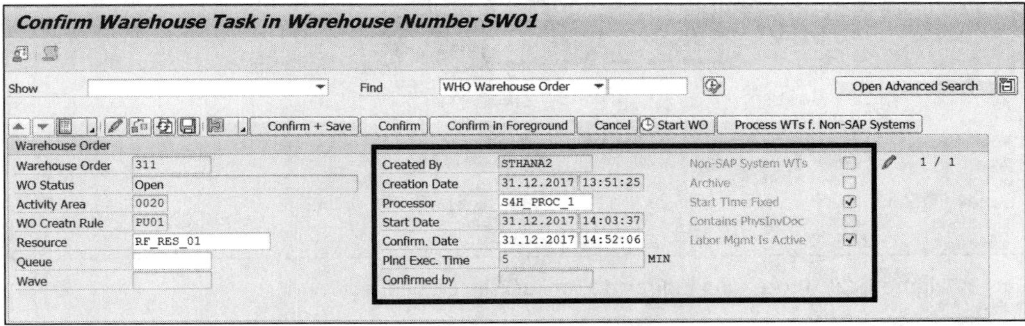

Figure 19.27 Confirming the Active Warehouse Order in Labor Management

Embedded EWM creates the executed workload automatically when a labor-management-relevant document is completed. Some of the documents for which executed workload can be created include a warehouse order, VAS, indirect labor tasks, and so on.

The executed workload can be changed from the embedded EWM warehouse monitor via Transaction /SCWM/MON. Choose the **Labor Management • Executed Workload** node, and select the **Change Executed Workload** and **Mass Change Executed Workload** methods.

For indirect labor tasks, execution time can be added manually or recorded by the system when the indirect labor task is confirmed. When an indirect labor task is completed, the executed workload is created by embedded EWM. It can be monitored using the embedded EWM warehouse monitor, and its data can be used during creation of employee performance documents. The start and end of the indirect labor task can be recorded using radio frequency devices or using Transaction /SCWM/ILT, as shown in Figure 19.28. In the transaction screen, the processor can click on the **Set Start Time** button when starting the task and on **Set End Time** when ending. If any exception occurs while completing the indirect labor task, it can be captured by the processor using an exception code.

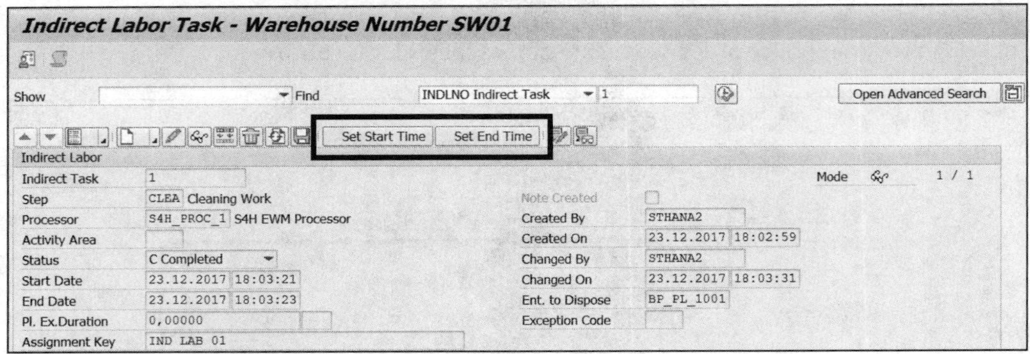

Figure 19.28 Processing Indirect Labor Tasks in Embedded EWM

19.6 Employee Performance

Employee performance evaluation and analysis is an important aspect of any warehouse's operations. Using embedded EWM, you can measure an employee's performance by comparing the executed workload with the expected duration of activities to be performed by a processor. In this section, we'll review the creation and calculation of employee performance using performance documents.

Embedded EWM uses performance documents to calculate, save, and forward performance data to a connected HR system for bonus payout calculation. A performance document contains the planned and actual execution duration of the assigned executed workload by a processor; this information is used to determine the efficiency and utilization of an employee. The performance document can be created in embedded EWM via **SAP Easy Access** path **Logistics • SCM Extended Warehouse Management • Extended Warehouse Management • Labor Management • Employee Performance • Employee Performance Overview**. A performance document is created for a valid embedded EWM processor, representing a warehouse employee. The processor's advanced search options include fields such as **Processor**, **Processor Group**, **Team Lead**, **Processor Number**, and **User Name**.

> **Tip**
>
> To create a performance document for a processor and transfer it to an HR system, it's important to assign a supply chain unit and HR business system to the processor master data.

A performance document is created by selecting the processor for which the performance document is to be created and clicking the **Create Performance Document** button. In the **EWL** field, the start and end time of the executed workload are used to create the performance document. In addition to creating the performance document, you can also add multiple executed workload items performed by the processor over a period of time to the processor document.

The performance amount to be given to the processor for the executed workload can be calculated using the **Calculate Performance Document** button.

The status of the performance document can be changed or displayed in the performance overview screen. You can delete performance documents with statuses **Created**, **For Approval**, or **Approved**. A performance document can undergo various status changes based on the actions carried out on the performance document.

If the performance document has the **Created** status, then it can be set to the **For Approval** status using the **For Approval** button if it's sent for approval to an HR person and again reversed back to **Created**. If the status of the document is **For Approval**, it can be changed by an HR person to **Approved** using the **Approved** button, and it can be reverted to **For Approval** as well. If the performance document is **Approved**, it can be sent to the HR system either manually using the **Transferred Manually** button or using a report, and it can't be canceled. If the document has been transferred, it can be set to the **Deleted** status using the **To Delete** button and can be reverted to the **Transferred** status.

The performance document can be transferred to a connected HR system. These documents are used by companies to pay out performance-based bonuses. A performance document is transferred to the HR system as an external wage component of an employee. It can be transferred via **SAP Easy Access** path **Logistics • SCM Extended Warehouse Management • Extended Warehouse Management • Labor Management • Employee Performance • Send Performance Document to HR**, as shown in Figure 19.29. Multiple search criteria are used for selecting the performance document to be sent to the HR system for bonus payout. The criteria can either be employee-specific data (e.g., processor, processor group) or team lead or performance-document-specific data (e.g., performance document number, document validity date, HR system, and personnel number).

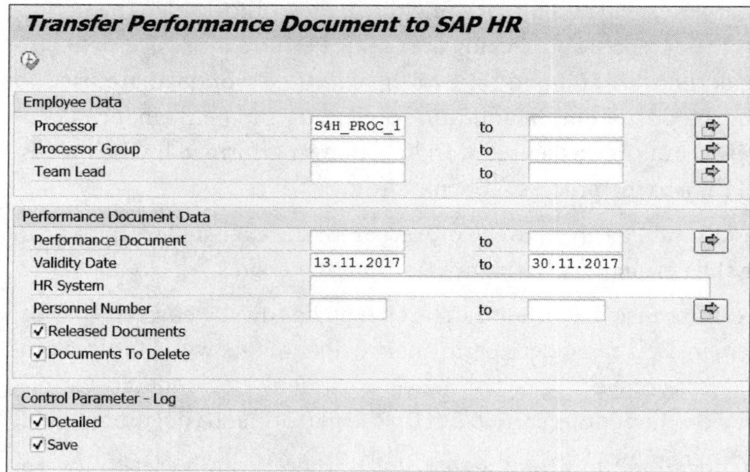

Figure 19.29 Report to Send Processor Performance Document to HR System

> **Note**
>
> The Maintain Performance Documents app allows you to create and maintain performance documents, as well as interface the performance data to the HR system for performance-based payout.

19.7 Summary

This chapter introduced the concept of labor management. We discussed how to plan labor times and resources in the warehouse by classifying, measuring, planning, and simulating warehouse activities. We also discussed how to compare and evaluate the performance of your warehouse employees based on engineered labor standards. You can evaluate performance on an individual level or based on teams or shifts. You should now understand the key concepts in labor management and be able to configure labor management in your warehouse. In the next chapter, we will cover value-added services.

Chapter 20
Value-Added Services

When organizations perform extra services for products received into or sent from the warehouse, these are called value-added services. These services, such as oiling, cleaning, fuming, and the like, enrich the value of a product. In this chapter, we'll discuss value-added services in embedded EWM in detail.

Value-added services (VAS) are services that organizations carry out a on the products they receive into or issue from a warehouse. Some examples of VAS include kitting, labeling, and packaging. These activities are carried out by sending the product to special work centers known as VAS work centers. VAS activities are carried out in the VAS work center, and consumption of auxiliary packing material (e.g., shrink wrap) used for carrying out VAS activities can be monitored in the warehouse. VAS processes can be carried out during inbound, outbound, or internal warehouse processes in embedded EWM.

Section 20.1 introduces VAS in embedded EWM, and Section 20.2 briefly discusses the structure and execution of a VAS order. Section 20.3 introduces the settings required to execute VAS activities in the warehouse. Section 20.4 introduces the process variants with which a VAS order can be created and executed while carrying out goods receipt, goods issue, and internal warehouse orders. Section 20.5 introduces the concept of auxiliary materials used to carry out VAS activities in a VAS work center. Finally, Section 20.6 covers printing VAS documents in embedded EWM.

20.1 What Are Value-Added Services?

Consider a situation in which a company wants to pack and label its goods in a customer-specified manner before shipping to prevent being fined by the customer for a compliance issue. In such a situation, in which some added work/service is to be done with a product before it's moved into or out of the warehouse, VAS are carried out in embedded EWM. Using a VAS process in embedded EWM enables organizations to document VAS activities executed on products.

A VAS order is carried out in the VAS work center where the services are carried out. The order is created in the warehouse request document in embedded EWM. You can use VAS execution in the work center to monitor the time required to carry out VAS activities, which can be billed to the client. In this section, we'll explain the structure of a VAS order created in embedded EWM and how it's processed in the VAS work center.

In Section 20.1.1, we'll explain the business context in which VAS can be used in real-world scenarios. In Section 20.1.2, we'll explain the processes carried out in the system as well as VAS-related documents with which value-added activities are carried out on inbound, internal, and outbound processes in embedded EWM and decentralized EWM.

20.1.1 Business Process

American company Alpha Medicals receives an order from one of its customers based in Mexico. The order sent by the customer requires Alpha Medicals to provide the products not only packed into appropriate packaging but also sterilized before being packed into cases for delivery. Stock that will be delivered to the customer is to be picked from the source bins of the supplying warehouse by the warehouse workers, sterilized at dedicated work centers, and packed in the desired packaging material to create finished product cases. To ensure that the warehouse worker applies the additional sterilization on the products before packing them, Alpha Medicals has implemented VAS so that embedded EWM proposes a process to the warehouse worker before packing the products. This ensures that required VAS can be applied on the products before packing the products in cases. The following steps are involved in applying these value services on the products in the warehouse involving VAS (Figure 20.1):

1. The warehouse receives a warehouse request document for outbound delivery to supply the requested products to the customer after performing the required VAS.
2. The warehouse-request-related warehouse task is assigned to the warehouse worker so that the worker can pick, pack, and stage the stock at the staging bay.
3. The system provides the warehouse worker with a task to move the products to the VAS work center based on the VAS setup for the products, so that the final of the VAS can be applied to the products.

4. The warehouse worker picks the products, carries them to the VAS work center, and applies the VAS.
5. After the products have been packed into shipping handling units (HUs) they are moved to the staging area. The packed goods pallets are then loaded onto the transportation units (TUs) and goods issued out of the warehouse.

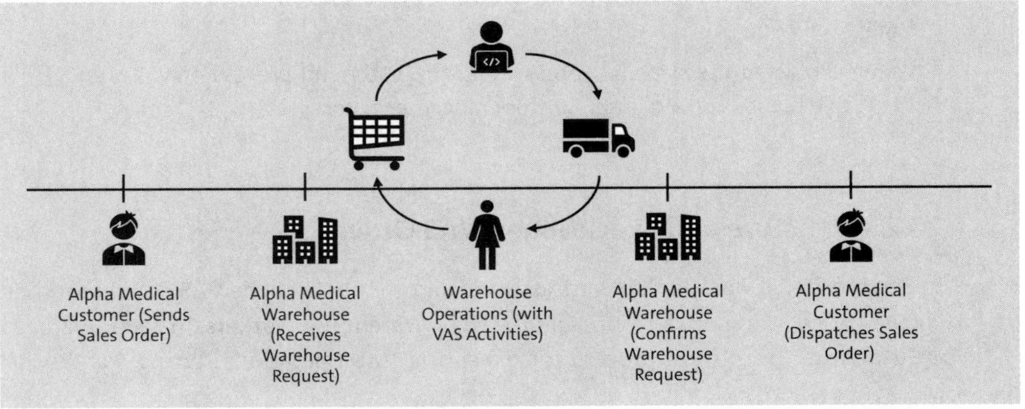

Figure 20.1 Business Flow in Value-Added Services Process

20.1.2 System Process

The system flow, including the documents data required, to execute VAS for outbound processing in embedded EWM and decentralized EWM is as follows:

1. An outbound delivery order is created in embedded EWM that contains information about the products to be delivered to the external customer by Alpha Medicals.
2. As soon as the outbound delivery order is created in embedded EWM in the previous step, based on the VAS master data set up in the system, a VAS order is also created per line item of the outbound delivery order, which contains the data about the VAS that will be done on the products in the VAS work center.
3. The outbound delivery order items in the previous step have an attached VAS order, so the picking warehouse task created for the warehouse worker directs the warehouse worker to carry the product to the VAS work center.
4. The warehouse workers are allocated the warehouse orders to pick the products for the outbound delivery order and deliver them to the VAS work center.

20

5. A warehouse worker performs VAS activities on warehouse products based on the VAS order, which contains information about the products and the activities to be performed on them. These treated products are then packed in cases, placed on pallets, and sent over to the staging area so that they can be sent out to the customers on TUs.

Note

We've explained the system process using the outbound process only. It's equally applicable to inbound and internal stock movement processes.

20.2 Structure and Execution of VAS Orders

In Section 20.2.1, we'll explain various parts and elements of the VAS document that shows critical warehouse-related data used by warehouse workers. In Section 20.2.2, we'll discuss the system process for executing VAS operations during warehouse stock movements.

20.2.1 Structure of a VAS Order

The VAS order in embedded EWM can be created automatically when the warehouse request is created, or it can be created manually by the user based on the settings for VAS relevance, which will be covered in Section 20.3. The VAS order created for a warehouse request can be accessed via **SAP Easy Access** path **Logistics • SCM Extended Warehouse Management • Extended Warehouse Management • Work Scheduling • Value Added Services**. From this path, you can select the required transaction to view VAS orders created for the goods receipt process, goods issue process, kitting, or internal warehouse processes.

As shown in Figure 20.2, a VAS order has three main sections. The **Header Data** section contains header-level information for the VAS order, such as the VAS order number, overall processing status, warehouse request number and item, and so on. The next section displays the list of VAS activities that are to be carried out in the created VAS order and contains information derived from packaging specifications, such as product, process step, and so on. In our example, you can see VAS activities for oiling and packaging that are to be carried out for the warehouse request item in the **Activities** tab.

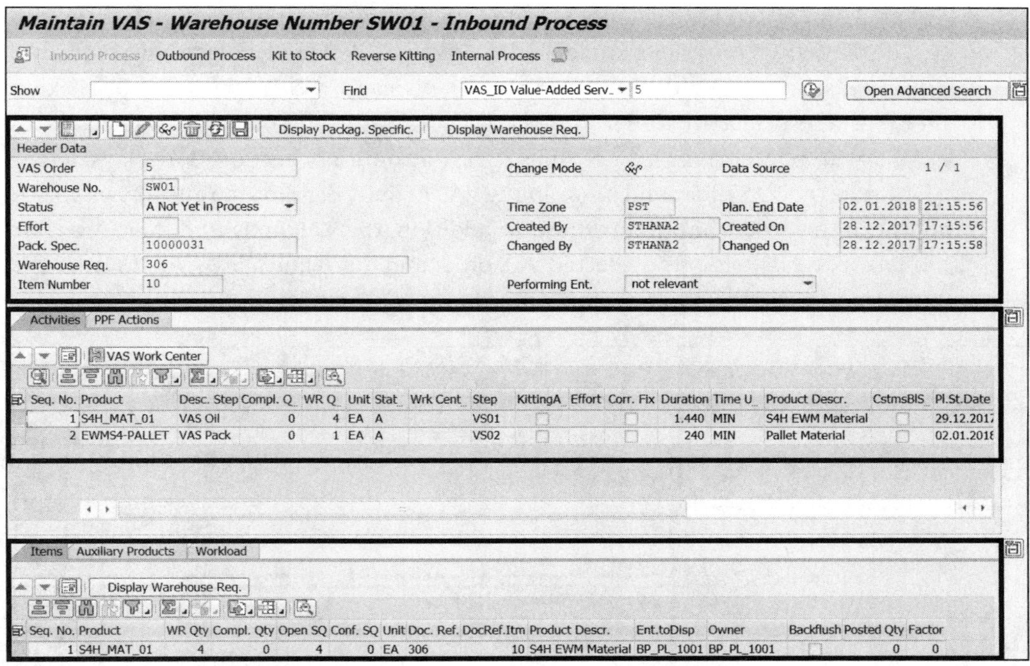

Figure 20.2 VAS Order in Embedded EWM

The last section on the transaction screen displays detailed data for the selected VAS activity. The **Items** tab displays the warehouse request item for which the VAS activity is to be carried out. The data in the **Auxiliary Products** tab is used to show the auxiliary products required to carry out the VAS activity for the warehouse request item. If labor management is active for the warehouse, and an external step is activated for labor management, then the data for workload execution for the processor is shown in the **Workload** tab.

20.2.2 Execution of a VAS Order in a VAS Work Center

Figure 20.3 shows a VAS work center screen, which contains four main sections. The top-left section ❶ contains the **Section/Bin/HU/Item** hierarchy of the VAS work center and the delivery product against which the VAS order is created. The top-right section ❷ contains various tabs and fields that allow you to perform HU processing and VAS activities at the VAS header, item, and activity levels. In the bottom-left section

❸, you'll find information about the **VAS/Activity/Item** order hierarchy. Here the system displays the VAS order number and VAS activity details in a hierarchical manner. You can display a VAS order by clicking on , display a VAS order activity by clicking on , and display a VAS order product by clicking on . You also can select a VAS auxiliary item by clicking on . Finally, the bottom-right section ❹ displays details of the selected VAS order and items in the **VAS Activity & Items** tab and allows you to complete the orders and items there. In addition, the **VAS Activity & Aux. Products** tab ❹ displays details of the selected VAS order and items and allows you to enter the quantity of auxiliary materials consumed in the VAS activity.

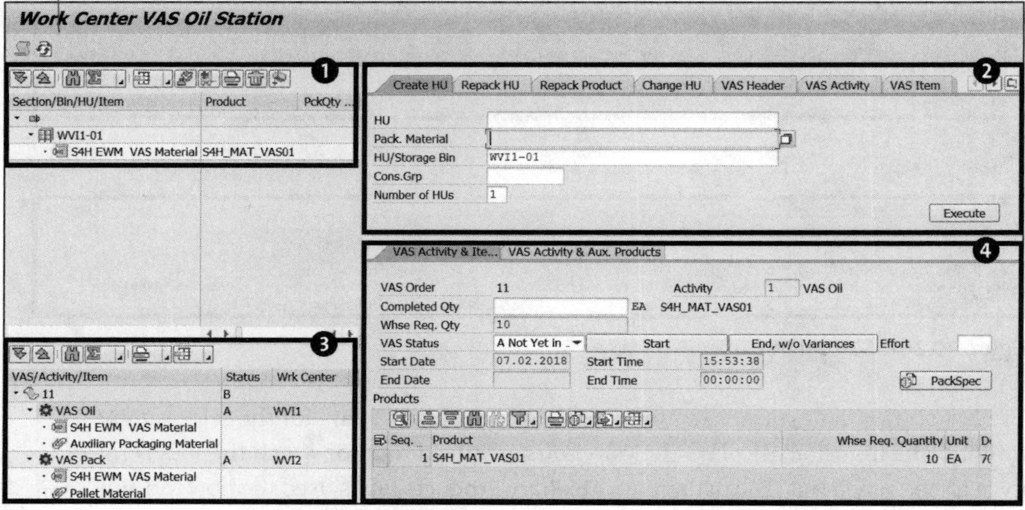

Figure 20.3 VAS Work Center Sections

After the delivery product is physically moved to the work center, you can open the VAS order in the VAS work center by using Transaction /SCWM/VASEXEC and using the VAS order number as a search criterion. If required, the warehouse worker can be handed the VAS order activity sheet, which can be printed by clicking on the **VAS Order** button. This sheet shows the details of the VAS order and its activities.

A work center worker can confirm the complete VAS order or individual VAS activities of the VAS order with or without variance. As the VAS activities of the VAS order are completed, they're confirmed by the warehouse worker in embedded EWM, as shown in Figure 20.4. Clicking on **Start** sets the VAS activity and header status to **B In Process**. If the VAS activity is completed without quantity variation, then clicking on

End, w/o Variances sets the VAS activity status to **C Completed-without Quantity Deviations**. If the VAS activity is completed with quantity variation, then entering the partially completed quantity in the **Completed Qty** field and clicking on **Save** sets the VAS activity status to **D Completed-with Quantity Deviations**. After all the activities of the VAS order are completed, the VAS order header status is changed to **Completed**.

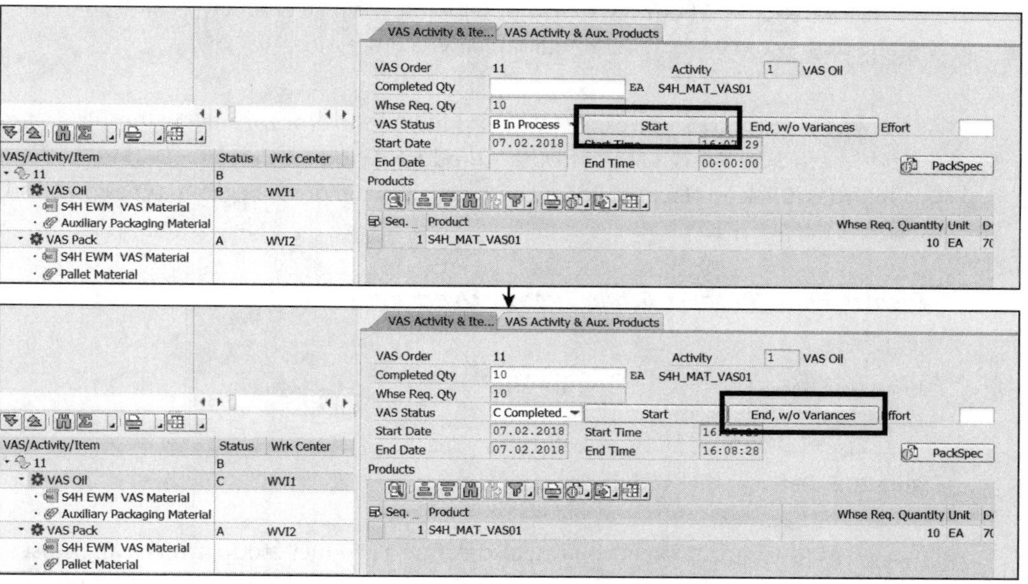

Figure 20.4 Executing the VAS Order Activity in the VAS Work Center

20

20.3 Configuring VAS

In this section, we'll explain the key configurations required for setting up the VAS process in embedded EWM. We'll also explain in detail how each configuration affects VAS processes.

20.3.1 Product Group Type and Product Group

Product Group Type and **Product Group** are configuration entries used across multiple processes in embedded EWM. These entries are used to group products that exhibit similar properties and must undergo similar processes, such as VAS or cross-docking in a warehouse.

> **Example**
>
> Suppose an organization has a variety of goods, such as jackhammers, screwdrivers, and so on, that require the added processes of oiling/packing and labeling to be done in the warehouse. They're assigned a common product group type and product group so they can be routed through similar VAS processing.

As shown in Figure 20.5, you can create a product group type for such materials under the IMG path **SCM Basis • Master Data • Product • Product Groups • Define Product Group Types**. Click on **New Entries** in the menu, add the product group type code, and save.

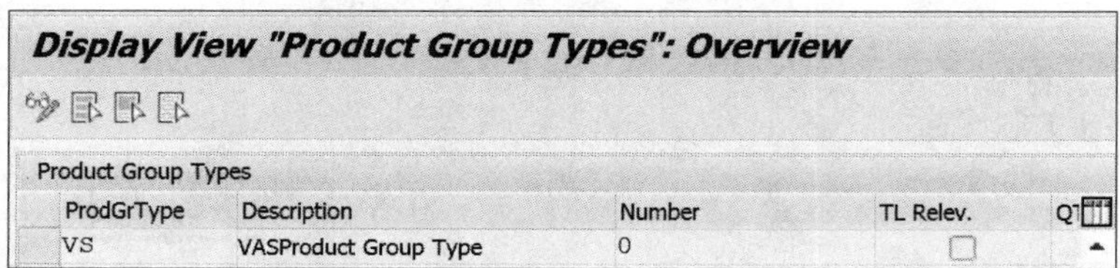

Figure 20.5 Defining the Product Group Type

For each product group type, you can also define a product group, which can be used to subdivide the product group type further to activate a warehouse product for special warehouse activities, such as VAS.

As shown in Figure 20.6, you create a product group for products in embedded EWM by navigating to IMG path **SCM Basis • Master Data • Product • Product Groups • Define Product Group.** Click on **New Entries**, add the **Product Group**, and save.

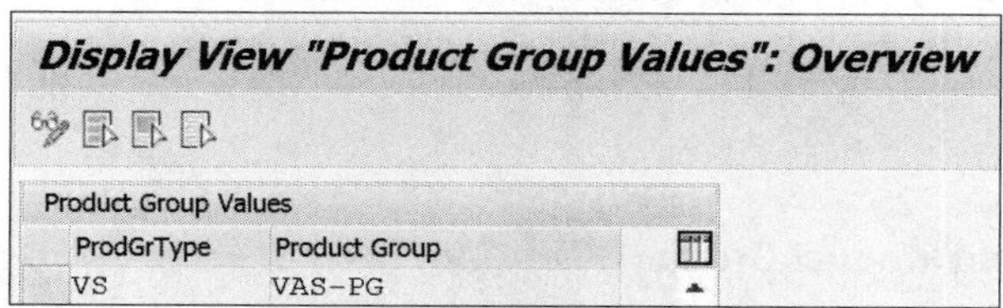

Figure 20.6 Defining the Product Group

To make a product relevant for the VAS process in embedded EWM, assign the product group type and product group to the product master in the **Properties 2** tab using Transaction /SAPAPO/MAT1, as shown in Figure 20.7.

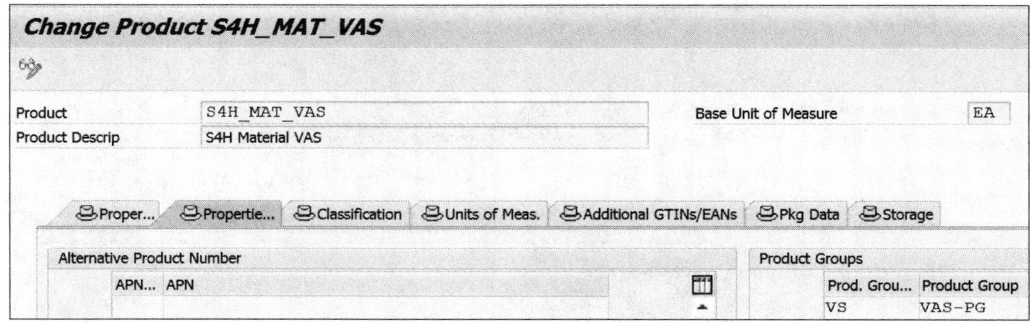

Figure 20.7 Maintaining the SAP Advanced Planning and Optimization Product Master for VAS Relevancy

20.3.2 Number Range for VAS Order

To enable the creation of a VAS order automatically or manually, you must first define a number range for VAS orders via IMG path **SCM Extended Warehouse Management • Extended Warehouse Management • Cross-Process Settings • Value-Added Services (VAS) • Define Number Range for VAS Order**. Provide the embedded EWM warehouse number for number range object **/SCWM/VASO**, and click on **Edit Interval** to create an internal number range for VAS orders.

20.3.3 Activate Order Management for VAS

To activate all the required order data areas, order data types, and order document management components for VAS, navigate to IMG path **Extended Warehouse Management • Cross-Process Settings • Value-Added Services (VAS) • Activate Order Management For VAS**, and click on the icon at the top of the screen.

20.3.4 Define Relevance for VAS

In this setting, set the relevance of VAS for a given document type and item type. Based on the settings defined here, the system can automate the creation of a VAS order during creation of a warehouse request. To define relevance for VAS, navigate to IMG path **SCM Extended Warehouse Management • Extended Warehouse**

Management • Cross-Process Settings • Value-Added Services (VAS) • Define Relevance for VAS, and set the control for when the system should create the VAS order for a combination of document type and item type, as shown in Figure 20.8.

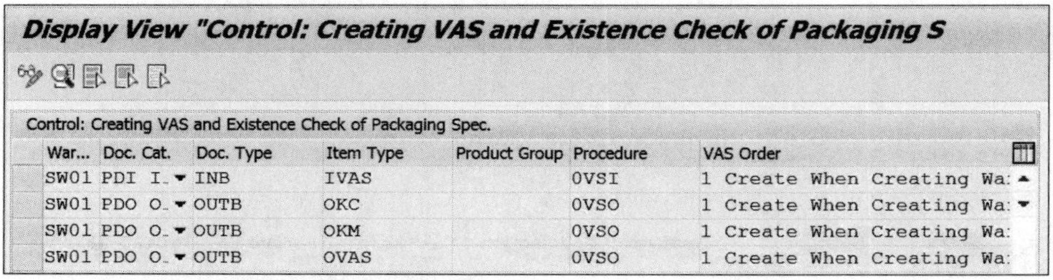

Display View "Control: Creating VAS and Existence Check of Packaging S

Control: Creating VAS and Existence Check of Packaging Spec.

War...	Doc. Cat.	Doc. Type	Item Type	Product Group	Procedure	VAS Order
SW01	PDI	I...	INB	IVAS		OVSI	1 Create When Creating Wa:
SW01	PDO	O...	OUTB	OKC		OVSO	1 Create When Creating Wa:
SW01	PDO	O...	OUTB	OKM		OVSO	1 Create When Creating Wa:
SW01	PDO	O...	OUTB	OVAS		OVSO	1 Create When Creating Wa:

Figure 20.8 Defining VAS Relevance

The following data is defined in this setting:

- **Packaging specification procedure**
  The value in the **Procedure** column contains the packaging specification determination procedure, which is used to determine the packaging specification required to generate a VAS order.
- **VAS order creation criteria**
  The **VAS Order** parameter controls in which processing step of a warehouse request a VAS order should be created. The options available for this setting are as follows:
  - **Do Not Create Automatically**
    The system should not create a VAS order automatically; it can be created manually.
  - **Create When Creating Warehouse Request/Warehouse Request Item**
    A VAS order should be created automatically with the creation of the warehouse request or when adding a new warehouse request item.
  - **Create at First Goods Receipt Posting**
    A VAS order can be created during the first goods receipt posting of a warehouse request.
- **Packaging specification existence check**
  The **PS Exist. Check** setting controls whether the existence check for the packaging specification is carried out by the system during warehouse request creation for VAS-relevant operations. There are three possible options available for this setting:

- **Do Not Conduct Existence Check**
  In this case, the system doesn't perform an existence check for the packaging specification while creating a warehouse request item.
- **Perform Existence Check (Error)**
  In this case, the system performs an existence check for the packaging specification. If it can't be found, then the system sets the warehouse request item status to **Inconsistent**. No further processing (e.g., goods receipt) can be carried out for the delivery.
- **Perform Existence Check (Warning)**
  In this case, the system performs an existence check for the VAS packaging specification. If it can't be found, then the system provides a warning message to the warehouse request. The delivery can still be processed.

- **Partner role**
  A warehouse request in embedded EWM can have multiple partners belonging to different partner roles. The **Partner Role** setting controls the partner used by embedded EWM to determine the right packaging specification for VAS.
- **Date/time type**
  The **Date/Time Type** setting controls which date/time in the SAP S/4HANA delivery item is used to determine valid packaging specifications.

20.3.5 Warehouse Number-Dependent VAS Settings

Next, enable certain settings at the warehouse level so that each embedded EWM warehouse can use individual control settings. Warehouse number-dependent VAS settings can be configured by navigating to IMG path **SCM Extended Warehouse Management • Extended Warehouse Management • Cross-Process Settings • Value-Added Services (VAS) • Warehouse Number-Dependent VAS settings**. Click on **New Entries** to add the warehouse number-dependent setting for the warehouse, as shown in Figure 20.9.

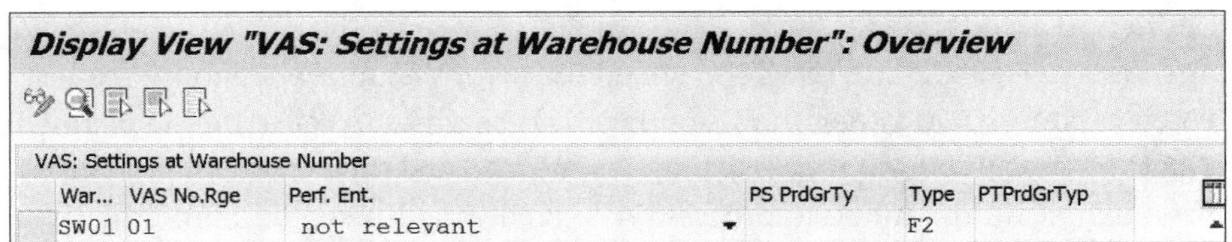

Figure 20.9 Warehouse Number-Dependent VAS Settings

The following settings are defined to set warehouse-specific VAS settings in embedded EWM:

- **VAS number range**
  VAS No.Rge is used to set the number range used for VAS order creation in the warehouse.
- **Performing entities**
  Perf. Ent. specifies which performing entities will carry out the execution of VAS activities at the level defined in the packaging specification.
- **Packaging specification product group type**
  The **PS PrdGrTy** setting is used to limit which packaging specification will be found for VAS processes and thus can be used as a filter parameter in VAS condition type OVSI for determining VAS packaging specifications.
- **VAS utility stock type**
  The **Type** setting enables you to enter the default stock type for the auxiliary product, which is used for carrying out VAS activities in the warehouse and for which you can post consumption postings based on utilization. Usually, a freely available stock type is used for consumption posting.
- **Planned time product group type**
  The **PTPrdGrTyp** setting is used to maintain the product group type, which is used to determine planned times for product VAS activities in the warehouse. To monitor the VAS orders in the warehouse monitor, check the planned start/end times of VAS steps and planned start/end times of VAS activities after goods receipt/goods issue in the warehouse.

20.3.6 Planned Times for VAS Activities

Planned times for VAS activities can be set at the delivery level or for each VAS activity. Let's go over some important settings required for setting up planned start and end times for the following VAS activities:

- **Define VAS fixed time**
  As shown in Figure 20.10, you define fixed times for VAS for a warehouse request. When creating a VAS order, the system uses these times to calculate the planned VAS start time (inbound process) and planned VAS end time (outbound process). For example, in the inbound process, VAS fixed time is used to define the time

from goods receipt to the time required to carry out the first VAS activity in the warehouse. Define VAS fixed time via IMG path **SCM Extended Warehouse Management • Extended Warehouse Management • Cross-Process Settings • Value-Added Services (VAS) • Plan Times • Define VAS Fixed Time**. Click on **New Entries**, add a combination of embedded EWM warehouse, document category, document type, product group, planned duration, unit of measure, and date/time type. Click on **Save**.

Display View "VAS Fixed Times": Overview

VAS Fixed Times

War...	Doc.Cat.	Doc. Type	Product Group	Duration	Unit	Date/Time Type
SW01	PDI Inbound D...			1	DAY	
SW01	PDO Outbound ...			0,500	DAY	

Figure 20.10 Fixed Plan Times for VAS Processes

- **Define duration of process step**

  As shown in Figure 20.11, you define a time interval for individual VAS process steps carried out for a warehouse request. When creating a VAS order, the system uses these times to calculate the planned VAS start time and planned VAS end time for each activity. They can be used later to monitor the VAS activities that are scheduled to be carried out in the warehouse monitor as well.

  The durations of process steps can be defined by navigating to IMG path **SCM Extended Warehouse Management • Extended Warehouse Management • Cross-Process Settings • Value-Added Services (VAS) • Plan Times • Define Duration of Process Steps.** Click on **New Entries**, add a combination of embedded EWM warehouse, product group, duration, and unit of measure. Save your entries.

20

Display View "VAS Duration of the Process Steps": Overview

VAS Duration of the Process Steps

War...	Step	Product Group	Duration	Unit
SW01	VS01		1	DAY
SW01	VS02		4,0	HR

Figure 20.11 VAS Duration for Process Steps

20.3.7 VAS Effort

The following steps define effort for a VAS order or activity, which can be used for reporting and information purposes while executing a VAS order:

- **Define effort for VAS order**
  As shown in Figure 20.12, you can define effort codes to capture special reasons associated with the execution of a VAS order. To set the effort for a VAS order, navigate to IMG path **SCM Extended Warehouse Management • Extended Warehouse Management • Cross-Process Settings • Value-Added Services (VAS) • Efforts • Define Effort for VAS Order**. Click on **New Entries**, enter the **Effort** code, and save.

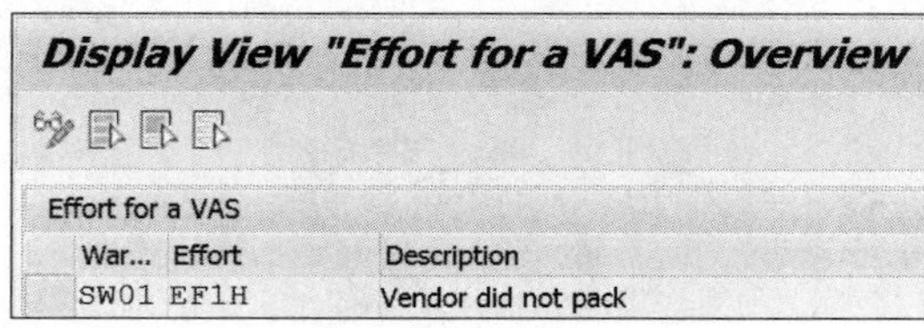

Figure 20.12 Defining VAS Effort

- **Define effort for VAS activities**
  As shown in Figure 20.13, you can define an effort code for an individual activity for a VAS order in the warehouse. A worker can specify the appropriate effort code to capture the special reasons associated with each activity of a VAS order. To set these codes, navigate to IMG path **SCM Extended Warehouse Management • Extended Warehouse Management • Cross-Process Settings • Value-Added Services (VAS) • Efforts • Define Effort for VAS Activity**. Click on **New Entries**, enter an **Effort** code, and save.

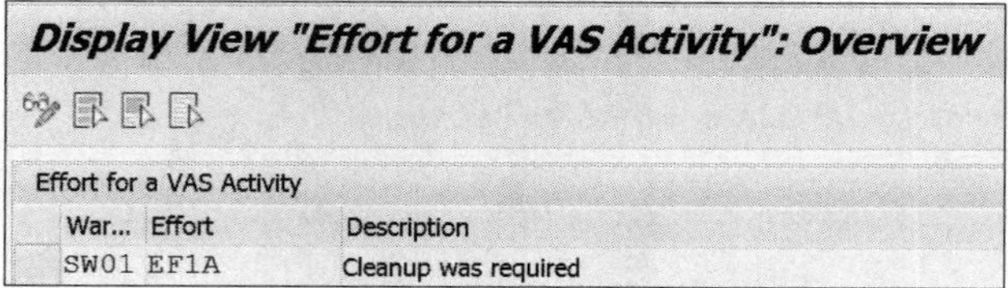

Figure 20.13 Defining Effort for a VAS Activity

20.3.8 Packaging Specification for VAS

A packaging specification is one of the most crucial master data objects used to create a VAS order in embedded EWM. The VAS activities are stored in a packaging specification that provides the activities that need to be carried out at each level of the specification and the required auxiliary products.

> **Note**
>
> For the system to create a VAS order, a valid packaging specification with condition records for determination needs to be set up in embedded EWM.

To create a packaging specification, use Transaction /SCWM/PACKSPEC, choose the VAS pack specification group, and enter the details in the individual sections in the next screen, as shown in Figure 20.14.

You can specify the activities that need to be carried out for a level of a packaging specification. When a VAS order is created, each of these levels will be adopted as activities that need to be carried out in the VAS order. Figure 20.14 shows a packaging specification for a product with one VAS step for oiling the product. In the next step, the product will be packed into a packaging material.

Assign the **External Step** in the **Warehouse** tab at each level, which maps the storage process step with the VAS activities that are to be performed for the product in the warehouse. The process step is mapped to the VAS work center where all VAS activities will be carried out.

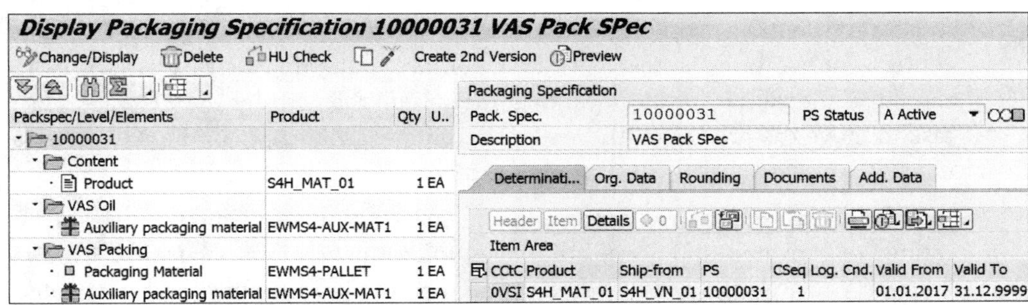

Figure 20.14 Creating the Packaging Specification for VAS

When the warehouse request is created, the VAS order is created if a valid condition record exists for the determination of packaging specifications for VAS. Depending on the business process, a condition record can be created for determination of packaging specifications for creation of the VAS order during goods receipt or goods issue or while executing kitting. Create a condition record in the **Determination** tab on the same transaction screen.

Example

In our example, the system will create a VAS order for inbound warehouse requests for which the delivery line item is S4H_MAT_01 and the ship-from party or vendor is S4H_VN_01, as maintained in the condition record for condition type 0VSI.

20.4 Process Variants for VAS

A VAS process can be used in multiple variants in embedded EWM while carrying out inbound, outbound, or internal warehouse processes. In this section, we'll review all the process variants that can be used to execute the VAS process in the warehouse.

20.4.1 VAS with Process-Oriented Storage Control

VAS can be used with process-oriented storage control, in which the HU moves across the VAS work center based on process steps defined in the storage control process. The storage control guides all the intermediate work centers through which the HU must travel, and the required VAS activities are performed at the required VAS work centers. The VAS order is created for the inbound or outbound delivery based on VAS relevance and packaging specifications. The system then creates the HU warehouse task to move the product to the VAS work center. Each activity in the VAS order is defined as a separate process step that's carried out in the VAS work center.

After completion of the VAS process, the final picking/putaway warehouse tasks are created or activated, and goods are moved to destination bins. Figure 20.15 shows how the VAS activities are performed in an inbound process with process-oriented storage control.

Tip

The storage process step for VAS should be defined as a rule-based step. The process step only becomes relevant if a valid VAS order exists for the delivery line item.

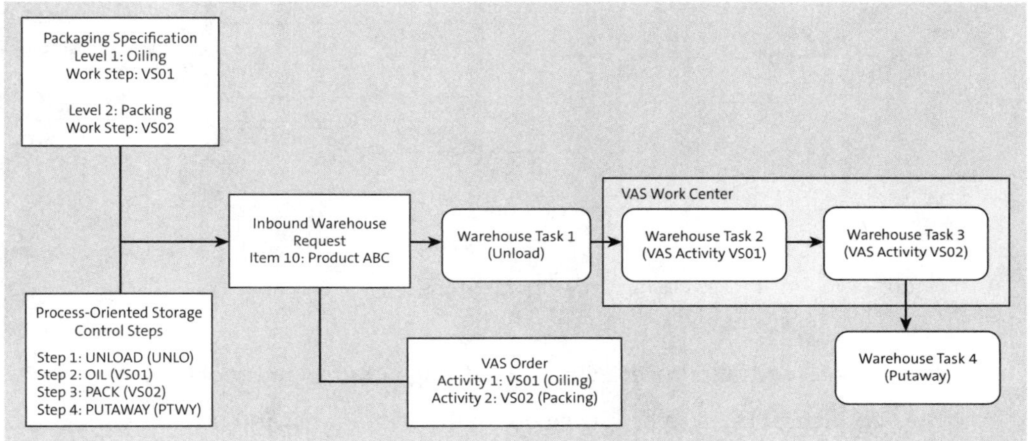

Figure 20.15 VAS Process with Process-Oriented Storage Control

20.4.2 VAS with Process Steps

The VAS process can also be performed without storage control by using the external process steps defined in the packaging specification in VAS. The destination work center is picked from the definition of the external process steps. The VAS order is created for the inbound or outbound delivery based on VAS relevance and the packaging specification. The system then creates a product warehouse task to move the product to the VAS work center as specified in the VAS order. Each activity in the VAS order is defined as a separate process step carried out in the VAS work center. The system creates a warehouse task for carrying out each of these activities.

After completion of the VAS process, the final picking/putaway warehouse tasks are created, and goods are moved to the destination storage bin. Figure 20.16 shows how the VAS activities are performed in an inbound process with process steps.

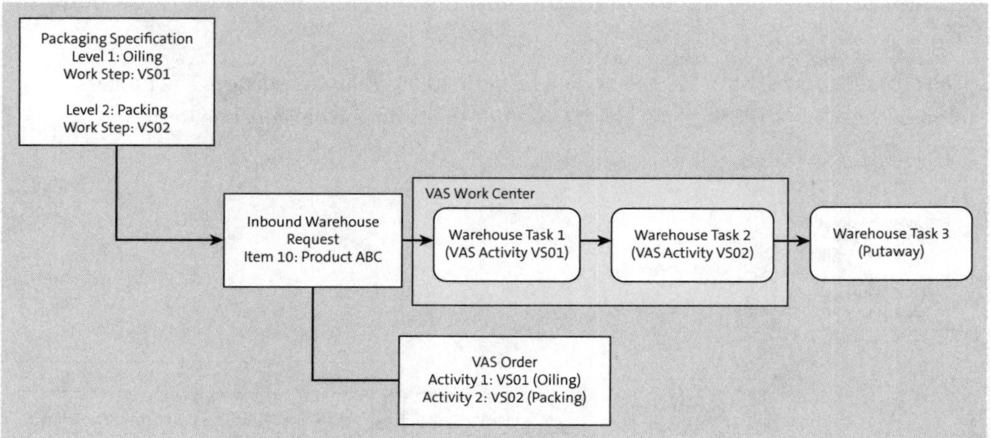

Figure 20.16 VAS Process Using Only Process Steps

20.4.3 VAS without Process-Oriented Storage Control or Process Steps

The VAS process can also be carried out in the warehouse without process-oriented storage control or process steps. In this case, the VAS order is created and printed for the warehouse operator to perform these activities in the VAS work center. When the VAS activity is completed, set the completion indicator in the VAS work center; the product is moved to the final storage bin or goods issue area. Figure 20.17 shows how the VAS activities are performed in an inbound process without process-oriented storage control or process steps.

Note

The following SAP Fiori apps are available to perform VAS operations for different warehouse processes:

- **Value Added Services (Internal)**
  This app allows you to perform VAS in a VAS work center for internal warehouse movement processes.
- **Value Added Services (Outbound)**
  This app allows you to perform VAS in a VAS work center for outbound warehouse movement processes.
- **Value Added Services (Inbound)**
  This app allows you to perform VAS in a VAS work center for inbound warehouse movement processes.

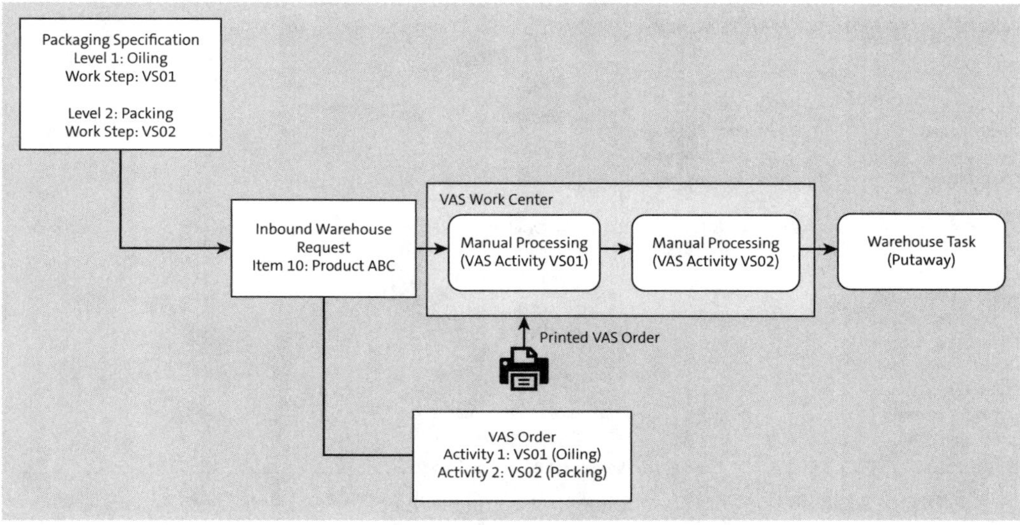

Figure 20.17 VAS Process without Process-Oriented Storage Control or Process Steps

20.5 Auxiliary Products in VAS

Warehouses use auxiliary products such as shrink-wrap, hangers, labels, and so on for carrying out VAS activities. These products are usually kept near the VAS work centers from which they're directly picked and used. If required, you can enable consumption posting of auxiliary products in the warehouse to monitor the stock of auxiliary products and refill them. For an auxiliary packaging material to be eligible for consumption posting, you must go to Transaction /SCWM/MAT1 and select the **Consumptin-Rel. VAS** checkbox on the **Whse Data** tab of the product master, as shown in Figure 20.18.

Auxiliary packaging material is kept in a VAS work center bin from which the material is picked and consumed. Thus, these bins are also called *consumption bins* for VAS work centers. This separation enables you to ensure that enough stock of auxiliary material is available for utilization in these consumption bins.

As shown in Figure 20.19, you can assign a source bin for storing auxiliary packaging material by navigating to **SAP Easy Access** path **Logistics • SCM Extended Warehouse Management • Extended Warehouse Management • Master Data • Assign Storage Bin for VAS Consumption Posting**. Click on **New Entries**, and add a VAS consumption bin for the combination of embedded EWM warehouse and VAS work center.

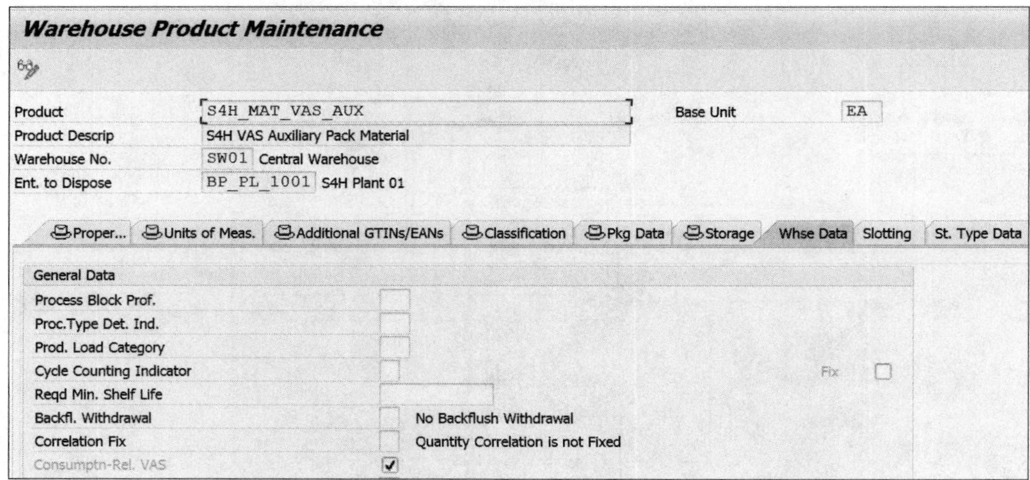

Figure 20.18 Activating Warehouse Packaging Products for VAS Relevancy

Display View "Assign Storage Bins for VAS Consumption Posting": Overvi

Assign Storage Bins for VAS Consumption Posting

War...	Work Cntr.	Storage Bin
SW01	WVI1	IVAS-01
SW01	WVI2	IVAS-01

Figure 20.19 Assigning VAS Consumption Bins to a VAS Work Center

The auxiliary packaging material is assigned at the required level in the packaging specification created for the VAS order. The actual quantity consumed for the auxiliary material is determined by the system by using the level quantity in the packaging specification. This quantity can be changed in the VAS work center manually in case of unplanned overconsumption or underconsumption by specifying the required value in the **Quantity to Be Consumed** field. The quantity of stock in the storage bin increases if you post a negative quantity for the auxiliary product and decreases if you post a positive quantity. The same quantity is updated in SAP S/4HANA. In standard SAP, movement types 291 and 292 are used for consumption posting in the SAP S/4HANA system. The example in Figure 20.20 shows the consumption of auxiliary products in a VAS work center.

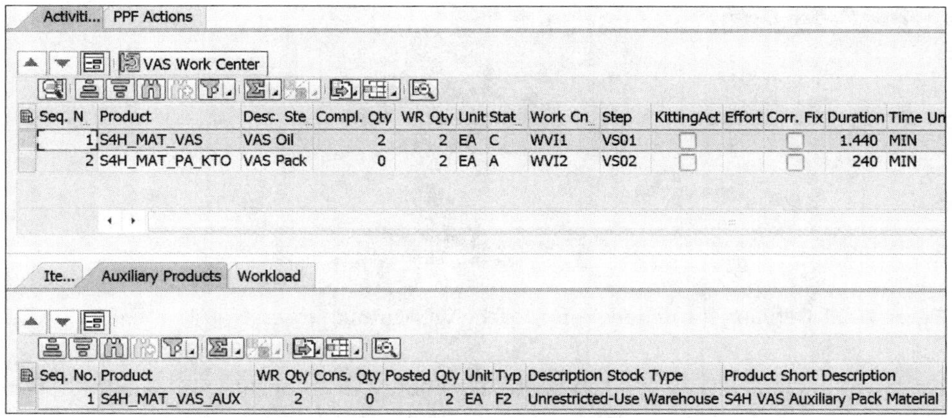

Figure 20.20 Auxiliary Product Consumption in a VAS Work Center

20.6 Printing VAS Documents

A worker can print the VAS activities for a product and use the printout as a guide to perform the activities in the VAS work center. This is particularly useful in organizations that don't want to use handheld or mobile devices for resource management. A printout of a VAS order also may be needed if you're executing a VAS order in the VAS work center without process-oriented storage control and process steps.

VAS orders are printed using the Post Processing Framework (PPF) of embedded EWM. You maintain the PPF settings for VAS printing by defining the action profile and action definition for a VAS order at IMG path **SCM Extended Warehouse Management • Extended Warehouse Management • Cross-Process Settings • Value-Added Services • Print VAS • Define PPF Action Profile**. Select the **/SCWM/VASORDER** action profile, as shown in Figure 20.21. The VAS orders can be printed using smart forms or Adobe PDF-based forms by selecting the required processing type for the /SCWM/PRINT_VAS action definition.

You can also define the schedule and start conditions triggering the PPF to print a VAS order via IMG path **SCM Extended Warehouse Management • Extended Warehouse Management • Cross-Process Settings • Value-Added Services • Print VAS • Define PPF Conditions**. Select the **/SCWM/VASORDER** action profile, and define the conditions by clicking on **Edit Condition** in the **Schedule Condition** and **Start Condition** tabs.

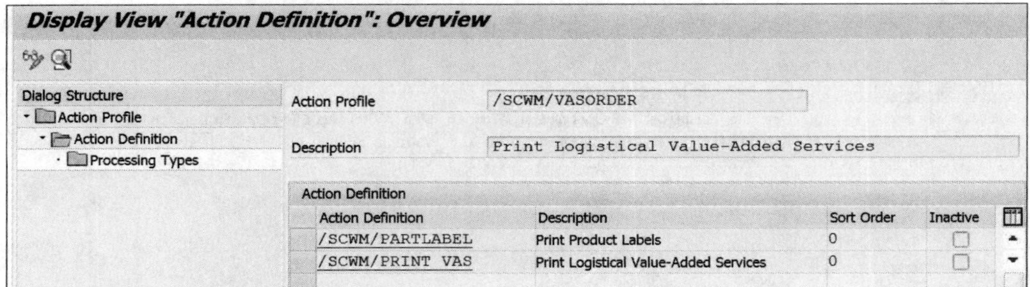

Figure 20.21 Defining the Action Profile for the VAS Output Process

As shown in Figure 20.22, you can configure when VAS orders are print via IMG path **SCM Extended Warehouse Management • Extended Warehouse Management • Cross-Process Settings • Value-Added Services • Print VAS • Define Time of Printing**. Set the time of printing of a VAS order for a combination of document category and document type for the embedded EWM warehouse.

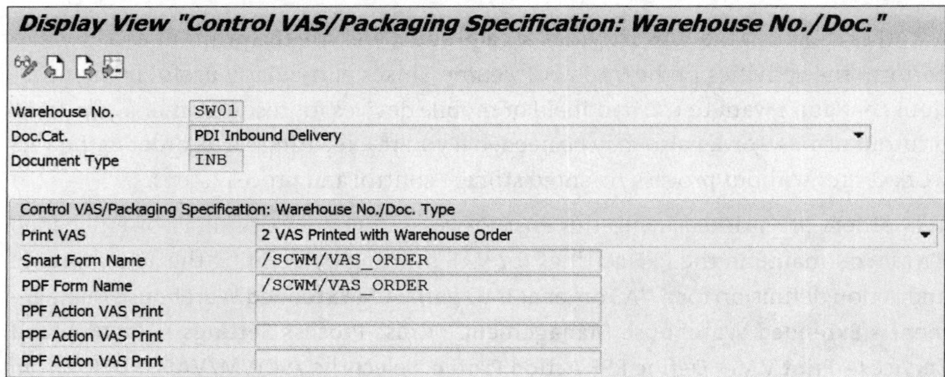

Figure 20.22 Defining the VAS Printing Time Setting

The following settings can be used to control when a warehouse order is printed:

- **Print VAS**
  This parameter controls whether the VAS order is to be printed just after creation of the VAS order or just after printing the warehouse order. If the latter is chosen, the printing of the warehouse order should be configured as a prerequisite; otherwise, the VAS order won't be printed.

- **Smart Form Name**
  This setting is used to provide the smart form name used for printing the VAS order.
- **PDF Form Name**
  This setting is used to provide the PDF form name used for printing the VAS order.
- **PPF Action for VAS Print**
  This setting is used to provide the PPF action used for printing the VAS order. If you want to print a VAS order just after creation, use the /SCWM/PRINT_VAS PPF action profile; if you want the VAS order to be printed after printing the warehouse order, use the /SCWM/PRINT_VAS_FROM_WO PPF action profile. A maximum of three such profiles can be specified for printing a VAS order for a combination of warehouse, VAS document type, and VAS document category.

20.7 Summary

This chapter introduced the concept of VAS in embedded EWM. We provided the settings and master data used for setting up VAS processes in embedded EWM. We also discussed various processes by which VAS can be executed in embedded EWM, such as with or without process-oriented storage control and external process steps. We also walked through a step-by-step flow of VAS processes in different stock movement scenarios. Finally, we discussed printing VAS orders for performing VAS activities. In the next chapter, we will discuss the process of preparing a kit.

Chapter 21
Kitting

A kit is a group of products always delivered together, and kitting is the process of building and assembling kits. Embedded EWM provides various operations for carrying out kitting, such as kit to order, kit to stock, and reverse kitting. We'll discuss these processes in detail in this chapter.

In any organization, many products are manufactured, stocked, and sold together. Some parts are managed individually, but some need to be grouped together with other parts to prepare a kit. Based on business requirements, kits can be created or consumed in inbound, outbound, and internal processes.

In this chapter, we introduce kitting in Section 21.1 and explain the use of kits in business operations. We also explain the types of kits and their structures. In Section 21.2, we discuss the process, configuration, and variants of the kit-to-stock process and do the same for the kit-to-order process in Section 21.3. Finally, in Section 21.4, we explain the process and configuration of the reverse kitting process.

21.1 What Is Kitting?

A kit's content can vary; for example, it can be a set of tools used for repairing heavy machinery or an assortment of products sold together in a retail store such as a TV set that consists of a television unit, remote, user manual, and so on. These groups of materials are called *kits* in embedded EWM, and kitting is the process of assembling these kits in the warehouse for storage or for sale.

In Section 21.1.1, we'll explain the business context in which kitting can be used in real-world scenarios. In Section 21.1.2, we'll cover the processes carried out in the system as well as kitting-related documents used for stocking, ordering, and reverse kitting in embedded EWM and decentralized EWM.

21.1.1 Business Process

Kits aren't created as master data in embedded EWM. The kit parts are defined as a bill of materials (BOM) in SAP S/4HANA. When a kit material is added to a delivery in embedded EWM, the BOM explodes in the logistics execution delivery. This delivery gets distributed to embedded EWM, and the embedded EWM system uses the delivery line items to get the kit structure. The kitting process is then carried out in embedded EWM based on the kit structure and packaging specifications, and the assembled kit is prepared either for storage or for shipping.

The following kitting processes can be performed in embedded EWM:

- Kit to order
  The kit-to-order process is carried out with reference to a customer sales order. This process usually is used when kits aren't stocked in the warehouse. Kit building and further processing are carried out after the customer sales order is sent from SAP S/4HANA to embedded EWM.
- Kit to stock
  In the kit-to-stock process, kits are prepared based on forecasted requirements so that they can be available at the time of order placement. Kit creation for kit to stock is carried out using a reference production order or through a manually created value-added services (VAS) order.
- Reverse kitting
  The reverse kitting process disassembles a finished kit into its components.

A kit consists of a kit header and kit components. The *kit header* is the main product sent to the end user and for which billing is carried out. Kit components are the materials used to create the higher-level product or the kit header. Kits can be of two types: simple or complex.

A *simple kit* consists of a header material and individual products as components. These component products are consumed as the process of kit creation is completed. Figure 21.1 shows a simple kit in which the kit header is the assembled kit for a TV set, and the kit components are individual materials such as the television unit, remote, and so on.

For a *complex kit*, the kit components are themselves kits that are made up of other kits, along with individual products. These are also called *nested kits* because they contain kits within kits. Figure 21.2 shows a complex kit for a TV set. The assembled TV set uses a remote kit that was created using a remote cabinet, batteries, and keypad.

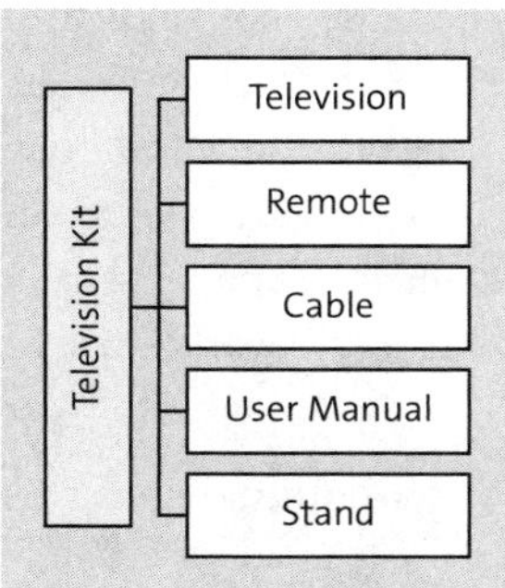

Figure 21.1 Simple Kit Structure Used in the Kitting Process

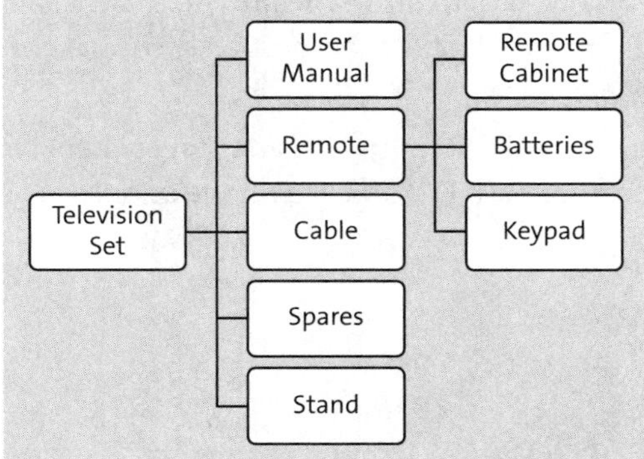

Figure 21.2 Complex Kit Structure Used in the Kitting Process

Note

Embedded EWM doesn't support working with complex kits, so we'll just cover the different kitting processes that can be carried out in the warehouse for simple kits.

21

Consider this example: American company Sun Electronics receives an order from one of its subsidiaries based in Mexico. The order sent by the subsidiary required Sun Telecom to provide a box that contains all the components of a TV, such as wire, signal transmitter, screen, remote, and so on, which are to be assembled by the subsidiary at its premise and installed as part of the subsidiary's finished stock. Stock that will be delivered to the customer is to be picked from the source bins of the Sun Electronics warehouse in a timely manner by the warehouse workers and packed in the desired packaging material to create a component pallet. To ensure that the warehouse worker picks the correct products and packing materials, Sun Electronics has implemented kitting so that embedded EWM proposes a process to the warehouse worker during the packing of products to ensure that all components are packed on the correct cases and then placed on the correct pallet before staging the pallets at the staging area. The following steps are involved in kitting products in the warehouse of Sun Electronics, as shown in Figure 21.3:

1. The warehouse receives a warehouse request document for outbound delivery to supply the requested kits to the subsidiary.
2. The warehouse-request-related warehouse task is assigned to a warehouse worker so that the worker can pick, pack, and stage the stock at the staging bay.
3. The system provides the warehouse worker a task to move the products to the kitting work center based on the packing master data for the products, so that the final kitted units can be created for the products.
4. The warehouse worker picks the products, packs them in kits, and stages them so that they can be loaded on the transportation unit (TU) docked on the door to take the product to the customers.

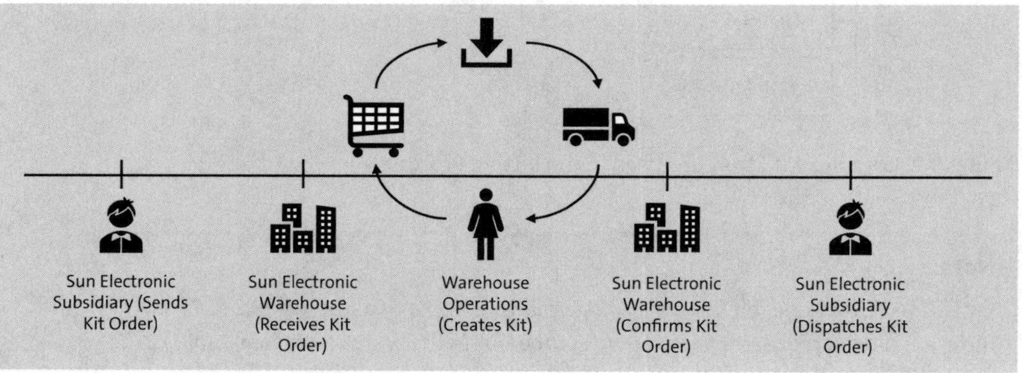

Figure 21.3 Business Flow for the Kitting Process

21.1.2 System Process

The following explains the basic system flow to execute kitting in embedded and decentralized EWM:

1. An outbound delivery is created in embedded EWM that contains information about the kitted product as well as the components required to create the kits.

2. The warehouse worker is allocated the warehouse orders to pick the products for individual components of the kits and deliver them to the kitting work center.
3. A warehouse worker creates kits based on the packaging specification, which contains the packed products as well the components inside them in the kitting work center.
4. The created kits are packed in pallets and sent over to the goods issue (GI) area where they are staged to be sent out to the customers on TUs.

Note

The following SAP Fiori apps are available to perform VAS operations for different kitting warehouse processes:

- **Value Added Services (Kit to Stock)**
  This app allows you to perform VAS in a VAS work center for the stock creation warehouse process.
- **Value Added Services (Reverse Kitting)**
  This app allows you to perform VAS in a VAS work center for the reverse kitting warehouse process.

21.2 Kit to Stock

In the kit-to-stock process, kits are assembled in advance before customer demand impacts the warehouse. This helps warehouses ensure more efficient processing and fulfillment of customer demands. The kit for a kit-to-stock process is assembled based on the production order created in SAP S/4HANA or directly in embedded EWM using a VAS order. We'll discuss kit creation from each of these processes in the following sections.

21.2.1 Kit to Stock Using a Production Order

As shown in Figure 21.4, creation of a kit is triggered using a production order created manually or automatically from planning. An inbound delivery is created in SAP S/4HANA for the kit header, and an outbound delivery is created for kit components when the production order is released.

The system first creates the outbound delivery for kit components, which is distributed to embedded EWM. Then, the inbound delivery for receipt of the finished kit is generated in SAP S/4HANA and distributed to embedded EWM. Using the Post Processing Framework (PPF), a VAS order is automatically generated in the inbound delivery to assemble the kits in the kitting work center.

After kitting is completed, GI is posted for kit components from the outbound delivery, and goods receipt (GR) is posted for the kit header from the inbound delivery. The GI and GR are also updated in the delivery documents in SAP S/4HANA, and the production order is updated accordingly.

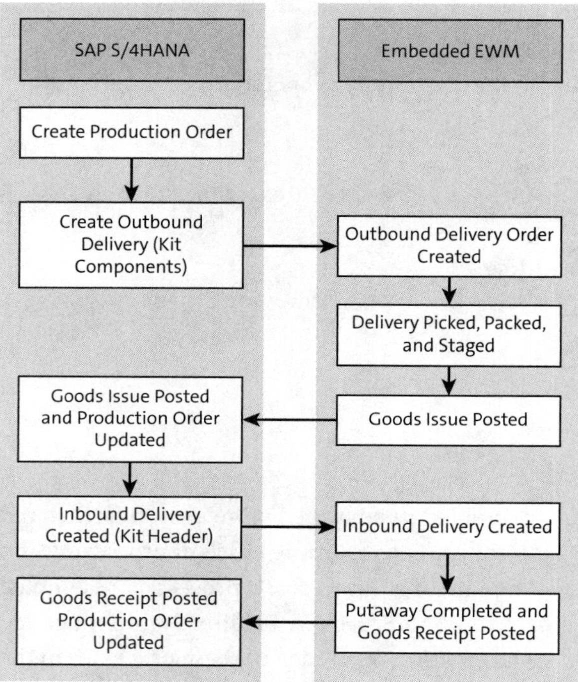

Figure 21.4 Process Flow for Kitting Using a Production Order

21.2.2 Kit to Stock Using a VAS Order

The kit-to-stock process also can be initiated directly from embedded EWM by creating a VAS order. You can also use a BOM during the creation of a VAS order to determine the proportionate number of kit components required for assembling the kit header product.

As shown in Figure 21.5, the process starts in embedded EWM with manual creation of a VAS order. To create a VAS order, navigate to **SAP Easy Access** path **Logistics • SCM Extended Warehouse Management • Extended Warehouse Management • Work Scheduling • Value-Added Services (VAS) • VAS for Kit Creation on Stock** or use Transaction /SCWM/VAS_KTS. Click on the **Create** button from the menu bar; select **Create with BOM** or **Create without BOM**; enter the VAS order type, parent product, quantity, child product, packaging specification, and so on; and save.

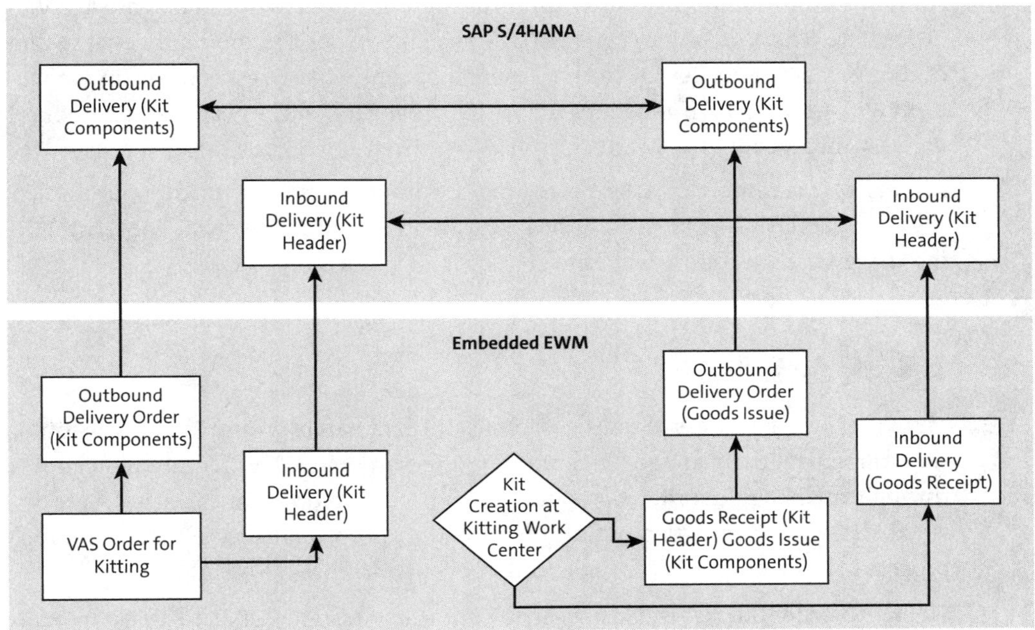

Figure 21.5 Kitting Process Initiated Using a VAS Order

The VAS order can be created with or without reference to a BOM. If you use a BOM, the system tries to find the BOM and explodes the kit hierarchy based on the BOM hierarchy. The total number of kit components are calculated based on the number of kits requested in the VAS order. When a BOM isn't specified, you must provide the kit header and component products, as well as the quantity of each, to create the kit.

You need to define a VAS order type for kit to stock. The VAS order type should be assigned to the document type and item type for inbound delivery and outbound delivery orders in embedded EWM. In addition, you need to create a packaging specification for the kit product and assign it to the VAS order type. To define a VAS order, navigate to IMG path **SCM Extended Warehouse Management • Extended Warehouse Management • Cross-Process Settings • Value Added Services (VAS) • Define Order Types for VAS for Kit to Stock**. Click on **New Entries**; enter the embedded EWM warehouse number, VAS document type, inbound and outbound document and item type, and stock types; and save.

If availability check is activated for the kit components, then the system tries to find available components and reduces the number of kits based on the confirmed kit components. If components can't be confirmed, the system doesn't create the VAS order. After the VAS order is created, the system creates the inbound delivery and outbound delivery order for the kit header and component, respectively, in embedded EWM, which in turn generates the inbound delivery for the header and outbound delivery for kit components in SAP S/4HANA as well.

After kitting is completed, GI is posted for kit components from the outbound delivery order, and GR is posted from the kit header. This ultimately posts the GI and GR in the logistics execution deliveries created in SAP S/4HANA as well.

21.3 Kit to Order

The kit-to-order process creates assemblies of kits based on immediate customer requirements if there are no kits in stock in the warehouse. This requirement comes through an open sales order. Components from the warehouse are used to create finished kits, which are issued out of the warehouse. You can execute the kit-to-order process in embedded EWM for sales orders created from SAP S/4HANA.

The kit-to-order process is usually carried out when it isn't feasible to invest in managing an inventory of assembled kits or the assembled kits can't be stocked due to product characteristics. In such situations, kits are assembled only when an open requirement is created in the system. The following points are applicable to kits created for kit to order:

- A kit is delivered in full to a customer. Thus, a complete motor with all individual components inside is delivered to a customer rather than a partially assembled motor.
- The kit header and kit components must have goods movement performed on the same dates.

- In case of a shortage, an internal stock transfer can be used to fulfill stock in the warehouse; the kit must be issued from the same warehouse.
- Kit prices are always calculated at the kit header level, rather than calculating the prices at the kit component level and adding them up at the kit header level.
- The kit header and kit component have a fixed quantity ratio as defined in the BOM structure. As soon as there is a change in component or header quantity, the revised kit quantities are calculated based on the defined ratio.

The process starts with the sales order created in SAP S/4HANA. The BOM is exploded for the kit material in the sales order. The delivery is created for the sales order and distributed to embedded EWM. The system creates picking warehouse tasks to execute picking for the kit components. These components are assembled into a pick handling unit (HU) to create the assembled kit and prepared to be shipped to the customer. There are three ways in which the kit-to-order process can be performed in embedded EWM for a sales order: create kits for kit to order during picking without a VAS order, create kits at a work center with a VAS order, or create kits at a work center without a VAS order. We'll discuss each of these processes in detail in the following sections.

21.3.1 Kitting during Picking

In this process, a kit is created during the picking of the kit components. This is suitable in the following cases:

- A detailed VAS process for kit creation isn't required. Instead, the kitting instructions required to carry out kitting in the warehouse can be set in free-text form in the warehouse request created in embedded EWM.
- Kitting doesn't have to be done in kitting-specific work centers. The assembled kits can still be brought to work centers for packing or repacking the finished kits.

A prerequisite for carrying out kitting during picking is to set the **Create Kit Item Automatically** indicator in Customizing of the item type of the kit header. The system uses this indicator to know if a kit must be created during the picking process. To do this, navigate to IMG path **SCM Extended Warehouse Management • Extended Warehouse Management • Goods Issue Process • Outbound Delivery • Define Item Types of Outbound Delivery Process**, and set the **Create Kit Item Automatically** indicator for the required item type.

While processing the delivery in embedded EWM, the warehouse tasks for kit components are generated for picking them from the source bin. Because the **Create Kit Item Automatically** indicator is set, the system creates a kit header item in the pick HU. Components are picked and assembled in a kit in accordance with the kitting instructions provided in the warehouse request. The warehouse task is confirmed, and GI is posted for the warehouse request. While posting GI, the system checks if the kits are complete; if everything is in order, GI is updated in SAP S/4HANA.

21.3.2 Kitting at a Kit-Specific Work Center

You can carry out kitting at a work center created specifically to carry out the kitting process. This is done using a VAS order, which provides steps for assembling kits and also records the duration and effort required to carry out VAS activities if labor management is activated. To enable creation of a VAS order for an outbound delivery order created for kit components, configuration for VAS must be completed as described in the previous chapter.

For the kit header, the GR movement type is maintained based on the item category for the kit header in IMG path **Logistics Execution • Extended Warehouse Management Integration • Outbound Process • Kit to Order • Set Goods Receipt Movement Type for Kit Headers**. This setting is required to determine the movement type posted for GR of the kit header in the warehouse. In standard SAP, movement type 521 can be used. In the same area, set the **KTO** checkbox for the item category of the BOM header if you want the BOM structure to be copied to the delivery for the kit-to-order scenario.

If you want the system to create an HU item automatically for the kit header in a pick HU created for the assembly of a kit, set the **Create Kit Item Automatically** indicator in the Customizing settings for outbound delivery items as described in the previous section. If this indicator isn't set, then create the kit header item in the pick HU manually in the work center.

You also need to create a packaging specification for the kit header material. This packaging specification is a mandatory requirement for creation of the VAS order. This packaging specification should have **Level Type** set to **Kitting**. Figure 21.6 covers the various steps involved in kitting at a work center using a VAS order.

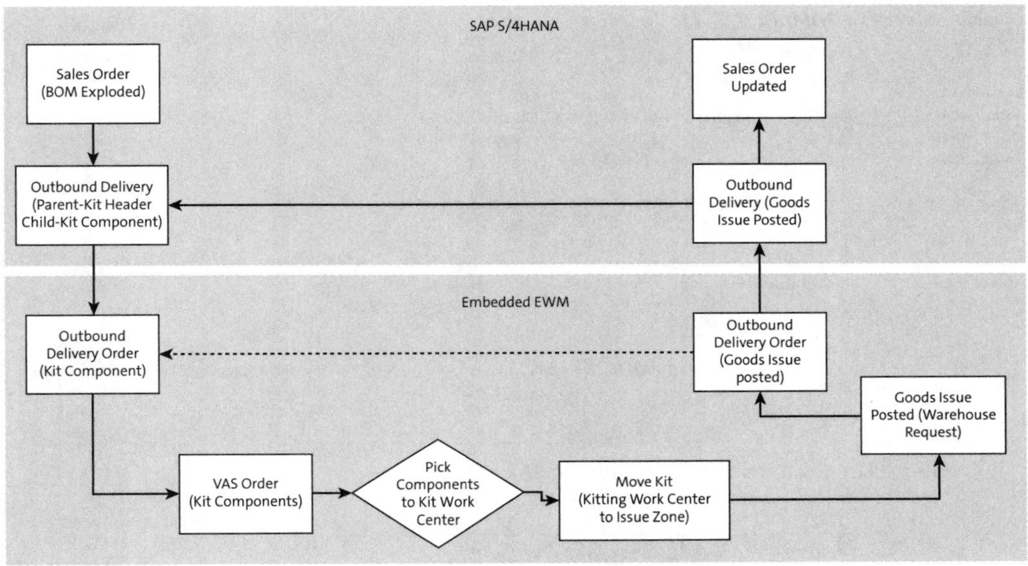

Figure 21.6 Kit to Order Using a SAP S/4HANA Sales Order

In detail, the steps involved in kitting a work center using a VAS order are as follows:

1. **Creation of sales order in SAP S/4HANA**
   As shown in Figure 21.7, the process begins with the creation of a sales order in SAP S/4HANA using a BOM. The BOM is exploded by the system, displaying the header and child components. You can create a sales BOM via **SAP Easy Access** path **Logistics • Sales and Distribution • Master Data • Products • Bills of Material • Bill of Material • Material BOM • Create**. Enter the product, plant, BOM usage, and validity, and press Enter. Then, enter the child products and quantity, and save the BOM.

2. **Creation of outbound delivery in SAP S/4HANA**
   Based on the sales order created in Step 1, as shown in Figure 21.8, an outbound delivery is created in SAP S/4HANA. The BOM structure is copied from the sales order to the delivery. This delivery is distributed to embedded EWM to create an outbound delivery order.

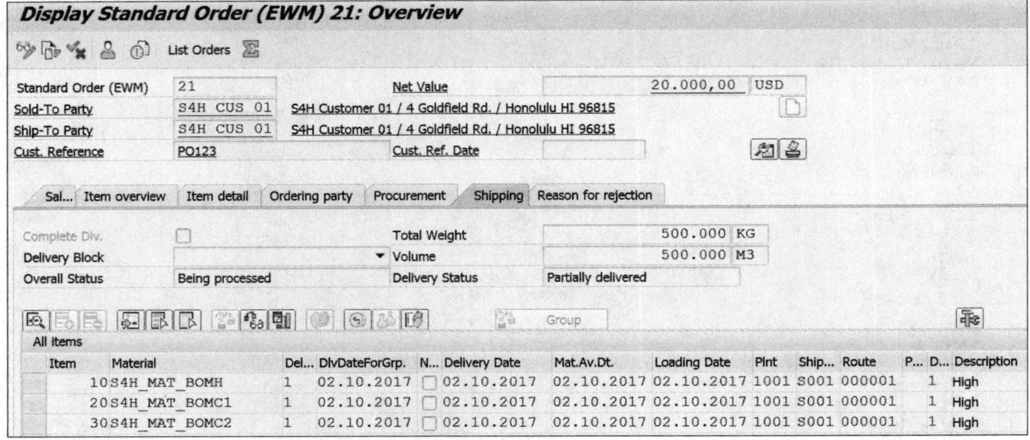

Figure 21.7 Creating the Sales Order in SAP S/4HANA

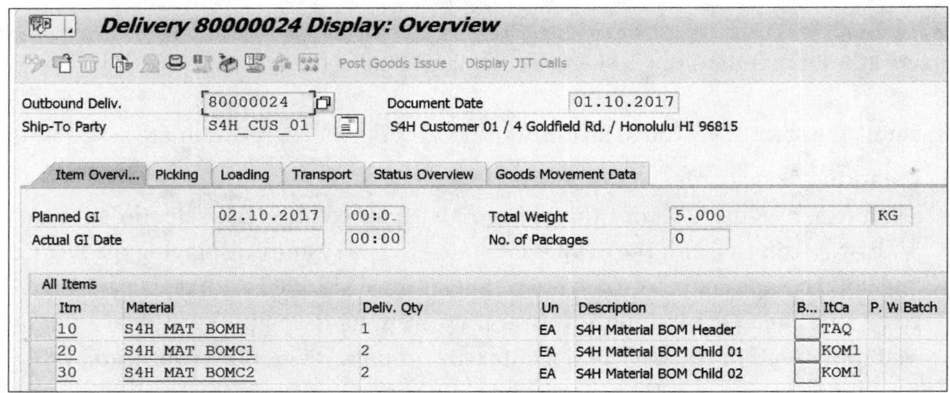

Figure 21.8 Creating the Outbound Delivery in SAP S/4HANA

3. **Creation of outbound delivery order for kit components**
   Based on the outbound delivery created in SAP S/4HANA, an outbound delivery order is created in embedded EWM. This outbound delivery order becomes the warehouse request in embedded EWM, which is used to create a kit using kit components from the warehouse. The kit structure is also copied into the delivery in embedded EWM. It's important to pick all quantities required for the kit components in the outbound delivery order to be able to post GI for the finished kit. As shown in Figure 21.9, the kit components are created in the outbound delivery order with a **+** sign in the **Level** column.

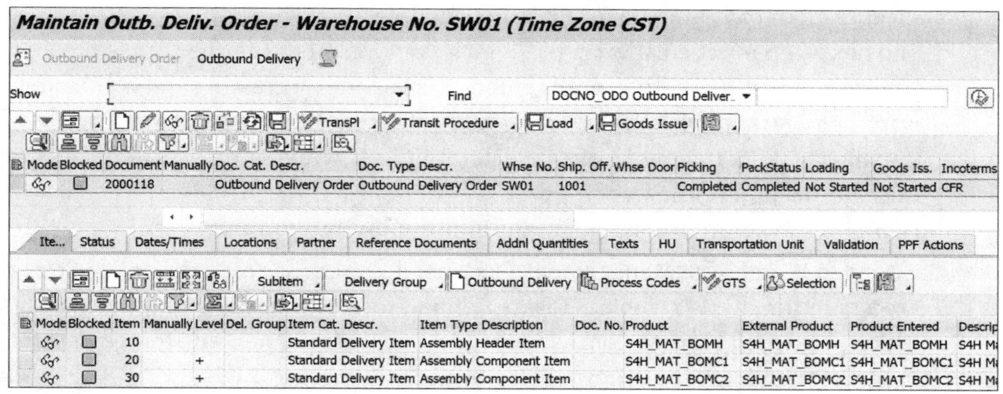

Figure 21.9 Outbound Delivery Order Created in Embedded EWM

4. **Automatic creation of VAS order for the kit header item**
   After the outbound delivery order is created, a VAS order is created for the kit header, as shown in Figure 21.10. The VAS order can be generated automatically or manually depending on the Customizing settings maintained in **Define Relevance of VAS Order**. You can see the created VAS order in the document flow of the outbound delivery order. The VAS order provides instructions for activities to be performed at the kitting work center and the external process step to move the components from the source bin to the kitting work center based on packaging specifications.

   As shown in Figure 21.10, the **KittingAct** checkbox is checked to show that the activity displayed in the VAS order is for kitting. This is determined based on the **Level Type** of **Kitting** selected while creating the packaging specification.

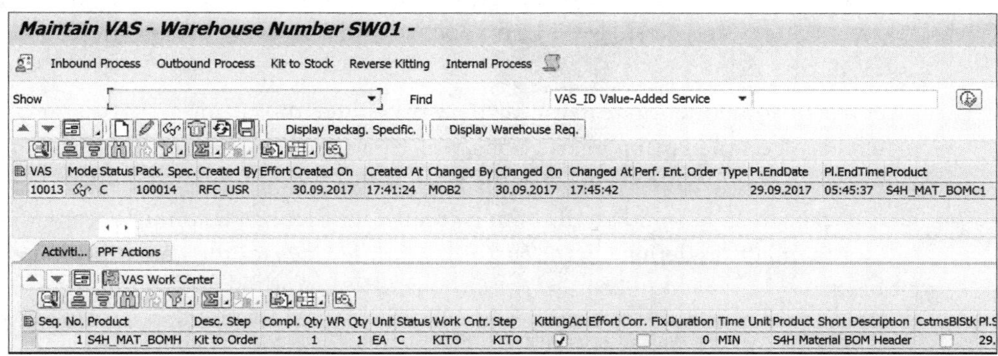

Figure 21.10 VAS Order Created for Kit Creation

5. **Picking of kit components for kit to order process**
   The next step in kit creation is picking kit components from the source bin and placing them in the kitting work center. This is done by creating and confirming warehouse tasks to pick the kit components in a pick HU. The source and destination bins of the warehouse tasks are determined using the settings maintained for the external process step.

   Define the external process steps determined in the VAS order via IMG path **SCM Extended Warehouse Management • Extended Warehouse Management • Cross-Process Settings • Warehouse Task • Define Process-Oriented Storage Control • Process-Oriented Storage Control Step**. Click on **Process-Oriented Storage Control** in the left-hand menu, as shown in Figure 21.11.

Display View "Process-Oriented Storage Control": Overview

Dialog Structure
- External Storage Process Step
- Process-Oriented Storage Control
- Storage Process - Definition
  - Assign Storage Process Step
- External Storage Process: Control p

Process-Oriented Storage Control

War...	External Step	Sour...	HUTGr	Whse Proc. Type	Dest...	Dest...	Dest. Stor. Bin
SW01	KITO			KITO	KTWC	0001	KIWC-01
SW01	OB02			3070			
SW01	OB03			3070			
SW01	OB04			3070			

Figure 21.11 External Process Step Setting for Kitting Using a Sales Order

6. **Creation of kit header in kitting work center**
   After the goods are moved to the kitting work center, you can access the kits there via **SAP Easy Access** path **Logistics • SCM Extended Warehouse Management • Extended Warehouse Management • Execution • Create Confirmation for VAS** or via Transaction /SCWM/VASEXEC. Enter the embedded EWM warehouse and kitting work center, and press Enter. This opens the kitting work center with the HU and VAS kit order.

   After the kit components are in the kitting work center, the kitting activity is completed based on the kitting instructions, which can be provided in the outbound delivery order and made available in the work center. As shown in Figure 21.12, the kit is packed in an HU, and an HU item is created for a kit header either automatically or manually as defined in the customization settings for the item type of the kit header.

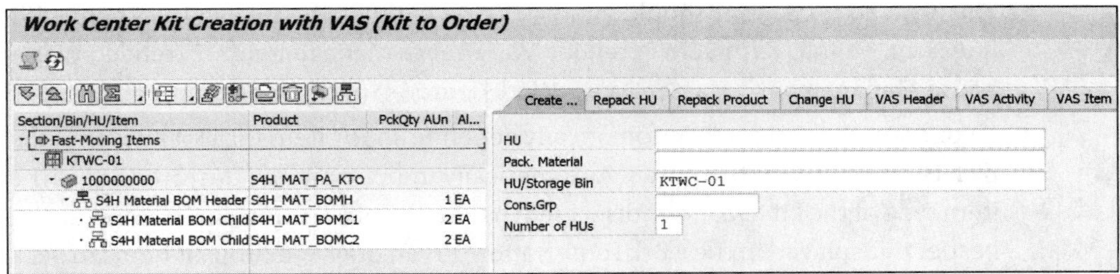

Figure 21.12 Created Kit Using a Sales Order in Kitting Work Center

7. **Moving the created kit from the kitting work center to the GI zone**
   After kitting is complete, the kit is moved from the kitting work center to the GI zone using HU warehouse tasks. If you're using process-oriented storage control, you can add additional steps, such as loading in the warehouse process.

8. **GI posted for warehouse request**
   After the GI is posted for the finished kit, the kit components are consumed, and the results of GI are also communicated to SAP S/4HANA.

21.3.3 Kitting at the Packing Work Center

The kit-to-order process can also be carried out to assemble a kit at the same work center where packing is performed. In such a case, you don't need to perform kitting in a special kitting work center; thus, a VAS order isn't required. In addition, because there is no packaging specification needed for creating the VAS order, you can't use it to display or print assembly instructions for the VAS order. You can refer to the text in the outbound delivery order or reference it by displaying it in the work center. The following configuration settings are required to carry out kitting at a work center without a VAS order:

- The relevance for VAS should be deactivated for the required document type and item type of the outbound delivery order if you don't want to create a VAS order. To do this, navigate to IMG path **SCM Extended Warehouse Management • Extended Warehouse Management • Cross-Process Settings • Value Added Services (VAS) • Define Relevance for VAS**, and deselect the **Relevance For VAS** indicator for the required item type. If you're using process-oriented storage control, then there should be a process step to move the HU to the work center where the kitting activity will be carried out.

- The work center layout should allow working with kits by setting the **Change Kit** indicator via IMG path **SCM Extended Warehouse Management • Extended Warehouse Management • Master Data • Work Center • Specify Work Center Layout**.
- If you want the system to automatically generate an HU item for a kit header in the pick HU, set the **Create Kit Item Automatically** indicator in the Customizing of the item type of the kit header, as discussed in the previous section. In this case, the kit header is displayed in the work center, and you can drag and drop kit items to pack them into the kit. If this checkbox isn't set, you'll need to generate the kit header item in the work center manually.

After you've configured all the prerequisites for the kitting process, the kit-to-order process can be executed by creating warehouse tasks for picking kit components for outbound delivery orders from source bin. Kits are assembled in a packing work center after components are picked in a pick HU. After moving a kit to the GI zone using HU warehouse tasks, the GI is posted for the warehouse request and communicated back to SAP S/4HANA, where the outbound delivery status is updated.

21.4 Reverse Kitting

Reverse kitting is the process by which an already present kit in the warehouse is disassembled into its components when the kit is no longer required. Reverse kitting is done by creating a VAS order for reverse kitting manually and can only be initiated from within embedded EWM.

To execute reverse kitting in embedded EWM, navigate to **SAP Easy Access** path **Logistics • Extended Warehouse Management • Extended Warehouse Management • Work Scheduling • Value Added Services (VAS) • VAS for Reverse Kitting** or use Transaction /SCWM/VAS_KTR. Click on the **Create** button from the menu bar, and select **Create with BOM** or **Create Without BOM**, as shown in Figure 21.13. Enter the VAS order type, parent product, quantity, child product, packaging specification, and so on, and then save.

You can carry out reverse kitting with or without a BOM. If a VAS order is created with a BOM, embedded EWM will explode a BOM based on the BOM defined in SAP S/4HANA system and populate the kit components. If a VAS order is created without a BOM, you need to specify the kit header and kit components manually.

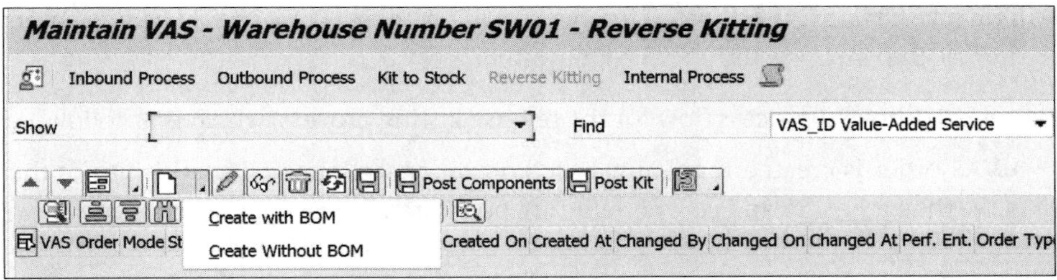

Figure 21.13 Creating a VAS Order for Reverse Kitting

Some prerequisites need to be met before starting the reverse kitting process:

- The VAS order type is defined for reverse kitting along with the assignment of the inbound delivery document type and item type for kit components and the outbound delivery order document type and item type for the kit header, as shown in Figure 21.14. The VAS order type for reverse kitting is defined in IMG path **Extended Warehouse Management • Cross-Process Settings • Value-Added Services (VAS) • Define Order Types for VAS for Reverse Kitting**.

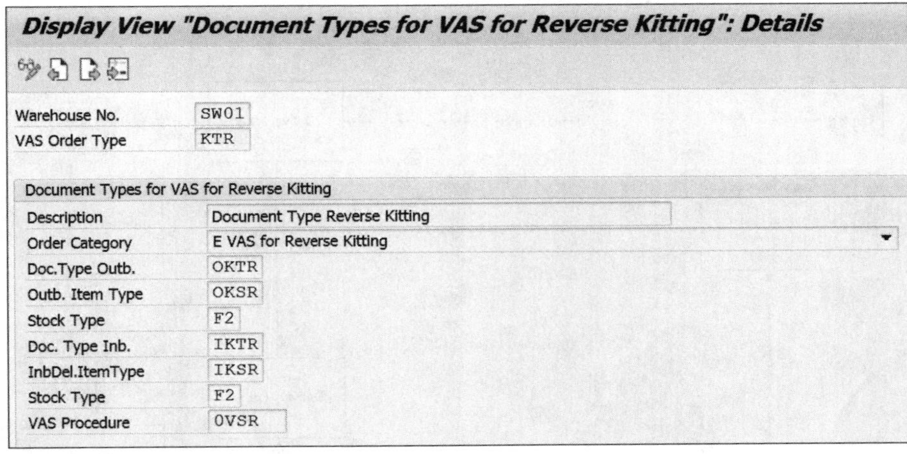

Figure 21.14 VAS Order Setting for Reverse Kitting

- A packaging specification is created for the kit product required to create the VAS order. The packaging specification should only be created at one level, **Kitting**, which will contain the activity that needs to be carried out for reverse kitting. Any other levels will be ignored.

- If reverse kitting is used with reference to a BOM, then a BOM should be present in the SAP S/4HANA system for the kit product.

Figure 21.15 shows a process flow for the reverse kitting process, which is as follows:

1. A VAS order is created manually. Based on order settings and availability of the BOM, the kit header and components are populated in the sales order.

> **Tip**
>
> You can also configure the system to perform an availability check for the kit header so that the VAS order can only be saved if the kit parts are available in the warehouse.

2. When the reverse kitting VAS order is saved, the system generates an outbound delivery order for the kit header and an inbound delivery order for kit components in embedded EWM.
3. The system communicates the deliveries created in Step 2 to SAP S/4HANA, creating outbound and inbound deliveries.

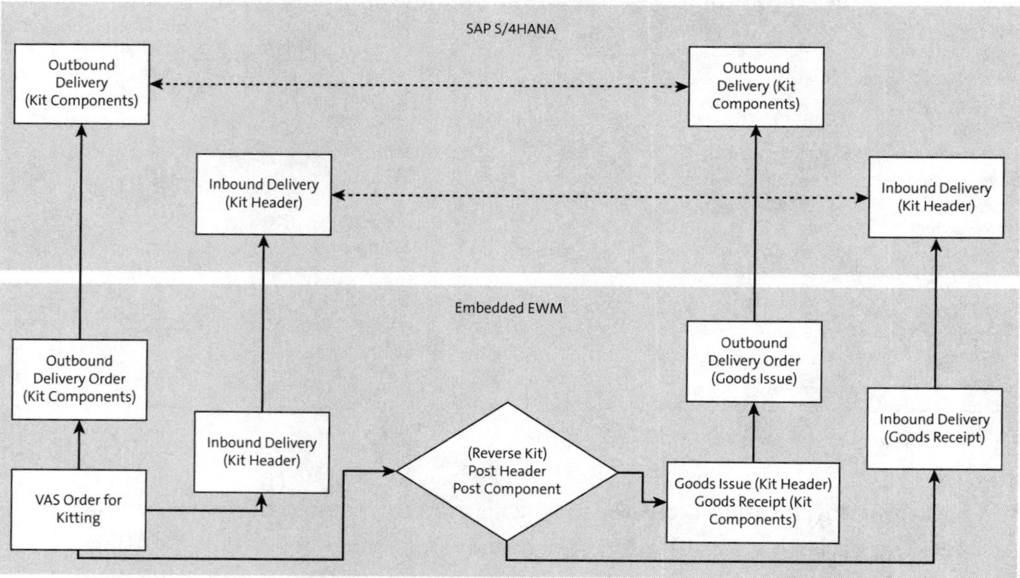

Figure 21.15 Process Flow for Reverse Kitting

4. A VAS order is created based on the packaging specification and updated in the document flow of both inbound and outbound delivery.
5. A warehouse task is created to pick the kit header from the source bin. Based on the destination bin set in the external process step of the reverse kitting activity in the packaging specification, the kit header product is moved to the reverse kitting work center.
6. The VAS activity is completed, goods issues is posted for the kit header, and goods receipt is posted for the kit components.
7. Based on the goods issue and goods receipt process in embedded EWM, goods movement information is communicated and updated in the inbound and outbound deliveries in SAP S/4HANA, thereby updating the stock quantities at the storage location level.

21.5 Summary

This chapter introduced basic concepts of kitting in embedded EWM using SAP S/4HANA. We explained in detail the various types of kitting processes that can be carried out in the warehouse, including kit to order, kit to stock, and reverse kitting. We also explained the process flow, prerequisites required for setting up each scenario, and the execution steps used for each. Finally, we provided detailed information about how VAS orders and packaging specifications play an important role in each kit-related process. In the next chapter, we will discuss cartonization planning.

Chapter 22
Cartonization Planning

In this chapter, we'll discuss cartonization planning, used in creation of planned shipping handling units (HUs). These HUs can be used as templates for creating shipping HUs during the picking and packing process.

Cartonization planning is used for creating planned handling units (HUs) based on information from product master data and outbound delivery orders such as weight, quantities, and volume. The planned shipping HUs are used as templates in the outbound process. Cartonization planning is usually done by a shipping officer to optimize the packaging of all delivery items that are going to customers on the same route at the same time. The warehouse worker completes the picking of goods in one or more pick HUs and then packs them into shipping HUs in a work center based on the results of cartonization planning.

In this chapter, we'll discuss the following: business use for cartonization planning in warehousing operations (Section 22.1), various configurations required to plan and execute cartonization planning in embedded EWM (Section 22.2), creating interim shipping HUs to plan and execute cartonization planning in various business scenarios (Section 22.3), and, finally, different ways to maintain planned shipping HUs in cartonization planning (Section 22.4).

22.1 What Is Cartonization Planning?

Cartonization planning is used for the creation of planned shipping HUs. *Planned shipping HUs* are different from regular shipping HUs in the sense that they don't exist in the warehouse physically but can be used to plan the creation of actual shipping HUs. A planned shipping HU still contains information about both the packaging material and the content to be packed. Planned shipping HUs can be created manually and automatically using cartonization planning. You can also create nested planned shipping HUs if a HU is packed in another HU.

In Section 22.1.1, we'll explain the business context in which cartonization planning can be used in real-world scenarios. In Section 22.1.2, we'll explain the processes carried out in the system as well as cartonization planning–related documents with which shipping HUs are created that act as templates for creating shipping HUs quickly in embedded and decentralized EWM.

22.1.1 Business Process

American company Alpha Medicals receives an order from one of its customers, Medimax Corporation Limited, based in Mexico. The order sent by Medimax contains various pharmaceutical products to be delivered in a timely manner and in appropriately packed pallets using the required packaging material. Stock to be delivered to the customer is to be picked from the warehouse of Alpha Medicals in a timely manner by the warehouse workers and packed in the desired packaging material so that the products don't get spoiled in transit. To ensure that the warehouse worker picks the requested products with the correct packing materials faster, Alpha Medicals has implemented cartonization planning so that embedded EWM proposes a template to the warehouse worker during packing of the products before staging the pallets at the staging area. The following steps are involved in faster packaging and shipment of products in the Alpha Medical warehouse involving cartonization planning, as shown in Figure 22.1:

1. The customer sends the order, and the warehouse receives a warehouse request document for the outbound delivery to supply the requested products to the customer.
2. The warehouse-request-related warehouse task is assigned to a warehouse worker so that the worker can pick, pack, and stage the stock at the staging bay.
3. The system provides the warehouse worker a template of the shipping HU based on the packing master data for the products, so that the final shipping HUs can be created in a faster manner for the products, and the time to stage them decreases. This is the part of the processes specific to cartonization planning.
4. The warehouse worker picks the products, packs them in the shipping HU, and stages them.
5. The shipping HU is loaded on the transportation unit (TU) docked on the door to take the product to the customers.

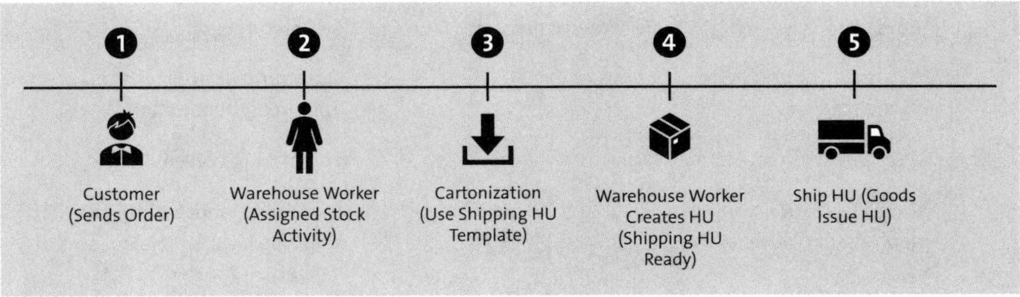

Figure 22.1 Business Flow in Cartonization Planning

22.1.2 System Process

An outbound delivery is created in embedded EWM. A shipping office clerk carries out cartonization planning to optimize the packaging of all delivery items that are to be sent to customers on the same route and that are planned to leave the yard at the same time. Using the results of cartonization planning, the shipping office clerk orders transportation capacity from the shipper. After the confirmation by the shipper, the shipping office clerk creates TUs and assigns them to the route and a door used for the route. With the automatic release of the waves, the warehouse activities begin. The system creates and prints warehouse orders, which are used as a work list for paper-based picking.

A warehouse worker takes the warehouse order printout and prepares a pick HU to be used for picking the products listed on the warehouse order printout. The warehouse worker carries out the picking for one or several pick HUs and brings the goods to the packing station, where they're consolidated and packed into shipping HUs, such as medium boxes, according to the cartonization planning results. The packer attaches shipping labels to the completed shipping HUs. The shipping HUs are then moved to the staging area. For staging, radio frequency (RF) devices are used.

When the truck arrives, it's checked in and directed to the door. The goods are loaded from the staging area into the truck. When the loading is complete, the shipping office clerk posts the goods issue, prints the delivery notes and loading lists, and hands them over to the truck driver. The shipping office clerk checks out the truck, and the truck leaves the door and the premises. The entire process is summarized in Table 22.1.

Steps	Business Process	System Process
Step 1: Outbound delivery created		Outbound delivery order is created in embedded EWM.
Step 2: Waves created		The picking wave is created.
Step 3: Cartonization planning performed		A shipping clerk creates planned shipping HUs for the outbound delivery order items that are shipped at the next truck departure.
Step 4: TU created	The shipping office clerk orders transportation capacity based on cartonization planning.	The shipping office clerk creates a TU with the external identifier and the route.
Step 5: Wave released		The system releases the wave, and then creates and prints warehouse orders.
Step 6: Goods picked	Warehouse worker creates and labels the pick HU. Goods are placed in the pick HU and moved to the packing station.	The pick HU is created, and the warehouse order is confirmed.
Step 7: Goods packed	A packer prepares a shipping HU according to the packaging proposal of cartonization planning. Goods are repacked from the pick HU into the shipping HU based on cartonization planning. Shipping HU labels are printed.	At the work center, the packer selects and scans the pick HU. The system proposes packaging material or shipping HUs for repacking. The packer confirms the repacking into the shipping HU. Upon confirmation, the system creates the shipping HU. The packer weighs and closes the shipping HU. Shipping labels are printed, and the system creates warehouse orders for staging.

Table 22.1 Cartonization Planning in Warehouse

Steps	Business Process	System Process
Step 8: Goods staged	The warehouse worker moves the shipping HU to the staging area.	The warehouse worker logs on as a resource, scans the shipping HU, and then confirms the open warehouse order for the shipping HU.
Step 9: Truck arrives at checkpoint and drives to the door	A truck arrives at the warehouse and is moved to the warehouse door.	The checkpoint clerk determines the door and confirms the truck arrival.
Step 10: Truck loaded	The warehouse worker moves the shipping HU to the truck.	The warehouse worker logs on as a resource and scans the shipping HU. The system determines the door for loading.
Step 11: Goods issue posted, and delivery note printed	Shipping clerk hands over the delivery papers to the truck driver.	Shipping office clerk posts goods issue and system prints the delivery papers.
Step 12: Truck leaves the warehouse	The truck leaves the warehouse.	The shipping clerk confirms the departure of the truck for the checkpoint.

Table 22.1 Cartonization Planning in Warehouse (Cont.)

22.2 Configuring Cartonization Planning

The following settings must be set up to implement cartonization planning and create planned shipping HUs in embedded EWM:

22

1. Define process profiles for cartonization planning. The process profile defines settings for when planned shipping HUs are created, such as during creation of warehouse orders or waves. It also defines the settings for creating shipping HUs during the picking and packing process. This is a warehouse-specific profile created via IMG path **SCM Extended Warehouse Management • Extended Warehouse Management • Goods Issue Process • Cartonization Planning • Define Process Profile for Cartonization Planning**, as shown in Figure 22.2. Click on **New Entries**, and define a process profile for your warehouse by entering the **Process Profile** name, **Description**, **Creation of Shipping HUs** settings, and transportation planning system settings.

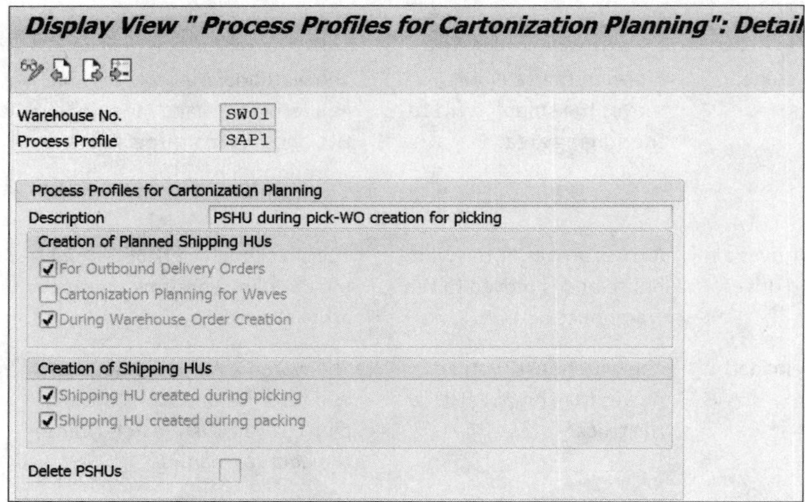

Figure 22.2 Defining the Process Profile for Cartonization Planning

2. Configure the process profile determination via IMG path **SCM Extended Warehouse Management • Extended Warehouse Management • Goods Issue Process • Cartonization Planning • Determine Process Profile for Cartonization Planning**, as shown in Figure 22.3. The process profile is determined using a combination of warehouse number, warehouse process type, and activity area.

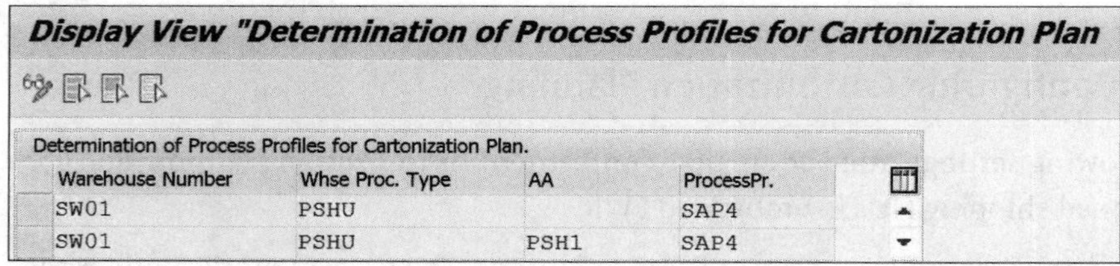

Figure 22.3 Determination of the Process Profile for Cartonization Planning

3. Define the algorithm profile, which the system uses to create planned shipping HUs, via IMG path **SCM Extended Warehouse Management • Extended Warehouse Management • Goods Issue Process • Cartonization Planning • Define Algorithm Profile for Cartonization Planning**, as shown in Figure 22.4. In this node, the algorithm for cartonization is defined for the warehouse by clicking on the **New Entries** button.

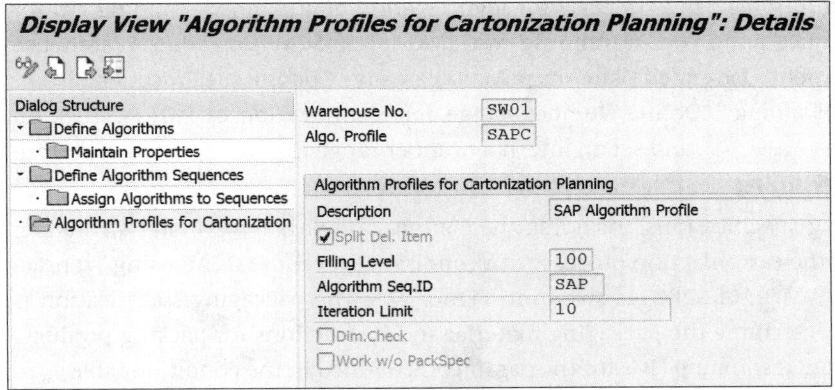

Figure 22.4 Defining the Algorithm Profile for Cartonization Planning

The defined algorithm is then assigned to an algorithm sequence to define the sequence in which algorithms are accessed. At least one algorithm must be assigned to the sequence.

4. Define an algorithm profile, and assign it to an algorithm sequence. The algorithm profile determines the logic for packing multiple items into planned shipping HUs.

   The following key data is used to define characteristics of the algorithm profile:

   - **Split delivery item**
     The **Split Del. Item** indicator allows the system to split the quantity in a delivery line item if it exceeds the planned shipping HU capacity.
   - **Filling level**
     The value in the **Filling Level** field is defined as a percentage and indicates the maximum percentage of volume up to which the packaging material can be filled while creating the planned shipping HU.
   - **Dimension check**
     If the **Dim. Check** indicator is set, the system checks the dimensions of the product being packed against the dimensions of the packaging material to check whether it can be packed in the HU created for that packaging material.

5. You can set an access sequence for determination of an algorithm profile based on various parameters such as warehouse process type, activity area, route, carrier, and so on. To do so, navigate to IMG path **SCM Extended Warehouse Management • Extended Warehouse Management • Goods Issue Process • Cartonization Planning • Define Access Sequence of Algorithm Profiles**.

22

6. Define a number range interval for identification of a planned shipping HU for your embedded EWM warehouse via IMG path **SCM Extended Warehouse Management • Extended Warehouse Management • Goods Issue Process • Cartonization Planning • Define Number Range for Identification of PSHUs**. Click on [Intervals], and set an internal number range that will be used in cartonization planning.
7. Packaging specifications, including the content and packaging material, are created for the cartonization process with condition procedure **0CAP** using Transaction /SCWM/PACKSPEC, as shown in Figure 22.5. The packaging specification is used to determine the packaging material and instructions for packing products into planned shipping HUs for the parameters defined in the condition table.
8. After the determination procedure for the packaging specification is assigned to the warehouse in embedded EWM, along with the cartonization work center layout, via IMG path **SCM Extended Warehouse Management • Extended Warehouse Management • Goods Issue Process • Cartonization Planning • Configure Cartonization Planning on Warehouse Number Level**, click on **New Entries**, as shown in Figure 22.6.

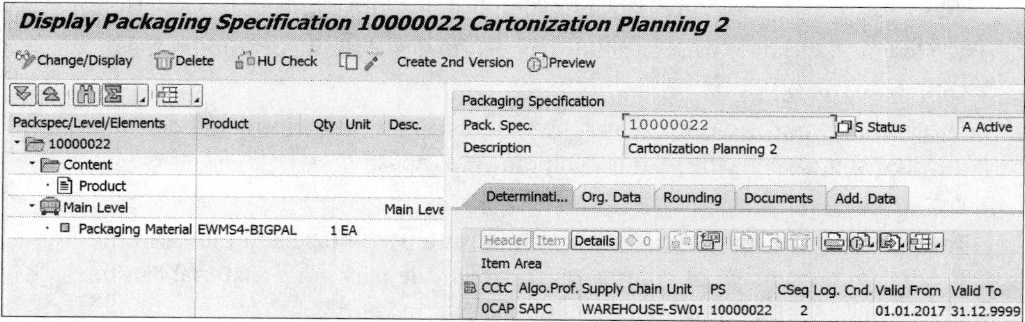

Figure 22.5 Packaging Specification for the Planned Shipping HU

Display View "Configure Cartonization Planning on Warehouse No. Level"

Configure Cartonization Planning on Warehouse No...

War...	Det. Proc.	Layout
SW01	0CAP	PSHU

Figure 22.6 Defining Cartonization Planning

22.3 Creation of Planned Shipping Handling Units

Planned shipping HUs are templates based on which shipping HUs can be created in embedded EWM during the picking and packing process. Planned shipping HUs don't physically exist in embedded EWM because they're used only for planning purposes. They can be created manually or automatically. If the quantity specified in the outbound delivery order is in the base unit of measure (BUoM), but the stock for the product is mostly stored with a special alternative unit of measure (AUoM), then the system uses the stock-specific UoM maintained in the product master data to carry out the cartonization planning.

The planned shipping HU is identified by a number with the prefix "$_", as shown in Figure 22.7, and it contains the following information:

- Planned shipping HU header
- Planned shipping HU item
- Additional planned shipping HU identifiers
- Reference document

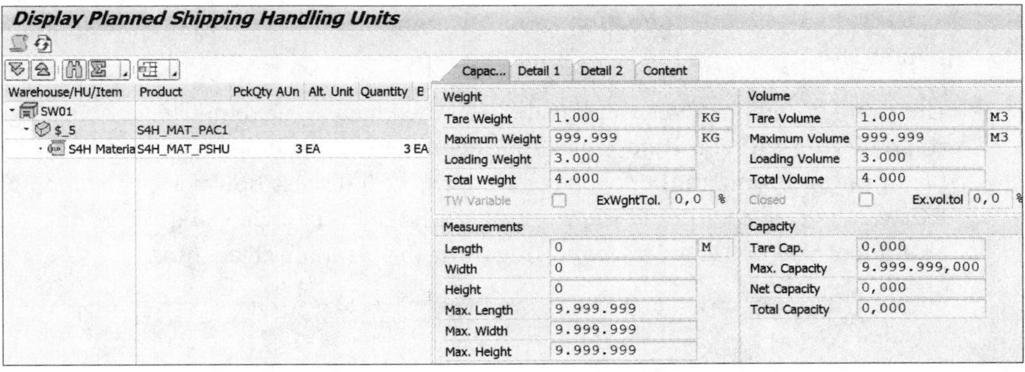

Figure 22.7 Planned Shipping Handling Unit in Embedded EWM

Planned shipping HUs can be created manually or automatically. They can be created automatically only if there is at least one active implementation of the cartonization planning algorithm business add-in (BAdI). You can access this implementation via IMG path **SCM Extended Warehouse Management • Extended Warehouse Management • Business Add-Ins (BAdIs) for Extended Warehouse Management • Goods Issue Process • Cartonization Planning • BAdI: Cartonization Planning Algorithm**.

The automatic creation process for planned shipping HUs includes the following steps:

1. For each created or changed outbound delivery order item, the system determines a process profile for cartonization planning and assigns it to the item. Automatic cartonization planning can be triggered for outbound delivery orders, for waves, and during warehouse order creation. We'll discuss each of these options in detail in this section.
2. The system groups the outbound delivery order items that can be packed together. During cartonization planning, the system processes each such group differently. The grouping is done based on the following factors:
   - Algorithm profile for cartonization planning
   - Consolidation group
   - Activity area
   - Wave (if you're doing cartonization planning for waves)

   Delivery items belonging to different process groups are always packed in different HUs.
3. The system executes the cartonization planning algorithm to create planned shipping HUs.

The planned shipping HUs thus created will then be used as templates for creating shipping HUs during the picking or packing process, depending on the process profile of cartonization. In the following sections, we'll discuss how planned shipping HUs can be created automatically for outbound delivery orders and waves during creation of warehouse orders for picking using the planning algorithms.

> **Note**
>
> The Maintain Planned Shipping HUs app allows you to create, maintain, and execute planned shipping HUs as templates for outbound warehouse requests in the warehouse.

22.3.1 Creation of Planned Shipping Handling Units for Outbound Delivery Order

Execute cartonization planning for outbound delivery order items by navigating to **SAP Easy Access** path **Logistics • SCM Extended Warehouse Management • Extended**

Warehouse Management • Work Scheduling • Cartonization Planning • Cartonization Planning for ODO. You can use this transaction to create, simulate, and delete planned shipping HUs based on the values selected in the **Execution Mode** drop-down.

Using simulation, you can simulate creating planned shipping HUs without saving them in the database. You can delete existing planned shipping HUs before starting to create new planned shipping HUs for outbound delivery orders. Creation of planned shipping HUs for the outbound delivery orders can also be performed in the background by scheduling report /SCWM/R_CAP_BACKGROUND using Transaction SM36. Various search criteria are available in the report selection screen, based on which outbound delivery order line items can be selected. For example, you can select deliveries by providing a time window for goods issue or departure from the yard or by picking deliveries for a specific ship-to party or carrier. The system will execute cartonization planning only for delivery items that aren't blocked and for which goods issue hasn't been initiated.

If the planned shipping HUs are already created for some of the quantity or the full quantity for the outbound delivery order item, then you can select the **Exclude Items with Planned Shipping HUs** indicator to exclude those items while creating new planned shipping HUs.

Embedded EWM allows you to carry out cartonization planning in outbound processing using a pallet algorithm. This functionality leverages the use of the package builder and provides more flexibility with the algorithms used for creating planned shipping HUs by allowing for mixed pallet building. Thus, instead of creating pallets for single products, the system can create pallets with separate layers for each product or create layers with mixed products. In each case, the system tries to use the complete HU capacity.

As shown in Figure 22.8, you can control the creation of mixed packages or layers by defining the attributes in the package building profile created via IMG path **SCM Extended Warehouse Management • Extended Warehouse Management • Goods Issue Process • Cartonization Planning • Package Building**. Click on **New Entries**, and select the required checkboxes to define package attributes in the **Package Builder Profile** section.

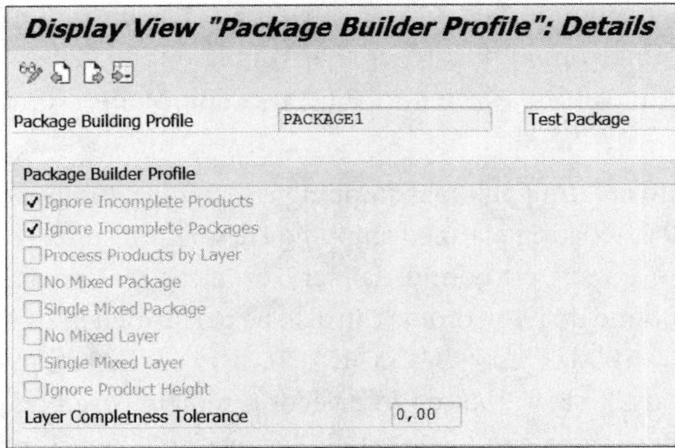

Figure 22.8 Define Package Builder

> **Note**
>
> The pallet algorithm used in embedded EWM for cartonization planning is also used in SAP Transportation Management for creation of freight units. This functionality is currently available only in embedded EWM in SAP S/4HANA and in SAP EWM 9.5, which is the latest SAP offering for standalone SAP Extended Warehouse Management.

22.3.2 Creation of Planned Shipping Handling Units for Waves

Using this process, embedded EWM can create planned shipping HUs for waves based on predefined algorithms. As discussed earlier, to trigger cartonization planning for items in outbound delivery orders, the **Cartonization Planning for Waves** checkbox should be selected in the relevant process profile. Embedded EWM tries to select the outbound delivery orders that have items or split items assigned to a wave. You can create planned shipping HUs for outbound delivery order items based on wave numbers and/or the time period or wave cutoff time for a specific warehouse number.

Creation of planned shipping HUs for waves can be done via **SAP Easy Access** path **Logistics • SCM Extended Warehouse Management • Extended Warehouse Management • Work Scheduling • Cartonization Planning • Cartonization Planning for Waves** or in the background by scheduling report /SCWM/R_CAP_WAVE using Transaction SM36.

If the planned shipping HUs already exist for the outbound delivery order items, then the system calculates the quantity of products not yet packed in a planned shipping HU for each selected outbound delivery order item. The system takes different actions based on the comparison between unpacked quantity and selected quantity. If the unpacked quantity is less than the selected quantity, then the system doesn't create a new planned shipping HU; otherwise, it does.

22.3.3 Creation of Planned Shipping Handling Units during Warehouse Order Creation

Embedded EWM allows users to use the planned shipping HUs created in the warehouse as pick HUs for picking warehouse tasks while creating warehouse orders for picking. The following settings need to be made in the system to execute picking with cartonization planning:

- To create the planned shipping HUs during warehouse order creation, you need to activate the **CAP Compatibility** setting in customization of the warehouse order creation rule. Embedded EWM can create planned shipping HUs for picking warehouse tasks during the creation of a warehouse order based on predefined algorithms.
- Define the setting to create pick HUs while executing pick warehouse tasks by setting the **Create HUs** and **Assign WTs to HUs** indicators in the packing profile assigned to the warehouse order creation rule.
- Define the start and end bins for the activity area via **SAP Easy Access** path **Logistics • SCM Extended Warehouse Management • Extended Warehouse Management • Master Data • Storage Bin • Assign Start/End Storage Bin for Activity Area**.

You can also use cartonization planning to create planned shipping HUs if you're using pick points in the picking process. However, the system only proposes pick HUs based on planned shipping HUs if all the HU warehouse tasks for carrying the stock from the source to the pick point are confirmed at the same time and if picking at the pick point is performed using RF. For two-step picking, you can use cartonization planning for planned shipping HU creation during the allocation step in the two-step picking process because they're created with reference to outbound delivery orders. Because the withdrawal warehouse tasks are created without reference to outbound delivery orders, you can't use cartonization planning during the withdrawal step in two-step picking.

The planned shipping HU created during cartonization planning also can be used as a template for creating shipping HUs or proposing packing materials for creating empty HUs while carrying out packing at a work center or using RF packing menu options. The empty HU can be created for packing goods into a shipping HU or used manually in the work center for repacking goods in the HU. The new HU may also be created while repacking HUs during consolidation or while repacking HU items during deconsolidation.

22.4 Managing Planned Shipping HUs in the Warehouse

The planned shipping HUs in the warehouse can be monitored in the embedded EWM warehouse monitor using Transaction /SCWM/MON. In the node hierarchy, navigate to the selection screen for displaying planned shipping HUs via **Outbound • Documents • Planned Shipping Handling Units**. You can use any of the following selection criteria to select the planned shipping HUs to display:

- Document or wave
- Shipment
- Partner

Embedded EWM provides an interface to maintain the created planned shipping HUs by navigating to **SAP Easy Access** path **Logistics • SCM Extended Warehouse Management • Extended Warehouse Management • Work Scheduling • Cartonization Planning • Maintain Planned Shipping Handling Units**. You can select the planned shipping HUs to be displayed for a warehouse by specifying the documents or planned shipping HUs.

The next screen displays the list of selected planned shipping HUs, as shown in Figure 22.9. The report provides various options such as creating, modifying, and repacking existing planned shipping HUs. To run the report, select the planned shipping HUs from the left-hand menu on the screen, select the available functions from the right-hand side, and click on **Execute**.

You also can create planned shipping HUs or simulate their creation from the report screen by clicking on [icon] and selecting the required action, as shown in Figure 22.10. For an unpacked outbound delivery order item with an open quantity greater than 0, select the **Automatic Cart. Planning** action to create planned shipping HUs. The system determines the cartonization profile and creates a planned shipping HU for the delivery item. The **Test Cart. Planning** option allows you to simulate the creation of planned shipping HUs. The system provides an option to select an algorithm profile to perform this simulation.

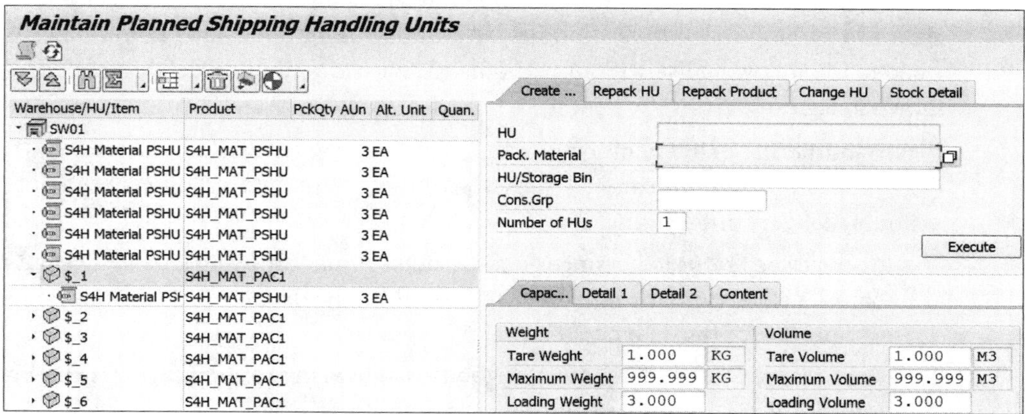

Figure 22.9 Searching Planned Shipping HUs Using Selection Criteria

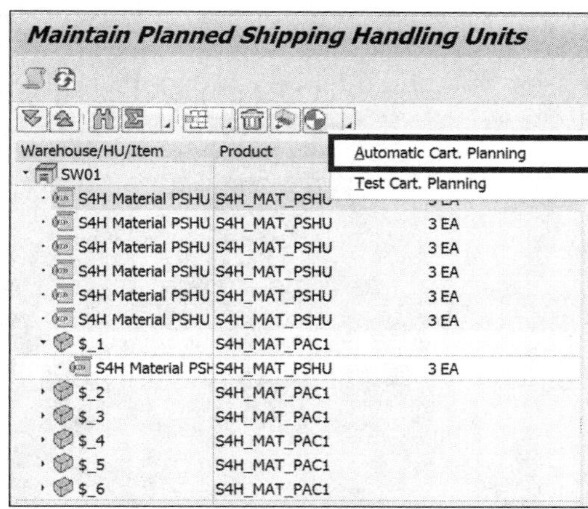

Figure 22.10 Maintaining Planned Shipping HUs

> **Note**
>
> To make any changes or carry out any action in an already-created planned shipping HU, it's important to define a cartonization work center with an appropriate cartonization work center layout.

The planned shipping HUs in the warehouse can be deleted on a regular basis, as well as on demand, by navigating to **SAP Easy Access** path **Logistics • SCM Extended Warehouse Management • Extended Warehouse Management • Work Scheduling • Cartonization Planning • Delete Planned Shipping Handling Units**. You can select the planned shipping HUs for deletion in a warehouse using the selection criteria provided in the following list, with or without reference to outbound delivery order, as shown in Figure 22.11:

- **With outbound delivery order**
  Planned shipping HUs can be selected with the appropriate subfilter of the outbound delivery order status:
  - **Goods Issue Status** (days since goods issue): Planned shipping HUs for the outbound delivery order can be selected based on the date on which goods issue was posted for the delivery item.
  - **Goods Issue Status** (date range of goods issue): Planned shipping HUs can be selected based on the date range for their goods issue dates.
  - **Archiving Status**: Planned shipping HUs can be selected based on outbound delivery orders marked for archiving.
- **Without outbound delivery order**
  Planned shipping HUs can be selected for outbound delivery orders that have already been deleted.

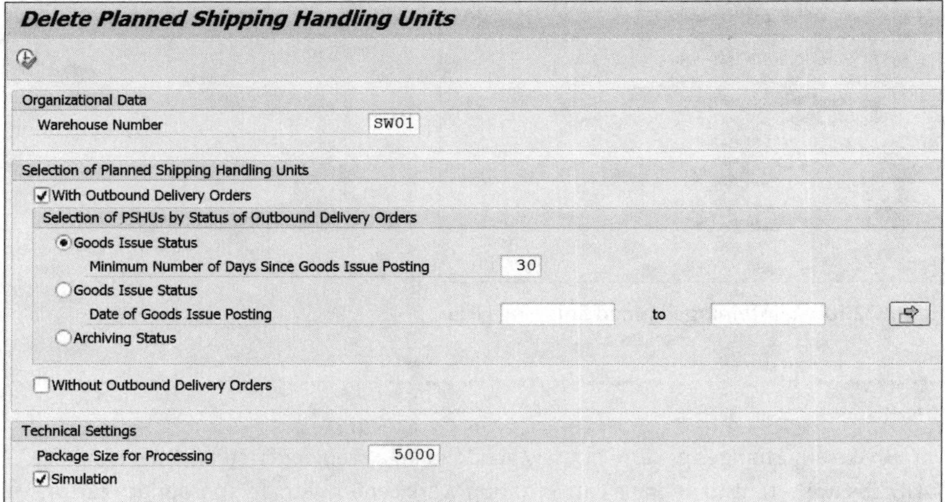

Figure 22.11 Deleting Planned Shipping HUs

It's important to note that embedded EWM provides a way to let you run the planned shipping HU deletion based on packages so that you can group several planned shipping HUs and execute their deletion in packages. This helps delete planned shipping HUs of a certain package even if another package faces deletion issues and isn't able to proceed with deletion. You can also simulate the deletion of planned shipping HUs in the system. This enables you to discover any issues with deletion without having to execute actual deletion.

22.5 Summary

This chapter introduced cartonization planning for creating planned shipping HUs. We specified the prerequisites required for setting up cartonization planning in embedded EWM, which can be used in picking and packing. We also explained various scenarios during which planned shipping HUs can be created: directly for an outbound delivery order, for waves, and in creation of planned shipping HUs during warehouse order creation. Use of planned shipping HUs during the picking and packing process was also explained in detail in this chapter.

Toward the end, we considered the other operations that can be carried out on planned shipping HUs, such as maintenance, monitoring, and deletion of obsolete planned shipping HUs. These sections on planned shipping HUs should help you use planned shipping HUs as effective templates to create pick HUs and shipping HUs during the picking and packing process in embedded EWM. In the next chapter, we'll discuss SAP Dock Appointment Scheduling.

Chapter 23
SAP Dock Appointment Scheduling

SAP Dock Appointment Scheduling is used to plan the arrival of vehicles in the warehouse efficiently. In this chapter, we'll discuss SAP's standard and user-friendly method for managing carrier appointments in embedded EWM using SAP Dock Appointment Scheduling.

One of the objectives of a busy warehouse is to make effective use of yard space and doors available to load and unload stock from different carriers during working hours without causing mismanagement and delays in warehouse processes. Carriers also want to improve on the way they coordinate the arrival and departure of transportation units (TUs)/vehicles in warehouses so that their vehicles don't have to wait unnecessarily in the yard. SAP Dock Appointment Scheduling provides an effective tool that can give visibility into vehicle management and planning for both the carrier and the shipping office.

In this chapter, we'll discuss the settings and workings of SAP Dock Appointment Scheduling with embedded EWM, starting with an introduction to SAP Dock Appointment Scheduling (Section 23.1), which is followed by a discussion of the fundamental building blocks and settings required to set it up for embedded EWM (Section 23.2) and how carriers can plan their own appointments using SAP Dock Appointment Scheduling in embedded EWM (Section 23.3).

23.1 What Is SAP Dock Appointment Scheduling?

The browser-based application called SAP Dock Appointment Scheduling divides the working time of the doors into meaningful slots and makes them visible to carriers so they can select a time slot for the arrival of a TU/vehicle in the warehouse. SAP Dock Appointment Scheduling allows carriers and warehouse users to plan appointments for incoming vehicles or TUs in the warehouse during loading and unloading. This allows carriers to more effectively plan their vehicles by reducing the waiting time in the warehouse. It also allows warehouse users to manage their workloads more effectively by streamlining the incoming and outgoing vehicles in the warehouse. SAP Dock Appointment Scheduling is available within embedded EWM, or it can be deployed as a standalone solution without using any embedded EWM functions.

In Section 23.1.1, we'll explain the business context in which SAP Dock Appointment Scheduling can be used in real-world scenarios. In Section 23.1.2, we'll explain the processes carried out in the system, along with documents related to SAP Dock Appointment Scheduling that are used to plan and execute TUs in embedded/decentralized EWM.

23.1.1 Business Process

American company Alpha Medicals receives an order from one of its customers, Medimax Corporation Limited, based in Mexico. The order sent by Medimax contains various pharmaceutical products that are to be delivered in a timely manner. Stock that will be delivered to the customer will be picked from the Alpha Medicals warehouse in a timely manner by the truck carrier so that it reaches the client facility in time. SAP Dock Appointment Scheduling is used to ensure the truck carrier arrives at the Alpha Medicals warehouse parking area on the correct date and time and docks its trucks at the correct docking location to maintain truck traffic in the parking lot without creating congestion in the warehouse yard. Carriers use SAP Dock Appointment Scheduling so they can—either directly or with the help of the Alpha Medicals yard administrator—book appropriate slots for their trucks to dock to the right doors in the yard so that stock can be loaded and goods issued to destination customers. This process in embedded EWM and its usage involves the following multiple steps:

1. Figure 23.1 depicts the dock appointment scheduling landscape of Alpha Medicals in which the truck carrier logs on to the Create Loading Appointments app and books appointment in the yard for arrival and departure.

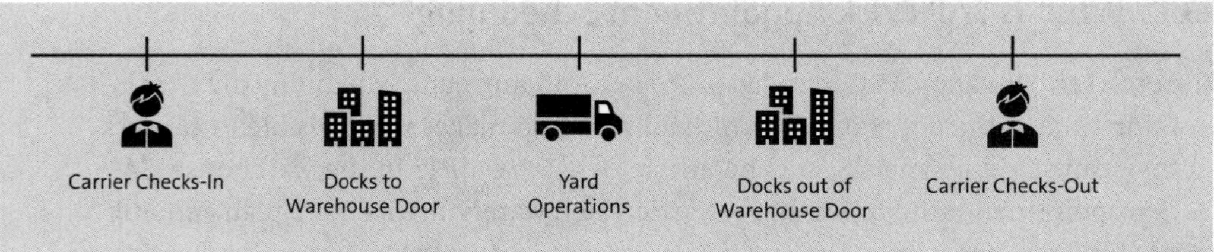

Figure 23.1 Business Flow for SAP Dock Appointment Scheduling

2. After the appointment is confirmed by the yard administrator of Alpha Medicals, the carriers get a confirmation of the same either via mail or directly in the Access Loading Appointment app.
3. Based on the allocated time schedule for truck arrival and departure, the carrier arrives at the warehouse, docks at that allocated parking lot, moves to the doors for loading the goods, and checks out using standard yard management features.

Based on this example, we've explained the series of processes carried out during the SAP Dock Appointment Scheduling processes. To optimize the frontend and make the frontend user friendly, SAP has provided the Process Loading Appointment app that can be used to carry out most of the preceding processes.

23.1.2 System Process

Process steps and documents that are created and used in embedded EWM using SAP Dock Appointment Scheduling are as follows:

1. The truck carrier books a stock handling activity appointment at the Alpha Medical warehouse so that the trucks can arrive in the warehouse without causing traffic congestion while maximizing truck usage time. After the appointment is booked, the truck arrives in the warehouse yard at the designated time and queues at the appropriate warehouse checkpoint.
2. After the truck arrives at the checkpoint, the truck status is set as **Arrived at Checkpoint** in SAP Dock Appointment Scheduling using the SAP Fiori app called Process Loading Appointments.
3. After the **Arrived at Checkpoint** status is set, a TU is created in embedded EWM, and its status is automatically set to **Arrival at Checkpoint**.
4. The logistics administrator of Alpha Medicals assigns deliveries to the TU that are to be carried together on this truck and assigns the TU to a door of the warehouse.
5. The preceding step sets the status of the TU as **Arrival at Door** in embedded EWM, which triggers the same status to SAP Dock Appointment Scheduling.
6. When the goods are ready to be loaded on the truck, warehouse workers load the goods from the goods issue staging area onto the truck. When loading is complete, the truck moves off the door to go out of the warehouse yard. The logistics administrator sets the status of the TU as **Departure From Door**. This status change is synchronously communicated to SAP Dock Appointment Scheduling, where the status of the truck is set as **Departure From Dock**.

7. After the truck moves out of the warehouse from the checkpoint, the status of the truck in embedded EWM is set to **Departure From Checkpoint**. This status change is synchronously communicated to SAP Dock Appointment Scheduling, where the status of the truck is set as **Departed From Checkpoint**.

Tip

It's worth mentioning that the SAP Dock Appointment Scheduling processes in embedded EWM have been enhanced over a period with the addition of a smart solution based on the Internet of Things (IoT), such as automatic number plate reading implementation to automate the check-in and check-out processes for trucks in warehouse.

To create and allocate appointments to the carriers, some important structures, such as docking locations, loading points, and the like, are created in SAP Dock Appointment Scheduling. This data can be created either from Transaction NWBC or using the SAP Fiori-based applications shown in Figure 23.2.

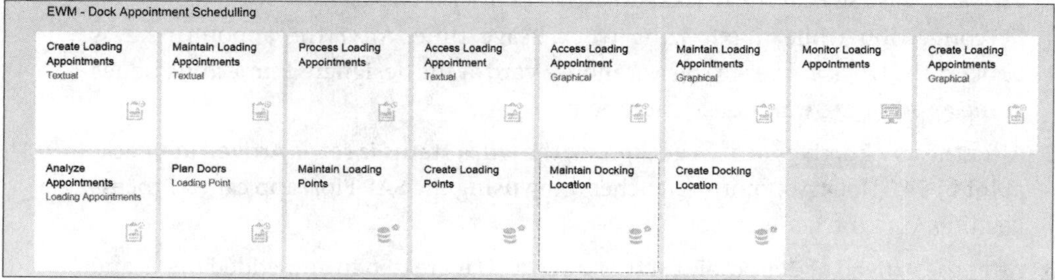

Figure 23.2 SAP Fiori Apps Used for SAP Dock Appointment Scheduling in Embedded EWM

23.2 Configuring SAP Dock Appointment Scheduling

In the following sections, we'll look at the fundamental building blocks of SAP Dock Appointment Scheduling and how to configure them. We'll also cover integrating SAP Dock Appointment Scheduling with embedded EWM.

23.2.1 Docking Location

A *docking location* represents a geographical location of a group of loading points, such as warehouses or distribution centers. If many loading points in geographical proximity have common characteristics such as time zone, address, and the like, then you can assign them to a docking location. The docking location is the embedded EWM warehouse if you're using embedded EWM integration with SAP Dock Appointment Scheduling. You can define whether the loading points are integrated with embedded EWM in the docking location.

Docking locations can be created by a user with the /SCWM/DAS_ADMINISTRATOR role. A docking location can be created via Transaction NWBC by navigating to **Dock Appointment Scheduling • Settings • Simple Setup • Create Docking Location**, as shown in Figure 23.3. You can also access the same options using the Create Docking Location app.

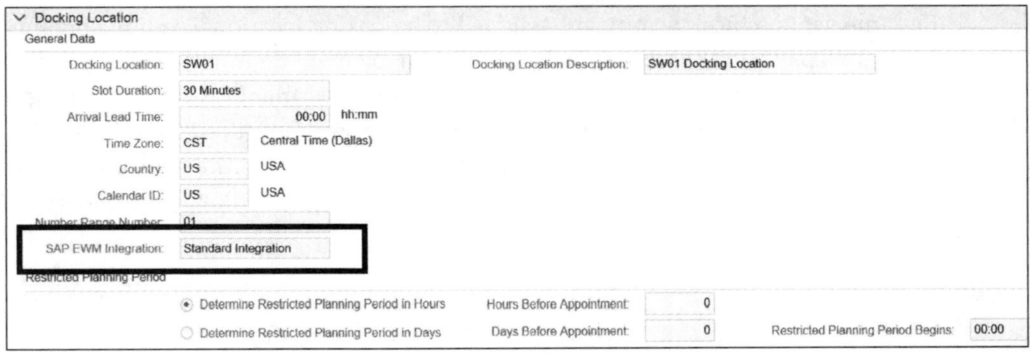

Figure 23.3 Defining the Docking Location for SAP Dock Appointment Scheduling

If you allow carriers to plan their appointments in SAP Dock Appointment Scheduling, they can do so at the docking location level, rather than at the loading point level. The system assigns the loading appointment to the relevant loading point.

It's also important to create a supply chain unit for the docking location in embedded EWM with the same name as the docking location. It can be created manually and assigned to business attribute **DL—Docking Location**, or the system can create it automatically for the docking location.

> **Note**
>
> The following SAP Fiori apps are available for docking location:
>
> - **Create Docking Location**
>   This app allows you to create new docking locations for SAP Dock Appointment Scheduling processing in the warehouse.
> - **Maintain Docking Location**
>   This app allows you to edit docking locations for SAP Dock Appointment Scheduling processing in the warehouse.

23.2.2 Loading Points

Loading points are docks in the warehouse that are used for identical business purposes, for example, for loading or unloading. As discussed earlier, loading points in the same geographical vicinity are assigned to a docking location. Loading appointments for TUs and vehicles are planned based on loading points. Loading points can be created via Transaction NWBC by navigating to **Dock Appointment Scheduling • Settings • Simple Setup • Create Loading Points**, as shown in Figure 23.4. You can also access the same options using the Loading Point app. The integration with embedded EWM must be identical for all the loading points belonging to the docking location and the docking location itself.

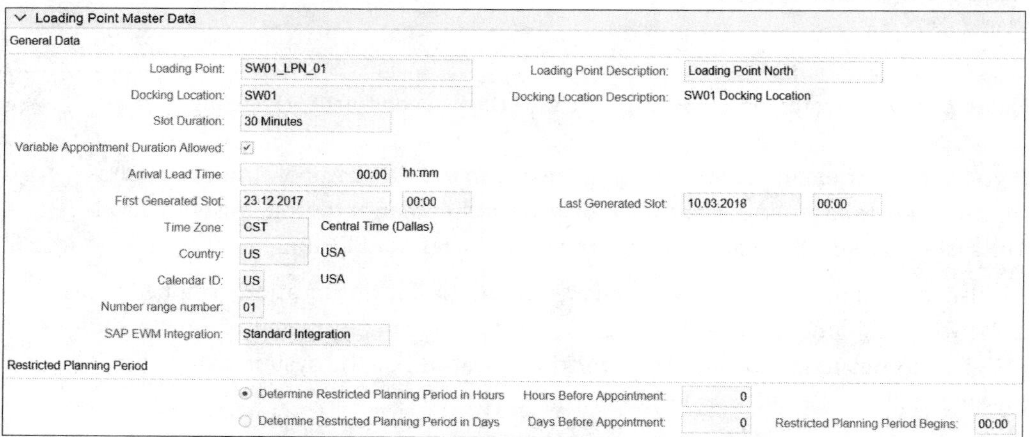

Figure 23.4 Defining Loading Points for SAP Dock Appointment Scheduling

If you're integrating SAP Dock Appointment Scheduling with embedded EWM, you must create a docking location for each warehouse and assign them to the embedded EWM warehouse. Each loading point is assigned to a supply chain unit in embedded EWM. If you don't assign an existing supply chain unit to the loading point or create a new one, then embedded EWM automatically creates a supply chain unit with the same name as that of the loading point. It uses the data entered for the loading point, such as name, address, time zone, factory calendar, and so on, to create the supply chain unit details. If an existing supply chain unit is assigned to the loading point, it must have the **LP—Loading Point** business attribute.

We'll talk more about integrating SAP Dock Appointment Scheduling with embedded EWM in later sections. The other data maintained for the loading point is as follows:

- **Time slots of loading points**
  Time slots are fixed durations of time used to plan time for the loading appointment. Time slots for loading points can be defined via Transaction NWBC by following the path **Dock Appointment Scheduling • Settings • Time Slots • Create Time Slots In Graphical View**, as shown in Figure 23.5.

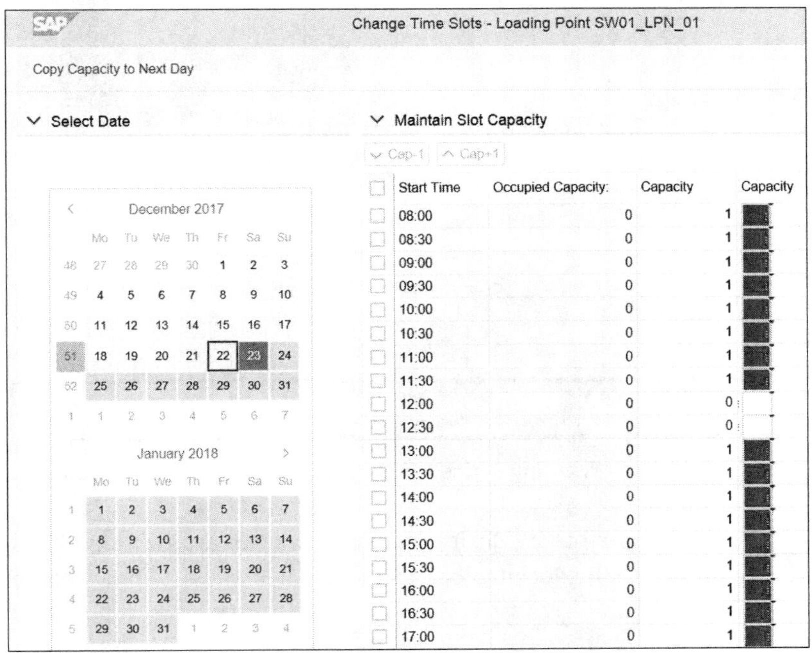

Figure 23.5 Defining Time Slots for Loading Appointments in SAP Dock Appointment Scheduling

In the input screen for creating time slots, provide the loading point, start time, finish time, and maximum capacity of TUs that can be docked at the loading point in a time slot, and then press Enter. The next screen displays the time slot definition.

You can also access the same options using the Create Loading Appointments app for creating time slots. If a slot duration is changed, then new slots are generated with the new slot duration without affecting originally generated time slots and appointments for the loading points. You can extend the time slot created to any number of future weeks by clicking on the **Copy Capacity to Next Day** option shown on the screen. In the popup screen that appears, enter the number of weeks and press Enter.

- **Restricted planning period**
  A restricted planning period is defined for the loading points in hours or days, as shown in Figure 23.6. For the restricted planning period, the appointment planners for the carriers can't reschedule or cancel their appointments but can make changes to simple details such as vehicle plate number. For any major changes, they must contact the warehouse administrator.

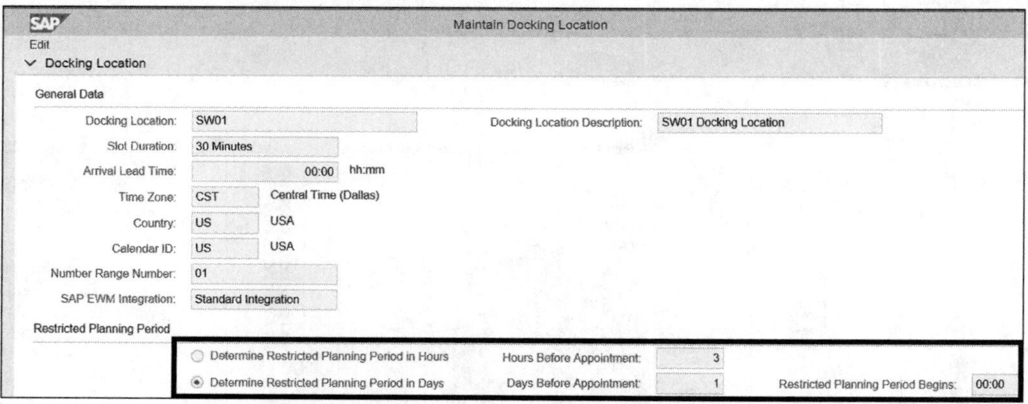

Figure 23.6 Defining a Restricted Planning Period for SAP Dock Appointment Scheduling

  If loading points are assigned to a docking location, you can assign a restricted planning period directly to the docking location, which will make it applicable to all assigned loading points.

- **Arrival lead time**
  The arrival lead time can be defined for loading points individually or for a docking

location to which loading points are assigned. Define the arrival lead time when a fixed time is required for each appointment to perform checks and paperwork at the checkpoint before the vehicle arrives at the loading point. The system adds the arrival lead time to the appointment time to calculate the time at which the vehicle should arrive at the checkpoint.

23.2.3 Appointment Management

You can create and manage a loading appointment for a loading point in SAP Dock Appointment Scheduling. The loading points can be inbound or outbound appointments, help the warehouse plan a vehicle's arrival in the warehouse, and help balance the load on warehouse doors. More than one loading appointment can be assigned to a time slot in embedded EWM if you can process loading and unloading activities from multiple TUs in the appointment duration. The SAP Dock Appointment Scheduling administrator can create loading appointments for a loading point even if no free capacity is available, but a carrier planner can't. It's possible to change the loading appointment if the vehicle hasn't yet arrived at the warehouse and move it to a different time slot, but only if you're not in a restricted planning period. You can also change the loading point for a loading appointment if the vehicle hasn't yet arrived at the warehouse and if the new loading point has the same docking location as the previous one. Loading appointments also can be canceled if needed.

Loading appointments can be created with different durations by assigning them to more than one time slot. The shortest loading appointment should be assigned to at least one time slot. The longest loading appointment should be assigned to a maximum of seven days. This time should include any time during which there is no warehouse worker available at the loading point. If docking locations are used to reserve appointments without specifying loading points, time slots, or both, then loading appointments have the **Provisional** status. These appointments don't consume any capacity at the loading point. After the loading points and time slots are specified, then the appointment status changes to **Planned**.

> **Note**
>
> You can schedule report /SCWM/R_DAS_DELETE as a background job via Transaction SM36 to delete old time slots and appointments. This helps manage transactional data volume in the system and improves system performance.

> **Note**
>
> The following additional SAP Fiori apps are available for appointment management:
>
> - **Maintain Loading Appointments**
>   This app allows you to edit loading appointments for SAP Dock Appointment Scheduling processing in the warehouse.
> - **Access Loading Appointments**
>   This app allows you to access loading appointments using textual and graphical forms for SAP Dock Appointment Scheduling processing in the warehouse.
> - **Analyze Loading Appointments**
>   This app allows you to analyze and process loading appointments for SAP Dock Appointment Scheduling processing in the warehouse.

23.2.4 Integration with Embedded EWM

SAP Dock Appointment Scheduling integration with embedded EWM allows you to manage deliveries in the warehouse using loading appointments. A loading appointment is created in SAP Dock Appointment Scheduling based on the planned arrival of a vehicle/TU in the warehouse. The loading appointment and its related TU/vehicle activity is sent to embedded EWM and can be viewed in Transaction /SCWM/TU for TUs and Transaction /SCWM/VEH for vehicles in embedded EWM. You must have SAP Business Client installed to use SAP Dock Appointment Scheduling.

You can monitor the TUs coming into and out of the warehouse based on loading appointments by using the shipping cockpit. The TUs consume the loading appointments and perform all steps, ranging from arrival at the checkpoint to departure from the dock in embedded EWM. You can plan deliveries in either SAP Dock Appointment Scheduling or embedded EWM if SAP Dock Appointment Scheduling integration is set up.

To integrate SAP Dock Appointment Scheduling with embedded EWM, the following settings must be made in SAP Dock Appointment Scheduling using Transaction NWBC or using an SAP Fiori app:

- A docking location must be created in SAP Dock Appointment Scheduling with the same name as the supply chain unit created for the warehouse in embedded EWM.
- Loading points must be defined and assigned to a docking location.
- Warehouse doors must be assigned to each loading point. Do this via Transaction NWBC by navigating to IMG path **Dock Appointment Scheduling • Settings •**

Simple Setup • Assign Doors to Loading Point. In the screen that appears, provide the loading point and embedded EWM warehouse number, and press Enter. Click on **Edit**, and assign the loading points to the warehouse doors displayed on the screen.

The following settings are required in embedded EWM to integrate with SAP Dock Appointment Scheduling:

- Define all settings required to perform basic shipping and receiving processes. These settings include creation of vehicles and TUs, setting up number ranges, and so on; they've been discussed in detail in Chapter 18.
- Create number ranges for loading appointments via IMG path **SCM Extended Warehouse Management • Extended Warehouse Management • Cross-Process Settings • Shipping and Receiving • Dock Appointment Scheduling • Define Number Range Interval for Appointment Numbers**, as shown in Figure 23.7. Click on Intervals, define a number range interval for appointments, and save.

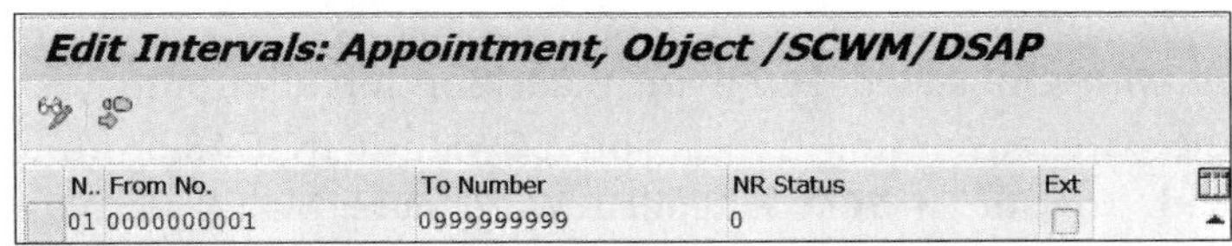

Figure 23.7 Number Range for SAP Dock Appointment Scheduling Appointments

> **Warning**
>
> The number range intervals of TUs/vehicles and appointment numbers must be different.

- Users should be assigned to appropriate roles to manage appointments for loading and unloading of goods. You also need to create a business partner for the carrier and assign it to the carrier role to allow carriers to book appointments directly in the system.
- The means of transport that needs to be entered in a loading appointment is created in Customizing by navigating to IMG path **SCM Extended Warehouse Management • Extended Warehouse Management • Cross-Process Settings • Shipping and Receiving • Dock Appointment Scheduling • Define Means of Transport**. Click on **New Entries**, and create the new means of transport.

- Additional reference document categories can be defined for use when creating loading appointments. These reference document categories can act as the basis for actions the system takes with the reference documents, for example, existence checks for packaging specifications. As shown in Figure 23.8, the reference document categories can be defined via IMG path **SCM Extended Warehouse Management • Extended Warehouse Management • Cross-Process Settings • Shipping and Receiving • Dock Appointment Scheduling • Define Reference Document Categories**. Click on **New Entries**, and create the document category.

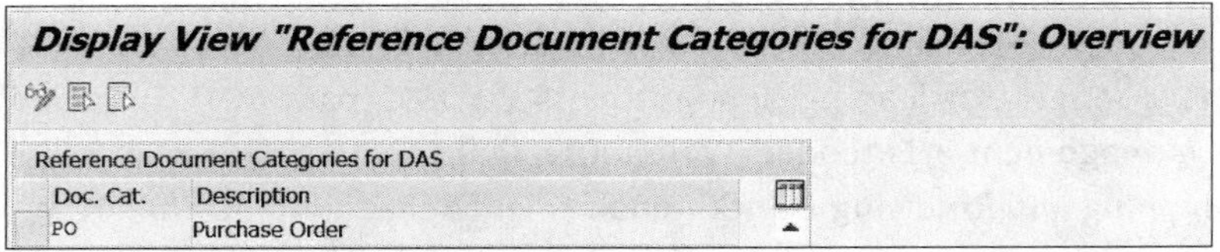

Figure 23.8 Defining Reference Document Categories for SAP Dock Appointment Scheduling

- Integration settings with embedded EWM are made for inbound/outbound appointments for the warehouse using Transaction /SCWM/SR_INTDAS or from **SAP Easy Access** path **Logistics • SCM Extended Warehouse Management • Extended Warehouse Management • Interfaces • SAP Dock Appointment Scheduling • Integration Settings for SAP EWM**. You can activate the creation of loading appointments for inbound or outbound TUs by selecting the required checkboxes, as shown in Figure 23.9. This allows appointments to be created as soon as deliveries are assigned to them.

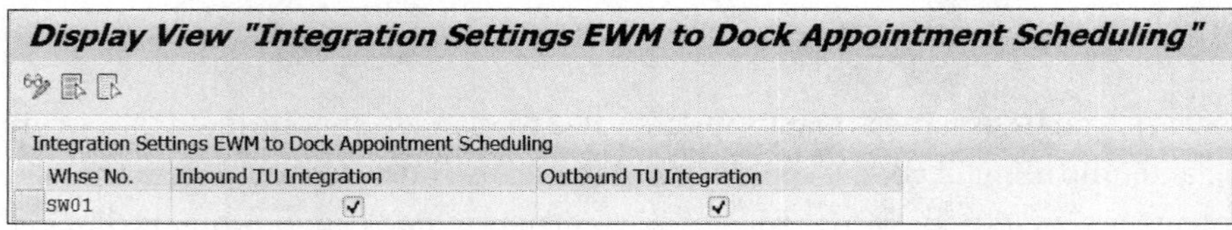

Figure 23.9 Integrating Embedded EWM with SAP Dock Appointment Scheduling

23.3 Planning for Carriers

As discussed previously, SAP Dock Appointment Scheduling provides a way to allow carriers working with appointment schedules to effectively manage their vehicle utilization. By collaborating with the warehouse, the carriers can prebook the loading appointments for their vehicles, thus reducing the amount of time their vehicles are standing idle in the warehouse, for example, waiting at a parking bay for an empty door. Carriers can also update the details of the loading appointment or cancel the appointment if it's not in the restricted planning window.

Define a carrier using Transaction BP with the business partner role of the carrier. The planner for the carrier is created as the business partner of type **Person** and is assigned the right role for authorization /SCWM/DAS_EXT_CARR_PLANNER. This step is required if the planner must be set up to book appointments on behalf of the carrier. To make a business partner a planner on behalf of the carrier, the carrier is assigned the planner business partner with the **Is Dock Appointment Scheduling Planner** relationship.

The carrier is provided limited authorization to plan and create new appointments. The system user for the carrier can then log in to embedded EWM and carry out appointment planning in SAP Dock Appointment Scheduling.

> **Note**
> The Plan Doors (Loading Point) app allows you to assign/unassign doors allocated to a loading point and to a TU for SAP Dock Appointment Scheduling processing in the warehouse.

23.4 Summary

This chapter introduced SAP Dock Appointment Scheduling and the business use of this application from the perspective of warehouse operators and carriers. We explained the building blocks and data elements required to set up SAP Dock Appointment Scheduling. This chapter also explains setting up the appointment planner for carriers. We also covered how SAP Dock Appointment Scheduling integration with embedded EWM can be carried out in both cases, whether the loading appointments originate in embedded EWM or in SAP Dock Appointment Scheduling. In the next chapter, we'll discuss the material flow system.

Chapter 24
Material Flow System

The material flow system provides a standard embedded EWM solution to manage automated warehouses for putaway and pick handling units (HUs). In this chapter, we'll discuss how embedded EWM can be connected directly to automated warehouses to streamline warehouse processes even further.

Warehouses often use automatic storage and retrieval systems to improve productivity in the warehouse and automate the movement of HUs without any manual intervention. Automatic storage and retrieval systems are mainly used in large warehouses that require a high rate of stock movement. An automatic storage and retrieval system consists of components such as a conveyer segment, an automatic forklift, transfer cars, storage racks, input/output systems, and so on.

As organizations grow, they implement advanced functionalities for optimized material flow in the warehouse. Automated warehouses provide one such optimization by using carousels, vertical lift modules, and automated storage and retrieval systems. These systems can handle a wide variety of loads at varying speeds, thus helping warehouses match the speed of order fulfillment with real-time order demand. These systems also reduce labor requirements for the warehouse.

Embedded EWM provides a standard solution called the *material flow system* to connect the system to an automated warehouse directly using programmable logic controllers. Section 24.1 introduces the material flow system and the advantages of using embedded EWM's material flow system over other third-party systems for integrating automated warehouses. Section 24.2 covers the core components in the material flow system and the configuration settings required to set up integration with an automated warehouse. With this information, you should be able to integrate automated warehouses with EWM using the material flow system and trigger telegram communication between embedded EWM and programmable logic controllers. Finally, Section 24.3 covers reprocessing acknowledged telegrams in embedded EWM in case of a system failure on the shop floor.

24.1 What Is the Material Flow System?

The material flow systems allow you to connect an automated warehouse to embedded EWM via programmable logic controllers. Because the material flow system communicates directly with the terminals exchanging information with automated conveyers, forklifts, and so on, no separate warehouse control unit is required for enabling communication between embedded EWM and the automated warehouse, as shown in Figure 24.1. Warehouse control units provide an interface to connect your warehouse management system (WMS) with automated warehousing components such as an automated storage and retrieval systems or forklift control systems. The warehouse tasks created in embedded EWM are subdivided into smaller tasks. These are passed on step by step via telegram communication to the programmable logic controllers responsible in each case. The automated warehouse uses these messages to execute warehouse tasks without the use of any third-party software.

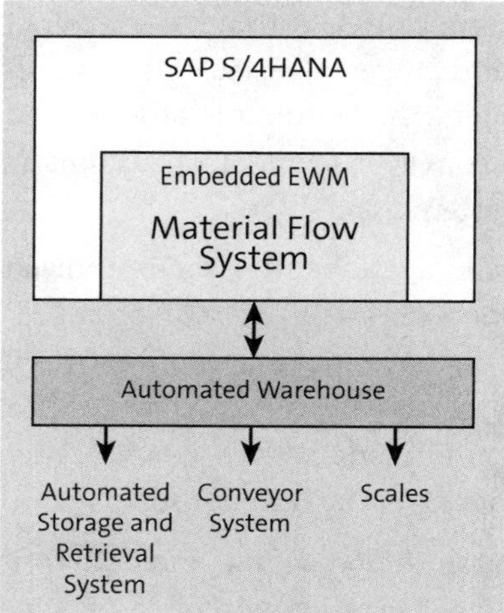

Figure 24.1 Embedded EWM and the Material Flow System Integration in SAP S/4HANA

In section Section 24.1.1, we'll explain the business context in which the material flow system can be used in real-world scenarios. In Section 24.1.2, we'll explain the processes carried out in the system and discuss documents related to the material flow system with which stock flow is carried out in conjunction with the material flow system in embedded EWM and decentralized EWM.

24.1.1 Business Process

American company Alpha Medicals receives an order from one of its customers, Medimax Corporation Limited, based in Mexico. The order sent by Medimax contains various pharmaceutical products to be delivered in a timely manner. Stock to be delivered to the customer is stored in bins of high rack storage in the warehouse. The products are picked by the warehouse worker and placed at the pick face area from where the warehouse workers place the stock on the automated belt system. Using barcode scanning and a stock removal process-oriented storage strategy, the material flow system delivers the goods to different packing stations. Packers then pack goods into HUs and place them onto pallets, which are then staged onto the staging area from where the goods are issued out of the warehouse.

Figure 24.2 depicts the automated warehouse of Alpha Medicals in which HUs are loaded in the infeed of the conveyers.

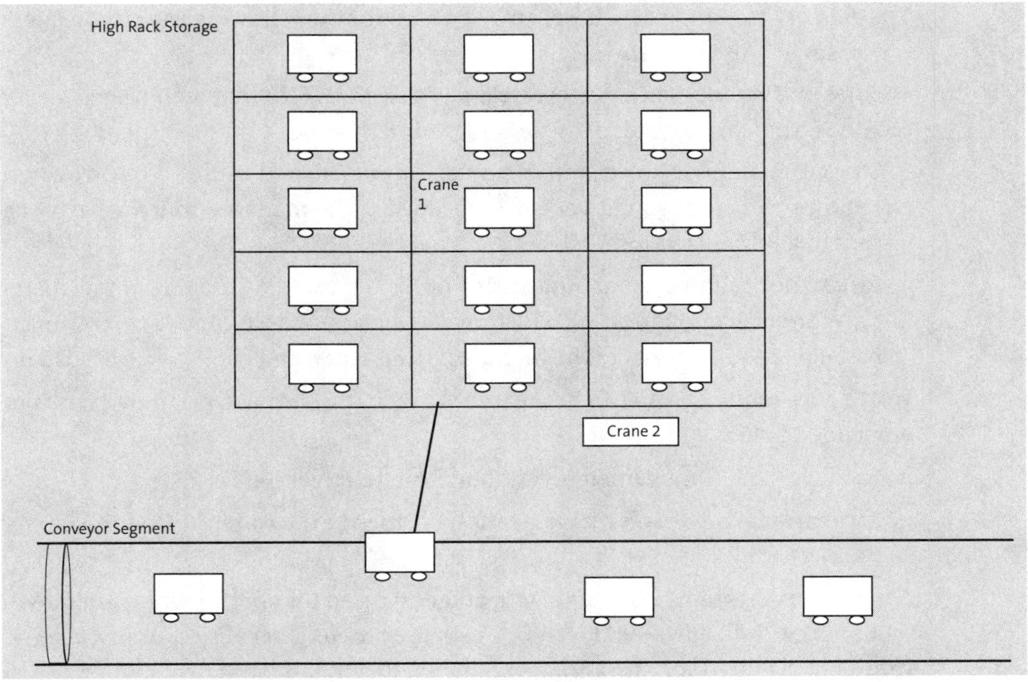

Figure 24.2 Automated Warehouse

Based on communication with the material flow system, the HU is carried to its destination bin through a network of conveyer segment lanes and drop points. The HUs then travel through a stacker crane, which can travel both horizontally and vertically. As in putaway, the material flow system is also used to pick pallets from high rack bins to the outfeed area of the conveyor segment, from where they're carried to a pick area or staging area in the warehouse.

24.1.2 System Process

The material flow system process comprises the following steps:

1. The material flow system interaction process starts with creation of a warehouse request document. The warehouse request document can be a delivery in SAP S/4HANA created for either inbound or outbound processing, or a warehouse request can be created for internal warehouse movement in embedded EWM.

   The delivery warehouse request can be created for the following various business processes in SAP S/4HANA:

   - **Sales:** A customer sales order is created in SAP S/4HANA that requires picking of goods from an embedded EWM–managed warehouse.
   - **Stock transfers:** A stock transfer order can be created in SAP S/4HANA that requires picking of goods from an embedded EWM–managed source plant to be sent to another location.
   - **Production staging:** A manufacturing order is created for staging of raw materials for production in the production staging area. These goods are consumed based on requirements in the manufacturing order, and goods issue is posted.

   Warehouse requests also can be created for various internal stock movements in embedded EWM:

   - For ad hoc stock movement from source bin to target bin
   - For rearrangement and reorganization of stock in the warehouse at the end of the day

2. A delivery is created in SAP S/4HANA and replicated for appropriate stock movement in the embedded EWM warehouse. The outbound delivery contains all relevant data required for stock movement: product, quantity, batch, and so on. In case of internal stock movements, the warehouse request is used as a base document to create follow-on documents.

3. Further processing as well as goods movement in embedded EWM is done based on the warehouse requests via creation of warehouse tasks.
4. After the initial handling of the stock is completed by the warehouse worker, and all associated warehouse tasks are confirmed by placing the stock on the automated stock movement belt, the material flow system creates stock movement tasks for packed products in embedded EWM. This leads to the automatic storage and retrieval system taking HUs to different areas of the warehouse and finally dropping them to the workers' handling bay, where the HUs are picked by either the workers or by robots and placed in the destination storage bin.
5. Depending on the number of route changes made by the material flow system for the HUs based on stock traffic, decongestion, and speed optimization parameters, the appropriate number of warehouse tasks are created and confirmed by the material flow system in embedded EWM, which keeps posting stock movements in the appropriate bins in embedded EWM.

Note

The basic difference between automated storage and retrieval systems and material flow systems is that an automated storage and retrieval system is a non-SAP automated stock movement system that interacts with embedded EWM using interfaces (e.g., IDocs) during warehouse task creation and confirmation communication.

The material flow system, on the other hand, is an out-of-the-box offering that interacts with embedded EWM and decentralized EWM for warehouse tasks creation and confirmation using native integration processes.

24.2 Configuring the Material Flow System

In this section, first we'll explain the different objects that, when defined, allow you to model the automated warehouse in embedded EWM. These objects work with each other to enable smooth functioning of the material flow system. Then, we'll discuss the basic configuration settings required to define and use these building blocks during execution of the material flow system in embedded EWM.

24.2.1 Building Blocks

The embedded EWM system controls the HU movement in an automated warehouse by interacting with one or more programmable logic controllers using warehouse tasks. Programmable logic controllers are linked to the embedded EWM system using communication channels. Embedded EWM warehouse tasks contain various stages for end-to-end material flow. The start and end of these stages are called *communication points,* through which messages called *telegrams* are interchanged between embedded EWM and programmable logic controllers. The connection between two communication points is called a *conveyer segment*. If a vehicle carries HUs between communication points and/or bins, it's represented as a resource.

To use the material flow system in embedded EWM, you need to perform some steps to set up its basic building blocks to map conveyor segments:

1. **Define a programmable logic controller.**
   Programmable logic controllers can be defined in embedded EWM via IMG path **SCM Extended Warehouse Management • Extended Warehouse Management • Material Flow System (MFS) • Master Data • Define Programmable Logic Controller**, as shown in Figure 24.3. Click on **New Entries** to create a programmable logic controller for your warehouse and define its attributes.

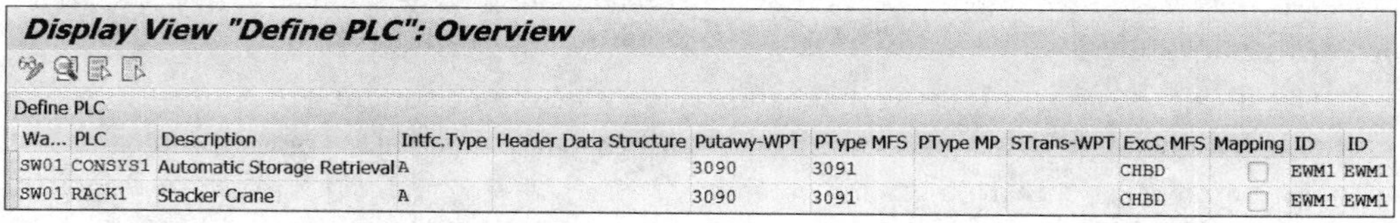

Display View "Define PLC": Overview

Define PLC

Wa...	PLC	Description	Intfc.Type	Header Data Structure	Putawy-WPT	PType MFS	PType MP	STrans-WPT	ExcC MFS	Mapping	ID	ID
SW01	CONSYS1	Automatic Storage Retrieval	A		3090	3091			CHBD	☐	EWM1	EWM1
SW01	RACK1	Stacker Crane	A		3090	3091			CHBD	☐	EWM1	EWM1

Figure 24.3 Defining Programmable Logic Controllers for the Material Flow System

Note

A *programmable logic controller* is a digital system that manages the movement of packed goods in automated warehouses using automated controls such as conveyors, stacker cranes, and so on. These automated controls that integrate with embedded EWM are defined in embedded EWM as programmable logic controllers. A programmable logic controller reads signals from connected input devices of an automated storage and retrieval system and uses control instructions to communicate with other devices such as sensors, motors, and so on.

The following fields are assigned for a programmable logic controller created for the warehouse:

- **Intfc. Type**
  A programmable logic controller is created for a programmable logic controller interface type, which is used to group together programmable logic controllers that communicate with embedded EWM in a similar way.
- **Putawy-WPT**
  The warehouse process type is used to carry out internal warehouse movements in the material flow system. The process category for the warehouse process type is **3–Internal Warehouse Movement**.
- **ExcC MFS**
  This is the exception code provided if the destination storage bin needs changing while confirming a warehouse task in the material flow system. The exception code must point to internal process code **CHBD**.
- **ID**
  This field is used to set the identification of the sender of telegrams to a programmable logic controller.

2. **Define a communication channel.**
   As shown in Figure 24.4, a communication channel can be defined via IMG path **SCM Extended Warehouse Management • Extended Warehouse Management • Material Flow System (MFS) • Master Data • Communication Channel**. Click on **New Entries**, and define a new programmable logic controller and communication channel for your embedded EWM warehouse.

Note

A communication channel is defined to create a link between the material flow system and programmable logic controller using an IP address and port. A communication channel contains various controls that drive the "to" and "from" interface communication using telegrams. These telegram messages are sent in a sequential manner. It often happens that the channel between the material flow system and the programmable logic controller is stuck or faces issues, due to which the telegram communication between them becomes asynchronous. You can restart or stop the communication channel between the material flow system and the programmable logic controller using the warehouse monitor.

Display View "Define Communication Channel": Details

Warehouse No.	SW01
PLC	CONSYS1
Comm.chan.	1

Define Communication Channel

Telegram Retries	3
Interval Tel. Retry	5
Highest Rec.Seq.No.	9999
Highest Rec.Seq.No.	9999
Fill Character	
HS Confirmation	A
HS Request	R
Handshake Mode	B Send Sender, Recipient, Telegram Type & Sequence Number
S/R Switch	☑
Max. Processes	1
Life Tel. Interval	30
Life Tel. Type	LIFE
Get Seq.No.	☐
Start Character	
End Character	
Telegram Length	0
Check Telegram	☐
ExcCode MFS	REST
Standard Error	
No Synchron.	☐

Figure 24.4 Defining the Communication Channel for the Material Flow System

3. **Define a communication point type.**
   After the communication channel is defined, the actual communication between the material flow system and programmable logic controller happens at the communication point. Each communication point is defined for a communication point type and a programmable logic controller. To define a communication point type, navigate to IMG path **SCM Extended Warehouse Management • Extended Warehouse Management • Extended Warehouse Management • Material Flow System (MFS) • Master Data • Define Communication Point Type**. Click on **New Entries**, and create a communication point type for the programmable logic controller and the embedded EWM warehouse.

4. **Define a communication point.**
   A communication point can be defined for a warehouse and programmable logic controller via IMG path **SCM Extended Warehouse Management • Extended Warehouse Management • Extended Warehouse Management • Material Flow System**

(MFS) • Master Data • Define Communication Point. Click on **New Entries**, and create a communication point for the programmable logic controller and embedded EWM warehouse.

As shown in Figure 24.5, a communication point is assigned to a storage bin in embedded EWM and can also be an ID point, end point, clarification bin, or scanner. When the HUs pass through a clarification point, the labels on the HUs are scanned, and a telegram is relayed from the programmable logic controller to embedded EWM. Embedded EWM triggers the action to find the destination storage bin and sends a new message to the programmable logic controller to move the HU to that bin. If you define a communication point for a clarification area, you can use it to reroute pallets to a storage type outside of the material flow system for further clarification. The pallet is brought back based on the decision made. The destination storage type and bin are provided in this setting, along with the warehouse process type used to create the task to move HUs to the clarification area.

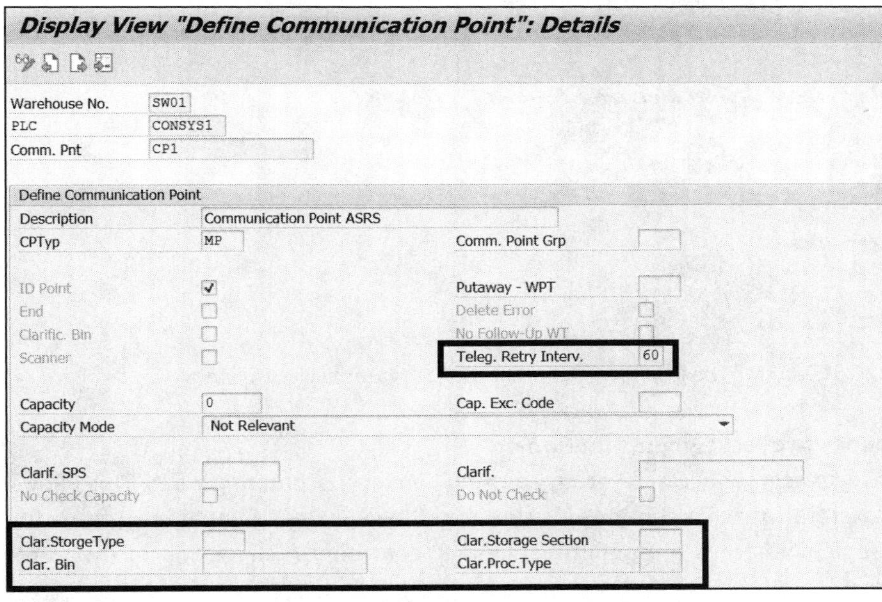

Figure 24.5 Defining the Communication Point

> **Note**
> An overview of communication points is provided in the warehouse monitor. Various actions, such as status requests, setting exceptions, and triggering telegrams for the communication point, can be taken using the warehouse monitor.

5. **Define a conveyer segment.**
   The conveyer segment represents a connection between two communication points over which HUs travel without any change in path. A conveyer segment can be defined with a capacity limit to restrict the number of HUs that can travel over the conveyer segment and an exception code to manage any capacity overflow. The system takes follow-up action as defined in the exception code. As shown in Figure 24.6, a conveyer segment can be defined via IMG path **SCM Extended Warehouse Management • Extended Warehouse Management • Extended Warehouse Management • Material Flow System (MFS) • Master Data • Define Conveyer Segment**. Click on **New Entries**, and create a new conveyor segment, along with its capacity and exception code.

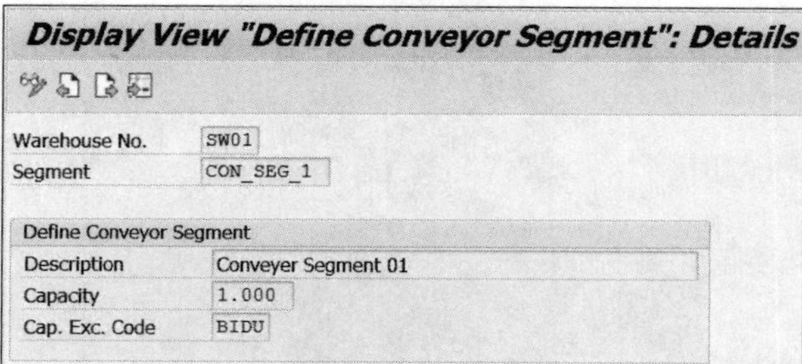

Figure 24.6 Defining the Conveyer Segment for the Material Flow System

6. **Group conveyer segments (optional).**
   Conveyer segments can be grouped using conveyer segment groups. This allows the system to take a combined action for all conveyor segments in a group, for example, if there is a programmable logic controller malfunction in the warehouse.

   The conveyer segments and conveyor segment groups can be overviewed in the **Material Flow System • Conveyor Segments** and **Material Flow System • Conveyor Segment Groups** nodes in the warehouse monitor. Using the button, you can assign an exception code to the segment or segment group to direct it to perform actions such as diverting the telegrams to some other programmable logic controller or draining the unconfirmed HUs to a drainage area.

7. **Define resource types.**
   A resource is used for performing stock movements in an automated storage and retrieval system and conveyor systems. It can be in the form of a transfer car or a crane to move the HU from one communication point to another. The material flow system resource type is used to group resources with common characteristics. Resources with common attributes are assigned to resource types, which can be defined via IMG path **SCM Extended Warehouse Management • Extended Warehouse Management • Extended Warehouse Management • Material Flow System (MFS) • Master Data • Define MFS Resource Type**. Click on **New Entries**, and provide a resource type and description.
8. **Maintain the material flow system resource.**
   Define the material flow system resource for a resource type in the warehouse via **SAP Easy Access** path **Logistics • SCM Extended Warehouse Management • Extended Warehouse Management • Master Data • Material Flow System (MFS) • Maintain MFS Resource**, as shown in Figure 24.7. Click on **New Entries**, and enter a resource ID with a description. A resource also can be assigned to a default queue from which it can pick up warehouse orders for processing.

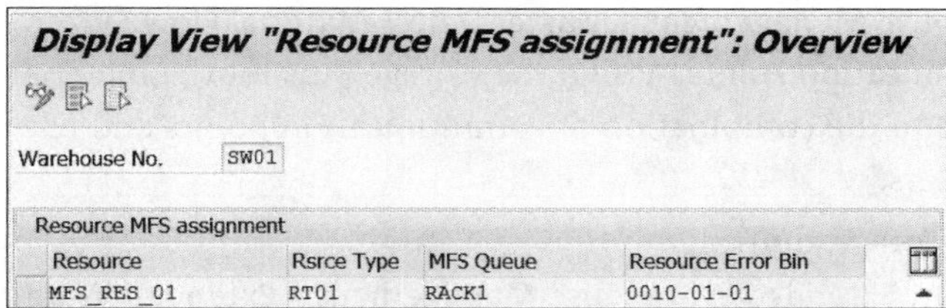

Resource	Rsrce Type	MFS Queue	Resource Error Bin
MFS_RES_01	RT01	RACK1	0010-01-01

Figure 24.7 Defining Resources for the Material Flow System

The resources available in the material flow system can be viewed in the **Resource** node in the embedded EWM warehouse monitor. Using the button, you can assign a user exception code to the resource and direct it to perform a particular follow-up action. In addition, you can recalculate warehouse tasks or trigger telegrams for the resources using the warehouse monitor.

24.2.2 Basic Configuration

After defining the building blocks of the material flow system, there are some other basic settings you need to make in embedded EWM:

1. **Assign the material flow system-relevant storage type role.**
   Assign **Automatic Warehouse (Controlled by MFS)** or **Automatic Storage Retrieval (Material Flow Control)** to the storage types used for mapping the automated warehouse via IMG path **SCM Extended Warehouse Management • Extended Warehouse Management • Master Data • Define Storage Type**. Click on **New Entries**, create a new storage type for the warehouse with the material flow system role, and save.
2. **Define storage groups for layout-oriented storage control.**
   Navigate to IMG path **SCM Extended Warehouse Management • Extended Warehouse Management • Material Flow System (MFS) • Storage Control • Define Storage Groups for Layout-Oriented Storage Control**. Click on **New Entries**, and create a new storage group for the warehouse and storage type. The storage groups are used for setting up communication points in the material flow system and are assigned to required storage bins created for the material flow system storage type.
3. **Assign the storage bins to a communication point.**
   Navigate to **SAP Easy Access** path **Logistics • SCM Extended Warehouse Management • Extended Warehouse Management • Master Data • Material Flow System (MFS) • Maintain Communication Points**. Assign the storage bins for the material flow system storage type to the combination of communication points and programmable logic controllers.
4. **Define layout-oriented storage control.**
   Navigate to IMG path **SCM Extended Warehouse Management • Extended Warehouse Management • Material Flow System (MFS) • Storage Control • Define Layout-Oriented Storage Process Control** to enable the material flow system to create warehouse tasks from the source bin to the destination bin using intermediate IDs and pick points for the material flow system. The goods are moved from the source to the destination bin in the warehouse via the intermediate storage group, for example, if the intermediate point is a transfer point. The goods can then be moved from the transfer point to the final putaway point.

5. **Enable warehouse order assignment**
   To assign warehouse orders to a resource and interleave warehouse tasks with a resource, appropriate queue types and queues must be defined for each programmable logic controller. Queues for the material flow system can be defined via IMG path **SCM Extended Warehouse Management • Extended Warehouse Management • Material Flow System(MFS) • Master Data • Define MFS Queue**. Click on **New Entries**, and create a new queue for the operative environment material flow system and the programmable logic controller name of the recipient for telegrams sent from embedded EWM.

6. **Configure actions.**
   To configure the actions the material flow system can take, define them via IMG path **SCM Extended Warehouse Management • Extended Warehouse Management • Material Flow System (MFS) • Telegram Processing • Define MFS Actions**. As part of follow-up settings, it's important to define which material flow system action will be determined by embedded EWM for a communication point type and telegram type. This can be configured via IMG path **SCM Extended Warehouse Management • Extended Warehouse Management • Material Flow System (MFS) • Telegram Processing • Find MFS Actions**.

7. **Define telegrams.**
   Telegrams represent the messages defined in embedded EWM. The programmable logic controllers and embedded EWM communicate using these telegrams. The structure of the telegram can be defined via IMG path **SCM Extended Warehouse Management • Extended Warehouse Management • Interfaces • Material Flow System (MFS) • Telegram Processing • Define Telegram Structure**. The telegram structure is defined for a programmable logic controller and programmable logic controller interface type. To create a new structure, click on the **Create New** button, and provide the structure name for the programmable logic controller interface type and telegram type for your warehouse.

8. **Generate application data.**
   As a final step, generate the application data to synchronize application data with Customizing data in the warehouse. To do this, navigate to **SAP Easy Access** path **Logistics • SCM Extended Warehouse Management • Extended Warehouse Management • Master Data • Material Flow System (MFS) • Generate Application Data**. Enter the warehouse number, and click on [icon]. The system should display a popup message confirming that application data was synchronized with Customizing data for the warehouse number.

While performing a putaway task in the material flow system section of the warehouse, the system creates warehouse tasks as defined in layout-oriented storage control to move goods through the bins created for communication points before the final putaway task is created. The building blocks of the material flow system and associated actions discussed in this section can be viewed in the embedded EWM warehouse monitor, as shown in Figure 24.8, by using Transaction /SCWM/MON and providing the warehouse number.

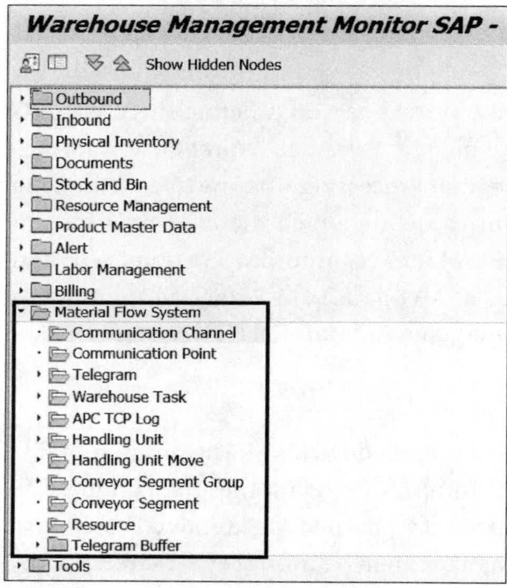

Figure 24.8 Nodes for the Material Flow System in the Embedded EWM Warehouse Monitor

24.3 Reprocessing Telegrams Using the Material Flow System Actions

In an automated conveyer segment of an automated storage and retrieval system, there can be many scenarios in which the automated conveyer belt may not function properly due to power supply issues, failure in the backend logic, and so on. This also affects the telegrams being sent between the material flow system and programmable logic controllers. To ensure asynchronous communication of the telegrams, they can be reprocessed with the correct time stamps when the issues in the automated storage and retrieval system are rectified.

Embedded EWM allows you to resend an acknowledged telegram manually in case of a failure. Using simulation, you can change input values for the telegram to simulate various test scenarios in which a telegram needs to be sent. You can display logs of telegrams received and sent from programmable logic controllers using the embedded EWM warehouse monitor. This overview is an important tool in case of message issues in the communication channel because it allows you to retrigger and simulate the telegrams using the button. It's also possible to view the warehouse tasks, warehouse order logs, telegram times, and so on for the selected telegrams using this node.

Resending an acknowledged telegram can be done using the embedded EWM warehouse monitor using Transaction /SCWM/MON. The telegram that needs to be present is selected in the **Material Flow System • Telegram • Other Methods • Resend Telegram** node. Choose , and select **Resend Telegram** for the selected telegram. To do so, navigate to **SAP Easy Access** path **Logistics • SCM Extended Warehouse Management• Extended Warehouse Management • Monitoring • Warehouse Management Monitor • Material Flow System • Communication Channel**, and click on **Start Channel**.

The prerequisite to trigger any reprocessing of telegrams in embedded EWM is that at least one communication channel must be started. When a communication channel is fixed to start the automated movement of HUs, EWM automatically sends all messages accumulated during the disconnection phase to a programmable logic controller. In any automated warehouse managed using the material flow system, it's always important to have both the messages and the acknowledgement of the messages received between the material flow system and programmable logic controllers. In adverse conditions when the programmable logic controller or rack feeder goes down, the acknowledgement of telegrams can't be sent back by the programmable logic controllers.

If embedded EWM doesn't receive acknowledgement of the telegrams, it tries again later based on the time specified in seconds in the **Teleg. Retry Interv**. field in the configuration for the communication point. There are various types of actions that the material flow system can take based on requirements. The action carried out by embedded EWM is executed by calling a function module assigned to the triggered material flow system action.

To define the material flow system action, navigate to IMG path **SCM Extended Warehouse Management • Extended Warehouse Management • Interfaces • Material Flow System (MFS) • Telegram Processing • Define MFS Action**. Click on **New Entries**, and enter an action ID for the new material flow system action and the function module that is called in embedded EWM when the action is called, as shown in Figure 24.9. The function modules assigned here are *synchronous function modules*, which means they're called as soon as the telegram arrives.

You can also assign an asynchronous function module to the material flow system action to denote an action that can be called asynchronously after the synchronous function module has executed. In this case, the programmable logic controller doesn't expect an immediate response for the action processing.

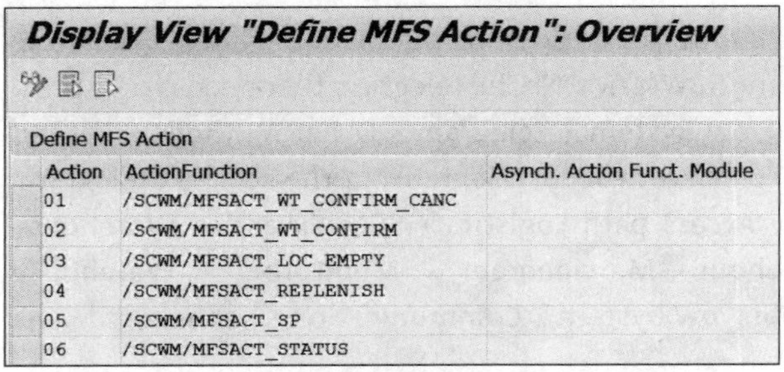

Display View "Define MFS Action": Overview

Define MFS Action

Action	ActionFunction	Asynch. Action Funct. Module
01	/SCWM/MFSACT_WT_CONFIRM_CANC	
02	/SCWM/MFSACT_WT_CONFIRM	
03	/SCWM/MFSACT_LOC_EMPTY	
04	/SCWM/MFSACT_REPLENISH	
05	/SCWM/MFSACT_SP	
06	/SCWM/MFSACT_STATUS	

Figure 24.9 Defining the Material Flow System Action

Embedded EWM triggers the material flow system action depending on the communication point type, resource type, and telegram type. You can set up the material flow system action determination via IMG path **SCM Extended Warehouse Management • Extended Warehouse Management • Interfaces • Material Flow System (MFS) • Telegram Processing • Find MFS Actions**. Click on **New Entries**, assign the material flow system action to the combination of fields for the warehouse (see Figure 24.10), and save.

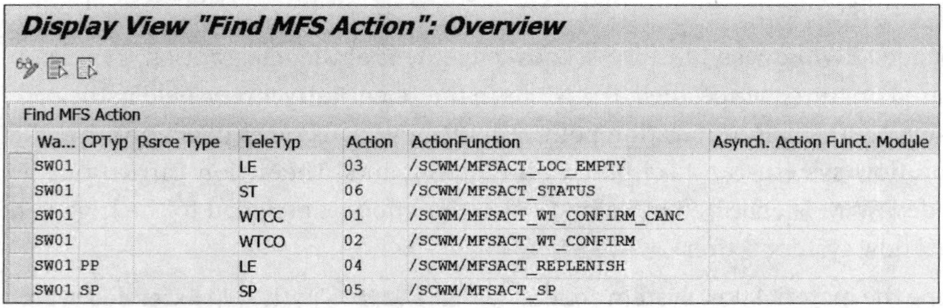

Display View "Find MFS Action": Overview

Find MFS Action

Wa...	CPTyp	Rsrce Type	TeleTyp	Action	ActionFunction	Asynch. Action Funct. Module
SW01			LE	03	/SCWM/MFSACT_LOC_EMPTY	
SW01			ST	06	/SCWM/MFSACT_STATUS	
SW01			WTCC	01	/SCWM/MFSACT_WT_CONFIRM_CANC	
SW01			WTCO	02	/SCWM/MFSACT_WT_CONFIRM	
SW01	PP		LE	04	/SCWM/MFSACT_REPLENISH	
SW01	SP		SP	05	/SCWM/MFSACT_SP	

Figure 24.10 Finding the Material Flow System Action

In addition to these standard processes used for reprocessing the telegrams, there's often a business requirement to process telegrams periodically in a custom manner. Logic can be configured, for example, to reduce unfilled bins in the warehouse or perform a specific action due to a maximum number of pending telegrams over a certain period of time. To do this, implement the Custom Logic for Periodic Action (/SCWM/EX_MFS_PERIOD_ACT) business add-in (BAdI) via IMG path **SCM Extended Warehouse Management • Extended Warehouse Management • Material Flow System (MFS) • BAdI for Material Flow System**.

Situations may arise during reprocessing in which the telegram received by the material flow system can't be reprocessed, and the function module defined for the determined material flow system action isn't executed properly. Any telegram that can't be tagged with a **Successful** processing status by the material flow system is set to the **Retry** status, and embedded EWM will try to execute the function module again based on the telegram retry interval time mentioned earlier.

Note

It's important to remember that not all function modules set telegrams to the **Retry** status. If a telegram is set to an **Error** status, then it must be investigated manually.

24.4 Summary

This chapter introduced the basic concepts and configuration of the material flow system in embedded EWM. We explained the elements in embedded EWM used to map an automated warehouse. We also discussed the process through which messages are communicated between automated conveyers/forklifts and embedded EWM. We explained how the material flow system handles exceptions that occur due to breakage or stock traffic on automated lines. In addition, we discussed using the material flow system for conveyer systems and how it's set up in the automated warehouse for putaway, picking, routing, and managing the HUs. You should now be able to set up and use the material flow system to manage your automated warehouses. In the next chapter, we will discuss integrating embedded EWM with other SAP products.

Chapter 25
Integration with Other SAP Solutions

Embedded EWM can be integrated with other SAP products, such as SAP Transportation Management and SAP Global Trade Services. In this chapter, we'll discuss using these integrations to optimize your end-to-end supply chain.

To manage certain business processes, an organization can integrate embedded EWM with other SAP solutions, such as SAP Transportation Management (SAP TM) and SAP Global Trade Services (SAP GTS). Each integration caters to supporting a specific business process, such as managing transportation, trade compliance, and so on.

Embedded EWM is integrated with many SAP applications and application components using direct and indirect integration. We've already discussed many of these integrated components thus far in this book, including master data, sales and distribution, purchasing, and production planning in SAP S/4HANA, as well as the material flow systems.

Organizations often need to have a connected supply chain so that warehousing, customs, and transportation are tightly integrated with each other, making real-time supply chain information available. This can be achieved in SAP S/4HANA by integrating embedded EWM with SAP TM and SAP GTS, thereby enabling organizations to keep track of interdependent supply chain processes using standard SAP solutions. Embedded EWM can also be connected with other applications, such as SAP BusinessObjects Business Intelligence (SAP BusinessObjects BI), SAP Environment, Health, and Safety Management (SAP EHS Management), and SAP Customer Relationship Management (SAP CRM). For the scope of discussion in this chapter, we'll cover integration of embedded EWM with SAP TM and SAP GTS.

In this chapter, we'll discuss the process and document flow between embedded EWM and other SAP applications and explain special business scenarios applicable to these integrations. Section 25.1 covers integration with SAP TM, which is used for optimizing both transportation and warehousing in the supply chain, and Section 25.2 covers integration with SAP GTS.

25.1 Integration with SAP Transportation Management and Embedded TM

Embedded EWM can be integrated with both embedded TM in SAP S/4HANA and standalone SAP TM using enterprise services. This requires SAP Process Integration (SAP PI) as an intermediate application to transmit the transactional documents between embedded TM and embedded EWM. In this section, we'll discuss the integration between embedded EWM and SAP TM. The process for integration is the same for embedded TM in SAP S/4HANA and standalone SAP TM.

In the following sections, we'll explain the integration of SAP TM and embedded EWM for the processes of delivery processing, using transit warehousing for third-party logistics, and warehouse billing for the purposes of calculating and billing warehouse services.

Note

Embedded EWM in SAP S/4HANA 1909 doesn't have indirect integration with SAP TM. In indirect integration, standalone SAP EWM can be connected with SAP TM using the LE-TRA component of SAP ERP. Embedded EWM only has direct integration with embedded TM as well as standalone SAP TM.

25.1.1 Configuring Integration with SAP Transportation Management

To integrate SAP TM with embedded EWM, it's important to complete the basic setup for freight order creation in SAP TM and the shipping and receiving component in embedded EWM. After this setup is completed, ensure that the following configurations are in place in both SAP TM and embedded EWM:

- **Integration configuration in SAP TM**
  SAP TM and embedded EWM communicate with each other using enterprise services. The enterprise services are triggered using the Post Processing Framework (PPF) output in both SAP TM and embedded EWM. For embedded TM and embedded EWM to trigger the services, you need to configure the following settings in SAP TM:
  - **Define means of transport in SAP TM to create transportation units (TUs) in embedded EWM**
    Define a means of transport in SAP TM, which represents the truck/trailer carrying deliveries into/out of the warehouse. Means of transport is defined via IMG

path **Transportation Management • Master Data • Resources • Means of Transport and Compartments • Define Means of Transport**. Click **New Entries**, and create a means of transport. When you plan the freight units on the freight order, the means of transport is assigned to the freight order. The assigned means of transport is communicated to embedded EWM when the loading/unloading instructions are sent by SAP TM to embedded EWM.

- **Activate the PPF action definition for sending loading/unloading instructions to embedded EWM**
  Activate the **Send Loading and Unloading Instructions (TOR_LDAP_REQ)** and **(TOR_LDAP_CNC)** action definitions for the **Actions for B2B Messages Related to Transportation Order (/SCMTMS/TOR)** action profile for the **Transportation Management (/SCTM/FOM)** application using Transaction SPPFCADM by unchecking the **Inactive** checkbox in the action definition.
- **Assign a PPF profile to the freight order type**
  The action profile for freight orders defined in the previous step is assigned to the freight order type via IMG path **Transportation Management • Freight Order Management • Define Freight Order Type** by clicking on **New Entries** in the menu, assigning the action profile in the **Output Profile** field, and saving it.

- **Integration configuration in embedded EWM**
  In addition to the previously mentioned configuration settings in SAP TM, the following configuration settings must be made in embedded EWM:
  - **Define means of transport in embedded EWM**
    You defined means of transport in the SAP TM system; you also define the means of transport, with the same name as that used in SAP TM, in embedded EWM via IMG path **SCM Extended Warehouse Management • Extended Warehouse Management • Master Data • Shipping and Receiving • Define Means of Transport**. Click on **New Entries**, enter the same code for **Means of Transport** as defined in SAP TM, and save it.
  - **Assign packaging material to means of transport in embedded EWM to create a TU**
    After the means of transport is defined, assign packaging materials to it via **SAP Easy Access** path **Logistics • SCM Extended Warehouse Management • Extended Warehouse Management • Settings • Shipping and Receiving • Link Between Packaging Material (TU) and Means of Transport**. Click on **New Entries**, and create a new means of transport with a particular packaging material.

- **Activate the PPF action definition for sending loading/unloading instructions to embedded EWM**
  For embedded EWM to interact with SAP TM, activate the action definitions, listed in Table 25.1, in the **Transportation Unit (/SCWM/TU)** PPF profile for the **Shipping and Receiving (/SCWM/SHP_RCV)** application using Transaction SPPF-CADM. Uncheck the **Inactive** checkbox for the action definition.

Technical Name	Action Definition Description
/SCWM/SR_SEND_TU	Send Message to FOM (Outbound Only): TU Contents Changed
/SCWM/SR_SEND_TU_FINAL	Send Message to FOM (Outbound Only): Loading Completed
/SCWM/SR_SEND_TU_FINAL_CANCEL	Send Message to FOM (Outbound Only): Reversal Loading Compl.
/SCWM/SR_SEND_TU_LDAP_NOTI	Send Message to TM

Table 25.1 Action Definitions for Integrated Transportation Units in Embedded EWM

- **Assign the PPF profile to TUs**
  You assign the action profile just defined to the TU via IMG path **SCM Extended Warehouse Management • Extended Warehouse Management • Cross-Process Settings • Shipping and Receiving • Define Control Parameters for Forming Vehicles/Transportation Units**. This is the action profile called when a TU is processed in embedded EWM. Click on **New Entries** to assign an action profile to a means of transport.

25.1.2 Delivery-Based Integration Process

In SAP TM, transportation planning is based on request documents in the form of inbound or outbound deliveries, which are planned using freight orders. In this section, we'll talk about outbound process planning with SAP TM. A freight order is sent to embedded EWM, which creates TUs. The warehousing-related steps are completed in embedded EWM, for example, unloading, loading, and so on. Embedded EWM then communicates the completion of warehousing activities to SAP TM, along with any discrepancies that were discovered, such as quantity deviations.

As shown in Figure 25.1, the following steps are performed in embedded EWM and SAP TM during the standard delivery-based integration process in an outbound scenario:

1. A sales order is created in the SAP S/4HANA system. Outbound deliveries for the sales orders are created in SAP S/4HANA. The delivery type is configured for integration with both SAP TM and embedded EWM. As soon as the delivery is saved in SAP S/4HANA, freight units are created in SAP TM, and an outbound delivery order is created in embedded EWM. Freight units are a sizable representation of orders/deliveries in SAP TM that are carried from a source location to a destination location without being subdivided further during the journey.
2. The freight units created for the outbound delivery order are planned in SAP TM. SAP TM creates the freight order for the planned freight units created with reference to the SAP S/4HANA delivery. The freight order represents planning of freight units from the source to the destination for means of transports such as trucks, vessels, trains, and so on. The **Load Planning** status of the freight order is set to **Load Plan Finalized**. SAP TM automatically sends loading instructions to EWM using the `LoadingAppointmentRequest` enterprise message.
3. When `LoadingAppointmentRequest` is received by embedded EWM, it creates a TU containing the distributed outbound delivery from SAP S/4HANA.
4. Warehousing activities are carried out in embedded EWM, and stock is moved to the staging area in the warehouse.
5. On arrival of the truck in the warehouse, the TU is checked in and docked at the warehouse door.
6. The truck is loaded and is ready for check-out from the checkpoint.
7. At check-out, the system automatically posts goods issue for the TU. Embedded EWM sends enterprise message `LoadingAppointmentRequest` to SAP TM. Outbound delivery in SAP S/4HANA is simultaneously updated with the goods issue status.

Tip

Delivery-based integration between SAP TM and embedded EWM, as explained in this section for the outbound process, is the same for inbound processes and stock transfer processes in SAP S/4HANA. The only differences are found in the initial request document for the outbound process and the stock transfer order.

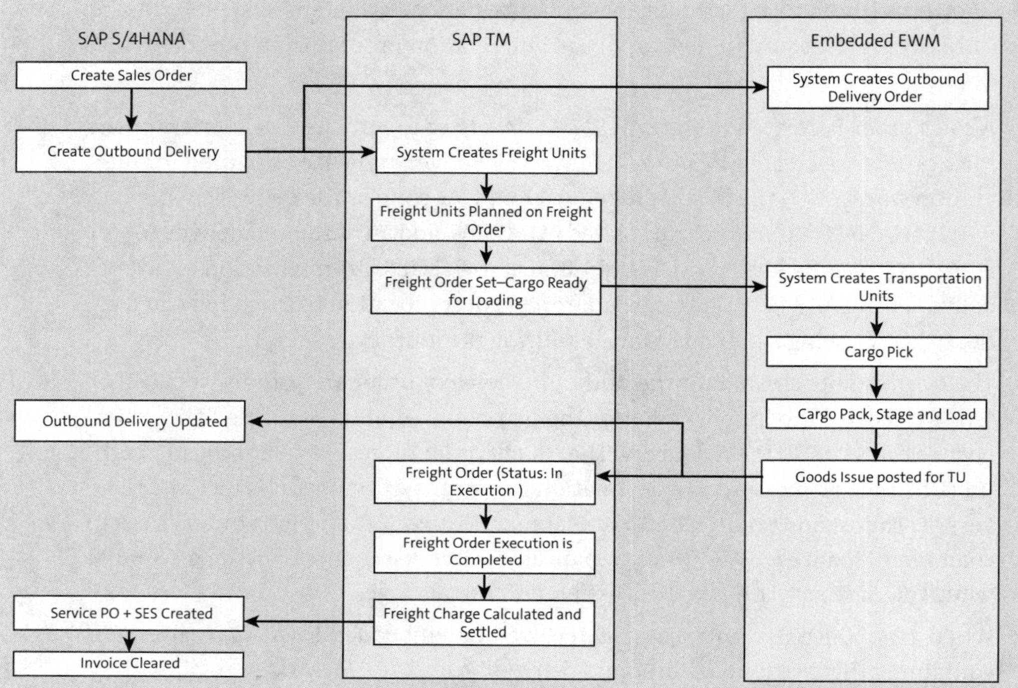

Figure 25.1 Process Flow between Embedded EWM and SAP TM in Outbound Scenario

25.1.3 Transit Warehousing

Transit warehousing can be used in scenarios in which stock is being transferred from the source to the destination via multiple intermediate warehouses. In such a scenario, these intermediate warehouses become transit warehouses. In this case, cargo isn't unpacked or put away in the intermediate warehouse. Stock is received and stored until it's moved to the goods issue area to be sent to the next intermediate stop.

The transit warehousing process includes the following process steps:

1. A customer service agent creates a forwarding order in SAP TM. The forwarding order represents the customer order created for a forwarding company.
2. The transportation planner creates or determines a route that contains a transit warehouse. A location can be made transit-warehouse-relevant if the warehouse number and a logical system of embedded EWM are entered in the location master data in SAP TM.

3. The forwarding order is planned in SAP TM. A freight order is created, based on which the stock is picked from the customer location and sent to the transit warehouse. The status of the freight order is set as **Ready for Transportation Execution**. After the truck reaches the embedded EWM warehouse, the transportation planner changes the status of the freight order to **Unload Plan Finalized**. SAP TM sends the unloading enterprise message `LoadingAppointmentRequest` to embedded EWM.
4. After embedded EWM receives the `LoadingAppointmentRequest` message, TUs, handling units (HUs), and inbound delivery for receiving the goods are created in embedded EWM.
5. The truck physically arrives in the warehouse, is checked into the warehouse yard, and is docked to the door. Embedded EWM sends back acknowledgement message `LoadingAppointmentNotification` to SAP TM. On receiving the message, SAP TM updates the freight order via which the TU was created in embedded EWM.
6. The truck is unloaded and goods receipt is posted for the deliveries assigned to the TU. This sends the `LoadingAppointmentNotification` acknowledgement message to SAP TM. The HUs are then brought to the bin in the transit warehouse or the staging area.
7. To complete the outbound process from the transit warehouse, SAP TM creates an outbound freight order from the warehouse to the gateway or next stop.

Note

The following SAP Fiori apps are available to perform transit warehousing using embedded EWM:

- **Handling-Unit Stock List**
  This app allows you to search, process, and report HUs for various operations (damage, lost, warehouse task maintenance, and processing) in warehouse which undergo transit using SAP TM.
- **Process Freight Order**
  This app allows you to view and process SAP TM freight orders containing transit warehouse deliveries for inbound and outbound processes using queries based on embedded EWM and decentralized EWM warehouses.
- **Prepare Loading or Unloading**
  This app allows you to view and process SAP TM freight orders containing transit warehouse deliveries for loading and unloading using queries based on embedded EWM and decentralized EWM warehouses.

25.1.4 Warehouse Billing

A warehouse billing process is used in embedded EWM to perform certain activities. In any transportation supply chain, only two possible types of organizations ship products from a source to a destination. An organization can be a *shipper* that sends products either using its own fleet or by outsourcing the service to a third-party logistics provider. Warehouse billing can be used by shippers for purchasing warehouse services from third-party vendors and paying the vendors for the services consumed over a given period. An organization can also be a *third-party logistics company* that receives the order for goods transportation and charges customers for any intermediate services. Third-party logistics players sell warehouse services to customers and bill them at regular intervals.

These services are settled on in an agreement in SAP TM. Periodically, the quantity of warehouse services used is transferred from embedded EWM to SAP TM. The system creates a service order in SAP TM, for which a charge is calculated and a settlement document is created. The charge calculation is done based on the charges agreed upon in the agreement. The document is then transferred to SAP S/4HANA to pay the external vendor.

The following features of warehouse billing can be used in embedded EWM:

- **Snapshot management**
  This process is used to capture embedded EWM data from transactional documents that are relevant to measuring actual warehouse services used. Warehouse services represent quantifiable attributes derived from business objects created in embedded EWM. These can be captured and transferred to SAP TM, for which a vendor can be paid at regular intervals. Data can be recorded as snapshots for the following business objects:
  - **Inbound deliveries:** Embedded EWM records data for the quantity of items received either partially or in full for the inbound deliveries created in the warehouse.
  - **Outbound deliveries:** Embedded EWM records data for the quantity of items issued and sent either partially or in full for the outbound delivery order from the warehouse.
  - **Warehouse tasks:** Embedded EWM records data for the number of warehouse tasks confirmed in the warehouse.

- **Warehouse billing measurement request management**
  This enables you to use SAP TM agreement data and determine the warehouse billing measurement services that should be used. In this process, embedded EWM automatically creates a warehouse billing measurement request when SAP TM sends agreement data to embedded EWM. In a warehouse billing measurement request, warehouse billing measurement services are assigned, for which warehouse billing measurements are captured for calculating the quantity of services performed in the warehouse. This information is later passed to SAP TM to calculate charges for warehouse services and settle them with the vendor.

  Service quantities for the following embedded EWM objects can be measured:
  - Number of documents
  - Product quantity
  - Weight
  - Volume
  - Number of bins
  - Number of HUs
- **Warehouse billing measurement management**
  After the warehouse billing measurement request is activated for capturing measurements, warehouse billing measurements are generated via **SAP Easy Access** path **Logistics • SCM Extended Warehouse Management • Extended Warehouse Management • Billing • Billing • Generate Billing Measurement**. Generated warehouse billing measurements can be displayed in the warehouse monitor using Transaction /SCWM/MON under the **Billing • Warehouse Billing Measurement** node. Warehouse billing measurements contain information about the quantity of services used, they're generated for a specific billing period in embedded EWM.

  After the warehouse billing measurement is generated for the warehouse billing measurement, it's transferred to SAP TM. The warehouse billing measurement is distributed using report /SCWM/WB_DISTRIBUTE_BM. After the warehouse billing measurement is transferred to SAP TM, its status is changed to **Distributed**.

  The completed services are then built using a service order in SAP TM. A settlement document is created for the service order and transferred to SAP S/4HANA, which creates a service purchase order and service entry sheets automatically. The vendor is paid for the warehouse services either by manual clearance from the finance department or by using Evaluated Receipt Settlement for automatic vendor payment clearance.

Decentralized EWM in SAP S/4HANA, on the other hand, allows you to make a record of warehouse services quantities that are part of the agreement in SAP TM. After successful calculation of the quantity of services performed for a warehouse that is linked to both decentralized EWM and SAP TM, the information can be sent back to SAP TM for charge calculation and service settlement document creation based on the services agreed to as part of the SAP TM agreement. This new feature enables you to perform the following two processes:

- Bill the customer a certain set of warehouse services based on the usage on a periodic and timely basis.
- Pay external vendors for warehouse services that can be obtained for a certain time period at a certain price.

Tip

The warehouse billing process in coordination with SAP TM is the same for both embedded EWM and decentralized EWM in SAP S/4HANA with no functional differences.

25.2 Integration with SAP Global Trade Services

SAP GTS is primarily used for managing export compliance, screening business partners and documents against sanctioned parties, and performing customs management. Embedded EWM can be integrated with SAP GTS for tracking bonded warehouse stock and creating interstate declarations for intercountry stock transfer. Bonded warehouse stock is the stock imported into a country, and duty is only paid on it if the stock is consumed in the importing country.

In this section, we'll explain the processes, integration, and use of embedded EWM integration with SAP GTS, facilitating the handling of import and export of goods using transit procedures, scrapping of goods based on custom approvals, and handling compliance of goods in warehouses.

25.2.1 Compliance Management in Outbound Processing with Embedded EWM

Embedded EWM integration with SAP GTS also can be used to check if delivery is relevant for export compliance in SAP GTS. A compliance check can be activated in SAP

GTS based on the company code, plant, and delivery types. SAP GTS carries out the following three checks on outbound deliveries and outbound delivery orders:

- **Legal control**
  Checks if a valid export license exists in SAP GTS for line items in the delivery.
- **Embargo**
  Checks if a partner function in the delivery has an embargo/trade block in GTS.
- **Sanctioned party list**
  SAP GTS allows screening of documents and business partners for people/organizations in a sanctioned party list. If the screening process results in a positive hit, then the document is blocked in SAP GTS, and a corresponding message is sent to embedded EWM.

The process for an outbound delivery is created in embedded EWM. The delivery is sent to SAP GTS to check if it's export-compliant. If the delivery is blocked in SAP GTS, then the status of the outbound delivery order is set to **GTS Check/Technical Error** or **GTS Check/Check, Not OK**; this status doesn't allow creation of an outbound delivery in embedded EWM. If the delivery document isn't blocked in SAP GTS due to any of these three reasons, embedded EWM allows completion of the picking process and creation of the outbound delivery. After the outbound delivery is created in embedded EWM, it's sent again to SAP GTS for an export control check. If the outbound delivery is blocked in SAP GTS, then the same status as discussed earlier is updated in the outbound delivery in embedded EWM; otherwise, embedded EWM allows goods issue to be performed for the outbound delivery, which is also updated in the outbound delivery in SAP S/4HANA.

The following configurations are required to set up compliance checks on outbound deliveries in embedded EWM:

- The **DGT: GTS Check** status type should be active in the status profile for item types in outbound deliveries. We discussed status profiles in Chapter 6.
- To enable compliance checks on outbound delivery orders in embedded EWM, navigate to IMG path **SCM Extended Warehouse Management • Extended Warehouse Management • Goods Issue Process • Outbound Delivery • Define Document Types for Outbound Delivery Process**. For the outbound delivery order document type and document category, select the **Legal Control GTS** checkbox as shown in Figure 25.2.

25

Figure 25.2 Compliance Check on the Outbound Delivery Order

If required, you can remove the SAP GTS lock in the delivery by clicking **GTS • Release GTS Lock** in the transaction screen for the outbound delivery order, as shown in Figure 25.3.

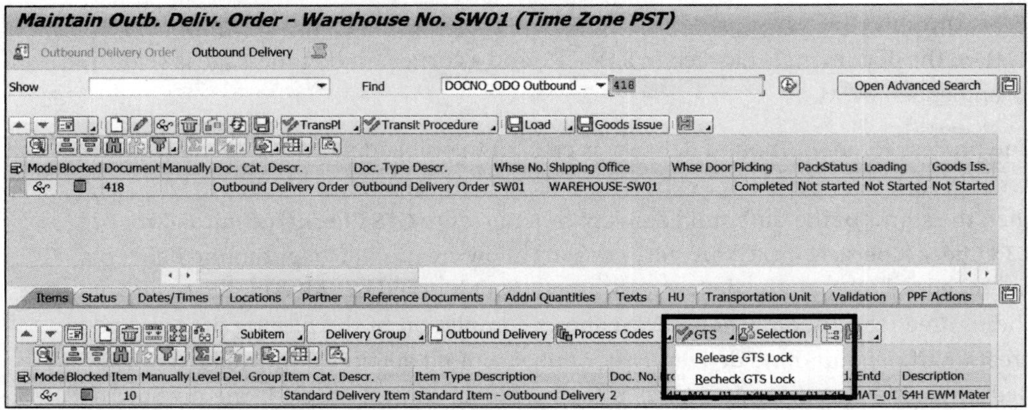

Figure 25.3 Managing SAP GTS Locks in Delivery in Embedded EWM

25.2.2 Transit Procedure

The transit procedure in SAP GTS allows you to shift customs handling during export and import scenarios so that the customs clearance takes place not when goods cross the border but when they arrive at their destination.

Embedded EWM can differentiate between deliveries relevant for transit procedures based on the reference document saved in the delivery information. These delivery documents are created with reference to other documents, such as sales orders, purchase orders, and so on. If any of those documents are transit-procedure-relevant, then based on system settings, the embedded EWM system determines the delivery also to be transit-procedure-relevant. After the determination of the transit relevance, the embedded EWM system can place either a custom block or a transit block on the deliveries until further approval.

Figure 25.4 shows the transit procedure in the inbound process. Goods are dispatched from India on a ship to company ABC in Germany in the European Union. This is considered an import into the European Union because goods are entering from a foreign country, which means that the receiving party can be eligible to pay a custom duty to the customs office to allow free circulation of goods in the European Union. To do this, the receiving company creates an import declaration. The import declaration can be created before or after goods receipt based on a country's legal regulations and/or business requirements. For countries in the European Union, the import declaration can be created before or after physical goods receipt in the warehouse; for countries such as the United States, it must be created at the port, before goods receipt in the warehouse.

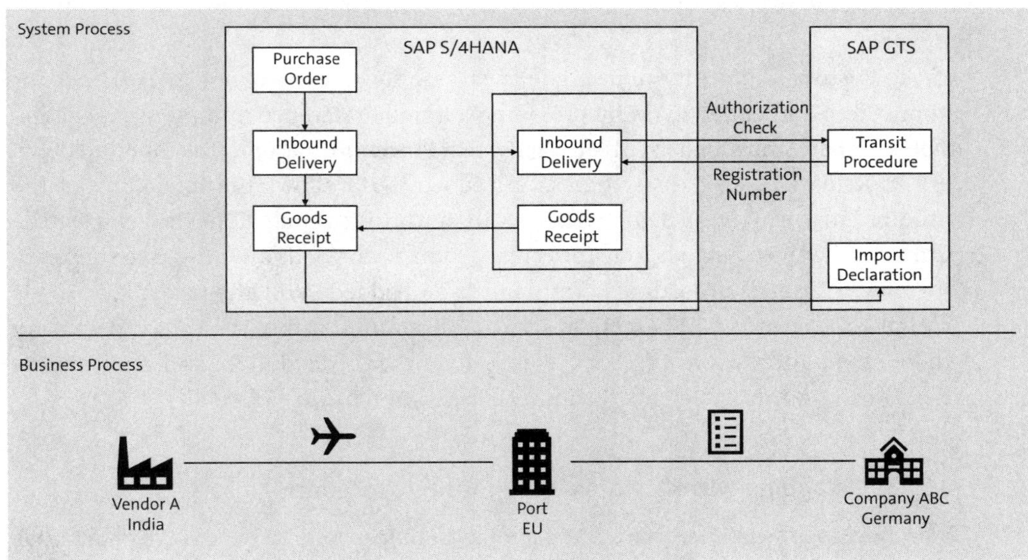

Figure 25.4 Transit Procedure in Inbound Delivery

In our example, the transportation vehicle arrives in ABC's warehouse with a delivery that's transit procedure-relevant. The delivery comes in with paperwork that holds the previous document type and document number, or they're manually added to determine transit-procedure relevance. This information also can be provided via an advanced shipping notification. It's mandatory to have an inbound delivery created before goods are received in the warehouse.

In customization settings, define the reference document categories via IMG path **Cross-Process Settings • Delivery Processing • Reference Documents • Define Reference Document Categories**. You should also assign the reference document categories that correspond to a previous document type to a transit procedure and set the transit-procedure-relevant indicator. To do so, navigate to IMG path **SCM Extended Warehouse Management • Extended Warehouse Management • Interfaces • GTS Integration • Define Previous Document Types**. Based on these customizations, embedded EWM determines that the previous document is relevant to the transit procedure and blocks the inbound delivery from goods receipt posting. Embedded EWM sends a message to SAP GTS about the delivery for which the transit procedure is to be performed. Based on this message, SAP GTS sends an Electronic Data Interchange (EDI) message to custom authorities to check whether unloading can be carried out.

If the customs authority allows goods receipt to be carried out, SAP GTS sends approval to embedded EWM by providing a unique reference number or a registration number. Embedded EWM sets the **Transit Procedure** status of the inbound delivery to **Released**. After this process, embedded EWM allows the unloading of the products in the inbound delivery. If customs authorities don't allow the vehicle to be unloaded because it needs a customs inspection, then goods are moved to safekeeping. SAP GTS sends unloading permission to embedded EWM after the inspection is complete. Embedded EWM sets the **Transit Procedure** status of the inbound delivery to **Released**. After goods receipt is completed in embedded EWM and replicated in SAP S/4HANA, you can create the import declaration in SAP GTS.

25.2.3 Scrapping with Customs Warehousing Procedure

Warehousing forms a key part of the supply chain process. To encourage companies to stay competitive in the global landscape, customs authorities provide tax-efficient options to importers by authorizing special customs procedures that help the importer by reducing import duties, taxes, and so on. In one such procedure, goods are moved to a bonded warehouse based on valid conditions that in turn provide economic benefits to the importer.

If a customs warehousing procedure is used in embedded EWM, it doesn't affect normal delivery processing. Embedded EWM sends goods movement and delivery information to SAP GTS via SAP S/4HANA. However, while scrapping in embedded EWM, you can send a request to customs authorities with permission to scrap via the integration. Bonded warehouses usually stock duty-unpaid goods, but this permission is required for scrapping both duty-paid goods and duty-unpaid goods. Scrapping occurs in embedded EWM when a posting change request is created in a customs warehouse. The following settings are required to set a warehouse and products relevant for customs procedures:

- Define a GTS system for the embedded EWM warehouse number via IMG path **SCM Extended Warehouse Management • Extended Warehouse Management • Interfaces • GTS Integration • Define GTS System for Warehouse Number**. Assign the GTS business system to your embedded EWM warehouse.
- Define a custom ID in embedded EWM by following IMG path **SCM Extended Warehouse Management • Extended Warehouse Management • Interfaces • GTS Integration • Define Customs ID**. Assign the custom ID to the warehouse number and the party entitled to dispose from **SAP Easy Access** path **Logistics • SCM Extended Warehouse Management • Extended Warehouse Management • Settings • Assign Warehouse Number/Party Entitled to Dispose to Customs ID**. This customs ID is also used to distribute the products relevant for customs warehousing procedures from SAP GTS to embedded EWM.
- The products that are part of the customs warehousing procedure in the customs IDs are distributed from SAP GTS to embedded EWM automatically by the system.
- To ensure that embedded EWM posts goods to scrap stock when the scrapping process is completed, create a scrap stock type in embedded EWM mapped to nonlocation-dependent stock type BB.

The process begins when a posting change request for scrapping is created in embedded EWM, which checks if the product in the delivery is relevant for customs warehousing. If it is, then the delivery is locked, and SAP GTS sends an EDI message to the customs authority for scrapping permission. After getting the permission, SAP GTS sends the scrapping reference number to embedded EWM, in which the posting change is unlocked and the posting change request processing continues. The warehouse tasks are created for the warehouse request, and the posting change is confirmed.

25.2.4 Safekeeping

Safekeeping is used for inbound deliveries in embedded EWM. The process of safekeeping is usually triggered as a follow-up to the transit procedure process. After the goods during inbound receipt follow the transit procedure process, safekeeping is triggered if further decisions need to be taken by the custom authorities. Until the decision of the customs authorities is conveyed to SAP GTS, the goods are moved to safekeeping. The different options available to the user are to import the goods and pay customs duty or include the products in the customs warehouse procedure. To configure this process, you must perform the following actions:

- Complete the configuration for the transit procedure for inbound deliveries as described earlier.
- Set the **Customs Block** indicator at IMG path **SCM Extended Warehouse Management • Extended Warehouse Management • Interfaces • GTS Integration • Define Previous Document Types**. This setting lets embedded EWM know if a document type and document number are relevant for customs block.
- Configure a new **Stock Type** with the **Customs Blocked** role via IMG path **SCM Extended Warehouse Management • Extended Warehouse Management • Master Data • Product • Define Stock Type** if you want to create a new stock type to identify customs-blocked stock. This allows the customs-blocked stock type to be assigned to delivery when the stock is posted to a bin containing customs-held stock.

The process begins when the inbound delivery is created in embedded EWM. The delivery has the previous document type and number either from the delivery in SAP S/4HANA or added manually in the inbound delivery in embedded EWM. If the reference document type is relevant to the customs block, then embedded EWM posts the stock to the stock type for the customs-block status. After the stock is released from the customs block, the stock is posted to unrestricted use in a putaway stock type.

25.3 Summary

This chapter introduced the integration of embedded EWM with other SAP applications: SAP TM and SAP GTS. We explained the process and document flow between embedded EWM and standalone SAP TM for delivery-based integration, along with the concepts of transit warehousing and warehousing billing. We also covered the integration of embedded EWM and SAP GTS, focusing on the use of the transit procedure and customs warehousing procedure in SAP GTS. We also explained how embedded EWM integration with SAP GTS can be set up to carry out compliance checks on deliveries in SAP GTS.

Appendix A
SAP Fiori Applications

SAP Fiori was introduced by SAP as a lightweight frontend solution based on SAPUI5 technology, which is also mobile-friendly. SAP Fiori provides a rich user-specific interface (UI) that can be customized for specific roles. It provides users with the ability to access SAP Fiori apps using multiple devices such as desktops, tablets, or smartphones. By providing a user-centric interface, SAP Fiori helps improve employee productivity by reducing training time and increasing mobility. For SAP Fiori apps to run, both frontend (UI) and backend apps must be installed in the SAP S/4HANA system.

SAP Fiori 2.0 is the next iteration of the SAP Fiori user experience (UX) with a new UI theme: Belize. The SAP Fiori frontend server 4.0 is required to run SAP Fiori 2.0 apps in SAP S/4HANA 1909. Using the viewport concept, the desktop has been expanded on both the left and right for a broader view and access to more information on a single screen. SAP Fiori launchpad is the single point of entry to access all apps.

You can perform all configuration, master-data-related, and transaction activities in embedded EWM using SAP Fiori apps. SAP S/4HANA 1909 provides various apps used for executing the different functionalities and processes in embedded EWM applications. Because SAP Fiori apps in embedded EWM are role-based so that users with specific roles can access them, we'll cover the list of all the SAP Fiori apps for various master data setup and embedded EWM processes in SAP S/4HANA 1909 and give snapshots of some important apps for each role.

A.1 SAP Fiori Applications for Warehouse Clerks

Several SAP Fiori apps are available for the SAP_BR_WAREHOUSE_CLERK_EWM role in embedded EWM. You can also create a new role using Transaction PFCG, assign a few of these SAP Fiori app menus to it (see Figure A.1), and assign the new role to a user in embedded EWM.

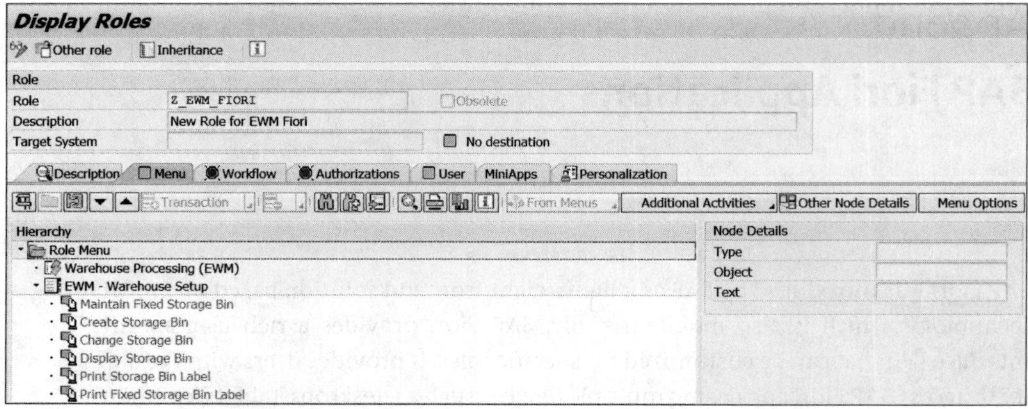

Figure A.1 Defining a New Role with the SAP Fiori Menu in Embedded EWM

The following SAP Fiori apps are available for the warehouse clerk role in embedded EWM:

- Analyze Differences
- Arrival and Departure – Transportation Units
- Assign Bin to PSA – Warehouse
- Assign Fixed Bins
- Assign Tolerance Group – Counting
- Assign Tolerance Group – Differences
- Cancel Picking
- Change Inbound Delivery
- Change Storage Bins
- Clear Production Supply Area
- Compare Stock – Inventory Management
- Confirm Warehouse Tasks
- Consolidate Stock
- Count Physical Inventory
- Count Physical Inventory – List
- Create Inbound Delivery

- Create Loading Appointments – Graphical, Access Loading Appointment – Graphical
- Create Loading Appointments – Textual, Access Loading Appointment – Textual
- Create Physical Inventory – Documents
- Create Posting Changes
- Create Storage Bins
- Create Warehouse Orders – Manual
- Create Warehouse Tasks – Handling Units
- Create Warehouse Tasks – Inbound Delivery
- Create Warehouse Tasks – Outbound Delivery Order
- Create Warehouse Tasks – Posting Change
- Create Warehouse Tasks – Product
- Create Warehouse Tasks – Warehouse Request
- Display Storage Bins
- Display Warehouse Tasks
- Display Workload – Goods Receipt
- Distribute Quantities – Merchandise Distribution
- Download Bins or Stock Items – Physical Inventory
- Handling-Unit Stock List – Transit Warehousing
- Load Transportation Units
- Load Workload Plan
- Maintain Correction Deliveries
- Maintain Docking Location, Create Docking Location
- Maintain Inbound Deliveries
- Maintain Indirect Labor Tasks
- Maintain Loading Appointments – Graphical
- Maintain Loading Appointments – Textual
- Maintain Loading Points, Create Loading Points
- Maintain Outbound Deliveries
- Maintain Packaging Specification

- Maintain Performance Documents – Employees
- Maintain Planned Shipping HUs
- Maintain Posting Changes
- Maintain Processor Work Schedule
- Maintain Product
- Maintain Products – Warehouse Data
- Maintain Resources
- Maintain Stock Transfers
- Maintain Transportation Units
- Maintain User Settings – Exception Code Profile
- Maintain User Settings – Radio Frequency
- Maintain Vehicles
- Monitor Loading Appointments
- Move in Yard – Transportation Units
- Outbound Delivery Orders
- Outbound Delivery Orders – Pickup
- Plan Doors – Loading Point
- Plan Doors – Transportation Units
- Plan Workload
- Post Consumption – Production
- Post Differences – Automatic
- Post Goods Issue – Unplanned
- Prepare Goods Receipt – External Procurement
- Prepare Goods Receipt – Production
- Prepare Loading or Unloading – Transit Warehousing
- Print Count Documents – Physical Inventory
- Print Fixed Bin Labels
- Print Inventory List – For Fire Department
- Print Storage Bin Labels
- Process Freight Orders – Transit Warehousing
- Process Goods Receipt

- Process Loading Appointments
- Process Physical Inventory
- Process Single Freight Order – Transit Warehousing
- Process Warehouse Tasks – Picking
- Process Warehouse Tasks – Putaway
- Process Waves
- Production Material Requests
- Rearrange Stock
- Replenish Stock
- Returns Initiation
- Reuse Lib for EWM
- Run Outbound Process – Deliveries
- Run Outbound Process – Transportation Unit
- Schedule Replenishment
- Shipping Cockpit – Execution
- Shipping Cockpit – Planning
- Stage for Production
- Unload Transportation Units
- Upload Bins or Count Results – Physical Inventory
- Upload Stock
- Value-Added Services – Inbound
- Value-Added Services – Internal
- Value-Added Services – Kit to Stock
- Value-Added Services – Outbound
- Value-Added Services – Reverse Kitting
- Warehouse Monitor

As shown in Figure A.2, any user with the warehouse clerk role can create and confirm a warehouse task using the Create Warehouse Task app. As you can see, the SAP Fiori app provides a simplified UX, which can be used in both desktop and mobile landscapes.

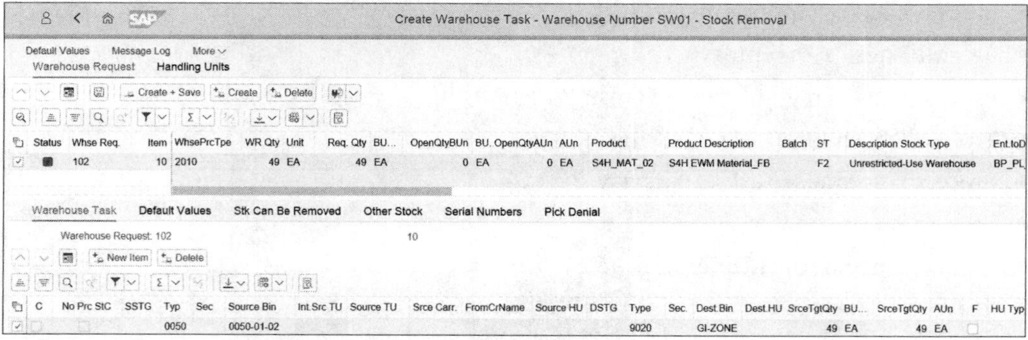

Figure A.2 Create Warehouse Task App

A.2 SAP Fiori Applications for Warehouse Shift Supervisors

SAP Fiori apps are available to any user with the /UI2/SAP_KPIFRW5_TCR_S role in the embedded EWM system. You can also create a new role using Transaction PFCG, assign a few of these SAP Fiori app menus to it, and assign the new role to a user in embedded EWM. These apps help you monitor warehouse key performance indicators (KPIs) for important decision-making.

The SAP Fiori apps available in embedded EWM and applicable to users with the warehouse shift supervisor role are as follows:

- Avg. Goods Issue Delay Time
- Avg. Wait Time in Yrd
- Deliv. GR Completion Outstanding
- Deliv. Itm Putawy Compl. Outstanding
- Deliv. Unloading Outstanding
- Delivery Arrival Overdue
- Gross Weight of Inbound Delivery Items
- Itms w/Incompl. Creation of Pick Task
- No. of Deliv. for Wave Pick Itms
- No. of Inbound Deliveries
- No. of Inbound Delivery Items
- No. of Outbound Deliveries
- No. of Outbound Delivery Items

- No. of Wave Pick Items
- Overdue Completion of Wave Pick Tasks
- Overdue Outbound Deliveries
- Overdue Outbound Delivery Items
- Perform ABC Analysis
- Pct. of Compl. Wave Pick Item Tasks
- Task Execution Performance
- Volume of Inbound Delivery Items
- Volume of Outbound Delivery Items
- Volume of Wave Pick Items
- Warehouse KPIs – Operations
- Weight of Outbound Delivery Items
- Weight of Wave Pick Items

An app used for displaying an outbound delivery order document is shown in Figure A.3.

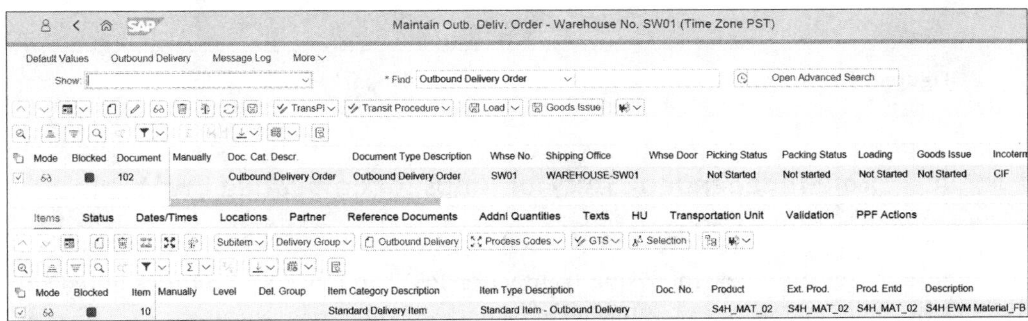

Figure A.3 SAP Fiori App to Display Outbound Delivery Order in Embedded EWM

A.3 SAP Fiori Apps for Warehouse Operatives

SAP Fiori apps are available to any user with the SAP_BR_WAREHOUSE_OPERATIVE_EWM role in embedded EWM. You also can create a new role using Transaction PFCG, assign a few of these SAP Fiori app menus to it, and assign the new role to the user in embedded EWM. The various SAP Fiori apps available in embedded EWM and applicable to users with the warehouse operative role are as follows:

- Deconsolidate Handling Units
- Pack Handling Units
- Pack Outbound Deliveries
- Pack Warehouse Stock
- Pick by Cart
- Process Value-Added Service
- Quality Work Center
- Test RF Environment

An app used for packing handling units is shown in Figure A.4.

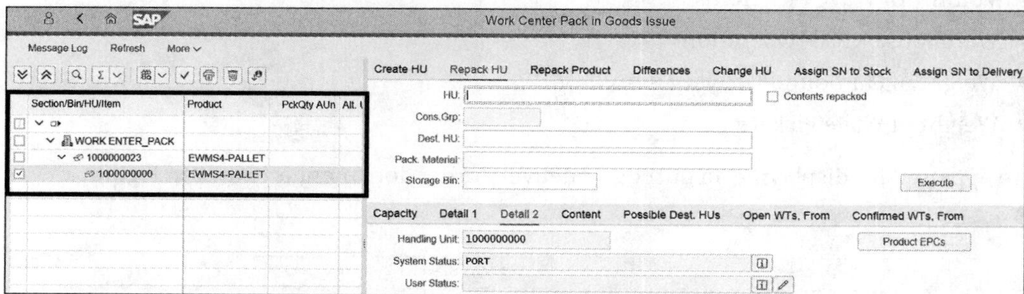

Figure A.4 SAP Fiori App in Embedded EWM to Pack/Repack Handling Units

A.4 Role-Independent SAP Fiori Apps for Embedded EWM

SAP Fiori apps are available to any warehouse workers using a custom-created PFCG role. You create a new role using Transaction PFCG and then assign the required SAP Fiori tile catalogs for the following apps in the **Menu** tab by clicking on **Transaction** and selecting the **SAP Fiori Tile Catalog** option. Next, you assign the newly created role to the user in embedded EWM. You can explore the various SAP Fiori apps that aren't specific to certain roles in the SAP Fiori Library at *http://s-prs.co/v500501.*

An app used for processing physical inventory documents is shown in Figure A.5.

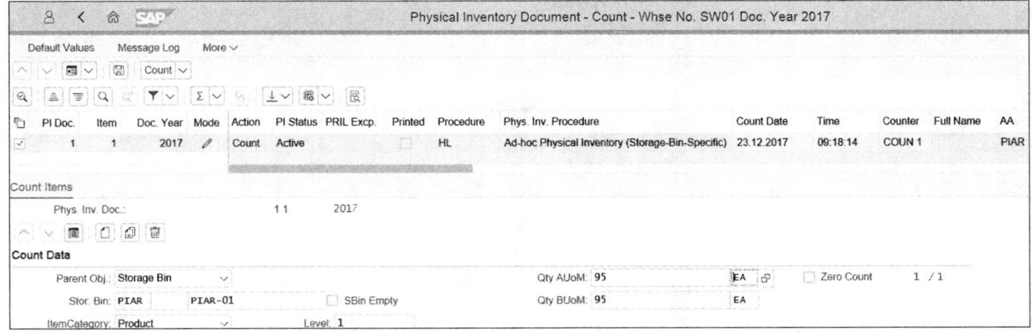

Figure A.5 SAP Fiori App for Bin-Specific Physical Inventory Count

Appendix B
The Authors

Namita Sachan is a senior SAP consultant at Capgemini UK with more than 11 years of experience with standalone SAP EWM, embedded EWM in SAP S/4HANA, SAP Global Trade Services (SAP GTS) and other SAP supply chain management solutions. She has worked with clients around the world in the United Kingdom, United States, and Europe. She has experience in multiple industry sectors and has worked on several SAP EWM implementation projects for mid-sized and large warehouses.

Aman Jain is a business process and architecture associate manager for Accenture United Kingdom and Ireland. He has more than 11 years of experience using SAP warehousing solutions for global clients in industry sectors such as consumer product group, oil and gas, automobile manufacturing, and communication technology. He has implemented multiple end-to-end greenfield projects for standalone SAP EWM, standalone SAP TM, embedded EWM and embedded TM in SAP S/4HANA, and other SAP S/4HANA supply chain applications. Aman is based out of Derby, United Kingdom, and lives with his wife, Namita, and son, Vihaan.

Index

A

B

C

D

G

H

I

M

R

T

U

V

W

Y

Z

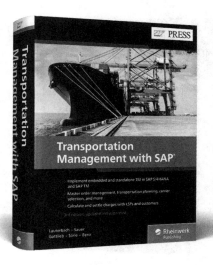